FISKE GUIDE TO COLLEGES 2027

FISKE GUIDE TO COLLEGES 2027

EDWARD B. FISKE

**former Education Editor of
the *New York Times***

**with Lisa Chambers
and
the *Fiske Guide to Colleges* staff**

Published by Sourcebooks
1935 Brookdale RD, Naperville, IL 60563-2773
(630) 961-3900
sourcebooks.com

Forty-third Edition

**Your comments and corrections
are welcome. Please send them to:**

Fiske Guide to Colleges
Email: fiskesupport@sourcebooks.com

Printed and bound in the United States of America.

DR 10 9 8 7 6 5 4 3 2 1

To Sunny

Contents

Index by State and Country

The colleges in this guide are listed alphabetically and cross-referenced for your convenience. Below is a list of the selected colleges grouped by state. Following this listing, you will find additional listings that categorize the colleges by their yearly costs of attendance and by the average debt accrued by students during their tenure at each school.

Index by Price

	PUBLIC	PRIVATE
$$$$	More than $14,500	More than $68,000
$$$	$12,000–$14,500	$62,000–$68,000
$$	$10,000–$12,000	$52,000–$62,000
$	Less than $10,000	Less than $52,000

Price categories are based on current tuition and fees and do not include room, board, transportation, and other expenses.

PUBLIC COLLEGES AND UNIVERSITIES

INEXPENSIVE—$

MODERATE—$ $

EXPENSIVE—$ $ $

VERY EXPENSIVE—$ $ $ $

PRIVATE COLLEGES AND UNIVERSITIES

* Although these are public institutions, Americans and other non-Europeans should compare the costs to out-of-state public schools, with the most selective universities approaching top U.S. private-college levels.

$$$$	More than $35,000
$$$	$29,500–$35,000
$$	$25,000–$29,500
$	Less than $25,000

Debt categories are based on the average amount of principal accumulated by *each undergraduate who borrowed during their tenure as a student*. Public and private institutions have been rated using the same criteria. Institutions for which data on average borrowing was unavailable have been omitted.

HIGH AVERAGE DEBT—$ $ $

VERY HIGH AVERAGE DEBT—$ $ $ $

The Best Buys of 2027

Following is an alphabetical list of 20 colleges and universities that qualify as Best Buys based on the quality of their academic offerings in relation to the cost of attendance.
(See page xxii for an explanation of how Best Buys were identified.)

Public	Private
Arizona State University	Brigham Young University
UC Irvine	California Institute of Technology
UC Riverside	The Cooper Union
University of Georgia	Grinnell College
Georgia Institute of Technology	Olin College of Engineering
University of Illinois at Urbana–Champaign	Pomona College
University of Maryland, Baltimore County	Princeton University
University of Minnesota Morris	Warren Wilson College
Purchase College, SUNY	Williams College
University of Washington	Xavier University of Louisiana

Introduction

FISKE GUIDE TO COLLEGES—AND HOW TO USE IT

The 2027 edition of the *Fiske Guide to Colleges* is a revised and updated version of a book that has been a bestseller since it first appeared more than four decades ago and is universally regarded as the definitive college guide of its type. Features of the new edition include:

- Updated profiles of 300+ leading colleges and universities
- Data on typical student debt
- "Sizing Yourself Up" college-fit questionnaire
- Guide to top preprofessional programs
- Listings for students with learning differences
- "Best Buy" colleges list
- Clear, concise statistical summaries
- Ratings for academics, social life, and quality of life
- "If You Apply To" admissions insights
- Guide to leading Canadian, British, and Irish universities
- **NEW:** Introduction to English-taught full-time undergraduate programs at top universities in Europe and Asia

Picking the right college—one that will coincide with your particular needs, goals, interests, talents, and personality—is one of the most important decisions any young person will ever make. It is also a major investment. Tuition and fees alone now average at least $12,000 per year at a typical public university and $45,000 per year at a typical private college. When room, board, and other expenses are thrown in, the overall tab at the most selective and expensive schools—absent financial aid—can approach $100,000 per year. Obviously, a major investment like that should be approached with as much information as possible.

That's where the *Fiske Guide to Colleges* fits in. It is a tool to help you make the most intelligent educational investment you can.

WHAT IS THE *FISKE GUIDE TO COLLEGES?*

Fiske Guide to Colleges mirrors a process familiar to any college-bound student and their family. If you are wondering whether to consider a particular college, it is logical to seek out friends or acquaintances who go there and ask them to tell you about their experiences. We have done exactly that—but on a far broader and more systematic basis than any individual or family could do alone.

In using the *Fiske Guide,* you should keep some special features in mind:

- The guide is **selective**. We have not tried to cover all four-year colleges and universities. Rather, we have chosen more than 300 of the "best and most interesting" of the country's 2,300 institutions—ones that students most want to know about—and written descriptive essays of 1,000 to 2,500 words about each of them. We have also, as of 2027, included a selection of international universities offering full-time undergraduate programs taught in English.

- Since choosing a college is a matter of making a calculated and informed judgment, this guide is also **subjective**. It makes judgments about the strengths and weaknesses of each institution, and it contains a unique set of ratings of each college or university on the basis of academic strength, social life, and overall quality of life. No institution is a good fit for every student. The underlying assumption of the *Fiske Guide* is that each of the colleges chosen for inclusion is the best place for some students but not a good bet for others. Like finding the right spouse, college admissions is a matching process. You know your own interests and needs; the *Fiske Guide* will tell you something about those needs that each college seems to serve best.

- Finally, the *Fiske Guide* is **systematic**. Each write-up is carefully constructed to cover specific topics—from the academic climate and the makeup of the student body to the social scene—in a systematic order. This means that you can easily take a specific topic, such as the level of academic pressure or the role of fraternities and sororities on campus, and trace it through all of the colleges that interest you.

HOW THE COLLEGES WERE SELECTED

How do you single out the "best and most interesting" of those 2,300 four-year colleges in the United States? Obviously, many fine institutions are not included. Space limitations simply require that some hard decisions be made.

The selection was done with several broad principles in mind, beginning with academic quality. Depending on how you define the term, there are about 200 "selective" colleges and universities in the nation, and by and large, these constitute the best institutions academically. All of these are included in the *Fiske Guide*. In addition, an effort was made to achieve geographic diversity and a balance of public and private schools.

Finally, in a few cases, we exercised the journalist's prerogative of writing about schools that are simply interesting. The tiny College of the Atlantic, for example, would hardly qualify on the basis of a superior academic program or national significance, but it offers an unusual and fascinating brand of liberal arts within the context of environmental studies for those who seek it. Likewise, Deep Springs College, the only two-year school in the *Fiske Guide*, is a unique institution of intrinsic interest.

HOW THE *FISKE GUIDE* WAS COMPILED

We asked school officials at each college or university selected for inclusion in the *Fiske Guide* to complete an online questionnaire. This questionnaire covered topics ranging from their perception of the institution's mission to the demographics of the student body. Administrators were also asked to recruit a small cross section of students to complete another electronic questionnaire with questions relating to what it is like to be a student at their particular institution.

The questions for students, all open-ended and requiring short essays as responses, covered topics ranging from the accessibility of professors and the quality of housing and dining facilities to the type of nightlife and weekend entertainment available in the area. By and large, students responded enthusiastically to the challenge we offered them. The quality of the information in the write-ups is a tribute to their diligence and openness. American college students, we learned, are a candid lot. They are proud of their institutions but also critical—in the positive sense of the word.

Other sources of information were also employed. Administrators were invited to send us any in-house research or other documents that would contribute to an understanding of the institution, and they were invited to comment on their write-up in the previous edition. Also, staff members have visited many of the colleges, and in some cases, additional information was solicited through published materials, such as the Common Data Set, telephone interviews, and other contacts with students and administrators.

The information from these various questionnaires was then incorporated into write-ups by staff members under the editorial direction of Edward B. Fiske, former Education Editor of the *New York Times*.

THE FORMAT

Each essay covers certain broad subjects in roughly the same order. They are as follows:

Campus setting	**Housing**
Academics	**Food**
Student body	**Social life**
Financial aid	**Extracurricular activities**

Certain topics are covered in all of the essays. The sections on academics, for example, always discuss the departments (or, in the case of large universities, schools) that are particularly strong or weak, while the sections on housing contain information on the types of accommodations offered (traditional dorms, suite- or apartment-style, single sex, gender neutral, etc.). Other topics, however, such as class size, the need for a car, or the number of volumes in the library, are mentioned only if they constitute a particular strength or weakness at that institution.

We paid particular attention to perennial and emerging issues such as underage drinking on campus, efforts by colleges to deal with growing concerns about mental health and sexual assault on campus, and initiatives aimed at increasing the socioeconomic, racial, and ethnic diversity of the student body. Also, we noted efforts that schools' administrations have been making to change or improve campus social and residential life through such measures as creating learning communities, restricting fraternities, and constructing new recreational facilities.

BEST BUYS

In the face of today's skyrocketing tuition rates, students and families in all economic circumstances are looking for ways to get the best value for their education dollar. To help out, the *Fiske Guide* has an "Index by Price" that groups public and private institutions into four price categories as well as an "Index by Average Debt" that indicates how much debt students who borrow typically incur by the time they graduate.

We also designate 20 colleges and universities—10 public and 10 private—as this year's Best Buys, institutions where it is possible for students to enjoy a quality academic experience at a relatively low cost. Most of these schools fall into the low/moderate categories for price and average debt, and their academic ratings range from three to five. Many qualify to be Best Buys because of innovative financial aid policies or a commitment to enroll a socioeconomically diverse student body. Look for the Best Buy graphic next to the college name. (An alphabetical list of all 2027 Best Buys appears on page xix.)

STATISTICS

At the beginning of each write-up are some basic statistics about the college or university—ones that are the most relevant to applicants. These include the address, type of location (urban, small town, rural, etc.), enrollment, and male/female ratio. We report the relative cost of the school, the percentage of students receiving financial aid of any kind (including loans), the percentage of students who procure loans, and the average debt incurred by students who borrowed. The percentage of incoming first-year students receiving Pell Grants is listed as an indication of the extent of socioeconomic diversity among the student body. Other statistics show the number of students who apply and the percentage of those who are accepted, the percentage of accepted students who enroll, the percentage of first-year students who graduate within six years, and the percentage of first-years who return for their sophomore year. For convenience, we include the telephone number and email address of the admissions office as well as the school's website.

Unlike some guides, we have intentionally not published figures on student/faculty ratios because colleges use wildly different—and usually self-serving—methods to calculate the ratio, thus making this particular statistic virtually meaningless.

Within the statistics, you will sometimes encounter the letters "N/A." In most cases, this means that the statistic was not available. In other cases, however, such as schools that do not accept federal financial aid or Pell Grants, it means "not applicable." The write-up should make it clear which meaning is the relevant one.

FISKE GUIDE POLICY REGARDING TEST SCORES

A special word needs to be said about the *Fiske Guide*'s policy regarding SAT and ACT test scores. For many years, the *Fiske Guide* regularly listed the range of scores for the middle half of enrolled first-year students—those between the 25th and 75th percentiles—on these tests for each college or university. We did so for two reasons: to help students assess their competitiveness as an applicant to a particular school and to give them a sense of how they might fit into the academic environment of the institution.

Several recent trends have now conspired to call into question the validity of admissions test data—and hence the reliability of using them for either purpose. Rather than publish inaccurate and misleading information, the *Fiske Guide*, beginning with the 2022 edition, has omitted any reporting of score ranges.

The most obvious recent challenge to the integrity of SAT and ACT score ranges has been the growing number of colleges that, for a variety of reasons, have stopped requiring applicants to submit test scores. Some of these schools are now "test-optional" (meaning that applicants have the choice of whether or not to submit scores), while others are "test-blind" (meaning that colleges do not look at scores even if applicants submit them). An estimated 1,800–2,000 of the 2,300 bachelor-degree-granting institutions in the U.S. fell into one of these categories. This trend was accelerated by the COVID-19 pandemic, which caused the widespread closing of testing sites and deprived hundreds of thousands of applicants of an opportunity to take the tests. With the easing of the pandemic, a number of colleges, including some of the most selective, have now reversed course and reinstated testing requirements.

After careful consideration, the *Fiske Guide* has made the decision to stop publishing test score ranges for each college and university for several reasons. First, unless the published score ranges reflect the scores of *all* first-year students, not merely those who were able to take the tests and chose to submit scores, the usefulness of these score ranges for assessing both an applicant's chances of admission and where they would fit into the academic environment of the school is seriously compromised. Incomplete and thus misleading scores serve no one's interest. Moreover, since it is likely that many students who choose not to submit test results do so because they have relatively modest scores, the result is to inflate a school's reported score ranges (something that has not gone unnoticed by schools pondering whether to go test-optional). Artificially high score ranges may also discourage students who might otherwise qualify for admission from applying in the first place. (One mitigating factor is that some test-optional colleges do request and report the test scores of all incoming first-years who took the tests after they have enrolled.)

Students applying to college in the next few years will be rightly concerned about how these trends will affect their chances of admission to a school of their choice. Such students should find comfort in the fact that since well before the pandemic, selective colleges in general have been placing less and less emphasis on test scores in making admissions decisions. Based on their own experiences, they have concluded that the combination of two other metrics—the level and consistency of applicants' high school grades and the rigor of curriculum they pursued—is by far the most reliable means to assess applicants' abilities. Increasingly, test scores, if they are referenced at all, are viewed primarily as confirmation of these other metrics.

In this context, an effective strategy for college-bound high school students seeking to estimate their admissions prospects at competitive schools would be to focus on the two factors that we know to be keys to their chances of admission: high school grades and whether they took advantage of the most challenging course offerings at their school. The *Fiske Guide* includes exclusive academic ratings for each school (see the section on Academic Ratings on page xxvii) as well as information on admissions selectivity. A school might be "highly selective" (up to 25 percent of applicants accepted) or "selective" (26 to 50 percent). Students seeking to gauge whether they would fit into the academic environment of a particular school can consult the school's write-up for information on academic advising, tutoring and mentoring programs, first-year seminars, and other programs to ease the transition to college in the first year. They can also read what students have to say about the level of competitiveness or supportiveness of fellow students. Retention and graduation rates are other useful clues.

Debate over the future role of SAT and ACT scores in college admissions—and their value for individual applicants—is playing out in the context of some broader social issues, including the extent to which admissions policies of selective colleges inadvertently perpetuate structural racism and economic inequality. Among other things, critics note preferential admissions for legacies and recruited athletes in niche sports such as lacrosse, crew, or golf that are played primarily by students from privileged backgrounds. Other suspect practices include the strategic allocating of merit scholarships to maximize tuition revenue and rapidly increasing pressure on students to apply through early decision, thereby surrendering their ability to negotiate a better financial aid package. Public discussion over these issues has been complicated by the June 2023 ruling by the U.S. Supreme Court ending the use of race and ethnicity in college admissions.

The role that SAT and ACT scores play in college admissions is at the center of these discussions. Supporters of testing requirements argue that since the tests, especially the SAT, were not curriculum-oriented, they offered colleges an independent way to identify "diamonds in the rough"—talented applicants, especially those from underrepresented racial or ethnic groups or from disadvantaged backgrounds, whose abilities might otherwise have gone unnoticed. Several previously test-optional schools that have reverted to requiring the tests have cited this as a reason. On the other hand, the enormous expansion of the $1 billion test-prep industry that has grown up around admissions tests has provided additional evidence that testing requirements give an edge on college admissions to privileged applicants with access to tutors and other sophisticated test prep, thus reducing the opportunities for those diamonds to glitter. Indeed, a wide body of research has shown that SAT and ACT scores track closely with socioeconomic data and may say more about a student's zip code than about their academic potential.

The decision to end the reporting of test score ranges in the *Fiske Guide* for the foreseeable future has been informed by all of the issues described here. How this policy might develop over the long term, however, remains to be seen, as the role of tests in the admissions process itself continues to evolve. No one knows what role the SAT and ACT will play in the "new normal" when colleges must make decisions without the benefit of testing for a majority of their applicants.

Applicants seeking information on the test score ranges of enrolled first-year students at particular schools can usually find it on the college website (search for "Common Data Set" as well as through the College Navigator feature of the National Center for Education Statistics website [www.nces.ed.gov/collegenavigator].)

For many years, the National Center for Fair and Open Testing (FairTest), a Cambridge, Massachusetts–based advocacy organization that is critical of standardized testing in general, has tracked the growth of "test-optional" colleges and universities. FairTest publishes a helpful list of such schools on its website (www.fairtest.org) that is constantly updated. **Since the test-optional field is changing daily, applicants should confirm the current policy of any school to which they are thinking of applying directly on the school's website.**

COLLEGE COSTS

Tuition and fees are constantly increasing at American colleges, but for the most part, the cost of various institutions in relation to one another does not change. Rather than put in specific cost figures that would immediately become out of date, we have classified colleges into four groups ranging from inexpensive ($) to very expensive ($$$$) based on estimated costs of tuition and fees for the 2025–2026 academic year and do not include room, board, transportation, and other expenses. The results for each college can be found in the "Index by Price" on pages xiii–xv. Separate scales were used for public and private institutions, and the ratings for the public institutions are based on the cost for residents of the state; out-of-staters should expect to pay more. If a public institution has a particularly low or high surcharge for out-of-staters, this is noted in the essay. The categories are defined as follows:

	PUBLIC	PRIVATE
$$$$	More than $14,500	More than $68,000
$$$	$12,000–$14,500	$62,000–$68,000
$$	$10,000–$12,000	$52,000–$62,000
$	Less than $10,000	Less than $52,000

In assessing the relative costs of various colleges and universities, it is important to keep in mind that the posted charges for tuition and fees are, in effect, "sticker prices." Every American who has ever walked into an automobile showroom knows that the price on the car window is not necessarily the amount they will end up paying, but rather the starting point for negotiations over matters such as trade-ins, financing terms, and so forth. The same rule applies to posted tuition and fee levels, especially at private colleges. Your cost at a particular college depends on a variety of factors, including your family's financial situation and how eager the school is for you to enroll. Some wealthy students will pay the full sticker price, but many others—often a substantial majority of others—will receive "discounts" in the form of merit- or need-based scholarships, loans, and other concessions. Likewise, students from disadvantaged backgrounds who manage to gain admission to expensive Ivy League or other elite universities can expect virtual free rides. Bottom line: Don't write off a school that you really like simply because the published sticker price looks out of reach. You might end up paying less at an expensive school eager to lure you with a generous financial aid package than you would at a school with lower tuition and fees but a smaller financial aid budget.

FINANCIAL AID

Since the first edition of the *Fiske Guide to Colleges* arrived over 40 years ago, the problems of financing college have become increasingly complex, mainly because of the seemingly relentless rise in the cost of education and some significant trends in financial aid. There has been a gradual shift from need-based to merit-based scholarships that favor middle-class students, as well as a tendency for schools to build higher loans and smaller outright grants into their financial aid packages. On the other hand, partly in response to public pressure to increase socio-economic diversity among their student bodies, a number of both public and private universities have begun to substitute grants for loans and even to eliminate tuition for low- and some middle-income students. Some colleges advertise that they are "need-blind" in their admissions, meaning that they accept or reject applicants without reference to their financial situation and also guarantee to meet the "demonstrated need" of all students whom they accept. "Demonstrated need" is itself a slippery term. In theory, the figure is determined when students and families fill out a needs-analysis form (e.g., the FAFSA and/or CSS Profile), which leads to an estimate of how much the family can afford to pay, frequently referred to as the "expected family contribution," or EFC. (Effective October 1, 2022, the FAFSA changed the term "expected family contribution" to "student aid index," or SAI.) Demonstrated need is then calculated by subtracting that figure from the cost at a particular institution.

In practice, however, what seems rather straightforward can be misleading. For one thing, colleges may make their own independent calculations about what families can afford to pay. Five different colleges may each give the same student five different numbers for what their demonstrated need is, and the differences can be significant. Some colleges say that they are need-blind in their admissions decisions but do not guarantee to provide the full financial aid required of all those who are accepted. Still others agree to meet the demonstrated need of all students, but they package their offers so that students they really want to enroll receive a higher percentage of their aid in the form of outright grants and a lower proportion in repayable loans. For example, if a school with a $50,000 annual price tag offers a financial aid package that includes $25,000 of grants and scholarships and $25,000 of "self-help" (institutional loans, Federal Direct Loans, a parent loan, or work study), that school can claim that it has met 100 percent of the student's demonstrated need, but at the end of four years, the student will still graduate with $100,000 of debt.

In order to test the sincerity of a school's promise to "meet 100 percent of demonstrated need," students might ask whether it has backed up that claim with other initiatives, such as replacing loans with grants in all financial aid packages (a welcome trend among many elite private colleges in recent years) or reducing or capping the amount of loans that families are expected to assume. Our write-ups often call attention to such initiatives. To get an idea whether the average student at a college graduates with a high amount of debt, check out our statistics on loans and debt (see "Student Loans and Average Debt Rating" on page xxvi).

Students and parents should not assume that their family's six-figure annual income automatically disqualifies them from some kind of subsidized financial aid. In cases of doubt, they should fill out a needs-analysis form to determine their eligibility. Whether they qualify or not, they may be eligible for a variety of awards made without regard to financial need.

For more information on the ever-changing financial aid scene, we suggest that you consult the companion book to this guide, the *Fiske Guide to Getting Into the Right College*.

STUDENT LOANS AND AVERAGE DEBT RATING

In today's academic climate, it is common for students and/or their families to borrow funds to assist with paying tuition and other college expenses. Therefore, a potentially useful piece of information is the proportion of students at each school who find it necessary to procure loans to finance their education. The student loan percentage considers any loan program used by students at any time during their tenure at an institution. Included are institutional, state, Federal Direct, and private loans certified by an institution, excluding parent loans. To ensure the most accurate information, schools submitted this data for students comprising their last graduating class. When available, this data was confirmed using the Common Data Set.

For a variety of reasons, the average debt carried by graduating seniors varies greatly from college to college as well as from student to student. Nevertheless, when considering a particular school, many prospective students will find it useful to know how much debt is typically incurred by students at that school. Thus the 2027 *Fiske Guide* lists the Average Debt Rating (ADR) for each school as reported in each institution's Common Data Set. The ADR is based on the average amount of principal accumulated by each undergraduate who borrowed during their tenure as a student. Using $29,500 as the median, we have organized the schools into four categories from low average debt ($) to very high average debt ($$$$). Both public and private institutions were rated using the same criteria. Institutions for which data on average borrowing was unavailable have been omitted.

DEBT RATING	AVERAGE CUMULATIVE PRINCIPAL PER UNDERGRADUATE BORROWER
$$$$	More than $35,000
$$$	$29,500–$35,000
$$	$25,000–$29,500
$	Less than $25,000

As previously noted at the end of the discussion of college costs on page xxiv–xxv, it is important when thinking about the cost of college to keep in mind your particular financial situation. Even if a school has high average debt levels, students who qualify for substantial financial aid packages may end up with little or no debt. Moreover, largely in response to the soaring cost of higher education, many U.S. colleges and universities, especially Ivy League or other elite private universities with substantial endowments, have begun replacing loans with grants in their financial aid packages—or even waiving tuition and fees entirely—for students from families whose annual incomes fall below certain levels, which can be as high as $200,000 or more. For students who qualify for such treatment, higher education can be a real bargain.

RATINGS

Much of the fierce controversy that greeted the first edition of the *Fiske Guide to Colleges* four decades ago revolved around its unique system of rating colleges in three areas: academics, social life, and quality of life. In each case, the ratings are done on a system of one to five, with three considered normal for colleges included in the *Fiske Guide*. If a college receives a rating higher or lower than three in any category, the reasons should be apparent from the narrative description of that college.

Students and parents should keep in mind that these ratings are by design general in nature and inherently subjective. No complex institution can be described in terms of a single number or other symbol, and different people will have different views of how various institutions should be rated in the three categories. The ratings should not be viewed as either precise or infallible judgments about any given college. On the other hand, the ratings are a helpful tool in using this book. The core of the *Fiske Guide* is the essays on each of the colleges, and the ratings represent a summary—an index, if you will—that flows out of the write-ups. Our hope is that each student, having decided on the kind of configuration that suits their needs, will then thumb through the book looking for other institutions with a similar set of ratings. Please note that these are **ratings**, not **rankings**. Rankings that list schools in numerical order—#1, #2, #18, #52, etc.—have an abundance of methodological and other flaws, but their overarching problem is that they purport to answer the wrong question: "What is the best college?" From the point of view of a college-bound student, the relevant question is: **"What is the best college for me?"** The three categories, defined as follows, are academics, social life, and quality of life.

Academics ✍

This is a judgment about the overall academic climate of the institution, including its standing in the academic world, the quality of the faculty, the level of teaching and research, the academic ability of students, the quality of libraries and other facilities, and the level of academic seriousness among students and faculty members.

Although the same basic criteria have been applied to all institutions, it should be evident that an outstanding small liberal arts college will by definition differ significantly from an outstanding major public university. No one would expect the former to have massive library facilities, but one would look for a high-quality faculty that combines research with a good deal of attention to the individual needs of students. Likewise, public universities, because of their implicit commitment to serving a broad cross section of society, might have a broader range of curriculum offerings but somewhat lower retention and graduation rates than a large private counterpart. Readers may find the ratings most useful when comparing colleges and universities of the same type.

In general, an academics rating of three pens suggests that the institution is a solid one that easily meets the criteria for inclusion in a guide devoted to the "best and most interesting" colleges and universities in the nation. An academics rating of four pens suggests that the institution is above average even by these standards and that it has some particularly distinguishing academic feature, such as especially rich course offerings or an especially serious academic atmosphere. A rating of five pens for academics indicates that the college or university is among the handful of top institutions of its type in the nation by a broad variety of criteria. Those in the private sector will attract academically high-achieving students, and those in the public sector are invariably magnets for the top students in their states. All can be assumed to have outstanding faculties and other academic resources.

In response to the suggestion that the range of colleges within a single category has been too broad, we have introduced some half steps into the ratings.

Social Life 💬

This is primarily a judgment about the *amount* of social life that is readily available. A rating of three chat bubbles suggests a typical college social life, while four chat bubbles means that students devote an above-average amount of time to socializing. It can be assumed that a college with a rating of five is something of a party school, which may or may not detract from the academic quality. Colleges with a rating below three have some impediment to a strong social life, such as geographic isolation, a high percentage of commuting students, or a disproportionate number of nerds who never leave the library. Once again, the reason should be evident from the write-up.

Quality of Life ★

This category grew out of the fact that schools with good academic credentials and plenty of social life may not, for one reason or another, be particularly wholesome places to spend four years. The term "quality of life" is one that has gained currency in social science circles, and, in most cases, the rating for a particular college will be similar to the academic and/or social ratings. The reader, though, should be alert to exceptions to this pattern. A liberal arts college, for example, might attract bright students who study hard during the week and party hard on weekends and thus earn high ratings for both academics and social life. If the academic pressure is cutthroat rather than constructive, though, and the social system is exclusive or elitist, this college might get an apparently anomalous two stars for quality of life. By contrast, a small college with modest academic programs and relatively few organized social opportunities might have developed a strong sense of supportive community, have a beautiful campus, and be located near a wonderful city—and thus be rated four stars for quality of life. As in the other categories, the reason can be found in the essay to which the ratings point.

OVERLAPS

Most colleges and universities operate within fairly defined "niche markets." That is, they compete for students against other institutions with whom they share important characteristics, such as academic quality, a particular religious or other mission, size, geographic location, and the overall tone and style of campus life. Not surprisingly, students who apply to College X also tend to apply to the other institutions—often referred to as "peer institutions"—in its particular niche. For example, "alternative" colleges such as Bard, Bennington, Hampshire, Oberlin, Reed, and Sarah Lawrence share many common applications, as do those with an evangelical flavor, such as Calvin, Gordon, and Wheaton (IL).

As a service to readers, we ask each school to give us the names of the colleges or universities that they consider to be their closest peer institutions and those with which they share the most common applications, and these are listed in the "Overlaps" section at the end of each write-up. We encourage students who know they are interested in a particular school to check out its peer institutions—and perhaps then check out the "overlaps of the overlaps." This method of systematic browsing should yield a list of 15 or 20 schools that, based on the behavior of thousands of past applicants, would constitute a good starting point for your college search.

IF YOU APPLY TO

Another helpful feature is the "If You Apply To" section at the end of each write-up. This is designed for students who become seriously interested in a particular college and want to know more specifics about what it takes to get in. It lists the admissions plans that the school offers: early decision, early action, and/or regular decision. If the college operates on a rolling-admissions basis—making decisions as the applications are received—this is also indicated.

The "If You Apply To" section advises students to check the school's website for the most up-to-date information regarding standardized test requirements. Additionally, we indicate whether the school accepts the Common Application and include information on any special instructions or unique components of the application that may be pertinent for students to know about.

For additional details about the application process, including ever-changing application deadlines, students should consult schools' websites, which will always contain the most complete and up-to-date information.

TIME TO RELAX

Students will find the *Fiske Guide* useful at various points in the college selection process—from deciding whether to visit a particular campus to comparing the institutions where they have been accepted. To make it easy to find a particular college, the write-ups are arranged in alphabetical order in the indexes. An "Index by State and Country," the "Index by Price," and the "Index by Average Debt" can be found on pages ix, xiii, and xvi, respectively.

While few people are likely to start reading at Adelphi and keep going until they reach Yale (though some tell us they did), we encourage you to browse. This country has an enormously rich and varied network of colleges and universities. There are dozens of institutions out there that can meet the needs of any particular student. Too many students approach the college selection process wearing blinders, limiting their sights to local institutions, the pet schools of their guidance counselors, or a parent's alma mater.

But applicants need not be bound by such limitations. Once you have decided on the type of school you think you want—a small liberal arts college, an engineering school, or whatever—we hope you will thumb through the book looking for similar institutions that might not have caught your eye. As already noted, one way to do this is to look at the overlaps of schools you like and then check out those schools' overlaps. Many students have found this exercise worthwhile, and quite frankly, we view the widening of students' horizons about American higher education as one of the most important purposes of this book. Perhaps the most gratifying remark we hear comes when students tell us, as many have, that they are attending a school that they first heard about while browsing through the *Fiske Guide to Colleges*.

Picking a college is a tricky business. But given the diversity and richness of U.S. higher education, there is no reason why you should not be able to find the right one *for you*. That's what the *Fiske Guide to Colleges* is designed to help you do. Happy college hunting!

COLLEGE ADMISSION PLEDGES

The college admissions process can be stressful for students and family members alike. For some lighthearted relief, we invite you to check out our fanciful College Admissions Pledges on pages 817–18. Enjoy!

Sizing Yourself Up

The college search is a game of matchmaking. You have interests and needs; the colleges have programs to meet those needs. If all goes according to plan, you'll find the right one and live happily ever after—or at least for four years. It ought to be simple, but today's admissions process resembles a high-stakes obstacle course.

Many colleges are more interested in making a sale than they are in making a match. Under intense competitive pressure, many won't hesitate to sell you a bill of goods if they can get their hands on your tuition dollars. Guidance counselors generally mean well, but they are often under pressure to steer students toward prestigious schools regardless of whether the fit is right. Your friends won't be shy with advice on where to go, but their knowledge is generally limited to a small group of hot colleges that everyone is talking about. National publications rake in millions by playing on the public's fascination with rankings, but a close look at their criteria reveals that they are, for all practical purposes, measures of institutional wealth.

Before you find yourself spinning headlong on this merry-go-round, take a step back. This is your life and your college career. What are you looking for in a college? Think hard and don't answer right away. Before you throw yourself and your life history on the mercy of college admissions officers, you need to take some time to objectively and honestly evaluate your needs, likes and dislikes, strengths and weaknesses. What do you have to offer a college? What can a college do for you? Unlike the high school selection process, which is usually predetermined by your home address, family income, or religious affiliation, picking a college isn't a procedure you can brush off on your parents or guardians. You have to take some initiative. You're the best judge of how well each school fits your personal needs and academic goals.

We encourage you to view the college selection process as the first semester in your higher education. Life's transitions often call for extra energy and focus. The college search is no exception. For the first time, you'll be contemplating a life away from home that can unfold in any direction you choose. Visions of majors and careers will dance in your head as you sample various institutions of higher learning, each with hundreds of millions of dollars in academic resources; it is hard to imagine a better hands-on seminar in research and matchmaking than the college search. The main impact, however, will be measured by what you learn about yourself. Piqued by new worlds of learning and tested by the competition of the admissions process, you'll be pushed as never before to show your accomplishments, clarify your interests, and chart a course for the future. More than one parent has watched in amazement as an erstwhile teenager suddenly emerged as an adult during the course of a college tour. Be ready when your time comes.

DEVELOP YOUR CRITERIA

One strategy is to begin the search with a personal inventory of your own strengths and weaknesses and your "wish list" for a college. This method tends to work well for compulsive list makers and other highly organized people. What sorts of things are you especially good at? Do you have a list of skills or interests that you would like to explore further? What sort of personality are you looking for in a college? Mainstream? Conservative? Offbeat? What about extracurriculars? If you are really into riding horses, you might include a strong equestrian program in your criteria. The main problem won't be thinking of qualities to look for—you could probably name dozens—but rather figuring out what criteria should play a defining role in your search. Serious students should think carefully about the intellectual climate they are seeking. At some schools, students routinely stay up until 3 a.m. discussing the value of deconstructing literary texts or the pros and cons of free trade. These same students would be viewed as geeks or weirdos on less cosmopolitan campuses. Athletes should take a hard look at whether they really want to play college ball and, if so, whether they want to go for an athletic scholarship or play at the less-pressured Division III level, where athletic prowess can give you an edge in getting accepted. Either way, intercollegiate sports require a huge time commitment.

Young women have an opportunity all to themselves—the chance to study at a women's college. The *Fiske Guide* profiles 10 such campuses, a vastly underappreciated resource on today's higher education scene. With small classes and strong encouragement from faculty, students at women's colleges move on to graduate study in significantly higher numbers than their counterparts at co-ed schools, especially in the natural sciences. Young men seeking an all-male experience will find four options in the *Fiske Guide*.

Students with a firm career goal will want to look for a course of study that matches their needs. If you want to major in aerospace engineering, your search will be limited to schools that have the program. Outside of specialized areas like this, many applicants overestimate the importance of their anticipated major in choosing a college. If you're interested in a liberal arts field, your expected major should probably have little to do with your college selection. A big purpose of college is to develop interests and set goals. Most students change their intentions regarding a major at least two or three times before graduation, and once out in the working world, they often end up in jobs bearing no relation to their academic specialty. Even those with a firm career goal may not need as much specialization as they think at the undergraduate level. If you want to be a lawyer, don't worry yourself looking for something labeled "prelaw." Follow your interests, get the best liberal arts education available, and then apply to law school.

Naturally, it is never a bad idea to check out the department(s) of any likely major, and occasionally your choice of major will suggest a direction for your search. If you're really into national politics, it may make sense to look at some schools in or near Washington, D.C. If you think you're interested in a relatively specialized field, say, oceanography, then be sure to look for some colleges that are a good match for you and also have programs in oceanography. But for the most part, rumors about top-ranked departments in this or that should be no more than a tie breaker between schools you like for more important reasons. There are good professors (and bad ones) in any department. You'll have plenty of time to figure out who is who once you've enrolled. Being undecided about your career path as a senior in high school is often a sign of intelligence. Don't feel bad if you have absolutely no idea what you're going to do when you "grow up." One of the reasons you'll be paying megabucks to the college of your choice is the prospect that it will expand your horizons and introduce you to fields that you never knew existed. Instead of worrying about particular departments, try to keep the focus on big-picture items, such as: What's the academic climate? How big are the first-year classes? Do I like it here? Are these my kind of people?

KEEP AN OPEN MIND

The biggest mistake of beginning applicants is hyperchoosiness. At the extreme is the "perfect-school syndrome," which comes in two basic forms.

In one category are the applicants who refuse to consider any school that doesn't have every little thing they want in a college. If you're one who begins the process with a detailed picture of Perfect U in mind, you may want to remember the oft-quoted advice, "Two out of three ain't bad." If a college seems to have most of the qualities you seek, give it a chance. You may come to realize that some things you thought were absolutely essential are really not that crucial after all.

The other strain of perfect-school syndrome is the applicant who gets stuck on a "dream" school at the beginning and then won't look anywhere else. With those 2,300 four-year colleges out there (not counting those in Canada and Great Britain), it is just a bit silly to insist that only one will meet your needs. Having a first choice is OK, but the whole purpose of the search is to consider new options and uncover new possibilities. A student who has only one dream school—especially if it is a highly selective one—could be headed for disappointment.

As you begin the college search, don't expect any quick revelations. The answers will unfold in due time. Our advice? Be patient. Set priorities. Keep an open mind. Reexamine priorities. Again, be patient.

To get the ball rolling, move on to the Sizing-Yourself-Up Survey.

FISKE'S SIZING-YOURSELF-UP SURVEY

With apologies to Socrates, knowing thyself is easier said than done. Most high school students can analyze a differential equation or a Shakespearean play with the greatest of ease, but when it comes to cataloging their own strengths, weaknesses, likes, and dislikes, many draw a blank. But self-knowledge is crucial to the matching process at the heart of a successful college search. The 30-item survey on the next page offers a simple way to get a handle on some crucial issues in college selection and what sort of college may fit your preferences.

In the space beside each statement, rate your feelings on a scale of 1 to 10, with 10 = Strongly Agree, 1 = Strongly Disagree, and 5 = Not Sure/Don't Have Strong Feelings. (For instance, a rating of 7 would mean that you agree with the statement, but that the issue is a lower priority than those you rated 8, 9, or 10.) After you're done, read on to "Grading Yourself" to find out what it all means.

FISKE'S SIZING-YOURSELF-UP SURVEY

Size

_____ 1. I enjoy participating in many activities.

_____ 2. I would like to have a prominent place in my community.

_____ 3. Individual attention from teachers is important to me.

_____ 4. I learn best when I can speak out in class and ask questions.

_____ 5. I am undecided about what I will study.

_____ 6. I want to earn a Ph.D. in my chosen field of study.

_____ 7. I learn best by listening and writing down what I hear.

_____ 8. I would like to be in a place where I can be anonymous if I choose.

_____ 9. I prefer devoting my time to one or two activities rather than many.

_____ 10. I want to attend a college that most people have heard of.

_____ 11. I am interested in a career-oriented major.

_____ 12. I like to be on my own.

Location

_____ 13. I prefer a college in a warm or hot climate.

_____ 14. I prefer a college in a cool or cold climate.

_____ 15. I want to be near the mountains.

_____ 16. I want to be near a lake or ocean.

_____ 17. I prefer to attend a college in a particular state or region.

_____ 18. I prefer to attend a college near my family.

_____ 19. I want city life within walking distance of my campus.

_____ 20. I want city life within driving distance of my campus.

_____ 21. I want my campus to be surrounded by natural beauty.

Academics and Extracurriculars

_____ 22. I like to be surrounded by people who are freethinkers and nonconformists.

_____ 23. I like the idea of joining a fraternity or sorority.

_____ 24. I like rubbing shoulders with people who are bright and talented.

_____ 25. I like being one of the smartest people in my class.

_____ 26. I want to go to a prestigious college.

_____ 27. I want to go to a college where I can get an excellent education.

_____ 28. I want to try for an academic scholarship.

_____ 29. I want a diverse college.

_____ 30. I want a college where the students are serious about ideas.

Grading Yourself

Picking a college is not an exact science. People who are total opposites can be equally happy at the same college. Nevertheless, particular types tend to do better at some colleges than others. Each item in the survey is designed to test your feelings on an important issue related to college selection. "Sizing Up the Survey" (below) offers commentary on each item.

Taken together, your responses may help you construct a tentative blueprint for your college search. Statements 1–12 deal with the issue of size. Would you be happier at a large university or a small college? Here's the trick: Add the sum of your responses to questions 1–6. Then make a second tally of your responses to 7–12. If the sum of 1–6 is larger, you may want to consider a small college. If 7–12 is greater, then perhaps a big school would be more to your liking. If the totals are roughly equal, you should probably consider colleges of various sizes.

Statements 13–21 deal with location. The key in this section is the intensity of your feeling. If you replied to number 13 with a 10, does that mean you are going to look only at schools in warm climates? Think hard. If you consider only schools within a certain region or state, you'll be eliminating hundreds of possibilities. By examining your most intense responses—the 1s, 2s, 9s, and 10s—you'll be able to create a geographic profile of likely options.

Statements 22–30 deal with big-picture issues related to the character and personality of the college that may be in your future. As before, pay attention to your most intense responses. Read on for a look at the significance of each question.

SIZING UP THE SURVEY

1. **I enjoy participating in many activities.** Students at small colleges tend to have more opportunities to be involved in many activities. Fewer students means less competition for spots.

2. **I would like to have a prominent place in my community.** Student council presidents and other would-be leaders take note: It is easier to be a big fish if you're swimming in a small pond.

3. **Individual attention from teachers is important to me.** Small colleges generally offer more one-on-one with faculty in both the classroom and the laboratory.

4. **I learn best when I can speak out in class and ask questions.** Students who learn from interaction and participation would be well-advised to consider a small college.

5. **I am undecided about what I will study.** Small colleges generally offer more guidance and support to students who are undecided. The exception: students who are considering a preprofessional or highly specialized major.

6. **I want to earn a Ph.D. in my chosen field of study.** A higher percentage of students at selective small colleges earn a Ph.D. than those who attend large institutions of similar quality.

7. **I learn best by listening and writing down what I hear.** Students who prefer lecture courses will find more of them at large institutions.

8. **I would like to be in a place where I can be anonymous if I choose.** At a large university, the supply of new faces is never-ending. Students who have the initiative can always reinvent themselves.

9. **I prefer devoting my time to one or two activities rather than many.** Students who are passionate about one activity—say, writing for the college newspaper—will often find higher quality at a bigger school.

10. **I want to attend a college that most people have heard of.** Big schools have more name recognition because they're bigger and have Division I athletic programs. Even the finest small colleges are relatively anonymous among the general public.

11. **I am interested in a career-oriented major.** More large institutions offer business, engineering, nursing, etc., though some excellent small institutions do so as well (depending on the field).

12. **I like to be on my own.** A higher percentage of students live off campus at large schools, which are more likely to be in urban areas than their smaller counterparts.

13. **I prefer a college in a warm or hot climate.** Keep in mind that the Southeast and the Southwest have far different personalities (not to mention humidity levels).

14. **I prefer a college in a cool or cold climate.** Consider the Midwest, where there are many fine schools that are notably less selective than those in the Northeast.

15. **I want to be near the mountains.** You're probably thinking Colorado or Vermont, but don't zero in too quickly. States from Maine to Georgia and Arkansas to Arizona have easy access to mountains.

16. **I want to be near a lake or ocean.** Oceans are only on the coasts, but keep in mind the Great Lakes, the Finger Lakes, etc. Think about whether you want to be on the water or, say, within a two-hour drive.

17. **I prefer to attend a college in a particular state or region.** Geographical blinders limit options. Even if you think you want a certain area of the country, consider at least one college located elsewhere just to be sure.

18. **I prefer to attend a college near my family.** Unless you're planning to live with your parents or guardians, it may not matter whether your college is a two-hour drive or a two-hour plane ride.

19. **I want city life within walking distance of my campus.** Check out the neighborhood(s) surrounding your campus. Urban campuses—even in the same city—can be wildly different.

20. **I want city life within driving distance of my campus.** Unless you're a hard-core urban dweller, a suburban perch near a city may beat living in the thick of one. Does public transportation or a campus shuttle help students get around?

21. **I want my campus to be surrounded by natural beauty.** A college viewbook will take you only so far. To really know if you'll fall in love with the campus, visiting is a must.

22. **I like to be surrounded by people who are freethinkers and nonconformists.** Plenty of schools cater specifically to students who buck the mainstream. Talk to your counselor or browse the *Fiske Guide to Colleges* to find some.

23. **I like the idea of joining a fraternity or sorority.** Greek life is strongest at mainstream and conservative-leaning schools. Find out if there is a split between Greeks and non-Greeks.

24. **I like rubbing shoulders with people who are bright and talented.** This is perhaps the best reason to aim for a highly selective institution, especially if you're the type who rises to the level of the competition.

25. **I like being one of the smartest people in my class.** If so, maybe you should skip the highly selective rat race. Star students get the best a college has to offer.

26. **I want to go to a prestigious college.** There is nothing wrong with wanting prestige. Think honestly about how badly you want a big-name school and act accordingly.

27. **I want to go to a college where I can get an excellent education.** Throw out the *U.S. News* rankings and think about which colleges will best meet your needs as a student.

28. **I want to try for an academic scholarship.** Students in this category should consider less-selective alternatives. Scholarships are more likely if you rank high in the applicant pool.

29. **I want a diverse college.** All colleges pay lip service to diversity. To get the truth, see the campus for yourself and take a hard look at the student-body statistics in the *Fiske Guide*'s write-ups.

30. **I want a college where the students are serious about ideas.** Don't assume that a college necessarily attracts true intellectuals merely because it is highly selective. Some top schools are known for their intellectual climate—and others for their lack of it.

A Guide for Preprofessionals

The lists that follow include colleges and universities with unusual strength in each of nine preprofessional areas: architecture, art/design, business, communications/journalism, engineering, film/television, dance, drama, and music. We also offer lists covering two of today's hottest interdisciplinary majors: environmental studies/science and international studies. In compiling the lists, we drew on data from the thousands of surveys used to compile the *Fiske Guide*. We examined the strongest majors at each college as reported in student and administrative questionnaires and then weighed these against the selectivity and overall academic quality of each institution. After compiling tentative lists in each subject, we queried our counselors advisory group, listed on page 813, for additional suggestions and feedback. To make the lists as useful as possible, we have included some schools that do not receive full-length write-ups in the *Fiske Guide*. Moreover, while the lists are suggestive, they are by no means all-inclusive, and there are other institutions in the *Fiske Guide* that offer fine programs in these areas. Nevertheless, we hope the lists will be a starting place for students interested in these fields.

If you are planning a career in one of the subjects in this section, your college search may focus largely on finding the best programs for you in that particular area. But we also recommend that you shop for a school that will give you an adequate dose of liberal arts. For that matter, you might consider a double major (or minor) in a liberal arts field to complement your area of technical expertise. If you allow yourself to get too specialized too soon, you may end up as tomorrow's equivalent of the typewriter repairman. In a rapidly changing job market, nothing is so practical as the ability to read, write, and think.

ARCHITECTURE
Private Universities Strong in Architecture
Carnegie Mellon University
Case Western Reserve University
The Catholic University of America
The Cooper Union
Cornell University
Drexel University
Howard University
Illinois Institute of Technology
Massachusetts Institute of Technology
University of Miami (FL)
Northeastern University
University of Notre Dame
Princeton University
Rensselaer Polytechnic Institute
Rice University
University of Southern California
Syracuse University
Tulane University
Tuskegee University
Washington University in St. Louis

Public Universities Strong in Architecture
University of Arizona
Arizona State University
University of Arkansas
Auburn University
UC Berkeley
California Polytechnic State University–San Luis Obispo
Clemson University
Georgia Institute of Technology
University of Illinois at Urbana–Champaign
University of Kansas
Kansas State University
Miami University (OH)
University of Michigan
North Carolina State University
University of Oregon
SUNY–University at Buffalo
University of Tennessee Knoxville
University of Texas at Austin
Virginia Tech
University of Washington

Arts-Oriented Architecture Programs
Barnard College
Bennington College
Hobart and William Smith Colleges
Pratt Institute
Rhode Island School of Design
Yale University

ART/DESIGN
Top Schools of Art and Design
Art Center College of Design
School of the Art Institute of Chicago
California College of the Arts
California Institute of the Arts
The Cooper Union
Kansas City Art Institute
Maryland Institute College of Art
Massachusetts College of Art and Design
Moore College of Art and Design
School of the Museum of Fine Arts (MA)
University of North Carolina School of the Arts
Otis College of Art and Design
Parsons School of Design
Pratt Institute
Rhode Island School of Design
Ringling College of Art and Design
San Francisco Art Institute

Large Universities Strong in Art or Design
Arizona State University
UC Davis
UC Irvine

UC Los Angeles
Carnegie Mellon University
Cornell University
DePaul University
Drexel University
Florida State University
The George Washington
   University
University of Kansas
University of Michigan
University of New Mexico
New York University
The Ohio State University
University of Oregon
Rochester Institute of
   Technology
University of Southern California
Southern Methodist University
Syracuse University
Texas Christian University
Washington University in
   St. Louis
Yale University

**Small Colleges and Universities
Strong in Art or Design**

Alfred University
University of the Arts (PA)
Bard College
Barnard College
Bennington College
Carleton College
Centre College
Champlain College
Emerson College
Eugene Lang College of Liberal
   Arts
Hampshire College
Loyola University New Orleans
University of North Carolina
   Asheville
Sarah Lawrence College
Scripps College
Skidmore College
Smith College
Southwestern University
Purchase College, SUNY
Vassar College
Westmont College
Wheaton College (MA)
Williams College

BUSINESS

**Large Private Universities
Strong in Business**

American University
Baylor University
Boston College
Boston University
Brigham Young University
Carnegie Mellon University
Case Western Reserve University
Chapman University
Cornell University
University of Denver
DePaul University
Drexel University
Elon University
Emory University
Fordham University
The George Washington University
Georgetown University
Gonzaga University
Hofstra University
Howard University
Lehigh University
Loyola Marymount University
Marquette University
Massachusetts Institute of Technology
University of Miami (FL)
New York University
Northeastern University
University of Notre Dame
University of the Pacific
University of Pennsylvania
Pepperdine University
Rensselaer Polytechnic Institute
Saint Louis University
University of San Diego
Santa Clara University
Seattle University
University of Southern California
Southern Methodist University
Syracuse University
Texas Christian University
Villanova University
Wake Forest University
Washington University in St. Louis

**Public Universities Strong
in Business**

University of Arizona
University of Arkansas

UC Berkeley
University of Colorado Boulder
University of Connecticut
University of Florida
Florida State University
University of Georgia
University of Illinois at Urbana–
   Champaign
Indiana University
University of Iowa
James Madison University
University of Maryland
University of Massachusetts Amherst
Miami University (OH)
University of Michigan
Michigan State University
University of Minnesota
University of New Hampshire
University of North Carolina at
   Chapel Hill
North Carolina State University
The Ohio State University
University of Oregon
Pennsylvania State University
Purdue University
Queen's University (Can)
University of South Carolina
SUNY–University at Albany
SUNY–Binghamton University
SUNY–University at Buffalo
University of Tennessee Knoxville
University of Texas at Austin
Texas A&M University
University of Utah
University of Virginia
Virginia Tech
University of Washington
William & Mary
University of Wisconsin–Madison

**Small Colleges and Universities
Strong in Business**

Austin College
Babson College
Bentley University
Bucknell University
Butler University
Clarkson University
Cornell College
DePauw University
Fairfield University

Franklin & Marshall College
Furman University
Guilford College
Illinois Wesleyan University
Ithaca College
Lake Forest College
Loyola University Maryland
Millsaps College
Morehouse College
Oglethorpe University
Ohio Wesleyan University
Providence College
University of Redlands
University of Richmond
College of Saint Benedict and
    Saint John's University
Skidmore College
Stetson University
Susquehanna University
Trinity University (TX)
Washington and Lee University
Westmont College
Wofford College

COMMUNICATIONS/ JOURNALISM
Private Colleges and Universities Strong in Communications/Journalism
American University
Boston University
DePauw University
Elon University
Emerson College
Fordham University
The George Washington
    University
Hofstra University
Howard University
Ithaca College
Loyola University New Orleans
New York University
Northeastern University
Northwestern University
University of Pennsylvania
Pepperdine University
Quinnipiac University
University of San Francisco
University of Southern California
Stanford University
Syracuse University

Texas Christian University
Washington and Lee University

Public Universities Strong in Communications/Journalism
University of Alabama
Arizona State University
University of Florida
University of Georgia
University of Illinois at Urbana–
    Champaign
Indiana University
University of Kansas
University of Maryland
University of Missouri
University of Nebraska–Lincoln
University of North Carolina at
    Chapel Hill
Ohio University
University of Oregon
University of Texas at Austin
University of Wisconsin–Madison

ENGINEERING
Top Technical Institutes
California Institute of Technology
California Polytechnic State
    University–San Luis Obispo
Colorado School of Mines
The Cooper Union
Florida Institute of Technology
Georgia Institute of Technology
Illinois Institute of Technology
Massachusetts Institute of
    Technology
Michigan Technological University
New Mexico Institute of Mining and
    Technology
Rensselaer Polytechnic Institute
Rochester Institute of Technology
Rose–Hulman Institute of Technology
Stevens Institute of Technology
Worcester Polytechnic Institute

Large Private Universities Strong in Engineering
Boston University
Brigham Young University
Brown University
Carnegie Mellon University
Case Western Reserve University

Columbia University
Cornell University
Dartmouth College
University of Denver
Drexel University
Duke University
The George Washington University
Gonzaga University
Howard University
The Johns Hopkins University
Lehigh University
Loyola Marymount University
Northeastern University
Northwestern University
University of Notre Dame
University of the Pacific
University of Pennsylvania
Princeton University
Rice University
University of Rochester
Saint Louis University
Santa Clara University
University of Southern California
Stanford University
Tufts University
Vanderbilt University
Villanova University
Washington University in St. Louis
Yale University

Public Universities Strong in Engineering
University of Arizona
Arizona State University
Auburn University
UC Berkeley
UC Davis
UC Irvine
UC Los Angeles
UC San Diego
UC Santa Barbara
Clemson University
University of Colorado Boulder
University of Connecticut
University of Delaware
University of Florida
University of Illinois at Urbana–
    Champaign
Iowa State University
University of Kansas
University of Maryland

University of Maryland, Baltimore County
University of Massachusetts Amherst
McGill University (Can)
University of Michigan
University of Minnesota
University of New Hampshire
New Jersey Institute of Technology
North Carolina State University
The Ohio State University
University of Oklahoma
Oregon State University
Pennsylvania State University
University of Pittsburgh
Purdue University
Queen's University (Can)
SUNY–Binghamton University
SUNY–University at Buffalo
SUNY–Stony Brook University
University of Tennessee Knoxville
University of Texas at Austin
University of Texas at Dallas
Texas A&M University
Texas Tech University
University of Toronto (Can)
University of Utah
University of Virginia
Virginia Tech
University of Washington
University of Waterloo (Can)
University of Wisconsin–Madison

Small Colleges and Universities Strong in Engineering

Alfred University
Bradley University
Bucknell University
Calvin University
Clarkson University
Harvey Mudd College
Lafayette College
Loyola University Maryland
Olin College of Engineering
Smith College
Swarthmore College
Trinity College (CT)
Trinity University (TX)
University of Tulsa
Tuskegee University
Union College

FILM/TELEVISION
Large Universities Strong in Film/Television

Boston College
UC Los Angeles
Chapman University
DePaul University
Drexel University
Elon University
Florida State University
Fordham University
Hofstra University
Indiana University
The Johns Hopkins University
Loyola Marymount University
University of Michigan
New York University
Northwestern University
Pennsylvania State University
Quinnipiac University
Rochester Institute of Technology
University of Southern California
Syracuse University
University of Texas at Austin

Small Colleges and Universities Strong in Film/Television

Bard College
California Institute of the Arts
Champlain College
Columbia College (CA)
Columbia College (IL)
Emerson College
Hampshire College
Hollins University
Ithaca College
Loyola University New Orleans
Occidental College
Rhode Island School of Design
Sarah Lawrence College
Purchase College, SUNY
Vassar College
Wesleyan University

PERFORMING ARTS—DANCE
Large Universities Strong in Dance

Arizona State University
UC Irvine
UC Los Angeles
Chapman University

Duke University
Florida State University
Fordham University
Indiana University
University of Iowa
New York University
The Ohio State University
University of Oregon
University of Southern California
Southern Methodist University
Texas Christian University
University of Utah

Small Colleges and Universities Strong in Dance

University of the Arts (PA)
Barnard College
Beloit College
Bennington College
Butler University
Connecticut College
Emerson College
Goucher College
Grinnell College
Hollins University
The Juilliard School
University of North Carolina School of the Arts
Oberlin College
St. Olaf College
Sarah Lawrence College
Skidmore College
Smith College
Purchase College, SUNY

PERFORMING ARTS—DRAMA
Large Universities Strong in Drama

Adelphi University
Boston University
Brandeis University
UC Irvine
UC Los Angeles
Carnegie Mellon University
Chapman University
DePaul University
Elon University
Florida State University
Fordham University
University of Iowa
Loyola Marymount University

University of Maryland, Baltimore
County
University of Minnesota
New York University
Northwestern University
University of Southern California
Southern Methodist University
Syracuse University
Texas Christian University
University of Washington
Yale University

Small Colleges and Universities Strong in Drama

Beloit College
Bennington College
Columbia College (IL)
Connecticut College
Cornell College
Denison University
Drew University
Emerson College
Eugene Lang College of Liberal Arts
Grinnell College
Hollins University
Illinois Wesleyan University
Ithaca College
The Juilliard School
Kenyon College
Knox College
Muhlenberg College
University of North Carolina School
of the Arts
Oglethorpe University
Otterbein University
Rollins College
Sarah Lawrence College
Skidmore College
Purchase College, SUNY
Vassar College
Wabash College
Wheaton College (IL)
Willamette University

PERFORMING ARTS—MUSIC
Top Music Conservatories

Berklee College of Music
California Institute of the Arts
Cleveland Institute of Music
Curtis Institute of Music
The Juilliard School

Manhattan School of Music
New England Conservatory
University of North Carolina
School of the Arts
Peabody Conservatory
San Francisco Conservatory
of Music

Large Universities Strong in Music

University of Alabama
Arizona State University
Brandeis University
UC Irvine
UC Los Angeles
Carnegie Mellon University
Case Western Reserve University
Chapman University
University of Cincinnati
University of Colorado Boulder
University of Denver
Florida State University
Indiana University
University of Iowa
Johns Hopkins University
University of Miami (FL)
University of Michigan
University of Nebraska–Lincoln
New York University
University of North Texas
Northwestern University
University of Oregon
Rice University
University of Rochester
University of Southern California
Southern Methodist University
Texas Tech University
University of Toronto (Can)
Vanderbilt University
Yale University

Small Colleges and Universities Strong in Music

Bard College
Bennington College
Carleton College
The Catholic University of America
Denison University
DePauw University
Gettysburg College
Gustavus Adolphus College

Illinois Wesleyan University
Ithaca College
Lawrence University*
Loyola University New Orleans
University of North Carolina
Asheville
Oberlin College*
University of Redlands
College of Saint Benedict and
Saint John's University
St. Mary's College of Maryland
St. Olaf College
Sarah Lawrence College
Scripps College
Skidmore College
Smith College
Purchase College, SUNY
Stetson University
Wesleyan University
Westmont College
Wheaton College (IL)
Wittenberg University

* These two schools are unusual because
they combine a world-class conservatory
with a top-notch liberal arts college.

ENVIRONMENTAL STUDIES/ SCIENCE

Allegheny College
American University
College of the Atlantic
Bard College
Bates College
Bowdoin College
Brown University
Bucknell University
UC Davis
UC Santa Barbara
UC Santa Cruz
Carleton College
University of Chicago
Clark University
Clarkson University
Colby College
Colgate University
University of Colorado Boulder
Colorado College
Connecticut College
Cornell University
Dartmouth College

Dickinson College
Eckerd College
The Evergreen State College
Florida Institute of Technology
Juniata College
McGill University (Can)
Middlebury College
University of Minnesota Morris
Mount Holyoke College
University of New Hampshire
University of North Carolina
  Asheville
Oberlin College
University of Oregon
Pitzer College
Prescott College
St. Lawrence University
Santa Clara University
University of the South (Sewanee)
Southwestern University
Stanford University
SUNY College of Environmental
  Science and Forestry
Purchase College, SUNY
Tulane University
University of Vermont
Warren Wilson College
University of Washington
Washington College

Wesleyan University
Whitman College
Williams College

INTERNATIONAL STUDIES
Allegheny College
American University
Boston College
Brandeis University
UC Santa Barbara
Carleton College
University of Chicago
Claremont McKenna College
Clark University
Colby College
Colorado State University
Connecticut College
University of Denver
Dickinson College
Drew University
Earlham College
Eckerd College
University of Edinburgh (UK)
The George Washington University
Georgetown University
University of Georgia
Goucher College
The Johns Hopkins University
Kalamazoo College

Lewis & Clark College
Macalester College
Middlebury College
University of Mississippi
Mount Holyoke College
New York University
University of North Carolina at
  Chapel Hill
Occidental College
University of the Pacific
Pomona College
Princeton University
University of Puget Sound
Rhodes College
University of Richmond
University of St Andrews (UK)
University of South Carolina
Stanford University
University of Toronto (Can)
Trinity College Dublin (Ire)
Tufts University
Tulane University
University of Utah
Vassar College
University of Virginia
William & Mary
The College of Wooster

Learning Disabilities

Accommodation for students with learning disabilities is one of the fastest-growing academic areas in higher education. Colleges and universities recognize that a significant segment of the population may be dealing with issues that qualify as learning disabilities, and the range of support services offered to such students is increasing. Assistance ranges from counseling services to accommodations such as tapes of lectures or extended time on exams.

Following are two lists—the first of major universities, the second of smaller colleges—that offer particularly strong services for LD students. If you qualify for such support, you should be diligent in checking out the services at each college on your list. If possible, pay a visit to the LD support office or have a phone conversation with one of the administrators. Since many such programs depend on the expertise of one or two people, the quality of the services can change abruptly with changes in staff.

Keep in mind also that many colleges are becoming increasingly skeptical of requests for LD services, especially when the initial diagnosis is made on the eve of the college search.

STRONG SUPPORT FOR STUDENTS WITH LEARNING DISABILITIES

Major Universities	**Small Colleges**
American University	Bard College
University of Arizona	Beacon College
Auburn University	Curry College
Clark University	Landmark College
University of Colorado Boulder	Lesley University
University of Connecticut	Loras College
University of Denver	Lynn University
DePaul University	Manhattanville University
Fairleigh Dickinson University	Marist College
University of Georgia	Marymount Manhattan College
Hofstra University	Mercyhurst College
Northeastern University	Mitchell College
Purdue University	Muskingum College
Rochester Institute of Technology	New England College
Syracuse University	St. Thomas Aquinas College (NY)
University of Vermont	West Virginia Wesleyan College
	Westminster College (MO)

A Note to the Reader

These are turbulent times for higher education in the United States—and for college admissions in particular. Since coming into office in January 2025, the Trump Administration has disrupted decades of collaboration between the Federal Government and research universities and forced hundreds of institutions to reduce their instructional and research budgets. It has sharply curtailed the inflow of international students, imposed caps on lifetime student borrowing and parent PLUS loans, and, following a U.S. Supreme Court decision, prompted institutions to abandon Diversity, Equity, and Inclusion (DEI) efforts aimed at expanding access to underserved populations. In several states, including Florida, North Carolina, and Texas, politicians have inserted themselves into curriculum decisions at public universities, raising concerns about academic freedom and faculty governance, especially in the social sciences.

At the same time, other forces are complicating the college admissions process itself. The Common Application allows students seeking a place in selective colleges to hedge their bets by applying to multiple colleges with ease. But that has made it harder for admissions officers to identify serious applicants who are likely to accept an offer. In response, some institutions—such as Washington University in St. Louis and Tulane University—have accepted high proportions of their students through an often confusing menu of early decision and early action options. While such a system helps colleges meet enrollment targets, it can disadvantage lower-income students who need to compare various financial aid offers before committing.

As a reader—and perhaps a high school senior—you may find all these changes daunting. That reaction is understandable. But let's step back and consider the broader landscape. The most striking feature of American higher education, unparalleled among developed countries, is its extraordinary diversity. There are about 2,300 nonprofit, baccalaureate-granting colleges and universities in the U.S., ranging from small liberal arts colleges off the beaten path to world-class urban research universities. Some are public, others private. Some identify as historically Black, single-sex, evangelical, or Roman Catholic; others focus on engineering, the environment, or Great Books. You name it!

Significantly, every one of these colleges is unique. Even schools that appear similar at first glance have different cultures and institutional personalities—shaped, among other things, by their academic philosophies, social values, extracurricular resources, and, crucially, their historical narrative. Think, for example, of the spirit of American ingenuity that informed Stanford's curricular foundations in science and engineering and found expression in the wide-open architectural style of its campus. Then compare it with the intellectualism that characterizes many of the older Eastern Ivies and continues to resonate in the centuries-old intimacy of a Harvard Yard. These institutional identities tend to endure even as schools evolve. When Yale and Vassar went co-ed, for example, the character of their student bodies and academic cultures did not noticeably change. To take an extreme example of such consistency, the fact that the University of Pennsylvania is a leader in service-learning can be traced to the lingering influence of its founder, Benjamin Franklin, the ultimate pragmatist, who lived three centuries ago.

Since its first edition more than 40 years ago, the *Fiske Guide to Colleges* has sought to help college-bound students navigate the wide range of options and complexities involved in choosing a school. At a moment when many are questioning the value of higher education in the first place, we continue to celebrate the diversity of U.S. higher education and its importance—not only for every student but for society as a whole. The *Fiske Guide* differs from other guides in its emphasis on narrative essays aimed at capturing the *distinctive cultures* and *institutional personalities* of the "best and most interesting" colleges in the country. The goal is to help you, the reader, determine which schools might serve your own unique goals, values, and interests.

A final note: In recent years, the number of U.S. college and university students participating in semester- or year-long study abroad programs has been growing. Some students have opted to obtain full bachelor's degrees from universities in English-speaking countries, and the *Fiske Guide* has long included detailed write-ups on schools in Canada, Ireland, and Scotland. With this edition, we are taking this interest in global education one step further. A new section on page 381 lists universities in *non-English-speaking countries* that offer full undergraduate programs *in English*. Check it out.

Happy college hunting!

Edward B. Fiske
Chapel Hill, NC

University of Aberdeen: See page 366.

Adelphi University

One South Avenue, Garden City, NY 11530

Situated in a comfortable Long Island suburb within shouting distance of Manhattan, Adelphi lets you taste urban life without being overwhelmed. Long established as an innovator in public health and the arts, Adelphi's strengths are professional programs grounded in the liberal arts. Almost all undergrads are New Yorkers, two-thirds are women, and 96 percent get some financial aid. Compare to Fairfield and Quinnipiac.

After going through a tumultuous time in the late 1990s, Adelphi has come into its own in the last 25 years. Enrollment has grown, more than 250 new faculty members have been hired, and the school has invested millions in infrastructure. Students will now find state-of-the-art equipment in physics and chemistry labs, new Steinway pianos in the music programs, and modern, smart classrooms with smaller class sizes. Student financial aid also has been expanded. "We are always changing and evolving, whether in research or in courses as new ones are created every day," says a psychology major. "The campus is very alive."

Originally founded as a prep school in Brooklyn in 1863, Adelphi morphed into a coeducational college in 1896 and in 1928 moved to Garden City, where it occupies 75 acres in an attractive residential suburb that boasts a Gothic cathedral and an abundance of stately homes. The campus is registered as an arboretum. A $34 million renovation of the Harley University Center added and enhanced dining and study areas, high-tech event spaces, and an art gallery.

General education at Adelphi follows what the administration calls PATH: preparation, awareness, transformation, and hands-on learning. Students are required to complete at least 30 credits through courses in the humanities, social sciences, natural sciences, mathematics, computing, and logic. First-year students take a writing seminar to hone their skills and another First-Year Seminar of their choosing. Other required courses include communications, quantitative reasoning, information literacy, and global learning and civic engagement. A new required course on examining race, racism, and justice was introduced in fall 2025. All students must also complete a capstone course or project.

Adelphi's most popular majors have a decidedly preprofessional bent: nursing, psychology, biology, and management. Communication sciences and disorders, exercise science, and social work are traditional strengths. The fine and performing arts are also notable, especially the theatre program. Joint bachelor's/graduate degree programs have been established in several disciplines, and a B.S./M.B.A. program in the business of science prepares students for executive careers in pharmaceuticals, tech, and other industries. In response to growing demand, a B.S. in artificial intelligence launched in 2025.

> **"We are always changing and evolving."**

Adelphi has "a relaxed but still serious environment," says a communications major. "The students are generally working hard, but it never feels too intense." Forty-one percent of classes have fewer than 20 students and none have more than 50. "All the professors are so helpful," says a sophomore, "constantly challenging you to try new things as well as see things from different perspectives." Adelphi's Career Center is said to be effective and the award-winning Bridges to Adelphi

Website: www.adelphi.edu
Location: Suburban
Private
Total Enrollment: 6,345
Undergraduates: 5,129
Male/Female: 33/67
Financial Aid: 96%
Pell Grant: 44%
Expense: Pr $
Student Loans: 55%
Average Debt: $
Applicants: 19,705
Accepted: 66%
Enrolled: 10%
Grad in 6 Years: 67%
Returning First-years: 82%
Academics: ✍ ✍ ✍
Social: 🗩 🗩
Q of L: ★ ★ ★
Admissions: (516) 877-3050
Email Address:
  admissions@adelphi.edu

Strong Programs:
Biology
Business
Communication Sciences and
  Disorders
Exercise Science
Nursing
Psychology
Social Work
Theatre

program offers career development and academic support to students with autism spectrum disorder.

Adelphi has increased its emphasis on experiential learning and student engagement in recent years. The Levermore Global Scholars program, open to students in all majors, takes an interdisciplinary approach to addressing global issues through special seminars, cultural excursions, activities at the UN headquarters in New York City, and opportunities for internships, study abroad, and service projects. All students can choose from more than 100 study-abroad programs. The SPARK Center, which stands for Scholars Pursuing Arts, Research and Knowledge, supports undergraduate scholarship and creative projects. Adelphi's Innovation Center research lab provides opportunities for students to collaborate with area businesses and nonprofits to explore leading-edge technologies. The Honors College offers a rigorous liberal arts program and living/learning community for exceptional students.

Eighty-eight percent of undergraduates hail from New York, while 4 percent arrive from foreign countries. A sophomore describes Adelphi students as "vibrant, outgoing, and dedicated," while a history major says, "Almost every aspect of the student body is diverse, from social interests all the way to cultural and ethnic backgrounds. There is something for everybody here." Ten percent of the students are Black, 23 percent are Hispanic/Latino, 14 percent are Asian American, and 3 percent are multiracial. Politically, a sophomore says, "Although hot-button issues are talked about, it is always an open discussion not met with hostility." Students grouse about the cost of tuition, but they also praise Adelphi's financial aid; 44 percent of students qualify for Pell Grants. Merit scholarships are worth an average of $24,900 each and more than 200 athletic scholarships are available.

"We have tailgates, a spring concert, and so many events happening all the time."

Despite several "comfortable and well-maintained" residence halls, a mere 20 percent of all undergrads live on campus. Gender-inclusive options are available, as are two first-year living/learning communities. Many students reside in university-arranged, off-campus apartments in Garden City. Campus dining gets mixed reviews. Mental health counseling access has been expanded to include a Peer Education Program, and students report feeling safe on campus.

Adelphi has been bolstering on-campus social life with an increase in free weekend and late-night programming aimed at encouraging students to stick around on weekends, and students are active in more than 90 clubs and organizations. "We have tailgates, a spring concert, and so many events happening all the time," cheers one student. Greek life plays a role, too, with 12 fraternities and sororities that attract 8 percent of the men and 12 percent of the women, respectively. Adelphi is a dry campus, and students say that the policy is strictly enforced. Students look forward to Spirit Weekend in the fall, the Winter Spectacular with ice skating and igloos, and Pantherfest in the spring. One student describes Garden City as "a very safe, low-key residential neighborhood." About half of students get involved in community service. The Center for Student Involvement offers discounted tickets to movies, Broadway shows, and professional sporting events.

Adelphi fields several competitive Division II teams (the Panthers) in the Northeast-10 Conference. The men's lacrosse team captured the national title in 2024 and 2025. Women's lacrosse and soccer are also strong. Among the school's club sports, eSports, ultimate Frisbee, soccer, Latin dance, and Bollywood dance are the most popular; half a dozen intramural sports are also available.

With its focus on creativity and innovation supported by small classes, personal attention, and hands-on learning, Adelphi has been thriving in the 21st century. Most students welcome the chance to play an active role in shaping not just their education, but the community as a whole. Says a junior, "We are a diverse student body with a wide range of students coming from all walks of life, but Adelphi feels like home."

Agnes Scott College

141 East College Avenue, Decatur, GA 30030

Combines the tree-lined seclusion of Decatur with the bustle of Atlanta. All-female school with exceptional facilities for a college of its size, Agnes Scott offers small classes, sisterhood, a richly diverse student body, and a more exciting location than some of its cohorts. Big emphasis on leadership and global learning. Socioeconomic diversity a priority.

Agnes Scott College, founded by Presbyterians in 1889, offers a small-town campus atmosphere and provides women with an intellectually challenging institution. The college produces skilled writers and artists, as well as mathematicians and scientists and continues to be one of the South's leading women's schools. The school focuses on delivering an innovative curriculum that cultivates globally-aware women leaders. ASC's climate as a small, single-sex institution leads to close relationships with the faculty and very involved students—both academically and socially. "We believe in the power of women, of deep thinking, of honor, of social justice, of learning for the sake of learning," asserts one senior.

The Agnes Scott campus sits on 100 acres in the historic district of Decatur, just outside of Atlanta. The well-maintained Gothic and Victorian buildings are surrounded by gardens filled with rare shrubs, bushes, and trees—all evidence of thriving alumnae support. The Bullock Science Center includes an X-ray spectrometer, nuclear magnetic resonance imaging equipment, and a scanning tunneling microscope. As part of a campuswide sustainability initiative, the college has renovated three residence halls earning one LEED Gold and two Platinum certifications.

In addition to outstanding STEM instruction, Agnes Scott provides students with solid grounding in the liberal arts, leadership, global learning, digital literacy, and professional success through an approach called SUMMIT. As part of SUMMIT, all first-year students participate in a two-day leadership immersion experience following orientation in the fall and then in the spring semes

> **"We are encouraged to find our own paths."**

ter, during a week known as Peak Week, embark on a faculty-led, global study tour to places like Grenada, Costa Rica, Paris, and the Navajo Nation. All sophomores are required to take an interdisciplinary SCALE course focused on leadership development, which includes spending Peak Week shadowing leaders of local business and nonprofit organizations, such as AT&T, The Atlanta Dream, UPS and the Atlanta Community Food Bank. Juniors and seniors select an Applied Career Experience during Peak Week to learn about topics and skills like data analysis, graphic design, or digital literacy. Each student also assembles her own board of advisors with faculty and staff members, a peer advisor, and a career mentor, and documents her progress throughout her four years with a digital portfolio. A junior praises SUMMIT for connecting students with "a group of people totally committed to making sure you get where you want to be."

Website: www.agnesscott.edu
Location: Small City
Private
Total Enrollment: 1,042
Undergraduates: 837
Male/Female: 0/100
Financial Aid: 100%
Pell Grant: 51%
Expense: Pr $ $
Student Loans: 62%
Average Debt: $ $ $
Applicants: 2,090
Accepted: 62%
Enrolled: 16%
Grad in 6 Years: 71%
Returning First-years: 81%
Academics: ✍ ✍ ✍
Social: 🍺 🍺
Q of L: ★ ★ ★ ★
Admissions: (404) 471-6285
Email Address:
admission@agnesscott.edu

Strong Programs:
Biology
Business Management
Creative Writing
English Literature
Neuroscience
Psychology
Public Health
Sociology and Anthropology

Academically, Agnes Scott delivers strong programs in public health, psychology, business management, English literature, and creative writing. In addition to STEM, popular majors include premed and prelaw. Aspiring engineers may complete their degrees through a 3–2 program with Georgia Tech, while nurses benefit from a dual-degree program with Emory. The College's Career Exploration Center plays a key role in guiding students to post-collegiate success.

The overall academic climate at ASC is rigorous but collaborative, and students are focused on learning first. "We are encouraged to find our own paths instead of competing for the same one," says a public health major. Adds a senior, "In every course, there is a cross-curricular approach. You will, at the end of your four years, be an excellent writer, speaker, and critical thinker." An honor system, enforced by a student judiciary, allows for self-scheduled and unproctored exams. Sixty-eight percent of classes have fewer than 20 students, which encourages close student/faculty interactions in the classroom. A sophomore says, "I cannot emphasize enough how invested Agnes Scott professors are in their students."

For those students wishing to leave Agnes Scott's idyllic campus behind for a time, there are study abroad options available at more than 150 universities in more than 50 countries. The Hubert Scholars Program combines experiential learning with humanitarian service either at home or abroad. Past Hubert scholars have mentored refugee girls in the local community and developed gender-equality education programs in Bangladesh. About two-thirds of students participate in research, and many present their results at an annual conference held in the spring.

Agnes Scott students "recognize the value of two very simple things: the value of diversity and the value of women's education," says a sophomore. Sixty-four percent of students are Georgia natives, 2 percent are international, and most of the rest hail from the Southeast. Despite the school's small size, its student body is hugely diverse; 29 percent are first-generation, 32 percent of ASC denizens are Black, 14 percent are Hispanic/Latina, 4 percent are Asian American, and 6 percent are multiracial. The school has made socioeconomic diversity a priority as well—an impressive 51 percent of current first-years are eligible for Pell Grants. A business management major comments, "I am challenged every day to think about the world from perspectives that I could never think about myself." Under the new Agnes Scott $100K Promise, all admitted undergraduates receive at least a $25,000 renewable merit-based scholarship.

Eighty-four percent of students live in Agnes Scott's six dorms, which are linked by tree-lined brick walks. "The residence halls are pretty nice. They have walk-in closets, lots of storage," says a student. All dorms have air conditioning. Juniors and seniors can live in Avery Glen, the college-owned apartment complex, while incoming students are assigned to one of two first-year dorms.

Students say that dining services staff is friendly and receptive to student feedback, and while the food is usually decent, options can be limited. They report feeling safe on campus, and one student says, "Campus security is very tight. There are always officers around keeping watch."

As for the ASC social scene, there are no sororities, but the college itself is a close-knit sisterhood. During the week, socializing tends to revolve around study groups, student club activities, and events planned by the campus programming board ("ProBo"), but when the weekend comes, social life moves off campus. "Parties at other colleges, nightclubs, bars, and off-campus restaurants are common places to find Agnes Scott students," says a senior. Enforcement of drinking policies falls under the honor code; students of legal age can enjoy alcohol in their dorms and at certain functions. Every October, students celebrate Black Cat week, a tradition since 1915 that marks the end of orientation and recognition of each new class and ends with a formal dance. Other traditions survive, too, such as the ring ceremony where sophomores receive the black onyx class rings that make them part of the ASC "Black Ring Mafia." Seniors who get into grad school or find jobs ascend to the top of the college bell tower, ringing the bell to share the good news.

Decatur (population 24,000) itself is not really a college town, but there are some attractions for Agnes Scott students. "There are nice little venues and coffee shops, very hip and fun," a student says. Convenient public transportation serves cultural landmarks and provides access to the social scene in nearby Atlanta. Many ASC students get involved with community service both on and off campus, with organizations like the DeKalb Rape Crisis Center, Hands Across Atlanta, and Best Buddies. Popular road trips include Stone Mountain and Six Flags or New Orleans for Mardi Gras.

Agnes Scott competes in the Division III Collegiate Conference of the South athletic conference. Scottie tennis has been the most successful of the school's six varsity teams, winning multiple conference championships, and softball and soccer are also competitive. Students stay active with a variety of recreational and intramural activities, such as Zumba, dodgeball, and club lacrosse.

Small but mighty, ASC stands out for the little touches that make students feel they're part of an intimate community, starting with pine-scented brochures sent to accepted applicants. One Scottie reflects, "Agnes Scott builds women who are fearless, who change the world, who question things and inspire others."

The college has renovated three residence halls earning one LEED Gold and two Platinum certifications, respectively.

If You Apply To ›

Agnes Scott: Early decision, early action I and II, regular decision. SATs or ACTs: optional. Accepts the Common Application. Accepts applications from students who were assigned female at birth as well as students who were assigned male or female at birth but identify as female, transgender, agender, gender fluid, or nonbinary.

University of Alabama

203 Student Services Center, Box 870109, Tuscaloosa, AL 35487

"Roll Tide!" still says a lot—but not everything—about Alabama, which is one of the fastest-growing public flagships in the country. Passion for the Crimson Tide is as strong as ever, but also look for strong honors programs, emphasis on undergraduate research, and pockets of professional excellence. Though its football team is among the nation's elite, 'Bama still lacks the academic luster of rivals University of Georgia and University of Florida.

The University of Alabama first earned its national reputation on the gridiron, but the state's first university (with roots all the way back to 1820) is committed to making an academic name for itself as well. In an effort to attract the South's best and brightest, UA has increased its emphasis on global perspectives, computer-based technologies, freshman learning communities, and undergraduate research and adopted a generous policy of merit scholarships, especially for out-of-state students.

'Bama's thousand-acre campus combines pristine brick, classical, revival-style buildings (a few of which survived the Civil War) with modern structures. One of the

A modern trolley service connects the 'Bama campus to the city's thriving downtown.

most stunning in the South, the campus boasts an expansive lawn and majestic trees and wraps around a shaded quadrangle, the home of the main library and "Denny Chimes," a campanile carillon that rings the Westminster Chimes on the quarter hour. Newer facilities include the Smart Communities and Innovation Building and the Alabama Intercollegiate Athletics Golf Facility.

The only course Alabama requires students to take during their first year is a two-term English composition sequence. Before graduation, students must also complete courses in natural sciences, math, humanities, and social sciences and either two semesters of a foreign language or one of computer science. Optional freshman learning communities allow students to take two or three academic courses together and a one-credit seminar taught by a full professor that ties the other courses together. All students may also enroll in the two-credit Academic Potential Seminar, which covers skills like personal responsibility, time management, and test preparation. Incoming first-years who are at the low end of UA's admissions spectrum may participate in the Crimson Edge Program, which requires an academic support class and includes specialized academic advising.

> **"Professors have been helpful, hands-on, and fully supportive."**

"The academic climate is rigorous, but manageable," says an operations management major. The university is organized into eight undergraduate colleges and schools, which together offer more than 80 undergraduate degree programs. Despite its size, 43 percent of classes have fewer than 20 students. The Culverhouse College of Business offers strong programs in marketing and management information systems. The College of Communication and Information Sciences is one of the country's top communication schools, while respected programs in the College of Human Environmental Sciences include food and nutrition and athletic training. Among STEM fields, metallurgical and materials engineering is noteworthy. The School of Music is a regional standout, drawing guest artists such as Wynton Marsalis, and the studio art and art history programs are well regarded. New College allows students to work with faculty to design their own interdisciplinary major. The most popular majors include business, social sciences, communication studies, journalism, and engineering. An accounting major says, "Professors have been helpful, hands-on, and fully supportive."

The Honors College serves 7,300 students and houses UA's three university-wide honors programs: computer-based honors, international honors, and university honors. "Honors classes can include a Habitat for Humanity course, Theory and Practice of Mentoring, or the one that takes the cake: the chocolate-tasting class," explains one participant. Honors students also get early registration privileges and the opportunity to write a senior thesis. The University Scholars Program provides qualified undergraduates whose objectives include master's or doctoral degrees an opportunity to begin graduate work during their senior year and become eligible for graduate fellowships and scholarships. Students recommend the Randall Research Scholars Program, which pairs undergrads with "leading research professors." Other offerings include the May interim term, when students spend three weeks focusing on one course in depth. About 13 percent of students choose to study abroad through more than 50 faculty-led programs around the world.

Forty-one percent of 'Bama's undergraduates are Alabama residents, and 1 percent are international students representing nearly 90 countries. UA students are "competitive but also very community centered," says a psychology major. Twelve percent of UA undergrads are Black, 2 percent are Asian American, 7 percent are Hispanic/Latino, and 4 percent are multiracial. Although UA traditionally leans right, one student notes, "all political beliefs are represented at the University." 'Bama awards nearly 275 athletic scholarships in 21 sports and has expanded the number of merit scholarships, which average $17,400. Consistent with its efforts to attract strong students from outside of Alabama, the school spends over $200 million on merit aid—more than double what it allocates to need-based scholarships and grants.

Although UA requires first-years to reside on campus, most students live in off-campus apartments in the Tuscaloosa area; only 27 percent remain in campus residence halls. "UA has the best dorms around!" cheers a public relations major. They're "like apartments, with typical units having four bedrooms, two bathrooms, and a common area and kitchenette," adds a junior. The living/learning communities get high marks for their tight-knit atmosphere. Students report that some campus dining halls are better than others, and one recommends the made-to-order fare at Bryant Dining, adding, "I would gladly eat at Bryant for the rest of my life." A senior says that sexual assault awareness is "not something that's swept under the rug." And the health and mental health services are lauded by a senior for being "quick, responsive, compassionate, and professional."

The Greek system plays an integral role in shaping social and political status both with the university and in the Deep South beyond. Thirty-one percent of men pledge fraternities and 45 percent of women join sororities, and a sophomore says, "Something is always going on in the mansions we call Greek houses." 'Bama Rush, in which predominantly white sororities coordinate outfits and dance routines to promote their chapters

"Any Alabama football game is a festival."

and attract the "right" kind of members, invites comparison to the spirit of a home football game. Repeated efforts by the administration to integrate 'Bama Rush have fallen short, but students say alcohol policies are well enforced. "I would not say Alabama has a party culture," offers an accounting major, "but more of a culture of tradition and pride." Those looking for alternatives will find everything from the annual Kentuck Festival of the Arts in Northport to Bible study groups among the school's 600-plus student clubs. "The Tapping on the Mound ceremony is a really special moment where students are recognized for their leadership and academic achievements," says a marketing major. A modern trolley service connects the 'Bama campus to the city's thriving downtown. Tuscaloosa is described as "an awesome college town," that is "mostly centered around the university." Advises a junior, "If Tuscaloosa is ever not enough for students, locations such as New Orleans, Atlanta, Nashville, and the Gulf of Mexico are all within four hours of campus for a weekend getaway."

'Bama football is a perennial Division I powerhouse. The annual Auburn–Alabama game—the Iron Bowl, one of the most intense rivalries in the nation—is the highlight of the school year. "Any Alabama football game is a festival," a sophomore says. Men's baseball, men's and women's basketball and cross-country, and women's gymnastics are all strong in the Southeastern Conference. 'Bama sports a number of solid nonathletic teams as well, including the Alabama Forensic Council, which consistently places in the top 10 in national competition, and Alabama Astrobotics, which has won nine national contests since 2012. Intramural and club sports draw 24 percent of students.

Although sports are still an integral part of the UA experience, the university's declared emphasis is now on technology, merit scholarships, global perspectives, and undergraduate research. It's an approach that's bringing in more serious, cosmopolitan students. Best of all, says one finance and marketing major, "The students are so friendly, if you pass someone on the quad and say 'Roll Tide,' you've pretty much made a friend for life."

If You Apply To ›

Alabama: Rolling admissions. Accepts the Common Application. Please consult Alabama's website for the most up-to-date information regarding standardized test requirements.

611 East Porter Street, Albion, MI 49224

Nestled in a rural town between Detroit and out-there Kalamazoo, Albion is a small private college that mixes experiential learning with a solid liberal arts education. Emphasis on civic engagement: think Gerald Ford, the moderate Republican president who is the namesake of Albion's signature institute for public service. Future doctors, lawyers, and businesspeople are set up for success.

Website: www.albion.edu
Location: Small Town
Private
Total Enrollment: 1,292
Undergraduates: 1,292
Male/Female: 46/51
Financial Aid: 100%
Pell Grant: 52%
Expense: Pr $ $
Student Loans: 74%
Average Debt: $ $ $
Applicants: 6,421
Accepted: 81%
Enrolled: 7%
Grad in 6 Years: 62%
Returning First-years: 71%
Academics: ✐ ✐ ✐
Social: 💬 💬
Q of L: ★ ★ ★
Admissions: (517) 629-0321
Email Address:
admission@albion.edu

Strong Programs:
Biology
Communication Studies
Economics and Management
Environmental Studies
Kinesiology-Exercise Science
Premed
Psychology
Public Policy

Michigan's Albion College, with the focus it places on community engagement and service, helps students achieve their goals through personal attention from professors, research, internships, and a devoted alumni network. Despite its small-town setting, the college has managed to attract an increasingly diverse student body. In the words of a mathematics major, "The culture of Albion College is centered around inclusion and helping people find out who they are."

One of three original chartered higher education schools in Michigan (and the first to go co-ed), Albion was founded in 1835 by the Methodist Church and located near the banks of the Kalamazoo River, about 90 miles west of Detroit. In addition to its newer Georgian-style architecture, the college has retained and restored several of its 19th-century buildings. The campus is spacious, with statuesque oaks and a beautiful nature center spanning more than 120 acres. The college's equestrian center is home to one of the largest indoor riding arenas in the United States. A new kinesiology lab opened in 2025, along with a renovated gymnasium and a new multicultural lounge.

Albion has a rich academic history and was the first private college in Michigan to have a Phi Beta Kappa chapter (1940). Students are required to take core courses distributed among humanities, natural sciences, social sciences, fine arts, and math. They must also satisfy requirements in environmental science, gender and ethnicity studies, and complete an experiential learning component. The first-year seminar is designed to provide a "stimulating learning environment" in a small-class setting; recent offerings include Ancient Aliens and Lost Civilizations, Fly Me to the Moon, and To Sleep or Not to Sleep. The academic climate is described as competitive in certain departments but generally positive. Sixty-nine percent of classes have fewer than 20 students, and professors are said to be interested in students' academic performance and their emotional well-being. According to a history major, "The professors help us out when we need help, and they are always there to support us."

Consistent with Albion's interest in developing civic leaders, the Gerald R. Ford Institute for Leadership in Public Policy and Service takes an innovative approach: Students participate in a simulation of city government in which they play the roles of community leaders. Visiting speakers include senators and congresspeople, governors and state legislators, and interest-group representatives. Albion's Wilson Institute for Medicine supports

"The culture of Albion College is centered around inclusion."

the popular premed program. Other established centers and institutes, dedicated to business and management, sustainability and the environment, social change, and teacher development offer courses, specialized academic advising, alumni networks, field trips, speakers, and other immersive opportunities that enhance the learning experience. "Take advantage of the academic institutes on campus!" urges a biology major. Albion's economics and management, psychology, and kinesiology-exercise science majors are well respected, as is the prelaw program. Other popular majors include biology and communication. The earth and environment department has combined the sustainability, environment, and geology departments into one inter-disciplinary department, which launched a new minor in environmental studies. Albion offers an engineering dual-degree program with Columbia and the University of Michigan. Albion has cut some language majors, sustainability studies, and a handful of others.

"With a smaller number [of students] you get a more personal learning experi-ence," a sophomore says of the academic environment. Albion's Foundation for Undergraduate Research, Scholarship, and Creative Activity (FURSCA), which pairs students from all disciplines with faculty mentors to conduct sponsored summer research or creative work, is highly commended by students. One participant, a bio-chemistry major, says, "My professor walked me through new and old techniques individually, so I feel much more independent in the lab than most." The experi-ence culminates in a public presentation during the annual Elkin R. Isaac Student Research Symposium, held every April. An honors program is available for highly motivated students. For those looking to take their educational experience to more distant shores, Albion offers more than 100 study abroad programs in over 40 countries.

Albion students "are funny, goofy, smart, athletic, and super generous," shares an English and education major. Michigan residents make up 73 percent of the student population, and 5 percent hail from abroad. "There are people from all races and back-grounds on campus," says a senior; currently, 16 percent of students are Black, 13 percent are Hispanic/Latino, 1 percent are Asian American, and 4 percent are multiracial. Politically, the stu-dent body is a relatively moderate mix of liberals and conservatives concerned with issues like racial and social injustice. "If you are closed minded you won't fit in here," warns a sophomore. There are a number of merit scholarships available, averaging $41,400, but no athletic scholarships. The Albion College Promise covers full tuition and fees for in-state students from families that make less than $55,000 per year. Fifty-two percent of first-year students are Pell-eligible.

"Take advantage of the academic institutes on campus!"

Since Albion is a residential college, 93 percent of students call the co-ed res-idence halls home, and the school "tries to offer a variety of living situations for students," reports a senior. The majority of the first-year class inhabits Wesley Hall. During their sophomore year, many students move to the suite-style rooms in Whitehouse Hall or Mitchell Towers; seniors occupy apartment-style housing called The Mae. Meals are served in the centrally located dining hall and are said to be "pretty good." A Starbucks café has been added in the library, and a Qdoba Mexican Eats has also opened on campus. Students rate campus security staff and counseling services—including career and mental health—highly.

Twenty-two percent of Albion men and 21 percent of the women belong to one of the school's six national fraternities and seven sororities. Greek parties draw large crowds, making them a primary part of many students' social lives. "Campus Safety monitors every party, and there is a curfew in place," notes a sophomore. Students 21 and older may consume alcohol in certain campus residence areas. A well-run union board organizes all sorts of activities—films, lectures, plays, comedians, and concerts—to keep students occupied in their spare time. On the weekends, Ann Arbor, East Lansing, and Chicago are frequent road- or train-trip destinations.

Students report that the town of Albion's annual Festival of the Forks is always highly anticipated, and the movie theater is free for students with a valid school ID. "Downtown Albion may be quaint, but it is growing and thriving with support from both the college and the community," comments a psychology major of the town that includes a brewpub, a bakery, a grocery store, a bookstore/coffeehouse, a

Albion offers an engineering dual-degree program with Columbia and the University of Michigan.

A new kinesiology lab opened in 2025, along with a renovated gymnasium and a new multicultural lounge.

community center, and a community theater. Students focus some of their energy by working for groups supported by the Student Volunteer Bureau, participating in "city clean-up day, Habitat for Humanity, and volunteering at nursing homes and schools," says a student. Some traditional events that offer a nice break from academics are the Day of Woden, which includes a picnic, DJ, carnival rides, and food trucks, held in the spring on the last day of class, and the KiKi Ball, a student fashion and talent competition.

"Athletics play a huge part in life at Albion," says a senior. The Britons football team competes in the Division III Michigan Intercollegiate Athletic Association and has won multiple conference championships. Other strong teams include men's lacrosse (the 2025 MIAA champs), women's basketball, men's and women's wrestling and equestrian. Hope College is a rival, as is Alma College. Some of the most popular intramural and club sports include basketball, pickleball, and disc golf.

"There are people from all races and backgrounds on campus."

At Albion College, professors are accessible and interested, academics are challenging without being overwhelming, and students feel supported and motivated. At the same time, an increased effort to connect students with real-world learning and service opportunities are garnering more applications from more diverse groups of students. In the words of one senior, "Even though Albion is a small school in a rural town in Michigan, we want to make a big impact on the world and make our school known."

If You Apply To ›

Albion: Early decision, early action, rolling admissions. Accepts the Common Application with supplement. SATs or ACTs: optional.

Alfred University

1 Saxon Drive, Alfred, NY 14802

Talk about an unusual combination: Alfred combines a nationally renowned and state-supported college of ceramics, a school of art and design, an engineering program, and a business school wrapped up in a small university of 1,400 undergraduates. The Finger Lakes is a region full of natural beauty, but it takes elbow grease to draw coastal types to the hinterlands of western New York.

Website: www.alfred.edu
Location: Rural
Private
Total Enrollment: 1,614
Undergraduates: 1,408
Male/Female: 48/52
Financial Aid: 84%
Pell Grant: 50%
Expense: Pr $
Student Loans: 86%
Average Debt: $ $

With about 1,400 undergraduate students, Alfred University isn't a bustling academic factory; it's a quiet, cloistered, self-described "educational village" in a tiny town wholly dedicated to the "industry of learning." The university, founded in 1836, boasts highly respected programs in art and design, as well as ceramic engineering. Innovation not only shapes the curriculum but also has a profound effect on campus life. Small classes and friendly competition support this diversity while encouraging individuals to succeed. Along with being able to handle the academic rigors of the college, students also have to weather brutal winters that dump snow by the foot on the region.

Alfred's campus consists of a charming, close-knit group of modern and Georgian brick buildings, accompanied by a stone castle. The Kanakadea Creek runs right through campus, and the town of Alfred (population 4,900) consists of two colleges (the other is Alfred State College) and a main street with one stoplight. There are a few shops and restaurants, but certainly no malls, parking lots, or tall buildings. Notable campus facilities include the 36 kilns in Harder Hall and the five telescopes at the Stull Observatory.

The university and its students share a no-nonsense approach to education. Although prospective students apply directly to one of four colleges and declare a tentative major, half of all requirements for a bachelor's degree are earned in the liberal arts college. Requirements are quite different in each school. However, the mix usually includes coursework in oral and written communication, quantitative reasoning, humanities, social and natural sciences, global perspectives, and health and wellness. All new students fulfill the one-credit Common Ground requirement, a series of discussions on diversity and inclusion.

Alfred, though private, is actually the "host" school for the New York State College of Ceramics, which is a unit of the state university system and comes with a relatively modest public university price tag. Ceramic engineering (the development and refinement of ceramic materials) is the academic cornerstone and the program that brings Alfred international recognition. All engineering programs are found within the Inamori School of Engineering, including uncommon majors in materials science and engineering, renewable energy engineering, and glass engineering science. The School of Art and Design's art department, with its programs in ceramics, glass, printmaking, sculpture, video, interactive media, and teacher certification, is also highly regarded. The College of Business gets good reviews from students and provides undergraduates with work experience through a small business institute where students have real clients. Art and design majors are the most popular, followed by mechanical engineering, business administration, and psychology. Newer degrees include a B.A. in computer science and a B.S. in biochemistry. Students are able to design their own interdisciplinary majors with personal guidance from top faculty members.

"I would say that Alfred is pretty competitive," says a junior. "The studio courses are challenging," adds a sophomore. Whatever their major, all students enjoy small classes, and the quality of teaching is reported as high. Most classes are taught by full professors, with graduate students and teaching assistants helping out only in lab sessions. "Most teachers have high expectations, resulting in greater student performance," says one junior. Alfred's academic advising and career planning services stress the university's commitment to helping undergrads plan their futures. Through the APEX (Applied and Experiential Learning) program, juniors and seniors can apply for up to $1,000 in funding to help offset costs associated with pursuing hands-on experiences like internships, apprenticeships, study abroad, and research positions. Faculty-led study abroad programs are offered during the May term and spring break, in addition to hundreds of exchange and affiliate programs, but only 3 percent of students study internationally. Seventy-five percent do research, often as senior capstone projects.

> **"I would say that Alfred is pretty competitive."**

Alfred students are "creative and like to be challenged," says a business administration major. Seventy-eight percent of the students at Alfred are from New York State, and 9 percent are international. Black students make up 7 percent of the student body, Hispanics/Latinos 11 percent, Asian Americans 2 percent, and multiracial students 4 percent. Half of first-year students are Pell-eligible, a notable number for a school of Alfred's size. Outstanding students can apply for many merit scholarships, averaging $23,600. There are no athletic scholarships.

Ninety percent of students live in campus housing, and no one seems to mind the three-year residency requirement because the rooms in the co-ed dorms are

(continued)

Applicants: 4,988
Accepted: 74%
Enrolled: 10%
Grad in 6 Years: 57%
Returning First-years: 72%
Academics: ✍ ✍ ✍
Social: 🗩 🗩 🗩
Q of L: ★ ★ ★
Admissions: (607) 871-2115
Email Address:
  admissions@alfred.edu

Strong Programs:
Art and Design
Business Administration
Ceramic Engineering
Glass Engineering Science
Materials Science and
  Engineering
Mechanical Engineering
Psychology
Renewable Energy Engineering

The Student Activities Board brings many diversions to campus, including musicians, comedians, lecturers, and movies.

large and comfortable. Upperclassmen have a choice of single rooms, suites, or apartments. Special-interest housing, such as Modern Language House and Unity House, is another option. The school has two dining halls, and students say the offerings include plenty of selections for vegetarians and vegans. "The dining facilities are very nice and well equipped, and the food is both diverse and edible," says a junior. Campus security is good, according to most students. "AU security will provide rides or walking escorts if you feel unsafe walking alone," a biology major says.

Alfred's location in the Finger Lakes region, almost two hours from Buffalo and an hour and a half from Rochester, is isolated. The other chief complaint is the chilly, snowy weather. Social life is a challenge due to the rural atmosphere and lack of Greek organizations, but the Student Activities Board brings many diversions to campus, including musicians, comedians, lecturers, and movies.

"[The town of Alfred has] a very close community."

Alfred is a dry campus, and students say the alcohol policy is largely respected and enforced in the dorms. "Alfred doesn't have too many problems with drinking that I have heard of," a student says. Because the university shares the town with Alfred State College, students account for 85 percent of the population, all of which makes Alfred a good college town and "a very close community," observes a biology major. The downtown scene provides students with an adequate number of movie theaters and eateries, and many students volunteer in the community. Every spring brings the annual Hot Dog Weekend, a big carnival-like event that fills Main Street with game booths, bands, and lots of hot dog stands.

Alfred's Division III Saxons are ominous opponents on the football, soccer, and lacrosse fields, and the softball team is a recent Empire 8 Conference champion. The equestrian team is competitive too. Many Alfred students are skiing, hunting, camping, and rock-climbing enthusiasts, and favorite road trips include Letchworth and Stony Brook state parks, as well as Ithaca, Rochester, Buffalo, and Toronto. Intramurals and club sports draw nearly half of the students, with soccer, basketball, and handball being most popular.

"Alfred University will prepare you to go into the real world," says a first-year. Although small and somewhat secluded, Alfred's world is a good choice for students who want to spend four years on the ABCs of arts, business, and ceramic engineering—just be sure to bundle up for the long, snowy winters.

If You Apply To ›

Alfred: Early action, regular decision. Accepts the Common Application with supplement. Applicants to School of Art and Design must submit portfolio. Please consult Alfred's website for the most up-to-date information regarding standardized test requirements.

Allegheny College

520 North Main Street, Meadville, PA 16335

An unpretentious cousin to more well-heeled places like Dickinson and Bucknell. Draws heavily from the Buffalo-Cleveland-Pittsburgh area. The college's powerhouse athletic teams feast on their Division III competition. Fraternities and sororities give Allegheny a robust traditional college life. If you've ever wondered what lake-effect snow is, you'll find out here.

Allegheny College is a down-to-earth Eastern liberal arts school boasting a rich history of academic excellence in an intimate setting. Administrators here understand the importance of providing students with real-world experience to complement their classroom work, and the school emphasizes communication skills. Allegheny's small size means students get plenty of personal attention, and despite the heavy workload, anyone struggling academically can easily find help.

Allegheny's 80-acre campus is tucked away in Meadville, Pennsylvania, 90 miles north of Pittsburgh. Founded in 1815 by local residents to bring New England–style education to what was then a new frontier town, the school is nestled in the Norman Rockwell–esque rolling hills of northwestern Pennsylvania. "The fall and the spring are beautiful," cheers a senior. "The snowy days are cold, but the trees always look amazing." The campus is home to traditional architecture and redbrick walkways as well as apartment-style housing for upperclassmen. A nationally acclaimed science complex supports strong programs, and the college also owns a 283-acre research reserve and an 80-acre protected forest. In 2020, Allegheny became the first college in the state to achieve carbon neutrality. The Allegheny Lab for Innovation and Creativity houses high-tech fabrication and computer labs, and the school's oldest building, Bentley Hall, was recently renovated.

Allegheny operates on two 15-week semesters each year, both featuring an Academic Programming Day when classes pause for college-sponsored programs, advising, and career counseling workshops. Allegheny's curriculum requires all students to complete at least one minor in addition to their major, each in a different division. Students also take at least one course in each of eight distribution areas: civic learning; human experience; international and intercultural perspectives; modes of expression; power, privilege, and difference; quantitative reasoning; scientific process and knowledge; and social behavior and institutions. Incoming students enroll in two first-year seminars that help them transition to college-level work and develop writing and speaking skills. Sophomores complete a communication-focused seminar, juniors take a seminar in their major field, and seniors pursue a capstone project, where they must orally defend a work of independent research.

Strong programs include environmental science and sustainability, economics, physical and biological sciences, computer science, and international studies (which offers a track in Middle Eastern and North African studies). Biology, psychology, environmental science, and business enroll the most students. Allegheny has added majors in software engineering, data science, industrial design, and public humanities. Accelerated and dual-degree programs include 3–2, 3–3, and 3–4 options leading to degrees in engineering, public policy and management, psychology, and several health professions.

"The classes can be challenging," warns a biochemistry and global health studies major. "But if you seek help from professors or student tutors, you won't fall behind." Students praise the faculty for their passion, knowledge, and accessibility. You won't find a teaching assistant at the lectern in any Allegheny classroom, and 84 percent of courses have fewer than 20 students. The college's honor code allows students to take unproctored exams.

The Maytum Center for Student Success works with students interested in study abroad, community service, and undergraduate research, and the school encourages students to have multiple experiences in these areas. The Career Education office helps students with career exploration, internships, and mentoring. Off campus, the college offers sponsored study-away programs in several U.S. cities and 15 countries, as well as semester internships and field-based research opportunities. Ten percent of students take part in some type of international experience. There's also an

> **"Hundreds of us are on campus every summer being paid to do research."**

Large-scale philanthropic events like Make a Difference Day and Service Saturdays are particularly popular.

on-campus independent study option and a three- or four-week Experiential Learning term in May that allows students to pursue short-term study abroad programs and internships. Allegheny boasts an award-winning undergraduate research program—"Hundreds of us are on campus every summer being paid to do research," raves a junior.

Fifty-four percent of students hail from Pennsylvania, with sizable contingents from Ohio, New York, and California; 6 percent are international. A political science and women's gender and sexuality major describes the study body as "a mix of niche/quirky individuals with a big population of athletes." Black students make up 9 percent of the student population, Hispanics/Latinos 7 percent, Asian Americans 3 percent, and multiracial students 4 percent. Politically, a sophomore reports, the school "veers heavily left," and a student who hails from Puerto Rico shares, "It can be hard as a foreign student of color in a school with a predominant white community, this also being located in a very conservative area." But, adds the student, "Allegheny has done an excellent job at making all the students feel included and celebrating the differences." Forty-one percent of students qualify for Pell Grants. Merit scholarships averaging $34,800 are available, but there are no athletic awards.

Allegheny students live on campus for all four years, a requirement that a senior says "helps build community but also means that people live in a dorm room longer than they may want to." Options include all-first-year dorms, co-ed and single-sex halls, small special-interest houses, and apartment-style housing for juniors and seniors. Students are mostly satisfied with their on-campus food choices and note that food trucks are also a popular option. A student organization called Why Not Us? promotes sexual assault awareness and advocacy.

"Allegheny has done an excellent job at making all the students feel included."

According to an English lit and business major, "There are frats on campus and bars in town, so parties and drinking occur, but it's not a huge part of the college's social scene." School policies allow alcohol on campus for those of age. Fraternities and sororities draw 15 percent of the men and 22 percent of the women and provide a great deal of nightlife. The Office of Student Leadership and Involvement offers a campus theater series, free movies in the quad, and comedians, hypnotists, slam poets, and live bands. Homecoming and Springfest (a day full of bands, activities, and food) break up the monotony of studying, and midnight breakfasts help ease end-of-semester stress. When crossing the campus's Rustic Bridge at the start of the year, remember to look down—it's a long-standing Allegheny tradition for students to steal the 13th plank.

Downtown Meadville is a 10-minute walk from campus but isn't really a college town, although a junior points out, "There are some hidden gems, including great restaurants, a movie theater, and a bowling alley." It also has community playhouses, as well as hospitals, children's homes, animal shelters, and other organizations that benefit from the more than 60,000 hours of service students contribute each year. "We've really

"Parties and drinking occur, but it's not a huge part of the college's social scene."

gotten to know the local businesses and take pride in supporting our local community," says an English major. Large-scale philanthropic events like Make a Difference Day and Service Saturdays are particularly popular, and the school offers community-engaged learning classes. When students hit the road, they usually venture to factory outlets in nearby Grove City, or to the bright lights of Pittsburgh, Erie, or Cleveland. Nearby state parks, Conneaut Lake, and Lake Erie offer hiking, waterskiing, and boating in warm weather and cross-country skiing in the winter.

Athletics play a big role in Allegheny life, and the Wise Sport and Fitness Center gives students looking to break a sweat reason to cheer. About a third of students compete in Division III athletics, and the Gators field 23 varsity teams, most of which compete in the Presidents' Athletic Conference. Men's and women's track and field, women's cross-country, and men's golf and tennis are the most competitive teams. Thirty percent participate in club and intramural sports, with ice hockey, ultimate Frisbee, bowling, and fencing drawing the most interest.

Allegheny has recently reduced the size of its faculty and eliminated majors in geology, religious studies, and film and digital storytelling. Nevertheless, the college continues to augment its history of academic excellence with a growing emphasis on extracurricular experiences designed to produce well-rounded alumni. The campus's natural beauty and the genuine affection students feel for it and for each other remain unchanged. Students appreciate the value placed on individuality and involvement. "There is a space for everyone, and the academic opportunities are endless," says a happy senior. "The students that come out of Allegheny are well-rounded and although they carry their own beliefs, they have a great understanding of the world. I came looking for a great environmental science department, and I got exactly what I was looking for."

If You Apply To ›

Allegheny: Early decision, early action, regular decision. SATs or ACTs: optional. Accepts the Common Application with supplement.

Alma College

614 West Superior Street, Alma, MI 48801

The college that put the "Alma" back in "alma mater." As friendly a campus as you'll find, Alma savors its Scottish heritage and combines the liberal arts with strengths in health and preprofessional fields. Students are fairly diverse socioeconomically, but few out-of-staters enroll. If central Michigan eventually gives you cabin fever, join the hordes who go abroad. Bring your bagpipes.

A tiny gem on Michigan's lower peninsula, Alma College was founded in 1886 by Presbyterians with an ambitious fourfold mission: "To prepare graduates who think critically, serve generously, lead purposefully, and live responsibly." Located in the city dubbed "Scotland, USA," the college puts its strong Scottish Presbyterian heritage on display. "Every spring, the city of Alma holds an annual Highland Festival that draws participants from all over the world," explains an environmental health major. "Our marching band also wears traditional Scottish kilts to every football game." Alma offers a wide array of choices for its undergraduates, including distinctive programs in health and preprofessional fields, as well as plenty of opportunities to learn abroad.

Alma's campus, located an hour north of the state capital of Lansing, features 27 Prairie-style buildings of red brick and limestone surrounding a scenic central mall. Although Alma was founded in 1886, most of the buildings have been built or renovated in recent years. The new 78,000-square-foot Andrus Family Field House opened in 2025. There are lots of trees and open places to sit, at least in the warmer months.

Alma's general education requirements include a First-Year Seminar to help ease the transition into college and coursework in writing, math, and a foreign language.

(continued)

Social: 💬 💬 💬
Q of L: ★ ★ ★
Admissions: (800) 321-2562
Email Address:
 admissions@alma.edu

Strong Programs:
Biology
Business
Education
Integrative Physiology and
 Health Science
New Media Studies
Nursing
Political Science
Psychology

During their first two years, students take four Explore courses, one in each of the following categories: making and understanding the arts, self and society, applying scientific thinking, and engaging in equity and justice. An interdisciplinary seminar is required in the junior or senior year. A peer mentoring program places successful older students in contact with new students to help them adapt to the opportunities and expectations of the Alma community. Students accepted to the four-year Presidential Honors Program complete a two-credit honors seminar for each of their first two years, followed by an honors thesis or research project their junior and senior years.

The college offers nearly 50 majors, of which integrative physiology and health science, biology, business, new media studies, and political science are some of the strongest. The business program now includes five interdisciplinary concentrations covering analytics, leadership, sports management, operations, and environmental responsibility. Alma's most popular majors, by student enrollment, are business, nursing, psychology, and education.

> **"Alma College always involves students in the hiring process for new professors."**

A number of health-related preprofessional tracks are available, ranging from dentistry and optometry to physical therapy and sports medicine, in addition to preprofessional programs for engineering and law. Students interested in the Scottish arts find a range of opportunities to work with nationally known instructors of bagpipe and Highland dance.

According to a political science and economics major, "The academic climate at Alma is extremely lively and individualized to each student's unique perspectives and goals." Sixty-five percent of classes have fewer than 20 students, and many of them incorporate service-learning opportunities. Undergraduate research is big at Alma, too, with 39 percent of students pursuing an independent project under a professor's guidance or joining faculty projects. "Although academics are challenging, all of my professors have been more than happy to help and are very understanding," says a pre-physical therapy major. Adds an education and dance double major, "The quality of instruction is also impeccable, as Alma College always involves students in the hiring process for new professors."

Alma's student-centered philosophy is exemplified by the Alma Commitment, which offers a promise that students will graduate on time (within four or four and a half years, depending on the major) and a pledge that each interested student can undertake an experiential learning opportunity, such as an internship, research fellowship, or study abroad. All students are also eligible for up to $2,500 in funding for

> **"Politically, you will get a range of views."**

these opportunities. "The Venture Grant at Alma is really something special," says a business leadership and management major. Despite Alma's small size and rural surroundings, the terms "provincial" and "insular" just don't apply here. International study is highly encouraged, and 36 percent of students go abroad. Fittingly, Alma has a study abroad partnership with the University of Aberdeen in Scotland, along with programs in 13 other countries. During the one-month spring term in May, students enroll in a single intensive course; about a third of the courses offered involve off-campus travel. Additionally, the Posey Global Leadership Fellowship Program funds more than 30 fellowships each year for students to participate in international internship, research, and leadership experiences. "I've been on five continents in the past four years thanks to this program," enthuses an environmental science major.

"My fellow students at Alma College are driven, caring, and open to growth," says an education and dance double major. The campus is largely homogeneous, with 86 percent of the student population coming from Michigan and 5 percent from abroad. "Politically, you will get a range of views," says a senior. "There's a

During the one-month spring term in May, students enroll in a single intensive course.

lot of respectful debate." Black students account for 6 percent of the student population, Asian Americans 1 percent, Hispanics/Latinos 4 percent, and multiracial students 3 percent. Brainy types can vie for merit scholarships that average $31,000; there are no athletic scholarships.

Ninety-one percent of Alma's students reside in campus housing, and the college has invested $24 million in remodeling and modernizing the residence halls. First-years are assigned rooms in co-ed halls, while upperclassmen play the lottery and usually get suites. Other options include an international house, a Model UN house, and college-owned apartments in a historic, converted opera house downtown. For meals, students go to the all-you-can-eat Hamilton Commons or Joe's Place, a snack bar. "Dining services cater to athletes and therefore the entire school is very well-fed," remarks a senior. Career advising and mental health support are strong say students who also note that they feel safe on campus.

When it comes time to socialize, the Alma College Union Board provides plenty of on-campus fun. "We offer music performances, movie nights, speakers, student panels, and tons of events in the dorms," says a senior. Twenty-seven percent of the men and 28 percent of the women go Greek. Parties at Greek houses are registered and monitored by security officers who scan IDs and distribute wristbands; students say these policies help keep underage drinking in check.

Town/gown relations at Alma are strong, with a majority of students volunteering, taking part-time jobs, and otherwise getting involved in the community. When it comes to nightlife, though, one student says the small city of Alma (population 9,000) "does not offer too much to do," other than a movie theater and a few restaurants. The annual Highland Festival features traditional Scottish games, bagpipers, and dancing. "Kilts are even sold in the bookstore," adds a sophomore. Students with wheels will find diversions within easy reach, as Mount Pleasant, Saginaw, and the East Lansing campus of Michigan State are less than an hour away, and ski slopes are just a bit farther. In the warmer months, the beaches of two Great Lakes, Huron and Michigan, are two hours away.

The new 78,000-square-foot Andrus Family Field House opened in 2025.

"Our marching band also wears traditional Scottish kilts to every football game."

The Alma Scots compete in Division III as a member of the Michigan Intercollegiate Athletic Association. Alma offers 13 varsity sports—including an eSports program—and some of the strongest include wrestling, football, women's volleyball, and competitive cheer. "Though we are a D3 college, we tail gate like a D1 college," raves a political science and communications major. For nonvarsity types, there is an active intramural program—about 30 percent of the students participate. Alma's Model United Nations program is internationally known and a record holder for "outstanding delegation" awards at the National Model UN Conference in New York City, the longest streak of any college or university.

Alma challenges students to take their learning beyond the classroom and around the globe, and with caring faculty—and ample funding for off-campus experiences—students feel supported every step along the way. As one senior says, "The chance to get involved in campus projects and hands-on learning has really helped me grow and apply what I learn in the classroom to real life. These opportunities make Alma really unique and worth checking out."

Overlaps

Adrian, Albion, Aquinas, Hope, Kalamazoo, Olivet, Trine, Wooster

If You Apply To ›

Alma: Rolling admissions. Accepts the Common Application with Alma supplement. Please consult Alma's website for the most up-to-date information regarding standardized test requirements

3400 South 43rd Street, Milwaukee, WI 53234

At last, a college that evaluates students on what they can do rather than how well they can memorize. Forget oval blackening; students here show mastery in their chosen fields. Practical and hands-on, Alverno gives its all-female and economically diverse students the real-life experience necessary to succeed beyond graduation.

Website: www.alverno.edu
Location: City Outskirts
Private
Total Enrollment: 987
Undergraduates: 527
Male/Female: 1/98
Financial Aid: 95%
Pell Grant: 68%
Expense: Pr $
Student Loans: 86%
Average Debt: $ $
Applicants: 624
Accepted: 86%
Enrolled: 16%
Grad in 6 Years: 51%
Returning First-years: 61%
Academics: ✍ ✍ ✍
Social: 💬
Q of L: ★ ★ ★ ★
Admissions: (414) 382-6100
Email Address:
admissions@alverno.edu

Strong Programs:
Biology
Business
Communication
Education
Music Therapy
Nursing
Psychology
Social Work

If you're the type of student who obsesses over your GPA, take heed: At Alverno College, you can forget about earning an A. This Roman Catholic, women's liberal arts college emphasizes ability-based learning instead of letter grades. While its roots go back to 1887, Alverno came into its own in the 1970s with its distinctive approach to learning and, unlike other educational innovations of that era, has found a continuing niche. The student body is diverse—in age, background, and religion—and while the ability-based method centers on individual growth, the learning environment is highly collaborative. "Alverno is empowering," says a music therapy major, because it's all about "finding each student's gifts and celebrating them."

Alverno is located in a quiet residential area of Milwaukee. The parklike 46-acre campus is just 15 minutes from downtown and a 10-minute walk from shops and restaurants. The Sister Joel Read Center houses 73,000 square feet of science labs, multimedia production space, and computer facilities. Alexia Hall features a high-tech nursing simulation center, art and dance studios, classrooms, private study rooms, and a student commons area.

Alverno students are required to show mastery in eight key abilities: communication, analysis, problem-solving, valuing in decision-making, social interaction, developing a global perspective, effective citizenship, and aesthetic engagement. Students move through interdisciplinary progressive levels toward a degree by being "validated" in these areas. For example, a course in sociology might contribute to validation in communication and social interaction, as well as in making independent value judgments. The college offers detailed feedback rather than letter grades, and faculty find innovative, "real-life" ways to assess students' mastery of subject matter. First-year students take a First-Semester Seminar and introductory courses in the arts and humanities, science, psychology and social science, communication, and math. Religious studies aren't required, but a Catholic liturgy is available. Students are also required to participate in off-campus, credit-bearing internships through Alverno's highly acclaimed internship program—one of the longest-standing programs of its type in the country.

"The level of professionalism that Alverno students have compared to those at other colleges or universities is amazing," one junior says. Alverno's nursing, education, and social work programs are well established and among the most popular majors, along with psychology and liberal arts.

"Alverno is empowering."

Students praise the communication and music therapy programs as well. Many professors at Alverno teach all levels of classes, so the quality of teaching is consistent throughout a student's college career, and regular academic advising keeps students on track. Seventy-eight percent of classes enroll fewer than 20 students, and students have easy access to faculty. "The faculty and staff really care whether you are successful," says a student. "They want to see you achieve and are willing to go [above] and beyond to make sure you do." Roughly 22 percent of students participate in the honors program, which provides travel fellowships, research opportunities, and special events for qualifying students. Alverno also boasts a dedicated Career Studio that provides career planning and job search assistance to students and alumnae, including frequent networking and on-campus recruiting events with employers. "We couldn't have more help," one junior says. A small number of Alverno students study abroad, often heading out on short, 10- to 14-day trips that complement a semester-long course. Twenty-five percent of students undertake faculty-guided research projects.

"Students are extraordinarily driven, and they know what it takes to succeed in the real world," says a junior. Eighty-nine percent of Alverno undergraduates hail from Wisconsin, and a quarter are above the age of 24; less than 1 percent are international. Alverno is one of the most inclusive and diverse colleges in the state, particularly socio-economically: 68 percent of first-years are eligible for Pell Grants. Black students account for 19 percent of the student body, Hispanics/Latinas 42 percent, Asian Americans 5 percent, and multiracial students 4 percent. A quarter of students are Catholic. According to a sophomore, the political climate is "fairly liberal, especially in relation to immigration, prison reform, and women's and LGBTQ rights." Merit scholarships are awarded based on a personal evaluation of each incoming student.

A one-day orientation program serves all new students. The majority are commuters, though dorm rooms house 18 percent of students, who say the residence halls offer clean, spacious rooms with fully equipped lounges, laundry, and cooking facilities available on each floor. Male visitors are allowed, but they must sign in and be out by midnight on week-days. Dining services draw complaints for offering limited options (especially for those with dietary restrictions), inconvenient hours, and overpriced meals. Events like Love Your Body Week and Denim Day promote student wellness and prevention of sexual violence.

"Students . . . know what it takes to succeed in the real world."

Dozens of cultural, dance, theater, and other student groups are active on campus, and the school has an on-site childcare center and a fitness center. But most of the social life takes place off campus at local clubs, bars, restaurants, coffee shops, and nearby colleges. "Milwaukee is a thriving city of the arts—visual, theatrical, and performance—not to mention the festivals that go on every year," says one art education major. In addition to a Performing Arts Center, free outdoor concerts, and multicultural festivals, the city also offers professional sports teams, parks, and shopping centers. Students look forward to Alverno's annual homecoming festivities and Community Day, which allows students and faculty to participate in an annual day of service. "Many of our programs are family friendly and inviting for students with children to attend," explains a sophomore.

Alverno competes in Division III athletics, including basketball, cross-country, golf, soccer, and tennis. The Inferno softball and volleyball teams have been the most successful programs recently. An informal intramural program occasionally offers activities like kickball and board-game tournaments. One-credit wellness courses on skills ranging from yoga and meditation to self-defense and crochet are offered every semester.

Attending a school like Alverno promises an experience far afield in some ways from the traditional college world. The emphasis on real-world applications builds confidence in one's actual ability to perform rather than the ability to score an A. Diverse students and faculty are often on a first-name basis from the start and build relationships that help students cultivate their personal strengths. The result? In the words of one biology major, "My school is the most uplifting place that I've ever encountered."

Overlaps

Carroll University, Marquette, Mount Mary, UW–Milwaukee

If You Apply To ›

Alverno: Rolling admissions. Does not accept the Common Application. Admits students who consistently live and identify as women, regardless of biological sex, and female students who identify as nonbinary or gender nonconforming. SATs or ACTs: optional.

4400 Massachusetts Avenue NW, Washington, D.C. 20016

If the odds are stacked against you at Georgetown and you can't see yourself on GW's ultra-urban campus, welcome to American University. The allure of AU is simple: Washington, D.C. American's campus is an accredited arboretum in a suburban–like northwest Washington neighborhood with easy access to the Metro and endless internship opportunities. American is smaller and less selective than GW.

Website: www.american.edu
Location: City Outskirts
Private
Total Enrollment: 9,964
Undergraduates: 7,061
Male/Female: 37/63
Financial Aid: 78%
Pell Grant: 23%
Expense: Pr $ $
Student Loans: 51%
Average Debt: $ $ $
Applicants: 17,154
Accepted: 61%
Enrolled: 16%
Grad in 6 Years: 75%
Returning First-years: 88%
Academics: ✑ ✑ ✑ ✑
Social: 🗩 🗩 🗩
Q of L: ★ ★ ★
Admissions: (202) 885-6000
Email Address:
admissions@american.edu

Strong Programs:
Business Administration
Communication, Legal
  Institutions, Economics, and
  Government
Environmental Science
International Service
Journalism
Political Science
Public Relations

Located just a few miles from our country's seat of power, American University has been a breeding ground for the next generation of reporters, diplomats, lobbyists, political leaders, and policymakers since it opened its doors to graduate students in 1914 and undergrads in 1923. Students take advantage of AU's strong programs in the arts, sciences, and business and recognize that Boston and New York City are not the only tempting urban destinations for college students. "American University is a diverse, pulsing, and dynamic school driven by some of the best faculty, staff, scholars, and students in the world," a senior says. Thanks to phenomenal internships, a comfortable location, and a strong international focus, AU continues to attract students from around the world.

At the urging of Methodist bishops, AU was established by an Act of Congress in 1892 with the goal of training public servants, and it remains affiliated with the Methodist Church. Its 90-acre residential campus is situated in the northwest corner of Washington, D.C., in an upscale (and safe) area that's just minutes from downtown; free shuttle buses transport students to the nearby Metro (subway) station. There's a mix of classical and modern architecture. Flower gardens line the parking lots, and the quad has numerous sitting areas for reflection and study. The 70,000-square-foot, environmentally friendly School of International Service building is LEED Gold–certified. In 2018, AU became the first university in the United States to achieve carbon neutrality. AU has been boosting research efforts in the sciences with the 125,000-square-foot Hall of Science, housing four life sciences departments, and the Don Myers Technology and Innovation building houses high-tech laboratories, classrooms, and research space and achieved R1 status in 2025.

AU's core curriculum aims to develop students into lifelong learners who "apply their learning to building lives of purpose, service, and leadership." First-years begin by taking Complex Problems, a small-group seminar focused on analyzing a special topic, and a yearlong AU Experience sequence that acclimates them to university life. In addition to coursework in writing, math or statistics, and diversity, students fulfill Habits of Mind requirements that cover five areas, ranging from ethical reasoning to culture and aesthetics. Finally, all students complete a capstone course or project in their major. The core still leaves plenty of time for students to delve into experiential learning, and more than 90 percent of them do so, pursuing "internships, study abroad programs, and coauthored research with our diverse and driven faculty," explains an administrator, much of it facilitated by the school's relationships with hundreds of private, nonprofit, and government institutions. The Cornerstone program offers first-years a D.C. internship, a fall study abroad in Madrid, or a spring study abroad in Greece. All students can choose from over 100 other study abroad programs.

> **"I have had professors who were former chiefs of staff to congressmen and senators, ambassadors, [and] diplomats."**

In the classroom, "The climate is not cutthroat," says a political science and economics major. AU has outstanding programs in political science, international service, business, journalism, public relations, and environmental science. "I have had professors who were former chiefs of staff to congressmen and senators, ambassadors, diplomats, as well as many other professors who had extensive experience in these fields," adds the student. A popular interdisciplinary major in communication, legal institutions, economics, and government combines many of AU's traditional strengths, and students also have the option to design their own interdisciplinary major. In all, students may choose from nearly 80 programs. Three-year bachelor's degree tracks are available in international studies; public health; and politics, policy, and law; B.A./M.A. degree options are also available. One media arts and film major who's pursuing the dual degree says the program "lets me apply one class's credit to both my undergraduate and graduate requirements." Fifty-seven percent of all classes taken by undergraduates have fewer than 20 students. A four-year honors program offers a select group of entering students small seminars, special sections of many courses, and designated floors in the residence halls.

The Cornerstone program offers first-years a D.C. internship, a fall study abroad in Madrid, or a spring study abroad in Greece.

"Our students have knowledge in subjects, hobbies, and more that make them whole individuals with diverse interests," a sophomore says. AU prides itself on drawing students from every state and more than 100 foreign countries; just 19 percent of undergrads come from the D.C. metro region, and 5 percent hail from outside the U.S. "AU is a very international campus," observes one senior. Eight percent of undergraduates are Black, 14 percent are Hispanic/Latino, 7 percent are Asian American, and 6 percent are multiracial. A relatively high proportion—nearly two-thirds—are women. An economics and political science major says, "We lean liberal here at AU, [and] we are much more vocal about politics compared to the average college student." The university offers hundreds of merit scholarships, averaging $13,700, and $47,600 in athletic scholarships to new students.

More than two-thirds of AU students live in campus housing, which is guaranteed for the first two years. AU offers traditional, suite-style, and apartment-style options; students report that the quality varies. Living/learning options are available, including the two-year D.C. Community Impact Scholars program, which involves opportunities for service-oriented research. "LLCs can fulfill core requirements and are a great way to do so while building community," notes a public relations and strategic communications major. AU completely renovated its main dining hall, and the food gets generally good reviews. A junior says, "AU is an open campus and feels very safe," and educational programming on personal wellness and preventing sexual assault is extensive. Students also praise other support services from career advising to the Center for Well-Being and the Center for Student Belonging.

"We have anything socially that people are looking for."

"I like to call AU a jack-of-all-trades school because we have anything socially that people are looking for," cheers a senior. On-campus fun revolves around club activities and functions organized by the student government. The AU campus is officially dry, and a senior says, "Many of our students go downtown in D.C. to clubs, bars, or parties at other schools." Only a small portion of the student body goes Greek. The immediate area around AU has restaurants and shops, and D.C. offers ample entertainment, much of it free—the art house movie theaters, gallery openings, pro soccer games, and more. "You just jump on the Metro to get anywhere," says a communication studies major. A favorite annual event, AMFEST brings bands, free food trucks, carnival rides, and more to campus. Quad Scream, right before finals, is a tradition that also gets a shout-out from students. Popular road trips include Baltimore, Williamsburg, Richmond, and Ocean City.

The immediate area around AU has restaurants and shops, and D.C. offers ample entertainment, much of it free.

The American University Eagles compete in the Division I Patriot League. Without a football team, students are most enthusiastic about men's basketball.

Men's soccer, women's volleyball, and wrestling are also strong. Field hockey and women's swimming have brought home recent conference championships. Games against Bucknell, Holy Cross, and the Naval Academy highlight the schedule. Students also take part in more than 25 intramural and club sports, ranging from volleyball and ultimate Frisbee to sailing and eSports, which are divided into different levels of competitiveness.

AU is heaven on earth for news junkies. But even if you are not addicted to watching C-SPAN 24/7, AU and Washington, D.C., are still a top combo for a rich college life. The opportunities for real-world experience—in fields ranging from business to international studies to political science—are outstanding. But AU is small enough to keep students from feeling lost in the fast-paced world inside the Beltway. As a sophomore explains, "American is perfect for those looking for a city school and normal college experience mash-up."

If You Apply To ›

American: Early decision I and II, early action, regular decision. SATs or ACTs: optional. Accepts the Common Application with supplement.

Amherst College

220 South Pleasant Street, Amherst, MA 01002

Original home to the well-rounded, superachieving, gentle-person jock. Compare to Williams, Middlebury, and Colby. Amherst has always been a standout in part because there are four other local institutions in easy reach to add diversity and depth. Among the few liberal arts colleges with nearly as many men as women. National leader among elite privates in seeking socioeconomic diversity and moving away from legacy admissions.

Amherst was founded in 1821 when the president of Williams College decided that Williamstown was too remote. With a handful of Williams professors and students in tow, he relocated 50 miles closer to Boston and set in motion centuries of fierce rivalry. Amherst has traditionally been a bastion of New England's elite, but over the last several decades, it has done an about-face. It has used its $3.5 billion endowment to become a national leader in extending high-quality liberal arts education to a diverse student body. Indeed, about half of the student body in the 2024–25 academic year were domestic students of color. Emphasizing "freedom to explore," Amherst puts the spotlight on learning and allows students to focus not on racking up high grade point averages, but rather on becoming people who base their thinking on a strong foundation in the liberal arts. "If your education is really your first priority," says a sophomore, "then I don't think there's a better school."

Amherst's 1,000 acres overlook the picturesque town of Amherst and the Connecticut River Valley and offer a panoramic view of the Holyoke Range and the Pelham Hills. On campus, a plot of open land housing a wildlife sanctuary and a forest shares space with academic and residential buildings, athletic fields, and facilities. Amherst looks like a college is supposed to look, with trees and paths winding through the buildings to offer long, contemplative walks. While Amherst's predominant architectural style remains 19th-century academia—red brick is key—everything from a "pale yellow octagonal structure to a garish, modern dorm" can be found here. A $242 million makeover of the east side of campus included the construction of four new residence halls and the interdisciplinary Science Center. Amherst's process of transitioning to a Geothermal Energy System is expected to continue through 2026.

Amherst offers a dynamic open curriculum in the traditional academic disciplines and in numerous interdisciplinary fields, and students choose their program based on their own individual interests and plans for the future. To graduate, students must take a first-year seminar, declare a major at the end of sophomore year, and satisfy all major program requirements. First-year seminars, limited to 15 students and occasionally taught by two or more professors, help foster interdisciplinary approaches across topics and are offered in several subject areas. Forty-six percent of students choose to undertake a capstone experience.

The most popular of Amherst's 43 majors include mathematics, economics, psychology, computer science, and English. Students may create their own courses of study from Special Topics classes if the subject of their interest is not available. Amherst's unique Law, Jurisprudence, and Social Thought program is not a prelaw major; instead, it's an interdisciplinary study of the law, drawing on fields as diverse as psychology, history, philosophy, and literature, with a strong theoretical focus. A new Asian American and Pacific Islander studies major examines the history, culture, and lived experiences of immigrants from that part of the world. Amherst's membership in the Five College Consortium means that students can also take courses from partner schools Mount Holyoke, UMass Amherst, Smith, and Hampshire—a benefit that significantly expands students' options.

The academic climate at Amherst is intense, but the classroom environment is supportive, and interaction with faculty is encouraged. "I've had professors who stayed after class to talk through a single question, or who sent thoughtful feedback on papers that made me see my own ideas in a new light," says an economics and math major. Through the Take Your Professor Out program, students receive funding to invite their professors out for dinner off campus once per semester.

Amherst's commitment to academic flexibility extends beyond traditional coursework. Students report that it's easy to get involved with faculty research as early as your first semester, and many praise the Summer Undergraduate Research Fellowship, which comes with a stipend and housing for STEM research. The Meiklejohn Fellows program provides summer internships and research opportunities for low-income and first-generation students. One student cheers the Strategic Learning Center as "a game-changer" for students struggling with the transition to college and academic life. For the 42 percent of students who choose to study abroad, there are more than 150 programs in dozens of countries to choose from; participants are able to apply their financial aid packages to approved programs. Amherst also has a sister university in Göttingen, Germany, and another in Kyoto, Japan, where one of the college's colonial-style buildings has been duplicated.

"Amherst students are curious, well-balanced, and love a good laugh," says a sophomore. Only 12 percent of Amherst students hail from Massachusetts, and 13 percent are international. "The students care deeply about a wide range of topics, and there's a strong culture of awareness and engagement," says a sophomore, adding, "Amherst is also one of the most diverse communities I've ever been part of." Sixteen percent are Asian American, 14 percent are Hispanic/Latino, 9 percent are Black, and 9 percent are multiracial. As part of its ongoing efforts to increase diversity, Amherst no longer considers legacy status in admissions—a

"I've had professors who stayed after class to talk through a single question."

Amherst students pioneered the development of ultimate Frisbee in the mid-1960s.

"Amherst is also one of the most diverse communities I've ever been part of."

practice that gives preference to the children of alumni. Furthermore, admission is need-blind, and all financial aid is awarded based on need, meaning no merit or athletic scholarships. Amherst guarantees to meet 100 percent of admitted students' calculated financial need with loan-free financial aid packages, which has helped attract a substantial number of low-income and Pell-eligible students.

Housing at Amherst is guaranteed for four years, and 97 percent of students live on campus. "First-year housing is absolutely beautiful," raves a math and computer science major. "Rooms are well-sized, and most freshmen will end up in a double, although there are a few triples spread out across the first-year quad." Those who don't want to take their chances with the room draw can participate in Lip-Sync+, a competition in which the winners receive the first shot at a triple or suite. A new Student Center and Dining Commons is expected to open in fall 2026 and will provide everything "from healthy food to recreational and spiritual activities to spaces for community engagement and fun." Students agree that the campus feels safe, and mental health services "are really good," says an anthropology major.

Although frats are nothing more than a faint memory, social activities are conducted almost entirely on campus. They range from dorm study breaks to club events to low-key gatherings. "It's definitely not a school of 'Thirsty Thursdays,'" says a sophomore. "It's common to work on Friday up to dinner." Sports teams host most of the parties, which are generally open to all students, and a history and computer science major reports, "The college takes a realistic approach to handling student alcohol use." The Powerhouse, a building that originally served as a campus steam plant at the turn of the 20th century, has been converted into a nightlife venue. Students take full advantage of the Five Colleges membership and, says an English major, most "socialize across campuses." Seasonal festivals and Food Truck Fridays are favorite events and the Senior Dorm Storm, when students about to graduate "storm" the dorm where they lived as first-years, sharing stories with the current first-year students living there.

The town of Amherst offers "lots of local restaurants, cafes, and stores and is a five-minute walk from campus," says an economics major. "We also have a bus system (free to students!) that goes to the other four colleges in the consortium, Northampton, Springfield, and a nearby mall with Trader Joe's, Target, a movie theater, escape rooms, and more." Many students take part in community service projects, and the college funds roughly 150 summer public service internships every year. For the many outdoorsy types, good skiing in Vermont is not far, and Boston (an hour and a half) and New York (a little over three hours) are close enough to be convenient road-trip destinations.

Sports are taken seriously, both varsity and intramurals. The school has removed its century-old unofficial mascot, "Lord Jeff" (Lord Jeffery Amherst was a British general who sought to exterminate indigenous people), and introduced a new mascot, the Mammoth. Amherst competes in Division III, but the strong baseball team takes on Division I opponents as well. Men's soccer brought home the national Division III title in 2024; women's basketball has won two national championships in recent years, and men's and women's soccer and women's ice hockey have brought home recent New England Small College Athletic Conference titles. "We have an athletic rivalry with Williams dating back 200 years," says a senior, drawing fans from all corners of campus. Amherst students pioneered the development of ultimate Frisbee in the mid-1960s, when players were still using metal cake pan lids, and the college's intramural and club programs continue to be well supported.

"First-year housing is absolutely beautiful!"

In recent years, Amherst has been an outspoken proponent—and model—of the value of diversity and inclusivity for the liberal arts, and these institutional values are not lost on its students. "'Supportive' is the first word that comes to mind when I describe Amherst," says a film and media studies major. The lack of restrictive requirements, a cadre of professors who are focused on teaching, and a devoted alumni network make it clear why most students love their institution. Says a sophomore, "Amherst's culture values inclusion, community, and personal growth, and that's something I think really sets it apart from other schools."

If You Apply To ›

Amherst: Early decision, regular decision. Accepts the Common Application. Please consult Amherst's website for the most up-to-date information regarding standardized test requirements.

Antioch College

One Morgan Place, Yellow Springs, OH 45387

Part social activist, part granola, and part anarchist with plenty of none-of-the-above mixed in, Antioch is a haven for square pegs. After shutting its doors in 2008 for three years, Antioch returned to offering its signature co-op program: academic study interspersed with 11-week work experiences. March and protest to change the world, then get a job. Cool.

Antioch College has long been the poster child for the funky diversity that characterizes U.S. higher education. Since its founding in 1852 by abolitionist and social reformer Horace Mann, this small liberal arts college in the Ohio boondocks has nurtured outspoken and socially aware students who thrive under the rigors of refreshingly nontraditional education. In 1902, Antioch pioneered the concept of co-op education, in which students alternate time in the classroom with jobs in the "real world." It is one of only ten Federal Work Study colleges (see also Warren Wilson).

The college was forced to shut its doors in 2008 because of inept management, but in 2011, it reopened, phoenix-like, thanks to loyal alumni and others unwilling to allow Antioch's signature approach to education to become a footnote to history. As it grapples with inevitable enrollment and financial challenges, Antioch is relying on a new generation of pioneers—students included—to reinvent the college for the 21st century.

Antioch is located in the progressive village of Yellow Springs (population 3,700), which has grown up around the college and become a popular destination for weekend tourists, thanks to its restaurants, art, and music. The campus is a mixture of traditional and eco-friendly buildings in various states of repair, including the giant Main Hall that looks like Hogwarts. The campus includes a working farm and dozens of geothermal wells, and it abuts the 1,000-acre Glen Helen Nature Preserve that serves both hikers and science students looking for field experience.

The academic climate is informal and collaborative, with most everyone called by their first name, but the overall atmosphere is hardly laid-back. "Because we are on an 11-week quarter system, we do the same amount of work that most people do in a semester," explains a psychology major. "Then there's the workload of helping to run a new college. That can be very mentally taxing."

Antioch, which views itself as a laboratory for democracy, is governed by a Community Council.

In 1902, Antioch pioneered the concept of co-op education, in which students alternate time in the classroom with jobs in the "real world."

Classes tend to be discussion-based, and take-home tests are common. The faculty is highly regarded but small, which means that turnover can be a problem. "A department can go from rock solid to extremely fragile in a matter of weeks," says a junior. Antioch's general education program includes a core curriculum with distribution requirements, as well as mandatory courses on dialogues across difference, race/ethnic studies, gender/sexuality studies, and a class that prepares students for cooperative education. In addition, all students complete a capstone project for which they create and present original work based on their self-designed major.

"Students, staff, and faculty get elected and make important decisions for our school."

Rather than selecting preset majors, all Antioch students design their own degree plans, picking and choosing courses from broad areas that suit their academic interests and needs. The curriculum offers several areas of focus, including culture, power, and change; global studies and engagement; interdisciplinary arts; social innovation; and sustainability and the environment. Students praise the biomedical and other sciences. "We have well-equipped labs and do a lot of sustainability projects, such as learning about climate change, recycling, composting, and other things that would help save our planet," says a sophomore. A peer mentoring program supports first-year and first-generation students, while Early Alert and First Watch programs ensure that students do not fall through the cracks. Career and other counseling services are said to be caring but understaffed. Antioch, which views itself as a laboratory for democracy, is governed by a Community Council. "Students, staff, and faculty get elected and make important decisions for our school. Our shared governance is pivotal to Antioch," says one denizen.

Under Antioch's flagship co-op program, students engage in full-time cooperative education experiences, generally off campus, for three or four quarters throughout their time at the college. "By the time you graduate, you have four amazing jobs on your résumé," gushes a sophomore. Each student is assigned a co-op advisor to help with the nearly continuous job hunt, which is eased by Antioch's extensive network of alumni. The downside: With students constantly coming and going, it is sometimes hard to maintain friendships and engage in extracurricular activities. Antioch has no study abroad program, but about 10 percent of students do co-ops in foreign countries.

Antioch students tend to be independent spirits. "We're all self-motivated and driven," says a first-year. "We're weirdos and proud." The student body is fairly diverse geographically, with 67 percent coming from out of state, but rural Ohio is an unlikely destination of choice for many students of color, and there are no international students. "It's an adjustment, especially if you're coming from a diverse area," says a junior. Black students currently make up 12 percent of the student body, Hispanics/Latinos 17 percent, American Indians 2 percent, Asian Americans 5 percent, and multiracial students 7 percent—but with such a small student body, these figures can shift significantly with each incoming class. "Our campus is almost entirely 'liberal' with a mixture of Marxists, Democrats, and Socialists," claims a student. "There are maybe two Republicans in the student body." A huge 77 percent of first-years are eligible for Pell Grants. The college offers a handful of merit scholarships, but most financial aid is need-based.

"Students can work on the farm and later eat their work."

Antioch operates a single dining facility with an all-or-nothing meal plan—19 meals a week or cook for yourself—and much of the food is supplied by local farmers and the student-staffed campus farm. That means, as a junior points out, that "Students can work on the farm and later eat their work." Students are required to live on campus in one of two residence halls or apartments until they are within a year of graduation. "There is no trouble finding housing," says a first-year. "Everything is very comfortable." Antioch was the first college to have a Sexual Offense Prevention Policy (SOPP) mandating verbal consent at every step of a sexual encounter, and entering students receive SOPP training during orientation. "We were famously mocked for it on *SNL*, but the rest of the country has slowly been following along," notes a political economy major.

In the absence of Greek organizations, social life tends to be rather low-key. "There's hiking, movies, two bars, and plenty of art and music events to attend both on campus and off," says a history major. Other diversions include the Camelot bike ride and quarterly dances before students head off on their co-ops. Dayton is 30 minutes away, Columbus and Cincinnati one hour. All sports at Antioch are intramural.

Antioch College is happily back on its feet but showing some growing pains. "We lose a lot of students due to the stressful environment," says a junior. "I think once we understand our institutional personality and promote it, we will have better retention rates." For many students, however, Antioch's search for an updated identity for the 21st century is part of what makes the place exciting. "Almost every person here has a different idea of what Antioch needs to be," observes a psychology major. "A perk of coming here is that you get to lend your hand in deciding what that will be."

If You Apply To ›

Antioch: Early decision I and II, rolling admissions. SATs or ACTs: optional. Accepts the Common Application with supplement. Application includes option to indicate gender identity and preferred pronouns. Art applicants must submit portfolios.

University of Arizona

1200 East University Boulevard, Tucson, AZ 85721

Tucson is an increasingly popular academic destination, and not just because of the scenic mountain views. A large and highly regarded honors college attracts top students, as do excellent programs in the sciences, arts, engineering, and business. Generally viewed as a cut above ASU in academic quality. Offers generous merit scholarships to eligible out-of-staters. Bring plenty of shorts and sunscreen.

With a campus that's encircled by mountain ranges and the beautiful Sonoran Desert, lined with palm trees, and set against a backdrop of stunning Tucson sunsets, it's no surprise that students at the University of Arizona love to hang out at the Mall. Not the shopping center, mind you, but a huge grassy area in the middle of campus where 41,000 Wildcats gather between classes. Despite its size, students are quick to point out that Arizona has a strong sense of community. "On an average day, people are having picnics, walking their dogs, playing games, tanning, etc., on the Mall," says a senior. With all the natural beauty that surrounds them, many Wildcats simply purr through four satisfying years.

Architecturally, Arizona's campus distinguishes itself from the city's regiment of adobe buildings with a design that seems a study in the versatility of red brick. Old Main, the university's first building, is into its second century, but it has plenty of modern neighbors, including high-tech science facilities, such as the $85 million Applied Research Building and the $99 million Grand Challenges Research Building,

(continued)

Enrolled: 18%
Grad in 6 Years: 68%
Returning First-years: 83%
Academics: 🖉 🖉 🖉
Social: 🗩 🗩 🗩 🗩
Q of L: ★ ★ ★ ★
Admissions: (520) 621-3237
Email Address:
admissions@arizona.edu

Strong Programs:
Biomedical Engineering
Business Management
Hydrology and Atmospheric
   Sciences
Legal Professions and Studies
Management Information
   Systems
Nursing
Physiology
Psychology

Arizona's battle cry, "Bear Down!"— frequently heard at sporting events—dates back to 1926.

which houses labs and research space for interdisciplinary programs. Eager shutterbugs can pore through photographer Ansel Adams's personal collection at the first-rate Center for Creative Photography. The campus offers three state-of-the-art recreation centers, and the Student Success District centralizes health and wellness, tutoring, and academic advising services, in addition to providing access to library and technology resources like 3-D printers.

Arizona's general education curriculum incorporates opportunities for students to engage in interdisciplinary learning, showcase their work in e-portfolios, and reflect on their experiences. In addition to a first-year writing requirement and a one-credit general education capstone course, students complete coursework that focuses on different Perspectives (Artist, Humanist, Natural Scientist, and Social Scientist) and Attributes (Diversity and Equity, Quantitative Reasoning, World Cultures and Societies, and Writing).

Arizona, whose origins date to 1885, has 20 colleges and hundreds of undergraduate majors. Sciences are the school's forte—the astronomy department is among the nation's best. Students have access to leading astronomers, including those who have created instruments to help NASA's James Webb Space Telescope peer deep into the universe. The small but rigorous College of Architecture, Planning, and Landscape Architecture is a national leader in sustainable planning for arid regions. Programs in management information systems, nursing, law, hydrology and atmospheric sciences, and physiology are particularly well regarded, and the English and history departments are also standouts. The university also offers the first B.A. degree in law in the country. New majors include public relations and pharmacology and toxicology.

"The professors and teaching assistants are incredibly supportive."

"The academic climate is challenging but rewards student initiative and hard work," comments a history major. Some first-year courses are taught by graduate students, and 28 percent of all classes enroll fewer than 20 students. "The professors and teaching assistants are incredibly supportive and always willing to assist students who require help," says a computer science major. Students also praise the THINK TANK tutoring program that operates out of several academic buildings and residence halls for academic support.

Arizona's Student Engagement and Career Development office connects students with real-world learning experiences, whether through courses that involve experiential learning components or through out-of-classroom opportunities like internships and fieldwork. "The U of A is very strong in research, and they have specific programs to help undergrads get involved," reports a senior. Career educators in the LifeLab assist students with career planning. The W.A. Franke Honors College offers one of the nation's largest and most selective honors programs, serving more than 3,900 students. In addition to offering a variety of honors courses, the college features smaller classes, personalized advising, and the Honors Village living/learning community. For those seeking new vistas, there are study abroad programs available in more than 60 countries.

"The energy is so high all of the time," says a senior of the campus tenor. "It is a very loud, rowdy bunch of extremely passionate people." Out-of-staters constitute 48 percent of the undergraduate student body; another 8 percent hail from foreign countries. Hispanics/Latinos account for 28 percent, Black students 4 percent, Asian Americans 5 percent, and multiracial students 5 percent. "People have all kinds of political views," says a junior. Merit scholarships averaging $12,900 and hundreds of additional

"Our institutional personality is a mix of academic excellence and laid-back vibes."

scholarships are available to eligible students; out-of-staters with decent GPAs enjoy more generous merit scholarships here than at some of Arizona's biggest competitors.

Through the Arizona Native Scholars Grant, the university covers all fees for Native Arizona resident undergraduates seeking their first bachelor's degree. Still, the president has called for cuts in financial aid and an end to the tuition-guarantee program that locks in rates for eight semesters. Stay tuned.

A senior says rooms in Arizona's 23 residence halls are "first come, first served," but all are generally well maintained: "The U of A gives students the option to live in communities based on religious affiliation, major, nationality, or anything else that student asks," reports a student. Less than 10 percent of undergraduates live in the dorms; some first-years and most older students flock to the abundant and less expensive apartments near the school. Several restaurants are located in the student union food court and sprinkled around campus, but many students express a desire for more traditional dining halls and healthy choices. Regarding safety, a student says, "Recently, safety has become a topic of concern. Many students want to see improvements to ensure everyone feels secure."

Despite the high percentage of off-campus residents, students stream back to campus on weekends for parties, sports, cultural events, and other activities organized by more than 400 student clubs and organizations. Eleven percent of the men belong to fraternities, and 16 percent of the women join sororities; students say Greek groups have an outsize influence on the social scene. The campus is technically alcohol-free, though some question whether the frats have gotten the message. Homecoming, with its Homecoming Olympics competition between student orgs on the Mall and its massive bonfire, is always a crowd-pleaser. "Dusk music festival is a must-go," adds one senior. On Reading Day, the day before final exams begin, the university offers free snacks and stress-relieving activities like yoga, meditation, and coloring. "Tucson is a place that has something for everyone," says a care, health, and society major. "We have a unique desert climate, beautiful views, and Tucson itself has amazing food and culture," adds a journalism major. Students enjoy the city's shops, restaurants, bars, and various dance clubs, not to mention easy access to hiking and other outdoor activities. Phoenix is less than two hours away.

U of A student athletes compete in 18 sports in Division I of the Big 12 Conference. The Wildcats men's baseball, men's and women's tennis, men's golf, and the triathlon team have won conference titles in the last few years. Football and basketball enjoy national prominence and provide great weekend entertainment, especially when the opposing team is big-time rival Arizona State. As one Wildcat points out, "Every time we play against ASU in any sport, there are T-shirts, stickers, and people asking, 'A-S-who?'" Arizona's battle cry, "Bear Down!"—frequently heard at sporting events—dates back to 1926, when a campus football hero, fatally injured in a car crash, whispered his last message to his teammates: "Tell them, tell the team to bear down." Nearly 100 years later, the enigmatic slogan still appears all over campus.

The University of Arizona offers a wide variety of academic options along with spectacular weather. "Our institutional personality is a mix of academic excellence and laid-back vibes," says a junior. "We embrace diversity and creativity, making our campus a dynamic and inclusive place to learn and grow." And with so many out-of-this-world programs on offer, as another student shares, "Students get way more than a degree out of attending the University of Arizona."

"Dusk music festival is a must-go."

Overlaps

Arizona State, CU Boulder, Grand Canyon, Indiana University, Northern Arizona, San Diego State, University of Oregon, University of Washington

If You Apply To ›

Arizona: Early action, rolling admissions. SATs or ACTs: optional. Accepts the Common Application with supplement.

Arizona State University

1151 South Forest Avenue, Tempe, AZ 85287

ASU is the largest university in the nation—with ambitions to welcome even more students, make innovative use of AI, and increase socioeconomic diversity. Locations in the metro Phoenix area attract plenty of out-of-staters who like the idea of seeing the sun every day. Administration's emphasis on offering an education to anyone who wants one and is qualified to succeed makes the professional schools and Barrett, The Honors College, the best bets. Strong student support services.

Website: www.asu.edu
Location: City Center
Public
Total Enrollment: 71,541
Undergraduates: 60,276
Male/Female: 51/49
Financial Aid: 88%
Pell Grant: 37%
Expense: Pub $ $ $
Student Loans: 37%
Average Debt: $
Applicants: 70,928
Accepted: 90%
Enrolled: 22%
Grad in 6 Years: 70%
Returning First-years: 87%
Academics: ✍ ✍ ✍
Social: 🗩 🗩 🗩 🗩 🗩
Q of L: ★ ★ ★ ★ ★
Admissions: (480) 965-7788
Email Address:
admissions@asu.edu

Strong Programs:
Architecture
Art
Biological and Biomedical
 Sciences
Business
Education
Engineering
Health Professions
Journalism

With a history that dates to 1885, Arizona State University has transformed itself over the last decade into the nation's largest public university. With no pretense of modesty, this mega-university, situated in a desert oasis that is one of the nation's fastest-growing metro areas, describes itself as the model for a New American University—one where "massive innovation" is the norm and where an interdisciplinary culture is seen as the best means of developing "world-changing ideas." ASU's stated goal is to serve any Arizona student qualified for college-level work, and in the process, it has become a national model of how to navigate the emerging demographics of U.S. higher education. ASU became the first university to broker an agreement with OpenAI to provide students with unlimited access to ChatGPT. Research spending is up, as are student retention and graduation rates. It offers additional learning locations throughout Arizona, as well as in California, Hawai'i, Washington, D.C., London, and Bermuda. Students appreciate the breadth of learning experiences they receive. "I love how my professors integrate ethics into science lectures and plant biology into philosophy readings," says a happy biology major.

The most populous of ASU's four campuses, Tempe offers a beautiful blend of palm-lined walkways and contemporary urban architecture. It is home to the College of Liberal Arts and Sciences, business, art and design, and engineering programs. Fifteen minutes by light rail brings you to the Downtown Phoenix campus, which looks like it sounds. It houses journalism, nursing, public service, and law programs and has a young professionals feel. The Polytechnic campus, a converted Air Force base, specializes in science and technology and boasts a desert arboretum, while West Valley campus has the feel of a liberal arts learning community, with a large central lawn and a focus on interdisciplinary, collaborative studies. Each of the four campuses has a Pat Tillman Veterans Center, which brings together academic and student support services that serve the university's continually growing enrollment of veterans and their dependents. In addition, the ASU Local program allows students to pursue hybrid degrees, taking online courses and participating in hands-on learning experiences two days a week at satellite locations in Los Angeles, Long Beach, and Chula Vista, California; Yuma, Arizona; and Hawaii and Washington, D.C.

The academic star at ASU is Barrett, The Honors College, a selective school-within-a-school living/learning community that is home to more than 7,000 students from every school and college across all four campuses. Most of these denizens reside in a cloistered complex on the Tempe campus that was designed by students, faculty, and staff working with nationally renowned architects. The nation's first four-year residential honors college within a major public university, Barrett has more than 50 dedicated faculty members who oversee students' ambitious honors projects. "There is no sense of competition among these honors students," marvels a junior. "Instead the students and faculty want to see everyone thrive academically and personally."

ASU has 16 colleges and schools and more than 400 undergraduate degree programs. Regardless of major, all students must fulfill general education requirements that include courses in nine areas: humanities, arts, and design; social and behavioral sciences; natural sciences; quantitative reasoning; math; American institutions; governance and civic engagement; global communities; and sustainability. The most popular majors are in business, management, and marketing; engineering; biological and biomedical sciences; and health professions. More than 40 new programs have been added in the past two years. The School of Sustainability, part of the College of Global Futures, emphasizes the study of land use and planning models that minimize environmental harm. The Walter Cronkite School of Journalism and Mass Communication enjoys state-of-the-art facilities and a strong national reputation, while the Herberger Institute for Design and the Arts features nationally recognized majors in architecture, art, design, music, dance, fashion, and the Sidney Poitier New American Film School. The sciences (including biochemistry, chemistry, geology, and biology) and social sciences boast first-class facilities, notably the largest university-owned meteorite collection in the world. All students can participate in Dreamscape Learn, a new virtual-reality experience that teaches students by putting them in the middle of a story. The School of Earth and Space Exploration is a leading center for research in astronomy and astrophysics. Anthropology benefits from its association with the Institute of Human Origins's Donald Johanson, who discovered the 3.2-million-year-old fossil skeleton named Lucy. ASU also offers the largest teacher preparation program of any American university.

Engineering programs, especially microelectronics, robotics, and computer-assisted manufacturing, are sure bets; the facility for high-resolution microscopy allows students to get a uniquely close-up view of atomic structures. ASU offers a B.S. in artificial intelligence in business, and many programs include courses and instruction on how to leverage artificial intelligence technologies in many fields, disciplines, and majors. The Fulton Schools of Engineering, composed of eight discipline-specific schools, offer a traditional engineering education with an emphasis on designing and creating innovative and entrepreneurial solutions. Future engineers can opt for a B.S. degree or, for those with broader interests, a B.A. The Ira A. Fulton Schools of Engineering eProjects program brings students, faculty, and industry together to find solutions to real-world problems.

"The students and faculty want to see everyone thrive academically and personally."

"The academic climate at Arizona State University will challenge you to think and create," says a journalism and mass communication major. "There is a lot of hands-on experience and in-person ways to get things done." Faculty members are expected to do both teaching and research, preferably with a practical emphasis, and students say professors are approachable and supportive. Thirty-nine percent of undergraduate classes have fewer than 20 students. The university has made serious efforts to provide students with strong support services, and it's working: A forensic psychology and communication major raves, "The student support services are large and in charge!" The Student Success Center connects new students with upperclassmen and graduate students for weekly coaching sessions on topics like time management, finances, and health and wellness. Incoming first-years who are undecided on a major participate in the Major and Career Exploration program, which involves seven-week courses offering opportunities for hands-on career exploration. ASU has drawn national attention for its innovative and patented eAdvisor system that keeps students on track to meet degree requirements and is backed up by a corps of full-time professional advisors. The

4 percent of ASU students who choose to study abroad have access to more than 300 programs in some 65 countries worldwide.

Sun Devils are "a very hard-working, dedicated, inviting group of people," says a finance major. Sixty-six percent of ASU students are Arizona residents, while 8 percent come from abroad. Twenty-seven percent of the undergraduate student body is Hispanic/Latino; Black students contribute 4 percent, Asian Americans 9 percent, and multiracial students 5 percent. Politically, says a senior, "most of the time things stay neutral." ASU offers merit scholarships averaging $9,400 to qualified students and awards roughly 400 athletic scholarships annually to athletes in 24 sports; 37 percent of students qualify for Pell Grants. ASU is committed to helping Arizona residents get a top-quality education. The Obama Scholars Program and the Arizona Promise Award—all part of the ASU Advantage Program—make tuition-free attendance possible.

"The academic climate . . . will challenge you to think and create."

Twenty-four percent of ASU students live in the co-ed dorms, which a student says are "overall nice," and the Mill Avenue Student Housing project opened in 2025, adding over 800 new beds in a LEED Silver-certified building. Students don't have to buy a meal plan, no matter where they live, and they praise the variety of options. Some complain about the campus's "walk-only zones" that prevent students from using bikes (of which there are thousands), skateboards, or other modes of transportation in certain high-traffic areas. Students say campus security is sufficient, and the Devils in the Bedroom student group helps promote awareness regarding sexual assault prevention.

"Since we have four campuses, there's four times as much to do," says a senior. On campus, notes a junior, "There are events hosted by the Programs and Activities Board, including movie nights, career fairs, and paint and sip." ASU's Greek system attracts 8 percent of the men and 11 percent of the women. The campus is officially dry, so many students head off campus on weekends—often far off campus. Those with cars have easy access to the mountains of Northern Arizona, the lakes on the outskirts of town, and the natural beauty of the Grand Canyon. "Tempe itself has a lot of available activities, such as paddle boarding, attending a Broadway touring show, fine dining, and night life," enthuses a senior. Devils in Disguise, an annual, student-run day of service, sends students out to complete various volunteer projects in the community.

"The student support services are large and in charge!"

"ASU has an incredible amount of school spirit," says a junior. Arizona State's Division I athletics department—supported by a fee required of all students in exchange for free access to athletic events—is consistently ranked among the nation's best. ASU began competing in the Big 12 Conference in 2024, and the football team won the championship that year. Women's triathlon has won multiple national championships. Volleyball was a recent conference winner, and men's wrestling and women's golf are also highly competitive. The men's and women's swimming and diving teams swept the 2025 national championship. Teams are known as the Sun Devils after a meteorological phenomenon, and the biggest rival is the University of Arizona, normally referred to simply as "that school down south." The first-rate Sun Devil Fitness Complex hosts dozens of intramurals and the huge club sports program, which boasts more than 50 club teams.

Arizona State may seem like an overwhelmingly big school, but students say they quickly find their community here. "What characterizes ASU is the ability to be involved in so many different communities," says a senior, "to be exposed to such diversity that is only found on a large university campus." To its credit, ASU likes to pride itself on how many students it accepts, not how many it turns away, and on its strong student support services. For those not intimidated by its sheer immensity, ASU may be a good place to earn a degree while enjoying a four-year relationship with the sun.

University of Arkansas

1 University of Arkansas, Fayetteville, AR 72701

U of A is a Southern public research university on a level with Alabama, LSU, and Ole Miss. Fayetteville prides itself on being a relatively progressive city in conservative Arkansas. With roots in agriculture, U of A has more recently developed strong programs in business, engineering, architecture, and other professional fields. Its most popular program takes the field on Saturday afternoons in the fall as wild hogs.

The flagship public institution for the state, the University of Arkansas is a nationally competitive, student-centered public research institution. First-year enrollment has increased substantially in the last decade, driven in part by expanding research capacity and new campus investments. Dedicated to "the importance of academic freedom, right to free speech, [and ensuring] that students, faculty, and staff from all backgrounds feel a sense of belonging," the school is thriving. Newer construction includes a state-of-the-art Studio and Design Center, and the Institute for Integrative & Innovative Research, where researchers tackle complex problems in health, food systems, data, and materials. A one-of-a-kind semiconductor facility and the Anthony Timberlands Center for Design and Materials Innovation opened in 2025.

The Arkansas campus is nestled among the mountains, lakes, and streams in the northwest corner of the state. "Come to a Razorback game in the fall when the leaves are changing," says one student, "and you will be totally won over." The community is friendly and safe, and the moderate climate means recreational opportunities abound in all seasons. The U of A is on its way to becoming one of the most bicycle friendly campuses in the country with the new Fayetteville Traverse loop, an 18-mile nature trail that weaves its way through the core of the campus and connects to existing community trails. Architectural styles on campus range from modern concrete to collegiate Gothic buildings constructed during the Depression, including the stately brick Old Main, dating to 1875, which once housed the entire university.

Established as a land grant institution in 1871, the U of A serves over 26,000 undergraduates and includes 10 colleges and schools and more than 50 research and outreach centers. U of A's core requirements include credits in English, history, math, humanities, fine arts, science, and social sciences. All students complete a capstone. The more than 4,000 undergrads who join the Honors College complete research or creative work culminating in an honors thesis. "Do it if you can," raves a first-year student. "You get first pick on classes, more scholarships to go abroad, and first pick on housing." The Sam M. Walton College of Business offers three of the strongest majors on campus: marketing, finance, and supply chain management. Other popular disciplines include nursing, industrial

Website: www.uark.edu
Location: Small City
Public
Total Enrollment: 28,115
Undergraduates: 26,292
Male/Female: 44/57
Financial Aid: 29%
Pell Grant: 23%
Expense: Pub $
Student Loans: 45%
Average Debt: $ $
Applicants: 30,549
Accepted: 74%
Enrolled: 22%
Grad in 6 Years: 71%
Returning First-years: 86%
Academics: ✍ ✍ ✍
Social: 🗨 🗨 🗨 🗨
Q of L: ★ ★ ★
Admissions: (479) 575-5346
Email Address: uofa@uark.edu

Strong Programs:
Architecture
Creative Writing
Finance
Industrial Engineering
Marketing
Nursing
Psychology
Supply Chain Management

engineering, psychology, English (particularly creative writing), and studio art. The Bumpers College of Agricultural, Food, and Life Sciences is home to the Center of Excellence for Poultry Science, a national leader in research on poultry epidemiology. The Fay Jones School of Architecture and Design's architecture program is also notable.

U of A's academic climate is "laid-back, but still demanding," says a senior. To help ease into the college transition, students recommend ROCK Camp, an optional summer orientation weekend, as well as the tutoring services of the Student Success Center. "Most of my professors are super approachable and really want you to succeed," says a marketing major. While a healthy portion of large lecture classes are taught by teaching assistants, 38 percent of classes enroll fewer than 20 students. Undergraduates in all disciplines are encouraged to conduct research, and 34 percent do so, often with generous funding. "Getting involved in campus research is very easy and often just requires talking to an enthusiastic professor with room in their lab," says a biology major. Sixteen percent of students opt to study abroad, which is available in over 50 countries.

"The students are cool and you'll definitely find a group to fit into," promises a computer science major. "There are people here from states like Colorado or Indiana, to different countries like Korea or Pakistan." Forty-four percent of undergraduates are Arkansas residents, but students attend from all 50 states; 1 percent are international. Black students make up 4 percent of the student body, Hispanics/Latinos 12 percent, Asian Americans 3 percent, and multiracial students 5 percent. One student says the political climate leans Republican, but a variety of political views are visible on campus. Arkansas awards thousands of merit scholarships each year, averaging $5,300, as well as roughly 400 athletic scholarships in 19 varsity sports. The New Arkansan Non-Resident Tuition Award gives scholarships to incoming students from neighboring states who meet certain academic requirements, but the largest increases in scholarship funding are designated for students from Arkansas. The Arkansas Transfer Achievement Scholarship allows graduates from two-year colleges in the UA System to transfer to the U of A at the same two-year tuition rate.

"Most of my professors are super approachable and really want you to succeed."

Fifty-four percent of all undergrads at Arkansas live in the residence halls; most move to Greek houses or other off-campus places after their first year. Students can join the Lead Hogs program if interested in learning about leadership and involvement opportunities. Campus dining generally receives positive student reviews. Campus police are said to be effective, and they have a presence at Greek parties. A senior reports, "The Title IX office has stepped up and improved procedures and outreach" related to the issue of campus sexual assault. Aside from a team of counselors to assist with mental wellness, the health center's Marrs Relaxation Room offers calming music, massage chairs, and even guided meditations for students who need a break.

"There is definitely a party culture, especially with Greek life and on football weekends, but it's not the only way to have fun," says a senior. Arkansas's Greek chapters attract 23 percent of the men and 41 percent of the women. School-sponsored Cardinal Nights offer alternative programming on Fridays, and students look forward to the annual spring carnival. Dickson Street, the core entertainment district in the town of Fayetteville, connects the university to Fayetteville's downtown historic district and is full of restaurants and bars. Students like to hike and go camping, and as a bonus, says a junior, "because our campus is pretty hilly in some parts, the freshman 15 doesn't exist!" Students are also big on community service, volunteering through local

"Because our campus is pretty hilly in some parts, the freshman 15 doesn't exist!"

programs. Those with cars (and students gripe about lack of parking) will find Dallas, Tulsa, Oklahoma City, Memphis, and St. Louis all within a six-hour drive.

The Razorbacks (wild hogs) compete in the Southeastern Conference, and the beloved Hog Call "Wooo Pig Sooie!" rings out during football and basketball weekends, although according to one senior, "No matter the time, place, or situation, it is always considered appropriate to call the hogs." Red Razorback logos are all over town. Other powerhouse teams include baseball, softball, track and field, and women's soccer. Recreational sports are also popular with 53 percent of students participating.

Southern hospitality has led to more students flocking to the state for a solid education at a bargain price. "It's a school where you'll feel supported, challenged, and included all at the same time," cheers a senior. Northerners may feel outnumbered, and those who frown on football should keep their feelings to themselves. But all students here look forward to graduation day, when their names will join those of more than 220,000 other alumni, engraved into the nearly four-mile network of sidewalks on campus.

If You Apply To ›

Arkansas: Early action, rolling admissions. Accepts the Common Application with supplement. Please consult Arkansas's website for the most up-to-date information regarding standardized test requirements.

Atlanta University Center

Atlanta is viewed as the preeminent city in the country for bright, talented, and successful Black people. It became the capital of the civil rights movement in the 1960s—a town described by its leaders as "too busy to hate." Atlanta evolved in the 1970s to become known as the "Black mecca of the South," it economically burgeoned to "Olympic City" in the 1990s, and it currently reigns as the hub of Black Hollywood.

At the heart of this storied culture is the Atlanta University Center (AUC), the largest Black educational complex in the world. The center consists of two undergraduate colleges (Morehouse and Spelman) as well as two that offer graduate degrees (Clark Atlanta University and the Morehouse School of Medicine) on adjoining campuses in the center of Atlanta, three miles from downtown. Two other institutions, Morris Brown College and the Interdenominational Theological Center, are no longer members. Students at the affiliated schools can enjoy the quiet pace of their beautiful magnolia-studded campuses or plunge into all the culture and excitement of this most dynamic of Deep South cities.

AUC, serving roughly 10,000 students, is home to a myriad of unique offerings, including Spelman's Innovation Lab; Morehouse's cinema, television, and emerging media studies major; Clark Atlanta University's Center for Innovation and Entrepreneurial Development; and Morehouse School of Medicine's Satcher Health Leadership Institute. The four component institutions have educated numerous generations of Black leaders. The Reverend Martin Luther King Jr. graduated from Morehouse, while his grandmother, mother, sister, and daughter all attended Spelman. Both schools gained national reputations at a time when they were among the best of the few colleges to which talented Black students could aspire. Even now, when the options are almost limitless, alumni continue to send their children back for more.

The six original schools—all but the medical school—became affiliated in 1929 using the model of California's Claremont Colleges, but the remaining members are fiercely independent. Each has its own administration, board of trustees, and academic specialties, and each maintains its own dorms, cafeterias, and other facilities. There is cross-registration among the institutions (Morehouse students, for example, go to Spelman for drama and art courses) as well as with Georgia State and Emory University. The governing body of the consortium, the Atlanta University Center, Inc., administers a centerwide dual-degree program in engineering in conjunction with Georgia Tech, and it runs campus security, a student crisis center, and a joint institute of science research. There is also a centerwide service of career planning and placement, where recruiters may come and interview students from all four institutions.

Dating and social life at the coeducational institutions tend to take place within the individual schools, though Morehouse, a men's college, and Spelman, a women's college, maintain a close academic and social relationship. The Morehouse–Spelman Glee Club takes its abundance of talent around the nation, and its annual Christmas concert on the Spelman campus is a standing-room-only event.

Morehouse and Spelman (see full write-ups) constitute the Ivy League of historically Black colleges and universities (HBCUs). The following is a sketch of the other institution within the AUC system offering undergraduate degrees, Clark Atlanta University.

CLARK ATLANTA UNIVERSITY (WWW.CAU.EDU)

Formed by the consolidation of Clark College, a four-year liberal arts institution, and Atlanta University, which offered only graduate degrees, CAU is a comprehensive coeducational institution that offers undergraduate, graduate, and professional degrees as well as nondegree certificate programs. The university draws on the former strengths of both schools, offering quality programs in the health professions, public policy, and mass communications (including print journalism, radio and television production, and filmmaking). Graduate and professional programs include education, business, library information studies, social work, and arts and sciences. CAU is the only private, independent graduate research institution in the HBCU community and the only HBCU member of the Georgia Research Alliance. The university enrolls 3,700 full-time undergraduates; about two-thirds come from out of state, and 77 percent are women.

Morehouse College

830 Westview Drive SW, Atlanta, GA 30314

Along with sister school Spelman, Morehouse is the most prestigious of the historically Black schools. Alumni list reads like a Who's Who of Black leaders. Best known for business and popular 3–2 engineering program with Georgia Tech. Built on a Civil War battlefield, Morehouse epitomizes the new South. "Morehouse Men" share a special bond.

Website: www.morehouse.edu
Location: City Center
Private
Total Enrollment: 2,372
Undergraduates: 2,372
Male/Female: 100/0
Financial Aid: 71%
Pell Grant: 54%
Expense: Pr $
Student Loans: 63%
Average Debt: $ $ $ $
Applicants: 5,510
Accepted: 52%
Enrolled: 24%
Grad in 6 Years: 53%

Founded in 1867 by Baptist ministers to educate formerly enslaved people and other Black men, Morehouse College has the distinction of being the nation's only historically Black, four-year liberal arts college for men. Top students come to Morehouse because they want an institution with a strong academic program and a culture that focuses equally on developing global leaders and fostering a sense of brotherhood among students. In today's challenging political climate, Morehouse's president stated in 2025, "What Morehouse will do in this moment in time is really prepare students to compete in an inclusive meritocracy." Notable alumni include the Reverend Martin Luther King Jr., Senator Raphael Warnock, Samuel L. Jackson, and Spike Lee. Says a psychology major, "Morehouse is a college of young, assertive, ambitious Black men."

Located near downtown Atlanta, the Morehouse campus was built on 66 acres that were once a Civil War battlefield. The campus is home to 42 buildings, many of them historic, including the Martin Luther King Jr. International Chapel. The college has continued to evolve over the last decade as it has enriched its academic program, conducted a successful national fund-raising campaign, increased student scholarships and faculty salaries, and improved its physical plant. In 2024, Google opened a new high-tech Google Annex Classroom at Morehouse.

Morehouse's general education program includes not only coursework in four major disciplines (humanities, natural sciences, math, and social sciences) but also the study of "the unique African and African American heritage on which so much of our modern American culture is built." A cornerstone of that study is a scheduled series of campuswide assemblies called the Crown Forum, which brings in community leaders and national figures from an array of industries for special presentations, artistic performances, and dialogues on topical issues. Students must attend at least six Crown Forum events per semester for six semesters to graduate. The academic climate at the House can get intense: "Morehouse offers an academic structure that is both competitive and rigorous," states a first-year. Fifty-four percent of the classes have fewer than 20 students, and students say their classmates strive to be the best in the classroom but take time to support each other too. A sense of mentorship pervades the campus, and students consider the school's full breadth of counseling services to be quite strong.

Undergraduate programs include the traditional liberal arts majors in the humanities and social and natural sciences, but as a rule of thumb, the more preprofessional your plan, the better Morehouse fits. While STEM fields have been traditionally strong at Morehouse, business and economics have risen in prominence, and business administration is now the most popular major. Engineering, another popular choice, is actually a 3–2 program in conjunction with Georgia Tech and other larger universities. Economics, biology, English, and political science are popular majors. The cinema, television, and emerging media studies major is growing, and a major in Chinese studies is available. Notable minors include journalism and sports, sustainability, and neuroscience. Programs that receive less favorable reviews from students are art and drama, and the administration admits that some of the humanities offerings could use strengthening. A four-year honors program is available for the highly motivated, and research opportunities in the sciences abound, including a research partnership with NASA. Thirty-one percent of students study abroad in more than 200 programs worldwide.

Seventy-two percent of Morehouse students come from outside the state, with the majority hailing from Southeast and Mid-Atlantic states; less than 1 percent come from other nations. Ninety-eight percent are Black, and one student attests, "Many students are here to get a greater understanding of their heritage and to promote it." Fifty-four percent of incoming first-years are eligible for Pell Grants. Merit scholarships averaging $6,900 are available, in addition to many scholarships for athletes. Morehouse now accepts transgender students who self-identify as male; however, enrolled students who transition to self-identifying as females would be asked to leave because, as administrators explain, being a men's college is central to Morehouse's identity. Morehouse has come under fire in recent years over how it has handled allegations of sexual misconduct and accusations of a "hypermasculine" culture.

Most new students are required to live on campus, and 53 percent of students live in campus housing; upperclassmen find their own off-campus accommodations. Some students grumble that campus housing is "too small" and "not well maintained." For first-years, students recommend Graves Hall, the college's oldest building, constructed in 1889. Themed residential academic programs are available for students interested in the arts, business, global learning, and STEM. The meal

> **"Morehouse is a college of young, assertive, ambitious Black men."**

> **"Many students are here to get a greater understanding of their heritage and to promote it."**

(continued)

Returning First-years: 86%
Academics: ✍ ✍ ✍
Social: 🗩 🗩 🗩 🗩
Q of L: ★ ★ ★ ★
Admissions: (844) 512-6672
Email Address:
 admissions@morehouse.edu

Strong Programs:
Biology
Business Administration
Chinese Studies
Cinema, Television, and
 Emerging Media Studies
Economics
English
Political Science
Pre-engineering

Homecoming week is a joint effort with Spelman and is one of the nation's largest at a historically Black college or university (HBCU).

plan at Morehouse is mandatory for students living on campus and draws its share of complaints as well, although dining services have expanded recently to include fast-food options and a coffee shop.

Morehouse's membership in the Atlanta University Center expands students' academic, social, and extracurricular options, particularly with neighboring Spelman College. Homecoming week, for instance, is a joint effort with Spelman and is one of the nation's largest at a historically Black college or university (HBCU), with events like pep rallies, hip-hop and R&B concerts, step shows, and a jazz brunch drawing thousands of alumni and community members. Spelman women have been known to quip, "You can always tell a Morehouse man, but you can't tell him much." Morehouse's fraternities, which sign up just a small fraction of the students, hold parties, though most students concur that "drinking is not a big deal here." Community service is an important emphasis, through student organizations as well as service-learning courses. Going out on the town in Atlanta is a popular evening activity, and on-campus football games, concerts, movies, and religious programs all draw crowds.

The Maroon Tigers compete in the Division II Southern Intercollegiate Athletic Conference. The basketball, track and field, and cross-country teams have enjoyed the most success; in 2025 the boxing club became the first HBCU to compete in the USA Boxing national championship. And the intramural program allows students a chance to become the superstars they know are inside them. During football season, students road-trip to follow the games at Howard, Hampton, and Tuskegee Universities.

Benefiting as it is from the surge of interest in HBCUs, Morehouse is well equipped to serve the contemporary heirs of a distinguished tradition. Morehouse students don't just attend Morehouse. They become part of a prominent and proud network of Morehouse Men who share the bonds of having had the Morehouse experience. Graduates find that alumni stand ready and willing to help them with jobs and other opportunities as they work to effect positive change in their communities and the world.

Overlaps

Davidson, Florida A&M, Furman, Georgia State, Howard, Millsaps, Rhodes, Spelman

If You Apply To ›

Morehouse: Early decision, early action, regular decision. SATs or ACTs: optional. Accepts the Common Application. Accepts applications from students who live and self-identify as male.

Spelman College

350 Spelman Lane SW, Atlanta, GA 30314

With a strong tradition of academic excellence, Spelman is a historically Black women's college that draws students from all corners of the country. Particularly strong in the sciences with noteworthy emphasis on undergraduate research. Wooded 39-acre Atlanta campus adjacent to brother school Morehouse offers easy access to urban attractions. Has dropped varsity sports to emphasize lifelong physical fitness.

As one of only two surviving Black women's colleges in the United States (along with Bennett), Spelman College holds a special appeal for Black women seeking to become leaders in fields ranging from science to the arts. Students flock here for that something special that predominantly white institutions lack: a supportive environment with first-rate academics and a tight-knit sisterhood where Black women can develop self-confidence and leadership skills before venturing out into the wider world—exactly the reasons for the national resurgence of interest in historically Black colleges and universities (HBCUs). "It's a true sisterhood," enthuses a psychology major. "The bonds are everlasting. There is no one on this planet who will know what you're going through except for your Spelman sisters."

Spelman was founded in 1881 by Sophia B. Packard and Harriet E. Giles, two pioneers in women's education from New England who were concerned with the lack of educational opportunities for Black women. John D. Rockefeller was an early funder, and the school was named in honor of his wife, Laura Spelman Rockefeller, and her parents, who were longtime activists in the antislavery movement. Spelman was traditionally the starting point for teachers, nurses, and other Black female leaders. Today's emphasis is on getting Spelman grads into boardrooms, courtrooms, and engineering labs. Honing women for leadership is the main mission, and that nurturing takes place on a classic collegiate-green campus sitting on 39 lush acres in an urban setting with a $506 million endowment. The new Campbell Center for Innovation and the Arts, located just outside the campus, is designed to foster connections between higher education and the Westside Atlanta community.

These are heady times for Spelman. Although it finds itself competing head-on with the Seven Sisters and other prestigious and predominantly white institutions that are eager to recruit talented Black women, the college is holding its own. Spelman offers a well-rounded liberal arts curriculum that emphasizes the importance of critical and analytical thinking and problem-solving. Usually, by the end of sophomore year, students are expected to complete 40 credit hours of core requirements, including English composition, foreign language, mathematics, African diaspora and the world, international or comparative women's studies, wellness and health, and computer literacy. In addition, first-years are required to take a First-Year Experience course, and sophomores must take Sophomore Year Experience.

Spelman's established strengths lie in the natural sciences (especially biology) and the humanities, both of which have outstanding faculty. Biology is among the most popular majors, as are psychology, political science, and health sciences, one of the fastest-growing offerings, along with a minor in food studies. Over the last decade, the college has greatly strengthened its math and science offerings; extensive undergraduate research programs in these areas provide students with publishing opportunities, and many end up attending grad school. In fact, Spelman leads the nation in the number of Black women who go on to earn Ph.D.s in STEM fields. Premed and prelaw programs are strong, and the 3–2 dual-degree program in engineering in cooperation with Georgia Tech is also a standout. The Women's Research and Resource Center specializes in women's studies and community outreach.

"The academic climate is very competitive," says an English major. "The school is made up of the top students from around the country, and the courses are designed to be a challenge for the best of the best." Individual attention is the hallmark of a Spelman education. Many faculty members are Black and/or female and thus excellent role models, ones the students find very accessible. "The professors here genuinely love what they do," says a sociology major. Except for some of the required introductory courses, classes are small; 57 percent have fewer than 20 students. Through the Spelman MILE (My Integrated Learning Experience), all students complete internships or undergraduate research projects in their majors. Students who want to spread their wings can venture abroad through a variety of programs in 40 countries, or try one of the

> **"It's a true sisterhood. . . .
> The bonds are everlasting."**

Website: www.spelman.edu
Location: City Center
Private
Total Enrollment: 2,653
Undergraduates: 2,653
Male/Female: 0/100
Financial Aid: 82%
Pell Grant: 45%
Expense: Pr $
Student Loans: 48%
Average Debt: $ $ $ $
Applicants: 12,023
Accepted: 25%
Enrolled: 24%
Grad in 6 Years: 78%
Returning First-years: 94%
Academics: ✍ ✍ ✍
Social: 🗩 🗩 🗩 🗩
Q of L: ★ ★ ★ ★ ★
Admissions: (800) 982-2411
Email Address:
  admiss@spelman.edu

Strong Programs:
African Diaspora Studies
Biology
Economics
Health Sciences
Mathematics
Political Science
Premed
Psychology

Spelman leads the nation in the number of Black women who go on to earn Ph.D.s in STEM fields.

domestic exchange arrangements with Barnard, Wellesley, Smith, and others. The Global STEM and Multidisciplinary Studies Research Program prepares students who are accepted into the program to "be globally engaged" upon graduation by pairing them with an international mentor and placing them in a research lab or field experience abroad.

"Spelman's personality is definitely 'Black Girl Magic,'" cheers a biology major. "We exude positivity, happiness, and success." Spelman's reputation continues to attract high-achieving, goal-oriented Black women from all over the country, including a high proportion of alumnae children, and the school has become increasingly selective. Twenty-five percent of students come from Georgia, and less than 1 percent come from abroad. Ninety-seven percent are Black; American Indian, Hispanic/Latina, Asian American, and white students combine to make up 3 percent of the student body. The political atmosphere is liberal, and according to a history major, "Hot topics on campus include the gentrification of the city of Atlanta (particularly the West End neighborhood that the campus is located in), women's rights, and issues related to the preservation of Black lives." Spelman offers a limited number of merit scholarships, and 45 percent of first-year students receive Pell Grants. There are no athletic scholarships.

Fifty-four percent of students live on campus in Spelman's 11 residence halls. Older halls add to the school's historical charm; students recommend that first-years check out Howard-Harreld Hall. Students report that there are more juniors and seniors who would like to live on campus than there are beds to accommodate them. The meal plan is mandatory for campus dwellers, and the food gets average reviews. A psychology major says the school's security efforts, gated campus, and Title IX procedures help students "feel protected" on campus.

"The academic climate is very competitive."

In part because of the Atlanta University Center, students have plenty of chances for social interaction with other nearby colleges, especially Morehouse. "Students mingle in the student centers of all four schools all the time, especially on Fridays," one denizen explains. Spelmanites also take advantage of the big-city nightlife; they attend plays, symphonies, and the hot Atlanta nightclubs. Lenox Square is popular for shopping. "Atlanta is a great college town!" gushes one junior. About half of the students get involved with service opportunities in the city. Sororities are present but only in small numbers. The attitude on drinking leans toward the conservative. Says one student, "No alcohol on campus—period." The most anticipated annual events include sisterhood initiation ceremonies, homecoming, and the Founders Day celebration. Varsity sports have been replaced with a general fitness and nutrition program that features an extensive list of physical activities such as running and yoga. An intramural program includes basketball, flag football, soccer, and volleyball.

Spelman College has spent more than 140 years furthering the education and opportunities of Black women. It has adapted its curriculum to meet the career aspirations of today's youth, built up its bankroll, and successfully met the recruitment challenge posed by diversity efforts at other universities. As elite an institution as ever, Spelman is staking its future on its ability to provide a unique kind of education that gives its graduates a competitive edge in the 21st century. As one satisfied student says, "If there is any place that a student can be academically enriched, it is here."

Overlaps

Agnes Scott, Bates, Clark Atlanta, Hampton, Howard, Vassar, Wellesley, Xavier University of Louisiana

If You Apply To ›

Spelman: Early decision, early action, regular decision. SATs or ACTs: optional. Accepts the Common Application. Accepts applications from students who consistently live and self-identify as women, regardless of their gender assignment at birth.

College of the Atlantic

105 Eden Street, Bar Harbor, ME 04609

A small college that sits on an island along the coast of Maine, COA is a haven for community-minded, environmentally conscious students who would rather save the world than make a buck. Lacks many of the usual trappings of college life, such as sports teams and Greek life. But with roughly 350 undergrads, it makes its distinctive blend of smallness and diversity an academic and social virtue. Students get lots of hands-on experience and are able to get involved in shaping the direction of the school.

College of the Atlantic attracts rugged individualists concerned with the world's pressing issues, notably climate change, social justice, and food systems. Students "chart their own educational path under the umbrella of human ecology—the study of the relations between humans and their natural, cultural, built, and technological environments." COA bucks the national obsession with growth—seeing smallness as the key to education—while taking a personalized approach to teaching and learning. "I chose COA because I found no other school that gave me as much freedom to create my own educational path," says one sophomore.

The 37-acre campus, covered in lush flowers, vegetable gardens, and lawns, sits on Mount Desert Island (pronounced "dessert") along the shoreline of Frenchman Bay and adjacent to the magnificent Acadia National Park. In addition, the college maintains two offshore island research centers, a remote wilderness center, two organic farms, a 100-acre wooded protectorate, and wood-pellet-heated "green" dorms. Founded by ecologically conscious local residents in 1969 around the concept of "human ecology," COA's mission is reflected in the facilities: Sustainability is prized, and the college uses environmentally responsible materials as much as possible.

Instead of traditional academic departments, COA has three broad resource areas: environmental sciences, arts and design, and human studies. "Learning happens during lectures, but the majority of it happens outside the classroom," says a junior. "We learn from observation and experience, sucking up every ounce of knowledge we can from real-world experiences." Students may choose to concentrate on more narrowly defined

> **"The majority of [learning] happens outside the classroom."**

topics within human ecology, such as climate change and energy, environmental law and politics, educational studies, farming and food systems, or sustainable business. With advisors and resource specialists, each student designs an individual course of study. The natural sciences are stellar, with excellent instruction in marine science, field ecology and natural history, and food systems and sustainability. For the entrepreneurially minded, the Hatchery is COA's sustainable business incubator, offering eligible students academic credit, a variety of resources, and 10 weeks to develop a business venture and build a prototype. The emphasis is on interdisciplinary exploration, and the most compelling ideas get a $5,000 grant from the college along with a year of professional services.

Student life at COA is intense and semicommunal, beginning with a five-day outdoor orientation for first-years. Before graduating, students must complete 40 hours of community service, a 10-week off-campus internship, and a 10-week senior project. Other requirements are few: First-years must take a writing course, the human ecology core course, and two courses are required in environmental

Website: www.coa.edu
Location: Rural
Private
Total Enrollment: 348
Undergraduates: 341
Male/Female: 28/71
Financial Aid: 98%
Pell Grant: 28%
Expense: Pr $
Student Loans: 55%
Average Debt: $ $ $
Applicants: 476
Accepted: 70%
Enrolled: 23%
Grad in 6 Years: 69%
Returning First-years: 85%
Academics: ✍ ✍ ✍
Social: 🗩 🗩
Q of L: ★ ★ ★
Admissions: (800) 528-0025
Email Address:
 inquiry@coa.edu

Strong Programs:
Climate Change and Energy
Creative Arts
Environmental Law and Politics
Environmental Studies
Human Ecology
Marine Science
Sustainable Food Systems

sciences, human studies, and arts and design. Sophomores must submit a writing portfolio for evaluation. All students incorporate research into their studies and complete a capstone project. "The college owns two offshore research islands that students live on during the summer to conduct research on seabirds and marine mammals while also expressing themselves through visual arts," shares one junior of the school's Islands Program. Ninety-seven percent of all classes have fewer than 20 students, and since the student body is so small, students can become close to faculty members. "The professors here are unbelievably invested in and concerned for students and growing their understanding, skills, and ways of life," says a junior. In addition to traditional grades, students receive in-depth written evaluations of their work. They must reciprocate with a self-evaluation of their performance.

COA offers regular study abroad programs in Mexico's Yucatán Peninsula and in Vichy, France. In the Yucatán, students do ethnographic, agricultural, or scientific research of their own choosing. In France, they take literature, philosophy, politics, and/or art classes. Both programs include a strong language immersion component. COA also supports student participation in other study abroad programs through partner institutions such as the EcoLeague. Fifty percent of students go abroad during their time at COA.

"COA is funky. We are a collection of eclectic personalities, people from diverse backgrounds and interests who come together with shared values and goals for a sustainable, peaceful future," says one sophomore. Fourteen percent of students are native to Maine, and the student population has a strong international aspect—22 percent of students come from nearly 50 countries—driven by the school's affiliation with the Davis United World College Scholars Program, an international scholarship program. The student body is roughly 1 percent Black, 4 percent Hispanic/Latino, 1 percent Asian, and 2 percent multiracial, and women outnumber men more than 2 to 1. "Students of color may have a hard time fitting in," muses a sophomore. The college's governance system gives students and administrators almost equal voices in how it's run; anyone may raise concerns, vote on policy changes, or contribute their opinion on the hiring of new faculty at the All College Meeting. The overtly liberal student body isn't shy about speaking out on global issues either. "One of the things we have the least diversity in is politics, and so it can be quite difficult for a student with an opinion that varies from the majority," opines a senior. Roughly half the students receive merit scholarships, worth an average of $12,800.

With the opening of two new residential buildings in the past five years and the purchase of multiple off-campus townhouses, COA has been working to address a housing crunch created by an expanding tourism season that has driven up prices and limited the availability of rental housing in and around Bar Harbor. Roughly 80 percent of students now live in college-owned housing. Dining fare in the TAB ("Take-a-Break") Dining Hall and the Sea Urchin Café gets generally high praise. "The chefs make nearly all the meals from scratch, including daily homemade bread, stir fries, curries, and so much more," according to one student. The university has expanded mental health counseling, and students say COA "is a safe campus situated in a safe town in one of the safest states in the U.S." All students are required to take bystander intervention training once a year to learn strategies for preventing sexual assault.

Bar Harbor is a tourist community that "nearly shuts down in the winter," according to one student, although they do enjoy the coffee shops, bakeries, restaurants, and movie theaters that stay open. Students get to know the townspeople through community service. On-campus activities include open-mic nights, talent shows, concerts, dances, and, during the winter, "weekly Fireside Fridays with free cookies, hot chocolate, and coffee," says a sophomore. There are no fraternities or sororities—"this is an alien concept to us," says a student. Instead, many kick back at small off-campus house parties, which often revolve around potluck meals, since most campus dining services are closed on weekends (the school began trying out a weekend meal service in 2025). Drinking is permitted on campus for those of legal age, only in private student rooms, but students agree that alcohol has little influence on the social scene.

There are no varsity sports (not even ice hockey), but the college provides all students with a membership to the local YMCA, where many students sign up for programs and sports including soccer and water polo, and badminton. Outdoor programs, which take students hiking, sailing, cross-country skiing, and rock climbing in the wilds of Maine, are very active, plus "there is the entirety of Acadia National Park to explore," adds a junior.

> "[We have] weekly Fireside Fridays with free cookies, hot chocolate, and coffee."

College of the Atlantic is a place where Earth Day really is cause for celebration—a school that has, "for lack of a better word, a bit of a hippie vibe to it," says a junior. It's where students have been known to cut class to march on Washington and where everyone who wants to, from students to trustees, jumps into frigid Frenchman Bay at the beginning of the fall term to swim the stretch of water between the school's pier and a neighboring island. "COA is a place fully based in people and relationships, not institutions and rules," says a senior. "So much is possible here because COA very intentionally puts a lot of power in front of the students to build their own experience and curriculum."

If You Apply To ›

COA: Early decision I and II, early action, regular decision. SATs or ACTs: optional. Accepts the Common Application with supplement. Application includes space for applicants to describe their gender identity.

Auburn University

Auburn, AL 36849

Sweet Home Alabama, where the skies are so blue and the spirit of football lasts year-round. Auburn was once called Alabama Polytechnic Institute, and today AU's programs in engineering, agriculture, and the health fields are still among its best. AU's down-home, small-town atmosphere may feel claustrophobic to those from outside the Deep South. As for the role of football, the $14 million scoreboard says it all.

Founded in 1856, Auburn University is a public land grant university that excels in professional and technical fields such as architecture, engineering, and agriculture. But the school also welcomes students with frenzied athletics, warm and cozy hospitality, and Southern charm. "It truly is a family atmosphere. We are here to learn and help each other," says one happy Tiger.

The town of Auburn, which grew up amid miles of forest and farmland largely to serve the university, is called the "loveliest village of the plain," a moniker taken from a line in an Oliver Goldsmith poem. The campus stretches for nearly 2,000 acres, graced by mossy trees, lush lawns, and majestic colonnades. Most buildings are red-brick and Georgian in style, with some more modern facilities grouped in a compact central location. Newer facilities include the Kreher Preserve and Nature Center's Environmental Education Building.

(continued)

Applicants: 55,056
Accepted: 46%
Enrolled: 24%
Grad in 6 Years: 82%
Returning First-years: 95%
Academics: ✎ ✎
Social: 🗨 🗨 🗨
Q of L: ★ ★ ★
Admissions: (334) 844-6425
Email Address:
admissions@auburn.edu

Strong Programs:
Agriculture
Architecture
Business
Environmental Science
Finance
Hospitality
Marketing
Mechanical Engineering

The annual Iron Bowl pits Auburn against Southeastern Conference archrival Alabama.

Auburn's core curriculum includes courses in the humanities and fine arts, science and mathematics, and social sciences. A writing-in-the-disciplines program bolsters every major with significant writing instruction. To ease the transition into college life, first-years undergo the two-day Camp War Eagle orientation. Auburn's SKILL Program provides academic coaching for students with learning differences and ADHD. The academic climate varies by department, and a senior says, "Rather than students competing with each other for higher grades, they are more willing to help their classmates through tutoring or group study sessions." Regardless of the rigor, students say professors generally go the extra mile for them. "Although I have not liked every teacher I've had, every teacher has taught me something new and useful," reasons a junior.

The engineering, architecture, agriculture, and pharmacy programs are stellar. Auburn boasts a first-of-its-kind program in wireless engineering for students who want to design network hardware or software for cell phones and other mobile devices. The Ginn College of Engineering also offers aerospace engineering, and Auburn has produced six NASA astronauts. The most popular majors include finance, marketing, mechanical engineering, and nursing science; the environmental science, pharmacy, and interior architecture programs also draw attention. Accelerated degree programs in numerous fields allow eligible students to count approved graduate hours toward both a bachelor's and a master's degree with the goal of completing both in as little as five years.

"The academic climate of Auburn is based heavily on professional development," says an accounting major, so the co-op program, which provides pay and credit in several professional fields, is increasingly popular. Five interdisciplinary areas identified as "strategic research clusters" compete for millions of dollars in special funding, which means more opportunities for undergrads to assist faculty with research in areas including health disparities, pharmaceutical engineering, climate and earth systems science, omics (yes, it's a word) and informatics, and scalable energy conversion science and technology. Opportunities for undergrads to work with faculty on research are abundant and 24 percent of students do. Eight percent of students join the Honors College, which culminates in a Senior Year Experience that may involve a traditional thesis, enhanced study abroad, service learning, or other capstone project. Fifteen percent of students study in over 35 countries on faculty-led expeditions. Closer to home, the Rural Studio program sends students in the College of Architecture, Design, and Construction to live in economically underserved Hale County, Alabama, to design and build innovative community buildings and homes for locals.

> **"Every teacher has taught me something new and useful."**

"Auburn students have real Southern charm, but they are also cultured and diverse in interests and backgrounds," says a junior. Indeed, 58 percent of Auburn undergraduates are Alabama natives, and many are second- or third-generation legacies. Black students account for a mere 4 percent of the largely homogeneous student body, Hispanics/Latinos represent 5 percent, Asian Americans make up 3 percent, and multiracial students add 3 percent; 2 percent hail from foreign countries. The conservative tone of this public Bible Belt campus makes it hospitable for more than 30 Christian student groups. "Half of Auburn students love politics and enjoy the political process, while the other half wouldn't know where their polling place was if you gave them a map," quips one senior. In an effort to increase diversity and address racial disparities on campus, Auburn has quadrupled the amount of money that it allocates to need-based financial aid for incoming first-years in the past decade. The university also awards merit scholarships averaging $8,500 and more than 400 athletic scholarships in 17 sports.

The majority of Auburn's 24 residence halls are co-ed by floor, but there are several single-sex halls; 18 percent of undergrads live in college housing. First-year students compete for rooms on a first-come, first-served basis with returning students, and the dorms fill up fast. "Get on a waiting list ASAP," advises a junior. The university helps those moving off campus find apartments and roommates. Twenty-seven percent of Auburn men join fraternities, and 47 percent of women join sororities, perhaps because chapters get space in the best dorms. Students grumble about the mandatory—and pricey—meal plan, but, says an exercise science and nutrition major, "The Edge at Central Dining is the newest dining hall edition featuring nine different food stations that have a huge variety to accommodate all allergen and dietary restrictions as well as different cultures and cuisines."

Aside from varsity sporting events and off-campus fraternity and apartment parties, students enjoy school-sponsored concerts, free movies, and plenty of intramural leagues. "Social life is great whether you are Greek or not," says a first-year. The campus is officially dry, except on game days, and students say the alcohol policy is enforced. "Auburn has a very family atmosphere, so the tailgating is spread out and family-oriented," says a junior. Long-standing traditions include Hey Day, when everyone wears a name tag and walks around saying, "Hey!" Students participate in a variety of community service programs, frequently as part of service-learning courses.

"Social life is great whether you are Greek or not."

Auburn is a football powerhouse with pockets as deep as its location in the South and values to match. On fall Saturdays, nearly 90,000 screaming fans turn the campus into Alabama's fifth-largest city, and the rallying cry "Warrrrr Eagle!" rocks the place each time an Auburn back runs to daylight. The annual Iron Bowl pits Auburn against Southeastern Conference archrival Alabama. Other solid Tigers teams include men's basketball, baseball, softball, golf, and women's equestrian. Aubie, the official tiger mascot, has won a record 11 titles (mascots compete in national championships too) at the UCA Cheer and Dance competition. The Auburn Recreation and Wellness Center is a 240,000-square-foot facility containing everything from weight-training areas to a virtual golf simulator and an outdoor leisure pool.

The Auburn Creed, a beloved tradition, states a belief in the value of "work, hard work," and Auburn is working hard to increase the caliber of its students and academic programs. "At Auburn, you're encouraged to unlock your full potential," says one senior, "with resources readily available to support your journey toward excellence."

Overlaps

University of Alabama, Clemson, University of Florida, Florida State, University of Georgia, University of Mississippi, University of South Carolina, University of Tennessee Knoxville

If You Apply To ›

Auburn: Early action I-IV, regular decision. Accepts the Common Application with supplement. Audition required for music, dance, and theater applicants. Please consult Auburn's website for the most up-to-date information regarding standardized test requirements.

Austin College

900 North Grand Avenue, Sherman, TX 75090

The second most famous institution in Texas with Austin in its name. Half the size of Trinity (TX), runs neck and neck with Southwestern to be the leading small liberal arts college in Texas. Combines the liberal arts with strong programs in business, education, science, and health, including premed. Don't look for the 'Roos on a map of the city of Austin. The college is just north of Dallas.

Website: www.austincollege
.edu

Location: Small City

Private

Total Enrollment: 1,214

Undergraduates: 1,162

Male/Female: 49/48

Financial Aid: 100%

Pell Grant: 41%

Expense: Pr $

Student Loans: 55%

Average Debt: $ $ $ $

Applicants: 5,282

Accepted: 48%

Enrolled: 14%

Grad in 6 Years: 67%

Returning First-years: 79%

Academics: ✍ ✍ ✍

Social: 💬 💬 💬

Q of L: ★ ★ ★

Admissions: (903) 813-3000

Email Address:
  admission@austincollege.edu

Strong Programs:
Biochemistry
Biology
Business Administration
Healthcare Administration
Kinesiology
Neuroscience
Psychology
Public Health

In a long-standing tradition, students go for a midnight plunge in the campus fountains on their birthdays.

For historical reasons over which reasonable persons can and do disagree, the Kangaroo has become the symbol of all things Austin College. All first-year students receive #RooNation T-shirts at orientation, and students hold a trick-or-treat alternative known as 'Roo Boo for local children. The college was founded by a Presbyterian missionary in 1849 with a land grant from early Texas matriarch Emily Austin Bryan Perry (sister of "Father of Texas" Stephen F. Austin). Its continuous ties to the Presbyterian Church (USA) are evident in the emphasis on values in core courses and high participation in service activities. Faculty and staff here even serve students breakfast at 9 p.m. the night before finals. It's just another example of the personal style that is typical of this charming Southern institution, which also boasts preprofessional programs, most notably premed, that are among the strongest in the state. "This university is truly such a unique place and can offer you opportunities that you never even expected," raves a senior. "It will truly change your life."

Austin College's 100-acre campus is in a residential area in the city of Sherman (population 45,000), an hour's drive from Dallas, and at the heart of the burgeoning North Texas technology corridor. The campus is designed in the traditional quadrangle style and comprises beige brick buildings, tree-lined plazas, decorative fountains, and an impressive 70-ton sculptured solstice calendar. Residence halls are conveniently located about 200 yards from most classrooms, which eases the pain of early morning classes. The IDEA Center for hands-on learning in the sciences features laboratory classrooms as well as a $1 million, 24-inch telescope and astronomical image camera in the building's domed observatory.

The core curriculum begins with a first-year seminar. Each professor who teaches the course becomes the mentor for the 20 first-years in their class. Then students select from courses in humanities, social sciences, and natural sciences, as well as classes that focus on writing skills, quantitative literacy, and global diversity. Students must complete one major and a minor or a double major to graduate. Additionally, all students satisfy an applied learning requirement by completing an internship, practicum, or similar experience. Adds one senior, "Austin College is very good for volunteering. Every year, they offer the Great Day of Service, where we can sign up for different places around Sherman to volunteer." During the January term, students focus on just one course, and many use that time to study abroad or undertake off-campus internships.

> **"This university can offer you opportunities that you never even expected."**

When it comes time to apply to grad school, premed, predentistry, and prelaw students at this little college have some of the highest acceptance rates of any Texas school. A BA2PA track has been added for undergrads who are interested in entering the M.S.–physician assistant program. Those pursuing the healing arts benefit from strong programs in neuroscience, public health, biochemistry, and health care administration, and a minor in mindfulness and health studies. An interdisciplinary philosophy, politics, and economics major includes a research capstone. The noteworthy Austin Teacher Program allows students to earn both a bachelor's and a master's degree in five years. Business administration, psychology, biology, and political science are the most popular majors. For students who want to dive into global education, the Jordan Family Language House is home to the first-year Global Living Learning Community, where 20 new students can immerse themselves in a variety of modern languages. A cooperative engineering program links the college with other schools.

"The academic climate is one of growth, curiosity and stepping outside your comfort zone," says an international relations major. Sixty-eight percent of all classes have fewer than 20 students. "[Professors] will go the extra mile to make sure you completely understand whatever the topic or subject is," says an English major.

The college also offers independent study and departmental honors programs. The Posey Leadership Institute offers seminars and courses, and a minor in leadership studies is available. For field biologists, AC maintains five research sites in Grayson County, including the Sneed Prairie Restoration Project. Students are able to conduct faculty-mentored undergraduate research across all disciplines and can choose to study abroad in programs offered in more than 60 countries.

"Austin College students have a greater sense of purpose in everything they are doing," says a senior. Ninety-two percent of students hail from the Lone Star State, with 1 percent from abroad. Hispanics/Latinos comprise 29 percent of the student body, Black students 8 percent, Asian Americans 9 percent, and multiracial students 5 percent. Politically, an English major notes a diverse range of views and credits the school for "trying to teach our students how to be a part of a healthy democracy." AC offers merit scholarships worth up to $33,000 but no athletic scholarships.

Eighty-five percent of undergraduates live on campus, and all are encouraged to do so for their first three years. "Housing is above average," a business administration junior says, although it can be "quite competitive," adds an English major. Residence halls are co-ed, except for one all-female and one all-male dorm. Juniors and seniors choose from suites, flats, and cottages. Dean Hall is a popular choice for first-years, despite (or perhaps because of) its reputation as being loud and social. As for campus dining, "The cafeteria has really stepped it up recently," cheers one student. "There are always a lot of options, and the food is genuinely good." The Pouch Club, an on-campus joint, serves pizza and burgers, as well as beer and wine for those of legal age. Students report feeling safe on campus thanks to thorough campus security and sexual assault prevention programs.

Most of the social life is either on or near campus. "There is always something to do, from smaller activities and club meetings to big dinners and guest speakers," a junior says. Twenty-one percent of the men and 27 percent of the women belong to local fraternities and sororities, respectively. Students can have alcohol in their rooms if they are 21 or older. Spring Carnival is an annual event, and Kangapalooza brings a big-name musician to campus each year. In a long-standing tradition, students go for a midnight plunge in the campus fountains on their birthdays. Popular weekend excursions are a drive to Dallas or to the college's 28-acre recreational spot on Lake Texoma (a half hour north). Of Sherman, one junior says, "There are super cute coffee shops, bookstores, antiques malls, and parks all around town."

The Kangaroos compete in Division III, and the women's water polo team captured recent back-to-back Collegiate Water Polo Association national championships. Other solid teams include women's basketball, men's soccer, and men's and women's swimming and diving. The recreational sports program draws a third of the students, with flag football, volleyball, and soccer proving popular.

At this college with roots in the Presbyterian Church, students praise the preprofessional programs and the intimate, supportive environment. "There's a more personal touch in the connections that I make every day, whether that's with other students or the faculty," says a satisfied biology major. "I truly feel seen and have been proven and told I belong here." And while Sherman may seem to be a sleepy little place, Austin College is definitely hoppin'. (Sorry.)

Austin College boasts preprofessional programs, most notably premed, that are among the strongest in the state.

"There's a more personal touch in the connections that I make every day."

If You Apply To ›

Austin: Early action I and II, regular decision. SATs or ACTs: optional (only considered if a student elects them to be used in admission review). Accepts the Common Application with supplement.

231 Forest Street, Babson Park, MA 02457

The only college in the *Fiske Guide* devoted entirely to business. Babson is the birthplace of entrepreneurial studies—which continue to define the campus ethos. Only 10 miles from college student mecca Boston and tougher to get into than ever. About two-thirds the size of Bentley, its closest competitor, and nearly a third of students are international. The one college in Massachusetts where it is possible to be a Republican with head held high.

Website: www.babson.edu
Location: Suburban
Private
Total Enrollment: 3,332
Undergraduates: 2,709
Male/Female: 56/44
Financial Aid: 34%
Pell Grant: 18%
Expense: Pr $ $
Student Loans: 35%
Average Debt: $ $ $ $
Applicants: 9,381
Accepted: 17%
Enrolled: 39%
Grad in 6 Years: 93%
Returning First-years: 95%
Academics: ✍ ✍ ✍
Social: 🗨 🗨
Q of L: ★ ★ ★
Admissions: (781) 239-5522
Email Address:
  ugradadmission@babson.edu

Strong Programs:
Accounting
Business
Business Administration
Economics
Entrepreneurship
Finance
Marketing

Babson is a pioneer in the study of entrepreneurship, dating to the 1970s—a time when people thought it couldn't be taught. Here, hands-on experience is the norm; students get school funding to start businesses during their first year and may hone their stock-picking skills by managing part of the college's endowment. Always the foremost business college in the Boston area, Babson attracts budding tycoons and entrepreneurs from around the globe. "If you want to be successful and be surrounded by people who will push you to be your best, this is the place to be," says a junior.

Founded in 1919 by financier Roger Babson, the college sits on 370 acres near the sedate Boston suburb of Wellesley. The campus features open green spaces, gently rolling hills, and heavily wooded areas. Buildings are gently shaded, and parking lots (filled with expensive foreign cars) are discreetly hidden. Architecturally, the campus is mainly neo-Georgian and modern. Park Manor West doubles as a first-year residence hall and the home of the Schlesinger Innovation Center, offering an amphitheater, classrooms, and collaboration spaces. The Herring Family Entrepreneurial Leadership Village provides a space for faculty, students, staff, and partners to come together for living/learning experiences and educational experimentation.

Although Babson is a business school, with that as its only academic major, students take business classes blended with coursework in the liberal arts and sciences. Babson's core curriculum emphasizes three major components. In the first, the yearlong Foundations of Management and Entrepreneurship course, first-year students split into groups to develop start-up business plans; each group gets up to $3,000 in seed money from the college to get their concept up and running. At the end of the year, the business is liquidated, and profits go to charity. Former FME groups have developed Babsonopoly (a Babson-themed version of Monopoly), published children's books, and sold solar-powered smartphone chargers. Second, sophomores take Socio-Ecological Systems, a cotaught course where they imagine sustainable solutions to real-world challenges. Finally, the Advanced Experiential course pairs juniors and seniors with an outside company or nonprofit organization for a semester-long, business-oriented project.

> **"No one blinks an eye when a student is walking around campus in a suit."**

All Babson students major in business and may select from 24 concentrations, such as business analytics, operations management, real estate, or even identity and diversity studies or literary and visual arts. (The Sorenson Visual Arts Center has painting, ceramics, and sculpture studios; labs for photography and digital art; a student art gallery; and workspace for artists-in-residence.) The school recently added technology entrepreneurship. Finance, economics, and marketing are the most popular concentrations, along with the entrepreneurship program, one of Babson's strongest, bringing in venture capitalists and executives from such companies as Dunkin' and Jiffy Lube for how-to lectures.

In the classroom, Babson relies on the case-study approach more typically employed by M.B.A. programs. Students break into groups or act as officers of pseudo corporations to address specific business situations and solve marketplace problems. "The academic climate is mostly collaborative, because there are group projects in almost every class," says a student. Just 19 percent of classes have fewer than 20 students, but others rarely exceed 50. "Professors know your name and know what your struggles are in the class," shares a junior. Accounting students may take graduate classes at Babson in the summer and fall after finishing their bachelor's degrees, letting them sit for the CPA exam about one year earlier than most other programs. The Center for Women's Entrepreneurial Leadership promotes women in business and offers scholarships, special events, and networking opportunities. Babson offers more than 100 global study programs around the world, and 63 percent of students participate; students in the Honors Program are required to do so. "Study abroad is basically baked into the Babson experience," says a junior. Not all programs are business oriented; the London Theatre Program, for example, focuses on arts appreciation.

Babson students are go-getters. "We enjoy comparing how full our Google calendars are," says one senior, and another student adds, "No one blinks an eye when a student is walking around campus in a suit." Black students make up 5 percent of the undergraduate student body, Hispanics/Latinos 17 percent, Asian Americans 13 percent, and multiracial students 3 percent. Massachusetts residents comprise 24 percent, while 28 percent are international. No one seems to care much about politics, or at least most prefer to avoid political discussions. "Students with financial constraints would definitely find a challenging time fitting in," cautions an accounting student, because "there is a lot of wealth on this campus." Merit scholarships averaging $23,900 are available; there are no athletic scholarships.

Babson guarantees housing for four years, and 76 percent of undergraduates live in campus housing, resulting in high demand for singles and suites. "The suite-style living is awesome," says a first-year. "It allows you to live with a bunch of your best friends but still have separate singles to sleep in." After the first year, rooms are assigned by lottery, with standing based on credits earned; housing policies are gender inclusive. At the main dining hall, you'll find sushi, make-your-own stir-fry, vegan stations, and other options, which receive average reviews. Security gets high marks, and the student-led Alliance for Sexual Assault Prevention organization is active in raising awareness about campus sexual assault.

Social life is centered on campus during the first two years through participation in more than 100 student organizations; after that, most students are 21 and have cars, so they head to the clubs and bars of Boston proper, about 20 minutes away. "Boston offers a very vibrant social scene for upperclassmen," confirms a senior. The Campus Activities Board brings in comedians, organizes bingo nights, and throws parties, as do Greek organizations, which attract 11 percent of the men and 17 percent of the women. "We never have any Friday classes, so Thursday and Saturday are the big party nights," explains a sophomore. Underage drinking on campus is treated with a three-strike policy, and the third offense gets violators kicked out of the dorms. Favorite campus festivals include alumni weekend (great networking opportunities) and Spring Concert, when bands come to play.

The "very affluent" town of Wellesley has shops and restaurants, and there is a subway stop. Students can take the T's Green Line into the city to explore Quincy Market or the campuses of Harvard, Northeastern, Emerson, and Boston Universities. The school sponsors trips to Celtics and Red Sox games. Wellesley is also home to Wellesley College, and it's not unheard of for Babson students to socialize with

"Professors know your name and know what your struggles are in the class."

Wellesley women; Babson also offers cross-registration at Wellesley and neighboring Olin College of Engineering. Popular road trips include the beaches of Cape Cod and Martha's Vineyard, the ski slopes of Vermont and New Hampshire, and the bright lights of New York City and Montreal.

While making money may be the most popular form of competition at Babson, students recognize the importance of keeping their bodies in competitive condition too. Popular intramural and club sports include volleyball, rugby, and ice hockey, and on the varsity level, the Beavers play in Division III. Any match against archrival Bentley and soccer games against Brandeis and Colby draw crowds. The men's ice hockey team is formidable, and men's and women's basketball, lacrosse, and alpine skiing are frequent title contenders.

"Thursday and Saturday are the big party nights."

At Babson, students embrace entrepreneurship as an ethos and are willing to work hard for what they want. One student calls it a "grind culture," but finds it "inspiring." After all, learning how to balance work with everything else that's important in life is a prerequisite to climbing the corporate ladder or becoming the next groundbreaking industry leader. And thanks to small classes, strong faculty connections, a laser-like focus on entrepreneurial leadership, and plenty of hands-on experience, students leave Babson well equipped to begin scampering up those rungs.

If You Apply To ›

Babson: Early decision I and II, early action, regular decision. SATs or ACTs: optional. Accepts the Common Application with supplement.

Bard College

30 Campus Road, Annandale-on-Hudson, NY 12504

A dominant presence in the world of nontraditional liberal arts colleges, Bard offers what is arguably the most innovative range of academic programs anywhere. Like Reed on the West Coast, combines unabashed individuality with rigorous traditional academics. Former president Leon Botstein, a sometimes controversial polymath known by all simply as "Leon," has championed the liberal arts in countries around the world.

Bard College has come a long way since its 1860 founding by 12 men studying to enter the seminaries of the Episcopal Church. Those pioneers would no doubt be surprised at the eclectic mix of students now running around Annandale-on-Hudson. The idea that Bard is strictly a school for artists and social science majors has largely disappeared, and the result is a school with a wide range of intellectual depth. Having expanded its mission beyond undergraduate and graduate education to also encompass support for the arts, secondary education reform, and the development of partnerships that bring education to underserved areas around the globe, Bard has earned a well-deserved national, even international, profile. Administrators explains Bard's focus as a "combination of rigorous liberal arts education with a strong emphasis on creativity, civic engagement, and interdisciplinarity." To succeed in such a dynamic environment, one student advises, "You don't need perfect grades. You just need an adventurous spirit, an ambitious attitude toward self-improvement, and an ability to evaluate your experiences and capabilities."

Bard's campus occupies 1,200 well-landscaped acres in New York's Washington Irving country on the shores of the Hudson River. Each ivy-covered brick building stands out—especially the dorms, which range from cottages in the woods to Russian Colonial in style. Renowned architect Frank Gehry designed the stunning, $62 million Fisher Center for the Performing Arts, which provides teaching and performance space for everything from opera to improv. Montgomery Place, a 380-acre estate and National Historic Landmark adjacent to the main campus, provides additional facilities for programs in the arts, humanities, and environmental sciences. Bard is currently building a new Performing Arts Lab, designed by Maya Lin (of Washington, D.C.'s Vietnam Memorial fame), with new studios for dance and theater, which is scheduled to open in 2026.

Despite Bard's reputation for nonconformity, the list of requirements is extensive, including ten distribution requirements. Classes are small and seminar style, and first-years show up three weeks before classes start for the Workshop in Language and Thinking, where they read extensively in several genres and meet in small groups to discuss reading and writing. (A literature major calls L&T "the best three weeks of my life.") The First-Year Seminar introduces the intellectual, artistic, and cultural ideas at the core of a liberal arts education. During Citizen Science, a ten-week program taken during one of their first two semesters, students "work to access, validate, and integrate scientific findings into their daily lives by using real-world examples." In the spring of the second year, students declare a major through Moderation, a midway review of performance when students submit a portfolio of work, write reflective papers, and discuss their proposed study plans with a faculty board. "It feels exciting to take that step and think about how my classes are leading into the bigger projects I want to do," says a psychology major. In junior year, preparation for the Senior Project begins. Students create original work as evidence of mastery in their field or fields, and their Senior Project is reviewed by a faculty board.

With authors such as M. Gessen, Francine Prose, and Dinaw Mengestu teaching at Bard, literature and written arts are among the school's best programs. Bard was one of the first to grant a B.A. in visual and performing arts and boasts one of the finest studio programs in the country; photography is one of the toughest majors to get into, and the film and electronic arts program is well regarded. Bard established what administrators believe is the first collegiate program in human rights. Environmental and urban studies is also strong. There is a five-year, dual-degree conservatory program for music students, and although Bard is far from pre-professional, it does offer combined programs of its own and with other schools in finance, engineering, public health, and a number of other fields.

> **"Students are more eager to engage in discussions about what they just learned in class."**

Bard's academic climate is "intellectual and consistently challenging," says a senior, but students agree that the atmosphere is collaborative. "Students are more eager to engage in discussions about what they just learned in class than they are likely to discuss what grades they received on the most recent exam," says a sociology and human rights major. Eighty-one percent of classes have fewer than 20 students, and if students want more individual attention, they can devise a syllabus for their own tutorial and find a professor to sponsor it. Professors receive outstanding reviews for their expertise and personal touch. Says a senior, "Professors value the students as individuals first."

A semester-long program in New York City lets students study biology and medicine at Rockefeller University, and spots are reserved for Bard students as Summer Undergraduate Research Fellows. Also located in New York City, Bard's Globalization and International Affairs program merges advanced coursework in global affairs

(continued)

Enrolled: 18%
Grad in 6 Years: 74%
Returning First-years: 85%
Academics: ✐ ✐ ✐ ✐
Social: 🗩 🗩 🗩
Q of L: ★ ★ ★ ★
Admissions: (845) 758-7472
Email Address:
  admission@bard.edu

Strong Programs:
Environmental and Urban
  Studies
Film and Electronic Arts
Literature
Music
Photography
Political Studies
Studio Arts
Written Arts

Bard is currently building a new Performing Arts Lab, designed by Maya Lin (of Washington, D.C.'s Vietnam Memorial fame).

with internships at leading public, private, and nonprofit agencies. All students study away or study abroad, and options are available in nearly 50 countries around the globe. To expand liberal arts instruction overseas and to help nurture emerging democratic societies, Bard has developed partnerships with educational institutions in locations as diverse as Berlin, Lithuania, Kyrgyzstan, South Africa, and the West Bank, as well as among prison inmates in the U.S.

Bard students tended to march to their own drummer in high school. "Many struggle their first year, when they realize everyone is just as unique as they are," says one senior. While the school has its share of extremely wealthy children of media moguls and Hollywood actors, Bardians take pride in diversity, whether socioeconomic, racial, geographical (69 percent are from out of state, with 17 percent from foreign countries), or ideological. "Bard students are very engaged, so social and political issues are a big part of campus life," says a studio arts major. Black students make up 7 percent of the student body, Asian Americans 3 percent, Hispanics/Latinos 16 percent, and multiracial students 7 percent. Merit scholarships averaging $15,200 are available, but there are no athletic awards. Bard offers an early-decision application option in which students can take the Bard Entrance Examination, demonstrating their academic ability by answering 16 essay questions and submitting three 2,500-word essays on a range of scholarly topics that are graded by professors.

Three-quarters of Bard students live on campus; first-years and sophomores are required to do so. Residence halls vary in style, explains one student: "Some are old Victorian mansions, some are new modern buildings that are eco-friendly, one looks like a castle, and others are big cement monsters from the 1950s." Many upperclassmen move off campus; to help ease their commute, Bard runs a shuttle to the nearby small towns of Red Hook and Tivoli (cumulative population 11,000), which are home to a variety of restaurants, bars, and other conveniences. Much of the fresh produce used in campus dining comes from Bard's own student-operated farm. Students say they feel safe on their rural campus, and for mental health care, "The Counseling Center is accessible and free," says an art history and computer science double major.

All Bard students are automatically made members of the student government, and cocurricular life is run by students; there are more than 150 different clubs. "There isn't a big party culture like at larger schools," says a senior, "but there are always student-led concerts, art shows, film screenings, and performances to go to." The Student Activities Board plans the Club Fair, at the beginning of the year, "which is a great way to see everything happening on campus and get involved," notes a studio arts major. Spring Fling, a festival with music, food, and performances, is also a popular annual event. There are no fraternities or sororities, and when it comes to alcohol, policies are focused on safety and respect, although underage drinking in the dorms is taken seriously. Bard's hometown of Annandale-on-Hudson is 20 miles from the crafts and antiques meccas of Woodstock and Rhinebeck, and not much farther from the ski slopes of the Catskills and the Berkshires. Having a car helps, although New York City is just 100 minutes away by train.

The Raptors compete in 18 Division III sports and are members of several conferences, including the Eastern College Athletic Conference, the Liberty League, and the College Squash Association. Track and field, soccer, basketball, cross-country, swimming, tennis, and men's volleyball have been strong in recent years. Bard is not a jock school, but one student notes, "There are plenty of pseudo jocks and intellectuals in good shape." Forty percent of the students get involved in intramurals. Across campus, miles of trails stretch through the woods along the Hudson. "If you like the woods, it's amazing," muses an anthropology major. "If you like the city, you'll go stir-crazy."

Thanks to a $500 million challenge grant from George Soros, Bard is looking forward to expanding programs that reach far beyond the arts. Students should come prepared to work hard and have their minds opened. "The Bard culture is a weird mixture of apathy and activism, arts and sciences, quirkiness and coolness," says a senior. "However, the one real thing that unites Bard is an ability to be self-driven and independent. Bard students are not followers, but establish their own paths."

If You Apply To ›

Bard: Early decision I and II, early action, regular decision. SATs or ACTs: optional. Accepts the Common Application.

Barnard College

3009 Broadway, New York, NY 10027

The most selective women's college in the country, Barnard is academically right up there with Wellesley, and the workload is on par with Pomona and Swarthmore. Step outside and you're on Broadway; across the street lies Columbia University, whose academic riches are yours for the taking. Barnard women are a little more artsy, outspoken, and city-ish than their counterparts at Columbia.

Barnard students get the best of both worlds—the small, close-knit atmosphere of a leading liberal arts school along with the limitless opportunities of Columbia University, the undergraduate division of the Ivy League research institution just across Broadway. And as a college for women, the school "embraces its responsibility to address issues of gender in all of their complexity." Whether they are passionate about art, urban studies, or computer science, women seeking a high-energy, empowering environment with top-notch academics are likely to find a niche here. "We are a college full of women who are unafraid to be leaders," says a senior. "Barnard is a place where women can express themselves and do hard things."

Barnard was founded in 1889 by suffragists in response to Columbia's refusal to admit women and was strategically named after a recently deceased Columbia president. Its campus is on the Upper West Side of Manhattan in the Morningside Heights neighborhood, just blocks from Riverside Drive, with its lovely path parallel to the Hudson River for running or biking. Trees and other greenery shade grand prewar apartment buildings, and grassy medians break up the wide expanse of Broadway itself. Barnard's architecturally diverse buildings are more modern than Columbia's, and in recent years, the college has invested to upgrade labs, classrooms, and the residence halls. The LeFrak Foundation Center for Well-Being opened in 2024 and serves as a centralized hub for all wellness-related initiatives across campus, including physical, financial, and mental health.

Barnard competes head-to-head with Columbia in admissions, an interesting dilemma because Barnard is an affiliate college of Columbia University, along with the engineering school, the medical school, the business school, and, of course, Columbia College. In general, women looking for a more traditional "rah-rah"

Website: www.barnard.edu
Location: City Center
Private
Total Enrollment: 3,229
Undergraduates: 3,229
Male/Female: 0/100
Financial Aid: 33%
Pell Grant: 20%
Expense: Pr $ $ $ $
Student Loans: 23%
Average Debt: $
Applicants: 11,836
Accepted: 9%
Enrolled: 69%
Grad in 6 Years: 93%
Returning First-years: 97%
Academics: ✍ ✍ ✍ ✍ ✍
Social: 🗩 🗩 🗩
Q of L: ★ ★ ★
Admissions: (212) 854-2014
Email Address:
admissions@barnard.edu

experience may prefer Columbia. Some students apply to Barnard as a back door to Columbia, which is harder for women to get into, but Barnard's admissions officers have become adept at sniffing out Columbia wannabes. Those who opt for Barnard like the fact that advising and housing are better more personalized on their side of Broadway and value its distinctive approach to educating women. Once enrolled, Barnard students share a first-year orientation program with Columbia, where they mix together in small groups and take tours of the campus and city.

Barnard's Foundations curriculum is designed to enable students to gain general knowledge in a range of academic disciplines, develop critical-thinking and communication skills, and spend more of their time exploring other areas of interest or pursuing cocurricular opportunities that enhance their major. First-year students must take a writing course, a first-year seminar, and a physical education class. In addition to standard distribution requirements, students must fulfill Modes of Thinking requirements in six areas, such as Thinking Technologically and Digitally, Thinking Locally, and Thinking about Social Difference. A senior project or thesis ensures academic depth within the major.

Barnard's most popular majors are economics, psychology, history, computer science, political science, English, biology, and neuroscience (there's a healthy contingent of premeds). Architecture, human rights, anthropology, computer science, architecture, and the visual and performing arts, especially dance, are also well regarded. Barnard boasts strong support for budding writers and is a hotbed of new talent. Women's, gender, and sexuality studies draws praise as well. The Athena Center for Leadership Studies offers workshops, mentoring programs, internships, guest speakers, and other special features. Several 4+1 pathways allow students to earn a bachelor's degree from Barnard and a master's degree from Columbia in public health, engineering, international and public affairs, and other areas in just five years. A dual-degree program is available with the nearby Jewish Theological Seminary, and music students may apply to take classes at Juilliard and the Manhattan School of Music. About a quarter of the students study abroad in their choice of more than 35 countries.

> **"Barnard is a place where women can express themselves and do hard things."**

After the first year, Barnard students may cross-register for courses at Columbia and vice versa; in certain majors, some required classes are only offered at Columbia, where the academic climate can be more competitive, with a stronger "stress culture," says a physics major. "It's quite easy to get bogged down with too much work," adds says a junior, "but Barnard also tries to emphasize the importance of mental and physical well-being." Many students come to Barnard because of its low student/faculty ratio. Sixty-seven percent of classes have fewer than 20 students. Another plus: Barnard has no graduate teaching assistants. In fact, Barnard professors enjoy Columbia's proximity almost as much as undergraduates, and each year one-third of the full-time faculty teaches in graduate departments throughout the university. Still, faculty members focus on their teaching responsibilities to undergraduates first, and a political science and art history major notes that because "professors have designed their classes on topics they are basically experts on, lectures and discussions are incredibly engaging."

> **"There is no shortage of amazing opportunities outside of the classroom."**

The basketball team were three-peat Ivy League champs in 2025.

Undergraduate research is also a priority at Barnard, especially in the sciences, and often occurs within guided internships, colloquia, and seminar courses. "From research in labs to internships at the Met, there is no shortage of amazing opportunities outside of the classroom for Barnard students in New York City," cheers a junior. Three-quarters of students complete internships before they graduate. Beyond Barnard, the career center hub that connects students with internship, career, and other postgraduate opportunities, receives positive reviews.

Barnard students "are intelligent, hardworking, and they care deeply about the world around them," asserts a sophomore. Twenty-two percent of Barnard students are New York natives, and 16 percent are international. Asian Americans make up 22 percent of the student body, Black students 6 percent, Hispanics/Latinas 14 percent, and multiracial students 8 percent. Students are mostly liberal and politically active. Barnard does not offer merit or athletic scholarships, but it does commit to a need-blind admissions process for domestic first-year applicants and to meet admitted students' full demonstrated financial need. A math major points out, "Access Barnard is an excellent resource here, which serves our first-generation, low income, and international students."

Barnard guarantees four years of housing to enrolling first-years, and 73 percent of students live in the dorms, which have come a long way in recent years: There's an 18-story Barnard dormitory tower, plus one dorm complex and eight off-campus apartment buildings. Nonresidents must be signed in by a resident, and entries are always guarded, so students say they feel safe. "The dorms are pretty big, and we also have a lot of choices when we become upperclassmen, so we can pick housing for the living style that suits us individually," reports a sophomore. All students must buy a meal plan, which may also be used at Columbia. "The college has created a Being Barnard program that teaches students how to recognize sexual assault and how to handle it both as a potential victim and as a passerby," explains a junior.

> **"We can pick housing for the living style that suits us individually."**

When it comes to social life, students tend to divide their time between the campus and the city, "but it's most common for students to actually leave campus for fun," explains a sophomore. "There is always something happening in NYC, so students want to take advantage of concerts, events, parties, clubs, bars, etc." Traditions include Big Sub in the fall, when a 700-foot-long sub sandwich is assembled throughout campus and everyone grabs a piece, and Midnight Breakfast the night before finals begin, when deans and administrators serve up eggs and waffles in the student center. Barnard women interested in Greek life are allowed to join sororities at Columbia, and alcohol is permitted in residential spaces for those of legal age. Many of the city's cultural offerings are free to students with their school ID. Road trips are infrequent, as not many students have—or want—cars, but when they happen, destinations range from Washington, D.C., to Boston, easily reached by train and plane.

Barnard athletes compete in the Division I Ivy League conference alongside their peers enrolled at Columbia, and archery, tennis, track and field, soccer, and fencing are popular and competitive. The basketball team were three-peat Ivy League champs in 2025. Columbia's marvelous gym, co-ed intramurals, and club sports are also available; the women's ultimate Frisbee and rugby clubs are particularly popular with Barnard students.

Students see Barnard as having "the supportive community of a small liberal arts women's college, the resources of a large research institution through Columbia, and the infinite opportunities of New York City right outside the gates," in the words of one proud Barnard woman. It's a winning combination that turns out well-rounded students ready to leap toward the future.

First-year students must take a writing course, a first-year seminar, and a physical education class.

Once enrolled, Barnard students share a first-year orientation program with Columbia.

Overlaps

Brown, Columbia, Pomona, Smith, Swarthmore, Wellesley, Wesleyan, Yale

If You Apply To ›

Barnard: Early decision, regular decision. Accepts the Common Application with supplement. Accepts applications from students who consistently live and identify as women. Please consult Barnard's website for the most up-to-date information regarding standardized test requirements.

Bates College

2 Andrews Road, Lewiston, ME 04240

Bowdoin got rid of its frats; Bates never had them, and therein hangs a tale. With its long-held tradition of egalitarianism and sense of community, Bates is a kindred spirit to Quaker institutions such as Haverford and Swarthmore. A four-week spring term helps make Bates a leader in studying abroad. Boasts a pioneering debate team. Blue-collar Lewiston is not a draw, but New England countryside is within arm's reach.

Founded by abolitionists in 1855, Bates College takes pride in its heritage as a haven for seekers of guidance, freedom, and justice, and it aims to help students find a broader purpose for their lives. The college's 4–4–1 calendar offers ample opportunity for study abroad, even for just four weeks at year's end. Its small size also means student/faculty interaction is plentiful, and close friendships are easily formed. "Bates has this really specific blend of intellectual curiosity, unpretentiousness, and social consciousness," says a senior.

The Bates campus features a mix of Georgian and Federal buildings and Victorian homes spread out over the grassy lawns of Lewiston. Over the last two decades, Bates has transformed its campus core: The college has converted two former student residence halls into key academic buildings, renovated historic Victorian homes into student residences, turned one of the country's earliest college football fields into a multisport turf field, and opened a state-of-the-art science center for the biology, chemistry, and neuroscience departments.

Bates emphasizes a broad-based education in the liberal arts. In addition to a writing-intensive first-year seminar, students take at least one class in each of five Modes of Inquiry: analysis and critique, creative process and production, historical and social inquiry, scientific reasoning, and quantitative and formal reasoning. All students select a major and a second area of study, which may be a minor, a second major, or a general education concentration (GEC). Bates's GECs consist of four interrelated courses structured around a central theme, such as Class, Inequity, Poverty, and Justice; Globalization; and Queer Studies. More than 75 concentrations are available, and they may fall within one department or program or may be designed by faculty from different disciplines. "One unique part of Bates is that just about all seniors write a thesis," says a chemistry major.

While Bates was a pioneer in not requiring standardized tests for admission, that doesn't mean its standards are lax. "The academic climate at Bates is rigorous but deeply collaborative," says an American studies and gender and sexuality studies major. "There's a strong emphasis on critical thinking, discussion-based learning, and making connections across disciplines." The most popular majors include psychology, politics, economics, history, and environmental studies, and these are also among Bates's best. The music and art departments benefit from the Olin Arts Center, which houses a performance hall, gallery, recording studio, art studios, and practice rooms. Interdisciplinary programs at Bates include rhetoric, film, and screen studies; earth and climate sciences; and gender and sexuality studies. Professors teach all courses, including lab and discussion sections, and 61 percent of classes enroll fewer than 20 students. "Spending time outside of class with the professors made me realize the sheer amount of

> **"Bates has this . . . blend of intellectual curiosity, unpretentiousness, and social consciousness."**

talent (often hidden underneath the professors' humility) we have in the faculty," a biology and English major says.

For those whose horizons extend beyond the charms of Lewiston, Bates offers study abroad opportunities in more than 80 foreign locations, and 65 percent of students take advantage of them. Bates's 4–4–1 calendar allows for a four-week short term at the end of the academic year, and students may use this term to focus on a single subject of interest, frequently off campus. Recent examples include geological fieldwork in the Northern Rockies; marine biological studies at stations on the coast of Maine; and art, theater, and music studies in New York City and Europe. Community engagement "is a central part of the Bates experience," says a sociology and theater major. "There are Community Engagement Courses in every single department for every class year [that] allow students to interact with the community." Research opportunities, including funded options, abound. "Two of my friends received the Otis Grant to spend 60 days backpacking through Italy in an attempt to 'debunk the Literary Sublime,'" shares a senior.

Ninety-one percent of Bates students come from Maine, 10 percent arrive from foreign countries, and many others hail from Massachusetts, California, and New York. "My peers are inquisitive, curious about the world, and often drawn to interdisciplinary ways of thinking," a student says. The administration has slowly been making Bates more diverse, and Black students currently account for 4 percent of the student body,

Hispanics/Latinos 10 percent, Asian Americans 7 percent, and multiracial students 8 percent. "Social and political issues are a regular part of campus life," opines a senior, including discussions about racial justice, labor rights, climate action, and the Israeli–Palestinian conflict. There are no merit or athletic scholarships available, although the college does guarantee to meet 100 percent of the demonstrated financial need of all students.

Ninety-two percent of Bates students live on campus, as housing is guaranteed for four years, and singles, doubles, triples, quads, and suites are available. "Housing is great here," a student raves. Students report that the campus dining hall offers tasty fare, with several stations ranging from brick-oven pizza and pasta to a vegan bar. Students say campus security is visible and more than adequate. "Given the nature of a small campus, students know a majority of the officers' names and do not feel intimidated to approach them about a problem," explains a history major.

Weekend diversions mostly occur on campus. "Whether it is parties, comedians, movies, or bands, there is always something to do," a student says. The Chase Hall Programming Board, run by students, plans many of the social events, including an annual gala. Without a Greek system, college alcohol policies are fairly loose, a student says. Barbecues and clambakes are big when the weather is nice, and the annual Winter Carnival includes a ski shredding competition, ice skating, and the Puddle Jump, where a hole is cut in the ice on Lake Andrews and students plunge in. In Lewiston (population 37,000) "there's a growing arts scene, local cafés, a few great bookstores, and access to outdoor spaces like Thorncrag and the Androscoggin River trails,"

cheers a senior. Students with cars can easily road-trip to the outlet stores in Freeport and Kittery, Maine. Other popular destinations include Bar Harbor in Acadia National Park or "Portland for great food," says a senior.

Bates's 31 varsity Bobcat teams compete in Division III, except for the ski team, which is Division I. Everyone gets excited for matches against Bowdoin and Colby, especially when it comes to basketball, football, and lacrosse. The women's rowing team has won five national championships in the last decade. The intramural program, organized by students, is "strong and spirited" and attracts many participants, with ice hockey, ultimate Frisbee, soccer, and rugby being among the favorites. Bates is home of the famed undergraduate debate organization the Brooks Quimby Debate Council. Founded in 1855 when completing a public debate was a graduation requirement, the team was one of the first in the nation to go co-ed and to include Black students.

If you can stand the cold and the silent, starry nights, Bates can be a good choice. With caring professors, a small student body, a focus on the liberal arts, and a free-spirited culture, students quickly become big fans. "Bates is not flashy or overly polished. It's thoughtful, sometimes scrappy, and always evolving," says a senior. "If you're looking for a place where you can ask big questions, be challenged, and still feel grounded in a real community—Bates could be a great fit."

If You Apply To ›

Bates: Early decision I and II, regular decision. SATs or ACTs: optional. Accepts the Common Application.

Baylor University

1311 South 5th Street, Waco, TX 76798

The largest and best-endowed Baptist university anywhere, Baylor has become one of the top research universities. Atmosphere is avowedly Christian. Lots of school spirit, especially at Saturday afternoon home football games. LGBTQ+ policies have been controversial. Baylor's motto—Pro Ecclesia, Pro Texana (For Church, For Texas)—says it all.

Baylor University offers students a solid Christian-influenced education at a bargain price. The university was founded in 1845 by the Union Baptist Association of Texas and named after a cofounder, 10 months before Texas became a state, and its Baptist tradition fosters a strong sense of community among students and faculty. The school's strategic plan has transformed the university by lowering the student/teacher ratio, renovating residence halls, and investing in resources to become a top-tier research university while enhancing its Christian identity. "Baylor's commitment to academic excellence and an incredible alumni network ensures a great education and a chance to get a job," lauds a junior.

The 1,000-acre Baylor campus abuts the historic Brazos River near downtown Waco, Texas (population 140,000). The Georgian architectural style emphasizes the gracious tradition of the aristocratic Old South, and the central part of campus, the quadrangle, was built when Baylor moved from Independence, Texas, in 1886. The campus has been witness to a number of renovations and new construction, including the Mark & Paula Hurd Welcome Center, the $185 million Foster Basketball Pavilion, and the Fudge Football Development Center.

Core requirements in the College of Arts and Sciences include a standard distribution of coursework in several liberal arts areas as well as two religion courses and two semesters of Chapel, ranging from a traditional worship service to Chapel experiences where students identify communities and connections that resonate with them. All new students take a New Student Experience course in the fall, and everyone completes a Cultural Events Experience. The Honors College oversees the honors program (which offers opportunities for course integration and independent research) and the University Scholars Program (which waives most distribution requirements).

Of Baylor's more than 130 undergraduate degrees, some of the most popular include nursing, biology, health science studies, and accounting. Computer science, communication sciences and disorders, business, psychology, and neuroscience programs are well regarded. More unusual options include institutes focusing on environmental studies and childhood learning disorders, a minor in military studies, and a major and minor in Great Texts, an interdisciplinary program exploring "the richness and diversity of the Western intellectual heritage." The archaeology and geosciences departments benefit from fossil- and mineral-rich Texas prairies. Students can opt to study abroad through over 100 programs on six continents; study and intern semesters in London, Scandinavia, and Singapore are also available.

Students say that Baylor's greatest strengths are a sense of community rooted in its emphasis on Christianity, as well as the faculty's focus on teaching and research. Baylor's hefty $2.2 billion endowment is the largest among the nation's Baptist-affiliated schools. Administrators strive to keep classes small—49 percent have fewer than 20 students. Full professors often teach first-year courses, and opportunities for mentored research abound. "While a lot is expected of us, professors are willing to help, and students work together to help one another excel," says an environmental health science major.

The students at Baylor are "kind, servant hearted, and faithful beings," says a political science major. Sixty-one percent of undergraduates are Texans, and 18 percent are Baptist; 3 percent are international. Black students account for 6 percent of the student body, Hispanics/Latinos 18 percent, Asian Americans 9 percent, and multiracial students 5 percent. The university has launched several initiatives to increase and support diversity on campus, including cultural competence training for students, faculty, and staff and programs supporting first-generation students. Students vie for numerous academic scholarships, averaging $17,800, and more than 400 athletic scholarships in 19 varsity sports.

As might be expected on such a conservative, religious campus, dorms are single sex and have limited visitation privileges, which draws complaints from many of the 31 percent of students who call them home. The Faculty-in-Residence program houses one faculty member in each residence hall who plans special events and supports "learning and faith development." Upperclassmen look off campus for cheaper housing with private rooms and fewer rules, but there has been a push for more students to stay on campus with the recent construction of three residence halls with apartment-style rooms. Students say they feel safe on campus with frequent police patrols. Based on its religious tenets, Baylor has received an exemption from some federal protections relating to LGBTQ+ students. Nevertheless, the university has affirmed its responsibility to serve the needs of all students regardless of sexual orientation or gender identity and, says a public health major, "I believe we are moving in positive directions at Baylor to make nontraditional students feel more welcome on campus."

As described by a junior, "The social scene varies on campus, You can find groups of very committed religious students, to groups who party often." Eighteen percent of Baylor's men and 34 percent of the women belong to a fraternity or sorority. "Greek organizations are a big part of the culture at Baylor," reports a student. Alcohol is not served on campus or at campus-sponsored events. Students may also join more than 330 other student organizations, most of which involve a community service requirement. "Common Grounds, an on-campus coffee shop, hosts concerts most weekends," says one student. "The movies are popular (a ticket costs $5 with a student ID)." Easy road trips include Dallas, Austin, San Antonio, Bryan/College Station, and beaches at Galveston, South Padre Island, and Corpus Christi. Most destinations are within a two-and-a-half-hour drive, students say, making a set of wheels a big help, if not a necessity.

On Dia del Oso (Day of the Bear), classes are canceled for a day in April in favor of a campuswide celebration.

"[Baylor students are] kind, servant hearted, and faithful beings."

The archaeology and geosciences departments benefit from fossil- and mineral-rich Texas prairies.

Highlights of Baylor's social calendar include Dia del Oso (Day of the Bear), when classes are canceled for a day in April in favor of a campuswide celebration. Christmas on 5th Street, organized by Student Life, gives students an opportunity to enjoy the annual Christmas tree lighting, concert, and other holiday festivities. The school claims to have the largest collegiate homecoming parade in the nation.

When it comes to football, remember: You're in Texas. The Division I Baylor Bears play in the $266 million McLane Stadium. First-years wear special custom jerseys to games and take the field before the players, then sit together as a pack. "It's a very awesome part of the freshman experience," one student says. But recently it's the basketball teams that are generating the most excitement.

"While a lot is expected of us, professors are willing to help."

The women's team advanced to their 21st straight NCAA tournament in 2025, and the men have been regularly a top three seed in the past few years. Acrobatics and tumbling have claimed 10 consecutive national titles. Big 12 Conference winners include football and men's and women's tennis, and men's and women's track and field are also strong. For weekend warriors, the McLane Student Life Center offers one of the tallest rock-climbing walls in Texas. The university maintains a small marina for kayaking and paddleboating, and several lakes with good beaches, fishing, and watersports are nearby. Popular intramurals include flag football, sand volleyball, and tennis; 36 club sports are another big draw.

"Baylor's personality is rooted in a blend of faith, tradition, and ambition," says one student. "It's a place where people help someone they have never met, and where thousands show up for football games and worship services." Baylor is unique in that the university is actively wrestling with how to live out its Christian mission in a changing world. Students looking to focus on strong academics, community involvement, and discovering their vocational calling may find Baylor a perfect fit.

If You Apply To ›

Baylor: Early decision, early action, regular decision. Accepts the Common Application with supplement. Please consult Baylor's website for the most up-to-date information regarding standardized test requirements.

Beloit College

700 College Street, Beloit, WI 53511

A small Midwestern college known for passionate students and a global focus, Beloit has emerged as a national leader in blending the critical thinking and other core values of the liberal arts with career preparation. Wisconsin location makes Beloit easier to get into than comparable schools in sexier places. Well-known anthropology and creative writing programs are among the best in the nation.

Beloit College remains dedicated to the liberal arts and sciences but is increasingly focused on connecting its brand of liberal education to career preparation and professional success, encouraging students to pursue diverse hands-on learning experiences. Known for attracting liberal freethinkers in the 1960s and '70s, the school has steered back toward the mainstream but still emphasizes inclusion, understanding, and the world beyond the United States. Advises an education major, "To really enjoy Beloit, you should be open to new ideas, concepts, and people."

Beloit was founded by transplanted New Englanders in 1846 when Wisconsin was still a territory. Its 40-acre campus is a Northeastern-style oasis an hour's drive from Madison and Milwaukee and less than two hours from Chicago. Academic and administrative buildings sit on one side, with residence halls on the other. Nineteenth-century Federal and Romanesque architecture dominates, with a few modern facilities mixed in, like the LEED Platinum–certified Sanger Center for the Sciences. The Powerhouse, the college's 120,000-square-foot student union and recreation center, is located in a repurposed power plant on the Rock River, adjacent to campus.

In the absence of core requirements, students complete three writing-intensive courses, a quantitative reasoning class, one intercultural literacy course, and a capstone experience. In addition, Beloiters tackle classes across five domains that focus on systems, arts, behavior, the universe, and texts. To satisfy an "Experience" requirement, students may undertake an internship, an entrepreneurial or research project, or a designated course with a similar component, such as field work or travel.

Beloit's five schools—Business, Environment & Sustainability, Global & Public Service, Health Sciences, and Media & the Arts—offer integrated majors and minors. Each school links curriculum with career-focused advising and programming, preprofessional experiential learning opportunities, and specialized credentials. Beloit has also created Impact Beloit to help connect students to community-based learning and internship opportunities. Business and economics, anthropology, and creative writing are signature programs, and the geology, international relations, theatre, and dance programs are also popular and well regarded. Biology, psychology, and sociology enroll high numbers too. Among the more distinctive options are a museum studies minor, enhanced by hands-on experience in the college's Wright Museum of Art and Logan Museum of Anthropology, which was established in 1894 and emphasizes social justice in museum practices. Notable interdisciplinary offerings include a performing and applied arts program uniting concentrations in dance, design and technology, music, and theatre performance. A 3–2 engineering dual degree is available with WashU in St. Louis and Rensselaer Polytechnic Institute, and a 3–1 or 4–1 nursing dual degree is available on the Beloit campus through a partnership with Edgewood College.

"There is . . . an atmosphere of meaningful collaboration."

The academic milieu is described as challenging but not competitive. "Students are expected to do significant work—papers, research, symposiums—but there is also an atmosphere of meaningful collaboration," says one student. Teaching is the faculty's priority, and 72 percent of classes have fewer than 20 students. "If you're struggling, your professors are there for you no matter what," says a biology major. The Advanced Mentoring Program matches each incoming student with a faculty mentor. Beloit teems with practical cocurricular experiences. "Boundary Waters, a summer course at the Coe College Wilderness Field Station in the Boundary Waters of Minnesota, is great for those interested in writing, environmental studies, social justice," praises a critical identity major. "One of the coolest learning opportunities on campus is our Center for Entrepreneurship [in Liberal Education]," says an international relations and psychology major, where facilities include an art gallery, TV and media lab, recording studio, and a MakerLab. Budding scientists may conduct biological and biomedical research at Northwestern and Rush Universities in Chicago. Students who wish to study or do research abroad can choose from programs in 60 countries.

Students at Beloit are "open-minded, curious, passionate, friendly, and supportive," observes a senior. While Beloit may not be as far-out as it once was, the student body is still decidedly liberal. Twenty-one percent of students hail from Wisconsin, and 13 percent come from abroad. "We are a diverse campus," says a

(continued)

Financial Aid: 98%
Pell Grant: 29%
Expense: Pr $ $ $
Student Loans: 87%
Average Debt: $ $ $
Applicants: 3,853
Accepted: 63%
Enrolled: 9%
Grad in 6 Years: 71%
Returning First-years: 81%
Academics: ✏ ✏ ✏
Social: 🗩 🗩 🗩
Q of L: ★ ★ ★ ★
Admissions: (608) 363-2500
Email Address:
admissions@beloit.edu

Strong Programs:
Anthropology
Business Management
Creative Writing
Critical Identity Studies
Health Sciences
International Relations
Museum Studies
Performing and Applied Arts

Traditional Bell Runs involve running from the quad to a bell and back—sans clothing.

first-year student. "Everyone is a part of the community, and you aren't left out." Hispanics/Latinos represent 18 percent of the total, Black students 8 percent, Asian Americans 2 percent, and multiracial students 5 percent. The Sustained Dialogue program encourages conversations about diversity and identity. Merit scholarships averaging $42,800 are available, and the school has launched the Beloit College Commitment, which offers cost benefits for qualifying students who hail from the eight counties surrounding the college. Beloit also guarantees academically qualified residents of several states that it will match the in-state tuition rate of the flagship public university in their home state.

Eighty-six percent of Beloit students live in on-campus housing facilities, where they're required to remain for three years. Fraternities attract 13 percent of the men, and sororities draw 10 percent of the women. Numerous special-interest houses cater to those interested in world languages, the arts, anthropology, and other disciplines, as well as to student organizations. As for meals, "They have fixed our main complaint, being the food," cheers a first-year. Two new campus dining venues have opened: DK's is a popular breakfast and lunch spot offering a mix of fresh and grab-and-go options. The renovated main dining hall, Hamiltons, now "takes a farm-to-fork approach," with some ingredients sourced from a student-run urban garden. Mental health support receives student praise. "They offer unlimited free sessions at the Health & Wellness Center as well as free online therapy services," reports a junior.

> "If you're struggling, your professors are there for you no matter what."

Social life is almost entirely campus-based. "On the weekends, there are always events going on such as lectures, music groups, movie showings, theater productions, dance shows, and parties," says one junior. Highly anticipated annual events include the Folk and Blues Fall Music Festival, which brings jazz, reggae, folk, and blues bands to campus, and Spring Day, when classes give way to "food trucks, bouncy houses, and different attractions for us to have a chill day," says a senior. An on-campus pub, C-Haus, draws budding musicians who perform for their fellow students. And while the school enforces state drinking laws, it's "not overly strict" says a senior. Traditional Bell Runs involve running from the quad to a bell and back—sans clothing.

Beloit (population 37,000) is a small, historically industrial city and a river walk connects the campus to downtown and its restaurants, bars, shops, and a popular farmers market. "Groups such as Habitat for Humanity, Beloit Interaction Committee, and the Outreach Center work hard to integrate students into the community," says a sophomore. When in need of a change of scenery, Beloiters take off for Chicago or the college town of Madison, easily reached through a regional bus service. For the outdoors-minded, "We have a boathouse very close to campus [where] we can go kayaking, canoeing, make s'mores, and much more," enthuses a senior.

Sports at Beloit are played more for fun than glory, unless, of course, it's a football game against rival Ripon College. The school offers 20 sports and 10 Division III Buccaneers squads, now including men's and women's ice hockey. Standouts in the Midwest Conference include baseball, which won its third straight title in 2025, and women's soccer and lacrosse. Intramural ultimate Frisbee draws around a hundred players and spectators, and intramural basketball, volleyball, and soccer are also popular.

> "The college has provided me with skills I will use for the rest of my life."

Beloit is a bundle of contradictions: a small liberal arts college in the heart of Big Ten state university country and an academic program that has an East Coast rigor but a laid-back classroom vibe reflective of the friendly spirit of the Midwest. "There are endless opportunities, and the staff and faculty are so down-to-earth and kind," says a satisfied senior. "I feel supported, and I think the college has provided me with skills I will use for the rest of my life."

Beloit created Impact Beloit to help connect students to community-based learning and internship opportunities.

Overlaps

DePauw, Knox, Lake Forest, Lawrence, Macalester, Oberlin, St. Olaf, Wooster

Bennington College

One College Drive, Bennington, VT 05201

Known for top-notch performing arts, an impressive list of alumni authors, and lavish attention on every student. Arts programs rely heavily on faculty who are practitioners in their fields. Slightly less competitive than Bard, more competitive than Hampshire and Sarah Lawrence. With just over 700 undergraduates, Bennington is one-third the size of most liberal arts colleges.

Bennington College is a school where architects are teachers, biologists sculpt, and a sociologist might work on Wall Street. According to the college's commencement statement, which is read annually at graduation, a Bennington education "seeks to liberate and nurture the individuality, the creative intelligence, and the ethical and aesthetic sensibility of its students." Since its founding in 1932, Bennington has pioneered self-directed education and emphasized fieldwork and personal relationships with professors—an approach that sets it apart even from other liberal arts colleges of similar (read: small) size. Says a junior, "The academic climate is unconventional in that students have a lot of influence in what classes are offered because we can talk to professors when they are planning classes for upcoming terms."

Bennington sits on 440 acres at the foot of Vermont's Green Mountains. The campus was once an active dairy farm, and a converted barn houses many classrooms and administrative spaces. But don't let the quaint New England setting fool you. The Dickinson Science Building boasts high-tech equipment for aspiring chemists, biologists, environmental scientists, and geneticists. A renovation of the central Commons building added new student social spaces, larger dining facilities, and ADA-accessible classrooms.

Thanks to its focus on John Dewey–style experiential learning, Bennington's academic structure differs from that of a typical college or university. Rather than selecting from preset majors, students design their own cross-disciplinary course of study (known as their "Plan"). "The plan process is unique in that you get an assigned faculty committee that helps you define your path within the areas of study that you want to pursue," explains a drama and politics senior. There are some academic requirements, including the Field Work Term, in which students spend six to seven weeks each year conducting an internship or other work experience in a field of interest and a location of their choice. "The quality of instruction prioritizes learning experience and the process of it rather than the result," says a music, Japanese, and drama student. "That's why we don't take grades. I love that." Students receive narrative evaluations (although they do have the option to request grades, too). Even Bennington's application process is nontraditional. In lieu of the Common Application, prospective students may choose to submit a "dimensional application"—an open-form application that allows them to choose any materials, in any format, that they believe best convey why they are well suited to attend Bennington.

> "The academic climate is unconventional in that students have a lot of influence in what classes are offered."

Website: www.bennington.edu
Location: Small Town
Private
Total Enrollment: 870
Undergraduates: 761
Male/Female: 25/75
Financial Aid: 96%
Pell Grant: 35%
Expense: Pr $ $ $
Student Loans: 64%
Average Debt: $ $ $
Applicants: 2,996
Accepted: 45%
Enrolled: 12%
Grad in 6 Years: 71%
Returning First-years: 82%
Academics: ✍ ✍ ✍
Social: 🗨 🗨 🗨
Q of L: ★ ★ ★ ★
Admissions: (800) 833-6845
Email Address: admissions@bennington.edu

Strong Programs:
Architecture
Cultural Studies and Languages
Literature and Writing
Mathematics
Psychology
Society, Culture, and Thought
Visual and Performing Arts

The First-Year Forum is a yearlong advising program that acclimates students to Bennington's approach to academics. The most popular areas of study include visual and performing arts, especially drama and music; society, culture, and thought; cultural studies and languages; and literature and writing. Computer science and mathematics are strong, too, although they attract a smaller number of students than many of the college's programs. A notable offering in architecture is heavily arts-oriented. "Half of the students here do work in the arts," says a sophomore. Consistent with Bennington's judgment that traditional academics have become "insular and self-perpetuating," the Center for the Advancement of Public Action invites students to put the world's most pressing problems at the center of their education via classwork and hands-on workshops. Closely related are the "pop-up mini courses" that faculty offer in response to unfolding events or current cultural phenomena. Recent topics of these three-week courses have included The War in Ukraine and Confronting Fascism in the Wake of an Insurrection. Cross-registration options at nearby Williams College expand students' access to course offerings; 16 percent of Bennington students study abroad.

"To a significant extent, it is up to the student how much effort they invest in class projects and how much they engage with independent projects," explains a political science and theater student. Sixty-two percent of courses enroll fewer than 20 students. Without academic departments, the faculty works to provide students with a well-rounded academic foundation. "The prospect of engaging in meaningful research projects under the guidance of renowned faculty members was incredibly appealing to me," says another political science student.

"The quality of instruction prioritizes learning experience and the process of it rather than the result."

Curiosity and excitement about exploration and experimentation will take you far here. "We are an open-minded community, willing to learn and unlearn, willing to speak up—not all of us of course," admits a junior, "but a significant number." Just 5 percent of undergrads are from Vermont, and 12 percent are international. Racial and ethnic diversity are a challenge: Black students account for 4 percent of the student body, Hispanics/Latinos 9 percent, Asian Americans 2 percent, and multiracial students 6 percent. Women make up 75 percent of undergraduates, but students report that the campus is diverse in terms of gender identity and sexual orientation. Thirty-five percent of first-year students are eligible for Pell Grants, and merit scholarships worth an average of $43,400 are awarded to qualified students; no athletic scholarships are available.

As Bennington lacks traditional departments, requirements, and even faculty tenure, it's not surprising that the school also eschews traditional dorms. "No one calls our houses dorms because they are just like houses with big common areas and community spaces, which are always filled with people and events," remarks a computer science and math student. Virtually all students live in one of these co-ed houses; a dozen are white New England clapboard, and six are more modern. Each house holds 30 to 40 people with two appointed chairs to govern house affairs. "The food here is great, with many options and lots of locally sourced ingredients," shares a senior. Students say the campus is generally safe, and student services have improved, especially for mental health counseling. "We have around six therapists on campus, each one is focused on a different approach," reports a junior.

"All students are invited to the big house parties that happen on Fridays and Saturdays."

With no Greek system, social life happens in the residential houses. "All students are invited to the big house parties that happen on Fridays and Saturdays. The themes are fun and creative, and everyone gets dressed up," explains a creative writing student. "There's no pressure to drink or smoke, but many do." Students say

Bennington's rugged location is ideal for outdoor adventures.

The Center for the Advancement of Public Action invites students to put the world's most pressing problems at the center of their education.

campus alcohol policies focus on keeping them safe rather than punishing them. Students look forward to Sunfest, "our on-campus music festival that takes place every May and is super fun," raves one student. For Rollerama, the college turns part of its huge Visual and Performing Arts complex into an indoor roller rink. And during the last week of each term, when (in lieu of final exams) students present their work to faculty, the ringing of the Commons bell at midnight calls weary students to the dining hall, where professors, staff, and the college president serve up French toast and other breakfast favorites.

Although the vibe on Bennington's campus is liberal and cosmopolitan, the neighboring town of the same name—four miles away, with a population of 15,000—is far more conservative, typical of rural New England. "The coffeehouse in town is a ten-minute walk from campus and often hosts music nights and DJ nights for students," says a senior. The area also offers some good restaurants and galleries and a lake with a public beach. Students can find their way into the community through volunteer work in local schools and homeless shelters.

Sports aren't a big focus, and Bennington has no varsity teams. Even so, 25 percent of students compete in intramural and club sports, with soccer, dodgeball, volleyball, and badminton proving the most popular. Bennington's rugged location is ideal for outdoor adventures, and an active outdoor collective takes students hiking, rock climbing, white-water rafting, and camping. Ski slopes beckon in the colder months.

As the first school in the nation to grant the arts equal status with other disciplines, Bennington offers a novel, participatory, and hands-on approach. Whether they're painters or writers, musicians or scientists, sculptors, dancers, or some combination thereof, what Bennington students have in common is self-motivation and a real thirst for knowledge. Says one student, "If you want an education you can shape yourself and you want that education to transcend your homework and the classroom, this is a great place to go to school."

Overlaps

Bard, Emerson, Hampshire, Mount Holyoke, NYU, Oberlin, Sarah Lawrence, Skidmore, University of Vermont

If You Apply To ›

Bennington: Early decision I and II, early action, regular decision. SATs or ACTs: optional. Accepts the Common Application.

Bentley University

175 Forest Street, Waltham, MA 02452

Bentley means business—studying it, that is, in the context of strong liberal arts. Offers both B.S. and B.A. degrees and helps 90 percent of its students land career-oriented internships. Boasts a scenic colonial-style campus with easy access to Boston and Harvard Square.

Bentley University is a midsized New England university that excels at turning out students who are committed to taking their place among the ranks of future business leaders. "Bentley prepares its students for the workplace by giving them comparable experiences socially, academically, and—most importantly—professionally," says a sophomore. With the university's solid courses in business, state-of-the-art facilities, dedication to the liberal arts, and emphasis on service learning, students find much to admire.

Bentley, which was founded in 1917 by Harry Clark Bentley, a prominent accountant, is situated on 163 acres in suburban Waltham, Massachusetts, just

Website: www.bentley.edu
Location: Suburban
Private
Total Enrollment: 4,738
Undergraduates: 4,433
Male/Female: 61/39
Financial Aid: 82%
Pell Grant: 18%

(continued)

Expense: Pr $ $ $
Student Loans: 52%
Average Debt: $ $ $ $
Applicants: 11,012
Accepted: 45%
Enrolled: 21%
Grad in 6 Years: 87%
Returning First-years: 93%
Academics: ✍ ✍ ✍
Social: 🗩 🗩 🗩
Q of L: ★ ★ ★
Admissions: (800) 523-2354
Email Address:
ugadmission@bentley.edu

Strong Programs:
Accounting
Computer Information Systems
Data Analytics
Economics-Finance
Management
Marketing

The powerhouse women's basketball team has won the Northeast 10 Conference championship in each of the last four years.

minutes west of bustling Boston. The dominant architectural style is Georgian, and the majority of campus buildings are classically built in red brick. The Bentley campus has three tiers. The north campus revolves around academics and features a library, "smart" classrooms, and high-tech labs and academic centers. The main campus centers on student life and is anchored by the 70,000-square-foot student center. The south campus focuses on recreation and includes the Dana Athletic Center and Bentley Arena. Residential housing is spread throughout each tier of the campus.

Bentley has long been committed to producing well-rounded business students who want to make a positive difference in the world, and this is reflected in the curriculum, which offers both B.S. and B.A. tracks. Although certain requirements vary based on which track a student is on, all students complete the core curriculum, grouped under four areas of study, beginning with Foundations for Success, including the Falcon Discovery Seminar that is designed to help first-year students with their overall adjustment to college. Their seminar instructor also serves as their academic advisor for the first three semesters. Other required courses fall under Business Dynamics, to develop an understanding of how successful businesses operate, and Business Environment, which focuses on processes and systems. Context and Perspectives is the arts and sciences core covering categories such as Scientific Inquiry; Institutions and Power; and Value, Ethics, and Society.

Not surprisingly, Bentley's most popular majors are finance, marketing, economics-finance, management, and accountancy. Students seeking a B.S. degree have their pick of more than a dozen disciplines, including majors in professional sales, computer information systems, and data analytics, while those interested in B.A. degrees can select from such fields as English, international affairs, sustainability science, health studies, and film and media studies. New business majors include artificial intelligence for innovation, business law, public relations, and experience design. The finance and technology (FinTech) major offers opportunities for students in this highly innovative field. A recently added liberal arts major in psychology integrates business and science.

> **"Bentley prepares its students for the workplace."**

"Bentley is competitive in a sense because we are all career-driven and want to do well in similar fields, but there is also a great sense of camaraderie," says a sophomore. Twenty-two percent of classes have fewer than 20 students, but none have more than 50, and group work is routine. "A majority of Bentley professors and lecturers come from industry," says a corporate finance and accounting major. "This presents a very unique opportunity to get an early taste of on-the-job, real-world expectations." Students rave about Bentley's career services. "It really does take stress away when you have that extra helping hand sourcing interviews/opportunities, teaching you the basic skills, checking in, etc.," says a senior.

As befits the university's focus on the corporate world, most undergraduates complete at least one internship. Students speak highly of the study abroad program, in which nearly half participate. The Cronin Office of International Education offers semester, summer, or weeklong faculty-led programs in more than 25 countries; many programs include internship and service-learning opportunities. The top 10 percent of students in each entering class are invited to participate in the honors program, which tackles a variety of topics—from the ethics of genetic research to analyzing complex financial crises—all in a seminar setting that is designed to promote discussion and debate.

"Bentley students are a remarkable blend of drive, motivation, and sociability," says a marketing major. Although half again as large as rival Babson College, Bentley's undergraduate student body is less diverse. Still, a junior says, "The Claudette Blot Multicultural Center offers mentor/mentee programs, a preorientation program for first-year students of color, and student-led organizations for men and women of color." Forty percent of Bentley undergrads are from Massachusetts, and 14 percent are international. Black students account for 5 percent of the student body, Asian Americans 10 percent, Hispanics/Latinos 14 percent, and multiracial students 3 percent. Bentley has a conservative tenor, but for students, social and political issues generally take a back seat to classes and internships. Merit scholarships are available, and talented athletes vie for more than 200 athletic scholarships in 18 sports. Through the BentleyFirst program, Massachusetts residents who are the first in their families to go to college and whose family incomes are less than $135,000 per year can attend Bentley for the same tuition rate as the state's flagship public university, UMass Amherst.

The university's student residences include apartments, suites, and traditional dormitories and house 73 percent of the student body. Six percent of students participate in living/learning communities, in which service learning is a big emphasis. In fact, 24 percent of all students do volunteer work through the Bentley Service-Learning and Civic Engagement Center. The dining hall food is not a selling point, but a junior says, "Meals at Bentley have improved over time." Students report feeling safe on campus thanks to an active police patrol, 24/7 safety escorts, and "Title IX staff who are in constant contact with students and put on various events throughout the year," says a junior.

"A majority of Bentley professors and lecturers come from industry."

Students say the social scene begins on campus and spills out into the surrounding areas. "There is so much involvement in Bentley's 100-plus organizations," says one student. "A group is bound to have an event on any given day." Sponsored events include the annual Back to Bentley and Spring Day festivals and activities put on by various cultural groups, like Latin dance night. Practically the entire student body shows up for Super Bingo, "which is like normal bingo, but with awesome prizes like TVs and iPhones," explains a sophomore. The Greek system attracts 11 percent of the men and 19 percent of the women, and Greeks and sports teams host frequent off-campus parties, but neither group dominates the social scene. Students of legal age may have alcohol, but "peer pressure is not an issue" for those who prefer not to imbibe, according to an accounting major.

Waltham (population 66,000) may not have the cachet of nearby Boston, but students say it has the basic amenities every college student craves: restaurants, bars, shops, and salons. "Overall, Waltham does not play a huge role in a Bentley student's daily way of life," comments one student. Those seeking a bit more action take the campus shuttle to Harvard Square or the T (subway) to the city, where students can mix and mingle with peers from other local colleges and universities. Jaunts to the beaches of New Hampshire, the ski resorts of Vermont, and weekend trips to the Cape make for popular diversions as well.

"There is so much involvement in Bentley's 100-plus organizations."

Competition at Bentley is not confined to the classroom; the university also fields men's and women's varsity teams at the Division II level and a competitive Division I men's ice hockey team. The powerhouse women's basketball team has won the Northeast 10 Conference championship in each of the last four years. Other solid Falcon teams include men's basketball, women's field hockey, and football. Students get fired up anytime rivals Babson and Bryant take the field, and there is the predictable T-shirt reading, "Friends don't let friends go to Babson." Popular intramural and club sports include basketball, ice hockey, volleyball, and equestrian.

"Bentley is a school that will simulate the real world as much as possible so that its students graduate prepared!" cheers one enthusiastic junior. Like the university

Overlaps

Babson, Boston University, Bryant, UConn, Fairfield, UMass Amherst, Northeastern, Providence

itself, Bentley students have a keen sense of who they are and where they're headed. For those students charting a course into the upper echelons of corporate America, Bentley may be the first step to a long and fruitful career.

Boston College

140 Commonwealth Avenue, Chestnut Hill, MA 02467

One of the main reasons that Boston is the ultimate college town. Set on a quiet hilltop at the end of a T (subway) line, BC is a close second to Notre Dame in the pecking order among true-blue Roman Catholics (though many students clamoring for a spot are not aware of its religious ties). An estimated 70 percent of students identify as Roman Catholic, compared to 50 percent at Georgetown and 80 percent at Notre Dame.

Website: www.bc.edu

Location: Suburban

Private

Total Enrollment: 14,726

Undergraduates: 9,654

Male/Female: 47/53

Financial Aid: 67%

Pell Grant: 13%

Expense: Pr $

Student Loans: 38%

Average Debt: $

Applicants: 34,779

Accepted: 16%

Enrolled: 43%

Grad in 6 Years: 91%

Returning First-years: 96%

Academics: ✍ ✍ ✍ ✍

Social: 🗩 🗩 🗩 🗩

Q of L: ★ ★ ★

Admissions: (617) 552-3100

Email Address:
 admission@bc.edu

Strong Programs:
Biology
Business
Economics
Film Studies
Finance

Boston College, one of the largest Roman Catholic schools in the country, is a study in contrasts. The academics and the athletic teams are both well respected. The environment is safely suburban, yet barely 20 minutes from Boston, the hub of the Eastern Seaboard's college scene. The Jesuit influence on the college provides a guiding spirit for campus life, but the social opportunities still seem endless. Despite the paradoxes (or perhaps because of them), students at BC enjoy a rich college experience.

Don't let the modest name fool you. Boston College is actually a research university with nine schools and colleges. It has three campuses: the main campus at Chestnut Hill, the Brighton campus across the street, and the Newton campus a mile and a half away. The dominant architecture of the main campus (known as "the Heights") is Gothic Revival, with modern additions over the past several years. There's lots of grass and trees, not to mention a large, peaceful reservoir (perfect to jog around) right in the front yard. The university recently completed a multiyear master plan that doubled the size of the main campus with a new dorm, a field house, a recreation center, and other facilities.

Boston College was founded by the Society of Jesus (Jesuits) in 1863 to teach the offspring of Irish immigrants. Today, the school prompts students "to explore the big questions and challenges them to ask: What difference will I make? How will my knowledge serve the world?" To discover answers, the Core Curriculum requires courses not only in literature, natural science, history, philosophy, social science, and theology but also in writing, mathematics, the arts, and cultural diversity, in addition to specific requirements set by each undergraduate school. Students in arts and sciences must also show proficiency in a modern foreign language or classical language before graduation. First-years are required to take a writing workshop in which each student develops a portfolio of personal and academic writing and reads a wide range of texts. About a quarter of students participate in the Capstone Program.

The schools of arts and sciences, management, education and human development, and nursing award bachelor's degrees. Finance, economics, biology, and communication are the most popular majors. Programs in management, nursing, international studies, film studies, and theology are particularly well regarded. BC recently launched a new undergraduate major in human-centered engineering, the university's only engineering program at any level. Outside the traditional classroom at the McMullen Museum of Art, students find exhibitions, lectures, and gallery tours. The Music Guild sponsors professional concerts throughout the year, and music students emphasizing performance can take advantage of facilities equipped with Steinways and Yamahas. Theater majors find a home in the 600-seat Robsham Theater Arts Center, which produces eight student-directed productions each year.

BC students are serious about their work, but not excessively so, helping to create a collaborative atmosphere. "If you are better at science than your roommate, you will help her out," states one senior, "and perhaps when it comes time to fulfill your philosophy core requirement, her love of Plato will get you through the class." Forty-nine percent of classes have fewer than 20 students, and professors are praised for their passion and knowledge, as well as their accessibility. "I have certainly been challenged by my professors but also supported, since they consistently make themselves available outside of the classroom," says one history major. The Jesuits on BC's faculty (about 45 out of 923) exert an influence out of proportion to their numbers. "The philosophy, theology, and ethics departments are the most important in setting the tone of the campus, because they encourage the students to be open-minded," says a first-year.

"I have certainly been challenged by my professors but also supported."

Students searching for out-of-the-ordinary offerings will be happy at BC. The PULSE program provides participants with the opportunity to fulfill their philosophy and theology requirements while engaging in social-service fieldwork at any of about 35 Boston organizations. The program reinforces the Jesuit emphasis on community service and sometimes inspires students to major in those areas. Forty-three percent of Boston College undergraduates study internationally by the time they graduate. BC offers nearly 60 academic programs in more than 30 countries around the world, as well as three-week summer study abroad programs. Students participating in the Undergraduate Faculty Research Fellows Program spend an average of 100 hours per semester assisting faculty with serious research, for which they are paid an hourly wage.

BC's campus is replete with sporting events, movies, festivals, concerts, and plays.

Twenty-four percent of BC undergraduates come from Massachusetts and 7 percent from abroad. Catholics comprise about 70 percent of the student body. Black students constitute 5 percent, while Asian Americans make up 11 percent, Hispanics/Latinos 13 percent, and multiracial students 5 percent. "The student body is a socially conscious, environmentally responsible, academically oriented group on the whole," offers one student. "There is a pervasive spirit of compassion that runs through the student body here." Indeed, the Jesuit appeal for tolerance means that students can find support and interaction even when approaching hot-button issues that orthodox Catholicism frowns upon, such as homosexuality. Nearly 300 athletic awards are doled out annually; merit scholarships are worth an average of $26,400. Additionally, BC observes need-blind admissions and meets the full demonstrated need of accepted students.

"The dorms are comfortable and spacious."

Eighty percent of BC students live in campus housing. When students are admitted, they are notified whether they will get on-campus housing for three or four years; most juniors with three-year guarantees live off campus or study abroad, then return to campus for their final year. The city of Boston has a fairly reliable bus and subway system to bring distant residents to campus; the few students who drive to school are required to show that they need to park on campus. "The dorms are comfortable and spacious," says an international studies major. Students pay in advance for a certain number of dining hall meals, served à la carte. "The food is expensive," notes one student, "but it is great quality." The Bystander Intervention program is intended to combat the issue of campus sexual assault.

BC's campus is replete with sporting events, movies, festivals, concerts, and plays. As at other Jesuit institutions, there is no Greek system at BC, and "the social life is much more inclusive" as a result, according to a senior. Those of legal age can drink on campus but are only allowed to carry in enough beer or wine for personal consumption. Spiritual retreats occur throughout the year at BC's own retreat center on the Charles River, 30 minutes from campus, and one student says, "Volunteer work is huge." Bars and clubs in Boston ("the college town of all college towns," cheers a junior) are another big draw, along with Fenway Park. On weekends, especially in the winter, the mountains of Vermont and New Hampshire beckon outdoorsy types.

Division I athletic events, especially football games, become social events, too, with frequent tailgate and victory parties. The traditional Eagles football contest with the Fighting Irish of Notre Dame is jokingly referred to as the "Holy War" and makes for a popular road trip. BC meets fierce competition from Atlantic Coast Conference rivals Duke, Miami, Virginia Tech, and others. Boston University is the archrival when it comes to ice hockey, a sport in which BC is a powerhouse. The men's team reached the "Frozen Four" in 2024; six former team members from both the men's and women's teams participated in the 2026 Olympics. Men's and women's soccer, basketball, fencing, and golf and women's lacrosse have recently reached NCAA playoffs. Intramural sports are huge here. Nearly half of BC undergrads participate in 40 intramural and club sports, from basketball and volleyball to skiing and rugby. Students even get the day off from classes to line the edge of campus and cheer Boston Marathon runners up "Heartbreak Hill."

Since its founding as a Jesuit institution, Boston College has been committed to "educating students who will use their knowledge, talents, and abilities in the service of others." BC students spend four years fine-tuning the art of the delicate balance, discovering ways to make old-fashioned morals relevant to life in the 21st century, and finding time for fun while still tending to their academic performance.

Overlaps

**Boston University,
Georgetown,
Harvard, NYU,
Notre Dame, Tufts,
UVA**

If You Apply To ›

BC: Early decision I and II, regular decision. Accepts the Common Application with supplement. Apply to particular school or program. Please consult BC's website for the most up-to-date information regarding standardized test requirements.

Boston University

233 Bay State Road, Boston, MA 02215

One of the nation's largest private universities and namesake to a city that boasts many other four-year colleges. Location adjacent to Fenway Park is the promised land for hordes of students from all over the world seeking a funky, artsy, youth-oriented urban setting that is less in-your-face than New York City. More selective than in the past and comparable to NYU.

Boston University, founded originally by Vermont Methodists in 1839 before being officially chartered in Boston in 1869, is an integral part of the city it calls home. The school's ample collection of nondescript high-rises stretches along bustling, four-lane Commonwealth Avenue (which now has the city's first protected bike lane)—and so do thousands upon thousands of students. From aspiring actors, musicians, journalists, and filmmakers to future scientists, doctors, dentists, and entrepreneurs, BU seems to offer something for everyone. A junior says, "You definitely walk away from BU with a sense of accomplishment and individuality."

The BU campus is an urban campus with the tree-lined side streets featuring quaint Victorian brownstones. The Center for Computing & Data Sciences is a 100 percent fossil-fuel-free building. BU continues its commitment to diversity, equity, and inclusion through the Newbury Center, which supports and celebrates first-generation undergraduates in all areas of campus life, and the Thurman Center for Common Ground, the Center for Gender, Sexuality, and Activism, and the LGBTQIA+ Student Resource Center are spaces for students of all races, religions, orientations, and ethnicities to participate in intercultural dialogues.

BU's university-wide general education curriculum, the BU Hub, requires students to complete coursework focusing on diversity, civic engagement, global citizenship, digital communication, and innovation among other areas to help them thrive in the future. The BU Cross-College Challenge, the BU Hub's signature feature, gives juniors and seniors the chance to collaborate with a small team of classmates and faculty from across the university on an interdisciplinary project.

BU's 10 undergraduate schools and colleges offer more than 300 majors and minors; business administration, communications, economics, engineering, computer science, and psychology are the most popular. "All of the academic programs I've encountered have an accomplished faculty that brings real-world experiences into the classroom," says a political science major. Recently added majors include Holocaust, genocide, and human rights studies, Korean language and literature, and Turkish cultural studies. The College of Communication combines theory with hands-on training—some of it by adjunct professors with day jobs at major newspapers and TV networks. It also houses the nation's first center for the study of political disinformation. The well-regarded School of Theatre benefits from the 250-seat, flexibly designed Booth Theatre. The College of Arts and Sciences offers more than 80 majors and special advising for premed and prelaw students. Many students in the Sargent College of Health and Rehabilitation Sciences go on to earn graduate degrees from the college's highly ranked physical and occupational therapy programs.

The Questrom School of Business, one of BU's top programs, offers an honors program for sophomores and concentrations in such areas as law, innovation and entrepreneurship, and business analytics. BU's Innovate@BU initiative connects students with resources to help them turn entrepreneurial ideas into action. Future employers of students in the School of Hospitality Administration offer internships in exotic locales such as Sydney and Shanghai. The College of Engineering, known for its biomedical engineering program, boasts a high-tech robotics lab. Students in the School of Visual Arts may show their work in one of three campus galleries. The cross-disciplinary Faculty of Computing & Data Sciences offers a B.S. degree in data science. Fifty-nine percent of classes have fewer than 20 students, and students say the academic climate encourages both cooperation and competition. "While I am consistently challenged, I do not feel overwhelmed by the workload," says one senior.

Students laud the First-Year Student Outreach Project, which brings new students to campus a week early to do community service. For a break from brutal Boston winters, BU offers more than 180 study abroad programs, including internships, field work, research, language study, and liberal arts programs, in 20 countries; 35 percent

> **"[The] accomplished faculty . . . brings real-world experiences into the classroom."**

Website: www.bu.edu
Location: City Outskirts
Private
Total Enrollment: 28,929
Undergraduates: 18,041
Male/Female: 41/57
Financial Aid: 56%
Pell Grant: 23%
Expense: Pr $ $ $ $
Student Loans: 34%
Average Debt: $ $ $ $
Applicants: 78,769
Accepted: 11%
Enrolled: 37%
Grad in 6 Years: 89%
Returning First-years: 95%
Academics: ✍ ✍ ✍ ✍
Social: 🎉 🎉 🎉 🎉
Q of L: ★ ★ ★
Admissions: (617) 353-2300
Email Address:
  admissions@bu.edu

Strong Programs:
Biomedical Engineering
Business Administration
Communication
Computer Science
Economics
Hospitality Administration
International Relations
Theatre

The First-Year Student Outreach Project brings new students to campus a week early to do community service.

of students typically participate. The Kilachand Honors College is a four-year undergraduate living/learning community that offers students the small classes, close interaction with faculty, and communal atmosphere of a small liberal arts college along with the resources of a major urban research university.

According to a biology major, BU students are "really cool nerds: smart, but also fun." Sixty-two percent of BU undergrads are from out of state, and another 21 percent come from abroad. Asian Americans make up 21 percent of the population, Hispanics/Latinos 11 percent, Black students 6 percent, and multiracial students 5 percent. Students report that low socioeconomic diversity is one of the biggest social issues on campus. "It is a diverse student body in all aspects. People come from all different walks of life, states, and countries," comments a political science major. BU has introduced several initiatives to address affordability: The university now guarantees to meet 100 percent of domestic students' demonstrated financial need and promises that if tuition increases, need-based scholarships will also increase by the same percentage. Loans are not included in financial aid packages for incoming first-years who are eligible for Pell Grants. In addition to need-based aid, BU offers merit scholarships averaging $31,700 each year as well as over 300 athletic scholarships in 18 sports.

> **"People come from all different walks of life, states, and countries."**

BU's Innovate@BU initiative connects students with resources to help them turn entrepreneurial ideas into action.

Typically, 66 percent of BU students live in campus housing, which is guaranteed for four years and selected via a lottery system. "Freshman/sophomore dorms are fairly typical, but housing gets better as you get to be a senior," explains a psychology major, and some of the newest facilities are like "luxury apartments." Meal plans are flexible, and one of the six dining halls on campus is kosher. There's also a farmers market and a food court with national chains like Starbucks and Panda Express. "For being in an urban area, I feel extremely safe on campus," reports one senior. The Sexual Assault Response and Prevention Center provides prevention-based programming and support and advocacy for survivors.

"The social scene at BU has a lot to offer," a student says. "We always have on-campus events every day of the week, including the weekends. If we don't feel like staying on campus, we can just hop on our Boston trains and be anywhere in the city within minutes." With less than 1 percent of the men and just 11 percent of the women joining fraternities and sororities, Greek life has little influence on the social scene. Parties happen off campus, including at neighboring schools, and policies regarding underage drinking on BU's campus are reportedly strict. Owing to Boston's pervasive Irish heritage, St. Patrick's Day is an occasion for revelry. The Splash student activity fair and homecoming in the fall are favorite annual events, along with comedy nights that bring big-name comedians like Colin Jost, Vanessa Bayer, and Hasan Minhaj to campus once a semester. Lobster Night, where the dining halls serve up whole lobsters, is always a big hit. Road trip options include Cape Cod, Cape Ann, and Providence, Rhode Island. Even better, "Fenway Park, downtown, Lansdowne Street, and Boston Common are all within walking distance," says a marine biology major.

> **"We always have on-campus events every day of the week, including the weekends."**

BU doesn't field a football team, so hockey season is the athletic high point of the school year. Most Terrier teams compete in the Division I Patriot League, and among the solid teams are men's and women's soccer, men's basketball, lacrosse, and rowing, and women's softball, field hockey, and rowing. BU has won numerous titles in the annual Beanpot men's ice hockey tournament, which pits BU against Harvard, Northeastern, and archrival Boston College. The Head of the Charles regatta, which starts at BU's crew house each fall, draws college crew teams from across the country. Of the dozen or so intramural sports offered, by far the most popular is broomball, which is like ice hockey on sneakers, with a ball instead of a puck and a broom instead of a stick; students may also compete in 37 club sports.

Boston University shamelessly urges students to just "Be You" (ahem), and most are happy to do so, but they warn that being successful here requires a certain degree of initiative. The eponymous university of the ultimate college town is "a great place, with lots of academic and social opportunities, but it's not for the timid student," remarks a geophysics and planetary sciences major. "You have to be pro-active about finding out what's going on around campus so that you can find your niche."

If You Apply To ›

BU: Early decision I and II, regular decision. Accepts the Common Application with supplement. Apply to particular school or college. Applicants to fine arts programs must submit a portfolio or audition. Please consult BU's website for the most up-to-date information regarding standardized test requirements.

Bowdoin College

255 Main Street, Brunswick, ME 04011

Rates with Amherst, Williams, and Wesleyan for liberal arts excellence and pioneered in not requiring the SAT. Bowdoin's science programs are especially strong, including its unique interdisciplinary offerings in environmental studies. Outdoor enthusiasts benefit from proximity to the coast of Maine. Not as large as some of its peers, with less overt competition among students.

Named after former Massachusetts Governor James Bowdoin II, a hero of the American Revolution who had a hand in stopping Shays' Rebellion, Bowdoin College has sought since 1794 to make nature, art, and friendship as integral to the student experience as the world of books. This is, after all, the alma mater of the great American authors Longfellow and Hawthorne. In fact, when new students matriculate, they sign their names in a book on Hawthorne's very desk. Bowdoin's "belief that the developments of our minds and imaginations should benefit society is a cherished value that connects the community across generations," say administrators. Though the New England winter can be frigid, students are quick to point out that good food and friendships help make the campus a warm and welcoming place.

Bowdoin's 215-acre campus sits in Brunswick, a coastal town in Midcoast Maine. Hidden amid the pine groves and athletic fields are 120 buildings in styles from German Romanesque, colonial, medieval, and neoclassical to neo-Georgian, modern, and postmodern. The historic Harriet Beecher Stowe House, in which the famed author wrote Uncle Tom's Cabin, has been carefully renovated and now houses faculty offices. Other buildings have been updated and newer construction includes Barry Mills Hall, which houses the digital and computational studies program, and the Gibbons Center for Arctic Studies.

To graduate, Bowdoin students must complete courses in five distribution areas that emphasize issues vital to a liberal education in the 21st century: mathematical, computational, or statistical reasoning; inquiry in the natural sciences; difference,

Website: www.bowdoin.edu
Location: Small Town
Private
Total Enrollment: 1,872
Undergraduates: 1,872
Male/Female: 48/52
Financial Aid: 58%
Pell Grant: 20%
Expense: Pr $ $ $ $
Student Loans: 18%
Average Debt: $
Applicants: 13,265
Accepted: 7%
Enrolled: 54%
Grad in 6 Years: 95%
Returning First-years: 97%
Academics: ✐ ✐ ✐ ✐ ✐
Social: 🌑 🌑 🌑
Q of L: ★ ★ ★
Admissions: (207) 725-3100
Email Address: admissions@bowdoin.edu

power, and inequity; international perspectives; and visual and performing arts. First-years have their choice of small seminars, which emphasize reading and writing; recent topics have included Exercises in Political Theory, Writing and Generative AI, The Art of Sportswriting, Modernity at Sea, and America in the World. One senior says the seminars "give you a good sense of what you really need to work on to succeed at Bowdoin." All incoming first-years receive a MacBook Pro, an iPad, an Apple Pencil, and access to a range of course-specific software.

Academic strengths include the sciences, particularly environmental studies, earth and oceanographic science, neuroscience, and computer science. Thanks to a $50 million grant from alumnus and Netflix founder Reed Hastings, Bowdoin launched a new Initiative for AI and Humanity in 2025 to help students grapple with issues related to emerging technologies. Bowdoin also offers a rare concentration in Arctic studies (its mascot is the polar bear). Students can participate in Arctic archaeological research in Labrador, Canada, or ecological research at the Bowdoin Scientific Station on Kent Island in the Bay of Fundy. The Schiller Coastal Studies Center, located just 15 minutes away on a 118-acre plot on Orr's Island, provides additional opportunities for multidisciplinary, field- and lab-based research on critical coastal and climate issues. Digital computational studies and English are also well regarded, and students say the popularity of government and legal studies, biology, and mathematics is well deserved. Dual-degree programs in engineering are available through Caltech, Columbia, Dartmouth, and the University of Maine.

> "My professors are intelligent, fun, passionate, and open-minded."

"Students take their schoolwork seriously, and the work is difficult," says a government and economics double major, while a math major adds, "professors have many office hours set aside to help students." Sixty-five percent of classes have fewer than 20 students. Professors teach all Bowdoin classes—there are no graduate students here and thus no teaching assistants—and their skills in the classroom are highly praised. "My professors are intelligent, fun, passionate, and open-minded," says a first-year.

Before school begins, the entire entering class takes preorientation hiking, canoeing, kayaking, or community service trips that teach them about the people and landscape of Maine. Service learning, coordinated by the McKeen Center for the Common Good, is increasingly an emphasis at Bowdoin; 58 percent of students volunteer with local community groups. "Undergraduate research opportunities abound," says a sophomore English major. And it's common for juniors and seniors to conduct independent studies with faculty members, then publish their results in professional journals. Sixteen percent of seniors complete yearlong honors projects. Nearly half the students study abroad through more than 100 programs offered in more than 50 countries.

Sporting events against Colby are exciting, and the annual hockey matchup draws crowds of alumni and locals alike.

Just 10 percent of students hail from Maine, and 8 percent are international. Black students make up 5 percent of the student body, Hispanics/Latinos 15 percent, Asian Americans 11 percent, and multiracial students 9 percent. On this liberal campus, "Many students are outdoorsy, athletic, a little preppy—but everyone has an interest and a passion that might surprise you," a mathematics major says,

> "Many students are outdoorsy, athletic, [and] a little preppy."

"and most people have friends from all different social groups on campus." In 1970, Bowdoin became the first leading college to make SAT scores an optional part of the admissions process, shifting the emphasis to a student's whole body of work. Additionally, Bowdoin employs a need-blind admissions policy, meets the full demonstrated financial need of all admitted students, and has eliminated loans from its financial aid packages, replacing them with scholarships.

Ninety-four percent of Bowdoin students live in college-owned housing, where first-years start off in quads, with two double bedrooms and a shared common room, in renovated historic residence halls. After that, students may apply to live in "College Houses," many of which used to be fraternity houses before Bowdoin phased out Greek groups nearly 30 years ago. Students give rave reviews to dining services, especially the lobster bake that kicks off each school year and the offerings for vegans and vegetarians. "Bowdoin's food is restaurant quality, and the menu is different every day," cheers a senior. Several student groups are active in raising awareness around issues of sexual violence, and a government major praises the "Safe Ride" system that provides campus-run on-call vans for a lift home (within a one-mile radius of campus).

"Bowdoin is a work hard–play hard kind of place," says a junior, and social life mostly centers around two groups: sports teams and College Houses. "We have a system of eight College Houses that host all types of events—academic, cultural, and parties—that are open to all students at the college," explains a junior. "This sense of inclusivity ensures that people do not feel the pressure to drink." Hard liquor is prohibited. Students look forward to homecoming in the fall and Ivies, a weekend blast of fun before spring finals, including a concert that brings major performers to campus.

One student says Brunswick (population 22,000) is "a great, quiet college town." America Reads and Counts Tutoring Program and various mentoring offerings help build bridges between students and local residents. A car comes in handy for the 15-minute drive to the shopping outlets of Freeport (including L.L.Bean's flagship 24/7 factory store) or the 30-minute trip to Portland for a "real" night out. Students can also opt to take a school shuttle, the inexpensive Metro Breez bus, or the nearby Amtrak train to these destinations or to Boston, a little more than two hours away. Ski bums will find several resorts within easy reach.

"We have a system of eight College Houses that host all types of events."

While the long winters can be grueling, they do bring out school spirit, especially when Bowdoin's hockey teams take the ice. The Polar Bears compete in the Division III New England Small College Athletic Conference. Sporting events against Colby are exciting, and the annual hockey matchup draws crowds of alumni and locals alike. Sports teams that have excelled recently include women's basketball, volleyball, field hockey, and rugby, men's and women's lacrosse, and tennis. Adds one senior, "Bowdoin Football is notoriously bad, but we love them anyway." Also popular are club sports, intramurals, and recreational activities, including those organized by the student-run Bowdoin Outing Club, whose weekend jaunts range from rock climbing, skiing, and white-water rafting to fireside knitting and sledding.

Students who love the outdoors, even when it's cold, will find warm and inviting academics at Bowdoin, where close friendships with peers and professors are easily forged. "Everyone at Bowdoin agrees that it is a special place," says a senior sociology major. "The way it fosters our lifelong relationships with the school and with each other is what makes it unique."

Overlaps

Amherst, Brown, Dartmouth, Middlebury, Swarthmore, Wesleyan, Williams, Yale

If You Apply To ›

Bowdoin: Early decision I and II, regular decision. SATs or ACTs: optional. Accepts the Common Application with supplement. Bowdoin offers applicants the option to record a short video response to supplement their application materials.

415 South Street, Waltham, MA 02453

Founded in 1948 by members of the American Jewish community who sought to expand access to higher education, Brandeis is an elite institution seeking top students of all faiths and backgrounds. Academic specialties range from the natural sciences to music and Near Eastern and Judaic studies. Has one of the top programs in neuroscience at a midsized research university. Competes with Tufts in the Boston area.

Website: www.brandeis.edu
Location: Suburban
Private
Total Enrollment: 4,746
Undergraduates: 3,611
Male/Female: 43/57
Financial Aid: 68%
Pell Grant: 29%
Expense: Pr $ $ $ $
Student Loans: 38%
Average Debt: $ $
Applicants: 10,462
Accepted: 41%
Enrolled: 17%
Grad in 6 Years: 86%
Returning First-years: 87%
Academics: ✍ ✍ ✍ ✍
Social: 🌑 🌑 🌑
Q of L: ★ ★ ★
Admissions: (781) 736-3500
Email Address:
  admissions@brandeis.edu

Strong Programs:
Biochemistry
Chemistry
Eastern and Judaic Studies
Islamic and Middle Eastern
  Studies
Music
Neuroscience
Physics
Psychology
Theater

Brandeis was founded in 1948 as a nonsectarian Jewish university three years after the end of the Holocaust, at a time when many elite universities restricted access to Jewish faculty and students. The only nonsectarian Jewish-sponsored college in the nation, it was named for Louis Brandeis, the first Jewish justice on the U.S. Supreme Court and a fierce defender of free speech who famously asserted that the remedy for harmful speech is "more speech, not enforced silence." Brandeis has always had a reputation for intense progressive thought, and it is being recognized as a rising star among research institutions, hosting more than 30 on-campus research centers and expanding its experimental- and service-learning offerings. Still, recent economic stressors and declining enrollment in comparison with other elite universities have resulted in administrative layoffs. Nevertheless, the university appears to be maintaining its Jewish identity while also attracting a well-rounded, eclectic group of students from all backgrounds.

Set on a residential hilltop nine miles west of Boston, Brandeis's attractively landscaped 235-acre campus boasts an abundance of distinctive buildings. The music building, for example, is shaped like a grand piano; the theater looks like a top hat. The 24-hour Shapiro Campus Center includes a student theater, offices for student clubs, and bookstore. The Shapiro Academic Complex houses the International Center for Ethics, Justice, and Public Life as well as the Mandel Center for Studies in Jewish Education. A new state-of-the-art residence hall is slated for completion in 2027.

Undergraduates enter the School of Arts and Sciences, which offers more than 40 majors and 50 minors through its departments and interdepartmental programs. About half of the students graduate with double majors. The Brandeis core curriculum is rooted in a commitment to developing strong communication, digital literacy, foreign language, and quantitative-reasoning skills and an interdisciplinary and cross-cultural perspective. First-year students must take a writing seminar and attend at least one of several Critical Conversation events held throughout the year, in which professors from different disciplines discuss major issues in a moderated setting in an effort to "model civil discourse." Other Brandeis Core requirements include credits in health and wellness; life skills; diversity, equity, and inclusion in the U.S.; and difference and justice in the world.

Neuroscience, biochemistry, chemistry, and physics are top-notch programs; social sciences, biology, business, and psychology enroll the most students. The university caters to premed students with special advisors and access to internships and research opportunities. With the largest faculty in the field outside of Israel, Brandeis is virtually unrivaled in Near Eastern and Judaic studies; Hebrew is a specialty. The program in Islamic and Middle Eastern studies is strong too. A growing number of interdisciplinary programs are becoming increasingly popular, particularly the international and global studies major and the health: science, society, and policy major.

Brandeis also maintains a commitment to the creative arts, with strong theater offerings and a theory-based music program founded by Leonard Bernstein.

"Brandeis takes its academic integrity seriously," says a creative writing and English major, and the climate can be intense. Fifty-nine percent of classes at Brandeis have fewer than 20 students, and a junior says, "Professors are very accommodating and are good lecturers and discussion leaders." All incoming first-years are assigned a student advisor, an academic advisor, and a faculty advisor. "Peer advisors are super cool because they have lived through the Brandeis experience and are truly a wealth of information," explains an American studies major. The Kraft Transitional Year Program is a one-year academic program for promising students from educationally underserved populations that guarantees small classes, rigorous academics, and strong academic support.

> "Professors are very accommodating and are good lecturers and discussion leaders."

Rising sophomores and juniors have the opportunity to earn credit through study abroad related to their majors. Forty percent of undergrads take advantage of more than 200 off-campus programs offered in more than 50 countries, including two university-run programs: an economics program in Copenhagen and a studio art and art history program in Siena, Italy. Undergraduates have numerous opportunities to conduct original research with faculty, and some even publish their work in academic journals. The Justice Brandeis Semester allows groups of 10 to 15 students to earn credits while focusing on topics of personal interest, such as bio-inspired design, ethnographic fieldwork, or mobile app and game development. The linked courses feature fieldwork, internships, or research under faculty supervision.

An extensive intramural and club sports program draws over 40 percent of students.

"Brandeisians are friendly!" cheers a sophomore. "Everyone here is very warm and always willing to meet new people." Thirty-three percent of Brandeis undergraduates are from Massachusetts, and the population is otherwise heavily bicoastal, with sizable numbers of New York, New Jersey, and California residents. Nineteen percent hail from foreign nations. Three chapels on campus—Roman Catholic, Jewish, and Protestant—are situated so that the shadow of one never crosses the shadow of another. It's an architectural symbol that students say reflects the realities of their diverse campus community. One-third of undergraduates are Jewish, and the more than 200 Muslim students have their own dedicated prayer space, as do followers of Dharmic religions. Black students make up 6 percent of the student body, Hispanics/Latinos 9 percent, Asian Americans 18 percent, and multiracial students 4 percent. Social justice is a big emphasis on this liberal campus. "Students care a lot about women's rights, LGBTQ+ rights, intersectionality, race relations, and a number of other issues," explains a theater arts major. Brandeis now meets the full demonstrated financial need of all undergraduates and covers full cost of tuition for students whose families earn less than $75,000. It also offers merit scholarships averaging $15,000 to qualified students, although there are no athletic awards.

> "Students care a lot about women's rights, LGBTQ+ rights, intersectionality, race relations, and . . . other issues."

Housing options include traditional quadrangle dormitories, where first-years and sophomores live in singles, doubles, or triples. Juniors and seniors can opt for singles, suites, or apartment-style housing. "Housing on campus improves as you get older," one student observes. First-years and sophomores are guaranteed housing, while upperclassmen play the lottery each spring. Seventy-two percent of students live on campus, and the rest find affordable off-campus housing nearby. Campus dining gets average reviews. The food court in the Usdan Student Center provides decent

First-year students must take a writing seminar and attend at least one of several Critical Conversation events.

alternatives, and there are always kosher, vegan, gluten-free, and allergen-safe options. The university opened a prevention, advocacy, and resource center on campus aimed at addressing sexual harassment and violence.

"The social life is lively, with on-campus productions, events, and activities predominantly occupying students' free time," says an anthropology major. Brandeis hosts more than 200 student clubs; some of the largest include the Waltham Group (a community service organization), the Campus Activities Board, and Triskelion (an LGBTQ+ social group). Weekends often feature live entertainment at The Stein, the on-campus pub, or Cholmondeley's Coffee House (a.k.a. Chum's) and small dorm parties. Annual events include 'DEIS Impact, a weeklong social justice festival; the Springfest outdoor concert; and the 24-Hour Musical, in which students learn and produce an entire musical in just 24 hours ("It's a total disaster, but it's hysterical," says a sophomore). Also well attended are the homecoming soccer match and carnival and the Leonard Bernstein Festival of the Creative Arts.

The possibilities for off-campus diversion are nearly infinite, thanks to the proximity of Boston and Cambridge, which are accessible by the free Brandeis shuttle bus or a nearby commuter train. (A car is more trouble than it's worth.) Brandeis's host town, Waltham, has a diverse selection of restaurants and a cheap movie theater but otherwise receives lukewarm reviews from students. One global studies major asks, "Who needs Waltham for excitement when Boston is a short shuttle ride away?"

Though the school does not field a football team, the Judges (remember Louis?) athletic program gets a boost from its membership in the Division III University Athletic Association, a neo–Ivy League for high-powered academic institutions such as the University of Chicago, Emory, and NYU. The men's and women's tennis teams make regular NCAA tournament appearances, and men's and women's track and field and fencing are also strong. An extensive intramural and club sports program draws over 40 percent of students, and contests run nearly every day of the year.

> **"The social life is lively, with on-campus productions, events, and activities."**

Few private universities have come as far as Brandeis so quickly, evolving from the bare 235-acre site of a failed veterinary/medical school to a modern research university of more than 100 buildings, a $1.2 billion endowment, and ever-growing academic opportunities. From the outset, Brandeis has been a mirror of its often-turbulent times. Its identity was forged in the wake of World War II and the Holocaust, and it came of age during the civil rights and other social movements of the late 20th and early 21st centuries. As an avowedly nonsectarian community that intentionally embraces both Jewish and Muslim students, it has been buffeted by the same campus turmoil that has affected other elite schools in the wake of the Israel-Hamas war and other recent events in the Middle East. One student described Brandeis as "a haven for students who are seeking academic challenge and an environment where social justice is revered." Given its history, Brandeis can be expected to continue looking for new ways to balance its historic commitments to its Jewish identity with traditional and nonsectarian liberal arts courses, social justice mission, diversity, and open inquiry.

Overlaps

Boston University, Brown, Case Western, Cornell, UMass Amherst, NYU, Northeastern, Tufts, WashU in St. Louis

If You Apply To ›

Brandeis: Early decision I and II, early action, regular decision. SATs or ACTs: optional. Accepts the Common Application with supplement.

Brigham Young University

Provo, UT 84602

From the time they are knee high, members of the Church of Jesus Christ of Latter-day Saints (a.k.a. Mormons) all around the world dream about coming to BYU. Most men and some women do a two-year stint as a missionary. Strongest academic programs are all preprofessional. The atmosphere is generally mild-mannered and conservative, but BYU goes bonkers for its sports teams.

Brigham Young succeeded the martyred prophet Joseph Smith in 1844 as head of the much-persecuted Church of Jesus Christ of Latter-day Saints and subsequently led his fellow Mormon pioneers on their treacherous trek from Illinois to the "Promised Land" of Utah. Three decades later, in 1875, church fathers established an eponymous institution to fulfill Young's vision of "a good education unmixed with the pernicious atheistic influences that are found in so many of the higher schools of the country." It is a vision that lives on at Brigham Young University, where a sense of spirituality pervades most everything, where faith and academia are intertwined, and where life is governed by a demanding code of ethics that has even led to the disciplining of star athletes in midseason.

The church's values of prosperity, chastity, and obedience are strongly evident on BYU's 557-acre campus, where the utilitarian buildings, like everything else, are "clean, modern, and orderly." The campus lies on the western edge of the Rocky Mountains, 4,600 feet above sea level, between the shores of Utah Lake and Mount Timpanogos, offering breathtaking sunsets and easy access to magnificent skiing, camping, and hiking areas. Days begin early; church bells rouse students at 8 a.m. with the first four bars of the hymn "Come, Come Ye Saints." (The same bells also peal every hour throughout the day.)

The strict Honor Code covers everything from dating practices to academic honesty; no-no's include men wearing beards; the consuming of drugs, alcohol, and caffeinated tea and coffee (although caffeine in soda is allowed); and entering the bedroom of a member of the opposite sex. While students elsewhere might find the code burdensome, at BYU, it is a point of pride. Indeed, the school's commitment to church values is the reason most students choose it. "The students who attend BYU are unique," says a communications major. "Everyone is clean-cut, shaven, modestly dressed, and proper in their etiquette."

> **"[Provo is] a good college town for people who don't like bustling metropolises."**

The church's influence continues when students set their schedules; students must take five doctrinal foundations courses, and subjects include, of course, the Book of Mormon. In addition to an extensive liberal arts core, BYU requires students to demonstrate proficiency in math, writing (first-year and advanced), American heritage, global and cultural awareness, and advanced languages, a catch-all category that can be satisfied with coursework in a foreign language or in statistics, advanced math, or advanced music.

BYU's academic offerings run the gamut, from liberal arts and sciences to solid preprofessional programs in engineering, nursing, business, and law. Students say the strongest offerings include education, exercise science, the Clark Law School, and most departments in the Marriott School of Business, especially accounting. There are also degrees in public health promotion and ancient Near Eastern studies. Brigham Young boasts campuses in Idaho and Hawaii, a center in Jerusalem,

---

Website: www.byu.edu
Location: Small City
Private
Total Enrollment: 31,995
Undergraduates: 30,147
Male/Female: 48/52
Financial Aid: 66%
Pell Grant: 13%
Expense: Pr $
Student Loans: 18%
Average Debt: $
Applicants: 11,698
Accepted: 68%
Enrolled: 78%
Grad in 6 Years: 81%
Returning First-years: 91%
Academics: ✍ ✍ ✍
Social: 🗨 🗨 🗨
Q of L: ★ ★ ★ ★
Admissions: (801) 422-4104
Email Address:
 admissions@byu.edu

Strong Programs:
Accounting
Business
Education
Engineering
Exercise Science
Nursing
Prelaw
Public Health Promotion

and a large study abroad program—nearly 200 programs in more than 50 countries. More than half of the students interrupt their studies—typically after the first year— to serve two years as a missionary.

Students agree that the academic climate is demanding. "It is competitive," a senior reports, and "some courses are known for being extremely difficult to pass, such as American Heritage or Econ 110." First-year students are often taught by full-time professors, who generally get good marks. "Most professors have a passion for their subject and for teaching," says a student. General education courses can be quite large, although 45 percent of all undergraduate classes enroll fewer than 20 students, and registration can be a chore. The honors program, open to highly motivated students, offers small seminars with more faculty interaction and is "an excellent way to get more out of your college experience," one participant says. The strength of the faculty is one reason BYU has more full-time students than any other church-sponsored university in the United States, almost all of them undergraduates.

Not surprisingly, the typical BYU student is socially conservative. "The students are very academically and spiritually minded," confides a junior, who further describes students as "intelligent, friendly, and honest." Twenty-one percent of BYU undergraduates are from Utah. Many others hail from California and Idaho, and 3 percent come from more than 100 other countries. Hispanic/Latino students contribute 8 percent to the student body, Asian Americans 2 percent, Black students less than 1 percent, and multiracial students 4 percent. Tuition for church members is lower than for non-members, because Latter-day Saint families contribute to BYU through their tithes. Academic scholarships averaging $4,600 are available, as are hundreds of athletic scholarships in 21 sports.

"The students are very academically and spiritually minded."

Just 18 percent of BYU undergrads—primarily first-years—live in the single-sex residence halls. "The dorms are small but comfortable and very clean," says a student. Upperclassmen typically opt for cheaper off-campus apartments, which are also single-sex (remember the Honor Code?). When it comes to food, the student dining outlets on campus are described as adequate. "The school provides decent, affordable on-campus meal plans," says a senior.

Whether it's work with the unhoused or others in need, dances, firesides, concerts, plays, sporting events, or special activities within the campus religious wards (small groups of about 100 students), most of BYU's social life is organized through or linked to the church. Community service is big, with students visiting patients at hospitals and care centers, performing at local festivals, and building and refurbishing houses. Social life is carried out within the church's bounds of propriety and is given a lighthearted feeling with groups that encourage "creative dating and lots of dating, period," says a senior. There are no fraternities or sororities to provide housing or parties, which is just fine with most students, since alcoholic drinks are banned. Road trips include Vegas or southern Utah, and with the mountains being so close, you'll find plenty of skiing and camping. Provo itself has plenty of places to eat and shop. "Provo wouldn't really exist without BYU," says a student, and "it's a good college town for people who don't like bustling metropolises."

Physical fitness is big here, and the intramural facilities are some of the country's best, with indoor and outdoor jogging tracks; courts for tennis, racquetball, and handball; and a pool. Also important are Division I varsity sports. The church philosophy of discipline and obedience has worked wonders for Cougar teams, which plays in the Big 12 Conference. Men's basketball reached the Sweet Sixteen in 2024, and the football rivalry against the University of Utah provides some serious end-of-season intensity—ESPN has dubbed the BYU–Utah rivalry the "Holy War." One of the most popular courses offered at BYU is ballroom dancing, partly because many participants aspire to join BYU's award-winning dance team.

To most Americans, BYU probably seems old-fashioned or like a step back in time. But for young members of the Church of Jesus Christ of Latter-day Saints, that may be just what the elder ordered. "BYU's dedicated faculty, devout atmosphere, and beautiful, clean campus set it apart from all other universities," a satisfied senior says.

If You Apply To ›

BYU: Regular decision. Does not accept the Common Application. Ecclesiastical endorsement required. Please consult BYU's website for the most up-to-date information regarding standardized test requirements.

University of British Columbia: See page 355.

Brown University

75 Waterman Street, Providence, RI 02912

To today's stressed-out students, the fantasy of taking every course pass/fail seems like a dream come true. Nobody at Brown actually does this, but the pass/fail option, combined with the school's notable lack of distribution requirements, gives it the freewheeling image that students love. In reality, doing well at Brown is just as tough as at other Ivies. Scorned by conservatives as a hotbed of political correctness.

Brown University is a perennial "hot college," with an overwhelming number of happy students and many more clamoring to join their ranks. Once here, students receive not only a prestigious and quality education, but also a chance to explore their creative sides at a liberal arts and sciences college that does not idolize grades or preprofessionalism and shuns GPAs, required courses, and competitive attitudes among its undergraduates. Brown's environment and policies have drawn both praise and criticism over the years, but its students thrive on this discussion and lively debate. "Brown's open curriculum, though not for everyone, is incredibly liberating," says one student.

Founded in 1764 as the College in the English Colony of Rhode Island and Providence Plantations, Brown was renamed in 1804 after Nicholas Brown Jr., a major benefactor whose father—one of the school's founders—was a businessman with controversial ties to the slave trade. The school has established a memorial to slaves at Brown and a Center for the Study of Slavery and Justice. The university sits atop College Hill on the east side of Providence, and its 140-acre campus affords an excellent view of downtown Providence. Campus architecture is a composite of old and new—plenty of grassy lawns surrounded by historic buildings that offer students refuge from the city streets beyond. The neighborhoods that surround the campus lie within a national historic district and boast beautiful tree-lined streets full of ethnic charm.

Brown's faculty has successfully resisted the notion that somewhere in their collective wisdom and experience lies a core of knowledge that every educated person should possess. As a result, aside from completing courses in a major and a minimum of 30 courses total, the only university-wide requirement for graduation is "the ability to write well." All students must demonstrate that they have worked at least twice on developing their writing (once during their first two years and again as upperclassmen) by taking approved English or writing-across-the-curriculum classes or by documenting their writing work in any other Brown course. Students can take their classes one of two ways: for traditional marks of A, B, C, or No Credit; or for Satisfactory/No Credit. The NC is not recorded on the transcript, while the letter grade or Satisfactory can be supplemented by a written evaluation from the professor. A habit of NCs, however, lands students in academic hot water.

The most popular majors (or concentrations, as they are called here) are in the social sciences, computer science, economics, math, and biology. Neuroscience, computational biology, applied mathematics, classics, and environmental studies are some of the university's best concentrations, and students also praise political science, engineering, religious studies, and history—although one says, "As far as I know, all our academic departments are super strong (like oxen or Heracles)." Other top-notch programs include comparative literature, modern languages, and the writing program in the English department. Future doctors can try for a competitive eight-year liberal medical education program where students can earn an M.D. without having to sacrifice their humanity. Fields related to scientific technology have very good facilities, including an instructional technology center, while minority issues are the focus of the Center for the Study of Race and Ethnicity in America.

Those with interests in interdisciplinary fields will enjoy Brown's wide range of concentrations that cross departmental lines and cover everything from cognitive science to public policy to a program in business, entrepreneurship, and organizations. Students can create their own concentration from the array of goodies offered. Brown also offers group independent study projects, a popular alternative for students with the gumption to take a course they have to construct primarily by themselves, and a five-year dual-degree program with the Rhode Island School of Design (RISD), also located on College Hill. Students can cross-register for individual courses at RISD as well. "Brown provides amazing financial support for research opportunities through our UTRAs (Undergraduate Teaching and Research Awards)," says a junior. Adventurous students can choose to spend time in study abroad programs in 75 countries. Roughly 30 percent of undergrads study abroad, and others go overseas to complete independent research or internships during the summer. Brown leads U.S. research universities in the number of graduates who win Fulbrights.

> **"Brown's open curriculum, though not for everyone, is incredibly liberating."**

"Although the coursework is definitely rigorous, students are mostly only in classes that they really want to be in, and therefore it leads to an enjoyable, relaxed climate," explains a computer science major. Brown prides itself on undergraduate teaching and considers skill in the classroom as much as the usual scholarly credentials when making tenure decisions. An applied math and biology double major says, "Professors come to Brown interested in engaging with undergrads and being part of our experience, so they're really accessible." The advising system reflects the administration's commitment to treating students as adults. It pairs each first-year with a professor and a peer advisor, and a computer science major says, "This duo is great," especially because peer advisors offer "informal advising, social advice, and class advice." Resident counselors in the dorms are also available to lend an ear. "CareerLAB and BrownConnect are super helpful resources for finding jobs and internships," cheers a junior.

Brown considers skill in the classroom as much as the usual scholarly credentials when making tenure decisions.

Brown offers nearly 90 special first-year seminars annually, capped at 20 students each and taught by faculty in all disciplines. "First-year seminars enable you to experience niche, in-depth seminar classes right away, along with your larger, introductory lecture courses," explains a sophomore. Overall, 68 percent of undergraduate classes have fewer than 20 students. Even so, particularly popular courses are usually jammed with students, and often there aren't enough teaching assistants to staff them effectively. Some, especially writing courses in the English department and studio art courses, can be nearly impossible to get into, although the administration claims that perseverance makes perfect—in other words, show up the first day and beg shamelessly.

"Brown students are very independent, which is an important quality for navigating our unique curriculum," says a sophomore. With a mere 6 percent of undergraduates hailing from tiny Rhode Island and 13 percent coming from foreign countries, geographical diversity is one of Brown's hallmarks. Consistent with the spirit of openness that defined Roger Williams's Rhode Island from the outset, Brown was the first Ivy League school to accept students from all religious affiliations. Today, Brown is a hot spot of student activism; nary a semester has passed without at least one demonstration about the issue of the day. Black students account for 8 percent of the student body, Hispanics/Latinos 12 percent, Asian Americans 23 percent, and multiracial students 8 percent. The LGBTQ community is also prominent. "Brown is one of the most conscious schools when it comes to identities, and students take the initiative to create spaces for people of all identities," observes a cognitive science major. Although Brown doesn't offer athletic or academic merit scholarships, it does practice need-blind admissions and guarantees to meet the full demonstrated need of everyone admitted with loan-free financial aid packages. Students whose families whose total annual income is $125,000 or less may be eligible for free tuition. The university also covers the cost of books for students on financial aid. Attendance is free for students whose family income is less than $60,000 annually.

> **"Brown provides amazing financial support for research opportunities."**

About half of the first-year students are assigned to one of eight co-ed Keeney Quad dorms, in "loud and rambunctious" units of 40 to 60 with several sophomore or junior dorm counselors. The other half live in the quieter Pembroke campus dorms or in a few other scattered locations. According to a sophomore, "Freshman accommodations are by and large quite plush." Options for upperclassmen include apartment-like suites with kitchens, special-interest houses, two social dorms, and Greek housing. Brown guarantees housing for all four years and requires students to live on campus through sophomore year; 75 percent of undergrads reside in university housing. Nearby off-campus apartments are becoming more plentiful—and more expensive—as the area gentrifies. Students appreciate the variety of accommodations offered at the two main dining halls and various smaller locations, one of which is vegetarian only, although the food gets middling reviews. "The larger the eatery is, the less flavorful food you can expect to get," observes a senior. Students say the campus feels safe, and one notes, "Brown emphasizes consent education and makes sexual health resources widely available."

> *The only university-wide requirement for graduation is "the ability to write well."*

"Much of the social life is on campus. I love that! You always feel part of the community," says an American studies major. More than a dozen a cappella groups, daily and weekly newspapers, political organizations, and "even a Scrabble club and a successful croquet team" represent just a few of the ways Brown students manage to keep themselves entertained. The university also sponsors frequent campuswide parties, dances, plays, concerts, and special events. The few residential Greek organizations tend to be considered much too un-mellow for Brown's taste—just 4 percent of the men and 2 percent of the women sign up. The nonresidential multicultural fraternities and sororities serve a more comprehensive student-life function, and parties are more likely to be

> **"Professors come to Brown interested in engaging with undergrads."**

held off campus by sports teams. Students report that alcohol policies focus on safety more than punishment. The biggest annual bash is Spring Weekend, which features plenty of parties and a big-name band on the Main Green. A favorite tradition involves a beloved music professor performing lively midnight organ concerts in a stately campus hall "on the four scariest nights of the year: the night before freshman classes start, Halloween, and the night before finals each semester," explains a denizen.

Providence, an old industrial city that has undergone a renaissance, is Rhode Island's capital, so many internship opportunities exist in state government. A few good music joints, lively bars, and several fine, inexpensive restaurants line Thayer Street. "Providence is a great place to see a concert or attend a festival," says a junior. For those interested in community service, the university's nationally recognized Swearer Center for Public Service helps place students in a variety of volunteer positions. Brown Community Outreach is, in fact, the largest student organization on campus. For a change of scenery, many students head to Boston or the beaches of Newport, each an hour away.

Brown does not have a reputation as an especially sports-minded school, and it cut several sports from its roster in a controversial move to focus its efforts on making its remaining 34 varsity teams more competitive. The Bears women's crew team has won multiple Division I championships, and men's soccer, lacrosse, and water polo have been competitive in the Ivy League Conference. Athletic facilities include an Olympic-sized swimming pool and an indoor athletic complex with everything from tennis courts to weight rooms. Thirty-seven club sports, plus intramurals ranging from softball and kickball to cornhole tournaments, offer a good mix of competitiveness and fun.

Ever since the days of Roger Williams, Rhode Island has been known as a land of tolerance, and Brown certainly is a 21st-century embodiment of this tradition. "Brown students build themselves up by building others up," says a physics and philosophy double major. "It's cool to be excited about anything here, and Brown students celebrate the talents of all of their peers." The education offered at this university is decidedly different from that provided by the rest of the Ivy League or, for that matter, by other top universities. Brown is content to gather a talented bunch of students, offer a diverse and imaginative array of courses, and then let the undergraduates, with a little help, make sense of it all. It takes an enormous amount of initiative, maturity, and self-confidence to thrive at Brown, but most students feel they are up to the challenge.

Overlaps

Amherst, Harvard, Oberlin, Penn, Pomona, Princeton, Wesleyan, Yale

If You Apply To ›

Brown: Early decision, regular decision. SATs or ACTs: required. Accepts the Common Application with supplement.

Bryn Mawr College

101 North Merion Avenue, Bryn Mawr, PA 19010

Bryn Mawr has the most brainpower per capita of the elite women's colleges. Politics range from liberal to radical, and the honor code shapes the campus culture. Mawrters wear (or take) their intellectuality super seriously. The college still benefits from ties to nearby Haverford, though the relationship may not be as tight-knit as in the days when Haverford was all-male. A train station just off campus offers easy access to Philadelphia.

Leafy suburban enclaves are a dime a dozen around Philadelphia, but only one is home to Bryn Mawr College, a top-notch liberal arts school that happens to be for women. On this campus, students find a range of academic pursuits from archaeology to film studies to physics and a diverse yet community-oriented student body. Founded in 1885 by a Quaker businessman, Bryn Mawr (which means "large hill" in Welsh) has evolved into a hotbed of intellectualism that prepares students for life and work in a global environment. Although students here abide by a strict honor code and participate in a host of long-standing campus traditions, they remain doggedly individualistic. "We are social-justice-minded, fiercely independent trailblazers who do not take no for an answer," asserts one sophomore. "I am absolutely certain that we will run the world someday."

Bryn Mawr's lovely campus is a path-laced oasis set among trees (many carefully labeled with Latin and English names) and lush green hills, perfect for an afternoon walk, bike ride, or jog. Just a 20-minute train ride from downtown Philadelphia, Bryn Mawr provides a suburban setting with a vital and exciting city nearby. The architecture is predominantly the collegiate Gothic style, a combination of the Gothic architecture of Oxford and Cambridge Universities and the local material, that Bryn Mawr was instrumental in establishing in the United States. Ten of Bryn Mawr's buildings are listed in the National Register of Historic Places. Variations on the collegiate Gothic theme include a sprinkling of modern buildings, such as Louis Kahn's slate-and-concrete residence hall.

The general education requirements include one semester of "quantitative" work; one semester in each of four "approaches to inquiry" (scientific investigation, critical interpretation, cross-cultural analysis, and inquiry into the past); two semesters of a foreign language; a power, inequity, and justice course; and the requirements of a major. Students are also required to take three credits of physical education, pass a swimming test, and complete the 10-week THRIVE program, which introduces first-years to the Bryn Mawr community and teaches life skills. In addition, all first-year students take a seminar named for alumna and Nobel Peace Prize laureate Emily Balch to develop their critical-thinking, writing, and discussion skills.

> **"We are social-justice-minded, fiercely independent trailblazers."**

Most departments are strong, especially the sciences, classics, archaeology, history of art, museum studies, and the foreign languages, including Russian and French. The growth and structure of cities major is a unique interdisciplinary program that blends coursework in urban studies, architecture, history, economics, and sociology, among other subjects. Combined degree programs, in which students earn both a bachelor's and a master's degree from Bryn Mawr, are available in a number of fields, ranging from chemistry and physics to classical and Near Eastern archaeology. The most popular majors are psychology, mathematics, literatures in English, biology, and sociology. Doing major work in music, fine arts, linguistics, religion, or astronomy requires a hike over to nearby Haverford College, Bryn Mawr's partner in the bicollege system, which allows students at each institution to take courses or even major or minor in programs offered by the other. Bryn Mawr and Haverford students cooperate on a weekly newspaper, radio station, orchestra, and other clubs and sports, and they may use facilities at each school, including dining halls and even dormitories. A free shuttle bus connects the campuses. Students may also cross-register with Swarthmore and the University of Pennsylvania; 95 percent of Mawrters take courses at these institutions or at Haverford at some point during their four years. Five-year dual-degree programs in engineering are offered in conjunction with Caltech, Columbia, and Penn.

Out of respect for their honor code, Mawrters refrain from discussing their grades, but they freely admit that they work hard to keep up with their rigorous

---

Website: www.brynmawr.edu
Location: Suburban
Private
Total Enrollment: 1,446
Undergraduates: 1,352
Male/Female: 0/100
Financial Aid: 84%
Pell Grant: 15%
Expense: Pr $ $ $
Student Loans: 44%
Average Debt: $ $
Applicants: 4,094
Accepted: 29%
Enrolled: 32%
Grad in 6 Years: 82%
Returning First-years: 92%
Academics: ✍ ✍ ✍ ✍ ✍
Social: 🍷 🍷 🍷
Q of L: ★ ★ ★
Admissions: (610) 526-5152
Email Address:
admissions@brynmawr.edu

Strong Programs:
Archaeology
Classics
Foreign Languages
Growth and Structure of Cities
History of Art
Museum Studies
Natural Sciences
Psychology

Bryn Mawr and Haverford students cooperate on a weekly newspaper, radio station, orchestra, and other clubs and sports.

courses. First-years and transfer students are initiated to the Bryn Mawr experience during Customs Week, which includes a variety of seminars and workshops, and Customs peer advisors support their transition throughout their first year. The quality of teaching at Bryn Mawr is unquestionably high, and faculty members are accessible, thanks to small class sizes and flexible office hours. "The professors here trust and respect the students and treat them as equals," comments a psychology major.

For those looking ahead to see what Bryn Mawr's steep tuition will buy in the long term, there is no lack of special academic programs with which to fill their résumés. The 360° Course Cluster program is an interdisciplinary experience that brings students from a variety of majors together to examine a central theme, like Europe from the Margins or Struggles for Global Health Equity, from multiple perspectives. Students take a cluster of two or three courses in a single semester and also complete a hands-on component, such as travel, fieldwork, or lab research. Thirty-three percent of students study overseas during their time at Bryn Mawr, choosing from about 70 programs in 30 countries. With easy access to a diverse variety of organizations in Philadelphia, 78 percent of Mawrters complete internships before they graduate. The Career and Civic Engagement Office connects students with internship and community service opportunities and offers guidance on networking, interviewing, and other professional skills.

> **"Each dorm is unique and has a character of its own."**

"Bryn Mawr tends to attract passionate, intelligent, kind, supportive, and involved individuals," says one student. The campus has a strong international flavor, with an impressive 13 percent of undergraduates hailing from abroad; only 12 percent are Pennsylvania residents. Black students make up 5 percent of the student body, Hispanics/Latinas 9 percent, Asian Americans 12 percent, and multiracial students 7 percent. "A lot of people are talking about race at Bryn Mawr, and also transgender issues," says one student. There are no athletic scholarships, but merit scholarships averaging $53,700 are available, and the school does guarantee to meet the demonstrated financial need of everyone admitted, including international students.

Roughly 90 percent of undergrads typically reside on campus, and housing is guaranteed for four years. "Each dorm is unique and has a character of its own," says a senior. "Many people liken the architecture to that of Hogwarts." Dorm features include hardwood floors, window seats, and fireplaces. Dining services, which receive rave reviews, offer plentiful, tasty choices as well as a nutritionist to assist students with dietary restrictions. A classical culture and society major says, "Public Safety are there to help and keep students safe."

Traditions are an important part of the campus social scene: "They play a big role in uniting all four classes and give students a role in the greater history of the college," says a student. The Elizabethan-style May Day festivities are held the Sunday after classes end in May. Everyone wears white, eats strawberries and ice cream, watches student plays, and dances around maypoles. Mawrters have been known to skinny-dip in the fountains and drink champagne on the lawn. The presentation of lanterns and class colors to incoming first-years on Lantern Night—and regal pageants, such as Parade Night and Step-Sing—fill life with a Gothic sense of wonder and school spirit. Bryn Mawr is located on suburban Philly's wealthy Main Line (named after a railroad), and the campus is two blocks from the train station, which provides students with convenient access to cultural attractions, as well as social and academic events at the nearby University of Pennsylvania and elsewhere in the city. "I consider our social life to be hanging out with friends, poetry slams, and watching plays and cultural shows," muses a junior.

> **"The Bryn Mawr experience is one of complete freedom to explore one's interests."**

Traditions are an important part of the campus social scene.

As for athletics, most Bryn Mawr Owls teams compete in the Division III Centennial Conference; field hockey, track and field, and crew are among the stronger teams. Club sports range from all-female teams to co-ed teams shared with Haverford, such as ultimate Frisbee and fencing, and intramurals are an option too.

Bryn Mawr is a symphony of contrasts: The campus is in suburbia but steps from a major city. Humanities programs are very strong, but science majors are also strong and enormously popular. The students are seriously intellectual and independent but revel in college traditions. The result is overwhelmingly positive. Says a student, "The Bryn Mawr experience is one of complete freedom to explore one's interests and individuality without the fear of being ostracized."

If You Apply To ›

Bryn Mawr: Early decision I and II, regular decision. SATs or ACTs: optional. Accepts the Common Application with supplement. Accepts applications from all individuals who identify as women, intersex individuals who do not identify as male, and individuals assigned female at birth who do not identify within the gender binary.

Bucknell University

One Dent Drive, Lewisburg, PA 17837

Bucknell, Colgate, Hamilton, Lafayette—all a little more conservative than the Ivy schools, and all a little less selective. Bucknell is the biggest of this bunch and, like Lehigh, offers engineering with a global touch. Bucknell's Greek system is strong, but students don't join until they are sophomores. The central Pennsylvania campus is remote but one of the most beautiful anywhere.

The students at Bucknell University strike a healthy balance between hitting the books and hitting the lively social scene on their pastoral central Pennsylvania campus. Yes, they tend to be preppy: "Bucknell students are mostly upper-middle-class, relatively conservative, and materially conscious. However, they are also highly motivated to succeed," says one student. With small classes, engaging faculty, and nice dorms, it's no wonder that students like this junior complain, "Four years at Bucknell go by way too fast."

In addition to being comfortable and friendly, Bucknell, founded in 1846 and named after an early benefactor, is physically beautiful. Located on a hill just south of quaint Lewisburg, the campus overlooks the scenic Susquehanna River valley. Grassy quads, shaded by leafy trees, are sprinkled among the Georgian-style buildings. The $38 million Academic East building houses laboratory space for engineering and scientific research, as well as the education department. Holmes Hall, a 79,500-square-foot facility, features high-tech labs and studios for Bucknell's management and art programs.

Students in Bucknell's College of Arts & Sciences and Freeman College of Management must complete general education courses in three areas—Foundational Experiences (including a writing-intensive Foundation Seminar), Disciplinary Exploration, and Disciplinary Depth—and must complete a culminating experience their senior year. In the College of Engineering, students take a common course their first semester that allows them to explore the intersection of multiple engineering disciplines through hands-on projects, and they undertake a capstone senior design experience as part of their curriculum. All first-year students are required to enroll in

The Campus Activities & Programs office and student organizations arrange everything from carnivals and hypnotists to religious retreats.

a Foundation Seminar that introduces them to college-level work and expectations, featuring such themes as Creative Dimensions: Exploring the Landscape of Arts and Media; Tackling Injustice: Agents of Change; and Myself and Others: Unraveling the Human Condition. In addition to faculty advisors, first-year students are assigned peer mentors who answer questions and connect them with campus resources and opportunities. The Center for Access & Success provides personalized mentoring for students enrolled in specific scholarship programs. Along with major-related requirements, each student must demonstrate competence in writing to graduate.

While Bucknell is known for engineering, management, and the natural sciences, students say academics are strong across the curriculum. "Bucknell does a great job acknowledging the changes in our society," enthuses a junior French and computer science double major. "We talk about the fast-growing technologies and what that means for our futures." The most popular majors are economics, political science, psychology, and biology. Other highlights include biomedical engineering; the animal behavior program, which benefits from an outdoor naturalistic primate facility for teaching and research; and environmental studies, which includes not only science courses but also classes in the humanities, social policy, and civil engineering. Management 101 is a favorite course among business students, who work together to create and sell a product and use the profits to fund community service projects. Newer majors include Arabic & Arab world studies, statistics, and business analytics.

> **"Bucknell students . . . are highly motivated to succeed."**

In the classroom, the emphasis is on discussion and group work. Professors facilitate the cooperative atmosphere and receive praise for always putting students first. "The professors' willingness to go out of their way to meet for one-on-one instruction is unrivaled," says a senior.

Thirty-seven percent of all Bucknell undergrads study abroad. Semester-long, faculty-led programs take them to England, France, Ghana, Greece, and Spain. Relationships with other colleges and universities enable students to choose from more than 400 other programs worldwide. The College of Engineering has one of the highest study-abroad participation rates for students in an engineering program, and it also offers a faculty-taught course that places engineering concepts into a real-world, global context. Department-specific honors programs attract top scholars, and many students participate in undergraduate research. "The STEM Scholars program allows incoming first years to get involved in research during the summer before their first year," says a senior. "Because of my early introduction to research, I have had so many opportunities, including presenting at the national ACS conference."

Twenty-three percent of students are Pennsylvanians. Racial and cultural diversity have been slow in coming say students, although "efforts to create more inclusion and equity have become more pronounced," comments a managing for sustainability major. Efforts include the Gateway Scholars Program that helps 20 first-generation students meet their financial needs without loans. Black students account for 4 percent of the student body, Hispanics/Latinos 9 percent, Asian Americans 4 percent, and multiracial students 4 percent, while international students represent 4 percent. "Bucknell tends to be more conservative than most schools," says a chemical engineering major, but social and political issues generally take a back seat here. Each year, Bucknell awards merit scholarships up to about $23,800, as well as more than 200 athletic scholarships.

> **"Bucknell does a great job acknowledging the changes in our society."**

Eighty-nine percent of undergrads live in university housing, as BU limits the number of seniors allowed to move off campus. Twenty-seven percent of students join the Residential Colleges (which a biomedical engineering major calls "fantastic for first-years"), choosing from among several themed living/learning communities focused on Arts, Discovery, Food, Global, Humanities, Languages and Cultures, Social Justice, and Society and Technology. Dining facilities offer an adequate variety, and a junior notes, "I am a vegetarian and have a lot of good options." Speak UP, a peer education group, holds mandatory workshops on sexual assault prevention and holds sessions throughout the year. The administration reports, "We have students—notably in computer science programs—who are conducting research on sexual assault data to evaluate and improve university processes and resources."

"Greek life or a sports team is nearly essential to have a social life here," a senior reports. Indeed, Bucknell's robust Greek system draws 31 percent of the men and 43 percent of the women, though rush is delayed until the start of sophomore year. Drinking at frat parties and a few bars close to campus is a pastime for many students of age, but the university offers plenty of alternatives. The Campus Activities & Programs office and student organizations arrange everything from carnivals and hypnotists to religious retreats, while the school-run Uptown nightclub offers bands, karaoke, pub nights, and other social events. "Friday nights are generally not a time to be in the library," confirms one student. Favorite traditions include

"Lewisburg is a charming little town."

the Fall Fest carnival that features a nationally known musical act, the Bison Sound concert with student performers, Greek Week, and the formal Chrysalis Ball in the spring. Also special are the Candlelight and Convocation ceremonies. "Convocation is an important tradition to Bucknell because you only pass through the Christy Mathewson Gates twice in your life: on your first and last days as a student here," explains a senior.

Lewisburg is small and rural, but Market Street has boutiques, restaurants, and an Art Deco movie theater serving up first-run flicks. "Lewisburg is a charming little town," says a senior. "There are fairs and festivals almost every weekend!" Through the Office of Civic Engagement, students have opportunities to volunteer and participate in service learning. When students get claustrophobic, New York, Philadelphia, and Washington/Baltimore are less than three hours away; the main campus of Penn State, in State College, Pennsylvania, is even closer.

The Division I Bucknell Bison have captured the Patriot League Presidents' Cup for the league's all-sports champion 18 times in 32 years. Men's and women's cross-country and track and field are perennially competitive, having combined for dozens of Patriot League championships. The rowing team has also won multiple titles. Other strong teams include women's soccer and men's and women's basketball and water polo. Basketball is a fan favorite, and Bucknell's biggest rivalries are with Lafayette and Lehigh. Intramural and club sports draw 31 percent of the students.

In the absence of diversity, Bucknell students get the best of several other worlds: excellence in engineering, management, and the liberal arts; abundant research opportunities; and a healthy social life. Another perk: "Students at Bucknell have a great sense of community that makes the school what it is," says one senior. "Everyone is proud to be a Bucknellian and is willing to help those around them." If you're seeking small classes and a supportive environment in a beautiful location, Bucknell may be a good fit.

Overlaps

Colgate, Davidson, Lafayette, Lehigh, Penn State, University of Pittsburgh, Villanova, William and Mary

If You Apply To ›

Bucknell: Early decision I and II, regular decision. Accepts the Common Application with supplement. Audition required for applicants to music program. Please consult Bucknell's website for the most up-to-date information regarding standardized test requirements.

Butler University

4600 Sunset Avenue, Indianapolis, IN 46208

Small, private university with an attractive campus near downtown Indianapolis and a relaxed Midwestern feel. Butler combines a strong liberal arts emphasis with hands-on learning. Strong in business, dance, and prepharmacy. Students are a homogeneous lot who share Indiana's trademark passion for basketball. Larger than DePauw, half the size of Northwestern.

Website: www.butler.edu
Location: City Outskirts
Private
Total Enrollment: 4,713
Undergraduates: 4,267
Male/Female: 40/60
Financial Aid: 99%
Pell Grant: 23%
Expense: Pr $
Student Loans: 50%
Average Debt: $ $ $ $
Applicants: 9,471
Accepted: 85%
Enrolled: 13%
Grad in 6 Years: 80%
Returning First-years: 88%
Academics: ✍ ✍ ✍
Social: 🗩 🗩 🗩
Q of L: ★ ★ ★ ★
Admissions: (888) 940-8100
Email Address:
admission@butler.edu

Strong Programs:
Dance
English
Health Sciences
Journalism
Marketing
Prepharmacy
Sports Media
Communication

With the new Founder's College opening in 2025, Butler University now has seven colleges serving undergraduates in fields from communication, education, and liberal arts and sciences to pharmacy and health sciences, business, and the arts. Founders College caters specifically to historically underserved students in the Central Indiana area by providing affordable associate's degrees in subject areas related to business, youth and community advocacy, and healthcare. Like the other colleges, it promotes the Butler way of life, which emphasizes teamwork, tenacity, and sound fundamentals. Indeed, students here find their school's cozy campus and solid academics to be a slam dunk.

Butler was founded in 1855 as a "nonsectarian institution free from the taint of slavery" on property donated by Ovid Butler, a lawyer and abolitionist. Located five miles north of downtown Indianapolis in the city's historic Butler-Tarkington neighborhood, Butler's 300-acre campus is hailed as one of the most attractive in the Midwest for its parklike setting, which includes centuries-old trees, open landscaped lawns, curving sidewalks, fountains, a nature preserve, a prairie, a historical canal, a formal botanical garden, an observatory, and jogging paths. The first building, Jordan Hall, features Gothic architecture and has set the tone for subsequent buildings. Butler's Hinkle Fieldhouse, which opened in 1928, has reigned as one of the nation's great sports arenas for nine decades. The $100 million Sciences Complex boasts state-of-the-art labs, high-tech classrooms, and the Science Innovation Center.

As part of Butler's core curriculum, students enroll in two common elements: First-Year Seminar, a two-semester sequence in their first year, and Global and Historical Studies, a sophomore-year sequence of courses. In addition to a standard distribution of liberal arts and science classes, students must take a social justice and diversity course. They also complete the Butler Cultural Requirement, which involves attending eight campus events over four years, and the Indianapolis Community Requirement, which connects students to the local area through off-campus community service. Incoming students looking to make friends before the start of their first semester can sign up for one of several optional preorientation programs that range from volunteering in Indianapolis to learning how major sporting events like the Indianapolis 500 and Super Bowl are organized.

"The academic climate is rigorous."

"The academic climate is rigorous," says an elementary education major, who recommends the exploratory studies program for "anyone who is stuck on what they want to study in college." The university's most popular majors include marketing, finance, biology, journalism, education, health sciences, and preprofessional tracks in pharmacy and physician assistant studies. Other solid offerings include dance (especially classical ballet), international business, English, especially the creative writing track, and sports media. Students in the risk management and insurance major learn how to mitigate and manage risks and can get hands-on experience through the school's student-run insurance company. New majors include nursing, public health, data science, kinesiology, neuroscience, and a B.F.A. in acting. Butler now offers three-year degree tracks for more than 40 academic majors. Half of all undergraduate classes enroll fewer than 20 students, and the majority of classes taken by first-years are taught by full professors. "Professors have a tendency to deviate from the normal lectures, notes, papers, and exams and allow us to take a more hands-on approach," comments a psychology and Spanish major.

The University Honors Program is designed to foster a diverse and challenging intellectual climate; students take four honors courses, participate in special honors events, and research and write a thesis. About 30 students are selected each year for the Butler Summer Institute, where they produce an original research or creative project under the guidance of a faculty mentor and with the support of a $4,500 stipend. Forty percent of students travel to far-flung locales around the globe, choosing from more than 300 study abroad options in over 50 countries, including Australia, Ireland, Germany, Ghana, and India.

"Generally, Butler's students are understanding, open-minded, kind, and wonderful," says a computer science major, adding, "For many people, Butler is less diverse than their high schools, which can be a culture shock." Forty-nine percent of Butler students come from Indiana. Black students account for 5 percent of the student body, Hispanics/Latinos 7 percent, Asian Americans 4 percent, and multiracial students 4 percent; another 1 percent are international. Most students come from middle- to upper-class families.

"We are mostly a 'bubble' because students don't really leave campus unless they need to go to a store or downtown Indy."

While there is not usually much overt political activism on campus, the lack of diversity and the cost to attend are common student complaints. Merit scholarships averaging $22,100 are as numerous as athletic awards.

Sixty-eight percent of students live in university-sponsored housing, with all but seniors and commuters required to do so. Options include dorms, university-owned houses and apartments, and Greek houses; first-year residence hall Residential College has undergone a $20 million renovation. "We only have two dining halls on campus, and they get mixed reviews," shares a senior. And while Butler is "not in the best part of town," students report feeling safe on campus: "Butler is a very tight-knit community, and we all look out for each other," says a junior. Adds a first-year, "All students are able to connect with a mental health professional through the counseling and consultation services program for free."

"Greek organizations and sports teams set the tone for social life," says a student; 27 percent of the men and 35 percent of the women go Greek. Although the university allows alcohol on campus, students say the social scene doesn't revolve around booze. "Butler students think they know how to party, but compared to state schools like IU and Purdue, that's laughable," remarks one senior. More than 200 student organizations coordinate social activities throughout the week, and a junior observes, "We are mostly a 'bubble' because students don't really leave campus unless they need to go to a store or downtown Indy." Favorite annual traditions include the Block Party and Bulldog Bash that welcome students at the start of the year, and Homecoming in the fall. Students seeking a change of pace head off campus and into the Broad Ripple neighborhood or downtown Indianapolis, where bars, restaurants, museums, cultural events, and professional sports are plentiful.

Butler fields 20 Division I teams (the Bulldogs), and all but one compete in the Big East—the football team is a member of the Pioneer Football League. Aside from basketball, the men's and women's soccer, cross-country, and track and field teams are strong. Intramurals are popular, especially basketball, soccer, volleyball, and flag football, and more serious students may also compete in numerous club sports. Butler's varsity and club-level eSports teams compete in the swanky Butler Esports Park.

Butler University strives to provide students with a strong undergraduate liberal arts experience and access to professional programs of "local impact and global reach." Students have taken note of the school's revamped programs, improved facilities, and focus on personal attention. Butler is "a school with the resources of a large school and the environment of a small school," says a satisfied first-year student. "It truly feels like a home away from home."

If You Apply To ›

Butler: Early action, rolling admission. SATs or ACTs: optional. Accepts the Common Application with supplement. Art applicants must submit portfolio.

California Colleges and Universities

California's three-pronged system of universities and community colleges has long been viewed as a model of excellence by other public higher education institutions nationwide and even around the world. The system offers a wealth of educational riches, including world-class research universities, enough Nobel Prize winners to fill a couple of classrooms, and colleges on the cutting edge of everything from film to viticulture. Underlying the creation of this remarkable system was a commitment to the notion that all qualified Californians, whatever their economic status, are entitled to the benefits of a college education.

The California system is composed of the 10 University of California (UC) and 22 California State University (CSU) campuses. It also includes more than 100 two-year community colleges that offer associate's degrees, pathways to transfer into four-year institutions, and even several specialized bachelor's degree programs. Governor Gavin Newsom has supported substantially increased funding for all three systems and vowed to limit the proportion of nonresident students on UC campuses to no more than 18 percent of the student population. The Tuition Stability Plan essentially locks in the tuition rate and student services fee for new first-year and transfer students at UC universities for up to six years for California residents and nonresidents alike. The UC system also has a Native American Opportunity Plan (UCNAOP) that covers tuition and student services fees for California residents who belong to federally recognized Native American, American Indian, or Alaska Native tribes.

ADMISSIONS REQUIREMENTS

Admissions requirements for the three systems and the institutions within them vary. Community colleges are open to virtually anyone who is 18 years old or older or who has a high school diploma or equivalent. To be considered for admission to a CSU or UC campus, applicants must complete a minimum of 15 yearlong college-preparatory courses in seven subject areas (referred to as "a-g courses"), including two semesters in the fine or performing arts. Applicants will be eligible for admission to the CSU system with a 2.5 or higher "a-g" GPA (3.0 for nonresidents); some lower GPAs are considered with supplemental factors. Applicants to a UC university must earn a 3.0 "a-g" GPA (3.4 for nonresidents) or better. GPA for eligibility is calculated using only 10th- and 11th-grade results. Choice of major continues to be an important factor for some campuses, and students interested in popular majors such as engineering and computer science are wise to take advantage of the opportunity to list an alternate major. Neither the UC nor CSU schools consider SAT or ACT scores in the admissions process.

UNIVERSITY OF CALIFORNIA (UC)

The UC system boasts more than 290,000 students, 240,000 faculty and staff, and 2 million living alumni. Although one university system, each of the nine undergraduate UC campuses (UC San Francisco offers only graduate and professional degrees) offers a full range of academic programs, and each has its own distinctive character. The newest member, Merced, opened in 2005 as the first American research university to be founded in the 21st century. In response to record-breaking application numbers, the UC system announced its 2030 Capacity Plan in 2022, which aims to increase enrollment by 23,000 students by the end of the decade. However, in June 2025, the U.S. Department of Justice opened an investigation into the UC system regarding some of the goals in the 2030 Capacity Plan.

In making admissions decisions, UC employs a "comprehensive review" process that takes into consideration not only curriculum and grades but also leadership, special talents, and the educational opportunities available to each student. To apply for admission to the University of California, students complete an application available at admission.universityofcalifornia.edu. The application is standardized across all UC campuses, making it easy for an applicant to apply to multiple campuses. For each campus selected, students must choose a major and, in some cases, an alternate major. There is an $80 application fee ($95 for international applicants) for each campus. To enhance their chances of gaining admission to at least one campus, prospective students are encouraged to use this application to apply to more than one school. They should understand that each campus to which they apply reviews their application using its own methodology and criteria. Decisions are thus campus-specific, and each university's admissions office is not aware of an individual applicant's other choices. Applicants who rank in the top 9 percent of all California high school students or the top 9 percent of their own California high school, but who are not accepted to any UC campus, will be offered a place at another campus if space is available.

UC Merced is described in the following paragraph. Full profiles of the other eight undergraduate UC universities follow this overview.

UC Merced (full-time enrollment 9,000) is the newest addition to the UC system. Opened in 2005 with a mission of bringing public higher education to one of the state's underserved areas, Merced is expanding rapidly and has established itself as a comprehensive research university. Faculty are bringing in substantial research funding, especially in the biological sciences. In 2025, UC Merced earned the prestigious R1 Carnegie Classification, recognizing its very high level of research activity. The campus, which sits on the shore of Lake Yosemite surrounded by green fields and considerable land set aside for conservation, boasts an environmentally friendly design and has a small-town feel. Merced offers more than 60 undergraduate academic programs through its three schools: engineering; natural sciences; and social sciences, humanities, and arts. It has a diverse student body, with students of color making up 86 percent of the undergraduate population, and a higher proportion of students from low-income and first-generation backgrounds than any other UC campus. It boasts a strong counseling and support system. Merced has the highest acceptance rate of any UC campus (90 percent) and draws relatively few students from out of state.

CALIFORNIA STATE UNIVERSITY (CSU)

The California State University system is separate from the University of California and constitutes the largest system of comprehensive four-year public institutions in the U.S.

The system serves 22 campuses and seven off-campus centers and caters to more than 471,000 students a year. And while many of the campuses serve mainly commuters, Chico, Humboldt, Monterey Bay, Cal Poly–San Luis Obispo, and Sonoma stand out as residential campuses. While a solid liberal arts education is offered in CSU institutions, the emphasis is often on career-oriented professional training; the system produces large numbers of engineers, nurses, and teachers for California's workforce. Size varies dramatically, from more than 30,000 full-time students at **Northridge** and **Long Beach** to fewer than 8,500 at several other campuses, like **Channel Islands** and **Monterey Bay**. Each campus has its strengths, although in many cases, a student's choice of school is dictated by location rather than by academic specialties. For those with greater flexibility, some of the more distinctive campuses are profiled in the following paragraphs.

Chico State (full-time undergraduate enrollment 14,000), situated in the beautiful Sacramento Valley, draws a large majority of its students from outside a 100-mile radius and continues to become more selective in its admissions. The on-campus undergraduate life is strong, and the social life is great. **California Polytechnic at San Luis Obispo** (22,000), colloquially known as Cal Poly–San Luis Obispo or Cal Poly SLO, is the toughest Cal State university to get into. It provides excellent training in the applied branches of such fields as agriculture, architecture, business, and engineering. **California Polytechnic Maritime Academy** (800), located 30 miles northeast of San Francisco in Vallejo, integrated with Cal Poly SLO in 2025. It specializes in marine transportation, engineering, and maritime technology and boasts the 500-foot training ship *Golden Bear*, which serves as a classroom. **Fresno State** (24,000), located in the verdant Central Valley, has one of the few viticulture schools in the state outside of UC Davis, and undergraduates can work in the school winery. Yosemite, Kings Canyon, and Sequoia National Parks are nearby.

San Diego State (35,000) is the balmiest of the campuses, with a more residential, outdoorsy, and campus-oriented social scene. "You could go for the weather alone—some do," says one former student. Contrasted with most other CSUs, athletics are very important, and the academic offerings are almost as oriented to the liberal arts as at its neighbor, UC San Diego. San Diego State is highly selective for students from out of the area.

San José State (23,000), located in the heart of Silicon Valley, boasts strong programs in computer science and engineering (including aerospace) as well as amazing internship opportunities for students right in its backyard. **Sonoma State** (5,800) situated just north of San Francisco in the wine-growing capital of the state, has become increasingly popular, with strong programs in computer science, creative writing, and electrical engineering, as well as a concentration in wine business strategies within the business school. The Hutchins School of Liberal Studies allows students to complete their lower-division general education requirements in small (15 students) seminar-style classes that emphasize critical examination and excellence in written communication. The housing and student life buildings are gorgeous.

California Polytechnic at Humboldt (5,300), colloquially known as Cal Poly–Humboldt, is perched at the top of the state near the Oregon border in the heart of the redwoods. Humboldt's forestry and wildlife departments have national reputations, and the natural science departments are strong. Students have the run of excellent laboratory facilities and Redwood National Park. Many in-staters come here to enjoy the rugged coastline north of San Francisco. **CSU Monterey Bay** (8,200) is one mile from the beach, and 52 percent of students live on campus. It offers an interdisciplinary focus with a global perspective, opportunities for internships, and a unique Capstone Festival featuring the culminating projects of graduating seniors, credential candidates, and master's students.

Sacramento State University (24,000) is recognized as a Hispanic Serving Institution (HSI) and an Asian American Native American Pacific Islander Serving Institution (AANAPISI). It has been ranked as the second most diverse college in the Western United States (*Wall Street Journal*, 2023), and it proudly houses the nation's first-ever Black Honors College that provides a rigorous and specialized educational experience focused on Black history, life, and culture.

The California State University application system features a single application for all 22 campuses that is available at https://www.calstate.edu/apply. Applicants must indicate the term they are applying for and their preferred campuses and majors.

Admission criteria are influenced by the student's location, with priority often given to students coming from local high schools or community colleges. Due to increasing demand, all campuses are becoming increasingly selective, especially for popular majors. There is a $70 application fee for each campus.

Consistent with the state's rich cultural and ethnic diversity, nine UC universities and at least 21 CSU campuses are recognized as Minority Serving Institutions (MSI) under a federal program designed to support accredited institutions of higher learning that serve significant populations of racial or ethnical minority or low-income students. Such designation makes these institutions eligible for targeted federal funding under the Higher Education Act of 1965 aimed at improving educational outcomes and closing achievement gaps for underrepresented populations. Among other things, funds can be used for curriculum and faculty development, technology updates, and academic supports such as tutoring and mentoring.

By creating supportive environments for students from the targeted groups, the MSI program has been credited with expanding access and improving graduation rates and economic mobility among students from underserved communities. Recent changes in federal policy, however, have caused UC and CSU to lose millions of dollars in MSI funding and put much of this progress at risk. Readers can determine whether a particular university is an MSI and in what category by consulting the university's home page.

110 Sproul Hall, Berkeley, CA 94720

Like everything else at Berkeley, the academic offerings at this flagship of flagship universities can be overwhelming. With 30,000 full-time undergraduate overachievers crammed into such a small space, it is no wonder that the academic climate is about as intense as you can get at a world–class public university. Don't expect to be on a first-name basis with your professor in Intro Bio.

Berkeley. Mention the name, and even down-to-earth students get stars in their eyes. Students who come here want the biggest and best of everything, though sometimes that idealism runs headlong into budget cuts, tuition increases, and housing shortages. Never mind. Berkeley is where the action is. If you want a quick indicator of Berkeley's academic prowess, look no farther than the parking lot. The campus is dotted with spots marked "NL"—spots reserved for resident Nobel laureates. There are seven of them on the current faculty. Then there are the hundreds of Guggenheim fellows, Pulitzer Prize recipients, MacArthur geniuses, and Fulbright scholars. Is it any wonder that this radical institution of the '60s still maintains the kind of reputation that makes the top private universities take note? The social climate at this mother of UC schools, founded back in 1868 as the state's land grant university, is not as explosive as it once seemed to be, but don't expect anything tame on today's campus. It has often been at the epicenter of the Free Speech movement. Flower children and granola chompers still abound, as do fledgling Marxists, young Republicans, and body-pierced activists.

Spread across more than 1,200 scenic acres on a hill overlooking San Francisco Bay, the Berkeley campus is a parklike oasis in a small city. The startlingly wide variety of architectural styles ranges from the stunning classical amphitheater to the modern Berkeley Art Museum and Pacific Film Archive sheathed in stainless steel. Large expanses of grass dot the campus and are just "perfect for playing Frisbee or lying in the sun." The oaks along Strawberry Creek and the eucalyptus grove date back to Berkeley's beginnings more than 150 years ago. Sproul Plaza, in the heart of the campus, is one of the great people-watching sites of the world.

Of course, Berkeley is not only gorgeous; it's also academically intense. "Everyone was the top student in his or her high school class, so they can't settle for anything less than number one," says one student. Another says bluntly, "Expect very little sleep." Although half of all undergraduate classes have fewer than 20 students, a handful of introductory courses, particularly in the sciences, enroll as many as 1,000, and professors, who

> **"[Berkeley students] can't settle for anything less than number one."**

must publish or disengage from the university's highly competitive teaching ranks, devote a great deal of time to research. After all, Berkeley has made a large part of its reputation on its research and graduate programs, many of which rank among the best in the nation.

Berkeley makes a good case for trickle-down academics. As a political science major explains, "This system has allowed me to hear outstanding lectures from amazing professors who write the books we read while allowing far more personal attention from the graduate-student instructors." Another student opines, "It's better to stand 50 feet from brilliance than five feet from mediocrity." Evidence of such gravitational pull is seen in the promising curricula designed specifically for first- and second-year students that include interdisciplinary courses in writing,

---

Website: www.berkeley.edu
Location: Small City
Public
Total Enrollment: 41,757
Undergraduates: 31,574
Male/Female: 43/55
Financial Aid: 55%
Pell Grant: 20%
Expense: Pub $ $ $ $
Student Loans: 25%
Average Debt: $
Applicants: 124,245
Accepted: 11%
Enrolled: 46%
Grad in 6 Years: 93%
Returning First-years: 97%
Academics: ✍ ✍ ✍ ✍ ✍
Social: 🗩 🗩 🗩 🗩
Q of L: ★ ★ ★
Admissions: (510) 642-3175
Email Address: N/A

Strong Programs:
Architecture
Business
Economics
Engineering
Mathematics
Molecular and Cell Biology
Political Science
Sociology

public speaking, and the history of civilization and an offering of small student seminars (with enrollment limited to 18) taught by regular faculty. Despite these attempts at catering to undergraduates, the sheer number of students at Berkeley makes it difficult to treat each student as an individual. As a result, such things as academic counseling can suffer. "Advising? You mean to tell me they have advising here?" asks one student.

Each of Berkeley's six undergraduate colleges or schools has its own set of general education requirements, which are generally not extensive, and a set of breadth requirements, which expose students to disciplines outside of their major. All students, however, must take English composition and literature and one term each of American history and American institutions, as well as fulfill an American cultures requirement—an original approach (via courses offered in several departments) to comparative study of ethnic groups in the United States.

Most of the departments at Berkeley are noteworthy, and some are about the best anywhere (like engineering and architecture). Business, economics, political science, sociology, mathematics, physics, chemistry, history, and English are just a handful of the truly dazzling programs. Berkeley offers eight departments and eight interdisciplinary programs in engineering; electrical engineering and computer science are the most popular. Interdisciplinary study and research are common across the sciences, such as the biological sciences division's programs in integrative biology and molecular and cell biology.

Special programs abound at Berkeley, though it's up to the student to find out about them. Students may study abroad on fellowships at one of 50 centers around the world or spend time in various internships around the country. If all you want to do is study, the library system, with more than 14 million volumes and more than 20 branches, is one of the largest in the nation and maintains open stacks. The DARE (Diversifying Access to Research in Engineering) program helps connect undergraduates with research opportunities in engineering and computer science, focusing particularly on supporting women and students from underrepresented groups.

> **"Social life at UC Berkeley is killer!"**

Although most Berkeley students are California residents, 14 percent come from out of state, and 10 percent come from foreign nations. Thirty-five percent are Asian American, 2 percent are Black, 22 percent are Hispanic/Latino, and 7 percent are multiracial. The university provides a variety of programs to promote diversity and inclusion, including the Center for Race and Gender and a peer education program for preventing sexual violence. Despite Berkeley's liberal reputation, recent trends have inched toward conservatism. Business majors and fraternity members outnumber young Communists and peaceniks these days, though the school does produce many Peace Corps volunteers. Merit scholarships averaging $8,900 are awarded to qualified students, and athletic scholarships are available.

Berkeley's highly prized residence halls have room for only 28 percent of the students, and new students receive housing priority. After that, the Cal Rentals is a good resource for finding an apartment in town. Many students live a couple of miles off campus, and several student-housing projects have opened in recent years, offering a variety of rooms in low-rise and high-rise settings. In the absence of a mandatory meal plan, everybody eats "wherever and whenever they wish," including in the residence halls.

If the housing shortage gets you down, the beautiful California weather will probably take your mind off it, as will the never-ending social opportunities. "Social life at UC Berkeley is killer!" exclaims one geography major. More than 1,200 student clubs and groups are registered on campus, which ensures that there is an outlet for just about any interest and that no one group will ever dominate campus life. Only 3 percent of the men and 5 percent of the women join fraternities or sororities. Weekends are generally spent in Berkeley, hanging out at the many bookstores, coffeehouses, and sidewalk cafés, heading to a fraternity or sorority party, or taking advantage of the many events right on campus. Berkeley is a quintessential college town ("kind of a crazy little town," says one anthropology major), and of course, there's always the people watching; where else can an individual meet people trying to convert pedestrians to strange New Age religions or revolutionary political causes on every street corner? Nearby Telegraph Avenue is famous (notorious?) for such antics every weekend.

Many students use the weekend to catch up on studying, but when they want to get away, the BART public transportation system provides easy access to San Francisco, by far one of the most pleasant cities in the world and a cultural and countercultural mecca. The Bay Area boasts myriad professional sports teams as well, including the Golden State Warriors, the Oakland A's, the San Francisco 49ers, and the San Francisco Giants. Get access to a car, and you can hike in Yosemite National Park, ski and gamble in Nevada, taste wine in Napa Valley, or visit the aquarium at Monterey. But be advised that a car is only an asset when you want to go out of town—students warn that parking in Berkeley is difficult, to say the least.

> **"At Berkeley, it is worse to be dull than odd."**

Division I varsity athletics have always been important here, and the university is a top producer of Olympic athletes. Men's gymnastics, men's crew, and men's and women's swimming are strong performers in the Pac-12. The Golden Bears basketball team has surged in popularity, and just about everyone turns out for the football team's "Big Game," where the favorite activity on the home side of the bleachers is bad-mouthing the rival school to the south: Stanford. Intramurals and fitness programs are enhanced by an extensive recreational facility and gorgeous weather year-round.

The common denominator in the Berkeley community is academic motivation, along with the self-reliance that emerges from trying to make your mark among more than 30,000 talented peers. Beyond that, the diversity of town and campus makes an extraordinarily free and exciting college environment for almost anyone. "It makes one feel free to dress, say, think, or do anything and not be chastised for being unorthodox," explains a student. "At Berkeley, it is worse to be dull than odd."

Overlaps

UC Davis, UCLA, UC San Diego, UC Santa Barbara, Harvard, University of Southern California, Stanford, University of Washington

If You Apply To ›

Berkeley: Regular decision. SATs or ACTs: not considered. Does not accept the Common Application. Apply to a particular college, school, or program. Application includes optional question about gender/sexual identity.

UC Davis

1 Shields Avenue, Davis, CA 95616

The closest thing to a cow college in the UC system, but with cultured, pedigree cows. Described by the New Yorker as "the MIT of American fermentation." Premed, prevet, food science—you name it. If the subject lives and breathes, you can study it here. A small-town alternative to the bright lights of UC Berkeley and UCLA. As is often true at science-oriented schools, the work is hard.

Website: www.ucdavis.edu
Location: Small City
Public
Total Enrollment: 38,685
Undergraduates: 31,484
Male/Female: 39/57
Financial Aid: 76%
Pell Grant: 32%
Expense: Pub $ $ $ $
Student Loans: 31%
Average Debt: $
Applicants: 98,869
Accepted: 42%
Enrolled: 16%
Grad in 6 Years: 86%
Returning First-years: 93%
Academics: ✍ ✍ ✍ ✍
Social: 🗩 🗩 🗩
Q of L: ★ ★ ★ ★
Admissions: (530) 752-2971
Email Address:
  undergraduateadmissions@
  ucdavis.edu

Strong Programs:
Agriculture
Animal Science
Biological Sciences
Biotechnology
Engineering
Environmental Science
Food Science
Studio Art

The hub of the university is a central area known as the Quad, one of many grassy open spaces outfitted with hammocks.

At the University of California Davis, environmental science and most everything that has to do with animals, agriculture, winemaking, or biological science are noteworthy. The Aggies' cup truly runneth over. Originally established in 1905 as the University Farm, the campus maintains its sprawling, verdant beauty, replete with native and imported forestry, charming bike paths, and mooing cows. But lest you assume this environmentally oriented university is full of quaint country folk right out of American Gothic, think again. UC Davis is a major research university and has become an international leader in the agricultural, biological, biotechnical, and veterinary sciences.

Located 20 miles west of Sacramento and 73 miles north of San Francisco, the 5,300-acre campus is located along the Capitol Corridor, skirting the Sacramento–San Joaquin Delta watershed. It features a 100-acre arboretum and hundreds of buildings with a blend of architectural styles, from traditional dairy barn to the modern Sciences Laboratory building with its rooftop greenhouse. The hub of the university is a central area known as the Quad, one of many grassy open spaces on campus outfitted with hammocks, perfect for soaking up the abundant California sunshine. The 75,000-square-foot Shrem Museum of Art devotes one-third of its space to education.

General education requirements aim to equip students with a breadth of knowledge to complement the expertise they develop in their chosen fields of study. UC Davis students are expected to address four core literacies: quantitative, scientific, civic and cultural literacy, and literacy with words and images.

Biological sciences, economics, managerial economics, psychology, and an interdisciplinary program in neurobiology, physiology, and behavior are among the campus's most popular majors. Animal science, engineering, and biotechnology are strong, and the agriculture program is one of the best anywhere. The school is "the number one choice for any prevet," according to one student, and it's great for premeds too. The food science major is also stellar and not for the faint of heart or those afraid of chemistry. It was Davis scientists who discovered how to optimize grape growing for California's wine industry. They devised the method for creating orange juice concentrate and came up with the idea of a machine-harvestable "square tomato." UC Davis's World Food Center is dedicated to innovating food production methods for improved human health and environmental sustainability. Studio art is also among the top in the nation.

"You really feel a sense of community when you're here."

Academically, "Davis can be challenging, but it challenges students in the right way," comments a biopsychology major. "Everyone is extremely helpful, and it doesn't seem impossible to do your best here." Many introductory courses are quite large, and students complain that the average class size is on the rise, but UC Davis also offers more than 200 small first-year seminars taught by the best instructors. The quality of teaching can vary considerably, according to students, although "most professors are willing to hold extra office hours and make time for the students," says a psychology major.

Faculty members here are expected to do top-level research as well as teach, giving undergraduates the chance to work directly with professors and grad students as assistants in first-class research groups. The University Honors Program is for academically talented first-year and transfer students who want to enhance their education through special courses. Roughly 15 percent of students study internationally, frequently through the 50-plus programs designed and led by faculty in more than 30 countries. "You can study abroad essentially wherever your heart desires for as short as one month or upward of a year," cheers one senior. The innovative UC Center Sacramento and the Washington Program give undergraduates academic credits for courses and internships in state and federal governments, respectively.

"Students at Davis are friendly, and you really feel a sense of community when you're here," observes one senior. Ninety-four percent of undergraduates hail from California, and 13 percent come from abroad. Black students account for 2 percent of undergrads, Asian Americans 31 percent, Hispanics/Latinos 25 percent, and multiracial students 7 percent. The university's Office of Campus Diversity, Cross-Cultural Center, and academic success centers for students of various ethnicities help support diverse populations. Campus hot topics include social justice and sustainability. Davis awards merit scholarships averaging $8,300, and there are more than 300 athletic awards.

"Davis . . . challenges students in the right way."

Thirty percent of undergraduates live on campus, and 90 percent of first-years choose to do so. Campus housing is secure, well maintained, and includes a number of living/learning community options. "Dorms are really nice and new and air-conditioned," a student says. Three meal plans for the three dining halls offer a wide range of options, including vegan and kosher items at every meal. Food trucks are positioned around campus at lunchtime, and a weekly on-campus farmers market provides ready access to fresh produce. A senior notes, "Our fraternities, sororities, and student government have taken steps to address sexual assault and promote a stance against it."

Davis scientists discovered how to optimize grape growing for California's wine industry.

"Davis has a good social scene, but you have to put in the effort to find places and events you like," says a design major. Active drama and music departments provide frequent entertainment, and the 1,800-seat Mondavi Center for the Performing Arts features international and local groups. There are more than 800 student clubs, and fraternities and sororities attract 5 percent of the men and 6 percent of the women. While alcohol is allowed in the dorms for those of age, a senior says the party scene "can get dull, so a lot of students like to go out of town" for more vigorous nightlife. Major annual social events include Lawntopia, a student-run music festival; Picnic Day, in which alumni join current students in a massive outdoor shindig; nearly three months of cultural celebrations every spring; and the Whole Earth Festival, "an earthy, tie-dyed sort of event." Health and environmental consciousness run high here, and bicycles are the main form of transportation across the incredible 100 miles of bike paths that crisscross the campus and environs. "Bicycles are the norm at Davis. Don't come without one," advises one psych major. The university also sponsors sustainability projects and promotes such novelties as contests between residence halls for the lowest heating and electric bills.

"Dorms are really nice and new and air-conditioned."

In between quizzes and cram sessions, the surrounding communities offer a welcome change of pace. With its tree-lined streets and quiet nights, the city of Davis itself is small but has enough restaurants, activities, and entertainment to keep those who want to stay close to campus happy. The relationship between the college and town is one of unusual cooperation (partly because the students, who make up half the population, like to vote in local elections). A car can come in handy if you are looking for an urban night out in Sacramento (20 minutes) or a big-name show in San Francisco (a little more than an hour). Undergrads who lack wheels of their own can get around town for free on the student-run Unitrans bus system or head to UC Berkeley via an intercampus shuttle. Beaches are a two-hour drive from the campus, and the ski slopes and hiking trails of Lake Tahoe and the Sierra Nevada mountains are a little closer.

Major annual social events include Lawntopia, a student-run music festival.

Most of UC Davis's 25 Division I varsity teams (the Aggies) compete in the Big West Conference. Men's basketball is a fan favorite, and women's basketball and cross-country have brought home conference championships. The annual Causeway Classic football game against rival Sacramento State stirs passions, as do recreational sports: Students are active in nearly 40 club sports and more than 25 intramurals. Given the Mediterranean climate, outdoor activities are popular, and almost everyone does something athletic—jogging, softball, tennis, swimming, or Frisbee—if only to break up their studies with a different kind of competition.

Proud of its small-town atmosphere, UC Davis is not for the lazy or faint of heart. As one student says, "There's no free ride. You are going to have to work for everything you get." And most students get a lot out of their four or more years at UC Davis. It's the ideal spot to combine high-powered work in science and agriculture with that famous easygoing California lifestyle.

If You Apply To ›

Davis: Regular decision. SATs or ACTs: not considered. Does not accept the Common Application. Apply to a particular college, school, or program. Application includes optional question about gender/sexual identity.

UC Irvine

260 Aldrich Hall, Irvine, CA 92697

Irvine sits in the midst of one of the nation's biggest suburbs, combining funky, modern architecture with a studious, preprofessional student body. Premed is the featured attraction, along with computer science and engineering. Not quite as close to the beach as Santa Barbara—but close enough for students to enjoy it regularly.

Website: www.uci.edu

Location: Suburban

Public

Total Enrollment: 35,982

Undergraduates: 29,515

Male/Female: 43/56

Financial Aid: 77%

Pell Grant: 38%

Expense: Pub $ $ $

Student Loans: 32%

Average Debt: $

Applicants: 122,706

Accepted: 29%

Enrolled: 19%

Grad in 6 Years: 87%

Returning First-years: 94%

Academics: ✍ ✍ ✍ ✍

Social: 🗩 🗩

Q of L: ★ ★ ★

Admissions: (949) 824-6703

Email Address: admissions@uci.edu

On the surface, UC Irvine's clean, contemporary campus appears to be home to students who study diligently in the busy library, wear sensible shoes to class, and at least try to resist that double shot of espresso at the busy coffee shops around campus. But that image starts to dissipate as soon as you hear that bizarre noise: "Zot! Zot! Zot!" Then a UCI student explains that "it's the sound that an anteater supposedly makes when it swipes an ant with its tongue." Hey, any school that has a marauding anteater as a mascot can't be completely straitlaced. The university is, however, serious about its reputation as a school with stellar programs in science, technology, and the arts.

Located in the heart of Orange County and founded in 1965, UCI is among the newest of the UC campuses. While enrollment is up and the administration anticipates further expansion, according to one English major, "It is the perfect size." UCI is liberally supplied with trees and shrubs from all over the world. Futuristic buildings are arranged in a circle around 21-acre Aldrich Park, "giving it the appearance of a relaxed art school," says one observer. Undergraduates have long quipped that UCI stood for "Under Construction Indefinitely." Newer campus additions include the Mesa Court Residence Hall expansion and the Mesa Court Community Center, which is expected to be completed in 2026.

UCI's general education requirements involve three courses each in writing; science and technology; social and behavioral sciences; and arts and humanities. Students also fulfill requirements in foreign language; quantitative, symbolic, and computational reasoning; multicultural studies; and international/global issues. Optional first-year seminars, limited to 15 students each, create a more intimate environment in which to adjust to academic life at a research university. Students may choose from more than 85 majors, and the Campuswide Honors Program is available for top students; several individual departments offer honors programs as well.

A "premed mentality" reigns at Irvine, and the School of Biological Sciences is the best academic division; undergraduate degrees in nursing science and pharmaceutical sciences are also notable. The university houses multiple medical research centers focusing on areas like aging and dementia, neurological disorders, and spinal cord trauma. The most popular majors include psychology, biology, business, and engineering. The computer science department is bolstered by a fast-growing major in computer game science. The Claire Trevor School of Arts offers nationally ranked programs in dance, drama, music, studio art, and music theater, and the school's Beall Center for Art and Technology enables students to explore the relationship between digital technology and the arts and sciences. An interdisciplinary major in social ecology combines criminology, environmental and legal studies, and psychology and social behavior and strongly emphasizes faculty/student relationships. Languages are solid at UCI, and a creative writing program is gaining national recognition.

Like most of the other UC campuses, UCI is on a 10-week quarter system, so the pace is fast and furious. "UCI is fairly competitive, and the courses are moderately rigorous," says a junior, but students are also said to be "surprisingly cooperative." Getting into required classes can be difficult at times, and "Graduate students teach lower-division writing courses," says one student, adding that "many classes are overcrowded, leaving little room for personal attention." Even so, 46 percent of undergraduate classes enroll fewer than 20 students.

Ninety-two percent of undergraduates are in-staters, the majority from Southern California and many of those from wealthy Orange County—although an impressive 51 percent of incoming first-years are first-generation college students, and 38 percent qualify for Pell Grants. Twelve percent hail from foreign countries. The campus leans liberal, but students are generally not as active in political or social causes as their peers at some other UC campuses. Students of color account for more than two-thirds of the student body, with Asian Americans representing 37 percent, Hispanics/Latinos 27 percent, Black students just 2 percent, and multiracial students 6 percent. One senior notes, "Cultural groups seem to segregate from each other," although several initiatives and events, including the Cross-Cultural Center, the Community Roots Festival, and the Deconstruction Zone Series, are designed to educate and engage the campus community in diversity, social justice, and cultural wellness. Merit scholarships averaging $10,200 are awarded annually, as are more than 130 athletic awards.

Forty-seven percent of undergraduates live on campus. Condominium-style dorms, both single sex and co-ed, are "exceptional compared to the high-rise dormitories of other institutions," says one senior. Others agree that the homey campus dwellings provide a good experience for new students. Although first-years are guaranteed on-campus housing for two years, 19 percent of them choose to live off campus, which can create a slight commuter-school atmosphere. Most upperclassmen opt for themed housing, fraternity and sorority houses, or off-campus dwellings, often on the beach.

One student remarks, "You have to find the social life on this campus. It won't find you." The 18 fraternities and 18 sororities attract a small percentage of students, and each has something going on every weekend. Students of legal age can unwind at the campus pub. The one event that brings everybody out is Celebrate UCI, a daylong, student-run festival featuring live performances, free food, carnival games and rides, and a car show.

The Claire Trevor School of Arts offers nationally ranked programs in dance, drama, music, studio art, and music theater.

"Graduate students teach lower-division writing courses."

Students may choose from more than 85 majors, and the Campuswide Honors Program is available for top students.

If life on campus is slow, beyond it is not. That's because UCI is located just 50 miles from L.A., five miles from the beach, and a little more than an hour from the ski slopes. Catalina Island, with beaches and hiking trails, is a quick boat trip off Newport Harbor; Mexico is two hours away. While some students treasure the city of Irvine's quiet setting, others lament its "lackluster, homogeneous communities" and conservative feel.

UCI fields 20 Division I Anteater athletic teams. Tennis and cross-country are perennial Big West powerhouses, and men's basketball is a recent conference champion. Men's volleyball and water polo are nationally ranked. There is no football team, but intramurals are extremely popular, as is the state-of-the-art campus recreation center. UCI's varsity eSports program for organized, multiplayer video game competitions is the first of its kind at a public research university.

> **"You have to find the social life on this campus. It won't find you."**

What lures students to UCI is its top-name professors, innovative academic programs, and the chance to be a part of its cutting-edge research. For those who come here prepared to keep their heads buried in a book for a few years, the reward can be an exceptional education. Where else can you study anteaters in the lab and then cheer them on in the gym?

If You Apply To ›

Irvine: Regular decision. SATs or ACTs: not considered. Does not accept the Common Application. Apply to a particular college, school, or program. Application includes optional question about gender/sexual identity.

UC Los Angeles

405 Hilgard Avenue, Los Angeles, CA 90095

Tucked into exclusive Bel Air with the beach, the mountains, and chic Hollywood hangouts all within easy reach. The adjacent town of Westwood is an ideal student hangout. Practically everything is offered here, but—no surprise, given its location in La La Land—the programs in arts and media are some of the best in the world. Less politically active than Berkeley but just as difficult to get into.

With 15 Nobel Prizes awarded to alumni and faculty, you might think UCLA is an intellectual brain trust. Or with a long list of well-known and highly accomplished alumni in the arts, film, and sports, maybe UCLA is some sort of incubator for truly talented and gifted people. Well, UCLA is all that and more. A superb faculty, a reputation for outstanding academics, and a powerful athletics program make this university a full-service place to study.

UCLA's prime location—sandwiched between two glamorous neighborhoods (Beverly Hills and Bel Air) and a short drive from the beach, Hollywood, the Sunset Strip, and downtown Los Angeles—makes it appealing for students who want more from their college experience than going to class. The beautifully landscaped, 419-acre campus features a range of architectural styles, with Romanesque/Italian Renaissance as the dominant motif, providing only one of a number of reasons students enjoy staying on campus. A wealth of gardens—botanical, Japanese, and sculpture—add a touch of quiet elegance. The campus is divided into North and South. The north part tends to house liberal arts departments, whereas the South tends to house math and science departments.

First-year students are encouraged to participate in a three-day summer orientation that provides workshops, counseling, an introduction to the campus and community, and a chance to register for classes. In fall quarter, first-years can begin a yearlong cluster of interdisciplinary courses on topics such as Environment and Sustainability or enroll in small-group seminars such as Perceptions of U.S. Abroad or Mental Illness and Movies. To graduate, first-year students are required to take (or test out of) quantitative reasoning and English composition courses. Lab science and a language requirement are necessary for a liberal arts degree, and all students must take a course on diversity. Students often have the opportunity to participate in capstone projects in which they must use the methodological training of their discipline and integrate what they have learned across topics and fields.

Strong programs abound at UCLA, which joined the UC system in 1919, and many are considered among the best in the nation. UCLA is well established in the STEM fields; the Samueli School of Engineering and Applied Science is highly regarded and sets the tone on campus, and biological sciences, mathematics, and chemistry are also strong. The School of Theater, Film, and Television is first-rate, and its students have the opportunity to study in Verona, Italy, with the Theater Overseas program. The popular Herb Alpert School of Music offers an institute of jazz performance and boasts legend Herbie Hancock among its distinguished faculty. Dance and design/media arts are standouts in the School of the Arts and Architecture. Sociology, psychology, political science, and economics enroll the most students.

"We are spoiled by incredible faculty at UCLA."

UCLA gets more applications than any other college in the country—more than 145,000 per year from prospective first-years—and the academic environment is intense, especially in STEM fields. Although 47 percent of all undergraduate classes have fewer than 20 students, required core classes, usually taken in the first two years, can be as large as 300 to 400 people, with smaller sections. Students warn that some profs are mainly interested in their research, but a political science major says, "We are spoiled by incredible faculty at UCLA—top researchers in their field and amazing lecturers." Two undergraduate research centers, one for the sciences and one for the arts, humanities, and social sciences, help students develop research skills and connect them with opportunities. "For more difficult classes, there are also TAs who can give you further instructions," notes an education and social transformation major. Faculty-led study abroad programs are popular, and "financial aid travels with you," according to a junior.

"UCLA students love a challenge," says a computer science major. "They are also very invested in building up their peers and the community around them." While 81 percent of undergraduates are California residents, a linguistics and psychology major says, "The student body at UCLA is quite diverse." Asian Americans account for 30 percent of UCLA's student population, Hispanics/Latinos

"The student body at UCLA is quite diverse."

24 percent, Black students 3 percent, and multiracial students 8 percent. Seven percent are international. The political atmosphere is liberal; UCLA is one of the few universities in the nation with a gay fraternity and a lesbian sorority, and students often advocate for social justice issues. Merit scholarships are available, averaging $9,300 each, as well as athletic scholarships. Thirty percent of incoming students are Pell-eligible.

Sixty percent of undergraduates, including almost all first-years, live on campus in the residential area known as "the Hill"; first-year students are guaranteed four consecutive years of university housing, and the dorms get great reviews. Residential learning communities with a faculty member in residence are an option for those who wish to bond with classmates over shared interests. Three residential dining

(continued)

Grad in 6 Years: 93%
Returning First-years: 97%
Academics: ✎ ✎ ✎ ✎ ✎
Social: 🗩 🗩 🗩
Q of L: ★ ★ ★
Admissions: (310) 825-3101
Email Address: N/A

Strong Programs:
Biological Sciences
Dance
Design and Media Arts
Engineering
Mathematics
Music
Theater, Film, and Television

Spring Sing, a campuswide student talent show presided over by celebrity judges, is a favorite tradition.

halls, along with seven restaurants, and snack bars serve meals that students rave about. "I have friends who attend other universities who will visit me just so they can eat UCLA's food," says a senior. UCLA has its own police department that keeps the campus safe, and a junior says, "Our Title IX officer is actively working to spread awareness [of sexual assault] and connect those affected with the right resources." Adds a senior, "Mental health services are pretty easy to find."

Consistent with UCLA's huge enrollment, there is no shortage of social options on campus. "The social scene is as active as the academics," cheers a senior. "Sometimes I wonder how people manage studying so hard and 'partying' hard." Eleven percent of men and 12 percent of women join one of UCLA's nearly 60 fraternities and sororities, and a senior says Greek life "is a fun way to get involved and meet people, but it does not monopolize social life." The university's alcohol policy is similar to that of other UC schools—open consumption is a no-no. Top-name entertainers, political figures, and speakers of all kinds come to the campus; film and theater presentations are frequent, and the air is thick with live music. Spring Sing, a campuswide student talent show presided over by celebrity judges, is a favorite tradition. Volunteer Day is a big deal here, too, and attracts more than 2,000 student volunteers annually.

> "I have friends who attend other universities who will visit me just so they can eat UCLA's food."

With all the attractions of the City of Angels at UCLA's doorstep, social life is hardly confined to campus. "There is constantly a variety of different concerts, plays, art shows, comedy shows, and festivals in L.A. that students can take advantage of," says a junior. The hopping Westwood neighborhood, which borders the university, has at least 15 movie theaters and scores of coffee shops and affordable restaurants, although the shops tend to cater to the upper class. The beach is five miles away, and the mountains are only a short drive. Although public transportation is cheap, it's also relatively inconvenient (although new bus routes have eased this somewhat). The easiest solution is to live close to campus and ride a bike.

The UCLA Bruins have won a staggering number of collegiate titles, including 124 Division I team national championships. Basketball is a crowd-pleaser—the women won the 2026 NCAA title—and women's soccer, men's and women's water polo, softball, and men's volleyball are all strong. The Bruins football team has played more games in the Rose Bowl than any other school—it's their home field! Along with crosstown rival USC, UCLA moved to the Big Ten Conference in 2024, and UCLA fans regard their intracity rivalry with enthusiasm. Beat USC Week, the week leading up to the football game between the two, is an event, featuring a bonfire, concert, and blood drive. About a third of students compete in club and intramural sports.

"Although everyone is striving for excellence, UCLA allows everyone to experience life," muses a junior. "That means taking time to prepare for exams and do it well, while also making time to play beach volleyball at Sunset Rec with all of your friends." A leading research center, over 140 fields of study, distinguished faculty members, and outstanding athletics make UCLA one of the most prestigious universities in the nation. And despite the huge size, students still feel they are part of a tight-knit community bubbling with Bruin pride.

Overlaps

UC Berkeley, UC Davis, UC Irvine, UC San Diego, UC Santa Barbara, Harvard, Stanford, University of Southern California

If You Apply To ›

UCLA: Regular decision. SATs or ACTs: not considered. Does not accept the Common Application. Apply to a particular college, school, or program. Application includes optional question about gender/sexual identity.

UC Riverside

900 University Avenue, Riverside, CA 92521

One of the most diverse UC schools, one of the least difficult to get into, and offers a more personal touch. UCR's traditional strengths in the sciences are bolstered by expanding opportunities for undergraduate research. Since many students commute, social life is relatively tame. While some complain of a lack of nightlife in Riverside, they readily agree that activities on campus make up for it.

Lacking the big-name reputation and booming athletic programs of many other UC schools, UC Riverside has chosen to place its emphasis on something that not all universities consider to be an overwhelming priority: the student. "At UCR, belonging, motivation, and sustainable progress for students, the region, and the world are real," say administrators. Riverside offers strong academic and cocurricular programs, and a richly diverse community. "Students are well taken care of and get personal attention," says one satisfied senior. Though part of the UC system, UC Riverside is a breed apart.

Located 60 miles east of Los Angeles, UCR is surrounded by mountains on the outskirts of the city of Riverside. The beautifully landscaped, 1,200-acre campus consists of mainly modern architecture, with a 160-foot bell tower (with a 48-bell carillon) marking its center. Wide lawns, clusters of oaks, and a botanical garden make ideal spots for relaxing between classes. Acres of citrus groves form a half-circle on the outer edges of campus and perfume the air. New construction includes the School of Business building, featuring an auditorium, classrooms, and more, as well as new North District student housing that opened in fall 2025.

All students are required to meet extensive "breadth requirements" that include courses in English composition, natural sciences and math, humanities, and social sciences. Some majors include a foreign language requirement. The campus libraries have an impressive four million volumes, an interlibrary loan system within the UC system, and hundreds of electronic databases, including a specialized science fiction research collection. UCR's California Museum of Photography is located in downtown Riverside and accessible online.

Decades ago, researchers at the Citrus Experiment Station in Riverside perfected the growing methods for the imported navel orange, making discoveries to protect the fruit from disease and pests and saving California's citrus industry. Riverside continues to excel in plant biology and entomology. But the campus has grown since its founding in 1954 to include excellent programs spanning a number of disciplines. The biological sciences program is

> **"The professors are usually happy to help students, as are the teaching assistants."**

UCR's most prestigious and demanding, especially the medical biology track. The Bourns College of Engineering, which has strong majors in computer science, computer engineering, and environmental engineering, is also quite selective. Creative writing is notable, and Riverside is one of few U.S. schools that offers an undergraduate major in public policy. Business administration, biology, psychology, and sociology are the most popular majors, and new majors have been added in actuarial science, Black studies, robotics engineering, among others. A number of 4–1 B.S./M.S. degrees are also available.

Students say the academic climate is cooperative. "Instead of being super competitive," says a student, "I see more students working together to get the job done."

Website: www.ucr.edu
Location: Small City
Public
Total Enrollment: 25,564
Undergraduates: 22,080
Male/Female: 46/51
Financial Aid: 74%
Pell Grant: 46%
Expense: Pub $ $ $
Student Loans: 45%
Average Debt: $
Applicants: 57,714
Accepted: 77%
Enrolled: 12%
Grad in 6 Years: 76%
Returning First-years: 88%
Academics: ✍ ✍ ✍
Social: 🎉 🎉
Q of L: ★ ★ ★
Admissions: (951) 827-3411
Email Address:
  admissions@ucr.edu

Strong Programs:
Biological Sciences
Computer Engineering
Computer Science
Creative Writing
Entomology
Environmental Engineering
Plant Biology
Public Policy

Currently, 27 percent of undergraduate classes have fewer than 20 students. Research is an institutional priority for faculty, and the quality of instruction can vary. Still, UCR has a tradition of undergraduate and faculty interaction; 32 percent of undergrads conduct research, and a wide range of research grants are available during the academic year. "The professors are usually happy to help students, as are the teaching assistants," says a psychology and education major. The University Honors Program offers exceptional students further academic challenges, in addition to extracurricular activities and special seminars for first-years. Talented student singers, dancers, and actors can earn stipends for performing in the community through an arts outreach program. Faculty-led, five-week summer study abroad options are expanding, and through the UC system, students have access to more than 150 international programs in over 40 countries.

Ninety-five percent of UCR undergraduates are from California, mainly L.A., Riverside, San Bernardino, and Orange County; 3 percent are international. "UCR is one of the most diverse universities in the nation," a political science major says, which creates "a blended environment of different cultures, nationalities, and social statuses." Indeed, Asian Americans account for 36 percent of the students, Hispanics/Latinos 40 percent, Black students 4 percent, and multiracial students 5 percent. A hefty 46 percent of first-time first-year students receive Pell Grants. As part of the UC commitment to diversity, UCR's Costo Hall houses centers for various ethnicities, for women, and for LGBTQ students. The political atmosphere is liberal, and a junior comments, "The student body is pretty chill and open-minded." Numerous merit scholarships averaging $5,600 are doled out every year, as well as more than 200 athletic scholarships in 17 sports.

Housing is relatively easy to obtain, but the quality varies greatly. "While West Lothian looks like a prison, Pentland Hills is like a resort," says one student. Thirty-four percent of undergrads live in college-owned housing. Construction is ongoing on the massive North District development, which will eventually add about 6,000 beds, new dining and athletic facilities, and other mixed-use spaces to accommodate the university's growing student population. A number of academically oriented living/learning communities are popular with first-years, who are guaranteed housing. Campus dining is generally described as adequate. Students say they feel safe on campus; security measures include an escort service, patrolling security officers, and regular training on sexual assault prevention and intervention.

"UCR has grown immensely over the past few years."

Fraternities and sororities attract 3 percent of the men and 4 percent of the women. "There is always something going on, whether it be a concert, lecture, or sorority/fraternity party," one sophomore says. Campus hangouts, including the renovated and expanded Barn, have live bands and comedy nights, and a cultural arts program brings professional shows to campus. Every Wednesday, the campus can enjoy a "nooner," where the music department puts on free concerts and lectures during lunch. Returning students are welcomed back every year with a campuswide block party, and the Spring Splash concert brings in hot bands. University Village is a commercial center offering a movie theater, restaurants, and an arcade right on the edge of campus. Riverside weather is temperate except during the summer months, when the heat and haze combine to make a trip to the ocean look really inviting. The coast is only about 45 minutes by freeway and the desert an hour east. Big Bear and numerous ski resorts are also within an hour's drive.

The Riverside Highlanders compete in the Division I Big West Conference in 17 sports, and the men's soccer and women's golf teams have been successful in recent years. A recreational program in men's and women's karate has turned out national champions. A student recreation center offers a health-club atmosphere with sand volleyball, weight and workout machines, and intramural sports, including perennially popular basketball and soccer leagues.

All in all, Riverside is expanding and becoming stronger, albeit not without some growing pains, including tuition and living costs. But it still offers more personal attention to its students than many of its larger, sister UC campuses. "UCR has grown immensely over the past few years," one sophomore says. "The emphasis for the future is to establish a name for UCR, to let the nation know what a wonderful university this is."

If You Apply To ›

Riverside: Regular decision. SATs or ACTs: not considered. Does not accept the Common Application. Apply to a particular college, school, or program. Application includes optional question about gender/sexual identity.

UC San Diego

9500 Gilman Drive, La Jolla, CA 92093

Applications have increased 70 percent at this seaside paradise. UC San Diego now rivals better-known Berkeley and UCLA as the Cal campus of choice for top students. Eight undergraduate colleges break the university down to a more manageable size. Best known for science, engineering, and the famed Scripps Institution of Oceanography.

Set against the serene beauty of La Jolla's beaches, UC San Diego invites students to catch as much relaxation time as they do study time. But San Diego, established in 1960, is now the research star of the UC system, and its faculty rates high nationally among public institutions in science productivity. And within each of the eight undergraduate colleges, a system that offers undergraduates more intimate settings, students are honing their minds with the classics and the cutting edge in academics. San Diegans tend to be more mellow than the average Southern Californian, and the students here follow suit. But UC San Diego is bubbling with intellectual energy and the healthy desire to be at the top of the UC system.

San Diego's tree-lined campus sits high on a bluff overlooking the Pacific in the seaside resort of La Jolla. The predominant architectural theme is contemporary, with a few out-of-the-ordinary structures, including a library that looks like an inverted pyramid. Another tinge of the postmodern is the nation's largest neon sculpture, which wraps around one of the high-rise academic buildings and consists of seven-foot-tall letters that spell out the seven virtues superimposed over the seven vices. Work is ongoing on a significant campus expansion that will add several new academic and residential facilities, including the Theatre District Living and Learning Neighborhood, with around 2,000 new beds for undergrads, classrooms, restaurants, and retail space.

UC San Diego's eight undergraduate colleges have their own sets of general education requirements, their own personalities, and differing ideals on which they are based. Revelle College, the oldest, is the most rigorous and mandates that students become equally acquainted with a certain level of coursework in the humanities, sciences, and social sciences, as well as fulfill a language requirement. John Muir College allows more flexibility in the distribution of requirements.

Website: www.ucsd.edu
Location: City Outskirts
Public
Total Enrollment: 42,178
Undergraduates: 33,844
Male/Female: 44/53
Financial Aid: 78%
Pell Grant: 36%
Expense: Pub $ $ $ $
Student Loans: 31%
Average Debt: $
Applicants: 134,455
Accepted: 27%
Enrolled: 20%
Grad in 6 Years: 86%
Returning First-years: 94%
Academics: ✍ ✍ ✍ ✍ ✍
Social: 🗩 🗩 🗩
Q of L: ★ ★ ★ ★
Admissions: (858) 534-4831
Email Address:
  admissionsreply@ucsd.edu

Strong Programs:
Biology
Chemistry

Thurgood Marshall College was founded to emphasize and encourage social awareness. Like Revelle, it places equal weight on sciences, social sciences, and humanities, but it also stresses a liberal arts education based on "an examination of the human condition in a multicultural society." Earl Warren College has developed a highly organized internship program that gives its undergraduates more practical experience than the others do. Eleanor Roosevelt College devotes its curriculum to international and cross-cultural studies. Sixth College focuses on art, culture, and technology, with the aim of preparing students to work collaboratively and enjoy working in their communities. Seventh College focuses on large-scale, global issues—such as climate change, mass migration, new technologies—and interdisciplinary approaches to addressing "A Changing Planet." At Eighth College, students take Critical Community Engagement courses to gain an "understanding of factors that have historically led to discrimination, structural and institutional racism, social exclusion," and other challenges. Prospective students apply to the university but must indicate their preferred college.

UC San Diego's programs in science, engineering, and computer science have global reputations and are "not for the faint of heart," says one student. The engineering school, notable for offerings like structural engineering and nanoengineering, is particularly competitive, and a limit to the number of students who can declare these majors means acceptance usually requires an A average and top test scores in entry-level courses. The nearby Scripps Institution of Oceanography is also excellent. Biological sciences (the most popular majors) and chemistry are strengths, but you really can't go wrong in any of the hard sciences. Although the humanities and social sciences are not as solid in comparison, international studies, psychology, and cognitive science are also popular. Students may also devise their own majors. Twenty-one percent of students study abroad; San Diego's five-week, faculty-led Global Seminars in the summer are especially popular.

> **"We enjoy extracurricular activities, but academic excellence is our priority."**

San Diego operates on the quarter system, which means students cram three or four courses into 10 weeks. Science students in particular find the workload intense. The quality of research done by the faculty, a handful of whom are Nobel laureates, is extremely high, and students have ample opportunities to assist with research, sometimes as early as their first year. Students say the typical scenario of research over teaching is not as common at UC San Diego. Even so, given the large class sizes—27 percent of undergraduate courses enroll more than 50 students—"you end up teaching a lot of the material to yourself," according to an anthropology major.

A theater major notes that the university's academic intensity "does not mean that all the students here are nerdy. We enjoy athletics and extracurricular activities, but academic excellence is our priority." San Diego ranks highly among public colleges and universities in the percentage of graduates who go on to earn a Ph.D. and in the percentage of students accepted to medical school. Ten percent of undergraduates are from states outside of California, and 11 percent are international. Representation of students of color is high, with 35 percent of the student body being Asian American, 27 percent Hispanic/Latino, 2 percent Black, and 6 percent multiracial. Diversity education includes a Cross-Cultural Center for students, faculty, and staff that provides activities, brown-bag luncheons, and programs on race relations. Merit scholarships averaging $13,600 are available, and the university offers more than 200 athletic scholarships.

> **"The residence halls are very nice, with all the amenities."**

Each of the UCSD colleges has its own housing complex, with either dorms or apartments. Most first-years live on campus and are guaranteed housing for their first two years. "The residence halls are very nice, with all the amenities," says an animal physiology major. Dorm residents are required to buy a meal plan, and their Dining Dollars are good at any of the campus's nearly 20 eateries. Overall, 48 percent of undergraduates live on campus; by junior year, students usually decide to take up residence in La Jolla proper or nearby Del Mar, often in beachside apartments. That can be costly, but if you are willing to relinquish the luxury of a five-minute walk to the beach, a short commute will bring you relatively affordable housing.

"La Jolla is a rich, conservative, retired, white, snobbish community," one sophomore says. "Not a college town!" Cars are, of course, an inescapable part of Southern California life, and owning one—many people do—makes off-campus living even better. "No car equals no fun," one international studies major says, although trying to park on campus can be difficult. Mexico is a half-hour drive (even nearer than the desert, where many students go hiking), and the two-hour trip to Los Angeles makes for a nice weekend jaunt.

For those looking to stay closer to campus, the Pacific Beach and downtown San Diego, with its zoo, Sea World, and Balboa Park, are all only 12 miles away. Torrey Pines State Natural Reserve is great for outdoor enthusiasts. "Most students hang out at the dance clubs, jazz bars, and great restaurants in the Gaslamp Quarter," says a senior. The university offers more than 750 student organizations, and 14 percent of the men and 14 percent of the women join a fraternity or sorority. The campus is dry, but some students claim that lax RAs and good fake IDs make for easy underage drinking. Although campus life is relatively tame, everyone looks forward to university-sponsored festivals, including the Open House, UnOlympics, and the Reggae Festival. The biggest annual event pays tribute to a hideously loud and colorful statue of the Sun God, which is the unofficial mascot for this sun-streaked student body. The Sun God Festival has drawn big-name performers such as Drake and Wiz Khalifa.

Although San Diego will never be mistaken for a sports-crazed school à la USC, UCSD's Tritons now compete in the Division I Big West Conference. Volleyball, water polo, soccer, basketball, and tennis teams have traditionally been the strongest. The school's club surfing team has won seven national championships. For weekend warriors, classes are available in windsurfing, sailing, scuba diving, and kayaking at the nearby Mission Bay Aquatic Center. Most students participate in one intramural league or another, and according to one, if you're not on a team, "you're not a true UC San Diego student."

The students at UC San Diego are exceptionally serious and out for an excellent education. But the pace (study, party, relax, study more) and the props (sun, sand, Frisbees, and flip-flops) give the rigorous curriculum an inimitable flavor that undergraduates would not change. Indeed, many believe they have the best setup in higher education: "a beautiful beachfront environment that eases a life of academic rigor."

Overlaps

UC Berkeley, UC Santa Barbara, UCLA, U of I at Urbana–Champaign, University of Michigan, UVA, University of Washington, UW–Madison

If You Apply To ›

San Diego: Regular decision. SATs or ACTs: not considered. Does not accept the Common Application. Apply to a particular college, school, or program. Application includes optional question about gender/sexual identity.

552 University Road, Santa Barbara, CA 93106

Willpower is the watchword at UC Santa Barbara. On a beautiful day with the sound of waves crashing in the distance, that's what it takes to hang in there with pen, paper, laptop, or book. Fairly or not, Santa Barbara is known as the party animal of the UC system. In the classroom, science is the best bet. Free spirits should check out the unusual College for Creative Studies.

Website: www.ucsb.edu
Location: Suburban
Public
Total Enrollment: 25,609
Undergraduates: 22,674
Male/Female: 41/57
Financial Aid: 72%
Pell Grant: 32%
Expense: Pub $ $ $
Student Loans: 28%
Average Debt: $
Applicants: 110,266
Accepted: 33%
Enrolled: 14%
Grad in 6 Years: 83%
Returning First-years: 93%
Academics: ✍ ✍ ✍ ✍
Social: 🗩 🗩 🗩 🗩
Q of L: ★ ★ ★ ★
Admissions: (805) 893-2881
Email Address:
  admissions@ucsb.edu

Strong Programs:
Chemical Engineering
Chemistry
Economics and Accounting
Environmental Science
Global Studies
Marine Biology
Physics
Sociology

For students at UC Santa Barbara, California's famed beaches serve as both classroom and playground. On weekends, sun-worshipping students grab surfboards and don bikinis and head to the water for some serious fun. During the week, those same students can likely be found studying technology rather than tan lines. "On a nice sunny day, the beaches and grassy areas will be flooded with students," says a first-year student, "but most of them are there with a book."

UCSB provides a comfortable mixture of work and play that is unique even in the UC system. Located just a stone's throw from the beach, UC Santa Barbara's 1,000-acre campus is bordered on two sides by the Pacific Ocean with a clear view of the Channel Islands. On the landward side are a nature preserve and the predominantly student community of Isla Vista, and five miles to the north lie the Santa Ynez Mountains. The campus, which joined the UC system in 1944, features mainly 1950s Southern California architecture with an atmosphere to match.

UCSB's general education program features the usual distribution requirements and coursework in writing, European traditions, world cultures, quantitative relationships, and ethnicity. Not surprisingly, the marine biology department stands

> **"The workload is definitely strenuous at times."**

out among the university's best, capitalizing on the school's aquatic resources; chemical engineering, physics, and chemistry are also well regarded. The Bren School of Environmental Science and Management is home to world-renowned faculty and has boasted six Nobel Prize winners in economics, chemistry, and physics. The most popular majors include sociology, psychological and brain sciences, communication, and global studies. The economics and accounting program is strong, and the courses are geared toward taking and passing the CPA exam, so graduation is usually followed by a mass recruitment by California's big accounting firms. The College of Creative Studies offers an unstructured curriculum to about 400 self-starters ready for advanced and independent work in the arts, math, or the sciences. The interdisciplinary global studies major, another noteworthy option, combines language study with global history, culture, economics, and politics.

"The academic climate of UC Santa Barbara is very collaborative," says one sophomore, but "the workload is definitely strenuous at times." Fifty-six percent of all undergraduate classes have fewer than 20 students, but teaching is a hit-or-miss affair, according to one junior: "Many of the professors are more interested in their research than teaching a class." On the flip side, many opportunities are available for undergrads to assist professors and get involved in undergraduate research. For those who seek time away, Santa Barbara is the headquarters of the UC system's Education Abroad Program, which sends students to any of 120 host universities worldwide; 17 percent of UCSB students study abroad.

UCSB students, 91 percent of whom are California residents, are traditionally public-spirited and laid-back. "There are some who aren't the most academically focused, but for the most part, I'd say the students are great at balancing their academic and social lives while getting involved in helping the community," says one mechanical engineering major. Asian Americans contribute 20 percent of the student body, Black students make up 2 percent, Hispanics/Latinos account for 28 percent, and multiracial students add 8 percent; 9 percent are international. The campus vibe is decidedly liberal. "Some of the biggest political issues on campus have to do with the environment. As a coastal area, UCSB is very susceptible to pollution," explains one student. Merit scholarships averaging $10,700 and more than 200 athletic scholarships are available for those who qualify.

University housing, which includes both dorms and privately run residence halls, is comfortable, well maintained, and much sought after. "Our on-campus housing is amazing, right in front of the beach," a junior says. "They come fully furnished, with high-speed Internet, cable, telephone lines, and a great atmosphere." Thirty-eight percent of students, most of whom are first-years, snag on-campus housing. Meals in the dorms are available to residents and nonresidents alike and are, according to most students, more than simply edible. "Great food and tons of it!" cheers one student. While students say they feel safe on campus, one oft used motto is "four years, four bikes," because of the frequency of bicycle thefts. Regarding campus sexual assault, "The school has provided as many resources as it can, really," says a chemical engineering major, and it "does its best to prevent it."

> **"Some of the biggest political issues on campus have to do with the environment."**

"It is really easy to get involved and make friends through campus activities," says a sophomore. "Additionally, the social scene off campus is really thriving in the community of Isla Vista." Neighboring Isla Vista has welcomed its student population—after all, most of its population is UCSB students. Students in turn are very active in the community. The fraternities and sororities, which attract 7 percent of men and 13 percent of women, are known for their philanthropy. The campus is dry, and one student says, "Drinking alcohol on campus is pretty well regulated and not easy to do." Movies and concerts are also available, and the mountains, Los Padres National Forest, and L.A. are all an easy drive away. The annual Extravaganza is an all-day free concert, and students are known to go wild on Halloween and dress up for the entire weekend. "Halloween is our claim to fame," boasts one student.

All of UCSB's varsity teams (the Gauchos) compete in Division I, and the most successful include soccer, water polo, baseball, volleyball, swimming, and basketball. A never-ending rotation of intramurals is available on and off the beach, and about a quarter of the students participate. Ultimate Frisbee is also quite popular, as well as nationally competitive.

Sure, UCSB students love to play, but that's not why most come to this coastal institution. "If there was anything that I would like to improve, it would be the lingering reputation UCSB has as a party school," observes one student. "This reputation is more of a relic from times past." That said, UCSB students also know a good thing when they see it: Not everyone gets to spend four years near the beach and come away with a degree.

Overlaps

UC Berkeley, UC Davis, UC Irvine, UCLA, UC San Diego

If You Apply To ›

Santa Barbara: Regular decision. SATs or ACTs: not considered. Does not accept the Common Application. Apply to a particular college, school, or program. Application includes optional question about gender/sexual identity.

1156 High Street, Santa Cruz, CA 95064

From its flower-child beginnings, UC Santa Cruz has wandered back toward the mainstream. The yoga mats and surfboards still abound, and Sammy the banana slug is still the mascot, but students are a lot more conventional than their predecessors. The emphasis continues to be on environmental stewardship, community engagement, and teaching students how—not what—to think. Inadequate student housing is a huge problem.

Website: www.ucsc.edu
Location: Small Town
Public
Total Enrollment: 19,101
Undergraduates: 17,251
Male/Female: 45/50
Financial Aid: 52%
Pell Grant: 31%
Expense: Pub $ $ $
Student Loans: 37%
Average Debt: $
Applicants: 71,696
Accepted: 66%
Enrolled: 9%
Grad in 6 Years: 75%
Returning First-years: 88%
Academics: 🖋 🖋 🖋 🖋
Social: 🗩 🗩 🗩
Q of L: ★ ★ ★ ★ ★
Admissions: (831) 459-4008
Email Address:
  admissions@ucsc.edu

Strong Programs:
Biology
Community Studies
Computer Engineering
Computer Game Design
Environmental Studies
Linguistics
Marine Biology
Robotics Engineering

UC Santa Cruz, still a baby in the UC system, was born during the radical '60s when it reigned as the ultimate alternative school, a place that consciously rebelled against the stodginess of educational institutions. The founding vision of an integrated learning environment remains to this day, and every undergraduate affiliates with one of the residential colleges. Progressive thought continues to flourish, as does a strong academic program that strives to focus on undergraduate education. Students still come to UC Santa Cruz to do their own thing.

The campus, among the most beautiful in the nation, is set on a 2,000-acre expanse of meadowland and redwood forest overlooking Monterey Bay. Bike paths and hiking trails wind throughout the redwood-tree-filled campus, and the beach is a quick drive away—or a spectacular bike ride or scenic hike. The buildings range from 1860 Cowell Ranch farm structures to the award-winning, modern residential colleges, whose styles range from Mediterranean to Japanese to sleek concrete block. Thanks to a unique building code, nothing

> **"Racial, ethnic, and cultural diversity is celebrated and strongly encouraged by the majority of the students here."**

may be built taller than two-thirds the height of the nearest redwood tree. The 26,000-square-foot Digital Arts Research Center serves as a social and intellectual hub for UC Santa Cruz's Arts Division. Newer additions to campus include the 35,000-square-foot Kresge College Academic Center, housing multiple departments and classrooms. UC Santa Cruz's Coastal Science Campus is home to expansive greenhouses, the Ocean Health Building, and more centers that support research and teaching on coastal conservation, ecology, climate change impacts, and similar concerns.

UC Santa Cruz's academic offerings range as widely as its architecture and feature both traditional and innovative programs, but overall, the emphasis is on the liberal arts and sciences, and a majority of the students eventually go on to graduate study. To graduate, students must fulfill a standard set of distribution requirements, in addition to taking one of three "perspectives" courses focused on environmental awareness, human behavior, or technology and society, and a course on creative process, collaborative endeavor, or service learning. A disciplinary communication requirement helps students develop writing skills specific to their chosen field of study. All seniors complete a capstone experience.

Led by marine biology and biology, the sciences are UC Santa Cruz's strongest suit. Science facilities include state-of-the-art laboratories; the Institute of Marine Sciences, which boasts one of the largest groups of experts on marine mammals in the nation; and the nearby Lick Observatory for budding stargazers. UCSC's Baskin School of Engineering offers strong programs in robotics engineering and computer engineering. The computer game design B.S. is noteworthy as the first such major in the UC system, and linguistics is strong. Students in STEM fields may benefit from research or internship opportunities coordinated through the university's satellite campus in Silicon Valley. UCSC offers more than the average number of interdisciplinary programs, including feminist, Latin American/Latino, and critical race and ethnic studies; environmental studies and community studies are standouts. The most popular majors are computer science, psychology, business management economics, and computer engineering. New majors are available in creative technologies and Latin American and Latino studies. While most students pursue traditional majors, the possibility is still there for eclectically minded students to pursue "history of consciousness" or just about anything else they can get a faculty member to OK. The Italian Studies major has been discontinued. Thirty-two percent of students engage in faculty-guided undergraduate research. Study abroad is available in more than 46 countries through 420 available options; field study and internships are also encouraged. More than 30 percent of students also participate in some form of community service and volunteer work.

"Courses are very rigorous," warns one undergrad. Though the curriculum is demanding and the quarter system keeps the academic pace fast, the atmosphere is noncompetitive. Classes can be large, with 35 percent enrolling more than 50 students, but most professors at UC Santa Cruz are there to teach. "I've been very impressed with how accessible professors are," says a sophomore. "Whether it's via email or regular office hours, I feel very comfortable talking to all of my professors."

"Before I came here, I was told that UCSC was a 'hippie-dippie' college," says one student, "but it's not true at all." Even so, UC Santa Cruz remains the most liberal of the UC campuses and, according to one student, is "still a school with a social conscience." Ninety-three percent of undergraduates are Californians, though the university always manages to lure a few Easterners; 2 percent are international. Asian Americans account for 24 percent, Hispanics/Latinos 29 percent, Black students 2 percent, and multiracial students 9 percent. "Racial, ethnic, and cultural diversity is celebrated and strongly encouraged by the majority of the students here," reports a politics major. One-third of incoming first-years qualify for Pell Grants. Merit scholarships, which average $8,000 each, are available, but there are no athletic scholarships.

> **"I was told that UCSC was a 'hippie-dippie' college, but it's not true at all."**

In an effort to become what one official calls a "near-perfect hybrid" between the large university and the small college, campus life revolves around the residential colleges, each of which has dedicated faculty fellows and support staff. Some dorms have their own dining halls, including at Rachel Carson College, where a recent renovation nearly doubled the available seating. Dining halls are said to have reasonably good food; students may also opt to join a food co-op. The CARE (Campus Advocacy, Resources, and Education) office provides education on issues of sexual assault and support to survivors. The university provides housing for more than half of undergraduates but guarantees it for only one year. Finding subsequent accommodations in the Santa Cruz rental market—among the most expensive in the nation—can be frustrating. While a renovation of Kresge College added 400 beds in 2023, the school announced in summer 2025 that construction of the Heller Drive development, a major housing project aiming to add 2,900 more beds, was delayed and wouldn't begin until 2027.

A dozen fraternities and sororities attract 5 percent of the men and 6 percent of the women, respectively. Students 21 and over are allowed to drink alcohol on campus, although not in public areas, and parties must be registered. Around 200 student organizations on campus cover a wide range of interests. The beach and resort town of Santa Cruz, with its boardwalk and amusement park, is only a 10-minute bike ride away, although pedaling back up the hill takes much longer.

Those looking for city lights can take the mountainous highway to San Jose (35 miles away) or the scenic coastal highway to San Francisco (75 miles), or ride a bus to either city. Monterey, Big Sur, the Napa Valley, and the Sierras are easily accessible by car.

Although UC Santa Cruz fields only a handful of varsity teams, which slug it out in Division III, students love their school mascot, Sammy the banana slug. Men's and women's cross-country, men's and women's volleyball, women's soccer, and men's swim and dive have performed well in recent years. Participation in intramurals and club sports is widespread, with soccer, volleyball, and basketball drawing the most students. Sailing and scuba diving are among the many physical education classes offered.

UC Santa Cruz is a progressive school with a gorgeous campus and innovative academic programs where the main focus of education is undergraduates. Many students are concerned that it is growing too fast, and an ambitious proposal for future expansion has threatened its heretofore cozy relationship with local citizens. Still, as long as the university retains its belief in "to each his or her own"—and students can find a place to live—it will remain uniquely UC Santa Cruz. Where else do you get to rally around a banana slug?

If You Apply To ›

Santa Cruz: Regular decision. SATs or ACTs: not considered. Does not accept the Common Application. Apply to a particular college, school, or program. Application includes optional question about gender/sexual identity.

California Institute of Technology

1200 East California Boulevard, Pasadena, CA 91125

If you're a Caltech student looking for tips on how to win a Nobel Prize, just ask a professor who already has one. A small, West Coast bastion of STEM research and teaching, Caltech looks for hardworking students with grit, wide-ranging intellectual curiosity, and a propensity for jaw-dropping pranks.

The California Institute of Technology counts 47 Nobel Prize winners among its faculty and alumni, and students' demanding courseload means plenty of opportunities to tap into that brilliance. Expectations are high; the school seeks to develop leaders who "collaborate across disciplines, launch new fields of study, and expand human knowledge." In fact, "Techers" are fond of saying that "the admissions office doesn't make mistakes," and it's not unheard of to take time off to deal with stress and avoid burnout. "The atmosphere promotes a love of science, learning, and discovery that is truly exhilarating," says a biology major. No doubt about it—if you prefer particle physics to partying, Caltech is a good place to be.

Caltech's 124-acre campus is located in Pasadena, a wealthy suburban city less than 15 miles from downtown Los Angeles. "It's not a college town at all," says a senior. Yet students can easily get to L.A., as well as the San Gabriel mountains, the Pacific Ocean, and the desert. Outside the classroom, at least, tranquility prevails, with olive trees, lily ponds, and plenty of flowers breaking up clusters of older Spanish mission-style buildings. Leafy courtyards and arcades link these with what one student describes as more modern, "block institutional" structures. The Beckman Auditorium (affectionately dubbed "The Wedding Cake" due to its round shape and conical roof) features spaces for performing arts, lectures, films, classes, and entertainment events. The new Resnick Sustainability Center offers research centers and teaching labs dedicated to innovation in climate science, water resources, and ecology and biosphere engineering.

Caltech's mission, one official says, is "to train the creative type of scientist or engineer urgently needed in our educational, governmental, and industrial development." After all, it was here that Albert Einstein abandoned his concept of a static cosmos in favor of the expanding-universe model. This is also where physicist Carl Anderson discovered the positron. With these luminaries as their models, students plunge right into the extensive core institute requirements, which include math, physics, chemistry, biology, science communication, computer science, two introductory lab terms, and 11 terms in the humanities and social sciences. The pass/fail grading system for first-year students goes a long way toward easing the acclimation period for new arrivals, but one computation and neural systems major opines, "It's very easy to feel imposter syndrome." The honor system, which mandates that "no one member of the Caltech community shall take unfair advantage of any other member," helps discourage unfair tactics to get better grades.

Founded in 1891, Caltech made its name in physics, and students say that program remains strong; it's also one of the most popular majors, along with computer science, mechanical engineering, electrical engineering, chemistry, bioengineering, and math. Students praise the geological and planetary sciences department for being "flexible with students and having excellent field trips," says a first-year. Caltech's $4.7 billion endowment is one of the largest among the nation's tech schools, and regardless of major, students benefit from state-of-the-art STEM facilities, including the Beckman Institute, a center for fundamental research in biology and chemistry, and the forthcoming Ginsburg Center for Quantum Precision Measurement. "Getting involved in research is extremely easy," says an astrophysics major, and over 90 percent of undergraduates do, including 80 percent who receive paid 10-week Summer Undergraduate Research Fellowships, which offer the chance to get a head start on their own discoveries with help from a faculty sponsor. Many summer fellows publish results from their endeavors in scientific journals.

"The atmosphere promotes a love of science, learning, and discovery."

Despite Caltech's reputation for ubiquitous brilliance, "Most of the professors here are more focused on research than on teaching so a lot of the teaching falls to the TAs," says an astrophysics major. Caltech operates on a quarter system, and coursework tends to be heavily theory-based. Students describe the academic climate as "extremely intense." One junior notes, "The speed at which material is taught is very fast!" But another says the intensity is also "positive, because there is a lot of rapport between students when it comes to helping each other academically." Students praise Caltech's smaller class sizes—71 percent have fewer than 20 students. "It's really easy to get to know professors, TAs, and other students across the whole campus," says a sophomore.

Caltech students "are some of the most determined, smartest, resilient people I have ever met," observes a mechanical engineering major. Thirty-one percent of Techers come from California, and 14 percent hail from foreign nations. Thirty-six percent of undergrads are Asian American, Hispanics/Latinos make up 17 percent of the student body, Black students just 5 percent, and multiracial students 9 percent. "We aren't too involved with politics or social issues," says an astrophysics major. "Part of this stems from the fact that we are too busy with work all the time!" But a physics major adds, "The LGBTQ community is well supported and very present on campus." All financial aid is awarded based on need—meaning no merit or athletic scholarships—and Caltech guarantees to meet the full demonstrated need of all

(continued)

Academics: ✍ ✍ ✍ ✍ ✍
Social: 💬
Q of L: ★ ★ ★
Admissions: (626) 395-6341
Email Address:
ugadmissions@caltech.edu

Strong Programs:
Bioengineering
Chemistry
Computer Science
Electrical Engineering
Geological and Planetary
 Sciences
Mechanical Engineering
Physics

It was at Caltech that Albert Einstein abandoned his concept of a static cosmos in favor of the expanding-universe model.

admitted students. Most students with family income of less than $100,000 can expect a no-loan financial aid package that covers tuition, fees, housing, and food, and most students with family income of less than $200,000 can expect an aid package that covers the tuition.

Caltech undergrads are required to live on campus for the first two years, and most remain in housing that one student calls "comfortable and convenient" for all four years. There are no fraternities or sororities, but the campus's eight co-ed "houses" inspire a loyalty worthy of the Greeks. "Housing is the most special thing about Caltech: We are sorted into houses in a fashion similar to rushing, except that everyone gets into a house," explains a computer science major. During Rotation Week, first-years spend an evening visiting each house, indicating at week's end the four they like the most; the Office of Residential Experience then sorts them into houses. The four older houses, which have been renovated, offer single, double, and triple rooms, while the newer ones have doubles. Each dorm has a dining hall, and those who live on campus must buy a meal plan, which a junior calls "quite expensive for the quality of food." Special plates are prepared daily for those with specific dietary needs. During an annual, student-led Title IX Summit, students plan solutions and strategies to prevent sexual violence.

"While The Big Bang Theory may paint Caltech as a very nerdy place (which we are some of the time), we have deep-rooted traditions with the house system that allow us to have a really enriching social life here," says a physics major. As the social center of Caltech life, each house takes a turn hosting at least one themed party during the year, which can be elaborate. "In the past, students have built moats and even a working rollercoaster for these parties," says a junior. Caltech requires any house or organization hosting a party to hire a professional bartender, who checks IDs. Other than house parties, students say, social life is pretty tame, since everyone is so busy with their schoolwork. "Ask any local bartender for a Caltech Cocktail and you will get three ounces of straight water," quips a sophomore. Some students head off campus—to Old Pasadena, nearby schools like USC, Occidental, and the Claremont Colleges, or to downtown L.A., easily reachable on the Metro's gold line. Additionally, cheers a junior, "There are awesome hikes near campus, beautiful beaches, and cool national parks like Joshua Tree nearby!"

"Getting involved in research is extremely easy."

Even with ample off-campus diversions, many Caltech students still prefer to make their own fun. The annual Pumpkin Drop (on Halloween, of course) involves immersing a gourd in liquid nitrogen and then dropping it from the library roof so that it shatters into a zillion frozen shards. On Ditch Day, classes are canceled. "The seniors of each house will plan an entire day of activities (all based on a theme, of course)" for the underclassmen, says a sophomore. "That could include things like scavenger hunts or escape rooms or even taking them off campus to the beach." During finals week, stereos blast "The Ride of the Valkyries" at seven o'clock each morning, just the thing to get you going after that all-nighter. Caltech also has a storied history of practical jokes. The most fabled student prank occurred during the 1984 Rose Bowl game, when UCLA played Illinois. A group of Caltech whiz kids spent months devising a radio-control device that would allow them to take control of the scoreboard in the second half to gain national exposure for Caltech by flashing pictures of their school's mascot, the beaver, and a revised score that had Caltech trouncing MIT.

"It's really easy to get to know professors, TAs, and other students."

As for Caltech's actual athletic exploits, some of the most successful of the school's 16 Division III teams include men's and women's tennis, men's soccer, men's track and field, and women's swim and dive. Perhaps more popular than varsity competition, though, are the intramural matches between the houses in several sports every year. Another favorite is the annual design competition that is the culmination of Mechanical Engineering 72, in which student-built robots must complete tasks while traversing an obstacle course.

Caltech students must learn to thrive under intense pressure thanks to the school's tremendous workload and somewhat quiet social life. But students say they appreciate the freedom to think and explore—and the trust administrators place in them through the honor code. Offers a sophomore, "I would describe Caltech as [having] a driven student body, with high standards and goals, that still likes to have fun and enjoys being in such an amazing location!"

If You Apply To ›

Caltech: Early action, regular decision. Accepts the Common Application with supplement. Students have the option of submitting published scientific research papers and letters from research mentors. Please consult Caltech's website for the most up-to-date information regarding standardized test requirements.

Calvin University

3201 Burton Street SE, Grand Rapids, MI 49546

A leading evangelical Christian institution that ranks high on the private college affordability list. About a quarter of the students are members of the Christian Reformed Church. Archrival of Michigan neighbor Hope and Illinois cousin Wheaton. Best known in the humanities and as one of the few Christian universities with engineering. Big emphasis on study abroad and investing in new sports, including football.

Calvin University takes seriously its mission to equip students to "understand complex issues from a Christ-centered perspective . . . defend their beliefs, and . . . express their creative solutions in a global culture." Along with Wheaton College in Illinois, it is regarded as one of the country's top evangelical colleges. Though no one is required to attend the school's daily chapel services, classes stop when worship starts, and most students view Christian values as central to the academic experience. "Whether having prayer or devotionals to start class, Bible studies with my track team, worship nights, or just tying conversations back into faith, everything comes back to faith here," says an exercise science major.

Calvin was founded in 1876 as the educational wing of the Christian Reformed Church in North America. After outgrowing one of its first homes, the school bought a tract of land on the edge of Grand Rapids and built its present campus. Calvin spreads out over 400 beautifully landscaped acres that include three ponds and a 100-acre woodland and wetland ecosystem preserve used for classes, research, and recreation. Most facilities are less than 50 years old and were designed by a student of Frank Lloyd Wright. Newer construction includes a soccer stadium, eight-lane track, and football building, along with a major renovation of the Hekman Library.

The Calvin Core consists of four components: Foundations (Christian thought and engagement); Competencies and Skills (writing, health, and world languages); Knowledge and Understanding (coursework in a broad range of liberal arts and science disciplines); and Cross-Disciplinary Integration (coursework that helps equip students to be global citizens). In addition, Calvin LifeWork is an optional program that teaches skills like financial literacy and career readiness to prepare students for success after college.

Website: www.calvin.edu

Location: Small City

Private

Total Enrollment: 3,184

Undergraduates: 3,002

Male/Female: 49/51

Financial Aid: 99%

Pell Grant: 24%

Expense: Pr $

Student Loans: 46%

Average Debt: $ $

Applicants: 5,723

Accepted: 71%

Enrolled: 21%

Grad in 6 Years: 74%

Returning First-years: 87%

Academics: ✍ ✍ ✍

Social: 🗨 🗨 🗨

Q of L: ★ ★ ★ ★

Admissions: (800) 688-0122

Email Address:
admissions@calvin.edu

Calvin's competition with Hope College is one of the great rivalries in Division III athletics.

Most students view Christian values as central to the academic experience.

"Rigorous scholarship, responsive teaching, and space for scholarly disagreement and discussion" characterize Calvin's academic climate, says a biochemistry major. Preprofessional programs, such as engineering, education, business, and nursing, are among the most popular majors. Philosophy, English, and religion are also regarded as strong. Calvin is the only Christian college in the U.S. to offer a comprehensive Asian studies program, which includes courses in Chinese, Japanese, and Korean language, history, and culture. Five-year bachelor-to-master's programs are offered in accounting and in speech pathology and audiology.

"Students at Calvin passionately strive to live for others and to live out their calling for God," says an exercise science major. Calvin is founded on the belief that every subject—even the sciences or mass media and popular culture—can be approached from a Christian perspective, and faculty members work hard to integrate faith and learning. "Topics like ethics or the synthesis of religion and science are addressed in my classes," explains an engineering major. In the absence of teaching assistants, professors are expected to reserve about 10 hours per week for advising and assisting students, outside of class. Thirty-nine percent of the classes at Calvin have fewer than 20 students and only a few have more than 50. Students give high ratings to peer tutoring and career counseling. "Our mental health services are amazing as well," boasts a psychology major.

> **"[Calvin offers] rigorous scholarship, responsive teaching, and space for scholarly disagreement."**

Learning also takes place outside of the classroom through internships and practicums, and more than 80 percent of students complete at least one internship before they graduate. Students involved in the Calvin Prison Initiative, which provides a Christian liberal arts education to incarcerated people at Handlon Correctional Facility, praise it as "integral and essential to fulfilling Calvin's mission." About 15 percent collaborate with faculty on research projects. For the 23 percent of students who choose to go abroad, Calvin offers dozens of faculty-led off-campus programs in such locales as Britain, Peru, Hungary, and Washington, D.C., in addition to programs offered in conjunction with partner institutions. "Study abroad is a major part of Calvin," enthuses a junior, calling it "crucial in my Calvin experience."

Though Calvin still has a strongly Dutch heritage, students who are members of the Christian Reformed Church now account for just 25 percent of the student body. "I believe that Calvin is becoming increasingly diverse each year," observes an elementary education major. Sixty percent of students are Michigan natives, and 15 percent are international. Black students constitute 5 percent of the total, Hispanics/Latinos 4 percent, Asian Americans 4 percent, and multiracial students 3 percent. "There are debates on campus revolving around the hot topics debated among all churches, including LGBTQ acceptance and rights, abortion, and women in the church," says a sophomore. Even so, a senior adds, "Calvin is extremely intentional about making all students feel loved and welcomed no matter their background." Eligible Calvin students receive scholarships based on academic merit, worth an average of $21,500 annually; there are no athletic awards.

> **"Students at Calvin passionately strive to live for others and to live out their calling for God."**

Calvin requires undergraduates to live on campus for two years, and students say there's no problem getting a room. For their first two years, students bunk in residence halls—each of which has separate wings for men and women—in four-person suites with two bedrooms connected by a shared bathroom. "The suites are typically set up with two freshmen on one side and two sophomores on the other," explains a nursing major. Juniors can choose between residence halls and on-campus apartments, and many seniors opt to move off campus. Calvin offers three intentional living/learning floors, "which provide a place for students passionate about the arts, outdoor recreation, racial justice, etc.," says a human resource management major. Students report "the food is good enough to be picky" at the dining facilities, and most praise the variety available. Safety is highly rated.

There isn't a big party culture on campus, but a senior points out, "Being so close to downtown Grand Rapids and with many students living off campus there are still the classic college events happening." On campus, students find a wealth of entertainment, including movies, speakers, concerts, and dances. The Cokes and Clubs event "allows 50-plus student organizations to gather on the central lawn. Incoming students receive a bottle of Coke, of course, [and] information about each club to facilitate involvement from the start," describes a senior. Hardy souls look forward to the Cold Knight Plunge, where hundreds of students voluntarily jump into the frozen Seminary Pond each winter, led by the college president and university pastor. Downtown Grand Rapids offers "many good restaurants, museums, parks, art exhibitions, concert venues, and fun activities," says a psychology major. Road trips include the beaches of Lake Michigan (a 45-minute drive) or Chicago (three hours distant). Spring break trips see a number of students traveling to places like Mississippi and Louisiana to complete service projects.

> **"I believe that Calvin is becoming increasingly diverse each year."**

Calvin fields a robust Division III athletic program that competes in the Michigan Intercollegiate Athletic Association (MIAA). Particularly competitive Knights teams include men's and women's basketball, men's swimming and diving, women's volleyball, men's and women's cross-country, and men's and women's soccer. Calvin's competition with Hope College is one of the great rivalries in Division III athletics, and current students and alumni alike rally together for the annual basketball game. The intramural program offers leagues and tournaments in sports ranging from pickleball to ultimate Frisbee and flag football.

Those who come to Calvin University are looking to build community with friends and faculty members who share their passion for faith-based academics. Says a marketing and English double major, "Calvin is curious, bold in faith and also inviting of other perspectives, seeks social justice, and actually engages problems that it notices."

Overlaps

Cedarville, Cornerstone, Dordt, Hope, University of Michigan, St. Olaf, Taylor, Wheaton (IL)

If You Apply To ›

Calvin: Rolling admissions. SATs or ACTs: optional. Accepts the Common Application with supplement.

Carleton College

One North College Street, Northfield, MN 55057

Less selective than Amherst, Williams, and Swarthmore, if only because of its out-of-the-way Minnesota location. Carleton retains its position as the premier liberal arts college in the upper Midwest. Predominantly liberal, but not to the extremes of its more antiestablishment cousins, and turns out lots of students who go on to get Ph.D.s. Students at Carleton excel at making their own fun, especially with Frisbees in hand.

Minnesota is many things: the land of 10,000 lakes, home to the massive Mall of America, birthplace of lore from Hiawatha to Paul Bunyan, and proud parent of

The school's powerhouse ultimate Frisbee club teams have won several national championships.

the Mississippi River. Beyond all that history-book stuff, tucked into a small town in the southeastern corner of the state is Carleton College, arguably the best liberal arts school in the Midwest. With traditions such as Friday Flowers, when students buy flowers on campus and "mail" them to their friends, you have the makings of an engaged, unique institution. "Carleton is quirky, and we're not afraid to embrace our quirk. In fact, we revel in it," says a biology major.

Carleton was founded in 1866 and named for an early benefactor. Surrounded by rolling farmland, Carleton's 1,040-acre campus is in the small town of Northfield, whose one-time status as the center of the Holstein cattle industry brought it the motto "Cows, Colleges, and Contentment." The campus boasts of fragrant lilacs in spring, rich summer greens, red maples in the fall, and a glistening blanket of white in winter. Lakes, woods, and streams abound, and you can traverse them on 15 miles of hiking and cross-country skiing trails. There's even an 880-acre arboretum. Carleton's architectural style is somewhat eclectic, with everything from Victorian to contemporary, but mostly red brick. Recent additions include Hasenstab Hall, home to the political science department, and a multiyear Student Life and Housing Plan to improve campus residences is ongoing. A new Student Health and Counseling Center opened in 2025, and the renovated Dacie Moss house, famed for its cookies that are available to students around the clock, reopened in 2025.

Carleton's top-notch academic programs are no less varied. The sciences—biology, physics, astronomy, chemistry, geology, and computer science—are among the best anywhere, and scores of Carleton graduates go on to earn Ph.D.s in these areas. Political science and international relations is a traditional strength; psychology and computer science are popular too. Engineers can opt for a

> **"Studying abroad is a big thing at Carleton."**

3–2 program with Washington University in St. Louis, and for geologists seeking fieldwork Carleton sponsors a program in Death Valley. Closer to home at the "arb," as the arboretum is affectionately known, students in the well-regarded environmental studies program have their own wilderness field station. In the arts, music and studio art majors routinely get into top graduate programs, and the college has expanded offerings in dance and theater. A minor in cross-cultural studies brings in international students to discuss global issues and dynamics with their American counterparts. Seventy percent of Carleton students spend at least one term abroad; offerings include roughly 20 faculty-led programs every year including offerings such as Cinema and Storytelling in Chile and Argentina. "Studying abroad is a big thing at Carleton," notes a physics major. "In fact, many students will go abroad twice." Seventy-seven percent of students conduct undergraduate research, and Carleton offers a rare summer research partner program in the humanities.

Distribution requirements ensure that a Carleton education exposes students not only to depth in their chosen field but also to "a wide range of subjects and methods of studying them," administrators say. All students must show proficiency in writing and a second language while fulfilling requirements in the areas of humanistic and social inquiry, literary/artistic analysis, the arts, science, and quantitative reasoning. There's also a Global Citizenship requirement, under which students must take one course on international studies, one course on intercultural domestic studies, and a first-year Argument and Inquiry Seminar. In their final year, all students complete a senior comprehensive project (known around campus as "Comps").

With highly motivated students and an "entirely rigorous" workload, according to a biology major, Carleton isn't your typical mellow Midwestern liberal arts college. The trimester calendar means finals may be just three months apart, and almost everyone feels the pressure. "I often joke that the hottest social spot at our school is the library," says a linguistics major. The six-week Christmas vacation is Carleton's way of dealing with the cold winters, offering more opportunities for off-campus studies or externships, a program unique to Carleton in which students can job shadow or focus on project-based work with alumni. Sixty-seven percent of classes have fewer than 20 students, so Carls are expected to participate actively. Carleton's faculty members are accessible and committed. "Almost every single professor has gotten to know me well because the classes are so small," says a psychology and German major. As part of its extensive advising program, Carleton assigns a "liberal arts advisor" to work with entering students for their first two years before they declare a major in the spring term of sophomore year.

"Students here have a sense of adventure and curiosity," says a senior. Nineteen percent of Carleton students are Minnesota residents, and 12 percent are international. More than half of the out-of-staters are from outside the Midwest, with both coasts heavily represented. Black students account for 6 percent of the student body, Hispanics/Latinos 10 percent, Asian Americans 10 percent, and multiracial students 9 percent. While students note limited racial diversity, a junior says, "The people at Carleton are some of the most welcoming people you will ever meet, and I personally haven't felt alienated based on my identities as a person of color and first-generation student." The Carleton campus is decidedly liberal ("Anyone who has very conservative views may have a hard time fitting in," remarks a junior), concerned with issues including climate change, gender and racial equality, and LGBTQ rights, and students are active in the local community. Carleton meets the full demonstrated financial need of all enrolled students, and all financial aid is need-based—a few merit scholarships averaging $8,000 are available but there are no athletic scholarships.

Ninety-seven percent of Carleton students live on campus, and housing is guaranteed for all four years; those who wish to live off campus must receive approval to do so. On-campus options range from comfortable old houses to modern hotel-like residence halls. "All dorms are quite livable and not all that different," says a first-year. Dorms are co-ed by room, but there are two halls with single-sex floors. Several college-owned "interest" houses, situated in an attractive residential section of town close to campus, focus on themes such as social activism and the outdoors. All campus residents must submit to a meal plan, and, a junior says, with "two dining halls plus three cafés, there are lots of options to choose from!" Students can also use their meal plans at neighboring St. Olaf. Students praise the mental health and career services, and say the campus is safe.

> "Almost every single professor has gotten to know me well because the classes are so small."

There are no fraternities or sororities. "If you are expecting some next level, Greek-life-esque parties until 5 a.m., you are going to be wildly disappointed," warns a junior. "But that doesn't mean there aren't any parties," clarifies another student. Carleton's social life tends to be relaxed and informal. Different clubs sponsor dances, free movies, and special events like Comedy Night. Students say there is no pressure to drink on campus. Popular annual events include the Midwinter Ball and the Spring Concert, known as "Sproncert." One distinctive Carleton tradition is the regular kidnapping and dramatic reappearance of a plaster bust of Friedrich Schiller, the Romantic philosopher and buddy of Goethe—such as dangling from a helicopter over homecoming football games.

Northfield itself is a history-rich town with a population of about 21,000. A favorite town event is the annual reenactment of Jesse James's failed bank robbery in 1876. "Northfield is quaint," a sophomore says, with vintage stores, coffee shops, restaurants, and a handful of bars and breweries. Students often frequent St. Olaf's campus and a popular coffee shop called Goodbye Blue Monday. Minneapolis–St. Paul, 45 minutes to the north, is a popular road-trip destination. First-year students aren't allowed to have cars on campus, but daily bus service is available.

The Knights compete in Division III athletics. Men's and women's cross-country have won multiple Minnesota Intercollegiate Athletic Conference titles in recent years, and men's and women's soccer, tennis, and track and field are also competitive. "Carleton's rivalry with St. Olaf is present in every sport," says one student. "Carls have recently resorted to calling St. Olaf 'Northfield Community College!'" The school's powerhouse ultimate Frisbee club teams have won several national championships. About three-quarters of the students compete in 24 club and 14 intramural sports, including broomball in the winter. While not an intramural sport, a popular tradition on campus is Rotblatt, a game described as "softball on steroids" and unique to Carleton. "Played once each spring, this marathon softball game begins at sunrise and lasts one inning for each year of Carleton's existence. It is Rotblatt tradition for players to both bat and field with a beverage of their choice in one hand."

"Carleton's rivalry with St. Olaf is present in every sport."

It can be cold in Minnesota, in a face-stinging, bone-chilling kind of way. And the classes are far from easy. But Carleton is a warm campus where students toe the line between individuality and community. At Carleton, says one student, "It isn't about getting the degree; it's about having an impactful experience where students learn more about themselves and the world they live in."

Overlaps

Amherst, Bowdoin, Macalester, Northwestern, Pomona, Swarthmore, University of Chicago, Williams

If You Apply To ›

Carleton: Early decision I and II, regular decision. SATs or ACTs: optional. Accepts the Common Application with supplement.

Carnegie Mellon University

5000 Forbes Avenue, Pittsburgh, PA 15213

The only premier university equally strong in both technology and the arts, Carnegie Mellon is a national leader in blending interdisciplinary and practical education. Applications continue to increase, so it must be doing something right. Shares its urban neighborhood with a variety of cultural and academic institutions, including the University of Pittsburgh. Working hard to reduce student stress levels.

Website: www.cmu.edu
Location: City Center
Private
Total Enrollment: 15,533
Undergraduates: 7,564
Male/Female: 50/50
Financial Aid: 48%
Pell Grant: 15%
Expense: Pr $ $ $
Student Loans: 29%
Average Debt: $ $ $
Applicants: 33,941
Accepted: 12%
Enrolled: 46%
Grad in 6 Years: 94%

Students at Carnegie Mellon don't have to choose between soaking up the high drama of Shakespeare and plunging into the fast-paced tech world. The university is known for both its science offerings and strong drama and music programs. But scholars "aren't just restricted to one lane," says an official—Carnegie Mellon continues to strive to offer both its technical and liberal arts students a well-rounded education that requires a lot of hard work but promises great rewards.

Tracing its origins to 1900, when industrialist Andrew Carnegie founded a technical school for the children of Pittsburgh's blue-collar workers, Carnegie Mellon was formed by the merger of Carnegie Institute of Technology and the Mellon Institute in 1967. Its self-contained, 157-acre campus is attractively situated in Pittsburgh's affluent Oakland section. Next door is the city's second-largest park and its major museum, named after—you guessed it—Andrew Carnegie. Henry Hornbostel, who attended the École des Beaux-Arts in the 1890s, designed the campus using a plan that is a modification of the Jefferson plan for the University of Virginia, with the Beaux-Arts device of creating primary and secondary axes and grouping buildings around significant open spaces. Buildings are designed in a Renaissance style, with buff-colored brick arches and piers, tile roofs, and terra-cotta and granite details. Newer construction includes the Highmark Center for Health, Wellness and Athletics, and an automated lab, complete with AI-encoded instruments, that is available for undergraduates to use.

Carnegie Mellon has seven constituent colleges that offer undergraduate and graduate degrees: the College of Fine Arts, the Dietrich College of Humanities and Social Sciences, the College of Engineering, the Mellon College of Science, the School of Computer Science, the Tepper School of Business, and the Heinz College of Information Systems and Public Policy. Each college has its own distinct character and admissions requirements. All the colleges, however, share the university's commitment to interdisciplinary and practical education, which shows the relevance of the liberal arts while stressing courses that develop technical skills and good job prospects. Students interested in humanities and social science can major in applied history, professional writing, or information systems, for example, instead of traditional disciplinary concentrations.

Most departments at Carnegie Mellon are strong, but exceptional ones include engineering, computer science, architecture, and drama. The undergraduate business program focuses on the technical aspects of management and quantitative decision-making. The most popular majors are computer science, business administration, electrical and computer engineering, and mechanical engineering. Initiatives aimed at connecting art and technology include the BXA Intercollege Degree Programs and the Integrative Design, Arts, and Technology network, which offers interdisciplinary minors like game design, animation and special effects, and innovation and entrepreneurship.

Courses are "extremely rigorous with many hours expected outside of the classroom," says one student. Students at Carnegie Mellon work hard, no doubt about it, and many complain that the academic environment encourages a serious culture of stress, but the university has taken steps to try to counteract that. Every day includes a designated "meeting-free" time for students, allowing them time to study or participate in student activities. A mechanical and biomedical engineering double major notes that there is a "mindfulness room" that serves as "a space for students to relax and take a break from schoolwork" (and get weekly visits from trained therapy dogs) and that students are encouraged to use campus counseling services "even if it is just to discuss stress and how to manage a new environment." Students also recommend the Academic Development Office, and one says, "There is absolutely no stigma against tutoring or outside resources." Sixty-eight percent of classes have fewer than 20 students, and professors rate highly with most students. "Some professors are better than others at lecturing, but I have not encountered a professor that doesn't care about the course," says an electrical and computer engineering major.

Students looking to hone their professional skills will find ample opportunities, including five-year dual-degree options, co-op programs, and advising and other resources within the Career and Professional Development Center. Research opportunities are available across the curriculum, as are several types of grants and fellowships to fund them. Those interested in service learning can get involved with the university's extensive outreach efforts to improve youth STEM education in the local area. Study abroad options are plentiful and include the university's established undergraduate campus in the Arabian Gulf nation of Qatar, but many students have difficulty fitting study abroad into their rigorous schedules.

"CMU is for people who know what they want to do," asserts one student. Despite the university's core emphasis on interdisciplinary, well-rounded education,

> **"[Courses are] extremely rigorous with many hours expected outside of the classroom."**

(continued)

Returning First-years: 98%
Academics: ✍ ✍ ✍ ✍
Social: 🗩 🗩 🗩
Q of L: ★ ★ ★
Admissions: (412) 268-2082
Email Address:
  admission@andrew.cmu.edu

Strong Programs:
Architecture
Art
Business Administration
Computer Science
Drama
Information Systems
Mechanical Engineering
Music

One event that brings everyone together is the Spring Carnival, a four-day weekend festival.

Carnegie Mellon remains one of the most fragmented campuses in the nation. Students divide themselves between actors, designers, and other artsy types and engineers, scientists, and architects. "Most CMU students own up to their identities as nerds, whether they be of the drama, history, or science variety," says a math major. In any case, students here are all high achievers and are united in their quest for a good job after graduation.

Once a largely regional institution, drawing mostly Pennsylvania residents, Carnegie Mellon now counts 86 percent of its full-time undergraduate students from out of state, including 23 percent from foreign countries, and they've eliminated legacy preferences in admissions. Half are students of color, including 33 percent Asian American, 4 percent Black, 9 percent Hispanic/Latino, and 5 percent multiracial. Students report that campus politics lean liberal, but most students don't get actively involved in social or political matters. The university says it remains committed to need-blind admissions and guarantees to meet the full demonstrated financial need of students. The school introduced the CMU Pathway Program in 2025, which covers full tuition for students whose families make $75,000 or less and loan-free financial aid for students whose families earn $100,000 or less. Some merit scholarships are available averaging $14,400, but there are no athletic scholarships.

Housing is guaranteed for undergraduates all four years if they stay in the university housing system, and half do so. Upperclassmen get first pick, so the popular university-owned apartments fill up fast, but there are a number of residence halls specifically for first-year students. The quality of each dorm varies, says a junior, but "the facilities are all very livable." The best dorms for first-years are Stever House—the first LEED-certified residence hall in the U.S.—Donner, Resnik, and Morewood Gardens. "Instead of buffet-style dining halls, we have several themed eateries that you can pick from," explains a sophomore, and meals are described as satisfying. Students report feeling safe on campus, thanks to a comprehensive security program, but one comments, "There is not enough campus conversation or emphasis on the issue of sexual assault."

> **"I have not encountered a professor that doesn't care about the course."**

With all the academic pressure at Carnegie Mellon, it's a good thing there are so many opportunities to unwind, especially with the entire city of Pittsburgh close at hand. "Pittsburgh is a great place to go to college," cheers a junior. "Whatever type of evening you're looking for, Pittsburgh has it." Nearby Oakland has coffeehouses, inexpensive films, dances, and concerts, and the downtown area (just 20 minutes away by bus) offers a rich social scene, with opera, ballet, symphony, concerts, and sporting events.

The Greek system provides the most visible form of on-campus social life, with 7 percent of men and 7 percent of women joining fraternities and sororities, and the school offers late-night events and concerts too. Those of legal age are allowed to have alcohol in their rooms, but according to one student, "Drinking takes place mostly off campus." One event that brings everyone together is the Spring Carnival, a four-day weekend festival. Student groups build themed booths and design, build, and race buggies made of lightweight alloys. Members of the student-run "Scotch 'n' Soda" theater organization also present a show.

> **"We have several themed eateries that you can pick from."**

As for sports, the Carnegie Mellon Tartans compete in the Division III University Athletic Association. The Kiltie Band, clad in kilts honoring Andrew Carnegie's Scottish heritage, rallies the crowd during home football and basketball games. In recent years, men's and women's golf and cross-country, men's indoor track and field, and women's soccer have performed well in their respective national championship tournaments. Students also participate in 47 intramural and club sports.

Carnegie Mellon appeals just as much to those yearning for the bright lights of Broadway as it does to those pursuing the glowing computer screens of the scientific and business worlds. And with a broad range of liberal arts and technical courses available to explore, there's no doubt students leave with a well-rounded education—and an impressive diploma. Students more interested in specializing in one field than being exposed to many may fare better elsewhere, but most who opt for Carnegie Mellon agree that the demanding environment is well worth it.

If You Apply To ›

Carnegie Mellon: Early decision, regular decision. Accepts the Common Application. Apply to particular school or college. Please consult Carnegie Mellon's website for the most up-to-date information regarding standardized test requirements. Arts programs require a portfolio or audition.

Case Western Reserve University

10900 Euclid Avenue, Cleveland, OH 44106

CWRU has most of the offerings available at Carnegie Mellon or WashU in St. Louis, but somehow it hasn't quite found its deserved niche in the national consciousness. Students in the know sing its praises, especially since CWRU is less difficult to get into than other institutions of comparable, or even lesser, quality. Students get an outstanding technical education with solid offerings in other areas.

Cleveland's Case Western Reserve University has much in common with Pittsburgh's Carnegie Mellon. Both are the product of mergers between a technical college, known for excellence in engineering, and a more traditional university, focused on the arts and sciences. Both are located in erstwhile Rust Belt cities that have long since reinvented themselves through technology, medicine, education, and advanced manufacturing. And both tend to attract brainy students more concerned with studying than socializing. While CWRU has received less national attention than Carnegie Mellon and WashU, a senior calls it "a university on the rise": Applications have increased 60 percent in the past decade, and the school has become more selective. CWRU has also increased its investment in the arts, humanities, and social sciences, with an aim toward helping students connect these disciplines with their technical studies.

CWRU is located on the eastern edge of Cleveland at University Circle. This 550-acre area of parks and gardens is home to more than 50 cultural, educational, medical, and research institutions, including the city's museums of art and natural history, its botanical gardens, and Severance Hall, home of the Cleveland Orchestra. Campus buildings are an eclectic mix of architectural styles, and several are listed on the National Register of Historic Places. The Peter B. Lewis Building (or "PBL," as it's known around campus), designed by Frank Gehry, is home to the Weatherhead School of Management and features undulating walls similar to those of Gehry's Guggenheim Museum in Bilbao, Spain. The Tinkham Veale University Center ("the Tink") meets LEED Silver standards and serves as a hub for campus dining, special events, and more than 200 student organizations, while the Sears think[box] is a fabrication lab designed to support cross-disciplinary entrepreneurial innovation. Two new residence halls for sophomores opened in 2024.

The product of the 1967 marriage between Case Institute of Technology and Western Reserve University, CWRU has four undergraduate schools: the College of

Website: www.case.edu
Location: City Center
Private
Total Enrollment: 11,366
Undergraduates: 6,391
Male/Female: 52/48
Financial Aid: 98%
Pell Grant: 18%
Expense: Pr $ $ $ $
Student Loans: 42%
Average Debt: $ $
Applicants: 37,082
Accepted: 38%
Enrolled: 12%
Grad in 6 Years: 87%
Returning First-years: 92%
Academics: ✑ ✑ ✑ ✑
Social: 🗩 🗩
Q of L: ★ ★ ★
Admissions: (216) 368-4450
Email Address:
  admission@case.edu

Strong Programs:
Biomedical Engineering
Business and Marketing

Arts and Sciences, the Case School of Engineering, the Bolton School of Nursing, and the aforementioned Weatherhead School; all also offer graduate programs. All CWRU students must complete a common set of general education requirements in which students take classes involving written and oral communications, quantitative reasoning, and wellness, as well as moral and ethical reasoning, global perspectives, human diversity, and local and global engagement. Students must also submit a senior capstone experience portfolio. According to a biomedical engineering major, "CWRU is a collaborative environment that allows students to excel in their own way."

CWRU's strongest programs include engineering—especially the biomedical and mechanical kind—nursing, business and marketing, computer science, and psychology. The school's polymer science major is one of the few such undergraduate programs in the country. Strengths in the College of Arts and Sciences include music (a joint program with the nearby Cleveland Institute of Music), anthropology (especially medical anthropology), and biology. Combined bachelor's and master's programs are popular, as is the Preprofessional Scholars program, which gives top first-year students conditional acceptance to CWRU's medical or dental schools, assuming satisfactory progress through prerequisite courses. Fifty-two percent of all undergraduate classes enroll fewer than 20 students. "The quality of instruction is variable," says a biology major, "but the majority of instructors are very good and willing to help at any time."

> **"CWRU . . . allows students to excel in their own way."**

Undergraduate research is highly encouraged, and 50 percent of students conduct research as part of senior capstone projects or independent studies. Thirty percent of students take part in study abroad, often in faculty-led programs during winter, spring, or summer breaks. For help with academic and career planning, every undergraduate is assigned a faculty advisor as well as a "navigator," a staff member who assists them throughout their four years. "A navigator is a great resource for nonmajor-specific questions relating to campus resources, academic resources, club suggestions, etc.," explains a first-year.

> *Every undergraduate is assigned a faculty advisor as well as a "navigator," who assists them throughout their four years.*

A senior says CWRU students are "driven, high achievers" who often "feel the need to prove themselves." Eighteen percent of CWRU's students are Ohio natives, and international students represent a strong contingent at 11 percent. Black students make up 6 percent of the student body, Asian Americans 30 percent, Hispanics/Latinos 12 percent, and multiracial students 5 percent. Students describe the political climate as low-key, with liberals and conservatives both well represented on campus. Eligible students receive scholarships based on academic merit that average $29,000, but there are no athletic awards. The university has adopted a need-aware admissions policy that includes a commitment to meet the full demonstrated financial need of incoming first-years.

Students are required to live on campus for their first two years, and 71 percent of all undergrads live in campus housing. Each first-year student participates in one of four residential colleges. "First-year rooms are adequate but nothing special," says one student, but upperclassmen rave about the amenities in the university's apartment-style suites. Dining-hall fare is "not Mom's cooking every night, but it's not bad," reasons one student. Some upperclassmen opt for off-campus apartments within walking distance of campus. "As it is an urban campus, crime does occasionally happen in the surrounding area or (rarely) on campus," reports a psychology major. "The school takes many strong measures to keep students safe, including many security officers and free rides across campus at night."

> **"[Students are] driven, high achievers."**

As for social life, says a junior, "Case is not ideal for anyone who prioritizes a vibrant social scene, but students who enjoy being social and going to parties/bars are able to find enough opportunities." On campus, there are dances, concerts, and movies. Fraternities and sororities draw 16 percent of the men and 14 percent of the women, but students report that Greek groups here are more focused on philanthropy than partying. Popular campus traditions include the Springfest carnival to celebrate the end of classes and "Study Overs," where students gather during finals week for free food, massages, study groups, and more. The annual sci-fi movie marathon is a rite of passage, while Engineers Week features a fuel-cell-powered car competition.

CWRU is located five miles from downtown Cleveland, which provides ample opportunities for internships, volunteer work, dining, and entertainment. "We're surrounded by museums and cultural institutions, which become a part of our education," enthuses a history major. "It's very budget-friendly," adds a senior. The city features the Rock & Roll Hall of Fame, and—in the warmer months— major league baseball games at Progressive Field. Convenient RTA train passes are included in student charges for a reasonable price, but having a car can be helpful, especially for road trips to nearby cities in Ohio or for longer jaunts to Chicago.

Although sports are not a major focus on campus, the Spartans field 17 Division III teams, and the annual football game against Carnegie Mellon is big. Baseball and softball are recent University Athletic Association champions, and men's and women's cross-country, men's tennis, and women's soccer are nationally competitive. Twenty-four percent of students participate in at least one of the intramural and club sports available, ranging from volleyball and ultimate Frisbee to ice hockey, badminton, and fencing. The 26-mile Hudson Relay, held the last week of the spring semester to commemorate CWRU's relocation from Hudson to Cleveland, pits teams of runners from the four classes against one another, with each person running a half mile.

A rigorous, science- and engineering-oriented research university, CWRU also devotes noteworthy attention to the student experience. "CWRU's personality is friendly and spirited," says a senior. "People can be self-deprecating and make a lot of jokes about Cleveland's bad weather, but the campus community itself is warm and inviting." With challenging academics, preprofessional programs, and research opportunities across all disciplines, students here are well-equipped to excel in their future careers.

> *The school's polymer science major is one of the few such undergraduate programs in the country.*

> **"[Cleveland is] very budget-friendly."**

Overlaps

Carnegie Mellon, Emory, Johns Hopkins, Ohio State, University of Michigan, University of Rochester, Vanderbilt, WashU in St. Louis

---

If You Apply To ›

CWRU: Early decision I and II, early action, regular decision. SATs or ACTs: optional. Accepts the Common Application with supplement. Music, theater, and dance require audition or other supplemental material.

The Catholic University of America

620 Michigan Avenue, NE, Washington, D.C. 20064

There are other Roman Catholic–affiliated universities, but this is The Catholic University. Catholics make up more than two-thirds of the undergraduate student body here (versus roughly half at nearby Georgetown). If you can't be in Rome, there is no better place than D.C. to work and play. CUA even has a Metrorail stop right next to campus. Academic freedom is the norm except in theology.

Website: www.catholic.edu

Location: City Center

Private

Total Enrollment: 3,993

Undergraduates: 2,971

Male/Female: 47/52

Financial Aid: 58%

Pell Grant: 24%

Expense: Pr $ $

Student Loans: 60%

Average Debt: $ $ $ $

Applicants: 6,714

Accepted: 83%

Enrolled: 13%

Grad in 6 Years: 80%

Returning First-years: 87%

Academics: ✎ ✎ ✎

Social: 💬 💬 💬

Q of L: ★ ★ ★

Admissions: (202) 319-5305

Email Address:
cua-admissions@cua.edu

Strong Programs:
Architecture
Business
Engineering
Music
Nursing
Physics
Politics
Psychology

Campus Ministry offers numerous opportunities to engage in faith and service through frequent community service events.

Founded in 1887 under a charter from Pope Leo XIII, The Catholic University of America was the brainchild of U.S. bishops who wanted to provide an American educational institution where the curriculum was guided by the tenets of Roman Catholic thought. Over time, the university has garnered a reputation as a research-oriented school that also provides a strong undergraduate, preprofessional education and an appreciation for the arts. The challenges of declining enrollment and changing demographics and social attitudes in the past decade has sparked renewed debate on campus about whether CUA is marketing itself as "too Catholic" and making itself less welcoming to prospective students in the process. "Our authentic Catholic background rules our academics, campus activities, and institutional offices all over campus," says a senior.

Catholic University's campus comprises 176 tree-lined acres, an impressive layout for an urban university, and houses 34 research facilities. Buildings range from ivy-covered limestone and brick to ultramodern, giving the place a true collegiate feel. A new nursing and sciences building opened in 2024.

CUA is one of the few schools in the country that began life as a graduate institution (others are Clark University and The Johns Hopkins University), and grad students still account for a respectable portion of the student population. Nine of its 11 schools admit undergrads. Specific graduation requirements vary by program, but all undergraduates participate in the First-Year Experience, an introduction to CUA's brand of liberal arts guided by the Catholic intellectual tradition.

> **"[Students are] extremely humble and dedicate their college careers to giving back to others."**

Assigned to Learning Communities of about 18 classmates, students take core classes in philosophy, theology, and English, and they receive one-on-one academic advising throughout the year. First-years also join their Learning Communities for out-of-class activities and group excursions into the city.

Students have excellent options in almost any department at CUA. In addition to politics, which is one of the most popular majors and sets the tone on campus, business, engineering, and architecture are strong. The physics department enjoys a modern vitreous-state lab, a boon for both research and hands-on undergraduate instruction. The School of Nursing is one of the best in the nation and CUA has added an accelerated nursing B.S. program. The Benjamin T. Rome School of Music, Drama, and Art is well known for its music offerings, including a joint degree that combines music with business. The National Catholic School of Social Service offers a bachelor of social work degree.

In the classroom, "The academic climate is rigorous but manageable if students put effort into class," says a politics major. Fifty-eight percent of classes have fewer than 20 students, which means individual attention from faculty members is common. According to a junior, "Professors are eager to explain confusing concepts and encourage students to persist." About 60 percent of faculty members are Catholic (the Vatican requires that figure to be at least 50 percent). CUA's chancellor is the archbishop of Washington, mass is held on campus daily, and Catholic churches across the country donate a fraction of their annual collections to the university. One corollary of being the only Catholic school with a papal charter is that faculty in Cannon Law, Theology, and Philosophy take special oaths and are approved by the Vatican.

Top students are invited to enroll in the University Honors Program, which features challenging seminar-style classes and the option of living in a dedicated honors community. Nearly a third of students take advantage of a wide variety of education abroad programs in more than 75 locations around the globe. The flagship Rome Center, jointly operated by CUA and an Australian counterpart, sponsors programs for liberal arts and architecture students, as well as a three-week summer program for the First-Year Experience. Eighty percent of students complete at least one internship at organizations ranging from NASA and the National Institutes of Health to the Smithsonian Institution. "Every year, our campus hosts a University Research Day, where classes are canceled and the entire day is dedicated to presentations, showcases, and discussions about student research," says a politics and philosophy major. Students give mixed reviews to career counseling services.

CUA students are "extremely humble and dedicate their college careers to giving back to others," comments a junior. Catholicism is clearly the tie that binds the student body, with 69 percent of students identifying as Catholic. Most students are also conservative, although some socially liberal causes are gaining traction on campus; students report that the administration's insistence on single-sex dorms, refusal to recognize LGBTQ student groups, and ban on speakers who have expressed pro-choice views have been controversial among the student body. "It is hard for a lot of students to reconcile their own personal set of beliefs with the Catholic identity of the school, which can be said even for many of the students who are Catholic themselves," remarks a politics major. Ninety percent of undergraduates are from outside D.C.; 3 percent arrive from foreign countries, and most of the rest hail from the Northeast. Six percent are Black, 23 percent are Hispanic/Latino, 3 percent are Asian American, and 5 percent are multiracial. Catholic University maintains a need-blind admissions policy, and all applicants are considered for merit scholarships, which average $31,200. No athletic scholarships are available.

> **"Professors are eager to explain confusing concepts and encourage students to persist."**

Sixty-one percent of undergraduates live in the 16 single-sex residence halls, which are intended to foster an environment of virtuous living. On-campus housing offers a variety of options ranging from the traditional to suites and apartments. "Most of the residence halls are nice and comfortable enough to make your own impermanent home," says a politics major. Campus fare is a mixed blessing: "The dining is unlimited, which is awesome for big appetites," says one student. "The problem is that it's overpriced and bland." Shuttle buses and safety escort services are provided as part of campus security, and students agree that they feel safe on campus, as long as they are careful. The Peer Educators Empowering Respectful Students (PEERS) group helps to raise awareness about sexual assault prevention. For mental health services, says one student, "The counseling center has great therapists with qualified backgrounds."

When students want to explore the city, they need only walk to the Brookland-CUA Metrorail stop adjacent to campus and then enjoy the ride. Capitol Hill is 15 minutes away and the stylish Georgetown area, with its chic restaurants and nightspots, a half hour. "Because we're in the city, most students would rather get dressed up to go out to a bar than to a house party," observes a senior. CUA does not have a Greek system, and most students agree that school policies are effective in curbing underage drinking. On campus, students have their choice of more than 100 clubs and organizations. Campus Ministry offers numerous opportunities to engage in faith and service through frequent community service events, student retreats, summer mission trips, and other programs. Six percent of students regularly participate in community service. Annual activities on campus include Fall Festival, the Capital Fest concert featuring a well-known band, Mistletoe Ball, Founders Day Ball, and Cardinalpalooza, a popular celebration of the end of the academic year.

> **"Because we're in the city, most students would rather get dressed up to go out to a bar than to a house party."**

CUA's Cardinals compete in Division III. The women's cross-country team, men's soccer, and men's swimming regularly bring home Landmark Conference championships, and other recent winners include women's outdoor track and field, women's golf, and men's basketball and baseball. Intramural and club-level programs attract plenty of interest, too, especially flag football, pickleball, and kickball.

When the idea of a Catholic university was first raised, the man who would become the university's first rector, Bishop John Joseph Keane, argued for an institution that would "exercise a dominant influence in the world's future" with a superior intellectual foundation. Now, nearly 140 years later, CUA offers students a wealth of preprofessional courses spanning the arts and sciences. Even as it grapples with how best to express and uphold its Catholic identity, the university remains dedicated to its mission of providing "scholarly research, education, and service in the light of the Catholic intellectual tradition."

If You Apply To ›

Catholic: Early decision I and II, early action, regular decision. SATs or ACTs: optional. Accepts the Common Application. Music applicants must audition.

Centre College

600 West Walnut Street, Danville, KY 40422

Centre may not be the most famous institution of higher learning in Kentucky, but it is certainly the best, and it offers college the way it used to be—football games, Greek row, and a gaggle of decades-old traditions. Likes to put learning into practice in real-world settings and offers the closeness between students and faculty that comes with a student body of 1,400. Compare to Sewanee, Rhodes, and Davidson.

Website: www.centre.edu
Location: Small Town
Private
Total Enrollment: 1,407
Undergraduates: 1,407
Male/Female: 48/52
Financial Aid: 98%
Pell Grant: 34%
Expense: Pr $ $
Student Loans: 56%
Average Debt: $
Applicants: 3,157
Accepted: 65%
Enrolled: 11%
Grad in 6 Years: 85%
Returning First-years: 84%
Academics: ✐ ✐ ✐
Social: 🗩 🗩 🗩
Q of L: ★ ★ ★
Admissions: (800) 423-6236
Email Address:
admission@centre.edu

Centre College, the only independent school in Kentucky with a Phi Beta Kappa chapter, has produced two-thirds of the state's Rhodes scholars over the last 50 years. The school is a throwback to the way college used to be, with Friday night parties on Greek row and Saturday afternoon football games. Centre's small size offers an intimate classroom environment. And its liberal arts focus means that despite Centre's southern location, students are progressive, intellectual, and perhaps more well-rounded than their peers at neighboring schools. A psychology and philosophy major suggests, "If you want a college where you can explore different interests, build meaningful relationships, and be part of a tight community, Centre's a great choice."

Located in the heart of Kentucky Bluegrass country, Centre's campus is 40 minutes from Lexington and just over an hour from Louisville, close to major airports and enabling students to attend events and participate in internships in either city. Buildings are a mix of old Greek Revival and attractive modern structures. More than 14 of them are listed on the National Registry of Historic Places, a fact that's less surprising when you know that Centre, which was founded by local Presbyterian leaders and dates to 1819, is the 48th oldest college in the United States. The college is home to four LEED-certified buildings, and newer facilities include a 135,000-square-foot athletics complex featuring an aquatic center, an indoor track and turf field, and a nutrition and wellness center.

Centre's Doctrina Lux Mentis general education curriculum (named after the school's motto, Latin for "Learning is the light of the mind"), requires coursework in each of the college's three academic divisions: arts and humanities, social studies, and science and mathematics. Students begin with a two-course sequence in the first year that emphasizes written communication in the fall and oral communication in the spring. A third course, taken junior or senior year, focuses on interdisciplinary thinking and serves as a capstone experience. Additionally, all students complete two experiential learning components, such as independent research or community-based learning.

"The academic climate is definitely challenging, but also really supportive," says a sophomore. Centre's most popular majors are business, economics and finance, international studies, mathematics, and psychology. Other strong programs include engineering, politics, neuroscience, and English. Art is solid, too, and glassblowing enthusiasts will find one of the few fully equipped undergraduate facilities for their pursuit in the nation. Sixty-nine percent of classes have fewer than 20 students. "Professors make use of the small class sizes to prompt interesting and involved discussions between students," says a math major.

> **"The academic climate is definitely challenging, but also really supportive."**

Approximately 52 percent of students perform collaborative research with faculty, and 85 percent take advantage of Centre's extensive study abroad programs. Centre runs 20 semester-long programs for students in all majors in 13 countries in addition to several shorter options offered during the January term. A study-away semester in Washington, D.C., or New York combines coursework with internships. A psychology major highly recommends the college's career services: "They provide constant assistance and support in the job-search process."

"Centre is surprisingly diverse for a college in the middle of Kentucky," says a sophomore. Fifty-six percent of Centre students hail from Kentucky, and 4 percent are international. Black students represent 6 percent of the student body, Asian Americans 7 percent, Hispanics/Latinos 7 percent, and multiracial students 4 percent. "I would say we have a 50–50 to 60–40 liberal-conservative split regarding political alignment," estimates a math major. Increasing diversity among faculty and staff has been a particular focus of late. Centre offers merit-based awards averaging $36,900, but no athletic scholarships. The school guarantees to meet 100 percent of demonstrated financial need for students; 34 percent of incoming first-year students are eligible for Pell Grants.

Virtually all students live on campus, thanks to a four-year residential requirement that students say makes for a strong sense of community. But most note, as an English major says, "housing is variable between years." As students gain seniority, they get access to more living options. Suite- and townhouse-style accommodations are available for many upperclassmen, and small Greek houses are an option for some, but most members of

> **"Centre is surprisingly diverse for a college in the middle of Kentucky."**

Greek life live in the residence halls. Students dine in one main dining hall, Cowan, and three café-style eateries, as well as a grab-and-go shop option. Students give high ratings to campus safety.

"The social scene at Centre is pretty lively but not overwhelming," says a sophomore. Greek life attracts 52 percent of men and 47 percent of women, and their parties are open to all. "Alcohol is a large part of the weekend social life here for many students," says a senior. The Student Activity Council sponsors a variety of alternatives, such as free midnight movies at the local theater and events like comedians, karaoke, and laser tag. Students also get free admission to Centre's separately endowed Norton Center for the Arts, a palatial, 1,500-seat auditorium that brings major musicals, concerts, and other performances to campus.

Traditions loom large at Centre. Campus superstitions include the placing of pennies on the toe of the Abraham Lincoln statue for good luck on exams and

Students get free admission to Centre's separately endowed Norton Center for the Arts.

avoiding stepping on the Centre Seal so as not to fail them. At the annual Honor Walk, seniors are invited to present a "talent" (a coin) to someone who has made a significant impact on their lives during their college years. Much to the chagrin of successive grumpy administrations, students have continued to honor a tradition known as "Running the Flame" (remember that Latin motto?). "People streak through campus to a statue of the 'flame of learning,'" explains a junior. Community service through the Greek system, Habitat for Humanity, or other organizations draws two-thirds of the students. Danville (population 17,000) offers some small-town charm—"There are two local coffee shops and, surprisingly enough, a specialty tea store," says a student—but there is more to do in Lexington and Louisville, both within an hour's drive, and it's easy to get to the countryside for camping, fishing, and other outdoor pursuits.

Centre earned a repeat Southern Athletic Association's all-sports trophy in 2025. The school's football team has been around for more than a century, and while it now competes against regional opponents in Division III, that wasn't always the case. In 1921, the Colonels beat then-powerhouse Harvard six to zero, a triumph that has been called the greatest sports upset in the first half of the 20th century. Nowadays, Rhodes College and nearby Transylvania University are Centre's key rivals. Among the most competitive teams are women's basketball and soccer and men's swimming and diving and baseball. More than half of the student body participates in intramural sports, with flag football, soccer, and basketball drawing the most players.

Centre College often takes visitors by surprise. Although situated in a quaint, historic setting, much of the campus has a fresh, modern feel. Students come here for a well-rounded liberal arts education with plenty of real-world preparation along the way. "By the time I reached my senior year," recalls a math major, "I felt cultivated as a public speaker, a problem solver, and a leader." With faculty who care about forming lasting friendships with students and a commitment to providing hands-on learning opportunities, Centre offers a distinctive mix of tradition and modernity.

Overlaps

Davidson, Denison, University of Kentucky, Kenyon, University of Louisville, Rhodes, Sewanee, Transylvania

If You Apply To ›

Centre: Early decision I and II, early action, regular decision. SATs or ACTs: optional. Accepts the Common Application with supplement.

Champlain College

163 S Willard Street, Burlington, VT 05401

A small college with a unique "upside-down" approach to blending professional education and the liberal arts. Updated curriculum allows students more flexibility. Champlain's academic strengths are game design, cybersecurity, and computer science—whose students create a distinctive campus culture—as well as business and information technology. A good fit for students eager to get started in a career. Social life revolves around student-friendly Burlington, and nearby ski slopes beckon. Low graduation rate is a challenge.

Situated on a hill overlooking the scenic Vermont lake for which it is named, Champlain College has set out to reinvent the relationship between professional studies and the liberal arts through its so-called upside-down curriculum. Instead of following the traditional academic path—two years of general education courses followed by two years of in-depth study in a major—students at Champlain immediately pursue both their major and a "radically pragmatic, career-focused" liberal arts curriculum and then continue this pattern simultaneously for all four years. "Our majors are not static programs but living platforms of applied learning" with a strong focus on "technology literacy," describes an administrator.

The college, whose roots date to 1878, sits on 22 acres in the historic Hill Section of Burlington, adjacent to the University of Vermont. The core academic campus consists of a mix of lovely restored Victorian mansions and complementary modern structures of brick with slate roofs and green trim. The adjacent "lakeside" campus houses the Leahy Center for Digital Investigation, while a "downtown" campus, connected to the academic core by shuttle buses, provides housing and dining for 300 upperclassmen. The Center for Communication and Creative Media, a 75,000-square-foot facility, offers game and audio labs, studio spaces, and a traditional and digital photo lab. Two buildings on campus have been fully renovated to create a new STEAM (science, technology, engineering, arts, and mathematics) center on campus.

Champlain's curriculum puts the emphasis is on preparing students for the real-world workplace and, beginning in 2026, offers students more "choice, flexibility, and freedom from day one." Students choose a major (or two) and engage in hands-on, career-focused learning from the get-go and can take as many as six classes in their major during their first year. Those who are undecided may try classes in multiple majors.

> **"The upside-down curriculum we have is a great concept."**

"The upside-down curriculum we have is a great concept because instead of waiting to practice in your field, you're jumping in and being able to see and decide if this is the path for you," says a social work major. Full-time, paid co-op experiences with industry partners, through which students can work and earn credit, will be available beginning in fall 2026. Champlain also gives students a full year's worth of flexible credits to apply to their major. All first-year students participate in Champ 101, a 10-week program that helps ease the transition to college. Applied General Education requirements, including science, math, writing, and more, are "collaborative, exploratory, and investigative liberal arts courses" that align with the student's major and all students must complete a capstone. Students also participate in InSight, a four-year personal finance, career positioning, and well-being program built into the curriculum.

All classes are taught by professors or adjuncts, with no TAs. "There is so much hands-on and industry relevant material being taught by professionals," cheers a business administration major of the small classes, 85 percent of which have fewer than 20 students. Computer networking and cybersecurity, computer science, game art, and game design are highly regarded and popular programs, and the business school offers seven majors, from business administration to game production management. New degrees include a B.S. in digital humanities and sonic arts.

Virtually all students participate in internships—"It's very easy to find a great internship with a company who will probably want you back full time once you have graduated," cheers a junior. Study abroad plays an important role at Champlain. The college maintains international satellite campuses in Montreal, a major global center for the game industry, and Dublin. Roughly 30 percent of students take advantage of study abroad.

"The overall description [of Champlain] is 'gamer school,'" says a junior, and another describes the students as "very relaxed and focused on studying and academic performance over partying." Twenty-three percent of students are native

Website: www.champlain.edu
Location: Small City
Private
Total Enrollment: 2,046
Undergraduates: 1,609
Male/Female: 63/37
Financial Aid: 80%
Pell Grant: 24%
Expense: Pr $
Student Loans: 65%
Average Debt: $ $ $ $
Applicants: 3,549
Accepted: 87%
Enrolled: 11%
Grad in 6 Years: 63%
Returning First-years: 82%
Academics: ✍ ✍ ✍
Social: 🗩 🗩 🗩
Q of L: ★ ★ ★
Admissions: (802) 860-2727
Email Address:
  admission@champlain.edu

Strong Programs:
Business
Computer Networking and
  Cybersecurity
Computer Science
Digital Forensics
Game Art
Game Design
Game Programming
Psychology

Burlington, a small city of 44,000 residents, is near the top of everyone's list of best college towns.

The college maintains international satellite campuses in Montreal, a major global center for the game industry, and Dublin.

Vermonters, with the rest hailing mainly from the East Coast and Midwest. Black students account for 3 percent of the total, Hispanics/Latinos 8 percent, Asian Americans 4 percent, multiracial students 5 percent, and international students just 1 percent. Men outnumber women by a ratio of 3 to 2. Politics lean liberal, but some students would rather hit the slopes than a protest march: "There are many skiers and snowboarders, of course, and a great deal of people who care about the environment or social issues." The school awards merit scholarships averaging $18,600.

"Champlain's first-year residence halls are renovated Victorian mansions that have modern technology and safety features with the old charm preserved," explains a senior. Sophomores and upperclassmen can choose among well-maintained traditional dorms, some quite new, that feature tuning and repair facilities for bikes, skis, and skateboards, or they can live in an off-campus apartment hall or find their own off-campus digs. Overall, 82 percent of undergrads reside in college-owned housing. Students take their meals at a dining hall where the food gets lukewarm reviews, or students may opt for take-out at one of two on-campus à la carte cafés. As for student services, a junior says, "Our Career Collaborative, Student Health Center, and Counseling Center are strong but small resources."

> "It's very easy to find a great internship with a company who will probably want you back."

The social scene on campus is quiet. "We are focused on more chill hangouts over ragers and parties," says a business administration major. The college sponsors more than 50 student clubs and organizes a range of activities on and off campus, from bingo to bowling nights. Burlington, a small city of 44,000 residents, is near the top of everyone's list of best college towns. "The surrounding area is great for shopping locally sourced items, eating all around the world, coffee shops and ice cream as well as historical attractions and learning opportunities," says a junior. In addition to the Church Street pedestrian mall, just below the campus, there is a park and bike path that runs along the lake's waterfront. The campus is dry, and policies are enforced.

No one seems to mind that Champlain has no varsity sports (except for the eSports team). But it does have a mascot named Chauncey T. Beaver as well as plenty of intramural options for all skill levels, including soccer, basketball, and dodgeball, and a rugby club that competes against other schools. Not surprisingly for a school full of gamers, Humans vs. Zombies and Quadball (formerly known as Quidditch) are popular. Annual traditions include the Rail Jam skiing and snowboarding competition in the fall and the Spring Meltdown just before final exams, which "takes over our largest quad area with carnival food and games with raffles and amazing prizes," says a student. The end of the year brings the Game Development Senior Show, where graduating seniors show off their projects to the college community (and company recruiters).

Overlaps

UConn, Ithaca, University of New Hampshire, Quinnipiac, Rochester Institute of Technology, Roger Williams, University of Vermont, Worcester Polytechnic

Administrators at Champlain are sensitive about the fact that only 65 percent of entering students graduate within six years. One contributing factor, students suggest, is the need to plunge immediately into a professional field that may not be a good fit. Other students point to the heavy workload in some majors and the lack of cultural diversity as possible factors. Champlain "is heavily steeped in nerd culture," says a junior. "Escaping it is difficult on campus." But administrators are working hard to mitigate these stressors by adding more flexibility into the curriculum.

> "We are focused on more chill hangouts over ragers."

For gaming enthusiasts, techies, creatives, and other career-oriented students, Champlain is a small school with a big vision of how to refashion the relationship between professional training and the liberal arts. It offers a unique option for students who have a strong, focused interest in its professional majors and who are eager to press "start" on their careers. "We are doers," explains a junior. "Our motto, 'Audeamus' or 'Let Us Dare,' applies to pretty much everything we do at Champlain, either socially or academically."

If You Apply To ›

Champlain: Early decision, early action, regular decision. SATs or ACTs: optional. Accepts the Common Application with supplement. Some majors require portfolio submission.

Chapman University

One University Drive, Orange, CA 92866

Chapman sits at the hub of Orange County and a stone's throw from L.A. Has parlayed its O.C. location into burgeoning popularity in film, television, and the performing arts. Those without showbiz aspirations can opt for strong programs in business, communication studies, or biology. Disneyland is in the neighborhood, just a short bike or train ride away.

Although best known as a Southern Californian mecca for budding filmmakers to hone their craft, Chapman University continues to stake its claim as a comprehensive institution that happens to offer one of the nation's best film programs—rather than a film school that also happens to offer other majors. Chapman boasts stellar programs in business and has increased its emphasis on health sciences and technology. Programs like the Grand Challenges Initiative "enable students to tackle complex global issues through collaborative, cross-disciplinary projects." It also facilitates countless internships to send its students out into the workforce with real-world experience.

Founded in 1861 under the auspices of the Christian Church (Disciples of Christ), Chapman is one of the oldest private universities in California. Originally called Hesperian College, the school was renamed in 1934 in honor of C. C. Chapman, an Orange County entrepreneur and benefactor of the school. The beautiful residential campus, situated on 80 tree-lined acres, features a mixture of landmark historic buildings and state-of-the-art facilities. It is located in the historic Old Towne district of Orange, near outstanding beaches, Disneyland, and the world-class cultural offerings of Orange County and Los Angeles.

Regardless of major, all students complete a four-part general education program: a First-Year Foundations course taken in the fall; six inquiry categories (natural science, quantitative reasoning, writing, social sciences, values and ethics, and artistic studies); a Global Citizen cluster (two courses in global studies, one in civic issues, and a language course); and a mini-minor, minor, or second major. Chapman's first-year experience program, Fenestra (Latin for "window"), encourages students to approach their first year as a "window of opportunity"; the program involves a weeklong orientation and special workshops, field trips, and social activities held throughout the year.

The most popular majors are business administration, psychology, health sciences, and biological sciences. Dodge College of Film and Media Arts is a comprehensive, production-based school that offers such majors as news/broadcast journalism and documentary, writing for film and television, public relations and advertising, and creative producing, as well as internships and other active learning

Website: www.chapman.edu
Location: Suburban
Private
Total Enrollment: 8,883
Undergraduates: 7,242
Male/Female: 38/62
Financial Aid: 83%
Pell Grant: 19%
Expense: Pr $ $ $
Student Loans: 43%
Average Debt: $ $
Applicants: 15,634
Accepted: 65%
Enrolled: 16%
Grad in 6 Years: 82%
Returning First-years: 92%
Academics: ✐ ✐ ✐
Social: 🗩 🗩 🗩
Q of L: ★ ★ ★
Admissions: (714) 997-6711
Email Address:
admit@chapman.edu

Strong Programs:
Biological Sciences
Business Administration
Communication Studies
Creative Producing
Dance
Film and Television Production
Health Sciences
Psychology

opportunities. Emerging entrepreneurs can take advantage of a well-stocked portfolio of business programs through the Argyros School of Business and Economics. The Economic Science Institute allows for the study of experimental economics under the direction of Nobel laureate Dr. Vernon Smith and encompasses fields as diverse as finance, engineering, neuroscience, computer science, and philosophy, among others. Notable programs in music, theatre, and dance involve frequent national and international performance components. The Fowler School of Engineering offers undergraduate degrees in computer engineering, computer science, data science, electrical engineering, and software engineering. Integrated degree programs allow students to earn a bachelor's and a master's in five years in several disciplines, including pharmaceutical sciences.

"Regardless of the course of study you are taking at Chapman, you are going to have an in-depth and personalized education," says a creative producing major. Forty percent of classes have fewer than 20 students, and a psychology major says, "Smaller class sizes allow for better relationships between professors and students." First-years are taught by professors—there are no teaching assistants—and a broadcast journalism student says, "The quality of instruction is very high with a lot of industry professionals teaching the courses and being open and very supportive." Students interested in conducting faculty-mentored research can apply to the SURF (Summer Undergraduate Research Fellowship) program, which awards up to $4,000 in funding to selected fellows. An English and sociology major recommends the Honors Program, which allows students to "dive deeply into niche topics" as well as "build and teach their own classes to their peers." Those seeking a global learning experience can choose from semester-long study abroad programs, in addition to short-term, faculty-led travel courses and international summer internships. As for career services, a junior says, "I have had over five internships in two years, and most of that can be attributed to the responsiveness and knowledge of the Office of Career and Professional Development."

"My fellow students [are] very driven and collaborative," says a documentary major. "The student body is very diverse in terms of interests, geographically and politically." Sixty-six percent of Chapman's student body hail from California, and 3 percent are international. Black students constitute 2 percent of the population, Asian Americans 16 percent, Hispanics/Latinos 20 percent, and multiracial students 9 percent. Chapman's Cross-Cultural Center is open to all

students and the documentary major adds, "socioeconomically, the student body is much more diverse than it is perceived to be." Eligible undergraduates receive merit scholarships worth an average of $22,100, but since Chapman is a Division III school, there are no athletic scholarships.

Roughly 90 percent of students reside on campus and Chapman has a three-year housing requirement for incoming first-years who don't reside with a parent near the school. First-years are housed in residence halls based on their chosen academic program; one student explains, "This allows for students to know their peers on day one of classes and always have a study partner throughout the semester." Meals at the Randall Dining Commons are described as tasty and diverse. Campus safety receives positive reviews, and the CARES (Creating a Rape-Free Environment for Students) student organization is active in raising awareness about campus sexual assault.

"There is a party culture, but it is not a make-or-break part of your college experience," says an educational studies major of the social scene at Chapman. Twenty-three percent of the men join fraternities, and sororities attract 32 percent of the women; all members of the Greek community are required to perform community service, and Greek life doesn't dominate the social scene. A senior raves, "There are tons of things to do in the area, especially since we have professional sports teams, concerts, theme parks, and the beaches." Every year, students flock to the homecoming celebration's chili cook-off and fireworks, the Fall Concert, the Spring Sizzle festival, and Midnight Breakfast during finals week.

The city of Orange (population 140,000) is a college town only in the technical sense of the term. "It's actually a very quiet city," says a junior. The Old Towne district is well known as "the Antique Capital of California," although several trendy restaurants, brew pubs, and boutiques have opened their doors in the last few years and are in walking distance of the campus. When students grow weary of the area, they take advantage of the pristine Southern California weather to explore the great outdoors or take trips to Disneyland, L.A., or San Diego.

> "[Nearby] we have professional sports teams, concerts, theme parks, and the beaches."

The Chapman Panthers compete in the Division III Southern California Intercollegiate Athletic Conference. Football, baseball, and men's and women's basketball are among the most competitive teams. The Chapman dance team has brought home several national championships in the last decade. Intramurals and club sports draw a quarter of the student body; intramural basketball and soccer are the most popular, and the men's club lacrosse team is nationally competitive.

Students at Chapman are expected not only to hit the books but also to actively express their creativity through hands-on learning, on-campus involvement, and forays into the real world. "Chapman is known for the people and the connections people make," says a senior.

Overlaps

UCLA, Elon, Loyola Marymount, NYU, Pepperdine, University of San Diego, Santa Clara, University of Southern California

If You Apply To ›

Chapman: Early decision, early action, regular decision. SATs or ACTs: optional. Accepts the Common Application. Art and talent-based programs require submission of a creative supplement.

College of Charleston

66 George Street, Charleston, SC 29424

A public school one-third the size of the University of South Carolina that blends a small-college feel with the advantages of a midsized, urban university. Compare to Elon University or James Madison University. Offers business, education, engineering, and the liberal arts and sciences. Location a feast for history and culinary buffs.

Whether sampling the traditional Lowcountry cuisine or delving into the wide range of courses offered at this historic liberal arts and sciences institution, students at the College of Charleston know they are getting a solid education based on creative expression, intellectual freedom, and hands-on learning experiences. Founded in 1770 as colonial South Carolina's first college, the school's original commitment to the liberal arts and sciences and to the citizens of the region has helped it become a well-respected institution throughout the Southeast. The tradition-rich location only adds to the experience, providing opportunities for research and internships and a robust social scene.

The College of Charleston was private at first and, after a number of identity changes, became a state university exactly 200 years later. Located in Charleston's

Website: www.cofc.edu
Location: Small City
Public
Total Enrollment: 10,325
Undergraduates: 10,093
Male/Female: 32/68
Financial Aid: 72%
Pell Grant: 23%
Expense: Pub $ $ $
Student Loans: 49%

(continued)

Average Debt: $ $ $
Applicants: 31,680
Accepted: 60%
Enrolled: 12%
Grad in 6 Years: 66%
Returning First-years: 82%
Academics: ✎ ✎ ✎
Social: 🌑 🌑 🌑 🌑
Q of L: ★ ★ ★ ★
Admissions: (843) 953-5670
Email Address:
   admissions@charleston.edu

Strong Programs:
Arts Management
Biology
Business Administration
Chemistry
Communication
Languages
Marine Biology
Psychology

famous Historic District, the campus features many of the city's most venerable buildings. More than 80 of its buildings are former private residences, ranging from the typical Charleston "single" house to the Victorian. The campus is within easy walking distance of the city's shopping and restaurant district and offers proximity to beaches. Cistern Yard, the area in front of Randolph Hall lined with moss-draped live oaks, is a student gathering point and the site of May graduation ceremonies. The campus has received countless awards for its design and has been designated a national arboretum and a National Historic Landmark.

The college's core curriculum is rooted in the liberal arts, sciences, and professional programs. The focus is on the development of problem-solving and critical-thinking skills, as well as taking an entrepreneurial approach to addressing global issues like climate change, social injustice, and economic inequality. Each student is required to satisfy credits in writing or English, history, mathematics or logic, social science, natural sciences, humanities, and foreign language. All new students attend Convocation, where they are introduced to the college's academic traditions, and first-years from underrepresented groups can participate in several support programs designed to ensure their successful transition to college. All new students take part in the First-Year Experience and choose between seminar and learning community options; sample seminars include Charleston Writers, Designing Your Life, and Gateway to Neuroscience.

Biology, chemistry, public health, and psychology are some of the strongest programs; many graduates go on to the Medical University of South Carolina, a few blocks down the street. Marine biology, communication, international studies, and arts management are also strengths. The historic preservation and community planning major uses Charleston as its classroom. The fastest growing majors are psychology, business administration, finance, communication, and marketing. New majors include nursing and health services administration and management. "Courses are challenging but always engaging," says a senior. Thirty-two percent of all classes enroll fewer than 20 students, and while students say the quality of instruction can be hit-or-miss, a communication major comments, "The majority of my professors have been unforgettable mentors to me and have played a critical role in my learning."

About 1,350 students enroll in the Honors College, where they are given a more demanding workload, including a culminating Bachelor's Essay that is undertaken with the support of a faculty mentor. The Office of Undergraduate Research and Creative Activities awards competitive grants to fund student/faculty scholarly projects. About 25 percent of undergrads study internationally;

> **"Courses are challenging but always engaging."**

the college sponsors more than 40 faculty-led study abroad programs, as well as upperclassmen spring break programs. Many performing arts majors take advantage of internships with Spoleto Festival USA, Charleston's annual international arts festival. The city's growing biomedicine, tech, and aerospace industries also provide opportunities for research and internships.

Dining services provide options for all types of diets, including vegetarian, vegan, and kosher fare.

According to an English major, the college's student body is "pretty accepting, artistic, and fun." Forty-six percent of students hail from South Carolina and another 2 percent from foreign countries. Two-thirds of undergrads are women, and the administration has been pushing to increase the proportion of students of color. The school is "not the strongest diversity in terms of socioeconomic and racial populations," says a psychology major. Currently, Black students account for 5 percent of the student body, Asian Americans 2 percent, Hispanics/Latinos 8 percent, and multiracial students 4 percent. Racial tension in the city of Charleston, known for its history as a major slave-trading port, has sparked "some protests and disagreements" on campus, says a junior, but overall, the political climate is left-leaning and usually relatively calm. The school's Center for the Study of Slavery in Charleston raises awareness of racial injustice and the legacies of slavery through research, public events, exhibitions, and other projects. The college offers merit scholarships averaging $13,200 and more than 130 athletic scholarships.

"On-campus housing at the College of Charleston is very nice, with choices between dormitories, apartments, or historic houses," says a student. Thirty-two percent of students live in college-owned housing, and students say more would stay on campus if there were space to accommodate them. Off-campus housing can get quite expensive, although the college leases multiple housing buildings within walking distance of campus in order to help ease the strain. Dining services provide options for all types of diets, including vegetarian, vegan, and kosher fare. "The omelets at Liberty are what I live for!" cheers a junior. As for security, "Being in the heart of a city can sometimes be overwhelming, but generally, campus feels safe," says one student.

Twenty-one percent of the men and 24 percent of the women belong to fraternities and sororities, respectively. "There are a few parties here and there," says a sophomore, while those of drinking age can head to bars on King Street. More than 240 student organizations help provide alternatives, and students enjoy Charleston's sporting events, concerts, and numerous festivals. As one student puts it, "The city is a social playground for college students. There are tons of restaurants, events to attend, and beautiful architecture to enjoy." The clap-clap of horse-drawn carriages bearing tourists is a routine sight. On weekends, students can head to beaches such as Folly Beach, Sullivan's Island, and Isle of Palms, which are minutes away. For those who don't mind a drive, there's "the Grand Strand," Myrtle Beach, 90 miles north, Savannah and Hilton Head to the south, and Atlanta to the west.

There is no football, but other athletic teams are popular, none more so than basketball. The College of Charleston is a Division I school, and several Cougar teams are competitive in the Coastal Athletic Association conference, including men's basketball, men's and women's golf, equestrian, and baseball. The sailing team is a top performer nationally. The intramural program offers eight team sports throughout the year, and basketball and soccer are the most popular, both in terms of participation and competitive fervor; around 25 club sports are also available.

The College of Charleston has become the best public liberal arts and sciences institution in South Carolina, propelled by its historic setting, an honors college, opportunities for internships and study abroad, and a healthy social life. "There's so much history here that you can't help but feel like you're making some yourself," muses an anthropology and biology double major.

"[The students are] pretty accepting, artistic, and fun."

Overlaps

Clemson, Coastal Carolina, Elon, James Madison, UNC Wilmington, University of South Carolina, Southern Methodist, University of Tampa

If You Apply To ›

Charleston: Early decision I and II, early action, regular decision. Accepts the Common Application with supplement. Application includes optional questions regarding preferred first name, birth sex, and gender identity. Please consult Charleston's website for the most up-to-date information regarding standardized test requirements.

5801 S. Ellis Ave., Chicago, IL 60637

Traditionally known as a haven for true intellectuals who enjoy nothing more than the chance to debate a fresh idea. The Common Core remains the intellectual heart of the school, and ongoing investments in academic offerings, dormitory life, the arts, and athletic facilities have helped cement UChicago's status alongside the top Ivies and Stanford.

Website: www.uchicago.edu
Location: City Outskirts
Private
Total Enrollment: 13,055
Undergraduates: 7,497
Male/Female: 54/46
Financial Aid: 87%
Pell Grant: 11%
Expense: Pr $ $ $ $
Student Loans: 11%
Average Debt: $ $ $ $
Applicants: 43,612
Accepted: 4%
Enrolled: 88%
Grad in 6 Years: 96%
Returning First-years: 99%
Academics: ✍ ✍ ✍ ✍ ✍
Social: 🌑 🌑 🌑
Q of L: ★ ★ ★ ★
Admissions: (773) 702-8650
Email Address:
 collegeadmissions@uchicago
 .edu

Strong Programs:
Biological Sciences
Economics
English
Environmental and Urban
 Studies
Global Studies
Mathematics
Physical Sciences
Political Science

The University of Chicago attracts students eager to move beyond the cliquishness of high school and the superficial trappings of Ivy League résumé building—the students are concerned about learning for learning's sake in addition to getting a job after graduation, though they're certainly successful at the latter. "'Life of the Mind' is taken very seriously," says a student. "The academic atmosphere extends beyond the classroom, and most people like it that way." Still, administrators have realized that in the 21st century, even the best schools cannot survive on intellectual might alone. To make UChicago more attractive, they've broadened the offerings in the core curriculum, expanded study abroad programs and career advising, and continue to focus on creating "an environment of open discourse and free expression." The result? Applications have increased sharply, and enrollment is surging. Says a first-year, "The fact that college here is a good time just makes us that much happier."

The university's 217-acre, tree-lined campus sits in Hyde Park, an eclectic community on Chicago's South Side, surrounded by neighborhoods on three sides and Lake Michigan on the other. One of 77 city neighborhoods, Hyde Park "is pretty intellectual," says one student, noting that "two-thirds of our faculty live here." Streets are lined with brownstones, rowhouses, and townhouses, giving way to luxury highrises with beautiful views as you get closer to the lake; the city's Griffin Museum of Science and Industry is within spitting distance. The campus itself is self-contained and architecturally magnificent. The main quads are steel-gray Gothic—gargoyles and all—and other buildings were designed by the likes of Frank Lloyd Wright, Eero Saarinen, and Mies van der Rohe. The Regenstein Library (known as "the Reg") is a national treasure, symbolically located in the heart of the campus. Next to the Reg is the Mansueto Library, a geodesic dome. Newer construction includes buildings for molecular science, public policy, the performing arts, and the residential commons.

Founded in 1890 thanks to John D. Rockefeller and Marshall Field's largesse, UChicago has historically drawn praise for its graduate programs, but in subsequent years, the undergraduate college has flourished, competing successfully with the likes of Stanford, Harvard, and Princeton. To that end, the university remains unequivocally committed to the view that a solid foundation in the liberal arts is the best preparation for future study or work. Thus, music students study musicology, but also learn calculus, along with everyone else. Regardless of major, 15 to 18 of a student's 42 courses fall under general education requirements called the Common Core, which is one of the most comprehensive sets of distribution requirements anywhere.

Other Core requirements include courses in the sciences and math, humanities, arts, social sciences, and a sequence of study in a specific civilization. There is a required writing tutorial as well. "The classes are difficult, but we're not at university for easy, certainly not at UChicago," says an economics major from England. The quarter system, pioneered by UChicago, means class material is presented over

10-week periods with the first term starting in late September and ending in mid-December. In practice, this means that students take more classes over four years than they would on a semester-based system, with virtually uninterrupted work through the year, punctuated by a long summer vacation and three exam weeks. A senior says, "It is important to practice time management in order to succeed. Once you get into the swing of things, however, everything is manageable." Seniors are also encouraged to do final-year projects. Classes are intimate, with 78 percent enrolling fewer than 20 students, and led by brilliant faculty members who've won Nobel Prizes, Guggenheims, and other prestigious awards. "Professors are at the absolute pinnacle of their field," says a senior, "giving every class the feel that you're on the cutting edge of every important conversation within your field of study."

The economics department, which has produced numerous Nobel laureates including Milton Friedman, is known as a bastion of free market economics and is one of UChicago's academic claims to fame. Popular majors include economics, biological sciences, political science, and English. Interdisciplinary majors in environmental and urban studies and global studies are notable. The university also prides itself on area studies programs, such as those focusing on East Asia, South Asia, the Middle East, and the Slavic countries. The Accelerated Medical Scholars Program allows exceptional undergrads to begin medical school during their fourth year, and similar joint-degree and professional options allow undergrads to engage with any of the university's other graduate and professional schools. The cross-subject molecular engineering major—the university's only undergraduate degree in engineering—focuses on "solving societal problems at the molecular level"; students delve into such topics as water conservation, quantum computing, and advances in biological immuno-engineering.

Students enjoy an abundance of research assistantships and opportunities for publication, even before they graduate. Students praise the three-year Trott Business Program, which offers workshops and specialized industry tracks. Through the Metcalf Internship Program, students have access to more than 4,500 fully funded internships that are offered exclusively to UChicago students. Established internships are available at the Argonne National Laboratory and Fermilab, both located in nearby suburbs, and at the UChicago-affiliated Marine Biological Laboratory in Woods Hole, Massachusetts. When Chicago gets too cold and snowy, students may take advantage of more than 80 study abroad programs, which reach most corners of the globe and include study at the university's centers in Hong Kong, Beijing, Delhi, and Paris. Financial aid applies to study abroad programs, and 40 percent of students take part. All students are assigned both an academic and a career advisor, and UChicago has one of the best career advising systems of any school.

Through the Metcalf Internship Program, students have access to 4,500 fully funded internships.

At UChicago, says a junior, "What brings together the student body is a love for learning and maybe just a bit of geekiness, whether that comes from a love of Plato or an obsession with big bang theory." Adds a senior, "We're also pretty known for being quirky—in a good way!" Ninety-one percent of undergraduates come from out of state, including many East Coasters with academic parents, while 14 percent are the first in their families to go to college. Twelve percent come from rural and small towns, and 19 percent are international. "There's a lot of diversity across all kinds of dimensions—geography, background, interests, politics," cheers a junior. "But what stands out the most is the diversity of thought." Several students point out that UChicago was a pioneer of free speech on college campuses, and "has successfully created a campus environment where all hot-button social and political issues are discussed," says an astrophysics major.

Admissions at UChicago are need-blind, and the university meets 100 percent of students' demonstrated need with financial aid packages that include grants instead of loans. The Odyssey Scholarship program offers generous financial aid packages, funding to support internships or study abroad, and other benefits to first-generation and lower-income students. Students from families earning less than $125,000 per year attend tuition-free. Socioeconomic diversity is slowly inching upward. The University of Chicago provides special academic and financial resources to veterans under the Federal Yellow Ribbon initiative.

New incoming students are required to live on campus for the first two years (transfer students only one year), and the school guarantees housing for four years. Fifty-eight percent of all undergrads live in the dorms, where "students are split into houses, which serve as smaller, more intimate communities that offer a very home-y feel," explains a political science major. All halls are co-ed, though some offer single-sex floors, and each dorm is different—some house fewer than 100 people in traditional, shared double rooms without kitchens, while another has 700 beds organized into colorful suites. "Hyde Park has tons of really cute, cheap apartments," reports one student, so many of the more "independent-minded" students move off campus. "As for the food, it's Chicago," deadpans a junior. "Of course the food is amazing." Campus safety and sexual assault are "something the school has taken extremely seriously," says a junior. And while the academic environment can be stressful, "we all take our mental health very seriously, and the school provides plenty of resources on that front," says a junior.

"Contrary to the old saying, this is not 'where fun goes to die,'" insists a junior, referencing a joking slogan once emblazoned on T-shirts that has dogged the university for years. "There's plenty of the typical college fun you'd expect to see on any campus." And according to a senior: "There is always some sort of event going on around campus, be it a theater performance or an a cappella show." Indeed, the university's a cappella scene is one of the tops in the country, and Chicago offers museums galore; world-class symphony, opera, and dance; the Second City comedy improv troupe (invented by University of Chicago undergrads); professional spectator sports; and plenty of clubs and bars. The university provides students with free, unlimited access to all parts of the city via public transportation, and Arts Pass offers free or discounted student admission to city art, theater, and cultural events. Cars are a nice luxury (if you can find a parking place). Road trips are infrequent, but one popular destination is Ann Arbor, about five hours away, for concerts and more traditional collegiate fun at the University of Michigan. Greek life has only a small presence on campus.

> "Professors are at the absolute pinnacle of their field."

Tradition is a hallmark at UChicago. Students have fond memories of first-year orientation, known as O-Week, an event administrators claim was invented at the university in 1934. Students celebrate the festival of Kuviasungnerk/Kangeiko ("Kuvia" for short), a winter week of early morning calisthenics and other activities, culminating in a Friday morning yoga session by Lake Michigan and a Polar Bear Run, where naked or seminaked Maroons dash across the academic quad. Each spring, students look forward to the Summer Breeze concert on the main quad and a four-day Scavenger Hunt ("Scav"). The humorous Latke-Hamantesh Debate "has been a tradition since 1946," says a senior. "Faculty members argue the merits of latkes versus hamantashen (potato pancakes vs. filled pastries), often using complex theories from their fields of study."

UChicago's Maroons compete in Division III, but, says a senior, "We don't really have many athletic rivalries anymore, so our main nemesis is Harvard, as they are our main intellectual and same school-color rival." Once a national football powerhouse, the school abolished the sport in 1939 only to bring it back in 1963.

Aside from hitting the gridiron or the basketball court, "even the varsity athletes are Phi Beta Kappa (that is, very smart) and involved with university theater," a junior marvels. In fact, athletes here have a higher overall GPA than the student body as a whole. Women's tennis and lacrosse have won recent division or conference championships. Other consistently solid programs include men's and women's soccer, women's basketball, and men's and women's cross-country. Intramurals draw 70 percent of undergrads, with students competing in sports ranging from the traditional (flag football, soccer, and volleyball) to the offbeat (inner-tube water polo, broomball, and archery). Numerous club sports are available as well.

The University of Chicago has moved well beyond the Spartan attitudes of former president Robert Maynard Hutchins, who led UChicago from 1929 to 1951 and once told members of the football team that was about to be abolished, "When I feel like exercising, I just lie down until the feeling goes away." A major national force for the liberal arts, he also once declared, "My idea of education is to unsettle the minds of the young and inflame their intellects." Conscious that it is younger and less moneyed than its Ivy League and Ivy-plus competitors, Chicago has taken on substantial debt over the last decade to invest in new facilities, academic programs, and student amenities, and the effort seems to be paying off. Among other things, undergraduate enrollment has increased by 43 percent since 2015. UChicago undergraduates today are certainly more social and more heavily involved in extracurricular activities than their predecessors, and the university draws strength from its role as a high-powered haven for superbright students, including those who lack the polished nonacademic credentials favored by admissions committees in places like Cambridge and New Haven. "The academic environment is not for everyone, but the University of Chicago never claimed to be," notes a computer science major. "This is a place where the driven come to thrive."

If You Apply To ›

UChicago: Early decision I and II, early action, regular decision. SATs or ACTs: optional. Accepts the Common Application with essay supplements and video profiles.

University of Cincinnati

2600 Clifton Avenue, Cincinnati, OH 45221

In most states, UC would be a big enchilada. But with Ohio State two hours up the road and Miami of Ohio even closer, Cincinnati has to hustle to get its name out there. A pioneer along with Antioch in co-op education, it offers quality programs in everything from engineering to art—and a historically competitive men's basketball team.

Many first-time visitors to Cincinnati are surprised to find an attractive and very livable city. As they traverse the city's hilly roads, they are in for another surprise—its university. Not only has the University of Cincinnati made its mark with its extensive research programs, but its signature experiential learning through cooperative education program, first established in 1906, is also the largest co-op offering of any public college or university in the country.

The compact campus is a mile uphill from Cincinnati's downtown area. Ultramodern buildings rise up next to traditional ivy-covered Georgian halls. Most

(continued)

Pell Grant: 19%

Expense: Pub $ $ $

Student Loans: 53%

Average Debt: $ $

Applicants: 34,285

Accepted: 85%

Enrolled: 23%

Grad in 6 Years: 75%

Returning First-years: 85%

Academics: ✏️ ✏️

Social: 🌑 🌑 🌑

Q of L: ★ ★ ★

Admissions: (513) 556-1100

Email Address:
 admissions@uc.edu

Strong Programs:
Architecture
Art and Design
Biological Sciences
Business Administration
Engineering
Music
Nursing
Prepharmacy

The university sponsors some events, such as the Red & Black Bash and the Sigma Sigma Carnival.

activities revolve around the university's "Main Street" in the center of campus. Newer buildings include the $93 million Arts and Sciences building and a recently opened indoor athletic practice facility.

Research has been a longtime forte. Campus scientists have given the world anti-knock gasoline, the electronic organ, antihistamines, and the U.S. Weather Bureau. But the university is perhaps best known for cooperative education, which allows students to earn while they learn. More than 40 programs across the Cincinnati curriculum offer the popular five-year professional-practice option, and about 3,500 students participate in co-ops each year. UC has taken steps to improve the quality of undergraduate education by strengthening its general education requirements to focus on critical thinking and expression, creating more than 100 learning communities for first-years, and expanding its honors program. "I enjoy how it is experience-based vs. just having to do more classes," says a mechanical engineering major. First-years must take English, math, and a contemporary issues class, and all students are required to complete a capstone experience. Other requirements vary by college.

The colleges of engineering; business; and design, architecture, art, and planning (the schools with the most co-op students) are the best bets at UC. The university's music conservatory, one of the top programs in the field, also offers electronic

> "It's a great little square mile. . . . Small campus, huge school."

media and broadcasting training, in addition to the strong musical theatre program. The colleges of nursing and pharmacy are well known and benefit from UC's health center and graduate medical school. The most popular majors are marketing, health sciences, psychology, and finance. Education students earn two bachelor's degrees: one in education and one in a liberal arts subject. The College of Medicine now offers a variety of undergraduate concentrations in public health. For the 13 percent of undergrads who choose to study abroad or work in international co-ops, opportunities are offered in more than 50 countries.

At UC, the academic rigor is largely a function of one's major; fields such as engineering and nursing require a substantially larger academic commitment. "I would say that the most rigorous courses are those that are nontraditional," offers one student, citing "study abroad, capstones, projects with corporate partners, and advanced topics classes." Some courses end up being quite large; just 33 percent of all classes have fewer than 20 students. "My professors are wonderful," cheers a fashion design major. "They even talk to us about how we feel about how our course is going and make changes according to feedback."

"We are your traditional hardworking college students," says a sophomore of UC's student body, 63 percent of whom participate in faculty-guided research. Seventy-two percent of undergraduates are native Ohioans, and 9 percent come from abroad. Black students make up 10 percent of the student body, Asian Americans 5 percent, Hispanic/Latinos 7 percent, and multiracial students add 5 percent. Diversity, equity, campus construction, and rising tuition are the hot topics on campus. "There are issues with the DEI programs potentially getting shut down that has caused tension on campus," says a student, while another explains, "We tend to spend a lot of money on new shiny buildings instead of retouching things that need improvement." The school offers merit scholarships averaging $6,200 and more than 250 athletic scholarships in 16 sports.

Twenty-one percent of UC students live in campus-owned housing. Many upperclassmen consider off-campus living far better than dorm life, and apartments can usually be found nearby. For meals, "Campus has three dining facilities, multiple fast-food restaurants in the university center, and a few cafés located in certain buildings," explains a senior. A marketing major adds, "Living in an urban environment means there are extra precautions that keep students safe."

Merchants have turned the area surrounding UC, called Clifton, into a mini college town with plenty to do. Although not a major metropolis like Chicago or Boston, the "Queen City" of Cincinnati (as in "Queen of the West") does offer an urban feel. "From sports to museums to Findlay Market to live music to parks to Kings Island—I am certainly never bored here!" enthuses a senior. Nine nearby bus lines take undergraduates into the heart of the city in minutes. On-campus activities include 550 student clubs, with everything from mountaineering to clubs in various majors. Fraternities and sororities attract 9 percent of the men and 7 percent of the women but are still the most active places to party on campus, usually opening their functions to everyone. "There are massive parties, if that is what you are interested in, but they are also easy enough to avoid if you are a nerd like me," says a mechanical engineering major. The university sponsors some events, such as the Red & Black Bash and the Sigma Sigma Carnival. Cleveland and Columbus make for good road trips.

Bearcat teams compete in the Division I Big 12. The men's basketball team, though recently inconsistent, has been histori-cally competitive, as is football, men's and wom-en's cross-country, women's basketball, and women's volleyball. Everyone mentions the annual "Crosstown Shootout" basketball game with Xavier University. Weekend athletes take advantage of UC's first-rate recreation center, and more than 50 club sports and a variety of intramurals are an option too.

> "The most rigorous courses are those that are nontraditional."

UC offers students a lively social scene, both on campus and minutes away in downtown Cincinnati. But cooperative education and experiential learning is the name of the game at this Ohio school, where the co-op program allows students to take their degrees out for a test drive before graduation and have a head start on their peers after it. "It's a great little square mile," says a satisfied communication major. "Small campus, huge school."

Overlaps

Bowling Green State, Indiana University, University of Kentucky, Miami University (OH), Ohio State, Ohio University, Purdue, Xavier (OH)

If You Apply To ›

UC: Early action, rolling admissions. SATs or ACTs: optional. Accepts the Common Application with supplement. Apply to particular program.

Claremont Colleges

In 1925, theologian and educator James A. Blaisdell had the vision to create a group of colleges patterned after Oxford and Cambridge in England—an "Oxford of the Orange Groves," as he elegantly put it. A century later, the five schools that comprise the Claremont Colleges thrive as a consortium of separate and distinct undergraduate colleges with two adjoining graduate institutions, a theological seminary, and botanical gardens. Like families, the colleges coexist, interact, and experience their share of both cooperation and tension. Ultimately, however, the Claremont Colleges consortium forms a mutually beneficial partnership that offers its students the vast resources and facilities one might only expect to find at a large university.

The colleges are located 35 miles east of Los Angeles on 546 acres in the suburb of Claremont (population 36,000), a peaceful, tree-lined neighborhood at the foot of the San Gabriel Mountains. The picture-perfect California weather has sometimes been marred by wildfire smoke and from smog courtesy of the neighbors in nearby L.A., but the smog level has declined dramatically in the past few years.

Of the five undergraduate colleges that make up the Claremont Colleges—Claremont McKenna, Harvey Mudd, Pitzer, Pomona, and Scripps—Pomona is the largest, with about 1,700 students. Each school retains its own institutional identity, with its own faculty, administration, admissions, and curriculum, although the boundaries of both academic work and extracurricular activities are somewhat flexible. Each of the schools also tends to specialize in a particular area that complements the offerings of all the others. Claremont McKenna, which caters mainly to students planning careers in economics, business, law, or government, has 11 research institutes located on its campus while Harvey Mudd is a liberal arts college specializing in engineering, science, and math. Pitzer, a classical liberal arts institution and the most socially progressive of the five, excels in environmental and sustainability studies, and at the all-women Scripps, the top majors include the social sciences, biology, and media studies. The oldest of the five colleges, Pomona ranks as one of the top liberal arts colleges anywhere and is strong across the board.

Collectively, the colleges share many services and facilities, including a student newspaper, a biological field station, a student health center, auditoriums, a 2,500-seat concert hall, a 350-seat theater, bookstores, a maintenance department, a business office, and a shared campus safety force. The Queer Resource Center, housed at Pomona but serving the whole community, is a model of collaboration between schools, and the EmPOWER Center provides the community with comprehensive support and educational resources on sexual assault, dating and domestic violence, and stalking. The Claremont library system makes two million volumes available to all students. Faculties and administrations are free to arrange joint programs or classes between all or just some of the schools. Courses are open to students from the other colleges (approximately 2,700 courses in all), but each college sets limits on the number of classes that can be taken elsewhere. Perhaps the best example of academic cooperation is the team-taught interdisciplinary courses, which are organized by instructors from the different schools and appeal to a mix of different academic interests.

The Claremont Colleges draw large numbers of students from within California, although their national reputation is growing. These days, about half the students hail from other Western and non-Western states, with a sizable contingent from the East Coast. The tone at the Claremont Colleges is decidedly intellectual, and graduate programs in the arts and sciences are more common goals than business or law school. Anyone who is bright and hardworking can find a niche at one of the five schools.

One student describes the town of Claremont as "a wonderful place if you're married or about to die." Indeed, the quiet local community ("the Village") has its share of senior citizens, but it also offers a flavor reminiscent of Ann Arbor (home to the University of Michigan), with quirky boutiques, coffee shops, truly remarkable candy stores, a Sunday farmers market, and eateries ranging from fine dining to diners and specialty bagel shops. There are even ice cream shops that freeze your ice cream with liquid nitrogen before your eyes—and it's all an easy walk or bike ride from any campus. Students report that the endless list of social activities offered at the colleges makes up for anything Claremont might lack. For hot times, Hollywood's glamour and downtown L.A. are within sniffing distance. The availability of shared Zipcars, rideshare services, and a Metro line make these and other locations easy to access. Nearby mountains and the fabled surfing beaches make this collegiate paradise's backyard complete. Mount Baldy ski lifts, for instance, are only 15 miles away, and you'll reach Laguna Beach before the end of your favorite album. For spring break, Mexico is cheap and a great change of pace.

On campus, extracurricular life maintains a balance between cooperation and independence. Claremont McKenna, Harvey Mudd, and Scripps field joint athletic teams, and the men's teams especially are Division III powers, due to the exploits of CMC athletes. Pomona and Pitzer also compete together with particular strength in water polo, track and field, and soccer. The popular Claremont Colleges Ballroom Dance Company has won multiple national collegiate championships, as has the perennially successful Claremont Colleges Debate Union.

Each of the five colleges has its own dorms, and since off-campus housing is limited in Claremont proper, the social life of students revolves around their dorms. Large five-school parties are regular Thursday, Friday, and Saturday night events. "In my opinion, Mudd's parties are the best because they always have themes," says a physics major. Claremont McKenna is said to have the most raucous party scene, while Pitzer hosts multiple music festivals throughout the year. There are no fraternities except for three local ones at Pomona, where joining is far from de rigueur. All cafeterias are open to all students, and most big events—films, concerts, etc.—are advertised throughout each campus. Day-to-day social interaction among students at different schools, be it for meals or dates, is not what it might be. Occasional political squabbles break out between liberal faculty and students at Pitzer and their conservative counterparts at Claremont McKenna. For the most part, students benefit not only from the nurturing and support within their own schools, each of which has its own academic or extracurricular emphasis, but also from the abundant resources that the Claremont Colleges consortium offers as a whole.

Claremont McKenna College

888 Columbia Avenue, Claremont, CA 91711

Watch your back, Pomona—this rising star is no longer content with being a social sciences specialty school. CMC is half the size of a typical liberal arts college and smaller than Pomona by about 300 students. CMC continues to develop its national and global reputation, and Californians now make up less than half the student body. Recently raised over $1 billion to put toward expanded science programs, faculty, and financial aid.

Claremont McKenna College's special niche in the Claremont College pantheon is top programs in government, economics, and international relations. In addition, CMC has 11 research institutes located on campus, which offer undergraduates ample opportunities to study everything from political demographics to the environment, and 60 percent do so. The arts and humanities are also available, but Claremont McKenna is better suited to those with high ambitions in business leadership and public affairs. "CMCers learn for the sake of doing," suggests one student. "The student body is incredibly passionate about applying what they learn to real world challenges."

The 135-acre (and growing) campus is mostly "California modern" in its architecture, with lots of Spanish tile roofs and picture windows that look out on the San Gabriel Mountains. Described by one student as "more functional than aesthetic," the physical layout fits right in with the school's practical attitude, although the public art collection at Claremont has been enriched over the past decade. Kravis Center is a state-of-the-art academic center that houses classrooms, seminar rooms, a computer laboratory, and faculty offices. Roberts Pavilion serves as an athletic, fitness, and events center.

CMC's extensive general education requirements include two semesters in the humanities; three in the social sciences; one each in the natural sciences and mathematics; and a senior thesis. All first-years take a First-Year Writing Seminar and a Freshman Humanities Seminar, and all students complete a capstone senior thesis. Claremont McKenna offers top programs in economics and government, but the international relations, psychology, and history programs are also considered strong. Interdisciplinary programs, such as the philosophy, politics, and economics major, are popular. Claremont recently raised over $1 billion—one of the highest fund-raising efforts ever for a liberal arts institution—to expand the campus, science programs, faculty, and financial aid. One result: CMC has launched the Kravis Department of Integrated Sciences, housed in the new Robert Day Sciences Center, which opened in fall 2025. A new integrated sciences major is structured around Health (genomics, systems biology, and health), Brain (brain, learning, and decision), and Planet (climate, energy, and the environment). The college also offers a popular 3–2 program in economics and engineering, a four-year B.A./M.A. program, and a 4–1 M.B.A. program in conjunction with the Claremont Graduate University.

"The academic climate is motivated, driven, passionate, engaged," says a public policy and philosophy major. Seventy-eight percent of classes have fewer than 20 students, and "professors put an emphasis on guiding conversations rather than leading them," says a psychology major. All first-years take part in a five-day orientation program that includes a Welcome Orientation Adventure (WOA!) trip and a reception with the president and department chairs. About 38 percent of Claremont

> **"CMCers learn for the sake of doing."**

McKenna students take advantage of study abroad programs offered in more than 55 countries, including Australia, Brazil, Costa Rica, and Japan. Participants in the Washington Semester can intern with the State Department, the White House, and lobbying groups. "The Soll Center for Student Opportunity is incredible for alumni connection, CV, and resume building," raves a junior. The college provides stipends through the Sponsored Internship and Experiences program, which allows students to pursue domestic and international internships, especially in their first and second summers.

CMC students "are super pre-professionally oriented," says an international relations and philosophy major. The student body is 41 percent Californian, with many other domestic students coming from the East Coast, and 17 percent of students are international. Asian Americans account for 17 percent of the student body, Hispanics/Latinos 15 percent, Black students 4 percent, and multiracial students 9 percent. CMC strives to be politically balanced, and a psychology major notes, "Students know how to share their opinions and how to disagree politely without causing harm." The school accepts domestic applicants on a need-blind basis and guarantees to meet the demonstrated need of all admitted students. It also awards a limited number of merit scholarships, which average $20,100.

Nearly all CMC students live on campus, and all residence halls are co-ed. Stark Hall, a substance-free dorm, gives students more living options. "Many of the rooms are pretty spacious and comfortable," shares a sophomore. A cluster of on-campus apartments equipped with kitchen facilities is a popular option for upperclassmen. As for food, says a junior, "[it's] delicious, and you have a choice of seven dining halls at all times and seven cafés (dozens of cuisines, sometimes even catered), at all hours of the day (from 6 a.m. until 2 a.m.)!" Students can eat in dining halls at any of the other four colleges. CMC has expanded its staff dedicated to assisting the campus community with issues related to discrimination, harassment, and sexual misconduct.

Most students agree that the social life at CMC is more than adequate, thanks to the five-college system. "Every Thursday and Saturday, there is always a larger party," says a first-year student. "Otherwise, dorm parties are very common, and

"Many of the rooms are pretty spacious and comfortable."

L.A. is accessible once you have a car after frosh year." The College Programming Board "actively promotes a safe drinking and bystander/responsibility culture." The mid-quad carnival and Pirate Palooza are favorite bashes, and Club Claremont plans on-campus events as well as outings for everything from surfing and skiing nearby to day trips to Disneyland and L.A. Ponding, another unusual CMC tradition, involves being thrown into one of the two campus fountains on one's birthday. The college sponsors an outstanding lecture series at the Athenaeum (a.k.a. "the Ath") on Monday through Thursday nights each week, as well as dialogue development and an emphasis on viewpoint diversity through its campuswide Open Academy. Before each lecture, students and faculty can enjoy a gourmet dinner together and engage in intellectual debates. Students also highly recommend road trips to Joshua Tree, Coachella, San Francisco, and Las Vegas.

Division III athletics are an important part of life at Claremont McKenna, and the school has an overstuffed trophy case to prove it. Men's and women's tennis and men's water polo have brought home national titles. Recent Stag (men's) and Athena (women's) conference champions include women's cross-country and volleyball, men's basketball, men's and women's golf, and softball. A third of the students play varsity sports, and CMC students tend to dominate the teams jointly fielded with Harvey Mudd and Scripps. Top rivalries include Pomona–Pitzer, both in athletics and academics, one student claims. Intramural offerings include cornhole, inner tube water polo, pickleball, and more.

CMC has embraced its mission to produce great leaders by providing students with ample opportunities for research and study abroad, as well as top-notch programs in government and economics. And with its incredibly successful fund-raising campaign, students are reaping the rewards with expanded opportunities for learning and real-world experiences. Claremont McKenna, says a sophomore, is "a school for people who are pre-professionally oriented, and really want to create change in the world by being responsible leaders."

Overlaps

Pomona, Stanford, UC Berkeley, UCLA, University of Southern California

If You Apply To ›

Claremont McKenna: Early decision I and II, regular decision. Accepts the Common Application with supplement. Please consult Claremont McKenna's website for the most up-to-date information regarding standardized test requirements.

Harvey Mudd College

301 Platt Boulevard, Claremont, CA 91711

Harvey Mudd may rank as the finest institution that few people outside of STEM-world have ever heard of. Renowned for encouraging women to go into engineering and other STEM areas, HMC challenges larger neighbor Caltech for sheer brainpower and tops it in access to outstanding faculty. Only Caltech sends a higher proportion of its graduates on for Ph.D.s. Offers more exposure to the liberal arts than most science- and technology-oriented schools, and a tight-knit community.

A top-ranked liberal arts college with a technical bent, Harvey Mudd College, established in 1955 and named for a founder, strives to give its students a sense of academic balance. Although it's a leading provider of high-quality programs in science and engineering (Where else can you take an introductory engineering class where you build your own underwater robot?), it also emphasizes a well-rounded education with knowledge in the humanities, social sciences, and arts. "Harvey Mudd is a nerdy, organic, stressful, and academically engaging college," says a first-year student. A senior adds, "I really think the culture and community at Harvey Mudd is my favorite part about this school."

HMC's mid-'50s vintage campus of cinder-block buildings, in the words of one student, "looks like an engineering college; it's very symmetrical and there's no romance." In addition, most buildings have small, square prism bricks, intended to accentuate architectural lines, that students have dubbed "warts"—not a very attractive picture. As part of a massive building campaign, however, the college has added a modern residence hall, the Shanahan Center for Teaching and Learning, and the $30 million McGregor Computer Science Center, which boasts a cutting-edge makerspace.

While most STEM-oriented schools tend to have a narrow focus, a math and computational biology major chose Harvey Mudd because "I can continue to study math and physics, and I can take diverse humanities and arts classes to broaden my perspective." The Common Core includes coursework in mathematics, computer science, and engineering; physics, chemistry, and biology (each with an associated laboratory); college writing (taught by faculty from all departments); humanities, social sciences, and the arts; and an Impact course that explores the intersection of

Website: www.hmc.edu
Location: Suburban
Private
Total Enrollment: 919
Undergraduates: 919
Male/Female: 49/51
Financial Aid: 70%
Pell Grant: 22%
Expense: Pr $ $ $ $
Student Loans: 44%
Average Debt: $
Applicants: 5,094
Accepted: 13%
Enrolled: 36%
Grad in 6 Years: 92%
Returning First-years: 96%
Academics: ✍ ✍ ✍ ✍
Social: 🗩 🗩 🗩
Q of L: ★ ★ ★
Admissions: (909) 621-8011
Email Address:
admission@hmc.edu

Strong Programs:
Biology
Chemistry

About 200 students stay on campus in the summer for 10-week research experiences.

HMC has one of the nation's best computer science programs and an award-winning math department.

STEM and society. "Your classes will be hard, and you will spend a lot of time on your studies, but it is definitely worth it," says a sophomore. Concerned that the core curriculum has indeed become too onerous, the administration has reduced the number of courses students are required to take in their first four semesters. Students praise the Academic Excellence programs, in which "upperclassmen work as tutors to help students in the General Ed courses during their first and second year," explains an engineering major. Sixty-two percent of classes have fewer than 20 people, and the absence of graduate programs means that undergraduates get uncommon amounts of attention, even from top faculty. "Professors really believe in you and your ability to grasp the content," says a computer science major.

Of the school's 14 majors, engineering enrolls the most students; computer science, mathematics, chemistry, and physics are other top choices. HMC has one of the nation's best computer science programs and an award-winning math department, and a combined major in computer science and mathematics is also very popular. Students interested in climate science can now major in biology and climate, chemistry and climate, or computer science and climate. Students rave about the Clinic Program, which drops real-life math, science, and engineering tasks (sponsored by major corporations and government agencies) into the laps of students. Recent sponsors have included NASA's Jet Propulsion Laboratory, Google, Microsoft, and Toyota. All students must either participate in the Clinic Program or complete original thesis-driven research in order to graduate. About 200 students stay on campus in the summer for 10-week research experiences, and a sophomore says, "In research positions, students are working one-on-one with the professors—they aren't washing beakers." Many students study abroad for a semester in their junior year in their choice of more than 20 countries.

"Harvey Mudd is a place full of nerdy people who love being nerdy," says a computer science major, "whether that be about hard science, math, or engineering, or about a music artist, book series, or anime." Forty-five percent of the students are homegrown Californians, and 11 percent are international. Black students represent 5 percent of the student body, Hispanics/Latinos 22 percent, Asian Americans 20 percent, and multiracial students 12 percent. A senior notes that

"The culture and community at Harvey Mudd is my favorite part about this school."

student groups like FEM Union (Female Empowerment at Mudd) and BLAM (Black Lives and Allies at Mudd) "have created spaces for discussions about issues of diversity and privilege." Merit scholarships averaging $13,800 help some with the hefty tuition bill, but as a Division III college, Mudd offers no athletic scholarships. It does, however, honor policies of need-blind admissions and covering 100 percent of students' demonstrated need with its financial aid packages.

Ninety-seven percent of undergrads live on campus, and students speak of a strong "dorm culture" on campus. "Each dorm has a proctor (think: the 'mom' or 'dad' of the dorm, usually a senior) as well as several mentors (the 'older siblings' of the dorm, who are mostly there for freshmen)," describes a computer science major. Mudd's dining options "are amazing," according to several students, and they appreciate their access to dining facilities at the other Claremont Colleges, which vastly expands their options. Career support and mental health services are said to be strong but also, "in high demand," says a computer science major.

Despite their heavy workload, most HMC students find abundant social outlets, even if it's just joining the parade of unicycles that has overrun the campus—not to mention skateboards, scooters, and freeline skates. "Harvey Mudd is very 'outsidey.' Not outdoorsy, but you'll always find people working or lounging in the sun," says a senior. Dorms host parties almost every weekend, a favorite being the Wild Wild West party, "where we fill a dorm courtyard with peanut shells and get a mechanical bull," says a physics major. While students do frequent the other Claremont campuses to socialize, it's Mudd's many traditions that really get them going. "Noisy Minutes occur every day for 15 minutes during finals week," says an engineering major. "Students are encouraged to come outside and be as loud as they can to help reduce stress. The dining hall then provides a late-night snack to help students continue studying." Engineering pranks are popular but must be reversible within 24 hours, as established by the honor code. "Pranking the president's house is one of the first things you do as a first-year student at Harvey Mudd!" enthuses a senior.

> **"Your classes will be hard, and you will spend a lot of time on your studies."**

Mudd fields varsity sports teams together with Claremont McKenna and Scripps, and the teams do extremely well. Men's water polo has brought home a national championship. Women's tennis, volleyball, and golf; men's and women's track and field; and men's swimming and diving are some of the strongest teams. Intramurals, also in conjunction with Claremont McKenna and Scripps, are even more popular. King among these is inner-tube water polo, which draws huge cheering crowds and, most importantly, removes the most difficult aspect of the sport—treading water.

HMC is right on the heels of Caltech as the best technically oriented school in the West. The college offers a gem of a technical education blended with a worthwhile amount of humanities and social sciences, and the administration seems serious about addressing the common student refrain that the heavy workload comes at the expense of time to reflect on what they are learning. HMC offers a welcoming attitude toward women and other groups traditionally underrepresented in STEM fields. As one student asserts, "Mudd is the college for students to be challenged like they never have been before and have the support to go through it."

Overlaps

UC Berkeley, UCLA, Caltech, Carnegie Mellon, Harvard, MIT, Olin College of Engineering, Stanford

If You Apply To ›

Harvey Mudd: Early decision I and II, regular decision. Accepts the Common Application with supplement. Please consult Harvey Mudd's website for the most up-to-date information regarding standardized test requirements.

Pitzer College

1050 North Mills Avenue, Claremont, CA 91711

Offers a haven for the otherwise-minded without the hard edge of nonconformity at places like Bard and Evergreen. Traditional strengths lie in the social and behavioral sciences, including innovative options such as secular studies. Students play a role in college governance. Far more selective than it was 15 years ago. A national leader in turning out Fulbright scholars.

As the most socially aware of the Claremont Colleges, Pitzer College offers students a creative milieu, abundant opportunities for intellectual exploration, and a sense of fierce individualism. It places a "strong emphasis on social justice, environmental sustainability, and intercultural understanding." Founded in 1963 and named for a benefactor, this small liberal arts and sciences school has changed with the times but continues to emphasize progressive thought, social responsibility, environmental sustainability, and an open social attitude. In the last 35 years, Pitzer students and

Website: www.pitzer.edu
Location: Suburban
Private
Total Enrollment: 1,195
Undergraduates: 1,195
Male/Female: 41/59

(continued)

Financial Aid: 38%

Pell Grant: 13%

Expense: Pr $ $ $

Student Loans: 30%

Average Debt: $

Applicants: 3,438

Accepted: 25%

Enrolled: 36%

Grad in 6 Years: 83%

Returning First-years: 94%

Academics: ✍ ✍ ✍

Social: 💬 💬 💬

Q of L: ★ ★ ★

Admissions: (909) 621-8129

Email Address:

admission@pitzer.edu

Strong Programs:

Biological Sciences

Economics

Environmental Analysis

Media Studies

Political Studies

Psychology

Secular Studies

The college boasts the Robert Redford Conservancy for Southern California Sustainability.

alumni have been awarded more than 300 Fulbright fellowships, and the school continues to attract top talent from around the world. "There is a priority to take classes and involve oneself in organizations that empower intercultural understanding," says a junior.

Even Pitzer's campus is, well, different. The classroom buildings are modernistic octagons, and the grass-covered "mounds" that distinguish the grounds "are perfect for sunbathing and Frisbee," says one student, and for lounging in Adirondack chairs beneath the palm trees. Drought-tolerant landscaping pervades the campus, and there is an organic garden. One interesting campus curiosity is the Grove House, a California craftsman-style house students saved from the wrecking ball decades ago and moved to campus. It houses a dining room, study areas, and art exhibits. Additional facilities include eight LEED-certified residence halls and the Nucleus West building, which houses the Natural Sciences Division of Pitzer and Scripps Colleges, a joint space where the colleges offer expanded and reimagined STEM courses.

In keeping with Pitzer's philosophy of student autonomy, each student has the maximum freedom to choose which classes to take. Instead of traditional academic departments, Pitzer has "field groups," which, as a political studies and Spanish double major explains, "allow for students to major in one subject area yet receive a holistic education." All students take a sequence of courses on social justice and intercultural exploration, and a lively first-year seminar program sharpens students' learning skills, especially writing. Students select from 40 majors, and they're also encouraged to design their own. Almost anything in the social and behavioral sciences is a sure bet, especially psychology. Environmental analysis, economics, biology, and sociology are other strong and popular programs. Pitzer is the first college in the country to offer an interdisciplinary program in secular studies, with courses such as secularism, skepticism, and irreligion. New majors include environmental sciences. Through cross-registration with the Claremont Colleges, Pitzer students can take advantage of a broader range of classes.

> **"The professors I have had are very down-to-earth and incredibly knowledgeable."**

The academic climate is "flexible, fluid, adaptable, and individualized," according to a psychology and dance major. Class size is generally small, with 77 percent of classes enrolling fewer than 20 students, which promotes close interaction between students and faculty. "The professors I have had are very down-to-earth and incredibly knowledgeable in their fields," says a sociology and gender/feminist studies major. Students play a large role in Pitzer's community government and sit on all policy committees, including those on curriculum and faculty promotion. The environment is a big focus here, and the college boasts the Robert Redford Conservancy for Southern California Sustainability. The Firestone Center for Restoration Ecology in Costa Rica is home to programs in science, language, and international studies and provides opportunities for research. Pitzer also runs its own study abroad programs in Brazil, Ecuador, Italy, Nepal, Vietnam, and Southern Africa, with over 50 programs in more than 30 countries; in all, 36 percent of Pitzer students go abroad. For students interested in new technologies, a computer science major suggests "taking advantage of consortium-wide clubs and resources," such as P-AI, a technical project incubator, and the Hive, which is "a wonderful resource for creatives," that offers collaborative and experiential liberal arts workshops.

Individualism is a prized characteristic among Pitzer students, and an Africana and media studies major describes them as "creative, intelligent, humanity centered, multi-disciplinary focused, passionate, and socio-politically aware." Forty-two percent of students are from California, and 9 percent are from foreign nations. Many come from wealthy backgrounds. Black students represent 4 percent of the student body, Hispanics/Latinos 12 percent, Asian Americans 13 percent, and multiracial students 10 percent. Students are heavily involved in volunteer work and cite "racism on campus, labor rights, immigration reform, environmental issues, and police brutality" as hot-button social and political issues. The school is committed to meeting 100 percent of enrolled students' demonstrated need, but it is not need-blind in its admissions. A limited number of merit scholarships worth an average of $5,800 are awarded to top achievers.

Eighty-five percent of students live in college-owned housing, and many find themselves in the newer, environmentally friendly dorms; the remainder hang their hats in "old but spacious" rooms. Boarders can choose from a variety of meal plans, and the food gets rave reviews, especially the fresh salad, sandwich, and fruit juice bars in the main dining hall. "The food is awesome: locally sourced, excellent variety, easy to be vegetarian," cheers a senior. Students say the Pitzer Advocates for Survivors of Sexual Assault student group has been a helpful campus resource. "Safety is a huge priority," declares a junior.

As for the social scene, "There are party pages that post events happening every weekend that students are hosting," says a senior. "Or each [Claremont] campus has a campus events affiliation where the colleges themselves host and fund the events/party." Pitzer has no Greek organizations, nor does it want any. Kohoutek, an alternative music festival, is the big annual event, featuring bands, food, and a "whole week of hoopla"; there is a rockabilly festival as well. "There is very heavy alcohol and weed usage on campus," says a junior. All parties that serve alcohol must be registered. As much as students enjoy the campus scene, some warn that without a car, things can get claustrophobic.

> **"The food is awesome: locally sourced, excellent variety, easy to be vegetarian."**

The Pomona–Pitzer football team has had winning seasons, and the school fields a variety of competitive Sagehens teams within the Southern California Intercollegiate Athletic Conference. Men's and women's water polo, men's and women's lacrosse, and football have won national or conference championships recently. Golf and men's basketball and swim teams also do well. Recreational sports thrive, with dozens of club sports, intramurals, and a hugely popular annual Humans vs. Zombies tag game that draws 500 participants across campus.

Pitzer College attracts open-minded students looking for the freedom to go their own ways. "As Pitzer students, we're always imagining outside of the box and imagining a more just and equitable world for everyone," says a senior.

> *A lively first-year seminar program sharpens students' learning skills, especially writing.*

Overlaps

Bates, Dickinson, Franklin & Marshall, Hamilton, Haverford, Occidental, Pomona, Scripps

If You Apply To ›

Pitzer: Early decision I and II, regular decision. SATs or ACTs: not considered. Accepts the Common Application with supplement. Application includes optional fields for gender identity and gender pronouns.

Pomona College

333 North College Way, Claremont, CA 91711

The finest liberal arts college in the West, and one of the few that Ivy-oriented Easterners will travel across the country to attend. Offers twice the resources of stand-alone competitors with access to the other Claremonts. A haven for the otherwise-minded, though not to the same extent as nonconformist neighbor Pitzer. Strong across the academic spectrum.

Website: www.pomona.edu
Location: Suburban
Private
Total Enrollment: 1,732
Undergraduates: 1,732
Male/Female: 44/56
Financial Aid: 58%
Pell Grant: 19%
Expense: Pr $ $ $ $
Student Loans: 19%
Average Debt: $
Applicants: 12,249
Accepted: 7%
Enrolled: 50%
Grad in 6 Years: 93%
Returning First-years: 98%
Academics: ✍ ✍ ✍ ✍ ✍
Social: 🗩 🗩 🗩
Q of L: ★ ★ ★ ★
Admissions: (909) 621-8134
Email Address:
 admissions@pomona.edu

Strong Programs:
Computer Science
Economics
International Relations
Mathematics
Neuroscience
Public Policy Analysis

Social life begins in the dorms, where study breaks, barbecues, and parties are organized.

Pomona College, located just 35 miles east of the glitz and glamour of Hollywood, is the undisputed star of the Claremont Colleges—"strongly rooted in Southern California yet global in its orientation"—and one of the top small liberal arts colleges anywhere. But the school's prestigious reputation doesn't go to the heads of Pomona's friendly students. "Students here are very open about different types of people—Pomona prides itself on its diverse community," chirps one Sagehen (the school's mascot).

The architecture is variously described as Spanish Mediterranean, pseudo-Italian, or, as a sophomore puts it, "a perfect mix of Northeastern Ivy and Southern California modern." One certainly notices more than one stucco building topped with a red tile roof on campus, as well as eucalyptus trees, canyon live oaks, and an occasional "secretive courtyard lined with flowers." The numerous open courtyards and gardens are popular study spots. By virtue of its location and beauty, Pomona's campus has served as the quintessential collegiate milieu in various Hollywood movies. Newer campus projects include Andrew Science Hall, which features a host of cutting-edge spaces and equipment, including a digital planetarium and electron microscope, and the $57-million Center for Athletics, Recreation, and Wellness.

Pomona was founded in 1887 by Congregationalists who wanted to import "New England–type" education to Southern California. In order to graduate, students must take at least one course in each of six Breadth of Study areas: criticism, analysis, and contextual study of works of the human imagination; social institutions and human behavior; history, values, ethics, and cultural studies; physical and biological sciences; mathematical and formal reasoning; and creation and performance of works of art and literature. The required Critical Inquiry seminar emphasizes thoughtful reading, logical reasoning, and graceful writing; students choose from more than two dozen offerings, with subjects such as Building the Future and Theatre in an Age of Climate Change. Students must also complete a senior exercise in their final year. A five-day first-year orientation program divides the new arrivals into groups of six to 12 students headed by a sophomore. "We provide a great deal of support in acclimating students to a college environment," says a senior. Economics, mathematics, computer science, and English are the most popular majors; international relations is well regarded.

"Pomona prides itself on its diverse community."

"Although classes can be difficult, students help each other out, and the classroom environment is an enjoyable one," offers one economics major. Students often form study groups in an effort to help one another through the demanding curriculum. One undergrad estimates the average student spends 20 to 30 hours a week studying outside the classroom. Classes are small—72 percent have fewer than 20 students—and "professors are not only amazing at the subject they teach but are also interested in getting to know and truly understand students outside of an academic setting," lauds a philosophy, politics, and economics major.

Educational enrichment opportunities abound at Pomona. Students can spend a semester at Colby or Swarthmore, pursue a 3–2 engineering plan with the California Institute of Technology or Dartmouth College, or spend a semester in Washington, D.C., working for a congressperson. Half of the students take advantage of 67 study abroad programs offered in more than 35 countries. Sixty-two percent conduct research mentored by a faculty member, and the Summer Undergraduate Research Program provides funding to more than 200 students to pursue such opportunities each summer. "Students and recent alumni are often featured as coauthors on papers in peer-reviewed journals," reports an administrator.

Pomona students "tend to be high-achieving, confident, verbal students with a fairly liberal political ideology," says a senior. "Students are laid-back in a very Southern California kind of way," adds another. Twenty-eight percent are

Californians, and a growing number venture from the East Coast; 17 percent come from abroad. Nine percent are Black, 17 percent are Hispanic/Latino, 19 percent are Asian American, and 9 percent are multiracial. There is a healthy mix of liberals and conservatives on campus, though the leftists are much more vocal. The student government is active, and the administration is credited with respecting students' opinions. One interesting way students voice their concerns is by painting the Walker Wall. Anyone is allowed to paint any message they want on the wall, and the school will even provide groups with the paint. Merit scholarships are available and average $9,200. Pomona is need-blind in admissions and meets the full demonstrated financial need of all those who attend. The college has replaced loans with grants in an effort to reduce the debt burden for families. The college also participates in the QuestBridge and Posse programs.

Virtually all Pomona students live on campus all four years. The 14 residence halls are co-ed, student-governed, and divided into two distinct groups. Those on South campus are family-like and fairly quiet, offer spacious rooms, and house first- and second-year students, while those on the North end have smaller rooms with a livelier social scene and house juniors and seniors. "Pomona's dorms are like palaces," says a student. The two newest residence halls, Dialynas and Sontag, are LEED Platinum–certified and feature suite-style apartments for upperclassmen. Oldenborg Center is a language dorm with wings for speakers of Mandarin Chinese, French, German, Japanese, Spanish, and Russian, and Pomona also has established language tables at lunch. "Pomona has three dining halls plus a café and a 'diner' space for students to eat," notes a junior. Boarders must buy a meal plan, and the food is good, with seafood certified by the Marine Stewardship Council, humanely raised beef and cage-free eggs, and ice cream for dessert every day. Students generally feel safe on campus. "The worst that usually happens are bike thefts," says a junior. Pomona also hosts the Claremonts' Queer Resource Center.

Social life begins in the dorms, where study breaks, barbecues, and parties are organized. There are movies several nights a week, and students also enjoy just tossing a Frisbee on the lawn. One student wanted to be sure that incoming first-years and transfers knew of the Coop's (student union) "best milkshakes west of the Mississippi," pool tables, and large-screen TV and gaming system. Students often spend Friday afternoons relaxing with friends over a brew at the Greek Theater. Pomona is unique among the Claremont Colleges in that it has three nonnational fraternities (two co-ed; there are no sororities). As for booze, "I haven't noticed any pressure to drink here," reports one student, but "alcohol is definitely present in the social scene."

"There's always a party at the 5cs!" says a sophomore of the five-college parties that happen nearly every weekend. "Students party hard, but study even harder," so during midterms and finals, the campus is a "social ghost town." Harwood dorm throws the five-college costume party every Halloween. "Pomona has so many traditions," says a psychological science major, among the most popular being "fountaining, where a group of your friends throw you in a fountain on campus for your birthday." The Nochella alternative music festival brings bands to campus. It helps to have a set of wheels here, although Zipcar and rideshare services are readily available. Every February or March, hundreds of students spend the morning at a nearby ski resort, then head to a local beach to swim, and end the day with an oceanside cookout.

There once was a time when the Pomona Sagehens were an athletic powerhouse; the football team even knocked off mighty USC on Thanksgiving Day back

"Although classes can be difficult, students help each other out."

"Pomona has so many traditions."

in 1899. In the last few years, the men's cross-country, women's water polo, and women's swimming teams have brought home national titles. Intense rivalry exists between the Claremont Colleges; basketball games between Pomona–Pitzer and CMS (Claremont–Mudd–Scripps) are "particularly heated." Pomona–Pitzer enjoys a lively rivalry with Occidental College as well. Intramurals, including hotly contested inner-tube water polo matches, attract many participants, and the Outdoor Education Center facilitates numerous outdoor adventures.

"Pomona offers a unique and desirable juxtaposition of rigorous academics and a comfortable social atmosphere," says a student. The strongest link in an extremely attractive chain, Pomona continues to symbolize the rising status of the Claremont Colleges in the world of higher education. There are few regrets about coming to Pomona. Says a senior, "We're in California. The sun is always shining. What's the problem?"

If You Apply To ›

Pomona: Early decision I and II, regular decision. Accepts the Common Application with supplement. SAT or ACT scores are not required.

Scripps College

1030 Columbia Avenue, Claremont, CA 91711

Scripps is easily the premier women's college on the West Coast, offering a commitment to women's education while interacting with co-ed institutions that are literally next door. Boasts strengths in social sciences, biological sciences, and the arts. Innovative Core Curriculum takes an interdisciplinary approach to learning.

Scripps College is a close-knit women's college where traditions include weekly tea and fresh-baked cookies, but thanks to its membership in the Claremont Colleges, it also has the diversity of a major research institution. Founded in 1926 by newspaper publisher Ellen Browning Scripps, the college continues to pursue her vision through its mission: "To educate women . . . so that as graduates they may contribute to society through public and private lives of leadership, service, integrity, and creativity." Students tend to be outgoing, articulate, and serious about their studies, though they still know how to have fun.

Scripps's scenic 32-acre campus, listed on the National Register of Historic Places, offers a tranquil, safe, and comfortable environment. The architecture is Spanish and Mediterranean, with tiled roofs and elegant, sustainable landscaping. A performing arts center provides permanent space for the Claremont Concert Orchestra and Concert Choir. In addition to a 700-seat theater, the center offers a music library, recital hall, practice rooms, faculty offices, and classrooms. The Lincoln Ceramic Art Building offers more than 5,000 square feet of work area and kiln yards.

> **"Professors encourage you to work in groups because more brains [are] always better."**

The required Core Curriculum in Interdisciplinary Humanities is a sequence of three courses focusing on ideas about the world and the methods used to generate them. In addition to Core, everyone takes courses in fine arts, letters, natural sciences, and social sciences—one of these classes must focus on gender and women's studies, and one must cover race and ethnic studies. All students also complete a senior thesis or project.

Popular majors at Scripps include psychology, politics, environmental analysis, biology, and media studies. The Williamson Gallery offers a state-of-the-art studio and freestanding museum-quality gallery for aspiring painters and sculptors. Premeds and STEM majors benefit from a joint science program for students at Scripps and Pitzer. Programs in area and ethnic studies, such as Middle East and North Africa studies and Chicanx/Latinx studies, are strong, and the feminist, gender, and sexuality studies department is also popular. The Scripps Humanities Institute offers seminars and lectures open to the general public along with fellowships for juniors; recently, the institute explored immigration policy and nationalism in the U.S. and abroad. The Scripps Presents event series also brings prominent writers, performers, visual artists, and activists to campus for public programming as well as student-only discussions and workshops.

The academic experience at Scripps emphasizes cooperation. "Scripps is a very supportive community," a junior says. "It is a place where professors encourage you to work in groups because more brains [are] always better." Seventy-five percent of classes have fewer than 20 students. "My professors are always up for a discussion, always willing to answer questions (even difficult ones), and always up to chat about how their day is going," says one student. When they're ready to branch out, typically in the junior year, more than 60 percent of Scripps students study abroad, choosing from more than 115 program options in 52 countries.

Forty-three percent of Scripps undergraduates are from California, and 4 percent come from other countries. Black students account for 4 percent of the student body, Hispanics/Latinas 11 percent, Asian Americans 14 percent, and multiracial students 11 percent. "The students here are diligent, thoughtful, and really down-to-earth," observes one politics major. Student organizations supporting Jewish, Asian American, Black, Latina, international, and LGBTQ students are available. Scripps Communities of Resources and Empowerment, known as SCORE, provides support and funding to student organizations that promote inclusion and social justice. Scripps meets 100 percent of admitted students' demonstrated financial need and has made more grant money available for students with the most need. The college also awards merit scholarships averaging $18,800 to top achievers but no athletic scholarships.

Virtually all of Scripps students live in one of the 12 "spectacular" residence halls, where options include singles, suites, and apartment-style living arrangements. A student says, "The dorms are gorgeous. They are well maintained and have lots of charm with French doors, balconies, or the occasional fireplace." First-years live in the same halls as sophomores, juniors, and seniors. The dining hall garners rave reviews as well: "The salad bar is gourmet, the bread comes from a local bakery, and the pizza is made in a wood-fired brick oven," cheers a bioethics major. "Don't get me started about the hot cookies!"

"With five undergraduate colleges literally across the street from each other, it is challenging not to have something to do."

Social life at Scripps centers on the residence halls, which take turns throwing parties. "Our social life is very much based on campus," explains a chemistry major. "With five undergraduate colleges literally across the street from each other, it is challenging not to have something to do—from movie screenings, art exhibits, concerts, special events like a carnival or the International Festival, and parties." Alcohol doesn't play a major role in Scripps social life, but the school does have a medical amnesty policy for underage students in need of emergency medical assistance. Traditions are important here, including the Matriculation Ceremony at the start of each year and the signing of Graffiti Wall by each class before graduation. For

Traditions are important here, including the Matriculation Ceremony at the start of each year.

The Scripps Presents event series brings prominent writers, performers, visual artists, and activists to campus.

students with cars, popular road trips include Pasadena, Mount Baldy, San Diego, and even Las Vegas and Mexico; students without wheels can hop on the Metrolink commuter train to downtown Los Angeles.

Athletic rivalries aren't the focus here, but Scripps does field joint teams with Claremont McKenna and Harvey Mudd, and when those teams face off against Pomona and Pitzer, students pay attention. All of the Stag (men's) and Athena (women's) teams compete in Division III, and the women's volleyball, tennis, and cross-country teams are especially strong. Intramural and club sports are also played jointly, and popular options include inner-tube water polo, basketball, pickleball, and volleyball.

With a winning combination of outstanding academics and personal attention, not to mention a cooperative, noncompetitive feel, Scripps offers the best of both worlds. Scripps students want to achieve great things, but not if that requires stepping on their classmates' toes. And just beyond campus, the other Claremont Colleges beckon, with additional parties, student clubs, intramural sports, and cross-registration privileges for a comprehensive college experience.

If You Apply To ›

Scripps: Early decision I and II, regular decision. SATs or ACTs: optional. Accepts the Common Application.

Clark University

950 Main Street, Worcester, MA 01610

Clark has a distinguished history that dates to the late 19th century. Clarkies bring a sense of mission and partnership to their relationship with this historic industrial town. The university is liberal, tolerant, and world-renowned in psychology, geography, and game design. Students pride themselves on being unique independent thinkers and making a difference.

Founded in 1887, Clark University has long played a pioneering role in American higher education. It is one of only three universities that began life as an all-graduate school on a German model (see also the Catholic University of America and Johns Hopkins). Clark is the only U.S. college that lured pioneering psychoanalyst Sigmund Freud as a lecturer, and his statue still stands in the center of the campus. Over the years, philosophy and, fittingly, psychology have been Clark's academic strengths, but today, it welcomes undergraduates of all backgrounds with small classes and no shortage of faculty attention. "High expectations, hands-on learning, and extraordinary access both to faculty and to off-campus learning and work opportunities encourage students to become autonomous learners," says the administration. In the words of one student, Clark offers "intensive world, workplace, and personal experiences" that "serve to push students to bring their college education into the real world."

Clark's compact, 50-acre campus has "enough ivy, tall maples, and collegiate brick buildings to make a traditionalist happy," even though it's located in the rather gritty Main South section of Worcester. Buildings range from remodeled Victorian-era residences—former homes of prosperous merchants—to the award-winning Robert Hutchings Goddard Library. Careful restoration has brought a renewed sense of history to the area. The new 70,000-square-foot Center for Media

Arts, Computing, and Design features virtual reality and robotics labs, a data science lab, a makerspace, and a video game library.

While Clark now serves primarily undergraduates, its graduate education roots are evident. Most courses are seminars, and 62 percent have fewer than 20 students. First-Year Intensives, required of all students and usually capped at 16, introduce them to the intellectual, social, and emotional growth they will experience in college. Often, the instructor acts as an academic advisor until the student declares a major. "The faculty are dynamic, often younger and earlier in their careers; many come from the professional world in addition to pure academia," shares a geography major. That said, in June 2025 Clark announced that in response to recent enrollment decline, it was planning to layoff 30 percent of its faculty and restructure some degree programs. Stay tuned.

Following the First-Year Intensive, the Clark Core curriculum includes nine additional requirements across the arts, science, history, language and culture, values, diversity and inclusion, written expression, systems analysis, and global perspectives. The goal is for students "to develop critical thinking skills, respect for other cultures and perspectives, and introduce students to new ways of seeing, thinking, and knowing humans and the natural world." Practice-based courses incorporate hands-on experiences culminating in a capstone project.

"[Clark offers] intensive world, workplace, and personal experiences."

Clark's psychology and geography departments continue to burnish their national reputations. As the birthplace of the American Psychological Association and the concept of adolescence, Clark is also strong in international development, social change, and environmental science. The new School of Climate, Environment, and Society advances interdisciplinary research around climate change. Popular majors include psychology, business, political science, and biology. Clark's Becker School of Design & Technology offers majors in game development, integrated graphic design, and eSports management. About 30 percent of seniors pursue an accelerated B.A./M.A. allowing them to earn a master's degree with the help of a full tuition scholarship.

"The academic climate on campus is rigorous, but in a way that reflects the students' own drive; we tend to feed into that rigor ourselves," explains a history and screen studies double major. Students say the small class sizes foster collaboration. "It's not hard to find study-buddies-turned-friends in your classes," says a senior. Twenty-six percent of Clark students spend at least one semester studying abroad at one of more than 50 available programs in 30 countries. Fifty-nine percent of students participate in undergraduate research, and students showcase their creative and research work at ClarkFest each semester. "Clark's identity is this perfect blend of two worlds," says a senior. "Research allows us to dive deep into our passions while liberal arts prevents us from becoming one-sided thinkers."

More than 130 student-run organizations offer endless concerts, improv, and theater shows.

"There is no typical Clarkie and that is what makes Clark, Clark," opines a psychology major. "Everyone has so many different interests that you cannot put a label on what kind of student goes here." One student describes Clark as "a conglomerate of very passionate and individualistic people who love collaboration." Thirty-six percent of Clarkies hail from Massachusetts, and international students make up another 6 percent.

"The faculty are dynamic, often younger and earlier in their careers."

Black students account for 5 percent of the student body, Hispanics/Latinos 13 percent, Asian Americans 7 percent, and multiracial students 5 percent. "There is a strong motivation for political activism," but "Clark students feel a need to support each other," says a political science major. While athletic scholarships aren't available, merit-based scholarships are. The Presidential Scholarship includes full tuition, housing, and meals for four years. Clark meets full financial need for

(continued)

Q of L: ★ ★ ★
Admissions: (508) 793-7431
Email Address:
   admissions@clarku.edu

Strong Programs:
Biology
Business
Geography
Interactive Media
International Development and
   Social Change
Political Science
Psychology

early-decision admits. "Clark's emphasis on financial support for lower-income students was also a major draw," notes a sophomore.

First-year students and sophomores at Clark are required to live in the residence halls. In all, 68 percent of undergrads live on campus in accommodations that are described as clean, comfortable, and "surprisingly big." The school is building new residences to accommodate a recent housing crunch. Campus dining gets average reviews for quality and diversity. "The secret is to use the spice and sauce rack as much as possible," confides an economics major. Students agree that the campus feels safe. Students report that it can be difficult to get an appointment with mental health counselors due to large demand.

Clark has no Greek life, but "sports teams kind of fill that partying gap," explains a senior. More than 130 student-run organizations offer endless concerts, improv, and theater shows, game nights, and other programs. First-year dorms are dry, but alcohol may be consumed in other dorms by those who are of age, and students say that alcohol policies emphasize safety over punishment. "Parties mostly happen off campus," notes a psychology major. "But students love to hang out in the green areas with friends." Coping with the frigid New England winters includes quaffing cups of hot chocolate and dreaming about Spree Day in April, when classes are canceled and students enjoy live music, food trucks, face painting, rock-climbing walls, mechanical bulls, and other festivities. Students also look forward to the annual International Gala, where students choreograph and perform dances representing different countries.

"Clark is a warm and accepting place."

Worcester, home to eight colleges, is "a city of hidden gems," says a student, offering restaurants with every conceivable type of cuisine, small clubs with live music, and the DCU Center, a 13,000-seat arena. Sixty-four percent of students mix with neighborhood residents through extensive volunteer programs coordinated by the Office of Community Engagement and Volunteering (CEV). "At most colleges, you would expect this to look more like 'volun-tourism' as opposed to addressing the needs of the community, but Clark's CEV office is headed by people who know the issues from a resident's perspective," says a senior. To get away, Clarkies head to Boston and Providence (both about an hour away), New York (three hours), or the rural wilds of Vermont, New Hampshire, and Maine.

The Clark Cougars compete in the Division III New England Women's and Men's Athletic Conference (NEWMAC), and the university fields 17 intercollegiate teams. Men's and women's soccer; women's rowing and volleyball; and men's lacrosse, baseball, and basketball are among the most competitive teams. About 41 percent of students participate in intramural and club sports; ultimate Frisbee, soccer, and basketball are popular options. In addition, Wellness Ambassadors, part of a skilled peer group, help students practice healthy habits.

Like Johns Hopkins and the Catholic University of America, Clark started out serving only graduate students but now offers a dynamic, undergraduate-focused educational environment. Clark continues to challenge convention, grounded in meaningful exploration and propelled by a mission to make a difference, while pioneering new teaching methods, pursuing new fields of knowledge, and finding new ways to connect thinking and doing. Through all this, a sense of community has remained a constant. Says a junior, "Clark is a warm and accepting place with students who hold the door open for others for just a little too long."

Overlaps

American University, Brandeis, Northeastern, Skidmore, Tufts, Vassar, University of Vermont, Wesleyan

If You Apply To ›

Clark: Early decision I and II, early action, regular decision. SATs or ACTs: optional. Accepts the Common Application. Application includes optional field for gender identity.

8 Clarkson Avenue, Potsdam, NY 13699

Clarkson lies on the edge of the Adirondack Park in Upstate New York, where the nearest major city is Ottawa. With an informal and close-knit atmosphere, Clarkson is one of the few small, undergraduate-oriented technological universities in the nation. Compare to Lehigh, Bucknell, and Union. Out-of-the-way location makes Clarkson easier to get into, but doing well is another matter.

At Clarkson University, engineering and ice hockey reign supreme. About half of the student body is enrolled in the engineering program, and the hockey teams are perennial contenders for top honors. Students here gain the "fundamental knowledge and hands-on experience they need to start their STEM careers," says an administrator, along with "the work ethic, grit, and drive that propel their lifelong success." Adds a junior, "We value academic integrity and success, but we also value failure, because it is in failure that we learn to grow."

The village of Potsdam, New York, is cloistered away between the Adirondacks and the St. Lawrence River. The campus relies mainly on modern architecture and lots of woods and wildlife. Academic buildings are connected by covered walkways that help take the sting out of getting around campus in the cold, snowy winters. Renovations across campus are ongoing, including the Schuler Educational Resources Center's Innovation Hub, which features labs, makerspaces, and group meeting rooms.

The university's general education program (Clarkson Common Experience) emphasizes four components: learning to communicate effectively; developing an appreciation for diversity; recognizing the importance of personal, societal, and professional ethics; and understanding how technology can be used to serve humanity. First-years (except those in the honors program) take a seminar that helps develop critical-thinking, reading, and writing skills. All students are required to complete a capstone professional experience, like a co-op, internship, research project, or thesis.

> "We value academic integrity and success."

Engineering isn't the only academic offering at Clarkson, but it certainly leads the way, and it represents the four most popular majors: mechanical engineering, engineering and management, civil engineering, and aerospace engineering. In the natural sciences, biology and biomolecular science are among the strongest offerings, along with environmental science and policy and environmental health science, which are bolstered by the extensive research and outreach activities of the Institute for a Sustainable Environment. The Reh School of Business is highly praised, too, and offers several majors, including distinctive programs in global supply chain management and innovation and entrepreneurship. All business students must have an international study experience and an internship in order to graduate, and first-year students actually start and run a business. The Lewis School of Health Sciences offers a bachelor of science in healthcare and unique direct-entry healthcare programs that guarantee admission into physical therapy, occupational therapy, and physician's assistant graduate programs.

Clarkson, which was founded in 1896, took its name from a local entrepreneur, prides itself on intimacy and personalized instruction; 48 percent of classes have fewer than 20 students, and 31 percent of students conduct research with a faculty mentor. "It is a high-pressure academic climate that causes a lot of stress but forces us students to thrive and overcome," says a finance major. "The professors

Website: www.clarkson.edu
Location: Small Town
Private
Total Enrollment: 2,939
Undergraduates: 2,189
Male/Female: 69/31
Financial Aid: 99%
Pell Grant: 20%
Expense: Pr $ $
Student Loans: 77%
Average Debt: $ $
Applicants: 6,661
Accepted: 77%
Enrolled: 10%
Grad in 6 Years: 75%
Returning First-years: 85%
Academics: ✍ ✍ ✍
Social: 🗩 🗩
Q of L: ★ ★ ★
Admissions: (315) 268-6480
Email Address:
admissions@clarkson.edu

Strong Programs:
Biology
Biomolecular Science
Business
Engineering and Management
Environmental Engineering
Global Supply Chain
  Management
Innovation and
  Entrepreneurship
Mechanical Engineering

understand what the further application of what we are learning could be and will usually go through examples of this in class," adds an aerospace engineering major. Students recommend taking advantage of the private, small-group, and drop-in tutoring services offered by the Student Success Center, and they uniformly praise the school's career services for contributing to the university's high job-placement rate. "The Career Center is there to help you from day one and will provide assistance on anything related to preparing you for your career," enthuses a senior.

Study abroad opportunities are available in nearly 30 countries, although just 6 percent of students participate. The growing honors program accepts more than 50 first-year students who undertake an intensive four-year curriculum. Several hundred students from all majors join teams in Clarkson's Student Projects for Engineering Experience and Design program, such as Formula SAE, concrete canoe, and robotics competition teams, which one student raves are "awesome!" For women interested in STEM fields on this male-dominated campus, the Women in Science and Engineering program enrolls about 25 first-year students into a residential living/learning program.

"Most students here like to have fun on the weekends and grind during the week," says an engineering and management major, and many are laser focused on postgraduation employment. Sixty-six percent of the student body is native to New York. Clarkson has trouble luring minorities to its remote locale, although efforts to change that are underway; Black students currently make up 3 percent of the undergraduate population, Hispanics/Latinos 13 percent, Asian Americans 2 percent, and multiracial students 4 percent. International students add another 4 percent. Students agree that the campus doesn't usually get too vocal about national political issues. Clarkson awards merit scholarships each year averaging $33,800. Forty athletic scholarships are offered, but only men's and women's ice hockey players need apply (it's Clarkson's only Division I sport).

"The Career Center is there to help you from day one."

Eighty-eight percent of students live in campus housing. Students are required to reside on campus all four years unless exempted to live in an off-campus Greek house. All first-years are housed in living/learning communities with students in their major or department, giving them the chance to study and learn together. Students say the quality of the dorms varies, but the on-campus apartments offer more gracious living. The dining facilities generally get average marks. "The food is very edible," says a student. "Even professors eat it."

The social scene is low-key, in keeping with Clarkson's "come-as-you-are" atmosphere. Residence halls and student clubs organize plentiful on-campus entertainment, and 12 percent of the men and 10 percent of the women join the Greek system. Drinking is permitted on campus for those of age, who also head to the handful of bars in downtown Potsdam, which one student describes as having "small-town charm with an Adirondack twist." With three other colleges nearby, the town caters to students. The extended snowy winters are great for snowboarders and ice climbers, and many students join the popular Outing Club to enjoy such outdoor adventures year-round. "The school has a fall and spring festival where they bring singers and entertainers to the school for a fun little festival," according to a sophomore. For those who crave the bustle of city nightlife, Ottawa and Montreal are each about an hour and a half away by car.

"Most students here like to have fun on the weekends and grind during the week."

When it comes to sports, "Clarkson revolves around hockey," says a junior. The men's and women's Golden Knights teams are perennially competitive in the Eastern College Athletic Conference and nationally, contending for the Division I championship with other blue-chip teams like St. Lawrence and Cornell. The annual game against archrival St. Lawrence has evolved into a popular two-day festival called Cold Out Gold Out, featuring live music, ice skating, horse-drawn carriage rides, and an alumni hockey match preceding the big game. Clarkson also offers 14 Division III sports. Women's volleyball is strong, and the men's Alpine and women's Nordic ski teams have brought home recent USCSA national titles. Most students take advantage of club sports and intramurals, with basketball, soccer, crew, and volleyball proving to be favorites.

"At Clarkson, we pride ourselves on being hardworking, innovative, creative, and very ambitious," comments a biology major. "We even hold friendly competitions each year to showcase and reward student innovation." Clarkson's bread and butter is its technological programs—particularly its slew of engineering majors—in which students gain ample exposure to the ever-growing variety of specialties. They also remember to have some fun along the way.

If You Apply To ›

Clarkson: Early decision, regular decision. Accepts the Common Application with supplement. Application includes optional field for gender identity. Please consult Clarkson's website for the most up-to-date information regarding standardized test requirements.

Clemson University

105 Sikes Hall, Clemson, SC 29634

Clemson is a technically oriented public university in the mold of Georgia Tech, North Carolina State, and Virginia Tech. Smaller than the latter two and more focused on undergraduates than Georgia Tech, Clemson serves up its education with ample helpings of school spirit and orange paint. Small-town location makes for a tight-knit campus, though also something of a hayseed image next to more sophisticated Carolina locales such as Columbia and Chapel Hill. Big on undergraduate research.

Nestled in the foothills of the Blue Ridge Mountains, Clemson University is a place where traditional Southern spirit continues to flourish alongside modern academics, big-time athletics, and state-of-the-art facilities. This public university, founded in 1889 as an agricultural college, has the ring of a private institution and features quality academics in technical and scientific areas such as engineering and biology. Tiger spirit is as strong as ever, as evidenced by the ubiquitous orange tiger paws that decorate the campus, and students here are happy to make tracks of their own.

CU's 1,400-acre campus is situated on what was once Fort Hill Plantation, the homestead of Thomas Green Clemson. The campus is surrounded by 17,000 acres of university farms and woodlands and offers a spectacular view of the nearby lake and mountains. Architectural styles are an eclectic mix of modern and 19th-century collegiate. Clemson Bottoms, half a mile down the road from the 80,000-seat football stadium, is home to the Calhoun Field Laboratory, a pastoral site dedicated to agricultural research that features a large, student-run organic garden. A fantastic resource for science enthusiasts and history buffs is the library's collection of first editions of the scientific works of Galileo and Newton. Douthit Hills is a $212 million residential village complete with dining and fitness facilities.

(continued)

Q of L: ★ ★ ★ ★

Admissions: (864) 656-2287

Email Address:
apply@admission.clemson
.edu

Strong Programs:
Accounting
Agriculture
Animal and Veterinary
  Sciences
Architecture
Biological Sciences
Engineering
Management
Psychology

The School of Architecture offers intensive semesters at the Overseas Center for Building Research and Urban Study in Genoa, Italy.

General education requirements include courses in advanced writing; oral communications; mathematical, scientific, and technological literacy; social sciences; arts and humanities; cross-cultural awareness; and science and technology in society. Biological sciences is Clemson's largest department, and computer engineering is among the nation's best in research on large-scale integrated computer circuitry and robotics. The School of Architecture offers intensive semesters at the Overseas Center for Building Research and Urban Study in Genoa, Italy. The accounting, animal and veterinary sciences, and agriculture programs are also well regarded. Management, biological sciences, psychology, marketing, and mechanical engineering are the most popular majors. Undergraduate teaching has always been one of Clemson's strong points, and for students interested in pursuing a liberal arts curriculum, the school has degrees in fine arts, philosophy, and languages and enjoys a strong regional reputation for its history program. Because of its prevailing technical emphasis, however, most students interested in the liberal arts head "down country" to the University of South Carolina.

Academically, the level of difficulty varies. "Classes are very competitive," says one junior. "While challenging at times, the coursework is stimulating and applicable." Professors run the gamut, but most receive high marks from students.

> **"While challenging at times, the coursework is stimulating and applicable."**

"Professors not only teach the classes but also make themselves available for tons of extra hours outside of the classroom," says a psychology major. Thirty-seven percent of the classes have fewer than 20 students. Fifty-four percent of undergrads take advantage of research opportunities during their time at Clemson. Ambitious students should consider applying to the Calhoun Honors College—the oldest honors program in South Carolina. Clemson also offers exchange programs in venues from Mexico to Australia.

Clemson's student body has a decidedly Southern air, as 59 percent of undergrads hail from South Carolina, with most of the rest from neighboring states; less than 1 percent come from foreign countries. The university has accepted large numbers of community college graduates in recent years. "Students are approachable and willing to help on any given day," says a marketing major. Black students make up only 5 percent of the student body, Hispanics/Latinos 9 percent, Asian Americans 3 percent, and multiracial students 4 percent. The average Clemson student is friendly and conservative, and though, as a public institution, the school isn't affiliated with any church, there is a strong Southern Baptist presence on campus. The university offers thousands of merit scholarships averaging $4,700 and more than 400 athletic scholarships.

First-year students are required to live on campus, and housing gets positive reviews, with several residence halls opening in the last few years, but just 8 percent of the students live in campus housing beyond the first year. Options include single-sex, co-ed, traditional, and apartment-style housing. Meals in Clemson's three main dining halls are satisfactory, according to students. "They have specials and even ask students to contribute recipes," explains one student. Students say they feel safe on campus thanks to diligent security officers. To address the issue of sexual assault, a senior reports, Clemson has implemented "awareness initiatives, events, and instructions on how to take action."

"At Clemson, the fun is mostly right outside our windows," says one student. "Whether it's a football game, a pep rally, a Residence Hall Association program, or one of our U-Nites Friday night activities, students always find something to do." Fraternities and sororities provide much of the social life, with 19 percent of Clemson men and 38 percent of women going Greek. The administration has introduced measures such as limiting fraternity members to bringing just one six-pack of beer to events in an effort to curb hazing, alcohol abuse, and other problems related to the Greek scene. The town of Clemson is small, with a handful of restaurants, bars, and shops, but many students love it. After class, many students hop on their bikes and head to nearby Lake Hartwell. The beautiful Blue Ridge mountain range is also close by for hiking and camping, and beaches and ski slopes are both within driving distance. Atlanta and Charlotte are only two hours away by car, and Charleston is four hours away on the coast.

Clemson has a high-powered sports scene and fields a number of competitive teams in the Division I Atlantic Coast Conference. The football team won eight of the last 10 ACC championships, including in 2024. Football fever starts with the annual First Friday Parade, held before the first home game, and on game days, the campus dissolves into a sea of Tiger orange, with pep rallies, cookouts, dances, and parties for the mobs of excited fans. The roads leading to campus are painted with large orange pawprints. So, too, are half the fans, making the stands in "Death Valley" look like an orange grove. Tiger fans are especially rowdy when the reviled University of South Carolina Gamecocks are in town; witness the traditional pregame pep rally known as Cocky's Funeral, during which "a giant cardboard 'chicken' is burned to the ground and free chicken sandwiches are given out to students," explains a senior. Known as the Palmetto Bowl, the annual South Carolina game has been played for more than a century. Baseball, men's and women's golf, and men's and women's soccer are also very competitive. A plethora of intramural and club sports are available too.

> "Students are approachable and willing to help on any given day."

Clemson is at its best serving those whose interests lie in technical fields. School spirit is contagious, fueled by a love of big-time college sports, and becomes lifelong for many Clemson students. Everyone can become part of the Clemson family, from Southern belle to Northern Yankee, as long as they're friendly, easygoing, and enthusiastic about life in general and the Tigers in particular.

Overlaps

Auburn, Coastal Carolina, University of Georgia, Georgia Tech, UNC Chapel Hill, North Carolina State, University of South Carolina, Virginia Tech

If You Apply To ›

Clemson: Early action, regular decision. Accepts the Common Application. Music and theater applicants must audition. Please consult Clemson's website for the most up-to-date information regarding standardized test requirements.

Colby College

4000 Mayflower Hill, Waterville, ME 04901

The northernmost venue for high-quality, private higher education in New England. Colby's picturesque setting is a short hop from the eastern seacoast or Maine's western lakes and mountains. No Greek life since the college abolished it over 40 years ago. An active, outdoorsy, community-minded student body in the mold of Middlebury and Dartmouth, and more buttoned-up than Bates or Bowdoin. Invented the monthlong January term.

Colby College draws students who like to push themselves, whether in the classroom, in creative pursuits, in volunteer work, or on skis. The city of Waterville, Maine (population 16,000), is a vibrant place to study; close friendships with peers and professors help ward off the long winter chill. Colby's top-notch study abroad program offers students an opportunity to explore the world, and even those who don't spend a semester or year away can get a taste during the month of January, when Jan Plan trips send Colby students far beyond the grip of Maine winters. "I was looking for a small college with a strong academic program and a sense of community, and this has proven true many times over," cheers a sophomore.

Website: www.colby.edu
Location: Rural
Private
Total Enrollment: 2,407
Undergraduates: 2,407
Male/Female: 49/50
Financial Aid: 49%
Pell Grant: 16%

(continued)

Expense: Pr $ $ $ $
Student Loans: 17%
Average Debt: $
Applicants: 19,187
Accepted: 7%
Enrolled: 46%
Grad in 6 Years: 89%
Returning First-years: 93%
Academics: ✍ ✍ ✍ ✍
Social: 🗩 🗩 🗩
Q of L: ★ ★ ★ ★
Admissions: (207) 859-4800
Email Address:
  admissions@colby.edu

Strong Programs:
Biology
Computational Biology
Computer Science
Economics
Environmental Studies
Global Studies
Government
Psychology

Students are required to live in college housing for all four years.

Colby sits high atop Mayflower Hill, with beautiful views of the surrounding city and countryside. Its 714 acres include a wildlife management area, miles of cross-country trails, and a pond used in winter as an ice-skating rink. Georgian architecture predominates, and the oldest buildings are redbrick with white trim and brass nameplates above their green doors. The more contemporary buildings lend a touch of modernity, and the Colby Museum of Art is renowned. The iconic Colby library tower is topped with a blue light proudly showing off the primary school color. Newer facilities include the $85 million Gordon Center for Creative and Performing Arts, which houses the departments of music, cinema studies, and performance, theater, and dance. Colby also has established centers for teaching, research, and artistic inspiration related to biodiversity on two islands in the Gulf of Maine, previously owned by the painter Andrew Wyeth and his wife, Betsy.

As a small college with a history of innovation and educational excellence dating to 1813, Colby encourages students to learn for learning's sake. Students must complete distribution requirements in English composition, foreign language, "areas" (courses in arts, historical studies, literature, quantitative reasoning, social sciences, and natural sciences), and diversity. Virtually all majors include a capstone experience. Colby was the first men's college in New England to admit women and the first college anywhere to establish a 4–1–4 academic calendar with a four-week January term between semesters. Students usually take three Jan Plan terms for credit to graduate, but many take four, using the month to pursue one intensive academic or career experience, such as a research project, internship, or study abroad. The COOT program (Colby Outdoor Orientation Trips), required of all first-years, involves three-day excursions by bicycle, canoe, or foot that introduce newcomers to the beauty of the Maine wilderness or to service or theater experiences.

> **"Critical thinking and effective communication are central to a Colby education."**

Colby students choose from 46 majors. Popular and well-regarded programs include biology, economics, environmental studies, government, and psychology. New majors have been added in Jewish studies and data science. Colby offers cross-disciplinary study at Davis Institute for Artificial Intelligence, the first such institute at a liberal arts college, with significant opportunities for faculty and student research. Students study oceanography through Colby's partnership with the Bigelow Laboratory for Ocean Sciences in East Boothbay, Maine. For would-be engineers, there is a joint 3–2 program with Dartmouth and 3–2 and 4–2 programs with Columbia. Classes are small and academics are demanding—"Critical thinking and effective communication are central to a Colby education," says a sophomore—but it helps that Colby's faculty is unusually devoted to undergraduate teaching and easily accessible. "Professors truly push us to think for ourselves and to deeply understand the material, not just memorize it," says a computer science major.

Study abroad is a serious emphasis at Colby, and the opportunities begin early. First-year students can apply to the Global Entry Semester program, whisking off to France or Spain with 20 or so classmates for the fall semester. Half of the school's majors have an international component, and nearly 70 percent of Colby students spend some time abroad. About a third of students conduct undergraduate research, and over 600 students present their work at the annual Colby Liberal Arts Symposium, "a day without classes where students engaged in research can present their work to peers and professors through presentations," explains a sophomore. DavisConnects provides career advising and guarantees every student access to at least one internship, research, and global experience, regardless of their ability to pay.

> **"Colby has three good dining halls, each with their own flair."**

Students describe Colby's student body as "a bit cliquey," with lots of "outdoorsy down-to-earth people." Says a sophomore, "It's pretty easy to strike up conversations or find people to hang out with." Although the proportion of Pell-eligible students has been rising in recent years, Colby is predominantly a white institution. "The administration has made strides in helping out the minority population on campus in my time," says a junior, "but there is a long way to go." Black students account for 5 percent of the student body, Hispanics/Latinos 8 percent, Asian Americans 10 percent, and multiracial students 7 percent. Just 7 percent of Colby students are from Maine, and 12 percent come from abroad. Politically, "Mayflower Hill is a very liberal space," says a sophomore. All financial aid at Colby is need-based, the college meets 100 percent of students' demonstrated need, and it has replaced student loans with grants in all its financial aid packages. The school now also covers full tuition for students whose families earn up to $75,000.

Students are required to live in college housing for all four years. "Our community advisor program is really focused on forming strong relationships in the dorm," says a sophomore. A residential complex in downtown Waterville offers a living/learning community focused on civic engagement for 200 juniors and seniors. "Colby has three good dining halls, each with their own flair, and makes an effort to source locally and sustainably," says a senior; a grab-and-go spot in the student union and a student-run coffee shop offer more options. First-years and sophomores take training workshops on sexual violence prevention, and one student remarks, "Colby makes its standards very clear to students." Mental health services "do a pretty good job," says a sophomore.

"Colby is quite geographically isolated, which limits the options for activities in the area and on campus," says a senior of the social scene. Colby may eschew fraternities and sororities, but parties in the senior apartments are a weekend staple and tend to be driven by sports teams. "Campus policies around alcohol are about creating a healthy drinking culture," says a junior. Fall Concert and Spring Concert bring well-known musical acts to campus once per semester. Another favorite—but

> "[Doghead is when] students party and stay up the whole night on St. Patrick's Day weekend."

not school-sanctioned—tradition is Doghead, "where students party and stay up the whole night on St. Patrick's Day weekend and watch the sunrise from the library steps together," says a senior. Downtown Waterville offers some good restaurants and bars, but otherwise it's "not the most active town for young people," opines a student. Popular Maine road trips include Portland, Freeport (home to the L.L.Bean factory and store), Mount Desert Island, and Sugarloaf Mountain (for skiing). Also easy to reach are the bright lights of Boston and Montreal.

The Colby Mules have come a long way since the first intercollegiate croquet game, played at Colby in 1860. Sports are Division III, except for squash and skiing, which are Division I, and solid programs include baseball; women's ice hockey, lacrosse, and Nordic skiing; and men's ice hockey, cross-country, and track and field. Games against Bates and Bowdoin draw crowds, especially the annual Bowdoin hockey match. A majority of the students participate in club and intramural sports; rugby, ultimate Frisbee, basketball, and badminton are some of the most popular.

Colby's traditional New England liberal arts small college feel and increasingly global focus combine to give students a modern yet traditional four-year experience, enhanced with long-standing traditions, abundant school spirit, and caring faculty members who focus on developing their students' minds. "People are encouraged to double major, study abroad, and try new things without being boxed into one path," says a computer science major. "If you take initiative, there's so much to gain."

Overlaps

Amherst, Bates, Bowdoin, Dartmouth, Hamilton, Middlebury, Tufts, Williams

If You Apply To ›

Colby: Early decision I and II, regular decision. SATs or ACTs: optional. Accepts the Common Application.

Colgate University

13 Oak Drive, Hamilton, NY 13346

With just over 3,200 students, Colgate is smaller than Bucknell and Dartmouth but bigger than Hamilton and Williams. Like the other four, it offers small-town living, close interaction between students and faculty, and many study abroad opportunities. Greek organizations and jocks are still well entrenched despite perennial administrative efforts to neutralize their influence.

Website: www.colgate.edu
Location: Rural
Private
Total Enrollment: 3,178
Undergraduates: 3,168
Male/Female: 43/56
Financial Aid: 50%
Pell Grant: 14%
Expense: Pr $ $ $ $
Student Loans: 21%
Average Debt: $ $ $
Applicants: 20,682
Accepted: 14%
Enrolled: 29%
Grad in 6 Years: 91%
Returning First-years: 93%
Academics: ✐ ✐ ✐ ✐
Social: 💬 💬 💬
Q of L: ★ ★ ★
Admissions: (315) 228-7401
Email Address:
  admission@colgate.edu

Strong Programs:
Computer Science
Economics
English
Environmental Studies
International Relations
Natural Sciences
Political Science
Psychology

While you may see the same Canada Goose jackets coming and going (and coming and going) as you stroll across Colgate University's campus, the students in them aren't all spun from the same cloth. "Most students at Colgate are freethinkers and open to new ideas," says a sophomore. From the herbarium to the Devonian fossils to the abundance of interdisciplinary courses, it's clear that Colgate has more to offer than just its picture-postcard setting. "Colgate draws students who want a high level of academic rigor and a top-tier liberal arts education," says one student. Adds another of the supportive environment among students and faculty, "You can take risks and be creative in your approach to academics without fear [of failure]."

Colgate's 13 founders started the school in 1817 with 13 prayers and 13 dollars. Their prayers were answered by soapmaking mogul William Colgate and his sons (think toothpaste), whose decades of philanthropic gift-giving to the fledgling university were enough to get the name changed in 1890 from Madison to Colgate. Today, the 575-acre campus sits on a hillside in rural New York, overlooking the village of Hamilton. Stately bluestone buildings peek out from tree-lined drives; lush green spaces are perfect for rugby, Frisbee, or other outdoor diversions, at least in the warmer months. Rolling hills and farmland surround the campus, making for stunning vistas all year long. The new Berstein Hall brings art and technology together and provides student project rooms, faculty research areas, and exhibition and performance spaces.

Aside from blazing a trail to rural New York, Colgate has led its peers in emphasizing interdisciplinary study. The faculty first established an interdisciplinary core program in 1928, and it's been a foundation of the curriculum ever since. Even now, all first-years take a seminar, capped at 18 students each, that introduces liberal arts topics, skills, resources, and ways of learning. Students choose from more than 40 topics, and seminar instructors double as academic advisors until students declare majors their sophomore year. Everyone completes four liberal arts core courses—Core Communities, Core Conversations, and Core Sciences—as well as courses emphasizing five liberal arts practices. Students also take classes in a range of disciplines that cover three broad areas: human thought and expression; social relations, institutions, and agents; and natural sciences and mathematics.

> **"You can take risks and be creative in your approach to academics."**

"The classroom atmosphere at Colgate places an emphasis on cooperation and collaboration over competition," says a Russian studies major. Students give high marks to Colgate's natural and social sciences programs, and economics, political science, psychology, and international relations are the most popular majors. Befitting Colgate's rugged location, there are five interdisciplinary environmental majors: environmental studies, environmental biology, environmental geography, environmental geology, and environmental economics. Seventy-one percent of classes have fewer than 20 students, and a geology major says, "The professors have been the most welcoming and dedicated people I've met in my life."

Classrooms and labs devoted to foreign language study help students gain comfort with another tongue—a good thing, since 53 percent of students study abroad. "Colgate is very good at sponsoring abroad programs. If the opportunity presents itself, take it," urges a senior. In addition to about 20 semester-long, faculty-led off-campus study programs (called "study groups"), Colgate offers five to eight "extended-study" travel programs that serve as two- or three-week extensions of regular on-campus courses. More than 100 other preapproved study abroad programs offer additional options. The Sophomore Residential Seminars program enables selected students to live together in the same residence hall and take a semester-long course that is capped off with a weeklong trip. "There are a lot of research opportunities at Colgate," says a computer science major, and over 80 percent of students get involved with it. Students have high praise for the Writing and Speaking Center. "It's an invaluable tool where peer consultants help students with both written and oral projects," explains a philosophy major. Colgate's Career Services office offers more than 200 formal recruiting partners. "So many students find internships and jobs through our amazing alumni network," says a classical studies and English major.

A senior says, "Students at Colgate are ambitious, driven, and intellectually curious," and students agree it is economically diverse. Twenty-two percent of students are New Yorkers, while 8 percent are international. Black students account for 4 percent of the population, Hispanics/Latinos 10 percent, Asian Americans 5 percent, and multiracial students 6 percent. Students credit the ALANA Cultural Center with "fostering a comfortable and friendly environment," but a senior says, "Colgate isn't really a politically active campus." Colgate does not award merit scholarships, but about 200 athletic scholarships are available in 13 sports. The university meets 100 percent of enrolled students' demonstrated financial need. Additionally, Colgate removed loans from aid packages for students whose annual family income is less than $175,000, and students whose annual family income is less than $80,000 attend tuition-free. Colgate has adjusted tuition costs to a percentage of annual income for students from families with annual income between $80,000 and $175,000.

"Colgate is very good at sponsoring abroad programs."

Ninety-three percent of Colgate students live in the residence halls, which range from traditional buildings with fireplaces to newer facilities that seem more like hotels. Students are housed in residential communities called Commons for their first two years and remain affiliated with their Commons throughout their four years. About 250 upperclassmen are allowed to live off campus each year. The main dining hall, Frank, serves up plenty of all-you-can-eat options that students mostly praise. "Is it Michelin Star? No. Will it sustain you for the next four years? Absolutely," opines a junior. Blue light call buttons around campus add to a general feeling of safety. A psychology major adds, "There is a large focus on mental health within the Colgate community, creating an open and encouraging space for students to discuss it honestly."

While Colgate has debated for decades doing away with fraternities and sororities, 30 percent of the men and 38 percent of the women join eight Greek life organizations. The university owns and manages all Greek housing, and recruitment is delayed until sophomore year. "There's almost always something happening on Friday and Saturday nights, especially within Greek Life," says a senior. And with more than 200 campus clubs and organizations, there are plenty of alternatives. "Cultural clubs often host food events featuring music, games, dancing, and traditional meals—which are always a hit," adds the senior. Students enjoy open-mic nights at the campus pub, Donovan's. "Springfest, Dancefest, Involvement Fair, Colgate vs. Cornell, jumping into Taylor Lake as a senior the week before finals are just a few true Colgate student traditions," relates a senior. Given the significance of the number 13 to the school's founding, every Friday the 13th is dubbed Colgate Day, a time to show off school spirit and pride. On the eve of graduation, seniors don their graduation robes for the Torchlight Ceremony, during which the graduating students process down the hill they walked up together during orientation.

In addition to a required four-day orientation, first-year students may participate in one of several preorientation programs, such as Wilderness Adventure, where groups of 8 to 12 canoe and hike in the Adirondacks. Hamilton is within walking distance of campus, but there's also a free bus that cycles through every half hour, especially nice in the depths of winter. The Palace Theater draws crowds with music, dancing, and a bar. There are also several alumni-owned shops and restaurants in the quiet town. For those with wheels, skiing is 45 minutes away, and the malls and city lights of Syracuse and Utica are roughly the same distance.

About a third of Colgate students enjoy facing off in intramural competitions and club sports, but students' most fervent cheers are reserved for Division I men's ice hockey against Cornell. "When Cornell comes to our rink, we throw Big Red gum on the ice, and they throw Colgate toothpaste on the ice [for matches at Cornell]," explains a junior. Women's ice hockey is a powerhouse, and the Raiders men's basketball and women's volleyball teams are recent Patriot League conference champions. Even weekend warriors may take advantage of facilities like the Sanford Field House, the Lineberry natatorium, and the Seven Oaks golf course.

> "Cultural clubs often host food events featuring music, games, dancing, and traditional meals."

Colgate led the way in interdisciplinary work and continues to do so now. What else has remained constant? A senior offers this assessment: "I think Colgate has embraced its identity as different from other liberal arts colleges in that we are not a crunchy granola hippie school, and we are not a socially progressive bastion of forward thinking. Colgate is what it is: a hidden gem in the Chenango Valley."

Overlaps

Boston College, Bowdoin, Bucknell, Colby, Cornell University, Dartmouth, Georgetown, UVA

If You Apply To ›

Colgate: Early decision I and II, regular decision. Accepts the Common Application with supplement. Please consult Colgate's website for the most up-to-date information regarding standardized test requirements.

University of Colorado Boulder

2055 Regent Drive, Boulder, CO 80309

Boulder is a legendary place that draws everyone from East Coast ski bums to California transplants. The scenery is breathtaking, and the science programs are first-rate. The University of Arizona is the only public university of similar stature in the Mountain West. Check out the residential academic programs.

Website: www.colorado.edu
Location: Small City
Public
Total Enrollment: 34,108
Undergraduates: 31,150
Male/Female: 52/48

Wild buffalo may be all but extinct on America's Great Plains, but they're in boisterous residence, proudly wearing black and gold, at the University of Colorado Boulder. A bevy of scholars' programs and residential academic programs give the campus a community feel, and students choose from a solid menu of academic offerings, including research experience, study abroad, and service learning. "There are so many ways to be active and engaged in your learning at Boulder," cheers a sophomore. And with nearly 300 days of sunshine a year, it's no surprise that CU Boulder Buffaloes are a happy herd.

Tree-shaded walkways, winding bike paths, open spaces, and an incredible view of the dramatic Flatirons rock formation make CU's 600-acre Boulder campus a haven for students from both coasts and for Colorado residents eager to pursue knowledge in a snowy paradise. The university was founded in 1876 as Colorado was becoming a state, and the campus includes about 200 classic rural Italian-style buildings and complexes built of Colorado sandstone with red tile roofs. City bus passes are included in the cost of tuition and fees, the campus Environmental Center facilitates sustainable culture and practices, and ongoing renovations and construction projects embody the university's commitment to sustainability and energy efficiency. Recent facility upgrades include the Renée Crown Wellness Institute, as well as a newly renovated performing arts theater and the new eSports gaming lounge in the student center.

Entering first-years and transfer students at CU Boulder choose from the following colleges, schools, and programs: the College of Arts and Sciences (which enrolls 70 percent of the students); the College of Music; the College of Engineering and Applied Science (the hardest to enter, students say); the College of Media, Communication, and Information; the Program in Environmental Design; the Leeds School of Business; the School of Education; and the Program in Exploratory Studies (which allows students to explore options before selecting a major). General education requirements cover three skills acquisition areas—written communication, quantitative reasoning and math, and foreign language—and three distribution categories: arts and humanities, natural sciences, and social sciences.

"You are always comfortable asking questions and asking for help."

"Unlike other highly competitive universities, there is a high level of collaboration," says an applied mathematics major. "Your classmates won't refuse to work with you, and you are always comfortable asking questions and asking for help." CU Boulder offers more than 4,500 courses each year in approximately 160 areas of study; psychology, finance, strategic communication, and integrative physiology are among the most popular majors. Outstanding programs include aerospace engineering sciences, physics, astronomy, chemical and biological engineering, computer science, music, business administration, and environmental studies. CU Boulder consistently ranks among the top universities in the country to receive NASA funding, leading to lots of opportunities for the design, construction, and flight of model spacecraft—and to several CU Boulder affiliates having worked as astronauts. A space minor is open to qualified students in any major. The Center for African and African American Studies supports teaching and research focused on the history and culture of people of African descent. The university also offers more than 50 bachelor's-accelerated master's degree programs, which allow students to earn two degrees in a shorter period of time. Forty percent of all undergraduate classes enroll fewer than 20 students, and a first-year says, "In my experience, professors and graduate student instructors alike have taken a keen interest in students' progress, success, and learning."

CU Boulder has tried to make its large campus seem smaller through specialized living/learning residential academic programs focusing on topics such as natural sciences and the environment, the arts, and engineering, which one senior says is "for freshmen essential for gaining a well-rounded experience at CU." The Presidents Leadership Class is a four-year scholarship program that provides promising students with leadership training, internships, volunteer opportunities, and visits with influential leaders. The Honors Program invites the top 10 percent of each incoming class in the College of Arts and Sciences to join. Multiple programs at CU Boulder support undergraduate research and community service opportunities, and the university sponsors over 400 study abroad programs in 70 countries around the world.

"Students are relaxed and explorative, curious and inquisitive, fun-loving and good-natured, focused and committed," says one Buffalo. Fifty-seven percent of CU Boulder's undergraduates come from Colorado, and 3 percent come from abroad.

CU Boulder's sorority chapters became the first in the nation to voluntarily make their houses dry.

Hispanics/Latinos account for 14 percent of the undergraduate population, Asian Americans 6 percent, Black students 2 percent, and multiracial students 7 percent. Social and political issues on campus include "wealth, liberalism, and inequality," according to one student. Qualified undergrads receive merit scholarships worth an average of $11,000, and more than 250 athletes receive scholarships in 10 sports. Additional programs provide debt-free financial incentives for qualified in-state students whose family income is at or below the federal poverty line. The university also guarantees incoming first-years that tuition and fees will not increase over their four years.

First-year students are required to live on campus, and 26 percent of all undergrads stay in university housing. "The older dorms are still in pretty good shape but aren't as nice as the newer dorms," a sophomore reports. Most sophomores, juniors, and seniors find off-campus digs in Boulder. An alternative to the main Center for Community dining center and 16 smaller dining locations is the Alferd Packer Restaurant & Grill, which takes its name from a controversial 19th-century folk figure known as the "Colorado Cannibal." Bon appétit. Generally, students say the campus is safe. CU Boulder offers nighttime transportation via a service called CU NightRide.

> **"Students are relaxed and explorative, curious and inquisitive."**

CU Boulder offers more than 4,500 courses each year in approximately 160 areas of study.

For the culturally minded, the university and the city of Boulder offer films and plays, the renowned Colorado Shakespeare Festival, art galleries and museums, and concerts by top bands. Denver is only 30 miles southeast, reachable by a free bus service. Most students get involved in community service, and the CU Engage center coordinates service-learning courses and community-based research opportunities. Eight percent of the men and 19 percent of the women go Greek, and fraternity and sorority parties have changed dramatically since CU Boulder's sorority chapters became the first in the nation to voluntarily make their houses dry. On campus, the ban on alcohol is taken seriously, and dorms are officially substance-free. Still, "The party scene is fairly large and has a lot going on most weekends," says a political science major. Day trips to ski resorts like Breckenridge and Vail largely replace weekend getaways here, but for those who've got to get out of the cold, Las Vegas isn't so far, says one student.

Physical exercise is a popular extracurricular activity at CU Boulder, especially the sort that involves sliding down snow-covered mountains. The massive Student Recreation Center features indoor and outdoor pools, a multipurpose turf gym, an ice rink, a climbing gym, and several multipurpose courts among other facilities. Varsity teams compete in the Division I Big 12 Conference as of 2024, and the Buffaloes men's and women's basketball, cross-country, and skiing teams are some of the strongest, along with women's soccer and lacrosse. Ralphie, the live buffalo who acts as CU Boulder's mascot, doesn't miss a game—and neither do many students. The club sports program, which boasts around 30 options, is highly competitive, regularly bringing home national titles in sports ranging from ice hockey and snowboarding to cycling and triathlon. Intramurals sign up about a third of the students each year.

> **"The party scene is fairly large and has a lot going on most weekends."**

Overlaps

University of Arizona, Arizona State, Cal Poly–San Luis Obispo, Colorado School of Mines, Indiana University, University of Oregon, University of Washington, UW–Madison

If you want to flex your muscles as well as your mind, look beyond the ivy-covered bricks and gray city skies endemic to so many Eastern institutions, and consider all the West has to offer instead. "The amount of resources students can utilize to further their education or gain experience in their field at CU and in the city of Boulder is immense and overwhelming," says one student.

If You Apply To ›

CU Boulder: Early action, regular decision. SATs or ACTs: optional. Accepts the Common Application with supplement. Music applicants must audition.

Colorado College

14 East Cache La Poudre Street, Colorado Springs, CO 80903

The Block Plan, a one-course-at-a-time academic schedule, is CC's claim to fame. It is great for in-depth study and short-term study abroad but less suited to academic projects that take an extended period of time. Colorado Springs is an ideal location at the base of the Rockies, which draw outdoor enthusiasts and East Coasters who like to ski. CC is the only top liberal arts college between Iowa and the Pacific.

Colorado College is one of the few U.S. schools offering one-course-at-a-time block scheduling. For more than a century, CC's focus on creative approaches to academics and its breathtaking location at the edge of the Rocky Mountains have drawn bright, independent liberal arts enthusiasts who also like to go out and play in the snow. "People don't come to CC because they want to make a ton of money or maintain the status quo," asserts a senior. "They come because they want to change the world, help others, and have a little fun."

Colorado's campus lies at the foot of Pike's Peak in the town of Colorado Springs. Many homes in the surrounding neighborhood are on the National Register of Historic Places, as are many CC buildings, including its first, Cutler Hall, and Palmer Hall, named after town founder William J. Palmer, a major force behind the establishment of the college in 1874. The prevailing architectural styles are Romanesque and English Gothic with some more modern structures thrown in. Newer construction includes the $52 million, 3,400-seat Robson Arena, hosting CC's Division I men's ice hockey team.

CC requires students to take courses focused on global cultures, issues of inequality (with respect to nationality, race, ethnicity, gender, class, and/or sexuality), natural sciences, and quantitative reasoning. Foreign language proficiency is also required. What really defines the academic climate, though, is the Block Plan (see also Cornell College in Iowa). Students take eight courses between late August and mid-May but focus on each one, in turn, for three and a half weeks. Some courses, such as those involving longer-term projects, are two blocks long. Four-and-a-half-day breaks separate the blocks. The plan helps students stay focused, eliminating the temptation to let one course slide so that they can catch up in another. But there are trade-offs. Students say it can be hard to integrate material from courses taken one at a time. There's also the danger of burnout, because so much material on a single subject is crammed into such a short span. An optional "half block" in January gives students a chance to explore niche academic interests or learn professional skills to become more competitive in the job market. In addition, an optional summer session offers three blocks.

The First-Year Program, consisting of a two-block sequence of courses with a student mentor and two advisors, helps students adjust to college-level academics, research, and the fast pace of the Block Plan. "CC is extremely collaborative," notes an environmental policy major. "However, it's extremely intense." Seventy-two percent of the classes have fewer than 20 students, and required courses are secured through a seniority-based system to determine who is enrolled and who is placed on a waitlist; seniors and juniors have higher priority for getting into classes that are intended for degree requirements. If you're going to take only one class at a time, it helps to like the teacher, and students say that's usually no problem here. "The professors are very accessible, and it is easy to have a good working relationship," says a history and political science major.

> **"[CC Students] want to change the world, help others, and have a little fun."**

The most popular majors at Colorado include business, economics, and society; computer science; political science; and psychology. The block schedule permits some classes at unique times and in unique places—for instance, astronomy at midnight or coral biology work in the Caribbean. The college's popular major in Southwest studies includes time at its Baca campus, 175 miles away in the historic San Luis Valley. Other interesting interdisciplinary programs include race, ethnicity, and migration studies. In addition to giving students the option to pick study abroad programs in a wide variety of countries, Colorado College faculty also teach both domestically and internationally throughout the school year and summer session. Roughly three-quarters of the students study off campus at least once during their time at Colorado.

Twenty-one percent of Colorado College students are in-staters, 6 percent are international, and the rest are from all over the United States. The school is trying to attract more diversity. Currently, 2 percent of undergrads are Black, 11 percent are Hispanic/Latino, 5 percent are Asian American, and 7 percent are multiracial. Groups like the Queer Trans Collective, Women's Wellness Collective, Hillel, and the Black Student Union provide support to students of varied backgrounds and viewpoints. "The general political orientation is extremely liberal," says a senior. The college meets 100 percent of admitted students' demonstrated financial need, and a limited number of merit scholarships, averaging $13,500, and a few athletic scholarships are available.

"CC is extremely collaborative."

Seventy-seven percent of students call campus housing home, and only seniors are permitted to live off campus. "The underclassmen dorms range from brand-new, almost luxury suites, to pretty old but full of character," says a senior. The "exceptional" dining facilities include a traditional, all-you-can-eat dining hall; a grill with American, Mexican, and sushi options; and an all-natural café and convenience store. The Student Organization for Sexual Safety raises awareness and addresses campus culture around issues like consent and sexual assault.

When the weekend comes, students unwind at parties in friends' rooms or seniors' off-campus houses. "There is a very large drug and alcohol presence on campus," reports a senior, "though it absolutely is not mandatory," socially speaking. The "low-key" Greek system attracts a small portion of students. Favorite traditions include the annual Llamapalooza music festival, a student-run fashion show, and the Arts and Crafts Fair. For those seeking a bit of urban culture, Denver and Boulder are a short drive away. Most CC students love heading off campus to ski or hike, either at nearby resorts or in Utah, New Mexico, or the Grand Canyon. First-year outdoor orientation trips help newcomers sort out the options, from backpacking and hiking to rafting, bicycling, and windsurfing. Students can even reserve a college-owned mountainside cabin. Service trips are sponsored during block breaks, and 67 percent of the students do some type of community service during their time at CC, often through community-based learning courses.

"It is easy to have a good working relationship [with professors]."

The Colorado College Tigers compete in two Division I sports—men's ice hockey and women's soccer—as well as 15 Division III sports. Basketball, lacrosse, swimming, and cross-country and women's volleyball are all competitive. The hockey rivalry with the University of Denver is huge. Students are also active in more than a dozen intramurals and 15 club sports.

The Block Plan made Colorado College what it is today, and the school continues to build on this reputation. As one senior underscores, "The intensive and demanding nature of the Block Plan calls for deep but quick thinkers [and] hard but patient workers." For those who are up to the challenge, CC offers a supportive environment, with a healthy dose of fun, where they can thrive.

Overlaps

Colby, Colgate, CU Boulder, Cornell College, University of Denver, Middlebury, WashU in St. Louis

If You Apply To ›

Colorado College: Early decision I and II, early action, regular decision. SATs or ACTs: optional. Accepts the Common Application with supplement.

1500 Illinois Street, Golden, CO 80401

Mines is the preeminent technical institute in the Mountain West. Getting in is not all that hard; getting through is another story. One-sixth the size of Texas Tech and best known for mining-related fields but strong in many areas of engineering. Men outnumber women by about 2 to 1. Golden provides easy access to the mountains and Denver. Graduates are heavily recruited.

If you're a bit of a geek whose only dilemma is what type of engineer to become, and you want to spend your scarce free time hiking, biking, and skiing with friends, then Colorado School of Mines may be the place for you. This public school's small size and rugged location endear it to the students who shoulder heavy workloads to earn their degrees. "There are often fun and entertaining conversations that could only be possible with the types of students here," says a mechanical engineering major. Just down the road from Coors Brewing Co., which taps the Rockies for its legendary brews, students at Mines learn to tap the same mountains for coal, oil, and other natural resources.

The school's 373-acre campus sits in the shadow of the spectacular Rocky Mountains in tiny Golden (as in gold mining), Colorado. Architectural styles range from turn-of-the-century gold dome to present-day modern, and native trees and greenery punctuate lush lawns. Among the newer additions to campus is the Beck Venture Center, which provides workspaces and funding for student, faculty, and alumni start-ups.

At Mines, the academics are rigorous. Core requirements include coursework in design and innovation, culture and society, success and wellness, student-led inquiry, and, of course, math, science, and engineering, with extra doses of physics, chemistry, calculus, and differential equations. In the first year, everyone takes CSM 101, a first-year advising and mentoring course. The required two-semester Cornerstone Design program helps develop communication, teamwork, and problem-solving skills. Because of Mines' narrow focus, the undergraduate majors—or "options," as they're called—are quite strong. There's plenty of variety, as long as you are into engineering; programs range from geophysical, metallurgical, and petroleum to chemical, electrical, and mechanical. Computer science, another popular choice, is the school's fastest-growing program. New majors include ceramic engineering and construction engineering. Mines has been investing more in humanities and social sciences, offering several minors in these areas. Courses in a student's option start in the second semester of sophomore year, and as seniors, all students complete a capstone requirement.

Pass/fail grading is unheard of at Mines, but failing grades are not. "Classes can be challenging at times," admits a mechanical engineering major, "but being surrounded by like-minded STEM students who want you to succeed is encouraging." Professors are qualified and helpful, and adjunct professors, who work in the fields they teach, draw praise for their practical knowledge. "Most of the teachers have industry experience and bring that into the classroom," a chemistry major says, but only 16 percent of undergraduate classes have fewer than 20 students.

Mines supplements coursework with a required six-week summer field session, enabling students to gain hands-on experience. About 20 percent of undergraduates participate in the McBride Honors Program, which includes seminars and off-campus

"Classes can be challenging at times."

Website: www.mines.edu
Location: Small City
Public
Total Enrollment: 7,302
Undergraduates: 5,931
Male/Female: 68/31
Financial Aid: 62%
Pell Grant: 15%
Expense: Pub $ $ $ $
Student Loans: 54%
Average Debt: $ $ $
Applicants: 11,436
Accepted: 61%
Enrolled: 23%
Grad in 6 Years: 82%
Returning First-years: 93%
Academics: ✍ ✍ ✍
Social: 🗩 🗩 🗩
Q of L: ★ ★
Admissions: (888) 446-9489
Email Address:
 admissions@mines.edu

Strong Programs:
Chemical and Biological
 Engineering
Computer Science
Electrical Engineering
Geophysical Engineering
Mechanical Engineering
Mining Engineering
Petroleum Engineering

activities that encourage them to think differently about the implications of technology. The WISEM program provides training, mentoring, and other support for women in science, engineering, and math. Typically, 10 percent of students study abroad, but the school also offers a First Year Semester Abroad in Antibes, France. Thirty-three percent of undergraduates participate in research with faculty members or on their own. "Career advising has some of the best faculty you can connect with," cheers a quantitative biosciences and engineering major.

Mines students "tend to be nerdier and there are a ton of introverts and outdoorsy people," says a senior. Established in 1874 to serve the emerging mining industry in the West, Mines is a state school, making it an especially good deal for homegrown students, who comprise 56 percent of the undergraduate student body. Three percent hail from foreign nations. Hispanics/Latinos represent 14 percent of the student body, Asian Americans 6 percent, Black students just 1 percent, and multiracial students 6 percent. Students are generally too wrapped up in academics to pay attention to political issues, according to a physics major. Merit scholarships averaging $8,400 are available to qualified students, and athletes may vie for athletic scholarships in 16 sports.

First-years are required to live in the residence halls; most students move off campus after the first year. A majority of buildings are co-ed, though the preponderance of men results in a few single-sex dorms. "All the residence halls have been refurbished and are looking better than ever," a sophomore says. Options for upperclassmen include college-owned apartments and off-campus condos and houses. There's only one cafeteria, Mines Market, and a junior says, "The vegetarian options are not very good unless you really like cereal and salad" (presumably at different meals).

"There are a ton of introverts and outdoorsy people."

There is life outside of the computer labs here. On campus, a junior says, "There is always a club putting together an event or just students throwing parties." Mines has an active Greek system, with fraternities and sororities attracting 13 percent of the men and 21 percent of the women. Rush is dry, and underage drinking is met with consequences. The social scene also includes homecoming and Engineering Days (E-Days)— five nights of events before finals start that include everything from a silent disco and lawn games to cardboard boat races and concerts. New student orientation features the traditional "M Climb," in which first-years hike up Mount Zion lugging a rock from their hometown, then "whitewash it and each other," says one participant. The rock is added to an M formation atop the mountain, and at the end of the year, "seniors return to take down a rock, completing the cycle."

The school's location at the base of the Rockies means gorgeous Colorado weather (make sure to bring sunscreen) and easy access to skiing, hiking, mountain climbing, and biking. Denver is also nearby, and aside from its museums, concerts, and sports teams, the city is home to many government agencies and businesses involved in natural resources, computers, and technology, including the regional offices of the U.S. Geological Survey and Bureau of Mines. Golden hosts the National Earthquake Center, the National Renewable Energy Laboratory, and, of course, the Coors Brewery. Road trips to Las Vegas or Texas provide occasional respite from the school's heavy workload.

Mines' 18 Division II varsity teams compete in the Rocky Mountain Athletic Conference. The men's track and field team is a recent national champion. Other competitive Oredigger teams include football, men's and women's soccer, and basketball. The intramural and club sports programs have grown dramatically, with the majority of students now participating.

While time spent in the classroom at Mines may be intense, for those who are focused on engineering, educational options don't get much better than those offered here. "Lots of companies recruit our students," says one senior, thanks to a stellar reputation in the fields of mining and engineering. A junior adds, "When you leave here, you're prepared for anything." Especially if you are an engineer.

Colorado State University

200 West Lake Street, Fort Collins, CO 80523

Known throughout the region for its prevet program, Colorado State turns out more STEM (science, technology, engineering, and math) graduates than any other Colorado campus. It lacks Boulder's glitz and glamour, but has a traditional college feel with a first-rate student center and strong ties to the local community.

Founded in 1870 as the Colorado Agricultural College, Colorado State University began with five students, two faculty members, and a mission "to serve society through teaching, research, and public service." Today, the university boasts approximately 1,700 faculty across eight colleges, as well as more than 240,000 living alumni, including state governors, corporate CEOs, Olympic gold medalists, teachers, researchers, and artists. Students here enjoy ample research opportunities, a slew of solid academic programs, and an unbeatable location.

Situated at the foot of the spectacular Rocky Mountains, CSU gives students easy access to abundant natural resources. The open space on the main campus reflects the university's heritage as a land grant institution. The Oval, a wide expanse of lawn encircled by towering elm trees, anchors the northeast corner of campus. Architectural styles range from Beaux-Arts to Renaissance Revival, and the campus features a spacious outdoor plaza, 32 acres of recreation fields, and stunning views of Long's Peak. The university also boasts a 1,400-acre foothills campus, a 1,600-acre agricultural campus, and the 1,200-acre mountain campus, which provide opportunities for hands-on learning and research.

All CSU undergrads complete a university-wide core curriculum that includes coursework in writing, quantitative reasoning, biological/physical sciences, arts/humanities, social/behavioral sciences, historical perspectives, global awareness, and three credits of courses that address diversity, equity, and inclusion. CSU offers more than 70 undergraduate majors, the most popular of which include business administration (especially the finance concentration), psychology, zoology, and biological sciences. Science and engineering are the university's main strengths, and the prevet program is distinguished. Computer science, ecosystem science and sustainability, and international studies are notable. New majors include livestock business management and hospitality and event management. Fort Collins has been a craft brewing hub for decades, and CSU's fermentation science major is a unique specialty. The performing arts have received a boost thanks to improved facilities, but the humanities are not as solid as other departments.

The academic climate can be competitive—especially in the preprofessional programs. "The courses are hard but manageable," a junior says. Thirty-two percent of classes have fewer than 20 students, and one student says, "If you express an

Website: www.colostate.edu
Location: Small City
Public
Total Enrollment: 26,260
Undergraduates: 22,979
Male/Female: 44/56
Financial Aid: 58%
Pell Grant: 20%
Expense: Pub $ $
Student Loans: 47%
Average Debt: $ $ $
Applicants: 38,465
Accepted: 89%
Enrolled: 16%
Grad in 6 Years: 67%
Returning First-years: 86%
Academics: ✍ ✍ ✍
Social: 🍺 🍺 🍺 🍺
Q of L: ★ ★ ★ ★
Admissions: (970) 491-6909
Email Address:
  admissions@colostate.edu

Strong Programs:
Biomedical Sciences
Business Administration
Computer Science
Ecosystem Science and
  Sustainability
Engineering
Fermentation Science and
  Technology
International Studies
Psychology

interest in their area of study, [professors] may invite you to do research in their lab, write a paper and be published in a major journal, or help you with graduate school applications—who knows!" A sophomore highly recommends the Key Communities living/learning program for first-years: "As a Key student, you take three classes with a cluster of 19 people whom you meet before classes start. This is so nice because you immediately have friends and people you know who also live in [the same hall] and can help you study." Qualified students can opt for the Honors Program to take honors seminars, receive specialized advising, and complete a senior thesis. Undergraduate research academies allow students to join a faculty-mentored, interdisciplinary team investigating a common problem or theme from different disciplinary perspectives. Overall, 26 percent of undergraduates participate in faculty research each year, and undergrads can study abroad in over 80 countries; many complete at least one internship.

"The students at CSU are friendly and accepting," says a junior. Sixty-three percent of CSU students are from Colorado, and 2 percent are international. Black students account for only 3 percent of undergrads, Asian Americans 3 percent, Hispanics/Latinos 16 percent, and multiracial students 5 percent. CSU is a politically active campus, with liberal and conservative viewpoints both well represented. Historically, "The biggest issues on campus are probably environmental issues," explains a student, "due mainly to our proximity to the Rocky Mountains." Thousands of merit scholarships averaging $5,200 are handed out each year, and athletes vie for nearly 200 scholarships in 14 sports. The CSU Tuition Assistance Grant provides financial support for in-state, low-income students.

"The students at CSU are friendly and accepting."

Twenty-seven percent of CSU students live on campus in residence halls and campus apartments; students may move off campus after their first year. "Residence halls are in great condition and more like a resort than the dorms we all picture from movies," says a student. Campus residents may choose from among a variety of meal plans, and the residence hall dining center provides an all-you-can-eat option. "The food is awesome," a student says. "I think it is as good as any restaurant in town." Students also report feeling safe on campus; security measures include a "safe walk" escort program and an active security staff.

The Greek scene attracts just 5 percent of the men and 6 percent of the women, so it's not a defining force in campus social life. "Campus activities, such as free movies or concerts, draw a large crowd," says one student, "while parties and other gatherings off campus do the same." The Lory Student Center hosts events on a regular basis, and more than 500 student clubs serve as a social outlet too. The CSU campus is dry, and "there is no tolerance for alcohol in the residence halls," notes a biochemistry major. "The policies are enforced."

"We have a huge homecoming with a bonfire, parade, and football game."

Fort Collins (population 170,000) is "a fun city that revolves around the school," says one junior. "There is a definite sense of community and support for CSU in the town," a senior adds. Students not only frequent the downtown bars, shops, and eateries but also can be found performing volunteer work or community service alongside the locals. Popular road trips include quick getaways to nearby ski resorts and hiking trails and longer treks to Utah and Nevada. Back on campus, students enjoy a number of traditions: "We have a huge homecoming," says one student, "with a bonfire, parade, and football game."

The CSU Rams compete in Division I as members of the Mountain West Conference, and the most competitive teams include men's basketball, women's volleyball, and men's and women's track and field. The University of Colorado is the hated rival—especially in football—and "the Rocky Mountain Showdown is probably the biggest event of the year," says a family and consumer sciences major. Popular intramurals and club sports include baseball, ice hockey, ultimate Frisbee, and eSports. The Student Recreation Center features an indoor track, a climbing wall, basketball and volleyball courts, cardio machines and free weights, and a host of other facilities for students who want to stay in shape.

Despite ubiquitous complaints about limited parking, rising tuition, and the need for more bike racks, students at Colorado State are quick to say why they appreciate their alma mater: "Because CSU rocks! It is an awesome school to go to and has lots to offer students of all ages and backgrounds," cheers a student. What's more, it's a "fun and beautiful place to be," says a junior, "and you know that your degree will mean something."

Columbia University

212 Hamilton Hall, New York, NY 10027

Once a high-powered Ivy League afterthought, Columbia now rivals the Ivy League's big three in selectivity. Applications have nearly doubled in the past 10 years for one simple reason: Manhattan trumps New Haven, Providence, Ithaca, and every other Ivy League city, with the possible exception of Boston, as a place to spend four years. The often overlooked engineering program is among the best in the nation for undergraduates. The heart of Columbia is still its Core Curriculum.

Students entering Columbia will, of course, expect the rigorous academic program they'll encounter at this Ivy League school, but they must also be streetwise, urbane, and together enough to handle one of the most cosmopolitan cities in the world. Columbia lets its students experience life in the Big Apple but serves as a refuge when it becomes necessary to escape from New York, allowing students to immerse themselves in the best academia has to offer, starting with the Core Curriculum. "Students here want a classical liberal arts education but do not want to live in a college bubble," says a first-year. Famous alums can be found in the highest echelons of their chosen professions, whether it be politics, literature, sports, or entertainment. Think Barack Obama. In 2025, Columbia found itself among the first universities targeted by the Trump administration, resulting in over $400 million in federal research funding being frozen. Columbia agreed to settle with the government and make several policy changes related to diversity, equity, and inclusion to restore the research funds.

The fifth-oldest university in the country, Columbia was founded under Anglican auspices in 1754 as King's College and renamed in 1784, after the American Revolution. With a total university-wide enrollment of more than 26,000 full-time students, says one of them, "It's easy to feel lost." Columbia's 6,600 traditional undergraduates are split into two divisions: the flagship Columbia College and the Fu Foundation School of Engineering and Applied Science. (The School of General Studies offers undergraduate education to part-time and nontraditional students. Sister school Barnard College, affiliated with Columbia University but governed by its own board of trustees, has an additional 3,000 students.) Columbia's campus has a large central quadrangle in front of Butler Library and at the foot of the steps leading past the statue of Alma Mater to Low Library, which is now the administration building. The redbrick, copper-roofed neoclassical buildings are "stunning," and the layout, says an undergrad, "is well thought out and manages to provide a beautiful setting with an economy of space."

The undergraduate experience at Columbia centers on its renowned Core Curriculum, a series of small, discussion-based seminars that explore "foundational texts, enduring documents, and exemplary experiments in literature, philosophy, history, music, art, writing, science, and more." While these courses occupy up to a third of the first two years and can become laborious, students generally praise them as worthwhile and enriching. "The Core truly unifies the school in a way that transcends most social limitations," says a first-year. Since being established in 1919, the college has expanded the diversity of the canon and now requires Core classes on non-Western cultures. According to a junior, some students find that the Core can "spark some interest in a subject they had never thought of before."

Two of the most demanding introductory courses in the Ivy League—Contemporary Civilization (CC) and Literature Humanities (LitHum)—form the basis of the Core. Both are yearlong and taught in small sections. CC examines political and moral philosophy from Plato to Camus, though professors have some leeway in choosing 20th-century selections. LitHum covers about 26 masterpieces of literature from Homer to Dostoyevsky, usually with some Sappho, Jane Austen, and Toni Morrison thrown in for alternative perspectives. One semester each of art and music history is required, and, while they are not given the same reverence as their literary counterparts, they are eye-opening all the same. Foreign language proficiency is required, as is a semester of University Writing, two semesters of science, "global Core" classes dealing in cultures not covered in the other Core requirements, and phys ed. Students at the School of Engineering and Applied Science complete approximately half of the Core Curriculum.

> **"[The campus] manages to provide a beautiful setting with an economy of space."**

Columbia is an intellectual school, not a preprofessional one, and even though a large percentage of students aspire to law or medical school, "we are mostly content to be liberal artists for as long as possible," says an English major. Even students in the School of Engineering and Applied Science pursue "technical education" with a liberal arts base. Almost all departments that offer undergraduate majors are strong, notably English, history, political science, economics, neuroscience, and computer science. Chemistry and biology are among the best of Columbia's high-quality science offerings. The earth and environmental science department owns 200 acres in Rockland County, home to many rocks and much seismographic equipment. The fine arts are improving, thanks to newer facilities and joint programs with schools such as the Juilliard School of Music. Many challenging combined majors are available, such as philosophy/economics and biology/psychology. There are 50 offerings in foreign languages, ranging from Czech to Persian to Urdu, and the East Asian languages and cultures department is one of the best anywhere. There is also an African American and African diaspora studies major and a women's and gender studies major taught in cooperation with Barnard. Students can take classes in any department at Barnard and graduate-level courses in several Columbia departments. A notable five-year bachelor's/master's program gives students access to the resources of the highly regarded School of International and Public Affairs and its multitude of regional institutes.

Students can take classes in any department at Barnard and graduate-level courses in several Columbia departments.

Columbia's workload is often stressful, and since most students are used to being top achievers, classmates can be intimidating to the faint of heart. A financial economics major offers this advice: "Prepare to be average and to be happy that you are an average student at Columbia." Student/faculty interaction is supported by one of the smallest student-to-faculty ratios in the country, and 59 percent of classes have fewer than 20 students. "Some of the professors are real leaders in their fields," says a philosophy major, who also cautions, "Many Core classes are taught by grad students, which has led to some less-than-ideal experiences for me." Additional interaction stems from professorial involvement in campus politics and forums and from the faculty-in-residence program, which houses professors and their families in spruced-up apartments in several of the residence halls. First-year students are assigned an academic advisor with whom they work for all four years, and they receive a departmental faculty advisor when they declare a major at the end of sophomore year. For students wishing to spend time away from New York, Columbia offers credit through more than 150 programs in 40 countries on six continents; about a third of students go abroad. Research is big here too, and undergraduates have the opportunity to work with professors in the sciences, humanities, and social sciences in over 200 research centers and institutes, although some have likely been impacted by the current political situation.

"In general, Columbia students are eager to learn, engaged with the world around them, and happy to explore New York City," says a sociology major. Seventeen percent of undergraduates come from New York, and 16 percent come from abroad. Students of color make up more than half of the undergraduate population: 8 percent are Black, 17 percent are Hispanic/Latino, 22 percent are Asian American, and 7 percent are multiracial. Columbia remains one of the nation's most liberal campuses, and an economics major notes, "Students take an active approach to solving the problems that face marginalized groups." The university awards financial aid based on need, meeting the full demonstrated need of all students, domestic and international, with grants instead of loans. Students coming from families with annual incomes below $150,000 and typical assets attend Columbia tuition-free.

Given the exorbitant nature of the New York housing market, 90 percent of Columbia students live in university housing, which is guaranteed for four years. Many rooms are singles, and it is possible to go all four years without a roommate. Carman Hall, one of three exclusively first-year dorms, is a popular choice for its private bathrooms. "Going into sophomore year, my roommate and I had a very bad lottery number," recalls one student, "but we were still able to get a room in an air-conditioned building with a view of the Empire State Building." First-year students are required to join one of three meal plan options and take most of those meals at John Jay. Dining options receive positive reviews, but for students who prefer to do their own cooking, several dorms have kitchens. The university has introduced a number of Title IX initiatives, including a comprehensive gender-based misconduct policy and the addition of a second sexual violence support center on campus. "Columbia has a robust Title IX investigation team," reports a senior. "I've never felt unsafe as a young woman walking around campus at night. We have guards in every dorm, a blue-light system, and campus patrols."

The social scene starts on the Columbia campus and spills over into the bustling streets of New York City. "We have the best of both worlds, because Columbia students can be a part of the vibrant on-campus community but also take part in New York's eclectic environment!" cheers one student. The challenge, others say, is finding time to relax and enjoy all the city has to offer. Rarely are there big all-inclusive bashes, the exceptions being the Tree Lighting celebration in December and spring's Bacchanal concert. "My favorite tradition is the Varsity Show, a more than 125-year-old tradition of a student-written musical that satirizes Columbia, the Ivy League, and current campus and world events," says a sophomore. Nine percent of the men and 13 percent of the women go Greek; the advent of co-ed houses has raised interest in Greek life, as has the arrival of sororities open to both Columbia and Barnard women. But Columbia is hardly a Hellenocentric campus. "I love that no one activity dominates the social scene," says a first-year. The Community Impact organization coordinates 27 local community service programs in which nearly 1,000 students participate.

Columbia athletics don't inspire rabid loyalty. "Columbia students are individualists," according to one sophomore. "This is not a school that rallies together at football games." Still, the Lions field 31 Division I teams. Men's and women's fencing have brought home national championships, while baseball, men's squash, and women's cross-country have claimed Ivy League conference titles. As an urban school, Columbia lacks team field facilities on campus; however, 100 blocks to the north is the modern Baker Field, home of the football stadium, the soccer fields, an Olympic track, and the crew boathouse. On campus, the Dodge Gymnasium, an underground facility, houses four levels of basketball courts, swimming pools, weight rooms, and exercise equipment. Dozens of intramural and club sports are available; men's and women's ultimate Frisbee are both nationally competitive.

> **"[Students] are mostly content to be liberal artists for as long as possible."**

"Columbia is definitely not a stress-free, friendly community, but it has its own charm," explains a senior. "The university is quintessentially New York: As a student, there are so many experiences to be had, but you really have to engage in the community and seek them out." Columbians are proud to attend college in New York City, and most would have it no other way.

Overlaps

Brown, UC Berkeley, Harvard, MIT, Penn, Princeton, Stanford, Yale

---

If You Apply To ›

Columbia: Early decision, regular decision. Accepts the Common Application with supplement. Please consult Columbia's website for the most up-to-date information regarding standardized test requirements.

University of Connecticut

352 Mansfield Road, Storrs, CT 06269

Squeezed in among the likes of Brown, UMass, Trinity, Wesleyan, and Yale—all within a two-hour drive—UConn could be forgiven for having an identity problem. Championship basketball teams have helped ignite Husky pride and boost selectivity. Storrs is nobody's idea of an exciting destination, but it does offer easy access to beautiful countryside.

Website: www.uconn.edu
Location: Rural
Public
Total Enrollment: 24,962
Undergraduates: 19,476
Male/Female: 45/55
Financial Aid: 69%
Pell Grant: 19%
Expense: Pub $ $ $ $

The top public university in New England and highly regarded nationally, the University of Connecticut has poured billions of dollars into new facilities and into expanding educational opportunities and research in STEM disciplines. Like many other schools, UConn is facing large budget cuts, in their case due to a projected $72 million deficit in 2026. There's talk about tuition increases and layoffs, and the university plans to increase enrollment by 4,000 over the next five years. Even so, UConn is the only public university in New England with its own law school, medical school, dental school, and school of social work—and undergraduates benefit indirectly from these resources. The glow of two nationally competitive basketball teams, a wealth of research opportunities, and more than 600 clubs and organizations make it clear why UConn moved well beyond its erstwhile "cow college" image.

UConn's 4,000-acre campus is about 23 miles northeast of Hartford. Building styles range from collegiate Gothic and neoclassical to half-century-old red brick. Dense woods surround the campus, which also boasts two lakes, Swan and Mirror. Ongoing renovations are the norm, sparking jokes about the "University of Construction," but the results are impressive. The 212,000-square-foot NextGen residence hall houses more than 700 students in several living/learning communities and features an innovative makerspace. The five-story, $95 million Engineering and Science Building and the $75 million Student Recreation Center are among the recent additions to campus.

Students say UConn's strongest offerings are preprofessional—business, engineering, education, pharmacy, and allied health, including nursing and physical therapy. The school's historic focus on agriculture is giving way to an emphasis on environment and ecology, including a strong program in coastal studies. Also notable are neuroscience, linguistics, history, human rights, and, of course, agriculture. (UConn was founded in 1881 as a farm school; it's where America learned to get more eggs per chicken by leaving the lights on in the coops.) Engineering is demanding, and, as at many schools, it has a relatively high attrition rate, with many students switching to the less rigorous major in management information systems. A special program in medicine and dentistry allows students to earn bachelor's degrees in any of UConn's more than 125 disciplines and guarantees admission to the School of Medicine or Dental Medicine if they meet all criteria.

UConn's academic atmosphere is described as moderately competitive and challenging, depending on a student's course of study. Core requirements include courses in four basic areas: arts and humanities, social sciences, diversity/multiculturalism, and science and technology. Students must also achieve competency in writing, quantitative skills, information literacy, a second language, and environmental literacy. Seminar-style writing classes are available to all first-years, and three-quarters also take at least one First-Year Experience course that guides them through the transition to college. The Academic Center for Exploratory Students helps first- and second-year students who still need to decide on a major. Students generally applaud the enthusiasm of their professors—and the graduate teaching assistants who administer tests, collect assignments, and run labs and discussion groups—but a senior grumbles, "Some lack the ability to connect with students and the skills to teach students effectively."

UConn's engineering, business, pharmacy, and honors students are required to undertake research projects, and each year, two teams of finance majors run their own $1 million portfolios for the student-managed investment fund. Students who aspire to graduate school in academic fields, rather than professional certification, may win grants to work independently under faculty members through the undergraduate summer research program. The students who qualify for the honors program gain access to special floors and dorms; several programs for disadvantaged students are also available. In addition, 15 percent of students participate in the study abroad program, which offers 275 options in more than 60 countries.

UConn students are "hardworking, responsible, intelligent, passionate, and inspirational," according to one psychology major. Seventy percent of UConn undergraduates are from Connecticut, and 7 percent are international. Many students choose to transfer to the Storrs campus after beginning coursework in their chosen major and earning 54 credits at one of UConn's four regional campuses. Eight percent of undergrads are Black, 17 percent are Hispanic/Latino, 13 percent are Asian American, and 5 percent are multiracial. There are cultural centers for

> "Students are very much concerned with what is going on today in our world."

> Dorms are all co-ed, and the entire campus, including outdoor areas, is equipped with Wi-Fi.

(continued)

Student Loans: 49%
Average Debt: $ $
Applicants: 55,479
Accepted: 52%
Enrolled: 15%
Grad in 6 Years: 83%
Returning First-years: 92%
Academics: ✍ ✍ ✍ ✍
Social: 🗨 🗨 🗨
Q of L: ★ ★ ★
Admissions: (860) 486-3137
Email Address:
  onestop@uconn.edu

Strong Programs:
Agriculture
Business
Coastal Studies
Education
Engineering
Nursing
Pharmacy
Physical Therapy

Black, Asian American, Latin American, and Puerto Rican students, as well as the Rainbow Center, a resource for LGBTQ students. "Students are very much concerned with what is going on today in our world," a student says. Eligible UConn students receive merit scholarships averaging $11,800, and hundreds of athletic scholarships are available in 18 sports. Persistence rates are notably high for a public flagship university, with 92 percent of first-years returning for their sophomore year and a six-year graduation rate of 83 percent.

Sixty-seven percent of the students live in university housing, which is available to all undergraduates. "All the dorms are very well maintained," says a senior. Dorms are all co-ed, and the entire campus, including outdoor areas, is equipped with Wi-Fi. Eight dining halls offer plenty of choices, including for vegetarians and vegans, though many students would just as soon visit the snack bar for some ice cream, freshly made with help from the cows grazing nearby. "The food at UConn each night is diverse, and a student can always find something he or she wants," one student says. A group of students are selected to live on a sustainable farm just off campus where they raise foods that are served in the dining halls. Students report feeling safe on campus. "Crime is so low we think it doesn't exist, the police don't bother anyone unless they have to, and we have a great system of security alerts," says a junior.

"The food at UConn each night is diverse."

"Social life is the best part of college life and includes clubs, frats, sports, and so much more," says one student. "As you get involved, you will be wicked busy!" Students 21 and over are allowed to possess no more than a six-pack of beer, one bottle of wine, or a small bottle of liquor. Underage students caught with booze may be evicted from campus housing. Late-night activities at the student union and other campus events provide a lot of alternatives to alcohol use. Fraternities attract 11 percent of the men, and sororities claim 13 percent of the women; members can live in chapter housing at the Husky Village. On weekends, there are buses to Hartford (only 30 minutes away), Boston, New Haven, New York, and Providence. Cape Cod and the Vermont ski slopes are within weekend driving distance. Favorite annual campus events include the mud volleyball tournament, carnival-style UConn Late Nights, midnight breakfasts during finals, homecoming, Winter Weekend, and Midnight Madness—the first official day of basketball practice. In addition to cheering for the Huskies, "it is good luck to rub the nose of the bronze statue of our mascot, Jonathan," says a sophomore.

The town of Storrs "is basically UConn," says one student. A recent downtown Storrs initiative offers shops, restaurants, and a town green, as well as additional living options available to students. The university provides transportation for students who volunteer in area schools and hospitals. Legend holds that UConn also offers one diversion most other colleges can't: cow tipping—that is, sneaking up on unsuspecting cows, which sleep standing up, and tipping them over. The administration contends that this is a myth, though students always claim to "know someone who did it."

UConn's teams are known as the Huskies (UConn. Yukon. Get it?), and in a state without any major league professional sports teams, UConn basketball routinely sells out the XL Center. The men's team were national champions in 2023 and 2024, and in 2025 the women's team notched their 12th national championship under legendary coach Geno Auriemma. Women's field hockey and men's soccer are also strong. Intramurals are offered at three levels, from recreational to competitive. Popular options range from underwater hockey and inner-tube water polo to basketball, volleyball, and flag football.

"As you get involved, you will be wicked busy!"

UConn continues to adapt its agricultural roots to the 21st century. Those seeking greener pastures will be hard-pressed to find a more dynamic public institution.

"We are a well-rounded campus with students from every background," a junior pharmacy student says. And if the school can successfully navigate its budget shortfall, it will continue to be a good time to be at UConn.

Connecticut College

270 Mohegan Avenue, New London, CT 06320

Like Skidmore and Vassar, Connecticut College long ago made a successful transition from women's college to co-ed. That means a slightly more progressive campus tenor than at, say, Hamilton or Trinity. The college is strong in the humanities, dance, and drama, and notable for its study abroad programs and funded internships. New London does not offer much, but at least it is on the water, and generous financial aid helps a lot.

Students at Connecticut College follow the example of their mascot, the camel—they take pride in drinking up and storing knowledge. The student-run honor code means finals are not proctored; they're even self-scheduled, whenever students prefer during a five-day window. "The honor code gives the freedom for the student to be responsible for their actions academically and socially," says an economics major. "It creates a respectful and trustful relationship between professors and students."

Placed majestically atop a hill, the Conn College campus sits within a 750-acre arboretum with a pond, wetlands, wooded areas, and hiking trails. It offers beautiful views of the Thames River (pronounced the way it looks, not like the "Temz" that Wordsworth so dearly loved) on one side and Long Island Sound on the other. The granite campus buildings are a mixture of modern and collegiate Gothic in style, with some neo-Gothic and neoclassical architecture thrown in for good measure. The college converted the main roadway through campus into a walkway and completed a renovation of the student center in 2025.

Conn was founded in 1911 as a women's college and went co-ed in 1969. The general education program, cleverly called Connections (get it?), lets students "build an integrated study plan that connects everything they learn and do at the College over four years, including coursework in their major, classes outside their major, study abroad and internships." Coursework includes two semesters of foundational courses, including a first-year seminar, an interdisciplinary ConnCourse, and two Social Difference and Power courses, followed by a series of thematically linked classes called an "Integrative Pathway." The senior year culminates with an integrative project that is presented at an All-College Symposium. Academics are definitely the focus here. "I'd consider the academic climate at Conn to be rigorous and intense but supportive all the same," says a film studies major. Much of that support comes from professors who are lauded for their accessibility and thoughtfulness.

> "I'd consider the academic climate at Conn to be rigorous and intense but supportive."

Website: www.conncoll.edu
Location: Small City
Private
Total Enrollment: 1,935
Undergraduates: 1,935
Male/Female: 39/61
Financial Aid: 99%
Pell Grant: 20%
Expense: Pr $ $ $ $
Student Loans: 46%
Average Debt: $ $ $ $
Applicants: 7,950
Accepted: 37%
Enrolled: 15%
Grad in 6 Years: 82%
Returning First-years: 90%
Academics: ✍ ✍ ✍ ✍
Social: 🗩 🗩 🗩
Q of L: ★ ★ ★ ★
Admissions: (860) 439-2200
Email Address:
admission@conncoll.edu

Strong Programs:
Biology
Chemistry
Dance
Drama
Economics

Conn's dance and drama departments are superb, and it's not uncommon for dancers to take time off to study with professional companies. Aspiring actors, directors, and stagehands may work on numerous on-campus productions and with the Eugene O'Neill Theater Institute, named for New London's best-known literary son. Chemistry majors may use high-tech gas chromatograms and mass spectrometers from their very first day. Conn also offers strong programs in biology, environmental studies, and international relations. Five interdisciplinary centers offer courses, certificates, and special programming in international studies, arts and technology, public policy and community action, the environment, and the study of race and ethnicity. The most popular majors are economics, psychology, English, and computer science.

To escape Conn's small size and occasionally claustrophobic feel, the Study Away/Teach Away (SATA) initiative allows groups of about a dozen Conn students and a faculty member to spend a semester living and working together at an overseas university in locations as far-flung as Italy, South Africa, Peru, and Vietnam. In fact, 36 percent of Connecticut College students study abroad through SATA and other college-approved programs offered in 40 countries. All students who participate in a set of career workshops are guaranteed an internship opportunity and may receive up to $3,000 in flexible funds to help cover housing or other costs. Opportunities for funded summer research with professors are also available.

"Connecticut College has a reputation for being a 'preppy' school; many of the students are very well-off," says a computer science major. Only 13 percent of students come from Connecticut, and 6 percent come from abroad. Black students make up 5 percent of the student body, Asian Americans account for 3 percent, Hispanic/Latino students add 12 percent, and multiracial students represent 4 percent. Students say there is a growing interest in activism on campus, and the political atmosphere is largely liberal. There are no athletic scholarships, but merit scholarships average $28,300 annually, and the college meets all admitted students' full demonstrated financial need. Loan reduction is available for students of highest need.

Nearly all students live on campus. Options include first-year-only and mixed-class housing, and dorms are run by seniors who apply to be "house fellows." Several specialty houses are dedicated to interests such as environmental awareness, substance-free living, quiet lifestyles, and international languages. "There is a great sense of house pride on campus," says one student. The campus boasts two dining halls that receive generally good reviews. "Students can make requests to dining staff by writing their thoughts on a 'napkin note' and pinning it to a provided bulletin board," reports a senior. A junior says that life on campus feels safe: "Campus safety officers patrol campus constantly." Another adds, "Conn has a local Green Dot program, which is really successful in educating the community about consent and destigmatizing discussions about sexual assault."

"The a cappella groups are the closest thing Conn has to Greek life."

Students keep busy with parties, movie nights, comedy shows, student productions, and dances—sometimes with out-of-town bands and DJs. "The a cappella groups are the closest thing Conn has to Greek life, the only major difference being their preference for practicing complex vocal arrangements over playing mindless drinking games," quips a sophomore. Students say the absence of Greek groups creates a more inclusive community. The alcohol policy falls under the honor code, and students take prohibitions seriously. Students anticipate the annual Floralia festival in the spring, when "students camp out in tents, eat lots of free food, and dance to music," says a junior.

Many students volunteer at the local schools, aquarium, youth community center, and women's center; a college van makes it easy to get to and from work sites. When

Many students volunteer at the local schools, aquarium, youth community center, and women's center.

The senior year culminates with an integrative project that is presented at an All-College Symposium.

students get the urge to roam, the beaches of New London and other shore towns are 20 minutes from campus. Trains go to Providence (Rhode Island), New York City, or Boston, while Vermont and upstate New York offer camping, hiking, and skiing.

The Conn Camels compete in 28 Division III sports, and men's ice hockey games against NESCAC rival Wesleyan draw crowds. Men's and women's soccer and men's swimming are among the stronger teams. Intramural and club sports range from floor hockey and squash to ultimate Frisbee and skiing. Between classes or at the end of the day, all students may use the natatorium's pool and fitness center and the rowing tanks and climbing walls at the field house.

On its friendly campus, Conn College encourages strong student/faculty bonds and takes pride in its ability to challenge—and trust—students, both in and out of the classroom. "Connecticut College promotes a sense of self-awareness and being able to be yourself in an environment that fosters creativity, acceptance, and community," reasons one junior. A classmate asks, "Who else has a dromedary camel as the mascot?!"

If You Apply To ›

Conn College: Early decision I and II, regular decision. SATs or ACTs: optional. Accepts the Common Application with supplement.

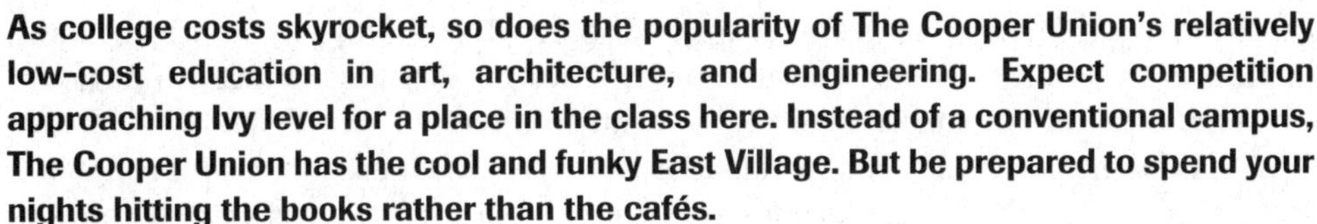

The Cooper Union

7 East 7th Street, New York, NY 10003

As college costs skyrocket, so does the popularity of The Cooper Union's relatively low-cost education in art, architecture, and engineering. Expect competition approaching Ivy level for a place in the class here. Instead of a conventional campus, The Cooper Union has the cool and funky East Village. But be prepared to spend your nights hitting the books rather than the cafés.

Since 2025, The Cooper Union for the Advancement of Science and Art has been taking steps toward returning to its tuition-free roots by ensuring graduating seniors pay no tuition. And if you manage to get accepted into this technical institute, you'll have access to some of the nation's finest academic offerings in architecture, engineering, and art. With the always vibrant East Village in the background and rigorous studying in the forefront, college life at The Cooper Union may seem to be faster than a New York minute. Whatever the pace, though, no one can deny that a CU education is one of the best bargains around—arguably the best anywhere.

The school was founded in 1859 by entrepreneur Peter Cooper, who believed that education should be "as free as water and air" and "accessible to all members of society without regard to gender, race, religion, wealth, or social status." With hefty contributions from Andrew Carnegie, J. P. Morgan, and various other fellow robber barons, the school was able to maintain its tuition-free policy and stay afloat in order to recruit poor students of "strong moral character." Trustees ended the famous policy in 2013, citing dire financial straits, but it now awards at least a half-tuition scholarship of about $22,300 to all undergraduates and seniors attend tuition-free. Its aspiration to reinstate full-tuition scholarships for all undergraduates by 2029 is on track.

Website: www.cooper.edu
Location: City Center
Private
Total Enrollment: 873
Undergraduates: 837
Male/Female: 46/51
Financial Aid: 100%
Pell Grant: 27%
Expense: Pr $
Student Loans: 30%
Average Debt: $ $ $
Applicants: 1,806
Accepted: 21%
Enrolled: 52%
Grad in 6 Years: 85%
Returning First-years: 92%
Academics: ✍ ✍ ✍
Social: 🌐

Students have their choice of around 80 clubs for everything from table tennis and jazz band to religion and drama.

The school's highly structured academic programs largely determine the core set of courses that students take.

In place of a traditional collegiate campus, Cooper offers two academic buildings and one dorm wedged between two busy avenues in the East Village, one of New York's most eclectic and exciting neighborhoods. The stately brick Foundation Building, home to architecture and art programs, is a beautiful historic landmark. The building's Great Hall was the site of Lincoln's "Right Makes Might" speech that turned him into a national political figure and the birthplace of the NAACP, the American Red Cross, and the national women's suffrage movement. The school also boasts the first academic building in New York City to achieve LEED Platinum status, the highest and most rigorous level of certification; known as 41 Cooper Square, the modern, nine-story building houses the engineering program and some art facilities. Built of brick and topped by a classic water tower, Cooper's dorm blends right in with the neighborhood. The high-tech IDC Foundation Art, Architecture, Construction, and Engineering Lab offers students access to advanced digital tools and fabrication equipment, while the new Civic Projects Lab provides work- and makerspaces for students and faculty.

Comprised of three schools specializing in architecture, art, and engineering, CU's curriculum is highly structured, and all students must take a sequence of required courses in their programs of study as well as in the humanities and social sciences. The first year is devoted to language and literature and the second to the making of the modern world; students can then choose from a range of electives after that. The nationally renowned engineering school offers both bachelor's and master's degrees in chemical, electrical, mechanical, and civil engineering. A B.S. in computer science is now available. The architecture school is "phenomenal—even unparalleled," in the words of one happy student. The art school, rather than offering individual majors, awards a bachelor of fine arts degree that encompasses a broad-based generalist curriculum in graphic design, drawing, painting, sculpture, photography, printmaking, film, and video. Students in any school can choose to pursue one of the few minors offered in the humanities and social sciences. All students must fulfill a capstone requirement: Engineers complete a senior design project and presentation, architects a yearlong senior thesis and presentation, and artists a senior exhibition.

The academic climate is "rigorous," says an architecture major. "You have to love it, at least some part of it." The workload is heavy across all programs, and collaborative group projects and study groups are common. Academic advising and counseling are available—as are peer mentors—but the school's highly structured academic programs largely determine the core set of courses that students take. Sixty-nine percent of classes enroll

> **"[The architecture school is] phenomenal—even unparalleled."**

fewer than 20 students—and, with a little persistence, they're not too difficult to get into. "The small size means the students get more intimate with visiting lecturers and faculty," says a junior.

Engineering students interested in long-term, interdisciplinary research can join a Vertically Integrated Project team, earning academic credit over multiple semesters while participating in faculty-led research on topics as diverse as smart cities, motorsports, and drones. Engineers can also participate in the popular Invention Factory summer program to build their own use-inspired inventions; prizes are awarded to the top projects, and all participants file provisional applications for U.S. patents. Roughly 10 percent of students find time to take their education global through a variety of study abroad programs. Closer to home, "career advising is very strong at Cooper Union," says a senior.

Strong moral character, while certainly welcomed, is no longer a prerequisite for admission, but an outstanding high school academic record most certainly is. CU students "range from being complete geeks who love math, science, and gaming to artsy and out-of-this-world," one student says. About half of undergraduates are from

New York State, and most of them grew up in the city; 11 percent are international. Asian Americans account for 31 percent of the student population, Black students 7 percent, Hispanics/Latinos 13 percent, and multiracial students 7 percent. The political climate depends on whom you ask, but a senior attests, "Cooper encourages you to speak up for what's right. After all this is what Peter Cooper fought for, and we will fight to always keep freedom of speech alive at Cooper Union."

The 15-story residence hall saves its occupants from commuting into the Village or cramming themselves into expensive apartments. The downside is that housing here is not guaranteed, and only 20 percent of the student body (mostly first-years) reside on campus. The facility is composed of furnished apartments with kitchens and bathrooms and is "in great condition and well maintained," says one resident, even if space can be tight. For those seeking off-campus housing, a first-year assures, "Few students have trouble finding an apartment, as leases are passed down from Cooper student to Cooper student." With no meal plan available, students cook for themselves, eat at the school cafeteria, or head for one of the myriad nearby delis and coffee shops. Students are mindful of potential safety concerns given the urban campus, and Cooper has expanded its education and training programs aimed at preventing sexual assault. Several students opine that mental health services could be improved.

> "The small [class] size means the students get more intimate with visiting lecturers and faculty."

In their downtime, students have their choice of around 80 clubs for everything from table tennis and jazz band to religion and drama. Many belong to professional societies, such as the American Society of Civil Engineers, and cultural groups are active on campus. Drinking is allowed during some school-sponsored events for students 21 and over, but "it's not a party school," states an architecture major. The few parties that do occur are typically small affairs at off-campus apartments. Annual events include the Culture Show, featuring multicultural music and dance, and the midnight breakfast, "where all clubs come together to form a feast for all students to eat and recharge before finals week," explains a senior. Nightlife and other social options are not far: The famed McSorley's bar is right around the corner, and nearby Chinatown and Little Italy are also popular destinations. The heart of Greenwich Village, with its abundance of theaters, art galleries, and cafés, is just a few blocks to the west.

> "Career advising is very strong at Cooper Union."

Cooper Union has no varsity sports, but it does sponsor a co-ed soccer team, which plays on nearby Randall's Island, as well as co-ed basketball and men's and women's volleyball teams that compete against other area schools. Students stay fit and participate in recreational activities in several different facilities in the city.

The Cooper Union offers an environment for survivors. Getting in is tough, and once admitted, students find that dealing with the onslaught of city and school is plenty tough as well. "You must learn to assert yourself and approach people to get what you want out of this education," warns an architecture major. But most students like the challenge and the rewards of Cooper's academic rigors. Thriving here requires talent, self-sufficiency, and a clear sense of one's career objectives. If you have it, says one happy senior, "This is definitely the place to be."

> *Cooper Union has been taking steps toward returning to its tuition-free roots.*

Overlaps

UC Berkeley, Carnegie Mellon, Columbia, Cornell University, NYU, Pratt Institute, RISD, School of the Art Institute of Chicago

If You Apply To ›

The Cooper Union: Early decision, regular decision. Accepts the Common Application with supplement. Apply to particular program. Art applicants must complete take-home test, architecture applicants must complete studio test, and engineering applicants must complete writing supplement. Please consult Cooper's website for the most up-to-date information regarding standardized test requirements.

Cornell College

600 First Street Southwest, Mount Vernon, IA 52314

The One Course At A Time model is Cornell's calling card. The main challenge: trying to lure top students to rural Iowa. Encourages students to do off-campus study in distant corners of the world. More accessible than Colorado College, which follows a similar academic model. Though primarily a liberal arts institution, Cornell has programs in business, engineering, and education.

Website: www.cornellcollege
.edu

Location: Small Town

Private

Total Enrollment: 1,078

Undergraduates: 1,078

Male/Female: 51/43

Financial Aid: 99%

Pell Grant: 36%

Expense: Pr $ $

Student Loans: 65%

Average Debt: $ $ $ $

Applicants: 2,522

Accepted: 80%

Enrolled: 14%

Grad in 6 Years: 62%

Returning First-years: 80%

Academics: ✐ ✐ ✐

Social: 🍷 🍷 🍷

Q of L: ★ ★ ★

Admissions: (800) 747-1112

Email Address:
admission@cornellcollege
.edu

Strong Programs:
Biochemistry and Molecular
  Biology
Business
Computer Science
Creative Writing
Education
Geology
Kinesiology and Exercise
  Science
Theatre

Cornell College attracts the type of student who seeks an intense yet flexible, self-designed program and a liberal, progressive atmosphere. It suits those who aren't satisfied with easy answers and thrive on loads of personal attention while focusing on one class and exercising disciplined study habits. "If you want a normal college experience, don't pick Cornell," warns one student, but "if you want to pour yourself into a class for three and a half straight weeks and feel exhausted but accomplished," Cornell may be just the right fit.

Aside from its distinctive schedule (shared only by Colorado College among major colleges), Cornell has one of only two U.S. college or university campuses listed in its entirety on the National Register of Historic Places. Cornell was founded in 1853, 12 years before the better known, similarly named Ivy League university. CC took its name from William Wesley Cornell, an iron tycoon and cousin of the other Cornell's Ezra. A pedestrian mall runs through campus, and the majestic clock tower of King Chapel looks over it all. The school's Cole Library is also the town of Mount Vernon's public library, one of few such libraries in the country. Cornell's student center, Thomas Commons, features an indoor-outdoor fireplace, classrooms and meeting spaces, and a glass-enclosed dining room with panoramic views of campus. Recent projects include an expansion and renovation of the Small Sport Center.

Cornell's core curriculum, called Ingenuity, combines distribution requirements in several liberal arts areas with opportunities for learning outside the classroom. In their first two years, all students take three discussion-oriented Foundations seminars, one of which is writing-intensive. The Ingenuity in Action component requires students to participate in at least two out-of-class experiences, such as internships, research or service projects, or study abroad—with funding provided by the college as needed. Most students complete a capstone experience in their major.

> **"At Cornell, a semester's worth of work is completed in a month."**

A sophomore explains block scheduling this way: "At Cornell, a semester's worth of work is completed in a month. This makes for a fast-paced class that is normally composed of a couple of papers, maybe some annotations, a midterm, a final, and a final project." A biology and Spanish double major adds, "Each class is pretty intense." If that sounds intimidating, it can be. But administrators say it also improves the quality of Cornell's liberal arts education by helping students acclimate to the business world, where "what needs to be done needs to be done quickly and done well." The One Course method also helps in academic advising—with grades every four weeks, signs of trouble are quickly apparent.

Cornell awards degrees in around 35 academic majors, as well as a group of preprofessional programs. In November 2025, however, Cornell College announced it would eliminate several liberal arts programs due to declining enrollment and student interest. The programs impacted include music performance, music education, classical studies, religion, as well as French and German studies; Spanish is being retained as a minor. The bachelor of special studies remains, which allows students to broaden or deepen their studies by building their own individualized major. Among the most popular majors are kinesiology, biochemistry and molecular biology, engineering, and studio art; other strong options include education, creative writing, business, theatre, computer science, and psychology. The college also offers preprofessional centers for health sciences, law and society, and literary arts. Classes are taught by full professors and are intimate, with 72 percent enrolling fewer than 20 students. Says a sophomore, "Professors spend all their time teaching and improving their courses to provide the best education possible."

Because of the unique One Course At A Time structure, "professors are able to offer off-campus study courses for up to a month that complements the course," says an administrator. Roughly 34 percent of Cornell students study abroad. Programs are also available in nearly 40 countries through partner providers. During the short breaks between courses, students can take advantage of symposia and athletic events. The Cornell Summer Research Institute offers an eight-week stipend for faculty-directed summer research projects, and 91 percent of students participate in some form of research. Career coaches at the Berry Career Institute help each student identify an individual path for their professional development.

"Professors spend all their time teaching and improving their courses."

"'Cornell weird' is a phrase that gets thrown around a lot, and it's accurate," says one student. "There is no singular way to describe a Cornellian other than unique." Thirty-one percent of students are homegrown Iowans, and 3 percent hail from other nations. Black students represent 8 percent of the student population, Hispanics/Latinos 11 percent, Asian Americans 4 percent, and multiracial students less than 1 percent. "Cornell starts with one huge disadvantage in terms of diversity: It's in the middle of a relatively small town in Iowa," admits one student. Politically, Cornell leans liberal. Thirty-six percent of incoming first-years qualify for Pell Grants. Merit scholarships of at least $35,000 are offered to qualified students, although there are no athletic awards.

Ninety-three percent of students live on campus. First-years enjoy completely renovated residence halls, while upperclassmen prefer the suite-style halls. Everyone eats together in Thomas Commons, where the food is "usually good," a junior says. Vegetarian options are always available. Student safety is taken seriously, students say, and, "Campus Security is very accessible, with an officer on call and on campus 24/7."

"Most of the social life happens on campus," says a psychology major. "Because everyone lives on campus, there is a lot of effort to make sure that there is always a lot to do and nobody has time to be bored." Local fraternities and sororities draw 20 percent of the men and 28 percent of the women; membership in a couple of fraternities is open to all genders, and in most sororities, any female-identifying student can join. "Some are completely dry or emphasize their commitment to service," reports one student, "while others are notorious for parties and jungle juice (never, ever drink jungle

"'Cornell weird' is a phrase that gets thrown around a lot, and it's accurate."

juice)." The Performing Arts and Activities Council is in charge of bringing entertainment to campus, which includes comedians, speakers, musicians, and hypnotists. Mount Vernon (population 4,500) is "small but very welcoming," says a student. Students either love the town's idyllic pace—a few local bars; an acclaimed restaurant; some funky shops; and a lot of peace, quiet, and safety—or long for more excitement. The latter is available in Cedar Rapids (home of archrival Coe College) or Iowa City (home to the University of Iowa), each less than half an hour away. Chicago is about four hours away.

On the field or on the court, Cornell's competition with Coe is always heated, especially when it comes to Rams football and basketball. "'Beat Coe' and 'Coe Sucks' have been emblazoned on Cornell fanwear since the 1920s," says one student of institutional history. "We have the archival records to back that up." Men's and women's track and field, men's basketball, lacrosse, and tennis are competitive in the Division III Midwest Conference, and women's volleyball has won several conference titles in recent years. Popular intramural sports include basketball, volleyball, and ping-pong.

Cornell offers a top-notch education, plenty of opportunities, and a supportive community. Flexibility and a sense of adventure are key to thriving in Cornell's One Course At A Time system. "Students must be able to adapt to a new environment very quickly—every block they have to remap their schedules to succeed in an entirely new course," explains a psychology major. "The block plan is not easy. Students who succeed on this plan are not afraid of the failures that are nearly inevitable, and they're excited for the opportunity to grow as a learner."

If You Apply To ›

Cornell College: Rolling admissions. SATs or ACTs: optional. Accepts the Common Application with supplement.

Cornell University

410 Thurston Avenue, Ithaca, NY 14850

Cornell University's reputation as a pressure cooker comes from its preprofessional attitude and a "we try harder" mentality. Spans seven undergraduate colleges—four private and three public—and tuition varies accordingly. Strong in engineering, architecture, and sustainability, world famous in hotel administration. Least difficult Ivy to get into and the farthest from an urban center. Once you're there, Ithaca is a great college town.

Cornell University has a long tradition of being the lone wolf among the Ivy League universities—not least for its stated ambition to become the finest research university for undergraduate education in the nation. The mixture within one institution of private and state-funded colleges and schools, preprofessional programs, and liberal arts results in, as one student says, "a diversity of opportunities in and outside the classroom."

Perched atop a hill that commands a view of both the city of Ithaca and Cayuga Lake, Cornell is breathtakingly scenic, with ravines, waterfalls, and parks bordering all sides of the campus. (As the saying goes, "Ithaca is gorges.") The Cornell Botanic Gardens, more than 3,500 acres of woodlands, natural trails, streams, and gorges, provide space for walking, picnicking, or contemplation. Cornell's superb library system consists of 20 libraries, including the beautiful underground Carl A. Kroch Library, featuring sky-lit atriums and renowned collections of Icelandic and Southeast Asian materials. The Johnson Museum of Art, designed by I. M. Pei, is one of the best university museums in the nation. The state-of-the-art Bill and Melinda Gates Hall houses high-tech research and teaching labs for computer and information sciences, while the LEED Platinum–certified Klarman Hall is dedicated to teaching, research, and education in the humanities.

Cornell was founded in 1865 and named for cofounder and telegraph mogul Ezra Cornell. At the undergraduate level, the university has four privately endowed colleges: architecture, art, and planning; arts and sciences; business (Nolan School of Hotel Administration); and engineering. Cornell is also New York State's land grant university and as such operates five other colleges under contract with the state: agriculture and life sciences, human ecology, the school of industrial and labor relations, the Brooks School of Public Policy, and the Dyson School of Applied Economics and Management, which, with Nolan, is part of the business school. New York residents at these "contract colleges" pick up their Ivy League degrees at an almost-public price (as in-state tuition at these schools is slightly steeper than SUNY rates). Prospective students apply to one of the eight colleges or schools through the central admissions office, and admissions standards vary by school. Each college sets its own general education requirements, but all Cornell undergrads take at least one First-Year Writing Seminar.

Cornell offers over 4,000 courses in nearly 80 fields of study. The most popular majors lie in the areas of computer science, engineering, business, biological sciences, and agriculture. The College of Architecture, Art, and Planning's offerings in architecture and fine arts are standouts. The College of Arts and Sciences boasts considerable strength in history, government, environment and sustainability, and just about all the natural and physical sciences. The English program has turned out a gaggle of celebrated writers, including Junot Diaz and the late Toni Morrison and Kurt Vonnegut. Foreign languages, required for all arts and sciences students, are strong (try taking Tamil, Zulu, or Nepali), and the performing arts, mathematics, and social science departments are considered good. Cornell was early among universities to add women's studies to the curriculum and continues to be an innovator with programs like China and Asia-Pacific studies, which requires a semester in China and another in Washington, D.C. The College of Agriculture and Life Sciences is highly ranked

> **"[Cornell has] a diversity of opportunities in and outside the classroom."**

and a good bet for anyone hoping to make it into veterinary school (Cornell's graduate College of Veterinary Medicine is among the best), while the School of Industrial and Labor Relations is the preeminent school of its kind. The College of Business offers more than a dozen noteworthy concentrations, including agribusiness management; finance, accounting, and real estate; and business analytics.

"The quality of teaching is top-notch," says one student who also cautions, "Some of the educators struggle to communicate their knowledge." First-year courses in the sciences and social sciences are generally large lectures, but overall, around half of the classes have fewer than 20 students. "There are many office hours held by teaching assistants, and professors make additional help extremely accessible," reports a computer science major.

Cornell academics are demanding and foster an intensity found on few campuses. "There is a competitive atmosphere, as students who attend Cornell are ambitious and passionate. However, this is a positive and motivating force," says one sophomore. To cope with the anxieties that the high-powered atmosphere can create, the university has one of the best psychological counseling networks in the nation, including an alcohol-awareness program, peer sex counselors, personal-growth workshops, and the student-led EARS (Empathy, Assistance, and Referral Service).

A co-op program is available to engineering students, and Cornell-in-Washington is popular among students from all seven undergraduate colleges. Students looking to study abroad can choose from hundreds of programs in 80 countries, including Indonesia, Belgium, Ireland, and Nepal; 31 percent of students participate. "The number of quality study abroad programs seems inexhaustible," says a sophomore. Roughly half of all undergraduates participate in a faculty-guided research

(continued)

Q of L: ★ ★ ★
Admissions: (607) 255-5241
Email Address:
  admissions@cornell.edu

Strong Programs:
Architecture
Engineering
Environment and Sustainability
Fine Arts
Government
History
Hotel Administration
Industrial and Labor Relations

Students celebrate the last day of classes—Slope Day—with a concert on Libe Slope.

experience during their four years. The Presidential Research Scholars program, open to undergraduates in all disciplines, provides as many as 200 selected students with up to $8,000 in funding to carry out individually designed research programs with the support of faculty mentors. More than three-quarters of students engage in community service opportunities coordinated by the Public Service Center and the Office of Engagement Initiatives.

What do Cornell students have in common? "We are cooler than the nerdy kids and nerdier than the cool kids," quips one senior. "We don't quite fit in anywhere else. We by and large didn't get into other Ivies, so compared to those students, we feel a need to validate and distinguish ourselves through hard work and a more robust social life." Thirty-six percent of Cornell's undergraduates hail from New York; another 9 percent are international. Black students constitute 8 percent of the student body, Hispanics/Latinos account for 14 percent, Asian Americans comprise 26 percent, and multiracial students add 6 percent. All first-years participate in discussion-based diversity workshops aimed at increasing dialogue and engagement. Upon graduation, nearly one-third of Cornell students attend graduate and professional schools.

Cornell is need-blind in admissions and meets the demonstrated need of all accepted applicants, but the proportion of outright grants varies based on income. Cornell caps need-based student loans at varying amounts based on family incomes above $75,000. The Cornell Installment Plan allows for payment of a year's or semester's tuition in monthly interest-free installments. The university does not award merit or athletic scholarships, but Cornell pledges to meet 100 percent of qualifying students' financial needs.

Fifty-two percent of Cornell's undergrads live in university housing; others try their luck off campus in Collegetown, a neighborhood abutting the southwest end of campus that is packed with student-oriented apartment buildings, restaurants, bars, and shops. Demand has kept the housing market tight and rents high, although options are increasing. "Housing was one of the main reasons I chose Cornell," says one junior. "I was able to essentially guarantee myself a single room even freshman year. My room was huge, and my dorm was quiet." North Campus residence halls, including four newer halls, are the home of all first-years and sophomores. Upperclassmen live in the West Campus house system in five living/learning "houses" with professors in residence, house chefs, and creative programming. Students on both campuses can opt to take one-credit Learning Where You Live courses taught in the residential communities. There are dorms devoted to everything from ecology to music, and cultural houses include the International Living Center, Latino Living Center, Ujamaa Residential College, and Akwe:kon, a program house focusing on American Indian culture (among the first facilities of its kind in the U.S.). Cornell's food service is reputedly among the best in the nation, with ten residential dining halls that function independently; one student enthuses, "The food is very diverse and super tasty!"

Despite the intense academic atmosphere—or maybe because of it—Cornell social life beats most of the other Ivies hands down. Once the weekend arrives, local parties, state parks, and ski slopes fill with Cornell students seeking to redress the balance between study and play. With about one-third of students pledging fraternities or sororities (but not until the second semester), these groups play a significant role in the social scene. "Social life at Cornell is really built around Greek life, especially for those under 21. Students who go Greek tend to have busy social schedules, and those who don't really need to find an organization they are passionate about," advises one student. Alcohol is part of the social scene, but one student says the university is "cracking down" on underage and high-risk drinking. First-years are not allowed to attend fraternity parties during the fall semester, and alcohol is banned from recruitment and new-member events in the spring. Students have their pick of roughly 1,000 student organizations—including clubs for Japanese drumming and Bhangra dancing—and there are innumerable concerts and sporting events throughout the year. Big events include Dragon Day (architecture students build a dragon and parade it through campus) and Springfest (a gathering on Ho Plaza). Students celebrate the last day of classes—Slope Day—with a concert on Libe Slope.

Cornell athletes have won their share of Ivy League team titles over the last decade and make regular Division I national championship appearances. Men's ice hockey is unquestionably the dominant sport on campus (its chief raison d'être being to defeat Harvard), and camping out for season tickets is an annual ritual. Men's lacrosse won the 2025 NCAA championship. Women's ice hockey, polo, and women's sailing are nationally competitive, and women's lightweight rowing has brought home several Intercollegiate Rowing Association titles. Cornell boasts the largest intramural program in the Ivy League, with more than a dozen sports, including nearly 100 basketball teams. The "four seasons of Ithaca" (rain, snow, slush, and drizzle) can make walking to class across the vast and hilly campus challenging, but with the first snow of the winter, "traying" down Libe Slope becomes the sport of choice for hordes of fun-loving Cornellians. Students head to Greek Peak Mountain for skiing, Cayuga Lake for boating and swimming, and countless places for hiking and watching the clouds roll by.

> **"Students who attend Cornell are ambitious and passionate."**

Like most other Ivy League universities, Cornell is a premier research institution with a distinguished faculty and outstanding academics. What sets it apart is its focus on preprofessional preparation for undergraduates and a student body that strives to combine high academic achievement with a vigorous social life—and, if you are in one of the state-sponsored schools, a break on tuition. One junior sums up the Cornell experience like this: "The people are passionate, the academics are rigorous, and the extracurricular activities are empowering."

> ### Overlaps
> Dartmouth, Harvard, Penn, Princeton, Stanford, Yale

If You Apply To ›

Cornell University: Early decision, regular decision. SATs or ACTs: required. Accepts the Common Application with supplement. Apply to individual programs or schools. Architecture applicants must interview. Applicants to design programs must submit portfolio.

University of Dallas

1845 East Northgate Drive, Irving, TX 75062

Bulwark of academic traditionalism in the Big D, with a Core Curriculum focused exclusively on Western civilization. The only outpost of Roman Catholic education between Loyola of New Orleans and University of San Diego. Generally shared religious and social values make for a strong sense of community. A compelling drawing card is the university's program in Rome, embraced by most sophomores.

While many universities around the nation have reexamined their Eurocentric core curriculums, the University of Dallas—the best Roman Catholic university

Website: www.udallas.edu
Location: Suburban
Private
Total Enrollment: 2,538
Undergraduates: 1,500
Male/Female: 45/55
Financial Aid: 99%
Pell Grant: 26%
Expense: Pr $ $
Student Loans: 47%
Average Debt: $ $
Applicants: 4,179
Accepted: 54%
Enrolled: 15%
Grad in 6 Years: 68%
Returning First-years: 81%
Academics: ✍ ✍ ✍
Social: 🗩 🗩
Q of L: ★ ★ ★
Admissions: (800) 628-6999
Email Address:
 admissions@udallas.edu

Strong Programs:
Biology
Business
Chemistry
Classics
English
Human and Social Sciences
Politics
Psychology

south of Washington, D.C.—remains proudly dedicated to a classic liberal arts education that fosters the study of "the great deeds and words of Western civilization." The campus tenor is conservative, but students say there are plenty of lively happenings to be found. Whether it's discussing Dante on the campus mall or cutting loose for the school's quirkiest event, a massive Groundhog Day party, one student says, "We are a seriously academic school, but the students still know how to have fun."

UD's 744-acre campus occupies a pastoral home in a Dallas suburb on top of what one student calls "the closest thing this region has to a hill." A major portion of the campus is situated around the Braniff Mall, a landscaped and lighted gathering place near the Braniff Memorial Tower, the school's landmark. Many campus buildings, including the tower, were designed by the midcentury modern architect O'Neil Ford. The primary tone of the buildings, like the surrounding North Texas landscape, is brown, and the dominant style, as described by one student, is "post-1950s, done in brick, typical Catholic—institutional." Even so, the campus boasts a beautiful chapel and a state-of-the-art science building.

Appropriately for a Catholic school, most eyes at UD look to Rome, where about 80 percent of undergraduates trek for the semester-long Rome Program, usually during sophomore year. The program "provides students with the unique opportunity to study at our very own Due Santi Campus, an idyllic countryside paradise a mere half hour south of Rome," enthuses a politics major. "We even have a working vineyard!" The program involves intense coursework, as well as trips to northern Italy and Greece. It is part of UD's four-semester Western civilization Core Curriculum, which includes philosophy, English, math, fine arts, science, American civilization, Western civilization, politics, economics, a serious foreign language requirement, and two theology courses (Understanding the Bible and The Western Theological Tradition). "The rigorous Core Curriculum provides a unifying basis for our strong community," says an English major. All students also complete a senior thesis or project, a comprehensive exam, and/or a senior seminar.

> **"The University of Dallas is very much like a coffeehouse. It is laid-back but intellectual."**

Students at UD, which was established in 1956 under the sponsorship of the Roman Catholic Diocese of Dallas, choose from 27 majors and 35 concentrations. Business, biology, English, politics, and psychology are some of the strongest and most popular majors. The business program draws on abundant internship opportunities in the Dallas/Fort Worth Metroplex. The politics major offers a concentration in political philosophy. Classics is, no surprise, a traditional strength, and a concentration in human and social sciences tackles 21st-century issues through theory and practical research in areas like anthropology, sociology, and social psychology. Premed students are well served by the biology and chemistry programs, as UD's medical school acceptance rate is over 80 percent. Other students take advantage of 3–2 dual-degree programs in nursing and electrical engineering, as well as 4 + 1 bachelor's/master's programs in several fields. The O'Hara Chemical Science Institute offers a hands-on, eight-week summer program to prepare new students for independent research.

"The University of Dallas is very much like a coffeehouse," muses one junior. "It is laid-back but intellectual; it is fun, and all your friends are there with you." The university uses no teaching assistants. "The professors are here to teach," says a politics and Italian major, "not to do research or write their own thing but to be with students." Sixty-four percent of classes enroll fewer than 20 students.

"A typical student at University of Dallas is a good student who is Catholic, conservative, and enjoys Irish music and beer," says a junior. Seventy-three percent

> *Seventy-three percent of UD students are Catholic, and many of them choose this school because of its religious affiliation.*

of UD students are Catholic, and many of them choose this school because of its religious affiliation. Fifty percent of undergraduates are Texan, and 1 percent are international. Twenty-eight percent are Hispanic/Latino, 7 percent are Asian American, 3 percent are Black, and 2 percent are multiracial. Most students are conservative and "think similarly about social issues such as gender and abortion," says one student, and there is not much political activism on campus. UD offers various merit scholarships averaging $31,500 but no athletic awards, as it is a Division III school.

Fifty-seven percent of students live on campus, where tradition and religious principle govern conduct. Students under 21 who don't reside at home with their parents must live on campus in single-sex dorms with strict visitation regulations. "The freshman dorms are a little old, but there is a great feeling of community there," says a junior. The sole dining hall is spacious and boasts a wonderful view of north Dallas. Still, the fast food and snacks at the Rathskeller are said to be better. Students say the campus is "extremely safe."

With no fraternities or sororities at UD, the Campus Activities Board sponsors most on-campus entertainment. Free movies, dances, and visiting speakers are usually on the agenda. Church-related and religious activities provide fulfilling social outlets for many students. During Charity Week in the fall, the junior class organizes a variety of fund-raising events. The biggest event of the year is Groundhog, a week of events celebrating Groundhog Day and culminating in a huge party at Groundhog Park, featuring "live bands, free food, beer for students over 21, and sports games throughout the day," explains an English major. Smaller off-campus parties happen frequently; on campus, a student warns, "The Office of Student Life runs a tight ship regarding alcohol." Students describe Irving (population 258,000) as "a suburb just like any other," but Dallas offers almost unlimited possibilities, including a full agenda for barhopping on Lower Greenville Avenue and food, craft breweries, and culture in the Bishop Arts District, both about 15 minutes away. The West End and Deep Ellum offer a taste of shopping and Dallas's alternative music scene. And for the more adventurous, Austin and San Antonio aren't too far away.

The University of Dallas is unusual for a Texas school in that its population does not salivate over football. But the Crusaders women's soccer and men's and women's basketball and golf teams are competitive in the Division III Southern Collegiate Athletic Conference. Club and intramural sports are well organized and sign up about a quarter of the students. The club rugby team (known in Groundhog tradition as the Hoggies) is particularly popular.

Although some students complain that UD's focus on Western liberal arts and its Catholic emphasis can feel academically limiting, most say they appreciate the sense of shared experience and strong tradition that defines their school. In the words of one senior, "Come here to have fun, build sincere friendships, work hard, and graduate with a deep sense of your place in the Western cultural tradition."

> *All students complete a senior thesis or project, a comprehensive exam, and/or a senior seminar.*

> **"The professors are here to teach, not to do research or write their own thing."**

Overlaps

Austin College, Baylor, Benedictine University, Catholic University, Franciscan, Hillsdale College, Rhodes, Texas A&M

If You Apply To ›

Dallas: Early action I and II, rolling admissions. SATs or ACTs: required. Accepts the Common Application with supplement.

6016 McNutt Hall, Hanover, NH 03755

The smallest Ivy and the one with the strongest emphasis on undergraduates and close-knit community. Traditionally the most conservative member of the Ivy League, it has steered toward more student diversity and more serious scholars, and made inroads reining in a long-standing party culture. Ivy ties notwithstanding, Dartmouth has much of the feel of places like Colgate, Middlebury, and Williams. Great for those who like the outdoors.

Website: www.dartmouth.edu
Location: Rural
Private
Total Enrollment: 6,742
Undergraduates: 4,474
Male/Female: 51/48
Financial Aid: 58%
Pell Grant: 20%
Expense: Pr $ $ $ $
Student Loans: 33%
Average Debt: $
Applicants: 31,656
Accepted: 5%
Enrolled: 69%
Grad in 6 Years: 96%
Returning First-years: 98%
Academics: ✍ ✍ ✍ ✍ ✍
Social: 🗨 🗨 🗨 🗨 🗨
Q of L: ★ ★ ★
Admissions: (603) 646-2875
Email Address: admissions .reply@dartmouth.edu

Strong Programs:
Biological Sciences
Computer Science
Economics
Engineering
English
Environmental Studies
Government
History

Unlike the other seven members of the Ivy League, which trace their roots to Puritan New Englanders or progressive Quaker colonists, Dartmouth College was founded in 1769 to educate Native Americans. The student body has always been the smallest in the Ancient Eight, and the school's focus on undergraduate education differentiates Dartmouth from its peers, though it does offer graduate programs in a range of academic subjects and professional areas. In 2023, it welcomed its first woman president—a leading cognitive scientist who emphasizes student health and wellness as well as fostering dialogue across the school. The college attracts plenty of hiking and skiing enthusiasts, and the Dartmouth Outing Club, the oldest in the country, is the most popular extracurricular organization. In recent years, Dartmouth has increasingly emphasized the importance of developing a global presence in its traditionally warm and inclusive community. According to one student, "We strongly value traditions, we like to have fun in our woodsy New Hampshire home, and at the same time, everyone is incredibly academically involved."

Dartmouth's picturesque campus is the most rural of the Ivies, and its winters may be the coldest (with the possible exception of those at Cornell). Set in the small town of Hanover, New Hampshire, which is bisected by the Appalachian Trail, the campus is arranged around a traditional New England green, bounded by the impressive library at one end and by the college-owned Hanover Inn at the other. Architectural styles range from Romanesque to postmodern, but the dominant theme is copper-topped colonial frame. The nearest big city, Boston, is two hours away, but major artists like Yo-Yo Ma routinely visit Dartmouth's Hopkins Center for the Arts, which recently reopened following a $123 million renovation.

Dartmouth's status as a member of the Ivy League means academic excellence is a given. First-years must take a writing-intensive seminar that involves both independent research and small-group discussion; about 75 are offered each year across different departments. Students must also demonstrate proficiency in at least one foreign language and take three world culture courses (one non-Western, one Western, and one Culture and Identity) and 10 courses

"The professors are truly the best out there for undergraduates."

from several distribution areas spanning the liberal arts and sciences. In addition, Dartmouth has a senior culminating activity—a thesis, public report, exhibition, seminar, production, or demonstration—that allows students to pull together work done in their major with a creative and intellectual twist of their own. Before arriving on campus for their first year, incoming students can opt to go on five-day pre-orientation trips with the Outing Club, getting to know their classmates while exploring the great outdoors.

Though Dartmouth students work hard, a linguistics major remarks, "It's never 'My success at the expense of yours.'" Popular majors include economics, government, engineering science, English, and history. Computer science offerings are among the best in the nation, thanks in no small part to the late John Kemeny, the former Dartmouth president who coinvented time-sharing and the BASIC language. The school offers a range of opportunities around environmental sustainability, including the Dartmouth Organic Farm, just three miles from campus, as well as the Institute of Arctic Studies, which offers courses in polar science diplomacy, Arctic Indigenous knowledge systems, and more.

Professors get high marks, perhaps because of Dartmouth's focus on undergraduates. The rural location also helps; faculty make a conscious choice to teach here, leaving behind some of the distractions afflicting their peers at more urban schools. "If you come to Dartmouth for only one thing, it would be the faculty," says an economics major. "The professors are truly the best out there for undergraduates." Fifty-eight percent of undergraduate classes have fewer than 20 students, and abundant research opportunities are available for undergrads. Female STEM students can participate in the WISP (Women in Science Project) program, which offers mentors, speakers, and even research positions for first-years. The EDGE Consortium, a coalition of universities partnering with the government and businesses to grow the American semiconductor industry, provides even more research projects and internships for those seeking careers in STEM fields.

But it's not only STEM students who benefit. "Dartmouth has an incredible amount of funding for research of all kinds," explains an English major. The Presidential Scholars Program provides one-on-one paid research assistantships with faculty. The Rockefeller Center's Policy Research Shop helps undergraduate public policy students write policy briefs for state legislators and government agencies in New Hampshire and Vermont.

"[Students here have a] true, true love for this school and a passion for learning."

The school's most notable eccentricity is the Dartmouth Plan, or "D-Plan"— four 10-week terms a year, including one during the summer. Students must be on campus for three terms during the first and fourth years and during the summer after the second year, but otherwise, if they're on track to graduate, they can take off whenever they wish. About 32 percent of Dartmouth undergrads take advantage of their "leave term" to study abroad, usually signing up for one of the college's more than 30 faculty-led programs. "There's an astronomy program that goes to South Africa, a linguistics program that goes to New Zealand and the Cook Islands, a theater program that goes to London," explains one happy participant.

Eighty-three percent of undergraduates hail from outside of New Hampshire, including 15 percent from other countries. Black students represent 6 percent of the student population, Asian Americans 13 percent, Hispanics/Latinos 10 percent, and multiracial students 8 percent. Consistent with its historical roots, Dartmouth continues to have a strong interest in recruiting and supporting Native American students, who currently represent 1 percent of the undergraduate student body. Students here have a "true, true love for this school and a passion for learning not simply for the grade but for the experience," says a senior. Students retain that passion after graduation, as Dartmouth has the most elaborate network of alumni organizations of any college in the country. Politically, an English major says, "there is a decent spread of opinions." Admissions are need-blind, even for students admitted from the waitlist, and the school meets the full demonstrated need of all admits. Dartmouth has eliminated student loans from all financial aid packages, and the college covers the cost of tuition for students from families with incomes below $125,000 a year. No merit or athletic scholarships are awarded; the Ivy League prohibits the latter.

Eighty-five percent of Dartmouth students live on campus in one of more than 30 dorms, which, in an effort to create a greater sense of community among undergraduates, have been organized into six House Communities, each led by a House Professor. "From suites to singles to apartment-style housing, it's easy to find housing on campus that will suit you," says an engineering physics major. Beginning in their first year, students can apply to live in one of nine living/learning communities, from the Sustainable Living Center to Global Village to various identity-based communities. Housing is guaranteed for first-years and sophomores. Because of the D-Plan, people are always coming and going, so it may be easier to find a new room or roommate than at schools on the semester system. Seniors may move off campus, where there are plenty of readily available options. Dining also offers a variety of choices, explains a senior: "There's one all-you-can-eat style dining hall, a couple of café locations (especially in the library) where you can get a quick coffee and pastry/sandwich, and few other locations with offerings ranging from fresh-made sushi to custom pasta to build-your-own smoothies to chicken tender quesadillas." Students say their rural campus generally feels safe but report that sexual assault has been a hot-button issue; the administration says it is addressing their concerns with efforts like the Sexual Violence Prevention Program. "Our mental health services used to be atrocious before COVID-19," says a senior, but "they have since improved."

"Social life primarily occurs on campus," says a senior. "There is college programming every Friday and Saturday night, including everything from roller-skating to pottery nights and comedy shows." Dartmouth's Greek system attracts 33 percent of the men and 33 percent of the women, who rush during the fall of their sophomore year. Although still the center of the school's party scene, fraternity parties are inclusive: "What's really unique about our Greek system is that it's open to the entire campus—if you have a Dartmouth ID card, you cannot be denied entry," explains a student. Dartmouth was one of the first schools to develop a counseling and educational program to combat alcohol abuse. More recently, the Moving Dartmouth Forward plan has banned hard liquor on campus. "While it can be annoying at times, I really do think the ban has been effective," reasons a senior. Parties and kegs must be registered, and the houses where they're being held are subject to walk-throughs by college safety and security personnel. "The Dartmouth Outing Club is very active, they have events and trips open to everyone all the time, and they are how many people find friends here," notes a senior. Good road trips include Montreal or Boston for a dose of bright lights and the big city or the White Mountains for camping. The DOC manages land grant cabins that may be rented for as low as one dollar a night.

"It's easy to find housing on campus that will suit you."

"I love Dartmouth's traditions, many of which revolve around the four seasons," says one senior. Major events include homecoming, which boasts a 75-foot-tall bonfire, and Winter Carnival, which involves ski racing at the college's skiway, located 20 minutes away, as well as snow-sculpture contests, a polar plunge, and partiers from all over the Eastern Seaboard. Spring brings Green Key weekend, an annual event featuring live music and parties. Community service is popular, and the Center for Social Impact sponsors immersion trips to places like New Orleans, Puerto Rico, and the Dominican Republic.

Dartmouth offers 35 Division I varsity sports. The Big Green football team was the Ivy League Champ in 2023 and 2024. Rugby and men's hockey also brought home Ivy League trophies in the 2024–25 season. Skiing and women's golf are also strong. The school also offers 33 club sports, including nationally competitive teams in sailing, skiing, figure skating, and ultimate Frisbee, and intramural sports. Dartmouth no longer has a physical education requirement for graduation and has replaced it with a wellness education requirement offering students flexibility in learning to support their physical and emotional health.

Dartmouth attracts outdoorsy, inquisitive, down-to-earth students who develop extremely strong ties to the school—and each other—during four years together in this quintessential rural New England setting. You'll have to be made of hardy stock to survive the harsh New Hampshire winters. But once you defrost, you may echo this satisfied economics and environmental studies major, who says, "I have found a home in the woods of New Hampshire and am very happy with my choice to come to Dartmouth!"

Overlaps

Brown, Columbia, Duke, Harvard, Penn, Princeton, Stanford, Yale

If You Apply To ›

Dartmouth: Early decision, regular decision. SATs or ACTs: required. Accepts the Common Application with supplement. Submission of a peer recommendation is strongly recommended. Application includes an optional question on gender identity.

Davidson College

405 North Main Street, Davidson, NC 28035

Traditionally styled as the "Dartmouth of the South." Goes head-to-head with Washington and Lee (VA) as the top liberal arts college below the Mason–Dixon Line, and Division I sports are an advantage. An early leader in the trend to replace loans with grants, it boasts a strong honor system that sets the campus tone. Small-town location is close to Charlotte and prime vacation spots.

Founded by Presbyterians in 1837 and named after a Revolutionary War hero, Davidson College combines the Southern tradition and gentility of neighbors like Rhodes and Sewanee with the academic prowess more common to Northern liberal arts powerhouses such as Dartmouth and Williams. It turns out more than its share of the region's political, education, legal, and other leaders. Often overlooked because of its small size and Carolina location, Davidson offers students strong interdisciplinary, international, and preprofessional programs, as well as a thriving social scene. A senior economics major boasts, "Davidson is the liberal arts school of the South."

Located in a beautiful stretch of the North Carolina Piedmont, Davidson's wooded campus features Georgian and Greek Revival architecture. The central campus is designated as a national arboretum, and college staff lovingly maintain a collection of the woody plants that thrive in the area. Davidson retains its original quadrangle, which dates from its founding, plus literary society halls built in the 1850s. New construction includes the Davidson College Stadium and Game Changers Field House.

In addition to classes in a range of liberal arts areas, core requirements at Davidson include coursework in a foreign language; cultural diversity; justice, equality, and community; first-year writing; and physical education. The most popular majors are economics, political science, biology, psychology, and English. Those whose academic interests lie outside the mainstream can work closely with select faculty members to pursue one of several majors established by the Center for Interdisciplinary Studies, such as Arab studies, bioinformatics, or global literary theory, or to design a major of their own. The interdisciplinary health and human values minor explores

Website: www.davidson.edu
Location: Small Town
Private
Total Enrollment: 1,867
Undergraduates: 1,867
Male/Female: 47/53
Financial Aid: 55%
Pell Grant: 22%
Expense: Pr $ $ $ $
Student Loans: 20%
Average Debt: $ $ $
Applicants: 8,114
Accepted: 13%
Enrolled: 48%
Grad in 6 Years: 91%
Returning First-years: 95%
Academics: ✍ ✍ ✍ ✍
Social: 🍷 🍷 🍷
Q of L: ★ ★ ★ ★ ★
Admissions: (800) 768-0380
Email Address:
admission@davidson.edu

the role ethical values play in defining problems as "medical" and worthy of scientific study. A 3–2 engineering program is available with Columbia University and Washington University in St. Louis.

Davidson's academic climate is "challenging and rigorous, but you're surrounded by a community of support," says a political science major. Seventy-four percent of classes have fewer than 20 students. Davidson's Honor Code allows students to take exams independently and to feel comfortable leaving doors unlocked. "The Honor Code is a cornerstone not just for academics but for all aspects of life at Davidson," says a student. Every entering first-year student agrees to abide by the code, and all work submitted to professors is signed with the word "pledged." Professors are highly lauded for being friendly and accessible, and with no graduate students around, opportunities to work with faculty members on research projects are plentiful.

The Sustainability Scholars Summer Program provides students with real-world projects that emphasize sustainability issues; students can be found in locations ranging from skyscrapers to community gardens. Students looking to sharpen their business or technical skills may take advantage of hands-on learning opportunities provided by the Hurt Hub for Innovation and Entrepreneurship. Study abroad programs, including 8 faculty-led and more than 125 partner programs, are available in countries from France, Germany, and England to Cyprus and Zambia. About 80 percent of students graduate with some international experience, whether it's coursework, service learning, research, or an internship.

> **"Davidson students are people who learn because they love to learn."**

"Davidson students are people who learn because they love to learn, not to perform intellectual ability but because of a genuine interest," comments an English major. While the school embraces its Presbyterian heritage, an Africana studies major says there is "a good amount of religious diversity" on campus. Twenty percent of Davidson students come from North Carolina and 11 percent from abroad. Black students represent 7 percent of the student body, Hispanics/Latinos 11 percent, Asian Americans 5 percent, and multiracial students 4 percent. "Politically, there's a left lean, but it's not significant compared to other liberal arts schools," observes a senior. The college practices need-blind admissions and, thanks to its highly touted Davidson Trust, guarantees to meet 100 percent of admitted students' demonstrated need through grants and student employment—eliminating loans from all need-based financial aid packages. Additionally, a limited number of scholarships averaging $40,800, and more than 100 athletic scholarships are available.

> *Davidson's eight fraternities, three sororities, and four all-female eating houses are the real center of social life on campus.*

Ninety-six percent of Davidson's students live on campus in co-ed or single-sex dorms. First-years are housed together and eat in Vail Commons, where the food is "average" but "accommodating to any dietary restrictions or needs, including religious needs," says a political science major. Seniors get apartment-style housing with private bedrooms. Many upperclassmen take meals at one of the fraternity or eating houses, which have their own cooks and serve meals family style. A limited number of upperclassmen receive permission to live off campus. Regarding campus safety and sexual assault, a senior reports, "I've seen more spaces emerge for conversation and support of sexual assault victims/survivors."

The Alvarez College Union provides a main gathering place, and students have around 200 clubs and organizations at their disposal, but Davidson's eight fraternities, three sororities, and four all-female eating houses are the real center of social life on campus.

> **"Davidson is the liberal arts school of the South."**

These nonresidential groups, which are housed in Patterson Court, charge dues that cover meals, parties, and other campuswide events. Fraternities claim 22 percent of the men, and sororities attract 40 percent of the women. The eating houses, each of which supports a different philanthropic cause, such as cancer and autism research, are not much different from Greek life. First-year women simply sign up for the eating house they want to join on Self-Selection Night, with no "rushing" allowed. And even if you don't join, "Greek life isn't elitist or exclusive. You can go to their open events, and you'll be encouraged to as well," explains a senior. The party scene is said to be low-pressure, and one student points out that "[alcohol] policies are tied into the Honor Code, so they are enforced." Davidson's first-year orientation includes the Cake Race, a tradition since 1930 that provides each runner with a cake they select based on the order in which they finish a (voluntary) 1.7-mile race. Another favorite tradition is Spring Frolics, a weekend of games, concerts, and free food.

The cozy town of Davidson (population 16,000) and the equally quaint neighboring town of Cornelius are common destinations for a relaxed night out, with coffee shops, cafés, beer gardens, miniature golf, and movie theaters. "For a college town, the town of Davidson shuts down pretty early," notes a junior. The college's 110-acre Lake Norman campus is ideal for sailing, swimming, and rowing. When those diversions grow old, North Carolina's largest city, Charlotte, is just 20 miles away, offering nightlife and other attractions. A car definitely helps here, as beaches and skiing are a few hours away in different directions. Public transit is an option, too, as is the college's shuttle service.

Davidson fields 21 varsity teams (the Wildcats), 19 of which compete in the Division I Atlantic 10 Conference. The nonscholarship football team plays in the Division I Pioneer Football League, and the wrestling team competes in the Southern Conference. About a quarter of students are varsity athletes. Basketball (one of the team's alumni is Stephen Curry), football, and men's golf are the most competitive programs. Intramural and club sports are varied and popular.

Despite its North Carolina location, Davidson has the look and feel of a New England liberal arts college, and it has recently begun to catch the eye of more top students who in the past might have limited their searches to schools farther north. From study abroad and independent research to a reception with the college president for graduating seniors, students here combine Southern tradition with forward thinking to make great memories, friends, and intellectual strides.

Overlaps

Amherst, Bowdoin, Duke, Middlebury, UNC Chapel Hill, Swarthmore, Wake Forest, Williams

If You Apply To ›

Davidson: Early decision I and II, regular decision. SATs or ACTs: optional. Accepts the Common Application with supplement.

University of Dayton

300 College Park, Dayton, OH 45469

Part of a cohort of Roman Catholic institutions in the Midwest that includes DePaul, Duquesne, Loyola of Chicago, Saint Louis University, and Xavier (OH). Drawing cards include engineering, entrepreneurship, education, and health sciences, as well as a pioneering program in human rights. Medium-size school with larger feel. The city of Dayton, home to the Wright Brothers, is enjoying a resurgence. UD's appeal is largely regional.

The entrepreneurship program dispenses $5,000 loans to participating sophomores to start their own businesses.

Anyone who thinks today's college students subscribe to postmodern cynicism should take a peek at Dayton, where optimism and Roman Catholic charity are thriving. Although its name suggests that it is a public university, Dayton was founded in 1850 by the Society of Mary (Marianists) and continues to emphasize that order's devotion to service. "Our Marianist curriculum encourages students to develop a critical mind, a compassionate heart, and to learn through doing" in a "welcoming and inclusive environment where students live and learn together in community," notes an administrator. To that end, Dayton continues to innovate new academic programs and has increased student funding for hands-on experiences like research and study abroad. "Perhaps the most identifying factor of UD is the sense of community that the entire student body and staff feel united by," shares a first-year.

Located two miles from downtown Dayton, the 423-acre parklike campus with a riverfront vista is bordered by a quiet suburban neighborhood. The more historic buildings make up the central core of the campus and blend architectural charm with modern technological conveniences. The historic UD Arena has hosted more Division I basketball tournament games than any other venue. The $51 million EPISCenter boasts labs where UD researchers and students work side by side with GE Aerospace scientists and engineers to create advanced electrical power technologies. A 95,000-square-foot innovation hub offers learning labs, classrooms, and opportunities for students to interact with local entrepreneurs. The Glass Center for the Arts is the first building on campus dedicated to the visual and performing arts, with a concert hall, art gallery, and experiential learning facilities for Flyer Media, including a TV studio and control room, and more.

The undergraduate curriculum, the Common Academic Program, is designed to equip students with the skills and experience to participate in a complex global society. The first-year experience course helps incoming students prepare for their academic careers and explore various majors. An experiential learning requirement was recently added and all students complete a capstone experience and public presentation their senior

> **"The most identifying factor of UD is the sense of community."**

year. UD students take full advantage of the strong offerings found in engineering (especially mechanical), business administration, biology, health sciences, and computer science; marketing, communication, and finance are among the most popular majors. The race and ethnic studies interdisciplinary program offers several minors, including Latinx and Latin American studies and Africana studies. Consistent with its religious mission, Dayton offers a major in human rights studies, the first of its kind, and a Human Rights Center. Recently, the school has added a neuroscience co-major, and several new minors in such fields as AI and data science, electrical engineering, and more. The entrepreneurship program dispenses $5,000 loans to participating sophomores to start their own businesses, with any profits going to charity; local entrepreneurs act as mentors. Through the Davis Center for Portfolio Management, finance students manage one of the largest student-run investment funds in the country, worth more than $80 million. Motivated students can earn two degrees at an accelerated pace through the Bachelor's Plus Master's program, choosing from two dozen available degrees.

A marketing major says, "The classes are challenging but allow me to be comfortable being uncomfortable." Forty-three percent of classes have fewer than 20 students. "Professors have been more than willing to work with students individually to make sure they feel confident, comfortable, and empowered to succeed," notes a business management major. Career services get good ratings for making sure students are well networked and for continuing to offer assistance to alumni at any stage of their careers. "The experiential learning opportunities are second to none at UD," raves a senior.

Qualified first-year and transfer students can be admitted directly into the University Honors Program, which features special activities and opportunities for fellowships and research. The University of Dayton Research Institute also offers students a chance to gain hands-on experience, and more than three-quarters of students participate in research. Study abroad options include academic and internship programs in such locations as Ireland, Spain, Ghana, and Ecuador. "Campus ministry provides opportunities for retreats, service-learning trips, cultural immersion, and outreach," adds a senior.

Fifty-four percent of Dayton's undergraduates are from Ohio, while 3 percent come from abroad. While UD "definitely isn't the most diverse," says one student, "that isn't to say that people cannot find their niche." Currently, 5 percent of students are Black, 7 percent are Hispanic/Latino, 2 percent are Asian American, and 4 percent are multiracial. Forty-three percent of the students are Catholic. Overt political activism is not common on campus, and several students call the political climate "neutral." Dayton doles out over 100 athletic scholarships each year, and merit-based academic awards average $30,300 per year. High school applicants who visit campus and file the FAFSA are eligible for a textbook scholarship of up to $4,000 ($500 per semester) if they choose to enroll.

> **"The classes are challenging but allow me to be comfortable being uncomfortable."**

About 35 percent of undergraduates live in university housing; those who live off campus generally live adjacent to it. Sophomores select suites or apartments, while upperclassmen take up quarters in the 400 university-owned houses, apartments, and townhouses that comprise the much-loved student neighborhood. Dining facilities offer full-service, casual restaurant-style menu selections that earn high marks along with a variety of cafés, delis, and convenience stores spread throughout the campus. Students report that campus safety is adequate. Students have access to Flyer Safe App, which makes it easy to contact public safety, and the Green Dot bystander intervention program has improved awareness of the issue of campus sexual assault. A well-being platform, YOU@Dayton, helps students navigate campus resources for academic, physical, and mental health.

The Red Scare student cheering section loves to intimidate opponents.

"The UD nightlife is fun between sporting events, activities like bowling and pool, formals, and other events across campus," says a senior. The student neighborhood serves as a sort of continuous social center. Up the Orgs activity fair "takes place on the first Friday of the fall semester and includes over 270 tables/booths for students to explore the different on-campus clubs, organizations, and student employment opportunities," explains a first-year. Greek organizations draw 5 percent of UD men and 11 percent of the women, "but it does not set the tone" for the school's social life, says an international studies major. More than 30 student groups are devoted entirely to service, and Christmas on Campus, when UD students host about 1,000 local elementary students for a night of crafts, games, and a visit with Santa, is one of the most student-involved activities.

> **"The UD nightlife is fun between sporting events, formals, and other events across campus."**

Students can check out free bikes through campus recreation, and a free city bus service links the campus with downtown Dayton. Just a short ride away are attractions like the Dayton Dragons minor league baseball team, the Dayton Art Institute, the U.S. Air Force's museums, a symphony in the Schuster Performing Arts Center, and free concerts at the Levitt Pavilion. Weekend excursions take aim at cities ranging from Louisville to Chicago to Indianapolis, as well as the restaurants, shops, and sports arenas of Cincinnati and Columbus.

The Dayton Flyers field 16 Division I men's and women's teams, and sports play a big role in campus life. "Dayton men's basketball is huge, and I love going to those games," raves a junior. Both the men's and women's basketball teams have reached the Elite 8 in recent years, and the Red Scare student cheering section loves to intimidate opponents. Football competes in the Pioneer League, women's golf plays in the Metro Atlantic Athletic Conference, and all other teams are in the Atlantic 10 Conference. Forty-four percent of the students participate in more than 30 club sports and the many intramural offerings.

As a midsized university where the undergraduates come first, Dayton has managed to maintain an exciting balance of personal attention, academic challenge, and all-American fun. The success of Dayton's attempts to provide its students with a high quality of life and a sense of cohesiveness is reflected in the strong social scene and family-like atmosphere among both students and faculty. "Community is said a lot at UD, and it's not a cliché or buzzword here," says a senior. "It is lived out daily."

Overlaps

University of Cincinnati, Indiana University, Marquette, Miami (OH), Ohio State, Ohio University, Saint Louis University, Xavier (OH)

If You Apply To ›

Dayton: Early action, regular decision. SATs or ACTs: optional. Accepts the Common Application with supplement.

Deep Springs College

250 Deep Springs Ranch Road, Highway 168, Big Pine, CA 93513

Picture 26 Ivy League–caliber individuals living and learning on a working ranch in a remote desert outpost—that's Deep Springs. DS is the most elite two-year institution in the nation, and the most unusual—and not just because of its free tuition. Occupies a handful of ranch-style buildings set on 50,000 acres on the arid border of Nevada and California. Students transfer to highly selective colleges after two years. After a century as an all-male school, Deep Springs has been co-ed since 2018.

Website: www.deepsprings.edu
Location: Rural
Private
Total Enrollment: 26
Undergraduates: 26
Male/Female: 50/40
Financial Aid: 100%
Pell Grant: N/A
Expense: Pr $
Student Loans: N/A
Average Debt: N/A
Applicants: 100
Accepted: 2%
Enrolled: 80%
Grad in 6 Years: 100%
Returning First-years: 93%
Academics: ✍ ✍ ✍ ✍
Social: 💬
Q of L: ★ ★ ★

If the thought of spending countless hours under the fluorescent lights of the classroom makes you grimace, you may consider getting your hands dirty at Deep Springs College. This two-year co-ed institution doubles as a working ranch. Students who are committed to "a life of service to humanity" enjoy a demanding and individualized education supplemented by the challenges and lessons of ranch life. Both, it seems, demand the same things: hard work, commitment, and pride in a job well done. Deep Springs students are also rewarded for their efforts in other ways: Tuition is free, as is room and board. Most Deep Springers have wide-ranging interests and have shunned acceptance at Ivy League schools to embrace the rigors of a truly unique approach to learning. "Spending hours in seminar, then going out to move wheel lines or milk a cow, gives a whole other dimension to my academic life that is both challenging and fulfilling," cheers a student.

California's White Mountains provide a stunning backdrop for the Deep Springs campus, set on a barren plain in Deep Springs Valley 5,200 feet above sea level, near the only water supply for miles around and 28 miles from the nearest town, a thriving metropolis known as Big Pine, population 1,875. The campus is an oasis-like cluster of trees and a lawn with eight ranch-style buildings that were built from scratch by the school's first class of students in 1917. The focal point is the Main Building, a venerable ranch-style structure with wide eaves that houses classrooms, offices, and the library. Faculty houses and the dining hall are grouped around the circular lawn a few yards away from the sole dorm, and the trappings of farm life surround the tiny settlement. The college operates an organic cattle ranch and 150-acre hay farm where they keep 200 head of cattle. A solar array produces twice as much energy as the college requires—except during peak summer times when the alfalfa needs irrigating. Meals are prepared and eaten in the Boarding House.

Founded in 1917 by industrialist L. L. Nunn, who made a fortune in the electric-power industry, Deep Springs today remains true to the three pillars of its charter: practical work, rigorous academics, and genuine self-government. In addition to coursework, students are required to perform 20 to 25 hours per week of labor, which can include everything from harvesting alfalfa to branding and herding cattle to cooking dinner. Applicants must be committed to the ideals of self-government, reflectiveness, frugality, and community activity. Those who are admitted can truly boast of being handpicked to attend: of the more than 100 applications received each year, only a handful of students are accepted. The two-round admissions process is intense, spanning months and involving several essays, letters of recommendation, and an on-campus admissions interview.

Student input carries a lot of weight at Deep Springs. Four student-body committees are an essential part of the school's self-governance pillar, and these groups play a determining role in admissions and curricular decisions, help choose the college's faculty, and even elect two of their own to be full-voting members on the board of trustees. A Spartan community code bans all drugs, including alcohol, and forbids students from leaving Deep Springs Valley while classes are in session, except for medical visits and college business. There are no phones and no Internet in the dorm, although there is limited Wi-Fi in the other buildings on campus. Significantly, these rules are all decided on and enforced by the student body, not the administration.

"[Deep Springs] academic life is both challenging and fulfilling."

Like almost everything else about it, Deep Springs has an unorthodox academic schedule: two summer terms of seven weeks each, and fall and spring semesters of 14 weeks each. Between 7 and 10 classes are offered every term. New students arrive in July to complete an intensive summer seminar that focuses on issues of ethics and governance and prepares students to read and write effectively for the fall. Currently, the only required courses are public speaking and composition. Students also take STEM classes during their first year and, in spring of their second year, write and give a speech detailing how they plan to live a life of service to humanity. The students control the academic program and quickly replace courses—and faculty—that do not work out. Philosophy, political science, and classics are among the most popular disciplines.

The faculty consists of three "permanent" professors—the humanities chair, the social sciences chair, and the natural sciences chair—who sign on for two years but can stay for up to six. Other courses are taught by the dean, the president, and visiting professors. With class sizes ranging from two to 14, there is ample opportunity for close student/faculty interaction. "There is nowhere to hide among only seven students in a heated discussion," notes a first-year. Close living arrangements have fostered a kind of kinship between faculty and students. "Faculty are generally accessible most hours of the day or night—as long as their porch lights are on, students can stop by to talk," says a student.

"Faculty are generally accessible most hours of the day or night."

The students "are the people who raised our hands when someone asked, 'Is there anyone who would be willing to do this?'" says a sophomore. With only 24 to 30 students enrolled at one time, demographics varies from year to year. Since everyone's tuition, room, and board are covered by a scholarship, students pay only for

(continued)

Admissions: (760) 872-2000
Email Address:
 apcom@deepsprings.edu

Strong Programs:
English
Philosophy
Physics
Political Science
Premed

In addition to coursework, students are required to perform 20 to 25 hours per week of labor.

indirect costs (books, travel, health insurance, and personal items). While most students come from upper-middle-class urban families, an increasing number qualify for additional, need-based financial aid to help cover these indirect costs. Almost all students transfer to prestigious universities after their two-year program, and 70 percent eventually earn a Ph.D. or law degree.

Rooms in the dorm are said to be spacious and comfortable, and a student explains, "The dorm includes a lovely common room with a library and a fireplace (the 'rumpus room'), as well as a gym, meditation room, multiple porches, and a backyard." Room selection and dorm maintenance is entirely the responsibility of the students, who also pitch in with preparing the meals. "Vegetarians are usually provided for, but we are a cattle ranch," notes one student. A committee of trained students, faculty, and staff runs workshops to educate the student body on preventing sexual assault and creating a safe, healthy climate on campus. For those seeking mental health services, Deep Springs provides access to free, unlimited 30-minute therapy sessions. As for security, the campus has a student-elected safety coordinator, wilderness trained student nurses, and a student fire chief keeping a careful eye on the campus. But one student warns, "Sometimes the bulls get loose."

"Vegetarians are usually provided for, but we are a cattle ranch."

Social life can be a challenge, especially with the isolation policy. Loneliness can be an issue. Still, one student says, "Often groups of people will go for a quick dip in the reservoir or sit on the front porch of the dorms to smoke and chat." Other common activities include pickup soccer games, hikes in the nearby mountains, horseback riding, and competitive gopher trapping in the winter months. Booj is "an impromptu, in-the-dark dance with music so loud you can't hear your own thoughts. Completely sober," says a student. During some years, students host their families and friends for Thanksgiving. End-of-term dinners, summer garden parties, and Sludgefest (an annual event involving cleaning out the reservoir) are time-honored Deep Springs traditions.

Critics of Deep Springs charge that DS cultivates arrogance and social backwardness among students who were too intellectual to be in the social mainstream during high school. While that charge is debatable, even supporters of Deep Springs confess to a love-hate relationship with the college. Although the interpretations may vary, one common thread winds through the DS mission from application to graduation: training for a life of service to humanity.

Perhaps more than any other school in the nation, Deep Springs is a community where students and faculty interact day-to-day on an intensely personal level and where the actions of each person affect everyone. Though the financial commitment is small, the personal commitment to this community is serious. "The level of responsibility and independence that students are required to have, and the ownership that they have over this educational project, is mind-blowing," remarks a sophomore. Urban cowboys and cowgirls who dream of riding into the sunset are in for a rude awakening. But for a select few, the camaraderie and soul-searching fostered in this tight-knit community can be life changing.

Overlaps

Amherst, Brown, University of Chicago, Columbia, Cornell University, Outercoast College, St. John's College, Yale

If You Apply To ›

Deep Springs: Regular decision. SATs or ACTs: optional. Does not accept the Common Application. Accepts applications from students of all genders and gender identities.

210 S College Avenue, Newark, DE 19716

Plenty of students dream of someday becoming Nittany Lions or Cavaliers—even Terrapins—but fewer aspire to be Blue Hens. The challenge for UD is how to win its share of students without the name recognition that comes from big-time sports. The state of Delaware is tiny, and only about a third of the students are in-staters. A manageable-sized public flagship where you won't be just a number.

The University of Delaware is a public gem that boasts solid academic programs, from engineering and nursing to art conservation and public policy. It also claims former president Joe Biden as an alum. Though lacking the national reputation of a big-time sports program, UD has been gradually attracting more and more out-of-state students who are looking for strong academics and hands-on experiences. "UD is a big school with a small-school feel," explains a first-year student. "There are limitless opportunities here, but it does not feel overwhelming. You see familiar faces everywhere, and the experience is very personalized."

Tracing its origins to a small private school founded in 1743 that turned out three signers of the Declaration of Independence, Delaware became a public land grant university in 1869. Its 950-acre Newark campus has an attractive mix of colonial and modern geometric buildings set among flowering and native plantings. The hub of the campus is a grassy green mall, flanked by classic Georgian buildings. The Mechanical Hall art gallery, one of three on campus, is home to the Paul R. Jones collection of African American art. Hotel and restaurant management students benefit from classes in a fine dining restaurant and a Courtyard by Marriott right on campus, which doubles as a learning and research facility. New facilities include a state-of-the-art research and teaching lab building devoted to research in psychology, neuroscience, biology and other sciences. Construction of a new $71 million residential complex on UD's Science, Technology, and Advanced Research Campus is underway.

> **"There are limitless opportunities here, but it does not feel overwhelming."**

To graduate, students must pass first-year English (critical reading and writing) and earn at least three credits of discovery-based or experiential learning, such as an internship, research, or study abroad. A required First-Year Seminar course, usually limited to 30 students, emphasizes class discussion, and a capstone experience is required during the senior year; other requirements vary by college.

Delaware's academic menu includes more than 150 undergraduate majors, ranging from the liberal arts and sciences to more professional programs like fashion merchandising and human relations administration. Psychology, finance, marketing, and communication are the most popular majors. Engineering, especially chemical engineering, is one of UD's specialties, and the school benefits from the close proximity of DuPont, the chemical giant that has been a major benefactor of the university. The Venture Development Center and the Delaware Innovation Fellows help students create businesses, nonprofits, and career paths. The School of Music is another attraction, with a 300-member marching band and several faculty members holding impressive professional performance credits. New majors include math and data science, cybersecurity engineering, applied physics, and more.

Classes tend to be on the large side, but 32 percent enroll fewer than 20 students. A senior calls the academic atmosphere "low pressure" and collaborative.

Website: www.udel.edu
Location: Small City
Public
Total Enrollment: 21,195
Undergraduates: 17,670
Male/Female: 39/61
Financial Aid: 70%
Pell Grant: 15%
Expense: Pub $ $ $ $
Student Loans: 59%
Average Debt: $ $ $ $
Applicants: 39,742
Accepted: 69%
Enrolled: 15%
Grad in 6 Years: 83%
Returning First-years: 92%
Academics: ✑ ✑ ✑
Social: 🗩 🗩 🗩 🗩 🗩
Q of L: ★ ★ ★
Admissions: (302) 831-8123
Email Address:
 admissions@udel.edu

Strong Programs:
Biological Sciences
Chemical Engineering
Engineering
Finance
Marketing
Music
Nursing
Psychology

The quality of teaching varies, but, for the most part, "If you want support here, all you have to do is show up to class and show that you are trying," says a medical laboratory science major. Students describe career preparation here as hands-on and useful. The Career Center "really wants us as students to experience everything that we might encounter in the real world before we get there," opines a biochemistry major.

UD created the nation's first study abroad program in 1923, and today 20 percent of students take part in programs offered in more than 40 countries, mostly for short-term, faculty-led courses during the monthlong winter session or summer break. Each year, more than 500 UD undergrads receive stipends to do summer research with faculty members. Students from any major can become Community Engagement Scholars, a four-year experience that incorporates special academic and career advising. Overall, about half of UD students participate in a service-learning opportunity. More than 600 new students enter the Honors College each year, which offers interdisciplinary colloquia, priority seating in honors sections of regular courses, personal attention, and extracurricular and residence hall programming.

Only 36 percent of undergraduates at Delaware hail from the First State, but one junior notes, "Students are all from the Tri-State, and we tend to all flock in groups." Three percent come from abroad, and racial diversity continues to increase; 6 percent of students are Black, 10 percent are Hispanic/Latino, 6 percent are Asian American, and 5 percent are multiracial. "I've met students that span the political and socioeconomic spectrum," states a public policy major. Merit and athletic scholarships are offered, with merit awards averaging $10,200. The First State Promise is a financial package for Delaware residents with family incomes of less than $75,000 that covers tuition costs at UD with grants and scholarships.

"If you want support here, all you have to do is . . . show that you are trying."

Thirty-seven percent of students live on campus, and first-year students are required to. UD provides housing options for students in every class year, though many juniors and seniors move into off-campus apartments. "Every dorm has its quirks—but every student will claim theirs is the best," laughs a senior. Honors students live together in designated residence halls, and certain academic departments require first-year students to reside in living/learning communities. Students in traditional residence halls must buy the meal plan; the food receives good reviews. To increase awareness about sexual assault issues, the Blue Hens CARE peer educators spread the word to students across campus about bystander intervention strategies. Students report that mental health services are strong.

"No matter the time in the night, there is always something going on," says a first-year. Fraternities attract 20 percent of the men and sororities 25 percent of the women; while the party scene is lively, most parties occur off campus. More than 400 student organizations coordinate regular on-campus events, and UD's two student centers, Perkins and Trabant, sponsor live entertainment, weekly trivia, and late-night events on Friday and Saturday nights. A favorite tradition is the candlelight ceremony that welcomes first-years to campus each fall, and popular annual events include homecoming celebrations on the central campus green, the Senior Fling concert in the spring, and Air Band, when, says a senior, "sororities and fraternities perform musical/dance interpretations of movie plots to raise money for UDANCE (our dance marathon for pediatric cancer)."

Main Street, the heart of downtown Newark (pronounced "New-ark"), is "easy walking distance," says a student. "There are tons of coffee shops, pizza places, a movie theater, bookstores, and shops—anything you could possibly want." For those seeking further excitement, New York, the Washington/Baltimore area, and Philadelphia are all within a two-hour drive. When the weather is warm, the beaches of Rehoboth and Dewey beckon, and in chilly months, the Pennsylvania ski slopes aren't too far.

"We are not a very athletics-oriented school, but we have a lot of school spirit," says a senior. Delaware's Division I Blue Hens joined Conference USA in July 2025 and now compete in the Football Bowl subdivision. Historically, men's lacrosse, women's field hockey, and men's and women's basketball teams are competitive, and the basketball teams enjoy a lively rivalry with Drexel. UD's varsity eSports team competes in the Perkins Student Center's sleek new Esports Arena, which can also be enjoyed by casual gamers. Recreational sports are popular; students have their pick of more than 35 club sports and 30 intramural programs.

> **"We are not a very athletics-oriented school, but we have a lot of school spirit."**

UD is a public flagship university that is large enough to offer something for everyone yet at a more manageable size than many of its closest competitors. With UD's traditional emphasis on out-of-classroom experiences, stimulating academic environment, and up-and-coming athletic teams, Blue Hens need never put all their eggs in one basket.

If You Apply To ›

Delaware: Early action, regular decision. Accepts the Common Application with supplement. Please consult Delaware's website for the most up-to-date information regarding standardized test requirements.

Denison University

100 W College Street, Granville, OH 43023

Denison draws more Easterners than Wooster and Ohio Wesleyan, and it fashions itself as a sort of Midwestern Haverford. Denison has a middle-of-the-road to liberal student body, fewer preppies than in years past, and one of the most beautiful campuses anywhere. Increasing popularity fueled by some distinctive majors and an innovative summer program that have helped create a more academically serious student body.

Denison University, tucked into the "quaint, small, and beautiful" village of Granville, draws "curious, down-to-earth" students from diverse backgrounds, according to one matriculant. Thanks to Denison's small size, there's ample opportunity to interact (and do research) with professors and to form close relationships with peers, as everyone focuses on the liberal arts. "Denison is a special place because it helps students figure out how their diverse interests intersect," says a politics and public affairs major. "This campus is a place where you are encouraged to keep doing everything you love."

Founded in 1831 to bring higher education to what was then the Northwest Territory, Denison was named after an early benefactor. The campus is set atop rolling hills in central Ohio. Huge maples shade the sloping walkways, which offer a panoramic view of the surrounding valley. Denison retained park architect Frederick Law Olmsted (designer of New York City's Central Park) for its first master plan back in the early 1900s. The Georgian style of many buildings—redbrick with white columns—also evokes shades of New England and its private liberal arts colleges. Recent campus additions include the 108,000-square-foot Michael Eisner Center for

(continued)

Academics: ✍ ✍ ✍
Social: 🗨 🗨 🗨 🗨 🗨
Q of L: ★ ★ ★
Admissions: (740) 587-6276
Email Address:
 admission@denison.edu

Strong Programs:
Biology
Computer Science
Data Analytics
Financial Economics
Global Commerce
Health, Exercise, and Sport
 Studies
Music
Philosophy, Politics, and
 Economics

Performing Arts (named for the former Disney CEO and Denison alum) and the Hoaglin Wellness Center.

Denison's general education requirements are comprehensive. In addition to a spate of coursework spanning the liberal arts and sciences, students take two first-year seminars and complete an "interdivisional requirement" by selecting a course from one of seven interdisciplinary programs, such as international studies or women's and gender studies. The power and justice requirement seeks to give students the ability to question their own place in the structures of power and privilege that constitute human societies. For help navigating the transition to college, most first-years sign up for optional Advising Circles, meeting weekly with a faculty advisor in groups of around 10 students.

Although biology, psychology, global commerce, and data analytics have the highest enrollment, students say some of the best majors are distinctive to Denison. The PPE major is effectively a triple major in philosophy, politics, and economics. The music department features a concentration in bluegrass designed by a faculty member who is an accomplished fiddler, while Denison's 350-acre biological reserve is a boon for biology and environmental studies majors. The financial economics; computer science; health, exercise, and sport studies; and theater programs are strong as well. "The academic climate at Denison is rigorous but manageable," says an international studies major. Sixty-eight percent of classes have fewer than 20 students, and individual attention is the norm. "There's curiosity embedded in the curriculum here," says a junior. "It's all about trying new things and finding new ways to cross disciplines."

> **"This campus is a place where you are encouraged to keep doing everything you love."**

Denison's award-winning undergraduate research program includes the signature Summer Scholar Program, which provides scholarships for about 120 students to stay on campus during the summer to complete 10 weeks of full-time research in collaboration with faculty members. Typically, more than half of the summer scholars are science students. Those with wanderlust can choose from more than 180 programs in 70 countries; overall, 80 percent of students go abroad, about a third of them in short-term, faculty-led programs. "I took a Denison Seminar on King Richard III where we got to travel as a class across England," cheers a sophomore. The school has invested $50 million in the Knowlton Center for Career Exploration, which one senior says "has become an incredible asset for students, helping them easily adapt to the ever-changing career landscape." Those considering a run for office may be interested in the Richard Lugar Program in Politics and Public Service, which includes courses on campus and culminates in a House or Senate internship in Washington. (The late former senator was a Denison grad.)

Greek organizations and other student groups host open parties in the senior apartments.

Denison students are "supportive, friendly, hard-working," says a biology major. Twenty-six percent of the population is homegrown, and 17 percent come from abroad. Black students constitute 5 percent of the student body, Hispanics/Latinos 7 percent, Asian Americans 4 percent, and multiracial students 4 percent. Denison is left-leaning, but one junior notes, "The students here are willing to have the difficult discussions about our world and society." Denison commits to meeting the full demonstrated need of all incoming first-years. The average merit-based financial aid award is $19,400, and there are no athletic scholarships.

> **"There's curiosity embedded in the curriculum here."**

Virtually all Denison students live on campus; the only ones allowed to live elsewhere are those commuting from home. (Another exception is the dozen Homesteaders, who live in three student-built, solar-paneled cabins on a sustainable farm less than a mile away and grow much of their own food.) Students generally live in dorms for the first three years and campus apartments their senior year, and they report that recent renovations have vastly improved the accommodations. Dining hall meals get good reviews. Educational programming for sexual assault awareness has increased, as has attention to student wellness. "From the new Hoaglin Wellness Center to Destress Fests, they've done a lot to make sure students are aware of all the health resources available to them," lauds an English major.

Given the residential nature of the campus, social life at Denison tends to revolve around student housing and clubs, although 20 percent of the men and 34 percent of the women join the Greek system. Greek organizations and other student groups host open parties in the senior apartments (a.k.a. the Sunnies) and in Moon Hall's social spaces (a.k.a. the Moonies) every weekend. Students report that regulations aimed at curtailing excessive drinking have improved the party scene: parties must be registered, have a sober host trained in safety, and offer food. School-sponsored events like guest speakers, plays, and concerts offer an alternative, and everyone looks forward to the D-Day and Doobie Palooza music festivals. Naked Week, held during National Eating Disorders Awareness Week in February, is another notable event. "This entails students streaking through a different quad on campus every night for a week in the spirit of body positivity," explains a sophomore.

Granville is a small, quiet town with four churches on the corners of the town's main intersection, and town-gown relations are said to be good. Granville has "amazing restaurants, cute boutiques, cozy coffee shops, and delicious Whit's custard," raves an English literature major. The Denison Community Association frequently sends students into Granville and nearby Newark to provide tutoring, mentoring, and other volunteer services. "Columbus is around 30 minutes

away, and there is a much larger social scene and party culture there if students are willing to head out there," suggests an international studies major. The school runs trips to the city's Easton Town Center, an outdoor shopping and dining mecca. Pittsburgh, Cleveland, Cincinnati, and Dayton are also close by.

Denison students are enthusiastic supporters of the Big Red, especially when rival Kenyon is in town, and Division III lacrosse games against Ohio Wesleyan always draw large crowds. The men's swimming and diving team is a perennial powerhouse, having claimed six national championships, and the men's tennis team won the 2025 NCAA championship. Men's and women's lacrosse and golf and women's swimming and diving are strong, too, along with baseball, women's fencing, and men's soccer. Intramurals and club sports remain hugely popular, with basketball, soccer, flag football, rugby, and ice hockey drawing the most interest.

Denison University aims to graduate independent thinkers who become active citizens of a democratic society. The school continues to value tradition—woe to the students who step on the school seal in front of the chapel, "who won't graduate in four years," warns a sophomore—while emphasizing the life of the mind. "Denison has grown more diverse, new programs have been introduced, and much of campus has been renovated," says a senior. "I wish I could experience it all over again!"

Overlaps

Bucknell, Colby, Colgate, University of Denver, Elon, Miami (OH), Ohio Wesleyan, Wake Forest

If You Apply To ›

Denison: Early decision I and II, regular decision. SATs or ACTs: optional. Accepts the Common Application.

2199 S University Boulevard, Denver, CO 80208

The only major midsized private university between Tulsa and the West Coast. DU's campus in residential Denver is pleasant, and admissions brochures shamelessly tout Rocky Mountain landscapes and healthy lifestyles. Senior faculty teach all core courses. A haven for skiing enthusiasts, business majors, and future diplomats, DU has become much more selective in recent years.

Website: www.du.edu
Location: City Center
Private
Total Enrollment: 8,510
Undergraduates: 5,750
Male/Female: 44/56
Financial Aid: 70%
Pell Grant: 15%
Expense: Pr $ $
Student Loans: 41%
Average Debt: $ $
Applicants: 18,785
Accepted: 77%
Enrolled: 9%
Grad in 6 Years: 76%
Returning First-years: 89%
Academics: ✍ ✍ ✍
Social: 🌑 🌑 🌑 🌑
Q of L: ★ ★ ★ ★
Admissions: (303) 871-2036
Email Address:
  admission@du.edu

Strong Programs:
Biology
Business
Computer Science
Engineering
Hospitality Management
International Studies
Music
Political Science

The oldest private university in the Rocky Mountain region, dating to 1864, the University of Denver is where former secretary of state Condoleezza Rice earned her B.A. in political science at age 19 and later returned for a Ph.D. in international studies. Her mentor was Soviet specialist Josef Korbel, father of the late secretary of state Madeleine Albright. So, it's not surprising that DU boasts strong programs in political science, international studies, and public affairs. Many students, however, opt for DU's business program, and the campus location offers ample opportunities for networking, skiing, and taking in the beautiful Colorado landscape. A first-year says, "DU students share a sense of adventure, risk-taking, and spending time doing what one values."

DU's 125-acre main campus is located in a comfortable residential neighborhood only eight miles from downtown Denver and an hour east of major ski areas. Architectural styles vary, and materials include brick, limestone, Colorado sandstone, and copper. Nearby Mount Blue Sky (14,265 feet) is home to the world's loftiest observatory, a DU facility available to both professors and students. Newer campus projects include the 500-bed, LEED Gold–certified Dimond Family Residential Village for first-year students, as well as the $64 million, 132,000-square-foot Community Commons, housing the campus's main dining hub, spaces for student organizations and special events, indoor and rooftop lounges, and academic advising services.

> **"DU students share a sense of adventure, risk-taking, and spending time doing what one values."**

Under the general education requirements, undergraduate students choose from a series of courses from the Common Curriculum that emphasize writing, quantitative reasoning, experiential learning, and cross-disciplinary inquiry. University rules stipulate that all core courses must be taught by senior faculty. Core courses are supplemented by a First-Year Seminar (limited to 15 students) that introduces students to college-level work and an advanced seminar that serves as a capstone to the curriculum model.

DU is known for business; the Daniels College of Business is home to the Knoebel School of Hospitality Management, one of the top hospitality programs in the country. Music, biology, engineering, and computer science have solid reputations. Psychology, finance, international studies, biological sciences, and marketing are among the most popular majors. The university has added a new major in kinesiology and sport studies and one in critical race and ethnic studies. Several dual-degree programs allow undergraduates to earn a bachelor's degree and an advanced degree from Denver's graduate schools in business, education, the arts, international studies, social work, and law.

Since DU operates on a quarter system, classes move quickly, and the workload can get intense. "I personally enjoy how rigorous the quarter system can be, because you are constantly learning something new," says an art history major. Students say small class sizes—54 percent have fewer than 20 students—make for a collaborative environment with plenty of support from faculty. DU is also recognized for its strong academic support services. A psychology major says, "The Learning Effectiveness Program has been amazing and given me the accommodations and resources I need to succeed."

DU's selective Honors Program accepts about 100 students each year who take a sequence of honors courses and complete a thesis or final project. Funded undergraduate research opportunities are widely available. Juniors and seniors have the chance to study abroad at no additional cost through the Cherrington Global Scholars program; 31 percent of Pioneers go abroad, and they say the over 100 available programs in more than 40 countries are an integral part of the DU experience. "DU fosters a global perspective in which students understand their role in and responsibility to the global community," says a psychology major.

"We have a funky mix of really preppy East Coasters and Midwesterners mixed in with all the laid-back outdoorsy people," says one student. Thirty-one percent of undergraduates come from Colorado, and 3 percent arrive from other countries. Black students account for 3 percent of the student body, Asian Americans 4 percent, Hispanics/Latinos 14 percent, and multiracial students 6 percent. The campus leans liberal, and students cite the environment and social justice as issues of particular concern. As one of the few private colleges in the West, DU is also among the most expensive in that region. But more than half of undergrads receive merit scholarships, which average $23,500, and more than 200 athletic scholarships are also available. "Students have relatively expensive hobbies like skiing, backpacking, and traveling," observes a senior. "I think individuals from low-income backgrounds have a hard time fitting in."

Forty-seven percent of undergrads reside on campus; students are required to spend their first two years in the residence halls. Students praise the five living/learning communities open to first years: "Being able to come onto campus and already have a structured and supportive group of people who shared a similar interest was incredibly helpful," a senior recalls. Most juniors and seniors opt for the decent off-campus quarters found within walking distance. Dining options in the Community Commons get rave reviews, and students report that dietary restrictions are easily accommodated. The university has increased staffing of its mental health counseling services, and a junior comments, "All leaders of student organizations receive training to reduce instances of sexual assault on campus and become better supporters of survivors."

> **"DU fosters a global perspective in which students understand their role in and responsibility to the global community."**

More than 100 student organizations offer on-campus activities for every interest. Fraternities and sororities draw 23 percent of the men and 20 percent of the women, but students agree that Greek groups don't set the tone for social life. "The campus is pretty quiet on the weekends because everyone is either in the mountains, downtown, or enjoying the sun at a neighboring park," explains a media studies major. "There is a lot to do aside from parties." Indeed, free access to the nearby light rail makes it easy to get downtown, where students enjoy "great shopping, festivals, events, concerts, phenomenal restaurants, and, for students over 21, one of the best microbrewery scenes," cheers a student. With consistently beautiful, sunny weather and great skiing, hiking, and camping less than an hour away in the Rockies, many DU students head for the hills on weekends, often on low-cost trips organized by the Alpine Club. The school's 724-acre Kennedy Mountain Campus, just over 100 miles from Denver in the Roosevelt National Forest, includes ten cabins and learning studios available for the DU community. Students also explore Estes Park, Mount Blue Sky, and Echo Lake.

Students unite when the powerhouse DU hockey team—which won a historic 11th national championship in 2026—skates out onto the ice, especially against archrival Colorado College. Other competitive Division I Pioneers programs include co-ed skiing, men's lacrosse, men's golf, and men's and women's soccer. Intramural and club sports are varied and popular. Each February, academics are put aside for the three-day Winter Carnival. Top administrators, professors, and students all pack off to Keystone, Winter Park, or another ski area to catch some fresh powder and see who can ski the fastest, skate the best, or build the most artistic ice sculptures.

Students like the University of Denver for its modest size, its friendly atmosphere, and the flexibility afforded by the albeit sometimes stressful quarter system. As the school pushes for a more ethnically diverse student body and improves its curriculum and facilities, the University of Denver is striving to become even better known for its intellectual rigor than for its gorgeous setting in the Rocky Mountains.

> **"We have a funky mix of really preppy East Coasters and Midwesterners mixed in with all the laid-back outdoorsy people."**

If You Apply To ›

DU: Early decision I and II, early action, regular decision. SATs or ACTs: optional. Accepts the Common Application.

DePaul University

1 East Jackson Boulevard, Chicago, IL 60604

Few universities have come so far, so fast. DePaul gets the nod over Loyola as the top Roman Catholic university in Chicago. Its Lincoln Park setting is like a Midwestern version of New York's Greenwich Village or Upper West Side. One in five undergraduates who report a religion are Roman Catholic. Especially strong in business, public relations, film, and the arts.

Website: www.depaul.edu
Location: City Center
Private
Total Enrollment: 18,579
Undergraduates: 13,231
Male/Female: 45/55
Financial Aid: 86%
Pell Grant: 31%
Expense: Pr $
Student Loans: 58%
Average Debt: $ $
Applicants: 31,266
Accepted: 76%
Enrolled: 11%
Grad in 6 Years: 68%
Returning First-years: 86%
Academics: ✍ ✍ ✍
Social: 🗨 🗨

The largest Roman Catholic university in the nation, DePaul University pursues the Vincentian mission of service and contributing to the "common good." Students claim the university's diversity and politically liberal leanings set it apart from rival institutions. "DePaul is characterized by its commitment to Vincentian values, which emphasize service to others, social justice, and community engagement," shares a business analytics major. Based in the heart of the city, DePaul is a feeder to Chicago's business community. A spate of campus construction has transformed it from the "little school under the El" to Chicago's version of NYU.

DePaul, which was founded by Vincentian fathers in 1898 and is named after the 17th-century French priest Vincent de Paul, has two residential campuses. The Lincoln Park campus, with its state-of-the-art library and student center, is home to the colleges of liberal arts and social sciences, education, and science and health; the theatre and music schools; and residence halls and recreational facilities. Lincoln Park itself is a fashionable Chicago neighborhood with century-old brownstone homes, theaters, cafés, parks, and shops. The Loop campus, so called because of the elevated train tracks that circle the area, is 20 minutes away by that train (a.k.a. the El or "L," depending on whom you ask) in downtown Chicago and houses the colleges of business, communication, computing and digital media, and law, as well as the School of Continuing and Professional Studies. The DePaul Center, a $70 million teaching, learning, and research complex, is the cornerstone of this campus. The renovated Sullivan Athletic Center and McGrath-Phillips Arena recently reopened.

All first-years take a course called Discover Chicago or its alternative, Explore Chicago, which introduces them to the city. "This class is one of the best things about DePaul. It's really fun and valuable," says a senior. Other common core courses include composition and quantitative reasoning, a sophomore seminar on multiculturalism in the United States, and an experiential learning program that requires an internship, research, study abroad, or service-learning experience. In their senior year, students create a final project.

DePaul's name is closely associated with Midwestern business and law, and undergraduates can find internships year-round with local legal and commercial institutions. The School of Accountancy and MIS is reported to be the most challenging department in the Driehaus College of Business. The College of Science and Health offers a health sciences program that prepares students for a variety of health care professions, and the Pathways Honors Program provides top students with specialized prehealth advising and summer research opportunities. The School of Cinematic Arts has teamed up with Cinespace Chicago, the city's premier movie studio, to create a learning environment that provides students with film and television production experience in the midst of a working studio. Other notable programs include theatre, game design, and animation. Combined, six-year bachelor's/law degree options are available in several fields, ranging from economics to Islamic world studies, and a number of five-year bachelor's/master's degree programs are also offered. The most popular majors include finance, marketing, psychology, and film and television.

Classes are often small, with 41 percent enrolling fewer than 20 students, and professors teach at all levels. The administration appoints student representatives from each school and college to faculty promotion and tenure committees. "The professors are generous meanwhile still assigning us rigorous work that is helpful for our understandings of concepts," says a business administration major. Clerics teach some courses and celebrate (voluntary) mass every day. In addition, the University Ministry hosts other religious services and leads programs to teach students about other faiths. The highly selective honors program includes interdisciplinary courses and a senior thesis. Thirteen percent of students participate in study abroad programs that take them to their choice of more than 40 countries around the world, including India, Ireland, Peru, and Switzerland.

"DePaul is both a city school and a commuter school," observes a psychology major, and as such, its student body is more self-sufficient and independent than most. Seventy-four percent of undergraduates hail from Illinois, and 4 percent come from foreign countries. Hispanics/Latinos represent 25 percent of the student body, Black students 8 percent, Asian Americans 12 percent, and multiracial students 5 percent. DePaul has a reputation for being politically liberal, and according to a senior, "Students are actively working to improve both DePaul and Chicago." In addition to academic merit scholarships, DePaul also awards scholarships to students who have artistic talent or strong leadership skills or those who participate in community service; such awards average $18,900 per year. Scholarships for athletes are available too.

With such a large commuter population, just 14 percent of undergraduates live in university housing. Those who do find the dorms comfortable and well maintained. "Rooms are good, no trouble getting them," says a first-year. The Lincoln Park campus includes six modern co-ed dorms and six townhouse and apartment buildings. At the Loop campus, a 1,700-bed residence hall includes a rooftop garden, fitness center, and

(continued)

Q of L: ★ ★ ★

Admissions: (312) 362-8300

Email Address:

admission@depaul.edu

Strong Programs:
Accounting
Animation
Business
Film and Television
Finance
Game Design
Psychology
Theatre

Combined, six-year bachelor's/law degree options are available in several fields.

"DePaul is both a city school and a commuter school."

"Rooms are good, no trouble getting them."

music, art, and study rooms. Campus dining receives lackluster reviews; many find the food overpriced. Students say they feel reasonably safe on campus but report that the Loop campus has experienced issues with crime in recent years. Campus safety officers regularly patrol the area and provide late-night rides home, and dorms require students to swipe ID cards at multiple points before allowing entrance. Nevertheless, "It's good to be wary near either campus at nighttime," advises a senior.

Fraternities and sororities draw just 3 percent of DePaul men and 6 percent of the women, respectively, and parties aren't a big part of campus life. Not surprisingly, with the school's proximity to Chicago's concert and comedy venues, restaurants, bars, clubs (especially on Rush Street), and sporting events, most social life occurs off campus. A music major says of the city, "There is everything to do here." In the warmer months, the beaches of Lake Michigan beckon students, while the university's huge annual outdoor Vinnie Fest "celebrates the university's mascot, Vincentian DePaul," explains one student, and includes music, food, games, and other festivities. Students find their groove for DemonTHON, an annual 24-hour dance marathon fundraiser benefitting Children's Miracle Network Hospitals.

DePaul competes in the Division I Big East Conference in 15 sports. Men's basketball is the headline story, beginning with the Blue Madness of each fall's first practice in October. The game against Notre Dame always draws a capacity crowd, though Loyola is DePaul's oldest rival. The men's tennis team has won a Big East championship, and women's basketball and softball are also competitive. Intramurals and club sports are big draws, as is the 123,000-square-foot Meyer Fitness and Recreation Center.

Expanding academic programs, a diverse student body, and all the opportunity of the city of Chicago make DePaul a dynamic university. Throw in the special bonds that students say they feel with fellow Blue Demons, and you have what one sophomore describes as "a unique atmosphere in which to learn and grow" in an urban setting.

Overlaps

Columbia College Chicago, U of I at Chicago, U of I at Urbana–Champaign, Loyola University Chicago, Marquette, Northwestern, Saint Louis University, Seattle University

If You Apply To ›

DePaul: Early action, regular decision. SATs or ACTs: optional (test-optional applicants are encouraged to submit optional personal essay). Accepts the Common Application.

DePauw University

204 East Seminary Street, Greencastle, IN 46135

DePauw is a small Midwestern liberal arts institution in the mold of Denison, Dickinson, Knox, and Ohio Wesleyan. Its Greek system is among the strongest in the nation. DePauw's Fellows and Honors Scholar programs are a major draw for career-oriented students looking to take their liberal arts experience to the next level. Almost all students study abroad.

Website: www.depauw.edu
Location: Small Town
Private
Total Enrollment: 1,892
Undergraduates: 1,892
Male/Female: 50/50

DePauw University offers a liberal arts education with an orientation toward experiential learning. The economics and management, communication, and natural sciences programs are strong. Students here are career-oriented and eager to take advantage of the rigorous classwork and ample real-world experiences. With an undergraduate population of nearly 1,900 students, close ties to classmates and faculty are a given. "If you want a school that pushes you intellectually while still feeling like home, DePauw is a solid choice," says a senior.

Founded in 1837 by the Methodist Church to export New England–style liberal education to what was then the frontier, DePauw is set amid the gently rolling hills of west-central Indiana. The lush green campus has a mix of older buildings and more modern redbrick structures. The DePauw Nature Park, about a mile away, is a well-kept, 520-acre park featuring nature trails and the LEED Gold–certified Prindle Institute for Ethics. DePauw has significantly upgraded its main campus in recent years, renovating its main library, opening a new first-year residence hall and a state-of-the-art dining hall, and improving its energy efficiency.

DePauw's first-year program helps students transition into college by combining academically challenging coursework with cocurricular activities and programs. Before arriving on campus, each student is assigned to a mentor group with 10 to 12 peers, an upperclassman advisor, and a faculty member who will teach their first-year seminar and serve as their academic advisor until they declare a major. By graduation, students must demonstrate competence in writing, quantitative reasoning, and oral communication and pass a course on power, privilege, and diversity. They must also complete at least two extended study experiences, which may include courses taken during the monthlong Winter or May terms, off-campus study, independent study or research, service-learning projects, or internships. "I've seen students in a variety of fields take on research projects that they can publish or present at conferences," says a senior.

> **"If you want a school that pushes you intellectually while still feeling like home, DePauw is a solid choice."**

Academically, the DePauw student body is as career-oriented as they come in a liberal arts college. The most popular majors include economics and management, communication, computer science, psychology, and English, and students may also design their own majors. DePauw's School of Business and Leadership is a rarity among liberal arts colleges. The Creative School offers degrees in visual and performing arts. The Institute of Music, one of the oldest in the country, offers a five-year dual-degree program in music performance/liberal arts. Students may supplement their coursework through eight academic centers offering cocurricular learning and professional development opportunities. Future reporters, editors, anchors, and producers will find a home in the Pulliam Center for Contemporary Media, which supplements DePauw's strong student-run newspaper, TV station, and radio stations. Seven other centers focus on management and entrepreneurship, ethics, technology, diversity and inclusion, civic engagement, student engagement, and 21st-century musicianship.

"The academic climate at DePauw is really engaging and collaborative," says a communications and global health major. Students say classes are challenging but well supported, with high-quality instruction from professors who "push you to think critically, communicate effectively, and lead with purpose," notes a senior. For exceptionally motivated students, Fellows programs in media, management, the environment, and science research offer a semester-long internship or research experience and opportunities to interact with top scholars and industry leaders on and off campus. Additionally, the Honor Scholars Program allows high-achieving students to embark on interdisciplinary study and complete a capstone thesis. Most DePauw students study off campus, often through short, faculty-led programs during the Winter and May terms; semester and yearlong options are also available.

"DePauw students are friendly, motivated, and supportive, with a tight-knit vibe," says a communications major. Fifty-two percent of students are from Indiana, and 23 percent are international. Students describe the school as "predominantly white," but campus diversity has grown. Black students now account for 6 percent of the student body, Hispanics/Latinos 8 percent, Asian Americans 2 percent, and

(continued)

Financial Aid: 77%
Pell Grant: 22%
Expense: Pr $ $
Student Loans: 82%
Average Debt: $
Applicants: 6,683
Accepted: 57%
Enrolled: 13%
Grad in 6 Years: 76%
Returning First-years: 90%
Academics: ✎ ✎ ✎
Social: 🗩 🗩 🗩
Q of L: ★ ★
Admissions: (765) 658-4006
Email Address:
  admission@depauw.edu

Strong Programs:
Communication
Computer Science
Economics and Management
English
Music
Natural Sciences
Psychology

The annual football game against Wabash College is the oldest small-college rivalry west of the Alleghenies.

multiracial students 3 percent. "It leans liberal, politically," says a senior. Merit scholarships averaging $37,400 are available, although there are no athletic scholarships.

All DePauw students live on campus, with few exceptions. Options include homey residence halls, suites, apartments, and college-owned houses, as well as Greek chapter houses. Additionally, says a senior, "We have two major living communities: the Healthy Living floor, if you are interested in a more tranquil dorm experience, or the Rainbow floor, if you are a member of the LGBTA+ community and would like to live with others in the community." Meals are served in Hoover Dining Hall and a few small cafés and grab-and-go options around campus. Forty-nine percent of DePauw's men and 44 percent of the women go Greek. That's not surprising, given that the first modern-day sorority, Kappa Alpha Theta, began here in 1870, and the university is home to the two longest continually running fraternities anywhere: Beta Theta Pi and Phi Gamma Delta.

"DePauw has a lively party culture that is open to all," says an economics major. Greek groups have worked hard to change the negative stereotypes of fraternities and sororities. A community council reviews allegations of misconduct, and rush is delayed until the spring semester so first-years can first get their feet on the ground academically. Around 100 student organizations offer ample alternatives, and students are active in about 20 volunteer programs.

The town of Greencastle (population 10,000) has a movie theater, a bowling alley, and several pizza places and restaurants. "It's not a bustling city," says one student, "but there's enough to keep you busy if you're looking for something low-key."

"DePauw has a lively party culture that is open to all."

In good weather, the DePauw Nature Park and several state parks offer hiking trails and lakes. Indianapolis is only a 45-minute drive, and St. Louis, Chicago, and Cincinnati make for good road trips. A cherished tradition is a takeoff on Indiana University's famed Little 500 bike race, itself a takeoff on the Indianapolis 500 auto race—teams of cyclists compete on a course that circles the heart of the DePauw campus.

Everyone gets excited about Division III varsity athletics, especially the annual football game against Wabash College, which is the oldest small-college rivalry west of the Alleghenies. The winner of each year's contest claims possession of the much-cherished, 300-pound Monon Bell, an artifact from the defunct Monon Railroad line. The Tigers football, field hockey, men's cross-country, women's basketball, and softball teams have all brought home North Coast Athletic Conference titles. Club sports and intramurals are growing in popularity, and students stay fit in the two-story Welch Fitness Center.

For a small school, DePauw offers a multitude of opportunities, balancing strong academics with a healthy dose of school spirit and a wealth of opportunities to lead—whether in one of the abundant extracurricular activities or by blazing a trail through study abroad. "It's the kind of place where your professors know your name, your classmates push you to be your best, and there's always something meaningful to get involved in, whether it's leadership, service, athletics, or creative expression," says a happy senior. "Even though it's a small liberal arts college, DePauw doesn't feel small in impact."

Overlaps

Butler, Denison, Knox, Miami (OH), Ohio Wesleyan, St. Olaf, Wabash, Wooster

If You Apply To ›

DePauw: Early decision I and II, early action I and II, regular decision. SATs or ACTs: optional (required for students applying to Honor Scholars and Fellows programs). Accepts the Common Application.

Dickinson College

272 W High Street, Carlisle, PA 17013

With traditions dating to the 18th century, Dickinson occupies a historic setting in the foothills of central Pennsylvania. Curriculum blends traditional liberal arts values with attention to international studies, foreign languages, study abroad, and sustainable development. With students of color, international students, and free spirits now more numerous, Dickinson is shedding its image as a preppy haven. Competes head-to-head with nearby Gettysburg.

Dickinson College won its charter in 1783, just six days after the Treaty of Paris recognized the United States as a sovereign nation, and this small liberal arts school has been blazing trails ever since. The moving force behind it was Dr. Benjamin Rush, the famous physician and signer of the Declaration of Independence who convinced John Dickinson, the then governor of Pennsylvania, to lend his name to the new school. Rush's founding mission was "to provide a useful education in the liberal arts and sciences." Now, administrators are also focused on global education, civic engagement, and attracting the best and brightest academic talent.

Almost all of Dickinson's Georgian buildings are crafted from local gray limestone, which lends pleasing architectural consistency. The 144-acre campus is part of the historic district of Carlisle, an economically prosperous central Pennsylvania county seat nestled in a fertile valley. A $19 million, LEED Platinum–certified residence hall houses 130 upperclassmen in single and double rooms. Dickinson has been a leader in sustainability education, and the college has achieved carbon neutrality.

To help students understand how the liberal arts fit into the broader world, Dickinson supplements standard distribution requirements with courses in multidisciplinary and cross-cultural studies, such as sustainability and U.S. and global diversity. It has created programs in food studies, justice studies, and health studies that have significant humanities components. The required First-Year Seminar introduces new students to college-level writing and critical thinking through interdisciplinary courses such as Ideas That Have Shaped the World, Storytelling with Food in France, and Natural Disasters and You. Sophomores choose from more than 40 majors, and 45 percent of seniors complete a capstone program.

> "Peers help each other become the best students they can be."

Dickinson is best known for its workshop approach to science education, its outstanding and comprehensive international education program, and the depth of its foreign language program, with more than a dozen languages offered, including Arabic, Chinese, Japanese, Hebrew, Italian, and Portuguese. The college's environmental studies and environmental science department is well respected. International business and management, one of Dickinson's most popular majors, involves coursework in economics, history, and financial analysis, as well as internships and overseas education. Other popular majors include biology, political science, psychology, English, data analytics, and international studies.

In addition, Dickinson offers certificates in food studies, social innovation and entrepreneurship, security studies, health studies, global preparedness (with the Army ROTC), and ballet (with the Central Pennsylvania Youth Ballet). Students can gain a hands-on understanding of human culture and behavior by studying archaeology in far-flung locations like Greece and Bolivia. Interdisciplinary programs such as neuroscience and workshop physics offer chances to carry out research with faculty

Website: www.dickinson.edu
Location: Small Town
Private
Total Enrollment: 2,277
Undergraduates: 2,270
Male/Female: 40/60
Financial Aid: 89%
Pell Grant: 12%
Expense: Pr $ $ $ $
Student Loans: 58%
Average Debt: $ $
Applicants: 7,258
Accepted: 42%
Enrolled: 21%
Grad in 6 Years: 80%
Returning First-years: 92%
Academics: ✍ ✍ ✍ ✍
Social: 🗩 🗩 🗩
Q of L: ★ ★ ★
Admissions: (717) 245-1231
Email Address:
  admissions@dickinson.edu

Strong Programs:
Environmental Science
Foreign Languages
International Business and
  Management
International Studies
Political Science
Psychology
Quantitative Economics
Workshop Physics

members. Dual-degree programs in engineering and law are available with partner institutions, and students interested in pursuing graduate studies in areas like business management and public health may partake in special advising programs.

Academics are demanding, but the environment is supportive. "Peers help each other become the best students they can be instead of trying to compete for the best grades," explains a sophomore. Sixty-five percent of classes have fewer than 20 students, allowing first-years easy access to their professors, who are highly rated by students. "I have had some of the most caring and intelligent professors," says a junior. The Advising, Internships, & Career Center receives positive reviews as well: "After each appointment, I feel enthusiastic and hopeful about my professional interests," cheers a neuroscience major.

Dickinson sponsors faculty-directed study abroad programs in 13 countries around the world and offers more than 50 partner programs on six continents; around half of the students participate. Options include academic year, semester, and summer programs; globally integrated courses that include a short-term international field experience; and specialized programs such as Mosaics, which combine domestic study with international study. Ninety-two percent of Dickinsonians complete an internship, externship, or research, service learning, or field-experience course. Thirty percent participate in community service projects.

At Dickinson, says a sociology major, "There are a lot of determined, passionate students who are committed to the concept of making these four years mean something." Twenty-nine percent of the student body hails from the Keystone State. Black students account for 4 percent of the student population, Asian Americans 5 percent, Hispanics/Latinos 8 percent, and multiracial students 5 percent; international students represent 12 percent. Dickinson has been enrolling a growing number of students of color and international students, especially through partnerships with the Posse Foundation, the Philadelphia Futures Foundation, and schools and foundations abroad, but some students note that the atmosphere on campus does not feel as much like an integrated, inclusive community as they would like. Dickinson awards merit scholarships averaging $26,800 but no athletic scholarships.

Dickinson students live in college housing throughout their four years. A senior reports that "freshman and sophomore housing is not typically as nice" as the accommodations for upperclassmen, which include small houses and apartments. Twenty-three percent of incoming students choose to participate in living/learning communities as extensions of the First-Year Seminar program. The organic college farm manages 80 acres and supplies produce to the dining hall, the college's in-town grab-and-go store and a local food bank and farmers market. It also serves as a living laboratory and work-study opportunity for students interested in sustainable development. Aside from the main cafeteria, there are café and snack-bar options, and "several provisions are met (e.g., kosher, vegan, nut-free, organic, gluten-free)," says a senior. At Denim Coffee at the Quarry, the college has partnered with a local coffee shop to provide gourmet brews and sandwiches. In response to student protests over inadequate handling of sexual assault cases, Dickinson's administration has made several amendments to its sexual misconduct policies, procedures, and reporting process.

"Whether it is a club, a sport, or a floor in your dorm, you must get involved in something to have a good social life," advises a political science major. Fraternities and sororities attract 8 percent of the men and 24 percent of the women, and they throw parties in houses that are owned and maintained by the college. Kegs aren't permitted in any college housing, and four underage drinking incidents will get you suspended.

"Drinking and parties are a large part of the social culture on campus, especially on the weekends," says a student. Each fall brings an arts festival and a well-attended drag show, and Springfest gives students one last blast before finals with a carnival and concert.

Carlisle is 20 miles from the Pennsylvania state capital of Harrisburg and has plenty of eclectic cafés, restaurants, shops, and festivals. "The town is very cute and fun to eat out and walk around in," says an English major. Big Brothers Big Sisters, the Alpha Phi Omega community service fraternity, and other programs help bring the school and community together. In the spring and early fall, beaches in Maryland, Delaware, and New Jersey beckon; they're just a two- to three-hour drive. Come winter, good skiing is half an hour away. Nature lovers will enjoy hiking the nearby Appalachian Trail. For those craving urban stimulation, the best road trips are to Philadelphia, New York, and Washington, D.C. All are accessible by bus or train—a good thing, since first-years can't have cars.

Dickinson students get riled up for any Division III Red Devils match against top rival Franklin & Marshall, and two annual football battles—the Conestoga Wagon game against Franklin & Marshall and the Little Brown Bucket match against Gettysburg—are popular traditions. A perennial champ, the men's lacrosse team has won several recent Centennial Conference championships; men's and women's soccer and track and field are also strong. About 42 percent of students take part in club sports; equestrian, ultimate Frisbee, and the Outing Club are the most popular. Recreational events like trivia nights and dodgeball tournaments are an option too.

Although Dickinson has been growing and evolving for more than two centuries, traditions remain strong. Seniors still share a champagne toast before graduation. And the steps of Old West, the first college building, are still used only twice a year—in the fall at the convocation ceremony that welcomes new students and in the spring for commencement. Dickinson continues to honor Rush's global vision, with its wealth of study abroad options and its demand that students cross the traditional borders of academic disciplines to grasp the interrelated nature of knowledge.

Overlaps

American, Bucknell, Connecticut College, Denison, Franklin & Marshall, Gettysburg, Lafayette, Skidmore

If You Apply To ›

Dickinson: Early decision I and II, regular decision. SATs or ACTs: optional. Accepts the Common Application with supplement.

Drew University

36 Madison Avenue, Madison, NJ 07940

From Drew's wooded perch in suburban New Jersey, Manhattan is only a 30-minute train ride away, and Wall Street, the UN, and Broadway are common destinations for Drew interns. Drew is the state's only prominent liberal arts college and one of the few in the greater New York City area. About two-thirds of the students are from Jersey, and Drew is still struggling to develop a national identity.

Founded more than 155 years ago as a Methodist university by Daniel Drew, a financier and railroad tycoon, Drew University has grown into a place where an emphasis on hands-on learning, research, and internships is just as important as performance in the classroom. The university encourages theater and the arts to thrive, promotes internships in New York City, and sends its students abroad for semester and monthlong educational ventures. As part of its reinforced commitment to global

Website: www.drew.edu
Location: Suburban
Private
Total Enrollment: 1,789
Undergraduates: 1,523
Male/Female: 44/56

There is a 21-and-over pub on campus, as well as two coffeehouses.

education, Drew has heavily recruited international students in recent years. As a junior explains, students here benefit from "both a traditional college experience and professional excellence due to our proximity to New York City."

The school occupies 186 acres of peaceful woodland in the upscale suburb of Madison and is known as the "University in the Forest." Fifty-six campus buildings peek through splendid oak trees and boast classic and contemporary styles, a physical reflection of Drew's respect for both scholarly traditions and progressive education. Recent campus renovation projects have included the Commons Dining Hall and the International Student Center.

In addition to an array of distribution requirements, Drew's general education program includes a first-year experience dubbed the Drew Seminar, the highlight of which is a daylong, faculty-led, course-related field trip to Manhattan. As part of an initiative known as Launch, first-years also take a workshop on career development and academic success in the spring. Launch guarantees all Drew students complete at least two hands-on learning experiences, such as internships, lab research, creative projects, New York City semester, and study abroad; students select their own mentorship team of faculty, counselors, and alumni to guide them through their four years. As seniors, students complete a capstone experience.

"The academic climate is well-balanced and constructive."

Political science is among Drew's strongest undergraduate departments, and future politicos can take advantage of off-campus opportunities in New York City, Washington, D.C., and London. Other popular majors include business, psychology, media and communication, and biology. Among recently added undergrad programs are cybersecurity, accounting, and finance, and the school has introduced B.S. degrees for some majors, as well as a new five-year B.A./M.S. in data science. The touted theatre arts department works closely with the Tectonic Theater Project in New York City and other theaters to produce plays that are written, directed, and designed by students. Several dual-degree programs allow students to earn a bachelor's from Drew and a graduate degree in areas like engineering, law, nursing, and medicine from Rutgers, Duke, Columbia, and other universities. Intent on using New York City as a classroom whenever possible, Drew offers seven intensive semesters—Wall Street, Broadway, the United Nations, Media and Communications, Social Impact, Contemporary Art, and Museums and Cultural Management—that take students into the city each week for real-world learning experiences.

"The academic climate is well-balanced and constructive, with an emphasis on doing well but without an unhealthy amount pressure," shares a political science major. Students take their academics seriously and rate their professors highly. Small class sizes and extensive enrichment opportunities allow students to develop personal relationships with faculty. "No student goes unnoticed; everyone bonds with a mentor on campus," says a sociology major. The Research Institute for Scientists Emeriti offers opportunities for students to do research with distinguished retired industrial scientists; 70 percent of students participate in some kind of research. Participants in the Baldwin Honors program take specialized classes, attend receptions with guest speakers, and complete an honors thesis. Drew's Center for Civic Engagement supports teaching, research, scholarship, art, and other university-based activities that benefit communities. Farther afield, Drew offers eight to 12 faculty-led study abroad TREC (Travel, Rethink, Explore, Connect) courses during winter, spring, and summer breaks each year, in addition to lengthier options through partner programs.

"Drew students are a welcoming bunch; we like new people, we like new ideas, and we like new ideals," observes a junior. About two-thirds of undergraduates are from New Jersey, and most attended public high schools; 11 percent are international. Eleven percent of students are Black, 7 percent are Hispanic/Latino, 4 percent are Asian American, and 4 percent are multiracial. "My favorite thing about Drew is that although people are politically and socially active, they are more interested in listening to what others have to say than in projecting their own opinions," says a senior. Thirty-six percent of new students receive Pell Grants. Merit awards average $22,700, but there are no athletic scholarships.

Seventy-eight percent of the students live in university housing, which is guaranteed for four years and includes both single-sex and co-ed dorms, theme houses, and, for upperclassmen, townhouses. A lottery gives housing preference to seniors and juniors, making room selection "an easy process," according to a sophomore. Most first-years reside in dorms situated at the back of campus, and 40 percent choose to take part in living/learning communities. Students report that a "massive renovation" to the Commons dining hall has vastly improved the quality of meals; "There's always something that I can look forward to eating," says a junior. As for safety, a senior says, "Campus is very safe, but Drew could be better at acknowledging sexual assault." On the other hand, says a junior, "We have an amazing career services and mental health team."

With no Greek life, a sophomore explains, "The athletic teams and theatre groups hold the most vibrant parties on campus," and for those who don't care to party, "Our Office of Student Activities supplements student-run programming by bringing in comedians, musicians, slam poets, and other performers every Thursday to engage the community." There is a 21-and-over pub on campus, as well as two coffeehouses. The Shakespeare Theatre of New Jersey is in residence on campus part of every year and offers both performances and internships. The long-standing First Annual Picnic, held on the last day of classes, provides an opportunity to enjoy free food, carnival games, and music.

"Drew students are a welcoming bunch."

About half of students volunteer in local and international activities such as Mentors at Drew and working with children in the Dominican Republic. The commuter town of Madison doesn't have the amenities of larger metropolitan areas, of course, but there are several unique shops and restaurants within walking distance of campus. One student says the town "is a nice college town according to my parents but not to students. Everything closes up pretty early." Nearby Morristown is more of a college place. New York City's Pennsylvania Station is less than an hour away by commuter train, and Philadelphia, the Jersey Shore, and the Delaware River are close by.

Interest in Drew's 25 Division III varsity teams has grown as the Rangers have become more successful. Women's tennis, men's basketball, and men's golf are recent Landmark Conference winners. The competitive men's and women's fencing teams parry with the likes of Duke and Cornell. Intramural and club sports range from basketball and floor hockey to rugby and eSports, and special recreation events like Hunger Games Dodgeball and the Rock Paper Scissors Tournament are student favorites.

"The athletic teams and theatre groups hold the most vibrant parties."

Drew offers its small body of students a wide range of opportunities, excellent access to the riches of New York City, and plenty of personal attention in a classic liberal arts structure. "I think Drew is like the coffeehouse of colleges," a theatre major muses. "There's always intellectual stuff going on, but it's very cozy." Not too bad for a school in the forest.

Overlaps

Drexel, Fairleigh Dickinson, Ithaca, Montclair State, Muhlenberg, The College of New Jersey, Rutgers, Ursinus

If You Apply To ›

Drew: Early decision I and II, early action, regular decision. SATs or ACTs: optional. Accepts the Common Application with supplement.

Drexel University

3141 Chestnut Street, Philadelphia, PA 19104

Drexel is a streetwise, no-nonsense technical university in the heart of Philadelphia. Like Lehigh, Drexel also offers programs in business and arts and sciences, and its most distinctive offering is the Westphal College of Media Arts and Design. A financial bargain compared to other leading technical schools, Drexel has adjusted its aggressive expansion plans of recent years in an effort to increase yield and graduation rates and plans to switch from quarters to a semester calendar in 2027. Check out the co-op program.

Website: www.drexel.edu
Location: City Center
Private
Total Enrollment: 16,687
Undergraduates: 12,201
Male/Female: 51/47
Financial Aid: 84%
Pell Grant: 26%
Expense: Pr $ $
Student Loans: 67%
Average Debt: $ $ $ $
Applicants: 37,314
Accepted: 79%
Enrolled: 8%
Grad in 6 Years: 78%
Returning First-years: 90%
Academics: ✍ ✍ ✍
Social: 💬 💬
Q of L: ★ ★ ★
Admissions: (800) 237-3935
Email Address: enroll@drexel.edu

Strong Programs:
Architecture
Business
Computer Science
Engineering
Film and Television
Game Design and Production
Nursing
Physics

For career-minded students who want to bypass the soul-searching of their liberal arts counterparts, Drexel University offers both solid academics and an innovative co-op program that combines high-tech academics with paying job opportunities—a mix that's particularly appealing in today's economic climate. The school dates to 1891, when Anthony J. Drexel, a Philadelphia financier and philanthropist, set up the Drexel Institute of Art, Science, and Industry to prepare young men and women to work in the emerging industrial society. Drexel began offering co-op education in 1919. "If you want a good job, you go to Drexel and you do co-op," asserts a student.

"Drexel's campus is impressive for its downtown Philadelphia location, with gardens and greenery on every block," says a student, "but the campus is woven tightly into the fabric of the city." The 123-acre campus, adjacent to the University of Pennsylvania, lies in what is now one of the most desirable parts of Philadelphia, with plenty of restaurants and stores. A multiphase neighborhood remake includes a $3.5 billion "Innovation Neighborhood" along the Schuylkill River rail yards that houses new research facilities and incubator space. The campus's older buildings are simple and fashioned of brick; most are modern and in good condition. Additional facilities include the Center City Campus for the College of Nursing and Health Professions.

> "Drexel's campus is impressive for its downtown Philadelphia location."

Cooperative education is the hallmark of Drexel's curriculum, which alternates periods of full-time study and full-time employment for four or five years, providing students with six to 18 months of job experience before they graduate. The co-op possibilities, which 95 percent of undergraduates take advantage of, are unlimited: Students can pursue co-ops virtually anywhere in the U.S. or in 28 other countries. Students in five-year programs spend their first and senior years on campus; the three intervening years (sophomore, prejunior, and junior) usually consist of six months of work and six months of school. A 10-week preparatory course, Co-op 101, covers such topics as skills assessment, ethics in the workplace, résumé writing, interviewing skills, and stress management. Most co-ops are paid, and the median six-month salary for co-op students is more than $22,000. And although some students complain that jobs can turn out to be six months of busywork, most enjoy making important contacts in their potential fields and learning while earning.

Grappling with a budget shortfall and declining enrollment in 2024, Drexel made staff cuts and is integrating several of its colleges and schools. The university plans to adopt a semester calendar beginning in August 2027, and new core curriculum requirements will be introduced, embedding interdisciplinary and experiential learning into all undergraduate majors. Until then, however, Drexel continues to operate year-round. "I would describe the climate as intense but manageable," says one senior. "Being on a quarter system is rigorous at times." Flexibility in requirements varies by college, but in the first year, everyone must take English composition, mathematics, and two one-credit courses: one that introduces students to university resources and one on civic engagement in the local community. Engineering majors must also complete the Drexel Engineering Curriculum, which integrates math, physics, chemistry, and engineering to make sure that even techies enter the workforce well-rounded and able to write as well as they can compute and design. Students enjoy the Hagerty Library, which offers a 24-hour study space and plenty of room for group work. What's more, each entering first-year is assigned a "personal librarian" charged with helping them make the best use of library facilities. Professors receive high praise from most and are noted for their accessibility and warmth. Says one student, "The only things that teaching assistants run are labs and study sessions." Forty-two percent of classes have fewer than 20 students.

The most popular majors are in business, engineering, health sciences, and computer science. Drexel's greatest strength is its College of Engineering and Computing, where the materials science, electrical, and architectural engineering programs are standouts. Other noteworthy programs include nursing, business, and the Westphal College of Media Arts and Design's majors in architecture, game design and production, and film and television; the College of Arts and Sciences is well recognized for theoretical and atmospheric physics. An honors college is available for those who seek an even more challenging experience, and about 8 percent of undergrads study abroad.

Drexel has long shed its reputation as an easy-admission commuter college. According to one sophomore, Drexel students are "not afraid of hard work because we do it all the time, even when we're exhausted." Fifty-four percent of the student body is Pennsylvanian, with another large chunk of students from adjacent New Jersey, and the campus tends to lean right politically. The international student population is 9 percent. Asian Americans account for 24 percent, Black students 10 percent, Hispanics/Latinos 9 percent, and multiracial students 5 percent. In addition to need-based financial aid, merit scholarships averaging $20,600 and around 200 athletic scholarships are awarded to qualified students. Community college graduates from Pennsylvania and New Jersey receive a 50 percent discount on tuition.

First-year students live in one of nine co-ed residence halls, including a luxurious high-rise, but most upperclassmen reside in nearby apartments or fraternity houses. Overall, just 19 percent of the students live in the dorms. Students say the two main dining centers offer a variety of "adequate" food. If all else fails, nomadic food trucks park around campus, providing quick lunches. Students are encouraged to use a shuttle bus between the library and dorms at night, and access to dorms, the library, and the physical education center is restricted to students with IDs, so most say they feel safe on campus.

With so many students living off campus and the city of Philadelphia at their disposal, Drexel tends to be a bit deserted on weekends. Friday-night flicks on campus are cheap and popular with those who stay around, and dorms sponsor floor parties. The dozen or so fraternities, which recruit 11 percent of the men, also contribute to the party scene, especially for first-years; the handful of smaller sororities attract 8 percent of the women. "Greek life is relatively small, so there are plenty of other ways to be involved socially," a senior says. "There's no pressure to drink," adds a communication major, and campus policies are strict; dorms require those of age to sign in alcohol and limit the quantities they may bring in.

Drexel's co-op program often undermines any sense of class unity and can strain personal relationships. Activities that depend on some continuity of enrollment for success—music, drama, student government, athletics—suffer most. "It's hard to get people involved because of the amount of schoolwork and co-ops," says one student. Even so, the university sponsors 18 Division I sports teams, competing in the Colonial Athletic Association. There is no football team, but the Dragons men's and women's basketball, crew, and wrestling teams are strong. "Our biggest rivalry is our feud with Delaware," admits one frenzied student. "We delight in sacrificing blue plastic chickens!"—Delaware's mascot. An extensive intramural program serves all students, and joggers can head for the steps of the Philadelphia Art Museum, just as Rocky did in the movies. Students take full advantage of their urban location by frequenting clubs, restaurants, cultural attractions, and shops in Philadelphia, easily accessible by public transportation.

Aspiring poets, musicians, and historians may find Drexel a bit disorienting. But future computer scientists, engineers, and other technical minds could get a fantastic jump-start on their careers, thanks to the university's unique approach to learning inside and outside the classroom. As one satisfied student explains, "The terms are intense, the activities unlimited, but Drexel graduates are surely among the most capable and motivated individuals I have ever met. When I graduate, I will be prepared and proud of it."

If You Apply To ›

Drexel: Early decision, early action, regular decision. Accepts the Common Application. Apply to particular school or program. Please consult Drexel's website for the most up-to-date information regarding standardized test requirements.

Duke University

2080 Duke University Road, Durham, NC 27708

What fun to be at Duke—face painted blue, rocking Cameron Indoor Stadium as the Blue Devils storm the court. The most prestigious private university in the South, Duke is academically competitive with the Ivies and Stanford but offers a distinctive brand with an emphasis on interdisciplinary and international perspectives and civic engagement. Strong in engineering and science as well as the humanities. DukeEngage service program dazzles. Generous in financial aid to neediest students, but not much socioeconomic diversity.

Duke University is one of the handful of elite U.S. colleges and universities where strong academics and championship-caliber sports teams manage to coexist. It might be south of the Mason–Dixon line, but it has long since outgrown its regional roots and stopped looking for models among certain ancient and prestigious Northeastern schools known for the erstwhile foliage on their walls. Faculty and students work across academic disciplines, travel the globe, and devote countless hours to implementing their school's motto of "knowledge in the service of society." Duke offers much to cheer about, says one senior, including "a diverse student body, challenging academics, world-renowned professors, research opportunities, and an immense amount of school spirit."

Founded in 1838 as the Union Institute (later Trinity College), Duke University is young for a school of its stature. It sprouted up in 1924 thanks to a stack of tobacco-stained dollars known as the Duke Endowment. Duke's campus in the North Carolina Piedmont is divided into two main sections, West and East, and with an additional 7,000 acres of adjacent forest, it offers enough open space to satisfy even the most diehard outdoors enthusiast. West Campus, the hub of the university, is laid out in spacious quadrangles and dominated by the impressive Gothic chapel, a symbol of the university's Methodist tradition. Constructed in the 1930s, West includes collegiate Gothic residential and classroom quads, the administration building, the huge Perkins Library, and the student union. East Campus, built in the 1920s, consists primarily of Georgian redbrick buildings. East and West are connected by buses that shuttle between them along wooded Campus Drive.

Students opt for one of two undergraduate schools: the Pratt School of Engineering and Trinity College of Arts & Sciences. The school's engineering programs—particularly electrical and biomedical—are national standouts. Natural sciences, most notably ecology, biology, and neuroscience, are also first-rate, and proximity to the Medical Center enhances study in biochemistry and global health. Duke's Sanford School of Public Policy offers an interdisciplinary major that trains aspiring public servants and future leaders of nonprofit organizations, government agencies, and other bodies that shape public life. Internships and apprenticeships are a big part of the program. Duke's English and dance programs are notable, but students say the language offerings can be weak. Duke has more than 60 interdisciplinary centers, including the Duke Global Health Institute, the Nicholas Institute for Environmental Policy Solutions, and the John Hope Franklin Humanities Institute. Computer science attracts the most majors, followed by public policy studies, biology, and economics.

Trinity College's curriculum, part of the traditional undergraduate coursework known as Program I, requires courses in five general areas of knowledge: arts, literature, and performance; civilizations; social sciences; natural sciences; and quantitative studies. Students must also fulfill requirements in six modes of inquiry, including foreign language; writing; research; ethical inquiry; science, technology, and society; and cross-cultural inquiry. All students complete three Small Group Learning Experiences: one seminar course during the first year, on topics such as Politics on Camera and How Hospitals Work, and two more as upperclassmen. Those who wish to explore subjects outside and between usual majors and minors may choose Program II, to which they are admitted after proposing a topic, question, or theme for which they plan an individualized curriculum with faculty advisors and deans.

When college counselors say Duke is hot, they're not referring to the boiling temperatures in the South. "The workload is heavy, but, because of the highly collaborative environment, it is manageable," says a public policy major. Seventy-one percent of classes have fewer than 20 students, and the university focuses resources on undergraduate education and having senior professors

> "The workload is heavy, but . . . it is manageable."

teach more classes. A senior says, "Faculty members are accessible, especially through a program called FLUNCH, where you are able to have a meal with a faculty member on Duke's dime." The highly regarded FOCUS program offers first-year students two linked seminars with no more than 18 students clustered around a single broad interdisciplinary theme, such as geopolitics and culture or science and the public; participants also live together in the same residence hall and attend weekly dinners with faculty. It is "an incredible opportunity to engage with the university's top professors," a senior reports. The Bass Connections program gives undergraduates a chance to work with faculty and graduate students in interdisciplinary, research-based project teams in areas such as global health and energy and environment.

Those who wish to see the world before embarking on their undergraduate career may apply to the Duke Gap Year Program; accepted students receive between $5,000 and $15,000 toward the cost of their chosen gap year program. More than half of

(continued)

Applicants: 51,795
Accepted: 6%
Enrolled: 59%
Grad in 6 Years: 97%
Returning First-years: 98%
Academics: ✍ ✍ ✍ ✍ ✍
Social: 🗩 🗩 🗩 🗩
Q of L: ★ ★ ★ ★
Admissions: (919) 684-3214
Email Address: undergrad-admissions@duke.edu

Strong Programs:
Biology
Dance
Ecology
Engineering
English
Global Health
Neuroscience
Public Policy Studies

Duke's undergrads study abroad, and there are ample opportunities for those who want a break from campus life without leaving the country. DukeEngage, an ambitious and innovative program backed by a $30 million endowment and unique among elite universities, supports students willing to spend summers working on projects ranging from building schools in Kenya to working with Gulf Coast flood victims. About a quarter of all undergrads participate in the program, which has become a centerpiece of the school's commitment to "knowledge in service to society."

The FOCUS program offers first-year students two linked seminars clustered around a single broad interdisciplinary theme.

"Students tend to be extremely driven, upper-middle-class, and focused on succeeding far after college," says one public policy major. Seventeen percent of Duke students are from North Carolina and qualify for tuition assistance, and the Northeastern corridor sends a fair-sized contingent, as does California. Eleven percent of undergraduates hail from overseas. Undergraduate women sometimes complain about the pressure they feel to demonstrate, in the words of a (female) former president, "effortless perfection" in all respects. Despite the unmistakable air of wealth on campus, about two-thirds of the students come from public high schools. Nine percent are Black, 11 percent are Hispanic/Latino, 22 percent are Asian American, and 7 percent are multiracial. Students of different ethnicities and races tend to "self-segregate," students say, producing little tension but also little interaction. The Center for Race Relations works to improve the way Duke educates its students about diversity and conflict resolution.

Duke admits students without regard to financial need and meets 100 percent of their demonstrated need. The university has eliminated loans from financial aid packages for families with incomes below $40,000 a year, and families from North or South Carolina with incomes below $65,000 receive grants for tuition, meals, housing and other fees; if local families' total income is less than $150,000, they receive full tuition grants. In addition to lots of athletic scholarships, the university also offers a small number of merit scholarships, including those offered through the Rubenstein Scholars Program for high-achieving, first-generation students from low-income backgrounds.

"Faculty members are accessible."

Duke undergrads are required to live on campus for three years; overall, 84 percent stay in university-owned housing. Students live in residence halls or quads that house both independent students and members of selective living groups such as fraternities. First-years all reside in dorms on the East Campus along with a faculty member and their family. "The dorms look like castles on the outside and feel like Harry Potter," says a junior, who adds that the new dorms "are like five-star hotels." Sophomores move to West Campus, where there are also special-interest dorms focused on themes such as women's studies, the arts, languages, and community service. Seniors can move off campus. Students give good ratings to campus security.

The university focuses resources on undergraduate education and having senior professors teach more classes.

Duke has been engaged in a massive physical expansion in recent years aimed at enhancing students' creature comforts, including a 72,000-square-foot, state-of-the-art Student Wellness Center. The glass-fronted Brodhead Center for Campus Life recently underwent an $80 million renovation, and the main dining hall, known to students as the West Union, offers options catered by local chefs and restauranteurs. Consistent with Durham's reputation as a foodie haven, the university boasts the most lavish and, students say, costly—the local term is "wuflation," a word invented by students based on the dining hall's name—dining on any college campus. Off-campus restaurants are linked to the Duke meal plan.

"Duke students are the type who will start a club if they are interested in something that nobody else is doing, work hard on a paper late into the night, and then go out Thursday, Friday, and Saturday," says a public policy major. Students agree that most social life takes place on campus or in surrounding houses and apartments. Although it has been pushed away from the center of campus, "the Greek scene dominates," says a history major. Fraternities and sororities attract 30 percent of the men and 42 percent of the women, respectively. Fraternity parties are open to everyone, and the free shuttle bus service that connects the school's various dorm and apartment complexes runs until 4 a.m. "There is a strong drinking and party culture on campus, though students are not pressured to participate," one sophomore reports.

Duke is also a culturally active campus; theater groups thrive, and the Nasher Museum of Art, with its world-class exhibits by Picasso, Calder, and El Greco, among others, has become a popular social hub. The Springternational festival brings in live bands and vendors peddling local crafts and exotic foods each spring, and the traditional Joe College Day has been revived as a daylong fall affair filled with food, arts and crafts, and music.

Durham is a small, working-class city that has had its share of racial tensions but also boasts a vibrant Black middle class and strong political leadership. Duke as an institution has been active in the community, especially in public schools, and hundreds of undergrads are involved in service learning, tutoring, and related activities. "Everyone is involved in volunteer work," says one student. Downtown Durham is booming, with old tobacco warehouses converted into restaurants, stores,

"Students tend to be extremely driven, upper-middle-class, and focused on succeeding."

offices, and apartments. The town is proud of its Durham Bulls, the local minor league baseball team, which coined the term "bullpen" and inspired the iconic 1988 baseball film Bull Durham. No one misses the irony of the fact that Durham, once known as the "City of Tobacco," now bills itself as the "City of Medicine."

Duke's official motto is Eruditio et Religio only to a few straitlaced administrators; everyone else knows it as Eruditio et Basketballio, which for practical purposes translates as "Go to hell, Carolina"—meaning UNC at Chapel Hill, Duke's archrival in the rough-and-tough Atlantic Coast Conference. At games, students transform into the legendary Cameron Crazies and get the best courtside seats, where they make life miserable for the visiting team. The Blue Devils won the national Division I men's basketball championship five times under fabled coach Mike Krzyzewski, who retired in 2022, and went to the Final Four in 2025. Sports-crazed Blue Devils erect a temporary tent city to vie for the best seats. This is far from roughing it—students form groups to hold their places so that some fraction can go to class and keep their peers who hold down the fort on track academically. "There is something magical about Duke basketball, and the feeling of being in the student section with the Cameron Crazies during the Duke–UNC game is something that can't be captured in words," gushes one fan. Men's lacrosse and women's golf are national powerhouses as well. The previously hapless football team now plays in a renovated stadium complete with luxury boxes for Iron Duke supporters and earns occasional bowl bids. Intramurals are big, with roughly 950 teams, and operate on two levels of competitiveness; more than 40 club sports are available as well.

Meandering around Duke's up-to-date campus, you can see the latest technology, but you can also hear the whisper of the Old South through those big old trees and stunning architecture. In addition to a sophisticated blending of old and new, Duke also does an impressive job combining sports and academia and producing students who almost define the term "well-rounded." With its distinctive blend of interdisciplinarity, internationalization, and civic engagement, Duke has fashioned a powerful new model for higher education in the 21st century.

Overlaps

Brown, University of Chicago, Columbia, Dartmouth, Harvard, Penn, Stanford, Yale

If You Apply To ›

Duke: Early decision, regular decision. Accepts the Common Application with supplement. Please consult Duke's website for the most up-to-date information regarding standardized test requirements.

801 National Road West, Richmond, IN 47374

Earlham is a member of the proud circle of solid Midwestern liberal arts colleges that includes Beloit, Grinnell, Kenyon, and Oberlin, to name just a few. Smallest of the group, but stands out for attracting a highly diverse student body to its conservative southern Indiana location. Earlham is distinctive for its Quaker orientation, welcoming environment, and international perspective.

Website: www.earlham.edu
Location: Small City
Private
Total Enrollment: 688
Undergraduates: 665
Male/Female: 46/49
Financial Aid: 95%
Pell Grant: 40%
Expense: Pr $ $
Student Loans: 47%
Average Debt: $ $
Applicants: 2,075
Accepted: 73%
Enrolled: 14%
Grad in 6 Years: 69%
Returning First-years: 77%
Academics: ✍ ✍ ✍ ✍
Social: 🗩 🗩 🗩
Q of L: ★ ★ ★ ★ ★
Admissions: (765) 983-1600
Email Address:
  admissions@earlham.edu

Strong Programs:
Biochemistry
Business
Computer Science
International Studies
Japanese Studies
Peace and Global Studies
Prehealth
Psychology

Earlham is a study in contrasts—a top-notch liberal arts college in a relatively conservative city that few could place on a map and an institution that in the 21st century remains true to the traditions of community, peace, and justice that are hallmarks of its Religious Society of Friends (Quaker) heritage. Earlham's curriculum and programs engage students with the world by exposing them to classmates from more than 50 nations and offering some 200 academic courses that incorporate an international perspective. In a "nod to our Quaker values of respect for persons, integrity, peace and justice, community, and simplicity," says an administrator, "students and faculty are on a first-name basis." Varied study abroad programs provide close faculty involvement and a thoughtful focus on cross-cultural perspectives. "We care about each other, and you will always be heard," says a computer science major. "You're learning how to think critically and act with purpose alongside people who are thoughtful and engaged."

Earlham was established in 1859 in the wake of the Great Migration of Quakers from Eastern states that took place in the first half of the 19th century. The college's 800-acre campus sits in the small, quintessentially Midwestern city of Richmond,

> **"You're learning how to think critically and act with purpose."**

just a short distance from Cincinnati and Indianapolis. Georgian-style buildings dominate, surrounded by mature trees and plantings, while the Japanese gardens symbolize the college's long friendship and closeness with Japan. Newer construction includes a $1 million renovation of the Runyan student center, which began in 2025.

To graduate, students must complete general education requirements in the arts, analytical reasoning, wellness, scientific inquiry, foreign language, and diversity. All students take a reading- and writing-focused first-year seminar and complete a capstone experience. Business, biochemistry, psychology, biology, and prehealth are some of the strongest and most popular programs. Accounting, engineering, computer science, and museum studies are also standouts. A wide range of interdisciplinary offerings includes peace and global studies, environmental sustainability, and Japanese studies, a field in which Earlham is a national leader. Preprofessional preparation and integrated learning programs are available in such areas as health sciences, education, business and entrepreneurship, and law and social justice.

A computer science major says the academic climate is "extremely supportive, thought-provoking, well-rounded and stimulating." Discussion facilitated by full-time professors rather than lectures or classes taught by teaching assistants is the predominant learning style here, and classes are small—80 percent have fewer than 20 students. "Students can build strong relationships with their professors, who are deeply invested in their academic and personal growth," says a math and business finance major. A quarter of the students join the honors program, which offers special seminars and an enhanced advising process.

The EPIC Advantage program provides every Earlham student with the opportunity to pursue an internship or faculty-guided research experience, on or off campus, typically during the summer before their junior or senior year, that's funded up to $5,000. Earlham offers study abroad programs in more than two dozen countries, including Ecuador, Germany, India, Japan, and New Zealand, most of which are managed by the college and 43 percent of students participate. In a Border Studies program, students live with families in Tucson, Arizona, and take courses focusing on United States–Mexico border issues. Popular May Term classes send students off campus with faculty for one-month intensive courses in various locations around the world. "One of my friends is spending several weeks in Germany with a professor studying ancient fossils in one of the most advanced DNA analysis labs in the world," says one sophomore. "His story is not uncommon for freshmen." About half of students eventually pursue postgraduate study, often after taking some time off for a job or to participate in volunteer or service programs.

Forty percent of the students are Hoosiers; impressively, another 18 percent hail from abroad. Eight percent are Black, with Hispanics/Latinos adding 6 percent, Asian Americans 2 percent, and multiracial students 5 percent. These days, just 3 percent of students are Friends, but traditional Quaker values still permeate this liberal campus. One student notes the contrasts at Earlham are visible within the largely liberal student body: "There are quite a few international students, but the general population of Earlham is white." The student muses Earlham "is uniquely diverse and not diverse at the same time." Merit scholarships averaging $32,000 are available for qualified students; there are no athletic scholarships. The INspire Earlham program offers free tuition to qualified Indiana students whose families earn up to $60,000; 40 percent of incoming first-year students are eligible for Pell Grants.

Ninety-two percent of Earlham students live on campus, with first-years occupying eight traditional residence halls. Mills Hall offers suite-style accommodations. Upperclassmen can opt to live in the dorms, the Campus Village Apartments, or one of 20 themed college houses. Dining facilities receive decent reviews. "Public safety is very strong," notes a studio art and art history major. While a senior offers, "Career advising and mental health services have actually improved" in the past four years.

There are no fraternities or sororities at Earlham, but on-campus activities abound. "Most everything happens on campus, which is great because everything is more open and accessible," a student says. Students enjoy improv comedy, a cappella music, equestrian programs, a lip-synch competition, fall and spring festivals, concerts, and sports. Student groups include numerous religious, ethnic, and cultural organizations, some of which also take the lead on throwing campus parties. Students 21 and over can consume alcohol, although only in their residence hall rooms, and a sophomore says, "While there are often parties on the weekend, it does not exclude you socially if you do not go." Traditions include a challenge for first-years to try to find the glass tomb in the Earlham Cemetery. On EPIC Day, students make presentations about internships or research they've pursued. Day trips to Cincinnati, Indianapolis, or Columbus and weekend visits to other nearby universities are popular diversions.

Though not a college town, the city of Richmond offers standard American and a variety of ethnic restaurants, as well as movie theaters, bowling alleys, golf, and a popular biking and running trail. "Richmond has great opportunities for volunteering or interning with NGOs but is less exciting if you are looking for a happening night life," reports a politics major. Fifty-six percent of students rack up many hours of volunteer service a year.

Earlham's 18 varsity teams (the Quakers) compete in Division III sports in the Heartland Collegiate Athletic Conference. Men's and women's soccer, men's tennis and baseball, and women's volleyball are strong. About a quarter of the students play club and intramural sports, with volleyball and pickleball the most popular.

Earlham students graduate ready to take on the world, thanks to the school's cooperative, can-do spirit, international perspective, and caring student/faculty community—and its commitment to a values-oriented education. "At Earlham," says a senior, "you can always find a space to be yourself and fight for the things you care about."

If You Apply To ›

Earlham: Early decision, early action I and II, regular decision. SATs or ACTs: optional. Accepts the Common Application with supplement.

Eckerd College

4200 54th Avenue South, St. Petersburg, FL 33711

There are few places more tempting to attend than a college with its own stretch of beach on the shores near Tampa Bay. Eckerd's only direct competitor in Florida is Rollins, which has a business school but is otherwise similar. Marine science, environmental studies, and international studies are among Eckerd's biggest draws. The student body is mainly from out of state, with an abundance of Yankee accents.

Attending Eckerd College demands a special sort of willpower. As an international business major explains, "We are right on the water, and it is like going to college in a resort." With free paddleboards, canoes, kayaks, boats, coolers, and tents always available for student use, it's a wonder anyone finds time to study. But study they do, as administrators continue to lure adventurous students to Eckerd with small classes, skilled professors, and a thriving social scene. "It's Eckerd's paradise-like setting that seals the deal for most prospective students," says a sophomore.

Founded in 1958 as Florida Presbyterian College and renamed 14 years later after a generous benefactor (of drugstore fame), Eckerd considers itself nonsectarian. Still, the school maintains a formal "covenant" with the major Presbyterian denomination, from which it receives some funds. The lush, grassy campus is on the tip of a peninsula bounded by the Gulf of Mexico and Tampa Bay, with plenty of flowering bushes, trees, and small ponds—it's not unusual to spot dolphins frolicking in the adjacent waters. Campus buildings are modern, and none are taller than three stories. Highlights include the $25 million, LEED Platinum–rated James Center for Molecular and Life Sciences and the state-of-the-art studios in the Nielsen Center for Visual Arts.

> **"We are right on the water, and it is like going to college in a resort."**

Autumn Term, Eckerd's version of first-year orientation, is a three-week term before the regular fall semester that introduces new students to the academic expectations and social responsibilities of the Eckerd community. First-years also take a Human Experience course in the fall, focusing on topics like justice, power, freedom, and global citizenship, and a First-Year Experience Seminar in the spring. In addition to standard distribution requirements, all students take one course each in environmental and global perspectives and complete at least 40 hours of community service before graduation; service opportunities are built into reflective service-learning courses that are offered in every major. Imagining Justice, the required senior capstone seminar, asks students to draw on what they've learned during college to find solutions to important issues. Seniors present their capstone work at a festival in the spring.

Eckerd students take their coursework seriously, but on the whole, a human development major says, "The atmosphere is relaxed. How could it not be when you can study and sunbathe at the beach?" Popular majors include environmental studies, marine science, animal studies, biology, psychology, chemistry, business administration, international studies, and creative writing. Wet subjects are especially strong. "The close proximity to the ocean gives [marine science] majors a great amount of hands-on, close-up experience," a student says. The Eckerd College Search and Rescue team, for instance, performs more than 500 marine rescues annually. Eckerd was a pioneer of the 4–1–4 term schedule, in which students work on a single project for credit each January. Every student has a faculty mentor, and there are no graduate assistants; 55 percent of classes have fewer than 20 students. "The professors are genuinely interested in what they're teaching, and you can see that passion through their willingness to work with students," says a marine science major.

Each year, 20 to 25 top incoming students are selected to participate in First-Year Research Associateships, receiving stipends of up to $1,000 to work side by side with leading professors on active research projects. A four-year honors program is also available. While St. Petersburg isn't exactly a college town, a side benefit to the school's location is the Academy of Senior Professionals at Eckerd College, a group of savvy senior citizens who mentor undergrads, work with professors on curriculum development, and lead workshops in their areas of expertise. Fifty-four percent of students study abroad, mostly during three-week terms in January and May. Programs are available in more than 300 destinations, including the school's study center in London.

A former Eckerd president once referred to the school's quirky students as "intellectuals in sandals," reports a junior. "I like the quote, and it really works." Another student says Eckerd attracts "friendly, liberal, free-spirited, and intelligent" students who enjoy the great outdoors and care about protecting the environment. Seventy-nine percent of the student body hails from out of state, with a large contingent coming from the Northeast; another 4 percent come from other countries. Hispanics/Latinos account for 10 percent of the student body, Black students 3 percent, Asian Americans 2 percent, and multiracial students 6 percent. Merit scholarships averaging $20,000 and athletic awards are available to qualified students.

> **"The professors are genuinely interested in what they're teaching."**

Eighty-seven percent of students live in the housing quads. First-years usually live in doubles or triples, while suite- and apartment-style residence halls are available for upper-class students. Most campus housing is gender neutral. Waterfront views and beach access are a given, and a sophomore notes, "We have many different types of themed housing, including pet-friendly, all-female, and health and wellness housing options." Vegan and vegetarian options in Eckerd's dining facilities are plentiful; the food generally gets average reviews. A management major explains that given the school's location near a tourist destination, "a security post at the entrance of the school provides a safer environment for students."

"Eckerd is a primarily student-run campus," says a junior, "and there are usually fun and interactive events that happen every Thursday, Friday, and Saturday." Students can partake in concerts, lectures, shows, and games arranged by the student activity board. There are no Greek organizations (a sophomore comments, "We have residence halls named after Greek letters, making fun of the tradition of having frats and sororities"), and weekend parties are usually held in the Kappa, Nu, and

Omega dorms. Kegs and glass bottles are prohibited on campus, and students 21 and over must wear wristbands at campus parties. Students and professors gather regularly for Fridays with Faculty and Friends to enjoy good conversation, food, and root beer floats in the campus pub. The last few weeks of the school year bring Springtopia, featuring major events like the Spring Ball and the Kappa Karnival, with rides, games, and cotton candy galore.

Off campus, students enjoy downtown St. Petersburg's First Friday block parties and Saturday Morning Market. Tampa and St. Pete also offer a Salvador Dalí museum—free for Eckerd students—and professional baseball, football, hockey, and soccer teams. The nightclubs and bars of Latin-flavored Ybor City are about 30 minutes away, and tempting road trips include Orlando's Walt Disney World and Universal Studios theme parks, Miami's South Beach, and that hub of debauchery on the delta, New Orleans.

> **"We have many different types of themed housing, including pet-friendly, all-female, and health and wellness."**

Varsity teams (the Tritons—after a Greek sea god) compete in the Division II Sunshine State Conference. "Men's basketball is the only sport that attracts lots of fans and spectators," a senior says, and for good reasons—the men's and women's teams are both frequent conference winners. The Triton Tip-Off pep rally helps kick off the season. Baseball and women's volleyball (both indoor and beach) are competitive, too, and the co-ed sailing team has claimed several recent divisional and regional titles. Eckerd doesn't have a football team, but popular club sports include rugby, lacrosse, soccer, and ultimate Frisbee.

Eckerd is committed to offering "experiential, service, and international learning" alongside the traditional classroom experience. That mission, combined with a focus on social justice and, of course, all the fun to be had in the Florida sun, gives Eckerd its distinctive flavor. As a sophomore puts it, "We have dogs, we have beaches, we have intense science labs, and tons of research opportunities. If you are serious about working hard and studying and getting tan while doing it, Eckerd is the right place to do it!"

If You Apply To ›

Eckerd: Early action, rolling admissions. Accepts the Common Application with supplement. Please consult Eckerd's website for the most up-to-date information regarding standardized test requirements.

University of Edinburgh: See page 369.

Elon University

100 Campus Drive, Elon, NC 27244

With tough in-state competition from the likes of Duke, Wake Forest, and the UNCs, Elon has put itself on the map with aggressive marketing, a classic colonial-style campus, and a culture of caring. Strong emphasis on global perspectives and active, experiential learning. A counterpart to University of Richmond with medium size, strong preprofessional programs, well-heeled student body, and popularity among Northerners.

Elon University derives its name from the Hebrew word for "oak," and at each year's opening convocation, entering students are given an acorn. Four years later, they are presented with an oak sapling at commencement. It's a charming tradition and a reminder of how things grow and change. With an emphasis on undergraduate research, internships, service learning, study abroad, and leadership—the five Elon Experiences—the university also provides its students with plenty of opportunities to mature intellectually and socially. "Finding a program that really matches your interest and getting involved in research is a great direction," urges a psychology and sociology major.

Elon was founded in 1889 and occupies a 690-acre campus in North Carolina's Piedmont region, and it is arguably the most architecturally consistent campus in the nation. Buildings are Georgian-style brick with white trim, and newer buildings have been adapted to modern architectural lines while maintaining this classic collegiate feel. On the north end of campus is Lake Mary Nell, home to an abundance of geese and ducks. Academic buildings are organized in five clusters: a historic quad near a fountain in the older section of the campus; the Lambert Academic Village; the School of Communications, a three-building quad; a business center; and a newly constructed Innovation Quad, home to engineering and other STEM programs. Other recent construction includes an EcoVillage with sustainable student housing. The East Neighborhood Commons residential building opened in 2024.

To graduate, students must complete a core curriculum that includes a broad range of liberal arts and science subjects as well as an interdisciplinary capstone seminar. All students must fulfill an Experiential Learning Requirement (ELR) by completing at least two of the five Elon Experiences. "I've found the critical thinking and reflection that comes from ELRs to be extremely beneficial for discussing my experiences and strengths in job interviews," says a journalism major. The university offers more than 70 undergraduate degrees, including nursing that also has an accelerated B.S. option. Business majors—especially finance, marketing, and accounting—are some of the strongest and most popular; students also flock to strategic communications and psychology. Programs in drama, education, and biology are strong. New majors include digital content management and neuroscience. The School of Communications is nationally recognized, and its cinema and television arts program benefits from two ultramodern digital television studios. Aspiring engineers may enroll in Elon's four-year engineering degree program or pursue a 3–2 dual degree with partner institutions like Virginia Tech, Georgia Tech, Penn State, and others. An accelerated 3–2.5 law dual degree program is also available.

Elon has an elaborate faculty-managed support system designed to ensure that first-year students don't fall through the cracks. Elon 1010 serves as an academic orientation for all first-years; students meet weekly in small groups with an academic advisor and an upper-level student. Students begin general studies with a course called The Global Experience, a seminar-style interdisciplinary class that investigates challenges facing the world. Fifty percent of classes have fewer than 20 students, which "makes it easier to learn and more intimate, with your professors knowing everyone," enthuses a policy studies major.

"We don't have the same level of academic rigor as other private liberal arts schools in the region," remarks an anthropology major, "but we make up for it with our focus on experiential learning." Twenty-six percent of undergrads engage in research with faculty and present their work at a research forum in the spring. Most students study abroad, thanks to the 4–1–4 academic calendar and more than 160 study abroad programs that students rave about. For career preparation, nearly all students complete internships, and students praise the career services office. Forty percent of students

Website: www.elon.edu
Location: Suburban
Private
Total Enrollment: 7,002
Undergraduates: 6,273
Male/Female: 40/60
Financial Aid: 77%
Pell Grant: 14%
Expense: Pr $
Student Loans: 34%
Average Debt: $ $ $ $
Applicants: 18,105
Accepted: 66%
Enrolled: 13%
Grad in 6 Years: 83%
Returning First-years: 90%
Academics: ✐ ✐ ✐
Social: 🗩 🗩 🗩
Q of L: ★ ★ ★ ★ ★
Admissions: (800) 334-8448
Email Address:
  admissions@elon.edu

Strong Programs:
Biology
Business
Cinema and Television Arts
Drama
Education
Finance
Marketing
Strategic Communications

> **"Elon's best asset is honestly its commitment to engaged learning."**

Twenty-six percent of undergrads engage in research with faculty and present their work at a research forum in the spring.

participate in Elon's Honors Program. That and Elon's eight Scholars programs, to which prospective students can apply alongside their admissions applications, are designed for exceptionally motivated students. They offer faculty support, scholarships, and peer networks, and current participants highly recommend them as being "profoundly impactful."

Given Elon's emphasis on out-of-classroom endeavors, students here have a lot going on. Twenty percent of undergrads come from North Carolina, and a finance major points out, "It truly lives up to its reputation of being a Northeastern school in the South, every other person is from either Massachusetts, New York, or New Jersey." Women outnumber men 3 to 2. Five percent of students are Black, 7 percent Hispanic/ Latino, 2 percent Asian American, 3 percent multiracial, and 2 percent international. Lack of racial and socioeconomic diversity is a common complaint, but students are now required to take a four-hour course on advancing equity. Politically, says a senior, the campus "certainly does lean liberal, but there are more conservatives here than you think." Fifteen percent of admitted first-year students are automatically awarded the Presidential Scholarship. Overall, merit scholarships average $10,200 per year, and the university awards more than 200 athletic scholarships.

"Elon students are pretty chill," says a sophomore. Sixty-nine percent of them reside on campus; they are required to do so for their first two years, and many choose to stay on campus for all four years. "The new dorms and apartments are gorgeous," says a senior. Options include traditional residence halls, university-owned apartments, and the Global and Colonnades neighborhoods, which feature two

"The new dorms and apartments are gorgeous."

dozen living/learning communities, such as Creative Arts, Gender and Sexuality, and Innovation. "Living in the LLC definitely made it easier to make friends," reports a first-year. Designed to bridge classroom learning with social experiences, these communities also serve to bring together diverse groups of students with common interests in a safe space; many participants in the Gender and Sexuality community, for instance, identify as LGBTQIA. Elon recently launched HealthEU, a wellness initiative to support student mental health. Those who move off campus find plenty of options within walking distance. Campus dining, which consists of three dining halls and almost 20 retail locations, receives good reviews for taste, variety, and accommodations for allergies and special diets. Campus security programs are said to be effective and include escort services, Safe Rides, and the Live Safe app to help students get home safely.

"Elon is over 60 percent Greek life and has only two bars in town," quips a junior of the social scene. "That tells you everything you need to know." Greek life attracts 20 percent of the men and 39 percent of the women. Students report that alcohol policies are loosely enforced. The Student Union Board hosts events every weekend, like bingo and trivia nights, a cappella concerts, and comedy shows. Favorite campus traditions include a weekly College Coffee, where students and faculty mingle over free breakfast—a tradition since 1984. An exercise science major says, "We have a Festival of Lights before winter break, and a holiday party at our president's house is a hallmark of the holiday season."

The tiny town of Elon is virtually indistinguishable from the university, but a first-year points out, "We are surrounded by bigger cities like Raleigh and Greensboro." Students do take an active role in the community through volunteer projects. Seventy-nine percent of students participate in community service, both domestically and abroad, and one student confirms, "Service is one of the bigger components of life as an Elon student." The nation-

"Elon is over 60 percent Greek life and has only two bars in town."

ally known Elon University Poll, which the school runs as a public service, tracks political and public policy issues. Road trips to the beach (three hours), the mountains (one hour), and Chapel Hill or Raleigh-Durham (less than an hour) are popular diversions.

Elon competes in the Division I Colonial Athletic Association and offers 17 Phoenix teams. Women's tennis captured its first CAA championship in 2025. Softball, women's track and field, and men's golf have also won recent conference championships. The intramural program covers more than 20 sports, including eSports, climbing, and hockey, and a successful club sports program lets students compete with other schools.

"Elon's best asset is honestly its commitment to engaged learning," says one student. By steadily ramping up its educational offerings, increasing and improving its facilities, and becoming more selective, this supportive liberal arts university is quickly outgrowing its local reputation. "Elon is a close-knit culture," says a senior, "that's focused on students and their overall well-being and success."

If You Apply To ›

Elon: Early decision, early action, regular decision. Accepts the Common Application with supplement. Application includes optional field for students who identify as part of the LGBTQIA community. Please consult Elon's website for the most up-to-date information regarding standardized test scores.

Emerson College

120 Boylston Street, Boston, MA 02116

Emerson is strategically located on Boston Common in the heart of Boston's Theater District and within walking distance of many of the city's major attractions. Specializes in communication and the arts. With roughly 4,000 undergraduates, Emerson is a smaller alternative to neighboring giants Boston U and Northeastern. Like most Beantown institutions, it is far more selective than it once was.

Those who aspire to a career in film, television, or marketing may want to start with a four-year stint in Boston. There they will find Emerson College, a small liberal arts school that offers strong programs in communication and the arts, as well as top-notch performance and production facilities. At Emerson, students take notes from professors who also happen to be working directors, producers, actors, editors, and writers. It's an approach that helps talented, city-savvy students find their voices. Emerson has turned out such notable alumni as actors and comedians Denis Leary, Jennifer Coolidge, Jen Kirkman, and Jay Leno. "If you are serious about surrounding yourself with creative people during your college years," says a journalism major, "this is the school for you." Prospective students take note: Getting into Emerson requires more than dreams. You'll need a solid academic record as well as plenty of talent.

Founded in 1880 by Charles Wesley Emerson, a minister, educator, and distant cousin of Ralph Waldo, Emerson is located on Boston Common in the middle of the city's Theater District, and much of the surrounding city is accessible by foot. The campus features a mix of traditional and modern high-rise buildings. The historic Cutler Majestic and Emerson Colonial theaters, the anchors of Emerson's urban campus, have been restored to their original grandeur. The 11-story Tufte Performance and Production Center features rehearsal spaces, a costume shop, a makeup lab, and television studios. Students here also have access to professional-grade equipment and digital labs, audio postproduction suites, radio stations (Emerson is home to the oldest noncommercial radio station in Boston), a multimedia newsroom, and a marketing research suite featuring eye-tracking technology and a two-way mirror for conducting focus groups.

Core requirements at Emerson consist of a combination of traditional courses and interdisciplinary seminars. All students must take courses in two areas: Foundations, which includes writing and oral communication, and Perspectives, which includes courses in aesthetics; ethics and values; history; literature; quantitative reasoning; diversity; world languages; and scientific, social, and psychological perspectives. Honors students take intensive seminars in their first three years and complete a senior thesis.

Undergraduates may choose from 27 majors in communication and the arts, ranging from stage and screen design technology and business of creative enterprises to communication disorders and journalism. Performance-related majors, such as musical theatre and theatre and performance, tend to be the most popular, along with business of creative enterprises, creative writing, and journalism. In 2025, Emerson opened the new School of Film, Television, and Media Arts in recognition of the college's strongest programs. An entrepreneurship minor features a business plan competition known as the E3 Expo (Emerson Entrepreneurship Exposition); students vie for thousands of dollars in start-up funds. Students at the Marlboro Institute for Liberal Arts and Interdisciplinary Studies, created when Emerson absorbed Vermont's Marlboro College in 2020, design their own interdisciplinary studies major tailored to their unique academic interests and complete a yearlong senior capstone project.

> **"The classes at Emerson are more challenging creatively than academically."**

"The classes at Emerson are more challenging creatively than academically," says a junior. A media arts production major agrees: "Students are encouraged to try new things and explore new mediums and apply for weird, wacky opportunities." Eighty percent of all classes have fewer than 20 students, and a political communication major says professors "give us real-world perspective and also always have an ear to the ground for those of us looking for internships."

For a semester-long program at Kasteel Well (in the Netherlands), students are housed in a restored, college-owned, 14th-century castle.

For those seeking a spotlight and stage in a different setting, Emerson offers several global study options, including a semester-long program at Kasteel Well (in the Netherlands), where students are housed in a restored, college-owned, 14th-century castle complete with moats, gardens, and a gatehouse. Each semester, about 200 students live at Emerson's Los Angeles Center on Sunset Boulevard in Hollywood, where they participate in internships with the likes of HBO, Warner Bros., Dreamworks, and the *Los Angeles Times*. Another semester-long program sends participants to Washington, D.C., for classes and internships. "Above all, cocurriculars are the backbone of an Emerson education," a film production major says. "Classes are thought-provoking, but nothing prepares you for the real world better than actually getting out into the field to practice as much as possible." In an effort to establish a global presence, Emerson's Global Portals initiative allows international students without U.S. passports to earn select Emerson degrees at partner universities in France, Switzerland, and Australia.

"The students at Emerson are artistic, passionate, and career-focused," says a student. Adds another, "We have a very large 'hipster' presence at our school." Twenty-two percent of undergraduates hail from Massachusetts, and most come from public high schools. Fourteen percent are international. Black students account for 6 percent of the student body, Hispanics/Latinos 13 percent, Asian Americans 5 percent, and multiracial students 5 percent. Despite a noticeable lack of socioeconomic and ethnic diversity, "Emerson is known for being extremely LGBTQ-friendly," says one senior. "Students are always championing liberal social causes." Emerson offers merit scholarships averaging $25,200 to qualified applicants, as well as scholarships to support underrepresented students. There are no athletic awards.

> **"The students at Emerson are artistic, passionate, and career-focused."**

Most undergrads reside on campus, since they are required to live in college housing for their first three years. After that, says a junior, "A lot of students take it as a rite of passage to move off campus." Several living/learning communities are available, such as Community Outreach, Digital Culture, and Writers' Block. The food receives middling reviews, and a junior says, "There isn't a wide variety for people with restrictions and allergies." Each building requires an ID to enter, and public safety officers regularly patrol the streets outside the buildings. "Emerson has had a rocky history with handling sexual assault," reports a junior. Although the college has taken steps to address concerns, another student explains, "The student body believes that there is still more to be done."

"While there is no shortage of on-campus events like comedy shows, performances, and club meetings, a lot of the traditional college nightlife tends to happen in the city or at someone's off-campus apartment," says a sophomore. More than 100 student organizations offer ample opportunity for involvement, as a theatre major explains: "There are magazines, television channels, theatre companies, and comedy troupes that publish, perform, and at times travel regularly." Popular annual festivities include the EVVY Awards, the largest student-run awards show in the country. Greek life, which attracts a mere 2 percent of Emerson men and 3 percent of the women, is a negligible influence at Emerson. Those seeking a more active party scene head to larger Boston universities on weekends. Students need only step

"Students are always championing liberal social causes."

off campus or hop on the T (Boston's subway system) to enjoy other diversions, including theater, museums, the Franklin Park Zoo, the Boston Public Garden, the Freedom Trail, the Boston Symphony Orchestra, and major league baseball at Fenway Park. A student says, "Emerson students live, study, work, and volunteer in almost every major neighborhood and area of the city."

Emerson fields 14 Division III athletic teams, and the Lions compete as a member of the Eastern College Athletic Conference and the New England Women's and Men's Athletic Conference. Solid teams include baseball, softball, basketball, cross-country, lacrosse, and soccer. Students also enjoy an active intramural program and take advantage of the 10,000-square-foot fitness center featuring state-of-the-art equipment, classes, and wellness workshops.

"Emerson prepares creative thinkers to get out into the workforce and make a difference," says one senior. While you are not guaranteed to become the next Oscar-winning director, the possibility is not that unreasonable at Emerson. And even if a lifestyle of fame is not for you, the excellent education, small classes, and attentive professors may teach you how to be the "star" of your own life story.

Overlaps
Bentley, Boston University, Butler, Chapman, Elon, NYU, Northeastern, Rollins

If You Apply To ›

Emerson: Early decision I and II, early action, regular decision. SATs or ACTs: optional (test-optional applicants are encouraged to submit an optional creative sample or portfolio). Accepts the Common Application with supplement. Additional materials required for applicants to performing arts, media production, comedic arts, and honors programs.

Emory University

201 Dowman Drive, Atlanta, GA 30322

Emory stands out from rivals like Duke and Vanderbilt thanks to its collaborative culture and international reach. Attracts a larger contingent from the Northeast than other Southern schools of its ilk. Business and premed are major draws, and its suburban Atlanta location offers internships, research, and real-world learning that's tough to beat. Also consider Oxford College, Emory's two-year, small-town liberal arts campus.

The Emory Experience Shuttle provides free transportation to popular neighborhoods and festivals.

Emory University is a favorite among students from both U.S. coasts and around the globe. They come for its size (big but not too big), location, national reputation, and, increasingly, for its diversity—students from more than 100 countries are represented on campus. One sophomore says, "Probably the best part of Emory [is] meeting people from all over the world and all different kinds of backgrounds." Even with the university's academic rigor, students say they feel supported in the classroom, and an atmosphere of Southern friendliness enhances the vibrant campus life.

Founded in 1836 in Oxford, Georgia, and relocated to Atlanta in 1915, Emory (named in honor of a Methodist bishop) is set on 631 acres of woods and rolling hills in the Druid Hills neighborhood of Atlanta. The campus spreads out from an academic quad of marble-covered, red-roofed buildings. Contemporary structures dot the periphery of the lush, green grounds. Emory has a world-class performing arts center and has expanded science and math research facilities, and updated first-year housing in recent years. The recently built three-story Emory Student Center houses the campus's main dining facilities, student organizations, and various multipurpose spaces.

Emory University offers applicants the choice between two different undergraduate experiences at two distinct campuses: Emory College in Atlanta, Georgia, and Oxford College, 45 minutes away in Oxford, Georgia. Emory College may be best for students who seek a standard four-year undergraduate experience at a research-focused institution that emphasizes academic independence and intellectual engagement. Oxford College,

"Probably the best part of Emory [is] meeting people from all over the world."

which enrolls about 1,000 students, is suited for those who seek academic rigor, interdisciplinary study, and to sharpen critical-thinking skills. Following two years of study at Oxford, all students continue as juniors on the Atlanta campus. Emory's distribution requirements span the liberal arts and sciences, aiming to develop competence in writing, quantitative methods, a second language, and physical education. All entering students take a first-year seminar that is limited to 15 students each and introduces them to college-level work.

Sixty-three percent of classes have fewer than 20 students. Just as Emory has invested in its physical plant, the school has focused on adding star faculty members to key departments, including Pulitzer Prize–winning poet Jericho Brown, all of whom teach undergraduates. "Faculty members make teaching a priority and set aside a significant amount of time for mentoring and helping students with both the course material and with life in general," says one student. Opportunities for mentored research are available in all fields, and the Halle Institute for Global Research and Learning awards fellowships to select undergraduates as part of their honors thesis or capstone project. A chemistry major notes, "Many students find research opportunities through professors they had during their freshman year."

Along with the sciences, business administration, nursing, biology, and neuroscience are among Emory's most notable majors. Offerings in biology and chemistry benefit from close proximity to Emory's health care enterprise, while a major in quantitative sciences allows students to combine the study of data science with one of 18 liberal arts tracks. Emory has close ties to the Carter Center (named for the late U.S. president, who for nearly 40 years participated in an annual town hall for first-year students). The English and creative writing program is nationally recognized. Emory has received a significant portion of Nobel laureate Seamus Heaney's archive, and its unique Irish studies program is said to rival those of Notre Dame and Boston College. A 3–2 dual-degree program allows students to earn a bachelor's degree at Emory and a bachelor's degree in engineering at Georgia Tech. Twenty-seven percent of students broaden their horizons through more than 100 study abroad programs spanning over 40 countries. The students who participate earn Emory credit and Emory grades, and they can receive Emory financial aid, scholarships, and grants.

"Though Emory is definitely not an easy school, and you have to work hard to earn your grades, overall, everyone manages to find a good balance between classwork, extracurriculars, and socializing," says a senior. Fifteen percent of undergrads hail from Georgia (more than a quarter are from the Southeast and 25 percent from the Mid-Atlantic region); 16 percent come from more than 100 countries around the world. A quarter of incoming students identify as Asian American, 10 percent as Black, 12 percent as Hispanic/Latino, and 4 percent are multiracial. Many students do service work through Volunteer Emory. Emory meets the full demonstrated need of all admitted students without loans, and the new Emory Advantage Plus program ensures that undergraduates from families with incomes up to $200,000 will pay no tuition. Merit scholarships worth an average of $30,800 are awarded annually, but there are no athletic scholarships.

Fifty-seven percent of Emory students live in campus housing; first-years and sophomores are required to do so. "The accommodations for first-years are really nice because all of the rooms have been renovated recently," reports a theater studies major. Lucky juniors and seniors may hang their hats in the one- to four-bedroom Clairmont Campus apartments, which boast such luxuries as private bedrooms, a washer-dryer in each unit, a rec center, and a heated, outdoor, Olympic-sized pool. In addition to the dining halls, there are small cafés, grills, and food courts on campus. Meals get fair reviews. When it comes to combating sexual violence, one student says, "Emory is very big on education and prevention."

> "Faculty members set aside a significant amount of time for mentoring and helping students."

"Most social life takes place on campus, but we are so close to Atlanta nightlife that many students choose to explore the area," says a student. Fraternities and sororities attract 23 percent of the men and 21 percent of the women, so, of course, Greek parties are abundant. Other options include concerts, Theater Emory shows, and other events organized by the Student Programming Committee. Alcohol isn't allowed in the first-year dorms, and "anyone caught will definitely suffer consequences," a first-year warns. A very popular highlight of the social calendar is Dooley's Week, a spring festival in honor of the "Spirit of Emory" (the school's unofficial mascot), Dooley, a skeleton who reportedly escaped from the biology lab more than 100 years ago. If Dooley walks into your class, the class is dismissed, and the week culminates with a costume ball in his honor. First-year halls also have Songfest, a competition where residents make up spirit-filled song-and-dance routines.

Just 20 minutes away, Atlanta offers a multitude of diversions, from major league sports to plays at the Fox Theatre, exhibits at the High Museum of Art, marine wildlife at the Georgia Aquarium, and shopping at Lenox Square. Upperclassmen enjoy the Atlanta bar scene, and some local dance clubs host college nights. The Emory Experience Shuttle provides free transportation to popular neighborhoods and festivals. Road trips include Stone Mountain, Athens, Savannah, and the beaches of Florida and the Carolinas.

Emory doesn't field a varsity football team, but the Eagles have produced a number of Division III national champs in recent years, including men's and women's swimming and diving and women's golf in 2025. Tennis and soccer are also strengths. Emory competes against academic powerhouses such as the University of Chicago and Carnegie Mellon in the University Athletic Association conference. Many students join at least one intramural or club sports team at either a competitive or a recreational level. Popular options include basketball, flag football, soccer, crew, and lacrosse.

> "We are so close to Atlanta nightlife that many students choose to explore the area."

While many Southern schools suffer from a regional provincialism, that isn't true at Emory, which blends a focus on teaching and research to nurture creativity and turn out leaders who are highly sought after in the working world—and by local

Overlaps

Duke, Georgetown, Johns Hopkins, Penn, Vanderbilt, WashU in St. Louis

and international postgraduate law, medical, and business programs. As one satisfied student concludes, Emory offers "high academic quality and rigor" yet "still has the hospitality and charm of a Southern school."

Eugene Lang College of Liberal Arts

65 West 11th Street, New York, NY 10011

Home to about 1,400 street-savvy, freethinking urbanites, Eugene Lang College is a popular alternative to much larger neighbor NYU in Manhattan's chic Greenwich Village. Emphasis on progressive critical inquiry pursued in seminar settings. With the city as its campus, Lang offers a less cohesive sense of community than traditional small liberal arts schools. Long-standing international perspective and strength in arts and humanities still predominate. Low graduation rate and declining enrollment are challenges.

Website: www.newschool.edu/lang

Location: City Center

Private

Total Enrollment: 1,391

Undergraduates: 1,391

Male/Female: 21/71

Financial Aid: 92%

Pell Grant: 30%

Expense: Pr $ $

Student Loans: 50%

Average Debt: $ $ $ $

Applicants: 2,627

Accepted: 83%

Enrolled: 15%

Grad in 6 Years: 55%

Returning First-years: 74%

Academics: ✍ ✍ ✍

Social: 🗩

Q of L: ★ ★ ★

Admissions: (800) 292-3040

Email Address: lang@newschool.edu

Strong Programs:
Culture and Media
Economics

Students seeking a typical college experience—large lectures, rowdy football games, and rigid academic requirements—would do well to steer clear of Eugene Lang College of Liberal Arts, The New School's undergraduate liberal arts college. That's because Lang offers small seminars, individualized academic programs with minimal required coursework, and not a single varsity sport—not to mention an urban campus that reflects the quirky and kinetic atmosphere of Greenwich Village. "We don't want to become business leaders but instead teachers, community organizers, thinkers, professors, and writers," a junior says. In fact, say administrators, Eugene Lang seeks to take advantage of its distinctive urban setting to produce students who are "intellectually curious, socially conscious, and continuously striving for personal and academic growth."

Lang fits right in amid the brownstones and trendy boutiques of one of New York's most vibrant neighborhoods. The school's main hub is a single five-story building between Fifth and Sixth Avenues on West 11th Street, although students make use of all 16 of the buildings that The New School occupies along lower Fifth Avenue. The New School's library is small, but students have access to the massive Bobst Library at NYU, which is just a few blocks away, as is the excitement of Greenwich Village and Washington Square Park. The 16-story University Center offers state-of-the-art facilities, including "smart" classrooms, design studios, a residence hall, and an auditorium. A new student center opened recently on 13th Street that houses the student-run New School Free Press, the university radio station, and various other offices and shared study spaces.

> "The texts we work with are pretty dense and challenging."

The New School was founded in 1919 by a band of progressive scholars that included John Dewey, Charles Beard, and Thorstein Veblen. A decade and a half later, it became a haven for European intellectuals fleeing Nazi persecution, and over the years, it has been the teaching home of many notable thinkers, including Buckminster Fuller and Hannah Arendt. Created in 1975, the undergraduate college was renamed 10 years later for Eugene Lang, a progressive philanthropist who made a significant donation to the school. In addition to Lang, today's New School includes a graduate program in social research, a school of management, and various arts and music programs, most notably Parsons School of Design. At night, the Schools of Public Engagement are host to a huge assortment of public lectures and performances, as well as continuing education courses. Like many colleges, however, the New School is grappling with budget shortfalls and announced it would merge some programs and cut others, including anthropology, history, and sociology. Other restructuring changes are expected to continue in 2026.

(continued)

Journalism and Design
Literary Studies
Politics
Psychology
Theater
Urban Studies

The two most distinctive features of Lang are the small classes and undergraduates pursuing their own path of study with minimal general education requirements. Students take one year of writing and choose one required first-year seminar from a broad-based menu; the seminar also incorporates workshops on nonacademic concerns and study skills and is taught by a professor who serves as students' faculty advisor. Additionally, all students take two University Lecture courses, choosing from three categories: Tools for Social Change, Introductions to Social Research, and Interdisciplinary Approaches to the Arts and Humanities. In their final year, students take on a senior capstone project that synthesizes their educational experience.

"The academic climate is pretty relaxed, but the texts we work with are pretty dense and challenging," says a culture and media major. Lang's most popular majors include literary studies, journalism and design, culture and media, and psychology; economics, theater, and politics are other strengths. Its city location enhances the urban studies program, and the writing minor is highly praised. While introductory language courses are plentiful, upper-level language offerings are limited. The college has, however, beefed up its offerings in global studies and added a minor called "code as a liberal art," which focuses on coding and computational systems in a liberal arts context. Thirty percent of undergrads take advantage of more than 40 joint B.A./M.A. and B.S./M.S. programs, including public and urban policy, international affairs, and arts management and entrepreneurship. "There is a large emphasis on research and studying not only core academic texts but also branching out into more alternative forms of learning," says a politics major. A large portion of the faculty consists of part-time adjuncts who hold other jobs in their respective fields. "I credit many professors with helping me navigate the professional world as I have gone to many of them for advice on getting internships, working in government, or discussing careers," praises a junior.

> **"I credit many professors with helping me navigate the professional world."**

The main academic complaint is the limited range of seminars, but outside programs and partnerships offer more variety. Students may enroll in approved classes in other divisions of The New School, and nearly 60 minors offered across the university provide opportunities to study topics like law and social change, sustainable cities, creative entrepreneurship, and capitalism studies. "As a New School student, you also have access to all of the studios and workshops at Parsons, like the metal shop and wood shop just to name a few," raves a senior. Lang's popular Civic Liberal Arts program offers courses that incorporate visiting fellows from community partners, the likes of which have included the *New York Times*, the Center for Traditional Music and Dance, and Brooklyn Grange. Twenty percent of students study abroad, and semester-long exchange programs are available with the University of Amsterdam, John Cabot University in Rome, and Sophia University in Tokyo, among others.

Lang attracts a disparate group of undergraduates, but many of them can be described as idealistic, independent, and politically progressive. "Most students have a passion for the social justice or political issues they are studying, and many do outside work with organizations related to their passions," explains a politics major. Seventy-one percent of students are female. Seventeen percent are from New York, and 11 percent come from abroad. Twelve percent are Black, 24 percent are

A multitude of cultural events, like Bollywood Night and Gospel Night, enhance campus diversity.

The New School's library is small, but students have access to the massive Bobst Library at NYU.

Hispanic/Latino, 8 percent are Asian American, and 8 percent are multiracial. Lang admits students regardless of their finances. Merit scholarships averaging $19,000 are offered.

The New School's residence halls accommodate roughly one-quarter of Lang students. A gender-inclusive housing policy assigns housing based on students' preferred gender pronouns. Off-campus dwellers live in apartments in the Village (if they can afford it), in Brooklyn (if they can afford it), or elsewhere in the New York City area. Students complain that food in the Dining Commons, while tasty and healthy, is too expensive, so most opt for the hundreds of delis, coffee shops, and restaurants that line Fifth and Sixth Avenues. The school reports they've increased the counseling staff, but students say some support services need to be made more accessible. The school struggles with a low six-year graduation rate of just 55 percent.

"Our lack of campus kind of makes all activity 'off campus.'"

Many students cite the school's location as one of its best features. "The city rules," reports a journalism and design major. The social network at Lang is quite small and, like many things, is left up to the student. "Our lack of campus kind of makes all activity 'off campus,' though we do have dances and club activities within the school facilities themselves," a junior says. On-campus activities tend to involve intellectual pursuits, such as poetry readings, open-mic nights, and working on the student newspaper and the literary magazine. A multitude of cultural events, like Bollywood Night and Gospel Night, enhance campus diversity. Students generally avoid drinking on campus. Athletics barely register here, although the school does field a few club teams: men's and women's basketball and co-ed cross-country.

Despite the seeming lack of tradition and typical sense of college community, Lang's stock continues to rise. Students relish the freedom and independence they have here. For a student who yearns for four years of "traditional" college experiences, Lang would likely be a disappointment. But for those desiring an intimate education in America's cultural capital, Lang offers all the stimulation of the city it calls home.

Overlaps

Bard, Emerson, Fordham, NYU, Oberlin, Pace, Pratt Institute, Sarah Lawrence

If You Apply To ›

Eugene Lang: Early decision, early action, regular decision. SATs or ACTs: optional. Accepts the Common Application with supplement and two New School–specific essays.

The Evergreen State College

2700 Evergreen Parkway NW, Olympia, WA 98505

There's no mistaking Evergreen for a typical public college. Never mind its unconventional students; Evergreen's interdisciplinary, team-taught curriculum is unique. To find anything remotely like Evergreen, you'll need to go private and travel east to places like Hampshire or Sarah Lawrence. Accepts just about anyone who applies, and graduation rate is growing after several years of decline. Traditions show a sense of humor.

In "La Vie Bohème," the anthem of Jonathan Larson's rock opera *Rent*, one of the characters asks, "Anyone out of the mainstream / Is anyone in the mainstream?" At The Evergreen State College, the answer has always been a vehement "No!" The school's unofficial motto is Omnia Extares, Latin for "Let it all hang out." Founded in 1967 as Washington State's experimental college, Evergreen has narrative evaluations instead of grades and lacks formal majors and even departments. This system may sound strange, but it works for those seeking the freedom to chart their own course. Where else will you find a criminologist and a theater professor teaching a class together?

Evergreen lies in a fir forest at the edge of the 90-mile-long Puget Sound. The peaceful, 1,000-acre campus includes an organic plant and animal farm as well as 3,300 feet of saltwater beach. Most of Evergreen's buildings are boxy concrete-and-steel creations, though the Longhouse Education and Cultural Center is designed in the Native American style typical of the Pacific Northwest. The college has also built an Indigenous Arts Campus featuring a fiber arts studio and a carving studio. In keeping with Evergreen's progressive nature, all new building projects strive to comply with LEED standards.

At first glance, Evergreen's wide-open curriculum might look like Easy Street. The college operates on 10-week quarters, but the structure of learning is different. Instead of signing up for unrelated classes to fulfill distribution requirements, students enroll in a single coordinated, 12- to 16-credit "program" spanning several disciplines that are often team-taught by multiple professors. Recent program offerings include Advanced Computing and Machine Learning, Psychology and Popular Music, and Business Start-Ups. In addition to professor and self-evaluations, students must write an annual Academic Statement, reflecting on their academic experiences and goals. Upperclassmen may fulfill an Individual Learning Contract developed in partnership with a faculty sponsor, and many complete some form of capstone experience, such as a senior thesis.

"The academic climate at Evergreen is robust, collaborative, and engaging."

Students praise Evergreen's environmental and sustainability studies offerings, which span agriculture, ornithology, and marine science, among others. To supplement their coursework, environmental scientists may also study marine animals while sailing in Puget Sound, spend seven weeks at a bird sanctuary in Oregon, or trek to the Grand Canyon or the tropical rainforests of Costa Rica. The Native American and indigenous studies program is notable, and computer science and various arts programs—dance, writing, visual arts, and media arts—also get high marks. Regardless of what they study, students warn that while the integrated approach to learning may improve comprehension and deepen understanding, it likewise means a lot of work. "The academic climate at Evergreen is robust, collaborative, and engaging," says a junior. "It gives space for both self-directed learning and small learning communities." Many academic programs include a service-learning component, and several faculty-led study abroad programs are available.

Because Evergreen attracts nontraditional students and those who are older than the typical first-year college student, administrators take advising and career counseling seriously. And in the past five years, faculty members have been more involved in recruiting new students, leading to an enrollment increase of over 20 percent since 2020. First-Year Experience programs focus on developing skills for college success, such as study skills, health and wellness education, and academic planning. "A goal of the faculty here is to get to know each student personally and to understand their interests and goals," explains a political economy student. Another bonus: Because Evergreen doesn't award formal tenure, there's less pressure for professors to conduct research and publish their findings—and less to distract them from teaching undergraduates. Professors who do engage in research often involve students in their work, and students may apply for competitive Summer Undergraduate Research Fellowship stipends.

<table>
<tr><td>

Website: www.evergreen.edu
Location: Small City
Public
Total Enrollment: 2,176
Undergraduates: 1,993
Male/Female: 39/60
Financial Aid: 83%
Pell Grant: 45%
Expense: Pub $
Student Loans: 56%
Average Debt: $ $
Applicants: 1,300
Accepted: 96%
Enrolled: 26%
Grad in 6 Years: 42%
Returning First-years: 73%
Academics: ✍ ✍ ✍
Social: 🗩 🗩 🗩
Q of L: ★ ★ ★ ★
Admissions: (360) 867-6170
Email Address:
  admissions@evergreen.edu

Strong Programs:
Computer Science
Dance
Environmental Studies
Media Arts
Native American and
  Indigenous Studies
Visual Arts
Writing

</td></tr>
</table>

Faculty members have been more involved in recruiting new students, leading to an enrollment increase of over 20 percent since 2020.

"Greeners want to be open-minded, intelligent, and actually meaningful to the world in which they live," says a student. Eighty-six percent of Evergreen's students are Washington residents. Black students account for 7 percent of the student body, Hispanics/Latinos 15 percent, Asian Americans 2 percent, American Indians 4 percent, and multiracial students 8 percent. Forty-four percent of students are of a nontraditional age. Liberal views and student activism dominate the campus. "If you are someone who doesn't like high-energy debate, you may find yourself struggling to connect with the school," says a media studies major. Feminists in Solidarity Together, Food Not Bombs, T-Rex (a transgender group), and Black Cottonwood Collective (an anarchist group) represent just a small sampling of the student activist groups on campus. A hefty 45 percent of incoming first-years are eligible for Pell Grants, and the proportion of first-generation students has risen to 30 percent. A limited number of merit and athletic scholarships are available for qualified students. The statewide Washington College Grant provides free or reduced tuition for in-state students from low- and middle-income families who meet certain requirements.

> "If you [don't] like high-energy debate, you may find yourself struggling to connect with the school."

Nineteen percent of Evergreen students, mostly first-years, live on campus. Students appreciate the amenities in the school's apartment complexes but say the dorms need sprucing up. There's an efficient bus system to get nonresidents to class on time, though it helps to have a car. Evergreen's food service offers a wide variety of dishes. "We have the amazing student-run café, the Flaming Eggplant. They serve delicious, locally sourced food that caters to special diets," cheers one student. Students say campus security is good, and although instances of sexual assault are uncommon, one student says, "Evergreen needs to work on reconciling its progressive, liberal image with the way that assaults are actually handled."

> *The school's unofficial motto is Omnia Extares, Latin for "Let it all hang out."*

Given the pervasive individualism that flavors Evergreen, it's little surprise that the college lacks a Greek system. Still, the housing and student activities offices organize plenty of events—including open-mic nights, soccer and other field games, and parties. Student musicians are often at the center of the social scene, hosting on-campus performances or playing popular "house shows" off campus. "We are in a marijuana-legal state, but you cannot have pot on campus. As you can imagine, this is the most violated rule on campus," quips a religious studies student. The fall Harvest Festival on the college's organic farm is a favorite annual event.

Olympia (population 56,000), the state capital, hardly qualifies as a college town, but it is progressive and open-minded, with art walks through local galleries, coffee shops, clothing stores, co-ops, and a thriving music scene. "It's a rad little town with its own personality," says a junior. The college's outdoor program organizes mountaineering, backpacking, and rock-climbing trips and offers a wide range of gear for rent. Seattle (just over an hour away) and Portland and the rugged Oregon coast (two to three hours away) provide changes of scenery; everything is kept green and lush by the (interminable) rain, which stops in time for summer break and resumes by November.

> "[Olympia] is a rad little town with its own personality."

You may chuckle at Evergreen's mascot, an eight-foot clam named "Speedy" (a nod to the large geoduck clams found in Puget Sound), but the school has an active intercollegiate athletics program. Geoduck teams compete in seven sports in the NAIA Division II Cascade Conference, and men's soccer, men's track and field, and women's volleyball have enjoyed recent success. About a quarter of students choose to participate in recreational or intramural sports.

Evergreen remains one of the best choices for students who see traditional academic structures as too restrictive. Freed from requirements and grades, Greeners

Overlaps

Bennington, UC Santa Cruz, Hampshire, Lewis & Clark, Prescott, Sarah Lawrence, University of Washington, Western Washington

delight in exploring the connections between disparate disciplines at their own pace. It's a challenging task that requires an ability to focus, but for Greeners, the rewards lie in an education that is personally meaningful and that allows them to develop and express their own identities. "Here you can truly be whoever you want to be," says a junior. "There's really nothing to fit into. There is no box at Evergreen; there's just the experience of being here."

If You Apply To ›

Evergreen: Rolling admissions. SATs or ACTs: optional (test-optional applicants must submit essay). Accepts the Common Application with supplement.

Fairfield University

1073 North Benson Road, Fairfield, CT 06824

Strategically located in Connecticut on the Long Island Sound near New York City, Fairfield offers a classic Jesuit-style Roman Catholic education. Nursing and business are the biggest academic draws. Athletics have become more competitive and applications are up. Minimal diversity, socioeconomic and otherwise, is both a problem and an issue on campus. Lively party scene.

Like Boston College to the north and Georgetown to the south, Fairfield University was founded by the Society of Jesus (Jesuits) and offers a dynamic living/learning environment that combines solid academics, experiential learning opportunities in and outside the classroom, a boisterous social scene, and an abundance of community service projects. Religious and lay faculty alike promote traditional Jesuit religious and humanistic values to the largely preprofessional student body, and the absence of Greek organizations is never an obstacle to organizing a good party. The school's goal is to turn out graduates who combine a "broad understanding and respect for arts, humanities, and sciences" with "abilities and skills that emanate from mastery in at least one academic discipline." As a communication and theatre major puts it, "Fairfield is a place where your mind can flourish."

The physical beauty of the university's scenic, tree-lined campus just 60 minutes from Manhattan is a source of pride. Founded on two adjoining private estates in 1942, the administration preserves a lush atmosphere of sprawling lawns, ponds, and natural woodlands. Buildings are a blend of collegiate Gothic, Norman chateau, English manor, and modern. The university has been upgrading collaborative living and learning spaces in recent years. Among the newer additions are the $51 million on-campus multiuse Mahoney Arena, the LEED Gold–certified residential Bowman Hall, and Innovation Annex, a hands-on hub for engineering students. A new building for the Dolan School of Business includes a big data analytics lab, an entrepreneurship center, a gaming lab, and other high-tech tools.

Students may have difficulty finding time to savor the beautiful facilities. Everyone completes the Magis Core, a classic Jesuit-style liberal arts core curriculum that constitutes about a third of a student's total courseload. The core requires classes in math, natural sciences, history, social and behavioral sciences, philosophy and religious studies, literature, writing, visual and performing arts, modern and classical languages, and social justice. First-year students are introduced to Fairfield with a thorough orientation program that includes a series of seminars and events

Website: www.fairfield.edu
Location: Suburban
Private
Total Enrollment: 6,078
Undergraduates: 5,326
Male/Female: 42/58
Financial Aid: 60%
Pell Grant: 9%
Expense: Pr $ $
Student Loans: 64%
Average Debt: $ $ $ $
Applicants: 18,509
Accepted: 33%
Enrolled: 24%
Grad in 6 Years: 84%
Returning First-years: 91%
Academics: ✍ ✍ ✍
Social: 🗩 🗩 🗩 🗩
Q of L: ★ ★ ★ ★
Admissions: (203) 254-4100
Email Address:
  admis@fairfield.edu

Strong Programs:
Business
Communication
Engineering
Finance

The Presidential Ball in the fall is a favorite annual event.

A formal academic convocation in the first week of classes features a speaker chosen to reflect the school's Jesuit values.

throughout the fall term. A formal academic convocation in the first week of classes features a speaker chosen to reflect the school's Jesuit values.

Fairfield's main academic strengths—and most popular majors—are nursing, business (finance, marketing, accounting, and management), psychology, communication, and biology. Students enrolled in the Dolan School of Business have access

"Fairfield is a place where your mind can flourish."

to the state-of-the-art Business Experiential, Simulation, and Trading Floor classroom. Strong programs in engineering—especially mechanical, software, and biomedical—are supported by recent investments in STEM facilities. A minor in humanitarian action is an outgrowth of Fairfield's involvement as a founding member, along with Fordham and Georgetown, of the Jesuit Universities Humanitarian Action Network (JUHAN). Students can also join the JUHAN club to organize campus events raising awareness for humanitarian issues, participate in alternative spring breaks, and serve as delegates to the UN Youth Assembly.

In the classroom, says a social work major, "the academic climate is rigorous and collaborative." Forty percent of classes have fewer than 20 students. Furthermore, a senior says, "Professors push their students to look at things from different points of view and hold them to a high standard."

Students can study abroad through their choice of more than 50 programs. Fairfield administers its own programs in Australia, France, Ireland, Italy, and Spain, and several professors lead short educational tours for credit during the winter intercession, spring break, and the summer. Around 12 percent of students join the four-year honors program. Twenty-four percent of students carry out undergraduate research projects, and qualified students in biology, chemistry, and physics are guaranteed the opportunity to do so. The school's close proximity to New York City enhances Fairfield's strong internship programs.

A junior characterizes fellow students as "generally well-off, pretty smart, and a little rowdy." Seventeen percent of Fairfield undergraduates are from Connecticut, and 2 percent come from abroad. Sixty-one percent are Catholic. Politically, a senior offers, "There is a balance between liberal and conservative perspectives." Hispanic/

"Professors push their students to look at things from different points of view."

Latino students constitute 9 percent of the student body, Black students 1 percent, Asian Americans 2 percent, and multiracial students 2 percent. Only 9 percent of Fairfield first-years are eligible for Pell Grants, but the university has a program, Company Scholars, that offers full funding to a select group of first-generation Jesuit high school and Cristo Rey graduates. Still, lack of diversity is a nearly universal complaint among the student body with one saying, "It is majority white by a country mile." But a biomedical engineering major adds, "I do think Fairfield is trying to improve on this, and progress can be seen." A new LGBTQIA+ mentoring initiative offers students a choice of mentors and a chance "to delve into this aspect of their identity through monthly reflections," says an administrator. To help students with Fairfield's price tag, the school offers merit scholarships averaging $23,400 annually, as well as more than 200 athletic scholarships in 20 sports.

Fairfield's residence halls house 73 percent of the student body, and housing is guaranteed for all four years for full-time students. Several living/learning communities are available for undergrads of all levels and come highly recommended. As a senior reports, "That was huge in helping me make friends and get adjusted to college." Seniors can apply to live off campus, and the most popular options are the privately owned beach houses and apartments on Long Island Sound made available to students off-season. Meals in the main dining hall get good reviews for taste and variety.

In an effort to enhance the residential nature of the school and at the same time curb the number of rowdy beach parties along the Sound, the university has added more on-campus townhouses and apartments for upperclassmen. Nevertheless, a junior admits, "Fairfield has a good party culture, which is available but not necessarily obnoxiously in your face if you don't want to engage with it." Counseling services, career advising, and campus safety receive positive reviews. "Fairfield is proactive from day one about educating students about the issue of sexual assault," reports a junior.

Party culture notwithstanding, students find plenty of on-campus activities to keep them busy, including a growing number of student organizations to meet just about any interest. Sponsored events range from dances to hanging out at the campus coffeehouse to concerts. The Presidential Ball in the fall is a favorite annual event, along with the Clam Jam beach party with live music, kegs, and food trucks. The Campus Ministry draws a large following, with daily masses, annual retreats, and regular community service work, including many service immersion trips, both domestic and international.

"Downtown Fairfield is really cute."

As for the surrounding area, "downtown Fairfield is really cute, and there are many restaurants and shops," enthuses a nursing major, although another student says the town can feel a bit "snobby." Relations with local residents are sometimes strained, but even so, the campus bookstore moved downtown and is becoming a community meeting place. In keeping with Jesuit values, volunteerism abounds, with 54 percent of the student body performing community service. "Fairfield on Fire is a day devoted to service in neighboring towns that is such a huge, inspiring initiative," raves a junior. Road trips to New York (an hour by train) and Boston (two hours away) are popular.

The Stags compete in Division I and have won several Metro Atlantic Athletic Conference championships recently, including in women's soccer, volleyball, and rowing, baseball, men's golf, women's lacrosse, and field hockey. Men's and women's basketball both draw crowds, and the boisterous home-court fans, who come to games in full Fairfield regalia, have been dubbed the "Red Sea." Living up to the Jesuit commitment to sound mind and body, roughly half of the students compete in one of 29 intramural leagues and 23 percent play club sports.

"Fairfield University prioritizes setting students up for the future," comments a senior. "The university really pushes getting internships, networking, and anything that would help you with your future career." Although Fairfield is reflecting seriously on issues of diversity and how to create an inclusive social atmosphere on campus, it remains committed to its Jesuit ideals and to offering an undergraduate experience defined by close bonds with faculty, challenging academics, an emphasis on community involvement, and the holistic development of each student.

The university has been upgrading collaborative living and learning spaces in recent years.

Overlaps

Bentley, Boston College, Elon, Fordham, Holy Cross, Providence, Santa Clara, Villanova

If You Apply To ›

Fairfield: Early decision I and II, early action, regular decision. SATs or ACTs: optional. Accepts the Common Application with supplement.

University of Florida

Gainesville, FL 32611

It should come as no surprise that UF is a world leader in agricultural sciences. But add accounting, engineering, and Latin American studies to the list of renowned programs. Among Deep South public universities, only the University of Georgia rivals UF in overall quality. Top-shelf varsity sports teams are a year-round draw, and UF's party-school reputation remains intact. State political leaders working hard to limit faculty autonomy and promote conservative views in academic policymaking.

Website: www.ufl.edu
Location: Small City
Public
Total Enrollment: 45,339
Undergraduates: 32,857
Male/Female: 45/55
Financial Aid: 89%
Pell Grant: 21%
Expense: Pub $
Student Loans: 17%
Average Debt: $
Applicants: 73,557
Accepted: 24%
Enrolled: 42%
Grad in 6 Years: 91%
Returning First-years: 98%
Academics: ✍ ✍ ✍ ✍
Social: 🗩 🗩 🗩 🗩 🗩
Q of L: ★ ★ ★ ★
Admissions: (352) 392-1365
Email Address:
webrequests@admissions
.ufl.edu

Strong Programs:
Accounting
Business
Communications
Engineering
Journalism
Latin American Studies
Psychology

UF's strongest programs are those with a preprofessional bent, including engineering, accounting, and prepharmacy.

Set on 2,000 acres of rolling, heavily forested terrain in north-central Florida, the University of Florida is an athletic powerhouse whose leaders seek to gain the same level of national recognition for their academic offerings as well. With roughly 32,000 full-time undergraduates, the school is already massive and continues to become more so as it adds scores of new faculty in areas such as artificial intelligence, food security, big data, and drug discovery. Though it's a very large campus, students can find ample resources at their fingertips with a little effort. The state's flagship university, founded in 1853, has become more selective in its admissions and continues to try to temper its long-standing reputation as a party school.

UF's campus has more than 20 buildings on the National Register of Historic Places. Most are collegiate Gothic in style—redbrick with white trim. They're augmented by more modern facilities, such as Hernandez Hall, a 110,000-square-foot chemistry building. UF's research capabilities and equipment are likewise impressive and a boon to aspiring physicians and scientists. Cypress Hall is one of only a few residence halls in the nation designed specifically to accommodate students with severe physical impairments. Newer construction includes the $150 million Malachowsky Hall for Data Science and Information Technology, a high-tech hub for the university's expanding initiatives in artificial intelligence, data science, and cyber systems, and an expansion of the student health care center.

Academically, UF's strongest programs are those with a preprofessional bent, including engineering, accounting, and prepharmacy. To balance students' preprofessional coursework, the UF Quest general education program requires students to take a Quest Humanities course and a Quest Natural or Social Science course, along with engaging in experience-based learning. Popular majors include biology, computer science, psychology, and finance; entomology and Latin American studies are specialties. Among the new majors offered are Hebrew, Industrialized Construction Engineering, and Great Books and Ideas. Students also give high marks to the College of Journalism and Communications, which boasts the lavish Innovation News Center that houses the college's news, weather, and sports journalism. The Graham Center for Public Service trains students in languages, culture, and other skills vital to careers in public service.

> **"[Students are] very outgoing and friendly."**

Top incoming first-years are invited to apply to the Honors Program, where they live together in a residential college and take honors sections of standard academic subjects, most of which are limited to 25 students. The Innovation Academy offers another distinct living/learning opportunity for undergraduates with a spring-summer schedule, offering options for internships and research in the fall. It draws students from more than 30 majors with one common minor: innovation. Thirty-eight percent of UF's undergraduates conduct research, while 17 percent study abroad through university-sponsored, exchange, and affiliate programs in more than 50 countries.

Led by Governor Ron DeSantis, conservative politicians have pushed hard in recent years to centralize governance and alter the general education curriculum to emphasize conservative academic priorities. The Hamilton Center for Classical and Civic Education, for example, focuses on the Western canon and civic learning. Faculty members, however, complain that the university is undermining academic freedom, faculty governance, and other long-standing principles of higher education.

UF's academic climate is intense and collaborative. "Closer to midterms and final exams, [the] campus feels constricted and very tense, with everyone huddled in libraries. However, around football season, [the] campus tends to be more relaxed," says one political science major. Despite the university's huge size, half of all undergraduate classes have fewer than 20 students. Some students say they have to climb a mountain of bureaucracy if a course they need is full, but the administration has hired around 500 new faculty over the past few years to improve undergraduate student/faculty ratios. Professors often have deep professional experience and bring enthusiasm to their work, though students frequently find teaching assistants behind lecterns. A junior says, "The quality of instruction is somewhat low in introductory classes but ramps up significantly in more specialized courses."

Students describe their classmates as "very outgoing and friendly" and "leadership-oriented." UF is Florida's flagship university, and 85 percent of undergraduates hail from the Sunshine State, while 3 percent come from overseas. Black students represent 5 percent of the student body, Asian Americans 12 percent, Hispanics/Latinos 25 percent, and multiracial students 5 percent. Efforts to increase diversity among students and faculty have recently begun to face political headwinds. Students say there is a mix of political views on campus, and racial tensions can occasionally flare up. One first-generation student of color remarks, "It's great to be a Gator, but it's hard to not be represented on this campus." UF offers more than 250 athletic scholarships as well as thousands of merit scholarships averaging $3,200. The Machen Florida Opportunity Scholarship provides funds and resources for first-generation, low-income students.

> "It's great to be a Gator."

Undergrads typically live on campus during their first year but then move out after that; overall, 25 percent of students stay on campus. Dorms are described as comfortable, and a senior advises students "to live on campus for at least one year to really immerse oneself in the UF experience and for simple convenience." Dining halls get mixed reviews, but students agree that suitable provisions are made for vegetarians and vegans. Campus security draws praise thanks to a robust police presence and a late-night "Later Gator" transportation system. "The STRIVE center works to educate the student body against sexual assault and other sexual violence on campus," notes a sociology and women's studies major.

Students at UF have more than 900 student organizations to choose from, and a psychology major says, "Getting involved on campus takes time, but it's a surefire way to find a mini community in a university that can be dauntingly massive." Eighteen percent of UF's men and 25 percent of the women go Greek; rush is held before classes start in the fall and again in the spring. Students report that "elitism" of Greek groups and the outsize influence they have on campus life, especially student government, are common complaints. UF students have a well-deserved national reputation for knowing how to party, but the binge-drinking rate has fallen sharply as a result of tough enforcement of zero-tolerance campus policies, including a ban on drinking games. A senior points out that "off-campus parties are certainly a fixture" of the social scene, especially in the Midtown area across from the football stadium.

The men's basketball team won its third national championship in 2025.

Gainesville, a city of about 148,000 between the Atlantic Ocean and the Gulf of Mexico, largely revolves around the university. "Gainesville is an awesome, young town that is perfectly suited for college students who wish to relax and unwind," a student says. There are plenty of stores, restaurants, and bars, as well as a sports arena and the Center for Performing Arts, which brings in world-class symphony orchestras, Broadway plays, opera, and large-scale ballet productions. The university owns a nearby lake, which is "great for lazy Sundays" and more vigorous water sports, and there's a plethora of parks, forests, rivers, and streams for backpacking, camping, and canoeing. Orlando and the beaches of St. Augustine and Jacksonville are also popular destinations.

> "Off-campus parties are certainly a fixture."

Sports are a year-round obsession here, and the students go wild anytime the Division I Gators take to the court, field, or gridiron, especially when they're squaring off against rivals Florida State or the University of Georgia. The annual homecoming extravaganza, known as "Gator Growl," is billed as the biggest student-run pep rally in the country. The university fields 19 varsity teams, most of which compete in the ferocious Southeastern Conference. The men's basketball team won its third national championship in 2025. Men's and women's track and field and men's golf recently won national titles. Men's and women's swimming and diving, women's gymnastics, softball, and lacrosse have been conference champions. More than 40 intramural leagues and tournaments are offered, as well as nearly 50 club sports, and for those who don't want to join a team, the 60,000-square-foot fitness park offers aerobics classes, martial arts, strength training equipment, and squash and racquetball courts.

For some students, the university's political troubles are concerning, and some find its sheer size to be overwhelming. For others, the size is a drawing card that means plenty of opportunities to pursue their interests or find new ones. Combine great weather with nationally recognized programs in engineering and business and nationally ranked athletic teams, and it's easy to see why Sunshine State natives get juiced up about studying here.

If You Apply To ›

Florida: Early action, regular decision. SATs or ACTs: required. Accepts the Common Application. Apply to particular school within UF.

Florida Institute of Technology

150 West University Boulevard, Melbourne, FL 32901

Florida Tech is practically a branch of the nearby Kennedy Space Center, so aeronautical science, aviation, and aerospace engineering are popular specialties. The Atlantic Ocean is close at hand, making the school an ideal spot for marine biology and ocean engineering. The only geographical drawback is the occasional early-fall hurricane evacuation. Florida Tech is the smallest of the major technical institutions in the Southeast. Strong international flavor.

Students at the Florida Institute of Technology can explore the endless depths of the ocean or shoot for the stars. Located just 40 minutes from one of NASA's primary launch pads, Florida Tech is a child of the nation's space program and the only independent technological university in the Southeast. The school's subtropical setting is perfect for scientific research and study in oceanography, meteorology, marine biology, and environmental science. It comes as no surprise that some of the most cutting-edge work in space and water-related sciences happens here. The combination of academic excellence and a convenient central Florida location draws students to this high-flying and innovative school.

Founded in 1958 to meet the academic needs of engineers and scientists working at what is now the Kennedy Space Center, Florida Tech's 130-acre contemporary campus features a botanical garden and an aquatic center. Campus architecture ranges from traditional redbrick to modern. The L3Harris Student Design Center is a high-tech space that serves seniors working on capstone projects in engineering and science. Recent construction includes the $18 million Nelson Health Sciences building with expanded opportunities for undergraduate education and research in biomedical engineering and biomedical sciences; a new 5,600 square-foot eSports facility; and the $1.25 million Mertens Marine Center, which includes research and lab spaces for students training in marine sciences.

If you're considering Florida Tech, make sure you have a strong background in math and science, especially chemistry and physics. Everyone must take courses in communication, physical or life science, mathematics, humanities, and social sciences and demonstrate proficiency in the technologies pertinent to their chosen major. All majors include hands-on projects and capstone requirements. Almost all first-years take part in the University Experience course, which helps them adapt to college life. Popular majors include aerospace engineering, mechanical engineering, computer science, and aeronautical science. Sustainability studies is one of Florida Tech's fastest-growing majors; a new major in environmental science and sustainability launched in 2025, and astrobiology is the first undergraduate program of its kind. Prospective aviation students can major in aviation management, aviation meteorology, aviation human factors and safety, and aeronautical science—all of which are offered with or without a flight option. The flight school has a modern fleet of more than 40 airplanes and 11 flight-training simulators.

> "Many professors are deeply passionate about educating students."

The academic climate is rigorous, but Florida Tech students enjoy rising to the challenge. "Students here want to spend extra time in the library or take those unpaid undergrad research positions," asserts a senior. Forty-eight percent of the classes have fewer than 20 students, and the majority are taught by full professors. "Many professors are deeply passionate about educating students and making a positive impact on their lives," says a meteorology major. In a move designed to elevate its national standing, Florida Tech now offers faculty tenure. Students in the Honors College work to achieve one of three tiers of recognition, depending on GPA and the number of honors credits completed: Mercury (honors), Gemini (high honors), and Apollo (highest honors). Research opportunities are available at the Indian River Lagoon or on the RV Delphinus, a 60-foot research boat owned by the school. Established in collaboration with Apollo 11 astronaut Buzz Aldrin, the Aldrin Space Institute conducts research and development intended to support an eventual human settlement on Mars. The ProTrack cooperative education program allows students in the College of Engineering and Science to complete three semester-long paid work experiences. Study abroad options are available in Oxford, England, and other locales, although only 6 percent of undergrads take advantage of them. The Student Success and Support Center is called "invaluable" by a junior.

"We are a space school," comments a psychology major. "Everyone knows about and follows advances in space technology in some way." Forty-one percent of Florida Tech students are Florida natives, and at 12 percent, the school's international population is large. "It is a microcosm of intelligent people representing 100 countries," says a sophomore. Black students represent 5 percent of the student body, Asian Americans 3 percent, Hispanics/Latinos 17 percent, and multiracial students 3 percent. Women make up only a third of the student body. Florida Tech offers merit scholarships averaging $16,700 and more than 200 athletic scholarships.

Fifty-four percent of students make their home in Florida Tech's modern dorms, which an aviation management major calls "very comfortable." First-years are required to live on campus in large double rooms or suite-style accommodations. Four-student apartments are available to a small percentage of qualifying upperclassmen by lottery. The meal plan is an open, unlimited arrangement, and students give the food positive reviews

> "Everyone knows about and follows advances in space technology in some way."

for variety and diversity. "We have international nights every month," cheers a senior. "All the students love them (literally had escargot one day)."

(continued)

Academics: ✍ ✍ ✍
Social: 💬 💬 💬
Q of L: ★ ★ ★
Admissions: (800) 888-4348
Email Address: admission@fit.edu

Strong Programs:
Aerospace Engineering
Astrobiology
Aviation
Biomedical Engineering
Computer Science
Marine Biology
Mechanical Engineering
Ocean Engineering

Watching rocket launches from campus with a trained eye and a cold brew is a treasured pastime.

Watching rocket launches from campus with a trained eye and a cold brew is a treasured pastime. The Rat, a campus eatery with pool tables and big-screen TVs, is a popular hangout, and there are more than 120 active clubs and organizations on campus; gaming, sci-fi, and performance-oriented groups such as Pep Band are student favorites. Fraternities and sororities claim 9 percent of the men and 3 percent of the women, respectively, and students describe the party scene as moderate. "This is a smaller STEM school, so there aren't parties everywhere you turn, but they are there if you look for them," reports a construction management major. Homecoming and the annual International Festival are much-anticipated events.

Melbourne is "a nice little beach town," says a senior, and students spend much of their downtime surfing, fishing, sailing, and hanging out at the beach. "Everybody goes to the beach whenever they can, even just to do homework," explains a sophomore. Bikes and skateboards are popular modes of transportation around campus; dining halls and other common areas are equipped with skateboard racks. Public transportation in the area is limited, so students recommend having a car on campus. More diversions can be found in the abundant theme parks of Orlando or at the Kennedy Space Center, each within an hour's drive.

The Florida Tech Panthers field 15 varsity teams that compete in Division II. Men's and women's soccer and swimming, men's rowing, and volleyball are competitive. The university's Precision Flight Team, the Falcons, regularly wins awards from the National Intercollegiate Flying Association. The expanding intramural and club sports programs offer sports like soccer, flag football, and pickleball.

Whether it's surveying the sky 30,000 feet above or marine coral 50 feet below the surface of the sea, students at Florida Tech get hands-on experience that serves to sharpen the school's already specialized, high-quality academics—all in a small, more personal setting. The administration continues to focus on capital improvements, sponsor cutting-edge research, and embrace global diversity. And with beaches and amusements close at hand, students can have some real fun in the sun while they prepare for high-flying or low-lying careers.

Overlaps

Caltech, University of Central Florida, Embry-Riddle Aeronautical, University of Florida, Illinois Institute of Technology, Rensselaer, Rochester Institute of Technology, Stevens Institute of Technology

If You Apply To ›

Florida Tech: Rolling admissions. SATs or ACTs: required. Accepts the Common Application with supplement.

Florida Southern College

111 Lake Hollingsworth Drive, Lakeland, FL 33801

The oldest private college in Florida, FSC combines top-ranked Division II athletics, strong career-oriented programs, an active Greek system, and a picturesque campus that doubles as a Frank Lloyd Wright museum. Centrally located between Tampa and Orlando. Competes with Rollins and Eckerd among leading liberal arts schools in the Southeast.

Website: www.flsouthern.edu
Location: Small City
Private
Total Enrollment: 3,194
Undergraduates: 2,626
Male/Female: 37/63

Since its founding in 1885, Florida Southern College has been committed to providing students with a solid liberal arts foundation and exceptional signature programs. Students enjoy a bevy of academic choices, including outstanding preprofessional programs, extensive internship opportunities, and a vigorous study abroad program. They also appreciate the college's attractive setting and its mission to develop well-rounded graduates. The college is affiliated with the United Methodist Church, to which 3 percent of students belong.

Situated on 113 acres overlooking pristine Lake Hollingsworth, Florida Southern is home to the world's largest single-site collection of structures designed by iconic architect Frank Lloyd Wright. The campus features 12 original Wright structures, as well as the Usonian Faculty House, which the college constructed in 2013 based on Wright's 1939 design for single-family faculty housing and which serves as a museum and welcome center for the college's architectural tourism. Wright's Annie Pfeiffer Chapel is a popular meeting and performance venue. The campus also houses several buildings designed by Robert A. M. Stern, former dean of the Yale School of Architecture, including the Becker Business Building. The Weinstein Computer Sciences Center features high-tech classrooms, workshops, and study spaces.

Florida Southern's core curriculum is based on student learning outcomes in eight areas, ranging from critical and creative thinking to effective communication to personal and social responsibility. Most classes meet for four hours a week, with at least one of those hours fully devoted to engaged learning techniques such as debate, small-group discussions, case studies, and research. As part of the required Passport Program for student involvement, students attend a minimum of six events every year, choosing from more than 300 options across six Passport categories: school pride, learning beyond the classroom, fine arts, service and diversity, health and wellness, and pathways to profession.

FSC students may choose from more than 70 undergraduate programs. The most popular majors include business administration, psychology, nursing, biology, elementary education, computer science, and accounting; all are among the college's strongest programs. The premed program boasts an exceptional placement rate in medical, dental, and pharmacy schools nationwide. Unique at the undergraduate level, a major in citrus and horticultural science involves plenty of hands-on experience thanks to FSC's on-campus collection of citrus trees. In addition to seven majors, the Barnett School of Business and Free Enterprise offers minors in entrepreneurship, eSports management, and healthcare management. Dual-degree programs are available in engineering with Washington University in St. Louis and in pharmacy with Lake Erie College of Osteopathic Medicine.

"We have a very relaxed academic climate," says a senior. "FSC is a huge advocate for engaged learning, so we always end up working in groups, creating a very collaborative culture." Sixty-one percent of classes enroll fewer than 20 students, and students praise professors for their accessibility. "The faculty take time to get to know the students," comments a criminology major. Students are bullish about FSC's career services. Says an interpersonal and organizational communication major, "The Career Center is the best resource on campus. They offer résumé building, [mock] interviews, and many more things to help you with your future career."

All FSC students are guaranteed an internship, and 60 percent avail themselves of this opportunity. Students have interned with Charles Schwab, the Kennedy Center, OPEC, Fox News, the Walt Disney Company, NASA, and scores of other organizations. About a quarter of students go abroad, mostly through the Junior Journey program, which guarantees all full-time undergraduates a short-term travel-study experience, often at no additional cost. Students may embark on faculty-led trips in May or during academic breaks to domestic and international locales such as Alaska, the Bahamas, Spain, and Japan. Traditional study abroad options are available as well. Qualified students may enroll in the highly selective Honors Program, which offers specialized gen-ed courses. Forty-three percent of students carry out undergraduate research projects during their time at FSC, usually as part of a senior capstone course. More than 100 students present their research and creative projects every year at Fiat Lux (Latin for "Let there be light"), the college's annual celebration of undergraduate work.

(continued)

Financial Aid: 97%
Pell Grant: 26%
Expense: Pr $
Student Loans: 55%
Average Debt: $ $
Applicants: 10,874
Accepted: 59%
Enrolled: 10%
Grad in 6 Years: 69%
Returning First-years: 78%
Academics: ✍ ✍ ✍
Social: 🗩 🗩 🗩
Q of L: ★ ★ ★
Admissions: (863) 680-4131
Email Address:
 fscadm@flsouthern.edu

Strong Programs:
Accounting
Biology
Business Administration
Citrus and Horticultural
 Science
Computer Science
Elementary Education
Nursing
Psychology

> **"We have a very relaxed academic climate."**

The social scene is active on campus, with frequent cookouts, concerts, sporting events, and more.

Florida Southern students are "very down-to-earth and easy to get along with," says one denizen. Fifty-one percent of students hail from Florida; 5 percent are international. Black students account for 6 percent of the population, Asian Americans 3 percent, Hispanics/Latinos 15 percent, and multiracial students 4 percent. "While the school is mostly conservative (as one might expect of a school in central Florida), students are generally tolerant of their peers' political opinions," reports an environmental studies major. The college awards merit scholarships of up to $26,000 as well as talent awards and over 200 athletic scholarships.

Eighty-five percent of FSC undergrads reside in student housing. First-year students live together in dedicated residence halls, while upperclassmen may choose from a variety of living arrangements, including college-owned apartments within walking distance of the campus. According to one student, some residential buildings "could be updated to be more modern." The cafeteria serves up "average" fare, including special options for vegetarians and vegans. Students report feeling safe on campus, and the "Just Ask" initiative aims to educate the community on preventing sexual assault and gender-based discrimination.

> **"The faculty take time to get to know the students."**

The social scene is active on campus, with frequent cookouts, concerts, sporting events, a farmers market, and activities organized by more than 100 student clubs. "The school sponsors various bimonthly wellness trips that vary from paintball to snorkeling with manatees," adds a student. Twenty-two percent of the men and 26 percent of the women go Greek, and a junior says, "Greek life definitely defines the party culture, but parties are often very inclusive." Alcohol is prohibited on campus, and a senior notes that alcohol policies "are not always obeyed but are enforced." FSC offers a number of traditions, including Southern's Got Talent, Cram Jam during finals week, the Winter Wonderland festival (complete with a Christmas tree lighting and temporary Florida-style snow), and the end-of-year Fair-Well Festival.

Lakeland (population 115,000) offers eateries, malls, movie theaters, and a historic downtown district with unique shops and attractions. "Lakeland is a great college town!" cheers a junior. "There are plenty of hip stores and restaurants." Many students venture out into the local community to volunteer, often through Greek life programs, or to take part in off-campus church services. For those with access to wheels, popular road trips include excursions to the Gulf Coast's sandy beaches, Orlando's famed theme parks, or the Florida Keys.

> **"The Career Center is the best resource on campus."**

The Florida Southern Moccasins (the snake, not the footwear) field 22 varsity teams, most of which compete in Division II as a member of the Sunshine State Conference. In addition, three club sports compete at the varsity level: equestrian, eSports, and men's ice hockey. Among the competitive "Mocs" teams, men's swimming, women's lacrosse, men's and women's basketball, men's cross-country, baseball, and women's volleyball stand out. "Our athletes dominate Division II sports every year," boasts one student, and Rollins and the University of Tampa are the Mocs' chief rivals. Intramural sports and activities sign up 20 percent of undergraduates; the most popular activities include flag football, volleyball, basketball, floor hockey, and Wiffle ball.

Florida Southern has a lot going for it. Despite the ubiquitous college student laments of limited parking and so-so food, most are quick to point out that they have access to strong academic programs, championship athletics, and all the sun and fun a person could want. "Florida Southern College is a great community where students can grow academically, socially, and emotionally," says one senior.

If You Apply To ›

Florida Southern: Early decision, early action, rolling admissions. SATs or ACTs: optional. Accepts the Common Application with supplement.

222 South Copeland Street, Tallahassee, FL 32306

Located in Florida's Panhandle, FSU is far from the glitz of South Beach, though location in the state's capital is an asset. The College of Motion Picture Arts is among the best around, and business and the arts are also strong. Big emphasis on undergraduate research. Notable features for first-year students include several living/learning options, study abroad opportunities, and freshman interest groups. Interference in academic policy making by politicians has increased in recent years.

At Florida State University, you could have a Nobel laureate for a professor, study in one of the finest science facilities in the Southeast, or network at the state capitol. While the choices are plentiful here—"FSU has too many resources to list," raves a junior—the pace of life makes it possible to taste a little of everything: a wide array of solid academic options, blistering Florida sunshine, and plenty to do, from football to Tallahassee hangouts. "There is a relaxed feel to campus that makes FSU the cool, laid-back friend of the Florida university system," says a student.

FSU is located in the Florida Panhandle, with rolling hills, flowering azaleas and dogwoods, and a canopy of moss-draped oaks. Glistening Gulf of Mexico waters are only half an hour away. Situated on 485 compact acres, the main campus features collegiate Jacobean structures surrounded by plenty of shade trees, with some modern facilities sprinkled in. FSU recently opened the Interdisciplinary Research and Commercialization Building, a hub for collaboration and innovation in quantum science, engineering, and material science. As with other major public universities in the Florida state system, FSU is dealing with pressures from conservative state political leaders bent on shaping curricular and governance policies and limiting faculty independence.

All FSU students must take at least one general education core course in communication, mathematics, social sciences, humanities, and natural sciences, as well as meet a civic literacy requirement. Students can choose from nearly 200 undergraduate majors, the most popular of which are psychology, business-related majors (especially finance and marketing), criminology, and political science. The neuroscience major is strong, and other outstanding programs include theater, international affairs, and nursing. The English department and the College of Motion Picture Arts have consistently won national and international awards. Engineering programs are a joint effort with neighboring Florida A&M; the FAMU-FSU College of Engineering holds the distinction of being the country's only shared college of engineering. The B.S. in public health program is rapidly growing in popularity. The immersive Engage 100 program helps first-year students acclimate to FSU.

Students report that the academic climate varies by department and depends on how much students choose to challenge themselves, but a finance and management information systems major says an FSU education helps students "develop intellectual strength through rigorous academic coursework, acquire skills through learning and hands-on experiences, and demonstrate strong character by being involved in their community." Sixty-three percent of undergraduate classes have fewer than 20 students, and a psychology major says, "Professors and graduate instructors are amicable, welcoming, and express genuine interest in the success of their students." First-years can take advantage of living/learning communities (where students with similar interests or majors live together in the same residence hall) and freshman

> **"FSU [is] the cool, laid-back friend of the Florida university system."**

Website: www.fsu.edu
Location: Small City
Public
Total Enrollment: 35,799
Undergraduates: 29,271
Male/Female: 44/56
Financial Aid: 82%
Pell Grant: 25%
Expense: Pub $ $
Student Loans: 29%
Average Debt: $
Applicants: 78,272
Accepted: 24%
Enrolled: 31%
Grad in 6 Years: 86%
Returning First-years: 96%
Academics: ✏ ✏ ✏
Social: 🗨 🗨 🗨
Q of L: ★ ★ ★ ★ ★
Admissions: (850) 644-6200
Email Address:
admissions@fsu.edu

Strong Programs:
Computer Science
Criminology
Education
Fine and Performing Arts
International Affairs
Motion Picture Arts
Nursing
Psychology

interest groups (clusters of high-demand first-year courses that have been linked by a theme or academic program). LGBTQ+ housing options are also available.

Honors courses, usually limited to 20 students, offer gifted students the opportunity to rub shoulders with top faculty, and students highly recommend applying. "You can live with other honors students, take classes with motivated students, and push yourself to your greatest achievements," enthuses a first-year. Certain students can even earn their degrees in three years. About a quarter of undergrads conduct some sort of out-of-class research, and students highly praise the nationally acclaimed Undergraduate Research Opportunity Program, which connects first-years and sophomores to faculty research projects for two semesters. Internships and political jobs abound for tomorrow's politicians since the state capitol and supreme court are nearby. For those with wanderlust, FSU offers extensive study abroad programs in which 14 percent of students take part.

Perhaps not surprisingly, FSU's student body has a distinctly Floridian flavor: in-staters comprise 82 percent of the group and international students 6 percent. Seven percent of undergraduates are Black, 4 percent are Asian American, 24 percent are Hispanic/Latino, and 4 percent are multiracial. The students at FSU are a friendly mixture of small-towners and city dwellers, and political tastes vary as well. "Politically minded students have many opportunities to join marches, protests, and campaigns," says a sophomore. Merit scholarships averaging $3,900 are available to qualified scholars, and athletes vie for more than 350 scholarships in 20 sports.

Residence halls, some of which have just been built in the last few years, are primarily for first-year students, and 79 percent of them live there. The halls get good reviews, and a senior says each has "their own community vibe." After their first year, students generally move into the apartments and houses located within walking distance of campus; the city and campus bus systems are useful for those who live farther away. Students enjoy meals in the Suwannee Room, a grand Gothic dining hall built in 1913, and they can choose from nearly 30 other dining locations around campus as well. Students cite FSU's student-driven "kNOw MORE" campaign as helping to educate the community about preventing sexual assault, and FSU's Counseling and Psychological Services offers daily drop-in workshops via Zoom as well as other programs to support student mental health.

When they're not studying, FSU students keep busy with films, concerts, and small parties in the residence halls or off campus. Eighteen percent of the men and 25 percent of the women belong to Greek life; Greek social activities have been somewhat curtailed with the implementation of safety measures intended to reduce the hazards of underage and binge drinking. With over 750 student organizations, "There are so many ways to get involved here, from Greek life to identity-based student unions, there is no limit to the impact you can make as a student leader," says a senior. The Flying High Circus draws students as participants and viewers twice yearly. Many head out to Tallahassee's "beautiful bar patios, art parks, and cafés," says one junior, or to its hopping club scene for nightlife.

"Game day is something that you won't want to miss!"

FSU Athletic teams compete in the Division I Atlantic Coast Conference, where it has become quite a powerhouse. School spirit runs high during football season, and each game is heralded by the beating of the campus spirit drum. "Game day is something that you won't want to miss," raves a senior, noting FSU students get free tickets to home games. Women's soccer were national champs in 2025; recent conference winners include women's beach volleyball, softball, men's tennis, and men's and women's golf. FSU's newest sport is women's lacrosse, which was recently elevated to varsity status. The many popular intramural and club sports include pickleball, baseball, disc golf, fencing, and more.

Despite the maneuvering by politicians, Florida State still remains a solid choice for those seeking knowledge under the blazing Florida sun. The school's laid-back, cheery atmosphere is appealing to many, but make no mistake: Students here take their learning and their futures seriously. With so much on offer, it's no wonder some students say, "Wish we could stay forever!"

Fordham University

Rose Hill Campus: 441 East Fordham Road, Bronx, NY 10458
Lincoln Center Campus: 113 West 60th Street, New York, NY 10023

New York City's Fordham is riding high, even though it is still operating in the shadows of urban icons like NYU and Boston College. There is no better location than Lincoln Center in Manhattan, where the performing arts programs are housed. The Bronx campus is home to larger programs and adjacent to the New York Botanical Garden and Bronx Zoo.

At Fordham University, the tradition of the Society of Jesus (Jesuits) pervades all aspects of life, from the quality of teaching to the emphasis on personal relationships to the pursuit of both "wisdom and learning," which also happens to be the school's motto. Students benefit from two campuses: the gated Bronx community of Rose Hill and the Lincoln Center facility, just a short subway ride away from the heart of midtown Manhattan. They can also take advantage of the Fordham Internship Promise, which guarantees at least one internship, research experience, or other hands-on learning opportunity before graduation. Though 34 percent of the student population is Roman Catholic, there's plenty of variation in ethnic background and in students' political, social, and religious views. Fordham, which dates to 1841, is "more diverse than Boston College, less funky than NYU," says a German and English double major.

The 85-acre Rose Hill campus is an oasis of trees, grass, and Gothic architecture; it's close to the New York Botanical Garden and Yankee Stadium. Rose Hill is home to Fordham College at Rose Hill, the largest liberal arts school at the university, as well as the primary programs of the Gabelli School of Business. The campus center at Rose Hill, which combines fitness and dining facilities, student services, and event spaces, received a $200 million renovation. The Lincoln Center campus benefits from its proximity to the Juilliard School, the CBS and ABC television studios between 10th and 11th Avenues, and Lincoln Center itself, Manhattan's performing arts hub. A new Learning and Innovation Technology Environment Center opened on the Lincoln Center campus, offering recording studios, 3-D printers, and more. Shuttles run between the two campuses.

Undergraduate requirements include coursework in English, social and natural sciences, philosophy, theology, history, math/computer science, and fine arts. Students also complete four distinctly Jesuit Eloquentia Perfecta (or "perfect eloquence") seminars, including a capstone senior seminar on values. First-year students can opt to participate in Urban Plunge, three days of exploring the city's diverse neighborhoods and working on a team service project before the start of the fall semester.

> "Serving the City internships have given me the opportunity to get nonprofit experience while also getting paid."

Website: www.fordham.edu
Location: City Center
Private
Total Enrollment: 13,737
Undergraduates: 10,101
Male/Female: 39/61
Financial Aid: 92%
Pell Grant: 33%
Expense: Pr $ $ $
Student Loans: 52%
Average Debt: $ $ $
Applicants: 43,364
Accepted: 59%
Enrolled: 10%
Grad in 6 Years: 82%
Returning First-years: 89%
Academics: ✍ ✍ ✍
Social: 🍷 🍷 🍷
Q of L: ★ ★ ★
Admissions: (718) 817-4000
Email Address:
  enroll@fordham.edu

Strong Programs:
Biological Sciences
Communications and Media
Film and Television
Finance
Global Business
History
Psychology
Theatre

No matter where at Fordham you study, humanities are a good choice. Strengths at Rose Hill include history, philosophy, biological sciences, psychology, economics, and film and television, while at Lincoln Center, theatre, English, and communications shine. The most popular majors across the university are business administration, global business, finance, and psychology. The B.F.A. in dance is offered in partnership with the Alvin Ailey American Dance Theater; students must be accepted by both Fordham and the Ailey audition panel. Fordham's public radio station, WFUV, offers hands-on experience for aspiring deejays and radio journalists. The notable global business program at Lincoln Center engages students in courses about the global dimensions of business and requires a study abroad experience. Rose Hill offers 3–2 engineering programs with Columbia and Case Western Reserve, and both colleges have a 3–3 program with Fordham Law School as well as 4–1 accelerated masters programs in many majors.

"Fordham offers a good balance between academic rigor and a relaxed atmosphere," says a business administration major. Half of all undergraduate classes have fewer than 20 students, and professors are praised for bringing much-appreciated professional experience and real-world perspective to the lectern. Undergraduate research opportunities are available, some with funding. Business students often obtain internships on Wall Street or elsewhere in the Manhattan financial community. Students give high marks to the Career Center, and a sociology major cheers, "Serving the City internships have given me the opportunity to get nonprofit experience while also getting paid." For students who wish to travel, Fordham offers over 100 study abroad programs in more than 50 countries, including those offered by the university's London Centre.

A political science major says Fordham students are "open-minded and eager to learn about different cultures and perspectives" but are also "opinionated, assertive, and outspoken." This is, after all, New York City. Thirty-eight percent of undergraduates hail from New York State, and many of the rest are from elsewhere on the East Coast; 8 percent come from abroad. Black students make up 7 percent of the student body, Asian Americans 14 percent, Hispanics/Latinos 21 percent, and multiracial students 5 percent. The university supports a vibrant LGBTQ community, and while it leans left, there is a healthy variety of political views. "I was pleasantly surprised to find thriving artistic, intellectual, and alternative subcultures that I don't think Fordham advertises enough," offers a senior. Thirty-three percent of incoming first-years receive Pell Grants. Hundreds of merit and audition-based scholarships averaging $19,100 are available as well as athletic scholarships in 19 sports.

> "[Students are] open-minded and eager to learn about different cultures and perspectives."

Forty-three percent of Fordham undergrads live in the dorms, and those who snag rooms in the two high-rise residence halls near Lincoln Center are saved from the borough's greedy brokers and unconscionable rents. Both campuses offer living/learning communities; all incoming Lincoln Center students participate in the first-year experience integrated learning community, while first-years at Rose Hill can apply for the Manresa Scholars Program, which offers access to academic live-in tutors and a Jesuit priest in residence. According to a biological sciences major, the dining services "cater to many special diets, such as vegan, vegetarian, halal, or kosher." Both campuses are safe, students say.

Fordham's Campus Activities Board sponsors events like movies, concerts, and dances on both campuses; there is no Greek system. Says one student, "The social scene is approachable and community-based." Students are far more likely to head to nearby bars, clubs, performances, festivals, and cultural events. "New York City has so much to offer that I rarely hear of parties," says a communications major. But an English major says as students become juniors and seniors, "Clubs and sports 'houses' become the main party spots, with themed and seasonal events mirroring that of Greek life." The Rose Hill campus backs up against the Bronx Zoo, and Arthur Avenue, the Little Italy of the Bronx, "has some of the best food I've ever had in my life, and for great prices," says an English and theology major. Students look forward to the President's Ball in the fall and Spring Weekend, which features a major concert and the Under the Tent dance on Martyrs' Lawn at Rose Hill. Forty-six percent of students participate in Fordham's Center for Community Engaged Learning, which sponsors classes in which students learn with and from neighbors and local groups working to build stronger communities.

The Fordham Rams compete in Division I and the Atlantic 10 Conference (and the Patriot League for football), and its location near the Hudson River has helped to produce the women's rowing Metropolitan champs. The most competitive teams include men's water polo, football, and baseball, men's and women's basketball, and men's and women's soccer. The Lombardi Memorial Athletic Center (named for football legend Vince, an alumnus) supports club sports and intramurals. Perhaps Fordham's most unusual athletic endeavor is Riding the Ram. "Students are expected to climb on the granite blocks and sit on the bronze statue of the Fordham Ram at least once in their time here," explains a computer science major. "However, ride the Ram at your own risk, as you will be reprimanded if caught in the act."

"The social scene is approachable and community-based."

"Fordham University's institutional personality is marked by its rich history, blending academic excellence with a commitment to social justice and global citizenship," says a finance major. Its admissions, academic standards, and national profile are all inching up thanks to Fordham's idea that diversity and community can coexist, instilling confidence and pride in Fordham students and loyalty in the expanding alumni base. Says a senior, "I'd recommend anyone who's interested in the humanities and social sciences, isn't interested in the exclusivity of Greek life but still likes to have fun, and likes a smaller school feel to apply to Fordham."

If You Apply To ›

Fordham: Early decision I and II, early action, regular decision. SATs or ACTs: optional. Accepts the Common Application. Apply to particular school or program. Theatre and dance applicants must audition. Portfolio recommended for visual arts applicants.

Franklin & Marshall College

933 Harrisburg Avenue, Lancaster, PA 17603

F&M is known for launching hardworking preprofessional students. Faces tough competition from the likes of Bucknell, Dickinson, Gettysburg, and Lafayette for Pennsylvania-bound students. Known for natural sciences, business, government, and emphasis on civic engagement. Meets the demonstrated need of every student. Strong contingent of international students.

Franklin & Marshall College is set in one of the country's 50 largest metro areas, but you can still enjoy the serene hills of Pennsylvania's Amish country nearby. While the city of Lancaster has modernized beautifully, parts of this historic town look much the same as they did when two acclaimed but struggling colleges

Website: www.fandm.edu
Location: Small City
Private
Total Enrollment: 1,794
Undergraduates: 1,794
Male/Female: 49/51
Financial Aid: 76%
Pell Grant: 18%
Expense: Pr $ $ $ $
Student Loans: 60%
Average Debt: $ $ $
Applicants: 9,881
Accepted: 28%
Enrolled: 17%
Grad in 6 Years: 84%
Returning First-years: 90%
Academics: ✍ ✍ ✍ ✍
Social: 🗩 🗩 🗩
Q of L: ★ ★ ★
Admissions: (877) 678-9111
Email Address:
admission@fandm.edu

Strong Programs:
Biology
Business, Organizations, and
  Society
Computer Science
Creative Writing
Economics
Government
Neuroscience
Psychology

The biggest annual event is the Spring Arts Festival, held the weekend before finals.

decided to pool their resources. In 1853, Marshall College (named for Chief Justice John Marshall) merged with Franklin College (started in 1787 with a donation of 200 English pounds from Ben himself). These days, F&M is modernizing, too, particularly by bringing a more global and experiential learning to the curriculum while adding majors like data science and film and media studies. "We are Diplomats who champion freedom of expression," administrators say, referring to the school's varsity sports name that references Franklin's diplomatic career. F&M seeks to create "extraordinary opportunities for students to be the curators of their own academic experiences."

F&M's 200-acre campus is surrounded by a quiet residential neighborhood shaded by majestic maple and oak trees. The campus itself is an arboretum and boasts 65 buildings of mainly Gothic and colonial architecture. The Diplomatic Cafe and Hartman Green appeal to students seeking a study respite in the middle of campus. Other notable facilities include the Life Sciences and Philosophy Building and Martin Library of the Sciences. As part of a decade-long urban renewal project, the college has developed 28 acres of land, once home to aged industrial buildings and rail yards, into a North Campus for athletic fields and facilities. Other additions include the Lombardo Welcome Center.

First-year students are introduced to F&M's academic community through a required Connections seminar, an intimate course that teaches the skills of critical analysis, research, writing, and civil debate. Additional general education components include requirements in arts, humanities, language, social sciences, natural sciences, and world perspectives. F&M has long been known for being strong in the natural sciences; its computer science and creative writing programs are on the rise. F&M has an excellent reputation for preparing undergrads for medical school, law school, and other careers. Business, organizations, and society is the most popular major, followed by government, psychology, and economics. Students tout new programs, like the F&M in Harrisburg semester, which pairs government students with internships in state government. "It's an incredible opportunity for aspiring political science students," says a government major.

> **"[F&M professors are] generally very smart and a pleasure to learn from."**

Students uniformly describe the coursework as demanding, but a biology major adds, "Despite the intensity of the academics, there is not a strong sense of competition." The relatively small student body and intimate class sizes help create a feeling of community between students and professors, who are "generally very smart and a pleasure to learn from," says a government and history major. "It is easy to develop genuine, close relationships with them." Thirty-two percent of F&M students engage in directed research under the guidance of faculty, including students in the Hackman Summer Research Scholars program. In the summer, faculty-led study abroad programs head to countries such as China, Italy, Russia, and South Africa, and 28 percent of students study in locations around the world during their time at F&M.

A government major says his classmates are "very friendly, motivated, and involved." Twenty-six percent of students hail from Pennsylvania, and 17 percent come from foreign nations. Black students comprise 5 percent of the student body, Hispanics/Latinos 9 percent, Asian Americans 5 percent, and multiracial students 4 percent. While most students share a liberal point of view, "the average F&M student is politically informed but not necessarily active," says a senior. F&M students do, however, take an interest when it comes to extracurricular activities and social opportunities. The 100-plus clubs on campus attest to that, as does a high level of participation in community service activities. The school guarantees to meet 100 percent of admitted students' demonstrated need.

The college requires students to live in college-affiliated housing all four years, and housing options include residence halls organized into five College Houses, apartments, lofts, townhouses, and special-interest housing. The faculty-led College House system "gives students more of a homey feel, as there are things going on in your house every weekend," says a junior. First-years are placed into the same College House as other members of their Connections seminar. Boarders eat most of their meals in the campus dining hall under a flexible meal plan, but students are issued debit cards that they may use at a number of different food stops on campus. A senior reports, "F&M's student support services have grown increasingly strong in the last few years."

Four fraternities attract 3 percent of the men, and seven sororities attract 19 percent of the women. They are integral to the nightlife, although the residence halls and student organizations such as the College Entertainment Committee offer a range of alternatives, including concerts and comedians. But, says a junior, "Our social scene is much more dominated by Lancaster, which is a beautiful small city that is great to hang out in on the weekends." Ben's Underground, a popular student-run nightclub, and Hildy's, a tiny local bar, are also favorite meeting places. The biggest annual event is the Spring Arts Festival, held the weekend before finals, which includes live concerts, student air-band contests, art exhibits, games, booths, and barbecues. "Students jokingly call it 'The Coachella of Central Pennsylvania,'" says a junior. Another highlight is Flapjack Fest, when professors serve pancakes to students.

Lancaster, a historical and well-to-do city located in a larger metro area of more than 500,000, offers a 16-screen cinema, scores of shops and art galleries, a historic farmers market, brick-and-cobblestone streets, and a plethora of quaint restaurants and cafés. "Downtown is always a fun place to go if you can spend money," says a senior. Those with a hankering for contemporary action take road trips to Philly, Baltimore, Washington, D.C., and New York City.

> "Lancaster is a beautiful small city that is great to hang out in on the weekends."

With the exception of wrestling, which is Division I, F&M teams compete in Division III. The college boasts recent Centennial Conference championships in men's and women's lacrosse and men's golf. Varsity squads are called the Diplomats, a moniker that gained currency in 1935 when the football team nearly upset national powerhouse Fordham. The annual football game against Dickinson for the Conestoga Wagon trophy is always a crowd-pleaser. The college also offers a selection of four intramural sports and eight club sports, such as ice hockey, rugby, and ultimate Frisbee.

At Franklin & Marshall, a happy senior says, "We have a stellar reputation and the best faculty. An F&M education will prep you for any job, and alumni jump at the chance to help." The college's illustrious namesakes would no doubt be proud of the quality academics and ever-evolving opportunities at the institution that bears their names. "The world may not know us as well as other schools," says a junior, "but once you find us, we have a lot to offer."

Overlaps

Bucknell, Colby, Dickinson, Gettysburg, Hamilton, Lafayette, Lehigh, Penn State

If You Apply To ›

F&M: Early decision I and II, regular decision. SATs or ACTs: optional. Accepts the Common Application with supplement.

Furman University

3300 Poinsett Highway, Greenville, SC 29613

Furman's campus is gorgeous; the swans are a particularly elegant touch. With roughly 2,300 undergraduates, Furman is larger than Davidson and half the size of Wake Forest. Academic life includes a strong emphasis on off-campus experiences as well as undergrad research. Although traditionally conservative, Furman students are increasingly progressive and diverse.

Website: www.furman.edu
Location: Suburban
Private
Total Enrollment: 2,485
Undergraduates: 2,364
Male/Female: 42/58
Financial Aid: 99%
Pell Grant: 15%
Expense: Pr $ $
Student Loans: 36%
Average Debt: $ $ $
Applicants: 10,813
Accepted: 43%
Enrolled: 13%
Grad in 6 Years: 79%
Returning First-years: 91%
Academics: ✐ ✐ ✐
Social: 🍷 🍷 🍷
Q of L: ★ ★ ★
Admissions: (864) 294-2034
Email Address:
admissions@furman.edu

Strong Programs:
Biology
Business Administration
Chemistry
Communication Studies
Health Sciences
History
Politics and International
Affairs
Psychology

While deeply rooted in Southern culture and academic traditions, Furman University is seeking to be known as a place where strong liberal arts and sciences, not big-time athletic rivalries or a boisterous Greek scene, set the campus tone. Student diversity is still a work in progress, but a strong sense of community is well established. As one denizen puts it, "I would describe us as a 'Furman Family.'"

Furman's 750-acre campus is one of the country's most beautiful, with tree-lined malls, fountains, a formal rose garden and Japanese garden, and a 30-acre lake replete with swans and ducks. Flowering shrubs dot the well-kept lawns, which surround buildings in the classical revival, Colonial Williamsburg, and modern architectural styles. Many have porches, pediments, and other Southern touches, such as handmade Virginia brick. Lakeview Hall, a new $70 million dorm for first-year students, opened in 2024, and major renovations are ongoing to the North Village apartments that house third- and fourth-year students.

Founded by Southern Baptists in 1826 and named for a denominational leader, Furman operates under the "semester-plus" system. The school year begins in late August, and the first semester ends prior to the December holiday break. Students begin the second semester in January and then have the option of attending a three-week May Experience in (guess when). General education requirements include a first-year writing seminar and a series of core requirements that fulfill the

> **"Classes are not easy, but professors and academic sources are very accessible."**

following "ways of knowing": empirical studies, human cultures, mathematical and formal reasoning, foreign language, ultimate questions, and body and mind. Finally, students must fulfill global awareness requirements, which includes a class on identities, equity, and justice. The most popular majors include health sciences, communication studies, politics and international affairs, psychology, and history. Business administration is among the stronger programs, along with chemistry and biology. Students in the health sciences program have access to the innovative international health and nutrition program as well as a human performance laboratory. Internships and research opportunities are available through the Institute for the Advancement of Community Health.

Furman's academic climate is "rigorous and intentional," says a psychology and English major. "Classes are not easy, but professors and academic sources are very accessible for students." Seventy-five percent of classes have fewer than 20 students, helping students get to know faculty members well, and the Pathways advising program helps first-years and sophomores stay on track.

The Furman Advantage ensures that every undergraduate will have the opportunity to participate in research, an internship, or study abroad. "I was offered a paid, interdisciplinary research position within two weeks on campus my freshman year," explains a math major. Thirty-nine percent of undergrads conduct research, many assisting professors through paid Furman Summer Research Fellowships.

Furman typically sends one of the largest student delegations to the annual National Conference on Undergraduate Research. Internships are popular, and 40 percent of students study abroad through one of two dozen Furman-sponsored programs on five continents. "Some of our offerings consist of studying happiness in Copenhagen, art in London, Amsterdam, and Paris, and even studying 'slow food' in Italy," explains a business administration major. Entering first-years have the opportunity to travel in small groups to an island off the coast of Charleston, the mountains of North Carolina, or even China during the summer before they enroll.

Furman broke with the South Carolina Baptist Convention in 1992, but it's still in South Carolina, where religion ranks second only to football as a cultural institution. Thirty-four percent of students hail from South Carolina; 6 percent are international. A political science and communications major describes students as "driven and very focused on success." The administration has committed to erasing Furman's traditional image as the "Country Club of the South" and diversifying the school, and the Student Diversity Council promotes such efforts. "There's growing racial, ethnic, and religious diversity and some strong support systems for underrepresented students," reports a sophomore, "but it's not always seen in every space." Black students make up only 6 percent of the student body, Hispanics/Latinos 7 percent, Asian Americans 3 percent, and multiracial students 4 percent. Every year, Furman awards hundreds of merit scholarships averaging $31,900, plus 170 athletic scholarships in 18 sports.

Furman is a residential campus, with 97 percent of students living in university housing, and students enjoy the resulting camaraderie. "The residence halls undergo cyclical renovations such that no one dorm is in disrepair," says a junior. Furman is no longer a dry campus, although the alcohol policy is strictly enforced in first- and second-year dorms, where most students shouldn't be imbibing anyway. The atmosphere is more relaxed for students of legal drinking age, who may consume alcohol in North Village, a university-owned apartment complex of 10 buildings for juniors and seniors. Meal plan credits can be used in the dining hall or food court. "The dining hall is awesome," cheers a sophomore. "It has a good variety of food and is very healthy." Campus police help provide a relatively safe environment, and for mental health support, "Our counseling center is the strongest/most used support service on campus," says a junior.

When the weekend comes, "The social scene on campus is fun, yet not too rowdy," says a philosophy major. Furman's Student Activities Board sponsors "free movies, weekend trips, restaurant deals, and huge concerts," says a communication studies major. Fraternities claim 25 percent of the men and sororities 44 percent of the women, and off-campus Greek parties draw crowds. "Greek life does tend to dominate life on Furman's campus," reports one student. A senior says students also flock to the spring concert, which has brought such top artists as Ed Sheeran and Drake to campus. "One of my favorite traditions is on the last day of classes, when seniors jump in the fountain to say their goodbyes," shares a junior.

Off-campus, says a senior, "Downtown Greenville is such a great place! So many restaurants and shops, plus good nightlife." The Peace Center for the Performing Arts brings in touring casts of Broadway shows and other top-rated acts. Forty-four percent of Furman's students devote spare time to the Heller Service Corps, which provides volunteers to more than 50 community agencies and organizes the annual Exceptional Adults Valentine's Day Dance for adults with special needs. The best road trips are to the mountains of Asheville (only 45 minutes away), Atlanta (for the big city and shopping, about two hours), and Charleston or Myrtle Beach (four hours).

Furman's debate and mock trial teams are both nationally ranked and regularly compete in intercollegiate tournaments.

"There's growing racial, ethnic, and religious diversity."

Students begin the second semester in January and then have the option of attending a three-week May Experience.

Furman's athletic teams are the Paladins (after the fiercest warrior in Charlemagne's court), and they compete in the Division I Southern Conference. Conference champs have included men's basketball, men's and women's cross-country, and women's tennis. Students happily yell out the school's tongue-in-cheek cheer ("FU one time, FU two times, FU three times, FU all the time!") during football games against archrival Wofford. A quarter of the student body plays intramural and club sports, and Greek groups compete annually for the coveted All Sports Trophy. Furman's debate and mock trial teams are both nationally ranked and regularly compete in intercollegiate tournaments.

Three decades after severing its religious ties, Furman continues to evolve. It may call itself a university, but its educational approach is closer to that of a traditional college of liberal arts and sciences, emphasizing broad exposure to many fields, problem-solving, and experience-based learning. "Furman's personality is very community-driven, and students are highly involved," says a happy junior. "Furman is constantly changing and adapting, but it still keeps its tradition-based drive."

Overlaps

Davidson, Elon, Rhodes, Sewanee, University of South Carolina, Wake Forest, Washington and Lee, Wofford

If You Apply To ›

Furman: Early decision I and II, early action, regular decision. SATs or ACTs: optional. Accepts the Common Application with supplement.

George Mason University

4400 University Drive, Fairfax, VA 22030

The largest public research university in Virginia, George Mason offers an alternative to UVA for students seeking a solid research institution sympathetic to both conservative and progressive values. The main campus in the Washington, D.C., metro area is a boon for job and internship seekers. Big focus on overall student well-being. A quarter of undergraduates start out in community colleges.

Website: www.gmu.edu
Location: Suburban
Public
Total Enrollment: 27,893
Undergraduates: 22,532
Male/Female: 51/49
Financial Aid: 78%
Pell Grant: 36%
Expense: Pub $ $ $
Student Loans: 47%
Average Debt: $ $
Applicants: 25,234
Accepted: 88%
Enrolled: 20%
Grad in 6 Years: 68%

Located in the middle of the budding high-tech corridor of greater Washington, D.C., George Mason University's primary hub features a suburban campus and symbiotic relationship with the surrounding region that contrasts starkly with Virginia's two other major universities, which have operated for many years in the relative isolation of Charlottesville and Blacksburg. With centers of both conservative thinking and liberal and progressive values, George Mason has grown by leaps and bounds for the past two decades, largely because of its commitment to extend the benefits of higher education to as many Virginians as possible.

Founded in 1957 as an outpost of the University of Virginia designed to meet the growing educational needs of Northern Virginia, George Mason became independent in 1972. It sits on a 677-acre wooded campus 20 miles southwest of Washington, D.C., in suburban Fairfax, Virginia. Campus architecture is modern and homogeneous, with lots of brick, glass, and metal, and just about everything is within a 15-minute walk. The campus observatory is second in the area only to that of NASA. The 100,000-seat EagleBank Arena hosts both sporting and entertainment events. Although George Mason's campus doesn't have the colonial ambience or tradition of William & Mary or UVA, its namesake does have the same Old Virginia credentials. George Mason drafted Virginia's influential Declaration of Rights in 1776, and he later opposed ratification of the federal Constitution because there was no Bill of Rights attached.

George Mason University is growing up fast. Its physical plant is expanding, thanks largely to a small but increasing endowment, funding from the State of Virginia, and some public-private partnerships. The growth has included a new 25,000-square-foot Activities Building, with basketball courts, meeting areas, and a practice space for the pep band. Through the university libraries, students have access to nearly two million electronic resources and borrowing privileges of the Washington Research Library Consortium. The Mason Square campus, 15 miles east in Arlington, Virginia, is home to the Schar School of Policy and Government, the Costello School of Business, the Carter School for Peace and Conflict Resolution, and the Scalia Law School. A new innovation center opened there in 2025.

George Mason has standard general education requirements, but students who prefer to find their own way can design a major under the bachelor's in integrative studies, which teams small groups of faculty and undergraduates on projects that can be easily connected to the world outside the campus. Nontraditional students, such as those who are already in their career or serve in the military, have the option to translate their experience into college credit by designing their own degree in the bachelor of individualized studies program. All students must complete the Mason Apex, courses or sequences that require students to translate the entirety of their undergraduate academic experience into integrative, applied, or experiential projects.

> **"[Faculty members are] flexible, accommodating, and helpful."**

George Mason has had two Nobel laureates in its libertarian-friendly economics department, which is among its strongest. Not surprisingly, given the school's location, the Schar School of Policy and Government also receives accolades. Business-related majors are popular, along with information technology; computer science; criminology, law, and society; and psychology. Other notable majors include the nation's first conflict analysis and resolution major, fast-growing computer game design and cybersecurity engineering majors, and forensic science. George Mason established its College of Public Health in 2022, the first of its kind in Virginia. The Mercatus Center, which has been supported with tens of millions of dollars from billionaire Charles Koch and his late brother David, is nationally recognized for its espousal of free market economic principles.

The academic climate varies by program, students say, and 33 percent of classes have fewer than 20 students. All faculty members are required to teach, and according to a global affairs major, the majority are "flexible, accommodating, and helpful." George Mason's Center for the Advancement of Well-Being is a national leader. "GMU does a particularly good job of providing support and resources for off-campus, transfer, and adult students," notes a computer science major.

Students here are decidedly career focused: 85 percent enter the working world directly after graduation. A computer science major comments, "A lot of people here see their degree as a means to an end, and they care more about getting a good job after graduation than they do about getting perfect grades." George Mason offers its undergrads over 130 accelerated master's degree programs for those interested in graduate study. All students are welcome to participate in George Mason's strong undergraduate research program, and an Honors College is available to top achievers. The Smithsonian-Mason School of Conservation allows students to live on-site at the Smithsonian Conservation Biology Institute in Front Royal, where they study global conservation

> **"Nearly every aspect of Mason is developing at breakneck speed."**

(continued)

Returning First-years: 86%
Academics: ✍ ✍ ✍
Social: 🗨 🗨
Q of L: ★ ★
Admissions: (703) 993-2000
Email Address:
  admissions@gmu.edu

Strong Programs:
Biology
Business
Computer Science
Conflict Analysis and
  Resolution
Criminology, Law, and Society
Economics
Government
Psychology

George Mason established its College of Public Health in 2022, the first of its kind in Virginia.

issues and civic concerns. The Science and Technology campus in Manassas, Virginia, opened a new Life Sciences and Engineering building with specialized, high-tech labs and classrooms. For those seeking adventure in faraway places, the Global Education Office offers over 200 different study abroad programs in more than 60 sites around the world, including Mason's own campus in South Korea.

A quarter of incoming students start out at Northern Virginia Community College or other two-year institutions, and 16 percent of undergraduates are over the age of 24. As such, many commute. Ninety percent are from Virginia, and 6 percent are international. Black students account for 13 percent of the undergraduate population, Hispanics/Latinos 18 percent, Asian Americans 23 percent, and multiracial students 6 percent. Students point to the campus's diversity as a highlight of the George Mason experience. "I've learned about many different cultures here, and I don't ever feel singled out," reflects a senior. Students are politically aware and, being so close to D.C., have plenty of opportunities to get involved. Thirty-six percent of incoming first-years receive Pell Grants. Merit scholarships averaging $7,000 are available to those who qualify, as are hundreds of athletic scholarships.

George Mason's traditional status as a commuter school is changing. On-campus housing is guaranteed for the first year; 21 percent of students live on or around campus in university-sponsored housing, including 48 percent of first-years. "Housing is competitive, but the residence halls are generally nice," says a global affairs major. Those who want an active campus social life should consider a stint in the dorms, but first-year residence halls are dry, and you can get the boot if you're caught having a party with alcohol. All first-years living on campus have the opportunity to join one of more than a dozen residential learning communities based around academics, identity, or interests. Sophomores and upperclassmen get rooms on a first-come, first-served basis prioritized by class status. Campus dining facilities are plentiful and operate around the clock but receive mixed reviews. Students report that the campus generally feels safe. "We have apps that can alert others of your location and when you expect to arrive home and police escorts if students ever feel unsafe walking around campus," explains a junior.

"There are events happening every day on campus."

George Mason's Johnson Center, with its food court, movie theater, computer labs, student support offices, and study areas, is the center of on-campus social life. Two student unions, the Student Union Building and the Hub, offer additional options for socializing and studying. "Our student life offices are very active, and there are events happening every day on campus," says a junior. Just 3 percent of the men and 4 percent of the women go Greek. Patriots Day, Gold Rush, and Mason Day are major bashes, in addition to homecoming and International Week. On the weekends, students find a predictable assortment of malls and shopping centers in Fairfax, but off-campus parties and the sights and sounds of downtown D.C., Georgetown, and Old Town Alexandria beckon when the sun goes down. Best of all, these are only a short commute away via a free shuttle bus to the Metro. Those searching for alternative collegiate scenes take road trips to James Madison and UVA.

George Mason competes in the Division I Atlantic 10 conference, and the men's and women's basketball teams are the marquee programs. Any game against Virginia Commonwealth University draws a big crowd, and the budding Revolutionary Rivalry with George Washington is gaining momentum. Students are proud of the colorful pep band the Green Machine, directed by a beloved music professor known as Doc Nix. Patriots teams that have brought home conference titles include the women's track and field and softball teams and men's baseball team. Club sports and intramurals are growing in popularity.

"Nearly every aspect of Mason is developing at breakneck speed. We haven't hit our best yet," says one student. The name of George Mason may not have the cachet of George Washington, James Madison, or the other luminaries of Virginia history who have had universities named for them, but with improving academics, an ever-expanding physical campus, and the rich cultural and economic resources of Washington, D.C., Mason's namesake may be set to follow in their footsteps.

The George Washington University

1918 F Street NW, Washington, D.C. 20052

Half again as large as American University, George Washington University competes with its academic neighbor up the Metro's Red Line for students eager to savor the political and cultural riches of the nation's capital. Internships are readily available, and political communication major is a specialty. Visitors to its Foggy Bottom campus are excused if they cannot figure out where the university ends and the U.S. State Department begins. Among the most expensive private schools in the country.

Like Washington, D.C., itself, the George Washington University draws students from all over America—and from 130 countries around the world. It's a school "for students who want to study in the heart of a city where ideas make a difference." Upon arrival, they find a bustling campus in the heart of D.C., enriched with cultural and intellectual opportunities, including internships with the Smithsonian Institution, the U.S. Capitol, the Library of Congress, NASA, and other national treasures. GW offers a front-row seat to history as top political officials and influential leaders serve as frequent guest speakers and visiting professors, and it is the only school in the country to hold its commencement on the National Mall. "We are the students who will make change in the world, and we are at the center of the important things that are going on right now," says one confident junior.

GW was established in 1821 by an act of Congress as a testament to George Washington's dream of a national institution of higher learning in D.C. Today, as GW enters its third century, undergraduates experience life on primarily two campuses—the Foggy Bottom campus on Pennsylvania Avenue near the State Department and the Mount Vernon campus, three miles away in the Foxhall neighborhood. (A few other satellite campuses in the area serve mostly graduate students.) The Foggy Bottom campus has a mix of renovated federal row houses and modern buildings and is virtually indistinguishable from the rest of the neighborhood, while the wooded Mount Vernon campus spans 23 bucolic acres near Georgetown and includes athletic fields, tennis courts, and an outdoor pool. Students live and take classes on both campuses and travel between the two on the "Vern Express," a shuttle that runs 24/7 during the academic year. The 500,000-square-foot Science and Engineering Hall is the largest academic building in D.C. dedicated to STEM fields.

Incoming students may enroll in the School of Engineering and Applied Science, the School of Business, the Elliott School of International Affairs, the

Website: www.gwu.edu
Location: City Center
Private
Total Enrollment: 18,540
Undergraduates: 10,686
Male/Female: 36/64
Financial Aid: 89%
Pell Grant: 17%
Expense: Pr $ $ $ $
Student Loans: 32%
Average Debt: $ $ $
Applicants: 27,006
Accepted: 47%
Enrolled: 19%
Grad in 6 Years: 84%
Returning First-years: 92%
Academics: ✍ ✍ ✍
Social: 🗩 🗩 🗩
Q of L: ★ ★ ★
Admissions: (202) 994-6040
Email Address:
  gwadm@gwu.edu

Strong Programs:
Biology
Biomedical Engineering
Finance
Geography

Milken Institute School of Public Health, and the largest undergraduate division, the Columbian College of Arts and Sciences (which also houses the School of Media and Public Affairs and the Corcoran School of the Arts and Design). All undergraduates are required to complete a core curriculum in the following areas: natural or physical science, mathematics or statistics, social sciences, the humanities, global perspectives, and local/civic engagement, plus two writing-in-the-disciplines courses. Some of the strongest and most popular majors are international affairs, political science, business, and biology. GW's political communication major combines political science, journalism, and communication technologies and is one of the few undergraduate programs of its kind and benefits from its Washington location. Programs in public health, geography, biomedical engineering, interaction design, and archaeology are also well regarded. Several accelerated undergraduate/graduate degree programs are available, including a seven-year B.A./M.D., and new majors include data science, cognitive neuroscience, and interaction design.

"The academic climate is rigorous but not unbearable," says a first-year. Fifty-two percent of undergraduate classes have fewer than 20 students; professors handle lectures and seminars, and teaching assistants facilitate discussions or labs. Almost half of GW's faculty members divide their time between the halls of academia and real-world positions, many of them governmental. The professors "aim to not only teach the course content but to demonstrate how the skills and information learned [are] used in the specific field," notes a first-year student.

> **"We are the students who will make change in the world."**

For about 500 highly motivated students, the University Honors Program offers special seminars, dedicated advising, independent study, and a university symposium. Seventeen percent of students study abroad via 300 programs available in more than 60 countries, including GW-run programs in England, France, Spain, and Chile. The Center for Career Services hosts job fairs, offers career coaching, and connects students with internship opportunities. "Students intern at Capitol Hill (we call it hill-terning because of how common it is), the Kennedy Center, the Smithsonian, and many other local organizations," reports a junior. Volunteering is big, too, and 90 percent of students take part in more than 80 GW courses that combine academics with service work in the D.C. community.

Major annual events include the Fall Fest and Spring Fling carnivals, with free food and nationally known musical performers.

Students at GW "are all driven and have unique experiences," says a political communication major. Ninety-eight percent of undergraduates come from outside D.C., including 7 percent who hail from foreign countries. Eight percent are Black, 14 percent are Hispanic/Latino, 16 percent are Asian American, and 6 percent are multiracial. Many students come from wealthy backgrounds (pricey nights out on the town are a common diversion), and a senior comments that the campus "remains fairly segregated according to race and cultural background." As you might expect, political issues of all sorts are important here. "Student initiatives have led the university to become more green and sustainable," reports another political communication major. Merit scholarships are available, averaging $25,100, and athletes vie for over 100 awards. GW is need-aware, not need-blind, in its admissions.

> **"[The professors] aim to demonstrate how the skills and information learned [are] used in the specific field."**

Sixty percent of GW undergrads live in campus housing, which is required for the first two years. There are seven living-learning communities available to first-year students, including Civic House and the Somers Women's Leadership Program. The historic Thurston Hall residence has been overhauled with a new dining hall and a penthouse with views of the city. Still, reports a senior, "Most dorms are

Sixty percent of GW undergrads live in campus housing, which is required for the first two years.

converted apartment buildings that are old and in need of renovation." Those who move off campus typically find group houses in Foggy Bottom or go to fashionable nearby neighborhoods like Dupont Circle and Georgetown, just a short walk from campus. First-year students living on campus have an unlimited meal plan and can dine at on-campus cafés or at more than 100 off-campus vendors. Sophomores and above can opt in to a "Build-Your-Own" meal plan that offers a variety of price options. Given GW's open, urban campus, safety can be a concern, but one student says, "There are many services to ensure security," including the university's police department. A junior adds, "Student organizations like Students Against Sexual Assault (SASA), Allied in Pride, the Feminist Student Union, and others work very diligently to increase awareness of sexual assault and provide students with the tools to protect themselves and others."

"If you're bored at GW, you're doing something wrong," states one business administration major. "Whether it's on campus or off campus, there's always something to do." Seven percent of GW men and 12 percent of the women go Greek, and there are more than 475 student organizations on campus. Alcohol consumption is allowed on campus for those of legal age. Major annual events include the Fall Fest and Spring Fling carnivals, with free food and nationally known musical performers. And every four years, GW celebrates the beginning of the new U.S.

> "Students intern at Capitol Hill (we call it hill-terning because of how common it is)."

presidential term with a formal Inaugural Ball of its own in January. Popular weekend trips include the Blue Ridge Mountains and the beaches of Ocean City, Maryland, and Virginia Beach, Virginia. Philadelphia and New York City are easily accessible by bus or train, a boon because most GW students don't have cars.

While GW's official mascot resembles a certain Founding Father, its quirky, unofficial one is the hippopotamus. The university has dropped its longtime Colonials moniker following student protests over its association with, well, colonialism, and teams now do battle as the Revolutionaries. GW doesn't field a football team, but its 20 varsity teams are competitive in Division I Atlantic 10 Conference play. Men's and women's basketball make regular NCAA tournament appearances, and recent conference champions include men's and women's swimming and diving, women's cross-country, rowing, and softball. Twenty percent of undergraduates participate in 39 club sports and 11 intramural activities throughout the year.

Perhaps it's fitting that a university located in the nation's seat of government would generate complaints about red tape: "The simplest of problems for students could be fixed if we didn't have to go through so many hoops to just get an answer," grumbles one student. Still, despite the bureaucratic annoyances, GW continues to build its reputation by putting its location to good use. "The opportunities are endless," says a student. "Picking and choosing what you want to do is the hardest part." For students interested in urban living in the heart of the nation's political establishment, GW may fit the bill. But that bill could be hefty.

Overlaps

American, Boston University, Georgetown, University of Maryland, University of Miami (FL), NYU, Northeastern, University of Southern California

If You Apply To ›

GW: Early decision I and II, regular decision. SATs or ACTs: optional. Accepts the Common Application. Art and design applicants must submit portfolio.

37th and O Streets NW, Washington, D.C. 20057

For anyone who wants to be a master of the political universe, this is the place. Strong international and multicultural environment. Georgetown is the most academically prestigious of the Jesuit schools in the U.S. and one of the most tolerant of religious diversity. A national leader in actively confronting its historical links to slavery. Occupies a tree-lined neighborhood that is home to many of the nation's most powerful people.

Website: www.georgetown.edu

Location: City Center

Private

Total Enrollment: 15,731

Undergraduates: 7,200

Male/Female: 40/59

Financial Aid: 71%

Pell Grant: 14%

Expense: Pr $ $ $ $

Student Loans: 34%

Average Debt: $ $ $

Applicants: 26,131

Accepted: 13%

Enrolled: 47%

Grad in 6 Years: 95%

Returning First-years: 97%

Academics: ✍ ✍ ✍ ✍

Social: 🗩 🗩 🗩 🗩

Q of L: ★ ★ ★ ★

Admissions: (202) 687-3600

Email Address:
guadmiss@georgetown.edu

Strong Programs:
Foreign Languages
Government
International Affairs
International Business
International Economics
International Regional and
 Comparative Studies
Nursing
Theology

As the oldest and most selective of the nation's Roman Catholic schools, Georgetown University offers students unparalleled access to the corridors of power of Washington, D.C. Aspiring politicos benefit from the university's emphasis on public policy, international business, and foreign service. The national spotlight shines brightly on this elite institution, drawing dynamic students and athletes from around the world. A senior says, "Georgetown balances academics, social life, and faith in an all-encompassing college experience based on 'care of the whole person.'"

From its scenic location just blocks from the Potomac River, Georgetown affords its students an excellent vantage point from which to survey—and shape—the world. Established in 1789, the 104-acre campus reflects the history and growth of the first university in the nation to be founded by the Society of Jesus (Jesuits). The Federal style of Old North, which once housed guests such as George Washington and Lafayette and is now home to the McCourt School of Public Policy, contrasts with the towers of the Flemish Romanesque-style Healy Hall, a post–Civil War landmark on the National Register of Historic Places.

Although Georgetown is a Catholic university, the religious atmosphere is by no means heavy-handed, and the student body tends to be diverse and open-minded. Roughly half of the undergraduates are Catholic, but all major faiths are respected and practiced on campus. That's partially due to the pronounced international influence here.

"Students take their coursework very seriously."

The school's hefty endowment is the largest among the nation's Jesuit colleges and universities. Georgetown has worked to confront its historical ties to slavery by offering preferential admissions status and care for elderly descendants of 272 slaves who were sold in 1838 to keep its doors open. In addition to offering a formal apology, it has created an African American studies department and established the Institute for Racial Justice to understand and address systemic racial inequities. A Reconciliation Fund, established in 2022, sets aside $400,000 per year for projects that engage communities of descendants of those who were enslaved on Jesuit plantations.

Through its broad liberal arts curriculum, GU focuses on developing the intellectual prowess and moral rigor its students will need in future national and international leadership roles. All students must complete requirements in humanities, philosophy, theology, engaging diversity, and writing; other requirements are specific to each school. Optional Ignatius Seminars, which focus on educating the "mind, body, and spirit," give first-years the chance to form close relationships with professors and reflect on their work. Would-be Hoyas may apply to one of four undergraduate schools: Georgetown College for liberal arts, the School of Nursing and Health Studies, McDonough School of Business, and the Walsh School of Foreign Service. Prospective first-years declare intended majors on their applications. This means, among other things, intense competition within the college for the limited number of spaces in Georgetown's popular premed program. Those who are undecided declare a major in the sophomore year.

International affairs, international history, international economics, and regional and comparative studies are among the hottest programs, as evidenced by the late secretary of state Madeleine Albright's nearly 40-year tenure at the Walsh School of Foreign Service (SFS). For future diplomats, journalists, and others, SFS offers several five-year undergraduate and graduate degree programs in conjunction with the Graduate School of Arts and Sciences. Georgetown's most popular majors are found in the social sciences, business and marketing, life sciences, and foreign languages, literatures, and linguistics. Of course, the theology department is also strong. The business school balances liberal arts with professional training, which translates into strong offerings in international business as well as an emphasis on ethical and public policy issues. The School of Nursing and Health Studies runs an integrated program combining the liberal arts and humanities with professional nursing theory and practice. The Faculty of Literatures, Cultures, and Language Studies, a leader in its field, grants degrees in ten languages, as well as degrees in comparative literature.

Annual formals such as the Diplomatic and the Blue/Gray Ball inspire students to dress up.

"Students take their coursework very seriously," says a senior. "The courses are challenging, but it certainly isn't impossible to do well." Sixty-five percent of classes have fewer than 20 students. Georgetown likes to boast about its faculty, and it should. "The professors are outstanding and the teaching is first-rate," says an American studies major, and

"[Students are not] pastel polo and pearl-clad preppies from Long Island."

TAs are used only to lead discussion sections and recitations. The Office of Global Education offers more than 150 programs in around 55 countries.

A senior says GU students are not the stereotypical "pastel polo and pearl-clad preppies from Long Island." Ninety-eight percent come from states outside D.C., and another 13 percent are international. Black students make up 5 percent of undergrads, Hispanics/Latinos 6 percent, Asian Americans 16 percent, and multiracial students 6 percent. A student committee works with the vice president for student affairs to improve race relations and develop strategies for improving inclusiveness and sensitivity to issues of multiculturalism. Georgetown offers no academic merit scholarships, but it does guarantee to meet the full demonstrated need of every admit, and more than 300 athletic scholarships draw athletes of all stripes. The Georgetown Scholarship Program offers financial and academic support to eligible low-income students.

The Faculty of Literatures, Cultures, and Language Studies, a leader in its field, grants degrees in ten languages.

University-owned dorms, townhouses, and apartments accommodate 69 percent of undergrads, and "housing is extremely nice," says a senior. All dorms are co-ed, and some have more activities and a stronger community feel than others. The dining hall serves "steadily improving" but expensive fare, but numerous other options are available to grab-and-go around campus. GU students feel relatively safe, thanks to the school's ever-present Department of Public Safety and its walking and riding after-dark escort services.

Jesuits know something about secret societies and thus frown on fraternities and sororities at their colleges. The lack of a Greek system and the university's strict enforcement of the 21-year-old drinking age has led to a somewhat decentralized social life, which is not necessarily a bad thing. Alcohol is forbidden in undergrad dorms, and all parties must be registered. The dozens of bars, nightclubs, and restaurants in Georgetown—Martin's Tavern and the Tombs are always popular—are a big draw, but they can get pricey. Bulldog Tavern, a campus pub in the spectacular student activity center, is a more affordable alternative. Popular annual formals such as the Diplomatic and the Blue/Gray Ball inspire students to dress up and pair off.

"Social life is a major part of campus," says a student. "Kids can easily find their niche." Georgetown has a reputation as a gay-friendly campus, and regular events include OUTober, a month of LGBTQ pride and awareness events held in October.

With everything from the museums of the Smithsonian to the Kennedy Center, "Washington is an ideal place to spend your college years," says a student. "The city has everything students could want, including culture, shopping, museums, monuments, social life, and the clean and convenient Metro for transportation." Given the absence of on-campus parking, a car is probably more trouble than it's worth. Road trips are said to be infrequent.

"Housing is extremely nice."

Should you notice the hills begin to tremble with a deep, resounding, primitive chant—"Hoya Saxa Hoya Saxa"—don't worry; it's probably just another Georgetown basketball game. Hoya is derived from the Greek and Latin phrase hoya saxa, which means "What rocks!" Some say it originated in a cheer referring to the stones that formed the school's outer walls. Recent Division I Big East champions include men's and women's soccer, men's lacrosse, and women's cross-country.

For anyone interested in discovering the world, Georgetown offers an outstanding menu of choices in one of the nation's most dynamic cities. Professors truly pay attention to their undergrads and the diverse students, who are "hardworking, diligent, caring individuals," says one sophomore. "Georgetown is a place where students of all backgrounds, all traditions, and all faiths come together for a common purpose of educating each other and making an impact on the world."

If You Apply To ›

Georgetown: Early action, regular decision. SATs or ACTs: required. Does not accept the Common Application. Apply to particular schools or programs.

University of Georgia

220 South Jackson Street, Athens, GA 30602

With early action applications at an all-time high, students in Georgia and elsewhere frequently choose UGA over highly selective private institutions. The HOPE Scholarship program provides generous financial support for top in-state students. Business, journalism, social and natural sciences, and engineering head the list of strong and sought-after programs. The college town of Athens boasts a great nightlife and is within easy reach of Atlanta.

A school that was previously known primarily for its dynamite football team and raucous parties, the University of Georgia has enjoyed a recent transformation into a widely respected research university with a high graduation rate. Top students who in the past would have looked to more prestigious universities are opting instead for UGA, which is now much tougher to get into. The state of Georgia uses lottery receipts to fund the HOPE Scholarship program, which covers 100 percent of tuition at UGA for all four years for full-time in-state students who finish high school in the state with a B average and maintain that average in college. But the school has widened its appeal beyond the state's borders. Today, "Georgia offers the most complete 'Southern college experience' in the South," raves a senior.

Founded in 1785 with the help of three Yale graduates, Georgia was the nation's first state-chartered university, although it didn't begin offering classes until 16 years later. (UNC was chartered later but wins bragging rights as the first public university to open its doors.) Its attractive 762-acre main campus is dotted with greenery and wooded walks. The older north campus houses the Morehead Honors College, the Terry College of Business, the School of Public and International Affairs, and the law school, and features 19th-century architecture and landscaping. The southern end of campus has more modern buildings, STEM facilities, and residence halls. The $140 million, six-building Business Learning Community complex features such high-tech resources as a trading room, a music business lab, and a business innovation lab.

UGA's core curriculum includes courses in world languages and culture, humanities, the arts, life sciences, and physical sciences, as well as quantitative reasoning and social sciences. First-Year Odyssey Seminars allow new students to study under a senior faculty member in a small, personalized setting while earning an hour of academic credit. All students must take part in a hands-on learning opportunity, such as research, study abroad, service learning, or internships, before they graduate. "The experiential learning requirement has made me explore things outside of what I am predisposed to and has expanded my horizons to more professional opportunities," enthuses a psychology major. UGA's Grady College of Journalism and Mass Communication is home to the prestigious Peabody Awards for broadcasting excellence, and the Terry College of Business is also noteworthy. A School of Computing and an Institute for Integrative Precision Agriculture opened in 2022. Ecology, public relations, international affairs, and engineering are also strengths; health-related programs are rapidly expanding. The most popular majors are biology, finance, marketing, and psychology. The Double Dawgs program enables students to earn both a bachelor's and a master's degree in five years or less; students may choose from some 265 combinations of degrees.

"Georgia offers the most complete 'Southern college experience' in the South."

A computer science and cognitive science double major describes UGA's academics as "tough but extremely collaborative." Large lecture classes are common, but after recent hires and new course sections, 45 percent of classes have fewer than 20 students. "Because of UGA's R-1 research status, we're able to garner a lot of industry leaders and cutting-edge researchers as our professors, which substantially elevates the climate and quality of instruction," says a management information systems major. Students find ample assistance with securing internships and jobs from the hands-on counselors in the Career Center.

The Center for Undergraduate Research Opportunities allows students to conduct a research or service project, write a thesis, or develop a creative work with close faculty supervision, awarding 500 scholarships per semester of $1,000 each. "Most students study abroad, usually in the sophomore to junior years," says a senior. In addition to courses at its campuses in Cortona, Italy, and Oxford, England, UGA offers over 130 programs in 77 countries, exchange programs with partner universities, and independent research and internship opportunities. The 2,900 students in UGA's highly regarded Morehead Honors College enjoy small classes taught by top professors, as well as special opportunities like Lunchbox Lectures and summer internships in Savannah, Washington, D.C., and New York City.

Eighty percent of UGA undergrads are Georgians, and 6 percent are international. A junior calls UGA students "friendly, approachable, and inclusive." Black students account for 8 percent of the student body, Asian Americans 13 percent, Hispanics/Latinos 8 percent, and multiracial students 4 percent. A junior points out that "Athens is a liberal town located in a conservative state," which balances out to a "reasonably moderate" political atmosphere on campus. Merit scholarships are available, and UGA also doles out over 400 athletic scholarships in 12 sports. As many as 100 top undergraduates are named Foundation Fellows, netting a full scholarship plus stipends for international travel and research.

(continued)

Average Debt: $
Applicants: 42,436
Accepted: 38%
Enrolled: 38%
Grad in 6 Years: 90%
Returning First-years: 94%
Academics: ✍ ✍ ✍
Social: 🗨 🗨 🗨 🗨 🗨
Q of L: ★ ★ ★
Admissions: (762) 400-8800
Email Address: apply@uga.edu

Strong Programs:
Agricultural Sciences
Business
Computer Science
Ecology
Engineering
International Affairs
Journalism
Public Relations

The Georgia–Florida football rivalry is the stuff of lore.

Sixty-six percent of Bulldogs live in over 30 residence halls, and first-year students are required to do so. "Each dorm caters to different personality types, bathroom preferences, and social environments," explains a public relations major.

There are five campus dining halls—each with its own specialty cuisine—and students drool over the delicious options; many choose to keep their meal plans even after moving off campus. "There is a dining hall called Snelling that is open really late so eating there past midnight is called 'Snellibrating' and you do it whenever something went well for you that day," says a senior.

When the weekend comes, students know how to have a good time. "There is something for everyone here at UGA, from the juggling club to a business frat or the ballroom dance club to Greek life," describes a dance and social work major. Fraternities and sororities attract 23 percent of the men and 34 percent of the women, respectively. Beyond that, there are more than 800 student organizations for students to choose from—"Get involved in major-specific clubs!" urges a marketing major. A favorite campus tradition is ringing the Chapel bell for athletic victories as well as personal accomplishments. "Hearing the Chapel bell ring is a heartwarming sound because you know that regardless of what's going on in your day, there's a Bulldog out there who has something worth celebrating," cheers one happy Dawg. Students might also ring the bell for the college's expanded resources and programming to support well-being, which get high marks.

The funky mix of shops, restaurants, clubs, and various music and cultural events found in downtown Athens is only a 10-minute walk from most residence halls. A junior enthuses, "Athens boasts a dynamic culinary scene, with a wide range of restaurants, cafés, food trucks, and farmers markets." Students enjoy getting involved in mentorship and volunteer programs in the Athens community, and philanthropic organizations like UGA Miracle, UGA HEROs, and Relay for Life are some of the largest student groups on campus. A car can be helpful (though a regular complaint is lack of parking), and popular road trips include the Florida and Carolina beaches and anywhere the Bulldogs are playing on a fall Saturday.

It's no stretch to claim that Athens residents worship UGA's perennially fierce football team. "Whether tailgating, hosting a watch party, or packing the student section, our students are committed to the Red and Black," says an English and public relations major. The Georgia–Florida rivalry is the stuff of lore.

The Bulldogs (remember that early Yale connection?) compete in the tough Southeastern Conference, and women's tennis and outdoor track and field were 2025 national champions. Swimming and diving, softball, and equestrian are especially competitive. Georgia's Debate Union enjoys consistent national success, and recreational sports are taken seriously, too, with more than 50 clubs and intramural sports available.

UGA's sheer size means you could coast through four years here as nothing more than a number. But with a little effort, that doesn't have to happen. First-year seminars, research projects, study abroad, and a strong culture of student mentoring offer the opportunity to graduate with a solid background in any number of areas and fond memories of Saturdays spent cheering on the Bulldogs—along with 93,000 of your closest friends. "The special culture of UGA is that it is top tier in both academics and football," says an agricultural and applied economics major. "UGA is really unlike any other place in terms of school spirit and sheer love for our school."

Overlaps

UC Davis, Clemson, University of Florida, Florida State, Georgia Tech, University of Minnesota, UNC Chapel Hill, UW–Madison

If You Apply To ›

Georgia: Early action, regular decision. SATs or ACTs: required. Accepts the Common Application with supplement.

Georgia Institute of Technology

North Avenue, Atlanta, GA 30332

As the South's premier technically oriented university, Ma Tech does not coddle her young. Students must contend with the sometimes mean streets of downtown Atlanta and fight through a wall of graduate students to talk with their professors. Big-time sports offer respite from the engineering focus. Tech's 60/40 male/female ratio is tempered by women from all-female Agnes Scott.

If you're looking for lazy days on the college green and hard-partying weekends, sorry! You won't find those at Georgia Institute of Technology, the South's premier tech university. What you will find are challenging courses that prepare you for a high-paying job as an engineer, architect, or computer scientist. "Tech is tough," reasons one student. "You have to want to be here." Even those who want to be there are happy to finally arrive at graduation day. What makes Tech a special place? "The fact that I survived it and got out with a degree," says a computer science major, only partially joking (we think).

Georgia Tech was founded in 1885 to promote industry in the post–Civil War South. Located just off the interstate in Georgia's capital city, Tech's 450-acre campus embraces 40 undergraduate residence halls, an aquatic center, a sports performance complex, and an amphitheater. Taking in the campus architecture is like traveling through time: building styles include the Georgian Revival and collegiate Gothic of the historic Hill District (listed on the National Register of Historic Places) and surrounding area, the International Style buildings constructed from the 1940s into the 1960s, the modernist structures of the 1970s and '80s, the postmodern facilities of the '90s, and the newly built high-tech facilities. All these styles coexist comfortably on a tree-filled, landscaped campus that serves as a green oasis in the midst of a dense urban environment.

Regardless of major, students must complete credit hours in writing; social sciences; technology, math, and science; arts, humanities, and ethics; political science and U.S. history; Georgia history; and wellness. Strong programs include math and computer science as well as most types of engineering, especially industrial, biomedical, aerospace, civil, and mechanical. The school of architecture has done

> **"I love a good challenge, and Tech is perfect for that."**

pioneering work in historic preservation and energy conservation. The architecture program's alumni include Michael Arad, designer of the September 11 memorial in lower Manhattan. Students in several disciplines complete a Capstone Design course, in which they work in teams to design, build, and test prototypes of products with real-world applications. Aside from the technical fare, Tech's business college is increasingly popular. The prelaw certificate is a boon to aspiring patent attorneys, as is the minor in law, science, and technology. Tech has plenty of liberal arts courses, but students say history, philosophy, and literature aren't the reasons why most students enroll.

Courses at Tech are "extremely rigorous," says a senior, at least in the sciences and engineering. "Grading on a curve creates hypercompetitive situations because your absolute grade is largely irrelevant—you just have to do better than most of the others." Classes tend to be big; 27 percent enroll more than 50 students. A computer science major warns that Tech is "absolutely horrible for things like freshman math classes. You're typically taught by TAs. Things get better as you progress and get to know professors." Faculty members have real-world experience; some are Nobel Prize winners or former NASA astronauts.

Website: www.gatech.edu
Location: City Center
Public
Total Enrollment: 26,279
Undergraduates: 17,626
Male/Female: 60/40
Financial Aid: 52%
Pell Grant: 13%
Expense: Pub $ $
Student Loans: 28%
Average Debt: $ $
Applicants: 59,789
Accepted: 14%
Enrolled: 46%
Grad in 6 Years: 94%
Returning First-years: 98%
Academics: ✐ ✐ ✐ ✐ ✐
Social: 🗩 🗩
Q of L: ★ ★
Admissions: (404) 894-4154
Email Address:
admission@gatech.edu

Strong Programs:
Aerospace Engineering
Architecture
Biomedical Engineering
Civil Engineering
Computer Science
Industrial Engineering
Mathematics
Mechanical Engineering

Tech's demanding workload means it's common to spend five years getting your degree. Students say the course selection process can be frustrating, and getting into required courses can be a struggle. One positive factor contributing to delayed graduation dates is the popular co-op program, through which more than 3,000 students earn money for their education while gaining on-the-job experience with more than 700 organizations worldwide. The university offers more than 90 exchange programs and 30 faculty-led study abroad programs; 56 percent of students have some sort of international study or internship experience by the time they graduate. Georgia Tech's innovative Vertically Integrated Projects program allows students to join student/faculty teams to work on large-scale, long-term, multidisciplinary research projects, earning academic credit over the course of multiple semesters. An honors program is available for the super motivated, and the Center for the Study of Women, Science, and Technology offers a living/learning community and research opportunities for women in STEM fields.

Most Georgia Tech students are too focused on school or their co-op jobs to care much about politics or social issues, although improving campus resources for mental health and the LGBTQ community has been a hot topic of late. According to a senior, "There are a lot of left-brain types here—high on the introspection and thinking, low on the social skills." And though they may be united in their pursuit of technical expertise, the campus is hardly homogeneous: Black students account for 8 percent of the student body, Hispanics/Latinos 9 percent, Asian Americans 35 percent, and multiracial students 5 percent. Sixty-seven percent of undergraduates hail from Georgia, and there are large contingents from California, Florida, and Texas; 8 percent come from abroad. To limit burgeoning enrollment, out-of-state applicants must meet somewhat higher criteria than their Georgia counterparts. Georgia residents who graduated high school with a B average benefit from the state's HOPE Scholarship, which covers about 94 percent of their tuition over four years, assuming they keep up their grades in college. In addition, Tech has eliminated loans for low-income Georgia residents. Merit scholarships are available, as are around 300 athletic scholarships.

Thirty-one percent of undergrads live in the dorms, where first-years are guaranteed a room. A senior says the quality of residence halls varies widely: "Some dorms are new, apartment-style, and nice. Others are foul dungeons." The campus dining halls offer "little variety and less quality," according to another student. Off-campus housing is generally comfortable, but parts of the surrounding neighborhood are sketchy. "Far too many cars are broken into or stolen," says one student. Campus police are said to be quick to respond to incidents. VOICE is a campuswide initiative working to address the issue of campus sexual assault.

"There are a lot of left-brain types here."

Being located smack-dab in the middle of "Hot-Lanta" does have its upside: an endless supply of clubs, bars, movie theaters, restaurants, shopping, and museums, both in midtown Atlanta and the Buckhead district. "Atlanta is not a college town," reasons a computer science major. "However, it is the best thing going in Georgia," with friendly, young residents, good cultural activities, beautiful green spaces, and a booming economy. The city also offers plenty of community service opportunities. Fraternities draw 20 percent of Tech's men, sororities attract 24 percent of the women, and members may live in their chapter houses. Alcohol flows freely at frat parties, but otherwise, students say, Tech's policies against open containers and underage drinking are strictly enforced. "There's not much in the way of social life here outside of the frats," says a senior. "You have your group of friends and you do your own thing." The best road trips include Florida's beaches, which are a half day's drive, and Athens, Georgia, for basketball or football games against the University of Georgia.

Tech's Division I varsity sports teams (the Yellowjackets) have become as big-time as any in the South, and when the weekend comes, students throw off their lab coats and become wild members of the "Rambling Wreck from Georgia Tech." The men's golf team has won multiple Atlantic Coast Conference championships, and baseball won the 2025 ACC title; men's and women's track and field and women's basketball are also competitive. About 40 percent of students participate in the university's 43 club and 20 intramural sports. Among Tech's many other traditions is "stealing the T," in which students try to remove the huge yellow letter T from the tower on the administration building and return it to the school by presenting it to a member of the faculty or administration. The addition of alarms, motion sensors, and heat sensors on the T has made the task more difficult but "certainly not impossible for a Georgia Tech engineer," says an electrical engineering major. And then there's the Mini 500, a 15-lap tricycle race around a parking garage with three pit stops, a tire change, and a driver rotation.

> **"Some dorms are new, apartment-style, and nice."**

Forget fitting the mold; the engineers of Georgia Tech are proud to say they create it. Self-direction, ambition, and motivation will take you far here, as will a fondness for highly complex software algorithms. And despite their complaints about the workload, the social life (or lack thereof), and the safety of their surrounding neighborhood, Tech students do have a soft spot for their school. Says one student, "I love a good challenge, and Tech is perfect for that."

If You Apply To ›

Georgia Tech: Early action I and II, regular decision. SATs or ACTs: required. Accepts the Common Application.

Gettysburg College

300 North Washington Street, Gettysburg, PA 17325

The "college by the battlefield" is strong in U.S. history—that's a given. The natural sciences and English are also noteworthy, and political science majors enjoy good connections in D.C. and Baltimore. Participation in undergraduate research and study abroad is notably high.

Whether the reference is to the Pennsylvania town steeped in Civil War history or the small, high-caliber college located in the famed battlefield's backyard, a certain pride and reverence are immediately evident when the name "Gettysburg" is uttered. This feeling is not lost on students at Gettysburg, who come to southeastern Pennsylvania to acquaint themselves with American history while gearing up for the future. "Gettysburg College, while holding tradition close, prepares students to enter a changing global environment," says a senior.

Gettysburg was founded in 1832 on land donated by famed abolitionist Thaddeus Stevens. Situated amid gently rolling hills, the college's 200-acre campus is "a historical treasure," an eclectic assemblage of Georgian, Greek, Romanesque, Gothic Revival, and modern architecture, plus several styles not easily categorized. One campus building—Penn Hall—was used as a hospital during the Battle of Gettysburg.

Gettysburg's curricular requirements include a First-Year Seminar that is limited to 16 students and a writing class; additionally, students take a first-year data and

The annual football game against Dickinson draws a good turnout.

society course and a Sophomore Seminar on communities and change. Students in all majors must complete a capstone requirement, such as a research project or senior seminar course. Five Guided Pathways provide interested students with an advising team and a thematic structure for their cocurricular experiences, allowing them to connect their activities with the skills they hope to strengthen. The excellent history department is bolstered by the school's nationally recognized and prestigious Civil War Institute and its minor in Civil War era studies. Also strong are the natural sciences, especially biology and health sciences, which are well endowed with state-of-the-art equipment. Political science; business, organizations, and management; health sciences, and psychology are the most popular majors. Students attending the Sunderman Conservatory of Music may double major or minor in another academic discipline, and a cooperative dual-degree program in engineering is available. New interdisciplinary majors include finance and public health policy.

"Gettysburg College has a rigorous academic climate," notes an economics major. "However, there is a strong support system." Sixty percent of classes enroll fewer than 20 students, and the small class sizes make for close student/faculty relationships. "Professors want to get to know their students," says an environmental studies major.

> **"Professors want to get to know their students."**

"They invite students to their houses, are available outside of office hours, and care for our well-being."

Undergraduate research is taken seriously at Gettysburg, with 55 percent of students participating. "The Cross Disciplinary Science Institute at Gettysburg allows students to have undergraduate research experience with professors during the summer, with a stipend and housing," explains a senior. For students in the natural sciences, the Cross-Disciplinary Science Institute offers a seminar series and opportunities for hands-on research in the lab. Most students complete at least one internship before they graduate. Around half of the students study abroad, choosing from more than 100 programs worldwide for the same price they pay for regular tuition back home. Gettysburg sponsors a United Nations semester through Drew University and a Washington semester.

Gettysburg students are "kindhearted, passionate, respectful, and open-minded," according to a health sciences major, and students laud the school for increasing diversity. Just 27 percent are native Pennsylvanians, and 14 percent are international. Black students represent 5 percent of the student body, Asian Americans 2 percent, Hispanics/Latinos 11 percent, and multiracial students 3 percent. Both sides of the political aisle are well represented, and a public policy major reports that "most members of the campus community can engage in productive, civil debate." No athletic scholarships are available, but merit-based academic scholarships average $32,600 per year.

All Gettysburg students are required to live on campus, with limited exceptions. First-years reside in traditional dorms; after that, options include suite- and apartment-style housing, fraternity houses, and theme houses, "which is a special way to foster community on campus," enthuses a senior who lived in the Blue Note Jazz House for three years. Dining options in the Dining Center (a.k.a. Servo), Bullet Hole, and Dive

> **"There are so many things to do it is often difficult to decide what not to go to!"**

receive enthusiastic reviews. "Student support services at Gettysburg are top notch," praises a senior, citing the availability of both career and mental health counselors. The Gender and Sexuality Resource Center holds numerous programs to support and increase awareness for the LGBTQ+ community.

Most social life happens on campus, and with over 140 clubs to choose from, a senior cheers, "There are so many things to do it is often difficult to decide what not to go to!" Twenty-eight percent of the men and 31 percent of the women go Greek;

rush does not occur until sophomore year. Students 21 and older are allowed to have alcohol on campus, and Greek parties are open to all students. "There is a party culture on campus, and it does not only involve Greek life," comments one student. Adds another, "We are not cliquey when it comes to our fun." The college sponsors alternative social events, including concerts, comedians, bingo, weekly Pub trivia, as well as bus trips to destinations like Washington, D.C., and New York City.

Gettysburg has "so many restaurants, places where local performances are put on, ghost tours, bowling, axe throwing, and more," raves a student. The orchards and rolling countryside surrounding the campus are peaceful and scenic, and there is a small ski slope nearby. "The Center for Public Service provides a lot of opportunities to make positive change in our community through volunteer work, immersion trips, and service projects," says an economics major; 73 percent of students actively volunteer. A prominent campus tradition is the First-Year Walk during orientation, where all first-year students walk through town to the National Cemetery following the same route that students took in 1863 to hear Abraham Lincoln deliver the Gettysburg Address. Today, an honored guest delivers the Gettysburg Address with remarks to the incoming class. Servo Thanksgiving, where faculty and staff serve students a holiday feast, the International Food Festival, and Springfest are other treasured traditions.

Gettysburg sponsors 24 varsity sports—12 for men and 12 for women—that compete at the Division III level as the Bullets. Men's and women's lacrosse, women's basketball, women's golf, and softball have performed well in the Centennial Conference. The annual football game against Dickinson draws a good turnout, and the Little Brown Bucket, mahogany with silver handles, is passed to the team that wins. Intramural leagues and campus recreation events are hugely popular, and Gettysburg also offers eight club sports.

At Gettysburg, students stay true to their slogan: "Do Great Work." A happy senior says, "Gettysburg does all they can to give you the experience you want, and we are so close-knit that you will never shake off the Gettysburg Pride." Students wanting personal attention from professors, solid academics, and an area rich with history might consider getting their education with a Gettysburg address.

Overlaps

American, Bucknell, Colgate, Dickinson, Franklin & Marshall, Lafayette, Muhlenberg, University of Richmond

If You Apply To ›

Gettysburg: Early decision I and II, early action, regular decision. SATs or ACTs: optional. Accepts the Common Application.

University of Glasgow: See page 371.

Gonzaga University

502 East Boone Avenue, Spokane, WA 99258

Best known for holding its own on the basketball court, Gonzaga is a medium-sized private university with a picturesque residential campus in an urban setting. Offers classic Jesuit education with rigorous core and emphasis on service, though less than half of undergrads are Roman Catholic. Less selective than Santa Clara or USD, comparable to USF, and Spokane, while not as cosmopolitan as Seattle or San Francisco, offers a relaxed, small-city vibe. Good bet for those who relish school spirit.

Website: www.gonzaga.edu
Location: Small City
Private
Total Enrollment: 6,896
Undergraduates: 5,137
Male/Female: 46/53
Financial Aid: 72%
Pell Grant: 8%
Expense: Pr $ $
Student Loans: 46%
Average Debt: $ $
Applicants: 8,759
Accepted: 82%
Enrolled: 17%
Grad in 6 Years: 86%
Returning First-years: 93%
Academics: ✑ ✑ ✑
Social: 🗩 🗩 🗩 🗩
Q of L: ★ ★ ★
Admissions: (800) 322-2584
Email Address:
admissions@gonzaga.edu

Strong Programs:
Accounting
Biology
Business
Engineering
Integrated Media
Nursing
Psychology
Special Education

Gonzaga's mascot is the Bulldog, and the student cheering section is naturally known as the Kennel.

Gonzaga University ("Gone-ZAG-uh") burst into the nation's frontal lobes in 1999 when its men's basketball team fought its way to the quarterfinals of the Division I tournament. Consistent success in the tournament since then has softened the Zags' image as a midsized David doing battle with Goliaths like UNC at Chapel Hill. What has lingered, though, is the image of a solid liberal arts university committed to the Jesuit ideal of "developing the whole person": mind, body, and spirit. According to a senior, "Gonzaga works to encourage an open mind but also to think critically about things. It also has a focus on leadership and emotional intelligence."

Founded in 1887 by the Society of Jesus (Jesuits) as a mission, the school takes its name from St. Aloysius Gonzaga, a 16th-century Italian aristocrat who joined the Jesuits and died while serving victims of an epidemic. The campus occupies 152 picturesque acres along the Spokane River, only a 15-minute walk from downtown Spokane. The Centennial Trail, a 37-mile paved bike path, borders the campus and river. Architectural styles range from the Romanesque College Hall to the sleek PACCAR Center for Applied Science. Newer additions include the Woldson Performing Art Center, the Integrated Science & Engineering facility, and the $60 million UW-GU Health Partnership building. The LEED Gold–certified Hemmingson Center boasts ample space for the student body association, student clubs and organizations, and the main dining hall.

> **"[Gonzaga] has a focus on leadership and emotional intelligence."**

Consistent with its Jesuit liberal arts tradition, Gonzaga requires undergraduates to complete an extensive core curriculum, beginning with a First-Year Seminar and ending with a Core Integration Seminar. Centered around the question of how students may "educate themselves to become people for a more just and humane global community," the core includes courses in English composition, communication and speech, and critical reasoning, with doses of philosophy and religious studies, literature, scientific inquiry, and mathematics. Writing, social justice, and global studies are emphasized throughout the core. Although Gonzaga is a Jesuit school and sponsors 16 spiritual retreats annually, there are no requirements to attend mass or chapel.

Gonzaga offers more than 50 undergraduate majors through the College of Arts and Sciences and the Schools of Business Administration, Education, Engineering and Applied Science, and Health Sciences. Students say some of the strongest programs are engineering, nursing, biology, psychology, and business. Seventy-eight percent of students participate in some form of experiential learning, including research and internships. Recently established programs include minors in health equity and robotics and majors in public health, biomedical engineering, data science, neuroscience, and women's, gender, and sexuality studies.

"We are students that are interdisciplinary and learn what is uncomfortable for us so that we will be able to grow into who we are meant to be," says a criminology major. While the workload can get challenging, "study groups are abundant and helpful," says a mechanical engineering major, and a senior notes professors "practically beg their students to get to know them through visiting office hours." Forty-one percent of undergraduate courses have fewer than 20 students, and the support resources, including the Career and Professional Development staff, earn high praise.

Top students may apply for the four-year Honors Program, and other special offerings include the three-year Hogan Entrepreneurial Leadership Program, open to high-achieving first-year students, and the Comprehensive Leadership Program, which provides a minor in leadership studies. Gonzaga's Army ROTC program (Bulldog Battalion) ranks as one of the best anywhere. The Gonzaga-in-Florence program, which a junior calls "transformative," allows students of any major to study at Gonzaga's campus in Florence, Italy, without delaying their four-year path to graduation. "At Gonzaga, it feels as if it's more of a 'where' will you study abroad than an 'if,'" says a nursing major, and indeed, 63 percent of students opt into more than 60 international programs.

> **"Study groups are abundant and helpful."**

"Gonzaga students are excited, passionate, service-driven, and open-minded," according to one history major. Five percent of Zags are from other countries, with the rest almost equally divided between Washingtonians and out-of-staters. Black students make up just 1 percent of the student body, while Hispanics/Latinos represent 14 percent, Asian Americans 7 percent, and multiracial students 8 percent. "There are a lot of white and affluent students here, which can be a bit of an adjustment if you are not both white and affluent," remarks a junior. Thirty-three percent of students identify as Catholic. Social activism on this left-leaning campus tends to revolve around issues of race, politics, and climate change. The school awards merit scholarships averaging $20,300 per year and 200-plus athletic scholarships.

Fifty-one percent of undergraduates reside in campus housing. First- and second-year students are required to live on campus and purchase a meal plan, but space for upperclassmen is limited, so most juniors and seniors find their own housing in the surrounding neighborhood. On-campus residence halls offer a variety of living styles, including both co-ed and single-gender corridors and floors and several living/learning communities. A senior explains that residence halls "range in how old they are and how nice some of the facilities are." Campus meals are primarily served in the COG dining hall, and a secondary education major says, "The dining facilities are amazing and the meals are occasionally great as well." Students report feeling safe on campus, and a senior says, "Campus security is helpful and quick to respond."

"There are off-campus parties each weekend students attend by word of mouth."

There are no fraternities or sororities at Gonzaga, but students say their absence has hardly put a damper on social life, either on or off campus. "There are off-campus parties each weekend students attend by word of mouth," informs a political science major. Still, students agree they don't feel pressured to drink. Underage students found in possession of drugs or alcohol may be required to take an awareness and safety program. The Hemmingson Center hosts a variety of social activities, including late-night programming on the weekends and the Den After Dark concert series. A favorite tradition is the choir's Candlelight Christmas concert that "creates such a warm and special environment during the Christmas season," shares a senior. With 230,000 residents, Spokane is the second-largest city in Washington but has the feel of both a tight-knit community and an active metro area. "Downtown has a vibrant nightlife filled with live music, dancing, and karaoke," says a senior.

The culture of Gonzaga places strong emphasis on issues of social justice and service. The school offers more than 100 community engagement courses, and 25 percent of all undergraduates participate in some form of community service. "Being involved in the community is a specific Jesuit trait that we all try to live out," says one student. During winter, spring, and summer breaks, nearly 200 students travel to sites across the nation to participate in community service projects, and the university produces many Peace Corps volunteers.

GU's 16 intercollegiate teams, known as the Zags or Bulldogs, compete in the Division I West Coast Conference. In the absence of football (shut down in 1941), basketball is both king and queen. The men's team was a recent national finalist. Men's and women's basketball, baseball, and women's soccer and rowing are recent conference champs. Intramurals and 30-plus club sports sign up students in droves. Outdoorsy types can take advantage of five ski areas within a 90-mile radius, and GU Outdoors sponsors adventures like rafting, hiking, and skiing excursions.

School spirit is a big deal at Gonzaga—mainly when it comes to sports and especially when the opponent is St. Mary's College of California. Since Gonzaga's mascot is the Bulldog, the student cheering section is naturally known as the Kennel. Students go through an elaborate process for tickets to big home basketball games that involves strategic social media posting and camping out in tents days before the opening tip. "It's insanity," confesses one sophomore, "but it's so much fun." A junior adds, "Every Zag should experience this at least once."

Overlaps

Cal Poly–San Luis Obispo, Creighton, Loyola Marymount, Marquette, University of Portland, Santa Clara, Seattle University, University of Washington

At Gonzaga, "spirit" takes on multiple meanings. Basketball may inspire the most vocal outpourings of school spirit, but students say the religious and humanistic values to which the university has long been committed run deep. "Gonzaga has a phrase called 'Zags help Zags,'" says a senior, "which means that there is always someone there to help support you through anything."

Gordon College

255 Grapevine Road, Wenham, MA 01984

Gordon is the most prominent Christian college in New England and competes nationally with Wheaton (IL) and Messiah, though it lacks the name recognition of the former. Not quite in Boston but close enough to be within easy reach. Extensive core curriculum shapes the undergraduate experience. Emphasis on integrating faith and learning.

Website: www.gordon.edu
Location: Suburban
Private
Total Enrollment: 1,298
Undergraduates: 1,241
Male/Female: 42/58
Financial Aid: 75%
Pell Grant: 22%
Expense: Pr $
Student Loans: 65%
Average Debt: $ $ $
Applicants: 1,913
Accepted: 86%
Enrolled: 22%
Grad in 6 Years: 68%
Returning First-years: 84%
Academics: ✍ ✍ ✍
Social: 🗩 🗩
Q of L: ★ ★ ★ ★
Admissions: (866) 464-6736
Email Address:
admissions@gordon.edu

Strong Programs:
Biblical Studies
Biology
Business
Education
Environmental Science and
Sustainability

Christian values are at the heart of almost all aspects of life at this New England college, where faith sets the tone for campus life inside and outside the classroom. Gordon College is unique in that it is the only Christian college of its type that has no formal denominational ties. Founded in 1889 as a missionary training school "to prepare the people of God to do the work of God," the college now sees its mission as preparing students to step "into a divided world confident in who God made them to be and prepared to make a difference." Always evolving, Gordon is sharpening its offerings across the board, from international education to accelerated learning and career-focused programs. "If you choose Gordon, you will be pushed to think beyond just your field of study, and you have the opportunity to grow a lot in your faith," says a finance and business major.

Gordon is located on Massachusetts's scenic North Shore, three miles from the Atlantic Coast and 25 miles from Boston. The campus sits on more than 485 forested acres, landscaped with flowers and boasting four large ponds. Most campus structures are Georgian-influenced traditional redbrick, except for the administration building, Frost Hall, an old stone structure modeled after a European castle that provides an eye-catching contrast. The Ken Olsen Science Center, an 83,500-square-foot science and technology center at the heart of the campus, is home to a fabrication lab, a vivarium, an aquarium, a human cadaver lab, and a biology greenhouse space.

"The academic climate is very interactive and friendly."

Religious commitment at Gordon is seen as the foundation of serious academic learning rather than a threat to free inquiry. Gordon's core curriculum includes distribution requirements in biblical studies and theology, the fine arts, humanities, social sciences, historical perspectives, natural sciences, math, and computer science. More than 35 programs have been added or redesigned to enhance career-focused academics. Additionally, says a junior, "Gordon has a program where students can create their own major by merging courses and requirements to create something that is unique to their interests." First-year students complete an outdoor education requirement, choosing between a 12-day expedition in the Adirondacks and a seven-week, campus-based course. They also take the Great Conversation, a writing-intensive first-year seminar that helps them learn how to integrate faith into their academic experience.

"The academic climate is very interactive and friendly," says a finance and business major. Gordon's most popular majors are business, psychology, biology, and communications. Biblical studies, music, education, environmental science and sustainability, and visual arts are also strong programs, although they may draw fewer students. A 3–2 engineering program, dual-degree nursing, and international affairs programs are also available. Sixty-four percent of classes have fewer than 20 students, and students say professors have high expectations but are helpful. "Having professors know you by name, where you're from, and your interests is something that makes Gordon a really special place," says a junior.

The Gordon Honors Institute encompasses four distinct four-year scholars programs, each providing hefty tuition support for high-achieving students: Global Honors Scholars, which offers honors seminars and travel experiences; A. J. Gordon Scholars, a personalized program culminating in a senior thesis or project; Dokes Ministry Scholars, an accelerated pastoral degree program in partnership with Gordon-Conwell Theological Seminary; and Clarendon Scholars, which focuses on urban leadership development. Additional honors opportunities include a yearlong great books seminar known as the Jerusalem and Athens Forum and the Pike Honors Program, which allows students to design their own majors. The college operates signature study abroad programs in Orvieto, Italy, and the Balkans. Gordon also partners with other programs to offer nearly 40 approved study locations. The Career and Connection Institute is working to expand opportunities for internships, mentorship, and preparation for graduate school and the workplace, while the Center for Entrepreneurial Leadership helps students launch their own start-ups.

Gordon is one of two top Christian schools that require undergraduate applicants to describe how their faith impacts their lives and to affirm that they recognize the Bible as "the Word of God and hence fully authoritative in matters of faith and conduct" (see also Wheaton College in Illinois). Gordon's trustees have reaffirmed the college's policy forbidding "homosexual practice." College operations slow on Sundays, although it's not required that students observe the Sabbath. Nevertheless, a junior opines, "I wouldn't recommend someone who does not identify as Christian to attend Gordon."

Gordon students are interested in "outdoor adventure, spiritual discovery, and overcommitment to both academics and extracurricular activities," says a psychology major. Thirty-nine percent of students are Massachusetts residents, and 9 percent are international. Asian Americans account for 3 percent of the student body, Black students 5 percent, Hispanics/Latinos 11 percent, and multiracial students 4 percent. Racial affinity groups on campus, including ALANA, ASIA, Afro Hamwe, and La Raza, are expanding, and a biology major says, "The events that they put on are huge learning opportunities." Students report that LGBTQ rights are a hot-button issue, although one student notes, "Because it's a Christian school, even the liberals aren't too liberal." Merit scholarships averaging $13,200 are offered to qualified undergrads, but athletic scholarships are not.

Eighty-nine percent of Gordon students live in the residence halls, which are clustered either around the central quad or on an area of campus known as the Hill. Men and women live in separate wings of the same buildings—often separated by a lobby or lounge. Students of the opposite sex are free to visit each other's rooms until 10 p.m. on weeknights and midnight on weekends. "Some of the dorms are old," reports one student, but adds, "they do have a great community." Permission to move off campus may be granted by petition, but the requirements for doing so are stringent. Students report that meals in the main dining hall, which overlooks a pond and doubles as a study area at night, are usually satisfying. Campus safety receives good ratings, and a student reports, "The college places an emphasis on strong student support including career advising, academic success and accommodations, and mental health services."

The Golden Goose talent show pitting all four classes against each other is a favorite tradition.

"I wouldn't recommend someone who does not identify as Christian to attend Gordon."

The college operates signature study abroad programs in Orvieto, Italy, and the Balkans.

Gordon's student-led Campus Events Council organizes activities like movie showings, dances, and coffeehouses held in Chester's Place, a student-run coffee shop with a pub atmosphere, named after a cat. There is no Greek system, and a senior says, "Gordon isn't a party school, but it is in an area where students can find pretty much whatever they are looking for." Students highly anticipate annual events like Christmas Gala and the Gordon Globes student film festival, during which students dress up and walk a red carpet. The "always hilarious" Golden Goose talent show, which pits all four classes against each other, is another favorite tradition. Drinking and smoking are forbidden on campus (and may result in suspension or expulsion); those who are 21 or older may drink off campus but are expected to do so responsibly. The town of Wenham offers "cute shops and restaurants along with other oddities—like used book stores, jewelry shops, and fresh markets," says a student, but another suggests getting a car.

For those who love the outdoors, Gordon's setting on rugged Cape Ann, a local tourist attraction, is ideal. The campus has cross-country ski trails and ponds for swimming, canoeing, and skating. The ocean is a quick bike ride away, nice beaches are available in many of the neighboring towns, and students frequently ski New Hampshire's nearby White Mountains. Volunteering through a prison ministry and in soup kitchens and local churches is popular, and domestic and international mission trips take students all over, including West Virginia, Northern Ireland, and India. Boston is 25 miles away by a five-minute drive to the T, the city's public transit system, so access to weekend diversions (and excellent internship opportunities) is relatively easy. Gordon students enjoy free entry to the city's Museum of Fine Arts.

> "Gordon is in an area where students can find pretty much whatever they are looking for."

Gordon's Fighting Scots compete in Division III athletics, and "a good portion of the student body comes out to the games" when the opponent is rival Endicott College, says a history major. Men's and women's soccer and women's volleyball have brought home Commonwealth Coast Conference championships, and men's and women's rowing are also competitive. About a third of the student body participates in club and intramural sports.

For many students, Gordon's combination of Christian values, strong academics, and a relatively relaxed atmosphere is a winning one. "Gordon doesn't feel like a cookie-cutter conservative Christian school that's out of touch with the wider world," says a sociology major. "Spirituality partnered with the liberal setting of New England makes Gordon a cool place where faith intersects with real-life issues."

Overlaps

Calvin, Eastern, Liberty, UMass Amherst, UMass Boston, Messiah, Westmont, Wheaton (IL)

If You Apply To ›

Gordon: Early action I and II, regular decision I and II. SATs or ACTs: optional. Accepts the Common Application with supplement. Applicants to music program must audition.

Goucher College

1021 Dulaney Valley Road, Baltimore, MD 21204

Strategically located near Baltimore and not far from D.C., Goucher is a modestly sized private liberal arts college that punches above its weight when it comes to ambitious academics. Offers excellent internships, a diverse student body, and plenty of personal attention. Strong in the sciences and communication. Distinctive requirement that all students spend time studying or working abroad makes for a globally oriented community.

Goucher's mission is to prepare students "for a life of inquiry, creativity, and critical and analytical thinking." There's a decidedly international bent to the Goucher experience, grounded in a robust study abroad program that sends students to far-flung locales around the globe. Says a senior, "Individuals who truly want to expand their mind and perspective through immersion in different cultures should seriously consider Goucher."

Formerly a staid women's college that was founded in 1885 and went co-ed way back in 1987, Goucher has a long-standing history of excellence. (The name comes from donors of its original campus in downtown Baltimore.) Phi Beta Kappa established a chapter on campus only 20 years after the college was founded, and Goucher ranks high among liberal arts colleges in turning out students destined for Ph.D.s in the sciences. Set on 287 landscaped acres in the suburbs of Baltimore, Goucher's wooded campus features lush lawns, stately fieldstone buildings (the fieldstone is mined from local quarries), and an equestrian field. The Athenaeum is the central gathering place, housing the library, an open forum for performances, exercise spaces, a café, and other vital college facilities. A new $50 million Science Center that will offer state-of-the-art labs and learning spaces is expected to open in 2027.

> **"Professors are able to give lots of individualized instruction."**

The Goucher Commons curriculum is designed to expose students to complex problem-solving through a multidisciplinary lens. All students must demonstrate proficiency in writing, data analytics, and a foreign language and take coursework focusing on environmental sustainability and race, power, and perspective. First-year students begin with a First-Year Seminar course, juniors study abroad, and seniors synthesize and reflect on their educational experiences by completing a capstone experience or research project.

Of Goucher's offerings, the science departments (especially biology and chemistry) are arguably the strongest, bolstered by resources like a nuclear magnetic resonance spectrometer and an observatory with a six-inch refractor telescope. The dance department is recognized as one of the best at a liberal arts school. Psychology, professional and creative writing, economics, and communication and media studies draw the highest enrollment. Newer majors include neuroscience, public health, digital arts, and engineering science. Unique minors include Arabic studies, historic preservation, and equine studies. For eager first-year students, Goucher offers accelerated three-year tracks in business management, computer science, data science, economics, and psychology.

Goucher academics "revolve around curiosity and learning more than grades," says a dance, gender studies, and integrative arts triple major. Faculty members here devote most of their time and energy to undergraduate teaching and have a good rapport with students. "Professors are able to give lots of individualized instruction and advice related to their field," explains a junior. Each first-year has a dedicated student success team to assist with academic advising, career skills, and the overall adjustment to college life, which is made easier by Goucher's trademark small classes and individual instruction. Students roundly praise the Academic Center for Excellence (ACE), which offers academic support services like study-skills workshops and supplemental instruction. Says a senior, "ACE contains some of the most calming, enlightened souls you'll encounter."

Goucher was the first college in the nation to require all its undergraduates to study abroad at least once before graduation. Over 100 programs are available in more than 40 countries. Most students head for foreign lands during their junior year, and the experience is expected to complement their major field of study. About half of students embark on semester-long programs, while the other half engage in three-week intensive courses offered during January term or summer. Students may apply their

Website: www.goucher.edu
Location: Suburban
Private
Total Enrollment: 985
Undergraduates: 926
Male/Female: 37/63
Financial Aid: 100%
Pell Grant: 39%
Expense: Pr $
Student Loans: 48%
Average Debt: $ $
Applicants: 3,682
Accepted: 78%
Enrolled: 10%
Grad in 6 Years: 57%
Returning First-years: 79%
Academics: ✎ ✎ ✎
Social: 🗩 🗩 🗩
Q of L: ★ ★ ★
Admissions: (410) 337-6100
Email Address:
  admissions@goucher.edu

Strong Programs:
Biology
Business Management
Chemistry
Communication and Media
  Studies
Computer Science
Dance
Environmental Studies
Professional and Creative
  Writing
Psychology

Students frequent the restaurants and bars in Towson, the small but bustling college town.

Goucher financial aid packages to study abroad. Many students opt to complete an internship or off-campus experience related to their major. Popular choices include congressional offices, museums, law firms, and media companies. Adds a visual and material culture major, "The research opportunities at Goucher have been great."

"The typical student is engaged with social justice, has a bit of an interesting fashion sense, and is pretty laid-back," describes a senior. Fifty-three percent of Goucher's students are homegrown Marylanders and 7 percent are international; most of the rest hail from over 35 states. Women still outnumber men by 30 percent. Black students make up 31 percent of the student body, Hispanics/Latinos 13 percent, Asian Americans 4 percent, and multiracial students less than 1 percent. The Center for Race, Equity, and Identity supports marginalized populations on campus and creates programming that encourages cross-cultural understanding. Students agree that progressive social activism is prevalent on campus. "People are consistently tabling, signing petitions, voicing their opinions, and getting involved," confirms a women, gender, and sexuality studies major. Goucher offers merit scholarships averaging $40,000 for those who qualify but no athletic scholarships. Thirty-nine percent of first-year students receive Pell Grants.

Eighty-four percent of students live on campus. Options range from new, hotel-like residences for first-years to senior apartments. Upperclassmen select housing through lotteries, and a sophomore says, "Most students get the rooms that they want. It's a very family-like atmosphere." Campus dining options, which include vegan and vegetarian fare, receive enthusiastic reviews. Says a senior, "We are dining pretty lavishly here." One student notes, "Sexual assault is not a taboo topic at Goucher, and many people feel comfortable talking about it." Another student points out, "We have counseling services and a student-run emotional wellness center."

Goucher has no sororities or fraternities, but the housing units hold periodic events, and the college hosts concerts, lectures, weekend movies, and more than 30 student clubs. "The social scene is fun but very low-key," says a sophomore. Neighboring Towson University offers a more traditional party scene. Alcohol is ever-present but not the hub of Goucher's social life. Major annual events include Gala and Get into Goucher Day, which is "a huge festival held every spring [with] inflatables, great food, live music, and all kinds of other cool stuff," explains a senior. Students frequent the restaurants and bars in Towson, the small but bustling college town, and a car is useful for visiting Baltimore. "The art scene nearby is incredible," raves a junior. Roughly half of students volunteer, many through community-based learning programs that tie hands-on service experience in the local area with academic coursework.

The Gophers field 20 varsity teams that compete in the Division III Landmark Conference. The co-ed equestrian team is nationally competitive, while men's and women's tennis and men's and women's track and field have been conference play-off contenders. Eighty-six percent of students participate in clubs and play on intramural teams, with ultimate Frisbee and volleyball being the most active. Students here can get creative with their recreational pursuits: the Humans vs. Zombies game originated at Goucher in 2005 and is still going strong.

Far from a stagnant place, Goucher is constantly rethinking its mission and redirecting its resources to broaden student experiences in a hands-on, global way. Goucher students are "dedicated toward improving the world," says a sophomore. "Students are here not only to get an education but to be able to contribute something to their community with it."

Phi Beta Kappa established a chapter on campus only 20 years after the college was founded.

Overlaps

American, Clark, Loyola University of Maryland, University of Maryland, McDaniel, Muhlenberg, Stevenson, Towson

If You Apply To ›

Goucher: Early action, regular decision. SATs or ACTs: optional. Accepts the Common Application.

1115 8th Avenue, Grinnell, IA 50112

Iowa cornfields provide a surreal backdrop for Grinnell's funky, progressive, and talented student body. With roughly 1,700 students, Grinnell is two-thirds the size of Oberlin. That translates into tiny classes and tutorials. Second only to Carleton as the best liberal arts college in the Midwest. Grinnell's biggest challenge is simply getting prospective students to the campus. The cornfields make for a tight-knit campus community with lots of future Ph.D.s.

"Go West, young man, go West," Horace Greeley said to Josiah B. Grinnell in 1846. The result of Grinnell's wanderings into the rural cornfields, about an hour from Des Moines and Iowa City, is the remarkable college that bears his name. Despite its physical isolation, Grinnell is an academic powerhouse on the national scene. Its $2.8 billion endowment, largely built on the stock-picking advice of erstwhile trustee Warren Buffett, is one of the largest of any liberal arts college.

Ever progressive, Grinnell was the first college west of the Mississippi to admit Black students and women and the first in the country to establish an undergraduate political science department. It was once a stop on the Underground Railroad, and its graduates include Harry Hopkins, architect of the New Deal, and Robert Noyce, inventor of the integrated circuit, two people who did as much as anyone to change the face of American society in the 20th century. The school's 120-acre campus is an attractive blend of collegiate Gothic and modern Bauhaus academic buildings and Prairie-style houses. (Architecture buffs should take note of the dazzling Louis Sullivan bank facade just off campus.) The $112 million Humanities and Social Studies Complex facilitates multidisciplinary collaboration and research.

True to its liberal arts focus, Grinnell mandates a first-semester writing tutorial, modeled after Oxford University's program, but doesn't require anything else. The roughly 35 tutorials, limited to about 12 students each, help enhance critical thinking, research, writing, and discussion skills and allow first-year students to work individually with professors. Recent offerings include Our Environmental Responsibility, Miss Americana and the Liberal Arts: The Taylor Swift Tutorial, and Queer African Stories. "Tutorials are fun, interesting, and a great introduction to the academic possibilities that Grinnell has to offer," one student says. When it comes to declaring a major, students determine their own course of study with help from faculty. To demonstrate the practical relevance of the liberal arts, Grinnell assigns an "explanatory advisor" to every first-year student to help them develop a sense of direction. They can then join any of seven "career communities," such as Education Professions and Business and Finance.

> **"The sciences are top-notch, with . . . graduate-level research at the undergraduate level."**

Departments in the social and natural sciences are strong, the latter bolstered by an influx of research grants. "Due to the college's enormous endowment, the sciences are top-notch, with the best equipment and graduate-level research at the undergraduate level," offers one student. Psychology, computer science, theater and dance, and foreign languages (including German and Russian) are among the most popular and strongest majors; economics, biology, and political science are also strong. Grinnell's admissions standards are high, and nearly one-third of graduates move on directly to graduate and professional schools. Students who don't mind studying, even on weekends, will be happiest here. Although the workload can be intense, a political science major says, "Virtually no one has the cutthroat attitude I've heard about at

---

Website: www.grinnell.edu

Location: Rural

Private

Total Enrollment: 1,725

Undergraduates: 1,725

Male/Female: 46/54

Financial Aid: 92%

Pell Grant: 19%

Expense: Pr $ $ $ $

Student Loans: 49%

Average Debt: $

Applicants: 9,758

Accepted: 15%

Enrolled: 31%

Grad in 6 Years: 88%

Returning First-years: 93%

Academics: ✒ ✒ ✒ ✒

Social: 🗩 🗩

Q of L: ★ ★ ★

Admissions: (641) 269-3600

Email Address:

admission@grinnell.edu

Strong Programs:
Biology
Computer Science
Economics
Foreign Languages
Political Science
Psychology
Theater and Dance

other schools." Sixty-three percent of classes have fewer than 20 students. Teaching is the top priority for Grinnell faculty members, and because the college awards no graduate degrees, there are no teaching assistants hanging around. "In general, profs are here to teach and have generous office hours," a sophomore says.

When the urge to travel arises, students may study abroad in the Grinnell-in-London program or in more than 100 other approved programs. Fifty-five percent of students spend some time away from campus, and financial aid extends to study abroad. The Grinnell-in-Washington program combines coursework with an internship in the nation's capital. Forty-five percent of students participate in undergraduate research, including the Mentored Advanced Project program, which enables them to work closely with a faculty member on scholarly research or the creation of a work of art. Co-ops in architecture, business, law, medicine, and 3–2 engineering programs are also available.

Grinnell is a bit of Greenwich Village in corn country. Despite the rural environment, the college attracts an urban clientele, especially from the Chicago area. Only 8 percent of Grinnellians are from Iowa, while 21 percent are international. "We're quirky, often hippie and liberal, though increasingly diverse," a student observes. The student body is 9 percent Hispanic/Latino, 10 percent Asian American, 5 percent Black, and 6 percent multiracial. Student groups such as the Intersectional Feminism Alliance, Social Entrepreneurs of Grinnell, and Grinnell Advocates (offering support for survivors of gender-based violence) help set the tone on campus. Admissions are need-blind, and the college meets 100 percent of admitted students' demonstrated need with loan-free financial aid packages. Merit awards averaging $21,300 are handed out annually, but there are no athletic awards. Grinnell policy dictates that at least 15 percent of every first-year class will be students whose parents did not go to college.

All students live in campus housing, which Grinnell guarantees four years. The residence halls are clustered into three areas: "East Campus is lovely but can be isolated and quiet, while South Campus is a sprawling warren usually known for being the hub of campus nightlife, and North Campus is a bit of a happy medium," explains a sophomore. All but two residence halls are co-ed, and after their first year, students participate in a sometimes stressful room draw. Meals in the dining hall are usually satisfactory, students say, although the options and hours can be limited. Safety on this rural campus is reported to be strong.

With no fraternities or sororities, all-campus parties revolve mainly around sports teams and the residence halls. "I liken the experience to that of a cruise ship," says one student, "in that the students all stay in one place and entertainment is brought to campus." Each dorm periodically sponsors a party using wordplay from its name in the title. For instance, James Hall puts on the Mary-Be-James party, for which everyone comes in drag. As for alcohol, a senior reports, "Grinnell is not a dry campus, but there are no bars on campus and there is no peer pressure to drink or culture of problematic drinking." Grinnell's social groups and activities range from the SciFi Association and the Queer Rainbow Super Team to improvisational workshops, poetry readings, symposia, concerts, and movies. Highlights of the campus calendar include semiformal Winter and Spring Waltzes, where "most people wear formals and look very nice, not a common occurrence at a school where comfort is the usual standard and women rarely wear makeup," notes one student. Titular Head is a festival of five-minute student films. During finals week, the library sponsors study breaks that have been known to feature free milk and cookies, choir sing-alongs, librarians reading their favorite picture books aloud, Bubble-Wrap-popping sessions, and other stress-relieving activities.

Grinnell (population 9,500) is "a small farming community with a nice down-town." The college's Service and Social Innovation Program works to bridge the town/gown gap by connecting students with more than 80 area nonprofit and community partners for service opportunities. Nearby Rock Creek State Park lends itself to biking, running, camping, kayaking, and cross-country skiing, and the Grinnell Outdoor Recreation Program sponsors a variety of pursuits, including off-campus trips and open rock-climbing sessions. There are a few bars and pizza joints down-town, but for those craving bright lights, Iowa City and Des Moines are within an hour's drive, and the college runs a shuttle service to them. Chicago and Minneapolis are each about four hours distant.

The Grinnell Pioneers compete in Division III athletics, and the men's basketball team has won national attention for an unusual run-and-gun offense that uses waves of five players like hockey shifts to wear down opponents. Recent conference champions include women's tennis and golf and men's and women's swimming. About a third of students play intramural sports, which offer competitive and non-competitive options.

Grinnell prides itself on its eccentricities. "We like being in the middle of Iowa, we like that you've probably never heard of us, we love that you won't come here because you want a big name." But there's no denying that Grinnell—a first-rate liberal arts college in an unlikely location—is a real gem of a school and one that is still relatively accessible.

Overlaps

Beloit, Carleton, Colorado College, Kenyon, Macalester, Oberlin, St. Olaf, Vassar

If You Apply To ›

Grinnell: Early decision I and II, regular decision. SATs or ACTs: optional. Accepts the Common Application.

Guilford College

5800 W Friendly Avenue, Greensboro, NC 27410

A rare school with Quaker heritage in the South, Guilford emphasizes a collaborative approach and is among the most liberal institutions below the Mason–Dixon line. A kindred spirit to Earlham in Indiana. With a notably high Black population and strong socioeconomic diversity, Guilford's signature program is community and justice studies. Presence of a cluster of older students enriches the campus culture.

If your idea of a rousing road trip is protesting in Washington, D.C., you'll likely find plenty of like-minded compatriots at Guilford College. Founded in 1837 by the Religious Society of Friends (Quakers), this left-leaning campus loves to debate just about any issue and get involved in the world around it. The student body is becoming more diverse in every respect, and campus inclusiveness is enhanced by a long-standing adult education program. "I'm proud to be part of a school that is very accepting and open," comments a sports management and marketing major. In 2025, Guilford successfully overcame a two-year academic probation period having balanced their budget and cut some staff.

Located on 350 wooded acres in northwest Greensboro, Guilford's redbrick buildings are mainly in the Georgian style. The school is the only liberal arts college in the Southeast with Quaker roots; it's the oldest coeducational institution in the South and the third oldest in the nation. During the Civil War, Guilford was one of a few Southern colleges that remained open—perhaps because it was also an

Website: www.guilford.edu
Location: Small City
Private
Total Enrollment: 978
Undergraduates: 945
Male/Female: 52/48
Financial Aid: 97%
Pell Grant: 58%
Expense: Pr $
Student Loans: 68%
Average Debt: $ $ $ $
Applicants: 3,775
Accepted: 84%

(continued)

Enrolled: 12%
Grad in 6 Years: 46%
Returning First-years: 65%
Academics: ✍ ✍ ✍
Social: 🗨 🗨
Q of L: ★ ★ ★ ★
Admissions: (336) 316-2100
Email Address:
   admission@guilford.edu

Strong Programs:
Biology
Business Administration
Community and Justice
  Studies
Criminal Justice
Exercise and Sport Sciences
Psychology
Religious Studies
Sport Management

All first-year residence halls have been renovated, and 200 solar panels have made the campus more environmentally friendly.

embarkation point on the Underground Railroad. All first-year residence halls have been renovated, and 200 solar panels have made the campus more environmentally friendly.

Guilford's general education program for traditional students, the Guilford Edge, emphasizes team-based, interdisciplinary projects. Guilford follows a 14-week fall term followed by a 14–3 spring term allowing for intensive course or off-campus experience. In addition to selecting a traditional, primary major, students identify a passion or issue that they explore in-depth, in the spirit of Quaker queries or questions. Guilford Edge also builds in comprehensive academic and career advising, campuswide events aimed at enhancing community spirit, and training in ethical leadership development that the college hopes will, among other things, boost applications and retention rates.

> **"I'm proud to be part of a school that is very accepting and open."**

"The college is centered on the Quaker values of community, diversity, equality, excellence, integrity, justice, and stewardship," explains a senior. Students say Guilford's most popular programs are also some of its best: business administration, psychology, exercise and sport sciences, biology, and sport management. Forensic biology and religious studies are notable as well, as are the peace and conflict studies and sustainable food systems majors. Business analytics is Guilford's newest major. The signature justice and policy studies department offers majors in community and justice studies and criminal justice. A unique, issues-based minor in principled problem-solving experience (PPSE) combines interdisciplinary coursework with hands-on learning that addresses a complex social issue. The PPSE topic changes regularly; one recent topic, Every Campus a Refuge, focused on how to mobilize college campuses to provide housing and other support to refugees during their initial resettlement. Classes at Guilford are small, with an average of 14 students, helping to create a more personal environment. A student says, "As long as students are willing to be challenged, they will be forming strong student and professor relationships."

Guilford believes that experiential learning adds immeasurably to classroom work, so faculty-mentored research and travel are important emphases. "In most classes, you will be doing some kind of hands-on learning, applying the knowledge you're learning to real-life situations," says a health sciences and chemistry double major. All first-year students are required to participate in an Integrative Experience, which begins with a seminar that helps hone their skills in time management, communication, and more. In addition to standard laboratory equipment, science students have access to a lake, an organic farm, and 220 acres of woodland property on campus, which provide a rich resource for fieldwork in environmental and sustainability studies. Guilford has several endowed funds that support student scientific research and travel, including an award for Women in Physical Science. The college offers study abroad in 75 nations; 25 percent of students participate.

In the words of a sophomore, Guilford students are "hardworking, brave, smart, and outgoing." They come from across the globe and a range of socioeconomic backgrounds; most are liberal and about 1 percent identify with the Quaker religious tradition. Seventy-eight percent of students are in-staters, and 1 percent are international. Black students represent 30 percent of the student body, Hispanics/Latinos 16 percent, Asian Americans 2 percent, and multiracial students

> **"The college is centered on the Quaker values of community, diversity, equality, [and] excellence."**

5 percent; 58 percent of first-years are eligible for Pell Grants. Guilford has made a point of enriching its student body by enrolling a sizable number of older students.

About 10 percent of full-time undergraduates are 23 or older and benefit from a large selection of evening classes and their own adult education orientation and counseling services. A junior says the population of adult students "adds a lot to classes because of their different life experiences." In an effort to promote affordability, Guilford promises to award every first-time applicant an automatic scholarship of at least $15,000 (and up to $27,000, depending on high school GPA) and guarantees that tuition will not increase over a student's four years. In addition, every student who lives on campus receives a $4,000 housing grant. As a Division III school, Guilford does not offer athletic scholarships.

All traditional students under the age of 23 are required to live on campus; Guilford's many older students are generally commuters and less involved in campus social life. On-campus apartments for juniors and seniors are comparable in price to off-campus digs. "The dining options on campus are fantastic," cheers a student. Campus safety gets good ratings too.

Guilford's social life revolves around student clubs and organizations, of which there are more than 50. "When the weather is nice, a lot of events happen outside, and it is easy to find people just lounging in the grass or down by the lake," says one student. Greek life is nonexistent, and alcohol is not allowed at college functions; nonetheless, there is a moderate party scene that students describe as "not toxic" and "very safe." Serendipity, a weeklong celebration of spring with student performances, games, lots of free food, big-name musicians, and a formal dance, is a beloved tradition. Beyond the campus gates, students find all of the essentials—Target, Starbucks, some clubs in downtown Greensboro (only 10 minutes away), the ethnic restaurants of Tate Street, and the college's Quaker Village. About a third of the students regularly volunteer in the community. Popular road trips include UNC at Chapel Hill (one hour), Asheville and the mountains (three and a half hours), and the famous Outer Banks beaches (four and a half hours).

> **"The dining options on campus are fantastic."**

Guilford's Division III athletic teams compete as the Fighting Quakers, and students cherish the oxymoron, as in their cheer: "Fight, fight, inner light! Kill, Quakers, kill!" Students root for the football team in the annual Soup Bowl against Greensboro College, while the men's golf team has brought home a slew of conference titles in recent years. The men's basketball, women's volleyball, baseball, and softball teams have also been successful. Intramural and club sports draw 20 percent of the students. Because of Guilford's emphasis on developing the whole person, physically, mentally, and spiritually, students are encouraged to participate in school-sponsored outdoor adventures, such as a ropes course, sailing, and whitewater rafting.

A popular Guilford mantra is: "How are you going to change the world?" And with students who'd rather get involved than sit back and watch, you can expect some pretty passionate answers to that question. It all goes back to Guilford's traditional Quaker goal of "educating individuals not only to live, but to live well." As one student explains it, "You will be pushed outside of your comfort zone in a lot of ways, but Guilford is also a place for growth."

Overlaps

Albright, Appalachian State, Elmhurst, Lipscomb, Lynchburg, UNC Greensboro, Roanoke, Wofford

If You Apply To ›

Guilford: Early decision, early action, rolling admissions. SATs or ACTs: optional. Accepts the Common Application with supplement.

800 W College Avenue, St. Peter, MN 56082

A touch of Scandinavia in southern Minnesota, GA is a guardian of the tried and true in Lutheran education. With Minnesotans comprising 83 percent of the students, GA is less national than cross-state rival St. Olaf. Extensive distribution requirements include exploring values and moral reasoning. Minnesota location makes for a friendly and homogeneous student body. And not many places have Hello Walk.

Website: www.gustavus.edu
Location: Small Town
Private
Total Enrollment: 1,845
Undergraduates: 1,844
Male/Female: 47/53
Financial Aid: 86%
Pell Grant: 27%
Expense: Pr $ $
Student Loans: 77%
Average Debt: $ $ $ $
Applicants: 5,294
Accepted: 62%
Enrolled: 15%
Grad in 6 Years: 77%
Returning First-years: 88%
Academics: ✍ ✍ ✍
Social: 🗨 🗨 🗨
Q of L: ★ ★ ★
Admissions: (507) 933-7676
Email Address:
   admission@gustavus.edu

Strong Programs:
Biology
Classics
Communication Studies
Economics
Music
Nursing
Physics
Psychology

Gustavus Adolphus College is named for Sweden's King Gustav II Adolph (1594–1632), who is credited with making Sweden a major European power and defending Lutheranism against the Roman Catholics. While the king's military victories earned him the title Lion of the North, he was also an advocate of education and culture. Save for the women now attending classes, King Gustav would probably feel at home at the college that bears his name, where a not-so-subtle Swedish influence pervades everything from the buildings to the curriculum. The college, founded by a Lutheran pastor as a parochial school in 1862, is the "epitome of Minnesota nice," says one sophomore admiringly.

The 340-acre GA campus is about 65 miles southwest of the Twin Cities. Not surprisingly, the prevailing architectural theme is Scandinavian, with mostly modern and semimodern brown brick buildings. Highlights include the 147-year-old Old Main and the centrally located Christ Chapel, with spires and shafts resembling a crown. Thirty bronze works by sculptor and alumnus Paul Granlund are strategically placed, and the 135-acre Linnaeus Arboretum and Interpretive Center offers plant study and retreats. The sidewalk running through the middle of campus is nicknamed the Hello Walk, because it's a tradition for students to greet one another as they pass—whether they know each other or not. A $70 million renovation and expansion of the Nobel Hall of Science nearly doubled the size of the school's natural sciences facilities.

> **"The courses require a lot of work both inside and outside the classroom."**

Under the Gustavus Challenge Curriculum, students fulfill standard distribution requirements in seven liberal arts areas, plus the First-Term Seminar, which covers critical thinking, writing, speaking, and recognizing and exploring values. Students must also complete a foreign language semester and a capstone course in their junior or senior year. A religious studies and philosophy class is also required. In addition to the core courses, first-year students must participate in a Signature Experience through study away, internship, faculty-guided research, or a course-based experience. A writing requirement is worked into students' major classes.

In the classroom, students find an academic smorgasbord, as GA aims to offer an education both "interdisciplinary and international in perspective." There are interdisciplinary programs in Scandinavian studies; gender, women, and sexuality studies; and environmental studies, to name a few, and if neither those nor traditional departments suffice, students may design their own courses of study. While biology, psychology, economics, and communication studies are among the most popular majors, nursing, physics, and classics are also strengths, and students give high marks to GA's premed advising program and its offerings in music. For the professionally minded, Gustavus offers 3–2 engineering programs with the University of Minnesota and Minnesota State in Mankato. Overall, academics at Gustavus are rigorous, but students say small classes make it easy to form dependable study groups, and classmates don't compete for grades. "The courses require a lot of work both inside and outside the classroom," says one junior. "Professors expect you to give your best every day, and in return they give you their best." Students find faculty members not just knowledgeable but also friendly, especially when they're serving up a free meal for students during Midnight Express, which precedes final exams.

In the summer term, Gusties may take concentrated courses on campus or pursue travel and co-op opportunities. The school sponsors study abroad programs at five colleges and universities in—surprise, surprise—Sweden, as well as others in non-Scandinavian haunts such as India, Malaysia, Australia, Russia, and Scotland, and 46 percent of students participate. The Nobel Conference brings Nobel laureates and other experts to campus for two days each October. Undergraduate research is a hallmark, and Gustavus Adolphus consistently ranks in the top 10 for papers presented at the National Conference on Undergraduate Research.

An elementary education major describes Gusties as "friendly, easy to talk to, energetic, and hardworking." For all its good points, though, this liberal arts college is hardly a model of diversity: 79 percent of students are white, 84 percent are Minnesotan, and 52 percent are Lutheran. The school is working hard to increase diversity, but that continues to be a challenge in its region. Black students currently account for 2 percent of the student body, Hispanics/Latinos 6 percent, Asian Americans 2 percent, and multiracial students 4 percent; international students add another 5 percent. Politically, the campus leans liberal but has its fair share of conservatives, and students report that environmental issues and women's and LGBTQ rights are frequent topics of discussion. Merit-based scholarships averaging $12,300 are available, but there are no athletic scholarships.

"[Dorms] stay full on the weekends and are well maintained."

On-campus living is required for all four years, and only about 11 percent of students receive permission to live off campus as seniors, which can be a source of frustration for upperclassmen. One student says the dorms "stay full on the weekends and are well maintained." Single rooms, apartment-style suites, and some college-owned houses are reserved for upperclassmen. The Crossroads International House is an option for students interested in languages and contemporary global issues. Students rave about the à la carte meal plan and especially about the Marketplace dining hall. In response to recommendations from a student task force, the administration has updated its sexual misconduct policies.

Ten percent of the men and 14 percent of the women go Greek, but GA's social life does not revolve around fraternities and sororities. "Saturday Night Lights puts on events like poker night, dances, game nights, etc., which always seem to be really fun and always include free food," says a junior. Because students 21 and older may drink in their rooms—with the door closed—underage students can get alcohol if they want it, but students say drinking isn't a popular pastime here. GA's many musical ensembles all perform together at the Christmas in Christ Chapel concert. The chapel holds 1,500 people and performances usually sell out. Sixty-eight percent of students participate in service projects, volunteering 15,000 hours each semester. Projects include working with children, the elderly, and the local animal shelter, as well as with Habitat for Humanity. The town of St. Peter has coffee shops and bowling, and the college offers periodic trips to Mankato, 10 miles away, and to the Twin Cities, for "real" shopping at the Mall of America or for a professional baseball, basketball, or hockey game.

"Any time, any sport—if St. Olaf is in town, the event is packed."

When it comes to athletics, "Any time, any sport—if St. Olaf is in town, the event is packed," says a lusty Gustie fan. GA competes in Division III, and the men's and women's tennis teams are perennial contenders for the national championship title. Men's and women's golf and swimming and women's ice hockey and volleyball have also been successful in Minnesota Intercollegiate Athletic Conference play. The college's forensics team is nationally competitive. A majority of Gusties participate in intramural and club sports, including rugby and cross-country skiing.

The Gustavus Adolphus campus may be gorgeous in the spring and fall and too cold in the winter, but it's warmhearted all year long. Small classes, one-on-one academic attention, a plethora of research opportunities, and an active campus social life go a long way toward making St. Peter, Minnesota, seem a lot less isolated. Says one senior, "Our core values of community, service, faith, justice, and excellence prevail both in and out of the classroom, and students commit themselves and their time here to such values."

If You Apply To ›

Gustavus Adolphus: Early action, rolling admissions. SATs or ACTs: optional. Accepts the Common Application with supplement.

Hamilton College

198 College Hill Road, Clinton, NY 13323

Hamilton is part of the network of elite, rural, Northeastern liberal arts colleges that extends from Colby in Maine through Middlebury and Williams to Colgate, about half an hour's drive to Hamilton's south. Hamilton is on the small side of this group and emphasizes collaboration with faculty. Need-blind admissions with no merit scholarships. Strong commitment to diversity and inclusion.

Website: www.hamilton.edu
Location: Rural
Private
Total Enrollment: 2,029
Undergraduates: 2,029
Male/Female: 45/55
Financial Aid: 91%
Pell Grant: 19%
Expense: Pr $ $ $ $
Student Loans: 43%
Average Debt: $
Applicants: 8,531
Accepted: 14%
Enrolled: 39%
Grad in 6 Years: 91%
Returning First-years: 95%
Academics: ✐ ✐ ✐ ✐
Social: 🌑 🌑 🌑 🌑
Q of L: ★ ★ ★
Admissions: (800) 843-2655
Email Address:
admission@hamilton.edu

Originally founded in 1793 as the Hamilton-Oneida Academy and chartered as a college in 1812, Hamilton took its name from Alexander Hamilton, who was an early trustee, and for much of its early life offered its male students a staunchly traditional education rooted in a classical curriculum—the school's motto is Socrates's first step to true wisdom: "Know thyself." In 1978, Hamilton merged with adjacent Kirkland College, the artsy, experimental women's college founded under its auspices a decade before. Particularly dedicated to transforming students into excellent communicators, "intellectual growth, flexibility, and collaboration are hallmarks of Hamilton's liberal arts education," and the college has increased opportunities for experiential learning and internships and is adding programs to develop students' digital fluency. "One thing [students] have in common is a passion for learning," raves a government major.

The original Hamilton campus features collegiate Victorian architecture rendered in rich, warm brownstone. By contrast, buildings on the original Kirkland campus and Burke Library on the Hamilton side consist mostly of boxy concrete structures of a 1960s "brutalist" vintage. Straddling the ravine that divides the two parts of today's campus is a student activities building with a diner, lounges, and areas for student and faculty relaxation. Surrounding the campuses are more than 1,300 college-owned acres of woodlands, open fields, and glens, with trails for hiking or cross-country skiing. The college has invested more than $374 million over the past 15 years in new and renovated facilities, including the Burke Library and Root Hall, an academic building at the heart of campus.

In the classroom, Hamilton is pure liberal arts. The open curriculum has no distribution requirements, but all students must pass at least three writing-intensive courses and a quantitative and symbolic reasoning course. The development of writing skills is a key area of focus in all majors. In an effort to reinforce its commitment to inclusion, the college requires that all majors feature relevant, mandatory coursework on social, structural, and institutional hierarchies. First-year orientation combines on-campus programming with adventure and service trips; more than 60 options are typically available, from participating in local arts events to working with refugee communities to kayaking on Lake Champlain. First-year students may also participate in an optional series of proseminars—classes of no more than 16 that require intensive interaction through writing, speaking, and discussion. Hamilton requires all students to undertake a senior project in their area of concentration.

Public policy and the natural sciences are among the strongest programs. Hamilton's Arthur Levitt Public Affairs Center, named for the former New York State comptroller, is a working think tank where undergraduates focus on leadership and social innovation. Biology, economics, mathematics, and computer science enroll the most students; world politics, neuroscience, environmental studies, Hispanic studies, and creative writing are also popular. Newer offerings include data science and Middle East/Islamicate worlds studies. Hamilton has "a rigorous, challenge-by-choice academic climate," explains an Africana studies and public policy major. Adds a cultural anthropology and creative writing major, "The College has academically surpassed my expectations, especially since I have discovered courses on topics such as American ghost stories and the history of print culture that I never expected to be available." Seventy-three percent of classes enroll fewer than 20 students, and professors are said to be friendly and dedicated to helping them succeed.

Every incoming student is assigned a faculty advisor, a career coach, and an ALEX (Advise, Learn, and EXperience) advisor who can assist them with course planning, off-campus learning opportunities, career exploration, and personal growth. "The Community Outreach and Opportunity Project (COOP) allowed me to intern for two consecutive years at a local nonprofit," lauds a sophomore, "exposing me to the issues in Utica and other nearby communities." Hamilton awards stipends to more than 300 students each year for summer research or internships. When the village of Clinton (population 1,600) gets claustrophobic, about 60 percent of students spend a semester or a year abroad through more than 100 programs. Students can also study off campus for a term in Washington, D.C., or New York City.

"Some might our call students overachievers, but I would say goal-driven," says a geosciences and Hispanic studies major. Twenty-six percent of Hamilton students are New York residents, and 8 percent are international. Black students constitute 3 percent of the student body, Hispanics/Latinos 10 percent, Asian Americans 9 percent, and multiracial students 6 percent. Although the campus is no political hotbed, students report that current issues (both local and global) receive ample attention from student activists. Consistent with Hamilton's commitment to socioeconomic diversity and its Division III status, there are no merit or athletic scholarships, but the college has a need-blind admissions policy and guarantees to meet 100 percent of admitted domestic students' demonstrated financial need.

All students reside on campus. Options range from stately old mansions and former fraternity houses converted into dorms to newer apartments that accommodate three

(continued)

Strong Programs:
Biology
Creative Writing
Economics
Government
Mathematics
Psychology
Public Policy
World Politics

"The Community Outreach and Opportunity Project (COOP) allowed me to intern for two consecutive years at a local nonprofit."

Feb Fest features snowshoeing, an ice-sculpture contest, and other winter activities.

"Some might our call students overachievers, but I would say goal-driven."

to four students each. While one senior calls the lottery system "a little bit of a crap-shoot until after sophomore year," the two sides of campus, Hamilton and Kirkland, feature distinct student cultures and a rivalry that students call "playful" and "endearing." Hamilton (nicknamed "the Light Side") tends "to be more sporty and outgoing," says a senior, while Kirkland (nicknamed "the Dark Side") attracts artsy free spirits. Campus dining options receive average reviews: "It is not the worst," deadpans a government major. Students say campus security and support services are effective.

Social life at Hamilton ranges from the campus's Little Pub, which occupies an old barn, to programming arranged by the campus activities board, such as comedy shows, a casino night, and concerts. "Greek life is not large," explains a senior; it draws 11 percent of the men and 14 percent of the women. Much of the social life does revolve around alcohol, students say, although stiff punishments are meted out to underage imbibers. "Class and Charter Day represents the one weekday in an academic year where almost all students put aside their academic endeavors to socialize, party, enjoy food trucks, and dance and sing along to a major visiting musical artist," says a creative writing major.

> **"Clinton is a quintessential small college town."**

While some students bemoan the rural location, a sophomore says, "Clinton is a quintessential small college town with gazebos, farmers markets, and a bustling coffee shop." The nearest small city, Utica, is only 10 minutes away by car. The college maintains a free jitney service for student transportation. "We are also not far from the amazing Adirondacks, which students enjoy visiting to hike, camp, and rock climb," says a senior. Given the long, snowy winters, such outings are often best enjoyed by skiers and other winter-sports enthusiasts. Other popular road trips include Syracuse and New York City, while Boston, Toronto, and Montreal are each less than five hours away.

In athletics, Hamilton offers 29 varsity sports teams (the Continentals) and is a member of the highbrow New England Small College Athletic Conference. Men's and women's ice hockey and men's basketball have been competitive in recent years. "One exciting event is the Citrus Bowl, an annual hockey game where all the students throw oranges onto the ice after Hamilton's first goal," says a senior. The extensive intramural and club sports programs draw high participation, especially in curling, volleyball, basketball, and ultimate Frisbee. Even some school traditions are athletically minded. Feb Fest features snowshoeing, an ice-sculpture contest, and other winter activities.

Hamilton students are, by necessity, hearty. They're used to the cold and the snow—and some may say that's what leads to the strong sense of community evident on campus. Many students agree that students and professors alike are motivated and driven to succeed but not at the expense of the warm friendships they build here. Says a senior, "At Hamilton, you will learn about sides of yourself you did not know existed and be encouraged to try whatever sparks your interest and joy."

Overlaps

**Amherst,
Bates, Bowdoin,
Colby, Colgate,
Middlebury, Vassar,
Wesleyan, Williams**

If You Apply To ›

Hamilton: Early decision I and II, regular decision. Accepts the Common Application. Please consult Hamilton's website for the most up-to-date information regarding standardized test scores.

1 College Road, Hampden–Sydney, VA 23943

The last bastion of the Southern gentleman and one of three all-male colleges in the nation. Feeder school to the economic establishment in Richmond. Picturesque rural setting evokes the old South. While some would argue that it is out of step with today's world, H–SC holds to its mission of asking what it means to be a "good man" in today's society.

Hampden–Sydney College was founded by Scotch-Irish Presbyterians in 1775 with the University of Edinburgh as its model and took its name from two 17th-century English patriots (John Hampden and Algernon Sydney). Seemingly a bit of an anachronism in a society increasingly focused on diversity, the all-male school still aims to expose its small student body to a broad liberal arts education, which is entirely focused on undergraduates. H–SC is one of only three all-male colleges in the nation and one of only two without a coordinate women's college (see also Wabash). "The student body is truly one brotherhood," says a mathematical economics major, "bound and forged by our Honor Code and Student Code of Conduct." Tradition reigns here, and students like to call themselves "Southern gentlemen." Of course, says another, there's plenty of not-always-gentlemanly fun to be had when you have 900 guys together.

Hampden–Sydney's 1,340-acre campus, surrounded by farmland and woods, features mainly redbrick buildings in the Federal style. The Pannill Center for Rhetoric and Communication houses the college's Rhetoric Program, writing and speaking centers, and student publications. The $40 million Pauley Science Center features state-of-the-art labs, classrooms, and interactive spaces.

To graduate, students must demonstrate proficiency in rhetoric and a foreign language, complete coursework in a range of liberal arts areas, and take at least three experiential learning courses, one of which must have a significant off-campus component, such as fieldwork, an internship, or travel abroad. All first-years participate in a special advising program, and 30 percent take first-year seminars linked to living/learning communities.

> **"Each student shares the common ground of being a Hampden-Sydney man."**

Most majors require a capstone course involving a 20-page research paper. The most popular area of study is the social sciences, followed closely by business and economics. The department offers three majors: economics and business, general economics, and mathematical economics. History, biology, and government are also popular, and physics is strong. The Wilson Center for Leadership in the Public Interest puts a public service focus on the study of political science, preparing students for government work and garnering high marks in return. The school's small size offers many opportunities to work closely with professors but has some academic drawbacks, including limited resources in some departments and fewer than 30 majors.

Students at Hampden–Sydney say there are no free passes when it comes to classwork, and the atmosphere can get competitive. "You really have to work hard," says a junior, "but most students are willing to put in that work in order to become better writers and thinkers." Classes are small; 67 percent have fewer than 20 students, and none exceed 40. Most H–SC professors live on campus and make themselves very available to students. Some even make house calls to find out why a student missed class. "Students are required to be in class or else they will fall subject to a withdraw-fail from the course," explains a history major.

Website: www.hsc.edu
Location: Rural
Private
Total Enrollment: 942
Undergraduates: 942
Male/Female: 100/0
Financial Aid: 80%
Pell Grant: 23%
Expense: Pr $ $
Student Loans: 62%
Average Debt: $ $ $
Applicants: 3,177
Accepted: 41%
Enrolled: 23%
Grad in 6 Years: 62%
Returning First-years: 83%
Academics: ✍ ✍ ✍
Social: 🗩 🗩 🗩 🗩
Q of L: ★ ★ ★ ★
Admissions: (434) 223-6120
Email Address:
  admissions@hsc.edu

Strong Programs:
Biology
Economics
Economics and Business
Government
History
Mathematical Economics
Physics
Rhetoric

Additional educational opportunities include the honors program, the summer research program (which is particularly popular among students in the sciences), and the TigerFund, which allows students to manage an equity fund. More than 100 study abroad options are available in 30 countries and revered institutions around the world, including Oxford, Cambridge, and the London School of Economics; 20 percent of students spread their wings in this way. Career services are said to be effective, particularly when it comes to connecting students with alumni for job opportunities.

"You really have to work hard."

"There is a wide range of personalities among the student body, but each student shares the common ground of being a Hampden–Sydney man," says a senior. Sixty-two percent of students are Virginia residents, and less than 1 percent come from foreign countries. Black students make up 7 percent of the student body, Hispanics/Latinos constitute 7 percent, Asian Americans add 1 percent, and multiracial students represent 5 percent. A history major reports, "Hampden–Sydney has certainly become more diverse in the last ten years and has worked to support students of all backgrounds and socioeconomic status." As a Division III school, Hampden–Sydney offers no athletic scholarships. There are, however, academic awards averaging roughly $26,900 for qualified students.

The annual spring Greek Week brings out the Animal House instincts of Hampden–Sydney's budding gentlemen.

Ninety-eight percent of students live on campus in traditional and apartment-style residence halls, and housing is guaranteed for four years. The renovated Whitehouse Quadrangle housing for first-years reopened in 2025. A dozen living/learning communities are available to choose from as well. The spacious dining facilities supply hungry students with "lots of options and good hours." Student support services receive good reviews, and a senior notes, "The counseling center members are often walking around campus to make themselves visible to all to ensure no student goes without the attention they need."

Students praise the close-knit atmosphere fostered by Hampden–Sydney's all-male status. "Our code of etiquette requires that we acknowledge people we pass on the sidewalk and reserve our phone calls and headphones for less populated areas,

"You come here for the school, not the town."

so we get to know each other on a personal level," explains one student. Hampden–Sydney's social nexus is the Circle, the site of the school's fraternities, which claim 27 percent of the students. "The social scene on campus is carried by two different groups: Greek Life and the College Activities Council," says a senior. The annual spring Greek Week brings out the Animal House instincts of Hampden–Sydney's budding gentlemen. "You don't need to be a brother of the fraternity or have a posse of women to get into a party," says a junior. But students warn that campus security will crack down on underage drinkers if parties get too wild. Student clubs offer another important outlet for socializing, and homecoming and various music festivals are also eagerly anticipated. Nearby women's colleges—Hollins, Sweet Briar, and Mary Baldwin—help mix up the social scene.

The TigerFund allows students to manage an equity fund.

Despite its lack of bright lights ("You come here for the school, not the town," one student points out), the nearby town of Farmville, population 7,500 and home to Longwood University, offers restaurants, stores, and a movie theater; it's just five miles from H–SC and provides numerous community service and outreach opportunities. Campus volunteers spearhead projects such as tutoring, highway cleanup, and Habitat for Humanity home building; 75 percent of students perform community service. When rural Virginia gets too insular, H–SC students can be found on road trips to the University of Virginia and James Madison University, Virginia's beaches, or Washington, D.C. The ski slopes of Wintergreen are within a two-hour drive.

Tiger football is big; students attend games in coat and tie, and alumni come out in droves for tailgating. H–SC's football rivalry with Randolph–Macon (not the former women's college!) is one of the oldest in the South. At the annual pregame bonfire, the college rallies to sing songs and hear student and faculty leaders vilify the enemy and extol "the garnet and gray." The basketball team is competitive, and the golf and lacrosse teams are nationally ranked. Sixty percent of students participate in intramural and recreational sports ranging from basketball and flag football to clay-target club and rugby.

Hampden–Sydney likes to tell new students that when they enter the campus gates, they're "joining a brotherhood older than America itself." The school's legacy as the 10th-oldest college in the United States may make it largely conservative and rather homogeneous. But 250 years of tradition, an unwavering commitment to the liberal arts, and a tight-knit student body also make for a rich—and definitely unique—undergraduate experience. Says a proud senior, "Hampden–Sydney College is one of the few institutions remaining where honor still means something to students."

Overlaps

Centre, Davidson, James Madison, Oglethorpe, Randolph–Macon, Roanoke, Sewanee, Virginia Tech

If You Apply To ›

Hampden–Sydney: Early decision, early action I and II, regular decision. Accepts the Common Application with supplement. Please consult Hampden–Sydney's website for the most up-to-date information regarding standardized test requirements.

Hampshire College

893 West Street, Amherst, MA 01002

NOTICE TO READERS: In April 2026, as the new edition of the *Fiske Guide to Colleges* was going to press, the Board of Trustees of Hampshire College announced that the 61-year-old liberal arts college would shut its doors at the end of the Fall 2026 semester. Like many other small private liberal arts colleges, Hampshire has struggled with serious enrollment, financial, and accreditation issues in recent years, and a fundraising campaign led by filmmaker and alumnus Ken Burns was not sufficient to save the institution. With Hampshire's closure, U.S. higher education has lost a refreshingly nonconformist college in which students, faculty, and the institution itself have consistently marched to their own academic beat.

Website: www.hampshire.edu
Location: Small Town
Private
Total Enrollment: 839
Undergraduates: 839
Male/Female: 28/41
Financial Aid: 100%
Pell Grant: 29%
Expense: Pr $ $
Student Loans: 54%
Average Debt: $ $
Applicants: 2,132
Accepted: 75%
Enrolled: 14%
Grad in 6 Years: 57%
Returning First-years: 78%

Passion reigns at Hampshire College. It's found in just about everything students do—from devising their own courses to starting new clubs to debating the most current social issues. There's no one way to do things at Hampshire, and the students revel in the freedom they have to direct the path of their education. "We love what we are studying because we get to choose what we are studying," says a third-year student focusing on sustainable agricultural methods. Without the yoke of traditional majors and the nail-biting stress of regular grades, Hampshire offers a virtually boundary-free exercise in intellectual exploration.

Located in the Connecticut River Valley of western Massachusetts, Hampshire's 800-acre campus sits amid former orchards, farmland, and forest. Buildings are eclectic and contemporary, and the school is proud of its bioshelter, arts village, and multisports and multimedia centers. Two nationally known museums—the Yiddish Book Center and the Eric Carle Museum of Picture Book Art—are located right on campus. The innovative Kern Center is the campus's "living building." Constructed entirely with local and regional nontoxic materials, the 17,000-square-foot building generates its own electricity and collects its own water. It's the latest in a series of sustainability efforts that also include converting the campus to 100 percent solar electricity.

The annual Spring Jam brings live bands to campus, and throughout the year, there's almost always a party going on.

Hampshire was created in 1965 by four nearby colleges—Amherst, Mount Holyoke, Smith Colleges, and UMass Amherst. Together the schools make up the Five College Consortium, through which enrolled students can take classes, join clubs, borrow books, eat food, play club sports, and more across all five campuses, which are connected by a free bus service. The goal of Hampshire was to reimagine liberal arts education. Instead of grades, Hampshire professors hand out narrative evaluations. With advisors, students create their own curricula, moving across, between, and outside of traditional academic areas to curate original courses of study. Degrees are obtained by passing through a three-part divisional structure, which takes the place of the traditional structure of a four-year program. The divisions move from exploratory to advanced, culminating in a yearlong thesis project. Students complete a series of examinations (a.k.a. "divisions")—not tests but portfolios of academic work, evaluations, and students' self-reflections on their academic development.

The first milestone, known as Division I, begins with one transdisciplinary seminar focused on a question of contemporary relevance in the sciences, culture and human experience, the arts and design, or race and power. Students take six other courses based on their own interest, and all first-year students commit to 40 hours of service or a semester-long equivalent. The second milestone, Division II, is when students devise a "concentration," Hampshire's version of a major. Division II includes regular discussions with faculty members, courses, independent study, and fieldwork or internships. Division III generally begins in the fourth year, when students complete a sizable independent study project centered on a specific topic, question, or idea, much like a master's thesis.

"We love what we are studying because we get to choose what we are studying."

Because of the division system, there are as many curricula at Hampshire as there are students. The common denominators are a rigorous workload, an emphasis on self-initiated study, close contact with faculty advisors, and the assumption that students will eventually function as graduate students do at other institutions. "The academic climate is not competitive because no two students study the exact same thing," explains a student. The importance of qualified, attentive faculty is not to be underestimated in an environment like this, and students heap praise on their professors. One says, "Professors have given me detailed and constructive feedback on my assignments, helped expand my thinking, and connected me with resources I never knew I needed."

Hampshire's flexibility is ideal for artists, and programs in film, video, and photography are dazzling. Communications, creative writing, psychology, biological sciences, and environmental studies are also good bets, and Hampshire was the first college in the nation to offer an undergraduate program in cognitive science. The college's Farm Center serves as a living laboratory for learning about sustainability, social justice, and community building. Internships and other real-world

"Professors have given me detailed and constructive feedback on my assignments."

experiences are highly encouraged. Twenty-five percent of students typically study abroad, and Hampshire offers more than a dozen of its own study abroad programs; students may also participate in programs through more than 150 institutions in nearly 50 countries. Befitting Hampshire's entrepreneurial nature, when it comes time for "Div Free" (as students call life after Hampshire), one in four students begin their own businesses, and a large percentage go on to graduate school.

"Hampshire prides itself on being quirky and weird," says a music composition, production, and audio engineering student. "Most students at Hampshire didn't quite fit in anywhere else and sort of found their group at this school." Just as Hampshire eschews letter grades, it also refuses to consider SAT or ACT scores in the admissions process. Twenty-eight percent of students come from Massachusetts, and 7 percent come from abroad. Seven percent of students are Black, 13 percent are Hispanic/Latino, 2 percent are Asian American, and 6 percent are multiracial—and most students would like to see these numbers rise. Hampshire's LGBTQ community is visible and vocal; 31 percent of students identify as trans/nonbinary or genderfluid. According to a philosophy student, "Political correctness doesn't even begin to describe" the social atmosphere. Take as examples the school's gender-neutral bathrooms and identity-based housing, which allows members of historically marginalized groups to live together. Aside from need-based aid, available merit scholarships average $59,000.

Nearly all undergraduates live on campus, and housing is guaranteed for all four years. First-year students live in dorms, while older students may move to one of more than 100 "mods"—apartments in which groups of four to 10 students share the responsibility for cleaning, cooking, and maintaining their space. But a student notes, "you will not be assigned a roommate unless you want one." Campus meals are diverse and include "many great vegan and vegetarian options," says one nano-technology student, not to mention great ice cream from local cows. Students can also get healthy options from Mixed Nuts, a student-run food co-op that is Hampshire's longest-running student group. Campus safety is good, students say, and sexual assault is addressed up front. "We have a loud and well-known consent culture on campus," says a student concentrating in geology and sustainability.

Not surprisingly, Hampshire has no fraternities or sororities, and on weekends, some students head for Boston, New York, Hartford, or, in season, the ski trails of Vermont and New Hampshire. But, says a third-year student, "Amherst is a college town, so there are lots of coffee shops, local businesses, restau-

"Hampshire prides itself on being quirky and weird."

rants." There are plenty of cultural resources within the Five College area, and the free buses to Amherst, Northampton, and South Hadley (all within 10 miles) are always crowded. The annual Spring Jam brings live bands to campus, and throughout the year, there's almost always a party going on, including the drag ball and the much-anticipated Halloween bash—an intense, all-campus blowout complete with fireworks. Perhaps the most unique tradition is when students complete their Division III requirements and ring the "Division-Free Bell" outside the library to celebrate with friends.

Hampshire is no place for competitive jocks, since many sports are co-ed and primarily for entertainment (there never was a football team here). Hampshire is affiliated with the United States Collegiate Athletic Association and is also a member of the Yankee Small College Conference. Students organize their own intramural teams and sports clubs (men's and women's soccer, basketball, and track and field are the biggies, and there's also the competitive Red Scare Ultimate Frisbee Team). The outdoors program offers mountain biking, cross-country skiing, and kayaking; equipment may be borrowed for free. The school also has its own climbing wall and cave, a gym with a solar-heated pool, and a co-ed sauna.

Hampshire's six-year graduation rate is low in comparison to other pricey, private liberal arts colleges, though not necessarily for bad reasons. Some students find the culture of individual study unnerving, if not stressful, or miss traditional college life more than they thought they would. Others, however, having taken full advantage of Hampshire's freedom to explore, discover a passion that might be their life's work and move on to pursue it at a larger school with more resources. At Hampshire, that's called success.

Overlaps

Bard, Beloit, Bennington, Clark, Knox, Pitzer, Sarah Lawrence, Warren Wilson

If You Apply To ›

Hampshire: Early decision I and II, early action, regular decision. SATs or ACTs: not considered. Accepts the Common Application with supplement.

Hartwick College

1 Hartwick Drive, Oneonta, NY 13820

Hartwick is known for its cozy atmosphere and ability to take good care of students. Combines liberal arts education with experiential learning opportunities. A general education program emphasizes hands-on learning, and a Three-Year Bachelor's Degree Program is an option. Reduced tuition cost by 60 percent in fall 2025 and has dedicated itself to student wellness. Bring your mountain climbing shoes.

Website: www.hartwick.edu
Location: Small Town
Private
Total Enrollment: 1,064
Undergraduates: 1,064
Male/Female: 39/61
Financial Aid: 97%
Pell Grant: 38%
Expense: Pr $
Student Loans: 85%
Average Debt: $ $ $ $
Applicants: 4,863
Accepted: 70%
Enrolled: 9%
Grad in 6 Years: 53%
Returning First-years: 74%
Academics: ✏ ✏ ✏
Social: 🍷 🍷 🍷 🍷
Q of L: ★ ★ ★
Admissions: (888) 427-8942
Email Address:
  admissions@hartwick.edu

Strong Programs:
Art
Biology
Business Administration
English
Music
Nursing
Psychology
Sociology

Hartwick College emphasizes community-centered learning, and in fall 2025, the school introduced a new identity as "The Life Balance College," spelling out a holistic approach to student well-being. The school's philosophy that learning isn't about memorization but about creating experiential knowledge and developing skills has expanded to include student support for maintaining a healthy life balance and financial well-being. To aid with the financial effort, Hartwick introduced a new, "transparent" tuition structure that aims to make the college more affordable and reduce the debt burden for its mostly homegrown student body. Students say they enjoy the comfortable atmosphere on this close-knit campus. "You will feel like you instantly become an active and important member of the community," assures one denizen.

Hartwick was founded way back in 1797 under the will of Lutheran pastor John Christopher Hartwick, and its campus has a New England feel with its ivy-covered, redbrick buildings and white cupolas, gables, and trim. The campus setting on Oyaron Hill, overlooking the city of Oneonta and the Susquehanna Valley, provides a breathtaking view, though the steepness of the campus may have some students wishing for the legs of a mountain goat. Facilities include a greenhouse, an herbarium, a biotechnology "clean lab," a graphics imaging lab, and a high-tech nursing simulation lab. The Baking Innovation Laboratory, offering food testing, research, and recipe development, provides students with hands-on learning opportunities. The new WICKed Esports Center is a competitive space for Hartwick's growing eSports experience.

> **"This college really cares about how their students are doing in their classes."**

Hartwick operates on a 4–1–4 academic calendar, with two 14-week semesters and a four-week January term, or J Term, in between. The FlightPath curriculum features a first-year program that includes a Wick Weekend orientation, a first-year seminar, a college writing course, and a 21st Century Skills course. All Hartwick students complete two wellness credits, and they are also guaranteed a career-related work experience, such as an internship, research project, or fellowship. The culminating capstone requires students to create a digital product and deliver an oral presentation.

The most popular majors are business administration, nursing, public health, and psychology. The English, biology, political science, music, and art programs receive high marks too. Growing computer science offerings include data science, cybersecurity, digital marketing, game development, and web design. The course catalog is necessarily limited by Hartwick's small size, but the Individual Student Program enables students to create their own major dealing with a particular interest as well as earn a bachelor's degree in three years. Students may also broaden their options by taking courses at nearby SUNY Oneonta.

The academic environment at Hartwick is described as collaborative and relaxed. "This college really cares about how their students are doing in their classes," explains a nursing major. Small class sizes are the norm. A political science and criminal justice major adds, "Being able to visit my professors outside of class, have conversations about life, careers, and academics, is invaluable." Individual tutoring and help sessions are offered, along with an innovative first-year early-warning program that identifies struggling students early and offers counseling.

Hartwick's emphasis on learning through real-world experiences is evident in the wide-ranging activities its students have pursued, often during J Term, such as studying politics in Greece, language and culture in Japan, or public health in South Africa. In fact, 75 percent of students take part in study abroad courses available in 25 nations around the globe. Well-funded global internship and research opportunities offer additional international experiences. The Griffiths Center for Collaboration and Innovation provides workspaces, labs, and classrooms where students can pursue cross-disciplinary innovation, entrepreneurship, and research opportunities. Seventy percent of students take community-based service-learning classes, which combine academic coursework with service opportunities in the Oneonta area. Participants in the Honors Program carry out four self-selected academic challenges, such as studying transcultural health in Cuba or the fashion industry in Italy, among other options.

Hartwick has improved its academic rigor in recent years, thanks to a focused recruitment program. "The students here are hardworking, well-rounded, driven, and accepting," says a junior. Seventy-six percent are from New York State, and most of the rest come from New England or the Mid-Atlantic states; 4 percent are international. Black students make up 11 percent of the student body, Hispanics/Latinos 10 percent, Asian Americans 2 percent, and multiracial students 3 percent. Thirty-eight percent of first-year students are eligible for Pell Grants. Students tend to be liberal but not particularly politically engaged; a sophomore says, "Hartwick is very accepting of student expression and even demonstration in regard to students' social and political beliefs." Hartwick lowered its tuition and fees by 60 percent in fall 2025 and offers annual scholarships up to $10,000, making the cost to attend comparable to that of most public four-year institutions in New York State.

"The rivalry of Hartwick and SUNY Oneonta is always fun."

All students except commuters reside on campus, most in traditional dorms, although suite-style options are available. Says a sophomore, "The dorms are all a comfortable size and are maintained properly." Upperclassmen may move into one of the fraternity or special-interest houses or into the coveted apartment community or townhouses. Hartwick's 256-acre Pine Lake Environmental Campus, located eight miles from the main campus, has cabins that are heated by pellet stoves and a lodge where environmentally conscious students can live in rustic style. Students give on-campus dining fair marks but praise campus safety officers. Career services are also good, and one student lauds the Belonging Center as "a great resource for students that would like to have one-on-one conversations with staff that can assist them in getting any help they may need while at Hartwick."

Hartwick's social scene is found both on and off campus, according to students. "There is somewhat of a party culture, with Saturday being the busiest because we aren't a dry campus," explains a junior. Students say the administration is tough about enforcing alcohol policies. Four fraternities and three sororities attract 8 percent of the men and 6 percent of the women. The school sponsors events like movies, comedians, and speakers many Friday and Saturday nights. Popular campuswide traditions include First Walk for first-year students and Last Walk for seniors. At Taste of Wick, held every semester, campus clubs and organizations set up tables to show students the various activities Hartwick offers. From campus, it's only a short walk, bike ride, or bus ride downhill into the small city of Oneonta, which "has so much to give to students," cheers a sophomore. "Main Street has many coffee shops, food places, and bookstores to explore." Hiking at Pine Lake and on the college's Table Rocks Trail system is also a popular pastime. Skiing is popular throughout the region.

As for sports, the Hartwick Hawks deliver plenty of excitement. The school's 21 varsity teams compete in the Division III Empire 8 Conference with women's tennis and field hockey and men's swimming and diving among the most successful teams. New offerings include men's volleyball and women's flag football. "The rivalry of Hartwick and SUNY Oneonta is always fun with the Battle of the Hills sporting events," says a sophomore. Intramurals are popular as well, especially soccer and basketball—20 percent of students take part.

Change is good, the sages say, and the folks at Hartwick would definitely agree. By focusing its efforts on reducing tuition, recruiting strong students, and emphasizing top-notch experiential learning, Hartwick is bolstering its image as a solid liberal arts college with a warmly welcoming community. "You can't walk more than 10 feet without seeing a familiar face, friend, or classmate," says one happy student. "That's what I really like about this school."

If You Apply To ›

Hartwick: Early action I and II, rolling admissions. SATs or ACTs: optional. Accepts the Common Application with supplement. Music applicants must audition.

Harvard University

University Hall, Cambridge, MA 02138

An acceptance here is the gold standard of American education. Reflecting its huge endowment, vast resources, and nearly four centuries of accumulated traditions, Harvard's very name has become synonymous with excellence in higher education. It takes moxie to keep your self-image under control amid all those overachievers, but most Harvard students can do it. ("I go to school in Boston.")

For nearly four centuries, the name Harvard has been synonymous with academic excellence, prestige, and achievement. The nation's first institution of higher learning (founded in 1636), Harvard University was named for clergyman John Harvard following his bequest of 400 books and half his estate. Despite ongoing political turmoil in which the university has battled the Trump administration's attempts to freeze billions of dollars in federal research funds, Harvard is still the benchmark against which all other colleges are compared. Seeking to "educate citizens and citizen leaders," it attracts the best students, the most academically accomplished faculty, and the most lavish donors of any institution of higher education nationwide. Sure, some academic departments at "Hah-vahd" may be smaller than others, but all have faculty members who have made a name for themselves and have written the standard works in their fields. Olympic athletes, concert pianists, and Rhodes scholars blend in easily here, ready to embrace the challenges and rewards only Harvard's quintessential Ivy League milieu can offer.

Spiritually as well as geographically, the campus centers on the famed Harvard Yard, a classic quadrangle of Georgian brick buildings whose walls seem to echo with the voices of William James, Henry Adams, Alain Locke, and other intellectual greats who trod its shaded paths in centuries past. Beyond the yard's wrought-iron gates, the campus is an architectural mix, ranging from the modern ziggurat of the science center to the white towers of college-owned houses along the Charles River. The Loker Commons student center provides a place for students to meet and philosophize over gourmet coffee or burritos of epic proportions. The massive, $1 billion Science and Engineering Complex across the river in Allston opened a few years back, and construction is ongoing on the new Allston location of the American Repertory Theater.

Under its "star" system, Harvard grants tenure only to scholars who have already made it—usually somewhere else—and then gives them free rein for research. (Critics say this system is short-sighted in that it rewards past and current academic accomplishment rather than nurturing future Nobel Prize winners and emerging academic fields.) "You can have unlimited contact with professors," notes a biology major, "but it must be on your initiative. This is not a small liberal arts college where people will reach out to you." Most professors teach at least one undergraduate course per year, and even the luminaries occasionally conduct small undergraduate seminars (including those reserved for first-years, which can be taken pass/fail). Harvard also sponsors faculty dining programs, such as Professors & Pastries and Classroom to Table, encouraging professors to chew on ideas and éclairs with students at residential houses and local eateries.

Harvard takes its undergraduate General Education (GenEd) or Core courses seriously, and senior faculty members are recruited to teach them. GenEd requirements include one course from each of four perspectives: aesthetics and culture; ethics and civics; histories, societies, and individuals; and science and technology in society. Additionally, students take an expository writing course, one quantitative reasoning course, and one departmental course from each of the three main divisions of the Faculty of Arts and Sciences: Arts and Humanities; Social Sciences; and Natural Sciences and the School of Engineering and Applied Science.

Harvard's best-known departments tend to be its largest; economics, government, computer science, applied mathematics, history, biological sciences, and psychology account for a large chunk of majors. But many smaller departments are gems as well: East Asian studies is easily top in the nation. The School of Engineering and Applied Sciences, with its interdisciplinary approach, claims about one in five undergraduate concentrators. Under the leadership of Henry Louis Gates Jr., the African and African American studies department has assembled the most high-powered group of Black intellectuals in American higher education. Smaller, interdisciplinary honors majors, to which students apply for admission, boast solid instruction and happy undergraduates too. These programs—social studies, history and science, history and literature, and folklore and mythology—are the only majors that require a senior thesis, although many students in other departments elect to do one. Harvard's visual and environmental studies department serves filmmakers, studio artists, and urban planners, and a major in theater, dance, and media is popular. Students can petition for individualized majors, typically during the sophomore year. And should you not find a class you are looking for, Harvard offers cross-registration with several of its graduate schools and MIT.

Incoming students are encouraged to explore a range of disciplines during their first year on campus. Seventy-two percent of classes have fewer than 20 students, but students uniformly complain about the overuse of teaching fellows (graduate students) for introductory courses in mathematics and the languages. TFs aren't all bad, though, says a junior: "They can give good advice, having just been in our position." Besides, it's easier to ask "dumb questions" of mere mortals than of the

> **"You can have unlimited contact with professors but it must be on your initiative."**

(continued)

Returning First-years: 98%
Academics: ✍ ✍ ✍ ✍ ✍
Social: 🗩 🗩 🗩
Q of L: ★ ★ ★ ★
Admissions: (617) 495-1551
Email Address: college@fas.harvard.edu

Strong Programs:
African and African American Studies
Applied Mathematics
Biological Sciences
Computer Science
East Asian Studies
Economics
Engineering
History

demigod professors. For many students, the most rewarding form of instruction is the sophomore and junior tutorial, a small-group directed study in a student's field of concentration that is required in most departments within the humanities and social sciences. Teaching of the tutorials is split between professors and graduate students, and the weight of each party's responsibility varies with the subject and the professor. With more than 200 study abroad programs available to choose from, 80 percent of Harvard undergrads indulge in some sort of international experience before they graduate.

The oft-made claim that "the hardest thing about Harvard is getting in" is right on target. Flunking out takes serious and sustained effort. Then again, Harvard can feel indifferent and antisocial. Brilliant overachievers who desire the occasional ego stroke might be better off at a top-notch small liberal arts college. All incoming first-years participate in a weeklong orientation, and optional preorientation groups, such as the urban, outdoor, and arts programs, help students acquaint themselves with one another and the Boston area. Although most students feel little competition, the academic climate is still intense. "The courses are difficult, particularly in the beginning as students make the transition from high school to college," says one student. Stressed-out students can count on help from a variety of quarters, including the various deans' offices, the Bureau of Study Counsel, the Office of Career Services ("dedicated to working with Harvard students and alums for the rest of their lives," claims a senior), and counselors associated with each residential house. The Radcliffe Institute for Advanced Study, which has evolved from the former Radcliffe women's college, affords undergrads access to a network of professional women, alumnae, and research fellows (both female and male). Sooner or later, all roads lead to Widener Library, where seemingly unlimited facilities lie in wait (and where snow-covered steps make prime sledding runs in the winter).

"The courses are difficult, particularly in the beginning."

Harvard does have one thing its $53 billion endowment can't buy: a diverse, high-powered, ambitious, and exciting student body. You will meet smooth-talking government majors who appear to have begun their senatorial campaigns in kindergarten and flamboyant fine arts majors who have cultivated an affected accent all their own. You will sample the intensity of Harvard's extracurricular scene, where 7,000 undergrads compete for leadership positions in a galaxy of extracurricular opportunities.

No one can tell you exactly what it takes to gain admission to Harvard (and if anyone tries, apply a large grain of sodium chloride), but here's a hint: superachiever academic records are the norm. And, of course, there are old-money types who probably spit up their baby food on a Harvard sweatshirt. (Many enter as sophomores when no one is looking.) As it is at other elite colleges, the practice of legacy admission preferences is now part of a national debate. Undergraduates come from all 50 states—85 percent are out-of-staters—although the student body is weighted toward the Northeast. Fifteen percent are international. About half of Harvard undergrads identify as students of color: Black students account for 9 percent, Hispanics/Latinos 12 percent, Asian Americans 24 percent, and multiracial students 8 percent. There are a few merit scholarships averaging $5,600, but no athletic scholarships; the university does practice need-blind admissions, and it meets the full demonstrated need of accepted students. For students who make the cut, Harvard is becoming more of a bargain in U.S. higher education. Families with annual household incomes below $200,000 are not expected to contribute to the cost of tuition. Families earning more than $200,000 may be eligible for tailored financial aid.

Virtually all undergraduates reside on campus, and every first-year class lives as a single unit in Harvard Yard, dining together at the beautifully renovated Annenberg

Hall. The older dorms provide spacious wood-paneled rooms, working fireplaces, and gentle reminders of Harvard's rich traditions. For their last three years, students live in one of 12 co-ed residential houses, built around their own courtyards with their own dining halls, libraries, and special facilities—from art studios to squash courts. Designed as learning communities, each house holds between 300 and 500 students, plus resident tutors and affiliated faculty members. Each house has a student council that plans social activities. Students are randomly assigned (with up to 15 friends) to a house. "The housing is one of the best parts of Harvard!" raves one student. Nine houses lie along the Charles River, while the other three sit a half mile away at the Radcliffe Quad. Some students consider the latter equivalent to a Siberian exile, especially during harsh Cambridge winters—although a shuttle does run regularly to the main campus.

Socializing at Harvard tends to occur on campus and in small groups. "It's certainly normal to spend Friday and Saturday nights studying," says a philosophy major. With the exception of the annual all-school First-Year Formal and the annual theme festivals each house throws, parties tend to be private affairs in individual dorm rooms. Students report that the legal drinking age is well enforced on campus.

The most distinctive and controversial aspect of social life at Harvard is the role of the so-called final clubs. These are exclusive and upscale social clubs that, while occupying their own buildings and in other ways completely separate from the university, play a significant role in the campus social life for the small minority of students who are "punched" for membership. The clubs have been engaged in a recurring struggle with Harvard's administration, which has condemned them as being out of place on the university's increasingly diverse campus. For many, the key to happiness in Harvard's high-powered environment is finding a niche, a comfortable academic or extracurricular circle around which to build your life. Outside activities include about 80 plays performed annually, a newspaper and several journals, and plenty of community service projects coordinated through the Phillips Brooks House Association student group.

"The housing is one of the best parts of Harvard!"

The possibilities of Harvard's social life are increased exponentially by Cambridge and Boston, where there are many places to have fun. Harvard Square itself is a legendary gathering place for tourists, shoppers, bearded intellectuals, and coffeehouse denizens. "Cambridge's Harvard Square is the perfect college town," a student cheers. "There are tons of shops, restaurants, and bars." The American Repertory Theater, transplanted from Yale in the mid-1980s, offers a season of professional productions and nearly as many professional student shows; its new location is expected to open in 2027. Cambridge also enjoys an exceptional selection of new and used bookstores, including, of course, the Harvard Bookstore and the mammoth Harvard Co-op, known universally as "the Coop." Boston boasts Faneuil Hall, the Red Sox, the Bruins, and more than 40 other colleges.

Most professors teach at least one undergraduate course per year.

Harvard has 42 varsity sports, which is the most of any Division I school and the most women's sports. The athletic facilities are across the river from the campus. Both the men's and women's squash and crew teams are perennial national powers, and men's ice hockey and women's lacrosse are also strong. Men's basketball has prospered in recent years under coach Tommy Amaker, a former Duke star. As for football, the team has been doing better in recent years, but the season always boils down to the Yale game, memorable as much for the antics of the spectators and marching band as for the fumbles of the players. Harvard Stadium, built in 1903, is the oldest in the country, and its layout helped determine the field size and rules of modern American football. Intramural sports teams are divided up by house, and each fall, league champs play teams from Yale the weekend of the game. Another fall highlight is the annual Head of the Charles crew race, the largest event of its kind in the world, where as many as 200,000 people gather to watch the racing shells glide by.

Nowhere but Harvard does the identity of a school—its history, its presence, its pretense—intrude so much into the details of undergraduate life. Admission here opens the door to a world of intellectual wonder, academic challenges, and faculty minds unmatched in the United States—but then drops students on the threshold. "I have quickly gained exposure to major theories in literature, psychology, anthropology, social sciences, and evolutionary biology," says a junior. That's the way Harvard is; what other kind of place could produce statesmen John Quincy Adams and John F. Kennedy, pioneers W. E. B. Du Bois and Helen Keller, and artists T. S. Eliot and Leonard Bernstein? Even its dropouts are movers and shakers (witness Bill Gates and Mark Zuckerberg). But caveat emptor: It is only the most motivated and dedicated student who can take full advantage of the Harvard experience.

If You Apply To ›

Harvard: Single choice early action, regular decision. SATs or ACTs: required. Accepts the Common Application with supplement.

Harvey Mudd College: See page 149.

Haverford College

370 Lancaster Avenue, Haverford, PA 19041

Quietly prestigious college of Quaker heritage. With an enrollment of about 1,400, Haverford is half the size of some competitors but benefits from its relationship with neighbor Bryn Mawr. Close cousin to nearby Swarthmore but not as far left politically. Exceptionally strong sense of community, with parklike campus amid the bustle of suburban Philadelphia. Honor code drives campus culture. A rare option if you want to play varsity cricket.

An overarching honor code covering everything from the classroom to the dorm room defines student life at Haverford College. Students schedule their own final exams and take unproctored tests. "The honor code, in some respects, is a self-selecting system which draws many students to Haverford. For this reason, nearly all students who come here share common values of trust, concern, and respect for others as well as academic integrity," says an econ major. Haverford may be smaller and less well-known than some of its peers, but it holds its own against the finest liberal arts colleges in the country. "In the academic and intellectual climate at Haverford, students are expected to care about ideas—of course—but also appreciate their importance and application in the outside world," offers a religion major.

Founded under the auspices of the Religious Society of Friends (Quakers) in 1833, Haverford functions much like a family. The campus consists of 216 acres just off Philadelphia's Main Line, an affluent area named after an erstwhile railroad, and resembles a peaceful, well-ordered summer camp. The densely wooded campus has an arboretum, duck pond, nature trails, and more than 400 species of shrubs and

Website: www.haverford.edu
Location: Suburban
Private
Total Enrollment: 1,427
Undergraduates: 1,427
Male/Female: 43/57
Financial Aid: 51%
Pell Grant: 14%
Expense: Pr $ $ $ $
Student Loans: 24%
Average Debt: $
Applicants: 7,341
Accepted: 12%
Enrolled: 43%
Grad in 6 Years: 90%

trees. Architectural styles range from 19th- and early 20th-century stone buildings to a sprinkling of modern structures here and there. The combination enhances the sense of a balanced community, bringing together two traditional Quaker philosophies: development of the intellect and appreciation of nature.

Haverford's curriculum reflects commitment to the liberal arts. General education requirements include courses in writing, language, and quantitative/symbolic reasoning, and students must complete two course credits in each of three "Domains of Knowledge," covering creative expression, the social/cultural world, and physical and natural sciences. Every Haverford student completes a senior thesis, project, or performance, partnering with a faculty mentor to do what amounts to graduate-level research. Math, biology, computer science, and economics are among the most popular majors, and the physics, psychology, and political science programs are also strong. There are more than a dozen areas of concentration—which are different from minors—that are attached to certain majors, including peace, justice, and human rights; biophysics; and Middle Eastern and Islamic studies.

> **"Students are expected to care about ideas—of course—but also appreciate their importance in the outside world."**

The Bi-College Consortium with Bryn Mawr, the nearby women's school, allows Haverford students to major in subjects such as art history, growth and structure of cities, and environmental studies. The relationship between Bryn Mawr and Haverford dates to the days when Haverford was all-male (it went co-ed in 1980), and today students from both schools cooperate on a weekly newspaper, radio station, orchestra, and other clubs and sports, and a free shuttle bus connects the campuses. About half of Haverford students take at least one course at Bryn Mawr each semester. The Tri-Co Philly Program brings Swarthmore into the mix and allows students to take two Philadelphia-focused courses in the city or cross-register for other classes. Cross-registration is also available at the University of Pennsylvania, and joint-degree programs are available with various institutions, including Penn, Caltech, Claremont McKenna, and Georgetown.

The academic workload at Haverford may be sizable, but students say the atmosphere is supportive. "We are extremely collaborative," explains a chemistry major. "I have never felt like anyone was competing with me over grades." Classes are small (72 percent have fewer than 20 students) and advising is ever-present: first-years are matched with professors who work with them from their arrival until they declare majors two years later, while upper-class "Customs people" are resources and mentors for living/learning groups of eight to 16 first-year students. Haverford's biggest strength may be its faculty members, who are unusually accessible—nearly a third of them live on campus. "Professors know students and communicate directly with them often," says a physics major. Haverford's Center for Peace and Global Citizenship—appropriate for a Quaker school—offers summer internships that emphasize the study and promotion of social justice and global issues. Nearly 70 study abroad programs around the globe attract a third of the students.

Haverford's distinctive honor code governs all aspects of campus life. "I can take my final exam at 3 a.m. on Founder's Green," says a junior as an example. The code, administered by students and debated and reratified each year at a meeting called Plenary, helps instill the

> **"I have never felt like anyone was competing with me over grades."**

values of "integrity, honesty, and concern for others." In good Quaker tradition, decisions are made by consensus rather than formal voting, and students play a large role in shaping college policy.

"You have to be some type of quirky to come to Haverford," says a chemistry major, but that's not a negative. A happy junior says, "I love my classmates:

(continued)

Returning First-years: 94%
Academics: ✎ ✎ ✎ ✎ ✎
Social: 💬 💬 💬
Q of L: ★ ★ ★ ★ ★
Admissions: (610) 896-1350
Email Address:
admission@haverford.edu

Strong Programs:
Biology
Computer Science
Mathematics
Peace, Justice, and Human
  Rights
Physics
Political Science
Psychology

> *Back in the 1850s, Haverford became one of the first colleges in the country to play cricket.*

they're curious, friendly, funny, whip-smart!" Only 13 percent of Haverford's students hail from Pennsylvania, but many are East Coasters nonetheless; 11 percent are international. Thirteen percent of students are Asian American, 12 percent are Hispanic/Latino, 4 percent are Black, and 10 percent are multiracial. Though the college is nonsectarian, the Quaker influence lives on in the form of an optional silent meeting each week. Students tend to be interested in progressive political and social ideas. Haverford meets the full demonstrated financial need of every admitted student and, for students from families with annual incomes below $60,000, has replaced loans with grants in its financial aid packages. Merit-based academic and athletic scholarships are not available.

Haverford's residence halls are spacious and well maintained, and most rooms are singles—even for first-years—so it's no surprise that 98 percent of all students live on campus. "While the dormitories are functional, they could benefit from updates," says an environmental studies major. All dorms are co-ed, but students may request single-sex floors. The school-owned Haverford College Apartments sit on the edge of campus and feature coveted one- and two-bedroom units, each with a living room, kitchen, and bathroom. "Under the Quaker ethos, we all eat under the same roof in the Dining Center," says a senior; special diets are easily accommodated, and meals receive average reviews. Campus security is good, owing in part to the school's location in the upscale Philadelphia suburbs, but the school is working to educate the campus community about gender-based violence and safe relationships. Regarding other services, a senior says, "We are lucky to have great services for mental health, career advising, and academic mentoring. You just have to be willing to reach out and ask for them."

Social life is mainly campus-based, although students do find opportunities to explore the surrounding area. "Ardmore is within walking distance and has a lot of cool restaurants and sweet shops—like Insomnia Cookies, which I think my team keeps in business," quips a senior. One campus group, Fords Against Boredom (FAB), "does trivia nights, bingo games, and other events on campus, but they also take students to the museums in Philly, to apple orchards in the fall, and to the King of Prussia Mall," explains a sophomore. "Haverford definitely has the best parties out of the three Tri-Co schools," boasts a junior, "so it's not uncommon to see Bryn Mawrters and Swatties catching the Blue Bus or Tri-Co Van to come to a Haverford party." Traditional events include the weekend-long, pre-exams Haverfest—a carnival-like festival with music, food, and games. On Pinwheel Day in the spring, "Some mystery group of students puts pinwheels all over Founder's Green and everyone skips class to spend the day outside," says a senior. Life in the close-knit, introspective environment that is Haverford can get stifling at times, but there are easy escapes. Downtown Philadelphia is just 20 minutes away by train. New York City, Washington, D.C., the New Jersey beaches, Pocono ski areas, and Atlantic City are only a couple hours away by car or train. About half of the students participate in volunteer projects coordinated by the Allen Office of Service and Community Collaboration.

"I can take my final exam at 3 a.m. on Founder's Green."

Haverford's rich athletic history dates back more than a century to 1905, when the school played Harvard in the first ever intercollegiate soccer game in the United States; Haverford has since racked up more soccer wins than any other school. The men's cross-country team is a perennial Division III national contender, and women's cross-country, volleyball, and lacrosse are competitive in the Centennial Conference. Back in the 1850s, Haverford became one of the first colleges in the country to play cricket, and the school still boasts one of the top collegiate teams. Despite a lively rivalry with Swarthmore, these Quakers have struggled to reconcile their peace-loving heritage with the desire to destroy opponents on the court or the field. For now, students root for their Black Squirrels and chant, "Fight, fight, inner light! Kill, Quakers, kill!" Intramural and club sports are popular, too, especially because participation counts toward the required six quarters of athletic credit.

Haverford students may be committed to the college's honor code and founding values, but the downside, according to one student, is that "students are challenged to meet an ideal set before them of creating the best community possible. For this reason, students are constantly criticizing themselves and the community as a whole to find ways of solving the problems facing them." See? Mom was right. With freedom comes responsibility.

If You Apply To ›

Haverford: Early decision I and II, regular decision. SATs or ACTs: optional. Accepts the Common Application with supplement.

University of Hawai'i at Mānoa

2500 Campus Road, Honolulu, HI 96822

One of the most accessible of the public flagships in the U.S.—at least when it comes to admissions—the University of Hawai'i at Mānoa pursues research and teaching in a uniquely cosmopolitan setting. Most undergrads are Asian Americans, Native Hawaiians, or other Pacific Islanders, and over half are in-staters. Astronomy, marine biology, and environmental studies are strong. Proximity to some of the world's best surfing an obvious plus.

One of the goals of the University of Hawai'i at Mānoa, which was founded in 1907, is to "serve as a bridge between East and West." UH Mānoa is one of the most ethnically diverse institutions in the country. Funding cuts imposed by the Trump administration have resulted in a loss of research grants and 90 outright terminations at the university. Even prior to the current political headwinds, the state's budget woes had impacted the university and students had complained of bulging classrooms and outdated facilities. Despite these challenges, a plant and environmental protection science major says, "Students, faculty, and community members are friendly and give off the Aloha Spirit."

The UH Mānoa campus occupies 320 acres in the Mānoa Valley, a residential Honolulu neighborhood. The architecture is regionally eclectic, mirroring historical and modern Pacific-Asian motifs, and is enhanced by extensive subtropical landscaping. The campus doubles as an arboretum with more than 4,000 trees and 500 species from all over the world. Situated within a few miles of the state capital and the city's major business district, the university provides excellent opportunities for students to interact with thought leaders, including mentorships and internships.

Core requirements are extensive: all students must take courses in math, humanities, social sciences, natural sciences, world civilization, and a foreign language or 'Ōlelo Hawai'i (Hawaiian). The First-Year program supports new students in their transition to the university by gathering diverse groups with similar interests to work and study together in Access to College Excellence academic learning communities made up of no more than 15 students. The Mānoa Writing Program, founded in 1987, is one of the oldest writing-across-the-curriculum programs in the country. Students are required to take five writing-intensive courses to graduate, but many take more.

Website: www.manoa.hawaii.edu

Location: City Outskirts

Public

Total Enrollment: 14,995

Undergraduates: 12,640

Male/Female: 40/58

Financial Aid: 47%

Pell Grant: 25%

Expense: Pub $ $

Student Loans: 36%

Average Debt: $

Applicants: 16,722

Accepted: 87%

Enrolled: 22%

Grad in 6 Years: 64%

Returning First-years: 81%

Academics: ✍ ✍

Social: 🗩 🗩 🗩

Q of L: ★ ★ ★

Admissions: (808) 956-8975

Email Address: manoa.admissions@hawaii.edu

UH Mānoa offers nearly 100 bachelor's degrees; among the best are astronomy, Pacific and Asian area studies, languages and the arts, ethnomusicology, and tropical agriculture. Astronomy and astrophysics benefit from the clear Hawaiian skies. It should come as no surprise that ocean-, climate-, and environment-related programs are also first-rate, with world-class facilities. The university takes pride in its programs in engineering, geology and geophysics, marine biology, international business, political science, travel industry management, and the School of Hawaiian Knowledge—the only college of indigenous knowledge at a major research university in the United States. The most popular majors, by enrollment, are in business, biology, psychology, and engineering. "The courses can be challenging based on what you take and the major you declare," says a senior. Forty percent of undergraduate classes have fewer than 20 students. Desirable classes and times are said to be difficult for first-years and sophomores to get into, although departmental academic advisors keep close tabs on whether students are on schedule to complete their degrees in four years. The Student Success Center offers academic advising, tutoring, and other support services. Professors receive generally favorable reviews. Says a biology and music double major, "Most [professors] are thoughtful and interested in the success of their students."

> **"Students, faculty, and community members are friendly and give off the Aloha Spirit."**

The two-tier Honors Program offers qualified first-years and sophomores the opportunity for general education courses in small, intensive classes, along with personalized academic advising and peer mentorship. Upper-class honors students are guided by faculty through independent, sustained research or creative work and must complete a final honors thesis. The Undergraduate Research Opportunities Program connects students in all disciplines with opportunities to engage in faculty-mentored research or creative projects. Participants present their work at a semester-end symposium. Students who tire of Hawai'i's endless beaches and beautiful sunsets can study abroad in locations around the world, including Asia, Australia, Europe, and South America.

Legend has it that if a rainbow appears during a game, UH Mānoa will win.

"Many students are very driven, but others are here to appreciate the island life," says a student. Sixty-three percent of undergraduates are in-staters, and 3 percent are from other countries. Hawai'i stands out among major American universities in that 34 percent of its undergraduates are Asian American and another 17 percent are of Native Hawaiian or other Pacific Islander descent. Black and Hispanic/Latino students each represent 2 percent of the student body, and 16 percent identify as multiracial. "The climate and diversity in Hawai'i allow for a greater and more open dialogue about race and culture," observes an English and history major. Political and social issues often take a back seat to academics and play, but among the more prominent concerns are the environment and Native Hawaiian rights. Especially promising students can compete for merit scholarships, which average $12,200 annually. The university also disburses roughly 250 athletic scholarships in 21 sports. The Mānoa Service Award offers $1,000 scholarships to current full-time students who complete 50 hours of volunteer work each semester.

Twenty percent of students live in campus housing, and those who apply by the May deadline are guaranteed a spot. Students recommend the Hale Aloha residence hall, consisting of four towers: 'Ilima, Lehua, Lokelani, and Mokihana; the rooms are compact but the hallways are active. If you're thinking about off-campus housing, take note: housing in Honolulu is scarce and expensive. Residential dining is located throughout the campus and serves diverse and adequate fare. "The Department of Public Safety has advertised more campus apps to help with safety so students can avoid getting into vulnerable situations," reports a history and economics double major.

> **"The courses can be challenging based on what you take."**

Because many students are commuters, UH Mānoa is sedate after dark, especially on weekends. Most social activity revolves around student clubs and, as one student explains, "simply being around the Campus Center, where you can find many students studying, socializing, or hitting the gym." Only 1 percent of the men and 1 percent of the women join the tiny Greek system. Drinking is not allowed in the residence halls. A couple of local hangouts provide an escape, and Mānoa Gardens, an on-campus bar, is also an option. Many students head off campus to enjoy "more beaches and hikes than one can handle," according to a sophomore. Lest anyone forget, some of the world's most beautiful resorts are less than a 20-minute drive away. Waikīkī Beach? Within two miles' reach. And round-trip airfare to the neighboring islands—including Maui, Kaua'i, and the Hawai'i Island—is reasonable. Favorite annual traditions include the homecoming fair and football game as well as the Aloha Bash, a big concert held every April featuring popular local bands.

UH Mānoa's athletic teams compete in Division I. The men's teams are known as the Rainbow Warriors, while the women's teams are the Rainbow Wahine, and legend has it that if a rainbow appears during a game, UH Mānoa will win. Twenty minutes before kickoff at every home football game, the team performs the Warrior Ha'a—their version of a traditional Māori dance. Men's and women's beach volleyball, men's and women's swimming/diving, and football are among the top draws. Intramural and recreational activities range from soccer and basketball to tai chi and snorkeling.

Students seeking warm weather and great surfing won't be disappointed, and those pursuing UH Mānoa's strong specialized programs undoubtedly benefit from the university's one-of-a-kind setting. But it's up to you, one student says, to get the best out of UH Mānoa. "The location allows mainland students to get a different cultural experience," adds another. "You're only young once—might as well be 20 in Hawai'i."

> *The campus doubles as an arboretum with more than 4,000 trees and 500 species from all over the world.*

> **"The location allows mainland students to get a different cultural experience."**

If You Apply To ›

UH Mānoa: Rolling admissions. SATs or ACTs: optional. Does not accept the Common Application.

Hendrix College

1600 Washington Avenue, Conway, AR 72032

Hendrix is in the same class of Southern liberal arts colleges as Millsaps and Rhodes. The most progressive of the three, Hendrix places a strong emphasis on international awareness and boasts colorful campus traditions. Arkansas is a tough sell, and the college accepts roughly half of all students who apply. About 50 percent of Hendrix students are from Arkansas, and most of the rest are Southerners.

For a school in the heart of the Bible Belt and Walton-land, Hendrix College, whose roots date to 1876 and took its name from a Methodist bishop, is surprisingly free-wheeling. In fact, it's among the South's most progressive liberal arts colleges. One goal is for its students to "lead lives of accomplishment, integrity, service, and joy." Academics are demanding but the atmosphere is laid-back. Students tend to be liberal—even radical—in their political and social views. Ironically, healthy dialogue

Male/Female: 49/51
Financial Aid: 98%
Pell Grant: 34%
Expense: Pr $
Student Loans: 51%
Average Debt: $ $
Applicants: 3,160
Accepted: 52%
Enrolled: 20%
Grad in 6 Years: 69%
Returning First-years: 78%
Academics: ✐ ✐ ✐
Social: 🗨 🗨 🗨 🗨
Q of L: ★ ★ ★ ★
Admissions: (501) 450-1362
Email Address: adm@hendrix
.edu

Strong Programs:
Biology
Computer Science
Economics and Business
English
Health Sciences
Neuroscience
Politics
Psychology

Undergraduate research is a priority, especially within the sciences, with 38 percent of students taking part.

about tough issues such as LGBTQ rights, the environment, and racial equity draws students together. "People here are passionate, intelligent, and fun," says a first-year. "They really want to change the world."

Hendrix's compact and comfortable campus stretches for 180 acres between the Ouachita and Ozark mountains. College land boasts more than 80 varieties of trees and shrubs and more than 10,000 budding flowers each spring. The main campus—with its own lily pool, fountain, and gazebo—occupies about one-fourth of the total acreage. The redbrick buildings are a mix of old and new, and a pedestrian overpass connects the main campus to the college's athletic facilities and a wooded fitness trail. The Miller Creative Quad combines arts facilities, including music practice rooms, a screening auditorium for the film studies program, and an art museum, with residential space on the upper floors housing 106 students.

Under Hendrix's general education program, first-years are required to take the Hendrix Immersion, a class that helps the transition to college life. The Capacities component involves requirements in writing, foreign language, quantitative skills, and physical activity, while the Learning Domains component requires coursework in six broad liberal arts areas. The Odyssey Program requires students to complete three experiences—which may be coursework, internships, or independent projects—selected from six categories: artistic creativity, global awareness, professional and leadership development, service to the world, special projects, and undergraduate research. "They give out tens of thousands of dollars a year to fund a lot of trips or learning experiences," raves a computer science and religious studies double major. All seniors must complete a capstone experience.

"Hendrix is very colorful and open to everyone."

Hendrix is strong in many areas, but natural and social sciences are definitely the school's forte. Popular majors include psychology, health sciences, computer science, and economics and business. The neuroscience and politics programs are notable, as are the premed and prelaw tracks. Students can also design their own interdisciplinary major, and a minor in comparative literature is now available. The Murphy Scholars Program draws participants from a broad range of majors, including the sciences, who are interested in deeper study of literature and language, awarding funding up to $4,000 to support independent projects. Doing well at Hendrix means keeping up with the intense workload, but students cite a collaborative atmosphere, and with 60 percent of classes enrolling fewer than 20 students, personal attention from faculty is the norm. "Professors care about their students and are willing to sit with each student until we grasp the concepts, regardless of how long it takes," says a history major. The school also offers dual-degree programs with Columbia and Washington University in St. Louis for aspiring engineers.

At Hendrix, undergraduate research is a priority, especially within the sciences, with 38 percent of students taking part; many get the chance to present original papers at regional and national symposia. Students also earn course credit for internships at U.S. embassies and organizations such as the National Institutes of Health and the U.S. Agency for International Development. About a quarter of students participate in a wide variety of opportunities to work, study, and serve abroad through Hendrix-sponsored programs in more than 10 countries from Costa Rica to Taiwan, and students have access to more than 300 partner exchange programs as well. For career preparation, Hendrix requires sophomores to participate in a three-day Career Term during winter break, in which students learn practical skills like interviewing and networking.

"Most students are liberal and eclectic, but all are respectful of political and social beliefs," says one student. Fifty-four percent of Hendrix students are from

Arkansas, and 2 percent come from abroad. Black students represent 7 percent of the student body, Hispanics/Latinos 8 percent, Asian Americans 3 percent, and multiracial students 5 percent. The Office of Multicultural Student Services seeks to enhance campus diversity, the lack of which is a common student complaint. Hendrix offers a variety of merit scholarships, averaging $30,300, to academically qualified students, but there are no athletic scholarships; 34 percent of incoming first-years receive Pell Grants. Through the Tuition Advantage Program, Hendrix will match the published in-state tuition at the flagship university in their home state for qualified students.

All students are required to live on campus, and only a few are granted exceptions each year, which students say adds to the sense of community. Residence halls offer "a classic dorm experience," says a senior, and Hendrix has recently completed extensive renovations to two historic student residence halls. Most upperclassmen take up quarters in on-campus apartments. As for dining, a politics and history major asserts, "The food is awesome. I absolutely love our Caf," and students report that plenty of choices are available for those with special dietary needs. Students also say they feel safe on campus, due in part to a visible security program and the close-knit nature of the campus. "Career advising and mental health [services] are great," says an anthropology and psychology major.

"Campus is lively on the weekends," says a senior, although another adds, "The social scene has had a decrease since my freshman year," with increased "strictness of being able to host a party." Greek life—a staple of most Southern schools—is conspicuously absent at Hendrix, and students are proud of their independence. The student-run Social Committee (SoCo) organizes campuswide events like concerts, dances, and parties, including the annual SoCo 54 disco-inspired party. The school has an amnesty policy for reporting emergency situations involving alcohol. Ample alternative programming is offered for those who don't wish to party. The Shirttail Serenade, a 100-year-old tradition that has evolved into a friendly dance-off, is held early in the fall semester. Donning white button-down shirts and dorm-specific paraphernalia (different colored shorts, crazy socks, glitter, etc.), teams of first-years from each residence hall perform dance routines while upperclassmen cheer them on.

Home to three colleges, Conway (population 73,000) is undergoing a revitalization and offers a growing number of shops and restaurants as well as Toad Suck Daze, a rollicking annual carnival downtown featuring bluegrass music. Little Rock, a 30-minute drive, provides more options. Popular road trips are Memphis (two hours by car) and Dallas and Oklahoma City (each a five-hour drive) for concerts and the like. For those who stay in town, the Volunteer Action Center coordinates participation in projects on Service Saturdays.

The Division III Hendrix Warriors field several competitive teams in the Southern Athletic Association; football, baseball, basketball, swimming, tennis, track and field, cross-country, and volleyball have been successful in recent years. Rivalry with Rhodes College is "strong but friendly," says one student. Intramural and club sports run the gamut from track and cross-country to dance. Hendrix College's Recreation and Wellness Department also provides opportunities for students, faculty, and staff to enhance their health and well-being through intramural programs, initiatives, and activities.

"Hendrix is very colorful and open to everyone," cheers a happy senior. Musician Jimi Hendrix—whose mug inevitably adorns a new campus T-shirt each year—once

> "[Hendrix gives] out tens of thousands of dollars a year to fund a lot of trips or learning experiences."

> "The food is awesome. I absolutely love our Caf!"

asked listeners, "Are you experienced?" After four years at Hendrix College, with small classes, an emphasis on research, and a laid-back atmosphere in which to test their beliefs and boundaries, students here can likely answer, "Yes!"

If You Apply To ›

Hendrix: Early action, regular decision. SATs or ACTs: optional. Accepts the Common Application with supplement.

Hiram College

11715 Garfield Road, Hiram, OH 44234

One of the smaller prominent liberal arts colleges in Ohio. Less known nationally than Denison or Wooster, Hiram draws the vast majority of its students from in state—and then sends them around the globe. Many classes are taught in seminar format, with ample undergraduate research opportunities. Unique academic calendar allows for off-campus learning.

Hiram College offers students a solid liberal arts education and plenty of opportunities to dive into a research lab, test out the corporate life, or travel the globe. In fact, all students are required to have a hands-on learning experience before they graduate. No matter where they hang their hats, students here enjoy a close-knit environment. "Most students know one another, word spreads fast, and small class sizes make for a very personalized academic experience," says a political science and international studies major.

Set on a charming hilltop campus that occupies the second-highest spot in Ohio, Hiram is blessed with an abundance of flowers and trees as well as a lovely view of the valley below. Hiram was founded in 1850 by the Disciples of Christ in a frontier area seen as "healthful and free of distractions." The prevailing architectural motif is New England brick, and many Hiram buildings are restored 19th-century homes. Science majors frequently work, study, and conduct research at the college-owned, 550-acre Barrow Biological Field Station a few miles away. Recent renovations include the student center, to bring back the campus bar, TJ's Dog House, and the Belichick Olympic Training Center, which includes new pickleball courts.

The Hiram Plan organizes the academic year into two longer 12-week sessions, each of which is followed by a shorter three-week term. Hiram's core curriculum is extensive. In their first year, students take two writing intensive seminars that focus on enduring questions. Juniors complete an interdisciplinary, team-taught Urgent Challenges course. Students are also required to take courses in eight Ways of Knowing, such as experimental scientific methods, social and cultural analysis, and understanding diversity. In addition, students satisfy an experiential learning component by studying off campus, conducting research, or working in an internship, and in the senior year, they complete and present a capstone project. Hiram also requires students to reflect on their career and other goals and on their progress at four points, starting in the spring of their first year. Thanks to the college's Tech and Trek mobile education program, every full-time, traditional student is outfitted with an iPad, an Apple Pencil, and a keyboard.

> **"Small class sizes make for a very personalized academic experience."**

At Hiram, all programs are solidly grounded in the liberal arts. Ethics is woven into accounting courses, and students are encouraged to couple preprofessional majors with more traditional humanities second majors or minors, such as computer science with performing arts. Most nursing graduates have a minor in biomedical humanities, a signature field in which Hiram was a national pioneer. The integrative exercise science and sport management programs are thriving. The sciences, especially biology, biomedical humanities, and chemistry, are strong, as is creative writing and the crime, law, and justice program. The Garfield Institute, named after the Hiram educator who went on to become the 20th U.S. president, offers a notable minor in public leadership. The most popular majors include accounting and financial management, education, psychology, and sport management. Dual-degree engineering programs are available with nearby Case Western Reserve as well as WashU in St. Louis. More than 20 three-year degree programs are also available. With 81 percent of classes enrolling fewer than 20 students, "Professors at Hiram use the smaller class sizes to challenge and inspire students to reach more goals," shares a biomedical humanities major, "whether those goals are educational or personal." Academic resources abound, including tutors, the writing center, and help from peers or profs.

Hiram's unique academic calendar allows ample time for off-campus endeavors. "The three-week semester is the perfect time for students to travel abroad and experience different cultures," explains a sophomore. Hiram coordinates two study away (domestic) or study abroad (international) programs each year, and during the summer the school offers opportunities at places such as the Northwoods Field Station in the wilds of Michigan's Upper Peninsula, where students choose courses ranging from botany and photography to geology and writing. Political internships are available in Washington, D.C. A four-year honors program is also available.

"Hiram students are willing to go out and explore," opines a junior. "Trying new things and being trailblazers is what Hiram is all about." Seventy-seven percent of Hiram students are in-staters. International students represent less than 1 percent of the student body. Black students constitute 11 percent, Asian Americans less than 1 percent, Hispanics/Latinos 9 percent, and multiracial students 3 percent. "We have a lot of diversity on campus," says a sophomore. Indeed, Hiram's **"Hiram is known for the 'Hiram Hi' because everyone is always greeting one another as they pass."** Intercultural Forum club is one of the largest and most active on campus, and the Office for Diversity and Inclusion offers peer mentoring and tutoring programs for first-generation students, among other services. A hefty 51 percent of first-years qualify for Pell Grants. In addition to need-based financial aid, Hiram awards merit scholarships averaging $10,300, but no athletic awards.

Most Hiram students—85 percent—live on campus, and everyone who wants a room gets one. "Hiram's housing process is determined by a lottery system, where the more credit hours a student has, the earlier they can pick their room for the next school year," says a sophomore. Most halls are co-ed, and upperclassmen who like their location can stay in the same room year after year. Thirty-six percent of students reside in living-learning communities. A majority of students live in two-person suites; the popular (and larger) triple and quad suites and the townhouse apartments are scarcer and usually claimed by upper-class students. Dining services receive good reviews, and expanded educational programming on sexual assault has been well received.

When the weekend rolls around, don't expect to find most Hiram students gathered around a keg; the college has cracked down on underage drinking, and participation in the school's two sororities and one fraternity is minimal. Parties thrown in suites and townhouses tend to be low-key. "The school does a pretty good job of providing activities to do on campus (most of the events involve free food!), but in the surrounding village, there isn't much to do," says a senior. Homecoming and Springfest are weeklong celebrations with diversions like "dive-in" movies at the pool and campuswide barbecues. Every spring brings Sugar Day, which celebrates students as they present their research and, a management major explains, "At the dining hall, there is pretty much nothing but sweets, which is kind of a pat on the back to the students that they're almost done with classes." Neighboring Garrettsville offers a few restaurants and bars, but those in search of a more active social scene make the 45-minute drive to Cleveland for concerts, professional sports, and the Rock and Roll Hall of Fame.

Hiram is hardly a mecca for budding athletic superstars, but it does have a decent Division III sports program, and its varsity Terriers play in the Presidents' Athletic Conference. Softball is a two-time NCAC conference champ. Additionally, men's volleyball and men's wrestling compete successfully in the Allegheny Mountain Collegiate Conference, and STUNT competes in the Great Midwest Athletic Conference. About half of the students play intramural and club sports, including volleyball, cornhole, and pickleball, and many enjoy the on-campus disc golf course as well. An excellent golf course lies three miles away, and good downhill slopes are about an hour distant.

Those looking for a school where anonymity is ensured need not apply. People here are so close that they share an equivalent of a not-so-secret handshake. "Hiram is known for the 'Hiram Hi' because everyone is always greeting one another as they pass," says a senior. Indeed, those seeking a friendly, all-American institution with a touch of internationalism might want to give Hiram a look.

If You Apply To ›

Hiram: Rolling admissions. SATs or ACTs: optional. Accepts the Common Application with supplement. Submission of a graded writing sample or essay is recommended.

Hobart and William Smith Colleges

300 Pulteney Street, Geneva, NY 14456

With a campus overlooking one of New York's picturesque Finger Lakes, HWS offers a distinctive balance of a strong liberal arts environment with strong career preparation and global perspectives. Takes pride in personal attention from full professors and a culture of community service. Lacks the name recognition of other elite New England liberal arts colleges, but that helps make it more accessible. Much of the social life takes place on campus, but skiing, sailing, and other outdoor activities beckon.

Website: www.hws.edu
Location: Small City
Private
Total Enrollment: 1,826
Undergraduates: 1,780
Male/Female: 46/53
Financial Aid: 97%
Pell Grant: 28%
Expense: Pr $ $ $

Hobart and William Smith Colleges began life as two separate, single-sex schools: Hobart College was founded in 1822 by Episcopal Bishop John Henry Hobart as an outpost for civilized and learned behavior on what was then a frontier, while William Smith College opened in 1908 and bears the name of a businessman who sought to extend education opportunities to women. They became a joint corporate—or "coordinate"—entity in 1943 that "prepares students to live lives of consequence."

The HWS campus stretches for 325 tree-lined acres and includes a forest and a wildlife preserve. Architectural styles range from colonial to postmodern, with stately Greek Revival mansions and ivy-clad brick residences and classrooms. The school boasts the renovated Adams Intercultural Center, a state-of-the-art performing arts building, two solar farms, and an entrepreneurial incubator space. The nationally ranked sailing team are among the students who enjoy the school's boathouse on the shores of Seneca Lake. If some students gripe about the "definitely cold" winters, a writing major adds, "There's something really peaceful and beautiful about campus in the snow—it's kind of magical in its own way."

For those willing to brave the Finger Lakes winters, the HWS curriculum begins with first-year students taking an interdisciplinary seminar constructed around a different interest; recent seminar offerings include Parched: The Past, Present, and Future of Water; Living with AI: Data, Society, and Machines that Learn; and Cooking, Cuisine, and Me. First-years in each seminar are assigned to the same orientation group, "so they are well acquainted before they start their first class together," explains an economics major. Students must also complete a major and a minor or second major and take four courses across key areas, including scientific and quantitative reasoning, artistic and creative expression, global and cultural connections, and ethical and social responsibility. All students conduct a senior capstone experience.

The most popular majors include business management and entrepreneurship, economics, media and society, and psychology. Environmental studies, biology, and architectural studies are strong, and the long list of minors includes aquatic sciences; bodies, disability, and justice; data analytics; and Italian studies. The Finger Lakes Institute gives students wide opportunities to work in various fields of scientific inquiry as well as public policy. HWS offers several dual-degree programs including a 3–2 joint degree engineering program with Dartmouth. Says one participant who's earning a physics and engineering degree, "It allows me to combine a well-rounded liberal arts education with a hands-on, technically focused engineering experience from a top-tier university."

> **"There are always visiting lecturers, speakers, and readings on campus for students to attend."**

"The academic climate is supportive without coddling," says an economics major. Adds a senior, "There are always visiting lecturers, speakers, and readings on campus for students to attend." The English major also offers a creative writing track, and students praise the Trias Writers in Residence program, "where visiting authors teach a creative writing class on campus." Small classes are the norm here: 67 percent have fewer than 20 students. Professors are praised for being accessible and engaging. "Professors treat students like peers and are open to any and all questions and challenges," says an environmental studies and geoscience major.

HWS students may take a term away from campus, and 60 percent do so, choosing from more than 50 study abroad programs, many of which are faculty led, and several new programs have been added ranging from Rome and Bali to Nepal. Seniors may elect to complete an honors project involving research, a critical paper, or an equivalent creative work in addition to written and oral exams on their projects. Students who complete the Pathways Program, a series of workshops and career counseling activities, are guaranteed an opportunity for a paid internship or research experience.

"I would describe my fellow students and friends as incredibly vivacious and eager to learn and engage with the community," says an international relations and Asian studies double major. Forty-one percent of the HWS student body are New Yorkers and 6 percent are international. Black students account for 7 percent of undergraduates, Hispanics/Latinos 11 percent, Asian Americans 3 percent, and multi-

> **"Professors treat students like peers and are open to any and all questions and challenges."**

racial students 4 percent. "Students feel comfortable expressing political opinions and thoughts," says a senior. Adds a junior, "When major social or political issues arise in the world, professors and faculty do an excellent job of addressing them thoughtfully." Merit scholarships averaging $34,200 are awarded to qualified students.

(continued)

Student Loans: 72%
Average Debt: $ $ $
Applicants: 5,904
Accepted: 64%
Enrolled: 15%
Grad in 6 Years: 77%
Returning First-years: 86%
Academics: ✍ ✍ ✍
Social: 🗨 🗨 🗨
Q of L: ★ ★ ★
Admissions: (800) 852-2256
Email Address:
   admissions@hws.edu

Strong Programs:
Architectural Studies
Business Management and
   Entrepreneurship
Economics
English
Environmental Studies
Media and Society
Psychology

The Winter Festival features horse-drawn carriages, huskies, food trucks, and fun activities for students.

At HWS, 91 percent of students live on campus and all may buy a meal plan. Housing includes lakefront residences, theme houses, and townhouses. Single-sex, co-ed, and gender-neutral options are available. Thirty percent of first-years opt to participate in living/learning communities. "It was helpful to have my classmates living in the same space as me," lauds an economics major. While no one raves about the dining hall fare, "the important thing is that they listen to our concerns," says a biology and environment studies major. When it comes to safety, a sophomore comments that campus security officers are "very efficient and helpful at all times." The counseling center, though it has been restructured to offer increased mental health care, receives mixed reviews. Career services, on the other hand, is universally lauded.

"The social scene at HWS is a lot of fun," cheers a junior. "While there is a party culture, what's great is that there's no pressure to take part." Six Hobart fraternities claim 13 percent of the men, who aren't permitted to pledge until sophomore year, and William Smith's sole sorority signs up 3 percent of the women. Underage students caught

"The social scene at HWS is a lot of fun!"

with booze must attend alcohol awareness classes and may face social probation. "Student Engagement also plays a big role in campus life, regularly organizing events that are open to everyone," says an international relations major. "One of my personal favorites is the Winter Festival, which features horse-drawn carriages, huskies, food trucks, and a variety of fun activities for students." Other annual traditions include Moving Up Day, which "celebrates the end of the academic year and HWS history," explains a student.

Geneva offers many amenities for students, including restaurants, bars, shops, concerts, and the Smith Opera House. All students are active in the community: collectively, HWS students contribute more than 30,000 hours of service each year, often through service-learning courses or one-day opportunities like Days of Service. Rochester, Ithaca, and Syracuse, all about 45 minutes away, make for popular road trips. Seneca Falls, birthplace of the suffrage movement, is also nearby. "Outdoor activities like hiking, swimming, or just spending time by the lake are common ways students connect outside of class," adds a physics major.

Students flock to Hobart hockey games as well as lacrosse matches against rivals Syracuse and Cornell. Varsity sports teams' mascots and colors reflect HWS's heritage: the Hobart Statesmen wear purple and orange, while the William Smith Herons sport green and white. Teams compete in Division III, except for Hobart lacrosse, which is Division I. Men's alpine skiing, basketball, football, sailing, and soccer and women's bowling, cross-country, field hockey, lacrosse, soccer, and squash are among recent conference champions, while men's ice hockey has won three straight national championships since 2023. The HWS Debate Team has had national and international success. Thirty percent of students participate in intramural and club sports.

HWS offers a unique kind of community along with a solid liberal arts education. "The HWS community is tight knit, as the smaller size offers an opportunity to get to know people through classes, clubs, dorms, and more," says a happy junior. "There are also ways to engage deeply with the surrounding community and reach beyond the college's walls. It is truly a special place."

If You Apply To ›

HWS: Early decision I and II, early action, regular decision. SATs or ACTs: optional. Accepts the Common Application.

Hofstra University

100 Hofstra University, Hempstead, NY 11549

Boasts a combination of suburban setting with ready access to the Big Apple. Hofstra has outgrown its commuter-school origins and offers a broad range of preprofessional and other academic programs. Well known as a lacrosse powerhouse. Has become more selective in recent years, but for many, it is still a backup to urban schools like BU and Northeastern.

Although it sits within striking distance of Manhattan concrete, Hofstra University occupies one of the loveliest campuses you'll find anywhere. Its bucolic setting is home not only to an accredited art museum and a nationally recognized arboretum but also to the school's blossoming preprofessional offerings. Whatever their field, Hofstra students enjoy special learning communities, research and internship opportunities, and first-year programs that help harried newbies get off to a good start. "It's a friendly environment that allows you to find your special niches, without forcing anything upon you," reflects an accounting and political science major.

Founded in 1935 with one building—the Dutch colonial mansion left in trust by Kate and William Hofstra on their 15-acre estate—the campus is now home to 117 structures on 244 acres. The suburban campus offers a parklike environment with a variety of architecture, from ivy-covered stone buildings to modern facilities with sleek angles and electronic signage, which surround open green quads. The campus is especially beautiful in the spring, when its 100,000 tulips, a tribute to the Dutch heritage of Hofstra's founders, are in bloom. Several buildings have undergone major renovations, and the Zarb School of Business has a 52,500-square-foot building boasting an incubator lab, a market research and behavioral science lab, and other amenities. The DeMatteis School of Engineering's 75,000-square-foot science and innovation center includes cutting-edge lab facilities for nursing, engineering, and computer science students.

> **"Most majors focus on ensuring that students are learning how to be a professional in their field."**

With more than 175 academic programs for undergraduates, Hofstra offers students plenty of career paths. Regardless of what major they choose, all undergrad students must complete distribution requirements, including coursework in humanities; natural sciences, mathematics, and computer science; social sciences; cross-cultural studies; and interdisciplinary studies. Students must also demonstrate their competence as writers, usually by taking the Writing Proficiency Exam in their first year.

With the DeMatteis School of Engineering and Applied Science and the Kalikow School of Government, Public Policy, and International Affairs, as well as joint undergraduate programs with its medical school, Hofstra has sought to model itself on much larger Northeastern universities like NYU and Syracuse. Traditional areas of strength include business, communication, engineering, and health sciences; marketing, accounting, journalism, television and film, radio production, and community health are particularly notable. Business students benefit from one of the largest simulated trading rooms in the New York area. Several dual-degree programs are available, pairing undergraduate degrees with corresponding master's degrees in such areas as physician assistant studies, labor studies, sustainability studies, and others. Nursing is now available as an undergraduate major from the Hofstra Northwell School of Nursing and Physician Assistant Studies.

Website: www.hofstra.edu
Location: Suburban
Private
Total Enrollment: 9,292
Undergraduates: 6,283
Male/Female: 42/58
Financial Aid: 84%
Pell Grant: 21%
Expense: Pr $ $
Student Loans: 57%
Average Debt: $ $ $ $
Applicants: 25,021
Accepted: 68%
Enrolled: 10%
Grad in 6 Years: 69%
Returning First-years: 84%
Academics: ✍ ✍ ✍
Social: 🗩 🗩 🗩
Q of L: ★ ★ ★
Admissions: (516) 463-6700
Email Address:
 admission@hofstra.edu

Strong Programs:
Accounting
Business
Communication
Engineering
Health Sciences
Journalism
Radio Production
Television and Film

"Most majors focus on ensuring that students are learning how to be a professional in their field, as opposed to being able to simply regurgitate the information," explains a junior. Forty-eight percent of undergraduate classes have fewer than 20 students, allowing for plenty of access to faculty. "The professors really care about your successes and often celebrate them with you," says a journalism major. Support services for students with learning disabilities are particularly strong and include accommodations as well as skill-development and coaching programs.

The First-Year Connections program offers new students a combined social and academic experience centered on small seminars (limited to 19 students) taught by senior faculty; recent seminars include Macro Freakonomics, Art in the Information Age, and The Mathematics of Elections. First-years may also enroll in clusters of thematically related courses, and several seminars and clusters have living/learning community options associated with them. The Honors College offers about 250 qualified entering students a multidisciplinary program with a special housing option. The university's 17 research centers facilitate opportunities for students to work with professors on scholarly projects, and internships in New York City are another popular pursuit. Students with wanderlust can take advantage of study abroad options around the world, including programs in Cuba, India, Italy, and Japan, and about 15 percent of undergrads do so.

"I wanted to make sure I wound up at a school where everyone brought something different to the table, and I definitely found it here," says a journalism major. Sixty-nine percent of undergraduates hail from New York, and 3 percent come from abroad. Black students account for 10 percent of the student body, Hispanics/Latinos 19 percent, Asian Americans 16 percent, and multiracial students 7 percent. Hofstra has hosted a trio of U.S. presidential debates, and a senior describes the political climate as "semi-intense" but "respectful." The university offers merit scholarships worth an average of $25,200 and over 100 athletic scholarships in 23 men's and women's sports.

"[Hofstra offers] an incredible number of clubs, in-dorm activities, and departmental organizations."

Thirty-eight percent of undergraduates live in university housing, which is guaranteed for all four years. Many dorms have been renovated in the last few years. Students have nearly 20 different dining options to choose from, and a health science major says, "Most meals are made to order, which ensures freshness and deliciousness." A junior reports, "The school takes safety very seriously, which is why we have five shuttle systems, including a night shuttle."

As for social life, "This is where Hofstra excels," boasts a sophomore, "offering an incredible number of clubs, in-dorm activities, and departmental organizations." Five percent of the men and 9 percent of the women go Greek, but they don't dominate the social landscape. Students of legal age are allowed to consume alcohol in their rooms; "parties are there if you're looking for them," says a junior. Hofstra is big on festivals, which include Fall Fest; a spring music festival; Irish, Italian, and Dutch festivals; and a long-running Shakespeare Festival that features performances on a stage that is purported to be the most authentic replica in the U.S. of the original Globe Theatre.

Hofstra's location 40 minutes east of New York City makes it easy to enjoy day trips and nights on the town, and the school organizes Explore Next Door events that take students to various neighborhoods, museums, shows, and sporting events. The two largest community service activities at Hofstra are Shake-a-Rake and Snow Angels, which send students out to do yard work and shoveling for elderly and disabled neighbors.

The Hofstra Pride compete in Division I and play an important role in shaping campus culture—especially the perennially powerful lacrosse and men's basketball teams. Men's soccer has become a powerhouse, winning four consecutive Coastal Athletic Association championships, including in 2024; volleyball and men's basketball are also strong. The dance team is nationally ranked, and the forensics, or debate, team has achieved national success as well. Roughly one-quarter of undergrads participate in the university's 25 club sports and 6 intramural leagues.

Opportunities abound at Hofstra, and the university continues to add resources—both curricular and extracurricular—to serve its diverse, career-oriented student body. As one junior puts it, "Many schools feel like buffets, where students are offered services and told to forge their own way to where they hope to be, while Hofstra caters directly to the individual student and asks what they can do to get a student from point A to point B." By connecting solid academics with hands-on learning experiences, the university seeks to put its students in a New York state of mind.

Overlaps

Boston University, University of Delaware, Fordham, NYU, Penn State, SUNY–Binghamton, SUNY–Stony Brook, Syracuse

If You Apply To ›

Hofstra: Early action I and II, rolling admissions. SATs or ACTs: optional. Accepts the Common Application with supplement.

Hollins University

7916 Williamson Road, Roanoke, VA 24020

One of the South's leading women's colleges, Hollins sits on the edge of Roanoke, the biggest city in southwest Virginia, where it has long been noted for creative writing, the performing arts, and its equestrian program. Social life often involves road trips to Virginia Tech and Washington and Lee, both about an hour's drive, or venturing into the great outdoors.

Traditions rule at Hollins University, Virginia's first women's college, founded in 1842 (and named after local donors) on a lush, 475-acre campus in the mountains. Each fall, students and staff hike up Tinker Mountain for skits, a picnic lunch, and a bird's-eye view of the changing foliage. During the holiday season, faculty and administrators sing carols outside students' residence halls. And after graduation, juniors inherit seniors' decorated gowns during Passing of the Robes. A few dozen male students can be found on campus, since Hollins offers 18 co-ed degree and certificate programs for graduate students. "A student should only attend Hollins if they want to be a part of a close-knit community that fosters creative minds and ambitious spirits," says a senior.

Described by the *New York Times* as "achingly picturesque," the neoclassical red-brick buildings at Hollins date back to the mid-19th century. There are some modern structures too, such as the Wetherill Visual Arts Center. Several buildings have been renovated in recent years, including Hollins Theatre, Dana Science Building, and a new student apartment village.

Hollins's Core Curriculum requires courses in quantitative literacy; foreign language; storytelling, myths, and narratives; diversity; and scientific reasoning as well as an interdisciplinary environmental course, an experiential learning element, and a life skills component, comprised of wellness, technology, financial literacy, and career development. Two terms of physical education are mandatory, and those looking to take advantage of Hollins's acclaimed equestrian program can earn PE credits with riding lessons. All new students take a required First-Year Foundations

Website: www.hollins.edu
Location: Suburban
Private
Total Enrollment: 673
Undergraduates: 661
Male/Female: 0/100
Financial Aid: 89%
Pell Grant: 38%
Expense: Pr $
Student Loans: 65%
Average Debt: $ $ $
Applicants: 2,827
Accepted: 68%
Enrolled: 10%
Grad in 6 Years: 70%
Returning First-years: 74%
Academics: ✑ ✑ ✑
Social: 🍷 🍷 🍷
Q of L: ★ ★ ★ ★
Admissions: (800) 456-9595
Email Address:
huadm@hollins.edu

The Signature Internship Program places upperclassmen in for-credit internships, offered by loyal alumnae across the country.

course and a Conflict & Collaboration class and participate in Orientation Week, which includes academic programming, a day of community service, and plenty of time to form friendships with new classmates. All seniors complete a capstone course or project.

Academics are the priority at Hollins. "[Classes are] very discussion-oriented, involving lots of questions back and forth from professor to student," says a first-year student. Of the school's 29 undergraduate majors, psychology, English, biology, business, and creative writing are the most popular. Public health is the newest. Students majoring or minoring in creative writing benefit from the nationally recognized Jackson Center for Creative Writing. Environmental studies and the visual and performing arts, especially film,

"[Classes are] very discussion-oriented, involving lots of questions back and forth from professor to student."

theatre, and dance, have good reputations too. Serious dance students can attend the American Dance Festival at Duke University to study intensively during the summer. Motivated students are encouraged to design their own majors. Classes are small, with 86 percent enrolling fewer than 20 students and none exceeding 40, and professors are well regarded. "We get lots of individual attention and extra help," says an art history and international studies major.

The Rutherfoord Center for Experiential Learning helps coordinate hands-on learning opportunities like study abroad, research projects, and internships, which students often pursue during the monthlong January Short Term. "Getting to work with your professors in the field and not just do research in a classroom setting is invaluable," praises an environmental science major. The Signature Internship Program places upperclassmen in for-credit internships, offered by loyal alumnae across the country. The Batten Leadership Institute, open to students of all majors, offers a certificate in leadership studies and opportunities for students to develop skills like effective conflict management, negotiation, and team building. The Entrepreneurial Learning Institute coordinates courses in applied entrepreneurship and other opportunities for students in all disciplines. In addition to a Hollins Abroad program in London, students may study through more than 20 affiliated programs around the world.

At Hollins, says an elementary education major, students "are supportive and don't tolerate drama. They want to see each other succeed." Sixty-three percent of undergrads are Virginians, and 6 percent hail from foreign countries. Black students make up 16 percent of the total, Asian Americans 2 percent, Hispanics/Latinas 12 percent, and multiracial students 3 percent. "There's a very large LGBTQ+ population on campus, so those issues are really important to everyone," says a senior, and campus politics lean liberal. Hollins hands out merit scholarships averaging $31,800 to qualified students but no athletic scholarships. Thirty-eight percent of incoming first-years qualify for Pell Grants.

Eighty-one percent of Hollins students live in the dorms; they have to, unless they're married, older than 23, or living at home in Roanoke with their parents. Options include traditional residence halls, several special interest houses, and the new apartment village. "Most of the dorms are beautiful historic buildings full of character and comfort," says a student. First-years live in Randolph and Tinker. Upperclassmen make their homes in Main, West, and East, which have 10-

"Most of the dorms are beautiful historic buildings full of character and comfort."

foot ceilings and hardwood floors, and some rooms also boast brass doorknobs, walk-in closets, and even fireplaces. Students chow down at Moody Dining Hall, which "just feels like a fast food joint," gripes a student. Other options are Greenberry's Coffee or the Hub. While the adjacent Roanoke neighborhood has its rough spots, "the campus is extremely safe," notes a junior.

"There isn't necessarily a loud party culture on campus," says a sophomore. Hollins shuns sororities, and sporadic student efforts to bring them to campus draw lively debate. To fill the gap, the school organizes mixers, concerts, dances, and second-run movies each weekend. Among campus traditions, students say Tinker Day is unique: "Who else would take an entire school day off to climb a mountain and eat donuts for breakfast?" asks one student. There's also a free shuttle to help students get around Roanoke (population 100,000). "Roanoke is a quaint city, not tall and towering but not small, either," says an English major. "There are local markets, a few clubs, a mall, and curious little local shops." As a result, road-tripping remains the preferred social option—to all-male Hampden–Sydney College, Virginia Tech, the University of Virginia, or Washington and Lee.

Hollins's on-campus stable, where students can board their own horses, comple-ments the school's top-notch equestrian program, which has brought home the Old Dominion Athletic Conference championship 21 times. The university also spon-sors eight other Division III sports. Although there are no intramural sports, the popular Hollins Outdoor Program offers hiking, spelunking, and other activities for all skill levels in the beautiful Shenandoah Valley and Blue Ridge Mountains. It also offers a certificate program that one student says "can help with getting jobs in National Parks and survival type jobs."

As the number of women's colleges continues to dwindle, Hollins remains com-mitted to the virtues of single-sex education. Students leave with confidence, critical-thinking skills, and intellectual depth, thanks to a solid grounding in the liberal arts. And the school's Southern heritage doesn't hurt, either. "Hollins is a great school that empowers women," says one senior. "It has made me independent."

Overlaps

Agnes Scott, Emory & Henry, Goucher, Hendrix, Meredith, Mount Holyoke, Roanoke, Sweet Briar

If You Apply To ›

Hollins: Early decision, early action, regular decision. SATs or ACTs: optional. Accepts the Common Application with sup-plement. Accepts applications from students who consistently live and identify as women, regardless of the gender assigned to them at birth.

College of the Holy Cross

1 College Street, Worcester, MA 01610

A tight-knit Catholic community steeped in the Jesuit tradition of service of faith and promotion of justice. Many students are the second or third generation to attend. Set on a hill above activity hub Worcester, an hour from Boston. Division I sports teams compete and win championships against schools 10 times Holy Cross's size.

Students at Holy Cross, founded in 1843 as the first Catholic college in New England, are devoted to the Society of Jesus (Jesuit) tradition of becoming "people for and with others." Students are driven by Ignatian principles of compassion and dignity for all humans. The College offers more than 90 community-based learning (CBL) courses that immerse students in the city of Worcester and the surrounding towns. The classroom focus is critical thinking and writing, but the school's proximity to several other colleges in the Worcester area means students can cultivate their social lives as well.

Holy Cross is located on one of the seven hills overlooking the burgeoning city of Worcester, and the 174-acre campus is a registered arboretum. The school's

Website: www.holycross.edu
Location: City Outskirts
Private
Total Enrollment: 3,127
Undergraduates: 3,127
Male/Female: 46/54
Financial Aid: 70%
Pell Grant: 20%
Expense: Pr $ $ $

(continued)

Student Loans: 41%
Average Debt: $
Applicants: 9,568
Accepted: 18%
Enrolled: 50%
Grad in 6 Years: 87%
Returning First-years: 95%
Academics: ✑ ✑ ✑ ✑
Social: 🗩 🗩 🗩 🗩
Q of L: ★ ★ ★ ★
Admissions: (508) 793-2443
Email Address:
  admissions@holycross.edu

Strong Programs:
Classics
Economics
English
Health Professions
Political Science
Psychology
Religious Studies
Sociology

The Fenwick Scholar program helps students design and carry out independent projects.

landscaping has won national awards. Architectural styles range from classical to modern. Newer structures include the Prior Performing Arts Center and City View Townhouses, which accommodate upperclassmen.

General education requirements at Holy Cross comprise 12 courses in nine areas spanning the liberal arts and sciences. Ideas and thinking are the focus, rather than preparation for a specific vocation. All first-year students participate in Montserrat, a comprehensive living/learning program named for the Spanish mountain where St. Ignatius began his spiritual journey. It centers on a small, yearlong seminar that students select from one of six clusters, each devoted to a specific theme: contemporary challenges, the divine, the self, the natural world, global society, and core human questions. Students live with other members of their cluster in the same residence hall and participate in cocurricular activities like special lectures, workshops, and field trips. "It was an eye-opening experience for me, and the friendships I made in my Montserrat class lasted throughout my entire four years," reflects a psychology major.

> **"The academic climate of Holy Cross is both rigorous and formative."**

Holy Cross boasts a high success rate for students getting accepted to medical school thanks in part to the strong health professions program. The economics, political science, psychology, and English programs are robust and popular. Students also give high marks to chemistry, physics, and sociology. One student described the classics department as one of the best-kept secrets on campus. As might be expected on a Jesuit campus, philosophy and peace and conflict studies are also popular. New majors have been added in neuroscience, critical race and ethnic studies, and architecture.

"The academic climate of Holy Cross is both rigorous and formative," says a math and religious studies major. Classes are small—64 percent have fewer than 20 students—which helps faculty members keep in touch with undergraduates. "I've been taught by a prosecutor, a U.S. Congressman, the American Meteorological Association's chief executive, public intellectuals, leading historians," marvels a political science and history major. Professors are praised for being willing to help. And students say the support they receive from each other is exceptional. One senior shares, "I have found notes in the Dinand Library with a positive quote or an encouraging message for the next student who sits there."

Holy Cross's popular CBL courses require weekly service with local volunteer, education, or health organizations in addition to time in the classroom; some courses focus on research that benefits local organizations. "I had the privilege of taking a CBL class my first year, during which I volunteered at a local health care facility," relates a senior. The honors program enables a small number of juniors and seniors to enroll in exclusive courses and thesis-writing seminars, while the Fenwick Scholar program helps students design and carry out independent projects. Each April, approximately 300 Holy Cross students participate in a four-day conference and present the results of their independent work. Forty percent of students pack their bags for a range of study abroad programs around the world, and the college strongly encourages yearlong programs. Two intensive study away programs, the Washington Semester and the New York Semester, combine an internship with a seminar course and an independent, research-based thesis or capstone project. Students praise the Center for Career Development, especially for its strong relationships with alumni.

While Jesuit ideals are an important element of the Holy Cross experience, students of all faiths are welcomed, and daily mass is not required. "We're an intellectually diverse school (atheists, devout Catholics, conservatives, liberals, etc.), but most students certainly come from New England and the Northeast," says a senior.

The chaplain's office runs several types of retreats for all faiths and reflective practices, including an optional five-day silent retreat. "The College celebrates every student's lived experiences, welcoming all races, sexual orientations, and gender identities," say administrators. Thirty-six percent of students are in-staters, and 1 percent are international. Black students make up 5 percent of the student body, Asian Americans represent 3 percent, Hispanics/Latinos account for 13 percent, and multiracial students add 4 percent. Social justice issues are a constant focus on campus, and the college sponsors many campuswide forums and panel discussions. Says a senior, "Because we offer so many opportunities for open discourse in and outside the classroom, we have a very respectful, encouraging intellectual climate." Holy Cross guarantees to meet admitted students' full demonstrated financial need. Students from families with annual incomes of $100,000 or less and typical assets receive full-tuition grants. Merit-based scholarships averaging $22,900 are available to top students, and athletes may vie for close to 200 athletic awards in 14 sports.

Eighty-eight percent of Holy Cross students live in the residence halls, where first-years and sophomores have double rooms, and juniors and seniors may opt for suites or apartment-style accommodations. Floors are single-sex; buildings are co-ed. First-years live on "Easy Street," in Hanselman, Clark, and Brooks Halls (on the college's central hill next to the Hogan Campus Center). Dorms receive decent reviews, especially for their size and storage space. Dining options include several campus eateries and the main dining hall; students rate the food as tasty and plentiful. Students say they feel safe thanks to regular campus security patrols and a safe-ride program, while the Counseling and Psychological Services office provides mental health support, which one student calls "extremely helpful and therapeutic."

Because, consistent with Jesuit tradition, there are no Greek organizations, dorm life takes center stage. The Campus Activities Board hosts various events, including karaoke, comedians, casino nights, and movie nights. Tradition is big at Holy Cross, cheers a senior; "whether it's the annual Pride Drag Show, the annual BSU fashion show, bingo hosted by CAB, or a sports game, there's always something to do." The Christmas tree lighting is a favorite event, and Spring Weekend brings well-known performers and a carnival. Additionally, says a psychology and sociology major, "the multicultural student organizations on campus are extremely active," offering cultural events with "great food and performances!"

"Volunteering is one way students live out the Holy Cross mission," a student says. The SPUD (Student Programs for Urban Development) is particularly popular and allows students to connect with others in the Worcester community. In the last decade, Worcester has blossomed into the fastest-growing city in New England and now features minor league baseball and hockey, nationally recognized small businesses, and world-class museums. A school shuttle service takes students to the orchestra, the DCU Center for athletic events and concerts, and the Worcester Art Museum. "Worcester is a vibrant city with lots of thrift shops and a fantastic food scene," says a senior. The college organizes trips to Boston, Providence, and New York City. There is also shuttle service to Worcester's Union Station, where students can connect to MBTA rail service to Boston as well as Amtrak routes.

Holy Cross's Crusaders compete in Division I athletics. "The annual Holy Cross vs. Boston College football game is always fun to attend," says a sophomore. The football and women's basketball teams have taken home Patriot League championships,

"We're an intellectually diverse school (atheists, devout Catholics, conservatives, liberals, etc.)."

"Worcester is a vibrant city with lots of thrift shops and a fantastic food scene."

and men's basketball, baseball, and ice hockey and women's lacrosse are also strong. A quarter of students participate in recreational sports. Holy Cross also competes nationally in moot court, mock trial, and mediation.

Holy Cross is keeping the faith—its emphasis on Catholicism and the Jesuit tradition, that is—as administrators place a renewed focus on academics, community, inclusivity, and its students' impact. "Holy Cross has prepared me to think critically, challenge the status quo, ask questions, and step outside my comfort zone to make changes in our world," cheers one senior. Indeed, the close-knit atmosphere offers students a multitude of opportunities to grow, serve others, and create lasting friendships.

If You Apply To ›

Holy Cross: Early decision I and II, regular decision. SATs or ACTs: optional. Accepts the Common Application.

Hood College

401 Rosemont Avenue, Frederick, MD 21701

Strategically located within striking distance of both D.C. and Baltimore, Hood offers an innovative mix of liberal arts and specialized career preparation. Big on technology, including a state-of-the-art trading room, and distinctive core curriculum stresses thematic study. Diverse student body.

Founded by the Reformed Church of the United States as a women's college way back in 1893, Hood College reinvented itself as a co-ed institution in 2003, and men now account for nearly 40 percent of undergraduates. Situated in historic Frederick, Maryland, Hood maintains a rich set of traditions, historical and otherwise, while taking full advantage of its location near two major cities. Students see their school's biggest strength in its people: students, staff, and faculty. "There are so many cultures and ethnicities and traditions to be shared," says one junior. "I love living here. I'm having the time of my life."

Hood's strikingly beautiful 50-acre campus features redbrick buildings and lush, tree-shaded lawns. Located at a major crossroads, the town of Frederick saw considerable action during the Civil War. Today, Hood is within an hour and a half of nearly 30 colleges and within minutes of a major National Cancer Institute research complex, high-tech firms, and small and large businesses.

> **"I love living here. I'm having the time of my life."**

On campus, technology programs, which are already important, get a further boost thanks to the Hodson Science and Technology Center. A state-of-the-art trading room allows students to practice using technology and analytical tools similar to those used on Wall Street. Newer additions include a 200-bed residence hall accommodating upperclassmen in suites and semi-suites.

Hood's core curriculum is composed of three parts: Heart, Mind, and Hands. Heart courses include a writing-intensive First-Year Seminar based on either hope, opportunity, obligation, or democracy, along with an English composition course. The Mind courses include a variety of arts and sciences options, including creative and performing arts, ethics, global languages, quantitative reasoning, and natural sciences. The Hands portion requires juniors or seniors to participate in at least one high-impact learning experience, such as an internship, study abroad, or undergraduate research.

In the classroom, says a sophomore, "hard work is required to do well." Hood's major strength lies in the sciences, especially the chemistry department and the biology department, with its special emphases on molecular biology, marine biology, and environmental science and policy. A semester-long coastal studies program takes students along the East Coast on a biological educational mission. Education, especially early childhood, and English are programs of note, as is a B.A. degree in law and criminal justice. The most popular majors are business administration, nursing, biology, psychology, and computer science. Five-year bachelor's/master's programs are available in business, environmental biology, biomedical science, psychology and counseling, and information technology. Only labs are taught by graduate assistants, and 74 percent of classes have fewer than 20 students. "The teachers want their students to succeed and are very accessible when students need help," cheers a math major.

If you really want to stimulate the brain cells, the four-year Honors Program features team-taught courses, a sophomore-year seminar on global issues that involves a community service project, and a senior seminar for which students choose both the topic and the professor. All students admitted to the Honors Program receive an automatic $2,000 scholarship. Internship opportunities include overseas jobs for language and business majors and legislative and cultural positions in Washington, D.C. Study abroad destinations include Ireland, Cyprus, Costa Rica, Morocco, and South Korea. The school's strong career resources give students a leg up on their next step in life, whether it be a job or graduate school.

In general, Hood students are "interested in their education and are serious and hardworking," says a sophomore. Nearly three-quarters of undergraduates call Maryland home, while 1 percent come to Hood from other countries. Eighteen percent of students are Black, 15 percent are Hispanic/Latino, 3 percent are Asian American, and 5 percent are multiracial. Students say the campus leans slightly left, politically speaking, and key issues include the environment and fiscal concerns. Forty-three percent of first-year students are eligible for Pell Grants. Hood provides merit scholarships worth an average of $28,900.

Hood's co-ed residence halls are well liked, with good-sized, air-conditioned rooms. The lottery system is based on seniority, and just over half of the students live on campus. First-year students live in dedicated first-year residence halls and can expect to be assigned to doubles (juniors and seniors can compete for singles and suites), and Spanish and French majors may apply to live in the language houses. In the college's two dining facilities, a senior says, "the meals are OK if you are not picky." Campus security receives praise: "I feel very safe on our small, homey campus with lots of lights at night and plenty of officers walking or driving around at all times," says one student.

Social life among the students is centered on the dorms, as each has its own personality as well as its own house council, rules, and social activities. Students report that although there is no Greek life, there are parties every weekend, along with movies, dances, and other forms of entertainment. The Whitaker Campus Center, with its table tennis and pool tables, grill and sandwich shop, bookstore, and meeting rooms, offers a great gathering place for residents and commuters 24 hours a day. Campus alcohol policies have been tightened, but drinking is generally not a huge part of the social life at Hood. "At parties and events, you have to show ID to get alcohol," one senior says. "If you don't like to stay on campus, there are restaurants, bars, clubs, malls, and coffeehouses within 10 minutes of the college by car," explains an English major. Scenic Frederick is described as small, safe, and beautiful. "Downtown Frederick is a very up-and-coming, artsy town," says one

(continued)

Chemistry
Education
English
Law and Criminal Justice
Nursing
Psychology

The school's strong career resources give students a leg up on their next step in life, whether it be a job or graduate school.

"Downtown Frederick is a very up-and-coming, artsy town."

Hood's core curriculum is composed of three parts: Heart, Mind, and Hands.

student. A one-hour car ride delivers students to the multiple diversions in Baltimore or Washington, D.C.

With over a century of history, Hood is rife with traditions. Some of the most important ones include the junior class ring dinner and formal, the May Madness festival and crab feast, a strawberries-and-ice-cream breakfast for seniors the morning of commencement, and the Hood "Hello"—the custom of greeting people you pass on campus. The Blazers compete in 22 Division III sports. Baseball and men's and women's basketball, track and field, and golf are among the stronger teams. Recreational and intramural sports attract 20 percent of undergraduates; popular activities include soccer, touch football, basketball, and the equestrian club.

Hood's mission statement seeks to prepare graduates to "lead purposeful lives of responsibility, leadership, service, and civic engagement." It does so with an eye to its past as well as the demands of a fast-changing social and professional environment. "The traditions are amazing," boasts a sophomore, "topped only by professors who care and friends you'll have forever."

If You Apply To ›

Hood: Rolling admissions. SATs or ACTs: optional. Accepts the Common Application with supplement.

Hope College

Holland, MI 49422

Hope has an in-between size—bigger than most small colleges but smaller than a university. It is evangelical in orientation, but less than 10 percent of the students are members of the founding Reformed Church in America. In addition to the liberal arts, Hope offers education, engineering, and nursing and makes undergraduate research a priority.

Each fall since 1898, around 36 Hope College students have spent up to three grueling hours engaged in "the Pull," an epic tug-of-war pitting even years against odd years as they stand assembled on the opposite end of a 650-pound rope, formerly across the 250-foot-wide Black River. This well-known annual tradition evokes the daily struggle Hope students face: maintaining their faith in a world eager to challenge it at every turn. The heritage of Hope's Dutch founders remains strong and visible on campus. "The academic programs, particularly the research and collaboration opportunities, far surpass those of Hope's rivals," opines a sophomore.

Hope was founded in 1866 with support from the Reformed Church in America and the biblical (Book of Hebrews) mission of becoming an "anchor of hope" for Dutch Calvinism in the West. It is situated on six blocks near downtown Holland, the tulip capital of the nation that was established by Dutch Colonialist Separatists, and a short bike ride from the shores of Lake Michigan. There's a lush pine grove in the center of campus, which features an eclectic array of buildings in architectural styles ranging from 19th-century Flemish to modern. A $6 million campus ministries building sits in the heart of campus as a reminder of the role of Christianity in the student experience.

Hope's general education program, designed around the themes "knowing how" and "knowing about," includes a first-year seminar that provides "an intellectual transition into Hope." Courses in expository writing, health dynamics, math and natural science, foreign language, religious studies, social sciences, the arts, and cultural heritage are also required; one class must have a focus on cultural diversity and one on international perspectives. All students take an interdisciplinary senior seminar in which they explore their beliefs, values, worldviews, and life goals in relation to the Christian faith. The FACES mentoring program helps underrepresented first-year students make the transition to college.

Among Hope's academic offerings, the sciences (especially biology and chemistry) stand out, with excellent laboratory facilities and faculty who are eager to involve students in their funded research. During the school year, undergraduates often conduct advanced experiments and even publish papers; come summer, more than 200 students receive stipends to participate in research full-time. Overall, 49 percent of undergrads get involved with research. Not surprisingly, a large portion of science majors go on to medical and engineering schools and Ph.D. programs. For those otherwise inclined, Hope's offerings in business and education are popular, and psychology, communication, and English are solid too. The Visiting Writers Series gives students an opportunity to interact with noteworthy authors. Recently added offerings include majors in environmental science and neuroscience.

"My school pushes the boundaries of academic rigor while still enabling students to be successful outside of the classroom," says an electrical engineering major. "Quality instruction is maintained by keeping classes exclusively professor-taught with minimal TA instruction." Classes are usually small. Students may study abroad in programs offered in more than 60 countries, and about half do so; options include semester-long exchanges and programs that combine classes with internships. The Boerigter Center for Calling and Career helps students explore the concept of vocation and find career and leadership opportunities through mentorship and networking events.

"This college often feels like 3,100 future CEOs vying for the #1 spot," says a senior, but students at Hope are "very outgoing, social, and friendly," says a business major. The student body is a rather homogeneous lot, with 68 percent hailing from Michigan and 3 percent coming from overseas. Black students account for 4 percent of the student body, Hispanics/Latinos 8 percent, Asian Americans 2 percent, and multiracial students 4 percent. Politically, according to a first-year, Hope "splits about 60/40 conservative/liberal in terms of the political orientation." LGBTQ rights, abortion, and gun control can be hot-button issues. Merit scholarships averaging $17,100 are available to qualified students, but there are no athletic scholarships.

Virtually all Hope students live in university-sponsored housing. Traditional dorms are arranged in first-year clusters by gender or co-ed by suite. "Dorms are fine, and I enjoyed them as a freshman, but most students opt for the college-owned apartment complexes and cottages surrounding the campus area," explains a student. On-campus students eat in one of two large dining halls where the fare—especially homemade bread and desserts—is tasty. "The STEP (Students Teaching and Empowering Peers) program focuses on peer education regarding sexual assault," says a senior. "They do a good job, but the school could always do more."

"The weekends are full and busy. The Student Activities Committee is the organization that makes the social life at Hope College thrive," says one student. The committee brings in comedians, bands, and hypnotists; shows movies in campus auditoriums; and plans the Spring Fling carnival, held on the last Friday of the academic year. Favorite annual traditions are the Nykerk Cup, which pits first-years

Favorite annual traditions are the Nykerk Cup, which pits first-years against sophomores in singing, acting, and orating competitions.

against sophomores in singing, acting, and orating competitions, and the Pull. Seven fraternities and eight sororities, all local organizations, claim 14 percent of the men and 20 percent of the women, respectively. Some parties do happen off campus, but those caught drinking on Hope's dry campus must atone by performing community service. Among the hundreds of student organizations are a variety of active religious life and service organizations.

Holland (population 34,000) is the site of spring's Tulip Time, one of the largest U.S. flower festivals. When Hope's cozy campus and the quaint town of Holland get too close for comfort, students find relief at the beaches of Lake Michigan ("definitely one of the highlights," says a junior) or drive 30 minutes to Grand Rapids, which offers some large-city amenities and good weekend rental deals at the ski slopes. Chicago and Detroit are other typical destinations for those trying to hit the road.

On the field and on the court, Hope's Flying Dutch and Flying Dutchmen are talented Division III competitors. Men's and women's basketball, men's soccer, and women's volleyball are strong, and the college has won a record number of Michigan Intercollegiate Athletic Association Commissioner's Cups, recognizing the conference's best overall sports program. Especially important are any competitions against Calvin (a century-old rivalry) and football versus Albion and Kalamazoo for the Wooden Shoes trophy. Hope's men's ice hockey team claimed its second-straight American Collegiate Hockey Association national championship in 2022. Intramural and club sports range from soccer and badminton to inner-tube water polo.

Hope's mission is "to educate students for lives of leadership and service in a global society." It's an institution with traditional Christian roots and an emphasis on undergraduates. "Hope is a place where students are challenged to become better students," says one senior, "but, more important, better people."

Overlaps

Albion, Alma, Butler, Calvin, DePauw, St. Olaf, Wooster

If You Apply To ›

Hope: Early action, rolling admissions. SATs or ACTs: optional. Accepts the Common Application.

Houghton University

1 Willard Avenue, Houghton, NY 14744

The Mid-Atlantic's leading evangelical Christian college. All students are required to take Biblical Literature and Introduction to Christianity, and most go to chapel three times a week. Perks include two honors programs and expansive indoor and outdoor equestrian facilities. Rural New York setting fosters an intimate sense of community, but when things get claustrophobic, students have ample possibilities for a semester away.

Website: www.houghton.edu
Location: Rural
Private
Total Enrollment: 735
Undergraduates: 721
Male/Female: 41/59

Located in the bucolic New York town that shares its name, Houghton University offers a solid, growing academic program and strong athletic teams while remaining committed to its core mission as a Christian liberal arts school. Founded in 1883 by Wesleyan Methodist minister William J. Houghton, the school relishes its Christian heritage and encourages students to do the same, saying, "Our Christian faith is present in the classroom and the chapel, but also in the athletic fields, residence halls, and practice rooms." Applicants must explain in their essays why they desire to be a part of a Christian academic community, and current students are expected to attend a set number of chapel services throughout the semester. These expectations help create true community on campus. A business administration major says, "Although we are a small Christian school, you will find people that you can connect with even though you both have different stories or backgrounds."

Houghton's scenic hilltop campus covers 1,300 acres of rural beauty, surrounded by vast expanses of western New York countryside. In addition to a 386-acre horseback-riding facility, the college has its own ski trails. The academic buildings are a mix of area "creekstone" (to use the local lingo) and brick. Recent renovations have included a complete update of the Chamberlain Reading Room and the creation of a campus Prayer Garden.

Houghton students complete general education requirements designed to provide a context and framework for the entire educational program. First-years must take Biblical Literature, Writing in the Liberal Arts, and a course titled Transitions, which helps students adjust to college and includes diversity training. Seniors complete a capstone seminar, project, or performance, depending on their major. Houghton is known for its equestrian studies program, and the music, education, and theology programs are also strong. The school's most popular majors include music, education, psychology, and communication. Other options include a 4–1 MBA program, a 3–4 Pharm.D. program with the University of Buffalo, a 3–1 nursing program with Indiana Wesleyan, and a medical early-acceptance program with the Lake Erie College of Osteopathic Medicine.

> **"Humble professors and supportive staff make doing hard things possible."**

Houghton's academic climate is "challenging and rigorous," according to a junior, but not overwhelmingly so. Adds an inclusive childhood education major, "Humble professors and supportive staff make doing hard things possible." Sixty-five percent of classes have fewer than 20 students, and most courses are taught by senior faculty, who students say do an outstanding job of fostering a sense of community. For instance, says a business administration major, "In my freshman year, one of my professors made us cinnamon buns before we took our final!"

Houghton offers two honors programs for incoming first-years. The London Honors program provides qualified students an intensive, hands-on experience in the humanities, along with study abroad experiences in the United Kingdom. The Science Honors in Puerto Rico program allows select students to engage with significant scientific problems in a hands-on, research-oriented environment and spend a culminating month in Puerto Rico. Houghton's Shannon Summer Research Institute, designed for students in math and the sciences, is also well regarded. Students can take advantage of off-campus study in a variety of programs throughout the year, including four-week Mayterm programs in such places as Europe and Central America.

Fifty-seven percent of students are from New York, and 8 percent are international. A senior describes Houghton students as "thoughtful and excited about going out and influencing the world in a positive way." Racial and ethnic diversity is limited: Black students account for 5 percent of the student body, Hispanics/Latinos 2 percent, Asian Americans 1 percent, and multiracial students 3 percent. Conversations "can get uncomfortable [involving] the topic of LGBTQ+ communities," says a senior, but "this does not mean they are not welcome." In 2023, the administration established the Kingdom Initiative to help foster positive and respectful dialogue among students around topics of cultural diversity "from a perspective that is distinctively and authentically Christian." Merit scholarships averaging $1,800 are available, and 44 percent of incoming first-years are eligible for Pell Grants.

Houghton's campus houses 85 percent of students. "Housing is fairly limited in terms of options, but all students are guaranteed a spot on campus," says one student. First-years and sophomores live in traditional residence halls, while juniors

(continued)

Financial Aid: 100%
Pell Grant: 44%
Expense: Pr $
Student Loans: 69%
Average Debt: $ $ $ $
Applicants: 1,041
Accepted: 89%
Enrolled: 23%
Grad in 6 Years: 67%
Returning First-years: 83%
Academics: ✍ ✍ ✍
Social: 🗨 🗨 🗨
Q of L: ★ ★ ★ ★
Admissions: (800) 777-2556
Email Address:
  admission@houghton.edu

Strong Programs:
Business
Communication
Education
Equestrian Studies
Music
Premed
Psychology
Theology

Hall Brawl, a week of friendly competitions between dorms, is a favorite tradition.

and seniors can apply for campus townhouses and apartments; all accommodations are single-sex. Dining options get good reviews for taste and variety. "They have started exploring the global stations, which include different food inspirations from other countries," says a senior. Students report feeling safe on their rural campus, and a political science major praises the Center for Student Success: "There are several professional counselors and therapists on staff, academic success coaches, and a well-equipped Office of Vocation and Calling."

"Most of the social life takes place on campus," explains an art major. Away from campus, an accounting major notes, "There is an overlook perfect for hiking; in the wintertime we have skiing and other fun stuff to do." The Campus Activities Board plans regular happenings, and dorm-identity events, film festivals, and concerts are popular. Seventy percent of students are involved in service projects such as Big Brothers Big Sisters, nursing home visitation, and local church outreach; the area surrounding the college is one of the poorest in New York State. Both the campus and the town of Houghton are dry. As a senior puts it, "Houghton is not a party campus, unless you count a group with tea and board games as a party." Students eagerly anticipate Purple and Gold Week, "where students compete in teams of purple and gold in fun games," explains a senior, as well as the SPOT talent show and Hall Brawl, a week of friendly competitions between dorms.

Houghton competes in Division III, and the men's and women's basketball teams both made NCAA tournament appearances recently. The men's tennis team has claimed the Empire 8 Conference title. Other competitive Highlanders teams (so named because of the campus topography) include women's field hockey and men's and women's cross-country. "Houghton is rivals with St. John Fisher, and the basketball games draw a lot of students," says a junior. Intramurals draw steady interest, with co-ed volleyball and inner-tube water polo being the most popular. The college also offers a variety of club sports.

"The basketball games draw a lot of students."

Students don't come to Houghton for the surrounding town of 1,700 souls, which is 30 minutes by car from the nearest city, or for the weather, which can be tough once winter sets in. But they do come, and for good reasons: there's little to distract them from their studies, their campus's natural beauty, and their spiritual growth. As one senior observes, "Houghton is foremost a Christ-centered institution." And within its tight-knit community, "If you would like to make a difference and have your voice heard, Houghton will give you that chance."

Overlaps

Eastern Nazarene, Geneva, Gordon, Grove City, Liberty, Messiah, Roberts Wesleyan, SUNY–Brockport

If You Apply To ›

Houghton: Rolling admissions. SATs or ACTs: optional. Accepts the Common Application with supplement. Music majors apply directly to music program.

Howard University

2400 Sixth Street NW, Washington, D.C. 20059

The flagship university of Black America and the first to integrate the Black experience into all areas of study. Strategically located in D.C., Howard depends on Congress for much of its funding. Preprofessional programs such as nursing, business, and architecture are strong. Sixty-seven percent of students identify as Black.

Contrary to the advice of early Black leaders such as Booker T. Washington, who argued in favor of technical training, Howard has promoted the liberal arts since its inception. This focus has served the school well; Howard's law school counts the late Supreme Court Justice Thurgood Marshall among its alumni, and Vice President Kamala Harris, the late Nobel Prize–winning author Toni Morrison, and actors Taraji P. Henson and the late Chadwick Boseman are graduates too. In recent years, Howard has strengthened its financial position and has been implementing a strategic plan structured around "Leadership for America and the Global Community." The four-part plan focuses on strengthening academic programs and services, promoting excellence in teaching and research, increasing private support, and enhancing national and community services.

Founded in 1867 by Union General Oliver Howard primarily to educate freed slaves, the university now operates five campuses and serves roughly 12,000 full-time students. Interestingly, Howard is one of a handful of universities in the nation supported partly by federal subsidies. In 2025, the White House released a new budget that would cut federal funding to Howard by $64 million, returning it to 2021 budget levels. Stay tuned. The 89-acre main campus houses most classrooms, dorms, and administrative offices, as well as the university center, the Founders, and undergraduate, medical, and dental libraries. The Howard Law Center is on the west campus near Rock Creek Park, the Divinity School is on a 22-acre site in northeast Washington, and there's also a 108-acre campus in suburban Beltsville, Maryland, and a campus in Silver Spring. Architecturally, the main campus is a blend of old and new, with numerous sculptures and murals created by Jacob Lawrence, Richard Hunt, Elizabeth Catlett, and Romare Bearden. Newer facilities include the state-of-the-art, 82,000-square-foot Interdisciplinary Research Building.

> **"Come to Howard ready to study."**

All students must complete general education requirements, which vary by school or college but uniformly encompass 17 credits in science, social sciences, humanities, computer literacy, math, languages, and one Afro American studies course. First-year seminars and various other special programs for first-year students are available in the undergraduate schools, such as communication, engineering, and arts and sciences. Seniors in arts and sciences must weather a comprehensive exam to graduate.

The school has excellent programs in business, political science, nursing, journalism, architecture, computer science, and psychology, and it has intensified offerings in Africana and diaspora studies. Other intriguing academic options are jazz studies, engineering (especially electrical engineering), and accelerated programs for a B.S. on the way to a medical or dental degree and a six-year B.A./J.D. law degree. The most popular majors are biology, communication, psychology, and political science. The Howard University Science, Engineering, and Mathematics Program, a multidisciplinary program involving nine departments, is designed to support underrepresented students pursuing degrees in STEM disciplines. Howard students can cross-register for courses at 13 other area schools, including American University, Georgetown, and GWU's Corcoran School of the Arts and Design.

In general, students say that the workload at Howard is demanding. "Some courses are more rigorous than others. But overall, this school is tough," says a junior. Another student adds, "Come to Howard ready to study." Forty percent of classes have fewer than 20 students. Most students agree that professors are ready and willing to help when asked, though academic advising is not Howard's strength. "Sometimes you may get professors who do not know how to break down anything," explains a psychology major. "Then it is your job to speak up and ask questions. You must ask questions because a closed mouth does not get fed!" Howard's prime D.C. location means that internship, co-op, and service-learning opportunities with all manner of government organizations, nonprofits, and corporations are practically limitless. Qualified students can apply for the Junior Experiential Learning Program, which helps them secure internships and other practical work experiences. The program also assigns

Website: www.howard.edu
Location: City Center
Private
Total Enrollment: 12,702
Undergraduates: 9,876
Male/Female: 26/74
Financial Aid: 93%
Pell Grant: 49%
Expense: Pr $
Student Loans: 72%
Average Debt: $ $ $ $
Applicants: 34,211
Accepted: 41%
Enrolled: 19%
Grad in 6 Years: 70%
Returning First-years: 91%
Academics: ✐ ✐ ✐
Social: 🗩 🗩 🗩
Q of L: ★ ★ ★
Admissions: (202) 806-2755
Email Address:
admission@howard.edu

Strong Programs:
Afro American Studies
Architecture
Biology
Business
Journalism
Nursing
Political Science
Psychology

Howard boasts the only all-Black collegiate swim team in the country (Northeast Conference champions in 2025).

each participant an alumni career mentor with experience in their field of interest who can assist with networking and career advice. Students can study abroad at one of the more than 200 institutions in 36 countries where Howard grants credit.

Eighty-two percent of Howard undergraduates hail from states outside of the District of Columbia, and another 7 percent are international. Black students represent 67 percent of the student body, Hispanics/Latinos 6 percent, Asian Americans 2 percent, American Indians 1 percent, and white 1 percent; 4 percent identify as multiracial. Nearly three-quarters are women. Many come from decidedly middle-class backgrounds, although 49 percent of first-years qualify for Pell Grants. Howard seems to be a very cohesive community, but career-minded and highly motivated students fit in best, students say, and most are politically liberal. "It's a very competitive school, from grades to fashion," says a junior. A range of renewable merit scholarships are available on a first-come, first-served basis to first-year applicants, and these awards average $15,500 per year. Transfer students are eligible for a separate pool of merit scholarships, and Howard also awards athletic scholarships. A deferred-payment plan allows families to pay each semester's tuition in three installments.

Sixty-eight percent of Howard's students are accommodated on campus, and facilities receive lukewarm reviews. "Housing at Howard is average in regards to availability, maintenance, and comfort," says one student. First-years get room assignments, while upperclassmen take their chances in a lottery. Many students live off campus purely to avoid the mandatory meal plan.

Weekends bring an assortment of social happenings to campus, many of which take place in the student center. On-campus parties and sports events are always big draws, but the restaurants and clubs in the nearby U Street corridor, the bars of Georgetown and Adams Morgan, and the Capital One Arena (home to the NBA's Wizards and the NHL's Capitals) also beckon and are easily accessible by public transit. Fraternities and sororities do not have their own housing or dining facilities, and only 1 percent of both men and women go Greek. Though small in numbers, one student says the Greeks are "an integral part of the university."

"You must ask questions [in class] because a closed mouth does not get fed!"

Athletics are also an important presence on campus, particularly Division I Bison basketball, soccer, and football. Howard boasts the only D1 all-Black collegiate swim team in the country, and its meets are a party with packed stands, a DJ, and poolside dancing. Both the men and women were Northeast Conference champions in 2026. Thanks to the largesse of basketball star Stephen Curry, it has developed one of only a few Division I men's and women's golf programs at HBCUs. The highlight of the season is always the grudge match with Hampton University to decide which school is the "true HU." Howard's homecoming is one of the best annual events, along with various Greekfests, concerts, and talent shows that current students, alumni, and community members enjoy together. Intramurals and club sports attract plenty of students, especially flag football, soccer, basketball, baseball, and tennis.

Among America's HBCUs, Howard stands out as the standard-bearer, a longtime center of excellence and leadership. Its scholarship and collections of artwork, rare books, manuscripts, and photographs are a repository of the Black experience, informing students' intellectual and personal growth. And with an increased focus on providing opportunities for real-world experience and service, Howard is sure to continue its long tradition of turning out Black leaders in all areas of society.

Overlaps

Clark Atlanta, Florida A&M, George Washington, Hampton, Morehouse, Spelman, Tuskegee, Xavier University of Louisiana

If You Apply To ›

Howard: Early decision, early action, regular decision. Accepts the Common Application with supplement. Please consult Howard's website for the most up-to-date information regarding standardized test requirements.

2112 Cleveland Boulevard, Caldwell, ID 83605

Got a map? You'll need a sharp eye to spot C of I, the *Fiske Guide*'s only liberal arts school between the Rocky Mountains and the West Coast. A new Do More in Four curriculum reduces the total number of required courses and utilizes a four-day week but still allows students to specialize in multiple fields. Two-thirds of the students are from Idaho.

With an emphasis on education and experiential learning, the College of Idaho, the state's oldest four-year university, offers students an opportunity to earn a solid liberal arts education through small classes in a small town. Outside class, the school's scenic environment allows sports and nature enthusiasts to explore freely before heading back into the classroom. At C of I, you'll be exposed to "hard work, great opportunities, and a healthy amount of fun," says a first-year student.

The college is in the town of Caldwell, where the atmosphere is calm and serene. For those looking for a little excitement, the state capital of Boise is a short drive from campus. Also nearby are some of Idaho's most scenic locations, such as beautiful mountains, deserts, and white-water rivers. The school, originally a Presbyterian college, first planted roots in downtown Caldwell in 1891 and then moved to its present site in 1910, where its nearly 30 buildings now occupy more than 50 acres.

The school's academic schedule is composed of 12-week semesters, spring and fall, separated by a four-week winter session, during which students can assist professors with research, take an internship, volunteer, or travel abroad. The college's Do More in Four curriculum allows students to take only four courses per semester, while every other college and university in Idaho requires

"We have a fantastic social scene."

five. Students choose to focus on one of four career sectors: Health and Scientific Research; Law, Policy, and the Public; Creative; and Business and Technology, and core course requirements include a first-year seminar, a civilization course, as well as classes focused on creative expression, human behavior, scientific reasoning, and quantitative analysis. Students must also complete an experiential learning requirement. With a four-day school week, "Focused Fridays" free up students for other learning pursuits, including research projects, art study, or internships and job shadowing. First-years sign an honor code and go through a weeklong orientation that includes an off-campus overnight stay at a lakeside camp.

"The workload can be relaxed or intense depending upon a student's desire for success," says one senior. Business, psychology, biology, and exercise science are among the majors recommended by students, and preprofessional programs, such as premed, prenursing, and prelaw, are also strong. New majors include biochemistry, criminology, and Spanish language for business, among others. The curriculum provides 3–1 opportunities for students to earn a master's degree alongside their undergraduate degree. Fifty-four percent of all classes at C of I have fewer than 20 students, and faculty are praised for their knowledge and accessibility. The college cooperates with the University of Idaho to offer a five-year course of study in engineering. Undergraduate research opportunities are available in all fields, and students present their findings at state and regional conferences. The college offers options for attending a foreign university or traveling overseas during the summer and winter breaks. Study abroad opportunities are available in nearly 60 countries.

Website: www.collegeofidaho.edu

Location: Small Town

Private

Total Enrollment: 1,080

Undergraduates: 1,031

Male/Female: 48/52

Financial Aid: 78%

Pell Grant: 28%

Expense: Pr $

Student Loans: 67%

Average Debt: $

Applicants: 3,650

Accepted: 49%

Enrolled: 15%

Grad in 6 Years: 63%

Returning First-years: 82%

Academics: ✍ ✍ ✍

Social: 🗩 🗩 🗩

Q of L: ★ ★ ★

Admissions: (208) 459-5305

Email Address:
admission@collegeofidaho.edu

Strong Programs:
Biology
Business
Environmental Studies
Exercise Science
Prelaw
Premed
Prenursing
Psychology

"Everyone seems like some kind of repressed genius trying to figure out their own existence, pursue stability, and create something meaningful," muses one student, adding, "There are also those who are more career-minded." Sixty-nine percent of the students are from Idaho and 11 percent come from foreign countries. Eighteen percent are Hispanic/Latino, 2 percent are Black, 2 percent are Asian American, and 5 percent are multiracial. Political issues receive plenty of attention on campus, and debates about the school's honor code are not uncommon among students. The college offers merit scholarships averaging $23,300 as well as more than 120 athletic scholarships. Not surprisingly, some of those dollars are set aside for skiers.

Sixty-three percent of students live on campus. "Residences are great, easy to decorate, and relatively big," says one student. Options include five traditional residence halls, two suite-style apartment buildings, and more than 20 rental houses. For meals, C of I provides "a grill, deli, salad bar, pizza, and vegetarian options" that are "to die for," according to one student. "Campus safety gets a 10 out of 10," says a junior. "There is an officer on duty 24/7 even over breaks and summer vacation."

Thirteen percent of men and 11 percent of women participate in the Greek system, which dominates campus social life. Students 21 and over are permitted to have alcohol on campus, in moderation (translation: no kegs). Annual social highlights include Winterfest, Spring Fling, and Homecoming week. Games against rival Northwest Nazarene also attract attention. "We have a fantastic social scene. We host events almost nightly," a student reports. Undergraduates can choose among more than 50 student clubs, and the arts are strong. Students of all majors participate in a wide range of instrumental and choral music, theater, visual arts, and other activities, and the choir has performed at Carnegie Hall and other venues around the country. "Finals breakfasts" offer something for bleary-eyed students to look forward to during finals week; at midnight on Tuesday, faculty and staff cook breakfast for students.

> **"Everyone seems like some kind of repressed genius trying to figure out their own existence."**

Caldwell, with about 73,000 people, is not a great spot for college students, but they get involved by helping out the local school district. Nearby Boise is a popular destination for shopping, dining, and cultural events, including a symphony orchestra, art museum, zoo, professional baseball and hockey, and the must-see World Center for Birds of Prey. Outdoor enthusiasts relish the fact that the C of I campus is just minutes away from world-class opportunities for skiing, hiking, camping, fishing, rock climbing, and white-water rafting. The student-run Outdoor Program offers trips, classes, and equipment rentals.

More than a third of students play for one of the college's 20 varsity teams, which compete in NAIA Division II. The Yotes ("We are the Coyotes") have earned team national championships in baseball, basketball, and skiing. For those who enjoy the game but might not make the team, there is an active intramurals program and the large Albertson Activities Center. "Intramurals are huge at our school," says a sophomore, drawing nearly half the students.

C of I has much to offer its Yotes. They enjoy a well-designed liberal arts education and personal academic attention on a campus striving to keep its offerings on the cutting edge. What's more, students here are encouraged to take an active role in the school's future. From creating traditions to upholding the honor code, a sophomore says, "We are involved in all aspects of campus life."

Overlaps

Alma, Boise State, Coe, College of Western Idaho, Cornell College, Earlham, University of Idaho, Idaho State

If You Apply To ›

Idaho: Early action I and II, regular decision. SATs or ACTs: optional. Accepts the Common Application with supplement.

601 East John Street, Champaign, IL 61820

Half a step behind Michigan and neck and neck with Wisconsin among top Midwestern public universities. U of I's strengths include business, communication, engineering, architecture, and the natural sciences. More than three-quarters of the undergraduates hail from in state. Huge Greek system.

Like many of its Midwestern neighbors, the University of Illinois, which dates to 1867, has its roots in agriculture. Three of the original 10 Morrow Plots, the oldest experimental fields in the nation, are a protected historic landmark in the middle of campus. Like most big, public universities, U of I has a plethora of choices, and with a strong Greek system and 1,000 clubs, social activities are more than plentiful. Homecoming weekend was invented at the University of Illinois, and whether cheering for the Fighting Illini, pledging a Greek organization, or celebrating Moms', Dads', or Siblings' Weekends, students here stir up a vibrant mix of school spirit and good times. Illinois's stellar academics and learning communities are up there with any of the country's public flagships. "There is a lot of pride and generations engraved into this university," says a sustainable design major.

Befitting one of the earliest land grant institutions, the Illinois campus was built in farm country between the twin cities of Champaign and Urbana. The flat, park-like campus was designed along a mile-long axis where trees and walkways separate stately white-columned Georgian structures made of brick. The impressive Illinois library system, one of the largest public university collections worldwide with more than 14 million physical volumes, makes it easier to keep up with classwork. A 225,000-square-foot computer science center and the physical education center are notable. Newer facilities include the Martin Softball Training Center, the Atkins Baseball Training Center, and the new Plant Biology Innovation Greenhouse.

> "There is a lot of pride and generations engraved into this university."

Illinois has 16 undergraduate colleges that together offer more than 150 undergraduate programs; if none of these strike your fancy, you may design your own. The general education program includes standard distribution requirements across a range of subjects; students may fulfill some requirements by taking interdisciplinary classes that explore three main "pathways," or real-world challenges facing today's society: Inequality and Cultural Understanding; Health and Wellness; and Sustainability, Energy, and the Environment.

Illinois supports excellent programs across the university, including the expansion of undergraduate minors campuswide. Engineering, business, communication, social sciences, architecture, education, industrial design, and the sciences—especially biological sciences, agriculture, and veterinary medicine—get high marks from students. A "CS + X" degree program allows students to combine the study of computer science with one of 12 other liberal arts fields, ranging from anthropology and advertising to chemistry and crop sciences, without having to go so far as double majoring. The initiative is a way for students to demonstrate both technical competence and career-related expertise to future employers. The interdisciplinary Beckman Institute for Advanced Science and Technology offers opportunities for undergraduate research in areas like intelligent systems and molecular science and engineering. Forty-three percent of undergrads conduct research during their four years.

Website: www.illinois.edu
Location: Small City
Public
Total Enrollment: 49,068
Undergraduates: 35,619
Male/Female: 52/48
Financial Aid: 68%
Pell Grant: 25%
Expense: Pub $ $ $
Student Loans: 38%
Average Debt: $
Applicants: 73,742
Accepted: 42%
Enrolled: 29%
Grad in 6 Years: 85%
Returning First-years: 95%
Academics: ✍ ✍ ✍ ✍ ✍
Social: 🗩 🗩 🗩
Q of L: ★ ★ ★
Admissions: (217) 333-0302
Email Address:
  admissions@illinois.edu

Strong Programs:
Architecture
Biological Sciences
Business
Communication
Education
Engineering
Industrial Design
Social Sciences

"Everything is intensive, competitive, and high paced," says a sustainable design major. "This is good but challenging." First-years and sophomores, who register last, may have trouble getting into necessary courses, but professors and academic advisors can usually help if needed classes are full, and students appreciate their dedication. Illinois has its share of stellar faculty, including Nobel laureates, National Medal of Science winners, and dozens of members of the National Academy of Sciences. "The quality of teaching is high with few exceptions," says a psychology major. "They are truly invested in our success," adds a senior. Even first-years stuck in large lectures (750 seats) will find some personal attention in the associated discussion sections, led by graduate teaching assistants. Thirty-nine percent of classes have fewer than 20 students. First-year Discovery Courses, seminars limited to 19 students, enable first-year students to interact closely with full professors. The Campus Honors Program includes faculty mentoring, intensive seminars, advanced sections of regular courses, and access to special resources. Twenty-four percent of undergraduates travel and study abroad, roaming 50 countries around the globe.

Eighty-three percent of Illinois undergrads are homegrown, and "the school is continuously getting more diverse," a sophomore says. Students come from multiple backgrounds and fit less into the stereotypical "Midwest" mold than one might think. Black students make up 5 percent of the student body, Hispanics/Latinos 14 percent, Asian Americans 23 percent, and multiracial students 4 percent, while international students account for 14 percent. Given the current political climate in the U.S., there are some hot-button issues, but one student opines, "What is the college experience without a little protest?" Merit scholarships averaging $5,800 and more than 200 athletic awards are doled out annually. The Illinois Commitment program provides free tuition and fees for four years for qualified in-state first-year or transfer students whose family income is $75,000 or less.

Half of all undergrads live in U of I's co-ed and single-sex residence halls, which range in size from 51 to 660 beds and are arranged in quadrangle-like groups. Some dorms are quite a hike from classrooms, veterans warn. The university offers 10 themed living/learning communities, such as WIMSE (Women in Math, Science, and Engineering) and Innovation LLC (entrepreneurship and creativity), that combine in-hall courses with specialized cocurricular activities. Each residence hall is a mini neighborhood, with dining halls, darkrooms, libraries, music practice rooms, computers, and lounges creating a sense of community. Chefs keep the food interesting, and campus safety maintains a visible presence. As for other services, a senior says, "There are a lot of resources, but it can be hard to find specific information."

"There is a big Greek life and party culture on campus," says a sophomore, and Illinois claims to have one of the largest Greek systems anywhere, with 87 chapters drawing 12 percent of the men and 18 percent of the women. Independents don't have to suffer boredom, though, as there are also roughly 1,000 registered student clubs and organizations, ranging from the ice hockey team to cultural affinity groups. "It's a very 'outside and do something' environment," a senior says. Though drinking is prohibited in the dorms, many regard campus alcohol policies as a "token gesture," a business major says. One student says, "I love Quad Day and believe that it's a great way to get involved in campus traditions." The Illini Union hosts bands, comedians, movies, trivia, karaoke, and other activities every week. The impressive Krannert Center for the Performing Arts serves as the area's cultural center, while Assembly Hall hosts national touring acts. Students get a discount at both facilities. For those who itch for the stimulation of a big city, the campus is just about equidistant from Chicago, Indianapolis, and St. Louis.

The Division I Fighting Illini compete in the Big Ten, and men's basketball and baseball have winning traditions. Men's golf and basketball are recent conference

Even first-years stuck in large lectures (750 seats) will find some personal attention.

"It's a very 'outside and do something' environment."

Homecoming weekend was invented at the University of Illinois.

champs, and women's gymnastics, soccer, and softball are solid too. The intramural program is extensive, with available facilities that include 16 full-length basketball courts, five pools, 19 handball/racquetball courts, a skating rink, a baseball stadium, and the Atkins Tennis Center. The majority of the student body participates in recreational sports. Illinois has a strong athletic program for students with disabilities, including wheelchair basketball, which was invented at the university.

While the University of Illinois may seem mammoth to some students, don't be scared off by this giant institution. Academic and social opportunities are incredibly diverse, and classroom sizes, while growing, are supplemented by smaller group discussions. The breadth of the programs offered combined with an active campus life makes for a well-rounded college experience. Says one happy advertising major, "At the end of my senior year, I could confidently say that I made friends for life, was supported by fellow students, and made connections that I will never forget."

<u>**If You Apply To ›**</u>

Illinois: Early action, regular decision. SATs or ACTs: optional. Accepts the Common Application with supplement. Apply to particular schools or programs. Music, dance, and theater applicants must audition.

Illinois Institute of Technology

10 W 35th Street, Chicago, IL 60616

Forget about cheerleaders, homecoming games, and other traditional trappings of college life. Illinois Tech is all about learning about technology, getting a degree, and landing a job. Academic focus is on engineering, computer science, and a bit of architecture thrown in for good measure. If your goal is a technical career in the Chicago area, look no further.

At the Illinois Institute of Technology, classwork and real-world experience promise to propel future engineers, architects, and computer scientists to the top of their fields. Students here engage in undergraduate research in state-of-the-art labs and gain practical work experience through abundant internship opportunities. The coursework may be hard, says a junior, but the effort "will pay off in the end" as students enter the workforce in high-paying technical jobs. And although students here tend to burn the midnight oil, they frequently escape to downtown Chicago for culture and much-deserved fun.

Illinois Tech's home is an urban, 120-acre campus designed by Ludwig Mies van der Rohe, the influential 20th-century architect who directed the architecture school for 20 years. Founded by a merger in 1940 but with roots dating to the 1890s, the school is just three miles south of Chicago's Loop and one mile west of Lake Michigan. Guaranteed Rate Field, home of the White Sox, is located directly across from the campus. Miesian-style buildings reflecting his rectangular "less is more" style are adorned by trees and grassy open parks. Crown Hall, which houses the College of Architecture, is a National Historic Landmark. The Kaplan Institute boasts high-tech labs, collaborative hubs, and makerspaces that allow students to work on cross-disciplinary projects and develop entrepreneurial ideas.

Along with humanities and social science courses, students must fulfill general education requirements that include mathematics, computer science, natural science, and engineering; writing is emphasized across the curriculum. All first-years

Illinois Tech's six-block campus sits in Bronzeville, a historically Black neighborhood on Chicago's South Side.

take an introduction to the professions seminar, which includes discussion of innovation, ethics, teamwork, communication, and leadership. Multidisciplinary, group-based learning is big here. Every student must complete two semester-long interprofessional projects that sharpen real-world skills.

Engineering and computer science are the most popular majors, and they set the tone at Illinois Tech. Every engineering department is first-rate. Architecture is also popular and highly regarded; the curriculum emphasizes a team approach that mixes third- through fifth-year students under the supervision of a master professor. "Architecture has a strong faculty," says one student, "and biomedical engineering is well funded." Agriculture and psychology are also among the most popular majors. Guided by an academic reorganization, the physical sciences have been bolstered, grouped together with career-oriented fields such as psychology and computer information systems. Illinois Tech was the first university to offer a B.S. in bioanalytical chemistry, and it has also added majors in artificial intelligence, food science and nutrition, and environmental chemistry. Accelerated master's programs enable students to earn both a bachelor's and a master's in five years. Dual admissions programs are available in pharmacy, optometry, and osteopathic medicine.

> "Architecture has a strong faculty, and biomedical engineering is well funded."

"IIT has somewhat of a stressful culture," warns an aerospace engineering major, although "professors and TAs are available and willing to help most of the time." Both the workload and the competition are fierce, but small class sizes allow for collaboration. Fifty percent of classes have fewer than 20 students. "A majority of the professors are very dedicated and knowledgeable about the topics they discuss," states a biochemistry major.

In addition to meeting outside of class to go over problem sets or for career direction, Illinois Tech students and professors often work side by side on research projects. The Lewis College of Science and Letters awards several $5,000 scholarships to undergrads to perform research work under the supervision of faculty during the summer. Engineering students make use of sophisticated labs and have access to independent research labs in Chicago. Two dozen on-campus research centers, such as the Pritzker Institute of Biomedical Science and Engineering and the Wanger Institute for Sustainable Energy Research, provide additional opportunities. The five-year co-op program—another possibility for hands-on experience—helps lead Illinois Tech students directly into high-paying jobs after graduation. Study abroad programs send students to more than 50 nations around the globe, including France, Greece, Chile, and Singapore; 10 percent of students—mostly architecture majors—participate.

"Many students are nerdy and antisocial," reports a senior, "but there are also many who are outgoing." In-state students account for 68 percent of the undergraduate population, and 14 percent hail from foreign countries. Black students constitute 6 percent of the student body, Hispanics/Latinos 28 percent, Asian Americans 16 percent, and multiracial students 4 percent. Students say International Fest is one of the year's most popular events, and the school sponsors a multitude of cultural awareness workshops and events on different diversity-related topics. "There are a lot of different political stances in the student body for sure," says one student. Merit scholarships averaging $30,900 are available to qualified students.

> "A majority of the professors are very dedicated and knowledgeable."

Forty-four percent of students live on campus, and first-years and sophomores are required to do so, although those who live with their families within a 20-mile radius of campus are allowed to commute. "The housing is very nice but expensive," says a biochemistry major, but there's little trouble securing a room. The Women in

Social Engagement learning community attracts female students who are interested in leadership, civic engagement, and social change. Some students live in apartments in the area; others inhabit one of the eight fraternity houses. The dining hall has several meal plans and a special vegetarian menu. Career and mental health services receive good reviews from students. "I really like how Career Services has career fairs very often," says a sophomore.

Illinois Tech's six-block campus sits in Bronzeville, a historically Black neighborhood on Chicago's South Side famous for nurturing the likes of Gwendolyn Brooks, Mahalia Jackson, and Herbie Hancock. The area is undergoing a revitalization, and the university connects students with local community organizations for volunteer work. Most students love exploring Chicago; the city skyline is beautiful and a veritable museum, with buildings designed by the likes of Frank Lloyd Wright, Louis Sullivan, and, of course, Mies van der Rohe. "Chicago provides educational opportunities, internship opportunities, and countless things to do," says one biomedical engineering major. Lake Michigan is within jogging distance, Chinatown is a walk away for lunch or dinner, and the school provides free shuttle bus service to downtown on weekends.

"There is not much going on in walking distance around campus," admits a senior. "However, with multiple train stations near campus, you can get to downtown within 20 minutes." Fraternities claim 8 percent of the men and sororities attract 10 percent of the women, and the Greek houses are dry. The Union Board offers movies, concerts, and comedians. Favorite events include Taste of the Quad, Homecoming, and Innovation Day, when student groups showcase their research and discoveries. Students can also take advantage of the city's ample nightlife or plan outings to museums, plays, or the Chicago Symphony.

In sports-crazy Chicago, Illinois Tech's Division III athletic teams (the Scarlet Hawks) are not much of a draw. Still, students praise the men's baseball and basketball teams, and the men's tennis team has won the Northern Athletics Collegiate Conference title. Men's and women's soccer and women's volleyball are also competitive. Several recreational sports are available for more casual athletes.

Heading off to Chi-town to take on the mammoth workload at Illinois Tech means hitting the books for hours and a fair share of all-nighters. But the payoff is undeniable. One student says bluntly, "This school is for people who want to make a lot of money after college." And while in school, they revel in the best of two worlds: a challenging academic climate and a great city in which to let off all that steam.

"I really like how Career Services has career fairs very often."

Overlaps

Carnegie Mellon, DePaul, Loyola University Chicago, U of I at Chicago, U of I at Urbana–Champaign, Marquette, Purdue, Rensselaer

If You Apply To ›

Illinois Tech: Early decision, early action, regular decision. SATs or ACTs: optional. Accepts the Common Application. Applicants to architecture program may submit optional portfolio.

Illinois Wesleyan University

1312 Park Street, Bloomington, IL 61701

IWU is a small Midwestern university with a penchant for creativity and the spirit of inquiry. The curriculum is basic liberal arts with additional divisions devoted to fine arts and nursing. An optional summer term allows students to travel or explore an interest. IWU's reputation is limited outside Illinois and surrounding states.

IWU's summer term gives students a chance to focus on a single intensive course or undertake research, a service project, or an internship.

Illinois Wesleyan University has its sights set on a special breed of student—the kind who isn't afraid to be many things at once. Students here are encouraged to pursue diverse passions, and IWU is a mecca for students who have preprofessional interests, especially those with unusual pairings like management and music. "What makes Wesleyan really stand out is its care and attention for each student as an individual," says a junior.

Founded in 1850, IWU occupies an 83-acre campus site in a north-side residential district of Bloomington. The heart of campus is the central quadrangle, and tree-lined walkways connect buildings that range in style from gray stone Gothic to ultramodern steel and glass. IWU's main classroom building, State Farm Hall, includes state-of-the-art classrooms and research spaces. The Petrick Idea Center, a new hub for innovation, creativity, and entrepreneurship, is expected to open in fall 2026.

Illinois Wesleyan's general education requirements expose students to a broad array of liberal arts disciplines and are intended to help them develop critical-thinking and writing skills, imagination, intellectual independence, social awareness, and sensitivity to others. All first-year students must take a Gateway Colloquium, a writing-intensive seminar-style class of no more than 16. First-years register for classes and begin

"IWU's academic climate is collaborative and explorative."

to reflect on their college experience during the Rising Titan summer orientation. They also attend the four-day Turning Titan orientation program, which involves an opening convocation, a common reading program, a day of community service, the Titan Carnival, and other events before classes begin in the fall.

Among the top programs in the College of Liberal Arts are biology, English, neuroscience, and math, and some of the most popular majors include business and marketing, nursing, accounting and finance, and psychology. The business administration department offers a Portfolio Management course in which students buy and sell orders overseen by a client board composed of university trustees. IWU's School of Nursing and Health Sciences is another big draw. The kinesiology and allied health major prepares students for careers in exercise science, physical therapy, cardiac rehabilitation, sports nutrition, and similar fields. The College of Fine Arts houses three separate schools of music, art, and theater; music and theater are the standouts, offering eight distinct majors between the two. New offerings include majors in data science and analytics, entrepreneurship, professional sales, and nutrition and health.

"IWU's academic climate is collaborative and explorative," says an accounting major. Adds a physics major, "We have a system where anyone can come into the physics conference room to do homework, study, hang out, the works. The professors will come into the room sometimes to just check in on us, and it has been amazing." Sixty-four percent of courses have fewer than 20 students. In addition to the usual fall and spring semesters, IWU has an optional summer term that gives students a chance to focus on a single intensive course or undertake research, a service project, or an internship. About 40 percent of students take advantage of the university's study abroad program, which sends them packing to their choice of more than 70 countries. Research opportunities are also plentiful, with around half of students taking part, and IWU hosts an annual student research conference that attracts scholars from all disciplines. Students praise advising and career services: "They push you past the expectations you set for yourself, and they guide you along the way," cheers a quantitative finance major.

At IWU, a finance major says, "Everyone has a sense of Titan pride that comes out in our mantra 'Titan Green Over Everything.'" Undergraduates here are largely the homegrown variety, with 84 percent hailing from Illinois and 5 percent from outside the country. Although IWU began admitting Black students in 1867, they still account for only 8 percent of the student body. Hispanics/Latinos represent 12 percent, Asian Americans 5 percent, and multiracial students 3 percent. Students here are generally liberal, socially conscious, and active in groups like Circle K, the Alpha Phi Omega service fraternity, and Habitat for Humanity. Merit scholarships averaging $33,000 are available to qualified students; there are no athletic scholarships.

IWU requires students to live on campus for three years, and two of the first-year residence halls have been renovated. A junior says, "Upperclassman dorms are newer and more spacious." Campus food is described as "nothing to rave about," although offerings for those with dietary restrictions have been improving. Most students say campus security is good, and the university's Consent Is Sexy campaign is helping push awareness of and discussions about sexual violence on campus. The Titan HEART initiative aims to raise awareness of suicide prevention and add mental health support resources.

Seventeen percent of the men and 21 percent of the women go Greek, and fraternities and sororities are the focus of IWU's social life. A student explains, "Most parties occur at frat houses, but the campus is so small that they are open to everyone." Alcohol policies allow drinking on campus for those of legal age. For alternatives, the Office of Student Activities sponsors free events in the student center almost every weekend, and academic departments and the Student Senate regularly bring guest speakers to campus. Each fall during homecoming, Greeks and dorm dwellers compete in the Titan Games to get appropriately psyched, and the Big Show brings major performers to campus in the spring. A junior recommends the Unity Gala, a formal-dress celebration "around the multifaceted identities and experiences" of students.

> "Most parties occur at frat houses, but the campus is so small that they are open to everyone."

Thanks to the proximity of Illinois State University—less than a mile away in neighboring Normal—IWU offers more than the typical small college town atmosphere. The area's total student population of about 25,000 provides students at tiny IWU with "the best of both worlds," says a senior. A first-year adds, "Some kids from big cities say there is nothing to do in Bloomington-Normal, but in my opinion, they are exaggerating." Options include nearby theaters, concert venues, coffee shops, bars, and a farmers market in warmer months. The best road trips are to Peoria or Urbana–Champaign (home of the University of Illinois) or to Chicago or St. Louis, each two and a half hours away.

The IWU Titans compete in the Division III College Conference of Illinois and Wisconsin. Football is well and good, but Titans men's and women's basketball really get students going. The men's golf team has won the CCIW championship several times, and men's lacrosse, women's golf, and baseball, softball, and volleyball are also strong. IWU's varsity eSports team is nationally competitive. The Fort Natatorium houses an impressive 14-lane swimming pool, and the swim team has had its share of stars. The small but active recreational sports program offers about a dozen club and intramural sports.

One of the Midwest's better-kept academic secrets, Illinois Wesleyan is at once cozy and diverse, loaded with opportunities for ambitious students with traditional or offbeat interests. As one junior advises, "The school provides a multitude of paths down which one can travel. IWU allows you to become who you want to be, but only if you let it."

Overlaps

Allegheny, Augustana (IL), Bradley, DePaul, U of I at Urbana–Champaign, Loyola University Chicago, Whittier, Wooster

If You Apply To ›

Illinois Wesleyan: Early action, rolling admissions. SATs or ACTs: optional. Accepts the Common Application with supplement. Music and theater applicants must audition or interview. Art applicants are required to submit portfolio.

107 South Indiana Avenue, Bloomington, IN 47405

Though men's basketball has traditionally been among IU's most famous programs, it's rivaled by the world-renowned music school and the distinguished foreign language and business offerings. IU enrolls more out-of-staters than the University of Illinois. Bloomington is a great college town, and most students live off campus after their first year.

Website: www.indiana.edu
Location: Small City
Public
Total Enrollment: 43,546
Undergraduates: 37,007
Male/Female: 50/50
Financial Aid: 59%
Pell Grant: 18%
Expense: Pub $ $
Student Loans: 38%
Average Debt: $ $
Applicants: 67,647
Accepted: 78%
Enrolled: 18%
Grad in 6 Years: 80%
Returning First-years: 91%
Academics: ✐ ✐ ✐ ✐
Social: 🗩 🗩 🗩 🗩
Q of L: ★ ★ ★ ★
Admissions: (812) 855-0661
Email Address:
 iub.admissions@iu.edu

Strong Programs:
Biological Sciences
Business
Computer and Information
 Technology
Dance
Education
Management
Marketing
Music

With just over 37,000 undergraduates on its enormous campus, Indiana University is the prototype of the large Midwestern school. With strong academics, a thriving social scene, and some of the best sports teams around, this top-notch public institution is a testament to Hoosier determination.

Located in southern Indiana's gently rolling hills, the 1,954-acre campus boasts architecture from Italianate brick to collegiate Gothic limestone to the distinctive style of world-famous architect I. M. Pei. Other unique campus features include fountains, gargoyles, an arboretum of more than 450 trees and shrubs surrounding two reflecting pools, a limestone gazebo, and the Campus River,

> **"The professors here are remarkable."**

a pretty creek that runs alongside a shaded path. Newer construction includes the Mies van der Rohe Building for the Eskenazi School of Art, Architecture + Design, the $17.5 million Ferguson International Center, which houses programs supporting international students and overseas studies, and a $23 million renovation of the Collins Living-Learning Center.

Founded in 1820, Indiana prides itself on its liberal arts education—many students have double majors or minors in programs across campus, and students are encouraged to explore their interests. General education coursework includes math, science, arts and humanities, social and historical studies, English composition, world languages and cultures, and additional requirements that vary by school.

IU's schools and colleges offer more than 200 undergraduate majors, interdisciplinary study, a design-your-own-major option, and substantial honors and research programs. The highly touted Kelley School of Business, with its respected global studies component, is among the most popular on campus, and the School of Education is also strong. Overall, the finance, media, marketing, accounting, and sport marketing and management majors enroll the most students. When it comes to the performing arts, the Jacobs School of Music is top in its field, setting the, ahem, tone for much of the campus, and the dance program is solid. The notable Media School gives students the language, communication, research, and technological skills they need to excel in media-related careers, while the O'Neill School of Public and Environmental Affairs is a top choice for those interested in public policy. The Hamilton Lugar School of Global and International Studies brings together language, area studies, and international studies programs to prepare students in the global competencies of the 21st century. The Irsay Institute, which conducts research and provides outreach education on health-related social sciences, is one of more than 100 research centers on campus.

Students describe the academic climate as rigorous but not cutthroat. "With 4,000 different courses per semester, a variety of intensity levels exists," says a marketing major. "There is a balance with room for both competitive overachievers and laid-back, carefree individuals." Students say they regularly share ideas with each other, and group projects are commonplace. Faculty members bring their research results directly to students, and some profs, especially in math and the sciences, bring undergrads into their labs to assist with ongoing projects. "The professors here are remarkable," says an art history major. As for advising, many students seem surprised by the personal attention they receive at such a large university, and they soon learn that many helpful resources are available to those students who seek them out. For those seeking study abroad opportunities, the university offers more than 380 programs in 70 countries and 17 languages for students in nearly every field of study; about 30 percent of students take part.

Fifty-five percent of IU undergraduates are from in state, and 5 percent are international. Black students account for 5 percent of the student body, Hispanics/Latinos 9 percent, Asian Americans 11 percent, and multiracial students 6 percent. And while IU does not guarantee that it will meet the full demonstrated financial need of every student, it does admit on a need-blind basis. Merit scholarships average $6,900 annually, and more than 300 athletic scholarships are available.

Housing is guaranteed to all incoming first-years and ranges from Gothic quads (co-ed by building) to 13-floor high-rises (co-ed by floor or unit). One student explains the housing situation this way: "All dorms have laundry facilities, cafeterias, computer clusters, and undergraduate advisors, and some even have special amenities like language-speaking floors." Learning communities—including both living learning centers and thematic communities—are popular with students who wish to explore common interests like civic leadership, public health, and the arts. Dining options range from all-you-care-to-eat to cafés featuring prepared and grab-and-go items, so students can find international and healthy menus sprinkled among the fast food. Alcohol is prohibited in the dorms, which may help explain why 70 percent of the student body lives off campus. Most off-campus residents choose apartments or small houses with big front porches within walking distance of the campus or the IU bus system. A number of student-driven initiatives, including Culture of Care, Step UP! IU, and It's on Us, are working to promote student wellness and safety on campus.

Although IU's more than 900 campus organizations host numerous events, the most active on-campus groups, in terms of social life, seem to be the Greeks, which attract 21 percent of the men and 20 percent of the women. Some complain of a polarized atmosphere. "There is a large separation between the Greek community and the rest of the student body," says a senior. With concerts, ballets, recitals, and festivals right on campus, students are not lacking for distractions. Indiana Memorial Union is one of the largest student unions in the nation, and the range of extracurricular organizations is also impressive. One of the most highly attended events of the year is the Little 500 bike race in the spring, modeled after the Indianapolis 500, when teams of IU undergrads race around a quarter-mile track; 2025 marked the 74th running of the race. The 36-hour Dance Marathon in the fall raises money for Riley Children's Hospital in Indianapolis. Various cultural centers and community partnerships provide plenty of opportunities for students to make a difference on campus and in the community.

Students say Bloomington (population 80,000) is a great college town. There are many excellent bars, shops, art venues, and ethnic restaurants, including one of the few Tibetan restaurants in the country. Locally, the area offers some impressive limestone quarries, miles of public forests, and three nearby lakes. Spelunkers will find heaven down below in the many nearby caves. Chicago, Cincinnati, Indianapolis, St. Louis, and even New Orleans are popular road trips.

One of the most highly attended events of the year is the Little 500 bike race in the spring, modeled after the Indianapolis 500.

"All dorms have laundry facilities, cafeterias, computer clusters, and undergraduate advisors."

"There is a large separation between the Greek community and the rest of the student body."

The O'Neill School of Public and Environmental Affairs is a top choice for those interested in public policy.

Although dozens of intramural and club sports are available, recreational sports pale in comparison with Division I varsity athletics here; basketball is an established religion in the state of Indiana. Students and faculty are all eligible for men's basketball tickets, but they've got to get requests in early. In recent years, the Hoosiers baseball and the men's and women's swimming and diving team have claimed Big Ten championships; the women's basketball team and men's soccer team have been contenders for national titles. The reinvigorated football team draws large cream-and-crimson crowds. Purdue has been IU's main athletic rival since 1891, and their football teams battle annually for the Old Oaken Bucket, found on a farm in southern Indiana in 1925 and alleged to have been used during the Civil War. The winner of the game with Michigan State takes home the Old Brass Spittoon.

Along with IU's reputation as a basketball powerhouse, it also provides committed students with stellar academics spanning a wide range of disciplines and a lively social scene. Those who don't mind its large size will find a welcoming atmosphere and ample opportunities for more intimate learning experiences, not to mention plenty of Hoosier pride.

If You Apply To ›

Indiana: Early action, regular decision. SATs or ACTs: optional. Accepts the Common Application with supplement.

International Universities

Do you thrive on new experiences? Like to meet new people? Want to learn about different cultures? You can do all that at a college or university in the United States, but if you really want to jump in with both feet, think about attending a school in a foreign country. For decades, many American college students have embraced study abroad as an enriching supplement to their undergraduate education. According to the Institute of International Education, more than 300,000 American students studied abroad in over 170 destinations worldwide during the 2023–24 academic year. Most of these students have taken advantage of short-term programs sponsored by their U.S. institutions—by spending a summer, a semester, or even a year overseas and earning credits that count toward their four-year degrees. Students routinely describe these experiences as academically transformative, culturally eye-opening, and personally inspiring.

In recent years, a small but growing number of American students have begun to look beyond such short-term programs and to consider obtaining their entire baccalaureate degrees from universities in other countries. The *Fiske Guide* has long described popular and well-established options that may appeal to American applicants seeking a full-time undergraduate experience abroad in Canada, the United Kingdom, and Ireland—among the most common destinations outside the U.S. for degree-seeking undergraduates. These days, however, Italy, Spain, and France, along with the UK, are increasingly popular destinations for American students abroad, together accounting for about 45 percent of all U.S. students who study overseas. And, in 2023–24, roughly 95,000 U.S. citizens were enrolled in full-degree programs outside the United States, pursuing fields ranging from business and economics to engineering, public policy, science, and the humanities.

In response to this growing interest, the *Fiske Guide* is widening its editorial lens to include a selection of institutions across continental Europe and parts of Asia, many of which are enrolling American undergraduates in meaningful numbers and offer baccalaureate degree programs taught in English.

Why is pursuing a degree abroad becoming more popular? The reasons are numerous. Globalization has made international education more visible—and more attainable. Moreover, shifting political and cultural pressures within the United States are prompting some students and families to look beyond our borders when considering college options. Heightened scrutiny of universities, debates over research funding and academic freedom, and uncertainty about long-term policy priorities have all contributed to a growing awareness that respected, high-quality alternatives exist outside American shores. For some students, international universities offer academic stability or a broader global perspective; for others, they provide a different educational philosophy or institutional culture that simply feels like a better personal fit. And, in many cases, these universities offer more affordable tuition.

The following sections examine Canada, Great Britain, and Ireland in more detail, followed by full-length articles on selected institutions, along with a discussion of the differences between American-style, four-year undergraduate programs and some of the European and Asian university offerings in countries ranging from France and Italy to the Czech Republic and Hong Kong.

Canadian Universities

Horace Greeley told ambitious young men of his generation to "go West." Today his admonition to young men and women seeking a quality college education at a relatively modest cost would probably be to "go North"—to Canada. A growing number of American students are discovering the educational riches that lie just above their northern border in this huge land of 40 million people that is known for its rugged mountains, bicultural politics, spirited ice hockey, and cold ale. As of 2024, around 8,100 American undergraduates were studying full-time in Canada. What's drawing them is easy to discern.

The top Canadian universities are the academic equals of most flagship public universities and many leading privates in the United States. Canadian campuses and the cities in which they are located are safe places, and unless one opts for a French course of study, there are no language and few cultural barriers. Canadian schools are strong on international exchange programs, and their degrees carry weight with U.S. graduate schools.

Canada has around 100 institutions of higher learning, ranging from internationally recognized research universities to the small undergraduate teaching institutions in the country's more rural areas. Most of the larger universities are located in highly urban centers, but some are situated in smaller towns where they dominate the life of the community. Most are almost literally next door to the United States, within 100 miles of the Canada–U.S. border. In this guide, we feature four of Canada's strongest universities: the University of British Columbia, McGill University, Queen's University, and the University of Toronto.

Institutions of higher learning in Canada were established from the earliest days of French settlement in the mid-17th century, making them some of the oldest in North America. The precursors to the public universities in Canada were the small, elite, denominational colleges that sprang up in Quebec, in the Maritimes, and later in Ontario. A few private denominational colleges and universities still exist in Canada, but most have been subsumed into affiliations or associations with the larger universities. Education in Canada, including university education, became the exclusive jurisdiction of provincial governments.

One of the key differences between Canadian and U.S. universities is that Canadian universities (and this is what they are, not "colleges") are primarily funded from public monies. Calculating the cost for an American to attend a Canadian university can be tricky. For one thing, the exchange rate between the U.S. and Canadian dollar fluctuates. Moreover, tuition and fee rates vary by field of study. The cost of pricey majors such as medicine and other hard sciences can easily be double or triple that of less expensive ones such as social work or theology. Canadian citizens, of course, pay far less than visitors from south of the border. Depending on the factors just described, tuition and fees at the four universities included in the *Fiske Guide* range from less than US $15,000 to more than US $70,000. For many U.S. students, education at one of the top Canadian universities is comparable to out-of-state rates at a flagship public university in the States.

Federal and provincial loans and grants that are readily available to Canadian students are generally not available to students from the United States and other countries. However, the majority of universities with competitive admissions, particularly those featured in the *Fiske Guide*, offer merit-based awards and scholarships to students of all nationalities. American students who attend leading Canadian schools can apply their U.S. student assistance funds, including Federal Direct Loans and Pell Grants.

The criteria for obtaining a degree are set by each institution, as are the admissions requirements and prerequisites. Unlike the United States, Canada does not offer nor require its own students to take a Canadian college entrance test. Some Canadian universities admitting students from the United States will ask for SAT or ACT scores along with high school marks from academic subjects in the last two or three years of high school. In general, top universities are about as selective as their American counterparts.

Application fees vary by institution, as do deadlines. Canadian universities are aware of the May 1 deadline operative in the United States, and they try to accommodate. Applications to the University of Toronto and Queen's University in Ontario are handled centrally through the Ontario Universities' Application Centre, although Queen's also accepts the Common Application as an alternative for students applying from the U.S. McGill and British Columbia handle their own applications directly. Canadian universities differ widely in the amount of credit and/or advanced standing they offer for Advanced Placement examinations or International Baccalaureate Higher Level examinations.

The following admissions requirements apply to applicants from an American school system. In recent years, many Canadian schools have relaxed their SAT and ACT testing requirements for applicants from the United States. Prospective students are advised to consult universities' websites or contact admissions officers directly for the most up-to-date information regarding testing requirements. Aside from SAT and ACT scores, the University of British Columbia bases admissions decisions on the average of eight full-year academic courses over the last two years of high school. McGill bases its assessment of American high school graduates on the overall record of marks in academic subjects during the final three years of high school and their class standing. Queen's looks at class rank. Toronto's Arts and Science faculties want a high grade point average. These universities generally have additional program-specific requirements for STEM fields that may be more stringent. ACT and CEEB Advanced Placement Examination scores are also considered.

It is hard to beat Canadian universities for the quality of student life. Although many students commute, most of the universities in Canada offer on-campus housing; some even guarantee campus housing for first-year students. Universities offer active intramural and intercollegiate sports programs for both men and women, and the usual student clubs, newspapers, and radio stations provide students with opportunities to get involved and develop friendships. As in the United States, student-run organizations are active participants in university life, with leaders serving on university committees and lobbying on issues ranging from creating more bicycle paths to keeping tuition low. Few Canadian campuses are troubled by issues of student safety or rowdiness. In the larger urban centers, Canadian campuses reflect the rich diversity of Canada's cultural mosaic, and most encourage their students to gain international experience by spending a term or a full year abroad.

Americans wondering about the currency of a Canadian degree in the United States should be reassured that top American and multinational companies—the likes of Chase, IBM, and Microsoft—actively recruit on Canadian campuses, as do American graduate schools.

The one thing that is different for U.S. and other international students intending to study in Canada is that they will have to obtain a study permit, equivalent to a visa, from Canadian immigration authorities as well as a passport. Getting a study permit is fairly straightforward for American citizens, but this slight bureaucratic hurdle is a reminder that Canada, for all of its similarities in language and culture with the United States, is still a separate country.

Universities Canada, a nonprofit organization representing Canada's colleges and universities, has more information at www.universitystudy.ca.

Canadian universities are currently playing host to about 10,000 American undergraduate and graduate students on their campuses, having become increasingly active in recruiting students from south of the border over the past two decades. Now, with research funds being cut at top U.S. institutions as they increasingly come under the Trump administration's microscope, some Canadian universities, including the University of British Columbia, have reported a jump in applications from American students in 2025. This is but one more reason why more young Americans may want to check out the "Canadian option." Canada, eh?

University of British Columbia

6200 University Boulevard, Vancouver, British Columbia V6T 1Z4

Natural beauty is the first thing that draws Americans to Vancouver—and Canada's premier western university. A similar scale to places like University of Washington but with two major differences—no big-time sports to unite the campus and limited dorm life. The university is active in recruiting overseas, which creates an international ambience.

What do three prime ministers of Canada, three provincial premiers, an astronaut, a world-renowned opera singer, and two Nobel Prize winners have in common? They are all graduates of the University of British Columbia. Founded in 1908, UBC offers students hundreds of solid programs, such as business, science, engineering, the social sciences, and fine arts, as well as ready access to beaches and mountains and a diploma with instant name recognition. Though the massive campus can sometimes feel isolating, students are nevertheless happy to be here in such illustrious company.

Located just 25 minutes from downtown Vancouver, UBC's striking Point Grey campus covers a peninsula that borders the Pacific Ocean and is bounded by an old-growth forest. Mountains—perfect for skiing—loom in the distance. Architectural styles are a mix of Gothic and modern, and students can enjoy a leisurely stroll through the university's botanical gardens. Notable campus facilities include the Kaiser Building (the central hub of engineering), the Barber Learning Centre, the Mitchell Thunderbird Sports Arena, and the Nest (a $106 million student union building). The university also has a smaller campus—UBC Okanagan—located in Kelowna, in the Okanagan Valley.

> **"Courses can be hard, but success is based on your interest and willingness to learn."**

UBC offers more than 260 undergraduate degree options, and popular majors include psychology, biology, English, and kinesiology. Programs in anthropology, First Nations and indigenous studies, and Asian studies are highly regarded and enhanced by the university's excellent Museum of Anthropology, which features one of the world's best collections of Northwest Coast First Nations art. Music majors benefit from the Chan Centre for the Performing Arts. Economics, geography, international relations, microbiology, and commerce are strong too. Additional programs include majors in applied animal biology, applied plant and soil sciences, geographical biogeosciences, and zoology.

First-year students are offered a wide array of programs, including Imagine UBC and Create UBC Okanagan, a first-day orientation. Arts One and the Coordinated Arts programs offer enriched, integrated approaches to broad interdisciplinary themes in arts and humanities. Qualified students can take advantage of Science One, featuring team-taught courses in biology, chemistry, math, and physics. The UBC study abroad program has more than 200 institutional partners in 40 countries, and co-op programs in engineering, science, arts, commerce, and forestry give students an opportunity to earn while they learn. In addition, honors and double-honors programs are available to superbrains and budding geniuses. Eighty-four percent of UBC undergrads participate in some form of enriched-learning experience, such as an internship or study abroad.

The academic climate is exactly what you would expect from a university of UBC's international stature. "Courses can be hard," says one student, "but success

Website: www.you.ubc.ca
Location: City Outskirts
Public
Total Enrollment: 59,150
Undergraduates: 47,856
Male/Female: 44/51
Financial Aid: 25%
Pell Grant: N/A
Expense: Pub $ $ $ $
Student Loans: N/A
Average Debt: N/A
Applicants: 43,992
Accepted: 63%
Enrolled: 51%
Grad in 6 Years: 84%
Returning First-years: 95%
Academics: ✐ ✐ ✐ ✐
Social: 🗨 🗨
Q of L: ★ ★ ★ ★
Admissions: (604) 822-8999
Email Address:
  international@askme.ubc.ca

Strong Programs:
Anthropology
Asian Studies
Commerce
Economics
First Nations and Indigenous
  Studies
Geography
International Relations
Microbiology

is based on your interest and willingness to learn." One student grumbles about his 8 a.m. philosophy lecture: "Who can focus on the big questions at that time of the morning?" Most classes have fewer than 50 students, while larger lectures are supplemented with smaller labs and discussion groups. Overall, the faculty receives good marks. "The professors are extremely intelligent people who are truly dedicated to their disciplines," says a junior. Academic advising is a mixed bag, with some students complaining that finding a knowledgeable advisor can be time-consuming.

With more than 40,000 undergraduates attending the Vancouver campus, it's no surprise that UBC's student population is a melting pot—nearly 30 percent come from outside Canada from 148 countries. "There is a huge diversity here that many smaller schools may lack," says a sophomore. The typical UBC student is bright, hardworking, and gregarious. Students of color are well represented (Asians make up the largest contingency), and the university encourages diversity through a series of special programs and active recruiting. Hot political issues include LGBTQ, women's, and human rights. The International Scholars program offers financial support, as well as special service projects, workshops, and other opportunities to top international students.

Roughly one-third of the students currently live on campus. A major expansion of on-campus housing, estimated at US $650 million, has taken place, and UBC guarantees a spot to all incoming first-time, first-year students. On-campus options include co-ed complexes (primarily for first-years), theme houses, university apartments, and family units for upperclassmen. A history major says on-campus living is worth it to "enjoy the community spirit." Those seeking off-campus accommodations must contend with Vancouver's pricey rental market. Hungry students will find an endless variety of meal options at the school's 45 dining locations, including "Japanese, Lebanese, Italian, and vegetarian" plates, according to one student. The Sexual Assault Support Centre provides support services and educational programming related to sexual violence.

"There is a huge diversity here that many smaller schools may lack."

On such a large campus, isolation is a real threat. "You need to get in touch with other students quickly when you get here or you could feel lost on such a big campus," says a first-year. Social life happens mostly on campus but largely "depends on the crowd you hang with," according to one student. For partying types, there are the requisite bashes, courtesy of UBC's small but active Greek scene—one of the few places where underage drinkers may sneak a sip of booze. Alternatives include university-sponsored events, such as movies and guest speakers. Popular campus events include Storm the Wall, long-boat racing, and the Arts County Fair.

Vancouver, with its population of 760,000, offers students countless opportunities, though one health science major says, "It isn't a college town. It is a well-developed semicosmopolitan city." Another adds, "Vancouver is one of the most livable cities in the world and UBC is located in the nicest, most beautiful part—it's not too hard to imagine what a pleasure it is to go to school here." Gorgeous weather draws students outdoors and to nearby beaches and mountains for in-line skating, snowboarding, and swimming. Eleven recreational sports leagues and multiple intramural events are a huge draw for students at the Vancouver campus; popular sports include sailing, skiing, and cycling. UBC has 36 varsity teams (the Thunderbirds), which have brought home more than 122 national championships—the most of any institution in Canada. Men's hockey won the Canada West championship in 2024. Men's and women's volleyball and swimming, along with women's ice hockey and field hockey, have been particularly competitive in recent years.

Spending four years at this mammoth university can be intimidating for the shy student. But for those willing to take control of their social lives, UBC offers an

Overlaps

UC Berkeley, UCLA, CU Boulder, NYU, Simon Fraser, University of Toronto, University of Victoria, University of Washington

impressive academic milieu. A history major offers this point of view: "I think that the school's biggest strength is its size; there are so many opportunities here."

If You Apply To ›

McGill University

845 Sherbrooke Street W, Montreal, Quebec H3A 0G4

The Canadian university best known south of the border. Though instruction is in English, McGill is located in French-speaking Montreal, a world-class city that has it all. Individualism is encouraged, and there's a strong international flavor. Just over 10 percent of students live in university housing, and anyone coming here will be on their own for housing after the first year.

With such strong preprofessional programs and a diverse student body, it's easy to see why enterprising men and women from around the world flock to McGill University, which was founded in 1821 by a bequest from Scottish merchant James McGill. But beware: this is not a cookie-cutter school, and fitting in actually seems to be discouraged. "McGill is a university where people are allowed to become individuals," a senior says. "Difference and creativity are celebrated here."

Montreal's climate alternates between hot summers and freezing winters. A junior describes McGill's 80-acre main campus as "an oasis in the heart of the city." Located in downtown Montreal amid the hustle and bustle, the campus provides students with ample green space and a welcome respite from the decidedly urban atmosphere of the city. A free outdoor skating rink adds charm in the frigid winter months. Campus buildings range from "Gothic-like" structures with vines growing up the sides to more modern structures. Trees and greenery dot the campus landscape, and the sprawling recreation trails of Mount Royal rise to its immediate north. Notable facilities include a $71 million life sciences research complex. The Schulich School of Music offers an ultramodern symphony and multimedia hall that functions as a recording studio, performance venue, and research studio. A short drive west of downtown, the Macdonald Campus occupies 1,600 acres of woods and fields on the shores of Lac St-Louis, providing unique opportunities for fieldwork and research.

To fulfill the university's general education requirements, students must first choose which discipline (or faculty) to enter. A senior says, "It is important to consider the university on the basis of which faculty you would be interested in, because they vary greatly and operate almost as independent units." First-year students must accumulate six to 12 credits in three of four disciplines, including languages, math and science, social sciences, and humanities, and declare a major before their sophomore year. Upon entering their major, students have a menu of course options that includes honors programs and double majors.

> **"Difference and creativity are celebrated here."**

The most popular majors are in the arts, health sciences, psychology, political science, and education, and the university's strengths also lie in preprofessional programs such as medicine, law, and engineering. The sciences receive uniform

Website: www.mcgill.ca
Location: City Center
Public
Total Enrollment: 40,531
Undergraduates: 28,167
Male/Female: 37/60
Financial Aid: 24%
Pell Grant: N/A
Expense: Pub $ $ $ $
Student Loans: N/A
Average Debt: N/A
Applicants: 38,135
Accepted: 48%
Enrolled: 40%
Grad in 6 Years: 85%
Returning First-years: 95%
Academics: ✍ ✍ ✍ ✍
Social: 🎭 🎭 🎭 🎭
Q of L: ★ ★ ★ ★
Admissions: (514) 398-7878
Email Address: N/A

Strong Programs:
Arts
Education
Engineering
Environmental Studies
Law
Medicine
Political Science
Psychology

praise, as does the School of Environment. A double-degree interdisciplinary program allows students to combine a bachelor of arts program with one in the sciences. Several programs help first-years with the transition to college, and some are tailored to international students, which includes those from the United States. For those who want to escape Montreal's brutal winters, there are internships; field studies in Barbados, Africa, and the Smithsonian Tropical Research Institute in Panama; and exchange programs with more than 150 partner universities around the world.

Regardless of major, students can expect classes to be demanding. "McGill has a very stressful and competitive atmosphere," a finance major says. Classes can be large—some introductory courses enroll up to 1,000 students (although 33 percent enroll fewer than 25 students)—and students must be willing to seek out professors and advisors. "The quality of teaching is generally above average," a student says. "Many of the professors are kind, intelligent, and devoted to their students." Students grumble that academic advising is a bureaucratic tangle. "There is way too much red tape, and dealing with the administration can be horrible," says one senior.

Forty-eight percent of undergraduates are Quebecers (or Québécois, as Francophones would say), and roughly a quarter are international, representing more than 135 countries—about 14 percent of undergrads come from the U.S. Indeed, McGill students are a diverse lot, and the only common thread among them seems to be their fierce independence. A geography major says McGill students are "hardworking, driven, very intellectual, and research-oriented." Environmental issues are a big concern, and students report that political and social issues receive ample attention on campus. Qualified students are eligible for merit scholarships and a limited number of awards for athletes. There is also a work-study program for those in need of financial assistance.

The university's traditional and alternative residence halls house about 11 percent of undergrads, primarily first-year students, in dorms, apartments, and shared facilities houses. Dorms run the gamut, but one recent acquisition is, according to a senior, a "four-star hotel, turned into a six-star dorm." Party animals will feel free to crank up the stereo in Molson or McConnell, while bookworms might be better suited for Gardner. Off-campus apartments are a popular alternative for upperclassmen, who take advantage of Montreal's clean, affordable housing. "The dining facilities are good," says a sophomore. Despite its urban location, the McGill campus is safe, and security receives positive reviews. "There are student organizations like 'Walksafe' and 'Drivesafe' that will walk or drive students to their residences at night regardless of where they are or where they are going," reports one student.

"McGill students are very sociable and love to party!" says one student. Though there are "considerable on-campus social activities, with many clubs and associations," many students venture off campus into Montreal for fun and adventure. "A cultural epicenter, Montreal is home to some of the world's best museums, galleries, restaurants, shops, and music," a senior says. "There are always free concerts and festivals all over the city throughout the year." Drinking is a popular pastime, but underage drinkers are few and far between since the legal age in Quebec is 18 and, a senior says, "McGill treats its students as mature, educated adults." Greek organizations sign up about 2 percent of the students, and McGill boasts Canada's first social fraternity for gay, bisexual, transgender, and progressive men. Well-attended campus events include homecoming, Winter Carnival, and Frosh activities during orientation week. New York City, Ottawa, and Toronto are popular road-trip destinations, and ski slopes are less than an hour away.

McGill students are a diverse lot, and the only common thread among them seems to be their fierce independence.

"Many of the professors are kind, intelligent, and devoted to their students."

The Schulich School of Music offers an ultramodern symphony and multimedia hall.

Men's and women's basketball and ice hockey, men's rugby, and men's and women's swimming are among the most popular varsity sports; men's rowing and women's artistic swimming have captured recent national championships. According to one student, "The McGill–Harvard rugby match is a must-watch." Intramurals offer would-be jocks an opportunity to blow off steam after classes and on weekends, with soccer and ice hockey attracting the most interest.

In recent years, the government of Quebec has been less than enthusiastic about funding its English-speaking academic gem, and large classes and mountains of red tape are undeniably part of the McGill experience. Nevertheless, most denizens seem happy. "The students who go to McGill are very invested in their academic life and are proud of their school," a student says.

If You Apply To ›

McGill: Rolling admissions. Does not accept the Common Application. Please consult McGill's website for the most up-to-date information regarding standardized test requirements.

Queen's University

99 University Avenue, Kingston, Ontario K7L 3N6

With about 21,000 undergraduates, Queen's is the smallest of the major Canadian universities. It is also the only one set in a metropolitan area of modest size. Engineering and business are the strongest areas of study, followed by nursing. Toronto and Montreal are both about three hours away. With 90 percent of its first-year students in the dorms, Queen's has a more active residential life than other Canadian universities.

Students at Queen's University approach work and play with equal zeal and enjoy a potent mix of school spirit and intellectual drive. Success requires energy and a willingness to get into the thick of things. "People who aren't interested in being a part of the school community are better off at a school that isn't such a big family," warns a sophomore. Solid academics, a pervasive school spirit, and long-standing traditions make life at this storied university unique—and demanding. "Getting into Queen's is just the first challenge," says a senior. "Succeeding at Queen's is another battle."

The 161-acre Queen's campus is located on the north shore of Lake Ontario, just minutes from the heart of Kingston, Ontario ("the limestone city"), and directly between Montreal and Toronto. "Almost all buildings are constructed using limestone," explains a senior. Historically significant buildings have been maintained, and "there are some modern buildings with a lot of glass to provide a bright and welcoming atmosphere." Ample greenery and open spaces provide students a place to stretch out under the sky and hit the books. The 80,000-square-foot Isabel Bader Centre for the Performing Arts features common teaching rooms and shared public spaces designed to encourage interactivity.

Established by the Church of Scotland in 1841 under a Royal Charter of Queen Victoria, Queen's University offers undergraduate degrees in a variety of faculties, including science, engineering, commerce, education, music, nursing, and creative arts. Academics are unilaterally solid, but the most demanding are engineering and commerce; health science and nursing are popular. The bachelor of commerce program was the first of its kind in Canada and provides students with an internationally focused liberal business education, enhanced by leadership modules and the integration of technology. The School of Computing offers bachelor of computing degrees in biomedical computing, cognitive science, and software design, as well as B.A. and B.S. degrees. Computing and the Creative Arts is a multidisciplinary program that allows students to use cutting-edge software programs for music, drama, art, and film production. General education requirements vary by program, but all students can expect to confront a rigorous series of core and elective courses. Students participating in programs at the Queen's Bader International Study Centre are whisked away to the university's campus in East Sussex, England, where they enjoy small classes and integrated field studies while residing in a 15th-century castle. In addition, there are exchange programs with more than 100 universities in 30-plus countries around the world. Queen's is considered a leader in study abroad; 20 percent of students participate. Opportunities for undergraduate research are abundant as well.

"The academic climate is quite competitive, and the courses are often theory-driven and require a substantial amount of work to prepare for class and complete assignments," says one senior. The general consensus among struggling students is that A's are hard to come by. "After working your butt off and reading stacks of textbooks, your grades pale in comparison to the marks of students at other universities," gripes a biology major. The QSuccess program helps orient first-year students academically and socially, and Bounce Back mentors offer academic support for first-year students who earn low GPAs in their first term. Participating students are paired with peer mentors who help them set goals and identify strategies for academic success.

> **"The academic climate is quite competitive."**

Bounce Back mentors offer academic support for first-year students who earn low GPAs in their first term.

Classes tend to be large for first-years and sophomores but dwindle in size as one approaches graduation. The majority of classes are taught by full professors, who receive praise for their accessibility and intelligence. "The teachers I have had have been thorough, challenging, and concerned about my success," says a junior. Office hours and special "wine and cheese" functions give students ample opportunity to mingle with faculty. Students report that there is little trouble getting into desired classes, and "there is lots of counseling available for students who need it."

Queen's students are an industrious, intelligent group, and most are used to academic success. School spirit runs high, and campus issues include rising tuition fees—and determining just who is responsible for the cost. Undergraduates come from every Canadian province and 97 countries; 77 percent are from Ontario and 8 percent are international. A sociology major says that "Queen's is very PC and inclusive, regardless of gender, race, religion, or sexual orientation."

> **"The teachers I have had have been thorough, challenging, and concerned about my success."**

Though there are no athletic scholarships, hundreds of merit awards averaging $7,000 are handed out annually. "I have had great help through scholarships and financial aid," relates a senior. "There is quite a lot of money for you. You just have to go after it." International students are automatically considered for available merit awards.

Ninety percent of undergraduates live in 18 residence halls, and all first-year students are guaranteed a place to hang their hats. Co-ed and single-sex dorms are available, and students say all accommodations are well maintained. A mandatory meal plan gives first-years a wide variety of foods to choose from, and the surrounding city also offers a plethora of dining options. After their first year, most students pack their bags and head off campus to the "student village," where comfortable apartments are available. Most Queen's students live within a reasonable walk of campus. Safety is practically a nonissue on campus; students report that they feel quite safe and that security is more than adequate.

Make no mistake about it, Queen's students know how to have a good time. One says, "Campus pubs and city pubs have both found their niche." On Thursday nights, students flock to the campus pub, the Underground, for a drink or two, while Saturday nights are reserved for city bars and nightclubs. The legal drinking age is 19, and kiddies will have a tough time skirting the law. "The bouncers in Kingston actually have a couple of brain cells and can spot a fake ID from 90 kilometers away," says a senior. Nonalcoholic alternatives include school-sponsored movies and extracurricular clubs (there are more than 300). "Extracurricular activities are a must, not an option!" says one student. Frosh Week is a favorite event, with "cheers that even the most blasé of students will be shouting out with pride by the end of the week." The school is steeped in Scottish tradition and modeled on counterparts in Edinburgh and Glasgow, and it's normal to see kilt-wearing bandsmen at important campus events.

> *The bachelor of commerce program was the first of its kind in Canada.*

Once the capital of Canada, Kingston is described as "very much a university town." The Royal Military College is nearby and downtown provides students with shops, clubs, museums, and movie theaters. The city's relative isolation makes it the favored stomping ground for students without wheels. Town/gown relations are good, and students are very active in the community. Toronto and Montreal (less than three hours away) are popular road trips.

> **"Extracurricular activities are a must, not an option!"**

With 13 varsity teams, more than 20 varsity clubs, and many recreational clubs, Queen's athletic program is not only the largest in Canada but also ranks with Harvard and MIT for the largest programs in North America. Competitive Gaels teams include men's and women's rugby, ice hockey, soccer, and volleyball. The annual "kill McGill" football game against rival McGill draws pigskin-crazed students from every corner of campus; homecoming is a lively affair. Intramural competition is fierce too, and nearly half of the students are involved on some level. A student says, "There is so much school spirit, sometimes it makes you sick."

Life at Queen's University is one of extremes. Though the academic climate can be tough and the winters long, students here find much to celebrate. "One of the great things about Queen's is that it's constantly growing and expanding to meet the needs of its students," says one senior, "but at the same time, it never loses sight of where it came from or what it stands for."

Overlaps

University of Alberta, University of British Columbia, Dalhousie, McGill, McMaster, University of Ottawa, University of Toronto, Western

If You Apply To ›

Queen's: Rolling admissions. Accepts the Common Application. Apply to particular program. Please consult Queen's website for the most up-to-date information regarding standardized test requirements.

University of Toronto

Toronto, Ontario M5S 1A1

With over 80,000 undergraduates, U of T is one of the largest institutions in the *Fiske Guide* and one of the biggest in the world. If ever there were a place where go-getterism is a necessity, this is it. In the absence of American-style school spirit, U of T students cut loose to find their fun in the city. Toronto is one of the most diverse and cosmopolitan cities in the world, with nearly half of its 3 million denizens born outside of Canada.

Website: www.utoronto.ca
Location: City Center
Public
Total Enrollment: 102,431
Undergraduates: 80,573
Male/Female: 38/50
Financial Aid: 20%
Pell Grant: N/A
Expense: Pub $ $ $ $
Student Loans: N/A
Average Debt: N/A
Applicants: 77,087
Accepted: 78%
Enrolled: 28%
Grad in 6 Years: 82%
Returning First-years: 93%
Academics: ✍ ✍ ✍ ✍
Social: 🗩 🗩 🗩
Q of L: ★ ★ ★
Admissions: (416) 978-2190
Email Address: future
.students@utoronto.ca

Strong Programs:
Biochemistry
Commerce
Computer Science
Engineering
Forensic Science
International Relations
Music
Physical Sciences

The intramural program is one of the largest in Canada, involving more than 20,000 students in more than 20 sports.

Students at the University of Toronto avoid getting lost in the shuffle by taking part in a unique residential college system that allows them to model their educational experience after their own personalities. Each college has a distinct character and appeal yet blends seamlessly into the university's overall academic milieu. And when it comes to academics, the U of T delivers, says a senior: "The students were likely at the top of their class in high school and are very competitive—more so than at Queen's or York universities."

The University of Toronto, founded by royal charter in 1827, is so large that it spans three campuses. The St. George campus in downtown Toronto features Gothic architecture and historic buildings. The suburban campuses in Mississauga and Scarborough feature more modern structures. A spate of new research buildings, athletic facilities, and student residences have opened in the last few years, including a new science building at Mississauga that administrators say is "one of the most energy-efficient biological and chemical laboratory facilities in North America." A new 23-story, 508-bed residence hall also opened on the St. George campus. As befitting such a gargantuan institution, the university's endowment is the largest of any Canadian college or university.

Students apply directly to one of Toronto's seven divisions—five of which are on the St. George campus—and choose from more than 700 undergraduate degree programs. The most popular programs include social sciences, math and physical sciences, humanities, commerce, management, and business administration. The health professions, agriculture, and engineering are big draws as well. New programs are available in city studies, climate change studies, and logic. The Faculty of Arts and Science offers a wide array of disciplines that span the arts, science, and business, while the Faculty of Music is the oldest in Canada and offers bachelor's, master's, and doctoral degrees in all of their programs. Distinctive learning options include First-Year Learning Communities and a wide range of research opportunities. Optional first-year seminars (called First-Year Foundations: The Ones Programs) are "a good transition from high school to university," says a senior, and give incoming first-years the chance to learn from leading faculty members in a less intimidating environment of around 25 to 50 students (a majority of classes have more than 200 students). Topics range from public policy to urban environments to geological fieldwork.

> **"During exam periods and the final weeks of each semester, the academic climate can become quite intense."**

Courses require a great deal of reading outside the classroom and are typically demanding. "During exam periods and the final weeks of each semester, the academic climate can understandably become quite intense," says one senior. Large lecture classes are accompanied by smaller tutorials, facilitating personal attention, and professors get high marks for their teaching skills and their smarts. "Even in classes of 1,500 students, professors have been consistently engaging and well-versed," says a student. Students who wish to venture farther afield can study, do research, or pursue internships abroad through around 170 exchange programs.

"Students are from all over the world and represent the full spectrum of values and backgrounds," says an anthropology major. "U of T is very diverse and the student body is generally intelligent, progressive, and open-minded." Twenty-nine percent of undergraduates are international—from outside Canada, that is, and roughly 2 percent are from the U.S. A large 53 percent of students identify as Asian, 6 percent as Black, 3 percent as Hispanic/Latino, and 3 percent as multiracial. The most significant issues on campus include "tuition fees, unequal pay, the environment, and critical social justice," according to one student. The Ontario Public Interest Research Group and Amnesty International attract sizable followings. A limited number of competitive academic scholarships are available for the most high-achieving international students.

Roughly 10 percent of students live in campus housing, and first-years are guaranteed rooms. "There are new buildings and historic old buildings that are beautiful," says an anthropology major. "They are cozy and comfortable and pretty well maintained." All of the dorms are affiliated with one of the seven colleges, which act as "local neighborhoods" and center on specialties, such as Buddhism, Celtic studies, and criminology. "Every cafeteria always has a vegetarian, vegan, halal, kosher, gluten-free, or dairy-free option," a junior reports. "Security is pretty good on campus, and our campus is in a good part of Toronto," a bioethics major says.

"Social life here revolves around the very energetic city in which the school is located," says a sociology and English major. Another student adds, "Social events are balanced between off-campus pubs, clubs, skating rinks, banquet halls, and stadiums to on-campus pubs, event spaces in Hart House, and student lounges." Toronto boasts great culture, super shopping, a clean and safe nightlife district—and the picturesque shores of Lake Ontario, lovely in warmer weather. The legal drinking age here is 19; students who are of age may have alcohol in their rooms but not in common spaces, and anyone caught violating local laws or the open-container policy is reported to the dean of the residence. But according to one student, "There isn't much of a party culture at U of T, because we are much more focused on studying." Students looking to unwind on campus will find plenty of school-sponsored events, such as movies and guest speakers, and while there are no fraternities or sororities, there is a club for nearly every interest. Students turn out in droves to celebrate Pride, reputedly the largest gay pride event in North America, along with Orientation Week, which includes wacky fun such as bed races between the colleges, and the annual Fireball formal dance.

Varsity sports are not a focus of campus life at Toronto, though ice hockey, volleyball, and basketball draw something of a following, especially when the opponent is Queen's University or Western University. The Varsity Blues women's swimming team, the men's and women's water polo, and the fencing teams are all competitive. The intramural program is one of the largest in Canada, involving more than 20,000 students in more than 20 sports, with 50-plus leagues and over 20 tournaments each year. Residence halls and groups of friends compete in everything from badminton to indoor cricket, karate, dodgeball, squash, and eSports. Students can also be found cheering the city's many professional teams, including the 2025 World Series–contender Blue Jays (baseball), the Raptors (basketball), and the Maple Leafs (hockey).

Toronto's biggest liability, its sheer and sometimes overwhelming size, may also be its biggest asset, students say—as long as they learn to speak up and proactively take advantage of all of the school's resources. Says a senior, "A prospective student should choose the University of Toronto due to its outstanding academic reputation and convenient location in the social hub of Toronto's downtown core."

The Faculty of Arts and Science offers a wide array of disciplines that span the arts, science, and business.

"Social life here revolves around the very energetic city in which the school is located."

Overlaps

University of British Columbia, UC Berkeley, UCLA, University of Chicago, Johns Hopkins, MIT, McGill, University of Michigan

If You Apply To ›

University of Toronto: Early action (only some programs; please consult the University of Toronto's website), regular decision. Does not accept the Common Application. Apply to specific program. Please consult University of Toronto's website for the most up-to-date information regarding standardized test requirements.

British and Irish Universities

If going to college in Canada sounds adventuresome, you may need even more moxie to venture overseas. But give it some thought. As one of the most popular overseas destinations (along with Italy and Spain), Great Britain currently has about 12,000 Americans enrolled in undergraduate degree programs, and another 25,000 per year are pursuing shorter study abroad stints. Hundreds more have found their way to the Republic of Ireland. Depending on your course of study, studying in Britain or Ireland may or may not turn out to be less expensive than a flagship public university in the U.S., but the top British and Irish universities offer a richer international experience, infused with historical and cultural perspectives, than you will find on this side of the Atlantic.

Before we go further, here's a word to parents and counselors: you may get queasy at the thought of sending your child across a 3,000-mile ocean, but a flight to Dublin or London is quicker than driving 10 hours to get to First Choice U. Once you're there, the cities are at least as safe as those in the U.S., and the small towns have a crime rate roughly equivalent to that of the town of Mayberry on *The Andy Griffith Show*. The best part for parents: you'll need to visit at least once—and preferably more.

For those who are hazy on their geography, England, Scotland, and Wales make up Great Britain; throw in Northern Ireland and the moniker changes to the United Kingdom. The Republic of Ireland, occupying the southern part of the Emerald Isle across the Irish Sea, used to be part of Great Britain but won its independence in 1921. Ireland is the closest European nation to the East Coast of the U.S. and the only English-speaking country in the eurozone. Britain and Ireland make the most sense for American students interested in studying English literature, history, foreign languages, and anything related to international studies. If medieval history is your passion, why not go to school where the remains of that long-ago world still dot the landscape? If you're looking for a career in international business, perhaps consider a country where the global village has been a way of life and you can make lifelong friends from around the world. Though Britain is an English-speaking country, it offers far better instruction in European and other languages than you can get in the U.S., and Ireland's favorable corporate tax rates have led U.S. companies such as Google, Microsoft, and Meta to make it their European headquarters (think internships). No matter what your academic interests, your classmates will include a cross section of nationalities that would be the envy of any North American institution. Most importantly, study in Britain and Ireland has the potential to be a life-changing experience that will broaden your horizons and deepen your understanding of our increasingly interconnected world. With cheap flights and trains readily available, travel to Continental Europe and beyond becomes second nature.

With all these benefits come some challenges. American students in Britain need to adjust to a different tenor of academic life than is found at U.S. colleges and universities. Students are treated as adults and expected to behave accordingly. The legal drinking age is 18, which obviates the need for fake IDs but puts the onus on students to behave responsibly. Dorms are generally the domain of first-year students; expect to find a "flat" (apartment) for subsequent years. "Sport" means playing, not watching. The student body will not come out on a Saturday afternoon for the big game for a simple reason: there are no big games. Most faculty members (a.k.a. tutors) are ready to help you if you are struggling with your studies, but only if you take the initiative. There is no dean of student hand-holding in British universities (nor do they offer landing pads for helicopter parents).

Americans thinking about studying in Britain and Ireland should also be aware of differences in the academic system "across the Pond." Most important: whereas American universities generally require students to sample a variety of fields for two years before choosing a major, British and Irish institutions expect students to identify a field of concentration before they set foot on campus. That's because students take their general education courses in high school. Thus students in Britain and Ireland take only two or three courses at a time, mostly related to their major. American-style distribution requirements are all but unheard of—good news for students who want to get out of those nasty math or foreign language requirements. But keep in mind that since British and Irish students tend to take courses only in subjects that seriously interest them, all classes are taught at a high level, even introductory ones. Moreover, although students get fewer hours in class, they are expected to put in more hours of study per course outside of class. Anyone who wants to change majors after a year or two may encounter difficulty.

Another important academic difference is that British and Irish universities evaluate applicants almost entirely based on academic credentials, with emphasis on demonstrated ability in their field of study. (Only St Andrews does holistic reviews.) No essays about page 236 of your autobiography or need to present yourself as a well-rounded overachiever who will enrich the campus environment. As one administrator put it, "We don't do social engineering." Along with Trinity College Dublin, the top British universities, especially the four "ancient" Scottish universities, are thus a good bet for U.S. students who may have the smarts to do Ivy League work but whose résumés do not include an Olympic medal or building a school in Belize during spring vacation. Standards are high. Recently, however, some British and Irish schools have relaxed their SAT and ACT testing requirements for applicants from the United States. Prospective students are advised to consult universities' websites or contact admissions officers directly for the most up-to-date information regarding testing requirements. Aside from SAT and ACT scores, some schools may require scores from AP exams. For the application essay, the British usually ask about commitment to your intended major and why you want to study it. They view American-style personal essays as fluff.

As with Canadian universities, the cost for an American studying at one of the leading Scottish and Irish universities will vary with fluctuating exchange rates. To complicate matters, tuition and fee levels vary not only across universities but also according to the course of study and academic level within each institution. Total tuition and fees among the five universities described in the *Fiske Guide* range from around US $25,000 to more than US $50,000 per year—roughly equivalent to the costs for out-of-state students at flagship public universities in the U.S. but less than the sticker price of many highly selective privates. The downside is that the sticker price is also the final price; academic scholarships are scarce and institutional financial aid all but nonexistent. British and Irish students, along with those from the European Union, generally receive government funding. Federal aid such as Federal Direct Loans and Pell Grants can be transported, but many, if not most, families will find themselves paying the full freight. For a searchable database of the few scholarships available for study in Great Britain, visit the British Council at britishcouncil.us/studyuk. One reason that financially strapped British universities have recently begun showing a greater interest in recruiting U.S. students is that they are a source of much-needed revenue. By and large, the academic bars for U.S. students are slightly lower than for native Brits.

If you are considering a British university, you may be picturing yourself in England, the most populous region of Great Britain that includes London as well as fabled universities Oxford and Cambridge. But here's the rub: the English have a system of higher education that makes degree study impractical in many cases. In England, undergraduate degrees are completed in three years, not four, and students are generally assumed to have completed 13 years of schooling rather than 12. As a result, the most selective English universities are difficult for American high school graduates to gain admittance, and the students who do get in will find themselves navigating a world more appropriate for juniors and seniors in college. One note on terminology: in Britain and Ireland, a program of study is called a "course." The British word for what we call a course is "module."

The **University of Cambridge** (cam.ac.uk) typically requires a minimum of five Advanced Placement scores in AP classes in subjects related to the program applied for, along with a high SAT or ACT score. The **University of Oxford** (ox.ac.uk) similarly requires either four top AP scores or three top AP scores and very high SAT or ACT score. In the past three years, Oxford accepted just 6.5 percent of U.S. students out of the over 2,500 who applied, and Cambridge accepted even fewer. The odds of admission to Oxford are lower than at any college in the U.S., including Harvard. Most American undergraduates at both Oxford and Cambridge are there for a second bachelor's degree after earning one from an American institution. Students with their hearts set on the Oxbridge institutions should consider them for graduate school, where both welcome Americans (and their dollars) in significant numbers.

Students will hear a similar story at the third-most recognized name in English higher education, the **London School of Economics** (lse.ac.uk), which enrolls about 5,000 undergraduates. The LSE says it will not normally consider U.S. students until they have a year of higher education under their belts. Less selective English institutions are more receptive to Americans, but once again, only those who feel certain of what they would like to study should apply. If you are in this category, there is one potential benefit to an English degree: the three-year degree program will save you a year of tuition bills.

So what to do? One answer is to cast your gaze on Scotland, England's less populous neighbor, where universities offer four-year degrees that are much better suited to the needs of American high school graduates. Scotland, which lies north of England, was an independent nation until 1706 and has its own parliament that exercises considerable power when it comes to domestic policy. It has an illustrious intellectual history and has produced the likes of Robert Burns, Robert Lewis Stevenson, George Orwell, and Muriel Spark. Scotland is more egalitarian in feel than England—less hung up on social class.

The Scots take great pride in their universities, which are central to their national identity and have deep historical ties with American higher education. The American-style liberal arts institution was imported directly from Scotland in the person of John Witherspoon, a graduate of the University of Edinburgh who was lured to the U.S. in 1768 to head Princeton University. With the model of his alma mater in mind, Witherspoon transformed Princeton from a small-time school for ministers into a broad-based institution that taught philosophy, history, geography, science, mathematics, and theology. Like their U.S. counterparts, Scottish universities offer four-year programs; thus, they represent something of a middle ground between the American system and that of Oxford and Cambridge with their three-year, entirely specialized programs. Scottish universities expect early specialization, but there is some room to explore fields outside your major during the first two years. One downside of studying in Scotland is its northern location, which makes for long winter nights. Scotland has also been historically regarded as a "dreich" corner of Britain—a Highland term referring to weather variously described as dull, overcast, drizzly, cold, misty, and miserable, or a combination thereof. Scottish higher education is noted for its four "ancient" universities—Aberdeen, Edinburgh, Glasgow, and St Andrews—each of which is profiled in the pages that follow.

There are seven universities in Ireland, but Trinity College Dublin is by far the most distinguished, and it is the only one that operates on a four-year system for undergraduates. TCD was founded in 1592 by Queen Elizabeth I as an Irish counterpart to Oxford and Cambridge to train Anglican clergymen. While TCD follows the Scottish system, its cultural ties remain distinctly English, and graduates who subsequently enroll in Oxford or Cambridge are automatically entitled to an "ad eundem" courtesy degree from the English university. Roman Catholics make up the overwhelming majority of students despite the fact that up until 1972, they needed special permission from church authorities to attend this bastion of Anglican scholarship.

Students applying to UK institutions should generally use the Universities and Colleges Admissions Service (UCAS, ucas.com), which functions like the Common Application group in the U.S. The UCAS form asks you to list all your courses and the grades you received in them as well as your SAT and/or ACT scores. It also requires an essay and a letter of recommendation. Most institutions will accept applications through the spring, though we recommend that you apply by the deadline for British students, January 15. The deadline for applying to Oxford and Cambridge or to apply to any program in medicine is October 15 for entrance the following fall. Many institutions have rolling admissions, another reason to apply early. A few institutions—Aberdeen, Glasgow, and St Andrews—now accept the Common Application as an alternative for American students. Applicants to Trinity College Dublin apply directly to the university, which has rolling admissions.

A high proportion of U.S. students currently enrolled in British universities come from families with international connections, such as close relatives living in other countries or diplomat parents, but prior international experience is by no means required. College in Britain is not for the faint of heart, but it can be richly rewarding for those with the initiative to take the plunge. After college in Britain, students will have the skills and savvy to succeed almost anywhere in the world.

University of Aberdeen

King's College, Aberdeen, Scotland AB24 3FX

Located in Scotland's third largest city, Aberdeen is the most accessible—and least competitive—of the four "ancient" universities. Notable for the flexibility of its curriculum and emphasis on independent learning. Major attractions include engineering, life and health sciences, and anything related to Europe. City of Aberdeen combines charm with the bustle of a small city. Outdoor enthusiasts will love the Scottish Highlands.

Website: www.abdn.ac.uk
Location: Small City
Public
Total Enrollment: 15,000
Undergraduates: 12,000

The University of Aberdeen was founded in 1495, three years after a certain well-known explorer sailed from Spain to the New (to him) World. Students seeking the flavor of old Europe will not be disappointed. With plenty of cobblestone streets and buildings made of ancient stone (it's the Granite City), the university has a distinctly medieval aura. It offers top-notch academics, a curriculum that is unusually flexible by UK standards, and a slice of life far richer than any U.S. institution can muster. "It's great fun and has a lot of opportunities," says a senior, "both academically and socially."

With a population of 230,000, the port city of Aberdeen is Scotland's third largest city. Once a hub for fishing, shipbuilding, and textiles, it is now a center for the thriving oil extraction business in the North Sea. With two universities—the other is Robert Gordon—it is the educational capital of Northeastern Scotland. Aberdeen is perched at a latitude roughly the same as Juneau, Alaska, but because of the Gulf Stream, winter temperatures are generally milder than those on the East Coast of the United States. December days are short in winter, but sky-gazers are often treated to glimpses of the fabled northern lights.

Most university buildings are concentrated in a quiet enclave known as "Old Aberdeen." The campus is crowned, literally, by a 16th-century tower in the shape of an imperial crown. Lightly traveled streets pass through the campus, and the multitude of green lawns and picturesque courtyards are ideal for lounging on sunny days. The university has invested $450 million in infrastructure and facilities over the past decade, including the Sir Duncan Rice Library, the Sports Village, the Aquatics Centre, and a $47 million Science Teaching Hub.

Academics at Aberdeen are organized across 12 schools that encompass disciplines in the arts and social sciences, life sciences and medicine, physical sciences, and business. The relative broadness and flexibility of the university's curriculum are more in line with the academic systems of Harvard, Melbourne, Hong Kong, and other top universities around the world than they are with Aberdeen's three "ancient" counterparts in the UK. Students

"It's great fun and has a lot of opportunities, both academically and socially."

are expected to sample a series of interdisciplinary Sixth Century Courses, such as Humans and Other Animals or Sustainable International Development, during their first two years. Other curriculum innovations are designed to encourage students to pursue interests outside their core disciplines—what might be called "electives" in an American context. Popular majors include English literature, biology, religious studies, environmental science, and a joint international relations/politics concentration. Engineering is also strong, especially for programs related to the oil industry. The Centre for Learning and Teaching helps faculty members find ways to enhance the learning experience, while the Student Learning Service helps students develop their academic skills.

With approximately 15,000 undergraduate and graduate students, Aberdeen is a medium-sized university by U.S. standards. "The academic climate at Aberdeen is largely collaborative. We do a lot of group work, and student interaction is really key," says a business major. Courses in the first two years generally consist of lectures supplemented by smaller weekly discussion sections. "In my first year, I was taught by a mixture of Ph.D. students and lecturers (professors). In my honours years, my lecturers were leading experts in their fields and widely published," says a student. Professors typically team-teach introductory "modules," with each covering the topics that are their specialty. As in other Scottish universities, students generally take only three subjects at a time in the first two years, with extensive reading and research outside of class generally taken for granted. "Often we are expected to come to class prepared to discuss certain topics but given no minimum reading assignment. The professor gives out a list of selected readings from which we can choose," explains a history major. Grades are typically determined by end-of-the-term evaluations with few intermediate assignments. At the end of their second year, students must typically pass exams in order to advance to "honors level," the equivalent of the junior and senior years of college in the States. Upper-level science students typically spend long hours in the lab. One nice feature: there is generally no limit to the number of students who can enroll in a particular course, thereby giving students the freedom to sign up for anything that strikes their fancy.

Students are expected to sample a series of interdisciplinary Sixth Century Courses, such as Humans and Other Animals or Sustainable International Development, during their first two years.

Overall, 73 percent of undergraduates hail from the UK, 6 percent come from the EU, and 20 percent arrive from abroad, adding to a community of more than 130 different nationalities. "We have a very international student body," says one senior. The political climate on campus is described as conservative and relatively subdued. Upon their arrival at the university, students partake of Freshers Week, when student organizations sponsor informational meetings. Aberdeen is a selective institution for U.S. students, though less so than the other "ancient" universities.

On-campus housing at Aberdeen is varied and guaranteed to all first-year students who apply before the deadline. A majority of the international students live in single rooms in the recently refurbished Hillhead Student Village, a complex of houses and flats that is about a 20-minute walk from the campus. Students may elect catered rooms (two meals per day) or self-catering, wherein they cook their own food with kitchen facilities generally located down the hall from the rooms. Many students choose to move off campus after their first year, and a variety of housing options are available near the campus. Only a few students own cars, as the university is within easy walking distance of the city center and the North Sea and is on a regular bus route.

> **"Often we are expected to come to class prepared to discuss certain topics."**

"Social life is great," raves one student. "There's always something going on." Another adds, "We have around 200 societies and sports clubs, and most students are involved in at least one." Since the drinking age in Britain is 18, social life at Aberdeen entails relaxed, legal consumption. You may find yourself doing what Britons call "the pub crawl," which means sampling the refreshment of several pubs before heading home in the wee hours. Popular campus social events include periodic formal balls, to which the men wear kilts and the women wear evening gowns. Perhaps the biggest event of the year is the Torcher's Parade, which is held every spring and features floats made by various student organizations. Sports are mainly for playing, rather than watching, with more than 50 sports clubs at students' disposal. Individual sports rather than team intramurals are the staple of weekend warriors, and students can purchase passes for various athletic facilities, depending on their interests.

Aberdeen is described by one student as "a fantastic college town!" The city center offers a variety of pubs and clubs to suit all tastes, as well as inexpensive cinemas, music, and theater. The city has plenty of old-world charm, and outdoorsy types will love the dramatic scenery that is everywhere in northeast Scotland. Picturesque cliffs overlooking the North Sea are within an easy bus or train ride.

> **"We have around 200 societies and sports clubs."**

Within a half-hour ride inland is the edge of the legendary Scottish Highlands and atmospheric Dunecht House, a 19th-century granite mansion where director Guillermo del Toro filmed part of 2025's *Frankenstein*, starring Jacob Elordi and Oscar Isaac. Famous castles abound in all directions, including the royal family's summer hideaway, Balmoral. For the Scottish version of the big city, Glasgow and Edinburgh are close by, and two hours on a plane will get you to most places in Western Europe.

Though Aberdeen may lack some of the conveniences of home, most Americans are happy they came. "Between classes on a sunny day, students will buy something from the bakery and sit on the grass amid 500-year-old buildings and cobblestone streets. It is such a carefree atmosphere with that special touch of Scottish tradition," says a satisfied history major. If you're the kind of person who likes to meet new people and learn about different cultures, you might thrive on the Aberdeen air.

Overlaps

Dundee, University of Edinburgh, University of Glasgow, Harvard, University of St Andrews

If You Apply To ›

Aberdeen: Rolling admissions. Accepts the Common Application with supplement. Apply to particular program. Please consult Aberdeen's website for the most up-to-date information regarding standardized test requirements.

University of Edinburgh

Old College, South Bridge, Edinburgh, Scotland EH8 9YL

With close ties to the city that created it in the 16th century, Edinburgh is the most prestigious of Scotland's major research universities. Combines deep roots in Scottish culture and history with the cosmopolitan flavor and cultural riches of a sophisticated capital city. Competitive admissions for top British students but better odds for Americans with Ivy-level academic credentials. More diverse student body than St Andrews.

The largest and best-known of the "ancient" Scottish universities, the University of Edinburgh is part and parcel of Scotland's most vibrant urban center. The city of Edinburgh is home to the Scottish Parliament, the national museum, abundant historical sites, winding streets, and countless restaurants and pubs. The university, like the city, has an unmistakable international feel, including long-standing connections across the pond. In addition to the likes of Charles Darwin and J. M. Barrie, eminent graduates include two signatories of the U.S. Declaration of Independence, Benjamin Rush and John Witherspoon.

Edinburgh is unique among the major Scottish universities in that it was founded (in 1583) by a municipality rather than under religious auspices. Its buildings are spread throughout the city, which, despite having about 525,000 residents, is really an overgrown town. The two main campus areas are known as the Central Area, home to George Square, the main library, and humanities courses, and King's Buildings, housing science and engineering courses. Public transport is good, but just about everything is within walking distance. The older university buildings are Georgian and tend to bear names from the Scottish Enlightenment (David Hume and Dugald Stewart), while more modern ones date to the '60s and '70s. The recently expanded and renovated Health and Wellbeing Centre operates as a hub for student health, counseling, residential life, and other services.

The university is organized around three colleges: Arts, Humanities, and Social Sciences; Science and Engineering; and Medicine and Veterinary. Edinburgh has traditionally been strong in the sciences, and historical ties to economists like Adam Smith and philosophers like John Locke have contributed to strong programs in those fields. English literature, international relations, veterinary medicine, international business, and law attract a lot of U.S. students, and computer science, linguistics, sociology, and history (Scottish and otherwise) are strong. Unlike in the U.S., the programs in veterinary medicine and medicine are five- and six-year programs, respectively, for undergraduates. Veterinary graduates can go on to practice immediately in the U.S. Research opportunities are available for undergraduates, including summer placements in animal biology through the Roslin Institute. Edinburgh also offers some 200 study abroad programs at leading universities around the world.

Applicants apply to study a particular subject, such as physics or English literature, but unlike the situation in the leading English universities, it is possible to make changes once enrolled. There is no core curriculum, and no one has to endure a class on science or any other subject in which they have little interest. Students normally take three courses for each of their first two years in a variety of fields and then concentrate on one or two subjects the last two years. Most courses involve a combination of lectures, which are taught by full professors, and weekly tutorials, or groups of 10 to 20 students led by tutors. Professors and tutors alike get generally high ratings from students. One student notes, "The faculty is very international."

Coursework throughout the year mostly involves essays, with final exams in late April or May accounting for most of the final grade. In their final year, all undergraduates complete a research project or thesis. The academic system is built around self-study. "As an American student, I find the academics very rigorous in comparison to my friends' at American universities, because all the work is independent even from the beginning of your first year," explains an English literature major. The academic pressure at Edinburgh is said to be intense, with little grade inflation, and although faculty members do not view their role as seeking out students who may need help, "professors and tutors are more than happy to help out when you ask," says one American denizen.

Edinburgh is the leading destination for top-performing Scottish students, who face tighter admissions standards than North Americans. Thirty-two percent of undergraduates hail from Scotland, 29 percent from elsewhere in the United Kingdom, 6 percent from the European Union, and the rest from other foreign countries. There are roughly 1,800 regular American undergrads and 900 postgrads. Edinburgh students tend to be more middle class than their counterparts at St Andrews, which is more upper class. Edinburgh is slightly more expensive than the other "ancient" Scottish universities but a bargain compared to the Ivies in the U.S. The university makes scholarships available to international students, and American students can use their U.S. student loans to attend. Given the nature of the student body, there is plenty of discussion of global issues. "Scotland is inherently left-leaning as a country," reports a language student, and recent student activism has focused on diversity, inclusion, and climate action.

About 20 percent of undergraduates live in university housing, and Edinburgh guarantees housing to all international first-year students. Many American and international students live in Pollock Halls, a collection of houses with mostly single rooms that are centered around a common cafeteria. Accommodations at Pollack are catered, meaning that residents get 14 meals per week in the cafeteria—breakfast and dinner during the week and brunch on the weekends. Students can also choose self-catered options in which they make their own cooking arrangements. Self-catered flats (apartments) generally consist of three to five students, each with an individual room, sharing a large common living and kitchen area. All university accommodations are described as clean and well maintained. Most students move off campus after their first year; the Student Union Advice Place will help you find a flat. "Edinburgh is a very competitive city when it comes to flat pricing," cautions a second-year American student, "and sometimes the cost of living for international students can be expensive." Cafeteria food is described as "fine but not that diverse," although several cheap cafés nearby offer alternatives. Students report that both the university and the city are safe: "Edinburgh has always made me feel secure," says one.

Since the university is so closely tied to the city, it's no surprise that social life takes place both on and off campus. "First-years tend to explore club life in the city center," explains an American student, "and as they get into their second and third years, the partying transfers homeward into flat parties." Two student unions, Teviot and Potterrow, offer cafés, coffee shops, and bars; on weekend nights, a large, open study area in Potterrow is converted into a nightclub for dancing. Frequent comedy nights, student productions, and pub crawls are other options. Since the drinking age is 18, the university has no school policy on the serving of alcohol. The city of Edinburgh offers its own menu of ancient and contemporary traditions. The Beltane Fire Festival, with roots in pagan times, celebrates the arrival of spring, and every

August, the city is host to the huge Fringe Festival, which draws artists and spectators from all over the world. Thanks to affordable trains and low-cost airlines like Ryanair and easyJet, trips throughout Britain and all over Europe are easy to arrange. "You get good at traveling," says one American undergrad.

The Edinburgh University Student Association and the Edinburgh University Sports Union combine to offer what one American describes as "just about every sport, charity, or special interest society/club conceivable." A fair is held during Welcome Week to give first-year students a sense of the options. Does the Chocolate Lovers Society sound tasty? Edinburgh's sports clubs, which compete against other Scottish and European universities in sports like rugby, soccer, and rowing, do well, but compared to varsity sports in the U.S., one student says, "the competition is laid-back." Most attention goes to the "very strong and popular intramural sports program, which, depending on the sport, has quite a high caliber of play." Many of the teams are co-ed, and there are eight levels of rugby. The Centre for Sport and Exercise boasts sports equipment, studios, weight rooms, a climbing wall, and archery ranges. In all, Edinburgh hosts more than 290 societies and more than 60 sports clubs.

Much of the fun of going to college in Scotland comes from taking part in centuries-old traditions, of which Edinburgh has an abundance. Various societies and degree programs sponsor weekly or monthly ceilidhs (pronounced "kaylees") or traditional Scottish Dance Nights. Robert Burns Night is a big deal, as is Guy Fawkes Night on November 5, when students set off fireworks **"Scotland is inherently left-leaning as a country."** throughout the city. Whereas American commencements feature students moving the tassel of their mortarboards from one side to the other, Edinburgh places a common cap on the head of each student in turn that contains a piece of the trousers of John Knox and a NASA emblem that accompanied an Edinburgh graduate on a space mission.

American students, especially those who are self-motivated, tend to do well at Edinburgh. "They are smart and well-traveled and tend to be independent thinkers," observes a faculty member. A philosophy and English literature major comments, "The university's culture is progressive, engaged, academic, and open." Another American transplant hails the fact that Edinburgh is "incredibly international but still Scottish," adding that "the bagpipes playing in the city streets, the ethereal castle, and the wee pubs constantly remind me where I am."

If You Apply To ›

Edinburgh: Rolling admissions for most programs. Does not accept the Common Application. Apply to particular program. Please consult Edinburgh's website for the most up-to-date information regarding standardized test requirements.

University of Glasgow

University Avenue, Glasgow, Scotland G12 8QQ

A major urban research university located in the bohemian section of a friendly and lively city. U of Glasgow is slightly smaller than U of Edinburgh and its atmosphere somewhat more laid-back. The West End is student-friendly, with lots of cafés and shops. Glasgow is a financial, cultural, and shopping center also known for its nightlife. Locals claim, "You can have more fun at a Glasgow funeral than at an Edinburgh wedding." Glasgow students get the point.

There are plenty of ceilidhs (pronounced "kaylees") or Gaelic social gatherings.

The second oldest of Scotland's major universities (after St Andrews), the University of Glasgow shares the history and culture of Scotland's largest city. Glasgow (population 650,000) was a major center of the 18th-century Scottish Enlightenment and the 19th-century Industrial Revolution, and it now ranks as Britain's largest financial center after London. The University of Glasgow was founded in 1451 with quarters in Glasgow Cathedral before moving to its own main campus in Gilmorehill in the city's West End in 1870. In contrast to the elitist traditions of the other "ancient" British universities, Glasgow pioneered in serving the educational needs of the growing urban and commercial classes and in 1894 became the first Scottish university to grant degrees to women. It's also "actively working toward becoming carbon neutral by 2030," say administrators.

Not surprisingly for a place with more than five centuries of history, the dominant architectural style on campus is brownish neo-Gothic, with a healthy mix of Victorian thrown in. The West End in Glasgow is a bohemian residential area with an abundance of restaurants, cafés, and shops catering to the college crowd. "The area is very student-oriented, with plenty of venues offering student discounts," reports one student. The city center, a 15-minute walk from the university, offers a multitude of historical sites and world-class museums as well as the best shopping in the UK outside London. Kelvingrove Park and the Botanical Gardens are down the street from the university's main gate. Through an ongoing $1.75 billion development plan, the university will double the 15-acre campus footprint by 2026. The university has already opened four state-of-the-art academic buildings: the JMS Learning Hub, the Advanced Research Centre, a new center for the School of Health and Wellbeing, and the Adam Smith Building for business students, with the new Keystone Building for engineering students underway.

"There is an air of camaraderie between students."

Students describe the academic climate as balanced and supportive. "There is an air of camaraderie between students," comments an archaeology major. "Some courses are more competitive than others, but overall it's not nearly as intense as I perceive some U.S. schools to be." The workload is said to increase noticeably in later years, but because students apply to study in a particular field, they "rarely find themselves in courses they would prefer to avoid," says a student. All undergraduates must participate in some level of research during their final two years. "The university loves to fund research or projects that will help it gain a spotlight, so never be afraid to apply for a scholarship if you have an ambitious idea!" urges a senior. First-year students enjoy a Fresher's Week, with headline musical acts, themed club nights, and sporting showcases, and a special orientation is also provided for international students.

Glasgow is the only Scottish university with the full range of both professional and academic offerings. The university is divided into four colleges: Arts; Social Sciences; Science and Engineering; and Medical, Veterinary, & Life Sciences. Befitting the alma mater of physicist Lord Kelvin (of absolute temperature fame), the sciences are strong, notably veterinary medicine, nursing, and geography. The economics department is proud that it turned out 18th-century economic philosopher Adam Smith. English language and literature is a traditional strength, and Glasgow maintains the only department of Scottish literature anywhere. Other popular programs include aeronautical engineering, data science and artificial intelligence, global security, and product design engineering. A newly launched liberal arts program offers a customizable, interdisciplinary curriculum that encourages critical thinking across humanities, social sciences, and natural sciences. Eastern European languages like Czech and Polish are specialties. Newer programs include international relations and an undergraduate degree in common law for students who intend to practice law outside Scotland. About half of the full-time U.S. undergraduates major in veterinary medicine; a five-year undergraduate degree is accredited by the Veterinary Medical Association.

Students describe faculty members as respected and knowledgeable. "Many professors practice in their fields daily, so they teach us not only the theory but also the practical application," explains a veterinary medicine major. Lectures are offered by full professors, and tutorials of about 15 students are occasionally handled by graduate students. Eighty percent of Glasgow undergraduates take advantage of semester-long or yearlong study abroad programs, especially through the Erasmus program, which allows students to take courses at European universities. A year of study abroad is mandatory for foreign language students during their third year. "The visa services in the Fraser building are useful as an international student," recommends a computing science student.

According to a sociology major, Glasgow students are "hip, hardworking, welcoming, and fun-loving." Consistent with the university's cosmopolitan setting and traditions, the student body is diverse with regard to nationality, race, religion, and socioeconomic backgrounds, and administrators report the university has launched a Reparative Justice program in partnership with the University of the West Indies. Twenty-two per-

cent of undergraduates are international, hailing from the U.S., India, China, the European Union, and dozens of other countries; 63 percent are native to Scotland, and the balance come from elsewhere in the UK. Support services for international students are strong. "You don't have an exclusive student body," reports a sophomore. "Dealing and working with people from different backgrounds is the norm." The university offers a range of merit-based scholarships and financial support schemes to make study more affordable and accessible for international students, including those from the U.S., and it also accepts U.S. federal loans, as determined by the FAFSA.

First-years usually live in university housing, which is not on campus but spread throughout the northwest sections of the city, and then move into readily available independent housing in later years. Overall, 85 percent of undergraduates live in college-owned housing. The residence halls are generally comfortable and well maintained; international students are guaranteed housing. As for dining, only one of the residence halls offers catered food, and it is located away from the main campus. The others are self-catered, which means that students cook for themselves (and save money) or savor the offerings of dining facilities sprinkled throughout the campus. "The on-campus dining is very good, and they have a range of foods from Indian to Scottish on various days," reports one denizen. Students describe campus security as good. "I always feel safe on campus," says an archaeology major. The Students' Representative Council (SRC) organizes various campaigns to educate the community on issues of sexual assault, gender equality, mental health, LGBTQ+ issues, and many other student concerns. The SRC also sponsors an annual

Raising and Giving week to aid volunteer organizations and raise awareness of volunteer opportunities. Social activism tends to be most vigorous when the issue involves cuts to the university budget and increases in tuition levels, although the war in Gaza has sparked protests, say students.

Social life is equally divided between on- and off-campus activities. Glasgow offers an abundance of quality restaurants, clubs, and pubs. There are plenty of ceilidhs (pronounced "kaylees") or Gaelic social gatherings, and the city sponsors an International Comedy Festival each March. Glasgow has a vigorous music scene that hosts an average of 130 music events every week. Much of the on-campus social life revolves around the two student-run university unions, the Glasgow University Union (GUU) and the Queen Margaret Union (QMU), which host student organizations, provide dining and social activities, and, of course, have their own bars. Since most students are above the drinking age of 18, underage imbibing is a nonissue. GUU favors sports, debates, and formal dances, while QMU is big on live music. With a name meaning "Dear Green Place" in Gaelic, Glasgow has over 90 parks and gardens to explore, with many housing some of the city's top attractions. Travel is a major attraction of studying in Scotland. "It's easy to get to visit Europe while studying in Glasgow with cheap flights and accommodations," reports one student. Loch Lomond, a 45-minute drive, offers watersports, hiking, and camping.

Intercollegiate debating is taken seriously, and the university has won the world championship several times. Glasgow is synonymous with sport. It was the European Capital of Sport in 2023, becoming the first city to take the title twice, and the city is hosting the 2026 Commonwealth Games. A majority of students belong to the Glasgow University Sports Association, and more than 4,000 students play in over 50 sports clubs. Competitive team sports include field hockey, rugby, soccer, basketball, American football, cricket, and many others, and recreational clubs are available for everything from cycling to skydiving to surfing.

Undergrads describe their experience living and studying in the West End of Glasgow as rewarding. One film/TV and theater studies major sums up her experience as follows: "The University of Glasgow is a rich and lighthearted university with a brilliant campus, hosting a rich and diverse student life." For students considering the school, she predicts, "These four years will be the best of your life!"

Overlaps

University of Aberdeen, Boston University, University of Edinburgh, King's College London, University of Liverpool, University of Manchester, NYU, University of St Andrews

If You Apply To ›

Glasgow: Rolling admissions. Accepts the Common Application with supplement. SATs or ACTs: optional, but please consult Glasgow's website for the most up-to-date information and other requirements.

University of St Andrews

College Gate, St Andrews, Scotland KY16 9AJ

The most international of Scotland's four "ancient" universities and one of the most popular overseas degree destinations in the world for U.S. students. Small by British standards and comparable in feel and stature to Brown. Major drawing cards range across English literature, international relations, history, the sciences, and modern languages. St Andrews is inseparable from the town, which boasts the famed "Old Course." With more than 600 years to gestate, traditions reign supreme.

Website: www.st-andrews.ac.uk
Location: Small Town
Public
Total Enrollment: 10,175
Undergraduates: 8,371
Male/Female: 38/62
Financial Aid: N/A

Harvard likes to brag about the fact that it was founded way back in 1636. Think that's old? Try 1413, the date Pope Benedict XIII issued a Papal Bull recognizing the University of St Andrews as Scotland's first university and the third in the English-speaking world. Set in a small ancient town on the North Sea opposite Norway, St Andrews is an ideal spot for adventuresome Americans who want a world-class education and an introduction to life outside North America. It now numbers roughly 1,600 Americans (19 percent of the student body). Success here requires a go-getter mentality. Support services are available, but students on this side of the Atlantic are accustomed to being treated like adults. "They don't hold your hand," says one U.S.

student, but another adds, "The university has such a long history and so many traditions that you really get a sense of community and continuity as soon as you arrive."

St Andrews is the only institution in the *Fiske Guide* whose most prominent landmark is the spot where a student was burned at the stake. In 1528, Protestant reformer Patrick Hamilton fell victim to the local archbishop. Tradition deems that if you step on the stones that mark that spot, you will fail your final exams, unless you submerge yourself in the North Sea just before dawn the first day of May as part of a tradition called the May Dip. Academic buildings are interspersed through the town's narrow medieval streets, and for all practical purposes, says one student, "The university is the town." Buildings are constructed of ancient stone and include the ruins of a 13th-century castle and a cathedral. Narrow alleys lead to secluded gardens and courtyards that add to the old-world charm. A number of academic buildings are perched on cliffs overlooking the North Sea, and white beaches are a two-minute walk from some of the dorms.

Though more flexible than most British universities, St Andrews is nevertheless best suited to those who arrive with clear academic goals in mind. "There are no general education requirements at St Andrews," say administrators. Instead, first-year students choose a specialty, and students typically take three courses, or "modules," per semester in each of their first two years and then opt for a single or double honors program in the final two years. (The course structure and/or number of class hours varies for students in the sciences, medicine, and arts and divinity.) "Year one entrants can change their chosen specialism at the end of year one if they have a change of heart," notes one student. First-year modules generally consist of three lectures per week with 100 or more students and a tutorial with 10 to 20, while honors-level (third- and fourth-year) courses are generally taught in seminar format. All undergraduate students complete an extended project or dissertation containing original research during their final two years. Fewer courses means less time in class but also significant outside reading and individual work. Modules typically end with papers or exams that account for most of the grade.

> **"You really get a sense of community and continuity as soon as you arrive."**

"The university is very competitive to get into, so this makes for an environment that is studious and academically driven," describes a management major. More so than in the United States, the onus is on the students to keep current with their rigorous workload. Nevertheless, the faculty gets high marks. "The lecturers expect a lot from their students," says an English and German major. Still, a physics major praises the amount of "contact hours" students have with professors, as classes "range from large, full class lectures to medium-sized workshops (working through questions with a third of the class) to the small tutorials, so there's always room to explore your understanding." Academic and personal support is available from Student Services, wardens (RAs) in the residence halls, and ramped-up career services that one student characterizes as "brilliant." Says a sophomore, "Roughly 60 percent of St Andrews students take part in some form of work experience or internship before the end of their time here."

Signature offerings at St Andrews include international relations, classics, art history, geography, economics, and physics. Psychology (especially neuroscience), English literature, history, and modern languages are strong, and the university is a world leader in the study of international terrorism. The most popular majors include medicine, international relations, psychology, and economics. Standards in foreign language are higher than in the United States, an opportunity but also a challenge. There are over 900 different degree combinations available. For example, a joint degree in Chinese studies allows students to study Chinese culture and language in combination with a second major in one of 14 fields, ranging from modern history to film studies. Students in the International Honours joint-degree program

(continued)

Pell Grant: N/A
Expense: Pub $ $ $ $
Student Loans: N/A
Average Debt: N/A
Applicants: 21,154
Accepted: 18%
Enrolled: 64%
Grad in 6 Years: 88%
Returning First-years: 99%
Academics: ✐ ✐ ✐ ✐
Social: 🗩 🗩 🗩
Q of L: ★ ★ ★
Admissions: (+44) 133 446 2150
Email Address: admissions@st-andrews.ac.uk

Strong Programs:
Art History
Classics
Economics
English Literature
Geography
International Relations
Physics
Psychology

Students in the International Honours joint-degree program spend two years at William & Mary in Virginia.

spend two years at William & Mary in Virginia and two years at St Andrews and earn degrees from both institutions. Faculty-mentored research opportunities are also on offer, and students praise the two-year Laidlaw Research and Leadership Scholarship for presenting internship and travel opportunities. Over 8 percent of undergraduates study abroad during their time at St Andrews.

St Andrews students are "diverse, multicultural, open, and friendly," says a mathematics major. St Andrews is one of the world's most international universities, with roughly a third of its students from Scotland, a quarter from other parts of the UK, and 42 percent from the rest of the world, including sizable contingents from Scandinavia, Eastern Europe, Asia, the Middle East, and, of course, the U.S. In fact, Americans represent the largest international group and are typically given a warm welcome, students say. Two percent of students are Black, 14 percent are Asian, and 7 percent are multiracial. Still, says a junior, "There is a pretty high population of wealthy, English private or boarding school graduates"—remember, Prince William and Catherine, Princess of Wales, met there—which lends a more conservative tenor to the campus than some Americans might expect. "St Andrews feels preppy but inclusive," muses an American third-year student, "and the endless string of social events tends to include things like formal balls, sailing races, and charity polo matches."

> **"[The environment] is studious and academically driven."**

While it is competitive for European students, who must be in the top 10th academically, it is more accessible for U.S. students who have the brains to make it into the Ivies but can't also throw a football or play a Liszt concerto. Tuition fees increase year-on-year inline with inflation, and the total cost of attendance is likely to be around $66,000 per year, with tuition currently around $42,000 for the liberal arts, while the medicine specialty runs around $50,000. Eligible U.S. students may be able to apply for Federal financial aid.

All undergraduate students complete an extended project or dissertation containing original research.

Housing is guaranteed for first-year students only, and students can request a single or shared room. After that, students generally move to one of the many flats (apartments) in town, which "can be tricky," says a senior. "Rent is expensive compared to nearby towns," which is a common student complaint that "the university is actively working to address," adds a junior. Forty-two percent of students reside in university housing, and those who do choose between the university meal plan or self-catering, in which they use kitchens in the dorms to prepare their own food. Catered and shared-bathroom halls are the most central and ancient, and students give the food generally positive reviews. Meals are served at specified times with standard portions, so don't expect the glitzy food courts or all-you-can-eat service typical in the States.

Given the symbiosis of town and gown, gathering with friends in local pubs is a favorite activity on weekends. "The university has its own club in the Student Union, which hosts themed nights as well as the monthly sports night," says an international relations major. The drinking age is 18 in Britain, and alcohol is certainly more out in the open than on American campuses. Black-tie balls and fashion shows are also staples, as are ceilidhs (pronounced "kaylees"), which feature traditional Scottish dancing akin to square dancing.

> **"[Students are] diverse, multicultural, open, and friendly."**

Like other Scottish universities, St Andrews offers "a society for everything you can think of," says a student. Interested in philosophical debate? A cappella singing? Belly dancing? Harry Potter? Stargazing from the university observatory? Then there's a society just waiting for you. The St Andrews debating society was founded in 1793 and continues to do well in international competitions. Political activism is muted, but the annual Charities Campaign raises roughly £80,000 a year for local charities.

As befitting a 600-year-old institution, St Andrews is rife with traditions. Red gowns, once the student uniform, are still worn on special occasions, but pubs remain forbidden to serve anyone wearing one. The aforementioned May Dip, aimed at purging oneself of academic bad luck, has roots in pagan times. One student explains that during Raisin Weekend in October, "Academic parents [third- and fourth-year students who 'marry' and adopt first-years] will dress their children up in funny costumes and send them on a scavenger hunt around town, doing silly, slightly embarrassing tasks." Students emerging from their last exam are greeted by their friends and doused with buckets of cold water.

"Every student I have ever talked to has shared their love for our lovely little university town above all else," shares a student. "[The] historical buildings and events, its traditions and beaches make the town a buzzing place to be despite being so little." The nearest road-trip destination is the medium-sized city of Dundee, about 20 minutes away, which offers shops, nightclubs, and movie theaters. "The public transport links in town are really good for students to get around and visit different places in Scotland," notes an English major. Scotland's two largest cities, Edinburgh and Glasgow, are about an hour away, and for outdoorsy types, the legendary Scottish Highlands are within easy reach. The Student Association helps with overseas travel.

Soccer, a.k.a. football, is the national sport, and students congregate to watch pro teams in the pubs or on the big-screen TV at the union. Women's field hockey, men's rugby, men's and women's soccer, golf, and water polo are among the school's most competitive sports teams, although these draw fewer spectators than do varsity sports in the U.S. Students tend to be much more enthusiastic about their "hall sport" competitions (the equivalent of intramurals in the U.S.), in sports ranging from rugby and ultimate Frisbee to shinty, a violent Scottish mix of field hockey and lacrosse. The fabled Old Course, where golf was invented in the 1500s, offers student discounts, but the sport is not as popular among students here as one might assume.

"St Andrews is a modern institution set in a medieval past," comments an ancient history major. "Students still embrace their gowns, walk the cathedral, and hang out on the beach below the castle." Although St Andrews comes the closest of any of the Scottish universities to having the feel of a liberal arts college, this is not the United States. Those who come here must be ready to adjust to a different way of life, and the tight identification of the university and the town can eventually make for a bit of claustrophobia. But these are small prices to pay for the richness of living abroad among the best and brightest from all corners of the globe. "The university's motto 'Ever to Excel' describes the institutional personality quite well," affirms a student. And with its hauntingly beautiful backdrop, says a zoology major, "You may only live here for a couple of years, but St Andrews will always be a home to you."

Overlaps

Boston University, Brown, Durham University, Georgetown, Trinity College Dublin, University College London, University of Edinburgh, University of Glasgow

If You Apply To ›

St Andrews: Rolling admissions. SATs or ACTs: optional. Accepts the Common Application with supplement.

Trinity College Dublin

College Green, Dublin 2, Ireland

The oldest four-year university in Ireland, Trinity College Dublin belongs to a peer group consisting of Oxbridge and the four "ancient" Scottish universities—albeit with a more European feel. Trinity combines rich academic offerings across the curriculum with life in one of the world's most vibrant capital cities. Traditions abound, academic and otherwise. Where else do honors students get the right to graze their sheep on the college green?

Website: www.tcd.ie
Location: City Center
Public
Total Enrollment: 18,852
Undergraduates: 14,095
Male/Female: 38/62
Financial Aid: N/A
Pell Grant: N/A
Expense: Pub $ $ $ $
Student Loans: N/A
Average Debt: N/A
Applicants: 20,061
Accepted: 34%
Enrolled: 74%
Grad in 6 Years: 95%
Returning First-years: 94%
Academics: ✍ ✍ ✍ ✍ ✍
Social: 🗩 🗩 🗩 🗩
Q of L: ★ ★ ★ ★
Admissions: (+353) 1 896 4500
Email Address: academic.registry@tcd.ie

Strong Programs:
Biological and Biomedical Sciences
Classics and Ancient History
English
European Studies
Global Business
History
Law
Political Science

Trinity participates in the U.S. federal student loan program and offers a number of scholarships, including one for U.S. students.

Founded in 1592 by Queen Elizabeth as an Irish Protestant counterpart to Oxford and Cambridge, Trinity College, the University of Dublin, is the largest and most distinguished of the seven universities in Ireland and one of the strongest anywhere. TCD was founded as the University of Dublin with the expectation that it would serve as "the mother of a university" and other colleges would grow up around it à la Cambridge and Oxford. Alas, this never happened, so for all practical purposes, Trinity College Dublin is the University of Dublin. Although best known for its offerings in the humanities and social sciences, Trinity is strong across the curriculum, including in new specialties such as nanoscience. The university has produced enough distinguished alumni to fill an encyclopedia (Jonathan Swift, Oscar Wilde, Samuel Beckett, Mary Robinson, and Sally Rooney for starters), and its students bathe in centuries-old academic traditions while enjoying life in one of Europe's most vibrant capital cities.

Trinity College Dublin occupies a 47-acre oasis in the heart of Dublin, within easy walking distance of the national museums, government buildings, and other major cultural attractions. "When you pass under the archway, you move from the bustle of the city to a traditional liberal arts setting, complete with rugby and cricket pitches,"

> **"[Dublin is] a compact and friendly city with lots to do."**

explains a sophomore. Most of the central buildings are built of light gray Georgian stone, including its iconic Campanile. The college's Old Library, with its oak-ceilinged Long Room, is home to the Book of Kells, an illuminated Latin manuscript of the Gospels that draws a steady stream of tourists onto the campus. The library, which has been in constant use since 1732, closed in fall 2023 for a three-year, $95 million restoration. Another library bears the name of James Ussher, the university's first student, who went on to make a name for himself by devising a Biblically based calculation that the world started at 6 p.m. on October 22, 4004 BC. A student describes Dublin as "a compact and friendly city with lots to do," while a first-year cautions, "Let's not go overboard. There is also a lot of rain."

Trinity is organized around three schools in each of the traditional areas: arts, humanities, and social sciences; engineering, math, and science; and health sciences. Unlike other universities in Ireland, Trinity offers a four-year undergraduate program parallel to the four "ancient" universities in Scotland. There are no "core" courses, but all students must complete an undergraduate research project in their final year. The college has traditionally been best known for its English and literature courses, along with history, political science, European studies, and international studies. Mathematics and the sciences are also strong, especially molecular biology, genetics, immunology, nanoscience, and chemistry. The Trinity Biomedical Sciences Institute is a state-of-the-art research facility, while the Trinity Long Room Hub accommodates research in the arts and humanities. The BESS program (Business, Economics, and Social Studies) and business, economics, philosophy, biology, and engineering are popular majors. Trinity has a strong interdisciplinary culture, and the Trinity Elective option encourages students to exercise their curiosity in a module (course) outside their specialty, such as film studies or globalization.

"The academic culture is rigorous with everyone in the library oftentimes," says a philosophy, political science, economics, and sociology major. The academic year runs for 11 weeks each in the fall and spring, followed by three to four weeks of exams. Students accumulate 60 credits per year through modules offering various numbers of credits, with strong weight given to final exams, although the balance of continuous and final assessment varies by module. A final-year capstone project brings 20 credits. "Academically, Trinity expects students to be self-motivated," says a law major. Lectures coupled with weekly tutorials are common the first two years but then give way to small seminars the last two years. An English major observes,

"There are regular continuous assessments, labs, tutorials, etc., to help students to learn. And lecturers are generally friendly and willing to answer questions students have." Each entering student is assigned a peer mentor and a personal academic tutor, not one of his or her professors, who will be available for personal, academic, and professional advice and, if necessary, become an advocate. "The SLD (Student Learning and Development) programme by TCD Library is extremely useful to get a handle on the academic structure," offers a global business major. American students can also sign up for the weeklong Trinity Smart-Start Program to help them get the hang of the university and its setting.

Trinity students are encouraged to take advantage of the nearly 300 foreign study options, including those with leading institutions in Australia, Canada, India, China, and Singapore; 30 percent take part. Trinity participates in the Erasmus Program with other European universities and has special relationships in the U.S. with such prestigious institutions as Brown, Chicago, and a dual B.A. program with Columbia. Dublin serves as the European headquarters for several major companies, such as Google, Airbnb, Microsoft, and Meta, which frequently recruit students for internships, summer jobs, and postgraduation careers.

As the top university in Ireland, Trinity is competitive academically. "My fellow students are highly motivated and very smart people," says a senior. "Moreover, the socioeconomic makeup of the college is very diverse." Thirty-four percent of undergraduates are international students from more than 120 nations, with the U.S. and Canada making up the largest group. Many U.S. students hail from elite public high schools and prep schools and have traveled abroad. Trinity is an ideal option for top students who are strong enough academically to qualify for Ivy League schools but who neglected to star on the soccer team or do community service in Bujumbura.

Trinity participates in the U.S. federal student loan program and offers a number of scholarships, including one for U.S. students. All students can try their luck in a series of competitive tests that sophomores can take just after Christmas known as the Foundation Scholarship Exams. More than 400 students typically sit for the exams, with about 90 becoming either "scholars" or "foundation scholars." Scholars become members of the university's governing board. Other benefits include five years of free or heavily discounted tuition, free accommodations and evening meals, and, best of all, the rumor goes, the privileges of carrying a sword into an exam and grazing their sheep on the campus green.

One drawback of Trinity's self-contained campus is the limited space for housing—only 33 percent of undergrads reside in university-owned facilities. Most first-year students live in Trinity Hall, a modern apartment building about 20 minutes away by bus. After that, preference for on-campus rooms goes to students in their final year. "There are, however, an abundance of private student housing/dorm companies in the city that cater to students from any institution," notes a junior. Strong public transportation makes access to affordable accommodations feasible, and the college's Global Room stands ready to help out. Given that residences include communal kitchens, Trinity offers no university-wide meal plan, "so students tend to be pretty self-sufficient when it comes to food," says an English major. Some head to the two main restaurants or smaller cafés on campus, which provide simple meals. And as a senior points out, given the school's prime location, "Trinity students are spoiled for choice in terms of eating establishments extremely close to the university." Despite its urban setting, the campus is said to be safe, and an engineering major comments, "Trinity has started to introduce sexual consent workshops to incoming students." As for mental health, financial, and housing student support services, a law major calls them "wonderful," adding, "There is also an

"Academically, Trinity expects students to be self-motivated."

entrepreneurial support service called Tangent that provides advisory services from industry professionals to current students who are creating business startups."

Extracurricular activities may not help you get into Trinity, but they play an important role in campus culture once you get there. "With over 120 societies, covering [academic] subjects, cultural, sports, and social interests, there is something to do for pretty much everyone," explains a law major. The most famous groups are the Philosophical Society ("the Phil"), which is the oldest debating club in the English-speaking world (1684), and its rival, the Historical Society ("the Hist"). The two clubs share a building, sponsor weekly public debates, and award medals to notable visiting speakers. The Metaphysical Society ("the Metafizz") also gives students a chance to show off how much they know about Plato or Bertrand Russell. The Student Union is active in campaigning for a variety of political and social causes; the strife in the Middle East has been a hot topic recently.

Social life takes place both on and off campus. Student societies are mandated to throw events once a month, so there is plenty to choose from every day of the week. The drinking age is 18, and most students attend "Pav Fridays," where the lively on-campus Pavilion Bar offers cheap beer and cider. Later in the evening, socializing usually spills out into the surrounding city and its vibrant music and cultural scene. As a senior puts it, "All of Dublin's nightclubs, bars, and pubs are pretty much a stone's throw away." (Where else can you go pub crawling in the footsteps of Bram Stoker, of *Dracula* fame, and James Joyce?) St. Patrick's Day is always a time to celebrate, but unquestionably the biggest event is Trinity Week. It starts on a Monday in the spring, when the new scholars are announced, given black robes, and invited to take on current scholars in a game of marbles on the steps of the chapel. Festivities culminate on Friday with the Trinity Ball, "an annual, black-tie mini–music festival that's organized by the Trinity Student Union," says a graduate student. "It's incredibly popular and tickets for it sell out immediately every year." Trinity is ideally located for travel to European and other destinations. "There are cheap buses from Dublin to any corner of Ireland," reports a senior. "It is also possible to fly to continental Europe or the UK for well under 50 euros."

> **"The Student Learning and Development programme is extremely useful to get a handle on the academic structure."**

Sports here are for playing, not watching, at the local, national, or intercollegiate level. Says a history major, "There is no school mascot or particular set of colors that students wear. People tend to do sport mainly as an extracurricular activity. It's not really a status symbol." Nevertheless, there are at least 50 club and intramural sports; men's rugby and women's field hockey are the most competitive club teams. Although the English invented rugby, students at Trinity started the first club, and the boat (rowing) club is also one of the oldest. The university does hire coaches for some intercollegiate sports, such as rugby and soccer, and team leaders are eligible for scholarships. The annual dodgeball tournament is also a highlight.

Trinity College Dublin combines strong academics with the benefits of a beautiful campus in the midst of a thriving capital city that is also a gateway to the rest of Europe. "You get a top-tier degree that costs less than most private colleges in the U.S. and gives you the international experience of a lifetime," comments one American denizen. "And I met the nicest, most interesting, and hilarious people—the Irish."

Overlaps

Brown, University of Cambridge, Columbia, University of Edinburgh, Imperial College London, NYU, University of Oxford, University of St Andrews

If You Apply To ›

Trinity: Rolling admissions. Does not accept the Common Application. Please consult Trinity's website for the most up-to-date information regarding standardized test requirements.

International Universities That Offer Full-Time Options in English for American Students

Some of you may be interested in broadening your search for international university options with English as the language of instruction but beyond English-speaking countries like Canada, the United Kingdom, and Ireland. To help you out, starting with this edition, the *Fiske Guide* has added descriptions of a few colleges and universities in continental Europe and Asia that you may want to consider. The schools included here enjoy strong academic reputations and offer instruction *in English*. Our goal is not to provide a comprehensive inventory of every international option (look for coverage of Australian institutions in a future edition of the *Guide*) but rather a curated starting point.

Pursuing a degree abroad can be an exciting and life-changing experience, but students and college counselors considering this option should understand the difference between the American university model and those of many international higher-education systems. U.S. colleges typically emphasize breadth, exploration, flexibility in choosing—or changing—majors, along with a set of general education requirements. By contrast, many international universities expect students to apply directly into a specific field of study from the outset, much like many of the UK schools presented in the previous section. In these systems, students tend to specialize earlier and follow a more prescribed academic path. Independence is often assumed, and administrative "hand-holding" is kept to a minimum.

Another key difference is time. Many undergraduate degrees abroad are designed to be completed in three years rather than four. In some European systems, American students who have not completed sufficient AP or equivalent coursework may be required to spend an additional "foundation" year taking preparatory courses to meet academic prerequisites. (International universities frequently offer these foundation programs, and some may be completed online.) Understanding these structural differences is essential before applying to an international school.

Broadly speaking, the international institutions included in this list fall into two categories. The first consists of English-language four-year programs at universities located outside of the United States. Schools such as the American University of Paris in France, University College Freiburg in Germany, and IE University in Spain operate on a familiar four-year bachelor's-degree model with some general education requirements and academic flexibility similar to that found at U.S. universities.

The second category includes three-year, European-style programs at international universities, where—for the most part—students apply directly into a specific field of study. Those included here offer programs taught in English. Changing majors at these institutions may require starting over or reapplying to a new program. Examples include University College London, Sciences Po in Paris, or Bocconi University in Milan.

Hybrids do exist. In the Netherlands, eight leading public universities offer small, U.S.-style liberal arts programs with a three-year degree model. Two of these, University College Utrecht and Erasmus University College, are profiled below. Constructor University, a small private institution in Bremen, Germany, offers a three-year degree that begins with a U.S.-style "Choice Year" before a deeper dive into single-subject study.

Outside of Europe, efforts to transplant the American liberal arts sensibility have been dicey, in large measure because advanced humanities and social sciences study is predicated on the values of Western-style democracy. NYU and a few other leading U.S. universities have tried in the last two decades with mixed success. For instance, NYU's degree-granting campus in Abu Dhabi, UAE, has received significant government support but also struggled with tensions linked to the Arab-Israeli conflict. NYU Shanghai, a small liberal arts college, has likewise faced cultural and geopolitical headwinds. In short, the realities of operating an international campus often extend beyond the classroom.

Though attending an overseas institution has challenges, many European and Asian universities charge tuition rates that are significantly lower than those at private colleges in the U.S.—and in some cases even lower than out-of-state tuition at large public universities. On the other hand, not all international universities participate in U.S. federal financial aid programs, including FAFSA or Title IV funding. Some accept U.S. Direct Loans; others offer their own scholarships, grants, or need-based assistance; still others expect families to pay out of pocket. Throughout this section, we flag these distinctions where possible, but families should be prepared to research funding options carefully and early in the application process.

The institutions highlighted here represent a growing set of viable, well-regarded alternative colleges or universities for American students who are globally minded, academically focused, and—in many cases—ready to commit early to a particular course of study in English. And, of course, this is a list for students with an adventurous spirit, a sturdy passport, and an eagerness to see the world.

INTERNATIONAL FOUR-YEAR ENGLISH-LANGUAGE DEGREE PROGRAMS

Austria—Central European University (approximately 1,400 total students; 250 undergraduates) is a small, selective international liberal arts university based in Vienna. Founded in 1991 by philanthropist George Soros, CEU was originally established in Budapest to promote open societies, academic freedom, and cross-cultural dialogue in Central and Eastern Europe before relocating to Vienna in 2019. The university offers three interdisciplinary bachelor's degree programs: a B.A. in culture, politics, and society; a B.A./B.S. dual degree in data science and society; and a B.A. in philosophy, politics, and economics. The programs can be completed in three years (for an Austria-accredited degree) or four years (for a degree accredited in both Austria and the U.S.). Academics are seminar-based and discussion-driven. First-year students must complete foundational courses in their chosen area of study; specific disciplines or specializations are narrowed down in year two; the third year may include study abroad as well as a thesis project to complete the Austrian bachelor's degree. Students who continue for a fourth year take more specialized courses in their major, including master's level classes and a variety of electives, and complete a capstone project to earn their American bachelor's degree. CEU enrolls an exceptionally international student body from dozens of countries (roughly 6 percent of enrolled students hail from the U.S.), and classroom conversations often reflect global political and social perspectives. The university is eligible for U.S. federal financial aid. (https://undergraduate.ceu.edu)

France—American University of Paris (approximately 1,100 undergraduates) offers a fully American-style, four-year liberal arts education in the heart of Paris. Accredited in the U.S. and located within walking distance of the Eiffel Tower and the Musée d'Orsay, AUP emphasizes small classes, close advising, and a broad general education core alongside majors in international business, global communications, politics, and the arts. The core curriculum includes integrative inquiry courses, critical thinking, writing and research, and quantitative reasoning. Students choose a course of study from more than 60 majors and minors and must complete a capstone project in their final year. With students hailing from more than 100 countries, AUP boasts classroom culture that feels genuinely global rather than study abroad temporary. U.S. federal financial aid is available. (aup.edu)

Germany—University College Freiburg (about 300 students) is a liberal arts and sciences institution within the wider University of Freiburg (about 22,000 students, 18 percent of whom are international), which sits at the edge of the Black Forest and near the borders of France and Switzerland in southwestern Germany—a setting often cited as one of the country's most livable. Founded in 1457, the University of Freiburg (which means "free town" in German) is one of Germany's oldest universities and has long been associated with humanistic scholarship and environmental research. UCF was founded in 2012 and offers a liberal arts and sciences program modeled on those found in America and the Netherlands. Over four years, students take shared core curriculum courses in English, which include key academic skills (writing, research, math), reflection and knowledge (science and theory), and responsibility and leadership. Interdisciplinary majors are offered in culture and history, governance, life sciences, and environmental and sustainability sciences. Students also have flexibility to take various electives—study abroad, internships, and courses from other majors. U.S. federal financial aid is not available. (uni-freiburg.de/ucf/)

Hong Kong—University of Hong Kong (about 19,000 undergraduates) is Asia's oldest English-language university serving undergraduates and one of the region's most prestigious public institutions. Founded in 1911 as an all-men's school, HKU admitted women a decade later. Located on Hong Kong Island with views of Victoria Harbour, it offers fully English-taught undergraduate instruction in a four-year format familiar to U.S. students (roughly 3 percent of undergrads are from North America). The university is especially strong in business, engineering, law, medicine, and the sciences and attracts a highly international student body. HKU's Common Core curriculum includes offerings in scientific and technological literacy, arts and humanities, global issues, Chinese culture and society, and artificial intelligence. Academic expectations are rigorous, and admission is competitive. HKU does not participate in U.S. federal financial aid programs. (hku.hk)

Spain—Universidad Carlos III de Madrid (approximately 18,000 total enrollment) is a public research university located just south of central Madrid, with main campuses in Getafe and Leganés and easy transit access to the city. Founded in 1989, UC3M has quickly built a strong international reputation, particularly in economics, engineering, law, and the social sciences, and now welcomes over 4,500 international students per year. Several bachelor's degrees are taught fully in English and follow a four-year structure familiar to U.S. students. For example, the international studies major requires a variety of arts and sciences courses in the first year (economics, comparative politics, sociology, and more) followed by three years of increasing specialization and electives as well as a final thesis in the fourth year. Coursework, especially in quantitative fields, tends to be structured and demanding. The student body is increasingly international, and faculty research strength shapes the classroom experience. UC3M participates in U.S. federal student loan programs. (uc3m.es/bachelor -degree/home)

Spain—IE University (over 10,000 students total), with campuses in Madrid and the historic city of Segovia, is Spain's most globally oriented private university and among its most selective. IE University was founded in 1973 by a group of ambitious entrepreneurs who aimed to "reinvent higher education." All bachelor's programs are taught in English and follow a four-year structure, with particular strengths in business, international relations, architecture, law, and data science. The academic culture is entrepreneurial and fast-paced, with mandatory internships and strong career placement. Students apply to a particular program and, in most majors, must complete several core competency courses in their first two years. Many programs include a required final project. Programs of note include the global bachelor in business administration, in which students start out in Madrid, spend their second year studying in Dubai, their third year in Singapore, and ultimately return to Madrid or can opt to spend the fourth year in New York City. Several dual, five-year degrees combine business administration with other options, such as international relations or fashion design. The student body is 75 percent international (11 percent of incoming students in 2025 were from North America), and classroom discussion mirrors American seminar style. IE participates in U.S. federal student loan programs (Title IV eligible). (ie .edu/university)

INTERNATIONAL THREE-YEAR ENGLISH-LANGUAGE DEGREE PROGRAMS

Czech Republic—Charles University (more than 24,000 undergraduates), founded in 1348 and located in Prague in the heart of the country, is one of Europe's oldest universities. Nearly half of all enrolled students are international. The university offers several English-taught, three-year bachelor's programs in fields such as economics, social sciences, computer science, and the humanities. Albert Einstein once taught here, and the university counts writers Franz Kafka and Milan Kundera as alums. Charles is also home to the Karolinum, one of the world's oldest surviving university buildings, originally established under Emperor Charles IV and still used for ceremonial and academic events today. Admission and academic expectations are rigorous, and programs tend to be more structured than at U.S. liberal arts colleges, although there are some flexible options, such as a bachelor's in liberal arts and humanities and an interdisciplinary program focused on philosophy, history, and cultural and social anthropology. Students in this program take core courses in the humanities and social sciences, complete comprehensive exams, and specialize through a selection of electives. U.S. federal financial aid is not available. (cuni.cz/UKEN-1.html)

England—University College London (about 25,000 undergraduates) is located in the Bloomsbury neighborhood in the heart of central London and is within walking distance of the British Museum and many of the city's other cultural landmarks. A new UCL East campus, at Queen Elizabeth Olympic Park, opened in 2022. Founded in 1826 as England's first secular university, UCL was also the first in the country to admit students regardless of religion and later among the first to educate women on equal terms. Today, it offers more than 400 three-year undergraduate degrees across a wide range of disciplines, with strengths in medicine, engineering, economics, architecture, and the sciences. Over 1,000 of all enrolled students are American. UCL has produced more than 30 Nobel laureates, and over 150 nationalities make up the student body. The academic culture is research-driven and self-directed, with fewer general education requirements than at U.S. colleges. For instance, students applying to the Arts & Sciences degree program must indicate a major and minor pathway when they apply, take roughly seven core courses ranging from math and data science to communications, and complete a foreign language requirement. Depending on the pathway they choose—Cultures, Health and Environment, Sciences and Engineering, or Societies—students then choose from among courses that run the gamut of arts and sciences. U.S. federal financial aid is not available. (ucl.ac.uk)

France—Sciences Po (about 6,700 undergraduates), based in Paris with additional regional campuses across France, is the country's premier institution for political science, international affairs, and public policy. Founded in 1872, the university is known for educating future leaders in government, diplomacy, journalism, and business; alumni include French President Emmanuel Macron. Undergraduate programs follow a highly structured, three-year European model, with students applying directly into a social science–focused curriculum and completing a mandatory year abroad, often spent studying, interning, or both. The Asia-Pacific, North America, and Mediterranean-Middle East minors are all taught in English and include a few core requirements as well as specialized courses in the major. The first year is typically based at one of Sciences Po's regional campuses, each with a geographic or thematic focus, before students transition to the Paris campus. Ten international dual degrees, which are four-year programs, allow students to graduate with two bachelor's degrees in conjunction with Sciences Po partners, including Columbia University, UC Berkeley, Luiss University in Rome, and others. Students pursuing this option spend the first two years at a Sciences Po campus and the next two years at the partner school. Academic expectations at Sciences Po are demanding, classroom discussion is intensive, and early specialization leaves little room for curricular wandering. Every year, around 1,300 students from the U.S. and Canada enroll, and overall, about half of the student body is international. For students passionate about politics, economics, or global affairs, Sciences Po offers a singularly immersive experience. U.S. federal financial aid is not available to undergraduates. (sciencespo.fr/en/)

Germany—Constructor University (about 2,000 students; 1,400 are undergraduates), formerly Jacobs University Bremen, is located in northern Germany just outside the historic port city of Bremen, not far from the North Sea. Founded in 2001, it was designed from the start as an English-language, research-oriented university with a fully residential campus and a distinctly international outlook. Students come from more than 120 countries, giving the campus a global feel. Roughly 4 percent are from North America. The university offers three-year English-taught bachelor's degrees in science, engineering, business, and social sciences, with an optional fourth year focused on research, internships, or study abroad. Academic expectations are high, classes are small, and undergraduate research is emphasized early. U.S. federal financial aid is not available, though generous merit scholarships help offset costs. (constructor.university/lp/study-in-germany)

Italy—Bocconi University (approximately 8,200 undergraduates), located in Milan in northern Italy, is widely regarded as Europe's leading university for economics, management, and policy studies. Founded in 1902 with an endowment from wealthy merchant Ferdinando Bocconi, and named for his lost son (much like Stanford University's origins), Bocconi is Italy's first university dedicated to economics, with 5,100 students coming from outside of Italy, and 53 percent of those enrolled in English-taught undergraduate courses. It has long been a training ground for business leaders, policymakers, and economists and counts numerous CEOs, finance ministers, and central bankers among its alumni. The Bachelor of Science programs follow the three-year model, with early specialization and a demanding academic pace, making Bocconi best suited to students who are confident in their academic direction from the start. Bocconi also offers a unique four-year world bachelor in business degree in which students spend their first year at the University of Southern California's Marshall School of Business, their second year at Hong Kong University of Science and Technology, their third year in Milan at Bocconi's main campus, and the fourth year at their choice of one of those schools; they graduate with three bachelor's degrees. The urban campus places students in the heart of Italy's financial and fashion capital, with strong ties to global employers. U.S. federal financial aid is not available. (unibocconi.it/en)

The Netherlands—Erasmus University College (roughly 600 students) is a specialized liberal arts and sciences college founded in 2013 within the greater Erasmus University Rotterdam (about 28,000 total students). EUR, located in the country's second-largest city and Europe's busiest port, is internationally renowned for business, economics, public policy, and the social sciences. Founded in 1913 and named for the 16th century humanist scholar Desiderius Erasmus, the university has built a reputation for applied research and global engagement. More than a quarter of its students come from outside the Netherlands, representing over 140 countries. Most bachelor's programs, including those offered by Erasmus University College, follow the three-year model and are taught in English, particularly in economics, international business, psychology, and public administration. EUC offers an interdisciplinary arts and sciences program in English that includes an Academic Core curriculum that will be familiar to American students. Core courses, taken in the first year, include humanities, social and behavioral sciences, life sciences, as well as economics and business. In the second year, students choose from 12 majors ranging from international law and culture and society to neuroscience. They also pursue various electives and complete a capstone project or thesis in the third year. EUC offers a separate department in economics and business, drawing on EUR's strengths in those areas. A dual degree with arts and a premed track are also available. The academic culture is serious and self-directed, with early specialization and fewer general education requirements than at U.S. colleges. Erasmus participates in U.S. federal student loan programs. (eur.nl/en/euc)

The Netherlands—University College Utrecht (about 750 students) is a highly selective residential liberal arts college located in Utrecht, in the central Netherlands, about 30 minutes from Amsterdam by train. Part of Utrecht University—one of Europe's oldest and most respected research universities, dating back to 1636—UCU was founded in 1998 and offers a three-year liberal arts and sciences curriculum taught entirely in English, featuring small seminars and close faculty advising. The emphasis is on exploration and flexibility, and students design individualized academic programs, choosing from over 200 courses across the humanities, sciences, and social sciences. In their first year, students take general academic skills courses involving writing, presentation, and methodology as well as a foreign language. They declare a major in the second year, choosing from more than 20 academic disciplines in humanities, social sciences, and science. During the third year, students work on their research thesis, "a sizeable academic paper" on a topic of their choosing. The campus is set on a former military base that now functions as a self-contained academic community, and the student body is notably international, with 68 percent of students coming from outside of the Netherlands. Courses are rigorous, and independence is key. U.S. federal financial aid is not available. (www.uu.nl/en/organisation/university-college -utrecht)

Singapore—National University of Singapore (about 30,000 undergraduates) is the country's flagship public university and one of the most highly ranked institutions in Asia and globally. NUS traces its roots to 1905, when it began as a small medical school. The institution as it stands today began in 1962 and has three campuses across Singapore—Kent Ridge, Bukit Timah, and Outram—offering students access to one of the world's most international and economically dynamic cities—not to mention an extraordinary culinary scene. With 16 colleges, NUS offers more than 60 undergraduate programs with instruction conducted in English and is particularly well known for engineering, computer science, business, medicine, and the sciences. Most bachelor's programs are completed in three years, although a four-year honors program is available in several majors and follows a more familiar American-style path. For example, majors in the College of Humanities and Sciences include a 13-course core curriculum featuring classes in humanities, science, writing, digital literacy, and Asian studies. Majors in the department are offered in everything from English literature and Chinese language to history and theater and performance studies. Academic standards are rigorous, and the school's programs "emphasize interdisciplinary learning and skill development." All students, including international students from 100 countries, engage in service learning, and the university's campuses emphasize sustainability. Admission is extremely competitive. U.S. federal financial aid is not accepted but loans and work-study opportunities are available. (nus.edu.sg)

MORE INTERNATIONAL LIBERAL ARTS UNIVERSITIES

Egypt—The American University in Cairo (Cairo) (aucegypt.edu)

England—Richmond American University (London) (richmond.ac.uk)

Greece—The American College of Greece (Athens) (acg.edu/about-acg/)

Greece—American College of Thessaloniki/Anatolia American University (Thessaloniki) (act.edu)

Italy—John Cabot University (Rome) (johncabot.edu)

Italy—The American University of Rome (Rome) (aur.edu)

Japan—University of Tokyo (Komaba campus) (u-tokyo.ac.jp/en/prospective-students/undergraduate/html)

Netherlands—Amsterdam University College (Amsterdam) (auc.nl/)

Switzerland—Franklin University Switzerland (Lugano) (fus.edu/academics/undergraduate-programs/majors)

INTERNATIONAL CAMPUSES OF U.S. UNIVERSITIES

Austria—Webster Vienna Private University (Vienna) (webster.ac.at)

China—NYU Shanghai (Shanghai) (shanghai.nyu.edu)

Germany—Bard College Berlin (Berlin) (berlin.bard.edu)

Japan—Temple University, Japan Campus (Kyoto) (tuj.ac.jp/ug)

Netherlands—Webster Leiden Campus (Leiden) (webster.nl)

South Korea—State University of New York (SUNY) Korea (Incheon) (sunykorea.ac.kr/en/)

Spain—Saint Louis University-Madrid (Madrid) (slu.edu/madrid)

Switzerland—Webster Geneva Campus (Geneva) (geneva.webster.edu)

University of Iowa

101 Jessup Hall, Iowa City, IA 52242

A bargain compared with other Big Ten schools such as Michigan and Illinois. Iowa is world-famous for its creative writing program and Writers' Workshop. Other areas of strength include health sciences, social and behavioral sciences, and business. Future scientists should check out the Research Fellows Program. The university is a regional draw, although more students are now arriving from outside the Midwest.

At first glance, one might dismiss Iowa as a standard-issue Midwestern State U. But look beyond the state's endless miles of fields and corn and you'll find one of the most dynamic schools in the country—and one of the best values to boot. Iowa is known for producing stellar nurses, future doctors, and, of course, wrestlers. Founded in 1847, Iowa was the first public university to admit men and women on an equal basis and the first to accept theater, music, and the other arts as equal to more traditional areas of academic research. The university has long been a major player in the creative fields, particularly writing, and its small-town atmosphere is just one of many reasons students nationwide flock to this "budget Ivy."

The 1,770-acre campus is located in the rolling hills of the Iowa River valley. Among its 300 major buildings is Old Capitol, the first capitol of Iowa, a National Historic Landmark and the symbol of the university. The primary architectural styles of the campus buildings are Greek Revival and modern. Notable recent facilities include a state-of-the-art, $31 million wrestling facility and a new Health Sciences academic building.

Seven of Iowa's 11 colleges offer either direct or delayed admission to undergraduates, with requirements varying by college. Liberal arts students must fulfill comprehensive requirements that include general education courses in the areas of communication and literacy; natural, quantitative, and social sciences; and culture, society, and the arts. The three-day On Iowa! program immerses incoming first-years in the campus culture and introduces them to popular activities and traditions. Optional First-Year Seminar courses help students hone their discussion skills in a small-group setting.

Iowa has a long tradition in creative arts and is the home of the famed Writers' Workshop, a two-year graduate program for emerging authors whose graduates have included Jane Smiley, John Irving, and Yaa Gyasi. The school also prides itself on its International Writing Program. "The English department is stellar," raves one English major. "It's possibly the best in the country—at least for creative writing." Iowa's programs in dance, music, and theater arts are also well respected. The university's on-campus hospital is one of the largest teaching hospitals in the United States. Undergraduates benefit from strong programs in the health professions, such as nursing, physician's assistant, and medical technician. The most popular majors are business, nursing, communication studies, and psychology. Iowa is also strong in education, physics and astronomy, hydroscience, and sustainability science. Combined degree programs permit students to earn degrees in liberal arts and their choice of business, engineering, nursing, or medicine. Agriculture, veterinary medicine, forestry, architecture, and animal science are only taught at Iowa's sister institution, Iowa State. New undergraduate programs include counseling and behavioral health sciences, entrepreneurship, and risk management and insurance.

> "Freshmen do tend to spend a majority of their time in large lectures."

Half of the classes have fewer than 20 students, and "freshmen do tend to spend a majority of their time in large lectures," says a senior. The level of academic rigor tends to depend on the program, and professors are a mixed bag, students report. "I have had a few really amazing teachers become mentors, and I've had more than a few terrible teachers who don't care," a journalism major says. The university's Four-Year Graduation Plan guarantees that students who fulfill certain requirements will not have their graduation delayed by unavailability of a needed course. The University Honors Program provides special academic, cultural, and social opportunities to qualifying students. A third of undergraduates participate in research; about 150 of them—across all disciplines—are chosen each year to be ICRU Research Fellows, earning scholarships of up to $2,500 to engage in faculty-mentored research. Undergrads who take advantage of study abroad programs can pack their bags for any of nearly 50 countries worldwide, mostly in UI-sponsored programs.

The football team is a national powerhouse and regularly appears in New Year's Day bowl games.

"Generally, students are very open-minded and kind," says an English major. Fifty-seven percent of undergraduates hail from Iowa, with most of the rest coming from contiguous states, especially Illinois; 1 percent are international. Black students account for 3 percent, Hispanics/Latinos 9 percent, Asian Americans 4 percent, and multiracial students 4 percent. Students describe the left-leaning campus as tolerant and supportive of a community atmosphere in and out of the classroom. In addition to more than 400 athletic scholarships, there are academic scholarships averaging $6,100 for eligible students.

"The residence halls range from hotel-like (Catlett and Petersen) to antiquated but charming (Currier and Hillcrest) to slightly gross (Burge, a.k.a. 'Dirty Burge,' and Mayflower)," explains a sophomore. All are co-ed by floor or wing. Twenty-eight percent of undergrads live in university housing; most students move off campus after their first year, often to apartments or houses adjacent to the campus. The "very nice" dining halls are "set up like food courts, with numerous options for varying ethnic and special tastes," says a senior. The student union includes a coffee shop, two cafeterias, and the State Room Restaurant. Regarding safety, a student notes, "The university talks a lot about preventing sexual assault and other forms of violence/intimidation."

Students often venture to Iowa City's lively downtown area, across the street from campus, which "is built with the college student in mind," a student says. "There are two university theaters right on campus, and many affordable cultural events take place at Hancher Auditorium. Mickey's, Sports Column, and George's are all popular hangouts with students." Fifteen percent of the men and 17 percent of the women belong to fraternities

and sororities, respectively. Policies against underage drinking are strictly enforced, and alcohol is only permitted at Greek events if there is a licensed, third-party vendor checking IDs, serving drinks, and providing security. "Students disobey the policy," says a student, "but there are fines and academic ramifications." Students look forward to the annual Iowa City Jazz Festival, homecoming, Dance Marathon, and Big Ten football, especially the game against Iowa State. For a change of scene, Chicago, Kansas City, or St. Louis are all within four to six hours by car, a short road trip by Midwestern standards.

Iowa's Hawkeyes compete in the Division I Big Ten Conference. The football team is a national powerhouse and regularly appears in New Year's Day bowl games. Hawkeye fans are serious about their team: "The whole town is basked in black and gold," a first-year says. The men's and women's wrestling programs enjoy a national reputation. Men's and women's basketball are also strong. Students are active in club sports and the extensive intramural program, which offers more than 40 individual, dual, or team sports; basketball, sand volleyball, and pickleball are some of the most popular intramural leagues.

Much more than a campus among the cornfields, Iowa is an ever-evolving university where scientific innovation thrives alongside artistic creativity in a relatively progressive college town. "No one has to be 'just an engineer' or 'just an artist,'" remarks an English major. The scope of Iowa's academic programs is broad and social activities abound—especially when it comes to rooting for their Hawkeyes.

If You Apply To ›

Iowa: Early action, regular decision. SATs or ACTs: optional. Accepts the Common Application with supplement. Applicants have the option of selecting preferred gender pronouns, preferred name, and sexual orientation.

2433 Union Drive, Ames, IA 50011

Agriculture and engineering are the twin pillars of Iowa State's curriculum, and the university is a magnet for preveterinary medicine students. Ames is a small city, and ISU must still endure barbs from certain snobby denizens of Iowa City. In truth, ISU is relatively cosmopolitan, with students hailing from more than 100 countries. While others retrench, ISU continues to innovate.

Love for Iowa State University runs as deep as its Midwestern roots. Strong programs in engineering, technology, agriculture, and animal science attract students from around the globe, enhanced by the close-knit, small-town atmosphere fostered at this school of more than 24,000 full-time undergraduates. At a time when many state universities are tightening the purse strings, Iowa State has expanded major research initiatives focused on areas like bioeconomics, food safety and security, artificial intelligence, and animal health—but it also announced in April 2026 it was cutting undergraduate programs in bioinformatics and computational biology, environmental studies, interdisciplinary design, religious studies, and women's and gender studies. It was also merging or consolidating some social sciences programs.

Iowa State opened its doors in 1869 with a focus on both classical and practical knowledge. Botanist and formerly enslaved scholar George Washington Carver was an early graduate (1894) and joined the faculty (a first-year scholastic leadership program has been created in his honor). The university has lavished attention on its parklike setting, located on a 1,984-acre tract in the middle of Ames, population 69,000. The campus, which boasts a combination of dignified old buildings and award-winning new ones, is a model of landscape design with numerous shady quadrangles with floral plantings and artwork that create a garden-like quality. History and tradition prevail, from the campanile, which serenades the campus with its carillon bells, to the huge public art collection, including murals by native Iowan Grant Wood and sculptures by Danish artist Christian Petersen. Much of the campus is closed to cars, largely for the benefit of walking and bicycling, as well as the swans and ducks that reside on Lake LaVerne. "The geese and the weather are the biggest menaces on campus," jokes a senior. "It's tough living in Iowa when the wind can blow you over or the snow will make your nose turn bright red, but it's all worth it when spring and fall come around, and the campus is gorgeous."

All undergraduates must take two semesters of foundational courses covering written, oral, visual, and electronic communication and demonstrate proficiency in English prior to graduation, in addition to taking a half-credit course on the use of the library and satisfying a three-credit require-ment in diversity. Other general education requirements vary by college. When Iowa State opened its doors in 1869 as a land grant univer-sity, agriculture and engineering ruled the academic roost, and these colleges still field outstanding programs in animal science, biological and agricultural engineer-ing, agronomy, and food science and technology. These days, though, the liberal arts are nearly as popular, and the College of Liberal Arts and Sciences is the largest of ISU's seven undergraduate colleges. Other colleges include business, design, veterinary medicine, and human sciences. Among the university's 100-plus majors, mechanical engineering is the most popular, followed by kinesiology and health, marketing, and finance. Programs in supply chain management; industrial, civil, aerospace, and software engineering; and elementary education are also strong.

> **"When spring and fall come around . . . the campus is gorgeous."**

Website: www.iastate.edu
Location: Small City
Public
Total Enrollment: 28,459
Undergraduates: 24,661
Male/Female: 55/45
Financial Aid: 66%
Pell Grant: 23%
Expense: Pub $
Student Loans: 55%
Average Debt: $ $
Applicants: 23,095
Accepted: 89%
Enrolled: 26%
Grad in 6 Years: 75%
Returning First-years: 88%
Academics: ✍ ✍ ✍
Social: 🗩 🗩 🗩 🗩
Q of L: ★ ★ ★
Admissions: (515) 294-5836
Email Address:
 admissions@iastate.edu

Strong Programs:
Agribusiness
Animal Science
Elementary Education
Food Science and Technology
Kinesiology and Health
Marketing
Mechanical Engineering
Supply Chain Management

Thirty-three percent of all undergraduate classes have fewer than 20 students. Despite the university's size, professors teach most classes. "I have never had a professor or TA who has not been willing to take the time out of their busy day to help me with a problem," says a kinesiology major. Academic and career counseling draw universal praise, too. Seventy-nine percent of first-year students join one of over 90 highly touted learning communities, taking a common set of classes or living together on the same residence hall floor. The Honors Program enrolls about 5 percent of students, who take special seminars, complete an independent honors research project or creative work, and have the option of living in honors housing. Just 5 percent of undergrads study overseas in programs offered in more than 40 countries. Fourteen percent take advantage of undergraduate research opportunities with faculty members.

Fifty-seven percent of ISU's undergraduates are Iowans, though all 50 states and more than 100 countries are represented. The atmosphere on campus is inclusive and respectful, and "people tend to keep their political ideas to themselves," according to an animal science major. International students make up 4 percent of the student body. Iowa State was the first co-ed land grant institution, but attracting students of color has proven more difficult: Hispanics/Latinos account for 7 percent, Asian Americans 4 percent, Black students 2 percent, and multiracial students 3 percent. "We have a lot of farmers and small-town Iowans," says a senior. "This is a pretty white campus." To improve diversity, ISU launched a $25 million campaign aimed at increasing the number of scholarships available for students of color, athletes, and student leaders. In addition to need-based financial aid and more than 400 athletic scholarships, thousands of merit awards, which average $5,700 annually, are available.

Thirty-one percent of students live in on-campus residence halls and apartments; most others find their own apartments near campus. Single-sex, co-ed, and suite-style dorms are available. "The dorms are sterile to begin with but students transform them into home with their own personal touch," explains a junior. Students dine at 26 campus locations, including four main dining centers. Campus safety receives good ratings, and students say educational and training efforts have been effective in raising awareness about campus sexual assault and violence.

"There is a bowling alley, a movie theater, and a special event called Iowa State after Dark."

Iowa State is not simply located in Ames. In many respects, it is Ames, but whether it qualifies as a college town depends on whom you ask. Des Moines, the state capital, is about 30 minutes away, and Iowa City, Minneapolis, and Chicago are other easy and enjoyable road trips. Socializing tends to stay on campus where, one student points out, "There is a bowling alley, a movie theater, and a special event called Iowa State after Dark, where they have a guest speaker and fun activities." More than 800 student organizations cater to just about any interest. Fourteen percent of both the men and women go Greek. Students of legal age are allowed to have alcohol on campus, and students report that alcohol policies are well enforced. Across the street from campus, Campustown offers several bars as well as a variety of cafés and international restaurants. One long-held tradition is campaniling, where students kiss under the campanile at the stroke of midnight.

Dubbed the Cyclones by a sportswriter who compared the football team to an "Iowa cyclone" after they upset Northwestern in 1895, these days Cyclone basketball is king; the men's and women's teams are usual invitees to the NCAA Division I tournament. The men's team has won the Big 12 title five times in the last decade. Football, wrestling, and men's and women's track and field and cross-country are also competitive. ISU's football stadium bears the name of Jack Trice, ISU's first Black athlete, who was fatally injured in a 1923 football game. "I literally cry almost every single game because you just feel like you are a part of something so large and amazing," enthuses a sophomore. Indeed, the passionate fans aren't only on campus; the whole state has gotten into Iowa sports, supporting the Cyclones from near and far. The Cyclones' rivalry with the University of Iowa's Hawkeyes is one of the strongest in the nation, and "Beat Iowa" paraphernalia is ubiquitous. The intramural program, which is one of the largest in the country, offers around 50 sports—and if that's not enough, students have their pick of more than 50 club sports too.

From its first class of 28 men and two women in 1869, Iowa State has taken to heart Abraham Lincoln's land grant ideal: to open higher education to all, to teach practical courses, and to share that knowledge beyond the borders of the school. According to one junior, it's this dynamic combination that draws "hardworking, kind students" from near and far.

If You Apply To ›

Iowa State: Rolling admissions. SATs or ACTs: optional. Accepts the Common Application with supplement.

Ithaca College

953 Danby Road, Ithaca, NY 14850

Ithaca offers an unusually wide array of programs for a smallish university. The common thread: solid preprofessional programs rooted in the liberal arts. Communications and music are traditional strengths, along with physical therapy and other health sciences. Crosstown neighbor Cornell adds curricular and social opportunities.

Located in the picturesque center of the beautiful upstate New York Finger Lakes region, Ithaca College was founded in 1892 as a music conservatory by a violinist. Since then, "a pedagogy founded on the concept of 'theory, practice, and performance' has distinguished IC's core approach to education." And it has led the way in showing how to combine hands-on preprofessional training in a wide range of fields, from communications and theatre to health sciences, with a solid grounding in the liberal arts. Ithaca has increased the number of business majors available and has added majors in education, screen studies, and race, power, and resistance. Ithaca's special approach to hands-on learning helps prepare students for life outside institutional walls. Says a stage management major, "Ithaca College has a unique institutional personality that really sets it apart, characterized by a vibrant sense of community and a deep-rooted spirit of creativity."

Ithaca College's campus, midway between Syracuse and Binghamton, lies on the city's southern hill overlooking Cayuga Lake. The college did not move to its present location, a sprawling 757-acre property, until the 1960s. The surrounding area is dotted with forests, rolling hills, some 150 waterfalls, and, of course, those ever-present gorges. Author Tom Wolfe dubbed the college "the emerald eminence at the fingertip of Cayuga Lake." Campus facilities afford students access to nearly 200 labs, smart classrooms, studios, practice rooms, and performance spaces, not to mention 560 acres of natural lands. A new $4 million NCAA-compliant, eight-lane track and field facility opened in 2025.

Ithaca has five schools—business; communications; health sciences and human performance; humanities and sciences; and music, theatre, and dance. Together, they offer more than 70 undergraduate majors and 70 minors. All students complete the Integrative Core Curriculum (ICC), which is designed to help them connect concepts

Each fall brings Applefest, a local downtown festival that celebrates the harvest, and in the winter, Chilifest helps students warm up.

across disciplines. All first-year students take a four-credit Ithaca Seminar during their first semester; recent examples of the nearly 100 offerings include Inquiring Minds Want to Know and Hello China: Preparing for the Future. These classes are limited to about 15 to 20 students each, and professors and students decide together how to use the fourth hour of instruction each week, covering topics related to the transition to college life, such as personal, social, and academic responsibility.

Ithaca is best known for its preprofessional programs—especially music, which dates to the college's founding. "The school attracts people who are interested in those fields even if they aren't planning on majoring in something within the arts,"

"Ithaca College has a unique institutional personality that really sets it apart."

a senior says. The school, which encompasses theatre and dance programs in addition to music, requires an audition, making it a destination for already accomplished performing artists. Professional programs in the School of Health Sciences and Human Performance range from speech-language pathology and public and community health to the highly regarded physical and occupational therapy programs. The Park School of Communications houses two of the college's most popular programs: television, photography, and digital media, and advertising, public relations, and marketing communications. The business school offers five undergraduate majors ranging from accounting to marketing and sport management. The School of Humanities and Sciences recently added a major in race, power, and resistance. The physician assistant program has a dedicated state-of-the-art facility in downtown Ithaca. Students who are undecided on a major enroll in the Exploratory Program, which helps them find an academic path through advising, workshops, and courses in a variety of fields. Cross-registration is available at nearby Cornell University, and Ithaca also offers a 3–2 physics and engineering program.

"Students frequently highlight the dedication of the faculty," says an integrated marketing communications major. "Instruction is not only high-quality but also highly personalized." Sixty-four percent of classes have fewer than 20 students, and professors are praised for their knowledge and enthusiasm. A sophomore says, "If you do struggle, as I have, there are lifelines in the form of TAs, free tutoring (in most cases), and persistent professor interaction." Research opportunities in the sciences and psychology are plentiful; students in other departments generally do research as part of an independent study course. Those seeking immersive real-world experience may apply for a semester-long program in Los Angeles that combines an internship with industry-related courses. Ithaca offers study abroad programs at the Ithaca College London Center and in more than 40 countries.

What defines a typical Ithaca student? A senior says they are "creative, driven, passionate, outdoorsy, and welcoming." Thirty-nine percent of Ithaca students hail from New York State; many of the rest come from elsewhere in New England, and

"Students frequently highlight the dedication of the faculty."

3 percent come from other nations. Black students represent 5 percent of undergraduates, Asian Americans 3 percent, Hispanics/Latinos 11 percent, and multiracial students 5 percent. Politically, the campus is liberal, and according to one student, "Hot-button issues include LGBTQ+ rights, the Black Lives Matter movement, climate change, and fighting anti-Semitism." The average offer of grants and scholarships per student is $24,900.

Eighty-five percent of Ithaca's students live on campus, thanks in part to the college's Circle and Garden Apartments, which have full kitchens and space for 630 upperclassmen in units that house two to six students each. Some students say room selection can be "competitive." First-year students participate in the First-Year Residential Experience. All students may choose to live in any of nine residential learning communities focusing on themes like multiculturalism, health and wellness, and outdoor adventure. A junior recommends learning communities as a way to "meet new people and become more involved in the Ithaca area." Campus residents can eat in any of the dining halls, each with a different daily menu and options for those with special dietary needs; the meals get mixed reviews. An advertising, public relations, and marketing major reports, "Campus is overall very safe—Public Safety has a noticeable presence on campus." Career advising and mental health counseling also get high marks from students.

Ithaca recognizes only academic fraternities and sororities, not social ones, but that doesn't slow down the campus social scene. "Between music school concerts, theatre performances, Student Activities Board movies, club events, open-mic nights, comedy shows, or athletic events, it is impossible to be bored on campus," one sociology major says. Nearly 200 student organizations also keep people busy. Students agree that the party scene is low-key, but the city of Ithaca caters well to college students, with a variety of coffee shops, bars and clubs, live music venues, a mall, a bowling alley, and movie theaters. "Ithaca is the best college town in the whole state!" cheers a junior. Each fall brings Applefest, a local downtown festival that celebrates the harvest, and in the winter, Chilifest helps students warm up. The area's hilly terrain provides abundant opportunities for hiking, biking, sledding, and skiing. Popular road trips include Syracuse and Binghamton, each an hour away, and New York City, Philadelphia, Boston, Washington, D.C., and Toronto, each between a four- and six-hour drive.

Ithaca fields 27 competitive Division III varsity athletics programs. The Bombers (a nickname dating back to the 1930s and whose origin remains, in the words of a university official, "likely lost forever in the mists of time") have claimed recent Liberty League conference championships in field hockey, men's basketball, women's lacrosse, men's and women's rowing, and more. The biggest annual athletic tradition is the "Cortaca Jug" football game that pits the Ithaca Bombers against rival SUNY–Cortland. (The winner gets the jug-shaped trophy, and the game is "the only Division III football game you can bet on in Vegas," boasts a sophomore.) More than 20 percent of students sign up for club and intramural sports; popular options include rugby, ultimate Frisbee, swimming, flag football, basketball, and volleyball.

If you can endure the harsh winters ("Come mid-February or so, we hate the snow!" gripes one senior), you'll appreciate the small size and personal attention characteristic of Ithaca College. "Everybody who is part of the Ithaca College community knows that they are part of something special," observes one student. "At other schools, you're a number. At Ithaca, we know your name."

> "Ithaca is the best college town in the whole state!"

Overlaps

University of Delaware, Elon, Emerson, Gettysburg, Marist, SUNY–Binghamton, Syracuse, University of Vermont

If You Apply To ›

Ithaca: Early decision, early action, regular decision. SATs or ACTs: optional. Accepts the Common Application with supplement.

James Madison University

800 S Main Street, Harrisonburg, VA 22807

JMU has carved out a comfortable niche among Virginia's superb system of public universities. More undergrads than UVA and three times as many as William & Mary. Strong in preprofessional fields such as business, health professions, and education. Undergraduates rule the roost. Football, basketball, and other warriors regularly punch above their weight.

Website: www.jmu.edu

Location: Small City

Public

Total Enrollment: 20,701

Undergraduates: 19,776

Male/Female: 43/56

Financial Aid: 58%

Pell Grant: 14%

Expense: Pub $

Student Loans: 43%

Average Debt: $ $ $

Applicants: 38,426

Accepted: 72%

Enrolled: 18%

Grad in 6 Years: 80%

Returning First-years: 92%

Academics: ✐ ✐ ✐

Social: 🌑 🌑 🌑 🌑

Q of L: ★ ★ ★ ★

Admissions: (540) 568-5681

Email Address:
  admissions@jmu.edu

Strong Programs:
Biology
Business
Education
Health Sciences
Health Services Administration
Nursing
Psychology
Sport and Recreation
  Management

Favorite traditions

include taking

graduation photos

with the various

campus statues

of James Madison

(or "JMaddy," as

he's been dubbed

by students).

No doubt about it: students at James Madison University get down to business. In fact, the school's business programs continue to garner national attention and attract top-notch students from coast to coast. The university has been growing at a steady rate, causing growth pains. But an emphasis on undergraduate teaching, close student/faculty interaction, and a warm and welcoming climate are still business as usual here. "JMU is comfortable—everyone has a place, you just have to find it," says a senior.

Founded as a teachers' college in 1908, JMU sits in the heart of the Shenandoah Valley, two hours from both Washington, D.C., and Richmond, Virginia. The university straddles Interstate 81, an outlet to several major East Coast cities. Three types of architecture make up the campus. The buildings on front campus have red-tile roofs and are constructed of a distinctive limestone block known as bluestone. Back campus has more modern, redbrick structures. The College of Integrated Science and Technology campus features modern beige buildings. Newer facilities include a three-story west campus dining hall and a 500-bed residence hall.

The General Education Program requires each student to take courses in several clusters, including Madison Foundations (comprised of critical thinking, communication, and writing), Arts and Humanities, The Natural World, American and Global Perspectives, and Sociocultural and Wellness.

> **"JMU is comfortable— everyone has a place, you just have to find it."**

The idea is to give students a basis for lifelong learning by challenging them to become active in their own education and to explore the foundations of knowledge. First-years are offered a variety of programs to help smooth their transition into the university. Outdoor Adventures, held before classes begin, give first-year students an opportunity to meet while hiking and climbing in the mountains.

JMU is recognized nationally for its College of Business, while education is also strong. In addition to health sciences, some of the most popular majors include health services administration, sport and recreation management, biology, nursing, and psychology. Undergraduates in the biology department have employed recombinant DNA technology to help develop organisms that produce biodegradable plastics, while a mathematical modeling laboratory helps undergrads solve real-world applied math problems. Also worth noting is the geology department's undergraduate summer geology field course in Ireland.

JMU's main mission is undergraduate teaching, and students say the classroom atmosphere is usually relaxed and supportive. Thirty-six percent of classes have fewer than 20 students, and a political science major reports that even in larger classes, "You feel like you can ask questions, get to know your professors one-on-one, and make connections." Student support services get high ratings. "The counseling center offers a student oasis and arts center where anyone can go free of charge to do yoga, rest, play relaxing games, make crafts, etc.," notes a senior.

Those looking for a more intense intellectual experience can apply for admission to the Honors College, which offers small classes and opportunities for independent study. Many upper-level programs encourage undergraduate participation with faculty research. JMU runs its own semester abroad programs in Belgium, England, Italy, Scotland, and Spain as well as dozens of short-term, faculty-led programs in more than 40 countries.

Students describe their classmates as cheerful folks who hold doors open for each other, and a junior says JMU students are interested in "finding lifestyles that they love instead of just jobs." Most undergrads attended public high schools, and 79 percent are from Virginia. In fact, there's a conscious effort to keep out-of-state enrollment below 30 percent; international students represent less than 1 percent.

Racial and ethnic diversity, although low, has been slowly on the rise; Black students currently account for 5 percent of JMU's student body, Hispanics/Latinos 9 percent, Asian Americans 5 percent, and multiracial students 6 percent. As for political inclinations, both sides of the aisle are represented, but an economics major says most students are "rather apathetic." JMU offers limited merit scholarships averaging $6,800 and more than 300 athletic scholarships.

Just 10 percent of students live on campus, but it's a requirement for first-years to do so. On-campus housing runs the gamut from the old high-ceiling variety to newer, air-conditioned dorms with fitness centers and apartments for sophomores. For upperclassmen, "Off-campus housing is extremely easy to find," reports a senior, "and there is a wide range of prices and amenities available." With 27 dining options on campus serving all sorts of dietary needs and preferences, students rave about the meal plan. "You're supposed to miss your mom's cooking when you go away, but I end up missing my college's food when I'm home," says one student. (We won't tell Mom.) According to a math major, JMU's Title IX office is "working hard to advance services," and the Campus Assault Response student group "is a great nonreporting resource for students" coping with sexual violence.

"Social life is really fun for a rural area," observes one student. "The students mostly gather at off-campus apartments via a bus system that runs into the late hours." Greek life attracts only 4 percent of the men and 5 percent of the women. The school cracks down on underage drinking on campus, and after three strikes, "students are asked to leave," says a student. Favorite traditions include the holiday tree-lighting ceremony, Spring Concert, the Madipalooza music festival, and taking graduation photos with the various campus statues of James Madison (or "JMaddy," as he's been dubbed by students). Most students find Harrisonburg a friendly, if not always lively, Southern town. As for road trips, the University of Virginia, almost an hour's drive to the south, is a top destination, but equally enticing are the many nearby natural delights of the Shenandoah Valley, including hiking, camping, and even skiing.

Sports fans here are known as the JMU Nation, and to say they are enthusiastic about their Division I Dukes (named after a popular university president) would be an understatement. Teams compete in the Sun Belt Conference, and building on recent successes in football and basketball, the school has been investing heavily in Olympic sports such as softball, volleyball, and women's lacrosse. These efforts are supported in part by mandatory student fees that rank among the highest of any public university in the country. Other successful teams have included tennis, golf, swimming and diving, and men's soccer. About half of the students participate in intramural and club sports. JMU's debate team ranks as one of the top public programs in the nation.

Though JMU still has a ways to go before establishing itself as a front-rank national university, it is making progress. The school is growing but not outgrowing its Southern charm. "The school spirit is really what sets us apart," says an elementary education major. "No matter where you go on campus, you are always going to find someone wearing purple and gold."

> "I end up missing my college's food when I'm home."

Overlaps

Appalachian State, Clemson, College of Charleston, George Mason, Grand Valley State, Illinois State, UVA, Virginia Tech

If You Apply To ›

James Madison: Early action, regular decision. SATs or ACTs: optional. Accepts the Common Application.

3101 Wyman Park Drive, Baltimore, MD 21218

With fewer undergraduates than its world-class academic reputation might suggest, Hopkins is a national leader in areas as diverse as biomedical engineering, international affairs, writing, and public health. Befitting its 19th-century origins as a graduate school, 80 percent of students engage in research. One of the first elite schools to eliminate legacy admissions, Hopkins has used a $1.8 billion grant for financial aid from billionaire alumnus Michael Bloomberg to enhance socioeconomic diversity.

Website: www.jhu.edu
Location: City Outskirts
Private
Total Enrollment: 17,419
Undergraduates: 5,664
Male/Female: 45/55
Financial Aid: 52%
Pell Grant: 16%
Expense: Pr $ $ $
Student Loans: 20%
Average Debt: $ $ $
Applicants: 45,895
Accepted: 6%
Enrolled: 47%
Grad in 6 Years: 94%
Returning First-years: 98%
Academics: 🖊 🖊 🖊 🖊 🖊
Social: 💬 💬 💬
Q of L: ★ ★ ★
Admissions: (410) 516-8171
Email Address:
 gotojhu@jhu.edu

Strong Programs:
Creative Writing
Engineering
Film and Media Studies
International Studies
Molecular and Cellular Biology
Music
Neuroscience
Public Health Studies

The first research university founded in America, in 1876, Johns Hopkins University took its name from its first benefactor, a Quaker entrepreneur whose $7 million bequest was the largest philanthropic gift in the U.S. up to that time. The university has garnered widespread acclaim for its exceptional professors, extensive resources, and abundant research opportunities. Though the university has a reputation for churning out premed students, this midsized Baltimore university has plenty to offer undergrads whose interests are decidedly nonmedical or nonscience based. Students who attend this elite university often collaborate while burning the midnight oil. "Walking through the library, all the group study spaces are routinely full of students studying together for exams, doing their homework, or simply chatting," notes a history major.

The arts and sciences and engineering schools are on the main Homewood campus, 140 picturesque acres in Baltimore's Charles Village neighborhood, just three miles north of the vibrant Inner Harbor. Tree-lined quadrangles, open lawns,

"The [January] classes are pass/fail and so much fun."

and playing fields make for an idyllic setting on the edge of a major urban center. The architecture on this urban campus is mainly Georgian redbrick, with several recently built, more modern structures scattered throughout. The Imagine Center and the SNF Agora Institute are new spaces where students are encouraged to explore options for their future and engage in inclusive dialogue about global democracy. Hopkins's School of Medicine and Peabody Institute are easily accessible from the Homewood campus via a crosstown shuttle. A 15,000-square-foot student center includes media and digital lounges, a performance space, and several dining options. The Hopkins Bloomberg Center, located near the White House in Washington, D.C., serves as the hub for students studying and working in public policy during a newly launched Hopkins Semester D.C.

At Hopkins, each major has its own distribution requirements; students entering the Krieger School of Arts & Sciences are required to take a first-year seminar and a writing course as well as courses in science and data; culture and aesthetics; citizens and society; ethics and foundations; and projects and methods. To help ease the transition to college, the university has developed and strengthened several student support resources in recent years. First-years are assigned an academic advisor, and arts and sciences students are encouraged to wait until at least their sophomore year to declare a major. During the optional January intersession, students can take courses or pursue independent study for one or two credits. "The classes are pass/fail and so much fun," cheers an international studies major, "everything from profiling mass murderers to a Harry Potter literature class!"

One in four Hopkins graduates head off for medical school, and public health studies is among the most popular majors, along with computer science, economics, and molecular and cellular biology. The Johns Hopkins Hospital and School of Medicine play such a major role in the identity of Hopkins that students sometimes fear they "overshadow the vibrant undergrad life that exists at Homewood." But administrators say the university is paying more attention to undergraduate programs and emphasizing interdisciplinary, cooperative approaches to the coursework, and students seem to agree. "I constantly learn about things that are done through the institution, and the core of it all is improving humanity," raves an economics and math major.

Engineering majors enjoy strong departments, such as biomedical engineering, mechanical engineering, chemical engineering, electrical and computer engineering, and computer science. New offerings include a major in systems engineering and a minor in energy. Students can receive a B.A. in creative writing through the Writing Seminars program, where they study with the likes of novelist Alice McDermott and poet Andrew Motion. The film and media studies program is notable, bolstered by the JHU-MICA Film Centre and industry connections. Students who are advanced in the performing arts and academics can pursue a dual degree with the university's Peabody Institute. Students can also choose from a cluster of related disciplines to design their own program. Most are generally happy with the quality of teaching, which is enhanced by small class sizes—78 percent of undergraduate classes enroll fewer than 20 students. "Professors teach at Hopkins because it is their passion," says a history major, "so the quality of instruction is incredibly high."

The well-developed graduate side of Hopkins proves to be a boon to undergraduates as well. The international studies program, for example, is enriched by its offerings at the university's Bologna Center in Italy, its Nanjing Center in China, and its Nitze School of Advanced International Studies in nearby Washington, D.C. The Hopkins Semester D.C. allows students to live, study, and work in the nation's capital while designing and completing a faculty-guided research project. About 10 percent of undergraduates study abroad in these and other locations across the globe. Undergraduate research is a Hopkins hallmark, with 80 percent of students having at least one research experience, and it's not only for STEM majors. "The history, political science, and international studies departments all have incredible professors and researchers always looking for undergraduate help," says a sophomore. The Provost's Undergraduate Research Awards offer funding and faculty support for research projects, and funding for unpaid or underpaid research and internships is available. The Clark Scholars Program provides special academic and networking opportunities to top engineering students. Sixty-two percent of undergrads engage with service organizations, community-based learning, and internships in Baltimore through the Center for Social Concern.

"The Hopkins student body is a vibrant tapestry of passion and diversity," muses an environmental science major. Geographically, many students come from the Mid-Atlantic region and New England; only 15 percent are Maryland natives, and 15 percent are international. Twenty-nine percent of undergrads are Asian American, 8 percent are Black, 19 percent are Hispanic/Latino, and 7 percent are multiracial. The proportion of first-generation students (about 18 percent) has more than doubled over the last decade because of a $1.8 billion gift for financial aid from business mogul Michael Bloomberg to ensure a Hopkins education is available to qualified students regardless of their ability to pay. "The political climate is generally apolitical as most students are too into their studies for politics," says a first-year student. At more than $13 billion, Hopkins's endowment is among the top 20 in the country. In addition to moving to a need-blind admissions process for domestic students, the university meets 100 percent of admitted students' demonstrated need with loan-free financial aid packages. Hopkins rewards the extraordinarily talented with hefty Hodson Trust scholarships worth about two-thirds of tuition annually, regardless of

"The quality of instruction is incredibly high."

need. More than 40 athletic scholarships are also awarded in women's and men's lacrosse, where Hopkins is a perennial national powerhouse.

Forty-six percent of undergrads live in student housing; first-years and sophomores are required to do so. "There are a variety of styles of dorms, including communal and suite-style, which allow for students to feel comfortable and empowered in their living spaces," offers a sophomore. For example, second-year students living in the Scott-Bates Commons, suite-style apartments, each get their own room and have access to the adjacent dining hall and campus bookstore. Most juniors and seniors choose to live in the plentiful row houses and apartment buildings that surround Hopkins. Campus dining gets positive reviews, as does security, thanks to the consistent presence of security personnel. The Sexual Assault Resource Unit student organization is active in raising awareness about sexual violence.

"While there may not be a huge party culture on campus, there is always some exciting event going on," cheers a public health studies major of Hopkins's social scene. The Hopkins Student Organization for Programming puts on numerous events, and fraternity parties can be found on the weekends; 22 percent of the men and 13 percent of the women belong to the Greek system. There are also more than 400 clubs and student organizations to pick from. Students speak fondly of the Lighting of the Quads celebration each winter, but the biggest and most popular undergraduate social event of the year is the student-organized Spring Fair. "Tons of Baltimore food vendors and shops line up on the quads, there is a concert, and the campus is generally full of merriment," says an international studies major.

In addition to on-campus events like guest lectures and performances, says a senior, "You have the whole city of Baltimore and its social scene to explore." One student explains the city's diverse bounty: "Students go to Station North for food, Mt. Vernon for street fairs and cherry blossoms, Fell's Point for cafés, Hampden for antique and vintage stores, Federal Hill for bars, and Inner

"Most students are too into their studies for politics."

Harbor for the National Aquarium and views of the harbor." Camden Yards, home of MLB's Orioles, is one of the best parks in the country. Annapolis is less than an hour away by car, while Washington, D.C., only an hour's train ride, also beckons. In the warmer months, a trek out to the Delaware and Maryland beaches takes the mind off the books.

When the nationally acclaimed Division I men's lacrosse team hits the road, students often take advantage of the opportunity to road-trip with them and cheer them on, with Loyola being a chief rival. Women's lacrosse is Division I as well, but the rest of the Blue Jays athletic program competes in Division III. Men's and women's cross-country, women's soccer, football, women's volleyball, and field hockey are all strong. The Johns Hopkins Undergraduate Debate Council has also had national success. A quarter of undergraduates compete in more than 40 intramurals and club sports.

With one of the world's premier medical schools, top science programs, and first-rate programs in areas as diverse as writing, international studies, environmental engineering, and philosophy, Hopkins is clearly among the best schools in the country. Students here take pride in the fact that they belong to the cream of the academic crop. "Hopkins is a place of discovery and exploration, and it really embodies creating new knowledge and expanding your horizons," says a junior. "It's a place for people who like to go the extra mile and find out something new."

Overlaps

University of Chicago, Columbia, Cornell University, Duke, Harvard, MIT, Penn, Yale

If You Apply To ›

Johns Hopkins: Early decision I and II, regular decision. SATs or ACTs: required. Accepts the Common Application with supplement. Biomedical engineering students must apply to that program.

1700 Moore Street, Huntingdon, PA 16652

Located in the middle of rural Pennsylvania and named after a nearby river, Juniata boasts one of the best undergraduate science programs among liberal arts colleges. Students are encouraged to customize their own education and to think globally. Peace and conflict studies is a specialty. All students receive merit scholarship at the time of admission, but not much diversity among students.

Set amid the ridges and valleys of central Pennsylvania, Juniata College's mission is to "empower students to develop the skills, knowledge, and values that lead to a fulfilling life of service and ethical leadership," and to that end, it offers students a tantalizing mix of academic flexibility, small classes, and surprisingly solid programs in the natural sciences. "The types of students who are attracted to Juniata are those who have a motivation to learn but are not interested in learning in the conventional way," says a psychology major.

Juniata's quiet 110-acre campus features a central stand of structures reflecting three architectural styles. The college was founded in 1876, and its landmark building, Founders Hall, is a colonial Revival structure, built of brick atop a stone foundation. Halbritter Center for the Performing Arts, Ellis Hall, and the von Liebig Center for Science are all Classical Revival buildings, the prominent pillars on each visible all over campus. The college also boasts a Beaux-Arts building, Carnegie Hall, originally built as a Carnegie library in 1907 and redesigned on the interior to house the college's art museum. Newer facilities include the Statton Learning Commons, which houses academic resources and support, including the library, tutoring, peer mentoring, the writing center, and digital learning.

Under Juniata's general education curriculum, all students complete coursework in five "Ways of Knowing" (creative expression, formal reasoning, humanistic thought, social inquiry, and scientific process) and four "Self and the World" courses (on the U.S. experience, ethical responsibility, local engagement, and global engagement) as well as a first-year composition class and a first-year seminar. As juniors or seniors, students take

> **"[Juniata students] are not interested in learning in the conventional way."**

one Connections course, which combines two ways of knowing and is team-taught by faculty from different departments. As a senior, every student creates a capstone project demonstrating their knowledge, skills, and personal reflections of their educational experience.

In lieu of preset majors, Juniata has flexible Programs of Emphasis (POEs). Each student works with two advisors to either shape an existing POE to fit their academic interests or to create an entirely new program. Approximately one-third of students take the latter path, designing their own customized POE. Of the more than 60 established POEs, some of the most popular are biology, biochemistry, environmental science, and psychology. The physics and chemistry programs are well regarded, and strong offerings in environmental science and wildlife conservation are enhanced by the college's field station at nearby Raystown Lake. "Juniata has long been known as a school for the natural sciences," says a senior. In addition, peace and conflict studies is one of the oldest and most comprehensive programs of its kind in the United States. Museum studies teaches students how to curate art (and provides internships at prestigious galleries around the nation). All programs are enhanced through local and global engagement learning experiences. New offerings include

Website: www.juniata.edu
Location: Small Town
Private
Total Enrollment: 1,220
Undergraduates: 1,190
Male/Female: 48/52
Financial Aid: 100%
Pell Grant: 34%
Expense: Pr $ $
Student Loans: 67%
Average Debt: $ $ $ $
Applicants: 2,779
Accepted: 79%
Enrolled: 17%
Grad in 6 Years: 74%
Returning First-years: 83%
Academics: ✍ ✍ ✍
Social: 🗩 🗩 🗩
Q of L: ★ ★ ★
Admissions: (814) 641-3420
Email Address:
  applications@juniata.edu

Strong Programs:
Biochemistry
Biology
Environmental Science
Museum Studies
Peace and Conflict Studies
Physics
Psychology
Wildlife Conservation

3–1 bachelor's and master's degree programs as well as undergraduate degrees in civil engineering, data science, business analytics, environmental engineering, strategic communication, and exercise science, among others.

A psychology major describes the academic atmosphere as "flexible but challenging." Sixty-four percent of classes have fewer than 20 students, which allows for plenty of interaction between professors and students. The Inbound program allows new students to spend a week on campus as part of a particular club or activity in order to "make their first few days of immersion into college life easier," says a student. Juniata has international exchange/study abroad agreements with colleges and universities in 24 countries. "Juniata makes it super affordable and possible for every student to go abroad, no matter what they're majoring in," cheers a sophomore. A majority of Juniata students also participate in community-engaged learning and faculty-guided research projects. "Juniata has an extremely strong focus on experiential learning," confirms a junior, adding "Research is done as early as second semester first year and is incredibly popular among all disciplines." The annual Liberal Arts Symposium features student research presentations, performances, and art exhibitions.

"Juniata students are empowered and outspoken," says a business analytics and communications major. Sixty-five percent of Juniata students hail from Pennsylvania, and 9 percent come from foreign nations. Black students account for 5 percent of the student body, Asian Americans 2 percent, Hispanics/Latinos 9 percent, and multiracial students 3 percent. A junior comments that while the school is still working to increase racial diversity, it has also "put a lot more effort into making people of color feel welcome." Adds another student, "Politically, we are pretty diverse." All students receive a merit scholarship at the time of admission, averaging $38,000. There are no athletic scholarships.

Juniata requires students to live on campus for four years. "Student housing isn't glorious," reasons a first-year, "but dorms are adequate." Two living/learning communities, Global Village and Eco House, are options for those interested in intercultural exchange and sustainable living. For grub, Juniata provides two main dining facilities, one buffet-style and one where meals are made to order, as well as several à la carte stops around campus. Students say their rural location feels safe. One student reports that the SPoT (Safe Place to Talk), which "does a lot of programs to promote safe sex and understanding of sexual assault and mental health awareness," is proving to be an effective source of support.

Social life is mostly on campus, and activities include live bands, trivia contests, dinners, and dances. "There are tons of events hosted by clubs all the time," says a chemistry major. Students of legal age may drink on campus, but students say the drinking and party culture is low-key, especially with no Greek life. Students enjoy a number of traditions, including Lobsterfest at the start of the year, Madrigal Dinner during the holidays, and Mountain Day, on which classes are canceled for the day and students attend outdoor activities at Raystown Lake ("Food, carnival games, kayaking, Slip 'N Slides, and the president's dog with a GoPro on—it is a great time," says a junior). During Human Mattress Dominoes, "we all drag our twin XL mattresses outside to fall like dominoes," explains a student. Huntingdon (population 7,000) provides the basic necessities as well as several restaurants, a movie theater, and a Mayfest street fair. Community service is popular, as are road trips to Penn State (40 minutes away), Baltimore, Philadelphia, and Pittsburgh.

The Juniata Eagles' 22 varsity teams compete in Division III. The women's volleyball team has dominated the Landmark Conference, winning 17 consecutive

"Research is done as early as second semester first year."

championships and three national titles since 2022. Men's volleyball, soccer, and both men's and women's swimming are strong too. Students are also active in club and intramural sports; the men's and women's rugby clubs and intramural basketball are among the most favored.

Although students sometimes complain about the limitations of attending a small college in a small town, most seem excited to be part of such an inviting academic institution. Those seeking "big football games, raging frat parties, and a vibrant urban setting" should look elsewhere, a senior observes. However, "if you are more interested in an intensive and personal academic environment with an extremely tight-knit and supportive community, then Juniata is the place for you."

If You Apply To ›

Juniata: Early decision, early action I and II, regular decision. SATs or ACTs: optional. Accepts the Common Application with supplement.

Kalamazoo College

1200 Academy Street, Kalamazoo, MI 49006

Kalamazoo College is a small liberal arts school that opens up the world to its students. A majority of them study abroad thanks to the ingenious K-Plan, a curriculum that allows them to study abroad for up to three academic terms. And if you need an extra boost to round out that résumé, there is an extensive career development program.

Kalamazoo College (colloquially known as K) may be a small school in America's heartland, but it makes studying abroad possible for a majority of students during their four years—creating a launching pad to the world. In addition to international education, the school's K-Plan emphasizes teaching, internships, and independent, faculty-guided research. Students are exposed to a demanding academic schedule and high expectations from faculty, but they say it's well worth the challenge. "Students at K really care about their studies," says an international and area studies major. "We enjoy writing, we enjoy discussion, and we enjoy critical thinking and inquiry."

Life on K's wooded, 65-acre campus centers on the Quad, a green lawn where students ponder their destinies and play ultimate Frisbee with equal ease. With its rolling hills, Georgian architecture, and brick-laid streets, the campus has the quaint look more typical of historic New England than of the nearby city of Kalamazoo, which, with surrounding communities, has 261,000 residents. Newer campus facilities include a $18 million LEED-certified natatorium, and two new residence halls are expected to open in 2027.

Founded in 1833 and formerly associated with the American Baptist Churches, Kalamazoo is the oldest private college in Michigan. Many first-years begin the year with a LandSea trip, which features a choice between three weeks of climbing, rappelling, canoeing, and backpacking in the mountains of the Adirondacks or a six-day camping experience just outside of town. By the end, they're convinced they can survive anything, including the rigors of a Kalamazoo College education and the long Michigan winters. Once on campus, they pursue a liberal arts curriculum that includes language proficiency, a first-year writing seminar, sophomore and senior seminars, as well as a senior integrated project—directed research, a creative piece, or a traditional thesis—basically anything that caps off each student's education in some meaningful way.

After their sophomore year, most of K's undergrads meet life's challenges with suitcase in hand, studying wherever their heart takes them, often for the same price as their campus tuition, room, and board. The college offers three-, six-, and nine-month immersive study abroad programs that are available to all students, regardless of major; all credit earned during study abroad transfers back to K. "Kalamazoo College does study abroad so well that it seems ridiculous not to take advantage of this opportunity," cheers a biology major. "They make it financially accessible and ensure that you won't fall behind by going abroad." Students recommend the study abroad options of 50-plus programs in more than 35 countries.

Back on campus, the academic climate of K's three 10-week terms "varies based on departments," says a biochemistry and Spanish major. "In the science departments, it is very intensive, competitive, and professional. In other departments, it feels more relaxed, experimental, and collaborative." The natural sciences are exceptionally good, and interdisciplinary programs in international and area studies, community and global health, and critical ethnic studies are also strengths. Psychology, biology, business, English, and biochemistry are the most popular majors, and students praise K's language departments. Professors, rated highly for their enthusiasm and accessibility, give students lots of individual attention. "Professors in your intended field will guide you through your four years here at K," attests a math major. Most students participate in career development programs like internships, "Hornet Huddles" with K alumni, and K-Trek trips to visit industries around the country.

> "Every student at Kalamazoo College is very driven whether that be academically or athletically."

"Every student at Kalamazoo College is very driven whether that be academically or athletically," muses a junior. Sixty-six percent of students come from Michigan and 4 percent from foreign nations. The student body is 16 percent Hispanic/Latino, 3 percent Asian American, 5 percent Black, and 5 percent multiracial. Many students crave more diversity on campus. The administration says it is continuing efforts to educate students on intercultural understanding. "The students at K are very politically active and vocal in their opinions," says a junior. Merit scholarships averaging $48,000 are available to qualified students. Athletic scholarships are not available.

Sixty-four percent of students live on campus. "Residential life on campus mostly involves underclassmen," notes a psychology major, "as the majority of the junior class is abroad and the senior class tends to live off-campus." The dorms are "big enough to live comfortably with another person," an economics and political science major explains. Dorms are divided by class year, and three dorms are available for first-year students. Dining services get mixed reviews. "The caf is generally pretty meh, but the late-night options are nice," offers a sophomore. Students give good ratings to campus safety, and while there are no Greek organizations, seven on-campus houses offer a more community-oriented atmosphere, including family-style dinners. For those who tire of campus life, "Off-campus housing is both cheap and located close to campus, so it is a popular option," reports a sophomore. Regarding student services, a psychology major says, "The student support resources are very strong, like the writing center and the mental wellness center."

> "The local music and art scenes are huge in Kalamazoo."

K's campus is always buzzing with social activities like movies, concerts, speakers, and other events. "House parties thrown by students occur on weekends," says

> *Dorms are divided by class year, and three dorms are available for first-year students.*

a junior, "as well as Western Michigan tailgating events, Greek life parties, athletic events, etc." Students agree that the atmosphere is pressure-free when it comes to alcohol. Students look forward to the Monte Carlo, "a casino-themed night with food and music," says a junior. In spring, the Day of Gracious Living happens when, without prior warning, classes are canceled, and students can choose to head to the beach, work on volunteer projects, or relax on campus. A majority of students get involved in the community through service-learning courses and student-led cocurricular activities, working with local partners to address issues such as neighborhood development, sustainability, prison reform, and migrant rights. "The local music and art scenes are huge in Kalamazoo, with many free performances all year and Art Hop every month," says a senior. In addition to the typical collection of restaurants, theaters, and bars, K students benefit from the physical proximity of Western Michigan University, where they may use the library or attend cultural events. Students "also can take a bus or train to other cities: Chicago, Grand Rapids, Ann Arbor, Detroit, etc.," notes a senior.

For those who equate college with athletics, K has something to offer—even if it's not nationally televised games or tens of thousands of screaming fans. With 22 varsity teams, the Kalamazoo Hornets have a long-standing rivalry with Hope College, culminating in the football teams' annual competition for the Wooden Shoes trophy. The outstanding men's tennis team has won the Michigan Intercollegiate Athletic Association conference championship 90 (!) times, most recently in 2025. The baseball team won its second consecutive conference championship in 2024. K offers intramural volleyball, soccer, and basketball, as well as several club sports.

Kalamazoo College is "an academically rigorous, small liberal arts college with an open curriculum and amazing travel opportunities," says a junior. The result, says a senior, is a student body defined by "open-minded, global citizens."

> ## Overlaps
>
> **Albion, Grand Valley State, Hope, U of I at Urbana–Champaign, University of Michigan, Michigan State, Western Michigan, Wooster**

If You Apply To ›

Kalamazoo: Early decision, early action, regular decision. SATs or ACTs: optional. Accepts the Common Application with optional writing supplement.

University of Kansas

1450 Jayhawk Boulevard, Lawrence, KS 66045

Often overlooked because of its heartland location, KU has the sophistication of the leading Big Ten universities but is much easier to get into. Stereotypes of Kansas to the contrary, Lawrence is not flat as a pancake. Offers a solid slate of professional schools and an honors program that is among the nation's best. Jayhawk basketball is legendary.

Despite its conservative Midwest location, the University of Kansas is a welcoming oasis of progressive activism and tolerance. The school courts extremely dedicated students with an impressive honors program that has helped raise its academic profile. With sound academics and extracurriculars, winning athletics, and a stellar social life, the University of Kansas has a bounty of opportunities for motivated Jayhawks. "We put a strong emphasis on research and individualism, which is awesome for students to break out of the set curriculum and explore what they are passionate about," says an international business major.

> **Website**: www.ku.edu
> **Location**: Small City
> **Public**
> **Total Enrollment**: 24,904
> **Undergraduates**: 19,555
> **Male/Female**: 47/53
> **Financial Aid**: 70%

(continued)

Pell Grant: 22%

Expense: Pub $ $

Student Loans: 47%

Average Debt: $

Applicants: 22,363

Accepted: 93%

Enrolled: 25%

Grad in 6 Years: 69%

Returning First-years: 86%

Academics: ✍ ✍ ✍ ✍

Social: 🗩 🗩 🗩 🗩

Q of L: ★ ★ ★ ★

Admissions: (785) 864-3911

Email Address: adm@ku.edu

Strong Programs:
Architecture
Business
Criminal Justice
Education
Engineering
Geology
Journalism
Music
Sociocultural Anthropology

Founded as a co-ed prep school in 1866, KU was one of the earliest public institutions to admit men and women equally.

Founded as a co-ed prep school in 1866, KU was one of the earliest public institutions to admit men and women equally; it began offering college level courses in 1869. The 1,000-acre campus is set atop Mount Oread—a hill that was once a crossing point for pioneer wagon trains—and spreads out on rolling green hills overlooking river valleys. Many of the buildings are made of indigenous Kansas limestone and are famed for their red roofs. But the real beauty of the campus lies in its landscape, particularly the breathtaking autumn foliage. The Dole Institute of Politics is home to one of the world's largest congressional archives and a World Trade Center memorial. A massive $350 million expansion of the campus's Central District features an integrated sciences building, a student union, and residence halls, among other facilities. The Gateway District at the north entrance of campus has seen renovations to the David Booth Kansas Memorial Stadium and the Anderson Family Football Complex.

Prospective KU first-years will automatically be considered for admission to the College of Liberal Arts & Sciences, where 49 percent of the undergraduate population is enrolled. To earn direct admission to one of the 13 other schools—ranging from Architecture & Design, Business, and Engineering to Health Professions, Nursing, Pharmacy, and Social Welfare—applicants need to include additional information, meet the schools' entry requirements, and, in some cases, pass prerequisite courses. As part of their degrees, all KU undergraduates must complete the university-wide KU Core 34 curriculum, which spans the entire undergraduate experience and culminates in a required capstone experience that varies by major.

> **"We put a strong emphasis on research and individualism."**

Some of the most notable undergraduate programs offered include criminal justice, sociocultural anthropology, education, geology, music, and health-related majors. The School of Journalism and Mass Communications perpetuates the legacy of famed journalist William Allen White, and the School of Engineering expanded with the opening of the interdisciplinary Earth, Energy, and Environment Center. Psychology, finance, journalism, and marketing are the most popular majors. Accelerated bachelor's/master's programs in several fields, ranging from environmental studies/urban planning to history of art, allow students to earn two degrees in five years.

"The academic climate is very flexible and supportive," says a microbiology major. Forty-six percent of all undergraduate classes have fewer than 20 students, and while teaching assistants do teach some classes, students often have access to leading professors early on. "My calculus course freshman year was taught by the head of the math department—showing that there isn't a time at KU where your academics and instruction are not made a top priority," says an architecture major. The Office of Student Affairs wins praise for its academic advising and its help with internships, disability services, and extracurriculars. "I have always had quick and easy access to career advising and school counselors as well," shares an accounting major.

Incoming first-years can apply to the University Honors Program, which provides more than 1,600 academically motivated students with in-depth courses, specialized advising, early enrollment, and financial support for opportunities like research projects. The study abroad programs draw 25 percent of students who may travel through 165 faculty-led, internship, direct enrollment, and reciprocal exchange programs in more than 70 countries.

"Students at KU are adventurous, outgoing, and supportive of one another," describes a senior. Fifty-seven percent of undergrads are from Kansas, and 6 percent are international. Black students account for 4 percent, Hispanics/Latinos 11 percent, Asian Americans 6 percent, and multiracial students 6 percent. Politically, "We are definitely a blue dot in a red state," says one student, but conservative views are well represented on campus too. "There are so many organizations that can help students find their niche," notes an environmental science major. KU grants four-year renewable merit scholarships averaging $8,000 to eligible first-years and athletes vie for 200 full and partial scholarships in 16 varsity sports.

Twenty-seven percent of undergraduates live in university-owned housing. Most students live off campus in Lawrence apartments, which are considered expensive only by Kansas standards. "Scholarship halls are a popular and affordable option, where about 50 students live together in a massive house," advises a senior. Students take their meals at 16 dining locations across campus, ranging from residential dining halls to retail cafés, coffeehouses, and snack shops. "The food is a good mix of different cuisines and is also healthy and nutritious," says a junior. One student explains, "KU SafeRide provides transportation for late at night, while Lawrence police and university police constantly patrol the streets." Additionally, the Sexual Assault Prevention and Education Center conducts training on consent and bystander intervention.

Greek life, which attracts 15 percent of the men and 24 percent of the women, is a conspicuous force in the social scene—and has been since 1873!—but doesn't control it. According to a behavioral neuroscience major, "KU is definitely a Midwest party school," but a human biology major cautions, "The university is a dry campus." About 500 organized groups keep things lively; other activities include movies, poetry readings, game nights, cultural events, and concerts. "The surrounding area has all sorts of different vibes," says a junior. "You can keep it very relaxed or have a loud and party-filled night." The university's bus system is much appreciated by tenderfeet, especially because that great big hill seems to double in size during the cold, windy winters.

With its myriad boutiques, restaurants, and bars and its active music scene, Lawrence is a favored destination for off-campus fun, and students also enjoy getting involved in the community through KU's Center for Community Outreach. "Lawrence is the American college town," asserts one enthusiastic Jayhawk. "Period." Topeka, the state capital, and Kansas City are each less than an hour's drive, and the area is also served by Amtrak.

KU varsity teams—the only ones in the nation that carry the name Jayhawks, who were antislavery pioneers in the 1850s—compete in the rough-and-tumble Big 12 Conference. "Our rivalries with Mizzou and K-State are insane," says one fan. Football and men's and women's basketball are regular powerhouses. James Naismith, who invented basketball, was KU's first coach (and the only Jayhawk coach to have a losing record). Women's volleyball, men's and women's golf, women's tennis, and men's and women's track and field are also competitive. Students take part in about 30 sports clubs and 30 intramural sports, the most popular of which is—you guessed it—basketball. Volleyball, soccer, and tennis are other student favorites.

Jayhawk traditions run deep. The school year kicks off with Hawk Week, the official welcome for new students. To demonstrate their team loyalty, thousands of students show up for the first men's and women's basketball practices of the season. This nocturnal tradition is lovingly labeled "Late Night in the Phog"—an allusion to the fieldhouse named after the late, great basketball coach Forrest "Phog" Allen. The traditional "Rock Chalk Jayhawk" KU cheer and steam whistle signaling the end of every class period are enough to bring a pang of nostalgia to the heart of even the most grizzled Kansas alum. "This is the only place to be a Jayhawk and we wear that on our chests loud and proud!" says a junior.

"There are so many organizations that can help students find their niche."

Overlaps

University of Arkansas, Indiana University, Iowa State, Kansas State, Michigan State, University of Missouri, University of Nebraska–Lincoln, University of Oklahoma

"This is the only place to be a Jayhawk and we wear that on our chests loud and proud!"

With nearly 200 undergraduate fields of study, Kansas's reputation (the nonbasketball one) continues to grow. Comprehensive study abroad programs, a distinctive honors program, and a robust sense of school spirit are just some of the reasons students choose to be Jayhawks. And as a satisfied sophomore points out, "Once you become a Jayhawk, you can feel the family and support everywhere on campus. We really care about one another and make sure our flock is ready to fly."

University of Kentucky

101 Main Building, Lexington, KY 40506

The state of Kentucky is better known for horses and hoops than for higher education, but its flagship public university, located in the heart of the Bluegrass, is working to change that. The University of Kentucky is always a championship contender on the basketball court of course, but its programs in business, engineering, health, and equine sciences are just as competitive. About a third of students come from out of state, mostly from Illinois, Indiana, Ohio, Tennessee, and Georgia.

Website: www.uky.edu
Location: City Center
Public
Total Enrollment: 30,341
Undergraduates: 23,338
Male/Female: 42/58
Financial Aid: 71%
Pell Grant: 26%
Expense: Pub $ $ $
Student Loans: 48%
Average Debt: $ $ $ $
Applicants: 31,517
Accepted: 93%
Enrolled: 22%
Grad in 6 Years: 71%
Returning First-years: 87%
Academics: ✍ ✍ ✍
Social: 🗨 🗨 🗨 🗨
Q of L: ★ ★ ★
Admissions: (859) 257-2000
Email Address:
 admissions@uky.edu

Strong Programs:
Business
Education

While the University of Kentucky Wildcats grab the most headlines, the university's claims to excellence stretch into outstanding medical and premedical programs, scientific research involving both professors and students, and a social calendar packed with enough Southern tradition to make even the most composed debutante's head spin. Over the last decade, UK has undergone a more than $2.3 billion campus transformation, much of it focused on student life, including more than $450 million in high-tech residence halls and the Gatton Student Center, complete with dining and a state-of-the-art fitness center. UK is a national leader in efforts to support first-generation college students and has established a dedicated living/learning community for them.

The University of Kentucky was founded in 1865 as the state's land grant university, and its campus contains a mixture of old and new, with traditional redbrick buildings that date back to the late 1890s and modern designs using contemporary glass and concrete. The well-maintained grounds are organized around comfortable parklike spaces influenced by Frederick Law Olmsted's design. The campus contains a vast number of mature trees and lawns set in a natural arrangement of open spaces, typical of the great land grant universities. Of course, UK's location in the heart of one of the finest horse-breeding areas in the world makes it a natural place for the Gluck Equine Research Center, a headquarters for research into horse diseases.

> **"I've had many professors whose lectures made me excited to go to class."**

UK's general education program, known as the UK Core, comprises the equivalent of 30 credit hours in 10 course areas that address four broad learning outcomes. Incoming students are encouraged but not required to take an academic orientation class called UK101, designed to help them adjust to college life. Students not ready to declare a major may test the academic waters in "Exploratory Programs" in a particular college. Business, engineering, and health, especially nursing and premed programs, tend to be UK's strongest fields, but several unique programs stand out. The equine science and management major prepares students for a wide range of careers in the horse industry by teaching both science and business concepts. Students studying prevet and animal sciences at UK will find coveted slots reserved for them at Auburn University and Tuskegee in the advanced veterinary medicine program, at in-state tuition rates. UK's Gaines Center for the Humanities is unusual in its study of public higher education, and the Patterson School of Diplomacy and International Commerce is one of the smallest yet most respected schools of its type in the country. The Lewis Honors College is housed in a dedicated quad of residence halls.

The academic climate is laid-back, but students shouldn't expect easy A's. Thirty-five percent of classes have fewer than 20 students, but lower-level "monster" science classes are common, and one student describes them as "extremely large and not at all personalized." When it comes time for course registration, a marketing major says students "have difficulty if they are freshmen because most of them have to take the same classes, and sometimes they don't get the right times—or the classes at all." It's hard to complete the engineering, health, business, and architecture programs in four years, students say. Internships and co-op programs also complicate—but enliven—the picture. The university has bolstered its advising services to provide more personalized attention and to better coordinate career and academic services. Teaching assistants and full professors teach about the same number of first-year classes, and students praise UK's faculty. "I've had many professors whose lectures made me excited to go to class," says a communication sciences and disorders major. Seventeen percent of students study abroad in more than 200 available programs, including 52 that are directed by UK faculty.

"UK students are typically self-assured, slightly competitive, and outgoing," says a psychology major, and according to a classmate, "Southern hospitality abounds." UK undergraduates hail from all 120 Kentucky counties and more than 100 countries; 33 percent are from out of state and 1 percent are international. The student body is predominantly white; Black students account for just 6 percent of undergrads, Hispanics/Latinos 7 percent, Asian Americans 4 percent, and multiracial students 4 percent. Diverse political views are represented on campus, but a senior says UK is "not really a politically charged university." Merit scholarships averaging $9,100 are offered to qualified students, as are more than 500 athletic scholarships.

"Southern hospitality abounds [at UK]."

The university has modernized all its residence halls and opened 14 new ones in recent years. Dorms are located on two parts of the campus—north and central—and offer suite-style rooms, with no more than four students sharing a bathroom. "Students get really nice amenities, like Tempur-Pedic mattresses, granite countertops, two sinks, and full-size closets," reports a student. The only downside of such plush accommodations, students say, is the hefty cost. Students are not required to live on campus, but 32 percent do so. Dining services get good reviews, and a communication major says, "There are so many options from sit-down, buffet-style to specialty cafés to fast food," as well as "worry-free zones" for students with dietary restrictions. The Green Dot Bystander Intervention program, designed to prevent sexual assault and domestic violence on college campuses, originated at the University of Kentucky and has been adopted by hundreds of colleges and universities across the country.

On campus, students enjoy movies, presentations, seminars, concerts, and athletic events. Nineteen percent of Kentucky men and 29 percent of the women go Greek, and fraternities and sororities offer numerous on-campus social activities as well as opportunities for volunteer work in the community. Students are not allowed to have alcohol on campus, except for special events that have been registered with the university. Students collaborate to mount one of the largest student-run philanthropies anywhere: DanceBlue. The yearlong fundraising effort culminates in a

(continued)

Engineering
Equine Science and
  Management
International Studies
Nursing
Premed
Prevet

DanceBlue is a yearlong, student-run fundraising effort that culminates in a 24-hour, no-sleeping dance marathon that benefits a local children's cancer clinic.

The equine science and management major prepares students for a wide range of careers in the horse industry.

24-hour, no-sleeping dance marathon that benefits a local children's cancer clinic and pediatric cancer research. Among the highlights of any student's career at UK are two one-month periods—one in the fall, one in the spring—when students spend afternoons at Keeneland Race Track enjoying the tradition of Kentucky horse racing.

Despite the limited diversity on campus, Lexington abounds with a multitude of ethnic eateries, as well as theaters, shops, and nightspots. The downtown area is within walking distance of campus. "Downtown Lexington has a great social scene, so lots of students will venture off campus for concerts, restaurants, festivals, farmers markets, etc.," says a senior. When it's time for a road trip, UK students head to Cincinnati or Louisville (one hour away) or to Atlanta or Chicago (six hours).

The best road-trip destinations, of course, are anywhere there's a steamy, noisy gym and a basketball team ready to do battle with UK's always-solid Wildcats. Home games at the legendary Rupp Arena—what one student calls "a magical experience"—are consistently packed by the Big Blue Nation. "In Kentucky, basketball is like a second religion," agrees another true-blue Wildcat fan. Football and women's basketball draw crowds too. The school fields 21 Division I teams in all, most of which compete in the Southeastern Conference (SEC). Intramurals range from soccer and basketball leagues to dodgeball tournaments and hot-shot contests.

> "In Kentucky, basketball is like a second religion."

"The culture of UK is unique because it has the competitive energy of the SEC, but it's not an overly Greek-focused campus and it does a great job of supporting every interest," comments a senior. Indeed, students here find plenty of solid opportunities, from specialties in equine and animal science to support for first-generation students to serious school pride. Whether it's screaming themselves hoarse for five players hitting the hardwood or for four-legged equines racing around an oval, for many students, the mix of collegiate craziness and old-world Southern hospitality found at the University of Kentucky is just what they want.

Overlaps

Indiana University, University of Louisville, Miami (OH), Ohio State, University of Tennessee Knoxville, West Virginia University

If You Apply To ›

Kentucky: Early action, regular decision. Accepts the Common Application. Please consult Kentucky's website for the most up-to-date information regarding standardized test requirements.

Kenyon College

104 College Drive, Gambier, OH 43022

Kenyon is a vintage liberal arts college plunked down in the middle of the Ohio countryside. More mainstream than Oberlin, more intense than Denison, and more selective than Wooster, Kenyon is best known for English and a small but distinguished drama program. Located in a tiny village where faculty and staff are the main residents. Swimming and diving teams make huge splashes.

Website: www.kenyon.edu
Location: Rural
Private
Total Enrollment: 1,732
Undergraduates: 1,732

The oldest private college in Ohio, Kenyon College provides students with an accessible and pure liberal arts experience that rivals those of leading East Coast institutions, with a goal being to "cultivate intellectual courage and humility in equal measure." Students here are proud of what they see as setting Kenyon apart from other liberal arts colleges. "One thing that unites us all is that we are passionate about something," explains one student. "Whether it be drama, physics, writing, activism—Kenyon students care!" Though highly selective, the college continues to build on its reputation as a supportive academic environment.

Kenyon's 1,000-acre campus sits on a hillside overlooking a scenic view of river, woods, and fields in a secluded village of roughly 2,500 residents. Old Kenyon, the college's original building, dating from 1826, is said to be the first collegiate Gothic building in America, and the campus is on the National Register of Historic Places. The campus also boasts a 500-acre nature preserve, featuring hiking trails and extensive perennial gardens. The 98,000-square-foot Chalmers Library is LEED Gold–certified, and three new apartment-style residences that will also be LEED Gold–certified are in the works.

The hallmark of Kenyon's academic philosophy is a fierce devotion to the liberal arts and sciences. While there is no core curriculum at Kenyon, all students must have proficiency in a second language and complete requirements in quantitative reasoning. A bevy of academic counselors, including upperclassmen and professors, help ensure that first-years stay on the right track. The culmination of each student's coursework at Kenyon is the senior exercise, which may take the form of a comprehensive examination, an integrative paper, a research project, a performance, or some combination of these.

English, a nationally renowned subject at Kenyon since the 1930s, is among the most popular majors, and it, along with the department of dance, drama, and film (which turned out the likes of Allison Janney and Paul Newman), sets the tone of campus life. Kenyon is the home of *The Kenyon Review*, a prestigious literary quarterly that offers internships to a few lucky students, and is a school about which alum E. L. Doctorow said, "Poetry is what we did at Kenyon, the way at Ohio State they played football." John Green, the giant of young adult fiction, is also an alum. Social sciences, biological sciences, and visual and performing arts round out the list of popular majors, and the modern languages and literatures and mathematics and statistics departments are also strong. Political science draws many undecided majors with its yearlong introductory class, Quest for Justice. The Integrated Program in Humane Studies concentration, the school's oldest interdisciplinary program, is also popular. Opportunities for independent study abound, such as a unique farming program that places students on nearby farms for fieldwork each week. Preprofessional opportunities include 3–2 engineering programs with several universities and high access to graduate programs in law, business, and medicine.

"The academic climate is rigorous but helpful and accepting," says a math and statistics major. Classes are small—70 percent have fewer than 20 students—and even the larger introductory courses use a two-part format in which students meet for lectures one week and split up for discussion sections with the professor the next. "Kenyon's professors are active researchers and exemplary teachers," says a math major. "They are passionate about their fields, and they love getting their students excited about the material as well." Many profs live close to campus, which enhances the close-knit environment. On-campus summer research scholarships in the sciences and humanities provide opportunities for collaborative research for aspiring scientists, scholars, and doctors. "Study abroad is a big program here," informs a sophomore, and 39 percent of students choose from nearly 200 programs in 50 countries, including Kenyon-sponsored programs in England and Italy.

Fourteen percent of students are Ohioans, one-third hail from New England and Mid-Atlantic states, and 12 percent come from abroad. Black students account for 2 percent of the student body, Hispanics/Latinos 8 percent, Asian Americans 4 percent, and multiracial students 6 percent, and the college is actively working to increase diversity. The liberal, friendly student body is politically engaged, especially when it comes to social justice issues, and a sophomore says, "Students at Kenyon thrive on open

> "Whether it be drama, physics, writing, activism— Kenyon students care!"

> "Kenyon's professors are active researchers and exemplary teachers."

Summer Sendoff is an outdoor concert celebrating the end of spring semester classes.

(continued)

Male/Female: 44/56
Financial Aid: 49%
Pell Grant: 13%
Expense: Pr $ $ $ $
Student Loans: 37%
Average Debt: $
Applicants: 7,736
Accepted: 31%
Enrolled: 18%
Grad in 6 Years: 82%
Returning First-years: 92%
Academics: ✍ ✍ ✍ ✍
Social: 🗩 🗩 🗩
Q of L: ★ ★ ★
Admissions: (800) 848-2468
Email Address:
admissions@kenyon.edu

Strong Programs:
Biological Sciences
English
Modern Languages and
  Literatures
Physics
Political Science
Psychology
Social Sciences
Visual and Performing Arts

conversation and do not silence opinions that contradict theirs." Kenyon meets the full demonstrated financial need of admitted students and awards merit scholarships averaging $19,500. Newman's Own Foundation Scholarships guarantee a loan-free education for 25 selected students with the greatest need who bring the qualities of creativity, community service, and leadership to Kenyon.

All students live on campus, with housing guaranteed for four years. First-years start in five dorms at the north end of campus, and most move to the south end the next year. Renovations and expansions are always in the works, but students say some accommodations still need improving. Rooms are selected via a sometimes-harrowing housing lottery. Everyone, including those in the apartments with kitchens, must buy the unlimited meal plan. "Kenyon is in an isolated area of Ohio and is generally very safe," a senior says. One student says of mental health counseling, "It can be difficult to book appointments due to the number of students in need."

Given the school's rural location, social life happens on campus, with more than 100 student clubs and a Greek system that draws 20 percent of the men and 28 percent of the women. The frats throw lively parties that are open to all, and a senior says,

> "If students embrace Kenyon, it is a quirky school that can be extremely rewarding to attend."

"Every student performance—sports games, public presentations, music recitals, art shows—is incredibly well attended." With its deli, market, coffeehouse, inn, restaurant, couple of bars, bank, and post office, Gambier is at least quaint, even if it causes some culture shock for urbanites. Students enjoy buying real maple syrup, fresh bread, and cheese from Amish farmers with stands on the main street on Saturdays. There are a few more options 10 minutes away in Mount Vernon, to which the college runs a daytime shuttle bus, and two small ski areas lie near campus. Columbus and Ohio State are a 45-minute drive south, and those seeking adventure farther from home sometimes road-trip to Cleveland (home of the Rock and Roll Hall of Fame), Cincinnati, Chicago, or even Canada.

Kenyon remains defined by its traditions, the most hallowed of which is renewed each year as incoming first-years sing college songs to the rest of the community from the steps of Rosse Hall. Departing seniors sing the same songs at graduation. On Matriculation Day each October, after a formal ceremony, first-years sign a book that contains the signatures of virtually every Kenyon student since the early 1800s. Summer Sendoff is an outdoor concert celebrating the end of spring semester classes.

Kenyon's varsity teams are known as the Owls. Men's and women's tennis and soccer are consistently competitive in the North Coast Athletic Conference, but the flagship sport is swimming. Kenyon's swimming and diving teams dominate Division III competition, with the men's team having won 34 national titles and the women's team claiming 25. The annual hockey game against Denison and soccer games against Ohio Wesleyan draw large crowds. Club and intramural sports attract 24 percent of the students with favorites including ultimate Frisbee, basketball, and volleyball.

Kenyon students are liberal, global thinkers who are as devoted to one another as they are to their studies and their traditions. *The Kenyon Review*, the legend of alumnus Paul Newman, and national-championship swimming give the college a distinctive identity. As one sociology major advises, "It can be tough at times dealing with the location or the intense academics, but if students embrace Kenyon, it is a quirky school that can be extremely rewarding to attend."

Overlaps

Colby, Grinnell, Hamilton, Macalester, Oberlin, Swarthmore, Wesleyan, Williams

If You Apply To ›

Kenyon: Early decision I and II, regular decision. Accepts the Common Application. Please consult Kenyon's website for the most up-to-date information regarding standardized test requirements.

2 East South Street, Galesburg, IL 61401

This friendly and progressive Illinois college was among the first in the nation to admit Black students and women. Offers a strong creative writing program, exceptional sciences, and a real-world atmosphere. More mainstream than Beloit and Grinnell and smaller than Illinois Wesleyan. With a hugely diverse student body of about 1,100, Knox offers an unusual degree of personal attention, even by the standards of small colleges.

With the unconventional Prairie Fire as its emblem, Knox College has long made a name for itself by breaking away from the conventions of the day. Founded by abolitionists in 1837 as the Knox Manual Labor College, this liberal arts college has a tradition of debate that extends beyond the Lincoln–Douglas event that occurred here in 1858. And through a warm, supportive academic community and emphasis on "putting knowledge into practice through real-world experiences," the college fosters a strong sense of individualism.

Located in the heart of the Midwest—midway between Chicago and St. Louis—the 82-acre campus has spacious, tree-lined lawns and a dynamic mixture of architecture that reflects the 164-year span of construction dates of existing buildings. Old Main, constructed in 1857, is a National Historic Landmark and the only building remaining from the 1858 Lincoln–Douglas debates. Newer campus projects include the Knight Living & Learning Center at Green Oaks, Knox's prairie campus.

Students say the academic relationships at Knox are infused with a spirit of cooperation and equality. Knox operates on an honor system that allows students to take tests unproctored in any public area. Beyond the classroom, students, faculty, and administrators make decisions on boards together, each with identical voting power. As part of Knox's Blaze a Trail first-year experience program, incoming students participate in new student orientation and take First-Year Preceptorial, a small seminar taught by professors from across the college that emphasizes critical analysis, writing, and class discussion. They may also join an optional living/learning community associated with their Preceptorial course. "The culture encourages open debate and hands-on projects, so you can try new things without feeling judged," says a junior.

> **"The culture encourages open debate and hands-on projects."**

All Knox students apply their learning to a real-world experience of their choice, such as independent research or creative work, an internship, community service, or study abroad, which serves as a capstone experience in their junior or senior year. What's more, through Knox's Power of Experience program, every student receives funding of at least $2,000 to support these experiences. The general education curriculum, known as Elements, spans coursework in the arts, sciences, humanities, and social sciences, through which students learn how to communicate in a second language, in numbers and symbols, and with people of diverse backgrounds. Creative writing and biology are among the school's strongest programs; the college's biannual literary magazine, *Catch*, has won several national and international awards, while biology attracts research grant money. Other popular majors include psychology, business and management, and computer science; the theater department is also notable. Knox offers 3–2 or 3–4 programs in engineering, nursing, medical technology, law, and architecture as well as a cooperative program with the George Washington University School of Medicine and Health Sciences.

Website: www.knox.edu
Location: Small City
Private
Total Enrollment: 1,116
Undergraduates: 1,116
Male/Female: 50/50
Financial Aid: 100%
Pell Grant: 32%
Expense: Pr $ $
Student Loans: 48%
Average Debt: $ $ $
Applicants: 4,899
Accepted: 71%
Enrolled: 11%
Grad in 6 Years: 68%
Returning First-years: 83%
Academics: ✍ ✍ ✍
Social: 🍺 🍺 🍺
Q of L: ★ ★ ★
Admissions: (800) 678-5669
Email Address:
  admission@knox.edu

Strong Programs:
Anthropology and Sociology
Biology
Business and Management
Computer Science
Creative Writing
Psychology
Theater

"The academic climate at Knox is fast-paced, as we have three semesters a year, but the faculty and peers are very supportive," says a biochemistry major. As part of Knox's trimester system, students are only required to take three courses per term, which keeps the coursework "very manageable," according to a biology major. Eighty-four percent of classes have fewer than 20 students, and a political science and economics major says, "The quality of instruction is very meaningful and sincere." Immersive terms give students the option of engaging in a hands-on exploration of a single field of study for an entire term; available subjects include clinical psychology, studio art, repertory theater, business start-ups, and fieldwork and community-building at the off-campus Green Oaks prairie restoration site. Knox offers more than 100 study abroad and off-campus programs around the world. Students praise Knox's academic advising system for helping them navigate the multitude of options; other student services, from career advising to mental health, receive high marks as well.

"Most students are open-minded, curious, friendly, and okay with big classroom discussions," comments a business and management major. Thirty-eight percent of students come from Illinois, and an impressive 27 percent hail from foreign countries. While Knox is not a hotbed of political protest, students here tend to be progressive and engaged in current events, and a commitment to diversity is evident across campus. Black students make up 6 percent of the student body, Asian Americans 4 percent, Hispanics/Latinos 13 percent, and multiracial students 5 percent. Thirty-two percent of first-years qualify for Pell Grants. Merit scholarships averaging $42,200 are available, but athletic scholarships are not.

Ninety-eight percent of students reside in campus digs. Most first-years live in recently "refreshed" single-sex suites, and a senior says the apartments and townhouses for upperclassmen are comfortable. Those who move off campus must obtain permission, which can be difficult. Dining services get good reviews, especially because the staff will "work with students to create new recipes and bring new products to Knox," explains a French and history major. Students rate campus safety as strong.

Five percent of men and 3 percent of women go Greek, and weekends are filled with on-campus club activities, cultural events, and fraternity parties, although all parties must be registered and alcohol-free. Students warn that the administration is quick to deal with underage drinkers. Annual events include the Knox Rocks music festival and International Fair, but a junior says Flunk Day is "the crown jewel of all Knox traditions." At 7 a.m. on a spring morning, Old Main's bell rings, seniors bang pots and pans, and classes are canceled to make way for lawn games, inflatables, food trucks, karaoke, and other rollicking festivities.

Galesburg is a small Midwestern railroad town, and the Amtrak station makes travel easy and relatively cheap. "Galesburg has everything you might need, including Walmart, Target, Marshalls, Wells Fargo, restaurants, thrift stores, and barber shops," reports a first-year. At one time, this city of about 30,000 was a center of abolitionism, and the honorary degree that the college bestowed on then-presidential candidate Abraham Lincoln was his first. For those interested in service, Knox was the first college in the country to establish an official Peace Corps Preparatory Program. Now, more than half of Knox students devote thousands of hours to community service every year. Nearby Lake Storey offers boating, water slides, and nature trails, and students looking for more excitement can travel to Peoria, about 50 miles southeast, or Chicago, about 200 miles northeast.

Prairie Fire athletics' 20 Division III teams generate enthusiasm, boosted by the school mascot, a fox named—you guessed it—Blaze. The women's basketball and men's and women's track and field teams are strong, playing in the Midwest Conference. Every fall, the football team endures lots of "hard Knox" against archrival Monmouth to bring home the highly prized Bronze Turkey trophy, a throwback to the time when the game was played on Thanksgiving Day. About 20 percent of students participate in intramural and club sports; basketball, volleyball, and ultimate Frisbee are the most popular.

As a Knox student, "You go to school in a small town in the Midwest, where the winters are bitter and the fall and spring are all too short," muses a junior. "But despite these challenges, Knox students focus their pride on their academics and the quality of their campus experience." The result is a close-knit community, an emphasis on hands-on learning, and an open-minded atmosphere fostered by Knox's notably diverse student body. "If you like knowing your classmates, having helpful resources, and working closely with teachers," says a satisfied business and management major, "Knox is a perfect fit."

If You Apply To ›

Knox: Early action I and II, regular decision. SATs or ACTs: optional. Accepts the Common Application with supplement.

Lafayette College

730 High Street, Easton, PA 18042

Geographically close to Lehigh but closer kin to Colgate and Hamilton and boasting a strong global orientation, including for engineering. Compare to Bucknell, Union, Swarthmore, and Trinity (CT), which also offer engineering. Attracts relatively preppy, sports-minded students who work hard and play hard. One of the smallest institutions to play Division I athletics.

Lafayette College has become one of the small elite liberal arts colleges with a huge presence abroad. A national leader in undergraduate faculty-mentored research, it ranks among the top colleges in study abroad participation, and its liberal arts curriculum mixes nicely with engineering in a small college atmosphere. Says one satisfied junior, "Lafayette is a place that believes that we can be leaders, scholars, athletes, and activists and that we don't have to choose just one."

Founded in 1826 and named for the famous marquis, Lafayette is situated on College Hill, a stately hill in Easton, Pennsylvania, just an hour and a half west of New York City and even closer to Philadelphia. The campus has an eclectic blend of architectural styles and more than 125 species of trees. Open, flexible learning and workspaces are a common theme in many Lafayette buildings, including the Skillman Library and the Acopian Engineering Center, which stays open all night and on weekends. Newer structures include the high-tech Rockwell Integrated Sciences Center, which boasts LEED Platinum certification, and a new residence hall.

A Common Course of Study includes a writing-intensive first-year seminar and courses in lab science, social sciences, mathematics, humanities, global and multicultural proficiency, and a foreign language. "The academic climate is rigorous and competitive but mostly prioritizes curiosity, learning, and engagement through activities such as research," explains an international affairs major. Engineering, psychology, social sciences, and biological and life sciences are among the most

Website: www.lafayette.edu
Location: Small City
Private
Total Enrollment: 2,775
Undergraduates: 2,775
Male/Female: 50/50
Financial Aid: 60%
Pell Grant: 10%
Expense: Pr $ $ $
Student Loans: 36%
Average Debt: $ $ $ $
Applicants: 10,193
Accepted: 32%
Enrolled: 22%
Grad in 6 Years: 88%
Returning First-years: 90%
Academics: ✑ ✑ ✑ ✑
Social: 🌑 🌑 🌑 🌑 🌑
Q of L: ★ ★ ★
Admissions: (610) 330-5100
Email Address:
admissions@lafayette.edu

The 1,000 Nights dance for first-years and the 100 Hours dance for seniors mark the number of days remaining until graduation.

Merit-based Marquis fellowships and scholarships covering full or half tuition respectively are available.

popular majors; nearly half of Lafayette's students major in STEM fields. Students in the four-year engineering and international studies dual-degree program earn a B.S. degree in an engineering field of their choice and a B.A. degree in international studies, choosing a foreign language of concentration in addition to completing an international experience. Programs in visual and performing arts have grown with the opening of the Williams Art Campus. The Dyer Center for Innovation and Entrepreneurship provides hands-on, multidisciplinary opportunities for collaboration in the liberal arts and engineering. Sixty-five percent of classes have fewer than 20 students. "It's easy to build real relationships with professors—I'm on a first-name basis with several," explains a computer science and economics major. The EXCEL program pays students who take research positions with faculty. "You can absolutely ask your professors about their work and even possibly shadow their lab/work," marvels a computer science and French major.

"Study abroad is a major part of the Lafayette experience—about two-thirds of students go abroad," says a junior. Students can pack their bags for programs offered in more than 50 countries. Options include several semester-long, faculty-led programs as well as short-term, faculty-led programs for credit during the January and May interim terms. Even engineering students are encouraged to explore foreign cultures; programs led by Lafayette faculty in Bonn, Germany, and Madrid, Spain, allow them to study abroad for a semester while maintaining normal progress toward their degrees. A government and law major comments, "There's a strong alumni network, and the Career Center does good work connecting students with alumni."

"Lafayette students are curious, competitive, engaged, active, and passionate," says a sophomore. Adds a mathematics major, "The student body is mostly white but there is an active community for students of color and lots of great resources for international students." Eighty-three percent of students are from out of state, and 7 percent are drawn from abroad. Black students account for 6 percent of the student body, Hispanics/Latinos 10 percent, Asian Americans 4 percent, and multiracial students 6 percent. A fairly diverse range of political views are represented on campus. Merit-based Marquis fellowships and scholarships covering full or half tuition respectively are available, and athletes vie for around 150 scholarships in 10 of the school's 23 varsity sports. Lafayette guarantees to meet the full demonstrated need of admitted students, and it has eliminated loans for students from families with total incomes less than $200,000.

> **"Study abroad is a major part of the Lafayette experience."**

Ninety-two percent of students live on campus, and housing is guaranteed for all four years. Possibilities include Greek houses as well as independent dormitories and college-owned apartments with a variety of living and eating arrangements. Housing is chosen via a lottery system, but most get into the dorm of their choice. Students laud the living/learning communities available. "We have the Art House, Dog House (where students train service dogs), and more," says a psychology major. Campus dining facilities get average reviews. "The counseling center is great here," says a junior, who adds, "the health center is not as good. It is a bit harder to get an appointment."

Greek life attracts 25 percent of the men and 34 percent of the women. All sororities and some fraternities are dry; most parties occur off campus. "There is a small party scene but it's easy to avoid if that's not your thing," confides a sophomore. The arts program brings a range of performers to campus, and the most important nonathletic event of the year is LafChella, a music and food festival featuring student bands and popular musical acts. The 1,000 Nights dance for first-years and the 100 Hours dance for seniors mark the number of days remaining until graduation.

For students with cars or those willing to hop a bus or train, Philadelphia and New York beckon on weekends; for a change of pace, there is also hiking the Appalachian Trail. Blue-collar Easton "can entertain you for four years, but you probably wouldn't want to live here the rest of your life," admits a senior. Adds a neuroscience major, "Downtown Easton is beautiful and has great food." Students look forward to Easton's annual garlic and bacon festivals. From College Hill and downtown to the South Side, the city also offers plenty of opportunities for volunteer work in schools, prisons, rehabilitation centers, hospitals, and environmental sites under the auspices of Lafayette's Landis Center for Community Engagement.

Division I sports add flavor to the Lafayette experience. The Leopards play in the Patriot League, and the field hockey, men's soccer, and men's basketball teams regularly vie for conference titles. The annual football game against nearby Lehigh, dating to 1884, is the most-played rivalry in college football. "I saw multiple people dressed up as Marquis de Lafayette," says a first-year. "The rivalry is real!" Students enjoy an extensive recreational program, including more than 30 club sports, several intramurals, and the massive Kirby Sports Center.

> "Lafayette students are curious, competitive, engaged, active, and passionate."

Students seeking close contact with professors, research opportunities, and a global outlook—and who aren't afraid of some serious study—might look at Lafayette. A first-year shares this anecdote: "I was once studying in a lounge area when a student I never met before saw my textbooks, explained that he had taken the course the year before, and proceeded to give me his number in case I had any questions throughout the semester." For those who desire a tight-knit, supportive community, that just about says it all.

<table>
<tr><td>Overlaps</td></tr>
<tr><td>Bucknell, Colgate, Franklin & Marshall, Gettysburg, Lehigh, Swarthmore, Trinity College (CT), Union</td></tr>
</table>

If You Apply To ›

Lafayette: Early decision I and II, regular decision. Accepts the Common Application. Please consult Lafayette's website for the most up-to-date information regarding standardized test requirements.

Lake Forest College

555 North Sheridan Road, Lake Forest, IL 60045

A small, selective, private college on Chicago's North Shore, Lake Forest generally attracts friendly, middle-of-the-road students. In the exclusive town from which the school takes its name, students find both a close-knit campus community and easy access to professional opportunities in nearby Chicago.

Located just 30 miles north of the downtown Loop, Lake Forest College offers excellent programs in business, biology, and psychology, along with abundant opportunities for study abroad and professional internships with organizations such as the Chicago Blackhawks, the Chicago Board of Trade, and the Shedd Aquarium. Academic improvements at Lake Forest are drawing attention; applications are up, and the school is attracting high-caliber students from across the nation and 80 countries. "Lake Forest College is a hidden gem," cheers a first-year student. "Opportunities are everywhere, but they require initiative. No matter your background or major, you can be an asset in any space."

Lake Forest was founded by Presbyterians in 1857 as an alternative to Methodist-oriented Northwestern University. With its mixture of century-old Gothic and

<table>
<tr><td>Website: www.lakeforest.edu</td></tr>
<tr><td>Location: Suburban</td></tr>
<tr><td>Private</td></tr>
<tr><td>Total Enrollment: 1,810</td></tr>
<tr><td>Undergraduates: 1,793</td></tr>
<tr><td>Male/Female: 43/57</td></tr>
<tr><td>Financial Aid: 99%</td></tr>
<tr><td>Pell Grant: 38%</td></tr>
<tr><td>Expense: Pr $ $</td></tr>
<tr><td>Student Loans: 51%</td></tr>
</table>

(continued)

Average Debt: $ $ $
Applicants: 5,358
Accepted: 57%
Enrolled: 14%
Grad in 6 Years: 78%
Returning First-years: 90%
Academics: ✑ ✑ ✑
Social: 🗨 🗨 🗨 🗨
Q of L: ★ ★ ★
Admissions: (847) 735-5000
Email Address:
 admissions@lakeforest.edu

Strong Programs:
Biology
Business
Communication
Entrepreneurship and
 Innovation
Finance
Health Professions
Neuroscience
Psychology

Several student organizations are devoted to community service, and Greek organizations sponsor blood drives, bake sales, and car washes.

modern glass structures, the college's 107-acre campus is storybook beautiful. Located on Chicago's North Shore in a wealthy, quiet suburb of 19,000, the campus has three contiguous parts divided by natural wooded ravines: North, Middle, and South. Each has a mix of residence halls and academic buildings. The state-of-the-art Donnelley and Lee Library offers a 24-hour computer lab, "smart" classrooms, and collaborative workspaces.

General education requirements include the First-Year Studies Program, featuring "very small classes designed to help freshmen integrate into the college," says an English major. "These courses are writing intensive and offer a variety of opportunities, including trips to Chicago for plays and museum visits." Students also complete two credits in each of three liberal arts areas (humanities, social and natural sciences, and math), two cultural diversity courses, and a senior studies capstone course.

Lake Forest's most popular majors include business, finance, biology, and data science. Psychology and English are popular as well. The school's two-year Health Professions Program "provides a valuable opportunity to explore various career paths within the health field," explains a senior.

> **"No matter your background or major, you can be an asset in any space."**

Accelerated and dual-degree programs—including three-year degree programs in philosophy and communication and dual-degree programs in law, engineering, pharmacy, accounting, and international studies—are available. Academic self-starters benefit from the self-designed major program.

The academic climate at Lake Forest "is relaxed and encouraging," says a communications major. Foresters especially enjoy the large doses of individual attention they receive from the faculty. "It has been really easy to communicate with professors whenever I had any questions or needed assistance on projects," confirms an English major. The Career Advancement Center offers symposia, workshops, and résumé clinics, and students benefit from the college's proximity to downtown Chicago, just an hour away by train. Many pursue internships in the city's business district, known as the Loop.

Each year, about 40 first-year students become Richter Apprentice Scholars, living together, working in a 10-week paid research assistantship during the summer before their sophomore year, and taking part in a weekly student/faculty colloquium. "I worked one-on-one with a professor on a data science research project, creating machine learning models," says a data science and economics major. "It was a great opportunity, especially as a first-year student." Study abroad is integral to the Lake Forest experience, and the school offers a choice of more than 250 programs in 70 nations. Students can apply their financial aid packages to approved semester-long programs.

About half of Lake Forest students hail from the Land of Lincoln, and 20 percent come from abroad. "Geographically, we proudly represent a truly global community," says a senior, and students are usually "creative, goal-oriented, successful, and caring," according to another senior. Black students make up 3 percent of the student body, Hispanics/Latinos 18 percent, Asian Americans 6 percent, and multiracial students 4 percent. Students say political debate is usually mild. Competitive financial aid packages are helping to bring more students from less-advantaged backgrounds to Lake Forest, and 38 percent of first-year students are Pell Grant-eligible. The college awards numerous merit scholarships averaging $32,900 but does not offer athletic awards.

Seventy-one percent of students live in the dorms, which they are required to do through their junior year. As the school grows, availability of housing, particularly single rooms, "has become a significant issue," notes a business major. "Some faculty residences have been converted into student housing, and the college has subleased apartments for off-campus living." Housing selection for upperclassmen is prioritized by seniority and GPA, "so there's a definite incentive to do well in your classes," says a senior. A fair number of students commute from home, and many seniors choose to stay on campus due to high rents in the surrounding area. Everybody eats in the central dining hall, where food is prepared to order at pizza, pasta, stir-fry, and other stations. Regarding campus safety, a senior says, "We have regular programming events and student panels dedicated to educating the campus on sexual assault." Mental health services are also strong. In addition to counseling, "There are many opportunities for group sessions, yoga and meditation events, and support groups that help students prioritize their well-being," notes a senior.

Most social life is campus-based. Some students complain that, as a communication major explains, "the social environment can be similar to high school because the college is so small." The Student Programming Board mixes things up by booking movies, comedians, and big-name bands, while the Garrick Players put on several productions per year. "Honestly," says a first-year, "some of the best nights happen right in the residence halls—movie marathons in the lounges, game nights, impromptu dance parties, or deep 2 a.m. conversations with friends." Greek life attracts 6 percent of the men and 7 percent of the women and their parties are open to all. Students say the party culture is relatively low-key, and underage students caught drinking on campus are strictly penalized. Everyone enjoys the semiformal Winter Ball, the annual Forester Day of Service, the Spring Concert, and the Drag Show lip-synch contest planned by PRIDE.

Lake Forest is wealthy and mostly residential, and one student says, "The town is actually in a forest, so the whole place is beautiful, and it feels like you live tucked away in a safe haven." There's a commuter train station five minutes away, and the Lake Michigan beach is just as close. The college also offers a shuttle service to local shops and movie theaters, though a car is helpful. Several student organizations are devoted to community service, and Greek organizations sponsor blood drives, bake sales, and car washes.

Division III Foresters athletics have begun to draw more attention from students. "We have 'Forester Fridays,' which are fun athletic events where people wear the school colors, red and black, and can participate in games, win prizes, and purchase Lake Forest apparel," cheers a senior. Men's and women's soccer, men's and women's lacrosse, softball, and football have been competitive in the Midwest Conference in recent years. Club and intramural sports programs include fencing, sailing, basketball, and men's and women's rugby.

Although Lake Forest's small size may feel confining to some, most students appreciate the college's collaborative atmosphere, increasing diversity, and healthy school pride. "Lake Forest is the kind of school where professors know your name," says a satisfied English major, "where you can explore multiple interests without being boxed into one path and where opportunities—like undergraduate research, campus jobs, leadership roles, and internships—are genuinely within reach from your first year."

Overlaps

Beloit, DePaul, Grinnell, U of I at Chicago, Knox, Lawrence, Loyola University Chicago, St. Olaf

If You Apply To ›

Lake Forest: Early decision I and II, early action I and II, regular decision. SATs or ACTs: optional (test-optional applicants must have an admissions interview). Accepts the Common Application with supplement.

711 East Boldt Way, Appleton, WI 54911

One of three small colleges in the nation that combine the liberal arts with a first-rate music conservatory (Bard and Oberlin are the others), and music of all kinds shapes the campus culture. Lawrence is half the size of Oberlin and comparable to Beloit and Grinnell, though Lawrence's personality is more mainstream than the others. Occupies a scenic bluff in northeastern Wisconsin.

Website: www.lawrence.edu
Location: Small City
Private
Total Enrollment: 1,378
Undergraduates: 1,378
Male/Female: 48/52
Financial Aid: 84%
Pell Grant: 20%
Expense: Pr $ $
Student Loans: 53%
Average Debt: $ $ $
Applicants: 3,270
Accepted: 64%
Enrolled: 17%
Grad in 6 Years: 76%
Returning First-years: 87%
Academics: ✍ ✍ ✍ ✍
Social: 🗨 🗨 🗨
Q of L: ★ ★ ★
Admissions: (800) 227-0982
Email Address:
  admissions@lawrence.edu

Strong Programs:
Biology
Economics
English
Government
History
Music
Physics
Psychology

Lawrence University is an unpretentious school that can appeal to both the left and right side of students' brains. For those with an analytical bent, there is Lawrence's uncommon physics program. More creative types can take advantage of the school's renowned Conservatory of Music. "I came to Lawrence because I found no other school where I could seriously study music and academics," says a senior. It's this eclectic, individualized approach to learning that attracts interested and interesting students from around the world. "Lawrence is, to me, founded on the idea that academics can be rigorous while also fun," muses a government major.

Lawrence's campus sits on a wooded bluff above the Fox River, perfect for long walks, jogging, or simply meditating underneath the trees. The pristine 88-acre campus reflects several architectural styles of the past 175 years, including Classical Revival, 1920s Georgian-inspired, and 1950s and 1960s institutional, unified by their limestone color. The award-winning Wriston Art Center and the Conservatory's Shattuck Hall of Music (both designed by Lawrence graduates) bring contemporary architectural touches to the campus. New facilities include the $38 million West Campus interdisciplinary building that includes the Trout Museum of Art, academic spaces, and apartments; the new Fox Commons in downtown Appleton provides apartment-style accommodations and collaborative spaces for business and entrepreneurship and prehealth students.

One of the first coeducational colleges established in the nation, Lawrence was founded in 1847 to educate German immigrants and Native Americans and was named after an early benefactor. While coeducation was shocking enough, innovators at Lawrence didn't stop there. Nearly 80 years ago, administrators introduced the First-Year Studies program, a required two-term course that focuses primarily on the great works of art, music, science, and literature of both Western

> **"Lawrence is founded on the idea that academics can be rigorous while also fun."**

and non-Western origin and gives all incoming students a shared intellectual experience. General education requirements at Lawrence include First-Year Studies, distribution requirements, and diversity, foreign language, and writing-intensive courses. All seniors—whatever their concentrations—are required to produce a final project demonstrating proficiency in their major field of study. As a linguistics major explains, the senior project means that "while everyone is working on something different, the whole senior class is engaged in meaningful discussions and exposed to unique challenges."

At the school's Conservatory of Music, the instrument collection includes an 1815 Broadwood piano identical to Beethoven's own Broadwood and a Guarneri violin. There are first-rate jazz ensembles along with classical and world music programs. The college offers a bachelor of music degree within its liberal arts environment, and students may opt to complete a five-year, double-degree program to earn both a bachelor of music and a bachelor of arts in another field. "Music is the unifying theme at Lawrence," says one student. "Almost everybody plays it or studies it or likes to listen to it and talk about it." Visual and performing arts are among the most popular majors, followed by biological sciences, social sciences, and psychology. The highly regarded physics department offers 3–2 engineering options with Columbia, Rensselaer, and WashU in St. Louis. Cooperative degrees in forestry and environmental studies, law, occupational therapy, and public health are also offered with such institutions as Duke, Marquette, and the Medical College of Wisconsin.

Small classes—79 percent have fewer than 20 students—make it "easy to connect and work closely with professors for a more personalized and thorough learning experience," says a geology major. Because of the three-term calendar, the academic climate is fast-paced and intense but also "extremely collaborative," a sophomore says. "As long as you stay on top of reading and notes, it is not overwhelming."

Students are encouraged to spend at least one term of their college career off campus, and 30 percent of undergrads do so. The university is known for its London Centre, which allows students to take classes "across the pond." Other off-campus programs include a Francophone seminar in Dakar, Senegal, and a marine biology term in the Cayman Islands. In all, more than 50 international programs are available in more than 25 countries. "There are so many opportunities for you to conduct your own research," say administrators, "whether you are a scientist, artist, musician . . . or maybe all three," and about 65 percent of students participate. The Lawrence University Research Fellows program pairs qualified students with Lawrence faculty or with alumni who are conducting research at tier-one universities across the country for 10-week research assistantships during the summer.

A senior describes Lawrentians as "forward-thinking, caring, and quirky." Twenty-nine percent of students hail from Wisconsin, and another quarter come from Illinois and Minnesota. At 11 percent, the international population is sizable. Black students make up 5 percent of the student body, Asian Americans 4 percent, Hispanics/ Latinos 12 percent, and multiracial students 5 percent. The political climate on campus is liberal and usually "calm," according to a sophomore. There are no athletic scholarships, but top achievers vie for merit scholarships averaging $34,400 each.

> "[Lawrence students are] forward-thinking, caring, and quirky."

Ninety-four percent of students live on campus, as four-year residency is required with few exceptions. "There are tons of options for housing: dorms, theme houses, group houses, lofts, etc.," explains a junior. On-campus students have a choice of meal plans and report that the food is diverse, healthy, and friendly to those with dietary restrictions. "Some of our produce comes from a student-run garden right across the street from the dining hall," says one student. To enhance safety, all on-campus parties hosted by student groups must be attended by at least one member who has been trained in bystander intervention.

Social life at Lawrence is mostly campus-based and as varied and eclectic as the students. Greek life attracts a modest 4 percent of the men and 3 percent of the women; students say the party culture tends to be laid-back. "Lawrence students aren't the kind to party every weekend, but we're also not the kind to never party at all," opines a sophomore. Thanks to the Conservatory, students can almost always count on there being some kind of concert or performance on any given day. The Winter Carnival and President's Ball, held in January, and LU-aroo, a student-organized music festival in the spring, are favorite annual traditions. The student-run Great Midwest Trivia Contest takes place during January each year; held since 1966, it's the longest-running trivia contest in the nation. Octoberfest is also a big weekend event, held in conjunction with the city of Appleton, which draws people in from nearby cities.

Relations between Lawrence and Appleton are good. "The town is safe and has lots to do," says a student, including "cafés, restaurants, shops, nightlife, performing arts, and farmers markets." Downtown Appleton is just one block from campus, but the nearest grocery store is a five-minute drive; the school provides regular shuttles to help students get around. Volunteerism is popular, and students regularly take part in activities such as tutoring at local schools. The best road trips are to Milwaukee (two hours), Green Bay (half an hour), and Chicago (four hours). Weekend seminars are held at Björklunden, the college's 441-acre estate on the shores of Lake Michigan.

> **"There are tons of options for housing: dorms, theme houses, group houses, lofts, etc."**

And what would a Midwest fall Saturday be without football? The Division III Lawrence Vikings draw good crowds. Baseball, women's cross-country, and women's soccer have won recent Midwest Conference championships, and men's cross-country and women's basketball are also competitive. The sparkling recreation center helps students fend off midwinter blues. Participating in a rousing game of intramural bubble soccer, where students are half encased in inflatable bubbles from head to waist, is a must for students, even if all you do is watch. Soccer, pickleball, and flag football are also popular.

With an outstanding liberal arts curriculum, knowledgeable and caring faculty, an administration that treats students like adults, and a charming country setting, Lawrence University is easily one of the better little-known schools in the country. "I've always felt that this school is a hidden gem," remarks a film studies major. And for students with a musical ear, Lawrence's symphony of offerings strikes just the right chord.

Overlaps

Beloit, Carlton, DePauw, Grinnell, Lake Forest, Macalester, Oberlin, St. Olaf

If You Apply To ›

Lawrence: Early decision I and II, early action I and II, regular decision. SATs or ACTs: optional. Accepts the Common Application with supplement. Music applicants must audition and complete additional requirements.

Lehigh University

27 Memorial Drive West, Bethlehem, PA 18015

Built on the powerful combination of business, engineering, and the humanities, Lehigh occupies a middle ground between techie havens such as Drexel and Rensselaer and liberal arts/engineering institutions such as Bucknell and Union. By graduation, students are primed for the global job market. Hillside campus means that students get plenty of exercise. A wrestling powerhouse.

Website: www.lehigh.edu
Location: Small City
Private
Total Enrollment: 6,866
Undergraduates: 5,813
Male/Female: 52/48
Financial Aid: 61%
Pell Grant: 24%

From the College of Arts and Sciences to the College of Business, Lehigh University combines the academic resources of a large research university with the collegial atmosphere of a much smaller institution. The school takes an interdisciplinary approach to education "that allows students to seamlessly integrate engaged research, global experiences, and entrepreneurship and innovation into the framework of their selected course of study." Since Lehigh's founding in 1865, much of its reputation has rested on its consistently strong engineering program at the Rossin College of Engineering and Applied Science, and the school has invested millions of dollars in recent years to enhance critical academic programs such as nanotechnology, biotechnology, bioscience, and optoelectronics. Says one engineering, arts, and sciences major, "Lehigh makes its students grow in so many ways—as a student, researcher, innovator, friend, and person."

Grand old oaks shade the buildings on Lehigh's 1,600-acre campus, which is tucked into the side of an eastern Pennsylvania mountain. The university spreads out over three contiguous campuses: the main Asa Packer Campus, named for Lehigh's businessman founder; the Goodman Campus, named for a donor; and the Mountaintop Campus, which formerly housed the research laboratory of now-defunct Bethlehem Steel. Architectural styles range from ivy-covered collegiate Gothic, including the historic Linderman Library, built in 1878, to modern glass and steel. Newer structures include the Business Innovation Building, which expands the existing Rauch Business Center with flexible, tech-supported classrooms and project spaces.

Distribution requirements are divided into four domains—the mathematical sciences, the natural sciences, the social sciences, and the arts and humanities. First-years take a Big Questions Seminar, focusing on some of the world's greater challenges, and two semesters of writing. Additionally, some degrees include a mandatory internship or capstone project. Finance, mechanical engineering, psychology, and biology are the most popular majors. Lehigh is big on connecting traditionally separate disciplines, so students interested in interdisciplinary study will find a wealth of options, including majors in arts and engineering, computer science and business, environmental engineering, and integrated business and health. Minors in engineering leadership and sustainable development are also available. "I love the flexibility that I have had with my major, and it is really cool that I have been able to study both engineering and psychology," says a senior. The College of Health, offering undergraduate degrees in community and global health and population health, is home to an array of programs, including health, medicine, and society. A number of 4–1 programs allow students to seamlessly earn a master's degree in financial engineering, education, public health and more.

Lehigh prides itself on offering innovative special programs, such as Interdisciplinary Capstone Design, which brings engineering, business, and arts students together to design and make products for sponsoring companies. The IDEAS (Integrated Degree in Engineering, Arts, and Sciences), computer science and business, and integrated business and engineering programs offer four-year honors curricula that allow students to blend two focus areas into a single course of study. Lehigh's Office of Creative Inquiry sponsors several interdisciplinary initiatives, among them the Mountaintop Summer Experience program, which gives roughly 175 students a chance to work in teams with faculty mentors on cutting-edge projects during the summer. Recent Mountaintop projects include developing a testing system for self-driving cars and designing an interface to track Pennsylvania's publicly traded companies. "Take part in the Mountaintop research over the summer," urges a psychology major. "It's really fun to be on campus then, and the programs are really cool." Co-ops allow students to spend eight months working for a major-related company—and getting paid to do so—while still graduating in four years. About 25 percent of students participate in more than 250 study abroad options offered in over 60 countries. Many students praise the Global Social Impact Fellowship and Iacocca International Internship programs, with one student calling the travel and experiences they afford "incredible and life-changing."

"Lehigh definitely provides an academically rigorous environment," says a biology major, and the students are ambitious—many pursue double majors and multiple extracurriculars—but the atmosphere is by no means cutthroat. "From

> **"Lehigh makes its students grow in so many ways—as a student, researcher, innovator, friend, and person."**

The Mountaintop Summer Experience program gives students a chance to work with faculty mentors on cutting-edge projects during the summer.

(continued)

Expense: Pr $ $ $
Student Loans: 48%
Average Debt: $ $ $ $
Applicants: 20,396
Accepted: 26%
Enrolled: 28%
Grad in 6 Years: 88%
Returning First-years: 94%
Academics: ✍ ✍ ✍ ✍
Social: 💬 💬 💬
Q of L: ★ ★ ★
Admissions: (610) 758-3100
Email Address:
admissions@lehigh.edu

Strong Programs:
Biology
Computer Science and
 Business
Environmental Engineering
Finance
Integrated Business and
 Engineering
Integrated Engineering, Arts,
 and Sciences
Mechanical Engineering
Psychology

group projects to late-night study groups in Linderman Library, I have always been able to find a classmate to help me in a variety of subjects," says a journalism major. Forty-six percent of undergraduate courses enroll fewer than 20 students, and a biology major says, "My professors are highly accomplished and can somehow explain very complex topics in a very simple way." Students praise the wide range of services made available to them, including mental health and career counseling. "The career center gets involved very early on in your first year," says a sophomore.

According to an accounting and finance major, students are "driven, passionate, fun, friendly, supportive." Twenty-five percent of Lehigh's students come from Pennsylvania, and many others hail from other Northeastern states; 6 percent come from more than 30 foreign countries. Black students account for 5 percent of the population, Hispanics/Latinos 11 percent, Asian Americans 11 percent, and multiracial students 4 percent. "There is a diverse range of political and social beliefs on campus," reports a first-year. Merit scholarships averaging $23,700 are awarded annually, and athletes vie for 200 scholarships in 25 sports.

Sixty-six percent of Lehigh students live on campus; first- and second-year students are required to do so. Accommodations are "either very homey or modern," says a sophomore. Many upperclassmen choose to live in apartment-style dorms, Greek houses, and off-campus apartments. Campus dining receives above-average reviews for taste and variety. Students note that the Office of Gender Violence Education and Support

"Take part in the Mountaintop research over the summer!"

has done much to educate the campus community, including rallies and prevention-awareness training.

An active Greek scene (18 percent of the men join fraternities and 25 percent of the women belong to sororities) fuels the campus social life. "Students who live off campus often host parties, and it creates a really great social scene," says one student. Although students agree that a drinking and party culture does exist, according to a finance major, "There isn't pressure from anyone to become involved in those activities." Plenty of on-campus social options are available too, says a business information systems major: "Lehigh After Dark events are always a huge hit and range from midnight breakfast bars and a massive carnival to massage therapy sessions and bingo nights." Favorite traditions include the Founder's Day celebration as well as bed races, the Turkey Trot, and other spirit activities during the week leading up to the big football game against Lafayette. "Personally, I love wingo," cheers a sophomore, "which is wings and bingo that's held once every two weeks." Locally and nationally, students volunteer roughly 65,000 hours each year.

The bustling campus has helped revive Bethlehem, a once-great steel town in the heart of the Lehigh Valley. "Bethlehem is a vibrant small city," says a first-year student. "There is a large arts culture, with regular concerts and festivals at the Steel Stacks and other locations." Students look forward to the city's Musikfest music festival in early August. For those with wheels, Philadelphia

"Lehigh After Dark events are always a huge hit."

is 50 miles to the south and New York City is 75 miles to the east. Skiers will appreciate the close proximity of the Poconos in the winter, while sun worshippers can enjoy the nearby Jersey Shore in the early fall and late spring.

The Division I Lehigh Mountain Hawks field a number of competitive teams. Lehigh's wrestling program is a perennial powerhouse, having brought home numerous Eastern Intercollegiate Wrestling Association championships, and the school recently launched a Division I women's wrestling program. Men's wrestling, women's basketball, and men's football are recent Patriot League champions; men's lacrosse and hockey are also strong. Fans flock to the annual Lehigh versus Lafayette football game, which was first played in 1884 and is the longest-standing rivalry in college football. "LeLaf is huge!" cheers a junior. The intramural and club sports programs offer nearly 30 sports to choose from, including ultimate Frisbee, men's ice hockey, and women's rugby.

Lehigh students proudly juggle rigorous classes and a packed extracurricular calendar in an environment that is well-balanced rather than intense. "Lehigh is in the Goldilocks zone," explains an economics major. "It is just small enough that it is easy to find and form a comfortable and intimate community but big enough that everyone can explore any and all of their interests."

If You Apply To ›

Lehigh: Early decision I and II, regular decision. Accepts the Common Application. Apply to particular colleges. Please consult Lehigh's website for the most up-to-date information regarding standardized test requirements.

Lewis & Clark College

615 South Palatine Hill Road, Portland, OR 97219

The West Coast's leader in international and study abroad programs. Politically liberal but not as far out as crosstown neighbor Reed. With Mount Hood visible in the distance (sometimes), there are a wealth of outdoor possibilities. Located in suburban Portland, within easy reach of the bustle of downtown.

The 19th-century explorers Meriweather Lewis and William Clark struck out from Middle America to find where the trail ended, and their travels took them to Portland, a green paradise by the Willamette River. The college that bears the explorers' names encourages students to explore too, helping them to "[think] of themselves as global citizens and environmental stewards." Since establishing its first overseas study programs in 1962, the college has sent thousands of students around the world to gain global perspectives in their fields of study. Back on campus, opportunities for academic exploration, research, and urban adventures abound in what the university describes as the "cool, progressive city of Portland, Oregon." Without a doubt, Lewis & Clark students receive, as one junior puts it, "an excellent, hands-on education."

Lewis & Clark, which produced its first graduates in 1873, boasts a gorgeous campus perched atop fir-covered bluffs overlooking the river. The campus is an old estate, complete with elaborate gardens, fountains, and pools, where cement is almost nonexistent and the roads are paved with cobblestones. The 50,000-square-foot Howard Hall, built as part of the college's commitment to sustainable development, earned a gold certification from the U.S. Green Building Council. Lewis & Clark draws 100 percent of its power from renewable sources.

Lewis & Clark requires that all students achieve competency in a foreign language and international studies; 45 percent of students fulfill these requirements by studying abroad for a semester or more. The college offers more than 30 study abroad programs each year, many of which are faculty-led, on six continents. Students may also study in New York City. In addition to the international studies and language requirements, students must complete courses in creative arts; culture, power, and identity; historical perspectives; natural sciences; and physical education and well-being. A required, two-semester first-year seminar helps ease new students into college life.

Website: www.lclark.edu
Location: City Outskirts
Private
Total Enrollment: 3,026
Undergraduates: 2,092
Male/Female: 37/63
Financial Aid: 99%
Pell Grant: 27%
Expense: Pr $ $ $
Student Loans: 42%
Average Debt: $ $
Applicants: 6,328
Accepted: 78%
Enrolled: 10%
Grad in 6 Years: 75%
Returning First-years: 86%
Academics: ✍ ✍ ✍
Social: 🗩 🗩 🗩
Q of L: ★ ★ ★
Admissions: (503) 768-7040
Email Address:
admissions@lclark.edu

Strong Programs:
Biology
Economics

Not surprisingly, one of the most popular majors at Lewis & Clark is international affairs; others include psychology, biology, sociology and anthropology, and environmental studies. There are multiple options for students seeking advanced degrees in collaboration with Lewis & Clark's Graduate School of Education and Counseling or Lewis & Clark Law School and 3–2 programs in engineering as well as a 4–2 partnership program in business and management. The Center for Community and Global Health offers premed and other health professions advising. Honors programs are available in most departments. The Rogers Summer Science Research Program teams students and faculty on research projects ranging from the evolution of spider venom to cybersecurity analysis. The Bates Center for Entrepreneurship offers a minor in entrepreneurial leadership.

Academically, "Classes are a mix in terms of difficulty, student participation, and amount of work," reports a student double majoring in psychology and rhetoric and media studies. First-years and graduating seniors get priority in the registration process, helping ensure graduation in four years.

> **"Classes are a mix in terms of difficulty, student participation, and amount of work."**

For those who plan out their requirements with their academic advisors but are unable to finish in four years, the college commits to paying for an additional semester of study. Professors get high marks for being knowledgeable and passionate. "The class sizes at L&C are fairly small and intimate, allowing you to have close connections with your professors," explains a sociology and anthropology major.

"Students here are socially conscious, motivated, and involved," says an international affairs major. Sixteen percent of undergrads hail from Oregon, and many of the rest are West Coasters seeking an emphasis on the liberal arts; the college is also a haven for well-off Easterners who see L&C as an escape from the social claustrophobia of the typical prep school scene. Six percent of students arrive from foreign countries. The campus is politically active and predominantly left-leaning. The student body is 5 percent Asian American, 3 percent Black, 13 percent Hispanic/Latino, and 9 percent multiracial. The Office of Equity and Inclusion aims to promote and expand campus diversity. Non-need-based financial aid awards average $28,900, but there are no athletic scholarships.

Lewis & Clark's residency requirement keeps students on campus for two years; 68 percent of all undergraduates stay in campus housing. "The most common room is a double, but there are also quads and singles, all of which have sufficient room,"

> **"Students here are socially conscious, motivated, and involved."**

reports a student. Owing to the college's hilltop location, lucky dorm residents have views of Mount St. Helens, Mount Hood, or the Portland skyline—at least when they are not fogged in. Students involved in performing arts, multicultural engagement, outdoor pursuits, and other programs can join living-learning communities. Dining halls cater to different diets, offering vegetarian and vegan options at every meal, and "the food can be tasty, but not always," says a student. L&C is located in a residential section of Portland, but safety is still a priority—residence halls have card-swipe entry systems and door alarms, and campus security officers are on duty 24 hours a day.

Fun-seekers at Lewis & Clark rely primarily on programs offered through Student Activities, such as on-campus movies, contests, dances, improv nights, and talent shows; there is no Greek life. Yearly events include the Fall Ball and Spring Fling dances and the International Fair, although one student grumbles, "There are no major traditions at Lewis & Clark. This can be disappointing." Students 21 and older are permitted to consume alcohol on campus, and students report that alcohol policies prioritize student safety. "There is not a huge party culture on campus, but it manifests in smaller kickbacks," says a senior.

Yearly events include the Fall Ball and Spring Fling dances and the International Fair.

Lewis & Clark requires that all students achieve competency in a foreign language and international studies.

The neighborhood immediately surrounding the college is pleasant, affluent suburbia, which means a few stores, restaurants, and bars. Students get involved in community service through a variety of campus organizations. The activity of Portland—mostly on Hawthorne Boulevard in the southeast section and in the Pearl District or on 23rd Street in the northwest quadrant—is 15 minutes away on the city's public transit system or the free campus shuttle service, the Pioneer Express. On the weekends and during breaks, College Outdoors sponsors trips to Mount Hood (great skiing, about an hour distant), the eastern Oregon high desert (two hours), or the coastal beaches (an hour and a half). Seattle and Vancouver, BC, three- and six-hour drives, are favorite road trips, as are San Francisco and Las Vegas when there's more time.

Pioneer teams compete in the Division III Northwest Conference, and the most successful teams include men's and women's cross-country, men's and women's tennis, and softball. Lewis & Clark has a well-organized intramural program. Ultimate Frisbee won its first national championship (men) and made it to national semifinals (women) in 2025, and basketball and volleyball are also student favorites. The L&C speech and debate team has won multiple national titles in recent years.

Lewis & Clark's many outdoor enthusiasts and champions of social causes thrive in the college's laid-back atmosphere. Students are entrepreneurial thinkers, knowledge-seeking pioneers—ones who would make the school's namesakes proud. "We constantly question and search for the answers," says a senior.

Louisiana State University

1146 Pleasant Hall, Baton Rouge, LA 70803

In the state famous for Mardi Gras, students come to LSU for a great time as well as a good education. Finding the former is a no-brainer. The latter can be had in everything from coastal sciences to cybersecurity and art to agriculture. LSU continues to make significant investments in infrastructure, with 77 percent of its undergraduate housing being recently constructed or renovated. It's the only university in the country with a live tiger residing on campus.

From abundant azaleas and Japanese magnolias and the smell of Cajun cuisine to the sororities' stately mansions and the "huge and legendary" rivalries with Alabama and Florida, few schools evoke the spirit of the South like Louisiana State University in Baton Rouge. The university offers solid programs in business, engineering, and the life sciences, and the academic profile of its students continues to rise, bolstering LSU's strong sense of community and school pride. "We are proud of our academic accomplishments, athletic victories, cultural richness, and innovation and want everyone to know," enthuses a junior. "#GEAUXTIGERS!"

LSU sits on 2,000 acres along the banks of the Mississippi River on the grounds of a former plantation. Most of the 250 buildings are Italian Renaissance in style, with tan stucco walls and red tile roofs. Lakes and sprawling oak trees dot the landscape, helping to diffuse the strong sun and temper Louisiana's legendary humidity. Recent campus projects include the newly renovated Huey P. Long

(continued)

Accepted: 73%

Enrolled: 23%

Grad in 6 Years: 69%

Returning First-years: 85%

Academics: ✍ ✍

Social: 🍷 🍷 🍷 🍷 🍷

Q of L: ★ ★ ★

Admissions: (225) 578-1175

Email Address:

admissions@lsu.edu

Strong Programs:

Biological Sciences

Business

Coastal Environmental Science

Computer Science

Construction Management

Engineering

Landscape Architecture

Music

Everyone looks forward to Fall Fest, which includes bands, food, and the LSU Tiger Girls Dance Team performing.

Field House, which houses the state's only undergraduate human anatomy and cadaver lab.

Founded in 1853, LSU was once an open-admissions university for state residents, but standards have gone up over the years, and with them the caliber of students. Students must complete a broad core curriculum with coursework in English composition, analytical reasoning, social sciences, humanities, natural sciences, and the arts. Entry-level classes can be large, but 43 percent of all undergraduate courses enroll fewer than 20 students. Especially motivated students may opt to join the Ogden Honors College to enjoy smaller class sizes and live in the Laville Honors House.

LSU students choose from more than 79 undergraduate degrees and tend to focus on practical majors that will help them get into graduate school or find jobs after graduation. "With two main libraries constantly filled with focused students, it's clear that academic excellence is a shared priority," says a political communication major, who describes the academic climate as "both rigorous and supportive." Popular majors include biological sciences as well as kinesiology, psychology, and mass communication. LSU's programs in landscape architecture, engineering (especially petroleum), physics, computer science, English, and music are highly regarded. Given LSU's location, its offerings in coastal environmental science, ecology, and agriculture are notable as well. The renowned, multidisciplinary LSU Center for Internal Auditing was the first university-based internal auditing training program to be established. Professors are lauded as "interactive and innovative." Research opportunities abound and include the President's Future Leaders in Research Program, which provides undergraduates the chance to work side by side with professors in a lab or in the field to learn what a career in that area might be like. Undergrads interested in study abroad can live and learn in over 100 locations in programs ranging in length from one week to one year.

> **"There is a strong Southern culture, but LSU is very diverse."**

"There is a strong Southern culture, but LSU is very diverse," attests a junior. Sixty-four percent of students are Louisiana natives, and 2 percent come from abroad. Black students make up 21 percent of the undergraduate student body, Asian Americans 5 percent, Hispanics/Latinos 11 percent, and multiracial students 4 percent. As for the political atmosphere, a senior says, "We have an area called 'Free Speech Alley' where anyone can express themselves with very little censorship." LSU's tuition is below the national average, and thousands of merit scholarships are available, averaging $6,600. LSU also hands out more than 500 athletic scholarships each year in 21 sports. Forty-two percent of incoming first-years qualify for Pell Grants, and the Pelican Promise Scholarship provides additional financial aid to low-income, Pell-eligible, in-state students.

Twenty-nine percent of students live on campus. Over the past decade, the university has invested more than $150 million in constructing or renovating housing facilities. Eighteen percent of first-year students choose to live in one of 10 residential colleges organized by academic interest. One sophomore explains, "From being able to knock on my neighbor's door and ask for help on homework to cooking in the kitchen with friends from class, it helped me bond with a smaller community." Meals at the dining halls receive average reviews, but a number of "delicious and inexpensive" eateries lie within easy reach of campus. Although crime can be a concern in Baton Rouge, a senior reports, "Campus safety is a priority, and our police department has increased night patrolling and self-defense classes since my first year." LSU also provides a transit system so that students don't have to walk alone after dark. Additionally,

> **"Anytime we play Ole Miss or Alabama, it is a special day in Baton Rouge."**

"LSU prioritizes student health and well-being," says a sophomore, "helping them de-stress by hosting events like therapy dogs in the libraries." One common complaint, however, is a lack of parking.

With nearly 500 student clubs, tailgating during football season, and the many nearby bars and entertainment venues in Tigerland, social life at LSU "is never-ending," enthuses a student. "No matter what your personality is there is something for you," says a marketing professional sales major. Nineteen percent of the men and 25 percent of the women go Greek. The administration has instituted several policy changes related to Greek life, including a ban on hard alcohol at all on- and off-campus Greek events, in hopes of reducing binge drinking, hazing, and other problems. "LSU has made an effort to educate and encourage victims and bystanders of hazing to speak out," says a senior. As for traditions, everyone looks forward to Fall Fest, which includes bands, food, the LSU Tiger Girls Dance Team performing, and a free spring concert featuring a big-name artist. Of course, Mardi Gras is also big. Road trips to New Orleans and the Florida beaches are common during spring break.

Tiger football is king in Baton Rouge—witness the 102,000-seat Tiger Stadium, the $28 million locker room that the *New York Times* described as "a purple-and-gold mash-up of a first-class airplane cabin and a sci-fi space station," and Mike the Tiger, the live tiger mascot that lives in a 15,000-square-foot habitat adjacent to the football stadium. Many students follow the team (and the fun) to Oxford, Mississippi (home of Ole Miss), or Auburn, Alabama (home of the Auburn Tigers). "Anytime we play Ole Miss or Alabama, it is a special day in Baton Rouge," cheers a junior. The Tiger baseball team is a dynasty, having brought home multiple Southeastern Conference titles and eight national championships, including in 2025. Women's basketball won the 2023 NCAA championship; women's gymnastics won the 2024 NCAA and 2025 SEC championships; and the Tiger Girls Dance Team claimed the 2024 UDA Nationals hip hop title. Women's soccer is also strong, as are both men and women's outdoor track. As for recreational sports, intramural soccer, flag football, and softball are popular.

LSU's trees and traditions date back 170 years, but the school continues to evolve in its efforts to attract a more academically motivated student body. "We like to have a good time, but we still get our stuff done when needed," says a junior. With the university's focus on experimental learning, discovery, diversity, and engagement, its academic profile is on its way to matching its athletic prowess. In the meantime, students are happy to laissez les bons temps rouler!

Overlaps

University of Arkansas, Auburn, Clemson, University of Louisiana, Oklahoma State, Southeastern Louisiana, University of Tennessee Knoxville, Texas A&M

If You Apply To ›

LSU: Rolling admissions. SATs or ACTs: optional. Accepts the Common Application. Application allows students to utilize preferred name, gender pronouns, and self-identified gender.

Loyola University Maryland

4501 North Charles Street, Baltimore, MD 21210

Vintage Jesuit school with a rigorous liberal arts curriculum, caring faculty, and a strong sense of community. Baltimore location a plus for those with "I don't want to miss anything" attitude. Same size as Providence, smaller than BC, Fordham, and other Roman Catholic schools in urban settings. No varsity football, but top-ranked lacrosse teams evoke plenty of school spirit.

Accelerated 3–1 and 4–1 programs are available in areas ranging from accounting to biological forensics and teacher education.

Four U.S. universities bear the name of St. Ignatius of Loyola, founder of the Society of Jesus (the Jesuits), but this one is the granddaddy of them all. Founded in 1852 (and the one that laid claim to www.loyola.edu), Loyola University Maryland combines the virtues of a residential campus with ready access to a major city on the Amtrak corridor. With a "big enough but not too big" feel, Loyola manages to strike a balance between real-world experience and the traditional Jesuit ideals of academic excellence, a liberal arts curriculum, and cura personalis (a.k.a. care for the whole person).

Loyola's Evergreen campus, the home to undergraduates, sits on 80 green and wooded acres in a residential area in northern Baltimore, about 15 minutes from the heart of the city. The academic Quad features the largest collection of collegiate Gothic buildings in Baltimore, including the Alumni Memorial Chapel with its lovely stained-glass windows. Architectural variety is provided by the Tudor-style Humanities Center, built in 1896; the contemporary Sellinger School of Business and Management, with its five-story glass facade; and the LEED Gold–certified Fernandez Family Center for Innovation and Collaborative Learning. The Karson Institute for Race, Peace & Social Justice provides professors, students, social justice workers, and activists an area to research and discuss issues regarding equality and justice. An in-progress addition to the Donnelly Science Center will offer sustainable teaching labs and spaces for student research.

Undergraduate academics at Loyola are organized around the triumvirate of the School of Education, the Sellinger School of Business and Management, and Loyola College, the school of arts and sciences. Consistent with Jesuit academic tradition, Loyola students pursue a core curriculum of 15 courses that encourages critical thinking across the liberal arts and sciences. Required classes include ethics and two diversity-designated courses. Messina is the university's first-year living/learning program, in which students enroll in two linked seminars, one in the fall and one in the spring, focused on one of four themes: The Visionary, Self and Other, Stories We Tell, and The Good Life. The courses are taught by their core advisor, and students benefit from additional Messina resources, including an upper-class peer mentor, and special programs, events, and excursions. "It makes new students feel like they are a part of the Loyola community and realize how many people care about them here," says a biology major.

> **"[Students] tend to work together on projects or while studying."**

The business program, which consists of nine majors ranging from accounting to sustainability management, is strong, as are most of the humanities. Finance, psychology, biology, and communication are the most popular majors. Other strong areas include forensic science, speech-language-hearing sciences, and engineering. A new B.S. in nursing launched in 2025. Accelerated 3–1 and 4–1 programs are available in areas ranging from accounting to biological forensics and teacher education. Students describe the academic program at Loyola as challenging but supportive. "Students are generally not competing against each other for the best grades but rather tend to work together on projects or while studying," says a senior. Forty-eight percent of classes have fewer than 20 students, and professors receive praise for their emphasis on teaching and getting to know students. "I cannot imagine what it would be like not to have a professor know my name," says a senior.

Each summer, 10 to 12 undergraduates are selected to work side by side with faculty from the eight natural and applied science departments to conduct research in the students' area of interest and participate in seminars. For top students, the Honors Program, Sellinger Scholars Program for business students, and Hyman Science Scholars for math, computer science, statistics, data science, or physics students provide an interdisciplinary route through a more ambitious core curriculum.

Around 60 percent of the students study abroad in their choice of more than 30 countries, usually for a semester during their junior year. Venues range from Bangkok, Dubai, and Singapore to Cape Town, Glasgow, and, of course, Rome. Loyola students are encouraged to engage in community service while abroad and to submit an Immersion Research Project upon return. "I studied in Cork, Ireland, and it was one of the highlights of my college experience!" cheers a senior.

Students at Loyola tend to be, in the words of one senior, "fairly preppy." Thirty-three percent of undergraduates hail from Maryland, and 2 percent come from other countries. Black students represent 12 percent, Hispanics/Latinos 15 percent, Asian Americans 4 percent, and multiracial students 5 percent. Forty-seven percent of undergrads describe themselves as Catholics. "Religion has a huge impact on campus," says one non-Catholic, who adds, "As a Christian, I love the fact that I can openly talk about my religion and that others accept my beliefs." Students cite women's and LGBTQ rights, immigration reform, homelessness, and hunger as popular causes on campus. Merit awards average $27,800, and Loyola offers more than 200 athletic scholarships in 13 sports.

Loyola students enjoy the spacious, modern residence halls, which are located west of the main campus and are connected by a pedestrian bridge spanning Charles Street. "One of the perks of Loyola's housing is that there are only a few traditional dorms," explains a psychology major. "Loyola has mostly apartment-style living," and it's possible to live in an apartment or suite with a kitchen and bathroom as early as the first year. Not surprisingly, 77 percent of students live on campus through senior year. There are 11 locations for on-campus dining, including a Starbucks in the Andrew White Student Center, which is a popular hub. While Loyola is an urban campus, an accounting major reports, "the Loyola police do a good job to make us all feel safe on campus."

Loyola has no fraternities or sororities, but given the proximity to Baltimore, this arrangement is just fine with students. "Most of Loyola's social life takes place off campus," says a student. "Bars and clubs are very close to campus, and the penalties for throwing a party in your room are pretty steep." That's not to say that on-campus life is monastic. "The campus is always buzzing with things like concerts and festivals," says an English major. The undisputed high point of the social calendar is Loyolapalooza, the spring festival held on the last weekend before final exams to celebrate the academic year. Students gather on the Quad for a concert, games, and food. A close second is the annual Black Student Association Fashion Show in the spring.

Fifty-two percent of students at Loyola get involved in community service, which plays a prominent role in campus life. "The passion for service runs very strong through the veins of Loyola," says a senior. The Center for Community, Service, and Justice connects students with opportunities ranging from one-time volunteer activities to semester-long service-learning courses. The city of Baltimore also offers an abundance of sights, including the famed Inner Harbor, with its many restaurants and museums, as well as major league sports. Loyola's neighbors include numerous other colleges and universities, including Johns Hopkins and Towson University. Baltimore "has plenty of young-adult neighborhoods and pockets of entertainment," reports an accounting major. Washington, D.C., an hour away by train, is a frequent weekend destination.

Loyola eschews varsity football, but the Greyhounds compete in the Division I Patriot League in eight men's and nine women's sports. Befitting the school's Maryland location, both the men's and women's lacrosse teams are consistently strong. Men's golf won their seventh conference championship in 2025. For those with more modest athletic ambitions, Loyola sponsors a variety of club sports teams and intramural events, as well as 40 outdoor adventure trips each year. Flag football, volleyball, and soccer are especially popular. The state-of-the-art Fitness and Aquatic Center features a well-equipped fitness center, a rock-climbing wall, a 14-lane pool, and other amenities.

Some Loyola denizens lament the absence of football and the dearth of on-campus parties, but such complaints seem a small price to pay for four years as part of a close-knit community that takes its humanistic, academic, and social values seriously. "We care for each other, and our Jesuit mission rings true in our day-to-day lives," says a senior. A classmate adds, "The good food, residence halls, and location don't hurt either."

If You Apply To ›

Loyola: Early decision I and II, early action, regular decision. SATs or ACTs: optional. Accepts the Common Application.

Loyola Marymount University

1 LMU Drive, Los Angeles, CA 90045

LMU is a university rooted in the Catholic intellectual tradition and known for its strategic Los Angeles location and world-class programs in film and television, business, engineering, and communication. Big international emphasis in film and theatre arts. Compare to Chapman, Santa Clara, and the University of San Diego. To take full advantage of L.A., access to a car is highly beneficial.

Website: www.lmu.edu
Location: Suburban
Private
Total Enrollment: 9,193
Undergraduates: 6,964
Male/Female: 48/52
Financial Aid: 90%
Pell Grant: 13%
Expense: Pr $ $ $
Student Loans: 35%
Average Debt: $ $ $
Applicants: 23,089
Accepted: 45%
Enrolled: 15%
Grad in 6 Years: 79%
Returning First-years: 89%
Academics: ✍ ✍ ✍
Social: 🗩 🗩 🗩
Q of L: ★ ★ ★
Admissions: (310) 338-2750
Email Address:
admission@lmu.edu

At Loyola Marymount University, one of the largest Catholic universities on the West Coast, students enjoy ideal weather year-round, a vast array of internship opportunities, and an academic lineup that includes strong programs in film and television, liberal arts and sciences, and business. "LMU is more than an academic institution," says a junior. "It is a community dedicated to helping students grow and thrive."

Established in 1911, LMU occupies a 142-acre campus perched on a bluff overlooking the Pacific Ocean and Marina del Rey in Westchester, a peaceful residential neighborhood of Los Angeles. Campus architecture is a mix of modern and modified Spanish Colonial Revival style, with orange-tiled roofs. The university is sponsored by three religious orders: the Society of Jesus (the Jesuits), the Religious of the Sacred Heart of Mary, and the Sisters of St. Joseph of Orange.

> **"LMU students care about their academic performance and seek challenges where they can."**

Campus highlights include the 24-hour Hannon Library, the $110 million, LEED Gold–certified Featherston Life Sciences Building, and the new Fitzpatrick Pavilion, boasting high-tech production and screening spaces for the film school.

LMU offers 56 baccalaureate majors and 57 minors in six colleges and schools. The general education requirements (known as the Core Curriculum) are designed to encourage intellectual breadth, tackling themes such as faith and reason; ethics and justice; culture; art and society; and science, nature, and society. Incoming students may take part in several programs designed to support the transition to college, including a first-year seminar, learning communities, and an honors program. Students also fulfill an experiential learning for mission requirement.

The most popular programs include psychology, marketing, finance, communication studies, and film and television production; these are also some of the university's best. Other strong programs include political science, international relations, journalism, entrepreneurship, computer science, engineering, and theatre arts. Students in the School of Film and Television have access to many resources, including a student-run production office, a television stage, and a film soundstage with a professional green screen (for those cool CGI effects!). Those in the Seaver College of Science and Engineering take part in national competitions to build rockets and race eco-friendly cars. New academic offerings include minors in cognitive science; LGBTQ studies; computer engineering; digital media, cultures, and industries; and a master's degree in entertainment leadership and management. Thanks to its L.A. locale, LMU offers experience-hungry students a plethora of internships, including opportunities at Disney, Sony Pictures, and Warner Bros. LMU also offers exchange, semester, and short-term study abroad options on six continents in a wide range of disciplines.

Much like nearby Tinseltown, LMU manages to be both competitive and relaxed. "LMU students generally care about their academic performance and seek challenges where they can," observes an economics major. Fifty-four percent of classes have fewer than 20 students, and while academic rigor and quality of instruction vary by program, students say student-faculty interaction is commonplace. "Professors are not only experts in their field, working for organizations like NASA and doing research with Olympians, but they truly care," shares a health and human sciences major.

LMU undergraduates hail from 48 states and 82 foreign countries; 61 percent come from California and 9 percent from abroad. LMU students have "a self-starter and go-getter attitude mixed with a passion for justice and advocacy," notes a senior. Black students represent 8 percent of the student body, Hispanics/Latinos 25 percent, Asian Americans 10 percent, and multiracial students 9 percent. A junior describes LMU students' political views as "involved in local and national issues that are relevant with the times but not to the point of hyper-partisanship." Merit scholarships averaging $11,600 are available for qualified students, and the athletically inclined vie for over 200 athletic scholarships in 14 sports.

About half of LMU students live on campus. Many first-years choose to participate in themed living/learning communities, including those dedicated to specific academic disciplines, first-generation students, and Ignatian leadership. The university offers a variety of dining options, with some reporting that the food has "vastly improved." Students describe campus security as good, and one senior comments, "LMU does a good job of informing students about sexual consent."

The social life at LMU takes place "both on and off campus," says one student. Student organizations and clubs frequently host activities, and Greek life influences the scene, too, attracting 17 percent of the men and 25 percent of the women. Students say there is little pressure to drink. Everyone looks forward to Fallapalooza, an outdoor music festival that "is such a great way to kick off the year," says a junior, and it's a tradition for your friends to toss you into Foley Fountain on your birthday. The university's Jesuit heritage promotes a commitment to community service, and about 70 percent of students take part, volunteering more than 200,000 hours of service every year in after-school programs, homeless shelters, health clinics, and other settings. The area of Westchester is "definitely not a college town," groans a sophomore. Fortunately, there's a lot nearby. "Many students like to go to the beach, Playa Vista, Venice, Manhattan Beach, or Santa Monica to get off campus," explains a junior. Popular road trips include San Diego, Santa Barbara, and Las Vegas.

LMU offers experience-hungry students a plethora of internships, including opportunities at Disney, Sony Pictures, and Warner Bros.

"[Fallapalooza music festival] is such a great way to kick off the year."

The university's Jesuit heritage promotes a commitment to community service, and about 70 percent of students take part.

Back on campus, LMU's varsity teams compete in the Division I West Coast Conference. Women's beach volleyball, men's soccer, women's water polo, men's water polo, softball, and men's golf are a few of LMU's nationally competitive teams who have recently won West Coast Conference titles and competed in the NCAA tournament. The Lions' rivalry with nearby Pepperdine always draws a huge crowd. Intramurals and club sports are popular and include flag football, soccer, basketball, dodgeball, and volleyball, among others. LMU's debate team is a standout, too, regularly placing high in national and international tournaments.

With its dynamic mix of solid academics, Jesuit and Marymount traditions, and thriving social life, LMU offers students substance and style. "Being a Jesuit school in Los Angeles, our students and faculty are catalysts for change and are always looking to make the world a better place," says a student. Whether you're an aspiring scientist, an emerging humanitarian leader, or a future filmmaker, Loyola Marymount University may be worth a look.

If You Apply To ›

LMU: Early decision I and II, early action, regular decision. Accepts the Common Application with supplement. Applicants to animation, dance, music, production (film and television), and theatre arts are required to submit a portfolio or audition; studio arts applicants have an option to submit a portfolio. Please consult LMU's website for the most up-to-date information regarding standardized test requirements.

Loyola University New Orleans

6363 St. Charles Avenue, New Orleans, LA 70118

Of the four Loyola Universities in the nation, this is the only one where you can go to Mardi Gras or Jazz Fest and then study the music, culture, and community you experienced the next morning in class. New Orleans (a.k.a. NOLA) is an ideal setting for this Roman Catholic, Jesuit university with strengths in business, communication, science, and nursing. NOLA's creative and cultural richness continue on campus.

Loyola University New Orleans is a liberal arts school founded in 1904 by the Society of Jesus (the Jesuits) that continues to enhance its rich tradition through extensive service-learning programs and a renewed commitment to diversifying the student body. The university has capitalized on its unique NOLA setting to develop excellent programs in the humanities, social and natural sciences, health, communications, business, and artistic and creative fields, with a preprofessional bent. "Our Jesuit identity separates us from other colleges," says a computer science major. "We are taught to fight for the poor and oppressed and be educated in all areas to become a holistic individual."

The school's attractive and well-kept 22-acre main campus, in the University section of Uptown New Orleans, mixes Tudor, Gothic, and modern structures. It overlooks acres of Audubon Park and, beyond, the mighty Mississippi River. Two blocks up St. Charles Avenue, Loyola's Broadway campus has an additional four acres. The renovated Monroe Hall features state-of-the-art science labs, including a nursing simulation lab, high-tech design studios, recording and production facilities, and a seventh-floor greenhouse. The Monroe Library houses approximately 500,000 volumes, an art gallery, and the Pan-American Life Student Success Center. A new energy-conscious seven-story residence hall opened in 2025.

The Loyola Core includes courses designed to develop skills in critical thinking, effective communication, quantitative reasoning, information literacy, and ethical reasoning. In addition to taking a First-Year Seminar that introduces them to college-level work and the Jesuit tradition of "thinking critically, acting justly," incoming students are assigned a "success coach" who provides academic guidance and helps instill life skills. Other aspects of Loyola's comprehensive first-year experience include a series of lectures and panel discussions, educational excursions, and service-learning projects.

The School of Communication and Design wins praise, as does virtually any program in the College of Music and Media, including majors in filmmaking, graphic design, jazz studies, and popular and commercial music that are increasingly sought-after in a city where these creative professions are defining specialties. Indeed, befitting its home in jazz capital New Orleans, music industry studies is one of the most popular majors, along with psychology, criminology and justice, and biology. Loyola's urban and electronic music production major is the first of its kind in the country, and students make use of state-of-the-art broadcast and recording studios. Nursing, finance, English, neuroscience, and prehealth are also strengths. Fast-growing majors include design, public health, and cybersecurity.

> "While we are right next to New Orleans, it doesn't mean that it's only party, party, party here."

Loyola's academic climate is said to be challenging, supportive, and vibrant. Sixty-one percent of undergraduate classes have fewer than 20 students, and students report that most faculty make an effort to get to know their students. "[Professors] are often very helpful outside of class, and their lesson plans are easy to digest," says another computer science major. Regarding counseling services, a first-year student explains, "Loyola takes mental health very seriously. Every week there is an anxiety workshop."

The University Honors Program gives high-achieving students access to small seminars, collaborative research projects with faculty, social activities, and a living-learning community of engaged and collegial scholars. Undergraduates can exercise their wings in study abroad programs available in more than 50 countries. With the help of the Office of Community Engaged Learning, Teaching, and Scholarship and the Career Development Center, students can make service part of their studies, and Loyola is a top producer of Peace Corps and Teach for America volunteers. Many students invest their sweat equity in the Loyola University Community Action Program, a student-led coalition of several organizations that take on issues such as hunger and homelessness. "There's also a lot of undergraduate research opportunities from professors that allow you to join their lab," says a senior.

Given Loyola's academic strengths, the student body is an interesting mix of creative types, social justice activists, and career-minded preprofessionals. "While we are right next to New Orleans, it doesn't mean that it's only party, party, party here," insists a computer science major. "There's always people working in the library or in the study nooks for their projects or papers." Forty-eight percent of Loyola undergraduates are Louisiana natives, and many of the remaining students are from the Southeast; 4 percent are international. Twenty-one percent are Hispanic/Latino, 21 percent are Black, 3 percent are Asian American, and 5 percent are multiracial. "There's multiple events meant to boost minority groups like women in STEM or the Black community," notes one student. Religion—specifically Roman Catholicism—has a significant influence on campus. Daily mass is open to the New Orleans community, and many students attend. Ten other religions are also represented on campus, and a sophomore explains, "The community is more alternative and liberal but that doesn't mean it's like a bubble. There are still many students with differing positions."

> "There's a lot of undergraduate research opportunities from professors that allow you to join their lab."

(continued)

Social: 💬 💬 💬
Q of L: ★ ★ ★
Admissions: (800) 456-9652
Email Address:
  admit@loyno.edu

Strong Programs:
Business
Criminology and Justice
English
Environmental Studies
Filmmaking
Finance
Music Industry Studies
Neuroscience
Psychology

Loyola's urban and electronic music production major is the first of its kind in the country.

Loyola awards merit scholarships averaging $25,200 each year, and athletic scholarships are also available. About a third of undergrads are first-generation college students, and 37 percent of incoming first-years are Pell-eligible.

Many Loyola students commute from home or off-campus apartments; 35 percent of undergraduates reside in campus housing. The transition to college is eased by themed living communities, which house classmates together in a common living space within one of the residence halls. Campus dining in the Orleans Room is described as adequate. "Occasionally they bring special chefs to make a feature dish," says a sophomore. Iggy's Cupboard is a free, student-run food pantry designed to address the issue of food insecurity on campus. According to a senior, "This is a very safe campus."

As for the social life, says a senior, "It's New Orleans. There's nothing else that needs to be said about its party culture." A philosophy major adds, "Loyola gives us lots of cool things to do on campus," including musical performances and sporting events. Fraternities and sororities are rarities at Jesuit schools, but at Loyola, 4 percent of the men and 10 percent of the women choose to belong. Major annual events include the "Sneaux" festival, which "features a petting zoo, a snow field, crafting stations, and multiple food booths," reports a student, the musical event Christmas at Loyola, and a crawfish boil in the spring. Loyola even takes the week of Mardi Gras off as a holiday. With so much bustling nightlife in the surrounding city, students report that not much underage drinking happens on campus. "New Orleans is such an exciting city to go to college in," enthuses a theatre arts major. "It has a super-cool culture of local shops and businesses"—not to mention the live music.

The Wolf Pack's teams compete in the NAIA Division I, most as members of the Southern States Athletic Conference. Men's and women's basketball, men's and women's swimming, and golf are competitive. Loyola's wellness program offers a range of fitness classes, intramurals, club sports, and other recreational activities for jocks and nonjocks alike. Basketball, flag football (no real pigskins at Loyola), women's volleyball, and co-ed eSports are popular pastimes.

Students at Loyola know how to pull together and draw strength from their faith as well as from the distinctive culture of New Orleans. Whether they're working closely with caring professors or relaxing with friends amid the Big Easy's boundless energy, students are satisfied with their choice. "Tulane may be bigger, but Loyola is more representative of New Orleans culture," concludes a computer science major. "You could say it has 'soul.'"

Overlaps

Lipscomb, Louisiana State, Loyola University Chicago, Rider, Seattle Pacific, Stetson, Valparaiso, Xavier University of Louisiana

If You Apply To ›

Loyola: Early action, rolling admissions. SATs or ACTs: optional. Accepts the Common Application with supplement. Audition, portfolio, and/or interview required for admission to the College of Music and Media.

Macalester College

1600 Grand Avenue, St. Paul, MN 55105

One of only a handful of leading liberal arts colleges in a major metropolitan city (two cities, in fact), Macalester offers an internationalist and multiculturalist view of the world. Carleton has a bigger national reputation, but the skill and diversity of the Mac student body are rising. The school also has the progressive capital city of St. Paul and easy access to Minneapolis, as well as a distinctive Scottish flavor.

Founded in 1874, Macalester College is an international island in the heart of the Great Plains. Students here actively participate in internships, volunteering, and service projects and are politically aware about all sorts of issues with local, national, or international import—from LGBTQ rights and immigration policy to divestment from fossil fuels. "Macalester has a long history of social and political advocacy, from the student body as well as the institution itself," says a junior. Bagpipes are heard frequently on campus (students can join free lessons), opening formal events and leading all major processions as a stirring reminder of the college's historic Scottish roots. Says one senior, "Bagpipes are like the Macalester anthem."

Macalester takes its name from a Scotsman named Charles Macalester, an advisor to Abraham Lincoln and other U.S. presidents. The college is located in a friendly, family-oriented neighborhood in St. Paul, Minnesota, one mile from the Mississippi River, which divides St. Paul from Minneapolis. Summit Avenue, a tree-lined street with the longest, best-preserved stretch of Victorian homes in the nation, forms the campus's northern boundary. The self-contained, 53-acre campus is arranged around Old Main, a splendid Victorian structure listed on the National Register of Historic Places. The unifying theme is red brick, the better to set off the octagonal Weyerhaeuser Chapel, constructed of black glass. Other notable facilities include the Janet Wallace Fine Arts Center (a.k.a. "J-Wall"), a $32 million theater and dance building and favorite study spot. A new residence hall and welcome center are scheduled to open in 2027.

Mac's general education requirements span the liberal arts and sciences and include courses around internationalism, cultural diversity, writing, and quantitative thinking. Every student completes a seminar-style First-Year Course and, in their senior year, a capstone experience, such as an independent research project, performance, artistic work, or other original work. In addition to international studies, Mac's academic strengths are also among the most popular, including economics, math, and biology. Psychology, computer science, and media and cultural studies are also student favorites. Eleven foreign languages are offered, and other notable programs include global indigenous studies and community and global health. Science facilities include an observatory and labs for electronic instrumentation and laser spectroscopy.

> "Macalester has a long history of social and political advocacy."

The academic climate is "deeply collaborative" and interdisciplinary, say students. "We love hearing about each other's passions and academic interests, which are often incredibly niche," says an English literature and creative writing major. Mac emphasizes small classes, and teaching and personal relationships are paramount. "The quality of instruction is incredible," raves an economics and political science major. "Professors will do things like recommend students for research positions that their colleagues offer based on that student's interests, as well as show up for athletic or extracurricular events and performances."

The late Kofi Annan, former UN secretary general and class of '61, typified one of Macalester's hallmarks: internationalism, not just in its curriculum and its student body but also in its emphasis on international, off-campus experiences. An impressive 54 percent of students go abroad to complete traditional coursework, independent research, and internships, choosing from 95 exchange and partner programs on six continents. Forty-one percent conduct undergraduate research, often in stipend-supported positions with Mac professors during the summer. Before graduation, about two-thirds of the students complete an internship, usually in the Twin Cities area, and almost all students get involved in volunteer work. As for students' well-being, "There is not a support service I want that Macalester does not offer," says a sophomore.

A psychology major says Mac "is a nerd school in the best way. Every student has their niche that they're super passionate and knowledgeable about." Students

Website: www.macalester.edu
Location: City Center
Private
Total Enrollment: 2,099
Undergraduates: 2,099
Male/Female: 42/53
Financial Aid: 89%
Pell Grant: 14%
Expense: Pr $ $ $ $
Student Loans: 52%
Average Debt: $
Applicants: 8,968
Accepted: 28%
Enrolled: 22%
Grad in 6 Years: 87%
Returning First-years: 92%
Academics: ✑ ✑ ✑ ✑
Social: 🗩 🗩 🗩
Q of L: ★ ★ ★ ★
Admissions: (651) 696-6357
Email Address:
  admissions@macalester.edu

Strong Programs:
Biology
Computer Science
Economics
Geography
International Studies
Mathematics
Media and Cultural Studies
Psychology

Popular annual events include when faculty and staff serve the students Midnight Breakfast before finals begin.

praise Mac's diversity. "You're more likely to have a classmate with a passport from another country than a Minnesota driver's license," says a junior. Seventeen percent of Macalester students hail from Minnesota, and the rest come from every state, and over 100 countries—15 percent hail from abroad. Seven percent of domestic students are Black, 13 percent are Hispanic/Latino, 9 percent are Asian American, and 10 percent are multiracial. Merit scholarships average $19,300; there are no athletic scholarships. Macalester guarantees to meet 100 percent of the demonstrated financial need of all admitted students.

First-years and sophomores are required to live in college housing; 57 percent of all students dwell in college-owned digs, which include traditional residences with single or double rooms as well as suites for upperclassmen. "There are a ton of housing options like language housing, quiet housing, food-specific housing, and more," enthuses a senior. Junior and senior residents of the Interfaith House and the Veggie Co-op prepare their own meals, while other students enjoy eating in the campus center. "It's really easy to hate on Café Mac, the one dining hall here," says a junior, "but honestly the food is much better than people give it credit for." Students praise campus security and the college's proactive approach to sexual assault and mental health awareness. "We are constantly holding dialogues, having discussions, bringing in outside speakers, and addressing policy," reports a junior.

Given the proximity to Minneapolis and St. Paul, much of Mac's social life takes place in the Twin Cities, although there are plenty of events on campus organized by the student-backed Program Board and other student clubs for those loath to leave. "There is no Greek life at Mac, so the parties normally happen off campus," says a sophomore. Popular annual events include when faculty and staff serve the students Midnight

> **"There is not a support service I want that Macalester does not offer."**

Breakfast before finals begin, Founders Day, Fall Ball, and the Brain Bowl football game against in-state rival Carleton. There are about a dozen other colleges and universities in town, and "being in the Twin Cities provides lots of opportunities to go explore," explains a sophomore, including plenty of bookstores, coffee shops, restaurants, bars, plus dance and jazz clubs and professional sports teams. Public transportation makes it relatively easy to get around. The Mall of America is nearby, though Mac students tend to tire of it quickly. For those with wheels, the best road trips include Chicago, Madison, and Duluth.

Competitive Division III Scots teams include baseball, basketball, football, women's water polo, and men's and women's soccer, cross-country, and track and field. Macalester has one of the oldest competitive debate programs in the nation, and the mock trial program is highly ranked nationally. About 60 percent of the students compete in intramural and club sports, including ultimate Frisbee, rugby, and ice hockey. "Whenever the weather's nice, students dot the lawns playing Frisbee, soccer, or cricket—yes, cricket!" says one student.

Macalester pairs high-powered scholarship with global perspectives informed by its Scottish heritage. Students here appreciate their freedom to grow within a supportive community. "There are so many different types of students, sports and clubs, areas of study, and organizations to be a part of, it's honestly crazy how much there is for such a small and intimate school," raves a senior. "Macalester is small, but it really doesn't feel like it."

Overlaps

Brown, Carleton, Grinnell, Middlebury, Oberlin, Smith, St. Olaf, UW–Madison

If You Apply To ›

Macalester: Early decision I and II, early action, regular decision. SATs or ACTs: optional. Accepts the Common Application with supplement.

168 College Avenue, Orono, ME 04469

A more affordable alternative for out-of-staters amid better-known New England public universities such as UMass, UNH, and UVM. Not coincidentally, UMaine is the least expensive—with less stringent admissions criteria—of the four. A popular marine sciences program flourishes here, as does engineering. UMaine is a global leader in the development of offshore wind power. Offers a solid honors program and one of the top varsity hockey programs in the nation. Aggressively recruiting out-of-state students.

At the University of Maine, over 7,000 undergraduates help themselves to a range of strong academic programs at a reasonable cost. As the state's flagship university, UMaine attracts top students to its marine sciences program. A friendly, medium-sized student body and an emphasis on undergraduate learning help create a cozy atmosphere that warms up the long Maine winters as students "engage in experiential learning, embrace ingenuity and exploration, and recognize that challenges are the gateway to progress." A biology major boasts, "We're competitive, we're focused on groundbreaking technology in our academics, and above all, we're focused on taking care of each other."

Situated on an island between the Stillwater and Penobscot Rivers, UMaine's campus covers 660 acres, centered on a large, tree-shaded grass mall. Architectural themes range from English academic to contemporary. Newer facilities include the Innovative Media Research and Commercialization Center, which contains a computer-driven 3-D router, a video production lab, and rich-media classrooms, the Versant Power Astronomy Center, home to the state's largest planetarium, and the $78 million Ferland Engineering Education and Design Center.

As Maine's only public research university, UMaine (founded in 1865) offers nearly 100 undergraduate majors and academic programs. The university is divided into the College of Education and Human Development; the Maine College of Engineering and Computing; the College of Liberal Arts and Sciences; the College of Earth, Life, and Health Sciences; and the Honors College (which now enrolls over 700 students)—as well as the Maine Business School and Graduate School. UMaine has a regional campus in Machias, situated on the Bold Coast, which enrolls close to 200 undergraduate students and offers specialized programs like integrative biology, outdoor recreation, and marine biology. Specific general education requirements vary from college to college, though all students must demonstrate writing proficiency and earn credits in physical or biological science, human value and social context, math (including statistics and computer science), and ethics. A capstone experience, such as a poster presentation or service project, is also mandatory.

> **"We're focused on groundbreaking technology in our academics."**

UMaine's engineering programs are some of the strongest and most demanding on campus. Other best bets include business, forestry, earth and climate sciences, and nursing. Marine sciences undergrads can spend a semester by the sea at UMaine's prominent Darling Marine Center, and UMaine's Climate Change Institute, one of the oldest climate research units in the United States, is renowned. The most popular majors include management, marketing, mechanical engineering, and psychology. The university offers more than 20 accelerated programs that allow students to earn both a bachelor's and master's degree in a minimum of five years, in

Website: www.umaine.edu
Location: Rural
Public
Total Enrollment: 8,203
Undergraduates: 7,449
Male/Female: 51/48
Financial Aid: 95%
Pell Grant: 35%
Expense: Pub $ $ $
Student Loans: 64%
Average Debt: $ $ $
Applicants: 14,044
Accepted: 97%
Enrolled: 15%
Grad in 6 Years: 55%
Returning First-years: 83%
Academics: ✍ ✍
Social: 🗩 🗩 🗩 🗩
Q of L: ★ ★ ★
Admissions: (207) 581-1561
Email Address:
umaineadmissions@maine.edu

Strong Programs:
Business
Earth and Climate Sciences
Engineering
Finance
Forestry Management
Marine Sciences
Nursing

fields as diverse as economics, information systems, and special education. Students describe the academic climate as cooperative and usually relaxed. Forty-two percent of all classes have fewer than 20 students, making it relatively easy to interact with professors. "I didn't know professors could be so attentive, intelligent, and dedicated to building their students' knowledge," attests a biology major.

Research is a key part of an undergraduate education at UMaine and is woven into many areas of the curriculum, as is real-world experience. First-year students looking for exposure to research in their first semester can select one of 13 optional, one-credit Research Learning Experiences in scientific fieldwork, nutrition, market research, and more. UMaine's Explorations program lets first-year students work with professionals in different areas before declaring their degree choices. SPIFFY, the student investment club, manages a $5.13 million, real-money portfolio. UMaine students may choose from over 100 study abroad programs in 50 countries.

Most undergrads hail from Maine and other parts of New England (making them immune to the frigid temperatures). "The common thread among UMaine students is their kindness," explains a senior. "In the winter, students will go around scraping the snow off other students' cars, even if they don't know them." Faced with a declining youth population in Maine, the university has been working hard to lure out-of-state students with several programs, including the Flagship Scholars Commitment Program, which allows eligible students to pay the same in-state tuition they would pay at their home flagship university. Such efforts are paying off—out-of-state enrollment is up. Racial diversity still has a long way to go: Black students account for 2 percent of the student body, Asian Americans 2 percent, Hispanics/Latinos 5 percent, and multiracial students 4 percent. International students add 2 percent. Students describe the political climate as balanced, with both sides of the aisle well represented. Merit scholarships average $9,200 a year for qualified students, and 195 athletic scholarships are available in 16 sports. Thirty-five percent of incoming first-years qualify for Pell Grants.

Forty-two percent of UMaine students live on campus; the rest seek shelter in Orono, nearby Bangor, or the sparsely populated area in between. Dorms are co-ed; some have gyms, computer labs, or apartment-style suites. First-years may opt to join one of eight living/learning communities organized around themes like nursing, engineering, and honors. "First-year residence halls are very well kept and have plenty of room," reports a student.

"The common thread among UMaine students is their kindness."

Meal options in the three main dining halls receive average reviews. "Campus feels incredibly safe to me," says one student. "The dorms are very well-secured and can only be accessed with our student ID cards."

Despite—or possibly because of—UMaine's relatively isolated location, the campus pulses with social life; more than 200 student groups and organizations plan plays, carnival nights, concerts, and comedy hours, with a different activity offered each night. Fraternities draw a small portion of students. Between local bars and clubs and frequent parties at Greek and off-campus houses, the party scene at UMaine is lively but, according to a senior, "not overwhelming if it's not your style." Everyone looks forward to Spirit Week and Maine Day of Service, a celebration focusing on beautification and giving back to campus that includes service projects, events, campuswide cookouts, and more.

A nursing major says the midsized town of Orono and the surrounding area have much to offer: "cute shops, cozy libraries, indoor and outdoor ice skating, music stores, bowling, movie theaters, a variety of restaurants, and vibrant museums." Buses to Bangor, 10 minutes away, run every 15 to 20 minutes, and popular road trips include Acadia National Park, skiing at Sugarloaf, L.L.Bean's 24-hour store in Freeport, and the real-life Mount Katahdin, which appears on L.L.Bean's logo. Those seeking big-city adventures enjoy Boston, four hours away, or Montreal, with its lower drinking age.

UMaine is the state's only Division I school, and athletic events are a big part of student life. Ice hockey reigns supreme, especially when rivals Boston College, Boston University, or New Hampshire are in town, and the Black Bears are perennial champions. Baseball and women's basketball have claimed America East conference titles in recent years. Women's soccer is also competitive. The sports club program has 31 sports, from alpine skiing to volleyball. The intramural program offers kickball, dodgeball, corn hole, and more.

> **"First-year residence halls are very well kept and have plenty of room."**

UMaine is a medium-sized school with a small-school atmosphere. Combine the state's natural beauty with an increased emphasis on top-quality facilities, more intimate student/faculty interaction, and innovations in admissions and it's no surprise that this campus is drawing more "Maine-iaks" each year.

Overlaps

UMass Amherst, University of New Hampshire, University of Rhode Island, South Dakota State, University of Southern Maine, University of Vermont, University of Wyoming

If You Apply To ›

Maine: Early action, rolling admissions. SATs or ACTs: optional. Accepts the Common Application with supplement.

Manhattanville University

2900 Purchase Street, Purchase, NY 10577

Previously a small liberal arts college, Manhattanville was recast as a university in 2024, expanding its course offerings. Located in the NYC area, the school occupies a former estate (complete with a castle) and is a quick train ride into Manhattan. Strong programs include education, psychology, and nursing. An increased emphasis on athletics continues to raise the school's profile. Sixty percent of students are women and 36 percent are Hispanic/Latino.

Founded in 1841 by the Sisters of the Sacred Heart as an all-women's boarding school, Manhattanville College was reclassified as Manhattanville University in 2024. Today it's a private, nondenominational, coeducational, liberal arts school with a mission to "educate students to be ethical and socially responsible leaders in a global community." The Atlas certificate program allows students to set goals, reflect on their academic and cocurricular experiences, and showcase their work in e-portfolios. But Atlas is just one way Manhattanville encourages individuality and personal growth. Personal attention is another. "The best perk of being part of [Manhattanville is that] it allows you to really connect with your professors," testifies a criminal justice major.

Manhattanville University pulled up stakes from its original location on Houston Street in New York City in the 1950s for a 125-acre estate in Purchase, New York. The estate is located in Westchester County, near the city of White Plains—home to several major corporations and just 28 miles from the Big Apple. Overlooking the central Quadrangle, which was designed by Central Park architect Frederick Law Olmsted, is the focal point of the campus: Reid Castle, a 19th-century replica of a Norman castle. The President's Cottage, built in 1860, has been converted into a modern Center for Design Thinking complete with a high-tech fabrication lab with 3-D printers.

Website: www.mville.edu
Location: Suburban
Private
Total Enrollment: 1,724
Undergraduates: 1,326
Male/Female: 40/60
Financial Aid: 99%
Pell Grant: 44%
Expense: Pr $
Student Loans: 66%
Average Debt: $ $ $ $
Applicants: 3,619
Accepted: 87%
Enrolled: 11%
Grad in 6 Years: 58%
Returning First-years: 74%
Academics: ✍ ✍ ✍
Social: 🗨 🗨 🗨

Art and design programs are enhanced by the proximity of New York City's many museums and galleries.

Manhattanville's general education program requires coursework in math, science, fine arts, social science, humanities, global studies, and a second language. First-year students take a seminar focused on ethics and social responsibility and two semesters of writing. Students also complete an experiential learning requirement, including internships, clinical placements, independent research, student teaching, and service learning. Seminar professors serve as faculty mentors, and all incoming students are also assigned academic advisors to help ease the transition to college life.

The university's strongest offerings include education, business (especially management and finance), and psychology, while communication studies and performing arts are also popular areas of study. Manhattanville's School of Education boasts a near-perfect pass rate for the New York State Teaching Exam. Enrollment in the School of Nursing and Health Sciences is growing rapidly, and the school has added a new major in imaging leadership. New majors have also been added in creative writing and literature, historical studies, and several areas of childhood and early childhood education. A popular sport studies major prepares students for a wide range of careers, such as sports business management, sport psychology, physical education, and sports journalism. Art and design programs are enhanced by the proximity of New York City's many museums and galleries. Students may choose from a bevy of five-year bachelor's/master's degree programs in several fields, cross-register for courses at neighboring Purchase College, SUNY, or opt to design their own major.

"Someone is always on the quad hanging out."

"The academic climate at school varies depending on the type of class and the professor you have, but overall it is good and very interactive," says a sociology major. Undergraduates enjoy regular access to professors, especially since 71 percent of classes have fewer than 20 students. Students give high praise to the academic support services offered by the Academic Resource Center, the Writing Center, the Center for Student Accommodations, and the Valiant Learning Support Program. Qualified first-years may apply for the Castle Scholars Honors Program for a more intensive curriculum. The university has study abroad options in 30 countries, and about 8 percent of students get involved in undergraduate research. The Center for Career Development helps secure internship placements at more than 350 locations in and beyond the New York Metro area, such as Mastercard, the Metropolitan Museum of Art, and U.S. Senate offices.

A communication studies major characterizes Manhattanville students as "diverse, friendly, and chill," and a classmate adds that the school "was recently recognized as a Hispanic Serving Institution." Indeed, Hispanics/Latinos represent the largest minority group, at 36 percent, in a college where most undergraduates (78 percent) are New Yorkers. Black students make up 11 percent of the student body, Asian Americans 3 percent, and multiracial students 3 percent; 3 percent of undergrads come from overseas. Students describe themselves as politically aware, and a junior says, "We are a community of social justice activists." Forty-four percent of first-years are eligible for Pell Grants. While there are no athletic scholarships, hundreds of merit scholarships averaging $23,500 are awarded to qualified students.

"A large portion of our school is made up of athletes."

Forty-five percent of Manhattanville's students live on campus in one of four residence halls, which have lounges, communal kitchens, and laundry rooms. First-years are assigned rooms that are "spacious and very comfortable" according to a student. Campus dwellers can choose from three different meal plans and can use their meal cards at the main dining hall, the Pub (a deli-type eatery), and vending machines. "There are plenty of options to choose from," a junior says. Students report feeling safe on campus.

The student programming board is working to improve the campus social life with weekend events such as dance parties, gaming tournaments, comedy and talent shows, movies, plays, and concerts. "Someone is always on the quad hanging out, playing spikeball, tanning with their friends, teammates, etc.," cheers a sport studies major. With no fraternities or sororities, off-campus parties are often hosted by sports teams, but a senior says Manhattanville "is not very much a party school." Every spring, students look forward to Quad Jam, an all-day concert and carnival. Another favorite tradition is Red Madness; "It's like *Dancing With the Stars* but with our athletic teams," explains a junior. There's also a Fall Fest and an International Bazaar, in which students give cultural performances and share ethnic foods.

Sixty-three percent of Manhattanville students contribute more than 30,000 hours of community service each year through more than 60 local and global programs. Purchase "is a great college town," says a first-year. Students frequently take the school's free bus to White Plains to enjoy a variety of restaurants, bars, and shops, and as one student points out, "Manhattanville is only 30 miles from New York City, so students can also go to the city for fun." Road trips include Rye Beach in the warmer months and upstate New York or Vermont for skiing in the winter.

Manhattanville has invested heavily in athletics in hopes of increasing its visibility, and one international student notes, "a large portion of our school is made up of athletes." Twenty-four Valiant teams (inspired by a 15th-century quote, "To the valiant of heart, nothing is impossible") hold their own in the Division III Skyline Conference. Men's and women's basketball, tennis, and men's soccer reached recent conference tournaments. Women's volleyball, softball, hockey, and lacrosse are also competitive. Intramural and club sports, ranging from flag football to volleyball, draw about a quarter of the students.

"Coming to Manhattanville's culture makes students the best version of themselves," a junior says. The familial atmosphere can get claustrophobic at times, but for those wishing to be part of a close but growing community where values matter, Manhattanville may be worth a look as it grows into its new identity as a university. In the words of one happy student, Manhattanville is "a community that allows you to be yourself, meet new people, try new things, expand your horizons, and overall a fun place to be."

Manhattanville's School of Education boasts a near-perfect pass rate for the New York State Teaching Exam.

Overlaps

Iona, Manhattan College, Marist, Mercy, Pace, Purchase (SUNY), Sacred Heart, St. John's University

If You Apply To ›

Manhattanville: Early action, rolling admissions. SATs or ACTs: optional. Accepts the Common Application with supplement. Auditions or portfolios are required for performing arts and visual arts applicants.

Marquette University

1250 West Wisconsin Avenue, Milwaukee, WI 53233

Marquette is a Catholic, Jesuit university situated near the heart of downtown Milwaukee. Service learning is a major emphasis. The student body is mainly from the southern Wisconsin/northern Illinois corridor, and the school draws a substantial number of Catholics. Relatively inexpensive, in keeping with its middle- and working-class roots. Compare to Saint Louis University and Loyola of Chicago.

At Marquette University, students practice what they preach. The college experience at this Catholic institution includes an emphasis on personal growth, civic

Student religious organizations are active, and students, faculty, and staff can attend mass every day of the week.

responsibility, and community service. The university continues to look for ways to affirm its traditions and values drawn from the Society of Jesus (the Jesuits) while at the same time expanding its global focus and connecting students with practical, real-world experiences. Service learning, which helps students put classroom theories to the test through volunteer work, is a cornerstone of campus life, helping to shape well-rounded students. "They all have a special mission or purpose," says a finance major. "They all want to make the world move in some way."

Marquette, which opened its doors in 1881 and takes its name from the 17th-century Jesuit explorer Jacques Marquette, occupies more than 90 acres of "concrete with interludes of grass and trees" just a few blocks from downtown Milwaukee.

> **"Marquette professors lead with the Jesuit value 'Cura Personalis,' which means caring for the whole person."**

While offering the advantages of an urban setting, its campus has plenty of open spaces suitable for throwing everything from Frisbees to barbecues. Most of the buildings are relatively modern, including a new $60 million home for the College of Business Administration that contains state-of-the-art connective technology. But Marquette is also the site of the St. Joan of Arc Chapel, which was built in France 600 years ago and later transported to Wisconsin. It is said to be the only medieval structure in the Western Hemisphere dedicated to its original purpose.

The Marquette Core Curriculum is structured in three parts. Foundations courses ground students in the theology, philosophy, and rhetoric of a Jesuit perspective. Discovery courses encourage an interdisciplinary approach, as students take four courses centered around a chosen theme, such as Crossing Boundaries and Exploring the Unknown. A final Culminating course helps students reflect on and apply what they've learned in the Core. Students who want to get a head start on the Marquette experience can opt to participate in the five-week Emerging Scholars Program, which offers credit and noncredit courses.

The most popular majors include nursing, biomedical sciences, psychology, and finance. Engineering programs and the social welfare and justice major are well regarded, as are more specialized majors in operations and supply chain management and bioinformatics. A senior raves about the school's Excellence in Leadership program: "I shadowed industry leaders, worked on a team capstone project, interviewed people with crazy titles, went on a week-long retreat. The program made me grow tremendously!" Through an affiliation with the Milwaukee Institute of Art and Design, two fine arts minors are available in studio art and graphic design. Marquette has its own museum, the Haggerty Museum of Art. Its highly popular service-learning courses, which draw more than 1,000 students every semester, connect participants with service opportunities in more than 130 community agencies. Overall, about three-quarters of Marquette students take part in some type of community service experience.

"Something unique about Marquette is our class sizes," attests a nursing major. Thirty-seven percent have fewer than 20 students, "allowing professors and students to create a trusting and encouraging atmosphere." The school's Jesuit influence is felt in the classroom. "Marquette professors lead with the Jesuit value 'Cura Personalis,' which means caring for the whole person," says a junior. "I feel like I'm being pushed to the best of my ability and being cared for mentally, spiritually, and academically."

Twenty-one percent of Marquette students travel each year for study abroad programs offered in more than 48 countries. The flagship Sibanye Cape Town service-learning program in South Africa is especially popular; participants combine their studies at the University of the Western Cape with two days of volunteer work per week in areas like education, public health, and economic development. The university is also home to the Les Aspin Center for Government in Washington, D.C., which allows students to take courses while participating in an internship with a federal government agency. Twenty-four percent of students assist faculty members with their research, and approximately 260 top first-year students per year join the University Honors Program.

Most of the undergraduate student body is from the Midwest, 34 percent from Wisconsin itself; 2 percent are international. In general, Marquette boasts a friendly collection of traditional, middle-class students. Student religious organizations are active, and students, faculty, and staff can attend mass every day of the week, but religious practice is left to the individual. According to a digital media and public relations major, "A lot of students are committed to exploring how their interests relate to social justice through volunteer work." Black students make up 5 percent of the student body, Hispanics/Latinos 16 percent, Asian Americans 6 percent, and multiracial students 3 percent. Marquette's successful Educational Opportunity Program enables low-income, disadvantaged students to have the benefit of a college education. Merit scholarships averaging $25,900 are available, as are athletic scholarships in 12 sports.

> **"[Marquette students] all want to make the world move in some way."**

Fifty-seven percent of Marquette students make their home on campus; residency is required for first-years and sophomores, except for commuters who live within 30 miles with a parent or guardian. All but two residence halls are co-ed, and there are more than 400 university-owned apartments (which come with a separate electric bill). Within the residence halls are five living/learning communities organized around academic and cultural interests. Dining reviews are mostly positive, with one senior noting, "The facility in the Commons is great, so much space for sitting and eating." Regarding security on this urban campus, a student says, "If you use your street smarts and the campus resources in place, you are entirely safe." The LGBTQ+ Resource Center supports students with an interest in LGBTQ and gender identity issues, and students are required to take yearly online training on sexual violence prevention. "They give us almost too many resources," opines a senior.

Social life takes place both on and off campus, and Greek life doesn't dominate the scene. "There is a significant party culture at Marquette, but not enough to call it a party school," says a senior. While Milwaukee is hardly a college town, and the wind from Lake Michigan is a regular complaint, students say there are many good things about being there, "from Bradford [beach], Brewers games, concerts, and breweries everywhere," touts a student. An old advertising slogan once claimed that

> **"[National Marquette Day] gets everyone out and makes it feel like a big state school."**

"Milwaukee Means Beer," and few Marquette students would disagree. They report that Marquette is stricter than most universities in enforcing the drinking age, especially in the dorms. National Marquette Day, a big pregame basketball pep rally, "gets everyone out and makes it feel like a big state school," says a senior, "but most of the time, [the social scene] is just people having fun all over campus in smaller groups."

The Golden Eagles Division I men's basketball is a powerhouse with four straight recent NCAA tournament appearances. Men's golf and women's volleyball teams are also highly competitive in the Big East Conference. A majority of students participate in roughly two dozen intramural sports and 46 club teams. Sports fans will be impressed with Milwaukee's Fiserv Forum, home to Marquette basketball and the NBA's Milwaukee Bucks. Nature lovers can head to Lake Michigan, a 40-minute walk from campus, or to Kettle Moraine, a glaciated region ideal for hiking and cross-country skiing. Chicago is only 95 miles away.

Students at Marquette are encouraged to engage not only in their own personal growth but also in the betterment of their local and global communities

Overlaps

Elon, U of I at Urbana–Champaign, Indiana University, Loyola University Chicago, Saint Louis University, University of Minnesota, UW–Madison, Villanova through service. Students say it's the supportive, familial atmosphere that makes them excited about those goals and that makes Marquette what it is. Confirms a senior, "Marquette students really are a community. Everyone supports everyone else."

University of Mary Washington

1301 College Avenue, Fredericksburg, VA 22401

Situated in historic Fredericksburg, Virginia, Mary Washington could be mistaken for one of Virginia's elite private colleges. A public liberal arts and sciences university, it offers a comparable amount of history and tradition albeit for a lower price. It's named for George Washington's mother and home to one of the few historic preservation programs in the country.

Website: www.umw.edu
Location: Small City
Public
Total Enrollment: 3,138
Undergraduates: 3,098
Male/Female: 36/64
Financial Aid: 88%
Pell Grant: 27%
Expense: Pub $
Student Loans: 46%
Average Debt: $ $ $
Applicants: 5,124
Accepted: 80%
Enrolled: 18%
Grad in 6 Years: 66%
Returning First-years: 84%
Academics: ✑ ✑ ✑
Social: 💬 💬 💬
Q of L: ★ ★ ★ ★
Admissions: (540) 654-2000
Email Address:
admit@umw.edu

Strong Programs:
Biology
Communication and Digital
 Studies
Education
Geography
Historic Preservation
International Affairs

Strolling among the University of Mary Washington's elegant buildings of red brick with white columns has led more than one pleased parent to declare, "Now this is what a college should look like." Indeed, for an aura of history and tradition, few schools stack up to this small college in Fredericksburg, a site of Civil War action and the boyhood town of George Washington. "Tradition is at the heart of UMW and is one of the many things that instills a sense of community here," says a junior.

The campus features classical Jeffersonian buildings, sweeping lawns, brick walkways, and breathtaking foliage. Founded in 1908 as the all-female branch of the University of Virginia, UMW went co-ed in 1970 and cut its ties in 1972. Recent renovations include a $24 million overhaul of Seacobeck Hall, now home to the College of Education, and a significant expansion of the Jepson Science Center.

Mary Washington has gained a reputation as one of the premier public liberal arts and sciences colleges in the country and seeks "scholars who are serious about academics, committed to an inclusive community and eager to contribute to the greater good."

> **"Research, especially in the science department, is great here at UMW."**

The core curriculum includes a diverse and global perspectives requirement, a digital-intensive course, a "Beyond the Classroom" component (research, a community engagement course, study abroad, or an internship), and an "After MW" component focused on career development. Students pledge to uphold the university's honor code and must take a discussion-based first-year seminar. Nearly every major requires students to complete a capstone project or take a senior-level seminar.

"The academic climate is very professional and supportive, with a flexible structure that allows for time invested in other activities," according to an international business major. Mary Washington's program in historic preservation is solid: "It's pretty unique and has great local partners for internships," says a senior. Among the sciences, biology and chemistry are favorites. The international affairs program benefits from the university's proximity to Washington, D.C., and communication and digital studies, geography, education, and theatre are also strengths. Popular majors include business and marketing, psychology, English, and computer science. New majors include applied mathematics and statistics, data science, and kinesiology. The close ties between students and faculty are a great source of pride. Fifty-seven percent of classes have fewer than 20 students, and with small class sizes, a political science major says, "We are able to fully participate and not be another number in a room of hundreds." Adds a biomedical science major, "The quality of the instructors is so outstanding that students can overcome any obstacles."

A biomedical science major cheers, "Research, especially in the science department, is great here at UMW." Philanthropic support has boosted undergraduate research, expanded full-ride scholarships for out-of-state students, and doubled the Summer Science Institute, which provides a stipend for a 10-week summer program. Eighty-five percent of students take on research projects, and about 13 percent participate in the university's honors program. Several departments offer grants for work abroad or in the U.S., and students rave about their study abroad experiences, available in more than 50 countries. "The career center on campus here is great for getting students prepared for any kind of internship or job," says a junior. The university's location, roughly an hour from both Washington, D.C., and the state capital, Richmond, is a handy asset for budding politicos.

An unusually strong sense of community characterizes everything from academics to campus life. Students are "kind, determined, and hungry for academic and cultural knowledge," comments an international business major. Eighty-nine percent of students are from Virginia and just 2 percent arrive from abroad. Black students make up 8 percent of the student population, Hispanics/Latinos 13 percent, Asian Americans 4 percent, and multiracial students 6 percent. "As an African American woman, I have never felt out of place," says a senior. "I had wonderful supervisors, club advisors, academic advisors, and friends who helped me make space for myself." Civic engagement is a priority, with students leading initiatives year-round to encourage voting. Says an accounting major from Texas, "Although I may have different hobbies or political views from my fellow peers, I've engaged in so much helpful dialogue that I'm very happy I came to UMW." Eligible undergraduates receive merit awards averaging $5,200, but there are no athletic scholarships.

Mary Washington has a two-year residency requirement, and 57 percent of students live in university housing. The residence halls offer singles, suites, and gender-neutral options. First-years are required to purchase a meal plan, and one senior reports, "Although the food was not my mother's home cooking, the dining environment and the international meals make students feel at home." A sophomore observes, "We have good support programs through the Office of Title IX, and there seems to be a general consensus among students that UMW is a safe place."

There is no Greek life, but, says a senior, "From Tuesday night bingo to live music events, there is always something happening on campus." Parties are generally thrown by sports teams. "Campus policies regarding alcohol are never punitive and always educational," says a senior. Favorite events include Devil-Goat Day, an all-day competition pitting graduation years against each other in a variety of field day–style events.

Nearby Fredericksburg has "a lively downtown [with] wine tastings, a cidery, as well as traditional bars with club dancing," shares a senior, while another adds, "There's also the Fredericksburg Nationals, our minor league baseball team, which has an awesome atmosphere (I'm not even a huge baseball fan)!" Fredericksburg also offers historic homes to visit, museums, bookstores, a mall, and plenty of restaurants. Students can drive to Richmond or D.C.

(continued)

Psychology
Theatre

Devil-Goat Day is an all-day competition pitting graduation years against each other in a variety of field day–style events.

"From Tuesday night bingo to live music events, there is always something happening on campus."

The international affairs program benefits from the university's proximity to Washington, D.C.

Instead of football, Mary Washington has an internationally known men's and women's rugby program, competitive eSports team, and well-established equestrian team. Its 18 Division III Eagles sports teams fly high in the Coast-to-Coast Athletic Conference, earning conference titles in women's swimming, men's and women's tennis, men's soccer, and women's volleyball. The 76-acre sports and field complex, complete with a newly renovated Olympic-size pool, is used for more than 20 club sports and a variety of intramurals, including basketball, no-tackle football, soccer, and pickleball.

UMW is "a school where you can get your degree and enjoy the campus and places around it at the same time," says a biomedical science major. With its history, traditions, small class sizes, and welcoming community, prospective students may find, as one happy senior did, "The best part about UMW is that the resources are ripe for the taking."

If You Apply To ›

Mary Washington: Early decision, early action, regular decision. SATs or ACTs: optional. Accepts the Common Application with supplement.

University of Maryland

College Park, MD 20742

The name says Maryland, but the location says Washington, D.C. Students in College Park can jump on the Metro just as they do at American or Georgetown. Maryland, the state's flagship campus, is nothing if not big, and savvy students will look to programs such as the Honors College and living/learning communities for some personal attention.

Website: www.umd.edu
Location: Suburban
Public
Total Enrollment: 37,175
Undergraduates: 29,078
Male/Female: 50/50
Financial Aid: 54%
Pell Grant: 16%
Expense: Pub $ $
Student Loans: 31%
Average Debt: $ $ $
Applicants: 60,042
Accepted: 45%
Enrolled: 10%
Grad in 6 Years: 89%
Returning First-years: 96%
Academics: ✍ ✍ ✍ ✍
Social: 🗨 🗨 🗨
Q of L: ★ ★ ★
Admissions: (800) 422-5867
Email Address: applymaryland@umd.edu

For good luck on exams, University of Maryland students rub the nose of Testudo, the school's terrapin mascot. But even without touching the storied statue, most students here feel lucky to be at a diverse school that offers a multitude of programs, from living/learning communities to special opportunities for first-year students, that make it feel smaller and more personal despite its daunting size. "With hundreds of different student organizations," says a senior, "students will always be able to find their niche."

Maryland's 1,340-acre campus embraces an array of architectural styles, including the Georgian brick buildings ringing the oak-lined mall at the heart of the campus. The 17,950-seat Xfinity Center hosts Terrapin basketball games and special university events. The $152 million Iribe Center for Computer Science and Engineering features six floors of specialized, high-tech labs. Among recent construction is a new $132 million Chemistry Building that includes 34 labs and 12 meeting rooms and new baseball and softball development centers.

Maryland, which dates to 1856, has earned a strong reputation for its engineering, computer science, and criminology and criminal justice departments, as well as the Smith School of Business and Merrill College of Journalism. The most popular majors are computer science, information science, finance, and public health science, and due to the popularity of computer science, the university has made it a limited enrollment program with specific guidelines for admittance. General education requirements entail a number of distribution areas, including professional writing, oral communication, diversity, and others. Students must also take two Big

Question courses in which they investigate significant issues in depth. For students at the extremes of the academic spectrum, there are departmental honors programs and the Honors College, as well as an intensive educational development and tutoring program. Students participating in individual studies can combine established majors and create their own programs.

Maryland's academic climate is "more collaborative than competitive," according to one student. Lower-level courses tend to be large and impersonal ("easy to hide in, even easier to skip"), but the corresponding weekly discussion sections led by teaching assistants offer personal attention. The situation improves by junior year, when classes of 20 to 40 students become the norm. "Professors are clearly well versed in their fields," says a biochemistry major, "but there is some expectation for students to teach themselves material." The university has put more emphasis on helping students make timely progress toward their degrees and has amped up experiential learning across nearly 300 courses. A two-day orientation, seminars, and course clusters are offered for incoming students, and 60 percent of first-years participate in more than 25 living/learning programs that provide experiential learning opportunities in more intimate settings. The First-Year Innovation and Research Experience (FIRE) program allows qualified students to join faculty-led research groups for research and mentorship experiences. One participant comments, "The FIRE program has really sparked and encouraged my interest in research." Internships in nearby Washington, D.C., and Baltimore are plentiful, and undergrads study abroad in dozens of countries, such as Costa Rica, Israel, and Sweden.

Seventy-six percent of undergraduates are Maryland natives, while New York and New Jersey are also well represented; 3 percent hail from foreign nations. Diversity is more than just a buzzword: 13 percent of students are Black, 11 percent are Hispanic/Latino, 24 percent are Asian American, and 5 percent are multiracial. Major social and political issues on campus revolve around greater awareness of racial and LGBTQ+ issues. Qualified undergrads receive merit awards averaging $7,100, and athletes vie for more than 400 scholarships.

Twenty-two percent of students live on campus in single-sex or co-ed dorms; first-years are guaranteed housing. While many juniors and seniors seek off-campus accommodations, those who stay on campus all four years will find that their digs improve as they gain seniority—upperclassmen have the option of on-campus apartments and suites. Even so, the quality of the dorms varies significantly based on their age, and a senior says, "The dorms are a gamble for a lot of money." Dining services get much better reviews. Campus safety features include front desks in the dorms that are staffed 24/7 and walking and riding escort services to transport students after dark. "The area has its rough spots, but it is constantly becoming safer," a sophomore says.

The university's reputation as a haven for those who prefer partying to studying is changing as students with better credentials apply, but there is still always something happening in the dorms and at local pubs. Students enjoy frequent school-sponsored concerts, movies, speakers, and Terps After Dark events, as well as the traditional football and basketball games and off-campus fraternity parties. "Social life is epic here," raves a history and education double major. Nine percent of men and 12 percent of women go Greek, and they have been known to incur disciplinary action by the administration, but they don't dominate the tone of campus life. As for drinking, "They say no tolerance, and in recent years, there have been crackdowns," says one student. Art Attack is a favorite annual event in which local artists share their crafts and national touring artists perform an evening concert. Other

"The FIRE program has really sparked and encouraged my interest in research."

Students enjoy frequent school-sponsored concerts, movies, speakers, and Terps After Dark events.

"Students here have a lot of school spirit. Terrapin pride runs rampant."

Students must take two Big Question courses in which they investigate significant issues in depth.

popular events include homecoming and Maryland Day, where "the campus mall basically turns into something that resembles a state fair," explains a junior. When Maryland's suburban campus feels too small, a few bucks and a few minutes on the Metro (Washington's subway system) brings Terrapins into downtown D.C. at a hare's pace; downtown Baltimore is a 40-minute drive.

Division I sports are a big deal here, and in a bow to the importance of television revenue, the Terrapins compete in the predominately Midwestern, 14-member Big Ten Conference. Despite the football team's disappointing record on the Big Ten stage, the Terrapins continue to achieve success: men's and women's lacrosse, women's field hockey, and baseball have claimed conference titles. Men's and women's basketball is also strong. "Students here have a lot of school spirit," a junior says. "Terrapin pride runs rampant." Around two dozen intramurals and more than 45 club sports draw roughly a quarter of the students.

The University of Maryland's overwhelming size is both a blessing and a curse. On one hand, "the diversity of the student body and the opportunities afforded are infinite," a sophomore says. On the other, largeness can translate into crowded dorms, big classes, parking problems, and other hassles. Still, most students agree that the university's range of academic programs, advantageous location near the nation's capital, and persistent school spirit make the Maryland experience worthwhile.

If You Apply To ›

Maryland: Early action, regular decision. Accepts the Common Application with supplement. Students who do not meet academic standards may submit additional information for consideration. Please consult Maryland's website for the most up-to-date information regarding standardized test requirements.

University of Maryland, Baltimore County

1000 Hilltop Circle, Baltimore, MD 21250

A midsized public university with the feel of a private. Strategically located in a suburban setting between Washington, D.C., and Baltimore, UMBC invests heavily in learning communities and other efforts to ensure that its undergraduates thrive. Nationally known for its selective Meyerhoff Scholars Program. Many student research options attract its diverse student body.

Since its founding in 1966, the University of Maryland, Baltimore County, has allowed students to take charge of their academic world, giving them access to academic and social resources and a thriving research agenda usually reserved for those attending mammoth public institutions or pricey private colleges. UMBC strives to instill in students values of advancing knowledge, economic prosperity, and social justice. "UMBC is a family," says a theatre and history major. "It's a community of scholars, but it's also a home for people of all backgrounds. Everyone wants to see you succeed."

UMBC's 500-acre suburban campus is located between D.C. and Baltimore, offering students access to an array of cultural attractions including restaurants, art galleries, specialty shops, and museums. In the past decade, the university has invested more than $420 million in new facilities and landscaping, including a LEED Gold–rated performing arts and humanities building, a 6,000-seat athletics arena and event center, the Interdisciplinary Life Sciences Building, the Center for Well-Being, and more than 3,000 trees.

All students complete general foundation requirements, including courses in the arts and humanities, foreign language, social science, math, and biological/physical science. The university offers several programs designed to help first-year students ease into college life, including First-Year Seminars that allow students to partner with faculty members to explore course material in an intimate, active learning environment. Students focus on creative and critical-thinking skills and written and oral communication and take part in faculty and peer critiques.

"UMBC students are encouraged to collaborate with their peers and grow together, tackling a problem, not each other," says a psychology and social work major. UMBC's most popular programs are also its strongest, including biological sciences, psychology, computer science, information systems, and engineering. Bioinformatics, theatre, and visual arts are also well regarded. The individualized study major gives students a chance to create their own majors. Students can also take advantage of established interdisciplinary programs in Asian studies, Africana studies, and global studies. Forty-three percent of classes have fewer than 20 students. "UMBC has excellent professors who enhance the material taught in classrooms by sharing their experiences in the field," touts a psychology major.

UMBC provides many ways for students to follow their academic, research, and entrepreneurial interests. The Alex. Brown Center for Entrepreneurship sponsors programs and courses to inspire entrepreneurial thinking among students and faculty. "Most of the professors offer opportunities for students to get involved in their projects and learn how to work in a research lab," says a biochemistry and molecular biology major. At UMBC's Undergraduate Research and Creative Achievement Day in the spring, budding researchers compete for undergraduate research awards of up to $1,500 and present their work to the entire campus. Thanks to the highly selective Meyerhoff Scholars Program, which addresses the shortage of diversity in the sciences and engineering, UMBC graduates more Black undergrads who go on to earn Ph.D.s in the natural sciences and engineering than any other American institution. Each year, the Shriver Center connects nearly 1,000 UMBC students with service-learning opportunities, while the Career Center places 2,000 students in internships, co-ops, and research positions. Study abroad programs are available in 60 countries.

UMBC students are "academic focused and not judgmental," says a Spanish major, while a social work and psychology major adds, "The student body is diverse, with people from all types of backgrounds." Ninety-three percent of students hail from Maryland, while 3 percent come from abroad. Black students account for 25 percent of the student body, Hispanics/Latinos 10 percent, Asian Americans 24 percent, and multiracial students 6 percent. The student body leans progressive, and issues such as "immigration, the Trump administration, and housing costs are a few of the main issues that often come up in conversation," says a senior. UMBC awards merit scholarships worth an average of $6,700 and athletic scholarships in 17 sports; 33 percent of incoming first-years qualify for Pell Grants.

Thirty-six percent of students live in campus housing, which is guaranteed for incoming first-years, but it "tends to fill up fast so it's best to get your application in early," advises a math major. Residential facilities receive average reviews.

(continued)

Accepted: 72%
Enrolled: 22%
Grad in 6 Years: 70%
Returning First-years: 85%
Academics: ✍ ✍ ✍
Social: 🗩 🗩 🗩
Q of L: ★ ★ ★
Admissions: (410) 455-2292
Email Address:
  admissions@umbc.edu

Strong Programs:
Bioinformatics
Biological Sciences
Computer Science
Engineering
Information Systems
Psychology
Theatre
Visual Arts

The highlight of the social calendar is Quadmania, a weekend festival in the spring with games, carnival rides, food trucks, and music.

Several living/learning communities connect students with similar interests and house them together in the residence halls. Students say off-campus housing is plentiful and cheap, although parking on campus can be a chore. Campus dining options include Starbucks and Chick-fil-A, a dining hall and the Commons, which offers a variety of fare, including international cuisine. As for security, "Campus is safe," says a student, "and you can call for an escort if you're feeling unsafe walking around."

Most students find their social niche through the many clubs and activities available, says a junior: "Whether it's movie night, bingo, the petting zoos, or a concert at the Event Center, there is always something for everyone." Each semester starts with a giant Involvement Fest, where students can learn about and join hundreds of organizations. Only 2 percent of the men and 7 percent of the women go Greek, and, says an art history and museum studies major, "The social scene overall is pretty calm. We are not a party school, at all." For luck, students rub the nose of a statue of the school's mascot, a Chesapeake Bay retriever named True Grit. "It's a classic tradition, and I'm a firm believer in its magic," cheers a junior. The highlight of the social calendar is Quadmania, a weekend festival in the spring with games, carnival rides, food trucks, and music. "Midnight Scream involves a lot of people coming out to one the fields at the beginning of Finals Week to scream out into the ether," shares a senior. For more urban adventures, downtown Baltimore is 10 minutes away and Washington, D.C., 40 minutes.

The UMBC Retrievers compete in Division I and field a number of competitive teams, including men's basketball, men's lacrosse, and women's volleyball. Men's and women's swimming and diving and women's softball have captured multiple America East conference titles. The Mock Trial team has made regular appearances at nationals. Intramurals and club sports sign up a quarter of the students, especially for soccer, basketball, and ultimate Frisbee.

Unlike the gargantuan University of Maryland at College Park, UMBC capitalizes on its smaller size by providing students with intimate learning communities, solid academics, and ample resources on a manageable scale. "UMBC is an open-minded environment with a special personality and activities for all types of interests," says a satisfied senior. "If you want to achieve something, this is the place to go."

If You Apply To ›

UMBC: Early action, regular decision. Accepts the Common Application. Please consult UMBC's website for the most up-to-date information regarding standardized test requirements. Visual and performing arts applicants must submit portfolio or audition.

University of Massachusetts Amherst

Amherst, MA 01003

A liberal mecca in cosmopolitan and scenic western Massachusetts, UMass boasts strong study abroad programs and an international flavor. Management and engineering are also strong. In addition to the resources of a major research university, offers ready access to privates Amherst, Hampshire, Mount Holyoke, and Smith via the Five College Consortium. Lack of big-time sports makes for a lower national profile than the likes of Michigan or UNC.

A leading flagship and land grant university with more than 150 years of tradition, the University of Massachusetts Amherst offers students a dizzying array of majors, extracurriculars, and social opportunities in a top college town, plus a strong honors program. UMass's membership in the Five College Consortium makes it a good choice for students who want to take advantage of the extensive resources and programs of a large research university while also experiencing the small-school atmosphere and intellectual rigor of four elite private colleges—all without emptying their wallets.

UMass's sprawling 1,450-acre campus is centered on a pond full of ducks and swans, while architectural styles range from colonial to modern. The school is located on the outskirts of Amherst, a city that combines the energy of a bustling cosmopolitan center with the quaintness of an old New England town while also catering to college life. UMass's library system is the largest of any public institution in the Northeast. The campus has undergone a spate of recent construction, including a major renovation of the university's original library building, Goodell Hall, which now houses the student services center. Ongoing projects include a computer sciences laboratory building and a sustainable engineering laboratories building.

UMass offers more than 115 undergraduate degree programs, and among them, management, engineering, and computer science are top-ranked, along with linguistics, food science, and nursing. Psychology, biology, finance, and computer science are the most popular majors. Agricultural sciences, public health sciences, and sport management also draw praise. New majors include statistics and data science, computational linguistics, environmental engineering, neuroscience, and film studies. Students seeking to stand out from the masses might consider the interdisciplinary major in social thought and political economy or the bachelor's degree in individual concentration, a design-it-yourself major. The Exploratory Track Program places undeclared first-years into one of seven academic advising tracks, based on the interests and academic strengths demonstrated in their admissions applications.

All undergraduates must complete courses in writing, basic mathematics and analytic reasoning, the biological and physical world, the social world, U.S. and global diversity, and an integrative experience. The writing requirement includes a first-year course taught in sections of 15 or fewer. Commonwealth Honors College offers qualified students special courses and sponsors interdisciplinary seminars, student gatherings, service projects, and a $192 million complex for gathering, advising, and program administration. UMass offers 300 study abroad programs in more than 65 countries worldwide and typically sends nearly a quarter of its undergrads globe-trotting. The Center for Student Business provides one of the most imaginative programs at UMass, allowing students to staff and manage seven campus businesses, learning how to work with others and resolve conflicts professionally.

UMass's intellectual and political climate is extraordinarily fertile for a large state university, and the school lends considerable research might to the Five College Consortium. The alliance allows students to attend UMass and take courses (for no extra charge) at the other four schools: Amherst College, Hampshire, Mount Holyoke, and Smith. Typically, 30 to 40 percent of the roughly 7,000 courses offered through the consortium are taken at UMass. The university is "definitely competitive," says a student. Twenty-seven percent of undergraduates participate in hands-on research with faculty. Full professors teach most courses, although some of the larger courses are broken down into smaller sections with graduate-level teaching assistants; overall, 47 percent of all undergraduate classes have fewer than

> "I have had some amazing, out-of-this-world professors."

The Bromery Center for the Arts brings nationally known theater, music, and dance performances to campus year-round.

20 students. "I have had some amazing, out-of-this-world professors," says a junior, "and some abysmal ones."

"We have nerds, jocks, theater buffs, hippies, and future CEOs," says a senior. Seventy-two percent of undergrads are in-staters, while 7 percent hail from abroad. Five percent of UMass students are Black, 14 percent are Asian American, 9 percent are Hispanic/Latino, and 5 percent are multiracial. The university has established cultural centers on campus, providing activities and support for students from different backgrounds, but racial equity is still an issue, students report. "There are always rallies about better programs and aid for minorities," says a senior. Merit scholarships averaging $8,300 are handed out each year, and athletes vie for over 200 athletic scholarships in 19 sports. UMass covers tuition and mandatory fees for in-state students from families with annual incomes of $75,000 or less and typical assets.

UMass has one of the largest on-campus housing systems in the country. Sixty percent of students are housed among seven residential areas. The Residential First-Year Experience assigns first-years to living/learning communities with peers who share common interests and experiences. Many first-years end up in the Southwest Area, a "huge, city-like complex" with five high-rise towers and 11 low-rise residence halls. "It is not a problem for students to get housing on campus; the only trouble is getting the housing that they want," says a student. Dining services get good reviews. A senior comments, "The campus is very self-contained, and so I have felt safe on campus even late at night." The UMatter at UMass program works to address issues of bias, sexual assault, hazing, high-risk drinking, and other community challenges.

UMass offers "a vast social life," says a student, with several social dorms, off-campus parties, and about 350 student organizations of all types. "On the weekends, we frequent the restaurants and bars in Amherst center, which is a lively—if small—college town," a chemical engineering major says. Both on campus and off, alcohol policies are strict and well enforced; off-campus parties are often registered with the university.

"Amherst center is a lively—if small—college town."

Seven percent of both the men and women belong to one of the more than three dozen fraternities and sororities, but they are somewhat out of the mainstream. The Bromery Center for the Arts brings nationally known theater, music, and dance performances to campus year-round. A free public transportation system allows maximum mobility, not only among the Five Colleges but also to nearby towns, which have several exceptional bookshops.

Settled in the Pioneer Valley and surrounded by the Berkshire foothills, Amherst is close to good skiing, hiking, and canoeing areas. It's also 90 miles west of Boston, 170 miles north of New York City, and 25 miles south of Vermont and New Hampshire, making a car useful.

Division I varsity sports are popular, especially men's and women's basketball; women's lacrosse, softball, and field hockey; and men's ice hockey. Most Minutemen and Minutewomen teams have competed in the Atlantic 10 Conference, but in July 2025, UMass became a full member of the Mid-American Conference, with hockey remaining in Hockey East. During a prior incarnation as an independent, the football team chalked up a 26–122 record and earned designation by the *New York Times* as "the nation's worst program." But with new leadership, new facilities, and the stability inherent in the move to the MAC, prospects for future gridiron success are on the upswing. With approximately 40 intramural offerings and nearly 50 club sports, recreational opportunities are extensive.

UMass is big enough to offer a vast number of academic and extracurricular opportunities, though at times it can feel impersonal and overwhelming. But with special residential programs that group students with similar languages, cultures,

Overlaps

Boston University, UC Santa Barbara, CU Boulder, UConn, Indiana University, University of Maryland, Northeastern, Penn State

and lifestyles, many students will easily find a home in Amherst. And as one junior cheers, "We have so many resources. If we don't have what you want, we'll give you the opportunity to create it!"

Massachusetts Institute of Technology

77 Massachusetts Avenue, Cambridge, MA 02139

If you're a science genius, come to MIT to find out how little you really know. No other school makes such a massive assault on the ego. Technology is a given, but MIT also prides itself on leading programs in economics, political science, and architecture, with unmatched undergraduate research opportunities. Those who don't study 24/7 can let off steam via the surprisingly extensive athletic offerings or by enjoying "the 'Tute's" prime location near downtown Boston.

Founded in 1861 as part of the country's rapid scientific and technological advances, the Massachusetts Institute of Technology continues to attract the brightest minds from near and far. MIT teachers and students have discovered many of the technological innovations that we take for granted, from electromagnets and radar to the decoding of the human genome. The school is a magnet for minds from Tim Berners-Lee, the Brit who invented the World Wide Web, to Noam Chomsky, the linguist and antiwar activist. Graduates have formed more than 25,000 companies that, among other things, employ a quarter of the workforce of Silicon Valley. While Harvard stuck to the English model of Oxbridge classical education, with its emphasis on Latin and Greek, MIT looked to the German system of learning based on research and hands-on experimentation. This emphasis is enshrined in the school motto—Mens et Manus, or Mind and Hand—as well as its muscular logo, showing a gowned scholar standing beside an ironmonger bearing a hammer and anvil. Intellect and craftsmanship pervade the classrooms, and students here are not so much taught as engaged and inspired.

MIT is located on 168 acres that extend more than a mile along the Cambridge side of the Charles River basin facing historic Beacon Hill and the central sections of Boston. The main campus of neoclassical architecture carved from limestone was designed by Welles Bosworth and constructed between 1913 and 1920. Since then, more modern designs in brick and glass have been added. The buildings have a utilitarian aura;

> **"[MIT] will take you right up to what you think your limits are."**

most are even known by number instead of by name. Athletic playing fields, recreational buildings, dorms, and dining halls are closely arranged on the campus and provide a sense of unity. Sculptures and murals, including the works of Alexander Calder, Henry Moore, and Louise Nevelson, are found throughout the campus. The university's Brain and Cognitive Sciences Complex is the world's largest neuroscience center.

All students must fulfill a set of General Institute Requirements consisting of a six-course "science core" that includes calculus and a lab and eight courses in the

Website: www.mit.edu
Location: City Center
Private
Total Enrollment: 11,657
Undergraduates: 4,489
Male/Female: 52/48
Financial Aid: 86%
Pell Grant: 20%
Expense: Pr $ $ $
Student Loans: 13%
Average Debt: $ $
Applicants: 28,232
Accepted: 5%
Enrolled: 86%
Grad in 6 Years: 96%
Returning First-years: 99%
Academics: ✐ ✐ ✐ ✐ ✐
Social: 🗨 🗨 🗨
Q of L: ★ ★ ★
Admissions: (617) 253-3400
Email Address: admissions@mit.edu

Strong Programs:
Architecture
Biology
Computer Science
Economics
Engineering
Management
Mathematics
Physics

humanities, arts, and social sciences; there's also an eight-credit physical education requirement. Students have a choice of focus in the basic science offerings. A basic biology course, for example, might emphasize either genetics or the environment. To fill much of their science core, many students will join one of three first-year Learning Communities that offer a coherent first-year curriculum, small classes, and common meeting spaces. Among these is the Experimental Study Group, which offers flexible, small-group seminars instead of traditional lectures and emphasizes peer-to-peer teaching. Not only can these communities offer support, but they can also engage geniuses who excel on exams without attending the lectures.

Once called Boston Tech and now colloquially referred to as "the 'Tute," MIT stresses science and engineering studies with a "concern for human values and social goals." Every science and engineering department is superb. The biology department is a leader in medical technology and the search for designer genes. Nevertheless, pure sciences tend to play second fiddle to the engineering fields that, along with computer science, draw the bulk of the majors. Electrical engineering and computer science are almost universally credited as tops in the nation. Students in these two areas may pursue a five-year-degree option, where they can obtain a professional master's degree upon completion of their studies. Biological engineering, chemical engineering, mechanical engineering, physics, and the aeronautics and astronautics department are also highly praised programs. The most popular majors include computer science and engineering, electrical engineering, mathematics, and mechanical engineering. New majors include climate system science and engineering and artificial intelligence and decision making.

For all of its emphasis on science and technology, MIT takes the arts and humanities as well as the social sciences—especially economics—seriously. Technology is, after all, the point where science and the humanities intersect over matters of values.

"Some professors really know how to engage the interest of the student."

Beyond that, the administration worries that engineers of the future will need first-rate technical skills coupled with a good understanding of technology's social context and marketplace. As one dean once put it, "Too many MIT graduates end up working for too many Princeton and Harvard graduates." Hence, the Sloan School of Management offers top-ranked undergraduate majors in management, business analytics, and finance. Even these programs, however, provide students with a rigorous, math-based education. Perhaps to help ensure that they will be able to make their future discoveries known, students must take four communication-intensive subjects. Architecture, political science, urban studies, linguistics, graphics for modern art, and holography—and just about anything else that can be linked to a computer—are strong, and the minority who major in these subjects receive enough personal attention to make any college student envious. "Some professors really know how to engage the interest of the student," says a senior.

A pass/no record grading system helps first-years adjust to "MIT brainstretching": in the first semester, freshmen receive grades of P, D, or F in all subjects they take. P means a C-or-better performance; D's or F's do not receive credit or appear on the permanent record. In the second semester, the P's are replaced by A, B, or C; D's and F's do not receive credit and are only noted internally. Grades or not, most students set themselves a breathtaking pace. "MIT is intense and will take you for quite a ride," a biology/premed student says. "The courses demand your full attention and a lot of extra work," another adds. Sixty-eight percent of all undergraduate classes have fewer than 20 students. MIT students have access to world-renowned professors and Nobel Prize winners who carry lighter teaching loads to allow them time for research. The Undergraduate Advising Center offers a team of professional "Institute Advisors" to support students from admission to graduation. The vast library system includes some one-of-a-kind manuscripts on the history of science and technology. One library is even open 24 hours a day, and "some students spend the majority of their time (awake or asleep) there," one student reports.

One of MIT's most successful innovations is the Undergraduate Research Opportunities Program, a year-round program that facilitates student/faculty research projects. Considered one of the best programs of its kind in the nation, it allows students to earn course credit or stipends for doing research. Ninety-three percent of students get involved with collaborative or independent research during their time at MIT. Relief from "tooling" (that is, studying) is found through the optional January Independent Activities Period, which offers noncredit seminars, workshops, and activities in fields outside the regular curriculum as well as for-credit subjects. Participation in the engineering co-op program, junior year abroad (including a major program at Cambridge University in England), or cross-registration at all-female Wellesley College are other helpful ways to get a change of pace.

"The average MIT student can be characterized as having a passion and singular drive for what they really want in life," offers a chemical engineering major. While MIT somewhat justly earned an image as a "conservative, rich, white boys' school" in the past, there is certainly enough racial and ethnic variety to beat that rap today. Black students account for 8 percent of the undergraduate student body, Hispanics/Latinos 14 percent, Asian Americans a hefty 35 percent, and multiracial students 7 percent. Women now comprise 48 percent of undergraduates. To further welcome diversity, MIT's application includes an optional question regarding gender identity and sexual orientation. Just 9 percent of students are residents of Massachusetts, and 12 percent are international. MIT is need-blind in its admissions and does not consider legacy or donor preferences; one in five students is the first in their family to attend college. Although there are no merit or athletic scholarships, MIT meets the full demonstrated financial need of all undergraduates—domestic and international. For students with family incomes less than $200,000 a year and typical assets, MIT ensures that scholarship funding from all sources will allow them to attend tuition-free.

> **"Some students spend the majority of their time (awake or asleep) [in the library]."**

Ninety-two percent of undergraduates live on campus, and all first-years are required to live in the dorms. Guaranteed housing is either single-sex or co-ed; the dorms are in the middle of campus, and most of the fraternities and living groups are a mile or less away across the Charles. Meal plans are mandatory for dorms that don't have kitchens and optional for equipped quarters. Frat members feast on spreads prepared by their full-time cooks, and the Kosher Kitchen provides some refuge for others. MIT has recently increased its Title IX staffing, training programs, and educational outreach in an effort to combat campus sexual assault.

MIT's social scene is varied. There are special lectures, campus movies, dances, parties, and dorm activities if one can escape the ubiquitous workload worming its way into the uneasy consciousness of a techie's every waking hour. The Rocket Team, the Guild of Bell Ringers, and a singing group called the Chorallaries are only a few of the diverse interests on this campus. Most on-campus drinking for 21-and-over students is relaxed and accepted, "as long as the alcohol does not result in unlawful behavior or cause any problems," a student explains. MIT's alcohol-prevention program is considered a national model, and drug-prevention initiatives are also comprehensive. The Greek scene attracts 41 percent of the men and 25 percent of the women. For those with the urge to roam, the multifaceted greater Boston metropolis sits only a few subway stops away. The student-friendly city boasts many restaurants, clubs, parks, shopping opportunities, and more than 40 other colleges.

When the MIT megabrains take a break, practical jokes, or "hacks" (described by one student as "practical jokes with technical merit"), are sure to follow. In past

> *MIT teachers and students discovered innovations ranging from electromagnets and radar to the decoding of the human genome.*

years, popular hacks have included dismantling a campus police car and reassembling its body at the top of the Great Dome (complete with a box of doughnuts on the seat), unscrewing and reversing all the chairs in a 500-seat lecture hall, and, of course, welding shut Harvard's gates. Hacking can also involve Harry Potter–style late-night explorations by students in the tunnels and shafts that run through restricted parts of the campus, a practice that's definitely frowned on by the school.

When not studying or hacking, these engineering jocks often turn into real jocks. MIT has 33 varsity sports, the most of any Division III school. Teams are known as the Engineers with an industrious beaver named Tim (if you can't figure it out, don't bother to apply) as their mascot. The women's swimming and diving and indoor and outdoor track and field each brought home national titles in 2025. Men's tennis and cross country are also competitive. Club ice hockey is popular, and even more popular is the extensive, well-organized intramural program (roughly 30 percent participate), with sports ranging from table tennis, billiards, and bowling to the more traditional basketball and volleyball. More than 30 instructional and competitive club sports are also available, and everyone has access to MIT's extensive athletic facilities.

Though students often wonder what life at a typical college would have been like, chances of survival and even satisfaction at MIT are excellent. Students are able to comprehend the incredible experience of attending one of the nation's leading academic powerhouses. A biology major puts it bluntly: "It will take you right up to what you think your limits are, and then MIT will shatter them and make you realize how great your potential is."

If You Apply To ›

MIT: Early action, regular decision. SATs or ACTs: required. Does not accept the Common Application. Application includes optional question regarding gender identity and sexual orientation.

McGill University: See page 357.

University of Miami (FL)

1252 Memorial Drive, Coral Gables, FL 33146

Football is a major reason UM is on the map, but it's hardly the only one. Renowned programs in marine science and music are big draws; business is also strong. Housing takes the form of a distinctive residential college system that includes living/learning opportunities. Attracts more Northerners than other leading Florida universities, with geographic reach continuing to expand.

Year-round sunshine and the colorful Miami culture could make even the most dedicated students forget why they are at college. But at the University of Miami, students can have their fun in the sun and get a solid education at the same time. The university, founded in 1925 by a group of Miami citizens who believed that an institution of higher learning was necessary for their growing community, boasts a boatload of strong programs, including red-hot preprofessional offerings. Sound academics, a diverse and energetic student population, and a subtropical climate create a perfect storm that attracts talented Hurricanes from far and wide. "At UM you will find diversity, tradition, unity, and rivalry," says one senior, "while getting an exceptional education."

Twenty minutes from Key Biscayne and Miami's beaches and 15 minutes from downtown Miami, the university's 239-acre campus is located in a tranquil suburb of Coral Gables and features tall palms, wide lawns, flowering vines, outdoor sculptures, and even a butterfly garden. The campus, centered around Lake Osceola, is architecturally eclectic, from postwar, international-style structures to modern buildings, most with open-air breezeways to let in the warm winds. Recent additions include the massive, $153 million Lakeside Village, composed of 25 interconnected buildings featuring suite- and apartment-style housing for 1,100 students, recreational and dining areas, a 200-seat auditorium, and other facilities.

UM's Cognates Program of General Education requires students to take at least three courses in each of three areas of knowledge: arts and humanities, people and society, and STEM (science, technology, engineering, and math). With nine undergraduate schools and colleges and more than 100 majors and programs, UM offers a broad range of preprofessional options as well as those across the liberal arts. The university has one of the nation's top programs in marine science, and its architecture and business programs are well regarded. UM was the first American university to offer a four-year undergraduate degree in music engineering. It has also developed a unique jazz program in the Frost School of Music. Accelerated degree programs in biochemistry and molecular biology, biology, chemistry, computer science, exercise physiology, Latin American studies, law, and marine geology receive high marks. The most popular majors are in the biological sciences, engineering, communication, and psychology. The Foote Fellows Honors Program provides high-achieving students with more academic flexibility, opportunities for faculty-mentored research, and additional experiences.

> "Everyone wants to get into the best graduate programs."

UM's academic environment manages to be "both competitive and collaborative," says a junior. "Everyone wants to get into the best graduate programs, but they want their peers to do so as well." Fifty-three percent of undergraduate classes have fewer than 20 students, and full professors do teach first-year students. Professors "are extremely accessible through office hours, and teaching assistants often reach out to students to help with workshops and extra study sessions," explains a business management major. For a change of pace, students take advantage of more than 80 study abroad options in dozens of countries, including 16 UM semester-on-location programs in France, the Czech Republic, South Africa, Italy, and elsewhere.

"The students at UM are culturally and academically diverse, with so many interests and passions," says one student. Sixty-six percent of UM's undergraduates come from out of state, including quite a few from the Northeast and upper Midwest. UM's student body is impressively diverse; Hispanics/Latinos account for a substantial 24 percent of the total, Black students 7 percent, Asian Americans 5 percent, and multiracial students 5 percent. International students, who represent 8 percent of undergraduates and more than 100 countries, play an integral role in the life of the university. Numerous merit scholarships, averaging $23,400, are available, as are over 200 athletic scholarships. The university meets 100 percent of the demonstrated financial need of all admitted students.

UM offers a distinctive system of residential colleges, modeled after those at Oxford and Cambridge. Each residential college has a live-in faculty member who works with staff to organize seminars, concerts, dinners, social events, and lectures, including guest speakers from all walks of life to discuss current issues. Generally,

(continued)

Financial Aid: 75%
Pell Grant: 14%
Expense: Pr $ $ $
Student Loans: 37%
Average Debt: $
Applicants: 53,954
Accepted: 19%
Enrolled: 24%
Grad in 6 Years: 84%
Returning First-years: 94%
Academics: ✍ ✍ ✍
Social: 🗩 🗩 🗩 🗩
Q of L: ★ ★ ★
Admissions: (305) 284-6000
Email Address:
  admission@miami.edu

Strong Programs:
Architecture
Biological Science
Finance
Health Science
Latin American Studies
Marine Science
Music
Nursing

SportsFest pits housing areas against each other in sports ranging from flag football to obstacle courses.

students give the dorms average marks; 36 percent of undergrads live on campus, and others bunk in off-campus apartments or commute. Finding healthy, tasty food on campus is easy. "Our food court is very diverse with just about every food option you can think of," says a senior. Students also report feeling safe on campus thanks to a robust security program that includes safety escorts, campus shuttles, and self-defense classes.

UM offers myriad social opportunities. "Miami is an incredible city, so there is always something fun to do with friends. The university is also constantly hosting activities on campus," reports a student. The Rathskeller, a popular meeting place on campus, is a student-run grill that offers food, entertainment, a venue for game-watch parties, and more. Campus alcohol policies are strict for underage students, and an art history major says,

> "The students at UM are culturally and academically diverse."

"The drinking and party culture on campus is not something that proves to be a massive issue." Off campus, however, frat parties and Miami's many bars, night-clubs, and festivals keep things lively. Fraternities account for 21 percent of the men, and sororities, with no housing of their own, attract 22 percent of the women. Students anticipate annual events such as Alumni Weekend and SportsFest, which pits housing areas against each other in sports ranging from flag football to obstacle courses. The biggest service event each year is Gandhi Day, during which hundreds of students spend the day doing community service.

Coral Gables (population 50,000) is not a college town. "We are a college in a big city," says a junior, which means access to events such as Miami's Art Basel and the Miami Open (tennis), as well as professional sports teams (Dolphins, Heat, Marlins, Panthers, Inter Miami CF). Those seeking to explore different culinary delights head to Coconut Grove, Wynwood, or Brickell. Public transportation and the Hurry Canes Shuttle service run in front of the residential colleges. On-campus parking is limited, but most students who can afford it recommend a car anyway. The best road trips are Key West, the Everglades, and, of course, UM football games against rival Florida State.

The Hurricanes compete in the Division I Atlantic Coast Conference. The most competitive teams are football, baseball, men's and women's basketball, men's and women's diving, tennis, and track and field. In a nod to Harry Potter fans, the extensive club sports program includes Quidditch, in addition to flag football, soccer, basketball, and more. The university also has a

> "Miami is an incredible city, so there is always something fun to do."

state-of-the-art recreation facility that includes an 18,000-square-foot fitness room and basketball, racquetball, squash, and tennis courts, plus an indoor pool and a juice bar.

It's hard to imagine a school in the Sunshine State without a generous allotment of fun, and UM is no exception. Still, students here are just as likely to search long and hard for the perfect instrumental phrase or mathematical proof as they are to scope out the perfect wave. Says one happy Hurricane, "The biggest complaint is that students don't have enough time in four years to access all the amazing things available."

The university has one of the nation's top programs in marine science, and its architecture and business programs are well regarded.

Overlaps

University of Florida, University of Maryland, University of Michigan, NYU, UNC Chapel Hill, Northeastern, University of Southern California, Tulane

If You Apply To ›

Miami: Early decision I and II, early action, regular decision. SATs or ACTs: required. Accepts the Common Application. Apply to particular schools or programs. Music and theater applicants must audition or submit portfolio.

Rather than disappear into the black hole of Ohio State, top students in the Buckeye state come here to feel as if they are going to an elite private university. Miami is the honors public university in one of the nation's most populous states. Twice the size of William & Mary, Miami has the same classic look but is much less selective. Miami's top draw is business, and its tenor is preppy/conservative. Bring your best clothes.

This Miami is about 1,000 miles from South Beach, but that doesn't mean it's without sizzle—the academic kind, that is. Tucked into a corner of Ohio, Miami University was founded in 1809 and takes its name from the Native American tribe that once lived in the Miami Valley region of the state. In recent decades, Miami has garnered national recognition as an excellent public university that has the traditional look and feel of a private, with a picture-perfect campus and high-caliber student body.

The university is staked out on 2,100 wooded acres in the center of an urban triangle of approximately three million people, encompassing Cincinnati and Dayton, Ohio, and Richmond, Indiana. The campus, one of the most architecturally homogeneous in the country, is dressed in the modified Georgian style of the colonial American period, and it remains as impeccably groomed as its sharply attired students. The school boasts a 40,000-square-foot indoor arena at the Miami University Equestrian Center. The $20 million McVey Data Science Building, designed to enhance interdisciplinary research and education, opened in 2024.

One of the oldest public universities in the country, Miami University was founded in 1809 to provide a classical liberal education and has never strayed from its central commitment to the liberal arts. All undergraduates must complete the Global Miami Plan for Liberal Education, which provides them with a background in a range of disciplines and includes requirements in intercultural competence, global perspectives, advanced writing, and experiential learning. Students must also fulfill a thematic sequence requirement by taking a series of related courses (usually three) outside their major, and they must complete a capstone experience their senior year. University Studies 101 is a one-credit course that helps integrate first-year students into the university community.

Popular majors include business and marketing, psychology, and strategic communication. Programs in nursing, architecture, education, kinesiology, interior design, computer science, and software engineering have traditionally been strengths. A unique major in emerging technology in business and design teaches students skills in coding, design thinking, artificial intelligence, augmented reality, product management, and more. The Center for Social Entrepreneurship helps students put their creativity and business savvy to use in solving persistent social problems. Gerontology is available as a major and a minor, and the Scripps Gerontology Center is one of the oldest of its kind in the country. Motivated as they are, nearly half of Miami students graduate with a double major or minor.

"The professors I have had have shaped my perspective on the world and life."

In the classroom, "Miami strikes a good balance between intensity and creating a positive working environment for students," says a strategic communication major. Professors are lauded for their knowledge and willingness to help. "The professors I have had have shaped my perspective on the world and life with their excellent

Website: www.miamioh.edu
Location: Small Town
Public
Total Enrollment: 17,248
Undergraduates: 16,276
Male/Female: 48/52
Financial Aid: 55%
Pell Grant: 12%
Expense: Pub $ $ $ $
Student Loans: 43%
Average Debt: $ $ $
Applicants: 39,580
Accepted: 75%
Enrolled: 14%
Grad in 6 Years: 80%
Returning First-years: 90%
Academics: 🖊 🖊 🖊 🖊
Social: 🗨 🗨 🗨
Q of L: ★ ★ ★
Admissions: (513) 529-2531
Email Address:
admission@miamioh.edu

Strong Programs:
Architecture
Business
Computer Science
Education
Interior Design
Kinesiology
Nursing
Software Engineering

instruction," says a political science major. Sixty-four percent of classes have fewer than 30 students, and most are taught by full professors, though graduate students do appear behind lecterns from time to time.

The three-week Winter Term allows students to take a class, study abroad, conduct research, or participate in an internship. Forty-three percent of all undergrads head for foreign climes. Miami's Dolibois European Center in Luxembourg offers summer, semester, or yearlong study and the chance to live with a local family. Other opportunities span more than 75 countries. The Inside Washington program sends students to the nation's capital to meet with high-profile figures and complete an internship. Undergraduate research gets a lot of attention at Miami too. The Undergraduate Summer Scholars Program gives 45 students a stipend of up to $7,000, a tuition waiver, and a project allowance to undertake a nine-week, faculty-mentored project. Each year, more than 2,000 Miami undergraduates work with professors on funded research, many starting as early as their first year. Ten percent of incoming first-year students are invited to join the Honors College, which entails more rigorous coursework, dedicated housing, a senior thesis, and other enrichment opportunities.

"Students here are ambitious, dedicated, and embody an attitude of success in the classroom and outside of it," observes a student. Racial and socioeconomic diversity are conspicuously lacking, although the university claims it is working to boost both; 3 percent of undergraduates are Black, 5 percent are Hispanic/Latino, 2 percent are Asian American, and 4 percent are multiracial. Two percent of students come from foreign countries, and 65 percent hail from Ohio. Miami has a long-standing reputation for wealth and conservatism, although a political science major reports that the student body is becoming "more evenly divided" between conservatives and liberals. Paul Ryan, the former Republican Speaker of the House of Representatives, learned his trickle-down economics here. The *New York Times* suggested that Miami appeals to Republican families as "a place unlikely to turn their children against them." Thousands of merit scholarships, averaging $11,600 each, and hundreds of athletic scholarships in 18 sports are awarded annually. The university also locks in tuition, fees, and room-and-board charges for four years.

Forty-six percent of the student body call the campus home, and residence halls are said to be comfortable and well maintained. First-year students join one of more than 30 theme-based living/learning communities (LLCs) and affinity communities, which center on interests such as the arts, leadership, premedicine, and shared cultural backgrounds. "My LLC provided me with an internship, the majority of my friends, and an ever-growing network within the first month of my first semester," reports a first-year student. Campus dining options are described as diverse, healthy, and usually tasty but overpriced. Students give good ratings to campus safety, and regarding sexual assault, one student says, "Student education, victim resources, and general awareness are widespread."

Twenty-three percent of the men and 31 percent of the women belong to fraternities or sororities, respectively, and the Greeks have a hard-partying reputation. Miami is known as the "Mother of Fraternities" because several national ones began here. Drinking at off-campus houses and local bars is a popular pastime, and a junior comments, "With a party culture this pervasive, it is simply not possible to prevent underage drinking." On-campus activities organized by Late Night Miami, such as movie screenings, musical performances, craft nights, and casino nights, provide a fun alternative but are not always well attended. Annual

Miami is known as the "Mother of Fraternities" because several national ones began here.

"My LLC provided me with an internship, the majority of my friends, and an ever-growing network."

University Studies 101 is a one-credit course that helps integrate first-year students into the university community.

"We have a public Ivy personality."

events include homecoming, Springfest, and continued rivalries with Ohio University. Miami offers more than 600 student organizations, and students log tens of thousands of hours of community service each year. Oxford (population 23,000) is a relatively quiet town with a decent bar scene, numerous restaurants, and local shops. For students who crave brighter lights and a bigger city, Cincinnati is about 35 miles away.

Miami's Division I RedHawks teams have won titles in football (Mid-American Conference championships), synchronized skating (national championship), field hockey, women's tennis, men's swimming and diving, and softball. Men's ice hockey games draw enthusiastic crowds. Miami Mock Trial consistently performs well at the American Mock Trial Association national championships. Intramurals and more than 50 club sports attract 30 percent of the student body, and popular sports include broomball, soccer, and sand volleyball.

With its strong emphasis on liberal arts and its opportunities for research, travel abroad, and leadership, Miami University effectively combines a wide range of academic programs with the personal attention ordinarily found only at much smaller, upscale institutions. As a senior put it, "We have a public Ivy personality."

If You Apply To ›

Miami (OH): Early decision, early action I and II, regular decision. Accepts the Common Application with supplement. Applicants may indicate if they are first-generation students or members of the LGBTQ community. Please consult Miami's website for the most up-to-date information regarding standardized test requirements.

University of Michigan

500 South State Street, Ann Arbor, MI 48109

U-M sits at the pinnacle of quality public higher education in the U.S., right up there with UC-Berkeley and UCLA. Academic strengths range across the board, from arts to engineering—with the long-standing honors program a special bonus for academic overachievers. Out-of-state families may need a second mortgage to handle U-M's pricey tuition.

One of the nation's elite public universities, the University of Michigan offers an excellent faculty, innovative research, dynamite athletics, and an endless number of special programs. Boasting more than 668,000 living alumni, it also produces more Fulbright scholars than any other U.S. university. "Michigan is a special place because it has a deep history and reputation," says a senior. "It is an excellent school, and no matter what degree you have, it is respected."

Situated on 3,279 acres, Michigan's campus is so extensive that newcomers may want to call on their GPS to find their way to class. The university is divided into two main sections. Central Campus, the heart of the university, houses most of Michigan's 19 schools and colleges. North Campus, which is two miles northeast of Central, is home to the College of Engineering; the School of Music, Theatre, and Dance; the Stamps School of Art and Design; and the Taubman College of Architecture and Urban Planning. Other campus areas include the Michigan Medicine main complex, containing three hospitals and multiple outpatient facilities, and South Campus, featuring state-of-the-art athletic facilities. A university bus system helps students get around. Architecturally, the main drag of campus features a wide range of styles, from the classical Angell Hall to the contemporary Michigan Ross School of Business. Recent construction includes the Leinweber Computer Science and Information Building. A new Central Campus Residential Development, scheduled to open in the fall of 2026, will add 2,300 new beds, along with a new dining facility.

Founded in 1817, U-M offers more than 700 active degree programs, including over 260 undergraduate majors, as well as individualized concentrations. No courses are required of all first-year students at Michigan, but all undergraduates must complete some coursework in natural sciences, social sciences, and humanities before graduation. Students in the College of Literature, Science, and the Arts (LSA)—Michigan's largest school, offering the most undergraduate majors—must also take courses in quantitative reasoning and race or ethnicity and complete a writing requirement.

For students with global interests, LSA's menu of 50 foreign languages includes several that can't be found at many other places, such as Dutch, Filipino, Hindi, Persian, Swahili, and Turkish. The College of Engineering and Ross School of Business are well respected, and the university's programs in health-related fields are also top-notch. Also worth mentioning are offerings in architecture, pharmaceutical sciences, education, art, music, and musical theatre. The most popular majors are computer science, business administration, economics, and psychology. Growing majors include kinesiology, community and global public health, and public policy.

Students describe Michigan courses as challenging but not overly competitive. "Academics come first, and everybody around you will be putting in the effort required to succeed," says a civil engineering major. Fifty-two percent of classes have fewer than 20 students, and one student says, "The professors here are intelligent and seem to enjoy teaching." Students report that there is excellent academic and career advising available. The University Career Center provides individual and group career counseling/planning and works with 950 companies annually in recruiting graduating U-M students. The LSA Opportunity Hub connects LSA students with liberal arts–oriented internships, practical workshops, alumni, and employers.

> **"[Michigan] is an excellent school, and no matter what degree you have, it is respected."**

Michigan's special academic programs seek to offer the best of both worlds—personalized attention and a large university setting. The university offers many themed living communities as part of the first-year experience, paired with an introductory course taught in the residence halls designed to support students through the transition to college; past programming has included movie nights, ice cream socials, rock climbing, and a trip to Michigan's Upper Peninsula to learn dog sledding. The university's long-established honors program, widely considered to be one of the best in the nation, offers qualified students honors courses and seminars, opportunities to participate in individual or collaborative research, and access to dedicated academic advisors. About 1,300 undergrads each year work outside the classroom with a small group of students and a research mentor through the Undergraduate Research Opportunity Program. Service-learning courses are plentiful, and students have the chance to study abroad in nearly 140 countries. Specific programs include a year abroad in a French or German university, a business program in Paris, summer internships in selected majors, and special short-term trips organized by individual departments.

North Quad is newer and the focal point for international and intercultural programming.

Fifty-two percent of undergraduates hail from Michigan, and 8 percent come from abroad. The student body is notably diverse for a Midwestern state university. Black students make up 5 percent of the student body, Hispanics/Latinos 12 percent, Asian Americans 18 percent, and multiracial students 6 percent. Michigan's Program on Intergroup Relations serves as a national model for supporting diversity on college campuses, offering a variety of intergroup dialogues, courses and workshops on social justice, and community outreach programs. There are large and well-organized Jewish and LGBTQ communities that are supported by Hillel and the Spectrum Center, respectively. Political issues flare up from time to time on campus. Michigan is the only public university in the state that meets the full demonstrated financial need of all in-state students, and Michigan residents with family incomes of $125,000 or less qualify for the Go Blue Guarantee of four years of free tuition. At more than triple the in-state tuition rate, U-M charges out-of-state students among the highest tuition and fees among U.S. flagship universities. Need-based financial aid is available to all applicants, who can also vie for hundreds of merit scholarships averaging $6,300, as well as over 700 athletic scholarships.

Residence halls at U-M traditionally have well-defined personalities. East Quad is the home of the Residential College, the Michigan Community Scholars Program, and the Gender-Inclusive Learning Experience. North Quad is newer and the focal point for international and intercultural programming. On-campus housing is said to be mostly comfortable and well maintained, and 25 percent of students reside there. "First-years are guaranteed housing, but not every sophomore is lucky enough to secure on-campus housing, and virtually no juniors and seniors get to live in the dorms," reports a student. Alternatives include fraternity and sorority houses, college-owned and private co-ops, and plenty of off-campus rentals. Campus residents take their meals at the many dining halls located inside residence halls. As for concerns about safety on campus, a student says, "Campus security is pretty good, and most people I know feel safe." The Division of Public Safety offers many services, including prevention and education programs, as well as a Special Victims Unit that specifically addresses instances of interpersonal violence, including sexual assault.

"Everybody around you will be putting in the effort required to succeed."

Detroit is a little less than an hour away, but most students become quite fond of the picturesque town of Ann Arbor. "Ann Arbor is a quintessential college town, with a wide range of cultural opportunities and ways for students to get involved," a sophomore says. A thriving music and performance arts community with over 29 ensembles in addition to several parks and gardens are available in the Ann Arbor area as well. A huge art fair held each summer draws craftspeople from throughout the nation and Canada. The Huron River and many lakes and swimming holes lie only a short drive away and seem to keep the summer-term population happy. Michigan winters, though, are known for being cold and snowy. Ten percent of the men and 16 percent of the women go Greek. As one sophomore says, "There is a large Greek party scene, and if that is what you are looking for, you won't be disappointed." Still, with more than 1,700 registered student organizations, other activities abound. For instance, the university's Solar Car Team has won numerous American Solar Challenge competitions.

"There is a large Greek party scene, and if that is what you are looking for, you won't be disappointed."

Division I football overshadows nearly everything each fall as students gather to cheer, "Go Blue." Attending football games is an integral part of the U-M experience, students say, and the Paul Bunyan trophy football competition with Michigan State and rivalry games against Ohio State are especially popular. Almost half of U-M's 29 varsity teams have brought home Big Ten championships in the past few years, among them football, field hockey, men's gymnastics, and women's golf. The men's basketball team won the 2026 NCAA title. Intramurals, which were invented at the University of Michigan, provide students with a more casual form of athletics, and more than 30 club sports and some 40 intramural offerings are also active.

The University of Michigan strives to offer its students a delicate balance between academics, athletics, and social activities. On one hand, this is an American college

Overlaps

UC Berkeley, UCLA, Cornell University, U of I at Urbana–Champaign, Michigan State, Northwestern, Ohio State, Stanford

with the usual interest in football and fraternities. But it's also a world-class research university with an excellent faculty and top-rated programs, intent on making America competitive in the 21st century. It's a good bet for assertive students who crave spirit and action as well as outstanding academics.

Michigan State University

426 Auditorium Road, East Lansing, MI 48824

Most people don't realize that MSU enrolls more full-time undergraduates than any other university in the state. Students can find a niche within any of more than 400 programs. MSU's self-contained campus is like a town unto itself, with a bus system available to get from one side to the other.

Website: www.msu.edu
Location: Suburban
Public
Total Enrollment: 46,487
Undergraduates: 38,406
Male/Female: 48/52
Financial Aid: 61%
Pell Grant: 18%
Expense: Pub $ $ $ $
Student Loans: 47%
Average Debt: $ $ $
Applicants: 62,138
Accepted: 85%
Enrolled: 18%
Grad in 6 Years: 81%
Returning First-years: 90%
Academics: ✍ ✍ ✍
Social: 🌑 🌑 🌑 🌑
Q of L: ★ ★ ★
Admissions: (517) 355-8332
Email Address:
admis@msu.edu

Strong Programs:
Agricultural Sciences
Biological and Biomedical
  Sciences
Business Management
Engineering

Michigan State's roots are agricultural. Founded in 1855 as the prototype for land grant institutions, it was the first university to teach scientific agriculture. Future engineers, plant scientists, and veterinarians still flourish here. So do those with wanderlust, thanks to study abroad programs on each of the world's seven continents. MSU's programs in natural sciences and multidisciplinary social sciences offer students the feel of a small liberal arts college and the resources of a large research university. "Resources here abound," says a senior.

The heart of the 5,200-acre MSU campus, north of the Red Cedar River, boasts ivy-covered brick buildings, some of which predate the Civil War and are listed on the National Register of Historic Places. This area houses five colleges plus the MSU Union and 10 residence halls. Across the river are the medical complex, newer residence halls, and two 18-hole golf courses. Most notably, MSU is home to the $730 million Facility for Rare Isotope Beams, a facility for nuclear physics research that is funded in partnership with the U.S. Department of Energy Office of Science and the state of Michigan. MSU opened the university's first free-standing multicultural center in 2025 and is in the process of completing a new Student Recreation and Wellness facility.

Michigan State students tend to be preprofessional and clear about their interests; the premed, prevet, and teacher education programs are strong, and the most popular majors include business, marketing, communication, journalism, various fields in the social sciences, and biological and biomedical sciences. Other popular options include engineering, supply chain management, environmental science, and hospitality business management; students in the latter program get real-world experience by staffing the university's hotel and conference center. To graduate, all students must satisfy university requirements in math and writing, complete a major, and take a minimum of 24 credits in the integrative studies program, which includes arts and humanities; social, behavioral, and economic sciences; and biological and physical sciences.

Academics at MSU get tougher as students advance through their majors, according to a junior. "Many of our courses are very competitive because they play a part in determining whether or not you are accepted into a specific program," adds a classmate. Classes are often quite large, and students say that, for the most part, professors are accessible and dedicated. A growing number of undergraduates take advantage of hundreds of group-based and individual research opportunities alongside faculty, and 70 percent of undergraduates complete an internship during their time at MSU. The Honors College is one of the oldest programs of its kind in the country and offers the intimacy of a small-college atmosphere. MSU has a strong international component as well, with upward of 300 study abroad options in more than 60 countries; 25 percent of undergrads take part.

"Students here are friendly and diverse," says an elementary education major. "We also have a large international population, which is really cool because it gives you the opportunity to get to know people and cultures from all over the world." Eighty-three percent of undergraduates are Michigan residents, and 9 percent are international. The university has a global alumni network of more than half a million Spartans, and more than 2,400 of them have served in the Peace Corps since MSU first partnered with the agency in 1961. Black students make up 7 percent of the student body, Asian Americans add 8 percent, Hispanics/Latinos constitute 7 percent, and multiracial students represent 4 percent. Scholarships are offered in 23 Division I sports, and thousands of students also receive grants and awards based on academic merit, which average $4,900 annually.

> **"[On game days] our large campus is filled from end to end with individuals sporting green and white."**

MSU requires students to live on campus for their first two years, and a sophomore says the residence halls and apartment communities are "very convenient and well maintained." Those seeking a traditional college experience can choose one of five huge "neighborhoods," each with three to 10 residence halls plus libraries, advising and tutoring services, health services, dining halls, and recreation areas. MSU is home to three degree-granting residential colleges geared toward public affairs, the humanities, and the sciences. Other living/learning programs, known by their catchy acronyms, include RISE (focus on the environment), MRULE (multiracial unity), and CORE (engineering). MSU's dining services dish out meals at 10 dining halls and two food courts; the Thrive at Owen dining hall serves food that is free of major food allergens.

MSU's Department of Police and Public Safety provides walking escorts for those who stay late at the library. Emergency telephones and other measures also aid student security, and East Lansing's bus system offers discounted night-owl rates for those living farther away. MSU's Sexual Assault Health Care Program provides supportive resources. Parking places on campus are in chronically short supply, and students complain about the tickets they receive as a result. Many students move off campus after their sophomore year because the city of East Lansing, just outside Michigan's capital, offers all the positive aspects of a large urban area (the population more than doubles when school is in session), along with the safety and community feel of a much smaller town. Twelve percent of the men and 13 percent of the women join Greek organizations, and according to one student, "The social life at MSU is very lively on the weekends." The University Activities Board brings in bands, dances, and comedians, and more than 1,000 student organizations hold various events. Second-run movies are also shown in Wells Hall.

> **"Many of our courses are very competitive."**

Weekends are dominated by Big Ten athletic competitions, with the MSU–Michigan rivalry especially fierce. "Our large campus is filled from end to end with individuals sporting green and white; alcohol-free tailgating is also available," says a junior. "Seeing 150,000 people in a space that usually has about 60,000 is

(continued)

Hospitality Education
Journalism
Marketing
Supply Chain Management

The Thrive at Owen dining hall serves food that is free of major food allergens.

The Honors College is one of the oldest programs of its kind in the country.

quite an experience." The men's basketball team is consistently strong, and women's soccer, cross-country, and gymnastics as well as men's ice hockey are recent conference champions. After more than six decades of standing guard at Kalamazoo Street and Red Cedar Road, the legendary statue of the school's mascot, affectionately known as "Sparty," was moved indoors to protect him from the elements. However, a replica of the Spartan statue stands outside and is guarded by students when Wolverines come to town. Students are still able to paint "the Rock," a large boulder donated by the class of 1873, to advertise campus events, birthdays, anniversaries, and the like. More than 20 intramurals and 27 club sports, from competitive cheer to water polo, also keep students busy.

With seemingly endless learning opportunities and an active social scene, future physicians, scientists, educators, and business leaders happily coexist at MSU in what one student calls a "diverse, friendly, and expressive" bunch.

If You Apply To ›

MSU: Early action, regular decision. SATs or ACTs: optional. Accepts the Common Application.

Middlebury College

Middlebury, VT 05753

Set in the picturesque and ski-friendly Green Mountains of Vermont, Middlebury is a magnet for students with serious interests in environmental and international studies. Known worldwide for its summer foreign language programs. Varsity and intramural sports play a big role in campus culture, which may help explain why Middlebury was the first college to play Quadball (formerly Quidditch).

For some, Middlebury College's campus, with its picturesque sunsets, excellent skiing, and rural Vermont charm, may bring to mind a resort. Middlebury is indeed a paradise for those interested in the environment, second and third languages, and a tight-knit community. But this school's intensive workload means four years here is far from a vacation. Middlebury "is the kind of place where someone will offer you their gloves in a snowstorm and then challenge your stance on neocolonialism in class two hours later," says an economics and film/media studies major. "Where you can go from hiking at sunrise to editing a film on Black resistance by sunset; where students dream big, fail often, and keep building anyway—because there's a shared understanding that the process matters just as much as the product."

The college's 350-acre main campus overlooks the village of Middlebury, Vermont, which a junior describes as a "small, quaint Vermont town of 9,200 people and five stoplights." The 1,800-acre mountain campus, site of the Bread Loaf School of English, the famed Bread Loaf Writers' Conference, and the college's Snow Bowl skiing facility, is nearby. Old Stone Row cuts across the campus, where the buildings evoke early New

> **"The faculty want to get to know their students as people."**

England mills. Marble and limestone academic halls and dormitories sit in quadrangles and feature views of the Adirondack and Green Mountains. Founded in 1800, Middlebury has achieved carbon neutrality and aims to use 100 percent renewable energy by the end of 2028. A new LEED Gold–certified residence hall opened in 2025.

Midd students take a discussion-based, writing-intensive First-Year Seminar with only 15 students; the instructor serves as advisor to those enrolled until they declare a major. In addition to satisfying distribution requirements in several liberal arts areas, students take classes in writing, cultures and civilizations, physical education, and, of course, their major. With all these requirements, it's no wonder students and faculty become close. "The faculty want to get to know their students as people and see them flourish in all that they do," says a political science major. About a third of students collaborate with faculty on research projects. During the four-week January term, students can narrow their focus to opportunities like a single intensive course or an internship. "The Center for Careers and Internships provides $1 million per year in funding to students hoping to take unpaid or underfunded internships over the summer," attests a senior.

Between June and August, Middlebury banishes English from its campus, and hundreds of students live, learn, and, ideally, think only in their chosen language. Especially strong are German, Chinese, Japanese, and Hebrew. Nearly everyone studies another tongue, and roughly 55 percent of students take advantage of Middlebury Schools Abroad in 32 cities around the globe or the over 40 partner universities in 16 countries. Students in the interdisciplinary environmental studies major choose one of 13 areas to focus on, such as conservation psychology, creative arts, and environmental history. Other highly touted Middlebury programs include English, international and global studies, international politics and economics, and architectural studies. Economics, computer science, and neuroscience are also popular. "Whether I'm learning about oligopolies in Econ or dissecting Gina Prince-Bythewood's cinematic style in Film, I'm being pushed to care deeply and think critically," says an economics and film and media studies double major.

"My fellow Midd students are sharp, passionate, quirky, and a little chaotic in the best way," says a first-year. "People here care—whether it's about climate justice, postcolonial literature, D3 hockey, or late-night a cappella rehearsals." Six percent of students come from within the state; 13 percent come from abroad. Seven percent of students are Asian American, 13 percent are Hispanic/Latino, 5 percent are Black, and 7 percent are multiracial. "Politically, the student body leans heavily to the left, though the school and student body are pretty good about embracing open-minded dialogue," comments a senior. In fact, Middlebury embeds conversations about privilege, power, and systemic issues throughout the curriculum, and all first-year students participate in JusTalks, a one-day, student-run program that facilitates workshops on systemic racism and other topics. Students note a socioeconomic divide on campus: "It's like a true middle class doesn't exist here," remarks a junior—but the college's need-blind admissions and 100-percent need-met policy help broaden access. Middlebury offers a handful of merit scholarships and no athletic scholarships.

Few Middlebury students live off campus (6 percent), since housing is guaranteed for four years. First-year students live in traditional residence halls tied to their First-Year Seminar courses and staffed by a dean. Upperclassmen can choose from a range of options, including suites, college-owned townhouses, the Environmental House (where residents cook all their own food), and other academic interest houses. The school's three dining halls get high marks for their tasty victuals, friendly staff, and accommodations for students with dietary restrictions. Students say they feel safe on campus—"It's hard to feel unsafe in rural Vermont," reasons one sophomore. Mental health services "are decent, but there's definitely room to grow," says a first-year, and the school is working on it: the college is putting a $4.9 million gift received in 2024 toward improving these services.

The Middlebury Pranksters ultimate Frisbee players have won the last three national championships.

"Midd students are sharp, passionate, quirky, and a little chaotic in the best way."

Middlebury embeds conversations about privilege, power, and systemic issues throughout the curriculum.

"The surrounding area does not offer much socially, so any social life happens pretty much exclusively on campus," says an English major. And while a senior says, "Middlebury definitely has a party scene," another adds, "There's also tons of events hosted by either student orgs or by the school itself." Middlebury's 200-plus student organizations offer ample variety to choose from. Those who stay on campus are treated to school-sponsored dances, plays, dance performances, trivia nights, or parties at the co-ed social houses. (Middlebury ousted fraternities and sororities in the mid-1990s.) Alcohol consumption is said to be common among underage students. "Winter Carnival is the absolute best weekend every year at Middlebury," raves a senior. The event includes ski and snowboard races, snow sculpture contests, theme parties, a giant bonfire, and a Winter Ball. Nocturne, which showcases student art, music, and activism, is also a favorite event. Feb Graduation—for students who graduate midwinter—"ends with the legendary ski-down, where graduates ski down the Middlebury Snow Bowl wearing caps and gowns," explains a film major. "It's surreal, hilarious, and kind of beautiful—a perfect representation of how quirky and tight-knit the community can be."

Off campus, Middlebury is "the quintessential New England town, straight out of Norman Rockwell." It has necessities such as restaurants, grocery stores, drugstores, hardware stores, and clothing shops, and 80 percent of students do volunteer work. The progressive, student-friendly city of Burlington is 45 minutes away, while Montreal is a three-hour drive, Boston four, and New York City five. Snow comes early here and stays late, but Middlebury's own Snow Bowl and Rikert Nordic Center, not to mention proximity to most Vermont ski slopes, make this a paradise for ski fanatics, a breed Middlebury attracts in large numbers.

> **"[After Feb Graduation], graduates ski down the Middlebury Snow Bowl wearing caps and gowns."**

Middlebury's powerful Panthers ice hockey teams—men's and women's—draw loyal fans from across campus and the local community, especially when archrival Norwich is in town. The college offers 31 Division III varsity sports and has won recent national championships in women's lacrosse and conference championships in field hockey, baseball, men's and women's tennis, and women's golf. About half of the student body is active in the large club and intramural sports program, which includes everything from a log-rolling club to rugby and soccer. The Middlebury Pranksters ultimate Frisbee players have won the last three national championships.

Midd students enjoy plenty of student/faculty interaction, tight-knit friendships, and excellent recreational opportunities in a beautiful setting. Add challenging academics to the mix, and Middlebury is a comfortable yet stimulating place to spend four years. As one multilingual international student beautifully puts it, "To me, Middlebury is thoughtful, tender, brilliant, and just chaotic enough to keep you on your toes. It's a community of people who aren't just trying to succeed in the world. They're trying to understand it, challenge it, and change it, starting right here."

If You Apply To ›

Middlebury: Early decision I and II, regular decision. SATs or ACTs: Optional. Accepts the Common Application.

1701 North State Street, Jackson, MS 39210

Millsaps is the strongest liberal arts college in the deep, Deep South and by far the most progressive. Its largely preprofessional students typically have sights set on business, law, or medicine and are well served by location in the state capital. Usually compared to Hendrix, Rhodes, and Sewanee. About half of the students come from out of state, generally from other Southern states.

Millsaps College, founded by Methodists in 1890 and named for early benefactor Major Reuben Webster Millsaps, was once thought of as a finishing school for well-bred Southern belles and gentlemen. Although less well-known outside the Deep South, it has long been one of the region's top liberal arts institutions. Affiliated with the United Methodist Church, Millsaps takes its motto, Ad Excellentiam ("toward excellence"), seriously. What characterizes the school is its focus on scholarly inquiry, spiritual growth, and community service. "Millsaps is the perfect package," says a first-year student, "strongly academic, small enough to build relationships, yet big-thinking enough to build the mind."

The college's 100-acre campus sits in the center of Jackson, on the highest point in the city. A mix of modern and traditional buildings is arranged around the Bowl, a sequestered glen surrounded by old-growth trees and shrubs that serves as a main student gathering place. Recent campus projects range from a new pickleball court to residence hall improvements.

Under the Compass Curriculum, all students complete coursework in Foundations (covering thinking and reasoning), Communication in Humanities, Problem Solving and Creative Practice, Integrative and Collaborative Learning, Our Human Heritage, and Explorations (covering a range of liberal arts subject areas). They also take at least one business course, and a writing across the curriculum initiative ensures that every student develops writing skills. By their fourth year, students must complete a Senior Reflective Essay and the Major Experience, which may involve research, a field- or community-based course, study abroad, an internship, or an honors project. Three-quarters of Millsaps students pursue faculty-mentored research.

> "The professors . . . push the students' academic boundaries."

Millsaps offers more than 40 majors and minors, including the option of a self-designed major. The Millsaps College Writing Program and creative writing are top-notch, and business is a strength. Although they enroll fewer students, the sociology/anthropology and religious studies programs are well regarded. The most popular majors are business administration, biology, accounting, and neuroscience. The college's prehealth mentoring program pairs students with practitioners in their chosen field, allowing them to earn credit for real medical experience. Other standout offerings include specialized instruction in medical Spanish and an interdisciplinary major in philosophy, law, and society. Cooperative agreements allow students to opt for nursing degrees in partnership with the University of Mississippi Medical Center, the University of Alabama at Birmingham, and Vanderbilt University. Millsaps also offers a premed program with William Carey University School of Osteopathic Medicine and pre-engineering in cooperation with Mississippi State, Auburn, and Columbia Universities.

"The courses are rigorous, as the professors continue to push the students' academic boundaries," says a sophomore. Most classes at Millsaps enroll fewer than

Website: www.millsaps.edu
Location: City Center
Private
Total Enrollment: 583
Undergraduates: 547
Male/Female: 54/46
Financial Aid: 100%
Pell Grant: 34%
Expense: Pr $
Student Loans: 86%
Average Debt: $ $ $
Applicants: 2,340
Accepted: 43%
Enrolled: 18%
Grad in 6 Years: 58%
Returning First-years: 58%
Academics: ✍ ✍ ✍
Social: 🗩 🗩 🗩
Q of L: ★ ★ ★
Admissions: (601) 974-1000
Email Address:
  admissions@millsaps.edu

Strong Programs:
Accounting
Biology
Business Administration
Creative Writing
Prehealth
Psychology
Religious Studies
Sociology and Anthropology

20 students, and none exceed 50. "The small classes have helped me really feel immersed in the materials, and my professors have been engaging and amazingly helpful," says a business and studio art major. Each year, a few select upperclassmen join the Ford Teaching Fellows Program, letting them work closely with a faculty member to learn about teaching—and paying them for their time in the classroom. For-credit internships are available with local businesses, in state government offices in Jackson, and at the teaching hospital and medical center across the street from campus. The college maintains a 4,500-acre biocultural reserve in the rainforest of the Yucatán Peninsula, which hosts courses exploring ecology, archaeology, and Maya culture. Twenty percent of Millsaps students study abroad in more than 50 nations.

Students at Millsaps are "energetic, smart, and corny," opines a psychology major. "I can always learn something new because of all the different cultures around campus." Sixty-three percent of students come from out of state, and 2 percent from foreign countries. Politically, "Millsaps has a long history of being responsive to social issues," says a government and politics major. Indeed, Millsaps was the first college in Mississippi to voluntarily open its doors to students of color, and it installed gender-neutral bathrooms on campus. Black students make up 23 percent of the student body, Asian Americans 3 percent, and Hispanics/Latinos 6 percent. Thirty-four percent of incoming first-year students are Pell-eligible. Qualified students are awarded academic merit scholarships averaging $29,500 each year, but there are no athletic awards.

Eighty-eight percent of students stay in campus housing—mostly, grouses a sophomore, because those who move off campus are subject to a 35 percent reduction in their merit-based financial aid. On-campus options include traditional, suite-style, and apartment-style halls, and a psychology major says, "Housing is average." The robust Greek system claims 57 percent of the men and 55 percent of the women; sophomore, junior, and senior men may live in one of four fraternity houses, but there is no sorority housing. "The Caf is clean and offers a large selection of food, including a vegan station," says a senior, but the quality of meals is hit or miss. "Millsaps has really emphasized sexual assault education," notes a biology major, and the issue "has been incorporated into the first-year curriculum."

"Millsaps is . . . the kind of college not usually found in the South."

"Greek life is the center of Millsaps's social life," a student explains, and the fraternity houses are usually open and rocking from Wednesday through Saturday nights. "On campus, we definitely have parties, but we also have cultural nights and festivals, welcome week, food trucks, pep rallies," attests a junior. When it comes to enforcing alcohol policies, "Campus police are very stringent," according to a senior. Major Madness is a favorite annual event, offering a week of campus entertainment and culminating in a weekend-long festival in the Bowl. "The South Asian Cultural Society hosts a Diwali celebration that much of the school turns up for," observes a sophomore. "There is a dance and lots of good food!" The city of Jackson also offers a wealth of options, including professional symphony, opera, and ballet, and the city is a nexus for Mississippi's legendary blues and "roots rock" musical traditions. Easy road trips include New Orleans, Memphis, and the riverfront casinos in Vicksburg, Mississippi; closer to campus, 10 miles to the north, is a huge reservoir that is popular for weekend water sports. For students who enjoy the great outdoors, the Natchez Trace offers easy access to wooded trails and bicycling paths.

The Millsaps Majors (remember Reuben) compete in the Division III Southern Athletic Association, so the school isn't nearly as sports crazy as most Southern campuses, but "we have a good rivalry with Belhaven, and many students show up to the games no matter the sport," says a math major. Women's basketball and golf and baseball have been competitive in recent years. Flag football and pickleball are favorite intramural sports. Everyone benefits from the 65,000-square-foot Hall Activities Center, which has facilities for weight training, aerobics, basketball, racquetball, squash, and volleyball.

In a state renowned for the traditions of blues, barbecue, old magnolia trees, and big-time football, this small, progressive school is an anomaly. "Millsaps is a magnet for accomplished students from strong backgrounds and the kind of college not usually found in the South," remarks a junior. Small classes ensure plenty of time to get to know fellow students and faculty members. That's one tradition that never gets old.

Overlaps

Albion, Austin College, Hendrix, Rhodes, Sewanee, Southeastern, Trinity University (TX)

If You Apply To ›

Millsaps: Early action, regular decision. SATs or ACTs: optional. Accepts the Common Application with supplement.

University of Minnesota

100 Church Street SE, Minneapolis, MN 55455

Not nearly as expensive as the University of Michigan or the University of Wisconsin if you happen to be from out of state. Strong programs include engineering, management, and health fields. Location in the Midwest's second-largest metropolitan area means easy access to internships and other off-campus opportunities. With a highly connected tunnel and skyway system to beat the cold, packing your woollies is optional. Check out the honors program.

The University of Minnesota, like the nearby Mall of America, can be overwhelming, given its seemingly limitless variety of offerings and gargantuan size. With 150 undergraduate majors across eight colleges, plus one of the largest study abroad programs in the nation, the U of M, founded in 1851, offers an abundance of academic choices. Enjoy all four seasons and dress for the winter. The university has a strong academic and career support program so students have help with the many choices.

The vast Twin Cities campus actually consists of two campuses with three main sections. The St. Paul campus encompasses the College of Food, Agricultural, and Natural Resource Sciences; the College of Biological Sciences; the College of Veterinary Medicine; and the College of Continuing Studies. The Minneapolis campus is divided by the Mississippi River into an East Bank and a West Bank that are home to the other colleges and most of the dormitories as well as most of the fraternities and sororities. Both campuses offer a blend of traditional and modern architecture, with columned buildings seated next to sleek geometric structures. The two campuses are five miles apart and linked by a free bus service. Academic facilities are excellent, beginning with the seven-million-volume library system, one of the largest in North America. A 1,200-acre arboretum is used for research and teaching, and the West Bank Arts Quarter makes a lively setting for the university's art disciplines. A new state-of-the-art chemistry building with 18 learning labs opened in 2025.

Minnesota's liberal education requirements call for students in all schools and colleges to complete a set of core distribution requirements and take courses that satisfy four of five themes. The first theme, Race, Power, and Justice in the United

Website: www.twin-cities.umn.edu

Location: City Center

Public

Total Enrollment: 38,986

Undergraduates: 29,812

Male/Female: 46/54

Financial Aid: 66%

Pell Grant: 29%

Expense: Pub $ $ $ $

Student Loans: 46%

Average Debt: $ $

Applicants: 41,357

Accepted: 80%

Enrolled: 22%

Grad in 6 Years: 85%

Returning First-years: 91%

Academics: ✍ ✍ ✍ ✍

Social: 🌢 🌢 🌢

Q of L: ★ ★ ★

Admissions: (800) 752-1000

Email Address: admissions@umn.edu

States, was updated in the wake of the 2020 murder of George Floyd by Minneapolis police and is now required of everyone, with the aim of increasing awareness of the need for systemic societal changes. Students are free to choose which three of the remaining four themes they wish to fulfill: Civic Life and Ethics, the Environment, Global Perspectives, or Technology and Society. First-years must take a writing course and four writing-intensive courses. The College of Science and Engineering is notable for its tutorial and internship options; the electrical and mechanical engineering programs are particularly strong and well subscribed. The Carlson School of Management is well regarded and offers majors in entrepreneurial management, international business, and other areas. Theatre arts is a standout in the College of Liberal Arts. Psychology, computer science, marketing, and finance are the most popular majors.

"The classes are relatively difficult," a junior says, but "it really depends on the subject." Just 36 percent of classes currently have fewer than 20 students, but the university is focusing more on undergraduates, bolstering academic advising and support services. Helpful teaching assistants are abundant, and professors receive high marks from most students as being approachable and knowledgeable. "The instructors have been exemplary due to their passion for the subject

> **"The instructors have been exemplary due to their passion for the subject matter."**

matter and commitment to their students," an archaeology major says.

The excellent honors program across all eight first-year colleges allows close contact with faculty members as well as leeway to enroll in certain graduate courses and seminars. The Undergraduate Research Opportunities Program provides scholarships of up to $1,800 for students to conduct research with faculty. Students find plenty of internship opportunities at the many corporations and government agencies in the Twin Cities area, and the university pushes its study, work, and volunteer abroad programs in nearly 100 nations.

Most U of M students are "motivated and hardworking," says a junior. Seventy-four percent of undergraduates are from Minnesota, and 6 percent hail from outside the U.S. Ten percent are Black, 7 percent are Hispanic/Latino, 13 percent are Asian American, and 5 percent are multiracial. Racial justice has been a major issue on campus since the Floyd murder. Merit scholarships averaging $5,900 are available, as are athletic awards in all major sports.

Twenty-three percent of undergraduates live in residence halls; there are nine traditional halls and three university-run apartment facilities. Students can also choose from 30 living/learning communities, such as Design House, STEM Diversity House, and Lavender House. "The only issue is finding affordable housing after freshman year," reports a journal-

> **"[U of M students are] motivated and hardworking."**

ism major. Campus security includes a free escort system for students, and the campus police department has collaborated with city officials to enhance street lighting and installed additional blue-light emergency response kiosks. As for dining on campus, dietary restrictions are easily accommodated at the university's seven residential restaurants, but meals are said to be hit or miss. "Fresh fruit and veggies are always available," notes a junior, who also adds (lest anyone fear the campus dietitians are excessively health-obsessed), "they have the best chocolate chip cookies."

"Most social life takes place right off campus," says one student, "but there are loads of activities available on campus, such as bowling, theater, late-night activities, and movies." The 1,000-plus student groups and the student union's live music dance club are good places to meet people. About 12 percent of students go Greek, and "Greek organizations definitely set the tone for the party and bar scene," says a senior. "Bars, houses, apartment complexes, dorms, and even neighborhoods are

The downtown areas of the Twin Cities are easy to get to by bus or light rail.

separated according to Greek participation (or lack thereof)." Spring Jam, a carnival weekend put on by the Greeks each April to raise funds for charity, is a huge event, described by one student as "homecoming in spring—but better."

Here, being "under the weather" can be a good thing, as campus designers found a way to get around—or under—wet or wintry conditions by linking many of the campus buildings with tunnels. For those who love winter, happy skiers and skaters become colorful spots all over the state's white backdrop. In the spring and summer, Minnesota's famed 10,000 lakes offer swimming, boating, and fishing. The down-town areas of the Twin Cities are easy to get to by bus or light rail, and there are scores of good bars, restaurants, nightspots, and movie theaters. The Twin Cities are also home to six professional sports teams, many of which offer discount days for students.

This is an athletically inclined bunch of students, as Division I varsity sports and intramural competition, which can go on well past midnight, are both popular. Students always hope the current season will be one in which the gridiron Gophers take home the roses in a bowl victory, but short of that, a win over Michigan for custody of the Little Brown Jug or Wisconsin for Paul Bunyan's Axe is cause for celebration. Women' and men's ice hockey, women's gymnastics, indoor track and field, and track and field have all won Big Ten conference titles in recent years.

"Most social life takes place right off campus."

Anonymity is easy at a university of this size, but there are ample opportunities to find academic and social communities that make the campus feel smaller. Then again, size does have its virtues in the countless array of campus resources. The University of Minnesota is ideal for those who appreciate an urban setting and a good, old-fashioned, button-up-your-overcoat winter.

Overlaps

U of I at Urbana–Champaign, University of Iowa, Marquette, University of Michigan, University of Minnesota Duluth, UW–Eau Claire, UW–Madison

If You Apply To ›

U of M: Early action I and II, regular decision. Accepts the Common Application with supplement. Please consult U of M's website for the most up-to-date information regarding standardized test requirements.

University of Minnesota Morris

BEST BUY

600 East 4th Street, Morris, MN 56267

The plains of western Minnesota may seem an unlikely place to find a liberal arts college—and a public one at that. UMN Morris is cut from the same cloth as Mary Washington, UNC Asheville, and St. Mary's College of Maryland. The draw: private college education at a public university price. Strong emphasis on environmental awareness and sustainability. Remote location pushes students to Minneapolis-St. Paul for city life.

The University of Minnesota Morris is more comprehensive than its small size might suggest. The first buildings on its 136-year-old campus were originally home to an American Indian boarding school, which was succeeded in 1910 by an agricultural school. Morris opened its doors in 1960, and since then, it has grown into a solid public liberal arts college. UMN Morris "strives to encourage students to push their limits and go out on limbs," says an English and history double major.

The 130-acre campus includes 32 brick-and-mortar buildings around a central mall. Two high-powered wind turbines, playfully named Bert and Ernie, generate

Website: www.morris.umn
.edu
Location: Rural
Public
Total Enrollment: 898
Undergraduates: 898
Male/Female: 47/52

(continued)

Financial Aid: 80%

Pell Grant: 43%

Expense: Pub $ $ $

Student Loans: 55%

Average Debt: $ $

Applicants: 2,956

Accepted: 75%

Enrolled: 10%

Grad in 6 Years: 63%

Returning First-years: 74%

Academics: ✍ ✍ ✍

Social: 🗩 🗩

Q of L: ★ ★ ★

Admissions: (888) 866-3382

Email Address:

admissions@morris.umn.edu

Strong Programs:

Biology

Business and Management

Chemistry

Elementary Education

English

Environmental Science and
  Studies

Native American and
  Indigenous Studies

Psychology

Campus traditions include the annual Circle of Nations Indigenous Association powwow.

about 70 percent of the university's power supplemented by solar arrays. The LEED Gold–certified Welcome Center is the first building in Minnesota (and the first on the National Register of Historic Places) to use energy-efficient chilled-beam technology.

Everyone at UMN Morris starts the Core Curriculum with two courses: the Intellectual Community seminar, which introduces students to college-level work and active interaction with faculty, and a college pathways course on academic strategies and well-being. Students then move on to five courses under Skills for the Liberal Arts (writing, world languages, quantitative reasoning), plus Morris Mission Themes, such as diversity, global perspectives, and civic responsibility. A capstone and experiential learning component— an internship or study abroad—round out the degree. The most popular majors are biology, psychology, elementary education, and business and management. Other strong programs: environmental science and environmental studies; Native American and indigenous studies, which benefits from the campus's unique history; English; chemistry; and computer science. Morris also has 4+1 programs in applied economics and mathematics.

"The academic climate is very welcoming and adaptive for the student," says a studio art major. "The professors are always talking about different opportunities, whether it's tutoring, meeting with them, or other opportunities outside of the classroom." Eighty-two percent of classes have fewer than 20 students, and students say they respect professors for their knowledge and real-world experience. "The professors all do research in their field, keeping up their expertise," notes an English and theatre arts major.

> **"The professors all do research in their field, keeping up their expertise."**

More than half of the students conduct research projects with faculty. "I recently participated in the Undergraduate Research Symposium," says a theatre arts major, explaining it's when students present their research to the broader campus community. "It's a really cool celebration of academics." Fifty-nine percent of students do volunteer work through the Office of Community Engagement. The Honors Program offers interdisciplinary honors courses and an honors capstone. UMN Morris continues to integrate study abroad opportunities into the curriculum, offering more than 300 options for students wishing to study overseas.

"My peers at Morris are driven, creative thinkers," observes a senior, while a junior adds, "We have a pretty diverse cultural makeup, and we have strong Christian, POC, LGBTQ+, and [international] student presences on this campus." Seventy-five percent of UMN Morris students are Minnesota residents, and 4 percent are international. The campus is more diverse than many other schools in the state: American Indians make up 13 percent, Hispanics/Latinos 8 percent, Asian Americans 1 percent, and Black students 2 percent, and 20 percent of students identify as multiracial. Both sides of the political aisle are represented on campus. Efforts to reckon with the campus's history as a Native American boarding school have drawn considerable attention, sparked by student demands to search the grounds for possible unmarked gravesites dating to that era. Honoring a policy that has been in place since 1909, a tuition waiver is available for American Indian students. Other financial incentives include the University of Minnesota Promise Scholarship, awarded to Minnesota residents with a family income that does not exceed $120,000; state residents with family incomes of $50,000 or less attend tuition-free. Merit scholarships averaging $4,900 are available, but there are no athletic awards. Forty-three percent of incoming first-years are Pell eligible.

About half of UMN Morris students live on campus in one of the six residence halls, which offer several living/learning communities, or in an apartment complex reserved for upperclassmen. "Most people have single rooms, and there is plenty of space on campus," reports a first-year. Students say the environmentally friendly Green Prairie Community residence hall is very nice, but others could use renovations. Many students opt for less expensive apartments and rental homes off campus. Dining options get mediocre reviews. UMN Morris's rural campus feels safe, according to students, and a senior says, "People are highly encouraged to speak out about sexual assault and report an incident." Mental health support is "particularly great for students," says a senior.

There is no Greek system, but "there is a bit of a party culture," says a senior. "Not Jersey Shore level, but students throw the occasional Halloween party and end of the year parties." Concerts, movies, presentations, shows, and campuswide games of Humans vs. Zombies or Hunger Games keep weekends busy, and roughly 120 student-led clubs and associations provide plenty to do. Campus traditions include the annual Circle of Nations Indigenous Association powwow and the tug-of-war competition between the two main first-year dorms; "Hundreds of students show up!" cheers a student.

Off campus, Morris is a "small but very friendly" town, says a student, with a couple of bars, coffee shops, smoothie shops, and plenty of parks and sport areas, plus a small music venue, ice rink, and bowling alley. The drinking age is strictly enforced but students say it's easy to find a sense of community both on and off campus. For those pining to get away, the nearest retail and restaurant chains are about 45 minutes away in Alexandria. Minneapolis-St. Paul, about three hours southeast, is also a popular destination.

> "There is a bit of a party culture—[but] not Jersey Shore level."

The Cougars compete in the Division III Upper Midwest Athletic Conference. Football, men's and women's basketball, and softball have claimed recent conference titles, and volleyball and soccer are also strong. Kickball, pickleball, volleyball, and knocker ball (a version of soccer where participants wear large inflatable spheres and knock each other down) are among students' favorite intramurals, and men's and women's rugby and ultimate Frisbee are popular club sports. The Regional Fitness Center or hiking and biking trails keep students active.

One of the smaller campuses in the University of Minnesota system, UMN Morris epitomizes the idea of "Minnesota nice." "It feels like Stars Hollow from *Gilmore Girls*," says a studio art major, "where you have that great sense of community with people you don't even have classes with." Tucked away from the state's big cities, some might find it isolated, but that means fewer distractions—and more time for reading, research, and friendship. "We are the University of Minnesota's gem on the prairie," says a senior. "We have the intimacy of a private school and the academic excellence of the state's largest educational institution, all for an affordable price."

If You Apply To ›

Morris: Rolling admissions. Accepts the Common Application with supplement. Please consult Morris's website for the most up-to-date information regarding standardized test requirements.

University of Mississippi

University, MS 38677

Located in the town of Oxford, Ole Miss is doing its best to put the state's problematic past behind it. Strong on public policy, international studies, and accountancy. The honors college is one of the best anywhere. Location near Faulkner's old hangouts is ideal for soaking up Southern literary traditions, and the beloved "Hotty Toddy" cheer continues to stoke school spirit, especially when Ole Miss takes on LSU and Mississippi State. Tailgating remains world class.

Website: www.olemiss.edu
Location: Small Town
Public
Total Enrollment: 24,042
Undergraduates: 20,448
Male/Female: 42/58
Financial Aid: 84%
Pell Grant: 20%
Expense: Pub $
Student Loans: 44%
Average Debt: $ $ $
Applicants: 33,363
Accepted: 97%
Enrolled: 19%
Grad in 6 Years: 72%
Returning First-years: 87%
Academics: ✍ ✍ ✍
Social: 🗨 🗨 🗨
Q of L: ★ ★ ★
Admissions: (662) 915-7226
Email Address:
   admissions@olemiss.edu

Strong Programs:
Accountancy
Arabic
Biomedical Engineering
Chinese
Education
International Studies
Pharmaceutical Sciences
Public Policy Leadership

Famed author William Faulkner grew up here and attended the university for three semesters before dropping out.

The University of Mississippi offers students an educational experience steeped in tradition and thick with school spirit. Although it originated as a reference to the wives of plantation owners, the nickname "Ole Miss" lives on as a term of affection among students and alumni. Mississippi's flagship university provides a host of academic programs, including a top-notch honors college and an innovative public policy leadership major, and supports a vibrant campus community.

Founded in 1844, the University of Mississippi's central campus occupies 850 acres of rolling land in the center of Oxford. The main campus consists of 200 buildings and a mix of architectural styles, including Greek Revival, Beaux-Arts Classicism, Georgian Revival, and modern. The white-columned Lyceum, which served as a hospital during the Civil War, is the campus's oldest building and now houses administrative offices. Newer construction includes the $175 million Duff Center for Science and Technology Innovation, the largest project in the university's history. A new softball complex opened in 2025.

All students must complete credit hours in English composition, mathematics, laboratory science, humanities and fine arts, and social and behavioral sciences; the curriculum has been revamped to include more critical thinking skills in first-year classes. Approximately 80 percent of first-year students sign up for the First-Year Experience, a seminar-style course that helps new students transition from high school into a successful college career. The Department of Writing and Rhetoric administers two mandatory composition courses for first-years.

Students say coursework is what you make of it and varies by program, but the atmosphere is collaborative. "The classes are definitely challenging at times," says one first-year student, "but doable with the right amount of work." Accountancy is one of the university's strongest and most popular majors; the university houses the American Institute of Certified Public Accountants Library. Programs in pharmaceutical sciences, biomedical engineering, education, Arabic, and Chinese are also strengths, and biological science and international studies are popular. The Center for Manufacturing Excellence "educates students on the fundamentals of accountancy, business, and engineering through the lens of manufacturing," while offering opportunities for internships with industry leaders such as Toyota, Deloitte, and SpaceX. The Center for Intelligence and Security Studies prepares students for careers in national security. The Lott Leadership Institute is a standout that offers a public policy leadership major and an innovative curriculum that combines the systematic study of public policy with the development of leadership qualities. "Conversational and debate classes are a change from the regular classroom, and Lott offers both," says one broadcast journalism major. Professors are highly rated across the university. "It is not at all uncommon for full professors to teach freshmen and even offer tutoring to freshmen during their office hours," explains a senior.

> **"The classes are definitely challenging . . . but doable with the right amount of work."**

Ole Miss offers numerous study abroad options, including 25 faculty-led programs, in such diverse locations as China, Greece, Ethiopia, Peru, and Thailand. Another option is the Croft Institute for International Studies, which accepts 70 students each fall. Participants study international politics, economics, and culture both in the classroom and via study abroad. Gifted students may apply for the nationally known—and highly competitive—honors college, where they take part in small, discussion-based honors courses offered in a number of disciplines, engage in community service, complete a senior thesis, and have access to foreign study fellowships. Roughly 1,700 students from 70-plus majors currently participate.

"Ole Miss students are ambitious, hospitable, and well-rounded," says one public policy leadership major. Forty-two percent of undergraduates are Mississippians, and 2 percent hail from abroad. Black students make up 9 percent, Hispanics/Latinos

6 percent, Asian Americans 2 percent, and multiracial students 3 percent. "The outside view of UM is that everyone is a sorority girl or a frat guy," a mathematics major complains. "We have people of all categories and cultures." Merit scholarships averaging $11,800 are awarded annually, as are more than 300 athletic scholarships in 21 sports. The university covers tuition, room, and board for Pell-eligible Mississippi residents who meet certain academic requirements.

Thirty-one percent of students live in the dorms, which are a hit-or-miss affair. "Some of the older dorms have seen better days," a student reports. Options include apartments, traditional residence halls, and residential colleges. Campus dining options are reported to be plentiful and tasty. "We offer several different dining halls," says a student, "some of which are all-you-can-eat and some of which are cafeteria-style." Campus security gets a thumbs-up too. "Ole Miss is the kind of place where people look out for each other," comments a student. "We have a campus police department that works diligently to make sure the campus is safe."

"Ole Miss students are ambitious, hospitable, and well-rounded."

The social scene is dominated by Greek life, which attracts 37 percent of the men and 54 percent of the women, although non-Greeks find plenty to enjoy as well. The Student Activities Association hosts a variety of on-campus activities each week, including movies, pageants, concerts, and multicultural events. Alcohol is forbidden from most areas of campus, and students say the school's policies are reasonably effective at curbing consumption. Campus worship organizations have a strong presence, and students can choose from among 300 student groups as well as volunteer opportunities in Oxford. One enthusiastic junior describes the city as "the best college town in the nation." Oxford has thriving arts and foodie scenes, and a senior says, "There are lots of locally owned businesses and restaurants that are unique to the area and very charming."

Famed author William Faulkner grew up here and attended the university for three semesters before dropping out. For 50 years, the university has hosted the Annual Faulkner and Yoknapatawpha Conference, the longest running academic event devoted to the work of an American writer. Although it lost out to the University of Virginia as repository of Faulkner's papers, Ole Miss operates Rowan Oak, Faulkner's home, and has a sizable collection of Faulkner materials. Blues legend B. B. King gave the university his personal record collection to help establish its Blues Archive, which is now one of the largest in the world.

The Department of Writing and Rhetoric administers two mandatory composition courses for first-years.

The Ole Miss Rebels compete in the gauntlet known as the Southeastern Conference, where they face the likes of Alabama's Crimson Tide, the Florida Gators, and the LSU Tigers. Women's golf and baseball are recent national champions; other solid teams include football, softball, and men's and women's basketball, cross-country, volleyball, and rifle. School spirit is on full display, especially when LSU is in town. On game days, frenzied fans gather on the Grove—10 acres of oak and maple trees in the center of campus—for tailgating, which draws more than 100,000 loyal supporters who pitch 2,500 tents and drink from red and blue cups (no beer cans allowed). Jackets, ties, and high heels are common, and food is sometimes served on silver trays. Says one happy Rebel, "The Grove is a place where people come together regardless of their differences to support our Ole Miss Rebs and share in a community that we all love." Rousing chants of the famous "Hotty Toddy" cheer can be heard throughout the football stadium just before kickoff—and just about anywhere else, for that matter. Dozens of intramural and club sports also prove to be popular diversions.

"Some of the older dorms have seen better days."

Overall, students here seem to be a contented lot, especially those in the honors college. It's clear that Rebel pride and the sense of community here are as strong as ever. Indeed, Ole Miss students have much to cheer about, including solid academics, game days in the Grove, and a healthy dose of school spirit.

If You Apply To ›

Ole Miss: Rolling admissions. Accepts the Common Application with supplement. Please consult Ole Miss's website for the most up-to-date information regarding standardized test requirements.

University of Missouri

Columbia, MO 65211

Renowned as home to one of the top journalism schools in the nation, Mizzou boasts the country's only commercial university–owned TV station as well as a National Public Radio outlet. Also strong in agriculture and plant science, the health sciences, business, and music. Comparable in size to Iowa and Iowa State, smaller than Illinois and Indiana. Columbia offers a vibrant social scene.

Website: www.missouri.edu
Location: Small City
Public
Total Enrollment: 27,256
Undergraduates: 22,978
Male/Female: 45/55
Financial Aid: 62%
Pell Grant: 26%
Expense: Pub $ $ $
Student Loans: 47%
Average Debt: $ $
Applicants: 24,490
Accepted: 78%
Enrolled: 31%
Grad in 6 Years: 75%
Returning First-years: 93%
Academics: ✍ ✍ ✍
Social: 🗩 🗩 🗩 🗩
Q of L: ★ ★ ★
Admissions: (573) 882-7786
Email Address:
mu4u@missouri.edu

Strong Programs:
Agriculture
Biological Sciences
Business
Constitutional Democracy
Engineering
Journalism
Music
Nursing

In 1839, the residents of Boone County, Missouri, raised enough money to create their state university in Columbia. Today, Missouri's flagship university has evolved into a top research institution and continues to uphold the belief of its founders in the great value of higher education that is accessible to all. A current 10-year "transformational" effort, MizzouForward, focuses on "faculty excellence, infrastructure growth, and student success" and includes up to 150 new faculty hires. Mizzou has also become a national leader in generating on-site renewable energy. "Students at Mizzou thrive on the hands-on learning approach that all of our degree programs offer, whether that's through internships, research labs, or even anchoring the news," says a junior.

The oldest public university west of the Mississippi, Mizzou occupies a 1,262-acre campus that doubles as the Mizzou Botanic Garden, featuring 42,000 plants and trees flanked by mansionlike fraternity and sorority houses. Francis Quadrangle, with 18 predominantly redbrick National Historic Landmark buildings, is the core of the campus. Central to this area are the 43-foot limestone columns of the original Academic Hall that was destroyed by fire in 1892. To the east of the columns is the original tombstone of Thomas Jefferson, which the Jefferson family gave to Mizzou (not UVA!) in the 19th century as a symbol of his championing of state-supported education. The eastern half of the campus consists of native white limestone buildings, most notably the Memorial Union, with its striking Gothic tower.

An array of general education requirements includes courses in three content areas: social and behavioral sciences; physical, biological, and mathematical sciences; and humanities and fine arts. Two writing-intensive courses are also required, and all undergrads complete a senior-year capstone course. Full professors teach the lecture courses at Mizzou, supplemented by a weekly discussion session led by a teaching assistant to go over material presented in class. Coined the "Missouri Method," an agribusiness management major explains, "Professors use real-world examples to tie heavy topics and theories to reality, helping us to make the connection." Owing to Mizzou's size, classes can fill up quickly, but the school guarantees the availability of coursework to complete a degree in four years.

With more than 300 degree programs and 13 schools and colleges, Mizzou offers a comprehensive set of choices for basic and advanced study. Aspiring journalists can get hands-on experience working on the *Columbia Missourian*, the local daily paper edited by J-school faculty members and students, or at KOMU-TV, the nation's only university-owned commercial television station. KBIA, Mizzou's National Public Radio station, is popular among journalism students and listeners alike. Agriculture is also nationally ranked, especially in the areas of agribusiness management and applied research for farm communities. The music program is noteworthy, and the College of Engineering maintains several strong undergraduate majors, including biological and computer science. The College of Business is competitive and features a five-year bachelor's/master's accounting program. Nursing is another popular major. A major in constitutional democracy prepares undergrads for careers in government, public policy, and law.

"The academic climate is a great mixture of competition but also support," says a political science major. Committed preprofessionals will be glad to know that Mizzou offers qualified first-years guaranteed admission to its graduate-level programs in medicine, law, veterinary medicine, nursing, and health professions. Mizzou is also one of the leading public universities for undergraduate research, allowing even first-year students to get involved. Students cite the Kinder Scholars D.C. Summer Program and study abroad as "a great way to get out and explore the world," says a junior. The 13 percent of students who study abroad can choose from programs in more than 40 countries. Additionally, the university sponsors Mizzou Alternative Breaks, service trips in which students work on volunteer projects in the U.S. and abroad during spring, winter, and weekend breaks.

"Professors use real-world examples to tie heavy topics and theories to reality."

"Mizzou's campus has a pretty Midwestern feel to it, so it's easy to talk to people, and most people are generally friendly," says a senior. Seventy-seven percent of Mizzou undergraduates hail from the Show-Me State, and just 1 percent are international. Black students account for 5 percent of undergrads, Asian Americans 3 percent, Hispanics/Latinos 6 percent, and multiracial students 4 percent. Politically, students report that both sides of the aisle are well represented, and several note, "It's a place where most students can find their people." Merit scholarships are available averaging $8,800, and athletes may compete for roughly 250 awards in 20 Division I sports. Missouri Land Grant scholarships cover full tuition and fees for Missouri residents who qualify for Pell Grants.

Ninety-four percent of Mizzou students live on campus, and first-years under age 20 are required to do so. "I loved my residence hall experience," says one sophomore. "I had a lot of space in my room and the closets were huge!" Residence halls have double rooms and are often crowded and lively. Single-sex halls, a few single rooms, and round-the-clock quiet floors are also available. About 30 percent of new students choose from among 100 Freshman Interest Groups, where 15 to 20 students with shared academic interests live in the same residence hall and enroll in three core classes together. All other undergrads living in the dorms participate in general and thematic living/learning communities. Mizzou's all-you-can-eat dining halls, coffee bars, and take-out stands offer good variety and accommodations for special needs. Mizzou opened a new student health center in 2024 and now offers a variety of mental health and wellness resources. "I like that many of our support services can be utilized remotely so they can be used just about whenever," says an international business major.

"[Mizzou is] a place where most students can find their people."

Students say Mizzou's social life is packed with options, including movies, the usual fraternity and sorority parties, 600-plus student organizations, shopping, eating out, and visiting great parks and hiking areas around town. Says a senior,

"There is always something going on at Mizzou, whether it be a free event being put on by campus or a social event happening in Greek Town." Twenty-eight percent of the men and 24 percent of the women go Greek. Mizzou is a champion of tough alcohol policies, and students have agreed to ban alcohol from all fraternities and sororities, making it one of the largest Greek systems in the nation to go dry. (The rule is lifted when alumni come home to visit!) "Mizzou's campus flows right into a lively downtown area filled with things to do, whether it's catching a concert at a local venue or grabbing frozen yogurt at Yogoluv," says one student. Students support the town by engaging in many hours of community service each year, and the community caters to them in return. Road trips to St. Louis, Kansas City, and Lake of the Ozarks offer a change of scenery.

The Missouri Tigers compete in the rough-and-tumble Southeastern Conference, and basketball draws big crowds. Women's gymnastics and volleyball and men's wrestling are strong. But the entire town turns out in black and gold for any football game. "Homecoming is the crown jewel of Mizzou tradition," cheers a journalism major. "The week is packed with major events like a parade, a massive canned food drive, the largest collegiate blood drive in the nation, and Fling, a spirited skit and dance competition." Other favorite traditions are the new students' Tiger Walk and the Senior Sendoff. Mizzou's popular intramural program has nearly two dozen sports and two skill divisions, attracting more than a quarter of the student body.

Mizzou is working hard to continue its trajectory as a school on the rise. "Mizzou is a place that challenges you to grow in every dimension—academically, socially, and professionally," lauds a journalism major. And like its students, the university continues to grow academically and culturally while sticking with its longtime strengths. One senior reflects, "We are a school rich in tradition but looking to the future."

> **"Homecoming is the crown jewel of Mizzou tradition."**

Overlaps

U of I at Urbana–Champaign, Indiana University, University of Iowa, Iowa State, University of Kansas, Kansas State

If You Apply To ›

Mizzou: Rolling admissions. Accepts the Common Application. Please consult Mizzou's website for the most up-to-date information regarding standardized test requirements.

Morehouse College: See page 36.

Mount Holyoke College

50 College Street, South Hadley, MA 01075

One of two women's colleges, along with Smith, that are members of the Five College Consortium in the scenic Connecticut River Valley of western Massachusetts. Less nonconformist than Bryn Mawr and Smith. MHC is strongest in the natural and social sciences and emphasizes leadership and professional experiences.

Mount Holyoke College pioneered women's higher education in 1837 and continues to pave the way as the leading gender-diverse women's college. The students who choose Mount Holyoke value achievement, leadership, inclusivity, and tradition.

While students occasionally complain about the heavy workload, most bring that challenge on themselves as they seek intellectual fulfillment within MHC's supportive, caring environment as well as hands-on professional experiences that sometimes take them far afield. "Mount Holyoke is a sisterhood," says a senior. "I have never before been surrounded by so many amazing, passionate women."

Mount Holyoke is located in the heart of New England on 700-plus acres of rolling hills dotted with two lakes, miles of hiking trails, and waterfalls. Modern glass-and-stone buildings stand alongside classic ivy-covered brick and sandstone structures. Campus highlights include the Japanese Meditation Garden and Teahouse, the Talcott Greenhouse, an art building with studios and a bronze-casting foundry, an 18-hole championship golf course, and an equestrian center. The 8,000-square-foot Fimbel Maker & Innovation Lab supports robotics, costume making, art history, architectural studies, and more.

The curriculum at this 189-year-old institution remains rooted in the traditional liberal arts and sciences. All students must take a first-year seminar; the college offers roughly 35 seminars each fall and five in the spring, covering a wide variety of disciplines and topics, such as Politics of the Self. The focus of these courses is developing skills in analysis and critical inquiry. Some also include field trips to museums or events in Boston, New York, or Washington, D.C.

Chemistry is a long-standing strength at Mount Holyoke, bolstered by top-of-the-line labs, a scanning electron microscope, and several nuclear magnetic resonance spectrometers. International relations, politics, environmental studies, and computer science are also strong. Popular majors include psychology, biological sciences, and English. Five-year dual-degree programs enable students to combine degrees from MHC with B.S. degrees in engineering from the University of Massachusetts Amherst, Caltech, or Dartmouth. There is also a five-year dual-degree program with the Graduate Institute in Geneva where students earn their B.A. from Mount Holyoke and complete an interdisciplinary M.A. in Switzerland for their fifth year. Many students find the Five College Consortium one of the school's greatest assets: 74 percent of Mount Holyoke students take at least one course offered through the consortium. A free bus service runs every 20 minutes between MHC and Amherst College, Hampshire, UMass Amherst, and Smith. As an alternative to pursuing a minor or second major, Mount Holyoke also offers the Nexus program, which builds in opportunities for internships, off-campus research, and public presentations, along with traditional coursework. Participating students select from one of nine preprofessional tracks, such as global business, nonprofit organizations, and data science.

"Mount Holyoke is a simultaneously intense and supportive academic environment," says an environmental studies major. "Most classes are discussion-based, even ones labeled lectures, and involve lots of student input," says an art history major. Personal attention from professors is a boon of the small classes. Although some of Mount Holyoke's intro courses have 50 or more students, 74 percent of classes have fewer than 20. The school's honor code makes possible self-scheduled, self-proctored final exams. Students say the Career Development Center's assistance with résumés, cover letters, and interview preparation is particularly effective.

Many students choose to take advantage of an optional January winter term to take a noncredit, nontraditional course or do an internship in major cities or points abroad. The Lynk curriculum-to-career experience guarantees all students funding for an internship or research opportunity, domestic or international, and offers students access to special resources, workshops, and networking opportunities with alums. "Lynk funding allows students to do work they want to do without

> "I have never before been surrounded by so many amazing, passionate women."

Website: www.mtholyoke.edu
Location: Suburban
Private
Total Enrollment: 2,182
Undergraduates: 2,164
Male/Female: 0/100
Financial Aid: 64%
Pell Grant: 25%
Expense: Pr $ $ $
Student Loans: 64%
Average Debt: $
Applicants: 5,226
Accepted: 36%
Enrolled: 27%
Grad in 6 Years: 84%
Returning First-years: 89%
Academics: ✍ ✍ ✍ ✍
Social: 🗩 🗩 🗩
Q of L: ★ ★ ★ ★
Admissions: (413) 538-2023
Email Address:
  admission@mtholyoke.edu

Strong Programs:
Biology
Chemistry
Computer Science
Economics
English
Environmental Studies
International Relations
Politics
Psychology

On Mountain Day, students wake up to ringing bells, classes are canceled, and everyone treks up Mount Holyoke to picnic and see the foliage.

sacrificing a summer of making money," cheers a sophomore. The Weissman Center for Leadership focuses on leadership development through three core programs: the Speaking, Arguing, and Writing Program, which helps students hone their rhetorical skills; Leadership and Public Service, which connects students with internships and other opportunities to explore careers in public service; and Community-Based Learning, which offers 25 to 30 service-learning courses every year as well as paid positions for students to work in leadership roles as community fellows and mentors. Thirty-four percent of MHC students spend time studying in another country. In addition to roughly 100 study abroad programs from approved partners, Mount Holyoke sponsors its own in France, China, Japan, and Costa Rica.

"MHC students are curious about others and about the world, driven and stubborn (in a good way), and genuinely warm and kind," says a senior. Twenty-four percent of students are Massachusetts natives, and a substantial 20 percent are international.

> **"MHC students are curious about others and about the world."**

Black students make up 5 percent of the student body, Asian Americans 7 percent, Hispanics/Latinos 10 percent, and multiracial students 5 percent. "We are a very leftist school," says a senior. "Gender equality, trans rights, bodily autonomy, equal pay, climate advocacy, racial equality, etc., are all very important to students." CAUSE (Creating Awareness and Unity for Social Equality) is a large and popular campus group dedicated to community building and student leadership. Mount Holyoke's financial aid packages meet 100 percent of applicants' demonstrated financial need. Merit scholarships are available, averaging $24,900, but there are no athletic scholarships.

> *The Lynk curriculum-to-career experience guarantees all students funding for an internship or research opportunity.*

Nearly all Mount Holyoke students live in the residence halls, which "all have their own personality, which makes it very difficult to choose sometimes," says one student. Most dorms are also very homey, with living rooms, TV lounges, and baby grand pianos; all serve milk and cookies (as well as healthier fare like hummus and vegetables) on school nights. Students from all four classes live together, and housing is guaranteed for all four years. Some residence halls also offer apartment-style living. Twenty-six percent of students opt to live in themed living-learning communities—which range from arts to outdoor adventure and the Shirley Chisholm community—named after the former MHC professor and the first Black woman elected to Congress. Meals in the Blanchard Community Center, the main destination for student life and dining, and campus security both get positive reviews. Counseling services "are quite available but have mixed reviews from people who use them," reports a geology major.

> **"A cappella is the football of Mount Holyoke."**

Social life on campus is described as "mellow" and inclusive, consisting of low-key parties, plays, concerts, speakers, and cultural events. "A cappella is the football of Mount Holyoke—we have six different groups who perform every semester and have significant followings in the student body," notes a senior. The Mount Holyoke College V8s (Victory Eights) are the oldest continuing female collegiate a cappella group in the United States. Students seeking a more "traditional" party scene typically head to UMass or other Five College schools. A computer science major says South Hadley (population 18,000) is "a bit isolated for people who really enjoy city life." The South Hadley Center has eateries, a pub, shops, and a movie theater. Road trips to Boston, Vermont, and New York City are popular when students can find the time.

> *Chemistry is a long-standing strength at Mount Holyoke, bolstered by top-of-the-line labs.*

"We have a multitude of traditions at Mount Holyoke that we take very seriously," comments a politics and religion major. Each class has a color and a mascot, and class spirit is huge, especially for the annual Junior Show and Convocation. Every fall on Mountain Day, students wake up to ringing bells, classes are canceled (even the library is closed), and everyone treks up Mount Holyoke to picnic and see the foliage. "In the spring, we have Pangy Day (short for Pangynaskeia, or 'cultivating the total world of women'), where students wrap a maypole, snuggle baby goats, and hang out in the sun with friends," explains a senior. The *Mount Holyoke News* is one of the oldest continuously running college newspapers in the country. Community service is an important emphasis, and 30 percent of students regularly volunteer.

In addition to academic pursuits, Division III Lyons athletics, such as basketball, cross-country, equestrian sports, field hockey, and lacrosse, are popular. The college encourages athletic participation with several competitive club sports and a state-of-the-art fitness center, although intramurals are not offered. Mount Holyoke's Model United Nations team frequently brings home top honors.

Mount Holyoke's diverse student body makes for a globally aware community, and its identity as a gender-diverse women's college nurturing future leaders promotes a culture where deep, personal relationships are the norm. Academic excellence and easy access to New York and Boston provide a small college atmosphere that's infused with art and culture. As one senior explains, "There is a unique bond and desire for empowerment on campus."

If You Apply To ›

MHC: Early decision I and II, regular decision. SATs or ACTs: optional. Accepts the Common Application with supplement. Accepts applications from students who are female, transgender, and nonbinary.

Muhlenberg College

2400 Chew Street, Allentown, PA 18104

There is a definite Muhlenberg type: ambitious, studious, and preprofessional. Muhlenberg is strong in premed, prelaw, pre-anything. Has a more humble, middle-class persona than Dickinson and Lafayette and boasts a challenging and supportive atmosphere. Takes its Lutheran values seriously but welcomes students of all or no religious backgrounds. Known for its performing and visual arts programs, business, and biology/prehealth.

Muhlenberg College is a small liberal arts school founded on solid Lutheran roots that takes pride in fostering a strong sense of community among undergraduates. With ample opportunities for hands-on learning and lots of support through an individualized coaching team, which assigns each student a career coach, a faculty advisor, and a college life coach, the school continues to attract the best and brightest to its preprofessional programs, including its top premed and predental programs. Put simply, says one senior, "Muhlenberg believes in students and their ability to learn."

Muhlenberg was established in 1848 and named after the founder of the Lutheran Church in America. Set on 82 parklike acres, the 'Berg campus is a combination of older Gothic stone structures and newer buildings in a variety of architectural styles that align with Muhlenberg's commitment to sustainability. The campus boasts a lovely chapel, the high-tech Trexler Library, a 40-acre biological field station and wildlife sanctuary, and a 64-acre arboretum with more than 300 species of wildflowers, broadleaf evergreens, and conifer trees. The Fahy Commons for Public Engagement and Innovation, a 20,000-square-foot, energy-efficient facility, houses the Office of Community Engagement, the Innovation & Entrepreneurship Program, and other academic spaces.

Muhlenberg's popular First-Year Seminars are small, writing- and discussion-intensive courses capped at 15 students. Recent offerings include The Art of Memory, Coming-of-Age Narratives, and Springsteen's America. All students complete one additional writing-intensive course, and courses to explore key content areas of the liberal arts in such areas as Representations and Creative Expression, Meaning and Value, Global Perspectives, and Intercultural Communication. Students also complete an experiential learning requirement and a capstone in their major.

Muhlenberg's reputation rests largely on its premedical program, which continues to attract large numbers of aspiring doctors. Majors in biology, public health, neuroscience, biochemistry, and chemistry are available, as are competitive early-acceptance programs in medicine with Temple and Boston University, a 3–4 optometry program with SUNY College of Optometry, and a 3–4 dentistry program with the University of Pennsylvania. The college's theater arts program is a national draw, and some alumni have gone on to star on Broadway. Science lab equipment at Muhlenberg is cutting-edge, and a comprehensive science major allows for a sampling of it all. The Living Writers course, offered once every three years, has brought a number of noted authors to campus, including Téa Obreht, Jonathan Franzen, and Zadie Smith. Theater is Muhlenberg's most popular major, followed by psychology, business and finance, and biology.

> **"Professors truly strive to have students understand and apply what they learn."**

Students describe the academic climate as serious, challenging, and encouraging. Seventy-seven percent of courses have fewer than 20 students, promoting a cooperative environment. "Professors truly strive to have students understand and apply what they learn to their everyday lives," cheers a junior. Advising is strong here too, and students may take advantage of programs like Alumni Week, which is organized around conversations and workshops with alumni in all industries. "The Career Center's team has helped me since freshman year to figure out what I want to do after Muhlenberg," says a media and communication senior.

The college offers four honors programs that provide early opportunities for internships, undergraduate research, and community engaged learning: the Muhlenberg Scholars Program, the Dana Scholars Program, the RJ Fellows Program, and the Shankweiler Scholars Program. Each program requires a culminating project or seminar in the senior year; 11 percent of students participate. Students speak highly of the college's array of service-learning course offerings, and 23 percent of undergrads conduct research with faculty. Those seeking international experiences may study abroad via 130 programs in countries around the globe; 32 percent do so, including in short-term, faculty-led programs, known as Muhlenberg Integrated Learning Abroad (MILA) in January and May. "MILAs have been a great opportunity," raves a math major.

Muhlenberg requires students to live on campus and guarantees housing to all undergraduates.

"Muhlenberg is basically the golden retriever of colleges: everyone is so sweet and friendly, but we are also hardworking and dedicated to our studies," muses a public health major. Muhlenberg draws 28 percent of its students from Pennsylvania

> **"Muhlenberg is basically the golden retriever of colleges."**

and many from adjacent New Jersey and New York; just 1 percent come from abroad. Black students account for 5 percent of the student body, Hispanics/Latinos 11 percent, Asian Americans 4 percent, and multiracial students 4 percent. Many students cite increasing the diversity of the student body and faculty as a top concern on this left-leaning campus. "There is an open political dialogue where students are encouraged to express their views without worry of backlash," says a junior. Merit scholarships averaging $27,200 are available, but athletic scholarships are not.

Muhlenberg requires students to live on campus and guarantees housing to all undergraduates. First-year students are able to live in one of three residence halls, "which is actually nice because it brings them all together in one area of campus," explains a senior. Upperclassmen praise the Muhlenberg Independent Living Experience townhouses and other suite-style options. Two dorms, Robertson and South, house 140 students in single, air-conditioned rooms overlooking Lake Muhlenberg. First-years choose from a seven- or five-day meal plan, and students rave about the food, the staff, and even the dining-hall ambience. "Our Wood Dining Commons is a cross between a ski lodge and Hogwarts," cheers one student. "There's even a fireplace!" Campus safety receives good ratings.

Most social life at Muhlenberg takes place on campus, and students say there's something to fit every interest. The Muhlenberg Activities Council provides comedians, current movies in the Red Door Café, live music, escape rooms, and bingo nights. Hillel is among the largest of the more than 120 student organizations, as are the theater and dance associations. Allentown offers a variety of restaurants, bars, and minor league sports, and a senior comments, "Muhlenberg's relationship with the surrounding community is definitely growing." Students get involved by volunteering as tutors and with groups such as Habitat for Humanity and America Reads. City buses stop on campus for trips to downtown Allentown, area malls, and other local activities. Students also venture to Philadelphia (60 miles) for nightlife and cheesesteaks, New York City (95 miles) for clubbing and theater, and farther out to Baltimore or Washington, D.C. Outdoorsy students can pick up the Appalachian Trail for a little hiking.

Nineteen percent of Muhlenberg men and 25 percent of the women pledge their undergraduate years to fraternities and sororities, respectively, and according to a junior, "Greek life is thriving if you want it but not thrust upon you in any way." Students report that the school takes its policies against underage drinking seriously. Big social events include homecoming and Midnight Breakfast, when faculty and staff serve late-night breakfast to students before finals. A favorite tradition is the candlelight ceremony during orientation where first-years write down their college goals, which they reopen in the days before graduation.

> **"Muhlenberg's relationship with the surrounding community is definitely growing."**

For the athletically inclined, the nicely alliterative Muhlenberg Mules compete in the Division III Centennial Conference with 23 varsity teams. Football, softball, and men's soccer have brought home conference titles in the last few years. Students say any contest against Johns Hopkins draws crowds. Muhlenberg's Life Sports Center offers a pool, a basketball court, other all-purpose courts, and a jogging track. Soccer, volleyball, and basketball are the most popular intramurals.

"It is an unspoken expectation on campus to hold the door for the person behind you, even if they are at a farther distance than would usually warrant such a gesture," explains a student. Small gestures of kindness are just one way in which Muhlenberg earns its reputation as a "community that cares"—it also offers students a warm, intimate academic milieu and plenty of support.

Overlaps

Emerson, Franklin & Marshall, Gettysburg, Ithaca, Lafayette, NYU, Skidmore, Syracuse

If You Apply To ›

Muhlenberg: Early decision I and II, early action, regular decision. SATs or ACTs: optional. Accepts the Common Application.

1400 R Street, Lincoln, NE 68588

Everybody knows Cornhusker football, but in other areas, Nebraska, the smallest public university in the Big Ten, flies under the radar. With less than a third of undergrads coming from out of state, has a corner on the market for Nebraskans. Business administration, psychology, finance, and foods, nutrition, and wellness studies top the list of majors. Given the state's demographic makeup, diversity is a challenge. Volleyball is an obsession.

Website: www.unl.edu
Location: City Center
Public
Total Enrollment: 21,086
Undergraduates: 18,390
Male/Female: 50/50
Financial Aid: 71%
Pell Grant: 25%
Expense: Pub $ $
Student Loans: 48%
Average Debt: $
Applicants: 17,841
Accepted: 87%
Enrolled: 30%
Grad in 6 Years: 67%
Returning First-years: 86%
Academics: ✍ ✍ ✍
Social: 🍷 🍷 🍷 🍷
Q of L: ★ ★ ★
Admissions: (800) 742-8800
Email Address:
admissions@unl.edu

Strong Programs:
Actuarial Science
Advertising and Public
   Relations
Animal Science
Business Administration
Early Childhood Education
Journalism
Nutrition, Exercise, and Health
   Science
Psychology

On crisp fall weekends, when spirits are high and the Big Red football arcs through the air, Huskers cheer and paint the town of Lincoln red and white in a show of appreciation for their alma mater. In fact, on home-game Saturdays, the stadium is the third largest "city" in the state, holding 5 percent of the population. Away from the stadium, students at the University of Nebraska–Lincoln have more reasons to cheer, with notable programs ranging from software engineering to digital humanities to PGA golf management.

Nebraska, chartered in 1869 as a land grant institution, spreads across two main campuses. The East Campus is home to the College of Agricultural Sciences and Natural Resources and the College of Law. Most entering students end up on the larger City Campus, surrounded by the bustle of downtown Lincoln and home to seven undergraduate colleges: architecture, arts and sciences, journalism and mass communications, business, fine and performing arts, engineering, and education and human sciences. On City Campus, the architectural style ranges from the modern Sheldon Art Gallery designed by Philip Johnson to the architecture building, which is on the National Register of Historic Places. There are also several grassy malls, an arboretum, and a sculpture garden. A third campus location, the Innovation Campus, serves as a research and technological hub where students can test their skills with real-world tools and projects.

Nebraska's 30-credit general education program, known as Achievement-Centered Education, is required of students in all majors and includes a senior-year capstone course. To help first-years get oriented, Big Red Welcome combines a new student convocation with entertainment, information booths, and food in a carnival setting. Nebraska's College of Agricultural Sciences and Natural Resources is known for its outstanding programs in animal science, food science and technology, and agribusiness. Journalism, actuarial science, and early childhood education are also traditional strengths. The school of music's opera program has received national attention, and the Johnny Carson School of Theatre and Film offers four undergrad degrees, including a B.F.A. in emerging media arts. The most popular areas of study are business administration, psychology, agriculture, communication/journalism, and engineering.

> **"The workload is fairly intensive if you want to get good grades."**

"The workload is fairly intensive if you want to get good grades," remarks an accounting major. Many classes are large; just 31 percent have fewer than 20 students. Graduate students teach some first-year courses, but top professors can be found inside the classroom too. "For a university this big, I think that the professors do a good job of making students feel valued," says a prenursing student. "It is hard to be recognized in classes with 100 students, but I don't think that the quality of teaching is any less. And there are always office hours for students."

The University Honors Program offers qualified students challenging coursework, research opportunities, and faculty mentors. The FYRE (First-Year Research Experience) program pairs first-years who have federal work-study awards with faculty members for up to five hours of collaborative research per week. Also, the UCARE (Undergraduate Creative Activity and Research Experience) program provides stipends for more than 400 students each year to participate in one-on-one research with a professor after the first year. The Raikes School of Computer Science and Management is a highly selective honors program that focuses on a curriculum in technology, business, and real-world projects and awards scholarships to participants. Study abroad opportunities are available in more than 70 countries and include nearly 40 faculty-led programs. Career Services shows students how to make a professional résumé, holds mock interviews, and hosts potential employers, among other activities.

A junior says Nebraska students' "social etiquette and values are high, embodying 'Nebraska Nice.'" A senior says the school leans liberal and adds, "Our students are incredibly politically active." Seventy-six percent of undergraduates hail from in state, and 3 percent come from abroad. Asian Americans make up 4 percent of the student body, Black students 3 percent, Hispanics/Latinos 10 percent, and multiracial students 4 percent. Many students say diversity—or the lack thereof—is an issue, but one notes, "UNL is a very inclusive space." Merit scholarships are available, with an average award of $8,000, in addition to more than 500 athletic scholarships in 19 sports.

Fifty percent of the students live in the university's single-sex or co-ed residence halls, and there's usually no trouble getting a room. "Most of the dorms are up-to-date and are pretty sizable, but there are a few that are smaller," explains a science education major. "There are options, however, for suite-style dorms that are available to everyone, including freshmen." First-years must live on campus, and many students move off campus after their sophomore year. Students praise the living/learning communities offered for first-years with common academic interests who live and take classes together. "I lived in a learning community my freshman year that helped me both find my major and make some of my closest friendships," enthuses a psychology major. As for dining, "As the pickiest eater in the world, the food was great," raves a junior. Students agree the campus feels safe. "UNL requires the entire student body and faculty/staff complete annual sexual misconduct prevention and response training," notes a music education major.

"A lot of the social life starts on campus but then moves off," says a communication studies major. "You meet people on your floor or in a club, and then you hang out and go out off campus." Fraternity and house parties, 500-plus student organizations, concerts and theater performances, the movies, eating out, visiting coffee shops and bars, and road trips to Omaha or Kansas City are just some of the activities that keep students busy. For many, the fall semester revolves around football weekends and postseason bowl games. Fraternities draw 29 percent of the men, and sororities attract 33 percent of the women. They offer both social events and a chance to get involved in the Lincoln community. Homecoming, Greek Week, the spring concert, and the Big Event (a major community service occasion) are among the most anticipated campus events.

"Lincoln is a great college town," exclaims one business administration major. Another student points out that the "thirty bars within a two-minute walk of campus" are appreciated by those of age, given the school's dry campus. Town/gown relations are good, and "the community is always eager for students to return in the fall," according to one premed student. Pachyderm enthusiasts will be delighted by the Nebraska Museum of Natural History's outstanding collection of prehistoric elephant skeletons. Beyond the town's sidewalks are miles of flat trails and plains, ideal for biking and cross-country skiing.

> "Social etiquette and values are high, embodying 'Nebraska Nice.'"

In a state with no major professional sports teams, Husker athletics play an outsized role. Football fans remain rabid despite losing records in the past few years. The women's volleyball team has won five national championships since 1995 and regularly draws record crowds, especially when chief rival Wisconsin is on the court. Women's bowling has also been a national champion, while baseball and softball have brought home conference titles. Men's and women's hoopsters frolic in the 15,500-seat Pinnacle Bank Arena. The annual Black Friday bowl game against the University of Iowa is the main football rivalry. And who hasn't heard of the classy Nebraska football fans and their hardworking mascots Herbie Husker and Lil' Red? "There is truly nothing like a Game Day in Lincoln, with the Sea of Red cheering on the football team," says a junior. Intramural sports are popular too, with flag football and basketball drawing the most participants; more competitive students can choose from 40 club sports.

At Nebraska, future agricultural experts mingle with techno whizzes, while teachers in training brush elbows with advertising mavens. Whether studying overseas, immersing themselves in internships, launching start-ups, or going wild on Saturday afternoons, students here know how to make the most of their time. Cheers one happy Husker, "The academic climate is led by the students, and our students have so much pride in our school that it's hard not to feel driven to succeed."

> ### Overlaps
>
> **Creighton, University of Iowa, Iowa State, University of Kansas, University of Minnesota, University of Missouri, University of Nebraska at Kearney, University of Nebraska Omaha**

If You Apply To ›

Nebraska: Rolling admissions. SATs or ACTs: optional. Accepts the Common Application.

University of New Hampshire

105 Main Street, Durham, NH 03824

UNH is a public university that looks and feels like a private college. Draws more than half of its students from outside New Hampshire. Well known for engineering, health, and life science programs—especially marine biology—and its business school is nationally ranked. UNH's focus is sharply on undergrads.

> **Website**: www.unh.edu
> **Location**: Small Town
> **Public**
> **Total Enrollment**: 12,393
> **Undergraduates**: 11,075
> **Male/Female**: 44/56
> **Financial Aid**: 91%
> **Pell Grant**: 21%
> **Expense**: Pub $ $ $ $
> **Student Loans**: 70%
> **Average Debt**: $ $ $ $
> **Applicants**: 21,175
> **Accepted**: 88%
> **Enrolled**: 14%
> **Grad in 6 Years**: 76%

Students at the University of New Hampshire know how to get their hands dirty, and this solid public institution provides them with countless opportunities to do just that. Founded as a land grant college in 1866, UNH's research mission has grown dramatically in recent years, yet the university remains a moderate-sized institution that emphasizes undergraduate instruction. Unlike at many large research universities, UNH faculty members teach all students, including first-years, and generally value teaching as much as they do their research. A love of the outdoors is a must, as is the ability to withstand long, cold winters. As they say around here, "Every day is a great day to be a Wildcat!"

The university's wide-open, grassy Durham campus is home to a mix of modern facilities and ivy-covered brick buildings. The sprawling lawns are surrounded by nearly 3,000 acres of farms, fields, and woods. During the past few years, UNH has invested in large-scale construction projects, including a recently completed $95 million expansion and renovation of the bioscience building, and renovations to Huddleston Hall include a major addition to house the new UNH Hamel Honors and Scholars College.

The university's core curriculum, the Discovery Program, includes general education requirements that apply across the board and mandate coursework in biological science; physical science; historical perspectives; world cultures; social science; fine and performing arts; humanities; and environment, technology, and society. First-year writing is also mandatory as part of a four-course writing-intensive requirement, as is a class in quantitative reasoning. All first-years take an Inquiry course involving an experiential learning component, and all seniors complete a capstone experience.

Interdisciplinary programs enhance UNH's emphasis on traditional academic offerings. A dual major allows students to pair a degree in sustainability with any other major, and minors range from leadership to green real estate to microbrewing. Engineering and business are among the most respected programs. The Paul College of Business and Economics is nationally ranked, offering a spate of majors and boasting multiple student-run organizations, one of which is the first student-run angel investment fund. Students entering Paul College participate in the First-Year Innovation and Research Experience, working in teams to develop business plans with guidance from peer advisors and alumni mentors. The marine, estuarine, and freshwater biology major is considered stellar, enhanced by UNH's proximity to the ocean and a brackish bay. Ocean engineering, bioengineering, homeland security, and a preveterinary advising program are also strengths. The most popular majors are business administration, psychology, communication, and nursing. New majors include mathematics education, public health, sustainability, and a 3–3 political science/law program.

> **"We have world–class professors, many of whom include students as research assistants."**

Students agree that the level of academic intensity varies by school and college, but the atmosphere is always busy. "On a normal day, I see students studying and working everywhere around campus, indoors and outdoors (when the weather permits)," says a business administration major. Classes are relatively small, with just 16 percent enrolling 50 or more students, and teaching assistants only facilitate discussion sections or labs. "We have world-class professors, many of whom participate in research and include students as research assistants," says a senior, and a junior notes that professors are accessible and "easy to speak to."

Research experience is a key emphasis at UNH, and 40 percent of undergraduates get involved before they graduate. The Hamel Center for Undergraduate Research engages around 300 students in its programs annually, including competitive, funded awards for student-led research in the U.S. and abroad. It also publishes *Inquiry*, UNH's online undergraduate research journal, and hosts the Undergraduate Research Conference, which showcases the scholarly work of more than 1,700 students annually. Additional opportunities include conducting research on NASA partner projects or at the Shoals Marine Laboratory six miles off the coast. Twenty-four percent of students broaden their horizons through more than 250 approved study abroad and exchange programs. The Semester in the City internship program sends civic-minded students to live together and work within social change organizations in Boston. The invitation-only Hamel Honors and Scholars College features small classes, personal mentoring, and optional honors-themed housing.

> **"Most of UNH's students care for the values of environmental stewardship, community connections, and Live Free or Die."**

"Most of UNH's students care for the values of environmental stewardship, community connections, and Live Free or Die," says one student, referring to the state's motto. While UNH is New Hampshire's flagship public institution, it has long been popular with out-of-staters, who make up 53 percent of its undergraduates;

(continued)

Returning First-years: 87%
Academics: ✍ ✍ ✍
Social: 🌢 🌢 🌢 🌢 🌢
Q of L: ★ ★ ★ ★ ★
Admissions: (603) 862-1360
Email Address:
admissions@unh.edu

Strong Programs:
Business Administration
Communication
Engineering
Homeland Security
Marine, Estuarine, and
 Freshwater Biology
Nursing
Psychology
Sustainability

The marine, estuarine, and freshwater biology major is enhanced by UNH's proximity to the ocean and a brackish bay.

international students add another 1 percent. As for racial and ethnic diversity, UNH has a long way to go. Black students account for just 1 percent of the student population, Asian Americans 3 percent, Hispanics/Latinos 4 percent, and multiracial students 3 percent. Politically, students are "engaged and vocal," says a senior. UNH's published tuition and fees for in-state are among the highest of any flagship university in the country. To ease the pain, the university offers hundreds of merit scholarships, averaging $7,200, and 215 awards are available for gifted athletes. The Granite Guarantee program gives free tuition to qualifying New Hampshire residents from low-income families.

Fifty-eight percent of Wildcats live in the school's co-ed residence halls, and accommodations are said to be generally comfortable. Most upperclassmen live off campus or in the two on-campus apartment complexes. More than a dozen themed living areas are available and are an increasingly popular option. Campus dining receives rave reviews, and students also give high ratings to campus safety. UNH is a national leader in efforts to prevent sexual assault on campus. In addition to its student-praised training programs and support services, UNH established the Prevention Innovations Research Center to develop evidence-based prevention strategies and policies.

UNH offers more than 200 student organizations covering just about any interest. "Get involved early on, as that will help you become acclimated to the campus," advises a social work and women's studies major. A great way to do that is through U Day, an event with booths and activities that introduces students to on-campus groups. Service organizations are popular, and 52 percent of students get involved with community service activities. The Campus Activities Board organizes weekend social events including dances, movies, bingo, and gatherings at local coffeehouses, and favorite annual events include homecoming and concerts in the fall and spring. Greek groups claim 15 percent of men and 10 percent of women. The party culture at UNH is lively, but Greek parties are subject to the university's no-tolerance alcohol policy, which evicts underage students caught with alcohol more than once from on-campus housing.

Less than a five-minute walk from campus is the beautiful little town of Durham, which caters to the student clientele. Its Main Street is lined with restaurants and coffeehouses, a grocery store, an ice-cream parlor, and a few bars. The free Wildcat Transit bus system takes students to cities in the Seacoast region, including vibrant Portsmouth, and the on-campus Amtrak station makes weekend escapes to Boston and Portland, Maine, easy—if students can find time off. (A generous winter break limits the number of days off during other seasons.) Still, says one student, "You can access the highest mountain in the Northeast, the beach, ski areas, and lake areas within two hours of UNH." Every four years, New Hampshire takes the spotlight when the state holds the nation's earliest presidential primary, making UNH a frequent destination for political candidates.

UNH has 20 Division I athletic teams, of which ice hockey is a fan favorite. Students celebrate the first Wildcats goal of each game by throwing a large fish onto the ice, and during games against its rival, the University of Maine, students wear white to "white out" the stadium. Men's football, skiing, and soccer and women's volleyball, cross-country, swimming and diving, skiing, and soccer are most competitive. Club and intramural sports enlist 27 percent of the student body. Broomball—played with broom-shaped sticks, balls, and sneakers on the ice—is very popular, as are activities organized by the Outing Club, including skiing, camping, fishing, and hiking. The Northeast Passage program, which is housed near campus in Durham, offers adaptive recreation programs for students and community members with disabilities.

New Hampshire's only major public university offers a huge variety of programs in a beautiful natural setting. That's one reason it attracts so many students from out of state. Another reason, a junior says, is that between smaller class sizes, community-oriented dorms, and welcoming student organizations, "You will feel like you're part of a very tight-knit community, even though there are 11,000 undergrads on campus, and you really have the chance to make your experience here whatever you want it to be."

The College of New Jersey

2000 Pennington Road, Ewing, NJ 08628

A public liberal arts institution in the mold of UNC Asheville or William & Mary. Also offers business, education, and engineering. With 95 percent of the students homegrown Garden Staters, TCNJ enjoys little draw beyond Jersey. On the other hand, it is now the state's second most selective institution, after a certain super-selective school up the road in Princeton. A smaller, more personal alternative to Rutgers.

The College of New Jersey is an up-and-coming public institution with special focus on undergraduates, an emphasis more commonly found at private schools. TCNJ offers professors focused on teaching and the encouragement of undergraduate research as well as a campus reminiscent of that of nearby Princeton University—minus the Ivy League price tag. Founded in 1855 as a teachers' college, it strives to provide students with opportunities in a host of other fields. The small size makes for closeness among students and faculty. Says one student, "TCNJ is really big on the 'community' feel."

TCNJ is set on 289 wooded and landscaped acres in suburban Ewing Township, six miles from Trenton. The picturesque Georgian colonial architecture centers on Quimby's Prairie, surrounded by the original academic buildings of the 1930s. A flock of Canada geese makes its home in one of the two campus lakes. Campus Town, a 12-acre, $120 million complex adjacent to the campus, features 612 apartments for upperclassmen, a campus gym, and retail shops and restaurants. The college recently completed the STEM Complex, a $96 million project that added the 89,000-square-foot STEM Building and renovated existing science and engineering facilities.

The College Core, TCNJ's general education program, requires coursework centered on three fundamental areas: intellectual and scholarly growth, social justice, and multidisciplinary perspectives. Incoming students participate in several programs to prepare them for college life and academics, including a summer reading program, welcome week, and a First-Year Seminar course, in which they take a small seminar on a topic outside of their intended major. First-years must also perform at least a half day of community service. All seniors complete a capstone requirement that varies by major.

Consistent with the school's origins as a teachers' college, education programs are well regarded; elementary and special education are particular favorites among

Website: www.tcnj.edu
Location: Suburban
Public
Total Enrollment: 7,231
Undergraduates: 6,942
Male/Female: 44/56
Financial Aid: 59%
Pell Grant: 24%
Expense: Pub $ $ $ $
Student Loans: 59%
Average Debt: $ $ $ $
Applicants: 12,766
Accepted: 62%
Enrolled: 19%
Grad in 6 Years: 86%
Returning First-years: 91%
Academics: 🖉 🖉 🖉 🖉
Social: 💬 💬 💬
Q of L: ★ ★ ★
Admissions: (609) 771-2131
Email Address:
  tcnjinfo@tcnj.edu

Strong Programs:
Biology
Business Administration
Elementary Education

(continued)

Finance
Marketing
Nursing
Psychology
Special Education

In the Mentored Undergraduate Summer Experience program, students spend eight weeks assisting faculty mentors with research and creative projects.

The school has no cap on out-of-state admissions, but only 5 percent of TCNJ's students are non-Jerseyans.

students. Early childhood and elementary education majors may pursue the urban education option, which prepares them to teach in urban schools and allows them to complete both a bachelor's and a master's degree in five years. The business school is strong, as are the natural sciences, especially biology. Other popular majors include finance, engineering, marketing, and nursing. Students in the engineering school can choose from eight majors, ranging from biomedical engineering to integrative STEM education. The college also offers a seven-year B.S./M.D. degree program with Rutgers New Jersey Medical School and a seven-year B.S./O.D. degree with SUNY College of Optometry.

Academically, TCNJ is competitive and getting more so. "The academic climate is somewhat intense," confides a sophomore. "Some students and professors try to downplay the competitive nature, but overall it's pretty driven." An honors program

"The academic climate is somewhat intense."

is available for those who wish to challenge themselves with even more rigorous academics. Thirty-five percent of undergraduate classes have fewer than 20 students, and none has more than 50. The college has no teaching assistants, and faculty members generally get high marks, though quality is said to vary by department. "My professors are very passionate about their work and field of study," says a psychology major. Many undergrads complete internships before they graduate. Students are able to get their passports stamped to study, intern, or volunteer overseas in dozens of countries. As part of the MUSE (Mentored Undergraduate Summer Experience) program, nearly 100 students spend eight weeks assisting faculty mentors with research and creative projects.

The typical TCNJ student is "overly book smart," according to one junior. The school has no cap on out-of-state admissions, but only 5 percent of TCNJ's students are non-Jerseyans, including the less than 1 percent who are international. The college has aggressively recruited students of color, and today, Black students account for 6 percent of undergraduates, Hispanics/Latinos 18 percent, Asian Americans 10 percent, and multiracial students 3 percent. "If you don't leave this school very well educated in political correctness, then you were obviously unconscious," says a marketing major, who praises the school for its diversity. Merit scholarships averaging $5,800 are available to qualified students. The Educational Opportunity Fund Promise Award covers full tuition and other expenses and provides specialized academic support services for qualifying New Jersey residents from disadvantaged backgrounds.

Dorm housing is only guaranteed for first-years and sophomores; overall, 44 percent of students live on campus. "Most of the dorms are really nice," says a student,

"TCNJ is really big on the 'community' feel."

"but a few are older and outdated." First-year students hang their hats in one of seven residence halls; after that, they can enter the lottery to secure spots in traditional residence halls, townhouses, or the Campus Town apartments. Many upperclassmen opt for nearby off-campus apartment complexes, which are plentiful. For meals, students head to 10 dining locations. The Anti-Violence Initiatives office encompasses training, counseling, and peer education efforts aimed at preventing sexual assault on campus.

Although suburban Ewing (population 36,000) doesn't really cater to students, funky New Hope, Pennsylvania, and preppy Princeton, New Jersey, are nearby; restaurants, bars, movie theaters—and, this being New Jersey, many malls—are within a short drive. Road trips to Philadelphia and New York, each about an hour away and accessible by train, are also highly recommended. Alcohol policies are strictly enforced; students 21 and over can enjoy adult beverages at the campus restaurant, Traditions, which also features a stage area for performances. Twenty-one percent of the men and 16 percent of the women belong to fraternities and sororities, which provide many of the off-campus parties. Campus programming includes dances, concerts, and movies. TCNJers look forward to several annual events, including homecoming, a Family Fest Day, and—the springtime favorite—Senior Week.

The College of New Jersey's 21 varsity teams (the Lions) are the pride of the New Jersey Athletic Conference and make frequent appearances in national Division III tournaments. Men's and women's cross-country and women's track and field, lacrosse, and softball have all taken home recent conference titles. Students rally around the football and basketball squads, especially when archrival Rowan comes to town. The college also offers intramural and club sport programs including flag football, basketball, golf, and pickleball.

The College of New Jersey is one of the few public liberal arts colleges with reasonable tuition and a location that offers a relaxed suburban haven within shouting distance of big-city opportunities. Not just for teachers anymore, TCNJ prides itself on the personal attention it devotes to students craving both professional preparation and a well-rounded education.

If You Apply To ›

TCNJ: Early decision, early action, regular decision. Accepts the Common Application. Music applicants must audition. Please consult TCNJ's website for the most up-to-date information regarding standardized test requirements.

New Jersey Institute of Technology

University Heights, Newark, NJ 07102

One of the few public polytechnic universities in the Northeast. Within New Jersey, NJIT occupies a middle ground between the behemoth Rutgers and smallish Stevens Institute, and nearly 90 percent of undergrads are state residents. Primarily offers engineering, computing, architecture, design, and business, and co-op option is popular. At nearly three to one, NJIT's gender ratio is skewed toward males.

The New Jersey Institute of Technology provides a solid STEM education that prepares students for an ever-changing global workplace. NJIT's challenging programs emphasize education, research, service, and (not surprisingly) economic development. The combination is enticing—as is the price tag, relative to the top-tier private technical institutes that are some of NJIT's closest competitors. Notes a junior, "This school has a very innovative tradition."

Founded in 1881 by local industrialists, NJIT's 48-acre urban campus includes more than 40 buildings ranging from Elizabethan Gothic to contemporary design. More recent additions include the $110 million Wellness and Events Center and the 10,000-square-foot Makerspace, which gives students hands-on design and manufacturing experience with top-of-the-line tools and technology.

Students complete general education requirements in college writing, cultural literacy, computer science, and math. All students take a First Year Seminar that introduces them to university life, and all seniors complete a capstone. NJIT is composed of five schools and colleges plus the Dorman Honors College, offering around 50 undergraduate majors. Computer science, mechanical engineering, information technology, and architecture are the most popular majors. Students earning their B.S. in business choose from five concentrations, from marketing to innovation and entrepreneurship. NJIT offers the only undergraduate forensic

The Student Activities Council plans events like laser tag, arcade days, and movie nights.

The Murray Center for Women in Technology offers scholarships, networking opportunities, and resources.

science program in the state, as well as prehealth and prelaw programs with an emphasis on technology.

"The overall attitude toward academics at NJIT is very serious, and people don't expect to just get by without putting many hours of work into their courses," says a mechanical engineering major, although some say the atmosphere can be low-pressure in certain fields. Thirty-two percent of classes have fewer than 20 students, and professors are given average to high marks. One computer science major offers this assessment: "I would say 10 percent of the professors I would never want to take again, 70 percent were fine, and 20 percent were incredible." Since most have worked in their industry, they can provide job information and networking opportunities. Career services also receive positive reviews.

NJIT's co-op program enables students to earn course credits while gaining paid work experience at tech companies and other organizations. Top first-year applicants are offered a spot in the Honors College, and about 700 undergraduates in all majors are enrolled. Perks include a dedicated honors dorm, research opportunities, and acceptance into accelerated premed and other prehealth programs. "If you're not in honors, get in touch with one of your professors that does interesting work, and work in their lab," advises one student. Study abroad is an option, but with their packed schedules, few students find time for it. Men make up roughly 70 percent of the student body, and a female biology major makes a common complaint: "The ratio of men to women in the school is shocking." The Murray Center for Women in Technology attempts to balance the scales, offering scholarships, networking opportunities, and resources.

> "Our personality is based around being smart nerds."

As New Jersey's technological public university, NJIT attracts students with wide-ranging interests. While some students characterize it as a "commuter school," a senior says, "Diversity extends beyond ethnicity; students come with varied political views, economic experiences, and life stories, which makes for dynamic conversations and learning." In-state residents represent 88 percent of the undergraduate student body, and international students add 6 percent. Ten percent of undergrads are Black, 29 percent are Hispanic/Latino, 20 percent are Asian American, and 3 percent are multiracial. One student praises the Educational Opportunity Program, saying, "If it weren't for them, I would not be here. They make it easy to be a minority." Thirty-eight percent of incoming first-years receive Pell Grants. The university awards merit scholarships averaging $14,900 to qualified students, and more than 100 athletic scholarships are also available.

NJIT's five residence halls accommodate 25 percent of the students. "Housing is pretty standard," reports a student. "You have a choice of suite-style or communal-style as a freshman." Upperclassmen move into on-campus fraternity or sorority houses or nearby off-campus apartments. Maple Hall, a newer apartment-style residential building, offers numerous single rooms and sustainable construction. Meals in Highlander Commons, the main dining hall, receive average reviews. Because of its urban location, safety is always a consideration at NJIT, but "public safety officers are always around," says an electrical engineering major. A sophomore adds, "The school supports speaking up about sexual assault" and provides ample resources for those who need them. As for mental health support, a biomedical engineering major recalls going through a hard time and says C-CAPS (the Center for Counseling and Psychological Services) "not only supported my emotional well-being but also helped me coordinate with professors to ease my coursework and extend assignment deadlines."

Newark is hardly a college town, yet it is undergoing a gradual urban renaissance, and several good restaurants are within walking distance. "Newark has something of a social scene during the day; at night, a trip to Jersey City or New York

City is usually a better bet," explains a senior. Forty percent of students regularly volunteer in the community. On campus, 5 percent of the men and 4 percent of the women join the Greek system. "For a tech school, the party culture is not bad," admits a first-year. HackNJIT, a 24-hour hackathon, is always well attended, and the Student Activities Council plans events like laser tag, arcade days, and movie nights. One of the best annual campus events is Spring Fest, which features bands, intramural games, carnival rides, and a semiformal. Most students agree that the administration's strict alcohol policies are effective. For more fun, the beach is an hour away.

NJIT students take pride in their athletic prowess, and the school is a member of the Division I America East Conference, competing mainly against Northeastern schools like SUNY–Stony Brook and University of Maryland, Baltimore County. Among NJIT's 17 varsity Highlanders teams, men's and women's basketball and tennis, men's soccer, and baseball are some of the most competitive. Soccer, basketball, and racquetball are the favorites when it comes to intramurals, and ice hockey, ultimate Frisbee, and bowling are some of the most active club teams.

"Our personality is based around being smart nerds," says a mechanical engineering student. Indeed, academics are the priority here; if the social life is less than electrifying, students don't mind. After all, they know highly skilled jobs will beckon after graduation. "You're going to get a good education for a low price and have many opportunities from the school," says a senior. Getting through NJIT is a challenge, but there's ample compensation available for alums in the technologically dependent workplaces of today—and tomorrow.

> **"Newark has something of a social scene during the day."**

If You Apply To ›

NJIT: Early action I and II, rolling admissions. Accepts the Common Application. College of Architecture and Design applicants must submit portfolio of creative work. Please consult NJIT's website for the most up-to-date information regarding standardized test requirements.

University of New Mexico

1 University of New Mexico, Albuquerque, NM 87131

UNM gives new meaning to cultural diversity. Studies related to Hispanic and Native cultures are strong, and in a land of picture-perfect sunsets, photography is a big deal. Even the mascot—Lobo—is Spanish. Technical programs are fueled by government labs in Albuquerque and Los Alamos, while the business school produces an outsized percentage of New Mexico's commercial elite.

The University of New Mexico's heritage stretches back to 1889 when New Mexico wasn't even a state, and the university's strengths are still rooted in the rich history of the American Southwest. New Mexico excels in areas such as Latin American and Southwest studies. Lest you think it is a typical state school, consider that many students are commuters or of nontraditional age. UNM also boasts the state's only law, medical, and architecture and urban planning schools.

Seated at the foot of the gorgeous Sandia Mountains in the lap of Albuquerque, the beautifully landscaped campus occupies nearly 800 acres and sports both Spanish and Pueblo Indian architectural influences, with lots of patios and balconies. The

Website: www.unm.edu
Location: City Center
Public
Total Enrollment: 17,465
Undergraduates: 14,468
Male/Female: 42/56
Financial Aid: 76%
Pell Grant: 43%

(continued)

Expense: Pub $ $
Student Loans: 36%
Average Debt: $
Applicants: 13,125
Accepted: 79%
Enrolled: 35%
Grad in 6 Years: 46%
Returning First-years: 75%
Academics: ✑ ✑ ✑
Social: 🌑 🌑 🌑
Q of L: ★ ★ ★
Admissions: (505) 277-8900
Email Address:
 unmlobos@unm.edu

Strong Programs:
Anthropology
Business
Chicana and Chicano Studies
Engineering
Latin American Studies
Native American Studies
Navajo Language
Studio Art

duck pond is a favorite spot for sunbathing, and the mountains, which rise majestically to the east, are visible from virtually any point on campus. Newer facilities include a $65 million building for physics and astronomy and interdisciplinary science.

UNM offers more than 4,000 courses in 12 colleges and schools, running the gamut from arts and sciences, education, and engineering to management, fine arts, and the allied health fields. Academic and general education requirements vary, but the core curriculum mandates courses in English, humanities, social and behavioral sciences, physical and natural sciences, math, fine arts, and a second language. Those reluctant to specialize can spend a few semesters in the broad University College, which offers bachelor of liberal arts and bachelor of integrative studies degrees. The Honors College awards a B.A. in interdisciplinary liberal arts. The Tamarind Institute, a nationally recognized center housed at UNM's College of Fine Arts, offers training, study, and research in fine-art lithography. Anthropologists may explore one of New Mexico's many archaeological sites, and engineers may join in major solar-energy projects. Other solid programs include Native American studies, Chicana and Chicano studies, and Latin American studies. Students may also minor in Navajo language.

The academic climate is "attentive and focused," according to an environmental science major. Students help one another study, and competition for grades is the exception rather than the rule. Roughly half of classes have fewer than 20 students.

"There are plenty of research opportunities." "Like many large state schools, you'll have a mixed bag of professors," observes an astrophysics major. First-Year Learning Communities and academic coaching help ease the transition from high school. Many classes are offered in late afternoon and evening sessions, and about half of the student body takes advantage of these after-hours options. Outside of class, "There are plenty of research opportunities," says a business major. Study abroad programs around the world beckon to 18 percent of undergrads.

UNM enjoys robust cultural diversity, even though the vast majority (85 percent) of students are state residents. "Sometimes it can be hard to fit in as an out-of-state student," admits one such first-year; "however, the people are really nice." High enrollment of students of color—51 percent Hispanic/Latino, 6 percent Native American, 4 percent Asian American, 3 percent Black, and 4 percent multiracial—reflects this cultural diversity. Two percent of undergraduates are from overseas. UNM hosts several centers and student groups, such as El Centro de la Raza and Nations at UNM, that support diversity and cultural activities. "Students here are pretty chill," says a journalism major. "We hang out, but for the most part, we are focused on school." The state-funded New Mexico Opportunity Scholarship covers tuition and fees for all in-state residents, regardless of income. Merit and athletic scholarships are available, and 43 percent of first-years qualify for Pell Grants. A relatively large 21 percent of undergraduates are age 25 or older.

The state-funded New Mexico Opportunity Scholarship covers tuition and fees for all in-state residents, regardless of income.

UNM has traditionally been a commuter school (and parking is a perennial complaint), although first-year students coming from outside a 30-mile radius of campus are required to live in the residence halls; 24 percent of students live on campus. Students say they are happy with the variety of food available to them. Some say safety can be a concern with UNM "being both an open campus and in proximity to a not great area of Albuquerque," explains a junior. As for mental health support, a first-year adds, "There are free services available 24/7."

"Social life takes place both on and off campus," a junior says. Alcohol, though banned from UNM residence halls, is readily available, according to most students, especially at Greek parties. Just 3 percent of the men and 3 percent of the women join the Greek system. Other students find their fun off campus in Albuquerque's clubs and restaurants. For the more socially conscious, the university sponsors Spring Storm, an outing of roughly 1,000 students who volunteer around the city on a Saturday. Annual social events include Welcome Back Days in the fall and Nizhoni Days, a weeklong celebration of Native American culture.

Albuquerque is New Mexico's largest city (with 560,000 residents), and it offers a variety of cultural attractions, including the nation's largest hot air balloon festival, a growing artists' colony, and concert tours to charm the ears. Santa Fe is an hour away. Those with cars take advantage of the state's natural attractions: the Sandias, the Carlsbad Caverns, and superb skiing in Taos, as well as excellent hiking and camping. For the archaeologically inclined, numerous Spanish and Native American ruins are within an easy drive.

> **"There are many cultural influences within the school."**

The UNM Lobos (Spanish for "wolves") compete in the Division I Mountain West Conference, and the men's football and basketball teams usually draw crowds, especially for "Rio Grande Rivalry" games against New Mexico State. The women's cross-country team is a regular contender for the national title. Recreational and intramural sports are popular; students flock to flag football, volleyball, soccer, and basketball.

UNM offers a sun-drenched location that satisfies—precisely because its academic climate is as relaxed as the rolling desert dunes. Furthermore, says a happy first-year student, "As a minority-majority school, there are many cultural influences within the school, making it unique from its architecture to its events."

Overlaps

Arizona State, CU Boulder, Eastern New Mexico, Highlands, New Mexico State, University of Texas at El Paso

---

If You Apply To ›

UNM: Rolling admissions. SATs or ACTs: optional. Does not accept the Common Application.

New York University

70 Washington Square South, New York, NY 10012

NYU's rise to a global brand has been breathtaking. The siren song of Greenwich Village now extends to the Tandon School of Engineering in Brooklyn, degree-granting campuses in Abu Dhabi and Shanghai, and a dozen academic centers around the world. Major draws include the renowned Tisch School of the Arts and the best undergraduate business school north of Penn.

With the world at its doorstep, New York University invites its student body to jump right in. Firmly planted in the heart of Greenwich Village, one of the most eclectic and energizing neighborhoods in New York City, NYU has set its sights on becoming the world's first truly global university, with campuses also in Abu Dhabi, UAE, and Shanghai, China, and 13 academic centers around the world. Its growing student body, burgeoning new facilities, and multiple opportunities for high-level internships and research projects have made it a top option for a rising number of students. "Our dorms are like city apartments, and our walk to class is on city sidewalks and across busy streets," says a business and political economy major. "Going to NYU prepares students to live and work in the real world."

It doesn't get more real world than the venue that NYU has called home since its founding in 1831. NYU has campuses and centers throughout the city but is

Website: www.nyu.edu
Location: City Center
Private
Total Enrollment: 49,667
Undergraduates: 27,778
Male/Female: 41/59
Financial Aid: 84%
Pell Grant: 20%
Expense: Pr $ $ $
Student Loans: 28%
Average Debt: $ $

(continued)

Applicants: 110,807
Accepted: 9%
Enrolled: 55%
Grad in 6 Years: 88%
Returning First-years: 96%
Academics: ✐ ✐ ✐ ✐
Social: 🗩 🗩 🗩
Q of L: ★ ★ ★
Admissions: (212) 998-4500
Email Address:
 admissions@nyu.edu

Strong Programs:
Business
Economics
Engineering
Film and Television
Global Liberal Studies
Journalism
Nursing
Politics
Visual and Performing Arts

The Gallatin School of Individualized Study offers students the opportunity to craft their own concentration.

primarily situated on Washington Square. Trendy shops, galleries, clubs, bars, and eateries crowd neighboring streets; SoHo, Little Italy, and Chinatown are just blocks away. Academic buildings—both modern and historic—blend with 19th-century brick townhouses surrounding Washington Square Park (the closest thing NYU has to a quad). NYU's library is one of the largest open-stack facilities in the country, with millions of volumes. Kimmel Center for University Life houses meeting space for hundreds of student organizations, plus areas for the frequent recruitment fairs and lectures from national and international leaders. It also holds the Skirball Center for the Performing Arts' 860-seat theater, which is the largest performing arts facility south of 42nd Street.

While it's common to associate NYU with the Manhattan skyline, at NYU Abu Dhabi, students are immersed in an international environment, encouraged to pursue their research interests with Abu Dhabi as a rich local resource and a launchpad for global inquiry. NYU Shanghai offers students an unparalleled opportunity to live and work in a world center of culture, finance, and innovation. From the banks of the Huangpu River to the futuristic skyline, Shanghai also offers a dynamic backdrop for academic pursuits and cultural immersion.

NYU's growing global reach is matched by the wide range of academic programs available at all the campuses but especially in New York City. Under the College Core Curriculum, first-years and sophomores take courses including foreign language, expository writing, foundations of contemporary culture, and foundations of scientific inquiry. The language offerings go far beyond the typical Spanish-French-German—among the choices are Arabic, Cantonese, Hindi, Modern Irish, Swahili, and Urdu—and NYU operates a language exchange program with other schools to create even more offerings. The Tisch School of the Arts trained such famed artists as Martin Scorsese, Pedro Pascal, Spike Lee, Donald Glover, and Maggie Rogers, and current undergrads continue to win many national student filmmaker awards. Tisch also boasts excellent drama, dance, photography, and television departments, and it's not uncommon to see students who haven't yet finished B.F.A. degrees performing in Broadway shows.

> **"Going to NYU prepares students to live and work in the real world."**

Wall Street's future bulls and bears graze at the Stern School of Business, where they benefit from the school's signature undergraduate business program, as well as unique degree offerings such as business and political economy and business, technology, and entrepreneurship. The Leslie eLab also provides space for aspiring entrepreneurs. Another favorite department among students (and the New York corporations who recruit them after graduation) is accounting, known for its high job-placement rate. In the College of Arts and Science, economics, English, journalism, history, politics, and global liberal studies win the highest marks from students. The Tandon School of Engineering, the Steinhardt School, the Silver School of Social Work, the College of Nursing, and the School of Professional Studies offer a bevy of career-based programs, including engineering, education, media, nutrition, and real estate. Steinhardt's offerings in music, music theatre, and music business are notable. Across the university, the most popular majors are in business, visual and performing arts, the social sciences, and computer science. The Gallatin School of Individualized Study offers students the opportunity to craft their own concentration. For those tempted to hang out around the Village for more than four years, there's a seven-year dental program and several five-year bachelor's/master's programs.

Finding a cheap New York apartment may be easier than sailing through NYU's challenging academics. Regardless of major, everyone is very focused on career preparation—it's never enough to just concentrate on your classes. "It's common for students to take on difficult course loads, along with a job or internship," explains a film and television major. Despite the university's mammoth size, 60 percent of classes taken by undergraduates have fewer than 20 students. Graduate students might lead foreign language sections, writing workshops, and the recitations that accompany lectures, but students still say teaching is usually top-notch and professors are reasonably accessible. "Surprisingly, most of our introductory courses are taught by really great and well-known professors," says one student.

Point to a spot on a world map and you'll likely hit a country hosting undergraduates from NYU, which sends more of them abroad than any other school. "At NYU, studying away is not a matter of 'if' but 'where,'" says a junior. In addition to its campuses in Abu Dhabi and Shanghai, the university has 13 academic sites in cities from Buenos Aires and Prague to Sydney and Tel Aviv, as well as exchange agreements with universities in other locations throughout the

> **"Most of our introductory courses are taught by really great and well-known professors."**

world. More than half of NYU undergrads study abroad, sometimes as early as their first year through the university's Liberal Studies. Locally, internships range from jobs on Wall Street to assignments with film industry giants. The career center is "amazingly personal and well run," says an econ major, and it has thousands of listings for on-campus jobs, full-time jobs, and internships. Students qualifying for first-year honors seminars study in small classes under top faculty and eminent visiting professors. An annual undergraduate research conference at the College of Arts and Science gives students the chance to present findings from their research.

An international politics major says NYU students are "high-achieving individuals, cosmopolitan, independent, self-driven, and confident." Thanks in part to the university's investment in student housing, 66 percent of undergraduates now come from outside New York State, including a substantial 26 percent from outside the United States. In-staters hail primarily from the city and nearby suburbs. Black students make up 7 percent of undergrads, Asian Americans 22 percent, Hispanics/Latinos 14 percent, and multiracial students 4 percent. On this generally liberal campus, social justice, immigration policy, the Israeli-Palestinian conflict, and rights of all kinds—LGBTQ, animal, human, and workers'—are important, students say. Although most financial aid is need-based, merit awards averaging $19,700 are available; athletic scholarships are not. Under the NYU Promise initiative, the university pledges to meet the full demonstrated need of incoming first-year students in New York, ensuring that families earning less than $100,000 with typical assets will not have to pay tuition.

Whereas NYU students once had to fend for themselves in New York's outrageous housing market, the university now guarantees four years of housing to all first-years (and most transfers) who seek it. Twenty-two residence halls, ranging from old hotels to a converted monastery, provide a wide range of accommodations. Most rooms have private baths and are larger, cleaner, newer, and better equipped than many city apartments, enticing 38 percent of students to

> **"[NYU students are] high-achieving individuals, cosmopolitan, independent, self-driven, and confident."**

stay in campus-owned housing. Opines a senior, "Housing is lovely although expensive, like everything else in Manhattan." First-year students reside largely in first-year residence halls, many of which have themed floors, and rooms are assigned by lottery each spring. The university provides free shuttle buses to dorms that are farther uptown or downtown. The dining halls offer extensive choices—from wraps to sushi to a dedicated kosher eatery. "The dining halls really try to accommodate everyone," says one student. Of course, downtown's array of ethnic restaurants also offers a variety of food at cheap prices.

NYU's library is one of the largest open-stack facilities in the country, with millions of volumes.

NYU has set its sights on becoming the world's first truly global university, with campuses also in Abu Dhabi, UAE, and Shanghai, China.

Because NYU is large and fairly decentralized, the Student Resource Center helps students navigate university resources and services. The university's Wellness Exchange provides students with a hotline that connects them with professionals who can help them address daily challenges or crises they may encounter, and S.P.A.C.E. (Sexual Misconduct Prevention, Assistance, Counseling, and Education) provides comprehensive resources and support. Students also meet with academic advisors—usually professors in their major department—at least once a semester. For concerned parents and students, NYU hosts a series of workshops on keeping safe, and programs like the NYU Trolley and Safe Ride Van Service provide door-to-door service for students until 3 a.m. "I always feel safe," says a linguistics major. "I can't walk more than one block without seeing an NYU security officer or an NYPD car just patrolling the area."

NYU's social life is divided between the campus and the city. "Students can be found all over the Village and NYC enjoying one of the most vibrant social scenes on the planet," enthuses a romance languages and psychology major. Many students march in the city's Halloween Parade, which takes over the Village, while most fall and spring weekends find a city-sponsored street fair somewhere nearby. On campus, there are concerts, movies, fraternity and sorority events (only 2 percent of the men and 5 percent of the women go Greek), and more than 300 clubs and organizations. Underage students caught with alcohol in public areas in the dorms may lose their housing. The rest take their chances with the notoriously strict bouncers at bars and clubs around Manhattan. The springtime Strawberry Festival includes free berries, cotton candy, outdoor concerts, and carnival amusements. The Violet Ball, a dinner/dance held each fall in the atrium of Bobst Library, offers an excuse to get dressed up. "We graduate at Yankee Stadium, which is incredible," cheers a senior.

While sports have not traditionally been a big emphasis at NYU, successful Violets programs include women's basketball and cross country (both 2025 national champs) as well as men's and women's fencing and swimming and diving, all of which compete in Division III. Roughly one-third of undergrads participate in intramural sports, which include flag football, bowling, and indoor cricket.

The heartbeat of New York City thumps day and night; NYU students thrive on all that energy and know how to capture it in their studies and social lives. "To be an NYU student is to be part college student, part New Yorker," a senior says. "Don't come here if you're not up to working hard and moving fast."

Overlaps

Boston University, UC Berkeley, Carnegie Mellon, Columbia, Cornell University, Northeastern, Penn, University of Southern California

If You Apply To ›

NYU: Early decision I and II, regular decision. Accepts the Common Application. Portfolio or audition required for some programs. Please consult NYU's website for the most up-to-date information regarding standardized test requirements.

University of North Carolina Asheville

1 University Heights, Asheville, NC 28804

Located in a picturesque mountain setting outside the progressive and arts-minded city from which it takes its name, UNC Asheville is North Carolina's contribution to the tradition of "public liberal arts" colleges. With 2,700 full-time, degree-seeking students, it is about half the size of William & Mary and somewhat smaller than Mary Washington. By Southern standards, a progressive university in a progressive city.

The University of North Carolina Asheville offers all of the perks that are generally associated with pricier private institutions: rigorous academics, small classes, and a beautiful setting. And it does it for a fraction of the cost. This public liberal arts and sciences university continues to integrate experiential learning into its traditional curriculum, emphasizing undergraduate research, internships, and service-learning experiences. According to a mass communication major, "We definitely lean into the culture of being a mountain school, a smaller school, and a liberal arts school."

Located in the heart of North Carolina's gorgeous Blue Ridge Mountains, the 360-acre campus lies in the middle of one million acres of federal and state forest near the tallest mountain in the East and the most heavily visited national park in the country. The campus was built in the 1960s when the university, whose origins go back to 1927, joined the UNC system. Much of the brick architecture reflects the style of that decade, although many of the buildings have been renovated in recent years, including a high-tech science and multimedia building. The Botanical Gardens at Asheville, adjacent to the main campus, features thousands of native plants and trees and serves as a wildlife refuge and study center for biology students. The STEAM Studio, located just off campus, brings together science, engineering, and art students in one collaborative, state-of-the-art makerspace.

Asheville's Core Curriculum is required of all undergraduates. In addition to first-year and senior-capstone liberal arts seminars, students must complete a course in Foundations of American Democracy and take courses in areas spanning the humanities, sciences, and mathematics. The most popular majors at Asheville are psychology, biology, health sciences, and environmental studies. As with several other campuses in the UNC system, UNCA has been experiencing enrollment declines and budget deficits. As a result, UNCA eliminated four departments with a low number of majors—religious studies, philosophy, drama, and ancient Mediterranean studies, or classics. French and German are now offered as minors. Students can continue to take advantage of Asheville's strengths as a global source of information for climate and atmospheric sciences—the NOAA National Centers for Environmental Information, the world's largest archive of climate data, and UNC Asheville partner NEMAC (National Environmental Modeling and Analysis Center), are both located in downtown Asheville. "UNC Asheville is a very environmentally friendly, artsy school," says a management major. A B.S. in astronomy has been added, the first and only degree of its kind in the UNC system. A joint B.S. degree in engineering (with a concentration in mechatronics engineering) with North Carolina State University is the only such program in the state.

Courses are challenging, but "UNC Asheville is laid-back and slower paced, which might be different for students who are used to competition and a faster-paced lifestyle," comments an economics major. Many classes have an average of 15 students, and a number of them have service-learning components. As a French and political science double major points out, "Our faculty's mentorship and close relationships are especially evident in undergraduate research." Research is indeed a key emphasis here: Asheville founded the National Conference on Undergraduate Research and has hosted the conference five times. Seventy percent of Asheville students will have an undergraduate research experience by graduation. The UNC Asheville honors program offers special courses—as well as cultural and social opportunities—to motivated students. Study abroad is an option too, in programs available in more than 50 countries. "Career advising is strong, and they constantly reach out to students about future plans," says a senior. The Career Center provides funding for students pursuing unpaid, off-campus internships.

> "UNC Asheville is a very environmentally friendly, artsy school."

Website: www.unca.edu
Location: Small City
Public
Total Enrollment: 2,700
Undergraduates: 2,676
Male/Female: 41/59
Financial Aid: 89%
Pell Grant: 37%
Expense: Pub $
Student Loans: 54%
Average Debt: $
Applicants: 7,378
Accepted: 92%
Enrolled: 11%
Grad in 6 Years: 54%
Returning First-years: 72%
Academics: ✍ ✍ ✍ ✍
Social: 🗩 🗩 🗩
Q of L: ★ ★ ★ ★
Admissions: (828) 251-6481
Email Address:
  admissions@unca.edu

Strong Programs:
Atmospheric Sciences
Biology
Environmental Studies
Health Sciences
Mass Communication
Music
Psychology
Visual Arts

The NOAA National Centers for Environmental Information and UNC Asheville partner NEMAC (National Environmental Modeling and Analysis Center) are both located in Asheville.

Fifteen percent of students come from out of state and another 2 percent from abroad. (The state limits its out-of-state admits to 25 percent.) Asheville has shed its early reputation as a hippie haven, but students still value individualism. "My fellow students are generally very smart, interesting, artsy, and have a variety of passions," explains a sociology major. Currently, the student body is 6 percent Black, 10 percent Hispanic/Latino, 1 percent Asian American, and 5 percent multiracial. Students say the campus is home to a strong LGBTQ community, and "students are also generally very liberal and left-leaning and try to build a welcoming environment," says a sophomore. Issues of environmental sustainability and the cutting of DEI programs get particular attention on campus. Asheville offers roughly 200 athletic scholarships as well as merit scholarships averaging $2,700; 37 percent of incoming first-years receive Pell Grants.

Fifty-five percent of the students live in the residence halls, which offer single and double rooms as well as suite-style options. "Housing is very nice and convenient but expensive," says a junior. Residential learning communities offer special residential and academic options for students with similar interests, such as the Cloud (for computer science and atmospheric sciences majors) and the Transfer Learning Community (for transfer students). For meals, students may eat dining-hall fare or grab

> "Our faculty's mentorship and close relationships are especially evident in undergraduate research."

something quick at retail outlets around campus, including at local food trucks. Students say they feel safe on campus, and the Health and Counseling Center also receives high marks. "We oftentimes have therapy dogs come to Highsmith Student Union and the students can hang out with them and pet them," cheers a senior.

Social life at Asheville is fairly low-key. Greek life is not an influential presence, with only 2 percent of the men and 1 percent of the women joining up. Most parties take place off campus, especially since RAs tightly monitor underage drinking in the dorms. "There is no tolerance for unsafe, underage, or unwise drinking," says a student. There are more than 60 student organizations, including the student newspaper, *The Blue Banner*. Several campuswide events bring the school together each year, including Rockypalooza, which kicks off the fall semester, the Turning of the Maples in October (featuring apple cider, maple cookies, and bluegrass music on the quad), and homecoming. During Greenfest, explains a student, the campus community gathers to "do outdoor service work on campus and attend informative talks about environmental issues."

The city of Asheville, long a haven for artists and an increasingly popular retirement destination, offers a tame but inviting nightlife, especially artsy West Asheville, where students hang out and enjoy the laptop-sized slices at PIE.ZZA pizza. The city

> "Housing is very nice and convenient but expensive."

has been named Beer City USA several times. Asheville is also home to a bevy of street performers, outdoor music festivals, and live entertainment events. For the many Asheville students with a hankering for the great outdoors, the university is surrounded by the Blue Ridge Mountains and the Smokies, where students can hike and rock climb; water buffs can go rafting and kayaking on the nearby rivers. Preorientation wilderness trips and urban excursions help build friendships among first-years. Those with cars can head to Greenville and Charlotte, one and two hours away, respectively.

The Division I Bulldogs boast Big South Conference teams in 16 sports. Men's and women's tennis and eSports have won their conference championships. Basketball is also successful. "We have a great rivalry with Western Carolina," says a health sciences major. Intramurals and club sports are at least as popular as the varsity sports (especially ultimate Frisbee and basketball), as are outdoor adventure trips and the on-campus challenge course and bike shop.

The STEAM Studio, located just off campus, brings together science, engineering, and art students in one collaborative, state-of-the-art makerspace.

Overlaps

Appalachian State, Christopher Newport, Furman, New College of Florida, UNC Charlotte, NC State, St. Mary's College of Maryland, Wooster

In September 2024, Hurricane Helene devastated western North Carolina, including Asheville. A year later, recovery efforts are ongoing but "the region's trails, rivers, and cycling routes are ready for adventure, and downtown galleries, shops, and restaurants are thriving," says a UNCA official. That includes UNC Asheville, where all the ingredients for a superior college experience lie in wait: strong academics, dedicated professors, and an administration that continues to push for excellence. It's a place to get the kind of liberal arts education and tight community usually associated with private colleges—but at the cost of a public university. "Everything feels connected here in the best way possible," says an enthusiastic senior, while a sociology major attests, "If prospective students enjoy good art, music, and interesting people, the school is a good fit."

If You Apply To ›

UNC Asheville: Early action, regular decision. Accepts the Common Application with supplement. Please consult UNC Asheville's website for the most up-to-date information regarding standardized test requirements.

University of North Carolina at Chapel Hill

Chapel Hill, NC 27599

Close on the heels of UVA as the South's most prestigious public university. With 82 percent of the spots in each incoming class reserved for in-staters, admission is selective but not impossible for out-of-staters who aren't 6'9" with a 43-inch vertical jump. Traditionally known for its success in basketball, UNC recently began investing heavily in football. Political interference in academic policies is a growing issue. Chapel Hill is a quintessential college town.

Welcome to "the Southern part of heaven," a place where the sky is Carolina blue and the academics are red-hot. As the flagship campus of the state university system, the University of North Carolina at Chapel Hill has earned its place among the South's most prestigious universities. The atmosphere here is a unique brand of Southern, a rowdy mixture of hard work, sports fanaticism, and traditions that seems to attract bright, serious, and fun-loving students from everywhere.

Chartered in 1789, UNC was the first public university in the United States to open its doors in 1795, and North Carolinians still take pride in Carolina's identity as "the University of the people." UNC's gorgeous and comfortable campus occupies 730 acres lush with trees and lawns and brick-paved walkways. The architecture ranges from Palladian, Federal, and Georgian to postmodern, with red brick the prevailing motif. The Old Well, the university's symbol, stands at the northern end of the campus.

The university's IDEAs in Action general education curriculum emphasizes the first-year experience, interdisciplinary learning, undergraduate research, and out-of-class experiences like internships and study abroad. The curriculum centers on developing skills in nine "focus capacities"—categories of courses that range from quantitative reasoning to ethical and civic values. In their first year, students take a College Thriving course, which eases the transition to college life. They also choose either a First-Year Seminar on a specialized topic, such as the Interplay of Music and Physics, or a First-Year Launch course that provides an introduction to a major. All

Website: www.unc.edu
Location: Small Town
Public
Total Enrollment: 27,423
Undergraduates: 20,123
Male/Female: 39/61
Financial Aid: 67%
Pell Grant: 17%
Expense: Pub $
Student Loans: 26%
Average Debt: $
Applicants: 66,535
Accepted: 15%
Enrolled: 45%
Grad in 6 Years: 91%
Returning First-years: 97%
Academics: ✐ ✐ ✐ ✐
Social: 🗩 🗩 🗩 🗩
Q of L: ★ ★ ★ ★
Admissions: (919) 966-3621
Email Address: unchelp@admissions.unc.edu

students take a Foundations of American Democracy class along with additional foundation and general education courses.

Chapel Hill offers around 75 undergraduate degree programs. Some of the strongest are communication and media studies, business administration, chemistry, sociology, English, global studies, and philosophy. Other popular majors include biology, psychology, economics, and computer science. The university has developed a broad range of opportunities to help students become entrepreneurial, including an entrepreneurship minor and the Carolina Case Challenge, a student-run competition that awards $1,500 in prizes each year for the best business plans. An applied sciences bachelor's degree offers tracks in materials engineering and environmental engineering, supplementing the offerings of the Department of Biomedical Engineering, a joint-degree program with North Carolina State University. The Board of Trustees recently bypassed the faculty and normal academic procedures to establish a new School of Civic Life and Leadership as part of an effort to promote conservative academic values, but the new school has struggled with high faculty turnover and other issues. State political leaders have also sparked controversy through increased involvement in governance and hiring policies and issues of academic freedom, especially in the social sciences.

"Although this is a prestigious university, I don't feel a sense of competition at all," says one sophomore. Academic and social life are governed by a student-run honor system. Forty-two percent of classes enroll fewer than 20 students, and access to registration is based on seniority. The Carolina faculty is, for the most part, top-notch. Professors keep regular office hours, and a history major says, "The majority of professors go out of their way to help students and make sure that they are learning everything they possibly can." Regarding career preparation, a senior cheers, "Our career services department on campus puts effort into each and every student."

> **"Our career services department on campus puts effort into each and every student."**

Undergraduate research is prevalent in all disciplines, and many students present their findings at professional conferences, publish results in academic journals, and win fellowships to support summer research in the United States and abroad. For those tired of the classroom rush, Research Triangle Park, a nearby research and corporate community and home of the National Humanities Center, employs many students as research assistants. UNC's robust study abroad program draws 28 percent of students and offers a wide range of options that include classes, internships, research opportunities, and service learning. Summer School, including the three-week "Maymester," provides undergraduates with diverse course options, some with off-campus travel or research opportunities not possible during the academic year. One-third of the students are involved in community service, many through a service-learning program for which they receive academic credit. Additionally, UNC's honors program is nationally recognized.

The annual Carolina Jazz Festival and Halloween Celebration on Franklin Street draw enthusiastic crowds.

"Carolina students are proud to attend this school, and they bleed Carolina blue," says one Tar Heel. Out-of-state admission is extremely tough; by statute, 82 percent of first-year undergraduates must be North Carolina residents. Six percent of all undergrads come from foreign countries. Big social and political issues on campus include multiculturalism, gender roles, and religion. Black students account for 7 percent of the student body, Asian Americans 16 percent, Hispanics/Latinos 10 percent, and multiracial students 5 percent. Women outnumber men on campus 3 to 2. UNC awards a limited number of highly competitive academic scholarships, along with over 400 athletic scholarships. What's more, the university is need-blind in admissions and commits to meeting

> **"Carolina students are proud to attend this school."**

the full demonstrated financial need of all admitted students—one of only two public universities in the U.S. to do so (see also University of Virginia). The Carolina Covenant program, which has served as a national model to universities seeking to increase socioeconomic diversity, offers scholarships, grants, and work-study as well as extensive mentoring and other support to qualifying students who are at or below 200 percent of the poverty level. UNC covers tuition and mandatory fees for undergraduate North Carolina residents whose family income is less than $80,000 per year.

First-year students are required to live on campus, and 43 percent of all undergraduates live in university housing, which "is an invaluable part of the experience," according to one student. Housing on the north side of campus offers old and recently renovated dorms; the south side offers several new housing options, which are a 15-minute hike from academic buildings (not to worry—there's a free campus shuttle). "The pickiest of the picky could be happy with Carolina dining services," says a first-year. Campus security is praised for its constant presence. "Sexual assault has become a very visible issue in the sense that people are more willing to talk about it," comments a sociology major, adding that the university has "taken steps to address the issue."

"'College town' in the dictionary should show a picture of Chapel Hill," boasts one senior. Franklin Street, the main drag in town that runs across the northern boundary of campus, offers ethnic restaurants, ice-cream parlors, coffeehouses, vegetarian eateries, bakeries, a dance club, a generous supply of bars, and the Varsity movie theater. Fraternities and sororities may account for only 7 percent of the men and 12 percent of the women, but they exert an influence far beyond their numbers. "Fraternities are a social hub, and many students flock to their off-campus parties," confirms one student. Between Greek life and other campus-sponsored activities, "There are always five or six things happening on any given day," says a political science major. FallFest kicks off the school year with an emphasis on the idea that you don't have to drink to have fun. The annual Carolina Jazz Festival and Halloween Celebration on Franklin Street draw enthusiastic crowds. And, as a senior explains, "We also have other fun traditions: students taking a sip from the Old Well, climbing up the Bell Tower, and streaking before finals (though we're not supposed to talk about that last one)."

Student and alumni enthusiasm for Tar Heel athletics is legendary, and the word "popular" doesn't do justice to the basketball games. A contest between Tar Heel hoopsters and NC State makes any Carolina fan's heart beat faster, but Duke takes the prize as the most reviled of all devils. The Tar Heels play in the 21,750-seat Smith Center, named for the late coach Dean Smith, one of the winningest college basketball coaches of all time. Starting with the 2024 hiring of former New England Patriots football coach Bill Belichick, UNC has begun investing tens of millions of dollars in hopes of becoming a force on the gridiron as well as the basketball court. Women's lacross brought home the 2025 national championship. Field hockey, men's and women's tennis, and women's soccer, baseball, men's cross-country, and golf are also highly competitive. Extensive intramural and club sports programs draw heavy participation; intramural basketball and soccer alone each boast rosters of more than 200 teams. The women's ultimate Frisbee team has won several championships. Those who crave fresh air can take advantage of the Outdoor Education Center's mountain bike trails, rope courses, and one of the longest double zip lines on the East Coast.

As a popular saying goes, "If God is not a Tar Heel, why is the sky Carolina blue?" It's a cute turn of phrase but also points to the passion that is well-known in these parts. As one of the best college buys in the country, UNC-Chapel Hill gives

"The pickiest of the picky could be happy with Carolina dining services."

students everything they want, both academically and socially. Current controversies over the preservation of academic freedom and other traditional values notwithstanding, North Carolina's flagship university, with its 231-year history, sustains an atmosphere of extreme pride, a love of tradition, and monumental school spirit. One first-year, full of that school spirit, says, "Southern hospitality blended with a high level of thinking, an overwhelming dose of friendliness and pep, and a spectacularly gorgeous campus make Chapel Hill my favorite place in the world."

If You Apply To ›

UNC at Chapel Hill: Early action, regular decision. Accepts the Common Application with supplement. Please consult UNC at Chapel Hill's website for the most up-to-date information regarding standardized test requirements.

University of North Carolina Wilmington

601 S College Road, Wilmington, NC 28403

Still overshadowed by Chapel Hill and the other biggies in the strong UNC system but making a name for itself. Strong in marine biology and other sciences. You won't see the Seahawks in the NCAA Final Four anytime soon, but you will be able to get to know your professors. Students tend to think of themselves as "hardworking beachgoers."

Website: www.uncw.edu
Location: Small City
Public
Total Enrollment: 14,297
Undergraduates: 12,983
Male/Female: 38/62
Financial Aid: 68%
Pell Grant: 25%
Expense: Pub $
Student Loans: 52%
Average Debt: $ $
Applicants: 20,393
Accepted: 64%
Enrolled: 21%
Grad in 6 Years: 71%
Returning First-years: 88%
Academics: ✍ ✍
Social: 🗩 🗩
Q of L: ★ ★ ★
Admissions: (910) 962-3243
Email Address:
 admissions@uncw.edu

Strong Programs:
Business Administration
Chemistry
Communication Studies

At the University of North Carolina Wilmington, the state's only coastal university, students enjoy extensive undergraduate research opportunities, a slate of solid sciences, and a close-knit community of individuals who like their modern academics mixed with a bit of old-fashioned Southern charm. "If a student is looking for a school where they can take a yoga minor with a biochemistry major and go to the beach at least once a day, this is the place," cheers a nursing major. The university's proximity to the ocean also provides a natural lab for the school's stellar coastal and marine sciences programs.

Founded as Wilmington College in 1947, UNCW moved to its present location in the heart of New Hanover County in 1961. The 660-acre campus is only minutes from Wrightsville Beach and historic downtown Wilmington and features Georgian architecture and designated conservation areas. These conservation areas are significant zones of natural beauty with their longleaf pines, oaks, dogwoods, and native magnolias. Notable campus landmarks include the clock tower, the library's Discovery Hall, Chancellor's Walk, and the campus life complex, which serves as the hub of the university community. In the past few years, UNCW has undertaken more than $460 million in campus construction with numerous buildings being built or restored, including four residence halls, a dining hall, a film studies building, a coastal engineering building, and the library.

> "Our university places a large emphasis on lab and fieldwork."

UNCW's University Studies curriculum requires students to complete coursework in three main categories—Foundations, Building Competencies, and Approaches and Perspectives—and to complete one approved Explorations Beyond the Classroom experience, such as an internship or a study abroad program. First-year students benefit from a range of special programs including a five-week Summer Bridge Program that gives them a jump start on taking core classes and utilizing campus resources. Many go on to take a first-year seminar, capped at 25 students.

"The general population at UNCW has a fairly relaxed attitude toward academics," attests a film studies major. Some of the most popular majors are in the health professions, business, psychology, communication studies, and biology. The university's strengths lie in the natural sciences, especially marine biology, chemistry, ecology, and other disciplines that form the core of the marine sciences. "Our university places a large emphasis on lab and fieldwork," says one geography major. UNCW also offers solid programs in film studies, creative writing, and cybersecurity. Coastal engineering, the first program of its kind in the nation, provides unique opportunities for research, including a state-of-the-art wave flume. First-years are taught by full professors, and a sophomore says, "You are more than able to receive one-on-one help from a professor or TA." Enrollments in introductory courses sometimes swell to more than 100, but 36 percent of all classes have fewer than 20 students.

More than 2,000 military-affiliated students are enrolled at UNCW, a veteran-friendly campus. Veterans Hall, a 145,000-square-foot facility, houses the College of Health and Human Services, Pharmaceutical Chemistry Program, and the Office of Military Affairs. For students yearning to experience new vistas, UNCW offers hundreds of approved study abroad trips in more than 50 countries. Students in the UNCW Honors College engage in living/learning communities, advanced coursework, and experiential seminars; honors students also "complete a thesis during their senior year that will be published as a part of the UNCW library collection," explains one member.

According to a marketing major, UNCW students are "hardworking beachgoers. Every student here is motivated but enjoys a little time off as well." Eighty-four percent of undergrads are native to North Carolina, and 1 percent are international. "Students come from all backgrounds in terms of race, socioeconomics, politics, and geography," says a junior. Black students represent 4 percent of the student body, Hispanics/Latinos 9 percent, Asian Americans 2 percent, and multiracial students 3 percent. Students describe a "relaxed" balance of liberal and conservative political views. "We're a coastal school, so many students are passionate about clean-water programs and recycling," reports a senior. Outstanding students can vie for nearly 700 donor-funded scholarships. Under UNCW's Support Opportunity Access Responsibility (SOAR) Scholarship program, high-achieving students from low-income families may receive grants and scholarships equaling at least the cost of in-state tuition and fees, in addition to federal loans or work-study funding if needed.

"How much better can a social scene get than the beach?"

All first-years and sophomores (except commuters who live at home with a parent or guardian) are required to reside on campus. Options range from traditional dorms to sophomore suites and apartments for upperclassmen. Most students who move off campus stay within a mile or so of the school. Campus eateries include Wagoner Hall, Dub's Café, the Shore, the Hawks Nest food court, and the Hub; students give the food positive reviews. "The food is delicious, and every student has at least one favorite dining hall," reports an elementary education major. "UNCW also does a great job of meeting dietary needs and restrictions." The career center gets high marks; students also praise campus police for keeping the area secure. "UNCW offers a strong mental health center that is available to students 24/7," says a nursing major.

When it comes to social life, a junior asks, "How much better can a social scene get than the beach?" Students look forward to homecoming, the communal Thanksgiving dinner called Wagsgiving, and the annual Oozeball mud volleyball

Students look forward to the communal Thanksgiving dinner called Wagsgiving and the annual Oozeball mud volleyball tournament.

First-year students benefit from a five-week Summer Bridge Program that gives them a jump start on taking core classes.

tournament. Additionally, "UNCWeekends puts something on every weekend for students both on and off campus," says a public health major. Fraternities and sororities attract 11 percent of the men and 9 percent of the women, respectively. The party scene is far from raucous, students report, and underage drinkers face stiff penalties if caught. Wilmington "offers a lot of really cool things to do, especially in the downtown district," says a student, and it has its share of restaurants, bars, and shops. Road trips include jaunts to Myrtle Beach, the Outer Banks, Washington, D.C., and the Appalachian Mountains.

UNCW fields 19 varsity teams that compete in Division I. Recent Coastal Athletic Association conference champions include men's and women's swimming and diving teams, men's basketball, and men's tennis. "Seahawk basketball is huge!" raves one first-year, especially when the College of Charleston is on the court. "Every time UNCW plays them, Trask Coliseum will be packed like a can of sardines and we get very loud," says a junior. Club and intramural sports are also popular, especially flag football, basketball, soccer, and ultimate Frisbee. UNCW men's rugby won its first-ever national title in 2025, while the university's surf team and club captured the East Coast Regional Championship. Sea kayaking and paddleboarding trips organized by Seahawk Adventures are other favorite diversions. The new outdoor sports complex provides enhanced spaces for general use, intramural sports, and sports clubs.

Despite complaints of limited parking and the lack of football, students at the University of North Carolina Wilmington are a happy lot. "Maybe it's because we're at the beach or maybe it's because we're in North Carolina," says a sophomore, "but one thing is for sure, UNCW is not a pressure cooker and nearly everyone is nice, welcoming, and contributes something of value to the community."

Overlaps

Appalachian State, College of Charleston, East Carolina, UNC at Chapel Hill, UNC Charlotte, UNC Greensboro, North Carolina State, University of South Carolina

If You Apply To ›

UNC Wilmington: Early action, regular decision. Accepts the Common Application with supplement. Please consult UNC Wilmington's website for the most up-to-date information regarding standardized test requirements.

North Carolina State University

Raleigh, NC 27695

NC State is a powerhouse in North Carolina's Research Triangle and beyond—just ask the thousands of graduates who have moved into jobs in the area. It has become more selective, and engineering, business, and biology are the most popular programs. Location in the state capital a mixed blessing given growing willingness of state legislators to meddle in academic and governance policies of their public universities. Compare to Clemson and Virginia Tech.

Website: www.ncsu.edu
Location: City Center
Public
Total Enrollment: 31,654
Undergraduates: 25,775
Male/Female: 50/50
Financial Aid: 63%

Whether you're looking for a stellar education or a top-rated athletics program, North Carolina State University offers students the benefits of a large school—highly regarded professors, a diverse student body, and plenty to do on weekends—while making sure that no one feels left out. "We're not some ivory tower where knowledge and discoveries live on a shelf," touts an administrator. "We know that when our graduates leave, they've had the opportunity to learn from top-notch scholars and mentors, conduct innovative scientific research, gain work experience with leading companies," and more.

Redbrick buildings, brick-lined walks, and cozy courtyards dotted with pine trees define the campus, founded in 1887. Holladay Hall has been designated as a historic site by the Raleigh City Council, while the ultramodern Hunt Library features a game lab, visualization studio, and digital production suites. For amusement, you can always stroll over and watch its robotic book retrieval system in action. NC State's Centennial Campus, a 1,105-acre, public-private research campus, is home to the $150 million Fitts-Woolard Hall, housing several engineering programs. The $45 million Wellness and Recreation Center boasts a 48-foot-tall climbing wall and top-of-the-line training equipment. The $160 million Plant Sciences Building is a hub of research and innovation and features extensive collaborative space. A permanent eSports gaming arena is expected to be completed in 2026.

General education requirements cover a broad range of liberal arts disciplines in addition to coursework that reflects interdisciplinary perspectives, develops writing skills, and engages students in-depth in an area that is clearly distinct from their major. A Foundations in American Democracy course requirement was added to all North Carolina state schools in 2025. An Exploratory Studies program provides guidance and counseling for incoming students to introduce them to possible majors. "The academic climate is relatively laid-back, and everyone is supportive," says an animal science major. Many classes are large, but faculty get high grades for being accessible and helpful during office hours. A biology major comments, "As with any university, NC State employs some outstanding faculty and some less-than-stellar professors who are more effective in the laboratory than in the lecture hall."

> "We're not some ivory tower where knowledge and discoveries live on a shelf."

NC State excels in the professional areas of engineering, architecture, business, agriculture, and the sciences, which are among the largest and the most demanding divisions. Not surprisingly, given its location in the heart of textile country, the university also boasts the largest and one of the best textiles programs in the nation. Business tops the list of most popular majors, followed by computer science, psychology, and biology. The College of Humanities and Social Sciences is the second largest school in the university, and solid nontechnical areas include communication, English, international studies, and social work. Notable programs are also available in genetics, forest management, biomedical engineering, sport management, and turfgrass science.

An important feature of NC State's approach to education is the cooperative education program, through which students in all schools can alternate semesters of on-site work with traditional classroom time. Twenty-two percent of students conduct undergraduate research. The university benefits greatly from its relationships with private industry through the state's high-tech Research Triangle Park, located nearby, as well as from cooperative ties with Duke and UNC at Chapel Hill. NC State offers close to 200 study abroad programs in more than 50 countries. In the University Scholars program, academic standouts live together and participate in weekly activities such as cultural events, honors classes, and outdoor recreation trips. In the University Honors Program, students enroll in small seminars, attend lectures and artistic performances, participate in high-impact cocurricular experiences, and have the opportunity to join a dedicated living/learning community.

NC State's star continues to rise as it becomes more selective. One student says the student body, a.k.a. Wolfpack, consists mainly of "hardworking and humble" North Carolinians; 87 percent are in-state students, and 2 percent are international. Six percent of undergraduates are Black, 9 percent are Hispanic/Latino, 10 percent are Asian American, and 5 percent are multiracial. Conservatism among students is not uncommon, but in general, according to a junior, "political and social activism are not widespread among the student body." Jocks and sports fans are visible, and

(continued)

Pell Grant: 19%
Expense: Pub $
Student Loans: 45%
Average Debt: $
Applicants: 44,043
Accepted: 42%
Enrolled: 32%
Grad in 6 Years: 80%
Returning First-years: 93%
Academics: ✍ ✍ ✍
Social: 🍷 🍷 🍷
Q of L: ★ ★ ★
Admissions: (919) 515-2434
Email Address: undergrad-admissions@ncsu.edu

Strong Programs:
Agriculture
Architecture
Biology
Business
Communication
Engineering
English
Textiles

Some ardent NC State fans storm nearby Hillsborough Street following game-day victories.

the university offers over 300 athletic scholarships. Those with outstanding academic qualifications can compete for merit scholarships averaging $5,700. The Pack Promise guarantees that every North Carolina resident admitted to NC State with a family income at or below 150 percent of the federal poverty level will receive an aid package that meets 100 percent of their demonstrated financial need.

Thirty-eight percent of students live on campus, which is a requirement for first-years, who choose between hall-style and suite-style accommodations. Eleven percent of students opt to reside in the school's 15 Living and Learning Villages, where they can live and socialize with others who share their interests, such as entrepreneurship and women's empowerment. "Not very many people stay on campus after their freshman year," reports a chemistry major. The dining halls feed all first-years and anyone else who cares to join the meal plan, and the food gets positive reviews. Campus safety also receives good ratings.

The 30 fraternities and 19 sororities attract 15 percent of the men and 18 percent of the women. The Greek scene provides much of the entertainment, but parties in dorms and at off-campus apartments are also popular. Alcohol policies are enforced, and if you're thinking about grabbing a brew, "don't try unless you're 21," warns a senior. A junior says, "There are always countless free events going on campus: concerts, festivals, free movies, or outdoor activities." Packapalooza, "a huge block party on Hillsborough Street with a free concert at the end," kicks off the academic year, and Wolfstock, a party and concert held on the Saturday before the last day of classes in the spring, closes it. Public transportation affords easy access to downtown, with its shops, restaurants, theaters, and night spots. Many students also like to head to the beach, which is about two hours away, or to the mountains for hiking or skiing, which is about a three-and-a-half-hour trip. Volunteering is popular too with 44 percent of students participating.

> **"There are always countless free events going on campus."**

Students love to cheer on their Division I Wolfpack teams, which do well in baseball, football, wrestling, gymnastics, men's swimming and diving, and women's cross-country. But basketball reigns supreme. Both the men's and women's teams, playing in the high-powered Atlantic Coast Conference, made it to the 2024 Final Four. Some ardent NC State fans storm nearby Hillsborough Street following game-day victories, especially those over archrival UNC at Chapel Hill. Indeed, the annual State versus Carolina football game always packs the stadium, and the never-ending call to "Beat Carolina!" permeates the campus year-round. Club sports and intramurals also thrive; offerings include cricket, flag football, disc golf, and, for those who are light on their feet, ballroom dance.

As in their other state universities, North Carolina political leaders have worked to limit the role of the faculty in shaping academic policies. That said, NC State has moved well beyond its origins as a land grant school focusing on agriculture and engineering. It has attracted a dedicated and friendly student body lured by an emphasis on learning beyond the classroom and inspired by the university's "Think and Do" slogan. NC State works well for those who can shoot hoops and for those who can calculate the trajectory of the same three-point shot.

Overlaps

**Appalachian State,
East Carolina,
Michigan State,
UNC Chapel Hill,
UNC Charlotte,
UNC Wilmington,
Purdue, Virginia
Tech**

If You Apply To ›

NC State: Early action, regular decision. Accepts the Common Application with supplement. Applicants to studio-based majors must submit a portfolio and additional essay. Please consult NC State's website for the most up-to-date information regarding standardized test requirements.

Northeastern University

360 Huntington Avenue, Boston, MA 02115

Northeastern is synonymous with experiential learning through hands-on professional and global experiences. By interspersing co-op jobs with academic study, students can get an edge in the job market while earning money and jump-starting their careers. Huge spike in applications and soaring ambitions have led to the creation of two additional undergraduate campuses in London and Oakland as well as first-year programs worldwide. With students always coming and going at the Boston hub, campus life can be uneven, but Northeastern has transformed its central university from blue-collar urban into Boston chic.

Long known for its co-op program and hands-on learning experiences, Northeastern University has become a top-tier institution. More selective than ever, NU has added new facilities and recruited big-name professors while continuing to combine liberal arts requirements with up to 18 months of challenging work placements. "Northeastern is a university that is focused on preparing for the future and gaining experience while attending college," cheers a health science major. "Northeastern cares about setting its students up for success in the postgrad world."

Northeastern's 73-acre Boston campus is an unlikely oasis located in the heart of the city, just minutes away from Fenway Park, shopping centers, nightclubs, cafés, Symphony Hall, and the Museum of Fine Arts. The campus's green spaces are interspersed with brick walkways, sculptures, and outdoor art. Older buildings are utilitarian gray brick, while newer structures are modern glass and brick. During inclement weather, students can be found navigating the underground tunnel system that connects many campus buildings. No longer a commuter college, NU has had the rare luxury for an urban institution of having erstwhile parking lots available for new construction. The state-of-the-art Interdisciplinary Science and Engineering Complex furthers NU's emphasis on applied—or, to use the local jargon, "use-inspired"—research.

Northeastern's core curriculum (known as NUpath) embraces writing-intensive instruction, mathematical/analytical thinking, and comparative understanding of religions and cultures. Students must take part in a first-year learning community, integrated experiential learning, and a capstone experience in their major. Woven into the Northeastern experience is its signature co-op program—which dates to 1909 and is the second oldest in the country. Seventy-five percent of students complete two co-ops, each four to six months in length. Working with a specialized co-op advisor, students may choose from more than 3,500 established co-op employer partners located in more than 149 countries, or they may propose their own co-op. Destinations range from nonprofits in Boston to a digital advertising agency in the Czech Republic, a children's occupational therapy center in Uganda, or even an Antarctic research station. Faculty members and dedicated co-op advisors prepare students for their co-ops with a special course beforehand, check in with them while they are out in the field, and organize academic reflection on the experience afterward. "The professors at Northeastern expect a lot from students but are happy to give support to students who ask for it," says a biomedical physics major. Fifty-one percent of classes have fewer than 20 students.

NU's undergraduate programs are housed in seven academic colleges, including the College of Arts, Media, and Design; the D'Amore-McKim School of Business;

> **"Northeastern as a university that is focused on preparing for the future."**

Website: www.northeastern.edu

Location: City Center

Private

Total Enrollment: 38,155

Undergraduates: 22,664

Male/Female: 43/57

Financial Aid: 69%

Pell Grant: 17%

Expense: Pr $ $ $

Student Loans: 44%

Average Debt: $ $ $

Applicants: 98,425

Accepted: 5%

Enrolled: 54%

Grad in 6 Years: 91%

Returning First-years: 97%

Academics: ✍ ✍ ✍

Social: 🗩 🗩

Q of L: ★ ★

Admissions: (617) 373-2200

Email Address: admissions@northeastern.edu

Strong Programs:
Architecture
Biological and Life Sciences
Business and Marketing
Computer and Informational Sciences
Engineering
International Business
Journalism
Social Sciences

the Khoury College of Computer Sciences; the College of Engineering; the Bouvé College of Health Sciences; the College of Science; and the College of Social Sciences and Humanities. The Explore Program offers experiential learning opportunities and academic advising to help undeclared students learn about potential majors and careers. Students with diverse interests may select from a slew of combined majors that cross disciplines, such as information science and cognitive psychology, political science and communication studies, and international affairs and cultural anthropology. Architecture and journalism are strengths, and the most popular majors fall under the categories of business and marketing, engineering, computer and information sciences, and health professions. The well-regarded international business program features an "expat year," in which students spend one semester studying at an overseas university and six months working at an international co-op. Health sciences students may pursue a six-year doctor of pharmacy degree, and several "PlusOne" programs allow students to earn a master's degree by completing an additional year of study. High-achieving first-year students may be invited to join the honors program to pursue more challenging coursework and live together in dedicated housing.

The Oakland, California campus, set on a lush 135-acre site on the edge of the Oakland hills, offers a small campus feel near San Francisco, Berkeley, and Silicon Valley. It was acquired in 2022 when Northeastern absorbed struggling Mills College, a women's college, to form a unique "bicoastal" institution of higher education. Now, administrators say, "Oakland is NU's West Coast hub for innovation, experiential learning, and frontier technology." Under the Dialogue of Civilizations program, faculty members take more than 1,200 students abroad each summer. If that or a co-op abroad isn't enough, at Northeastern's London campus, located at St. Katherine Docks, a bustling area near the Thames, students can take advantage of experiential learning in the center of the UK's hub for international relations, finance, and technology.

Northeastern students tend to be academically and professionally driven. "Very quickly, we are sent out into the real world to really understand what we are doing and where we want to go," muses a political science and international affairs major. "This causes us to mature quite quickly." Northeastern was founded in 1898 as a YMCA educational program to serve local students from diverse socioeconomic backgrounds. These days, only 16 percent of undergraduates are from Massachusetts, and 17 percent qualify for Pell Grants. Consistent with Northeastern's efforts to promote a global culture, 13 percent come from overseas. Asian Americans comprise 23 percent of the student body, Hispanics/Latinos 11 percent, Black students 5 percent, and multiracial students 7 percent. Merit scholarships averaging $12,700 are awarded annually, as are nearly 300 athletic scholarships.

All Boston students are required to live in university housing for their first two years. "Every first-year student on the Boston campus is placed in a Living/Learning Community based on anything from their intended major or career path to one of their favorite hobbies," notes a business administration major. After sophomore year, university housing is limited and offered on a space-available basis, so most upperclassmen rent privately owned apartments near campus. The dining halls offer "a lot of options and good food," according to students, who also speak highly of NU Public Safety: "I feel extremely safe on campus even though it is in the middle of the city," says one senior. Another adds, "All Northeastern students go through sexual assault and diversity training that gives us the tools to deal with these issues while on campus, as well as during study abroad and even during our co-op experiences."

When it comes to the social scene, hundreds of clubs and activities abound, but the continuous flow of students on and off the campus for co-ops can be disruptive. "I may see a friend one quarter in class and then not again for six months. It's hard to stay connected," a student explains. Fraternities attract 5 percent of the men and sororities 9 percent of NU women. Favorite traditions include the annual Husky Hunt, a 24-hour scavenger hunt around Boston. "One of the best things about Northeastern is the location," raves a senior. "There is always something to do in Boston," including a seemingly endless array of concerts, museums, clubs, and eateries. Catching a Red Sox game, with student tickets starting as low as $9, is a highlight. In the winter, the ski slopes of Vermont beckon, and in balmier weather, students are off to the beaches of Cape Cod and the North Shore.

Woven into the Northeastern experience is its signature co-op program—which dates to 1909.

Northeastern fields 19 Division I varsity teams (the Huskies) as part of the Colonial Athletic Association and the Hockey East Association. The biggest sports series of the year is the Beanpot Hockey Tournament ("Hockey is king here at Northeastern"), which pits Northeastern against rival teams from Boston College, Boston University, and Harvard. "It is all about bragging rights and pride, and the fans from the schools make it fun," reports a student. One T-shirt reads, "No—we don't want to B.U.," epitomizing the competitive nature of the sports teams in the Boston area. NU's men's and women's ice hockey, women's basketball, and men's baseball teams are recent conference champions, and the fleet-footed men's and women's track and cross-country teams regularly leave their opponents blinking in the dust. The recreation program offers more than 30 intramural options, and with 50-plus club teams, Northeastern is well represented in nonvarsity competition with other schools.

"Every first-year student on the Boston campus is placed in a Living/Learning Community."

Northeastern is a school on the rise. It has moved well beyond its origins as an open admissions commuter school and—through aggressive fundraising, an ambitious building program, and unabashed marketing—adapted its century of experience with co-op education to the emerging global economy. Northeastern students tend to be serious about their studies but learn to wear many hats. "We are employees at co-op, students in class, friends and roommates in our free time," explains one denizen. "We balance work and play while still meeting deadlines." Northeastern students graduate with a broad reservoir of experiences that they know will serve them well once they start scouring those job listings—both in the U.S. and around the world.

Overlaps

Boston College, Boston University, UC Berkeley, Columbia, Cornell University, NYU, Penn, Tufts

If You Apply To ›

Northeastern: Early decision I and II, early action, regular decision. Accepts the Common Application. Please consult Northeastern's website for the most up-to-date information regarding standardized test requirements.

Northwestern University

633 Clark Street, Evanston, IL 60208

The Big Ten is not the Ivy League, and Northwestern has more school spirit than its high-powered Eastern counterparts. Much more preprofessional than its nearby rival University of Chicago or any of the Ivies except Penn, NU is comparable to Duke and Stanford with an academic culture that encourages interdisciplinary work. World-renowned in journalism.

Website: www.northwestern
.edu

Location: Suburban

Private

Total Enrollment: 20,021

Undergraduates: 8,912

Male/Female: 46/54

Financial Aid: 87%

Pell Grant: 19%

Expense: Pr $ $ $ $

Student Loans: 29%

Average Debt: $ $ $

Applicants: 49,474

Accepted: 8%

Enrolled: 55%

Grad in 6 Years: 95%

Returning First-years: 98%

Academics: ✍ ✍ ✍ ✍ ✍

Social: 🗩 🗩 🗩

Q of L: ★ ★ ★

Admissions: (847) 491-7271

Email Address: ug-admission@
northwestern.edu

Strong Programs:

Chemistry

Education

Engineering

History

Journalism

Music

Radio, Television, and Film

Theater

Northwestern consistently has among the highest graduation rates for major football programs.

On Sunday nights before finals begin at Northwestern University, students are encouraged to let off steam with a campuswide "primal scream." The ear-shattering event illustrates two big themes at NU: students work really hard, but they also know how to let loose and enjoy themselves. This elite, top-tier university, the only private school in the Big Ten, boasts some of the most well-respected preprofessional programs in the country. Plus, Northwestern is ideally located just outside of Chicago. "I love being at a place where I can learn and have a great social life," says one student.

Northwestern, founded in 1851 by a group of Methodist ministers and businessmen to serve the former Northwest Territory (hence the name!), is situated on 231 acres about a dozen miles north of the Chicago Loop. An eclectic mix of stone buildings with abundant ivy, the leafy campus is set off from the town of Evanston and runs for a mile along the shore of Lake Michigan. Students migrate between the North Campus (techy) and the South Campus (artsy). The newer buildings are located adjacent to a 14-acre lagoon, part of an 85-acre lakefill addition built in the '60s. This area provides students with a prime location for picnicking, fishing, running, cycling, or just daydreaming. Recent campus additions include the 96,000-square-foot Ryan Fieldhouse, part of a larger $270 million sports complex.

Half of Northwestern's undergraduates are enrolled in arts and sciences, while the other half are spread out among five professional schools, all with national reputations. Indeed, students tend to identify more strongly with their school than with Northwestern as a whole. The Medill School of Journalism, the only such program at a top private university, sends student reporters out with iPads and video cameras as well as spiral notebooks.

"The academics are rigorous and will take some adjustment from high school."

The curriculum integrates multimedia techniques with the study of "audience understanding" and features internships at dozens of top newspapers, magazines, and television stations across the nation. There's also a four-year accelerated B.S.J./M.S.J. program. A dazzling electronic studio centralizes Medill's state-of-the-art broadcast newsroom and the communication school's radio/TV/film department. The School of Communication also houses a notable program in theater. The McCormick School of Engineering and Applied Science is strong in all aspects of engineering and pairs students with clients with practical problems. Five-year co-op options are available. The School of Music wants students who can combine conservatory-level musicianship with high-level academics; it offers a five-year program from which students emerge with two B.A. degrees. The School of Education and Social Policy is the only school of its kind in the country and competes with Vanderbilt for education majors. Students and faculty members alike are encouraged to range across traditional disciplinary barriers—a policy that has led to the creation of some entirely new fields such as materials science—and students are free to switch schools once they are enrolled.

Consistent with this approach, students say the university's best programs include the Integrated Science Program and Mathematical Methods in the Social Sciences, a selective program that gives students the technical skills to move into various areas of the social sciences. Strong arts and sciences departments include chemistry and history, although the humanities as a group are less strong. The social sciences (especially economics, psychology, and political science), journalism, neuroscience, engineering, and visual and performing arts enroll the most majors. Each of the undergraduate schools determines its own general education requirements, but broad outlines are similar. Each school requires a graduate to have coursework in "the major domains of knowledge"—science, mathematics and technology, individual and social behavior, historical studies, values, the humanities, and the fine arts. Incoming students take part in Wildcat Welcome, a weeklong orientation designed to ease the transition into college life.

Unlike most schools on a 10-week quarter system, Northwesterners take four (not three) courses each quarter, except in engineering, where five are permitted. "Students tend to be supportive and collaborative," says a senior, but "the academics are rigorous and will take some adjustment from high school." Virtually all undergraduate courses are taught by regular faculty members. Introductory courses are larger than most, but 76 percent of all undergraduate classes have fewer than 20 students. "The quality of teaching at Northwestern depends on the department and the professor," confides a senior, "but overall, I would say it's very high quality." The Office of Undergraduate Research helps students apply for research assistantships and faculty-mentored independent projects, often with the support of grants. About a third of students take a break from campus through their choice of 150 study abroad programs in 50 countries.

Upon graduating, NU students tend to pursue business fields like consulting and finance, with technology, education, and communication distant followers. "Many students are overachievers," comments a social policy major. "Many are goal- and career-oriented." Twenty-four percent of undergraduates hail from Illinois, and 12 percent come from overseas. Students of color represent a sizable contingent of the student body, with Asian Americans accounting for 21 percent, Black students 8 percent, Hispanics/Latinos 16 percent, and multiracial students 8 percent. Merit scholarships average $21,200, and more than 300 athletic scholarships are available in 19 sports. NU guarantees to meet the full demonstrated need of every admit and has eliminated need-based loans from its financial aid packages.

Fifty-five percent of all undergraduates reside in university housing, mostly in double rooms, although there are also singles, triples, and suites. "Housing varies significantly in quality at Northwestern," reports a journalism and political science major, and a classmate adds, "The nicer dorms on campus are competitive to get into." Several residential colleges, in areas like engineering, commerce and industry, and communication, bring students and faculty members together during faculty "firesides" or simply over meals. Fraternities and sororities also have their own houses. Most upperclassmen move off campus, but a senior cautions, "Housing in Evanston is expensive." Students can choose to eat at any one of six residential dining halls or a variety of restaurants and cafés on campus. "There is always at least one option for halal, kosher, vegan, vegetarian, gluten-free, or allergen-free needs," says a sophomore. Students generally feel safe on campus, but crime has been a concern in Evanston, especially after dark.

"Many students are overachievers. Many are goal- and career-oriented."

Much of the social life at NU is centered on the Greek system, with 14 percent of the men and 18 percent of the women joining up. Some students say finding a social niche can be tough, especially for those who aren't involved in Greek life, athletics, journalism, or theater. The school's alcohol policy is stiff but not always effective, "like the vast majority of campuses nationwide," says a student. The student government and Activities and Organizations Board sponsor an array of campuswide events, including theater productions, concerts, and movies. The 30-hour Dance Marathon and Dillo (Armadillo) Day, an end-of-the-year music festival with big-name artists, food trucks, a beer garden, and art installations, are popular annual events. Another tradition is upheld when representatives of student organizations slip out in the dead of night to paint their colors and slogans on a centrally located rock. In all, there are more than 500 student organizations, ranging from an African drum and dance ensemble to Adshop, an advertising agency that lets students hone their marketing skills by promoting local businesses. Suburban Evanston is "the restaurant haven of Chicago's North Shore," says a junior. A short stroll off campus brings you to the town's myriad restaurant options, trendy bars, and coffee shops with space to plug in a laptop and study, but most businesses close by 10 p.m. For culture or a night out, of course, Chicago is right across the border.

Wildcats Football and tailgate parties are a traditional way of bringing alumni back and rousing the students to support the smallest and only private school in the Division I Big Ten. Northwestern consistently has among the highest graduation rates for major football programs. In 2025, women's field hockey and golf brought home Big Ten championship titles. As far as facilities, NU is on par with many schools its size and larger, with the beautiful Norris Aquatics Center/Henry Crown Sports Pavilion and the Nicolet Football and Conference Center used for conditioning of varsity athletes. The student-sponsored intramural program provides vigorous competition among teams from dorms and rival Greek groups, and over 30 club sports are an option too. Northwestern also boasts one of the winningest debate teams in the country.

> **"The nicer dorms on campus are competitive to get into."**

Northwestern occupies a unique niche in U.S. higher education. It has the academics of the Ivies, the spirited atmosphere of the Big Ten publics, and, along with Duke, Stanford, and perhaps Vanderbilt, combines success in Division I sports with quality instruction. Northwestern students bask in their school's balance of challenging academics, preprofessional bent, and myriad opportunities to get off campus to learn and let loose.

If You Apply To ›

Northwestern: Early decision, regular decision. Accepts the Common Application with supplement. Please consult Northwestern's website for the most up-to-date information regarding standardized test requirements.

University of Notre Dame

Holy Cross Drive, Notre Dame, IN 46556

The Holy Grail of higher education for many Roman Catholics. ND's heartland location and 80-percent-Catholic enrollment make it a bastion of solid education and equally solid values, religious and otherwise. Offers business, science, architecture, and engineering in addition to the liberal arts. ND's personality is much closer to Boston College or Holy Cross than to Georgetown. Only school ever ranked #1 in both football and graduation rates.

Founded in 1842 by the French priest Edward Sorin from the Congregation of Holy Cross, the University of Notre Dame has come a long way from its fledgling days in a rustic log cabin. While described as "a Catholic academic community of higher learning," its students need not be affiliated with the Roman Catholic Church. Notre Dame takes pride in fostering a culture that values open discussion of religious, spiritual, and social issues, and it appeals to non-Catholics who are committed to social justice or seek a broadly spiritual dimension to their education. A soft spot for football doesn't hurt either.

With 1,250 acres of manicured quads, twin lakes, and woods, the university offers a peaceful setting for studying. The lofty Golden Dome that rises above the ivy-covered

Gothic and modern buildings and the old brick stadium, where Knute Rockne made the Fighting Irish almost synonymous with college football, are national icons. The university recently completed a $1.1 billion construction spree that added 20 new buildings in less than a decade, including several new academic buildings and residence halls. The nine-story Duncan Student Center overlooks the football stadium and boasts a career services center, dining facilities, a fitness center with a massive rock-climbing wall, and premium stadium seating for football VIPs. Notre Dame's $20 billion endowment is the largest of any of the country's Catholic colleges and universities.

Liberal education is more than just a catchphrase at Notre Dame. No matter what their major, students must take the First Year of Studies, one of the most extensive academic and counseling programs of any university in the nation. The core of the program is a one-semester writing-intensive university seminar limited to 20 students per section. The remainder of each first-year's schedule is reserved for the first of a comprehensive list of general education requirements covering writing and mathematics, natural science, theology, philosophy, history, social science, and fine arts. Academic and peer advisors are assigned to each student, as are tutors if necessary. Administrators are quick to point out that, due in part to the success of the first-year support program, a whopping 99 percent of first-years make it through and return for sophomore year.

In the College of Arts and Letters, highly regarded departments include English, theology, and philosophy. Physics and chemistry are tops in the College of Science, bolstered by the first-rate equipment in the Nieuwland and Jordan Science Halls. Within the engineering school, chemical engineering rules, while the Mendoza College of Business's accountancy program is ranked among the nation's best. Another standout is the School of Architecture's five-year undergraduate degree program, in which students spend their entire junior year in Rome. The most popular majors overall are finance, economics, neuroscience and behavior, and computer science. Students describe the academic climate as fairly competitive but not cutthroat by any measure. "The workload is very demanding," says a senior. "It requires the student to have very good time-management skills." Sixty percent of classes enroll fewer than 20 students, and students praise faculty members for being dynamic, personable, knowledgeable, and accessible. "The professors here care a great deal about their students, and it shows," says a biology major.

Notre Dame offers a variety of special academic programs and options. One of the most popular is the Program of Liberal Studies, in which students study art, philosophy, literature, and the history of Western thought within their Great Books seminars. The Summer Comprehensive Grant program awards up to $5,000 to students wishing to spend their summer focusing on independent research. Roughly 70 percent of undergrads take part in Notre Dame's extensive international study program, which includes opportunities at the university's Global Gateways in London, Dublin, Rome, Beijing, and Jerusalem.

With a predominantly lay board of trustees and faculty, Notre Dame remains committed to "the preservation of a distinctly Catholic community," and it has a more self-consciously Catholic identity than any other major research university, including Boston College and Georgetown. The president and several other top administrators are priests of the Congregation of Holy Cross, and roughly 80 percent of incoming first-year students identify as Catholic. Each dorm has its own chapel with daily masses, though attendance is not required. The main social issues discussed on campus include abortion; gender, racial, and LGBTQ issues; and faith. Black students make up 5 percent of the undergraduate student body, Hispanics/Latinos 15 percent, Asian Americans 6 percent, and multiracial students 6 percent. Despite its relative cultural homogeneity, Notre Dame recruits from

(continued)

Student Loans: 38%
Average Debt: $ $ $
Applicants: 29,942
Accepted: 11%
Enrolled: 62%
Grad in 6 Years: 95%
Returning First-years: 99%
Academics: ✍ ✍ ✍ ✍
Social: 🗩 🗩 🗩
Q of L: ★ ★ ★
Admissions: (574) 631-7505
Email Address:
  admissions@nd.edu

Strong Programs:
Accountancy
Architecture
Chemical Engineering
Economics
English
Finance
Political Science
Theology

Students must take the First Year of Studies, one of the most extensive academic and counseling programs of any university in the nation.

all over the country; 92 percent of the students are from states outside of Indiana, and 7 percent hail from other countries. Competitive merit awards average $10,100, and families with income up to $150,000 pay no tuition. The university meets full demonstrated financial need without resorting to loans. The Division I powerhouse deals out hundreds of athletic scholarships as well.

Eighty-two percent of ND students live on campus, which is required for their first three years. First-year students are assigned to a residence hall, mixed among the other classes, and they are encouraged to stay in the same one until graduation. Since ND has never had Greek organizations, the single-sex dorms become surrogate fraternities and sororities that breed a similar spirit of community and family. "The dorm culture is a unique part of ND's personality," comments a sophomore. Notre Dame has been co-ed since 1972, and parietal rules (midnight on weekdays, 2 a.m. on weekends) are still strictly enforced—and the subject of many student complaints. Students eat in the North or South dining halls or take their pick from 26 other restaurants, cafés, and to-go locations. As for safety, "The campus is self-contained and well-lit," reports a student.

ND's social life isn't as rambunctious as it once was, thanks to policies that forbid alcohol at campus social events. The rules relating to alcohol in the dorms are a bit more relaxed. For those who choose not to indulge, there are several groups dedicated to good times without alcohol. Most activities take place on campus and include parties, concerts, and movies. A popular event is the An Tóstal

**"Notre Dame football is
massive."**

(Gaelic for "the pageant") festival, which comes the week before spring finals and guarantees to temporarily relieve academic anxiety with silly games, free food, giveaways, music, and other activities. The annual Notre Dame Forum brings internationally known speakers to campus to address timely topics like sustainability and the Catholic Church's sex abuse crisis. Students are involved in the community through volunteer work—more than 10 percent of grads enter public service positions. The best outlet for culture is nearby Chicago, about 90 minutes away. South Bend, with a metro area population of 325,000, offers plenty of entertainment options as well.

Notre Dame competes in the Division I Atlantic Coast Conference (ACC) for all sports except football and ice hockey. There's nothing like Notre Dame football, with its proud gridiron heritage and legends from Knute Rockne and the Gipper right on down to more recent greats such as Joe Montana. ND's name may be French, but the spirit of the Fighting Irish reigns supreme. "Notre Dame football is massive," cheers a sophomore. It wasn't intentional—at least that's what they say—but the giant mosaic of Jesus Christ on the library lifts his hands toward the heavens as if to signal yet another Irish touchdown. Tailgate parties are celebrated events, occurring before and after the game. Aside from football, Notre Dame offers a solid all-around athletic program. Men's lacrosse and women's basketball have brought home recent ACC championships, and the co-ed fencing program has won four of the last five national titles, including in 2025. Die-hard jocks who weren't recruited for varsity teams will find plenty of company in ND's very competitive club and intramural sports. The Bookstore Basketball Tournament, the largest 5-on-5, outdoor hoops tournament in the world with more than 700 teams competing, lasts for a month.

From administrators to students, everyone here is considered part of the "Notre Dame family." Traditions are held in high esteem. For those looking for high-quality academics, a friendly, caring environment with a Catholic bent, and an excellent athletic scene, ND could be an answer to their prayers.

If You Apply To ›

ND: Early action, regular decision. Accepts the Common Application. Please consult Notre Dame's website for the most up-to-date information regarding standardized test requirements.

The college that invented nonconformity. From the Underground Railroad and coeducation to global learning and the modern peace movement, Obies have long been in the forefront of social progress. As at Grinnell and Reed, Oberlin's curriculum is less radical than its students. Oberlin is especially strong in the sciences, and its music conservatory is among the nation's best. The annual Drag Ball is quintessential Oberlin.

New and contrasting ideas are a way of life at Oberlin College, a liberal arts school where nonconformity is a cherished tradition and student activism continues to make occasional headlines. Founded in 1833 by abolitionist heirs of local Christian revivals, Oberlin was a stop on the Underground Railroad, and it was the first American college to admit students of color and grant undergraduate degrees to women in a coeducational program. That pioneering spirit endures. With academic options ranging from cinema studies to neuroscience, Obies thrive on higher thinking and exploring their talents. As one junior puts it, "Oberlin is its own brand of indie-cool, with a vibrant student community that is constantly connecting academics, people, and places in a way you could not possibly predict."

Oberlin's 440-acre campus mixes Italian Renaissance buildings (four by Cass Gilbert), early 20th-century organic stone halls, and some less inspiring 1950s dorms. The buildings rise over flatlands typical of the Midwest, which do little to stop brutal winter winds. The Allen Memorial Art Museum, sometimes mentioned alongside those at Harvard and Yale, features a brick-paved,

> **"Oberlin is its own brand of indie-cool."**

flower-laden courtyard and a fountain. The Oberlin College Science Center offers state-of-the-art classrooms, a science library, and laboratory space. A $140 million Sustainability Infrastructure Project included converting the entire campus to geothermal heating and cooling and allowed the school to achieve carbon neutrality in 2025.

There are no academic first-year requisites at Oberlin, but students must show proficiency in writing and math and take courses in arts and humanities, natural sciences and math, social sciences, and cultural diversity. Students must also participate in three January terms, during which they pursue monthlong projects, traditional or unique, on or off campus. About 40 different First-Year Seminar classes are available every semester, with enrollment limited to 14 students each, and although optional, almost all first-years sign up because "it's a great way to make friends," says a student. "It also introduces you to the Oberlin academic experience."

Oberlin's Conservatory of Music ranks among the nation's top performance schools; the voice, violin, and technology in music and related arts programs are especially praised. It is the oldest continuously operating music conservatory in the country, and Oberlin is one of only a handful of liberal arts colleges with a conservatory (see also Bard and Lawrence). The conservatory boasts 150 practice rooms, a substantial music library, and Steinway pianos—one of the world's largest collections. It enrolls about a fifth of Oberlin undergrads, who must audition to gain acceptance. Each year, about 40 students enter the Double Degree Program, earning both a B.M. and a B.A. in five (or fewer) years; these students must be admitted to both the college and the conservatory.

Website: www.oberlin.edu
Location: Small Town
Private
Total Enrollment: 2,883
Undergraduates: 2,869
Male/Female: 41/59
Financial Aid: 88%
Pell Grant: 9%
Expense: Pr $ $ $ $
Student Loans: 45%
Average Debt: $ $
Applicants: 10,529
Accepted: 34%
Enrolled: 20%
Grad in 6 Years: 81%
Returning First-years: 91%
Academics: ✍ ✍ ✍ ✍
Social: 🌑 🌑 🌑 🌑
Q of L: ★ ★ ★ ★
Admissions: (440) 775-8411
Email Address: college.admissions@oberlin.edu

Strong Programs:
Biology
Chemistry
Creative Writing
Dance
Economics
Environmental Studies
Music
Neuroscience

Oberlin has been a leader among liberal arts colleges seeking to promote their science offerings; biology and chemistry are two of the college's strongest departments, and environmental studies and neuroscience are well regarded. The creative writing and dance departments are notable, and students also flock to economics, politics, psychology, and computer science. Interdisciplinary and self-created majors, such as Africana, East Asian, Russian, Jewish, and gender studies, are popular—not surprisingly at such a liberal school. Technically inclined students can pursue 3–2 engineering degrees with Case Western Reserve, WashU in St. Louis, Columbia, and Caltech. One of Oberlin's more unusual offerings is ExCo, an experimental college that offers students and interested townsfolk the chance to teach and learn together. Most classes are taught by students, and topics can range from community organizing to knitting to salsa dancing and much more.

Students are as serious about academics as they are about politics and social causes, and heavy workloads are the norm. "Oberlin is academically rigorous, but they make up for it by having more support resources than most of us know what to do with," says a psychology major. "The average Oberlin syllabus will work in trips to our art museum, instruction in a local café, or a class taught in the campus's arboretum when the weather is nice." Seventy-eight percent of classes have fewer than 20 students, and a philosophy major says, "Professors are always open to a lot of feedback on how they teach and what classes look like." Most departments offer group and individual independent study opportunities and invite selected students to pursue demanding honors programs, especially during their senior year. Sixty-six percent of students conduct undergraduate research, and 80 percent study, intern, or do service abroad in Oberlin programs in Italy, Spain, and the UK or in 90 other affiliated programs.

Oberlin students are—in a word—passionate. An English, history, and French major describes them as "active, engaged, passionate, delightfully and thoughtfully quirky, and friendly." Ninety-one percent of undergraduates come from outside Ohio and 9 percent from abroad. But achieving diversity in rural Ohio has been a challenge: Black students account for 4 percent of the student body, Asian Americans 5 percent, Hispanics/Latinos 9 percent, and multiracial students 9 percent. Merit scholarships averaging $22,600 are available to qualified students, and Oberlin promises to meet students' full demonstrated financial need. For all its talk of nonconformity, Oberlin is also a model of political correctness. "Politically it is not the most diverse [campus] but we are very inclusive and honest," says a sophomore.

"Oberlin [has] more support resources than most of us know what to do with."

"One thing really unique about Oberlin is how collaborative and student-run a lot of the extracurriculars are," a junior notes. "There is a very active network of Major Committees and student life offices that are completely student-run so you can get involved by planning events, allocating funds, working with clubs to balance budgets, or even vote on which new faculty should be hired in a department."

Ninety-three percent of Oberlin students live in campus housing, including several program houses focusing on various foreign languages and cultural backgrounds. For five dollars, students can rent up to two original works from the art museum to decorate their rooms. A small number of upperclassmen are allowed to live off campus every year, and those who wish to do so must try their luck in a random lottery. Students may eat in any of four dining halls and various cafés. Six co-ops that comprise the Oberlin Student Cooperative Association, a roughly $2-million-a-year corporation run entirely by students, offer appealing alternatives to dining-hall fare. Regarding safety, students say they feel safe on campus but report that the administration's handling of sexual assault cases needs improvement to better support survivors. "Career advising and mental health are pretty standard," attests a sophomore.

Social life, like so much of the Oberlin experience, is lively and eclectic. Several house parties, plays, movies, and conservatory performances are planned each week. "Social life is based around live music," says a junior. "We go to a lot of concerts, and house parties usually book at least one campus band." A psychology major adds, "Our parties have less beer pong and more jazz bands." The midnight Organ Pump concerts in Finney Chapel each semester combine serious classical music with musical oddities, such as the school police blotter performed as Anglican chant. The Halloween concert is popular, as is the annual Drag Ball, in which half the student body comes in full drag. "It's very Oberlin, because it's all about challenging social norms," says a student. Since there's no Greek system, nothing is exclusive. "The open-mindedness of the student body extends to social life, so while people drink and do drugs, there is little pressure to partake," comments a senior.

The small town of Oberlin offers some good restaurants and local shops, although they tend to close early. "There's only really two square blocks of downtown," says one student, "but within it is basically everything that you need." When the urge to wander strikes, Cleveland is only 30 miles away. Although relations between ultraprogressive Oberlin and the town can be uneasy, Obies eagerly give back through volunteer activities at local schools, hospitals, and nursing homes.

"Our parties have less beer pong and more jazz bands."

The Division III Yeomen and Yeowomen (medieval terms for people who own and cultivate land that hearken back to the college's founding motto of "Learning and Labor") appear to be building a loyal fan base: the women's cross-country team is a perennial powerhouse, and men's cross-country and women's track and field have claimed North Coast Athletic Conference championships in recent years. Thirty percent of students compete in intramural and club sports.

Small in size, Oberlin's emphasis on global learning, research, and a vibrant liberal arts education makes it feel much larger. Students are more likely to discuss local poverty than the quality of cereal choices in the dining halls, and they can be found playing a Steinway or plugging away at astronomy. One Obie sums it up this way: "Oberlin is the epitome of a liberal arts school, and that is reflected in all of the ways students customize their learning experiences, from the topics they choose for papers and projects to how they demonstrate that they care about current events."

Overlaps

Carleton, Kenyon, Lawrence, Macalester, Northwestern, Reed, Vassar, Wesleyan

If You Apply To ›

Oberlin: Early decision I and II, early action, regular decision. Accepts the Common Application. Applicants to Conservatory of Music must audition or interview. Please consult Oberlin's website for the most up-to-date information regarding standardized test requirements.

Occidental College

1600 Campus Road, Los Angeles, CA 90041

Occidental is a streetwise cousin to the more upscale and suburban Claremont Colleges. Plentiful internships and study abroad give Oxy students real-world perspectives. Opportunities for undergraduate research are abundant. Oxy's innovative diplomacy and world affairs program features internships with UN agencies. Strong focus on diversity and social justice.

Half of Oxy students participate in some kind of community project, most through the Center for Community Based Learning.

Founded in 1887, Occidental College is one of a handful of small colleges located in a big city, in this case La La Land. But unlike the sprawling and impersonal City of Angels, Oxy emphasizes a strong sense of community and a decidedly diverse student population that seeks "to embrace difference and make a difference in the world." Notable attendees include former president Barack Obama. "Students dream big at Oxy," says a senior. "Whether a student wants a career in Hollywood or on Wall Street, everyone knows that it starts in the classroom."

Set against the backdrop of the San Gabriel Mountains, Oxy's self-contained Mediterranean-style campus is a secluded enclave of flowers and trees between Pasadena and Glendale, minutes from downtown Los Angeles. The McKinnon Center for Global Affairs features a two-story, LED-lit wall of sculpted glass with embedded interactive screens that display a shifting array of student and faculty research and coursework. Newer campus additions include a state-of-the-art music production center and an $18 million aquatic center.

Inside this urban oasis resides a thriving community of high achievers who don't for a moment believe that the liberal arts are dead or even wounded. Required first-year seminars are small, discussion-based classes centered on building foundational skills for college. All Oxy students must show proficiency in a foreign language and complete coursework in world cultures, fine arts, the preindustrial era, science, and math. In their final year, all students complete a senior comprehensive, or "comp," such as a project, paper, or exam that shows mastery in their field.

Many of Occidental's academic departments are excellent; economics, diplomacy and world affairs, psychology, biology, urban and environmental policy, politics, and computer science are among the strongest and most popular majors. "The

"Students dream big at Oxy." academic climate at Occidental is both rigorous and supportive," says a sophomore. The media arts and culture major, which offers concentrations in critical media and media production, is solid; students learn both theory and production skills and enjoy access to internships in L.A.'s film and entertainment industries. Several interdisciplinary majors, such as critical theory and social justice, are also strong. There are 3–2 engineering programs with Caltech and Columbia University. A 4–3 physical therapy program allows students to earn a Doctor of Physical Therapy degree at the Massachusetts College of Pharmacy and Health Sciences. Academics at Oxy are challenging, but the atmosphere is not competitive. Students say the teaching, in general, is excellent. Sixty-nine percent of classes have fewer than 20 students, and as academic advisors are responsible for about four students per class (16 total), personal relationships develop quickly. "Professors' office doors are always open for students if they need help in class or in life," confirms a senior.

Oxy encourages diverse learning experiences through independent study, internships, and study abroad. The college boasts an unusual UN program that allows students to intern with UN-related organizations while also taking classes and living in Manhattan for a semester. The Campaign Semester, offered every two years, gives students a chance to work full-time on political campaigns and then return to campus for a seminar where they reflect on their experiences. Students can study abroad or pursue international research or internships in programs offered in more than 50 countries. The Summer Research Program supports more than 125 student research projects in the sciences, social sciences, and humanities every summer, and many students publish and present their work.

"Students at Oxy are generally creative, smart self-starters and politically and socially engaged/opinionated," says a sociology major. Perhaps not surprisingly, students tend to be liberal, and the raging social concerns are "racial and social inequalities, environmentalism, and gender issues," according to one student. Thirty-eight percent of the students are from California, and 5 percent hail from foreign nations.

Black students make up 4 percent of the population, Hispanics/Latinos 18 percent, Asian Americans 16 percent, and multiracial students 10 percent. Merit scholarships average $21,000, but there are no athletic scholarships. Unlike many of its peers, Occidental stopped making a priority of pursuing wealthy applicants years ago and started investing in grants and scholarships for lower-income students of color. The college now meets the full demonstrated financial need of admitted students. The Barack Obama Scholars Program provides top achievers who have demonstrated serious commitment to public service with a two-year experience that includes academic-year seminars, two summers of funded opportunities, faculty and professional mentorship, and up to $10,000 in postgraduate support to help launch their careers.

The residence halls are small—almost all house fewer than 150 students—and co-ed by floor or room. First-years live together in five dedicated first-year halls, and students are required to live on campus and purchase a meal plan until their senior year, when they can opt to move off campus. Special-interest housing, like Food Justice House and Queer House, is popular. As of 2025, all residence halls have air conditioning. "The food is fresh and yummy!" cheers a student. "It's always changing and they bring in locally sourced produce." Resources related to sexual assault include the Project SAFE student group, which a senior says "has been absolutely wonderful in creating a safe and respectful campus."

While the bustle of L.A. often beckons on weekends, the Oxy campus provides its share of fun too, whether it be a "basketball game, concert, dance, or party," says one student. Greek organizations attract 1 percent of the men and 2 percent of the women, but they are neither selective nor exclusive; students choose which to join rather than being chosen, and the frats must invite everyone to their functions. As for alcohol, "like most other colleges, there is underage drinking even though this is illegal," says a junior. Dance Production—a decades-old tradition in which student dancers perform works by student choreographers—sells out both performances each year. Other big events include Apollo Night (a talent contest) and the Fall Fest and Spring Fest concerts, featuring big-name performers. You may want to keep your birthday a secret, or on that unhappy day, a roaring pack of your more sadistic classmates will carry you out to the middle of campus and mercilessly toss you in the Gilman Fountain. It's a tradition, after all.

"The surrounding areas of northeast Los Angeles provide for arguably the best places to be in the county when it comes to food, places to shop, and also relax," raves an economics major. Community outreach is important at Occidental and dates back to the mid-1960s, when the college opened its Community Literacy Center and one of the country's first Upward Bound programs for underserved students. Half of Oxy students participate in some kind of community project, most through the Center for Community Based Learning. When students become weary of the social life in the "Oxy fishbowl," they head for the bars, restaurants, museums, and theaters of downtown Los Angeles and Pasadena, where, one student notes, "You can find almost anything except snow." But the ski slopes of the San Gabriel Mountains are not far away, and neither is Hollywood nor the beautiful beaches of Southern California. A car (your own or someone else's) is practically a necessity, though the college runs a weekend shuttle service to Old Town Pasadena and other popular spots.

Oxy's 20 sports teams (the Tigers) compete in Division III. Women's basketball, men's and women's cross-country and track and field, men's and women's soccer, and men's water polo are some of the most competitive teams. Oxy's 125-year-old

An unusual UN program allows students to intern with UN-related organizations while also taking classes and living in Manhattan.

"The academic climate at Occidental is both rigorous and supportive."

All Oxy students must show proficiency in a foreign language and complete coursework in world cultures.

"[In Pasadena], you can find almost anything except snow."

football rivalry with Pomona–Pitzer ended in 2020 when the college discontinued the sport. The school's Io Triumphe ("Hurrah, O Triumph") nonsense chant, a tradition since 1905, has been mocked for nearly a century by rival Redlands, which made up a gibberish chant of its own in 1921. Oxy's small recreational sports program offers intramural soccer and basketball along with seven club sports; rugby and ultimate Frisbee are popular.

Occidental's creative, motivated, and diverse students are not here for the bright lights and beautiful people of Los Angeles; those are just fringe benefits. Instead, students are drawn to this intimate oasis of learning by professors who hate to see anyone waste one whit of intellectual potential. Advises one happy sophomore, "If you're someone who values creativity, close relationships with professors, and being in a city like L.A. while still having a tight-knit campus, Oxy really stands out."

If You Apply To ›

Oxy: Early decision I and II, regular decision. SATs or ACTs: optional. Accepts the Common Application with supplement.

Oglethorpe University

4484 Peachtree Road NE, Atlanta, GA 30319

Small wonder that brochures for Oglethorpe trumpet Atlanta as the college's biggest drawing card. In a region where most liberal arts colleges are in sleepy towns, Oglethorpe has the South's most exciting city at its fingertips. Highly diverse student body and extensive financial aid. Oglethorpe Idea stresses broad academic values, while interdisciplinary Core Program gives shape to the curriculum.

Founded in 1835, Oglethorpe University takes its name from the visionary founder of the state of Georgia, James Edward Oglethorpe. His idealism is well captured in the school's motto, Nescit cedere (He does not know how to give up), and in its ambition to become the first-choice university for high-achieving students in a region where it faces tough competition from much bigger names. Even as it continues to increase enrollment, the university remains committed to the Oglethorpe Idea and to connecting students with real-world experiences. Says a junior, "Although few outside of the Southeast have heard of it, this school provides a top-notch education."

Oglethorpe's 118-acre campus is strategically located in Brookhaven, one of Atlanta's safest and most popular inner suburbs, with a picturesque Gothic campus that gives a traditional college feel. The heavily wooded, slightly rolling terrain is perfect territory for walks or long runs, and the beautiful campus has served as the backdrop for numerous movies and TV shows. Oglethorpe's academic buildings and some residence halls are in the English Gothic style. Newer facilities include the Cousins Center for Science and Innovation, featuring laboratory-classrooms and workshops.

> **"The professors clearly show an interest and passion in their work."**

The university's guiding principle is the Oglethorpe Idea—a philosophy based on the conviction that education should help students make a life, a living, and a difference. All students take the sequenced, interdisciplinary Core Curriculum program at the same point in their college careers, providing them with a model for integrating information and gaining knowledge. In addition to requiring several liberal arts and sciences courses that help develop students' ability to reason, read, and speak effectively, the core asks them to reflect on and discuss matters fundamental to understanding who they are and what they ought to be.

Oglethorpe's most popular majors—business administration, biology, communication studies, and psychology—are some of its strongest, along with English, accounting, film and media studies, theater, and preprofessional advising for a variety of health and medical fields. Minors in urban leadership and nonprofit management are specialties. The art department offers tracks in film production, medical and scientific illustration, and photography. Aspiring engineers may take advantage of dual-degree programs with Georgia Tech and Kennesaw State, and future teachers can enroll in a dual-degree program with Mercer. New programs include actuarial science.

"I have never breezed through a class," says an art history major. "The academics are so rigorous." Oglethorpe's faculty may be demanding, but they're also friendly and helpful. "The professors clearly show an interest and passion in their work, which translates into their teaching," says a history major. Classes are generally small—a whopping 94 percent have fewer than 20 students. Students may sign up for a wide variety of study abroad programs, including short-term and faculty-led options. Sophomores and juniors interested in producing an independent honors thesis can apply for admission to the Honors Program.

What's an Oglethorpian like? "We tend to be open-minded, thoughtful, and intellectual," explains one student. Most come from public schools, and 84 percent are Georgians; 3 percent hail from abroad. Oglethorpe prides itself on being one of the first Georgia colleges to admit Black students. Currently, 20 percent of students are Black, 4 percent are Asian American, 30 percent are Hispanic/Latino, and 4 percent are multiracial. Socioeconomic diversity is also strong, with 41 percent of first-years receiving Pell Grants. "The diversity is one of my favorite things about our campus," cheers a senior. Notably, every admitted student who completes the FAFSA form receives a $500 grant, regardless of financial need. Merit scholarships are also available, averaging $39,400. In an effort to earn more national name recognition, Oglethorpe's Flagship 50 program pledges to match the in-state tuition rate of each U.S. state's flagship institution for incoming first-years who meet certain academic requirements.

Forty-one percent of Oglethorpe's students live on campus—and most love it. "The dorms are big and have nice furniture," says an accounting major. Most rooms are suites with private bathrooms, and some singles are available. Meals in the Petrel's Nest dining hall get mixed reviews, but one senior says, "The menus are regularly updated to incorporate seasonal ingredients and feedback from students." Students praise the school's mental health support.

The social scene on campus is active for a small school. "Our Student Government Association sponsors events like bubble soccer, food truck Fridays, Bob Ross art night, and more," explains a human resource management major. Students of legal drinking age are allowed to have alcohol on campus. Fraternities and sororities, which claim 7 percent of the men and 7 percent of the women, throw parties that draw big numbers. "Greek parties are really fun but much less raucous/drug-infused than parties at other schools like UGA and Georgia Tech," opines one senior. The campus celebrates its origins once a year during Oglethorpe Day with a footrace around the quad and a bold-name guest lecturer. Each holiday season brings a particularly unique tradition: the Boar's Head Ceremony, which celebrates a medieval scholar who halted a stampeding wild boar by ramming his copy of Aristotle down the animal's throat and also recognizes inductees of an academic honor society.

It's rumored that Oglethorpe barflies do more hopping than Georgia bullfrogs, and bars, clubs, and cafés abound within 10 minutes of campus. Students can also find excitement on the campuses of the dozen or so other colleges in the area or in downtown Atlanta. "There are always city events like free yoga that are just a short

(continued)

Strong Programs:
Accounting
Biology
Business Administration
Communication Studies
English
Film and Media Studies
Psychology
Theater

The campus celebrates its origins once a year during Oglethorpe Day with a footrace around the quad and a bold-name guest lecturer.

"Our Student Government Association sponsors events like bubble soccer [and] food truck Fridays."

The university's guiding principle is based on the conviction that education should help students make a life, a living, and a difference.

MARTA ride away!" enthuses a junior. Atlanta proper offers everything you can imagine—arts, professional sports (including basketball's Hawks, football's Falcons, and baseball's Braves), and entertainment (ride the Great American Scream Machine at Six Flags). Oglethorpe always has a big contingent going to Savannah for St. Patrick's Day and to New Orleans for Mardi Gras, and sunny Florida beckons too.

Oglethorpe's mascot, the Stormy Petrel, is a sea bird that flies in the face of storms. (James Oglethorpe was inspired by them on his first visit to Georgia in 1733.) Oglethorpe fields 16 Division III varsity sports. The men's and women's golf teams are powerhouses, and men's soccer and tennis are recent Southern Athletic Association champions. Men's and women's basketball games are popular. Intramural sports attract about 10 percent of the student body. The Georgia landscape makes possible a plethora of outdoor activities, including hiking at nearby Stone Mountain and boating or swimming in Lake Lanier (named for Georgia poet Sidney Lanier—Oglethorpe Class of 1860).

Though Oglethorpe is still working to achieve widespread name recognition, its diverse and growing group of students get all the attention they need from a caring faculty on a close-knit campus. And being in a large city like Atlanta provides anything else that might be lacking, ranging from great nightlife to internships and postgraduate employment with big-name corporations. In a sea of large Southern state schools, Oglethorpe stands out as a place where students rule the roost.

If You Apply To ›

Oglethorpe: Early action I and II, rolling admissions. SATs or ACTs: optional. Accepts the Common Application with supplement. Application includes optional questions on gender identity and preferred pronouns.

The Ohio State University

281 West Lane Avenue, Columbus, OH 43210

The biggest school in the Big Ten, Ohio State competes for top students not only with Michigan and Wisconsin but also with two other fine Ohio publics, Miami and Ohio U. Operates the mother of all college sports programs, which consistently racks up national titles and spills over into undergraduate wellness programs. Check out the top-notch honors program. Columbus, the capital of Ohio, has become an exciting city.

Envision a campus with 52,000 full-time students and too many opportunities to count. What might come to mind is The Ohio State University (and don't forget the "The"—it's trademarked), located in the heart of the state's capital, offering 15 colleges and more than 200 undergraduate majors. If those numbers aren't staggering enough, consider the fact that OSU has 36 varsity sports, 20 intramural sports, nearly 60 sports clubs, and the third largest campus in the nation. It also has an operating budget larger than that of the state of Delaware. While students cite the school's size as both a blessing and a curse, all seem to agree that at OSU, the sky is the limit for those with a desire to sample its academic and other resources.

This megauniversity stands on 1,665 acres in the middle of the city, just two miles north of downtown Columbus. "One part of the campus maintains a nostalgic air while another is relatively modern," observes a student. The grounds are nicely landscaped, and a centrally located lake provides a peaceful setting for contemplation and a break from all the surrounding activity. OSU's rich array of academic resources includes 12 libraries with nearly 10 million volumes. Across the Olentangy River from campus is a teaching and research farm associated with the College of Food, Agricultural, and Environmental Sciences. The Recreation and Physical Activity Center is the nation's largest facility dedicated to student fitness, wellness, and recreation. In the past decade, the school has opened several new buildings, including the Energy Advancement and Innovation Center—an interdisciplinary research center that serves as a hub for work on creating the next generation of smart energy system—and the Interdisciplinary Health Sciences Center.

Ohio State's general education curriculum gives students the flexibility to pursue minors or second majors. The university's commitment to liberal arts learning remains strong: all undergrads must satisfy requirements that include courses in writing, math, data analysis, arts and humanities, historical studies, social and behavioral science, and intellectual diversity, along with a capstone seminar. Some of the school's most celebrated departments include business, engineering, neuroscience, nursing, dance, and design; political science and education are also strong. OSU is internationally known for pioneering work in computer graphics and animation. The African American and African studies program offers one of the most extensive offerings of African languages of any U.S. university. Furthermore, the university has the nation's only ABET-accredited program in welding engineering and the nation's first undergraduate program in data analytics. The majors that enroll the most students include finance, psychology, marketing, and biology. A personalized study program enables students to create their own majors. Conservative politicians in Ohio have passed legislation targeting DEI programs, tenure, and other policies at universities in their state, and as a result OSU has announced it will cut several undergraduate majors, including medieval and Renaissance studies, music theory, and musicology, among others.

First-years may take advantage of numerous programs, including the First Year Success Series, covering topics like study skills and career exploration, and pre-enrollment programs like Buckeyes First (for first-generation students). Once the academic year is underway, they experience a variety of class formats and sizes, ranging from intimate first-year seminars to large lectures; overall, 39 percent of undergraduate classes have fewer than 20 students. "Classes demand a lot of atten-

> **"Classes demand a lot of attention, independence, and self-advocacy on the part of the student."**

tion, independence, and self-advocacy on the part of the student," comments a sport industry major. Teaching assistants hold smaller recitation sections of large lecture courses and deal on a personal level with students. Class sizes generally whittle down as students continue in their fields of study. At such a large institution, says a biomedical science major, "The quality of instruction varies based on the college, but the research orientation of the professors often enhances student connection and topic relevancy in the classes." About a quarter of undergraduates participate in research opportunities. OSU's honors program allows selected students to learn from top professors in small classes averaging about 25 students each. Columbus affords students access to internships with the state government and major tech and research organizations, including the IBM Analytics Solutions Lab and Battelle. Students can study abroad through 200 programs offered in more than 50 countries.

"Most students are extremely well-mannered, ambitious, open-minded, and obsessed with the Buckeyes," says a loyal sophomore. Seventy-one percent of Ohio State's undergraduates hail from Ohio, and most out-of-staters come from Illinois, Pennsylvania, California, New York, and New Jersey. Ten percent come from foreign countries. The student body is 8 percent Black, 6 percent Hispanic/Latino, 11 percent Asian American, and 5 percent multiracial. As for politics, a sociology and political science major opines, "Because we are such a large institution, there are people from all

(continued)

Enrolled: 22%
Grad in 6 Years: 88%
Returning First-years: 94%
Academics: ✍ ✍ ✍
Social: 🗨 🗨 🗨 🗨
Q of L: ★ ★ ★
Admissions: (614) 292-3980
Email Address:
 askabuckeye@osu.edu

Strong Programs:
Business
Dance
Design
Education
Engineering
Finance
Neuroscience
Political Science

Columbus boasts a symphony orchestra, a ballet, and professional hockey and soccer teams.

kinds of social and political backgrounds." Qualified students compete for merit scholarships averaging $7,600, and hundreds of athletic scholarships go to talented athletes each year. The Ohio State Tuition Guarantee sets and freezes rates for tuition, fees, and room and board for in-state first-year students in each entering class for four years.

The residence halls, which house 34 percent of Ohio State students, are located in three areas: North, South, and Olentangy (that is, those closest to the Olentangy River). First-years and sophomores are required to live in residence halls unless they are commuting from home, and first-years are scattered among each of OSU's 40-plus residence halls. A senior advises, "Make sure to look into the Scholars Program, which puts you in a learning community for four years with other people who have the same major or professional goals." About 20 percent of students opt to live in one of the 15 living-learning communities. Campus residents may choose from four meal-plan options, and the food gets mostly positive reviews.

"Most students are ambitious, open-minded, and obsessed with the Buckeyes."

Buckeyes ACT is a comprehensive program intended to combat sexual misconduct and relationship violence on campus. "Mental health services are really a highlight of OSU," says a political science major, while a senior adds, "Career coaching for free and tutoring for free have greatly enhanced my learning and helped me through tough semesters of classes."

OSU is a bustling place on weekends. "Social life is never-ending," cheers one student. With nearly 1,400 student organizations to choose from, it's hardly difficult to find something to get involved with. Various social events are planned within residence hall communities. The student union runs eateries, a tavern, movies, and other activities. Eight percent of OSU men and 12 percent of the women join fraternities and sororities. "Greek organizations do not dictate social life on campus," says a junior, and most partying happens off campus.

Such a large student market has, of course, produced a strip of bars, fast-food joints, convenience stores, bookstores, vegetarian restaurants, and you-name-its along the edge of the campus on High Street, and downtown Columbus is just a few minutes away. The fine public transportation system carries students throughout this capital city. "There are so many unique neighborhoods to explore," raves a junior. "I don't think I could ever try everything Columbus has to offer during my four years if I tried." Columbus boasts a symphony orchestra, a ballet, and professional hockey and soccer teams; OSU's D-Tix program offers students discounted or free tickets to cultural and sporting events. The city's central location in the state makes it easily accessible to Cleveland and Cincinnati. Outdoor enthusiasts can ski in nearby Mansfield, canoe and sail on the Olentangy and Scioto Rivers, hike the city's 19 metro parks, or camp in nearby Hocking Hills.

Ohio State operates arguably the most lavish—and successful—college sports program in the nation. The Buckeyes field 16 men's, 17 women's, and three co-ed varsity teams, from golf to gymnastics to riflery. (A buckeye, incidentally, is a small,

Overlaps

**University of
Cincinnati, U of I at
Urbana–Champaign,
University of
Maryland, Miami
University (OH),
University of
Michigan, Penn
State, Purdue,
UW–Madison**

"There is a lot of Buckeye pride at OSU!"

shiny nut that falls from Ohio's official state tree.) Recent national champions include women's ice hockey, synchronized swimming, and dance and co-ed pistol, while Big Ten champs include men's and women's tennis, women's swimming and diving, and football. "Football game culture is a huge draw to OSU every fall," says a senior. "The student section is very fun and has a ton of unique cheers and chants." Rivalries abound, although the annual gridiron contest with "That Team Up North" (Michigan's Wolverines) gets the most heated; preparations for the big game include "crossing out every letter M on all campus signs with red tape," explains a fervent fan. Many students take advantage of an extensive roster of club sports and an ambitious intramural program that boasts a dozen basketball courts and 26 courts for handball, squash, and racquetball.

OSU's sheer size is sometimes overwhelming to be sure, but students here seem to thrive on the challenge and excitement of a huge university. As one senior suggests, "Students who want to feel a big sense of school pride, enjoy sports and academics, enjoy ample options for career trajectory, and want a large school will enjoy OSU." Adds the student, "There is a lot of Buckeye pride at OSU!"

Ohio University

1 Ohio University, Athens, OH 45701

OHIO is roughly one-third the size of Ohio State and plays up its homey feel compared to the cast of tens of thousands in Columbus. The Honors Tutorial College is a draw for top students who want to work closely with faculty. Communication and journalism top the list of prominent programs that also include sports administration and health research; learning communities are plentiful. OHIO is not in the Big Ten, but the Mid-American Conference generates its own excitement.

With top-notch programs in journalism, business, health care, and engineering, Ohio University has become a competitive Research 1 public institution with a strong focus on professions, accessibility, and student success without shedding its small-town roots. Faculty interests range from dinosaur anatomy to rural diabetes rates. Students here love to hit the town for fun but are quick to hit the books as well. Those who choose to attend OHIO receive ample returns, says a senior, including "a quality education, lifelong friends, supportive faculty, and a beautiful campus."

Established in 1804 as the first institution of higher learning in the old Northwest Territory, Ohio University's main campus is located in Athens, which lies about 75 miles southeast of Columbus, the state capital, and was named after the ancient center of learning in Greece. Encircled by winding hills, the campus features neo-Georgian architecture, tree-lined redbrick walkways, and white-columned buildings all clustered on "greens," which are like small neighborhoods. Long walks are especially nice during the fall foliage and spring cherry blossoms seasons. All new construction and renovation projects over $2 million follow standards for LEED Silver or higher certification. OHIO's five regional campuses are located throughout the state.

The BRICKS (Building Connections, Reasoning, Integration, Communication, Knowledge of Inquiry, and Synthesis) general education curriculum involves two writing-intensive foundations courses, a standard set of distribution requirements, and an upper-level capstone course, and it incorporates interdisciplinary, intercultural, and hands-on learning. Students enroll in nine undergraduate colleges and one center for international studies. OHIO's most popular majors include psychology, nursing, marketing, and communication studies. Engineering and business are also strong. Experiential learning opportunities for students are a high priority for OHIO, and the institution offers multiple innovative programs, like training in virtual reality within the Scripps College of Communication to prepare students for their evolving fields. The Scripps College contains five distinct schools: journalism,

Website: www.ohio.edu
Location: Small Town
Public
Total Enrollment: 19,856
Undergraduates: 16,670
Male/Female: 41/59
Financial Aid: 88%
Pell Grant: 28%
Expense: Pub $ $ $
Student Loans: 57%
Average Debt: $ $
Applicants: 27,105
Accepted: 85%
Enrolled: 19%
Grad in 6 Years: 65%
Returning First-years: 84%
Academics: ✍ ✍ ✍
Social: 🗩 🗩 🗩 🗩
Q of L: ★ ★ ★
Admissions: (740) 593-4100
Email Address:
 admissions@ohio.edu

Strong Programs:
Business
Communication Studies
Education
Engineering

information and telecommunication systems, communication studies, media arts and studies, and visual communication. In addition, OHIO's competitive bachelor of science in nursing program stretches across multiple campuses.

OHIO students work hard, but a communication major says the academic environment is "open and inviting." First-years are often taught by full professors with TAs handling study sessions. OHIO supports more than 250 learning communities, in which 96 percent of first-year students participate; some have a residential component, but most do not. "Learning communities are paired with a professor in your area of study, so you can make connections in your program in your very first class," explains a journalism major. Just 27 percent of undergraduate classes have fewer than 20 students, but faculty make themselves as available as possible. "The professors are more than willing to help you learn if you are willing to ask," says a junior.

One of the advantages of an Ohio University education and something that sets the school apart from run-of-the-mill state institutions is the Honors Tutorial College. Founded in 1972, it's the nation's first multidisciplinary, degree-granting honors program modeled on the tutorial method used in British universities, notably Oxford and Cambridge. In the highly selective program, students pursue an individualized curriculum in their major field and spend much of their time in one-on-one weekly tutorials with profs. A separate OHIO Honors Program, open to students in all colleges, offers challenging small-group seminars and the option to complete honors projects in traditional classes. Co-op programs are available for engineering students, and nearly anyone can earn credit for an internship. The Provost's Undergraduate Research Fund provides financial support for undergraduate research, and students showcase about 850 research and creative projects at the university's annual Student Research Expo. The Office of Global Opportunities offers worldwide destinations for anywhere from one week to one year; 13 percent of students study abroad.

"Students at Ohio University are accepting, motivated, and enthusiastic about being Bobcats," says a communication studies major. Eighty-five percent of undergraduates are Ohioans, and 1 percent are international. Five percent of undergraduates are Black, 5 percent are Hispanic/Latino, 1 percent are Asian American, and 4 percent are multiracial. The student body's liberal leanings are pronounced in comparison to the conservatism of southeast Ohio. The OHIO Guarantee ensures a fixed rate for tuition, housing, dining, and fees for four years, while the OHIO Guarantee+ provides personalized graduation plans, career-readiness tools, and even additional financial support if students need extra time to graduate. For Pell-eligible local students, the President's Opportunity Promise covers the full cost of tuition and mandatory fees. The OHIO Excellence Awards program provides merit scholarships up to $6,500 and need-based grants for outstanding students, and the athletically gifted can vie for over 200 scholarships.

Forty-three percent of students live in campus housing. Five LEED-certified residence halls have been built in recent years, and one currently under construction will be the school's largest and serve as a center for community on South Green. Juniors and seniors usually move to nearby apartments or rental houses. Both campus dining halls have been renovated and receive positive reviews for working with students with food allergies; one location now accepts food stamps. OHIO has worked to improve mental health care services for students, including animal-assisted therapy, which is a part of the Survivor Advocacy Program.

Campus social life includes guest speakers and performers, plays, midnight movies, and other events. Only about 6 percent of the men and 4 percent of the women choose to participate in Greek life. The administration has attempted to

"You can make connections in your program in your very first class."

OHIO has worked to improve mental health care services for students, including animal-assisted therapy, which is a part of the Survivor Advocacy Program.

OHIO offers multiple innovative programs, like training in virtual reality within the Scripps College of Communication.

curtail underage drinking with a strict alcohol policy, and many students complain that OHIO's traditional party-school image overshadows the school's academic quality, but an accounting major concedes that "there is definitely a large party atmosphere." Students look forward to university-sponsored events such as homecoming and the International Street Fair, as well as unsanctioned events like the so-called fest season in Athens. "We are known for our street fests," says a journalism major. "Almost every Saturday in the spring has a party on a street." Court Street is dotted with bars and clubs. Volunteer opportunities, such as Habitat for Humanity and a local homeless shelter, are available through the Campus Involvement Center. Students also love to hike and camp at the nearby state parks and national forest or trek to Columbus for shopping.

Division I sports are a big draw at OHIO. The Bobcats field 16 varsity teams, and the Bobcat football team makes regular bowl game appearances. The men's basketball and baseball and women's volleyball, soccer, and softball teams are competitive too. The university also boasts a nationally ranked speech and debate team. OHIO offers more than 30 club sports, and 16 percent of students participate in those and intramurals each year; popular choices include flag football, rugby, and soccer, as well as a new precision flight team.

"We are known for our street fests."

Students say Ohio University has much to offer, from quality professors to a vibrant social life and a sense of community. "We are always looking out for one another," says a sophomore, "and we all love Athens—it has a special place in our hearts."

If You Apply To ›

OHIO: Early action, rolling admissions. SATs or ACTs: optional. Accepts the Common Application with supplement. Some selective programs, such as the Honors Tutorial, have specific criteria for admissions; please consult the Ohio University website for information.

Ohio Wesleyan University

61 South Sandusky Street, Delaware, OH 43015

OWU serves up the liberal arts with an emphasis on linking theory and practice. Has expanded campus housing, study, and hangout spaces in recent years as part of efforts to enhance the residential experience. Attracts students with preprofessional aspirations. Offers a variety of research, travel, and internship programs, notably New York Arts and Wesleyan in Washington.

Ohio Wesleyan University is a small school with a big commitment to providing its students with a well-rounded education. Established in 1842 and traditionally affiliated with the United Methodist Church, OWU now serves students of all faith traditions. Hallmarks of an OWU education include strong preparation for graduate and professional school, a solid grounding in the liberal arts, real-world experience, and an emphasis on having fun outside the classroom.

Situated in the center of the state and on the outskirts of Columbus, OWU's spacious 200-acre campus is peaceful and quaint. Several buildings are on the National Register of Historic Places. The architecture ranges from Greek Revival to colonial to modern, with brick academic buildings on one side of a downtown thoroughfare

(continued)

Student Loans: 73%
Average Debt: $ $ $ $
Applicants: 6,144
Accepted: 56%
Enrolled: 13%
Grad in 6 Years: 58%
Returning First-years: 85%
Academics: ✍ ✍ ✍
Social: 🗩 🗩 🗩 🗩 🗩
Q of L: ★ ★ ★
Admissions: (800) 922-8953
Email Address:
  owuadmit@owu.edu

Strong Programs:
Botany
Business Administration
Communication
Education
Exercise Science
Microbiology
Psychology
Zoology

In fall 2025, the university opened The 1842, a student hub that offers duckpin bowling, billiards, sand volleyball, pub food, beverages, and more.

that runs through the campus and dormitories and fraternities on the other side. Stately University Hall, with its majestic spire and bell tower, is the main campus landmark and houses the president's office and the 1,100-seat Gray Chapel, home to the largest Klais organ in the United States. In a significant expansion of campus housing, the university has opened three duplexes for living/learning communities, renovated a first-year residence hall, and built a new apartment village for seniors, an honors house, and a house of Black culture. Slocum Hall, which received an $11-million renovation, features a leaded glass ceiling and houses the admissions welcome center, career center, and the Slocum Reading Room.

OWU's general education curriculum is focused on capability-based courses and includes a problem-solving first-year seminar focusing on a complex global challenge. Students must also take a college writing seminar and at least one course in each of nine core competencies, or "power skills," that include the arts, sciences, communications, foreign languages, power and diversity, and more. The most popular majors are psychology, biology, business, and finance. Preprofessional education has always been Ohio Wesleyan's forte; the curriculum also includes majors in education, nutrition, and data analytics, and the highly popular zoology, botany, and microbiology majors are interesting alternatives to the traditional premed route. Nursing, dentistry, optometry, veterinary medicine, law, and public administration round out the list of preprofessional offerings. The Woltemade Center for Economics, Business, and Entrepreneurship caters to budding entrepreneurs, and the fine arts programs offer both professional and liberal arts degrees. Classes are small, with 53 percent enrolling fewer than 20 students, and an economics and psychology major says, "Professors want to see their students thrive and help them every step of the way."

All students are required to participate in the OWU Connection, supplementing their major with interdisciplinary learning, global perspectives, service learning, and practical experiences; students may fulfill these expectations by choosing from a number of pathways, such as special courses, study abroad, internships, and independent projects. "Our school offers a paid summer science research program for students interested in participating in research," says a psychology and biochemistry major. The Career Connection office guides students from every major and helps them to secure internships across the country. Students seeking financial support for such endeavors may apply for an OWU Connection Grant. The honors program offers qualified students one-on-one tutorials and a chance to conduct research with faculty members in areas of mutual interest. Students who desire careers in public policy and service may choose to pursue a semester-long internship through the Wesleyan in Washington program, while others may join the New York Arts program to spend a semester in Manhattan in apprenticeships with working creative professionals. The university's travel-learning courses, which append one to two weeks of travel to a regular semester-long class, are particularly popular.

"Our school offers a paid summer science research program for students interested in participating in research."

Seventy-four percent of students come from Ohio, and 6 percent are international. Students agree that diversity could be improved. "However, with the recent support for underprivileged students and better reach out to the community, the diversity is growing," attests a senior. Black students make up 9 percent of the student body, Hispanics/Latinos 6 percent, Asian Americans 2 percent, and multiracial students 4 percent. Liberals and conservatives are well represented on campus, and hot topics include racial, gender, and sexual equality. Forty-five percent of first-year students receive Pell Grants. Merit scholarships average $33,700 for qualified students.

Eighty-five percent of OWU students live in university-sponsored housing. All but one of the dorms are co-ed, and rooms are mostly doubles or apartment-style, four-person suites. All fraternities offer a residential option. "We have small-living units or SLUs, which are essentially themed houses," says a senior. "The members of these houses do house projects every semester for the campus and are an important part of the OWU community." Students enjoy numerous culinary choices, from 24/7, all-you-can-eat in the main dining hall to snacks from the college grocery store.

"There are many social events on campus," says a sophomore. "The school hosts functions like laser tag or roller-skating." In fall 2025, the university opened The 1842, a student hub that offers duckpin bowling, billiards, sand volleyball, pub food, beverages, and more. Part of OWU's commitment to mend its partying ways includes dry recruitment for Greek life and responsible host training for all events with alcohol so students understand all university policies. Greek membership attracts 24 percent of men and 16 percent of women. "There is definitely pressure to drink, because so many people do it every weekend," says one student. Among OWU's best-loved traditions are homecoming in the fall and the President's Ball in the spring. Day on the Jay, held at the beginning of the year and again at the end of the spring semester, is a carnival-like celebration with games, inflatables, and plenty of free food.

The city of Delaware (population 45,000) is "adorable," says one junior. "There are several small shops and restaurants that are also relatively diverse from Greek to regular pizza and burger joints." The Little Brown Jug, one of harness racing's Triple Crown events, takes place each autumn, bringing thousands of people to the city. Sixty-five percent of students devote more than 30,000 hours to community service annu-ally, through either service trips or local service projects like Bishop Scholars Tutoring, Unity Community Center, and Common Ground Free Store. "Because of the high amount of volunteering that OWU students do in Delaware, we have a fairly good relationship with the town," one student says. Ohio's capital and largest city, Columbus, is only 30 minutes away by car and offers many internship and job opportunities. Lakes, farms, and even ski slopes are within a few hours' drive.

OWU's Division III Battling Bishops are a North Coast Athletic Conference pow-erhouse. Men's and women's soccer, men's and women's basketball, women's field hockey, and men's and women's track and field are among the strongest teams. "We have a huge rivalry with Denison," says a psychology major. Sports fever carries over into intramural and club sports; ultimate Frisbee, rugby, and eSports draw the most enthusiasm.

Ohio Wesleyan offers a solid liberal arts education focused not on bells and whistles but on practical, career-related experience. "Ohio Wesleyan is a place where the education goes well beyond the classroom," says one student. "The family atmo-sphere and the opportunities that the college provides you enrich the entire college experience."

> **"The school hosts functions like laser tag or roller-skating."**

Overlaps

Denison, Kenyon, Miami (OH), Ohio Northern, Ohio State, Otterbein, Wittenberg, Wooster

If You Apply To ›

OWU: Early decision, early action, rolling admissions. SATs or ACTs: optional. Accepts the Common Application with supplement.

660 Parrington Oval, Norman, OK 73019

Tops among public universities in attracting National Merit Scholars, OU is strong in engineering and geology-related fields. Admissions are increasing, as are sponsored research awards. Check out the nationally recognized Honors College and the growing variety of living/learning options. Counseling services are a national model.

Website: www.ou.edu
Location: Small City
Public
Total Enrollment: 24,389
Undergraduates: 20,376
Male/Female: 48/52
Financial Aid: 95%
Pell Grant: 30%
Expense: Pub $
Student Loans: 44%
Average Debt: $ $ $
Applicants: 24,893
Accepted: 77%
Enrolled: 25%
Grad in 6 Years: 75%
Returning First-years: 90%
Academics: ✍ ✍ ✍
Social: 🗩 🗩 🗩
Q of L: ★ ★ ★
Admissions: (405) 325-2151
Email Address:
 admissions@ou.edu

Strong Programs:
Chemistry
Energy Management
Engineering
Entrepreneurship and Venture
 Management
History of the American West
Meteorology
Native American Studies
Petroleum Engineering

The University of Oklahoma has more to boast about than its powerhouse football program. Founded in 1890, OU has capitalized on its Great Plains location by cultivating strengths in petroleum and geological engineering, meteorology, and the history and culture of the American West. It has also worked to make itself, in the words of a first-year student, "a large university with a small-town vibe" by capping the size of first-year comp courses and establishing residential colleges. Couple that with a genuine friendliness among the student body, and it's easy to understand this favorite saying: "Sooner born and Sooner bred, when I die, I'll be Sooner dead!"

Located about 20 miles south of Oklahoma City, OU's 3,500-acre Norman campus features tree-lined streets and predominantly redbrick buildings. Many are historic in nature and built in the Cherokee Gothic or Prairie Gothic style. The Norman campus is home to 16 colleges; six medical and health-related colleges are located on the OU Health Sciences campus in Oklahoma City, and programs from colleges on both campuses are also offered at OU's Schusterman Center in Tulsa. The Sam Noble Oklahoma Museum of Natural History houses more than 10 million artifacts, including the oldest work of art ever found in North America—a 12,000-year-old lightning bolt painted on an extinct bison skull. Newer facilities include McCasland Hall, a residence hall featuring 560 beds for first-year students; the renovated Jones Family Welcome Center at Jacobson Hall; and the Brody Family Performance Facility, a state-of-the-art indoor practice facility for the golf program.

OU's general education requirements consist of coursework in communication (including English composition), natural science, social science, and arts and humanities. First-years start in their degree-granting colleges and have the opportunity to take a First-Year Experience course, choosing from options within the colleges. Students must also complete at least one upper-division course outside of their major and a capstone course, experience, internship, or research.

The most popular majors include business, engineering, communication and journalism, and psychology. The Gallogly College of Engineering offers a computer science program along with aerospace, civil, mechanical, and environmental engineering, among other degrees. The Mewbourne College of Earth and Energy provides programs in geology, geophysics, and paleontology, and its petroleum engineering program ranks among the best in the nation. OU is home to the largest school of meteorology and boasts the country's only meteorology/atmospheric science program within a National Weather Center. In the Dodge Family College of Arts and Sciences, the natural sciences, notably chemistry, are strong. The Price College of Business offers a dozen majors, including energy management, entrepreneurship and venture management, and healthcare business. Other well-recognized programs at OU include history of the American West and Native American studies majors and a minor in constitutional studies. The Rainbolt College of Education's rigorous teacher-certification programs integrate field experiences and mentoring to support growth.

> **"I have . . . never been in a class that requires little effort."**

"I have never had a course that is impossible," comments a psychology major, "but I have also never been in a class that requires little effort." Study groups are common, and students recommend academic tutoring and advising services. OU is one of the nation's few public universities to cap first-year English comp courses at no more than 19 students; overall, 41 percent of undergraduate classes have fewer than 20 students. In the past two decades, increased private support has helped the school attract and retain talented faculty. "Professors do a great job of engaging students and making the material easy to understand and fun to learn," says one sophomore. OU's recently expanded advising service offers support on topics ranging from financial and mental health issues to life skills.

The rigorous Honors College offers 1,800 students small classes with outstanding faculty members, independent study options, and opportunities to apply for competitive funded research programs, including the Honors Research Assistant Program. Students across the university compete for numerous funded undergraduate research and creative opportunities. Over 100 study abroad opportunities are available in 50 countries, including at OU's study centers in Arezzo, Italy, and Puebla, Mexico. Students are often able to apply their financial aid to study abroad, and scholarships are also available.

> "Professors do a great job of engaging students and making the material fun to learn."

A nursing major says OU students create a "lively, energetic, young, and studious" atmosphere on campus. Fifty-seven percent of undergraduates hail from the Sooner state, and 3 percent come from abroad. Black students account for 5 percent, Asian Americans 7 percent, Hispanics/Latinos 15 percent, American Indians 4 percent, and multiracial students 10 percent. A meteorology major describes the political climate as "open and accepting," with greater diversity of views than one tends to find in the rest of the very red state. Qualified students receive scholarships based on academic merit, with awards averaging $3,300; athletic scholarships are also available. OU offers a variety of special aid programs aimed at making the university more affordable for low-income students.

Twenty-eight percent of OU undergraduates live on campus, and the university is making living/learning communities a major focus. McCasland Hall, a new residence hall, opened in fall 2025, and another is scheduled to open in fall 2026. The residence halls are mostly occupied by first-year students, who can choose to live on specific academic floors or at the Honors College. Residential colleges modeled after those at Yale and Oxford also serve as living/learning communities and are the preferred option, along with the OU Traditions Square apartment community, for upperclassmen. Come mealtime, one student says, "Eating at the Caf is like eating dinner with the whole freshman class every night." Students say they feel safe on campus and praise programs like OU Advocates and required trainings for their efforts in sexual assault prevention.

> "Eating at the Caf is like eating dinner with the whole freshman class every night."

The OU social scene is vibrant and well balanced with on-campus activities and off-campus fun. Twenty-seven percent of men and 32 percent of women go Greek. Although the dorms and Greek houses are dry, off-campus fraternity parties are the highlight of weekends at OU. The "three-strikes" alcohol policy "has greatly cut down on alcohol incidents" on campus, says one student. Campus Corner, located right across the street from campus, is another source of nightlife, with several restaurants and bars as well as coffee shops and boutiques. Norman, population 128,000, is Oklahoma's third-largest city, and Oklahoma City is just 20 minutes away. OU's annual day of volunteering, the Big Event, sends more than 5,000 students into the community for a day of service. Favorite traditions include the

University Sing talent show, tailgating, and, of course, the annual road trip to Dallas for the OU–Texas football game.

OU is known for successful Division I athletics and is capitalizing on that reputation with its 2024 move to the Southeastern Conference. Sooner football brought home the Big 12 Conference title 14 times since 2000. "Every football game day, the town swells to over 500,000 people, and I consider game days an all-day festival," says a letters major. The women's gymnastics team has won three national championships in the past five years, and the softball team captured its historic fourth consecutive national title in 2024, the first program to four-peat as national champions in college softball history. The men's gymnastics and men's and women's basketball teams make regular NCAA tournament appearances, too. Recreational and intramural programs attract 16 percent of the undergraduate population, and flag football and basketball are especially popular.

"OU offers the classic college experience," says a senior. Indeed, students at Oklahoma have a lot to brag about. "The educational opportunities are top-notch," says one junior, and "a student can come from anywhere and find that they are part of something special." If you're searching for a school with plenty of spirit and a feeling of family, OU may be worth a look—sooner, rather than later.

If You Apply To ›

OU: Early action, regular decision. SATs or ACTs: optional. Accepts the Common Application with supplement.

Olin College of Engineering

1000 Olin Way, Needham, MA 02492

Olin opened its doors in 2002 with an innovative and forward-looking project-based curriculum and a commitment to turning out "technologists with soul." Wasted no time becoming an elite institution that competes head-to-head with Caltech and MIT for top students. Every enrolled student gets a hefty merit scholarship. Located in Needham, near Babson and Wellesley, on the outskirts of Boston.

Website: www.olin.edu
Location: Suburban
Private
Total Enrollment: 373
Undergraduates: 373
Male/Female: 52/48
Financial Aid: 81%
Pell Grant: 12%
Expense: Pr $ $ $
Student Loans: 30%
Average Debt: $
Applicants: 928
Accepted: 22%
Enrolled: 49%
Grad in 6 Years: 83%
Returning First-years: 99%

In the mid-1990s, leaders of the F. W. Olin Foundation began daydreaming about what "state-of-the-art" engineering education for the 21st century would look like. Two decades and $470 million later, they have their answer: the Franklin W. Olin College of Engineering. This elite engineering school aims to turn out farsighted graduates who are not only technically competent but who can "come up with innovative ideas and products." The curriculum is project-based, and students become as comfortable in the machine shop as in labs and classrooms. The founders also decided that rather than gradually building up the quality and reputation of their new school, they would invest in excellence from the get-go. By offering every enrolled student a merit scholarship of $10,000 per year for four years, Olin has succeeded in luring superbright students away from Caltech, MIT, and other engineering highfliers. Sure, the college lacks the rich tradition and reputation for research of more established institutions, but that doesn't seem to bother the more than 350 students who have latched on to perhaps the best deal in U.S. higher education.

Olin's 70-acre campus is located adjacent to Babson College in a pleasant suburb less than 15 miles west of Boston. The campus design is an innovative blend of the traditional and futuristic. Five buildings curve around a central green space, creating a sense of community and echoing the design of the traditional New England college. The modular classrooms set the stage for hands-on work, and there are plenty of meeting and public spaces to encourage the kind of collaboration called for in modern-day engineering.

Olin's innovative curriculum emphasizes science and engineering as well as business and entrepreneurship. Students choose from three majors—electrical and computer engineering, mechanical engineering, or a self-designed major in engineering with a concentration, such as bioengineering, computing, design, robotics, or sustainability. In addition, students must complete 30 credits of math and science and 28 credits of arts, humanities, social sciences, and entrepreneurship. The course catalog is thin, especially in liberal arts subjects, but students can and do take courses at nearby Babson, Wellesley, and even Brandeis.

> **"All of your classes are focused around projects that help teach you how to immediately apply a concept."**

Students start hands-on engineering right away with relatively simple projects, building mechanical systems intended to mimic animals or insects that hop in the first-semester Design Nature course. They then progress to more sophisticated challenges like Principles of Integrated Engineering, in which they build a project involving electronic, mechanical, and software components (such as an automatic cake decorator or a light-seeking flower pot). Concern for "engineering design" is built into every subject. Each student also completes one of two options—SCOPE (Senior Capstone Program in Engineering) or ADE (Affordable Design and Entrepreneurship)—for a yearlong, team-based senior capstone project in which they apply their knowledge to solving real-world problems in partnership with outside organizations or communities.

Courses are rigorous, but working in teams and across disciplines is the norm for faculty as well as students. "All of your classes are focused around projects that help teach you how to immediately apply a concept," says a mechanical engineering major. Grading starts after the first semester. Forty-nine percent of all classes have fewer than 20 students, and all are led by professors, with whom students are on a first-name basis. Prospective faculty members must go through an extensive interview and audition process, and once hired, none are ever granted tenure. Like their students, many of them have been lured from the likes of MIT because they like the challenge of helping to create what one of them termed "the model of engineering for the future." A first-year says, "Professors are usually very responsive to student questions, even after hours. You can also sometimes find professors eating in the dining hall with students."

First-year students participate in an interactive, weeklong orientation program that includes team-building exercises, meetings, and meals with faculty and advisors as well as a trip into Boston. The college also encourages students to engage in "Passionate Pursuits" via independent projects, for which they receive nondegree academic credit and, often, funding. A sampling of student projects includes rock climbing, guitar making, marathon training, gelato making, and Bhangra (Indian folk dancing).

> **"Professors are usually very responsive to student questions, even after hours."**

Olin offers several direct-exchange options as well as preapproved programs at approximately 40 institutions around the world. Most students conduct research with faculty members.

"Oliners are always doing interesting things," cheers an electrical and computer engineering major, "like spinning fire in our fire arts club, making dice for Dungeons and Dragons, or making something cool in our shop spaces." Seventeen percent of students hail from Massachusetts, and 6 percent come from abroad. Black students represent a mere 4 percent of the student body, Asian Americans 20 percent, Hispanics/Latinos 10 percent, and multiracial students 10 percent. Students appreciate the balanced male/female ratio as "very uncommon" for an engineering school. "We are very LGBTQ friendly," affirms a sophomore. "Politically, we're a

(continued)

Academics: ✍ ✍ ✍ ✍ ✍
Social: 🍷 🍷 🍷
Q of L: ★ ★ ★ ★ ★
Admissions: (781) 292-2222
Email Address: info@olin.edu

Strong Programs:
Electrical and Computer
 Engineering
Engineering
Mechanical Engineering

The admissions office invites approximately 250 applicants to attend one of three "candidates' weekends" in the spring.

bit weird. We're a very liberal-presenting place, but a lot of students don't actually engage in thinking about political issues." To make sure that it selects students who are a good fit for Olin's unique approach to engineering, the admissions office invites approximately 250 applicants to attend one of three "candidates' weekends" in the spring, where they learn about the school, take part in team projects such as building a weight-bearing bridge out of Styrofoam, and go through a 25-minute interview with a team that may include faculty, staff, students, and alumni. About 150 of these students are accepted, and about 40 are placed on a waitlist. In addition to awarding half-tuition scholarships, Olin guarantees to meet 100 percent of any remaining demonstrated financial need for all enrolled domestic students.

All students live on campus in Olin's two residence halls, first-years and sophomores in doubles in West Hall and upperclassmen in either doubles or suites in East Hall. Meal options in Olin's sole dining hall get average reviews, and a senior points out that the school "does exist in a food desert." Olin operates with a student-designed honor system that makes for unlocked rooms and take-home exams. "You can leave your laptop in the lounge, and it won't walk off," says a senior.

"The Student Activities Committee hosts some sort of schoolwide event every weekend."

When students aren't laboring over the latest Modeling and Simulation of the Physical World assignment, they tend to congregate on campus for fun. "There are parties in the residence halls, and the Student Activities Committee hosts some sort of schoolwide event every weekend," says a junior. There are no Greek organizations, and students say the social scene does not revolve around alcohol. The student orchestra has no conductor—or, as the joke goes, "not even a semiconductor." When the campus scene grows tiresome, "the surrounding area offers nothing," one student gripes of the town of Needham, so students often travel to nearby Babson (on foot) or Wellesley (by shuttle bus) to mingle. Aside from frequent visits to Boston, students enjoy road trips to Vermont or the beaches of Maine.

Students take advantage of volunteer opportunities, and the college organizes community-oriented events, such as a charity auction where students offer up everything from original artwork to haircutting services. Campus traditions "are very weird but have a certain charm," says a sophomore, who cites California day: "When the first proper snow of the year happens, the youngest Californian in the school sends out a poem about seeing snow for the first time and then the entire school goes out at midnight and runs around the center courtyard in swimsuits."

Although Olin does not offer varsity sports, two competitive club sports are available: soccer in the fall and ultimate Frisbee in the spring. In addition, "pickup leagues have evolved for soccer, Frisbee, football, and basketball," says a junior, and students are allowed to participate in intramural sports at Babson and Wellesley. Many students join extracurricular project teams that participate in competitions like Formula SAE, SAE Baja, and robotic sailing.

For those who have what it takes, Olin College offers a top-notch engineering degree at a bargain price. Pioneering Olin students have watched their school grow up and blossom, and they frequently take part in shaping its innovative approach to engineering education. Students here value interdisciplinary, project-based instruction, and they graduate inspired to shake up the workforce. As one junior comments, "Olin is pretty quirky, and we like to think we're different—passionate, weird, and doing fun things."

Overlaps

UC Berkeley, Caltech, Carnegie Mellon, Harvey Mudd, MIT, Rose–Hulman, Stanford, Yale

If You Apply To ›

Olin: Regular decision. Accepts the Common Application with supplement. Please consult Olin's website for the most up-to-date information regarding standardized test requirements.

1585 E 13th Avenue, Eugene, OR 97403

A flagship university of manageable size in a great location, UO is notable for its emphasis on the undergraduate educational experience in and out of the classroom. Liberal arts are more than just a slogan, and programs in the sciences, business, and communication are strong. Splashy sports program plays a big role in shaping campus life and culture. Lagging state funding ensures that it lacks the academic range of larger flagship universities.

As the most accessible of the West Coast flagship universities, the University of Oregon attracts brainy students who are proud of their often quirky ways. Bicycling is the main form of transportation, recycling is a requirement, and littering is déclassé. "I'd describe the University of Oregon as a place where you can find whatever you're looking for," describes a business administration major. "Whether you're into academics, the outdoors, sports, activism, or creative pursuits—there's truly something for everyone here."

UO's buildings date from as early as its founding in 1876 and are surrounded by the university's lush 295-acre arboretum-like campus, which boasts more than 4,000 trees representing nearly 500 species. Many academic buildings were built before World War II and represent a blend of classical styles, including Georgian, Second Empire, Jacobin, and Lombardic. A 160,000-square-foot, glass-and-steel facility is part of the Knight Campus for Accelerating Scientific Impact (funded in part by UO alum and Nike cofounder Phil Knight and his wife).

Oregon's academic calendar is organized by quarters, and its general education program consists of standard distribution requirements as well as one course exploring difference, inequality, and agency in the U.S. and one course on global perspectives. Each summer, the university offers IntroDUCKtion to new students, featuring opportunities for orientation, registration, and advisement. First-Year Interest Groups consist of 20 first-year students who take two lectures courses and one first-year experience seminar together around a common theme, such as Going Green and Path to Global Citizenship.

UO's professional schools—journalism, design, education, law, business, and music and dance—are highly regarded and considered more accessible to entry-level students than similar programs elsewhere. The most popular majors include business administration, psychology, general social science, and journalism/advertising. The College of Design offers sought-after programs in architecture, landscape architecture, and interior architecture—the state's only accredited degrees in these fields. In the College of Arts and Sciences, environmental studies is strong, and the science departments enjoy advanced resources and research opportunities in fields like nanotechnology, optogenetics, and neuropsychology. Pine Mountain Observatory, a field-study resource for astronomy and physics students located high in the Cascade Mountains, and the Oregon Institute of Marine Biology give students a chance for hands-on studies in their major. The interdisciplinary comics and cartoon studies minor is the first of its kind in the nation. The Sustainable Cities Initiative pairs students from a dozen academic programs (architecture, public policy, etc.) with community leaders to create innovative solutions to climate change.

"The academic climate at the University of Oregon is collaborative yet challenging," says an accounting major. "But it's not so competitive that you can't stand

> **"There's truly something for everyone here."**

Website: www.uoregon.edu
Location: Small City
Public
Total Enrollment: 22,554
Undergraduates: 19,430
Male/Female: 44/56
Financial Aid: 82%
Pell Grant: 23%
Expense: Pub $ $ $
Student Loans: 40%
Average Debt: $ $
Applicants: 40,021
Accepted: 88%
Enrolled: 14%
Grad in 6 Years: 71%
Returning First-years: 86%
Academics: ✐ ✐ ✐
Social: 🍷 🍷 🍷
Q of L: ★ ★ ★ ★
Admissions: (800) 232-3825
Email Address:
admissions@uoregon.edu

Strong Programs:
Architecture
Business Administration
Design
Education
Environmental Studies
Journalism
Music and Dance
Psychology

out if you put in the effort," notes a junior. Thirty-six percent of classes have fewer than 20 students. The quality of instruction varies, and it's not uncommon to find teaching assistants at the lectern, but a psychology and sociology major says, "All of my professors have been very passionate about what they are teaching."

Highly motivated undergraduates may apply to the Clark Honors College, a small liberal arts college with its own four-year curriculum that includes a senior thesis and opportunities for exclusive research assistantships. Student-run community internship programs provide credit for community volunteer work. Thirty-seven percent of undergrads study or complete internships abroad during their time at UO through more than 300 programs in 60 countries.

Only 54 percent of undergraduates are native Oregonians. International students account for just 1 percent of the student body. Asian Americans represent 7 percent, Black students 3 percent, Hispanics/Latinos 18 percent, and multiracial students 10 percent. "The political climate is skewed liberal all across campus," notes a sophomore. Numerous merit scholarships worth an average of $6,700 are available, as are more than 100 athletic scholarships in 20 sports. The Oregon Duck Tuition Guarantee keeps students' (including those from out-of-state) tuition fixed for up to five years without any increases or annual hikes. The PathwayOregon program covers tuition and fees for Pell-eligible Oregonians.

> **"It's not so competitive that you can't stand out if you put in the effort."**

Twenty-eight percent of UO students live in the university's 10 residence halls. First-years are required to reside on campus. A student says of the rooms, "They are pretty small, but I love the cozy feeling." There are several thematic living arrangements, including the Global Scholars Hall, the Clark Honors College, and Kalapuya Ilihi Hall, which is named for the native inhabitants of the Willamette Valley and offers communities for Native American and indigenous studies, social activism, art and design, and media and social action. Students can choose from five meal plans, and 14 dining venues serve up fresh, diverse menus. "The food on campus is actually amazing," says a sophomore. Students say they feel secure on campus, but some cite the growing homeless population just off campus as a safety concern. Even so, a senior reports, "There is a ride service called Duck Rides that can pick you up within a five-mile radius of campus and bring you back to your residence hall or off-campus apartment for free, no questions asked, to ensure students' safety." As for mental health services, a junior calls them "really solid— they offer a lot of helpful resources."

Eighteen percent of UO men and 16 percent of the women join Greek organizations, which provide living space, social diversions, and a wealth of leadership and community service opportunities. "The university plays host to a variety of concerts, culture nights, film viewings, guest lecturers, sporting events, and dances," a journalism major says. Students 21 and over may have alcohol in their rooms, but only with the doors closed. A junior says, "There are large parties happening around campus most nights of the week for people who would like to spend their time on such activities," but there is no pressure to do so. Everyone looks forward to the biannual Street Faire that brings local vendors to campus in the fall and the spring. "There is great food, local businesses, and artists, and everyone on campus gets to enjoy something different," explains a psychology major. Also popular, of course, is every home football game, where "thousands of students whoop and holler and scream their lungs out" for their Ducks.

"Off campus, there are tons of things to do, and due to our public transportation services, the city itself is pretty easy to get around," reports a journalism major. Eugene (population 178,000) offers plenty of popular hangouts, and according to one enthusiastic student, "Everything about Eugene is based around the Ducks!"

The one drawback is Oregon's weather: it rains and rains from late fall through spring. Still, the moist climate rarely dampens enthusiasm for the many expeditions available through the university's well-coordinated outdoor program, from rock climbing to skiing. An hour to the west, the rain turns to mist on the Pacific Coast; an hour to the east, it turns to snow in the Cascade Mountains. Those who stick around all year are rewarded with green, sunny summers.

UO's official mascot is a whimsical yellow-and-green likeness of Donald Duck. The athletic program is financially independent of the university, and the Ducks continue to dominate their Division I athletic rivals. They moved to the Big 10 in 2024, winning eight conference championships in the first year. The women's indoor track and field were national champions in 2025. Baseball, men's basketball, track and field, football, softball, and women's golf have had impressive successes as well. Duck fans love cheering on their teams, especially during the annual football game against archrival Oregon State, a grudge match that has been playing out since 1894. Intramurals are another time-honored pastime here, with flag football, basketball, soccer, and softball being the most popular.

"Everything about Eugene is based around the Ducks!"

The University of Oregon "is a place where you can explore different interests, meet all kinds of people, and really figure out who you are and what matters to you," cheers a junior. It offers ample opportunities for those with lofty ambitions to succeed. Indeed, UO's accessible academics, expert faculty, and abundance of social activities confirm that UO is all it's quacked up to be.

If You Apply To ›

UO: Early action, regular decision. SATs or ACTs: optional. Accepts the Common Application with supplement.

Oregon State University

1500 SW Jefferson Way, Corvallis, OR 97331

The biggest dilemma facing the typical 18-year-old Oregonian is whether to be a Beaver or a Duck. Choose Duck and hang with the ex-hippies in cosmopolitan Eugene. Choose Beaver and get small-town life with professional programs in business, engineering, and life sciences in Corvallis. Strong STEM focus, along with global emphasis.

Once known as Moo U, there's much more to Oregon State University than cows, fruits, and vegetables. One of the most accessible West Coast public universities, OSU is strong in many departments, including biotechnology, forestry, and engineering. As a land grant university founded in 1858, OSU offers abundant research opportunities and co-op work experiences, especially for students in STEM fields. Says one satisfied student, "Anyone would be lucky to be at Oregon State."

Located in the pristine but rainy Willamette Valley, OSU's campus is a mix of older buildings and more modern structures. In addition to the 500-acre main campus, OSU owns 13,000 acres of forestland near campus and numerous agricultural tracts throughout Oregon. Thousands of azalea and rhododendron bushes welcome springtime on campus with their colorful blooms, and summers are unfailingly sunny. Newer facilities include the PRAx, a center for the creative arts, and a new student health center.

Website: www.oregonstate.edu
Location: Small City
Public
Total Enrollment: 25,285
Undergraduates: 21,972
Male/Female: 51/49
Financial Aid: 67%
Pell Grant: 21%
Expense: Pub $ $ $
Student Loans: 43%
Average Debt: $ $

(continued)

Applicants: 30,293
Accepted: 77%
Enrolled: 20%
Grad in 6 Years: 70%
Returning First-years: 88%
Academics: ✍ ✍ ✍
Social: 🗨 🗨 🗨
Q of L: ★ ★ ★
Admissions: (541) 737-4411
Email Address:
osuadmit@oregonstate.edu

Strong Programs:
Agricultural Sciences
Business
Climate Science
Engineering
Forestry
Marine Biology
Natural Resources
Oceanography

The All-University Sing features musical numbers staged by fraternity and sorority members.

OSU operates on a quarter system, and its extensive Baccalaureate Core requires courses in a variety of areas, including skills; perspectives; and difference, power, and discrimination. One writing-intensive course is required as well. Perhaps the core's most innovative facet is its "synthesis" requirement, in which upperclassmen take two interdisciplinary courses on global issues in the modern world. The level of academic pressure varies by major, but even those in the various honors programs say they don't feel overworked. Although classes can be large, a merchandising management major says, "Professors are willing to spend one-on-one time to be able to make sure that you will succeed in their class."

OSU's College of Liberal Arts ranks with business and engineering as the largest on campus, but there are many more preprofessionals than poets. With the exceptions of history and English, the liberal arts—including such standard fare as sociology, economics, and philosophy—play second fiddle to more practical, technical fields. The business school offers some of the finest business-related programs in the state, and majors in forestry, natural resources, marine biology, oceanography, climate science, and engineering are strong drawing cards. Agriculture doesn't lure as many students as it used to, but excellent programs include agricultural sciences, animal sciences, and food science and technology. Adrenaline junkies and travel fans can major in tourism, recreation, and adventure leadership. Computer science, business administration, mechanical engineering, and psychology are among the most popular majors.

"Anyone would be lucky to be at Oregon State."

Students in the Honors College participate in small seminars with top professors and hands-on research, culminating in a senior thesis. Students in almost all majors can participate in the cooperative education program, which allows them to alternate terms of study with several months of work in a relevant job. Many research opportunities are available. Students who choose a semester abroad may select from 200 study abroad programs or research and internship opportunities in 70 countries around the world.

OSU students are "friendly and approachable," says a marketing and sustainability major, but mainly they share "a love for Oregon and what it has to offer." Fifty-four percent of undergraduates are from Oregon, and 3 percent hail from foreign countries. Just 2 percent are Black, 13 percent are Hispanic/Latino, 8 percent are Asian American, and 7 percent are multiracial. The Office of Diversity and Cultural Engagement sponsors several cultural resource centers, conferences, social justice retreats, and other diversity initiatives to support students from underrepresented backgrounds. Students come from "diverse socioeconomic and political backgrounds, and OSU does a good job of supporting the freedom of speech," explains a sophomore. Merit scholarships averaging $7,800 are awarded annually, as are more than 200 athletic awards in 17 sports. The Bridge to Success program allows roughly 3,000 in-state students per year to attend the university tuition-free.

First-year students are expected to live in college housing, though fraternity pledges have the option of living in their houses. Co-ed and single-sex options are available in the dorms, which house 17 percent of the students. "I loved living in my hall because it is where I made many friends; however, I much prefer living off campus because it is not as expensive," a student says. In addition to standard rooming situations, several living/learning communities in areas like engineering, outdoor adventure, and the environment are also options. "The food on campus is actually pretty good with lots of variety in various cultures," says a marketing and interior design major. Campus security and mental health support services get good reviews too.

"The whole community comes out and supports us during game days."

"Greek life is alive and well at Oregon State," says a sophomore, with 14 percent of men and 15 percent of women joining fraternities or sororities. Administrative efforts to make Greek parties safer include a ban on hard alcohol, a training program for students who wish to serve as sober party monitors, and a medical amnesty policy. Favorite campus traditions include the All-University Sing (featuring musical numbers staged by fraternity and sorority members) and the Dam Jam music festival in the spring. As for Corvallis (population 60,000), a senior says, "Corvallis is a little dry when it comes to outings, but OSU's clubs and activities make up for that." A popular student activity is complaining about the Willamette Valley weather: "People in the valley don't tan, they rust," warns one native. One reward for all the rain, however, is the abundance of flowers that bloom in all colors and shapes each May. Beautifully rugged beaches are less than an hour away, and some of the best skiing in the country can be found in the Cascade Mountains, two hours east. Hiking and rafting are nearby too, and camping on the coast provides more good times.

Cheering for OSU athletic teams keeps students Beaver busy, as does participation in 40 intramural leagues and 40 club sports. Benny Beaver, the school's former (and somewhat benign) mascot, has been replaced by a more aggressive beaver that students have dubbed the "angry beaver." Baseball, men's soccer, and men's and women's basketball and golf are highly competitive in the Pac-12 Conference and on the national stage. Oregon State's football rivalry with the University of Oregon dates back to 1894, and one student says, "The whole community comes out and supports us during game days."

While still a leader in agricultural education, OSU has expanded its reputation as a university that prepares students for successful futures in ever-evolving scientific, technical, and business fields. OSU doesn't scream for attention. Instead, it's content to be a "nice" college, in "a safe and pleasant little town," where professors are "helpful" and, even if everyone doesn't know your name, they'll let you stand under their umbrella whenever the skies open up.

Overlaps

Cal Poly–San Luis Obispo, Colorado State, Iowa State, University of Nebraska–Lincoln, Oklahoma State, University of Oregon, University of Washington, Washington State

If You Apply To ›

Oregon State: Early action, regular decision. SATs or ACTs: optional. Accepts the Common Application with supplement. Applicants have the option of identifying their gender, preferred name, and sexual orientation.

University of the Pacific

3601 Pacific Avenue, Stockton, CA 95211

The university's name dates from a time when there were no other U.S. universities near the Pacific. Still the only small, independent university in California north of L.A., it offers an eye-popping array of programs for an institution its size, including business, engineering, pharmacy, and education. The student body is just as diverse.

University of the Pacific was established in 1851 by Methodist ministers as California's first institution of higher education. Perhaps that's why it looks like 175 acres of New England plunked down in California wine country. With its stately combination of red brick and ivy, it could be mistaken for an East Coast liberal arts college. But instead of a blanket of snow, Pacific is surrounded by the lush greenery of the San Joaquin Valley. On campus, this increasingly competitive bastion of learning offers its 3,200 undergrads a solid and diverse academic program. "Our

Website: www.pacific.edu
Location: Suburban
Private
Total Enrollment: 5,900
Undergraduates: 3,125
Male/Female: 45/55

All students entering in their first year must complete two core seminars: problem-solving and oral communication and writing and critical thinking.

Pacific is surrounded by the lush greenery of the San Joaquin Valley.

school is very diverse, very academic focused, and does a great job at preparing you for graduate school," cheers an English major.

With majestic evergreens and flowering trees complementing collegiate Gothic buildings, Pacific's Stockton campus is home to six undergraduate schools, including the College of the Pacific, the university's liberal arts and sciences division. There is also a school of law in Sacramento, a superlative school of dentistry in San Francisco, a pharmacy school in Stockton, and the School of Health Sciences in Sacramento. A biological sciences building provides 56,000 square feet of space for the biological sciences department.

The university-wide general education program has four components: core seminars, a breadth program, a diversity and inclusion requirement, and fundamental skills. All students entering in their first year must complete two core seminars: problem-solving and oral communication and writing and critical thinking. In addition, students must complete six to nine courses in the breadth program and must demonstrate competence in writing, math, and reading. Strong offerings abound in the schools of engineering and business (with specialty concentrations in arts and entertainment management, business law, and entrepreneurship). The sciences, education, English, and international relations are also strong. A first-year says, "The best academic departments tend to be prepharmacy, predentistry, and the health, exercise, and sport science programs, because they do an astounding job of preparing students for their future professions."

> **"Our school does a great job at preparing you for graduate school."**

Students report that the academic atmosphere is relaxed. "Instead of students who do whatever it takes to be at the head of the class, everyone works together," says an international relations major. Forty-eight percent of the undergraduate classes have fewer than 20 students, and teaching assistants teach labs only. "The faculty members are very accessible," says one sophomore. The university guarantees graduation in four years (assuming the student follows all university guidelines), or it will pay for the extra schooling. Students are also guaranteed to have the opportunity for some type of experiential learning, and a number of internship and co-op programs are available. "Undergraduate research opportunities on this campus are amazing," enthuses an English major. An extensive study abroad program offers 200 choices in dozens of countries; international relations and global studies majors are required to spend at least one semester abroad.

Pacific students are "eager to learn but also want to experience learning outside of a classroom setting," says one first-year. Ninety percent of undergraduates are California residents, and 7 percent hail from foreign countries. As for ethnic diversity, Asian Americans account for 34 percent, Black students 3 percent, Hispanics/Latinos 29 percent, and multiracial students 6 percent. The school is middle-of-the-road to conservative, though politics in general play a small role on campus. "We're very open to all political, religious, sexual orientations, etc.," says a senior. Though not unusually expensive by national standards, the university price tag can seem steep when compared to the University of California system, so Pacific has stepped up efforts to compete, using merit scholarships averaging $25,400 annually as well as athletic scholarships in several sports. Thirty-eight percent of first-year students qualify for Pell Grants.

First-years and sophomores are required to live on campus, and 51 percent of all undergrads make their home in the residence halls. "Housing is generally pretty clean, and the sense of community is felt all across the halls," says one student. With three meal plans, two dining halls, and one fast-food-type facility, residents are well fed. A senior reports, "Campus security is pretty effective."

"There are some parties on campus, but most of them are off campus," opines a first-year. Just 5 percent of the men and 4 percent of the women go Greek, and the majority of Greek houses are designated substance-free. Students caught violating the alcohol policy must take an online course in alcohol education. Other social opportunities are offered by the Residence Hall Association, intramural and club sports, conservatory and drama/dance programs, campus movies, and nearly 200 student clubs. Annual campus festivities include the Tigerlands and Block Party concerts, described by a junior as "fun festivals we hold once a semester." For weekend excitement, Pacific students love to hit the road: within about two hours, they can be skiing, shopping in San Francisco, or surfing in Monterey. Stockton itself (population 322,000) offers shopping and plenty of fast-food joints as well as numerous volunteer opportunities.

> "Undergraduate research opportunities on this campus are amazing."

Pacific dropped football long ago, but the Tigers field several other competitive Division I teams. The women's volleyball team makes regular NCAA tournament appearances, and men's and women's basketball and water polo are also strong. The university also sponsors a solid speech and debate team.

Pitted against the state's immense public university system, Pacific stands out for offering major university opportunities in a small-college setting. The administration is striving to place more focus on its student body, which is becoming more top-notch and diverse. A political science major says, "When you come here, you instantly feel like you are surrounded by very friendly and loving people."

If You Apply To ›

Pacific: Early action, regular decision. SATs or ACTs: optional. Accepts the Common Application.

University of Pennsylvania

1 College Hall, Philadelphia, PA 19104

An Ivy League institution in name, Penn has more in common with places like Georgetown and Northwestern—where the liberal arts share center stage with preprofessional programs. At Penn, that means business, engineering, and nursing. Penn has something else other Ivies don't: school spirit. It's a good idea to apply early decision if Penn is your first choice.

Even in the fraught political climate of the mid-2020s, Benjamin Franklin would be proud of the way the university he helped create has surged. Once relegated to the bottom rungs of the Ivy League (and often confused with Penn State), the University of Pennsylvania is now the first choice for top students who see no conflict between high-level academics and having a life. The undergraduate College of Arts and Sciences—once on the university's back burner—is now central not only to its undergraduates but also to three other undergraduate schools that tap into its programs and course offerings. With a distinguished history that dates to 1740, Penn established the nation's first medical school, the first business school, the first journalism curriculum, and the first psychology clinic, and it is a pioneer in service learning and service research. In her inaugural address, a former president paid tribute to Franklin as "the ultimate visionary and pragmatist. Franklin thought education should be for the body as well as for the soul—that it should enable a graduate

(continued)

Accepted: 5%
Enrolled: 68%
Grad in 6 Years: 97%
Returning First-years: 99%
Academics: ✑ ✑ ✑ ✑ ✑
Social: 🗩 🗩 🗩
Q of L: ★ ★ ★
Admissions: (215) 898-7507
Email Address:
 info@admissions.upenn.edu

Strong Programs:
Anthropology
Biological Basis of Behavior
Business
Cognitive Science
Communication
Engineering
Management and Technology
Nursing

Juniors may apply to any master's program and begin completing graduate requirements during their senior year.

to be a breadwinner as well as a thinker, that it should produce socially conscious citizens as well as conscientious bankers and traders."

"Penn" is the university's traditional informal name. In recent years, "UPenn" has also emerged as a nickname, although this alternative is used more by outsiders than by students themselves. Penn's campus is situated in a tree-shaded, self-contained, 300-acre nest called University City, which is adjacent to downtown Philadelphia. Its more than 180 buildings range from Victorian Gothic to postmodern. There are very old structures, such as College Hall, and newer ones, such as Wharton's Huntsman Hall and Skirkanich Hall, home to Penn's bioengineering programs.

Penn's academic reputation has traditionally been wrapped up with its 12 graduate schools, especially the prestigious Wharton School of Business; the Annenberg School of Communication; and the well-known law, medical, and veterinary schools. (Penn claims to be the first university in the country to offer both undergraduate and graduate studies.) Three of the four undergraduate schools—engineering, nursing, and the undergraduate division of Wharton—are also professionally oriented and offer an education that's hard to beat anywhere. The undergraduate College of Arts and Sciences (a.k.a. "the College") provides students with high-quality instruction as well as the chance to run into a Nobel laureate here and there. The $237 million Amy Gutmann Hall is named for Penn's longest serving president (2004–2022) and serves as a hub for interdisciplinary collaborations.

> **"[Most professors] have developed a great teaching style."**

Finance is among the most popular undergrad majors, followed by economics and nursing. Penn's anthropology department ranks with Chicago's as tops in the country, while the management and technology program is also outstanding. Penn has earned applause in the field of cognitive and computer sciences because of its special program linking psychology, linguistics, and computers with philosophy. Another popular crème-de-la-crème interdisciplinary major, biological basis of behavior, combines psychology, biology, and anthropology. Students are allowed to design their own individualized majors, and they can hop from school to school—undergraduate or graduate—in doing so. Students in the Vagelos Program in Life Science and Management pursue studies in both the College of Arts and Sciences and the Wharton School, exposing them to research and development, biotech start-ups, managed care, and other related issues.

At the Wharton School (named after the 19th-century industrialist who founded it), the Joseph Wharton Scholars program emphasizes breadth in the arts and sciences. Another added plus that comes with a Penn undergraduate education is the opportunity for early entry (submatriculation) into the university's graduate programs. Juniors may apply to any master's program (continuing into the Wharton M.B.A. program is especially popular) and begin completing graduate requirements during their senior year. Penn offers no co-op programs and discourages full-time internships for credit, remaining true to the Ivy League belief that learning should be based in academic settings. Thirty percent of students explore more exotic classrooms by studying abroad at Penn's programs in Italy, Scotland, Japan, China, and Nigeria, among others. First-years are encouraged but not required to participate in a seminar program that explores various areas of academic interest and also in the Penn Reading Project, which involves student and faculty discussion of a common text.

Fifty-nine percent of undergraduate classes have fewer than 20 students, and while professors at Penn take their research responsibilities seriously, they are surprisingly accessible to first-years. "Most departments have fantastic professors who are tops in their field," says one student, "and have developed a great teaching style." The academic program at Penn is well supplemented by its huge and busy library, which houses more than six million volumes.

Despite all the preprofessional programs, Penn never lets its undergraduates stray too far from the liberal arts. The general education requirements in the College of Arts and Sciences mandate that students take at least one course in each of seven "sectors": society; history and tradition; arts and letters; living world; physical world; humanities and social sciences; and natural sciences and mathematics. Students must also complete one course in each of six "foundational approaches" areas, including writing, foreign language, quantitative data analysis, formal reasoning and analysis, cross-cultural analysis, and cultural diversity in the U.S. Strict academic policies and demanding professors exacerbate the academic pressure. "Penn is a competitive university," says one nursing major, "but is also intellectually stimulating."

> **"Penn students have historically been extremely involved with the local community."**

Thousands of faculty and students give expression to Benjamin Franklin's adage that service to humanity is "the great aim and end of all learning." To wit, Penn is a national leader in service learning and service research. Students work with local public school students as part of academic coursework in disciplines as diverse as history, anthropology, and mathematics. There are tons of opportunities to volunteer—from tutoring to Big Brothers Big Sisters to the Ronald McDonald House. "Penn students have historically been extremely involved with the local community and have taken the experiences they've had in the neighborhood with them to the real world," an economics and history double major says.

Eighteen percent of Penn undergraduates are Pennsylvania natives, and 13 percent are international. "There are all kinds of people with all kinds of personalities, interests, and backgrounds," says a student, "all of which makes Penn a vibrant place to live and study." Nine percent of undergrads are Black, 12 percent are Hispanic/Latino, 30 percent are Asian American, and 5 percent are multiracial. Penn admits students regardless of need—and meets full demonstrated need with loan-free financial aid packages—but does not offer any merit or athletic scholarships. Outreach programs target hundreds of schools and thousands of students from low- and middle-income families in an effort to improve socioeconomic diversity. Penn covers tuition for families earning $200,000 or less with typical assets and no longer considers the value of the primary family home among the assets used to determine financial aid eligibility.

> *Penn's anthropology department ranks with Chicago's as tops in the country.*

Fifty-two percent of all undergraduates live on campus and enjoy a wide range of living options in Penn's 15 co-ed "College Houses." The Quad, home to three of the houses, remains the hot spot, described as "well maintained and incredibly comfortable." Most College Houses offer living/learning programs for those who want to be surrounded by others with the same interests. Some upperclassmen move to the apartment-style accommodations in three high-rises across campus, but most head to nearby off-campus houses and apartments—"for the freedom, plus it's a lot cheaper," a junior says. Meal plans are required for first-years, and the food isn't all that bad for institutional fare. "The best kept secret on campus is the kosher cafeteria," says a finance and management major.

> **"Social life at Penn centers around frats."**

Undergraduates may work hard during the week, but in contrast to typical Ivy League achievers, they leave it behind them on weekends. "Social life at Penn centers around frats," a junior explains. "Parties freely serve alcohol to underage drinkers," according to another student, despite school policies dictating otherwise. More than two dozen fraternities attract 19 percent of the men, while sororities claim 17 percent of the women. The frats' exclusive claim to the houses along Locust

Walk, the main artery on campus, has been undone: after some controversy, it was determined that non-Greeks too must be able to live at the social nexus of the campus. Two big annual events at Penn are Spring Fling, a weekend "nothing short of absolutely incredible fun," and Hey Day, a century-old tradition where juniors, donning Styrofoam hats and carrying thin wooden canes, march down Locust Walk to officially become seniors, taking chomps out of each other's hats as they go.

Downtown Philadelphia is only a few minutes away by foot, car, or public transportation. Penn is located in the western part of town, once considered to be dangerous, but nowadays, as a senior explains, "There are a wealth of cultural resources at the tip of your fingers, and more and more students are able to find jobs in the Philadelphia area after graduation." Students frequent sporting events, South Street ("a miniature Greenwich Village"), and, of course, myriad bars and clubs. The city is home to several other colleges, and a student says, "There is a lot of social intermingling among the schools, and university students dominate the nightlife." Road trips include New York City, Washington, D.C., Atlantic City, and even Maine and Florida.

Penn is more sports-minded than most Ivy schools, and Division I football is the biggie. The team has grown accustomed to sitting on the top of the Ivy League and is at the nexus of widespread school spirit. Tickets are free for those with a student ID. The Penn–Princeton rivalry is always a crowd-pleaser. At the end of the third quarter of each home game, everyone in the stands begins belting out the lyrics of the Penn fight song, and when they get to "Here's a toast to dear old Penn," the students shower the field with burnt toast, "a moment that makes all Penn students proud," according to a senior. Aside from football, solid Quakers teams include men's and women's basketball, men's lacrosse, and women's field hockey and fencing. A bevy of intramurals and nearly 40 club sports bring thousands of less-seasoned athletes out to play each year, and all types of athletes benefit from the swanky track and weight-lifting facilities. Each spring, Penn hosts the prestigious Penn Relays, a track-and-field extravaganza that attracts the nation's best track athletes.

While its students work hard, Penn lacks the intellectual intensity of some of the other top Ivies, and you can detect preprofessional undercurrents. But most accept it for what it is: a first-rate university where you can live a relatively normal life in the heart of Philadelphia. Penn is one Ivy League university where no one apologizes for having fun. Says one sophomore, "There is a great balance between academics and social activities, which is rare in such highly competitive institutions."

Overlaps

Brown, Columbia, Cornell University, Georgetown, Harvard, Northwestern, Stanford, Yale

If You Apply To ›

Penn: Early decision, regular decision. SATs or ACTs: required. Accepts the Common Application with supplement.

Pennsylvania State University

201 Old Main, University Park, PA 16802

With a student body the size of a small city, Penn State is strong in fields from meteorology and business to film and television. The 1,800-student Schreyer Honors College is one of the nation's elite programs. Although its athletic programs have tended to grab most of the headlines, Penn State remains one of the premier public universities academically.

Living it up with over 40,000 fellow full-time undergraduates is probably not for the faint of heart. But those who can muster the energy to take advantage of Penn State's legendary school spirit and to navigate its vast sea of academic options will be rewarded with stellar programs in engineering, the sciences, and other fields appropriate to a land grant university.

With an eclectic architectural mix, including white-columned brick, stone, and some modern apartments, Penn State, which was founded in 1855 as the state's land grant university, continues to experience growth as major renovation and expansion projects proceed. New facilities and renovations are constantly underway. The $144 million Chemical and Biomedical Engineering Building is among the newer additions to campus. "Penn State just keeps growing and improving itself," says one student.

Penn State's general education requirements consist of 45 credits that include several communications and quantification courses as well as humanities, arts, natural sciences, social and behavioral sciences, and health and physical education courses. The incorporation of critical-thinking skills has been made a priority in the general curriculum. In addition, undergrads must enroll in courses on U.S. and international cultures. One helpful program offered to first-years is LEAP (Learning Edge Academic Program), which gives new students the benefit of a big university while making it seem small. Students in LEAP take a team approach by taking classes and living together. About 1,800 of the university's best and brightest are invited to participate in the Schreyer Honors College, which offers opportunities for research and an honors thesis as well as honors options in regular courses.

The most popular majors at Penn State fall under the categories of engineering, business, computer and information sciences, and social sciences. The university maintains strong programs in the scientific and technical fields such as earth sciences, engineering, forensic science, and life sciences, as well as nutrition and family studies. The meteorology program boasts alumni worldwide, including the founder of AccuWeather, an internationally renowned private forecasting firm. The College of Information Sciences and Technology is designed to prepare students for the digital age. The College of Agricultural Sciences has extensive facilities that include huge livestock barns. Its food sciences program is one of the best in the nation. Dairy products from the school's cows are sold at an on-campus store, and courses are offered in the production of its famous ice cream. Students can choose from more than 275 undergraduate majors spread over more than 20 locations statewide, including the College of Medicine and Dickinson Law, both located near Harrisburg, and Penn State Law on the University Park campus. Combined undergraduate/graduate degree options are available, as are engineering co-op programs, distance learning, and student-designed majors.

"The one thing about Penn State is that your academic experience is completely what you make it," counsels one student. Some of the intro-level lecture courses draw up to 400 students at University Park, yet most students seem to agree that classes are excellent and require your full attention. Students report that professors are accessible and engaging—when they are teaching; grad students frequently take on that responsibility. For cramming outside of class, the Penn State library system contains over 10 million volumes. About 16 percent of students study abroad through nearly 300 summer, semester, and full-year programs offered in roughly 50 countries.

"Penn State students are active, fun, and open-minded," says one student. Sixty-two percent of undergraduates are residents of Pennsylvania, with 9 percent hailing from foreign nations. More than half of Penn State's undergrads who finish

> **"Penn State just keeps growing and improving itself."**

The Dance Marathon, a student-run fundraiser, brought in $18.8 million for pediatric cancer patients in 2026.

at University Park began their education at one of the university's undergraduate campuses across the state. Many students note that race and diversity issues can be pronounced on a campus that is still pretty homogeneous for a public university: Asian Americans make up 8 percent of the undergrad population, Black students 5 percent, Hispanics/Latinos 9 percent, and multiracial students 4 percent. Hundreds of athletic scholarships are available in 29 varsity sports, as are thousands of merit awards, averaging $5,600.

First-years must live in the dorms, which students say are comfortable and located near classroom buildings and dining facilities. Overall, 35 percent of students live on campus; the rest find a home off campus, often in downtown apartments. "I loved living in the dorms," reports one public relations major. "I think it's part of the whole college experience, and I made some great friends along the way." The meal plan operates on a point system where you pay for what you eat. Stand for State is a comprehensive bystander intervention program covering sexual assault, drug and alcohol use, acts of bias, and mental health concerns.

> **"Penn State students are active, fun, and open-minded."**

"Social life at Penn State is huge," says a first-year. Seventeen percent of men and 20 percent of women go Greek. Partying at Penn State mostly happens at fraternities, but the administration has been focusing on measures to increase student safety and reduce dangerous drinking, hazing, and sexual assault, including imposing new rules for social events sponsored by Greek organizations. Greek Chapter Scorecards track conduct violations and disciplinary actions as well as academic performance, community service hours, and philanthropic fundraising efforts for every Greek chapter on campus. For social alternatives, the HUB (the campus union building) offers nonalcoholic entertainment, and more than 1,000 student organizations keep students busy too. Favorite annual events include the mid-July arts festival, the Dance Marathon—a student-run fundraiser that in 2026 brought in a record breaking $18.8 million for pediatric cancer patients—and, of course, homecoming.

The area around Penn State was dubbed "Happy Valley" in the 1930s because, largely due to the presence of the school, the area was less affected by the Great Depression. Sportswriters picked up on the term and still use it, and University Park students take advantage of the picturesque and peaceful locale by engaging in outdoorsy activities, including skiing and snowboarding at a nearby slope and sailing, canoeing, hiking, and renting cabins in Stone Valley. State College offers restaurants, bars, and cultural events such as symphonies, theatrical shows, and ballets, while the Bryce Jordan Center hosts top-notch performers. The town may be small, but according to a biochem major, "a majority of the students get involved in community service to maintain and constantly improve town relations."

> **"Social life at Penn State is huge."**

When thousands of alumni converge to cheer on their Nittany Lions (named after a type of local mountain lion) in blue and white, the festivities include tailgating replete with pregame parties and postgame revelry. As a member of the Big Ten, Penn State's foes include Michigan and Ohio State, both of which make great road trips. Nittany Lions teams have won over 80 national team championships in a wide variety of sports; the men's wrestling team brought home its fourth national title in a row in 2025. Women's volleyball, men's lacrosse, and men's and women's soccer are strong. There are three large gyms, a competitive-size pool, an indoor ice rink, and an extensive program of intramural and club sports for the recreational athlete, including a large angler's club.

Whether students want to major in meteorology, pursue cutting-edge research in AI, or dance 46 hours away for a good cause, Penn State's mix of scale, spirit, and

Overlaps

University of Delaware, Indiana University (PA), University of Maryland, Ohio State, University of Pittsburgh, Rutgers, Temple

substance shows it still lives up to its Happy Valley reputation. As one proud Lion explains, "Imagine a family of 40,000—the excitement, compassion, and sense of belonging."

Pepperdine University

24255 Pacific Coast Highway, Malibu, CA 90263

With stunning view of the Pacific Ocean, Pepperdine boasts what is arguably the most beautiful campus setting in American higher education. Proximity to L.A., only 35 miles away, contributes to its growing popularity. Pepperdine describes itself as a "Christian university," and students come ready to embrace its religious culture.

Given its picturesque setting that includes a beautiful surrounding seashore, Pepperdine University might seem like paradise for students seeking sunshine rather than study. But as a major Christian university, Pepperdine's prevailing philosophy is, as a communications major put it, that "God and the academic experience must be married," and it seeks to turn out graduates who will "lead purposeful lives as servant-minded leaders throughout the world." The result is an intimate learning environment that prides itself on moral integrity as well as high academic standards. Undergrads praise their educational opportunities, the strength of their school's spiritual community, and the vast sandy beaches beckoning below their hilltop campus.

There's no denying that Pepperdine's location, nestled in the Santa Monica Mountains about 35 miles northwest of Los Angeles, is a strong selling point. The 830-acre Malibu campus, to which the school moved from L.A. in 1972, overlooks the Pacific Ocean and features fountains, hillside gardens, mountain trails, and a 20-minute walk to the beach. Spanish revival architecture—cream-colored stucco buildings topped with red ceramic tile roofs—dots the landscape. The Phillips Theme Tower, a 125-foot-tall white stucco cross, stands 345 feet above sea level on the outskirts of campus and pays tribute to the university's Christian heritage.

Pepperdine was founded in 1937 by George Pepperdine, who established Western Auto Supply Company, a successful retail auto parts business. He was a lifelong member of Churches of Christ, and he dedicated his fortune to creating and endowing "a college that would provide the best education possible in an environment that celebrated faith-based principles," says an official. Campus life reflects an adherence to Christian values, from the prohibition of overnight dorm room visits by members of the opposite sex to the requirement that students attend Chapel—a faith exploration gatherings program for first- and second-year students. Drinking is also officially prohibited on campus. Most Pepperdine students like what one calls the "highly moral" atmosphere. "In comparison to other schools, Pepperdine students generally have a more religious foundation and thus have high standards of moral integrity," opines a student.

The academic programs of Seaver College, Pepperdine's undergraduate school, aim to prepare students to become "moral and intellectual leaders." Individual classes

> **"Pepperdine students generally have a more religious foundation."**

Website: www.pepperdine.edu
Location: Suburban
Private
Total Enrollment: 5,800
Undergraduates: 3,390
Male/Female: 40/60
Financial Aid: 93%
Pell Grant: 27%
Expense: Pr $ $ $ $
Student Loans: 36%
Average Debt: $
Applicants: 11,526
Accepted: 63%
Enrolled: 12%
Grad in 6 Years: 83%
Returning First-years: 88%
Academics: ✍ ✍ ✍
Social: 💬 💬
Q of L: ★ ★ ★ ★
Admissions: (310) 506-4392
Email Address: admission-seaver@pepperdine.edu

Strong Programs:
Biology
Business Administration
Economics
Integrated Marketing
  Communication
Journalism
Public Relations
Psychology
Sports Medicine

are demanding, as is the required Seaver Core program, which includes courses in English composition, speech and rhetoric, and a variety of liberal arts areas, such as creative arts, historical thinking, laboratory science, language and culture, and mathematical reasoning. Students must also take three religion courses. Faculty members are said to be accessible and responsive—not surprising when 69 percent of classes have fewer than 20 students. One student says professors "demand a lot from their students and expect a high standard and quality of work."

The Business Administration Division is the most popular at Pepperdine. The communication department, with majors including advertising, public relations, and journalism, is highly touted and boasts radio and television broadcasting studios. Psychology, integrated marketing communication, management, biology, and sports medicine are also popular. Dual-degree engineering programs are available in partnership with the University of Southern California and Washington University in St. Louis. The well-organized Career Center allows students to sign up for job fairs, interviews, and individual and group career-counseling sessions. Sophomores interested in international culture may spend a year at Pepperdine's own facilities in Buenos Aires, Florence, London, and elsewhere. Locations for summer study have included East Africa, the Galapagos Islands, Madrid, and Oxford. Roughly 80 percent of Pepperdine's undergraduates participate in short- and long-term study abroad programs.

Students embrace a wide range of political viewpoints on campus, but, as one denizen put it, "Pepperdine tends to shy away from political activism." Many students come from well-to-do California Republican families. Students have joked

"[Pepperdine's residence halls are] comfortable, convenient, and really quite nice."

that there's never a shortage of Porsches and BMWs on campus, but there is a shortage of places to park them. Still, the administration notes that about 18 percent of undergrads are first-generation students and 27 percent of students qualify for Pell Grants. Overall, 52 percent of undergraduates are California natives, and 8 percent come from abroad. Hispanics/Latinos account for 19 percent of the students, Asian Americans 15 percent, Black students 3 percent, and multiracial students 7 percent. The university awards merit scholarships averaging $16,900 to top achievers, in addition to about 300 athletic scholarships in 14 sports.

Sixty-one percent of undergraduates live in college-owned housing. A senior declares that Pepperdine's residence halls are "comfortable, convenient, and really quite nice." Housing options on the Malibu campus include single-gender suite-style houses, coed residence halls with single-gender suites, and coed apartment buildings with single-gender apartments. First-year students are typically assigned to suites with bathrooms, living rooms, and four double bedrooms. Some consider these arrangements crowded, but a junior says they "connect freshmen instantly to seven suitemates and friends." Despite the above-average cost of living in the Malibu area, many upperclassmen choose to live off campus. As for dining in the campus's nine venues, a senior says, "The meals are just OK."

Because the social scene in Malibu is pretty slack, with a 10 p.m. noise curfew and high price tags for everything, students typically head to L.A., Hollywood, Westwood, and Santa Monica for fun. "For a large proportion of students, academics and their social lives take priority over religious matters," says a public relations major. "Parties on weekends are well attended and probably draw a larger portion of students than church on Sunday." Roughly 21 percent of the men and 33 percent of the women join one of seven national fraternities or eight national sororities, respectively. Along with student government, they sponsor dances, movies, and other typical college activities, including the occasional illicit drink. "Pepperdine enforces a 'dry' campus," says one student. The Tyler Campus Center, housing the main dining hall, the bookstore, and more, serves as the main social center, and annual events including the Christmas tree lighting and Waves Weekend draw crowds.

Sports receive lots of attention at Pepperdine. The Waves compete in the Division I West Coast Conference and have won 10 NCAA team championships over the years. Competitive teams include men's and women's golf, men's and women's tennis, and women's swimming and diving. Students **"Parties on weekends are well attended."** enjoy participating in 12 club and intramural sports and have access to tennis courts, a swimming pool, and extensive physical education facilities that serve varsity jocks and weekend warriors alike.

Pepperdine has taken up the challenge of trying to marry the Christian focus of a Bible college with the academic rigor of a secular university—all in a location famous for being the home address for many of Hollywood's biggest stars. It's the rare place where a morning surf session might be followed by an ethics seminar—and both feel true to the spirit of the school.

If You Apply To ›

Pepperdine: Early decision, early action, regular decision. Accepts the Common Application. Please consult Pepperdine's website for the most up-to-date information regarding standardized test requirements and any additional application requirements for specialized programs.

University of Pittsburgh

4200 Fifth Avenue, Pittsburgh, PA 15260

As its home city has risen in stature, Pitt has become a hot commodity along with next-door neighbor Carnegie Mellon. A state-related university in the mold of the University of Cincinnati—not the state flagship, but strong in a host of preprofessional programs, especially in health fields. Pitt is among the nation's strongest in philosophy. Admissions is rolling, so apply early.

Pittsburgh long ago joined the ranks of the most livable cities in the United States. The University of Pittsburgh has matured, too, becoming a formidable public research institution. The school offers numerous opportunities for students pursuing medical, engineering, and business careers but leaves a great deal of room for exploration in the liberal arts. Students are encouraged to "lead lives of purpose and possibility" and carve out their own academic niche, either with multiple majors or with certificate programs. "I would describe Pitt as a powerhouse of academics and research, with a healthy amount of fun mixed in," says a junior.

Pitt began as a tiny, private educational academy in the Allegheny Mountains in 1787. Oh, how times have changed. The university, which became state-related in 1966, is adjacent to Carnegie Mellon and adjoins a 456-acre city park; it is part of the landscape of shops, museums, and galleries that make up Oakland, the heart of Pittsburgh's educational and medical center. Spacious, light-filled, contemporary buildings and generic modern office buildings make up the Pitt campus, but the architectural focal point is the iconic 42-story, neo-Gothic academic building, appropriately called the Cathedral of Learning, a national historic landmark. A new campus recreation and wellness center is expected to open in 2026.

Academic requirements in the Dietrich School of Arts and Sciences include

(continued)

Social: 💬 💬
Q of L: ★ ★
Admissions: (412) 624-7488
Email Address:
 pitt.admissions@pitt.edu

Strong Programs:
Bioengineering
Biological Sciences
Business
Computer Science
Engineering
Nursing
Philosophy
Psychology

writing, quantitative and formal reasoning, and foreign languages, as well as course-work in the humanities, social and natural sciences, and foreign cultures. First-year students undergo an extensive orientation before the fall term starts, take a one-credit studies seminar, and complete a course on diversity. Pitt offers guaranteed admission into a wide variety of graduate programs for outstanding first-year applicants. The Outside the Classroom Curriculum is an optional cocurricular program in which students build skills in leadership, reflection, service, and more.

With 16 undergraduate, graduate, and professional schools and more than 100 undergraduate majors across its five-campus system, Pitt rightfully claims to accommodate students with diverse needs. The excellent engineering and nursing schools attract high-caliber students. Premed students can watch transplants at the famed University of Pittsburgh Medical Center, one of the world's leading organ transplant centers. The rehabilitation science major prepares students for Pitt's highly competitive physical therapy program, which is tops in the country. The most popular majors include research and experimental psychology, biology, regis-tered nursing, and finance. The interdisciplinary politics and philosophy major is a unique offering.

Students describe coursework at Pitt as intensive but manageable; a chemistry major says, "With the rigorous material and courseload comes a lot of support from faculty and staff, so it all ends up balancing out." Forty percent of classes have fewer than 20 students, and a politics and philosophy major says, "Even though we have roughly 20,000 undergraduate students, class size does decrease as you get past the general education requirements and into the more program-specific courses." Pitt faculty members are often at the top of their fields, leading the way in areas like astronomical discoveries and medical advances.

> **"I would describe Pitt as a powerhouse of academics and research, with a healthy amount of fun mixed in."**

The academically motivated can pursue a distinctive, research-focused bachelor of philosophy degree from the excellent University Honors College. More than half of Pitt undergraduates participate in research facilitated by the university's 400 cen-ters, institutes, laboratories, and clinics. "There are so many opportunities to partic-ipate in personal projects and receive funding for these initiatives," cheers a history of art & architecture and microbiology major. For those who want to travel, the university boasts study abroad options in more than 60 countries; 26 percent of undergrads participate. Closer to home, Pitt is a partner with Carnegie Mellon University in the Pittsburgh Supercomputing Center. Students praise the Career Center's internship prep program, which places students in local internships after they've completed a set of workshops and other requirements.

> *More than half of Pitt undergraduates participate in research facilitated by the university's 400 centers, institutes, laboratories, and clinics.*

"The student body is fairly diverse and there are many student groups on campus for people to find their community," says a political science and economics major. Sixty-two percent of undergraduates are from Pennsylvania, and 4 percent hail from other countries. Black students account for 5 per-cent of the student body, Asian Americans 15 per-cent, Hispanics/Latinos 7 percent, and multiracial students 5 percent. "Socioeconomically and polit-ically it is more diverse," attests a computer and data science major. Pitt offers merit awards averaging $8,900 to incoming first-years, and more than 250 athletic scholarships are available in 19 varsity sports. Pell Grant recipients benefit from the Pitt Success Pell Match Program, which doubles the federal amount.

> **"There are many student groups on campus for people to find their community."**

Pitt continues to increase the amount of on-campus living space and guarantees housing for three years. Forty-one percent of students live in a variety of co-ed and single-sex dorms with all kinds of rooming situations, from singles to apartment-style suites. Seventeen living/learning communities for first years and several for upper-class students draw nearly a third of students. Hungry students may choose from two all-you-care-to-eat dining facilities, more than 25 on-campus retail dining locations, and several off-campus local spots. "After the recent renovations and changes to the dining hall, the food is really good," shares a senior. Campus safety is bolstered by a consistent police presence, and a sophomore notes, "The administration has shown that they're receptive and responsive to student concerns about issues like sexual assault." Several students note that other services, such as mental health care, are strong, but a junior notes, "students must reach out first."

Within minutes of Pitt's campus are shops, parks, museums, professional sporting events, and performing arts venues, and PITT ARTS provides students with discounted or free tickets for cultural events in the city. The university also grants students fare-free access to city buses. "Exploring the city has been one of my favorite parts of my Pitt experience. There's so much more to do and see outside of Oakland," says a senior. Another adds, "The city has a mix of quirky bars, dancing bars, and clubs for the 21+ crowd." On campus, students have more than 700 clubs and organizations to choose from, and 9 percent of the men and 12 percent of the women belong to the Greek system. "Greek life is not huge here," says one senior. Favorite annual events include Lantern Night in which alums welcome first-years with candles in small lanterns, as well as Bigelow Bash and Fall Fest, concerts that bring recognizable performers to campus. Adjacent Schenley Park offers jogging trails and green space. Ski slopes and mountain trails are not far away, and road trips to Penn State and Philadelphia, Boston, and New York City are popular.

> "The 'Backyard Brawl' (Pitt v. West Virginia) is our biggest Pitt football rivalry and game of the year."

The Pitt Panthers compete in the Division I Atlantic Coast Conference, and men's wrestling and women's volleyball have taken home recent championships. Men's basketball and men's and women's soccer are also strong. "The 'Backyard Brawl' (Pitt v. West Virginia) is our biggest Pitt football rivalry and game of the year," cheers a senior. "Usually, we sell out Acrisure Stadium for this game, and it is so much fun!" Approximately 42 percent of undergrads take part in intramurals and club sports; the most popular are basketball, volleyball, and flag football.

Pitt is a large university made to feel small. Its flexibility in adapting to students' needs and its commitment to community breed a kind of loyalty and pride that students say can't be found elsewhere. Case in point, one senior declares, "I have two separate friends who have our unofficial slogan, 'Hail to Pitt,' tattooed on them." Now that's commitment.

Overlaps

University of Delaware, University of Maryland, University of Michigan, Northeastern, Ohio State, Penn State, Purdue, Rutgers

If You Apply To ›

Pitt: Rolling admissions. Accepts the Common Application with supplement. Please consult Pitt's website for the most up-to-date information regarding standardized test requirements.

Pitzer College: See page 151.

Pomona College: See page 153.

503 S Broad Street, Clinton, SC 29325

A South Carolina liberal arts college that competes head-to-head with Wofford for students who want their education served up with plenty of personal attention. Business programs complement the focus on liberal arts. Scottish heritage adds flavor to the small-town setting. About two-thirds of PC students are from South Carolina.

Website: www.presby.edu
Location: Small Town
Private
Total Enrollment: 1,087
Undergraduates: 848
Male/Female: 50/50
Financial Aid: 99%
Pell Grant: 30%
Expense: Pr $
Student Loans: 68%
Average Debt: $ $ $ $
Applicants: 3,297
Accepted: 68%
Enrolled: 12%
Grad in 6 Years: 51%
Returning First-years: 80%
Academics: ✍ ✍ ✍
Social: 🗨 🗨 🗨
Q of L: ★ ★ ★ ★
Admissions: (800) 476-7272
Email Address:
  admissions@presby.edu

Strong Programs:
Biology
Business Administration
Computational Biology &
  Bioinformatics
English
History
Prepharmacy
Psychology

Consistent with the school's founding by clergyman William Plumer Jacobs way back in 1880 to educate orphans, Presbyterian College students strive to live up to the motto Dum Vivimus Servimus ("While we live, we serve"). Virtually all students volunteer while at PC. Increasingly, they are also logging research hours in the lab, traveling to far corners of the world, and trying out potential careers through internships. At the same time, they continue to pursue personal, spiritual, and academic growth as part of a "church-related liberal arts education."

Presbyterian College's campus sits on 240 acres in the South Carolina piedmont. The redbrick buildings are largely Georgian in style, with tall, white columns and lots of shade trees. Many structures are listed on the National Register of Historic Places, including the campus's most recognizable building, Neville Hall. The campus resembles Thomas Jefferson's University of Virginia, with buildings grouped around three plazas, which are perfect for reading, studying, or throwing a Frisbee. A new outdoor sports complex includes courts for pickleball and basketball.

PC's curriculum emphasizes the traditional liberal arts, with a range of required courses, as well as experiential learning: all students either study abroad, conduct independent research, or complete an internship before graduation. The required Compass program extends from first year through senior year, beginning with a First-Year Exploration course that focuses on critical thinking, academic skills, and personal exploration of vocation and calling. Sophomores take a course that helps them explore potential career paths. Students must also develop an electronic portfolio and participate in a senior capstone course.

"The coursework is intense at times but is not so intrusive that it devours all of a student's time," says a political science major. An honor code holds students accountable for their behavior and creates an atmosphere of mutual respect. Classes are small, with 68 percent enrolling fewer than 20 students, encouraging personal relationships with faculty.

> **"My professors have been so much more than just teachers to me."**

"My professors have been so much more than just teachers to me—they have become my friends, travel partners, mentors, and role models," enthuses an English and history double major. The most popular majors are business, biology, psychology, and sociology. These are also some of PC's strongest programs. Computational biology & bioinformatics is a rare offering for a college. High-achieving students desiring a degree in pharmacy can apply to the Early Entry Pre-Pharmacy Program, which allows them to earn a doctorate degree in six years through the PC School of Pharmacy. PC Flex provides a path for students in some majors to complete their four-year degree more quickly.

Options for off-campus study, in which 22 percent of students partake, include semester-long exchange programs as well as highly popular, short-term Maymester trips led by faculty to destinations such as Australia, Greece, South Africa, Fiji, and, of course, Scotland. The Center for Inquiry, Research, and Scholarship lets students collaborate with faculty in research. For eight weeks each summer, 10 to 25 Summer Fellows receive stipends to live on campus, undertake independent research guided by faculty, and present the findings of their work.

While a minority of students are Presbyterian, the campus atmosphere is distinctively Christian. "Our students practice servitude and Christian love in their daily lives," a senior says. Forty-two percent of undergraduates hail from states outside South Carolina, and 5 percent come from nations abroad. "The great thing about PC is that it's becoming more diverse," cheers a biochemistry major. Black students make up 17 percent of the population, Hispanics/Latinos 10 percent, Asian Americans 1 percent, and multiracial students 7 percent. Politically, reports a senior, "PC seems to be split between both major political parties." Merit scholarships worth up to $30,000 are handed out to eligible students, as are roughly 200 athletic awards.

Eighty-nine percent of Presbyterian students live on campus, where accommodations range from traditional rooms with hall baths to suites and apartments, and quality is said to vary. The two dining facilities on campus, a buffet-style dining hall and a food court, receive mixed reviews. "The Sunday buffet is awesome. After church, people from the community pay to eat in our cafeteria," says an English major. A senior notes that the campus feels safe, and the school's strict honor code means that "you can trust your neighbors at PC." Mental health care is strong, attests a senior: "They have given me helpful advice to manage my stress and anxiety."

"Our students practice servitude and Christian love in their daily lives."

Twenty-one percent of PC's men and 22 percent of the women join Greek groups, and "There are parties every Saturday night unless the school says otherwise," says one student. The school has taken a firm stand against underage and unsafe drinking: all frat parties must be registered and attended by sober party monitors, while staff check IDs and distribute under-21 wristbands at the door. For alternatives, the Student Activities Board hosts movie nights, coffeehouses, art nights, and other events on campus, and many students join clubs. Owing to PC's aforementioned motto, Student Volunteer Services is the largest organization on campus, routinely sending students to help at local orphanages, nursing homes, schools, and other facilities. Favorite annual traditions include Shuckin' and Shaggin', an oyster roast and dance in the fall, and Spring Fling, a weekend carnival. Students also look forward to the Christmas at PC concert and to the outdoor graduation ceremony under the oaks, complete with bagpipes. As for the surrounding area, "Clinton is not a very active town," says a business administration major, so students usually head to Greenville, Spartanburg, or Columbia (all within an hour's drive) when they want to get off campus for a bite to eat or shopping. PC is equidistant from South Carolina's mountains and beaches, providing many opportunities to enjoy the outdoors.

PC's 19 varsity sports teams compete in Division I. The college's mascot is the Blue Hose, a reference to the socks the first football teams wore. (While some students wear kilts during athletic events, most constrain such enthusiasm, says a junior.) Men's baseball is a recent Big South Conference winner, and other strong programs include women's wrestling, tennis, and basketball and men's soccer. Recreational sports are divided into three divisions, depending on how competitive you are. All students may take advantage of PC's 31-acre recreational facility, with lighted softball, football, and soccer fields, volleyball courts, a basketball court, a track, and an amphitheater.

Presbyterian College students take pride in the school's history and traditions, including its very own tartan. "When you are at PC you are family," says a sophomore. PC's church affiliation keeps students focused on service and on bettering the broader world, adding dimension to their classroom experiences. One Blue Hose sums it up this way: "PC is Southern, classic, timeless, and fun!"

Maymester trips are led by faculty to destinations such as Australia, Greece, South Africa, Fiji and, of course, Scotland.

The most popular majors are business, biology, psychology, and sociology.

Overlaps

Anderson, Clemson, College of Charleston, Furman, University of South Carolina, Winthrop University, Wofford

If You Apply To ›

Presbyterian: Early action, regular decision. SATs or ACTs: optional. Accepts the Common Application with supplement.

Prescott College

220 Grove Avenue, Prescott, AZ 86301

With its commitment to environmental studies, sustainability, and social justice in a liberal arts context, Prescott attracts students who love the outdoors and are looking for an alternative college experience. Unique academic calendar. Has ready access to northern Arizona and southern Utah's outdoor playground. College of the Atlantic is the only remotely comparable college in the *Fiske Guide*.

Website: www.prescott.edu
Location: Small City
Private
Total Enrollment: 465
Undergraduates: 202
Male/Female: 38/62
Financial Aid: 89%
Pell Grant: 41%
Expense: Pr $
Student Loans: 59%
Average Debt: $ $ $
Applicants: 140
Accepted: 99%
Enrolled: 17%
Grad in 6 Years: 40%
Returning First-years: 75%
Academics: ✍ ✍ ✍
Social: 💬 💬
Q of L: ★ ★ ★ ★
Admissions: (877) 350-2100
Email Address:
admissions@prescott.edu

Strong Programs:
Adventure Education
Arts and Letters
Critical Social Justice and
  Solidarity
Education
Environmental Humanities
Psychology
Sustainable Community
  Development

This tiny outpost in the wilderness of central Arizona is a perfect spot for the adventurous nature lover who wants to learn survival skills and likes studying outdoors. Where else but Prescott College could you major in adventure education or take courses like Backcountry Skiing and Avalanche Training, Ecopsychology, and Barrio Pedagogy? Before any Prescott student sets foot in a classroom, they head to the outback for three weeks of hiking and camping, or to the town of Prescott for service learning, research projects, and field trips. Wilderness Orientation and Community-Based Orientation offer an introduction to everything Prescott stands for: hands-on experience, personal and social responsibility, cooperative living, and stewardship of the environment.

Founded in 1966 and still one of the only private liberal arts college in Arizona, Prescott retains the air of a 1960s commune. Surrounded by national forest, the college's "campus" consists of a two-block-long handful of buildings in the small town of Prescott. The architectural style of the campus ranges from the historic to the modern. The largest of the college's buildings is the Crossroads Center, an all-green building, which houses the library, computer labs, classrooms, conference centers, and the Crossroads Café. The administrative building was once a convent; its chapel is now used for meetings, art shows, and performances.

Prescott's requirements for graduation are characteristically unorthodox. Instead of grades, faculty members give narrative evaluations, although students may elect to receive grades. And rather than accruing credits, students design individualized "degree plans" that outline the competence (major) and breadth (minor/ concentration) areas they will pursue and the Senior Project (thesis) they will complete to

> **"You can interact with your coursework in a way that's more meaningful to you."**

demonstrate competence (graduate). Students must obtain two levels of writing certification (college level and thesis level) and math certification, showing knowledge of college-level algebra. Students also take a set of required interdisciplinary Core Curriculum courses, which are cotaught by faculty from multiple fields. Prescott's personal touch even extends to graduation, a unique experience where a faculty member speaks about each student personally and then the student speaks on their own behalf.

Prescott bills itself as a college "for the liberal arts and the environment," and students tend to envision themselves becoming teachers, researchers, park rangers, wilderness guides, social activists, and the like. To design their degree plans, students start by selecting an area of study: adventure education, field ecology and conservation, critical social justice and solidarity, environmental humanities, or psychology. Those with eclectic interests can opt for interdisciplinary studies to blend courses from multiple areas. Each area of study offers several concentrations. In the standout environmental studies program, for instance, concentrations cover impressive breadth and depth, ranging from marine studies to natural history and climate justice. Adventure education, in which students learn everything from avalanche forecasting to rock climbing, is also a specialty. The teacher preparation program offers students teaching credentials in elementary and secondary education. Several programs have accelerated pathways in which undergrads can earn a master's degree tuition-free. Prescott does not offer a comprehensive program in advanced math, chemistry, physics, or foreign languages other than Spanish.

"People are inspired to work hard because their projects reflect their passions, not because they're worried about getting an A," observes one senior. A human consciousness major adds, "Because you're not cramming for the next test (I never took one here), you can interact with your coursework in a way that's more meaningful to you." There's no tenure track at Prescott, and publishing and research take a back seat to teaching, although students warn that the quality of instruction can be inconsistent. With virtually all classes enrolling fewer than 20 students, the academic atmosphere is intimate, to say the least.

Prescott's academic calendar consists of two 16-week terms, each of which is divided into four blocks. During each block, students pursue intense immersion in just one course for four weeks, a model designed to allow maximum flexibility for fieldwork, community-based studies, and outdoor learning. Students may spend a block in the backcountry of Baja California or the alpine meadows of Wyoming, for example, or in a local service clinic. Students can even take a one-month rafting trip down the Colorado River for credit. Though Prescott does not offer a traditional study abroad program, students are encouraged to take courses in marine biology and cultural studies at the Kino Bay Center for Cultural and Ecological Studies in Mexico, as well as a social justice course in Kenya; about half of Prescott students have an international experience by the time they graduate. "Prescott's campus has no borders," says a sustainable community development major. "There are so many opportunities to go abroad or be out in the field." Paid internships are available through partnerships with AmeriCorps and other organizations.

"There is a 'hippie' stereotype of PC students, but I think that image is slowly shifting," remarks a senior. Environmental issues still predominate among the liberal student body. Despite the challenges of low retention and graduation rates, Prescott's unconventional approach continues to entice students well beyond Arizona. Prescott's Changemaker Scholarship is bringing in more students by awarding guaranteed tuition scholarships worth up to $17,000 per year to every incoming undergraduate who enrolls in a degree program. About 31 percent of students are 25 or older. Currently, 73 percent of undergraduates are out-of-staters; less than 1 percent come from other countries. The minority population is small but growing, with Black students making up 4 percent of the total, Hispanics/Latinos 7 percent, Asian Americans 3 percent, and multiracial students less than 1 percent. Pell Grant recipients represent 41 percent of incoming first-years.

Twenty-six percent of full-time undergrads call the on-campus housing units—a grouping of eight-person townhouses known as the Village—home. The vast majority of students fend for themselves in the town of Prescott, a rapidly growing community of approximately 48,000 where almost everything is accessible by bicycle. The college assists with the apartment hunt by providing lists of available properties and by cosigning leases when necessary. The Crossroads Café, the only dining facility, draws praise for being tasty and fresh. "Omnivores, vegetarians, vegans, and gluten-free folk all love the food in the café," cheers one student. Additionally, "The café staff offer cooking lessons throughout the semester. There's also free community lunch every Wednesday."

Social life at Prescott is informal, often consisting of small, "mellow" off-campus parties. With fewer than 20 student organizations and no strong traditions to speak of, students say the campus doesn't offer much in the way of a social scene. "If you love the outdoors, Prescott is great. Do not come here for a social experience," advises an adventure education major. As for the townsfolk, students describe them as "a mix of artists, activists, students, locals, retirees, and ranchers." Those looking for nightlife can hit Whiskey Row, the town bar scene, or drive to Flagstaff (90 minutes) or Phoenix (two hours).

The college offers just one sport—cycling—which has won titles in road cycling, mountain biking, and cyclocross. For other sports, students often participate in city leagues. "Our school has bike jousting, juggling, barefoot soccer, ultimate Frisbee, and capoeira—none of which involve competing against other schools," says one student.

Prescott may not have the huge campus or financial resources that are typically associated with larger schools; however, the small classes and specialized programs appeal to a student who would not be interested in your "typical" college. As a senior explains, "Our passion and dedication to education spring from a deep inner desire to effect positive change in the world."

If You Apply To ›

Prescott: Rolling admissions. SATs or ACTs: optional. Accepts the Common Application with supplement.

Princeton University

Princeton, NJ 08544

Princeton is the smallest of the Ivy League's Big Three, which means plenty of attention from faculty and plenty of opportunity for rigorous independent work. Offers engineering but no business major. The affluent suburban location contrasts with urban New Haven and Cambridge. Residential college system modeled on Yale's provides a support network and a social alternative to long-standing eating clubs. Generous financial aid program covers full tuition, room, and board for about one-quarter of undergraduates.

Princeton occupies a distinctive niche among America's superelite universities. It is a major research university with a world-class corps of professors who, in the absence of lots of graduate and professional students, lavish their attention on a relatively modest number of talented undergraduates. Princeton has an engineering school as well as programs in applied science, architecture and public planning, and public policy and an Entrepreneurial Hub near campus, but it is basically an "arts and sciences university." The academic atmosphere across campus is dominated by commitment to the liberal arts—with a carefully structured set of core requirements and a heavy emphasis on independent study, including a mandatory senior thesis. A sophomore says, "What sets Princeton students apart is that they come here not just for an excellent education, but they come to share knowledge with others."

For better or worse, Princeton has been known as a bastion of exclusivity, although its undergraduates are now just as racially and ethnically diverse as any other Ivy League school. Still, university leaders are looking to make Princeton's particular brand of high-powered undergraduate liberal arts education available to an even more diverse group of students. Sensitive to faculty complaints that Princeton enrolls too many bright students whose main claim to fame is that they have learned to work the system, the admissions office is on the lookout for more students with demonstrated intellectual curiosity—including more STEM majors, creative types, and high-ability/low-income students. The administration has made major investments in the sciences, engineering, and creative and performing arts to enhance these efforts. The Emma Bloomberg Center for Access and Opportunity provides all students with mentorship and academic enrichment opportunities. Two of the center's programs aimed at supporting first-generation, low-income, and other underrepresented students include the Freshman Scholars Institute, which offers an academic and social introduction to Princeton over the summer before classes start, and the Scholars Institute Fellows Program that covers all four years.

Cloistered in a secluded but upscale New Jersey town, Princeton's architectural trademark is Gothic, from the cavernous and ornate university chapel to the four-pronged Cleveland Tower rising majestically above the treetops. Interspersed among the Gothic are examples of colonial architecture, most notably historic Nassau Hall, which served as the temporary home of the Continental Congress in 1783 and has defined elegance in academic architecture ever since. A host of modern structures, some by leading American architects Robert Venturi, Frank Gehry, and I. M. Pei, add variety and distinction to the campus, but the ambiance is still quintessential Ivy League at its best. The outstanding library facilities embrace five million volumes and provide 500 private study carrels for seniors working on those mandatory theses; there are another 700 enclosed carrels in other parts of the campus. Princeton's campus is self-contained, but those who venture outside its walls will find the surroundings quite pleasing. One side of the campus abuts quaint Nassau Street, which is dominated by chic (and pricey) boutiques and restaurants, as well as coffee shops and more affordable eateries. The other side of campus ends with a huge man-made lake that was financed by Andrew Carnegie so that Princetonians would not have to forgo crew. A new residence, Hobson College, is slated for completion in 2027. The new Princeton University Art Museum, designed by Sir David Adjaye, renowned designer of the National Museum of African American History and Culture in Washington, D.C., opened in 2025.

Princeton became the model for American-style liberal arts colleges after John Witherspoon was lured from the University of Edinburgh to become president in 1768. Today, Princeton is distinctive in its modest scale and its emphasis on undergraduates. Each student's Princeton experience begins with a week of orientation; hundreds of students participate annually in Outdoor Action, a few days of wilderness activities immediately preceding orientation. All first-year students are also assigned a faculty advisor. With fewer graduate students to siphon off resources or consume faculty time than at large research universities, undergraduates get the lion's—or should we say Tiger's!—share of both; at last count, 70 percent of Princeton's department heads taught introductory undergraduate courses. An economics major says, "I can open the newspaper and read my professor's article or turn on the TV and see him giving a speech, then go to a lecture to hear him speak, then go to his office to speak with him one-on-one." Two-thirds of new students work closely with senior faculty members by participating in the optional First-Year Seminar program, choosing from more than 75 options offered annually, ranging from Writing for Your Life to The Coming of Driverless Cars. Lovers of literature can study with poet Ilya Kaminsky, and nearly every other department has a few stars of its own. "We have some of the most brilliant professors in the world here," confirms a junior. Senior professors lead at least one or two of the small discussion groups that accompany each lecture course.

(continued)

Returning First-years: 98%
Academics: ✍ ✍ ✍ ✍ ✍
Social: 🗩 🗩 🗩
Q of L: ★ ★ ★
Admissions: (609) 258-3060
Email Address:
  uaoffice@princeton.edu

Strong Programs:
Architecture
Computer Science
Economics
Engineering
History
Mathematics
Philosophy
Public and International Affairs

> **"[Princeton students] come to share knowledge with others."**

Hundreds of students participate annually in Outdoor Action, a few days of wilderness activities immediately preceding orientation.

Every student must fulfill distribution requirements in culture and difference, epistemology and cognition, ethical thought and moral values, historical analysis, literature and the arts, social analysis, quantitative and computational reasoning, and science and engineering. Students also take a first-year writing seminar and must demonstrate proficiency in a language other than English. During their junior year, liberal arts students work closely with a faculty member of their choice in completing two junior papers—about 30 pages of independent work each semester in addition to the normal courseload. Princeton also requires every graduate to complete a senior thesis—an enterprise that serves as a culmination of their work in their field of concentration. As a result, "seniors develop close personal relationships with their thesis advisors," says one student. Alumni often cite the thesis as one of their best experiences at Princeton.

Naturally, given Princeton's small size, the number of courses offered is smaller than at other Ivies, but students still have many high-quality options and 76 percent of undergraduate classes have fewer than 20 students. Princeton's math and philosophy departments are among the best in the nation, and architecture, economics, history, public policy, English, physics, molecular biology, and romance languages are right on their heels. As part of a major effort to become a national center in the field of molecular biology, the university supports a sizable laboratory for teaching and research. Princeton is one of the few top liberal arts universities with equally strong computer science and engineering programs, most notably chemical, mechanical, electrical, and aerospace engineering. Operations research and financial engineering is one of the fastest-growing majors. One of Princeton's best-known programs is the prestigious Princeton School of Public and International Affairs, which offers a multidisciplinary, policy-focused major for undergraduates. A majority of students study abroad in 100-plus programs offered in more than 40 nations. For those wishing to postpone their entry into the university in favor of an international experience, Princeton's Bridge Year program covers the full cost of one-year service abroad programs in Bolivia, India, Indonesia, and Senegal.

> **"I can . . . read my professor's article or turn on the TV and see him giving a speech."**

"The courses are very challenging and rigorous," a junior reports, "but perhaps because of that, people are very cooperative. They realize that no one can really succeed alone." The university honor code, unique among the Ivies, allows for unproctored exams. A limited number of courses can be taken on the pass/fail option. Although the faculty gets high ratings for its academic advising, students are rather cool on the university's nonacademic counseling programs.

> *The administration has made major investments in the sciences, engineering, and creative and performing arts.*

"Our students are tight-knit, extremely hardworking, highly cooperative, and supportive of one another's activities," says an economics major. Eighteen percent of undergraduates are New Jersey residents, and 13 percent are international. Black students account for 10 percent of the student body, Hispanics/Latinos 9 percent, Asian Americans 23 percent, and multiracial students 7 percent. While diversity is present, the social atmosphere can be somewhat stratified. "As an African American, I can say that even the African Americans are subdivided based on economics, place of origin, and whether you went to public or private school," explains one senior. Although students report that there can be a general air of apathy around campus, administrators are quick to point to the numerous political organizations on campus as evidence of students' interest in political and social issues. Princeton undergraduates, both domestic and international, are admitted to the university without regard to their financial need, and those who qualify for aid receive generous support that covers their full demonstrated need. In fact, Princeton was the first university in the U.S. to replace loans with grants for all aid recipients. Most students from families with annual incomes of up to $150,000 do not pay tuition, room, or board and receive grants to assist with the cost of books and personal expenses. Most students from families with annual incomes up to $250,000 pay no tuition.

In an attempt to improve campus life and broaden the social options, Princeton has grouped its dorms into eight residential colleges, each with its own dining hall, faculty residents, and an active social calendar. Under this system, nearly all students live and dine with their residential college unit for all four years. Just 5 percent of undergraduates live off campus. The university's turn-of-the-century Gothic dorms may look like crosses between cathedrals and castles, but students say conditions on the inside are sometimes less glamorous. Some halls offer apartment- and suite-style layouts.

Princeton's eating clubs are its most firmly entrenched bastions of tradition. Run by students and unaffiliated with the school, they line Prospect Avenue and have, for more than a century, assumed the dual role of weekday dining hall and weekend fraternity. Of the 11, five admit members through an open lottery, but the others still use a controversial selective admissions process called bicker (because of the wrangling over whom to admit), to the chagrin of the administration and most students. While many of the clubs opened their doors to women back when Princeton went co-ed, two of the oldest and most exclusive—the Ivy Club and the Tiger Inn—remained all-male until 1991, when a court decision compelled them to admit women. Now, all the clubs are co-ed.

Catering exclusively to upperclassmen, the eating clubs provide a secure sense of community for their members. More than half of all sophomores join one of the clubs at the end of the year, becoming full-fledged members by the fall of their junior year. Annual dues vary; the most expensive is the Ivy Club, which charges its members over $12,000 a year. Financial aid covers eating costs for those who qualify and want to join. Unfortunately, the social options for those who choose not to join may feel limited. All too often the upper-level eating clubs steal the thunder from college-sponsored social events. As a result, "the underclassmen spend too much time pining for the day when they, too, can join the closest thing Princeton has to cliques," says one student. Some opt for life in independent dormitories or join the handful of Greek fraternities and sororities (not sanctioned by the administration) that have sprung up on campus over the past few years and have become feeders to particular eating clubs.

"Virtually all social life takes place on campus, both at the eating clubs and at dorm parties," says a sophomore. Princeton has the oldest licensed college radio station in the nation, plenty of journalistic opportunities, a prestigious debating and politics society (Whig-Clio) whose ranks have included James Madison and Aaron Burr, and a plethora of arts offerings. The McCarter Theatre Center, adjacent to campus, houses Princeton's

"Seniors develop close personal relationships with their thesis advisors."

Triangle Club, which counted Jimmy Stewart and Brooke Shields as members. The roundup of annual campus events includes lawn parties in the fall and spring and an international festival. Each year about 60 percent of students engage in volunteer activities such as tutoring, working in soup kitchens, or helping the elderly. Few students complain about boredom, and many praise the affluent town of Princeton for the parks, woods, bike trails, and, most important, the quiet and safety it offers students. Students rarely venture much farther than New York or Philadelphia, each one hour away (in opposite directions) on the train.

Athletics are a big deal at Princeton, both varsity and intramural. Several of the Tigers' 38 Division I teams have claimed recent Ivy League conference titles, among them football, men's soccer, women's cross-country, men's basketball, lacrosse, women's rowing, fencing, and golf. Women's rugby is the newest addition to the varsity roster. Dozens of club and intramural sports are available, ranging from archery to ballroom dancing to handball, and the eating clubs and residential colleges offer recreational athletic programs, too. Every spring students compete in the annual dodgeball tournament.

Princeton's unofficial motto is "Princeton in the nation's service and the service of humanity," and the oft-repeated notion that with privilege comes responsibility lives on as part of its culture. It's easy to be humbled at Princeton. Even the most jaded students must be awed and inspired when they think of those who've traversed the campus paths before them. While some may find the ambiance too insular, not many turn down membership in this very rewarding club.

If You Apply To ›

Princeton: Single choice early action, regular decision. Accepts the Common Application with supplement. Applicants must submit a graded, written paper, preferably from an English, social studies, or history class. Please consult Princeton's website for the most up-to-date information regarding standardized test requirements.

Principia College

1 Maybeck Place, Elsah, IL 62028

Prin is a tiny college in a tiny town about an hour from St. Louis. Most of its students, faculty, and staff are practicing Christian Scientists. Prin is mainly liberal arts, though business administration is a popular major. Sixty percent of students study abroad. Campus tenor is similar to other places like Pepperdine and Wheaton (IL) that take their religious values seriously.

Many students come to Principia College with a common bond—Christian Science. They shun smoking, drinking, drugs, and sex in favor of God and learning. Prin graduates are culturally, spiritually, and intellectually well-rounded, the product of a liberal arts education that promotes critical thinking and a broad worldview. Prin, founded in 1912 with the goal of "serving the Cause of Christian Science" (but with no formal ties to the Boston-based church), attracts a lot of international students. The historic campus is reminiscent of Harry Potter's Hogwarts, but the fictional school of wizardry never had a woolly mammoth to unearth as Prin once did. Says one senior, Principia "has a warm, calm, and cozy atmosphere that reminds me of a second home."

Principia's 2,600-acre campus, on limestone bluffs above the mighty Mississippi River, is a designated National Historic Landmark. The dominant architectural influences are colonial American, Tudor, and medieval, and many buildings—including most student housing—were designed by California architect Bernard Maybeck. A contemporary of Frank Lloyd Wright, Maybeck urged Principia trustees to bring the college to its current spot when they relocated from St. Louis in 1935. The College Chapel, whose bells ring out hymns every Sunday evening, is the symbolic center of campus.

In addition to coursework in their major, students must complete a broad range of distribution requirements in the arts, humanities, social sciences, and natural sciences, as well as two physical education courses and a bible course. All students participate in a first-year experience program their first semester, and all seniors must complete either a capstone course or a major-related internship. Of the roughly

20 majors offered, the most popular are communication and journalism, education, English, and biological sciences. Business administration, environmental studies, visual and performing arts, and religious studies are also strong.

Academics are challenging, but students can count on each other and their professors for help. "Most classes take advantage of group work in small teams," says a senior, and professors receive high marks. "Due to the small classroom style, faculty members are extremely accessible," says a business administration major. Sixty percent of Principia students participate in the five or six study abroad programs the school organizes each year. Each program enrolls 18 to 22 students, and sites are determined by academic subject and focus. Recent locations have included England, Spain, Greece, Nepal, and Finland. Others participate in a prairie restoration program, gather data for the study of the Mississippi River's aquatic life, or build solar cars to be entered in races around the world. "Career advising is very strong," cheers a music and global studies double major. "The opportunity for internships, especially for Christian Scientists, is huge as well."

> **"[Principia] has a warm, calm, and cozy atmosphere that reminds me of a second home."**

"We strive to be the most moral people we can be," says one junior. The minority population is small—11 percent of students are Black, 5 percent are Hispanic/Latino, less than 1 percent are Asian American, and 5 percent are multiracial. Still, an impressive 41 percent of students arrive from abroad, and 14 percent are from Illinois. Principia does not accept any governmental financial aid, so Pell Grants and the typical federal loans are not available to students, but the school does offer merit scholarships averaging $11,500, grants, and private, institutionally funded loans. No athletic scholarships are available.

All students live on campus, except for the few who are married or live locally with their parents. "The housing at Principia is superb, in the form of large, historical houses rather than the typical dormitory," says a senior. Students are expected not to be in wings where the opposite sex lives during "house hours" every night. First-years live in two modernized Maybeck houses with upperclassmen resident advisors trained to help new students adjust to college life. "Each house has its own sense of culture and traditions, and houses have brother-sister relationships as well as rivalries," explains a business administration and mass communication major. A sit-down pub and restaurant on campus provides a nice alternative to traditional dining-hall fare, but the food is a common complaint. Students agree that they feel safe on campus, citing the rural location and a strong security presence. Regarding mental health support, several students say it mostly comes from "empathetic professors."

> **"The opportunity for internships, especially for Christian Scientists, is huge."**

In addition to eschewing alcohol, tobacco, and drugs, students are also asked to sign a pledge of abstention from premarital and extramarital sexual relationships. "Those who sign the contract are committed to those morals for religious reasons," a political science major says. "It is a dry campus that takes violations of that very seriously," adds a sophomore. It goes without saying that Greek organizations are nonexistent; instead of partying, students keep busy at school-sponsored concerts, movies, dances, or intramural sporting events that pit one house against another. "On-campus events can be fun if people show up. It always depends on the involvement," says a first-year. Each house organizes its own annual celebration, international students show off their native cuisines at the Whole World Festival, everyone looks forward to Spring Formal, and in the fall, "Game of Homes is a competition between the different houses put on by student government for a cash prize," explains one student. The Public Affairs Conference is the oldest student-run event

A sit-down pub and restaurant on campus provides a nice alternative to traditional dining-hall fare.

All students participate in a first-year experience program their first semester.

of its type in the U.S., bringing in big-name speakers to give talks, lead workshops, and provide networking opportunities to students. "Elsah is not a college town," says a junior, complaining that "not much has changed" since the town was founded in 1853. Stores, restaurants, and movie theaters are about 20 minutes away in Alton, and St. Louis is about an hour's drive.

Principia's Panthers compete in Division III, and men's soccer and rugby and men's and women's tennis and basketball are especially competitive. Thirty-five percent of students play intramural and club sports; sand volleyball, basketball, and eSports teams are strong. Campus athletic facilities include a four-court indoor tennis center, a field house with gym and pool, and outdoor courts and running trails.

Prin students embrace the conservative environment at their Christian Scientist school. Gone are the pressures that take hold of most college students, and a political science major says it "promotes character development and personal growth." A strong international presence and study abroad opportunities give students a taste of what lies beyond this quaint rural campus, but in the meantime, a junior says, students enjoy the comfort of Prin's "supportive community of like-minded thinkers."

If You Apply To ›

Principia: Early action I and II, early decision, rolling admissions. Accepts the Common Application with supplement. Only college in the world that admits only Christian Scientists. Please consult Principia's website for the most up-to-date information regarding standardized test requirements.

Providence College

1 Cunningham Square, Providence, RI 02918

Strong Catholic atmosphere makes Providence more comparable to Notre Dame than to nearby Boston College or Holy Cross. Liberal arts emphasis rooted in a required two-year interdisciplinary Western Civilization sequence, though more than a third of the students eventually opt for business disciplines. Friars athletic teams do well in small but high-profile Big East Conference. No fraternities or sororities, but Providence is a vibrant college town.

As the nation's only college or university operated by the Dominican friars, Providence College, founded in 1917, wears its Roman Catholic and Dominican identities on its sleeve. Over 60 percent of students are Catholic; friars in habits walk the campus grounds; crucifixes adorn the walls of classrooms and offices; and St. Dominic Chapel stands tall in the heart of the campus. The school's mission is grounded in these identities, as it aims to "provide an education for the whole person—body, mind, and soul—that bridges the common divides between matter and spirit, God and creation, faith and reason." Students here enjoy solid offerings in the sciences and liberal arts—including a unique and rigorous two-year Western Civ course—and a tight-knit community of like-minded men and women.

Located only an hour's drive from Boston and just a few hours' drive from New York City, Providence College's 105-acre campus is situated in Rhode Island's capital city. The campus boasts open spaces, beautiful lawns, and student-centered facilities. The traditional brick and stone academic buildings, residence halls, and campus chapel coexist with several contemporary structures. The college's campus transformation project has added several new facilities over the past decade, among them the Ruane Center for the Humanities, a four-level addition to the Science Complex, and the $30 million Ryan Center for Business Studies. A new nursing and health sciences building opened in 2025.

The heart of Providence's Core Curriculum is a sequence of seminar-based classes that comprise the Development of Western Civilization program. This 16-credit course spans students' first and second years and introduces them to the seminal ideas and primary texts in history, literature, theology, and philosophy as well as the music and visual arts that shaped the Western world and other civilizations. Aside from DWC, students take additional coursework in theology, philosophy, natural science, social science, quantitative reasoning, and fine arts, and they must demonstrate proficiency in intensive writing, oral communication, diversity, and civic engagement.

Providence comprises four schools: arts and sciences, business, education and social work, and nursing and health sciences. The noteworthy School of Business draws over 40 percent of the students and offers some of the most popular majors, including marketing, finance, accountancy, and management. All School of Business majors share a common set of core courses to ensure that business graduates have a broad understanding of all essential business disciplines. Biology, psychology, the social sciences, and visual and performing arts are also popular choices, and the chemistry and biochemistry program is strong. Providence has added majors in nursing, health sciences, and neuroscience. The college also offers a combined degree program with the New England College of Optometry, which allows for completion of the B.A. and doctorate in seven years.

"The academic climate at Providence College is rigorous but supportive."

"The academic climate at Providence College is rigorous but supportive," says a junior. Fifty-three percent of the undergraduate classes have fewer than 20 students and are taught by tenured or junior faculty. A Spanish and global studies double major says, "Professors here go the extra mile for their students. They are enthusiastic and available to us." The Liberal Arts Honors Program offers students of high academic ability and initiative a more in-depth and rigorous version of PC's core curriculum, and small, seminar-style honors courses are offered in virtually all areas. Students have ample opportunity for experiential learning through internships and faculty-directed laboratory or field research. PC's Center for Global Education sends 40 percent of students to their choice of more than 40 countries, including Argentina, Italy, New Zealand, and South Africa.

Twelve percent of PC's undergraduates come from Rhode Island, and the remainder are mostly from the Northeast. Most students are "preppy, white, Catholic, and generally upper-middle-class," according to a sophomore. Just 2 percent are international. Black students account for 2 percent of the student body, Hispanics/Latinos 9 percent, Asian Americans 1 percent, and multiracial students 3 percent. Many students are vocal about social and political issues, particularly when it comes to religion and race. "We have a lot of outspoken liberals and closet Republicans at PC," observes a senior. The lack of racial diversity on campus draws near-universal concern: "I think it is felt very strongly among the minority students that we need more diversity on campus, even with all of our cultural clubs," says a junior. Merit scholarships averaging $25,700 are available to qualified students, as are athletic scholarships.

"There are free events for students to attend almost every day of the week."

Seventy percent of students live in the dorms, where conditions are said to be adequate and well maintained, if not spacious. Options include eight traditional halls, five apartment buildings, and a suite-style residence. Many seniors move off

(continued)

Enrolled: 19%
Grad in 6 Years: 86%
Returning First-years: 94%
Academics: ✍ ✍ ✍
Social: 💬 💬 💬
Q of L: ★ ★ ★
Admissions: (401) 865-2535
Email Address:
  pcadmiss@providence.edu

Strong Programs:
Accountancy
Biology
Chemistry
Education
Finance
Management
Marketing
Psychology

Annual traditions include Civ Scream, held at midnight on the eve of Western Civ finals.

campus into the surrounding neighborhoods. Campus dining is "good and constantly getting better," says a global studies major. "We have a good line of communication between administration and students, and I feel as if PC has implemented all that they can to keep students safe," says an English major.

A junior says the social life is varied and, "There are free events for students to attend almost every day of the week, including weekends." Absent a Greek presence, students find other ways to let off steam. Annual traditions include a spring concert featuring top national acts and Civ Scream, held at midnight on the eve of Western Civ finals: "The entire sophomore class circles around the quad and screams to let out their frustration over Civ. People do crazy things, and it is always something to remember," says a student. And although the college is in "kind of a run-down area," an English major says the city of Providence "is full of opportunities," including a mall, a movie theater, and a cultural district with all sorts of shops and eateries. Owing to the college's strong Catholic identity, community service and volunteer work are popular pastimes. The city is also home to six other colleges, which enhances the social scene. Popular road trips include treks into Boston and New York City.

The Providence Friars field 19 varsity teams, most of which play in the competitive Division I Big East Conference (hockey is part of the Hockey East Association). Highly ranked teams include men's and women's ice hockey, basketball, soccer, and cross-country, and women's volleyball and field hockey. "Basketball and hockey games are very important to PC students because we can show our school spirit," says a sophomore. Students get especially rowdy when rivals UConn and URI are in town. Many students get involved in intramurals and club sports, with flag football, softball, rugby, and lacrosse proving to be particularly popular.

Providence College appeals primarily to those students who want to challenge themselves academically without compromising their faith. Despite frequent complaints about the length and rigor of the Western Civ requirement and the lack of diversity, students here seem content with what the college has to offer and are proud to be part of the PC community. "PC is preppy and a great place to be," says a senior. "We have Division I school spirit but in a small-school atmosphere."

Overlaps

Boston College, Fairfield, Fordham, Holy Cross, Loyola University Maryland, Notre Dame, Stone Hill, Villanova

If You Apply To ›

Providence: Early decision I and II, early action, regular decision. SATs or ACTs: optional. Accepts the Common Application with supplement.

University of Puget Sound

1500 N Warner Street, Tacoma, WA 98416

Ask anyone in Tacoma about Puget Sound and they'll tell you that UPS (the college, not the package service) delivers solid liberal arts programs with a touch of business. Within easy reach of the Sound and Mount Rainier, the university specializes in all things Asia, including a nine-month university-sponsored trip. Compare to Whitman and Willamette.

A strong curricular emphasis on global awareness, supportive faculty, and a relatively laid-back atmosphere have raised the profile of the University of Puget Sound, transforming it from a regional liberal arts college in Tacoma to an undergraduate institution with national reach. The school's first-rate Asian studies program continues to draw students interested in cultural studies, Pacific Rim economics, and international travel, and the UPS community is as close-knit as ever. "People don't come here because they have heard of us before," says one contented senior. "They come here because they visit and they don't want to leave."

Founded by Methodists in 1888 to bring higher education to the region, Puget Sound is cradled by the Cascade Range and the rugged Olympics, with easy access to the urban energy of Seattle and the natural beauty of Mount Rainier. The 97-acre campus boasts carefully maintained lawns, native fir trees, and plenty of other greenery, thanks to the moist climate. Most buildings, with distinctive arches and porticos, were built in the 1950s and '60s. Additional facilities include an athletics and aquatics center and a 3,850-square-foot Sculpture House, with facilities for welding, woodwork, and painting.

Puget Sound's core curriculum, Grow, requires first-year students to begin with a connections course introducing them to the school, followed by a critical conversations seminar. Students go on to complete courses in three divisions: natural science and math, social sciences and historical perspectives, and artistic and humanistic perspectives, as well as demonstrate foreign language proficiency, and take a course on knowledge, identity, and power. All students also participate in at least one form of experiential learning before graduation. Two upper-level capstone courses, Connections, are all interdisciplinary and encourage students to develop an understanding of the interrelationship of fields of knowledge.

While navigating UPS's requirements, students may pursue a B.A., B.S., or B.M. (bachelor of music) degree. Some of the most popular majors are psychology, communication studies, biology, and business and leadership. African American studies is also strong. For classes in the environmental studies and sciences department, "You're often able to go on field trips with professors and working professionals," notes a senior. The university has developed a reputation as a jumping-off point to Asia—both literally and figuratively. Its curriculum stresses two of the fastest-growing fields in the region: Asian studies and Pacific Rim economics. Nearly one-third of Puget Sounders take at least one Asian studies course, and every other year, there's a nine-month, school-sponsored trip through Japan, Thailand, Korea, India, China, and Nepal, where participants study art, architecture, politics, economics, and philosophy. In all, more than 100 study abroad programs are available in more than 40 nations; 29 percent of students participate. Other special offerings include an honors program, the Business Leadership Program, and residence-based humanities programs.

Students say that while their peers are academically motivated and coursework can be challenging, the atmosphere at Puget Sound is "generally very relaxed and enjoyable, with professors always encouraging lots of interaction from students," explains a history major. Sixty-seven percent of classes have fewer than 20 students. "I have been so well taken care of by our professors, and I see them as instructors but also mentors," says a psychology major. Fifty percent of students participate in the plentiful opportunities for undergraduate research, which have ranged from examining bacteria on lizard eggs to summer fieldwork studying graffiti in Europe. Advising, which includes both academic and peer advisors, and career services receive positive reviews.

"Students at Puget Sound are definitely outdoorsy," says a Hispanic studies junior. "Lots of Birkenstocks and plaid. Politically liberal, for the most part." Most come from western states, with 29 percent hailing from Washington; less than 1 percent come from abroad. Black students make up only 3 percent of the student

> **"You're often able to go on field trips with professors and working professionals."**

An active Hawaiian student organization sponsors a luau each spring.

body, Hispanics/Latinos 11 percent, Asian Americans 7 percent, and multiracial students 9 percent. According to a junior, "There is a big push for more diversity on campus," and students are also concerned with LGBTQ rights, gender equality, and environmental issues. There are no athletic scholarships, but merit awards averaging $29,000 are doled out annually.

Seventy percent of Puget Sound students live on campus, and first-years and sophomores are required to do so. First-year students all live together, and after that students may live in Greek chapter housing, pursue a single room in the dorms, or apply for one of 60 university-owned houses, many of which focus on themes like outdoor leadership and music. "The surrounding neighborhood is happy to rent out houses to students who choose to live off campus their junior and senior years," reports a computer science major. Aside from the main campus dining area, students can chow down at three campus cafés and the Cellar, and meals get good reviews for freshness and variety. "We have a strong security team that takes sexual assault very seriously and has been good at communicating with the campus," comments a junior.

> **"Students at Puget Sound are definitely outdoorsy."**

Twenty-two percent of Puget Sound men and 14 percent of the women go Greek, though fraternities and sororities don't dominate the social scene and all Greek parties are alcohol-free. "Social life at UPS is fairly intimate. In my experience, people tend to hang out more off campus on the weekends, at people's houses and such," a philosophy major says. Popular school-sponsored activities include the Log Jam BBQ and club fair that kicks off the school year, the Foolish Pleasures festival of short student-produced films, and the Lumbershoot music festival in the spring (a play on Seattle's Bumbershoot). An active Hawaiian student organization sponsors a luau each spring, with "great food and lots of traditional dances." The Repertory Dance Group and Puget Sound Outdoors are among the most popular campus organizations. A few Tacoma bars and restaurants are within walking distance, and a junior says the university is working "to give students pipelines to the local community through volunteering and social justice programs, free and discounted museum passes, and more." With the mountains and beaches so close—Seattle is 30 minutes away by car, Portland two hours south, and Vancouver, British Columbia, three hours north—road trips are de rigueur. That's especially true during ski season, and the school rents out all the necessary equipment.

Students are fond of saying that Puget Sound's Division III varsity teams, the Loggers, "Kick Axe." Solid teams include football, men's and women's soccer and basketball, and women's crew. The school's archrival is Pacific Lutheran University. "Football and basketball games against PLU are a big deal and always packed," says a fan. About half of the students sign up for intramural and club sports, including favorites volleyball, soccer, and flag football.

Don't let UPS students' slacker-chic clothes and casual demeanor fool you. Puget Sound means serious study for students seeking immersion in the liberal arts and the natural beauty of the outdoors. As a molecular and cellular biology major explains, "The vibe is laid-back but purposeful at the same time. People who come to this school are passionate and love to share those passions with others."

Overlaps

Lewis & Clark, Occidental, University of Oregon, Seattle University, St. Olaf, University of Washington, Whitman, Willamette

If You Apply To ›

Puget Sound: Early decision, early action, regular decision. SATs or ACTs: optional. Accepts the Common Application with supplement.

610 Purdue Mall, West Lafayette, IN 47906

Purdue is Indiana's STEM university—with side helpings of business, health professions, and liberal arts. Compare to Kansas State and Big Ten rival Michigan State. Does better than most large universities in giving students hands-on opportunities such as internships and co-ops—and resisting tuition increases. Enrollment has increased 30 percent over the past decade. Flight technology and aerospace—and turning out future astronauts—are longtime specialties. Political tone leans conservative.

Successful Indiana colleges typically have three things in common: a solid agricultural program, a powerhouse basketball team, and a conservative student body. Purdue University has all of these—along with one of the nation's strongest engineering programs and the distinction of having awarded more bachelor's degrees in the field than any other institution. Purdue is also home to the nation's first computer science department, and its programs in pharmaceutical sciences, nursing, and management are top-notch. Budding classicists, dramatists, and literary critics might want to look elsewhere, but those seeking small-school friendliness with big-school spirit may be very happy to join the ranks of Boilermakers.

Purdue, founded in 1869 and named for its first major donor, is the main attraction in the small industrial town of West Lafayette, where the population triples when students return each fall. The campus features redbrick and limestone buildings arranged around lush, shaded courtyards. Newer facilities include the $64 million STEM Teaching Lab, which provides multidisciplinary laboratory classrooms for up to 15,000 undergraduates. Purdue is also home to Amazon's first ever brick-and-mortar location, where students can have textbooks shipped overnight for no cost.

Students apply to and enroll in one of Purdue's 10 colleges, and academic requirements vary by school and major. Typically, they include English, math, a lab science, and foreign language proficiency. Engineering is the most popular major, followed by business, computer science, and industrial engineering. Students flock to the five-year engineering co-op program, one of the most competitive on campus, because it marries classroom study with paid, real-world work. Additionally, Purdue offers a strong undergraduate program in professional flight technology, which includes hands-on training at the university's own airport. Purdue has produced more than 20 astronauts, including pioneers Neil Armstrong and Gus Grissom. A four-year program in retail management is available in partnership with the Fashion Institute of Technology (FIT) in New York. For those seeking to save money on their degree and pursue their post-graduation plans sooner, Purdue offers more than 20 "Degree in 3" programs in the Colleges of Liberal Arts and Education, through which students can earn a bachelor's degree in three years; options range from communication and history to sociology and special education.

"The academic climate is fairly competitive and intense," says a sophomore. Despite the university's size, 41 percent of classes have fewer than 20 students, and many first-year classes are seminar-style, taught by graduate students and academic advisors who help answer students' questions and provide career advice. "I've had some teachers who were phenomenal at connecting with the students and having them understand the concepts," one student confides, "and other teachers act like

> **"The academic climate is fairly competitive and intense."**

Website: www.purdue.edu
Location: Small City
Public
Total Enrollment: 49,120
Undergraduates: 41,893
Male/Female: 60/40
Financial Aid: 62%
Pell Grant: 16%
Expense: Pub $
Student Loans: 35%
Average Debt: $ $ $
Applicants: 78,745
Accepted: 50%
Enrolled: 29%
Grad in 6 Years: 83%
Returning First-years: 93%
Academics: ✍ ✍ ✍
Social: 🗩 🗩 🗩
Q of L: ★ ★ ★
Admissions: (765) 494-1776
Email Address:
  admissions@purdue.edu

Strong Programs:
Aeronautical and Astronautical
  Engineering
Agriculture
Computer Science
Management
Mechanical Engineering
Nursing
Pharmaceutical Sciences
Professional Flight Technology

they are presenting to an empty room." About a third of undergrads study abroad, and options are available for students in all majors in more than 60 countries. Undergraduates also participate in more than 2,000 research projects each year.

"The students here are very academically focused and driven," says a junior. "They have fun and relax on weekends, but everyone knows the reason we are here is to get a degree to be successful in the future." About half of Purdue's undergraduates hail from Indiana, although there is a healthy proportion of international students at 10 percent. Just 3 percent are Black, 15 percent are Asian American, 8 percent are Hispanic/Latino, and 5 percent are multiracial. Thousands of merit scholarships averaging $5,300 are awarded annually; athletes vie for roughly 250 scholarships in 18 sports. The Purdue Promise program grants financial assistance and specialized academic and leadership coaching to eligible Indiana residents from lower-income backgrounds.

Forty-two percent of students live in Purdue-owned housing, much of it off-campus, but almost all first-years live in residence halls, though they aren't required to, and Harrison Hall is said to be a good pick for newbies. "Some are definitely nicer than others," a sophomore admits. "Many of them still do not have air-conditioning." The notion of a "co-ed dorm" here means that men and women share a lobby. Those with a grumbling stomach are treated to tasty options on campus. "Our food is fantastic," cheers one junior. "It's all-you-can-eat." Walking and riding escorts and a visible security presence help students feel safe.

"There are also many great nearby restaurants within walking distance for all students."

"The social life typically takes place on campus," reports one philosophy major. Alcohol is prohibited in dorms, and "people have been kicked out of the residence halls for being caught with alcohol," says a sophomore. Greek life draws 13 percent of Purdue men and 17 percent of the women and offers many social opportunities. But there are other options, too, including sports games and more than 1,000 student organizations, ranging from the BBQ society to professional development clubs. "Outside of class, you can do anything from skydiving, paintball, choir, rock climbing, salsa dancing—anything. It's up to you," encourages a senior mechanical engineering major.

As far as college towns go, West Lafayette "would not exist if it weren't for Purdue," one student says. Another adds, "The surrounding area has a good social scene for those 21 [and over], with excellent bars and nightlife. There are also many great nearby restaurants within walking distance for all students." Harry's Chocolate Shop—a bar, not a candy store—is a longtime student favorite. Chicago and Indianapolis are favored weekend destinations for students with cars, and each spring, a week of fun and parties leads up to the Grand Prix go-kart races. Students also look forward to the Bug Bowl, an annual event sponsored by Purdue's entomology department, including cricket-spitting and cockroach races.

Purdue's "Boilermaker" moniker was coined by a sportswriter in 1891 describing how "the Burly Boiler Makers from Purdue" defeated Wabash College's football team 44–0. Boilermaker pride manifests itself at Division I games of all types, especially when the opposing team is Indiana University, known derisively as "that school down south," in the annual struggle for the Old Oaken Bucket. Every year, the winner adds a link to a chain on the bucket in the shape of either an "I" or a "P." Men's and women's basketball, golf, and swimming and diving are among the most competitive sports. Thirty-one club sports and more than 35 intramurals are a big draw for those looking for friendly competition. Solar car racing and Rube Goldberg machine contests are some of the more popular activities among STEM students.

With enrollment at an all-time high, Purdue students are discovering that learning is fun when academics are mixed with real-world experience and a healthy dose of school spirit. "Purdue has great academic programs, incredible organizational and social opportunities, and an awesome sense of community," says one enthusiastic sophomore. "Boiler Up!"

Queen's University: See page 359.

Quinnipiac University

275 Mount Carmel Avenue, Hamden, CT 06518

Aggressive expansion of programs and facilities has put Quinnipiac on the map of comprehensive New England colleges with a preprofessional bent. Less selective than Fairfield and Ithaca, with more dual-degree options. Business and health sciences are big attractions. Best known to the general public for its political polling and hockey prowess. Midway between NYC and Boston on Amtrak.

Over the last three decades, Quinnipiac University has tripled in size from a small liberal arts college to a full-fledged university with 6,000 undergrads, three dozen graduate programs, and nine academic divisions spread out over three campuses—a massive expansion that has helped increase the school's national prominence. With its strengths in health, business, and communications well established, the university has begun to carve out a niche for itself as a place where talented, preprofessional undergraduates can get on a fast track to advanced degrees and jump-start their careers.

Quinnipiac's 250-acre Mount Carmel campus sits adjacent to Sleeping Giant State Park, with its 1,700 acres of hiking and walking trails, 90 minutes from New York City and two hours from Boston. The university was founded in 1929 as a business school and took its name from the local Quinnipiac Native Americans. Traditional New England red brick dominates, and a large central quad is surrounded by the library, the student center, the admissions and financial aid office, and academic buildings. The three-building Evans College of Arts and Sciences Center features a spacious quad that overlooks Clark's pond and its family of resident swans. The 250-acre York Hill campus is just across Whitney Avenue and features the cozy Rocky Top Student Center, which resembles a European ski lodge and boasts panoramic views of the region. The 104-acre North Haven campus, located four miles from the Mount Carmel campus, serves as home to the Center for Medicine, Nursing, and Health Sciences, the School of Law, and the School of Education.

> **"Students will find courses challenging but reasonable."**

Quinnipiac's liberal arts philosophy is evident in its general education curriculum, which includes foundational courses in the sciences, social sciences, humanities, fine arts, writing, and intercultural understanding, as well as a capstone requirement in the senior year. All incoming students take a First-Year Seminar designed to help them practice critical thinking and inquiry.

Website: www.qu.edu
Location: Suburban
Private
Total Enrollment: 7,752
Undergraduates: 6,070
Male/Female: 39/61
Financial Aid: 83%
Pell Grant: 17%
Expense: Pr $ $
Student Loans: 65%
Average Debt: $ $ $ $
Applicants: 21,323
Accepted: 77%
Enrolled: 11%
Grad in 6 Years: 77%
Returning First-years: 87%
Academics: ✍ ✍ ✍
Social: 🗩 🗩 🗩
Q of L: ★ ★ ★ ★
Admissions: (203) 582-8600
Email Address:
   admissions@qu.edu

Strong Programs:
Engineering
Entrepreneurship
Film, Television, and Media Arts

Two annual concerts, Fall Fest and Wake the Giant, bring big headlining performers to campus.

Quinnipiac owns several media outlets, including a student-run radio station and television station.

Quinnipiac offers more than 100 majors; the newest include business analytics, data science, and sustainability and environmental policy. Nursing, health science studies, finance, and marketing are among the most popular. The School of Business's programs in entrepreneurship and finance are strong, while students in the School of Communications benefit from solid offerings in journalism and film, television, and media arts. Quinnipiac owns several media outlets, including a student-run radio station and television station. Seventeen engineering labs accommodate majors in civil, industrial, software, and mechanical engineering. Irish studies is a noteworthy minor; the university's Ireland's Great Hunger Institute houses one of the world's largest collections of art and literature dealing with the Great Irish Famine. A spate of combined undergraduate/graduate degree programs are available in such fields as business, communications, law, and social work; the entry-level physician assistant, physical therapy, and occupational therapy combined degree programs are particular specialties. The university's career-oriented student body makes the most of these opportunities: nearly a third of undergrads stay at Quinnipiac to complete an advanced degree in their chosen profession.

"Students will find courses challenging but reasonable," says a junior. Fifty-five percent of all classes have fewer than 20 students, and "there are no massive lecture halls," says one journalism major. There are no teaching or graduate assistants, either; all classes are taught by professors. "Professors are knowledgeable and have real-world experience that will help prepare you for your future career," notes a nursing major. Each school and college provides its own career development center, which students rate highly for assisting with internship and job placements.

Highly motivated students may enroll in the Honors Program, which features special seminars, close relationships with professors, and a slew of enrichment and leadership opportunities. Internships and clinical experiences abound: communications students may elect to spend their summer on production sets or on-air in Los Angeles, while political science majors have the opportunity to assist elected officials at the state capital or in Washington, D.C. The university is home to the renowned Quinnipiac Polling Institute, a national survey that polls registered voters about political races, state and national elections, and issues of public concern. Study abroad options include a highly popular semester program at University College Cork in Ireland; 35 percent of students take part in programs offered in 32 countries across the globe. "With so many different ways to go abroad (semester program, 10-day service trip, three- or six-week seminar), there is no reason not to take advantage and explore the world," urges a physical therapy major.

"Professors are knowledgeable and have real-world experience."

"A lot of students come here for a very specific program or a dual degree, which makes them very focused on maintaining high grades," observes a biomedical sciences major. Most students come from the Northeast, and a senior reports, "Quinnipiac has a reputation for recruiting affluent students." Thirty-six percent of undergrads hail from Connecticut, and 2 percent are international. The student body is 4 percent Black, 11 percent Hispanic/Latino, 3 percent Asian American, and 3 percent multiracial. Political and social issues aren't a huge concern on campus, students say. Qualified undergraduates receive merit awards averaging $24,400, and gifted athletes vie for nearly 200 athletic scholarships in 21 sports.

On-campus housing is required for incoming first-years and guaranteed for three years; 68 percent of students reside in school-owned housing. Most first-years and sophomores live on the Mount Carmel campus, while upperclassmen live on the York Hill campus in suite-style accommodations or in nearby houses or an apartment complex owned by the university. About a quarter of the students join the 19 available living/learning communities. Residents of the Grove hall collaborate on a "big idea" to problem-solve an issue with the local community over the course of the year. Students are required to purchase a meal plan; food options at the main dining hall (Café Q) and the Bobcat Den get average reviews. Campus security maintains a visible patrol on campus, and an occupational therapy major says, "Students are required to learn about sexual assault during their freshman orientation, and it's a serious topic that is reinforced throughout their time here."

The Quinnipiac social scene is bustling. The campus hosts a variety of events, including guest speakers, comedians, craft nights, and film screenings; there are also roughly 150 student clubs to whet the appetite. Thirteen percent of the men and 19 percent of the women join fraternities and sororities, which do not have dedicated housing. "Party culture is present," especially among Greek groups and sports teams, notes a senior, "but it is not over the top." Quinnipiac is a "wet" campus—students 21 or older are allowed to possess alcohol in the dorms—but underage drinkers face stiff penalties. Two annual concerts, Fall Fest and Wake the Giant, bring big headlining performers to campus.

When students tire of the campus scene, they trek into surrounding towns in search of fun. Hamden offers the usual mix of chain restaurants, movie theaters, and bowling alleys, and the university provides a free shuttle to New Haven (home of Yale University), where students enjoy the food and nightlife. Seventy-five percent of students choose to get involved in the local community through volunteer work. The great outdoors beckon too. "It's a rite of passage to hike Sleeping Giant State Park at least once during your time here," says an English major.

> **"Party culture is present, but it is not over the top."**

The Quinnipiac Bobcats field 21 Division I teams—seven for men and 14 for women—and most compete in the Metro Atlantic Athletic Conference. Men's and women's ice hockey play in the powerful Eastern College Athletic Conference—the perennial powerhouse men's team have brought home national championships, and nothing brings out the Bobcat faithful like the annual hockey match versus rival Yale. "The Yale rivalry is fierce, and student pride comes alive," says a student. Women's rugby has brought home national championships, while conference champs include women's golf, women's basketball, and baseball. Intramurals are popular and range from eSports to women's figure skating.

Quinnipiac's momentum is fueled by more than new facilities and programs—it's driven by a student body focused on turning education into action. With strong ties to professional schools, abundant experiential opportunities, and a location that puts New England's major cities within easy reach, the university continues to attract students seeking a direct route from college to career. Quinnipiac is demonstrating that bigger can also mean better.

If You Apply To ›

Quinnipiac: Early decision, early action, regular decision. SATs or ACTs: optional (required for some programs). Accepts the Common Application. Apply to particular program.

Randolph College

2500 Rivermont Avenue, Lynchburg, VA 24503

Randolph College pursues its traditional mission of strong liberal arts through a unique and creative curriculum. Students concentrate on two courses at a time and take a break on Wednesdays for special enrichment activities, academic and otherwise. Suburban location on the James River is rich in history.

Students take just two courses at a time, allowing for in-depth immersion in coursework and free time to pursue other educational opportunities.

With cherished traditions, cozy dorms, and challenging, seminar-based classes, Randolph College, named for early 19th-century Virginia politician John Randolph, who once fought a duel with Henry Clay, has preserved the best elements of its past while evolving into an institution relevant for today. The student-run Honor System has been in effect for more than 130 years. Its innovative TAKE2 curriculum makes Randolph the only college in the country where students take just two courses at a time, allowing for in-depth immersion in coursework as well as free time to pursue other educational opportunities. The college, which started out in 1891 as Randolph–Macon Women's College and went co-ed in 2007, offers students a place to be themselves. "Fitting in isn't what Randolph is about," says a sophomore. "One of our mottoes is 'Be an Original,' and you can see that throughout the school."

The college's 100-acre campus sits in the historic neighborhood of Lynchburg, on the banks of the James River. A brick wall around the campus's perimeter built in 1930 has become a symbol of the school, and many fondly refer to their time there as being spent "behind the Red Brick Wall." Graceful old redbrick buildings are covered with purple wisteria and linked by glass corridors called trolleys; the surrounding trees burst into riotous bloom each spring. Main Hall, dating from 1893, houses dorm rooms, classrooms, and faculty and administrative offices. The Maier Museum of Art has one of the best college collections of American art in the country. The Martin Science Building has been completely renovated, and Randolph opened a new Robotics and Mechatronics Lab in 2025.

Randolph's TAKE2 curriculum divides the academic year into four seven-week sessions, during which students take just two courses. Class periods are extended to allow more time for hands-on activities and group interaction. No classes are held on Wednesdays, giving students a midweek break to rest, study, or engage in extracurriculars, field trips, volunteer work, or internships. General education requirements cover traditional liberal arts subjects such as artistic expression, human experience, culture and identity, social and natural science, and writing. Incoming students take the First-Year Seminar, which examines how to maximize academic success. Every major culminates in a senior-year capstone experience, with an honors option available for highly motivated students.

"We want you at Randolph, you will always be at home!"

Biology, English, psychology, and sport and exercise studies are some of the most popular majors. Programs in history, studio art, and economics are also well regarded. New majors include robotics and mechatronics engineering, cybersecurity, and cognitive science. A program in American culture combines classroom study with guest speakers and travel to important historic or cultural sites. SUPER (Step Up to Physical Science and Engineering at Randolph) is an immersive STEM scholarship program for first-year students that includes a two-week residential academic program in the summer and specialized academic services and mentoring.

According to a senior, the workload at Randolph is "just heavy enough to promote academic growth but still reasonable enough to keep you sane." A senior praises the TAKE2 program but explains, "Since we only have two classes, the content is delivered at a faster rate." Since 84 percent of classes enroll fewer than 20 students, it's easy for students to form friendships with their professors. "Professors know what interests you," says a senior, "and are always open to helping out with finding jobs or internships."

All Randolph students are eligible to apply for a $2,000 RISE grant, which can fund research, international travel, and other academic pursuits. The eight-week Summer Research Program is "a fantastic opportunity for students to work with a faculty member on a topic that they are passionate about," says a history major; in addition to conducting research, participants attend a series of seminars with guest speakers, present their findings at a closing symposium, and get paid a stipend.

About a third of students study abroad. Randolph's two-week, faculty-led summer study seminars are a popular option; recent seminars have taken students to Italy, Iceland, and Korea. More than half of Randolph students secure off-campus internships, with organizations from the Chicago Lyric Opera to the National Gallery in London.

"Randolph walks to the beat of its own drum," says an elementary education major. Seventy-five percent of Randolph students hail from Virginia; 3 percent are international. Students of color have a notable presence, with Black students accounting for 24 percent of the student body, Hispanics/Latinos 9 percent, Asian Americans 3 percent, and multiracial students 3 percent. Socioeconomic diversity is strong, with 53 percent of first-years qualifying for Pell Grants. Students report that the political atmosphere is largely liberal. Randolph has reduced its sticker price by more than 30 percent. Merit scholarships average $16,800 per year, but there are no athletic awards.

> "Since we only have two classes, the content is delivered at a faster rate."

Seventy-four percent of Randolph students live in college-owned housing. And a global studies major calls the residence halls "pretty nice and comfy," although students gripe about the lack of air-conditioning in some dorms. Main Hall, a.k.a. "the Hilton," is the largest dorm, and its central location makes it the most convenient. After the first year, housing is selected by lottery, and college-owned apartments across the street from campus are the preferred option among upperclassmen. As for campus dining, a biology major says, "The actual dining hall is very nice; the food is mediocre at best." Security officers patrol continuously and take pride in knowing students by name. "Our counseling services are always full because they are so helpful," says an elementary education major of the mental health care available.

"The real social scene is inside the Red Brick Wall," says a sophomore. "We have a number of secret societies, clubs, and other social organizations." The Randolph Programming Board makes sure students have fun by hosting comedians, bands, and other entertainers, as well as talent shows and outdoor parties. For off-campus fun, students occasionally get away to other nearby colleges like Hampden–Sydney, Washington and Lee, and the University of Virginia. "Randolph allows drinking in your room, however you do have to be of age and not in the halls or lounges," warns a senior. There is no Greek life, but sports teams and other organizations offer a low-key party scene.

> "We have a number of secret societies, clubs, and other social organizations."

The town of Lynchburg (population 80,000) hosts two other colleges and has a shopping mall and some retail chains, but is otherwise "less than exhilarating," admits a biology major. Most restaurants and stores close early, but the college's coffee bar satisfies students' caffeine cravings. "We also have a lot of hiking and recreation options that are close by and affordable," offers a junior. Students often get involved in the local community via volunteering.

Randolph's WildCats compete in Division III, and the school's top rival is the University of Lynchburg. Recently, the women's tennis team has been most competitive, along with men's soccer, basketball, and track and field. But more than athletic contests, students look forward to Randolph traditions, such as the Even/Odd class-year rivalry, Ring Week (in which a first-year anonymously decorates the door of a junior and leaves small gifts all week, culminating in a scavenger hunt for their class ring), and the Pumpkin Parade (during which sophomores present lit jack-o'-lanterns to seniors, who show them off in an evening parade). The Never-Ending Weekend each fall includes both a formal and the annual Tacky Party, for which tasteless attire is de rigueur.

Overlaps

Bridgewater, Centre, Eckerd, Hendrix, James Madison, Old Dominion, Randolph-Macon, Wells

From going co-ed to expanding cocurricular opportunities to redesigning its academic calendar in support of a more balanced college experience, Randolph College is working hard to live up to its motto Vita abundantior (the life more abundant). Through all these changes, a student explains, Randolph's "core dynamic and value system" have remained the same: "Students still value respect and responsibility." And for students considering applying, cheers a happy senior, "We want you at Randolph, you will always be at home!"

University of Redlands

1200 E Colton Avenue, Redlands, CA 92374

If you like the thought of palm trees against a backdrop of snow-covered peaks, Redlands may be your place. As a "university," Redlands is double the size of Occidental and Whittier. The distinctive Johnston Center for Integrative Studies, an alternative living/learning program, makes an odd—albeit first-rate—contrast to the buttoned-down preprofessionalism of the rest of Redlands.

Amid the dozens of gigantic and well-known universities in the state of California stands the University of Redlands. With its innovative, alternative living/learning option and strong preprofessional emphasis, this versatile school, founded in 1907, is one of higher education's better-kept secrets and a place where students receive all the personal attention and intellectual stimulation they could want. As a public policy and political science major explains, the combination of "free-spirited" individualism and career-oriented professionalism means that "we definitely have two different vibes on campus."

The University of Redlands's 160-acre campus, covered in majestic oak trees, is designed around "The Quad," a large grassy area surrounded by a group of dorms that face one another. The two main landmarks are the Memorial Chapel and the Administration Building. Redlands's facilities are a mixture of older, historical columned buildings and more modern, renovated ones. The view from campus is breathtaking. Mountain ranges form the backdrop, and neighboring Big Bear Lake and Arrowhead ski resorts give endless getaway opportunities. Also nearby are the San Gorgonio Wilderness and Joshua Tree National Park.

Redlands's most distinctive attribute is the Johnston Center for Integrative Studies, an experimental living/learning community within the College of Arts and Sciences where students create their own course of study and are assessed by professor and self-evaluations rather than grades. The Johnston Center was established in 1969 to function as an alternative college within a traditional setting. With about 200 participants, it's one of the university's largest programs and offers unusual academic freedom: there are no departments, majors, or distribution requirements. Instead, students design contracts with professors for their entire plan of study. At the beginning of each course, students make up the syllabus by consensus and then set their own research and writing goals. Each student develops four-year goals—which are reviewed by a student/faculty board for direction and breadth—within one or more broad areas:

> **"Redlands feels like a small, close community with a global outlook."**

the social sciences, behavioral sciences, humanities, and fine and performing arts. One student explains, "Johnston Center students tend to be independent thinkers, self-motivated, and [don't] take classes just because they have to." Recent participants have designed degrees such as food in society, urban agriculture, and social behavior across cultures.

(continued)

Aside from Johnston, Redlands is noteworthy among liberal arts institutions in that it also offers preprofessional programs. The school of performing arts has brought together the conservatory of music with theater and dance. Premed/prehealth and prelaw students receive advising on requirements for graduate school, and 3–2 engineering degrees with Columbia University and WashU in St. Louis are available. Redlands has emerged as a national leader in science curriculum reform with innovative interdisciplinary offerings like human-animal studies and the health, medicine, and society program, which combines the study of natural science, medical humanities, public policy, global health, and more. Business is the most popular major, and the university also offers solid majors in global business and theater business. Psychology, audiology, and integrative studies are popular, too, and Redlands offers a Peace Corps prep program for those interested in volunteer work abroad. Regardless of major, all students must take a first-year seminar, participate in 80 hours of community service, and complete a capstone requirement, such as an internship or academic research. "One of the things I love most about the University of Redlands is the opportunity to do research with any professor," says a biochemistry and molecular biology major.

With its 4–4–1 calendar, Redlands affords students the option to take one immersive course each May, and some use the term to study abroad.

In Redlands's small, discussion-based classes, "Education becomes a conversation, and students' original ideas are not only allowed but encouraged," says a Johnston Center student. Sixty-four percent of classes have fewer than 20 students, meaning "interaction with professors is common and camaraderie is abundant," says a psychology and Spanish double major. With its 4–4–1 calendar, Redlands affords students the option to take one immersive course each May, and some use the term to study abroad. Students may embark on Redlands's signature program in Salzburg, Austria, or choose from more than 70 other options worldwide. The Redlands Promise guarantees that if incoming qualified students are unable to graduate in four years with the help of faculty advising, Redlands will cover the cost of additional courses needed for graduation.

"Interaction with professors is common and camaraderie is abundant."

"Redlands has a very personal, small-town sort of feeling," says a sophomore. "Everyone is so friendly and supportive." Seventy-five percent of undergraduates come from within the state, creating a mellow, Southern California atmosphere on campus; 1 percent hail from abroad. The climate is a definite plus, with temperatures rarely below 50 degrees. Hispanics/Latinos represent 43 percent of undergrads, Asian Americans 5 percent, Black students 5 percent, and multiracial students 6 percent. "Our school has grown more diverse and more politically active in my four years here," reports a senior, and the student body leans liberal. Redlands annually awards merit scholarships averaging $37,300 but there are no athletic scholarships. Thirty-five percent of incoming students are Pell Grant recipients.

Redlands is noteworthy among liberal arts institutions in that it also offers preprofessional programs.

Sixty-one percent of students live in the residence halls and on-campus apartments, most of which are co-ed, but the housing gets lukewarm reviews, although the largest on-campus residence, Anderson Hall, has been newly renovated. Students enjoy their food at the Table at Irvine Commons, the Launch Kitchen, or the Plaza Café & Market, part of the Hunsaker University Center, which has a "town square" atmosphere. Students praise Redlands's safety and its approach to sexual assault prevention.

"Greek life is a large part of our school but our administration has been cracking down on them so they may not be a thing for too long," reports a psychology major. Local fraternities and sororities claim 8 percent of the men and 15 percent of the women, respectively, and their generally well-controlled parties are open to all. "For traditions, one of the most beloved is decorating the Deacon statue," says a sophomore. "Deacon was the university's first live bulldog mascot, and now we have a statue in his honor." Students also look forward to the annual Spring Fest concert and the Asian Student Association's market night, which offers "great food and entertainment," cheers junior. The nearby city of Redlands offers a variety of coffee shops and restaurants, and students are highly involved in the local community. "The vibe downtown ranges from fancy to vintage to relaxed, so there's something for everyone," says a sophomore. Road trips to Los Angeles, Palm Springs, and San Diego are common.

The University of Redlands sponsors 21 intercollegiate Bulldog teams, all of which consistently vie for spots among the top of the Division III Southern California Intercollegiate Athletic Conference (SCIAC). Football, baseball, and men's and women's golf, softball, men's water polo, and track and field are competitive. Games against rival Occidental always draw crowds, and the "Och Tamale" school chant—a string of complete gibberish invented in 1921, supposedly in mockery of Oxy's own Latinesque nonsense chant—is a beloved school tradition ("Och tamale gazolly gazump!"). Nearly half of students participate in at least one intramural or club sport.

The University of Redlands is a lot of different things to a lot of different people. With nearly 180 full-time faculty members, it manages to be a liberal arts college, a preprofessional institute, and an alternative school all in one. The Johnston Center is clearly a path to travel for the innovative individualist, but even those who don't join Johnston can find what they want and need at Redlands, including a strong sense of community. "University of Redlands feels like a small, close community with a global outlook," says a sophomore. "And that's honestly the best part."

If You Apply To ›

Redlands: Early action I and II, regular decision. SATs or ACTs: optional. Accepts the Common Application. Application includes optional questions on gender identity. Applicants to music program must audition.

Reed College

3203 SE Woodstock Boulevard, Portland, OR 97202

Reed is a West Coast counterpart to Grinnell or Oberlin, mixing community-driven students with a rigorous curriculum. Sends huge numbers of grads on for Ph.D.s. Students who were unconventional thinkers in high school often find a sense of belonging at Reed. Honor Principle and annual springtime Thesis Parade epitomize Reed's culture of celebrating intellectualism.

Reed College is one of the most proudly intellectual colleges in the country. It's the place where the late Steve Jobs—cofounder of Apple—attended for a semester before dropping out to reshape the world and where students complain that the library, which closes its doors at midnight on Fridays and Saturdays, shuts down too early. Students receive lengthy and detailed written commentaries from professors on their work, which fosters continued dialogue and eliminates grade inflation. "Reed is the absolute best place for someone who likes to think, to read, to question, and to work," says a student. "It's a community of scholars." But also, says a sociology major, "Reed is like a rebellious nerd, a teenager who just discovered David Lynch and wants to be him."

Located in southeast Portland, Reed's 116-acre campus boasts rolling lawns, winding lanes, a canyon creek, and protected wetlands. Two thousand majestic arbors shade a mix of original campus buildings, constructed of brick, slate, and limestone in the Tudor Gothic style, as well as lodges in the homey Northwest Timber style and some more modern facilities, such as the Performing Arts Building. Recent construction includes the $27 million, LEED Platinum–certified Trillium residence hall ("it's like living in an IKEA," quips a student) on the north end of campus.

Founded in 1908 and named for a pair of Oregon pioneers, Reed emphasizes personal freedom and responsibility, especially through its Honor Principle. Nevertheless, the curriculum and academic requirements are remarkably traditional. First-year students must complete Humanities 110, a yearlong interdisciplinary course focused on society and culture from the ancient Mediterranean to pre- and post-colonial Mexico to the Harlem Renaissance. Designed to create a shared intellectual experience for new students, the class draws on instruction from 25 professors, including some of Reed's most senior and distinguished faculty. Students must also take courses in three "breadth" areas: arts and literature; social sciences; and natural, mathematical, and psychological sciences. Seniors are required to submit a research-based thesis to graduate, and on the due date, just after spring classes have ended, they march through campus in the Thesis Parade. This marks the beginning of Renn Fayre (originally "Renaissance Fayre"), a weekend-long celebration that involves a feast prepared by alumni, a softball tournament, live music, and fireworks.

"The academic climate can feel quite intense most of the time," explains a mathematics major, but an environmental studies major explains, "Reed prioritizes feedback on assignments more than letter grades," which alleviates some of the pressure. Reed's most popular majors include psychology, biology, computer science, and English. A major in comparative race and ethnicity studies draws from sociology, anthropology, history, and the arts. Dual-degree (3–2) programs are offered in engineering and forestry/environmental science. Students take full advantage of the range of academic options, which often keep them glued to their computers and study carrels. You'll never find a TA at the lectern or leading a group discussion here, so students rarely attend class unprepared for the lively intellectual banter that typically ensues between inquiring and active minds. A psychology major comments that professors "want to be at Reed, meaning that their top priority is teaching." Reed has improved its retention and graduation rates considerably in the last decade or two by becoming more selective in admissions, increasing on-campus housing for a stronger residential community, and bolstering student support services, including a popular peer tutoring program.

Despite Reed's small size—77 percent of the courses taken by undergraduates have fewer than 20 students—the school offers excellent research opportunities in the liberal arts and sciences. Budding physicists and environmental scientists can work with college staff at the 250-kilowatt Triga nuclear reactor after passing an Atomic Energy Commission examination. "It's grueling, but physics here is legendary," says a junior. Reed also has a tradition of respect for calligraphy that, among other things, inspired Steve Jobs to build first-rate graphics into Apple computers and, in the process, shape the look of every computer that followed. Eighty exchange programs attract 43 percent of students, taking them to their choice of 30 countries.

(continued)

Male/Female: 33/44
Financial Aid: 57%
Pell Grant: 15%
Expense: Pr $ $ $ $
Student Loans: 47%
Average Debt: $ $ $
Applicants: 9,431
Accepted: 25%
Enrolled: 13%
Grad in 6 Years: 72%
Returning First-years: 87%
Academics: ✐ ✐ ✐ ✐
Social: 🗩 🗩 🗩
Q of L: ★ ★ ★
Admissions: (503) 777-7511
Email Address:
  admission@reed.edu

Strong Programs:
Biology
Comparative Race and
  Ethnicity Studies
English
History
Interdisciplinary Studies
Mathematics
Physics
Psychology

> **"Reed is like a rebellious nerd, a teenager who just discovered David Lynch and wants to be him."**

First-year students must complete Humanities 110, a yearlong interdisciplinary course focused on society and culture.

Reed also offers domestic exchange programs with Howard and the Sea Education Association. Three-quarters of Reed's grads go on to graduate school, and a quarter eventually earn Ph.D.s.

Reedies are "amazing, fun-loving nerds who all have a very specific passion that they want to talk your ear off about," says a history major. While Reed attracts students from across the country, the student population draws heavily from California; only 10 percent of Reedies are in-staters. Eight percent hail from other nations. Eight percent are Asian American, 12 percent are Hispanic/Latino, 2 percent are Black, and 10 percent are multiracial. "The Multicultural Resource Center provides resources—guest speakers, lecturers, Tuesday Talks, and more—to keep diversity an ongoing discussion on campus," says an English major. A sophomore adds, "Queer students are very successful and safe here." As for the political climate, the atmosphere is liberal, and a dance and math major remarks, "Students love to have opinions here so every social issue going on in the world is talked about on campus." All financial aid at Reed is need-based, and the school covers 100 percent of admitted students' demonstrated need. Students from families earning under $100,000 receive free tuition, but just 15 percent of first-year students are Pell-eligible.

> **"Reed prioritizes feedback on assignments more than letter grades."**

> *The school's unofficial, tongue-in-cheek slogan is "Atheism, Communism, Free Love."*

About 68 percent of Reed students live on campus in comfortable rooms, some of which feature such homey touches as fireplaces or balconies, "which make it so it's not like living in a tiny box," says a senior. Reed's "neighborhood" housing model groups residence halls into distinct neighborhoods with specific programming, like workshops and social events. First-year students live together in designated neighborhoods, sophomores select neighborhoods based on their interests, and juniors and seniors live in upper-division neighborhoods. There are five language houses (Chinese, French, German, Russian, and Spanish), each of which is staffed with a native speaker. First-years and sophomores are guaranteed housing; upperclassmen seeking a taste of post-college independence must contend with Portland's pricey rental market. In the Commons dining hall, a student says, "The food is surprisingly good and diverse, and the kitchen is happy to help with any particular dietary needs." Mental health support receives positive reviews, as does campus security. "Reed's strongest support service is SHARE (Sexual Health, Advocacy & Relationship Education)," says a junior, "which offers consent education, contraceptives, and sober spaces for students."

"On campus, there are always small parties, or plays, or giant Student Union (SU) dances, or fire-dancing shows, or bands playing," says one student. Students describe Reed's alcohol policies, guided by the college's Honor Principle, as effective and well enforced. Students look forward to Paideia ("education" in ancient Greek), a week-long program of both practical and wacky non-credit classes mostly taught by students themselves before spring semester begins. Past Paideia offerings have ranged from personal finance to mushroom identification to burlesque. During the Owl Fight, students wrestle on the lawn over a 300-pound concrete sculpture of the Doyle Owl, the closest thing Reed has to a school mascot.

> **"Portland, Oregon, is one of the coolest, weirdest places in America."**

> *Reed emphasizes personal freedom and responsibility, especially through its Honor Principle.*

"Portland, Oregon, is one of the coolest, weirdest places in America, so of course it's a good social scene," raves a senior. The city boasts a diverse range of live music, literary events, and film screenings, as well as an eclectic array of shops, bars, and restaurants. Many students get involved in community service projects organized by SEEDS (Students for Education, Equity, and Direct Service). The mammoth Powell's Books downtown is about a 15-minute drive, and Oregon's coastal beaches, mountains, or high desert are all about two hours away—although finding time for road trips can be a challenge. The school also owns a ski cabin on Mount Hood that sleeps 15.

While Reed doesn't have varsity athletics, club teams in basketball, rugby, soccer, and ultimate Frisbee do compete with other clubs in the area. A variety of intramural and recreational sports are available for the less competitive, such as rugby, rowing, and curling.

Reed attracts seriously intellectual, unconventional students, but it is not without a sense of humor—the school's unofficial, tongue-in-cheek slogan is "Atheism, Communism, Free Love." If you're a lover of learning who prefers to start Saturday nights with your nose in a book and end them at an all-school dance party, this Portland school may be worth a look. As one satisfied senior puts it, "Reed gives you the education of an Ivy but the fun of a state school."

If You Apply To ›

Reed: Early decision I and II, early action, regular decision. Accepts the Common Application with supplement. Please consult Reed's website for the most up-to-date information regarding standardized test requirements.

Rensselaer Polytechnic Institute

110 8th Street, Troy, NY 12180

If you can spell Rensselaer, you've already got a leg up on many applicants. RPI is one of the nation's great technical universities—along with Caltech, Harvey Mudd, and MIT—and one of the most innovative. The beauty of RPI is the chance for hands-on learning and synergy between technology, management, and entrepreneurship. School spirit soars when Division I hockey teams take the ice.

It would be an exaggeration to say that technology has divine status at Rensselaer Polytechnic Institute, though the school's conversion of a Gothic chapel into a computer lab does hint in that direction. Still, technology remains omnipresent at this school, which pioneered the teaching of calculus via computer in the early '90s. RPI's Artificial Intelligence Multiprocessing Optimized System is the most powerful supercomputer housed at a private university, and the school has been hiring new faculty to support research and educational efforts in artificial intelligence and data analytics. Students attend class in high-tech studio classrooms where they work on team projects and collaborate to solve real-world problems. As the school says, "RPI defines an educated person as someone hungry to know how things work." Recent investments in residential life, off-campus learning opportunities, and career services continue to raise RPI's profile at home and abroad.

Set high on a bluff overlooking Troy, New York, Rensselaer's 275-acre campus mixes modern research facilities and classical, ivy-covered brick buildings dating to the turn of the 20th century. The cutting-edge Shirley Ann Jackson, Ph.D. Center for Biotechnology and Interdisciplinary Studies (named for the renowned physicist and former president of RPI) houses more than 400 researchers in biotechnology and related disciplines who work in such areas as regenerative medicine, bioinformatics, biocatalysis, and metabolic engineering.

In order to graduate, students must complete distribution requirements and attain "data dexterity," a requirement that administrators describe as "proficiency

The Grand Marshal oversees a boisterous weeklong carnival celebrating campus elections, during which professors are barred from giving tests.

in using diverse data sets to define and solve complex real-world problems." An initiative called the Arch requires all students to live on campus and attend a full academic semester the summer between their sophomore and junior year. The summer semester offers more than 210 courses, in addition to field trips, pop-up courses, career development workshops, and other activities. In their junior year, all students undertake a semester-long off-campus experience, such as an internship, co-op, research, or study abroad program.

Founded in 1824 by landowner and philanthropist Stephen Van Rensselaer, RPI made its reputation as one of the nation's premier engineering schools and continues to excel in traditional favorites such as mechanical and aeronautical engineering, as well as newer specialties like biomedical and environmental engineering. Architecture, computer science, and information technology are also strengths. RPI's Lally School of Management combines elements of a business school with the latest technical applications. Entrepreneurship is one of its specialties; budding entrepreneurs from all majors may participate in a support system for start-up companies. RPI is a national leader in the study and application of digital media and offers B.S. degrees in electronic arts and games and simulation arts and sciences. Industry semiconductor workforce courses allow students to learn from semiconductor researchers and leaders in top companies such as IBM, Applied Materials, and ASML. RPI has greatly expanded its humanities, arts, and social science offerings, and has added a B.S. in music. Students with long-term professional goals may take advantage of accelerated B.S./M.B.A. programs in engineering and business administration or science and business administration, or complete an accelerated B.S./M.D. in seven years.

> **"The professors here know the kinds of skills that students need to learn."**

"Rensselaer is rigorous," says a game and simulation arts and sciences major. "The professors here know the kinds of skills that students need to learn, and if the students aren't willing to put in the effort, they won't succeed." Roughly 85 percent of Rensselaer's full-time students are undergraduates, a high percentage for a top engineering school; because of this, RPI has worked hard to ensure that classes are smaller and more attention is paid to individual needs. A junior notes, "There's a strong sense of support among students; everyone kind of understands what you're going through." Forty-five percent of classes enroll fewer than 20 students. Students give high ratings to the drop-in tutoring services offered by the Advising and Learning Assistance Center. Thirty-seven percent of undergrads work on research projects with faculty members. Says a biological neuroscience major, "I was able to join a graduate lab during my first month on campus and have been completing Alzheimer's disease and cancer research ever since." Popular co-op programs in more than a dozen fields help students earn both money and credit. Study abroad programs are available in more than 20 countries.

"I usually describe RPI students as driven, smart, and a little quirky in the best way," says a civil engineering major. Nearly 70 percent of RPI students are male, but one female student says, "I have always felt supported in predominantly male groups." Thirty-nine percent of students are New Yorkers, while 7 percent are international. RPI is fairly diverse, with Asian Americans comprising 22 percent of the student body, Black students 5 percent, Hispanics/Latinos 11 percent, and multiracial students 5 percent.

> **"There's a strong sense of support among students; everyone kind of understands what you're going through."**

Politically, "folks are on the more progressive side of things," says a student. The biggest campus issue may be choosing the Grand Marshal, who oversees a boisterous weeklong carnival celebrating campus elections, during which professors are barred from giving tests. Merit scholarships averaging $34,500 are available, as are 40 athletic scholarships.

Fifty-seven percent of students live in university housing; first-years and sophomores are required to live in the residence halls, where they are supported by a team of faculty and peer advisors intended to create smaller, more tightly knit student communities. Most upperclassmen choose to move into less-expensive off-campus apartments. Meals served in the four campus dining halls get good reviews. A senior notes that RPI's recent restructuring of Title IX procedures "has made sexual assault a conversation people are really starting to have." Adds a senior, "RPI's mental health services are also fantastic. There are always fun events and de-stress activities each week to help students."

Socially, RPI "is more low-key and nerdy than wild," says a junior. Eighteen percent of men and 11 percent of women go Greek, but a sophomore says, "You don't have to be involved in Greek life to have a social life." Alcohol is not allowed in Greek housing or residence halls; an on-campus pub serves beer and wine to those 21 and over. With more than 200 student clubs and organizations, a mechanical engineering major says, "Whether you are into dancing, coding, playing video games, playing sports, modifying cars, or going on outdoor trips, there are plenty of social groups that offer what you are looking for."

Free shuttle buses run regularly from campus to downtown Troy. "Troy was a booming river-town in the early 20th century and has shifted towards being a tech hub, but it still has much of the classic charm," reports a senior. "There are lots of diners and restaurants as well as festivals and the Troy Farmer's Market every Saturday." Students frequently get involved with community service projects. Movie theaters are within easy reach, and for a taste of bigger-city nightlife, Albany is a half-hour drive. For more adventurous excursions, the Berkshires, Catskills, Adirondacks, Lake Placid, New York City, and Boston are popular destinations.

> **"You don't have to be involved in Greek life to have a social life."**

The athletic scene at Rensselaer revolves around hockey—the school's only teams playing in Division I. One of the biggest weekends of the year is Big Red Freakout, when all festivities center around cheering on the beloved Engineers. "Everyone wears red, the rink is packed, and it's one of the few times you really feel the whole campus come together," says a junior. Twenty-one varsity teams compete in Division III, and the men's and women's cross-country and men's football, baseball, and men's and women's tennis are strong. There are many intramural sports to choose from, but the most popular may be the Division 4 hockey team (meaning "I really don't know how to play this," says a junior).

The oldest school of science and civil engineering in the English-speaking world, Rensselaer is still providing cutting-edge technology to students constantly wondering how things work. Tech geeks aren't the only ones who will find a home at RPI with the expanded humanities offerings. RPI students work hard to attain their sought-after data dexterity, sometimes to the detriment of a social life, but they don't seem to mind. Says a civil engineering major, "There's a strong sense of independence here; people build their own paths, take on ambitious projects, and get involved in things because they're genuinely interested."

Overlaps

Caltech, Carnegie Mellon, Georgia Tech, Northeastern, Purdue, Rochester Institute of Technology, Stevens Institute of Technology, Worcester Polytechnic

If You Apply To ›

RPI: Early decision I and II, early action, regular decision. Accepts the Common Application. Apply to particular program. Please consult RPI's website for the most up-to-date information regarding standardized test requirements.

14 Upper College Road, Kingston, RI 02881

URI is a smallish alternative to UConn and UMass. With Boston, Providence, and vacation hot spot Newport within easy reach, there is plenty to do. Strong programs include engineering, marine sciences, nursing, and pharmacy. Enrollment and faculty ranks have been on the rise. More than half of URI's students are out-of-staters.

Website: www.uri.edu

Location: Small Town

Public

Total Enrollment: 14,377

Undergraduates: 12,757

Male/Female: 41/58

Financial Aid: 74%

Pell Grant: 26%

Expense: Pub $ $ $ $

Student Loans: 70%

Average Debt: $ $ $ $

Applicants: 26,987

Accepted: 72%

Enrolled: 15%

Grad in 6 Years: 72%

Returning First-years: 84%

Academics: ✑ ✑ ✑

Social: 🗩 🗩 🗩 🗩

Q of L: ★ ★ ★

Admissions: (401) 874-7000

Email Address:
admission@uri.edu

Strong Programs:
Business
Communication Studies
Engineering
Kinesiology
Marine Sciences
Nursing
Pharmacy
Psychology

No longer an unabashed party school, the University of Rhode Island has earned a reputation for challenging academics with an emphasis on innovation and interdisciplinary learning. URI offers an environment in which students engage in service learning, do research with top faculty, and find a heavy emphasis put on alternative styles of learning. "Our college is an amazing place to learn, prosper, and have fun," boasts one sophomore.

URI was chartered as a land grant school in 1888, and its 1,200-acre campus is in the small town of Kingston. Surrounded by farmland and only six miles from the coast, it is also within easy driving distance of cities such as Providence—the home to Brown, the Rhode Island School of Design, and several other colleges and universities—Boston, and New York. The main academic buildings at URI, a mixture of modern and "old New England granite," surround a central quad on Kingston Hill. At the foot of Kingston Hill lie the athletic buildings and agricultural fields. In 2025, URI kicked off a comprehensive plan to remake the campus with new facilities and pedestrian pathways over the next 20 years. First up are three new residence halls, the first of which is expected to open as soon as 2027.

New students initially enroll in the University College, which offers academic and career guidance, as well as advice on fulfilling general education requirements. All new students take URI 101, a one-credit course intended to acquaint them with support services, cocurricular activities, academic majors, and career options. After a year or two in University College, students choose more specialized colleges, such as the well-regarded College of Pharmacy, which offers a six-year Pharm.D. program. The engineering, business, and marine sciences departments are also strong, and the most popular majors include nursing, psychology, kinesiology, and communication studies. The five-year international engineering dual-degree program combines degrees in engineering and a foreign language with a year abroad for language immersion and an engineering internship. Students can earn up to four academic credits during the Winter J Term session in January.

> **"Students here are involved and outgoing."**

Academic intensity at URI tends to vary by program. Professors receive generally good marks for their teaching, but their accessibility can be hit or miss. "At times, it can be difficult to work with faculty," says a marine affairs major, who encourages students to "find a professor or faculty member who is invested in you and your studies." Thirty-seven percent of classes enroll fewer than 20 students. The Academic Enhancement Center, along with its Writing Center, provides peer tutorials, course-specific collaborative learning projects, supplemental instructional sessions, and special programs for high-risk students.

URI offers international exchange programs with universities in such diverse locales as Chile, France, Korea, and Norway, as well as domestic exchange programs with state colleges and universities. Twenty percent of undergraduates participate in the 200-plus available programs in more than 70 countries. Students interested in research can collaborate on projects with multidisciplinary teams of faculty through established research partnerships, such as the Partnership for the Coastal Environment. URI's Honors Program draws about 900 students with an honors colloquium and expanded research opportunities. The Center for Student Leadership Development offers a minor in leadership studies, as well as conferences, retreats, and workshops.

Although URI gives preference to in-state students who meet certain requirements, 52 percent of undergrads come from states outside Rhode Island; less than 1 percent arrive from foreign countries. "Students here are involved and outgoing," one junior says. Five percent of the student body is Black, 12 percent is Hispanic/Latino, 3 percent is Asian American, and 4 percent is multiracial. "There is no doubt about it that URI is a predominantly white institution," says one student of color, "but diversity comes in many shapes and forms. We are diverse when it comes to socioeconomic status, nationality, sexual orientation, political affiliation, gender, and many other ways." The university has been investing in resources to support diversity in recent years, and a senior says, "URI has great women's services as well as LGBTQ services." The academic profiles of the incoming class have risen, in large measure due to the Presidential and Merit Scholarship Programs for outstanding first-years. Merit awards average $6,100, and athletes vie for scholarships in 16 sports.

> **"We are 10 minutes from the beach and 30 minutes from Providence."**

Though most first-year students live on campus, 61 percent of all undergraduates choose to find off-campus digs near the beach. Most residence halls have recently been renovated—and more modern housing is on the way. The Brookside Apartments residence hall has added 500 beds for upperclassmen. "Some of the freshman dorms are gorgeous," one student reports. About 80 percent of first-years participate in living/learning communities in a variety of disciplines. Dining options include two dining halls, and students say the staff is accommodating of various dietary needs. "Campus security does rounds around campus throughout the night," notes a student.

Greek life attracts 24 percent of the men and 28 percent of the women. The campus coffeehouse hosts open-mic nights, and more than 120 student organizations provide a variety of activities. The student newspaper that covers it all has one of the most original names anywhere: *The Good 5¢ Cigar* (as in, "what this country needs is a really good five-cent cigar," a quip uttered by U.S. Vice President Thomas R. Marshall in 1914). Given the small size of the state, a fair number of students choose to head home on weekends. As for Kingston, it's a sleepy New England college town of 7,800; students get involved in the community through clubs or URI 101, which requires volunteer work. "There is nothing in Kingston," complains one student, "but we are 10 minutes from the beach and 30 minutes from Providence." Wakefield and Newport, both nearby, offer more entertainment, and fun road trips include Boston (90 minutes) and New York City (four hours).

Division I sports are big at Rhode Island, and basketball games are especially exciting. Midnight Madness (the team's first sanctioned practice of the year) is always well attended, and URI fans love it when the Rams defeat archrival Providence College. Recent Atlantic 10 conference champs include men's track and field, women's basketball, as well as women's sailing. URI also offers around 17 club sports and more than a dozen intramurals. A favorite student tradition is oozeball, an April volleyball tournament played in about two feet of mud. As befits the school's coastal locale, sailing draws much interest, and the club team regularly produces All-Americans.

URI offers students a large school feel in a small state. Consistent efforts by the administration to invest in campus upgrades and new educational opportunities have paid off, as evidenced by the changing face of the student body and their

Overlaps

UConn, University of Delaware, UMass Amherst, University of New Hampshire, Northeastern, Penn State, Syracuse, University of Vermont

accomplishments. Students here work hard to achieve good grades and lay the foundation of lifelong learning.

Rhode Island School of Design

20 Washington Place, Providence, RI 02903

The nation's best-known art and design school, RISD sits on a hillside adjacent to Brown. The campus offers easy access to downtown Providence, but it can't match the location of rival Parsons in New York's Greenwich Village. Offers 18 undergraduate majors in architecture, fine arts, and design. Industrial design is a specialty, and athletics are, well, quirky.

Website: www.risd.edu
Location: Small City
Private
Total Enrollment: 2,517
Undergraduates: 2,084
Male/Female: 29/71
Financial Aid: 36%
Pell Grant: 17%
Expense: Pr $ $ $
Student Loans: 34%
Average Debt: $ $ $
Applicants: 6,692
Accepted: 19%
Enrolled: 41%
Grad in 6 Years: 89%
Returning First-years: 95%
Academics: ✍ ✍ ✍ ✍
Social: 🗨 🗨
Q of L: ★ ★ ★ ★
Admissions: (401) 454-6300
Email Address:
 admissions@risd.edu

Strong Programs:
Architecture
Film, Animation, Video
Graphic Design
Illustration
Industrial Design
Painting

Founded in the late 19th century by a group of activist women to address the country's need for more artisans and craftsmen, Rhode Island School of Design has grown into a premier arts incubator. It's a place where today's artists and designers gather to share ideas and create tomorrow's masterpieces and architectural icons. In fact, the cofounders of Airbnb, Brian Chesky and Joe Gebbia, met and developed their creative instincts here. RISD (pronounced "Rizdee") grants degrees in virtually every design-related area, and like the varied curriculum, the students and their creations are as diverse as the colors on an artist's palette. One thing that everyone here shares is an intense workload and a highly competitive spirit. "RISD students are masochists," says one first-year.

Though you might expect an art school like RISD to occupy funky, futuristic buildings, the predominant look here is colonial New England. Set on the upgrade of College Hill, RISD is located at the edge of Providence's beautifully preserved historic district, adjacent to Brown University. Many campus buildings date from the 1800s and early 1900s; the mostly redbrick-and-white-trim group includes converted homes, a bank, and even an old church. Perhaps RISD's most prized facility is the RISD Museum, a superlative collection of roughly 100,000 works that includes everything from Roman and Egyptian art to paintings by Monet, Matisse, and Picasso.

While RISD looks traditionally New England on the outside, behind those historic walls lies something else entirely. First-year students take a common curriculum called Experimental and Foundation Studies, which acclimates them to RISD's approach to studio learning and group critiques. In addition to courses in their major, students

"RISD students are masochists!"

must complete coursework in the liberal arts (theory and history of art and design; literature; and history, philosophy, and social sciences) and a final-year project to graduate.

The most popular majors include illustration, industrial design, graphic design, architecture, film/animation/video, and painting. Students may choose to supplement their degrees with one of six concentrations in computation, technology, and culture; drawing; theory and history of art and design; history, philosophy, and the social sciences; literary arts and studies; and nature-culture-sustainability studies.

The Nature Lab allows for examining, exploring, and understanding patterns, structures, and interactions of design in nature. RISD also offers cross-registration and a dual-degree option with Brown for students seeking more diverse courses. A First Year in Florence option features studio and liberal arts courses that introduce students to RISD within the rich historical context of Florence, Italy.

Hands-on studio courses abound at RISD, and roughly three-quarters of classes have fewer than 20 students. "The academic atmosphere is competitive because we are passionate and collaborative because we need others' input for our work to be successful," explains a textiles major. Though highly selective, RISD will sometimes take a chance on academically underachieving high school graduates with special artistic promise. Still, while students at RISD don't "hit the books" in the traditional sense, the in-studio workload is considerable, and students warn that organizational and time-management skills are essential. Teaching here is said to be generally good, although it can be a mixed bag. "For the most part, I have had positive and supportive professors, but I have also had professors who lacked a sense of criticality," reports a senior.

During RISD's Wintersession, five weeks between the first and second semesters, students are encouraged to take courses outside their major. An international exchange program provides opportunities to study abroad at approved art institutions in 25 countries worldwide.

RISD students (referred to as "RISDoids") come to Providence to form a distinctly urban mix of styles and personalities. "We are the lost misfits who have found each other," says a senior. A mere 2 percent of students are native Rhode Islanders, not surprising given the state's small size, while an impressive 33 percent hail from foreign countries. The racial makeup of the campus is mixed, with Asian Americans representing 26 percent of the student body, Black students 5 percent, Hispanics/Latinos 8 percent, and multiracial students 5 percent. Students say the campus is liberal, open-minded, and inclusive. Some complain about the skewed male/female ratio, since "sometimes there is not even one male-identifying person in the classroom," according to an illustration major. Socioeconomic disparities can be a concern as well; one senior remarks, "I cannot afford to be as elaborate in my projects as most people can, wasting materials and going all out, but I find other ways." Tuition and fees here are steep, and although the school has been increasing its need-based financial aid, it does not guarantee to meet students' full need. A new two-week, on-campus First-Generation to College Pre-Orientation program aims to smooth the path to college for first generation students. Merit scholarships average $8,500, but athletic scholarships are nonexistent.

Sixty-eight percent of undergraduates reside in campus-owned housing, and all RISD residences are gender inclusive. First-years live together in a group of co-ed dorms known as the Quad. "All on-campus housing is well maintained, comfortable, and damn luxurious for dorms, with plenty of security," says one film major. "It's just grossly overpriced." Most upperclassmen move off campus to nearby apartments, many of which occupy floors of restored homes; RISD also owns an apartment building and some renovated colonial and Victorian houses. All boarders buy the meal plan, but campus dining receives mixed reviews. Some students have criticized the administration for handling sexual assault cases too lightly.

Despite a student body that looks like it could have been plucked from the streets of New York's Greenwich Village, RISD is not the place to come for a wild and funky nightlife. "Given the high level of commitment at RISD, there is not a large social life," laments an architecture major. "Many students are consumed by their studios, working until very late." The Tap Room inside Memorial Hall went dry years

A First Year in Florence option features studio and liberal arts courses that introduce students to RISD within the rich historical context of Florence, Italy.

"We are passionate and collaborative because we need others' input for our work to be successful."

The cofounders of Airbnb, Brian Chesky and Joe Gebbia, met and developed their creative instincts at RISD.

ago, but students 21 and over are allowed to drink alcohol within their private rooms in upper-class housing. There is no Greek life, and a painting major comments, "A RISD party is usually a group of five to seven friends drinking wine, listening to good music, and cooking together." Students head to Brown for more adventuresome parties, and Providence provides some social outlets as well.

"Many students are consumed by their studios, working until very late."

Though RISD isn't much for traditions, one big annual event is the Artists' Ball, a festive October dance party featuring eclectic and over-the-top student-made costumes. When claustrophobia sets in, students can flee to the RISD farm, a 33-acre recreation area on the shores of nearby Narragansett Bay. Boston and New York City are one and four hours away by train, respectively.

Though jocks are an endangered species at RISD, recreation opportunities are plentiful and one of a kind. There is no intercollegiate sports program in the ordinary sense, though there is a co-ed club ice hockey team, called the Nads (which, of course, inspires RISDoids to holler "Go Nads!") and a seven-foot-tall mascot named Scrotie (use your imagination). The men's basketball team competes locally, and the rowing team participates in regional regattas, including the Head of the Charles race in Boston. Other recreational sports range from soccer and ultimate Frisbee to sailing and skiing.

Students come to RISD committed to their crafts, and most march to the beat of their own drums as they rush from studio courses to gallery openings to exhibitions. They can be confident that their endless studio hours are designing a foundation for future success. "If you are a student who thrives under pressure, under constraints that are meant to fortify your critical skills," says one senior, "then RISD is the place for you."

If You Apply To ›

RISD: Early decision, regular decision. SATs or ACTs: optional. Accepts the Common Application with supplement. All applicants must submit a portfolio of their visual work.

Rhodes College

2000 North Parkway, Memphis, TN 38112

Goes head-to-head with Sewanee for the top spot in the pecking order of mid-South liberal arts colleges, with Rhodes the more progressive of the two that also has Memphis and its red-hot music scene. Natural and social sciences head the list of solid programs, and undergraduate research opportunities are plentiful. Strong honor system and commitment to community service.

Since 1848, Rhodes College has been instilling the timeless values of truth and honor in its students. The school's honor code means exams are not proctored and backpacks are left unattended in the cafeteria. Its small size gives everyone an opportunity to take on leadership roles in campus clubs and organizations, and people are generally friendly. Throw in the college's proximity to Memphis's world-famous Beale Street, barbecue, and the blues, and it makes for a winning combination.

Rhodes was founded as a Presbyterian school in Clarksville, Tennessee, and it moved to its 100-acre campus in Memphis in 1925. Located in the residential midtown section, Rhodes sits across from a 175-acre park housing the city's largest art museum, a golf course, and the Memphis Zoo. Whether new or old, all campus buildings are Collegiate Gothic in style, constructed of Arkansas fieldstone with leaded-glass windows and slate roofs. Thirteen of the original buildings are on the National Register of Historic Places.

The Rhodes general education curriculum features highly regarded three-course sequences known as The Search for Values in the Light of Western History and Religion, and Life: Then and Now. The Search sequence has been part of the Rhodes curriculum for more than 75 years. To receive a Rhodes degree, students must select one of the two sequences and demonstrate proficiency in 12 areas that form the foundation of the liberal arts, such as written communication, mathematical reasoning, and multicultural perspectives. A "sustained engagement" experience, such as an internship or study abroad—is also required. First-years take a yearlong seminar designed to ease the academic and social transition to Rhodes.

Rhodes is especially strong in the natural and social sciences, thanks to labs with state-of-the-art equipment. Business, psychology, biology, and computer science enroll the most students. Economics, international studies, English and creative writing, and chemistry are well respected, as is the music business program. Aside from traditional lecture-style classes, the college offers seminars, honors programs, one-on-one Directed Inquiry tutorials, and interdisciplinary majors. Rhodes also participates in a dual-degree program for engineers with Washington University in St. Louis. "The academic climate at Rhodes is vigorous," says a political science and French major. "Many of our classes are challenging, and it is nearly impossible to get by without making an active effort." Eighty percent of classes have fewer than 20 students, which means professors are more than talking heads. "Professors encourage you to really think about your future," comments a junior. "They're amazing sounding boards, mentors, and friends." Students also praise the career center for "offering personalized guidance, résumé workshops, and networking opportunities." Internship options abound.

Students who can't find what they want on campus may tap into a variety of study abroad programs, and 66 percent do so. The Buckman International Fellows program offers summer internships across the globe, including in South America, Africa, Europe, and Asia. A partnership with St. Jude Children's Research Hospital lets students conduct research there in the summers and continue their projects during the next school year; 44 percent of Rhodes students take part in undergraduate research.

"We have a rather artsy and service-oriented population," says a health equity major. Like Davidson and Hendrix, Rhodes tends to attract white, Southern, middle- and upper-middle-class students, although diversity is inching upward with students arriving from 48 states and 63 countries, "contributing to a rich tapestry of experiences and perspectives," according to an economics major. Thirty-five percent of students are Tennessee natives, and 10 percent are international. Black students represent 9 percent of the student body, Asian Americans 9 percent, Hispanics/Latinos 8 percent, and multiracial students 5 percent. The political atmosphere is "relatively liberal," comments a senior, while another says, "Students always have opinions but are almost always very respectful." Eligible students receive scholarships based on academic merit averaging $30,500. There are no athletic scholarships.

Rhodes requires on-campus housing for the first three years, where 70 percent of students live in air-conditioned dorms. Residence halls are open to all students except for West Village and East Village, where upperclassmen vie for rooms during the yearly lottery. Students eat in the Refectory, known as "the Rat" (officials assure us it's not a commentary on the food), or the Lynx Lair; the former has hot food

(continued)

Expense: Pr $ $
Student Loans: 55%
Average Debt: $
Applicants: 6,365
Accepted: 50%
Enrolled: 12%
Grad in 6 Years: 84%
Returning First-years: 91%
Academics: ✍ ✍ ✍
Social: 🗨 🗨 🗨
Q of L: ★ ★ ★ ★
Admissions: (901) 843-3700
Email Address:
  adminfo@rhodes.edu

Strong Programs:
Biology
Business
Chemistry
Computer Science
English
History
Music Business
Psychology

lines, and the latter offers fare such as wraps, sandwiches, and burgers, along with a well-stocked salad bar. "Our two campus dining facilities serve very edible food," reports one student, "and there is typically something for all tastes, preferences, and lifestyles." Students give good ratings to general campus safety. One student reports, "The school has made some policy changes regarding sexual assault and the protection of sexual assault victims." Regarding mental health support, a health equity major praises the counselors, adding, "Students get a certain number of free sessions so there are no barriers holding them back!"

Fraternities draw 30 percent of the men and sororities sign up 37 percent of the women. "The majority of campus social life revolves around partying and Greek life," says a biology major. Chartered buses provide rides to off-campus parties, many of which are sponsored by the Greeks, though independents are welcome to attend. Despite campus policies prohibiting underage drinking, students say those who are determined can usually find booze—if not at parties, then in other students' rooms. Students look forward to All Sing, a performance competition during Parents Weekend, and the three-day Rites of Spring concert draws crowds for the big-name headliner.

Lively and energetic Memphis has its fair share of college students, with three other four-year institutions in the area and a number of community colleges as well. There are plenty of clubs and bars, along with live music and arts organizations, volunteer opportunities, and internships. "Service is an integral part of the Rhodes experience," says a senior, with most students participating.

Rhodes fields 11 women's and 10 men's varsity Lynx teams, which compete in Division III. The women's lacrosse team has won nine straight Southern Athletic Association conference titles, and baseball, men's lacrosse, men's swimming and diving, women's golf, and men's soccer have also been successful in recent years. About a quarter of all students participate in intramurals and club sports, the most popular being basketball, soccer, and kickball. The Bryan Campus Life Center boasts squash and racquetball courts and a suspended indoor track. Rhodes's mock trial team holds the record for consecutive national championship tournament appearances and has won four times.

Rhodes College students relish the school's solid academics and rich Southern tradition. A happy computer science major boasts that it offers "a perfect liberal arts education." The school's reputation is rising within and outside the Southeast, and it is slowly becoming more diverse. What hasn't changed is the friendly vibe on campus and the eagerness of students, faculty, and staff to welcome you to the community.

"We have a rather artsy and service-oriented population."

Overlaps

Emory, Kenyon, University of Richmond, Sewanee, University of Tennessee Knoxville, Trinity University, Tulane, Vanderbilt

If You Apply To ›

Rhodes: Early decision I and II, early action, regular decision. SATs or ACTs: optional. Accepts the Common Application.

Rice University

6100 Main Street, Houston, TX 77005

One of the few top private colleges making serious efforts to keep tuition affordable. Rice is outstanding in engineering, architecture, natural sciences, and music, and it is a national leader in entrepreneurship studies. With around 4,600 undergraduates, Rice is smaller than many applicants realize. In lieu of Greek life, Rice has a residential college system like Yale and Princeton.

Founded in 1912 by Texas cotton mogul William Marsh Rice, Rice University has stayed true to its mission of providing unsurpassed programs in natural sciences, engineering, the arts, and humanities—with a price tag most families can afford. With its top-notch programs in the liberal arts and sciences and huge endowment (used to tamp down tuition), Rice is a good deal among top schools. It is the dominant university in the Southwest and second only to Duke in the entire South. Thanks to an aggressive growth plan, a nearly $2 billion building campaign, and generous financial aid, enrollment is soaring as the university continues to attract more and more top talent from around the country.

Rice was modeled after such disparate institutions as progressive, low-tuition Cooper Union and the more traditional Princeton University. Today, Rice boasts plenty of distinctive characteristics all its own. The predominant architectural theme of the campus, situated three miles from downtown Houston, is Spanish Mediterranean. A particular standout is the colorful Duncan Hall, designed by British architect John Outram. Newer facilities include the Brockman Hall for Opera, which features a 600-seat, European-style opera theater. But Rice's buildings are less notable than its trees—4,600 of them at last count, with the entire campus officially designated as an arboretum. About half of the trees are live oaks, with branches that spread high and wide and provide an unbroken canopy of shade from the searing Houston sun.

Rice has traditionally excelled in the natural sciences and engineering, and students majoring in these areas still dominate the student body. Architecture here is one of the finest undergraduate programs in the nation, and the physics and astronomy department works closely with NASA. Programs in computer science, engineering, kinesiology, and biosciences are popular, and economics and music are highly regarded. Rice launched an undergraduate school of business in 2021. Rice has a long tradition of encouraging double and even triple majors in such seemingly opposite fields as electrical engineering and art history. Under the area-major program, students can draw up proposals for independent interdisciplinary majors. All first-years participate in a writing program that is tailored, in part, to individual disciplines, as well as a diversity class and physical activity course. Other distribution requirements are flexible: students take three courses each in the humanities, social sciences, and natural sciences/engineering, choosing the courses that interest them most.

> "Students are almost always willing to help each other."

Courses are challenging, but for the most part, says a senior, "Students are almost always willing to help each other, creating a caring and supportive atmosphere." Everyone operates under the honor system, and most exams go unsupervised. Class size rarely presents a problem; 64 percent have fewer than 20 students. Faculty members receive high marks, and full professors often teach first-years. "One of my favorite things about Rice is how the professors are so invested in my learning," says a kinesiology major. Under the Mellon Fellow program, selected humanities and social sciences majors may work with a faculty mentor on an academic project that offers a summer research stipend. Sixty-eight percent of undergrads complete at least one research experience by the time they graduate. About a quarter of students participate in 150 study abroad programs offered in 60 countries.

Students describe their classmates as friendly and quirky, and a senior says Rice students are "intellectual, but not navel-gazing." Rice was founded to serve "residents of Houston and the state of Texas," and 38 percent of undergraduates still hail from the Lone Star State. Most of the out-of-staters are transplanted from California, Florida, the Northeast, and other Southern states; 14 percent come from other countries. Twenty-nine percent of undergraduates are Asian American, 17 percent are Hispanic/Latino, 8 percent are Black, and 6 percent are multiracial. "The political

Every undergraduate is assigned to a residential college in their first year, and they remain a member of that college for all four years.

climate at Rice is pretty liberal, especially for a Texas school," notes an engineering major.

Rice practices need-blind admissions (although it is need-aware for international students) and guarantees to meet the full demonstrated need of every admit. Merit scholarships averaging $19,100 are available to qualified students, and over 200 athletic scholarships are awarded each year. The ambitious Rice Investment financial aid program makes tuition free for low-income and middle-class students. Undergraduates with an annual family income of up to $140,000 receive full-tuition grants, and those whose annual family income does not exceed $75,000 also qualify for grants that cover room, board, and mandatory fees. Additionally, students with family incomes between $140,000 and $200,000 are awarded half-tuition grants. Need-based loans have been eliminated for all students who qualify for the Rice Investment. A junior points out that "Rice has improved low-income accessibility by training faculty and staff on how to support first-generation and low-income students."

Rice's founder did not approve of elitist organizations, which means fraternities and sororities are no-nos. Their functions are largely assumed by the 11 residential colleges, Rice's version of dorms, which 59 percent of students currently call home. The housing system is based on the British residential college model. Every undergraduate is assigned to a residential college in their first year, and they remain a member of that college for all four years—even if they choose to live off campus at any time. Students praise the residential college system for giving everyone a sense of belonging to a relatively small community. The quality of housing "varies from OK to super nice," according to one senior. Each residential college is connected to a "servery" (a.k.a. dining hall), and students can eat anywhere they please. "There's a wide variety of options, so you can be as indulgent or as healthy as you want," says a senior. Another student comments that "campus security is about as good as it can be in a big city like Houston." Among Rice's efforts to combat the issue of sexual assault on college campuses is a mandatory five-week, one-credit Critical Thinking in Sexuality course taken by all incoming first-years.

Social life is campus-based and revolves around the residential colleges, which frequently host themed, campuswide parties as well as private gatherings. "While Rice students can write algorithms and social commentary, they still know how to throw a good party," boasts one junior. Students 21 and over are allowed to have alcohol on campus. Other student organizations host activities like shows, dinners, and dances, too. Halloween brings a massive naked run, but the favorite annual tradition by far is Willy Week, which features a variety of festivities put on by the residential colleges, a university-wide water-balloon fight, and the highly anticipated Beer Bike, a relay race in which co-ed teams must speed around a bicycle track and chug water ("which used to be beer, before the drinking law changed," a student explains).

Houston has a bustling nightlife, but you'd better bring a car to enjoy it. The light-rail system makes it easier to get to the city, but it's still a challenge to get around—even with free transportation passes. The city offers ample opportunities for internships and volunteerism; 40 percent of students get involved in service learning. Galveston's beaches on the Gulf of Mexico are only 45 minutes away, and heading for New Orleans, especially in February, can make a great weekend trip.

Ardent football fans abound at Rice; tearing down the goalposts after home victories remains a happy Owls tradition. Baseball is a powerhouse, and women's basketball and cross-country are strong, too. All teams compete in the Division I Conference USA. Rice students go really wild for intramurals, which pit the residential colleges against each other—75 percent participate.

William Marsh Rice never lived to see the fruits of his bequest (sadly, he was chloroformed by his valet in an ill-fated conspiracy to claim his estate), but he would certainly be proud of the eponymous university that he created. "Rice is a welcoming place with an openness to new ideas and a willingness to explore," says an economics major. As the university grows, it remains to be seen whether it will be able to maintain the close relationships with faculty and the intimate quality of the residential experience that has made it special. But when students venture outside the campus for the last time, their Rice diplomas open doors to the corporate world. And thanks to Rice's efforts to keep tuition affordable, their wallets haven't been emptied.

If You Apply To ›

Rice: Early decision I and II, regular decision. Accepts the Common Application with supplement. Music applicants must audition. Architecture applicants must submit portfolio. Please consult Rice's website for the most up-to-date information regarding standardized test requirements.

University of Richmond

410 Westhampton Way, Richmond, VA 23173

Offers students a preprofessional climate rooted in the liberal arts. Though located in the South, there are plenty of Yankee and international voices on UR's forward-looking campus. Business and a unique school for leadership studies are featured offerings, along with a strong global emphasis, but working to diversify its strengths and reputation beyond business. Compare to Emory, or to Bucknell but with urban proximity. A national leader in digital humanities.

Students at the University of Richmond enjoy a healthy mix of Southern ambiance and intellectual rigor that includes small classes, close friendships, and lots of teamwork. A force for progressive liberal arts and sciences, it was a pioneer in leadership studies and continues to expand its international emphasis. In addition to being part of an academic co-educational college, students also are members of either Richmond College (men) or Westhampton College (women), and in the coordinate system, students take advantage of separate student governments, traditions, and dean's offices for advising and support.

UR's 350-acre campus is nestled amid rolling hills about 15 minutes from downtown Richmond, the state capital. The campus, notable for its stately pines and red-brick collegiate Gothic buildings, wraps around a 10-acre lake. Established in 1830, the university moved in 1914 to its present location on former plantation land. The intramural fields, two residence halls, and the Passport Café have been renovated, an extensive library renovation is underway, and a memorial to a burial ground for enslaved people was recently completed.

All Richmond undergraduates combine their major with a foundational curriculum that include six areas of inquiry: historical, literary and textual, natural science, social, symbolic reasoning, and visual and performing arts. Students also complete requirements in communication, qualitative data literacy, and power,

(continued)

Admissions: (804) 289-8640
Email Address:
admission@richmond.edu

Strong Programs:
Accounting
Biology
Business Administration
Health Studies
Leadership Studies
Philosophy, Politics, Economics,
 and Law
Political Science
Psychology

Favorite traditions include Midnight Munchies, when the dining hall stays open past midnight with a DJ spinning tunes the night before finals.

equity, identity, and culture. Everyone takes a First-Year Seminar with faculty drawn from across the university on topics ranging from bioethics to constitutional law. There are also wellness and foreign language requirements.

While the School of Arts and Sciences is the largest school on campus, business administration is the most popular major—UR boasts a top undergraduate business school. The university is actively building up its other offerings, especially in the sciences. Popular options include biology; leadership studies; and philosophy, politics, economics and law. The Jepson School of Leadership Studies draws on the liberal arts to educate students about how they can best serve society. About half of UR students take the foundation leadership course. UR is at the forefront of the digital humanities movement, and the Digital Scholarship Lab allows students to mine huge databases to generate new knowledge.

> **"Everyone is super excited to be a Spider and be on campus."**

One senior describes the academic climate as "competitive, but not in a toxic manner." Classes are usually small; 76 percent have fewer than 20 students. "Each professor knows their students by name, how they learn academically, and even their associated interests," says a rhetoric and communications studies major. Students are also enthusiastic about Career Development's programs, such as Spider Road Trips, which take students to major cities to learn firsthand about various industries and network for potential jobs and internships.

The Richmond Guarantee offers undergrads guaranteed funding of up to $5,000 for at least one summer research or internship experience. "I know that my internship experience, stemming from the Richmond Guarantee, will provide me with a competitive advantage," says a confident sophomore. Fifty-three percent of undergrads study abroad, choosing from 70 programs at partner universities worldwide. A senior who studied abroad in London reports, "I will never forget my time abroad and will value it forever. It even inspired me to apply to the University of Oxford for graduate school!" About 12 percent of sophomores participate every year in what one student calls the "especially sought-after" Sophomore Scholars in Residence program, a living/learning program that combines a yearlong interdisciplinary course, various opportunities for community-based activities and domestic or international travel, and a group capstone project in the spring.

"Everyone is super excited to be a Spider and be on campus," says a business administration major referring to the school's mascot, "students are diligent and hardworking but also know how to have fun." Nearly half of UR students hail from the Northeast, and only 16 percent are Virginians. International students account for 11 percent of the undergraduate population. Seven percent of students are Black, 6 percent are Asian American, 9 percent are Hispanic/Latino, and 4 percent are multiracial. The Student Center

> **"[The academic climate is] competitive, but not in a toxic manner."**

for Equity and Inclusion supports multicultural, LGBTQ, and first-generation students. A history and global studies major comments, "One of the most interesting things about Richmond is that we are not a particularly political campus." Despite its high sticker price, UR prides itself on being accessible, mainly because it practices need-blind admissions and guarantees to meet the full demonstrated financial need of domestic applicants. Richmond covers tuition, housing, and food for qualified in-state students whose families have annual incomes of $75,000 or less. The Richmond Scholars program awards merit scholarships equivalent to full tuition, room, and board to 25 top students in every entering class, while Presidential Scholarships, worth one-third of tuition, are given to up to 80 incoming students. Division I athletes vie for over 200 athletic scholarships.

Although Richmond does not have an on-campus housing requirement, 76 percent of undergraduates live on campus all four years. First-year students typically live in traditional doubles; suite- and apartment-style options are available after that. "Our residence hall rooms are above average for a college campus, and each room has its own heating and AC unit," says a senior. First-years can apply for the Richmond Endeavor living/learning program, which combines two academic courses with advising from a faculty mentor and a peer advisor. The Heilman Dining Center offers hot entrées as well as made-to-order paninis, pizza, pasta, and such; seven retail dining locations provide other options. "The food is to die for!" raves one gourmand. Students say they generally feel safe at UR, and they praise the Counseling and Psychological Services, with a senior noting, "Their 24-hour guarantee response time goes to show how much the university prioritizes mental health."

Students agree that Richmond is "a very social campus" with plenty of options for entertainment during the week and on weekends. Nonresidential fraternities and sororities attract 12 percent of men and 17 percent of women, but "Greek life only plays a small part of the overall social scene," explains a sophomore. The SpiderBoard sponsors regular movie nights, karaoke, and concerts. First-year students have Proclamation Night for Westhampton College and Investiture for Richmond College, during which they sign the honor code and write a letter to themselves, which is returned to them

"[Richmond is] a very social campus."

to open at the start of their senior year. Other traditions include the Ring Dance, a soiree "for the junior girls where they are given their rings," explains an English and leadership studies major, and Midnight Munchies, when the dining hall stays open past midnight with a DJ spinning tunes the night before finals.

Once viewed as a privileged enclave, UR has made a strong commitment to the city of Richmond. Eighty-four percent of students volunteer outside of class in programs coordinated by the Bonner Center for Civic Engagement. "Richmond has a ton of great restaurants," says an economics major, "so I made it my goal to try a new restaurant every weekend." The city also boasts art galleries, beautiful historic neighborhoods, and plenty of internship opportunities at local corporations and government agencies. For those wishing to get away, Williamsburg, Virginia Beach, and Washington, D.C., are not far, and nature buffs also like the river and the nearby backpacking, thanks to the proximity of the Blue Ridge Mountains and Appalachian National Trail.

The school's 17 varsity teams spin their webs in Division I. The Spiders are members of the Atlantic 10 Conference, with the exception of football, which joined in the highly competitive Patriot League in 2025. Recent conference champs include football, men's and women's lacrosse, men's and women's basketball, and women's golf. For the basketball rivalry with Virginia Commonwealth University, UR students "dress up as Spider-Man in the front rows of the game," says a senior. The university offers more than 40 active club sports as well as 18 intramural sports.

Students at Richmond certainly find plenty of programs to like. From first-of-their-kind academic programs to innovative out-of-classroom learning and networking opportunities, Richmond is working hard to push its vision of preprofessional education shaped by commitments to the liberal arts, leadership, and community involvement. Ultimately, says a junior, "Just walking around our campus, going into our buildings and facilities, and talking to the average student will give you a new appreciation of what higher education, and specifically a liberal arts education, can bring you."

Overlaps

Boston College, Colgate, Davidson, Villanova, UVA, Wake Forest, WashU in St. Louis, William & Mary

If You Apply To ›

Richmond: Early decision I and II, early action, regular decision. Accepts the Common Application with supplement. Please consult Richmond's website for the most up-to-date information regarding standardized test requirements.

300 W Seward Street, Ripon, WI 54971

Located where the Republican Party was born in 1854, Ripon is more middle-of-the-road than Beloit and Lawrence and similar in atmosphere to places like DePauw and Knox. With about 800 students, Ripon is the smallest of the five. Strengths are science, education, and communication. Required Catalyst curriculum focuses on developing real-world professional skills. Sixty-eight percent of students are in-staters.

Website: www.ripon.edu
Location: Small Town
Private
Total Enrollment: 762
Undergraduates: 749
Male/Female: 55/45
Financial Aid: 100%
Pell Grant: 36%
Expense: Pr $ $
Student Loans: 78%
Average Debt: $ $ $ $
Applicants: 1,974
Accepted: 80%
Enrolled: 13%
Grad in 6 Years: 62%
Returning First-years: 76%
Academics: ✍ ✍ ✍
Social: 🗩 🗩 🗩
Q of L: ★ ★ ★
Admissions: (800) 947-4766
Email Address:
  adminfo@ripon.edu

Strong Programs:
Biology
Business Management
Communication
Education
Exercise Science
History
Psychology
Sciences

Everything about Ripon College is small, aside from perhaps its academic ambitions. The school is in a tiny Wisconsin town, and there are just under 800 students, meaning "if you don't go to class, your professor will know," a first-year says. Winter brings bitter cold and lots of snow, but the warmth of personal relationships with peers and professors helps to compensate for the frigid temperatures. "Ripon is a school where you're surrounded by familiar faces," says a computer science and theater major. "It's impossible to get lost on this campus."

Founded in 1851 as a prep school, Ripon became a college in 1863. The school's 250-acre campus sits in a town of 7,800, about 20 miles west of Highway 41 between Fond du Lac and Oshkosh. It features tree-lined walks, wetlands, prairie, and woods, and a mixture of 19th- and 20th-century architecture lends a majestic feel. The Franzen Science Center has been fully renovated.

Ripon's Catalyst curriculum calls for students to complete five required seminar courses. Two courses in the first year and two in the sophomore year focus on developing basic academic skills that will prepare students for the Applied Innovation Seminar their junior year, in which they work in small teams with a faculty member to research, develop, and present solutions to large questions facing society. "The Catalyst curriculum enhances skills that employers are looking for," explains a sophomore. All Ripon students graduate with a concentration in applied innovation, and their academic transcripts attest that they have acquired skills in oral communication, writing, critical thinking, collaboration, quantitative reasoning, information literacy, interdisciplinary integration, and intercultural competence. In addition to the Catalyst courses, most students complete a senior seminar or thesis in their major.

> **"Ripon is a school where you're surrounded by familiar faces."**

A politics and government major describes the academic climate as "moderately relaxed" and the workload as "very reasonable." Ripon students delight in their small classes, 66 percent of which have fewer than 20 students, and report that student-initiated study groups are common. "Professors are able to give each student a great amount of personalized attention," cheers a mathematics and physics major. "Office hours are the best at Ripon—make use of them."

Ripon's strengths include the sciences, education, and communication; the most popular majors are psychology, exercise science and kinesiology, elementary education, and biomedical science. Students also give high marks to the premed and health sciences advising program. Newer offerings include majors in engineering and women's, gender, and sexuality studies. Motivated students with AP credits—or just the stamina to take an extra class each term—may finish in three years, thanks to Ripon's accelerated degree program. A 3–2 dual-degree program in engineering with WashU in St. Louis is another option, as is a 3–3 law program with multiple partner universities. In the Summer Opportunities for Advanced Research program, students are paid to perform 400 hours of research or artistic activities on campus and attend weekly professional development seminars. Students can take terms away from campus, in the U.S. or abroad, through programs organized by Ripon or partner providers, including a faculty-led program in Barcelona.

Ripon students are generally "laid-back, friendly, and positive people," says a student. Sixty-three percent come from Wisconsin, and most of the rest hail from elsewhere in the Midwest. One percent come from foreign nations. Black students account for 4 percent of the student body, Asian Americans make up 1 percent, Hispanics/Latinos add 11 percent, and multiracial students represent 2 percent. The college organizes a student diversity conference every April and other programs to support diversity and inclusion on campus. The town of Ripon's claim to fame is its status as the birthplace of the Republican Party, founded on February 28, 1854, to be exact, three years after the college. These days, a senior comments, the campus is "rather unusual in that there is a fairly equal split between Republicans and Democrats." The school offers merit scholarships worth an average of $29,800 but no athletic awards. Thirty-six percent of incoming first-years are eligible for Pell Grants. Ripon covers the cost of tuition for new in-state students whose families make less than $75,000 per year. In-state students with higher family earnings will pay no more than they would to attend the University of Wisconsin at Madison.

Ninety-six percent of Ripon students live on campus, since they must petition to live off campus. First-years are housed together; students may choose co-ed or single-sex halls, with doubles, singles, or suites. Students complain that some facilities need renovations or repairs. "A prospective student should not expect a state-of-the-art or modern living experience at Ripon," cautions a senior. Ripon has two main dining areas—the Commons, with a traditional hot-food line and made-to-order options, and the Spot, a pub-style hangout. A psychobiology major reports that "the quality of food has improved." Campus security receives good ratings, and according to a psychology major, most students "feel comfortable and safe" reporting incidents of sexual harassment or assault.

Social life is mainly concentrated on campus. Thirty-two percent of the men join fraternities, and 31 percent of the women pledge sororities. Members of Greek life are grouped together in the dorms and host parties in their rooms or lounges, where alcohol is permitted for those of age, but one student likens this to "having a party at your parents' house. You're allowed to do it, but you're constantly being watched." Underage drinkers face fines. Campus hangouts like the Spot and the Nest offer live music, comedy, game nights, art shows, and poetry readings. Favorite annual traditions include homecoming and the Springfest concert and carnival. The best road trips include nearby Oshkosh and Appleton or even Milwaukee and Madison. Chicago is a three-hour drive.

"Downtown Ripon offers many great restaurants, little shops, and a movie theater," says a first-year, but most places close early. About 81 percent of students get involved in community service in the local area, and at the start of each year, all the churches in Ripon come together to host a home-cooked potluck dinner for students. Though Ripon's winters can be bitterly cold, the college's location means that frozen lakes and a blanket of snow are a natural part of the winter landscape, and cross-country and downhill skiing, tobogganing, and ice skating are regular diversions. There is even some fervent cheering for dogsled and iceboat races. And when it's not winter ("for one month during the year," quips one student), nearby Green Lake offers boating, fishing, and other water sports.

Ripon's varsity teams (the Red Hawks) compete in Division III, and matches against Beloit and Lawrence usually draw excited crowds; the Lawrence–Ripon rivalry

"We are interactive. We are tight–knit. We are a community."

is one of the oldest in Wisconsin. Men's and women's basketball and track and field have claimed recent Midwest Conference titles. Intramural sports are popular, especially indoor soccer, volleyball, basketball, badminton, and cornhole. Ripon also boasts nationally ranked Ethics Bowl and Business Ethics Bowl teams.

Ripon College offers a strong grounding in the liberal arts, along with a peaceful, quaint, historical, and friendly community where you'll be much more than a number. "I am on a first-name basis with our dean and president, and it's not because I'm in trouble," a junior says. Though being at such a small place can be stifling, Ripon students aren't complaining. "We are interactive. We are tight-knit. We are a community," one student says. "We are Ripon."

If You Apply To ›

Ripon: Rolling admissions. SATs or ACTs: optional. Accepts the Common Application with supplement.

University of Rochester

252 Elmwood Avenue, Rochester, NY 14627

The name may conjure up an urban public university, but Rochester, located in an up-and-coming city, is a quality private university in the orbit of Carnegie Mellon, Case Western Reserve, Johns Hopkins, and WashU in St. Louis. The university has a scientific bent with a focus on research. Music is another strength. Innovative Take Five and e5 programs reward ambitious students with a tuition-free fifth year to explore new interests or pursue entrepreneurial projects.

Over the past decade, Rochester has focused on improving faculty-to-student ratios, made robust investments in facilities, and developed a curriculum that allows students to design their own paths. Add top-rate STEM programs to the combined benefits of having a music school, strong humanities offerings, and an art gallery, and today, Rochester ensures that students have freedom to explore while getting plenty of hands-on experience. The school has positioned itself as a respected and academically rigorous research university. Cheers one student, "It's a great fit for driven, curious students who are excited to chart their own path."

Founded in 1850 by a convention of Baptists, the University of Rochester occupies a snug 90-acre campus, which nestles up to a bend in the Genesee River two miles south of downtown Rochester. Although a few buildings are modern—the Wilson Commons student center designed by I. M. Pei, for example—most of the older structures come in Greek Revival and Georgian colonial styles. The Eastman Quadrangle, with the library and original academic buildings, adds to Rochester's stately look.

There are no general education subject requirements at Rochester other than a writing class, but students are introduced to the full range of liberal arts. The Rochester Curriculum focuses on three classic divisions of learning: humanities and arts; social science; and natural science, mathematics, and engineering. Students choose a major from one of these areas and complete a cluster of three courses in each of the remaining two divisions. Orientation Rochester-style lasts one week and includes a fall festival called Yellowjacket Weekend, designed to help new students "become fully integrated in the university community."

The university's 200-plus degree programs span the standard fields of study, but Rochester takes special pride in its famed Eastman School of Music, which is open to undergraduates. It also excels in the engineering and scientific fields, including biomedical engineering. Optics has long been a strength—naturally, given that the city of Rochester is home to Kodak, Xerox, and Bausch & Lomb. The university's Institute of Optics, the nation's first center devoted exclusively to the subject, is a leader in basic optical research and theory, and it awards about half of all optics degrees in the U.S. The most popular majors include psychology, computer science, applied music, and biological sciences. Economics, engineering, and health science are strong, and Rochester is one of the few schools that offers a degree in American Sign Language.

"The academic environment is collaborative rather than cutthroat," attests a business major. Students admit the academics are challenging but describe the atmosphere as helpful. "Many professors explicitly encourage working together on assignments and projects," says a brain and cognitive science major. Sixty-eight percent of classes have fewer than 20 students. Professors are praised for their skills behind the lectern as well as their passion. "Professors not only teach their respective topics, but they also do research and professional development to expand on their thinking and reasoning," notes an English major. Students also highly rate the Greene Center for Career Education and Connections.

For students whose educational ambitions can't be realized in just four years, two innovative programs offer up to an extra year of study at no extra cost. The Take Five Scholars Program allows students to spend an additional semester or year—tuition free—exploring interests outside their major or a topic they wish to study in greater depth. The Experiential-Five (e5) Program extends the same offer but with an entrepreneurial focus: e5 students pursue internships, undertake special projects, develop entrepreneurial plans, or launch a start-up. Overall, 95 percent of Rochester students get involved in experiential learning, including internships, research, and education abroad; opportunities include Research and Innovation Grants, which provide funding of up to $3,500, and the Journal of Undergraduate Research. Study abroad programs are available in over 40 countries.

"Students here are generally friendly, respectful, and open-minded," says a business major. "The campus community is also very LGBTQ+ inclusive, and people are supportive of each other's identities." Students appreciate the geographic diversity on campus: 24 percent of students come from foreign countries, while 39 percent hail from New York State. Many also come from New England, Florida, the Midwest, and California. Asian Americans make up 18 percent of the student body, while Black students account for 6 percent, Hispanics/Latinos 9 percent, and multiracial students 5 percent. A senior says, "There is always an active dialogue" about current social and political issues. For first-generation students, a political science major recommends checking out The Kearns Center: "It's an awesome resource." Eligible undergraduates receive merit scholarships averaging $13,300.

First-years and sophomores are required to live on campus, and 71 percent of all undergrads choose to do so all four years. "Dorms are comfortable, modern, high-tech, very generously sized, and well maintained," a senior says. New students are assigned to rooms—usually doubles—and upperclassmen can usually get suites or apartments through the lottery. In addition to a variety of co-ed and single-sex options, special-interest floors are available for enthusiasts of music, computers and

(continued)

Strong Programs:
Business
Computer Science
Economics
Engineering
Health Science
Music
Optics
Psychology

Wilson Day is an annual day of community service that places incoming students in more than 50 agencies throughout the city.

Experiential-Five students pursue internships, undertake special projects, develop entrepreneurial plans, or launch a start-up.

technology, anime, green space, and interclass living. Fare served in the dining halls receives high ratings from students, as does campus safety. "Rochester offers solid student support services," says a sophomore. "The University Counseling Center (UCC) provides well-organized mental health services, including free consultations with licensed therapists or psychiatrists."

Eight percent of the men and 10 percent of the women go Greek, and fraternities contribute heavily to the social life of Greeks and independents alike by sponsoring parties and concerts. Students of legal age are allowed to drink in designated areas of the campus, but students agree that Rochester is not much of a party school. "While there are many things to do in the city of Rochester, it seems that most of the social life occurs right on campus," observes one student. UR has its own set of movie theaters, and a cappella concerts always draw a crowd. Favorite annual events include Meliora Weekend—a combined parents weekend and alumni reunion named for the school's motto (Meliora means "ever better" in Latin) that features a carnival and a headline act, such as comedian Trevor Noah or *Hamilton* Tony-winner Leslie Odom Jr.—during homecoming; the holiday Boar's Head Dinner; and a spring fling known as Dandelion Day. Wilson Day is an annual day of community service that places incoming students in more than 50 agencies throughout the city of Rochester to paint houses, landscape, and play bingo in nursing homes.

Many students take the free campus shuttle into the greater Rochester area, where they may entertain themselves on the beaches of Lake Ontario, in the International Photography Museum at the Eastman House, or at the Rochester Philharmonic Orchestra. An unofficial Rochester tradition calls for each student to eat a "garbage plate" at Nick Tahou's, an infamous local dive, before graduating. In addition to frequent ski trips, favored out-of-town destinations include Niagara Falls, about 70 miles west, and, for the more venturesome, Toronto, 125 miles farther westward.

"Many professors explicitly encourage working together on assignments and projects."

Rochester's 23 varsity sports compete in the Division III University Athletic Association. Yellowjackets teams have captured recent conference or regional championships in field hockey, men's golf, men's and women's soccer, softball, and men's and women's indoor track and field. Roughly half of students participate in intramurals each semester. If intramural competition isn't your bag, Rochester has group fitness classes and a sports complex complete with indoor and outdoor tennis courts, a fitness center, an eight-lane pool, and an indoor track.

The University of Rochester is living up to its Meliora motto as its academic reputation improves with updates to the curriculum, the facilities, and just about everywhere you look on campus. Rochester seems to be winning its battle for a spot among the nation's leading private research universities. And if the city gets upward of eight feet of snow in the winter, one happy Yellowjacket points out, "it's great for winter sports or studying or even sleeping late on a snowy Saturday."

Overlaps

Boston University, Carnegie Mellon, Case Western, Cornell University, Johns Hopkins, NYU, Tufts, WashU in St. Louis

If You Apply To ›

Rochester: Early decision I and II, regular decision. SATs or ACTs: optional. Accepts the Common Application with supplement. Musicians apply directly to the Eastman School of Music.

Rochester Institute of Technology

1 Lomb Memorial Drive, Rochester, NY 14623

RIT is the largest of New York's major technological universities. The school is strong in anything related to computing, art and design, and engineering. In the city built by Kodak (remember them?), photography, imaging science, and film and animation are among the tops in the country. National leader in serving deaf and hard-of-hearing students. More relaxed feel than most technical schools.

Unlike many liberal arts colleges that prefer students test the academic waters before deciding on a major or future job plans, Rochester Institute of Technology's focus on career-oriented and technology-based academics from the get-go puts the spotlight on undergraduates. Established in 1829, RIT is more accessible than many of its closest competitors. Students who are geared up and ready to "go professional" will be more than satisfied with RIT's extensive co-op program. "One of our sayings is that RIT is home to thinkers, makers, and doers," describes a physician assistant B.A./M.A. student.

While the town of Rochester may sometimes seem like a reluctant host to weekend fun-seekers, it can hardly deny that it is, in fact, a college town; RIT shares the city with six nearby colleges. Its main campus, located on 1,300 suburban acres six miles from downtown Rochester, has its own distinctive style—redbrick buildings with sharp, contemporary lines. The Student Hall for Exploration and Development brings technology, art, and design under one roof. A new athletic facility and performing arts space are set to open in 2026.

RIT's general education program offers students considerable flexibility. Beyond a first-year writing course, required liberal arts credits vary by major; more than 80 academic minors have been added within the past few years. Unlike many universities, RIT allows first-year students to schedule significant coursework in their majors early on and spreads out liberal arts requirements over a more extended period. Those who are unsure of their academic path may enroll in any of the university's college-based exploration options before deciding on a major.

RIT specializes in carving out niches for itself with unusual programs, and majors are offered in more than 200 fields, from basic electrical and chemical engineering to packaging science and bioinformatics. Fortunately, applicants narrow the range of choices to a manageable size by applying to one of nine undergraduate colleges: Art and Design; Saunders College of Business; Golisano College of Computing and Information Sciences; Gleason College of Engineering; Engineering Technology; Health Sciences and Technology; Liberal Arts; Science; or the National Technical Institute for the Deaf. RIT is a leader in providing access and support services for deaf and hard-of-hearing students. Many hearing students choose to learn sign language as well.

"**RIT makes me want to work harder without making me feel like I won't succeed.**"

Predictably, majors in engineering and engineering technology are among the most popular at RIT, particularly mechanical engineering; computer science, game design and development, and a program that lets students design their own major also enroll high numbers. Photography is a signature program, and the film and animation and industrial design programs are well regarded. The College of Art and Design offers excellent programs in ceramics, furniture design, glass, and metals and jewelry design, and students have the run of Bevier Gallery, where visiting artists

Website: www.rit.edu
Location: Suburban
Private
Total Enrollment: 15,233
Undergraduates: 12,898
Male/Female: 65/35
Financial Aid: 99%
Pell Grant: 34%
Expense: Pr $ $
Student Loans: 70%
Average Debt: $ $ $ $
Applicants: 27,911
Accepted: 67%
Enrolled: 16%
Grad in 6 Years: 73%
Returning First-years: 89%
Academics: ✐ ✐ ✐
Social: 🗩 🗩 🗩
Q of L: ★ ★ ★
Admissions: (585) 475-6631
Email Address:
  admissions@rit.edu

Strong Programs:
Art and Design
Computer Science
Game Design and
  Development
Engineering
Film and Animation
Imaging Science
Industrial Design
Photography

provide firsthand instruction. Dozens of accelerated dual-degree options allow students to earn a bachelor's degree and a master's degree in five years. Undergraduates being the school's top priority, classes are kept relatively small—47 percent have fewer than 20 students—and the faculty develops new academic programs to fit career needs. An illustration major says, "If you're struggling with something [professors] are willing to take the extra time to help."

Students come to RIT to prove themselves, both in the classroom and through real-world experiences, so it's no surprise that students' schedules are demanding. "RIT makes me want to work harder without making me feel like I won't succeed," says a biomedical engineering major. Through RIT's co-op program, juniors and seniors can take one to two terms away from campus for full-time, paid positions that give them practical experience in their field, key networking opportunities with potential employers, and, often, inspired ideas to bring back to campus. The Simone Center for Student Innovation and Entrepreneurship helps students learn how to take an idea from conception to commercialization through coursework, consulting opportunities, and workshops. Students showcase their research and creative projects every year during Imagine RIT. Study abroad programs are available in more than 60 countries, including RIT's global campuses in China, Croatia, Kosovo, and the United Arab Emirates.

RIT students are quirky and comfortable in their own skin. "People wear bathrobes to class and knit during lectures and do interpretive dances on the quad," says a junior. "Whatever quirk you have, bring it here, because it makes us fun." Forty-eight percent of undergraduates are from New York State, the remainder coming largely from New Jersey, Pennsylvania, and Connecticut; 4 percent are international.

"We graduate with lots of lab/field/hands-on experience."

Six percent of students are Black, 10 percent Hispanic/Latino, 12 percent Asian American, and 6 percent multiracial. "The male-to-female ratio is still not where it should be," says one woman, "but this is a tech school, and 2 to 1 really isn't that bad." The large number of deaf students helps create a unique atmosphere. Politically, students tend to be aware of global issues, if not overtly active in them. RIT admits students without regard to financial need and offers merit scholarships averaging $18,800 to eligible students; 34 percent of incoming first-years receive Pell Grants. Only a few athletic scholarships are available.

Half of RIT students live on campus; first-years are required to live in the dorms, while upperclassmen sign up for the numerous campus apartments on a first-come, first-served basis. RIT offers a variety of special-interest houses and lifestyle floors, including "mainstream" floors where both deaf and hearing students live. Those who choose to live off campus take advantage of areas serviced by the school shuttle bus. Vegetarians, vegans, and carnivores alike will find on-campus meal options to be reasonably diverse. Campus security is "all over campus all of the time," says one student. Students seem to agree that mental health services could be more robust.

RIT's buzzing campus may seem at odds with its sedate suburban surroundings, and students say there's not much within walking distance of the campus. Downtown Rochester has more to offer, including minor league baseball, farmers markets, museums, and bookstores, and students also take road trips to Buffalo, Syracuse, and Canada. For those without transportation, there's always something to do on campus, courtesy of the more than 300 student clubs and organizations. Just 3 percent of the men and 2 percent of the women choose to go Greek. "RIT is not a party school," reports a senior, but favorite annual events include Brick City Homecoming, FreezeFest, and SpringFest.

RIT fields 21 Division III athletic teams. In addition, the Tigers—whose mascot is RITchie the Tiger—men's and women's ice hockey teams compete in Division I, and both are strong. Men's lacrosse has captured two national titles in recent years; men's swimming and diving, track and field, and cross-country and women's volleyball are also competitive. Sixteen percent of RIT undergrads participate in intramural and club sports, including esports, volleyball, and soccer.

RIT students are dedicated and career-oriented, yet they don't take themselves too seriously, which gives this demanding techie school a surprisingly relaxed feel. And best of all, says an imaging science major, thanks to an abundance of co-op education opportunities, "we graduate with lots of lab/field/hands-on experience." Indeed, self-motivated and focused, RIT students have their eyes on the future and are well prepared to meet it.

If You Apply To ›

RIT: Early decision I and II, early action, regular decision. SATs or ACTs: optional. Accepts the Common Application with supplement. Applicants to art, design, and film and animation programs must submit portfolio.

Rollins College

1000 Holt Avenue, Winter Park, FL 32789

The oldest postsecondary institution in Florida, Rollins is the marriage of a liberal arts college and a graduate business school that operates under the mantra of "applied liberal arts." A haven for out-of-staters who want their ticket punched to Orlando, with its abundant entertainment and professional opportunities. Famed alum Fred Rogers said, "Life is for service," and community engagement opportunities here abound.

Move over, Mickey Mouse. Hold up, Harry Potter. You're not the only attractions in central Florida. For students looking to hit the books under the ever-present Florida sunshine, there's also Rollins College. Located in a quiet suburb of Orlando, Rollins, which was founded in 1885 and named after a benefactor, offers students plenty of places to have fun and gain hands-on career experience. Dubbed "Rollins Gateway," the school's signature approach to education "combines our interdisciplinary curriculum with applied-learning experiences outside of the classroom and an integrated mentorship model" to empower students. "From the college's small class sizes to its beautiful campus and outstanding community, each piece of the puzzle felt more desirable than the last," says one happy first-year student.

Capitalizing on its location along the shores of Lake Virginia, Rollins's 80-acre campus combines the natural beauty of the lakeside with consistent, Spanish Mediterranean architecture. The Bush Science Center is a state-of-the-art, LEED-certified facility featuring research and instructional labs and student/faculty lounges. The Tiedtke Theatre & Dance Centre offers a theater, dance studio, costume shop, and more. Lakeside Neighborhood, an apartment-style residential complex for juniors and seniors, boasts such luxurious amenities as full-size beds, in-unit laundry machines, a café, a gym, and an outdoor pool.

The general education curriculum, known as Rollins Foundations in the Liberal Arts, seeks to help students develop skills relevant to any major or career, while preparing them for global citizenship and responsible leadership. Students are required to demonstrate competency in foreign language, mathematical thinking,

Website: www.rollins.edu
Location: Suburban
Private
Total Enrollment: 2,807
Undergraduates: 2,580
Male/Female: 39/61
Financial Aid: 94%
Pell Grant: 25%
Expense: Pr $ $ $
Student Loans: 38%
Average Debt: $ $ $ $
Applicants: 8,860
Accepted: 48%
Enrolled: 14%
Grad in 6 Years: 75%
Returning First-years: 85%
Academics: ✐ ✐ ✐
Social: 🗩 🗩 🗩 🗩
Q of L: ★ ★ ★
Admissions: (407) 646-2161
Email Address: admission@rollins.edu

Six dining facilities are located throughout campus, including a nautically themed, pub-style restaurant.

writing, and ethical reasoning. First-year students must take a fall-semester Rollins College Conference course, a small class of about 18 students, led by a professor-advisor who is assisted by two upperclassmen peer mentors. Students also complete five Foundations classes, with the first four courses coming from each division of the college: Humanities, Sciences, Social Sciences, and Expressive Arts. The final Foundations class is an interdisciplinary capstone that requires students to conduct original research on a global issue, which they present to the campus community at the Foundations Summit. There's also an Intercultural Competency requirement.

The most popular of Rollins's nearly 40 undergraduate majors include business management, communication studies, psychology, and computer science. Economics and biology draw large numbers, too. The chemistry department turned out a Nobel Prize winner, and the Annie Russell Theatre hosts productions staged by the well-known theatre department. A 3–2 accelerated management program allows qualified first-years to gain guaranteed admission to Rollins's top-ranked Crummer Graduate School of Business, leading to B.A. and M.B.A. degrees in five rather than six years. Accelerated bachelor's/master's programs are also available in human resources, public health, pre-engineering, applied behavior analysis and clinical science, liberal studies, strategic communications, and teaching.

> **"Professors make classes very discussion based so you are never being talked at in a lecture."**

"The academic climate is vigorous and challenging but with proper academic assistance from faculty," says a public policy and political economy major. "Professors make classes very discussion based so you are never being talked at in a lecture," adds a communication studies major. Rollins offers many opportunities to collaborate on research with faculty or pursue independent projects, participate in internships, and volunteer through service-learning classes. Nearly half of all undergrads study abroad at least once while at Rollins, taking off for programs in more than 50 countries all over the world. The four-year honors curriculum culminates in researching, writing, and defending a senior thesis.

The student body at Rollins is summed up by one senior as "diverse in interests, but lacking diversity culturally." A sophomore adds, most are "kind, welcoming, ambitious, committed to public service, and politically/civically engaged." Students report that both sides of the political aisle are well represented on campus, but the atmosphere doesn't usually get heated. Fifty-four percent of Rollins undergraduates are from Florida, and 9 percent hail from outside the United States. The student body is 6 percent Black, 19 percent Hispanic/Latino, 4 percent Asian American, and 5 percent multiracial. Merit scholarships average $24,800 for qualified students, and over 100 athletic scholarships are up for grabs.

Fifty-eight percent of the college's students live on campus in spacious co-ed dorms. "[Residence halls] are really nice," a student says, and feature "big rooms and hardwood floors." Another adds that, for those who prefer to live off campus, "there are plenty of houses and apartments near the campus that can be rented at a reasonable cost." Six dining facilities are located throughout campus, including a nautically themed, pub-style restaurant that treats diners to views of the lake, and the food receives positive reviews. A senior says, "Campus security is top of the line and super friendly."

> **"I would describe Rollins more as a bar/club school than a frat school."**

The Greek scene claims 16 percent of the men and 24 percent of the women, so there's always a party somewhere—often off campus. "I would describe Rollins more as a bar/club school than a frat school," insists a senior. The administration has clamped down on social excesses, with party monitors checking IDs and a student activity director attending each on-campus party. Penalties for underage drinking are strictly enforced. Beyond parties, the college's more than 100 student organizations are tailored to just about any interest. Students can paddleboard, sail, or wakeboard on Lake Virginia between classes, and there are also movies on Mills Lawn or "dive-in" movies at the pool, lip-synch contests, and live bands in the campus center. Fox Day in the spring is "a sacred tradition"—the president cancels classes for the day by placing a fox statue on the front lawn, and people head for the beach, hit the theme parks, or relax on campus.

"Winter Park isn't a typical college town," says one student. Adds another, "Rollins sits across the street from Park Avenue, a great street with a park, many restaurants, and boutique shops that offer discounts to students." Every first-year student participates in SPARC Day, Rollins's annual day of service held during orientation, and many students volunteer with community partners such as Habitat for Humanity and local schools. "Community service is a big part of the Rollins experience," comments a math and computer science major. Orlando's offerings include entertainment complexes and theme parks such as Disney's Magic Kingdom, EPCOT, Animal Kingdom, Universal's Islands of Adventure, and more. Popular road trips include Cocoa Beach, Miami, and Tampa.

Athletics are an integral part of campus life. Division II Tars teams (a nickname for 18th-century sailors) have claimed numerous national championships in men's and women's golf. The water ski team is a perennial national powerhouse. Other competitive teams include men's and women's soccer and men's and women's swimming, and women's sailing. Intramural sports are popular, too, with more than 20 leagues and events during the school year. Club sports teams have been formed for everything from eSports and paddleboarding to volleyball and dance.

Rollins students enjoy sand and sun, as well as a diverse academic climate and plenty of practical career preparation. As the oldest recognized college in the state of Florida, Rollins offers a rich legacy and smooth-as-silk Southern character. Says one sophomore, "It's a liberal arts school where you're challenged to grow personally and intellectually, and many students are passionate about making a difference."

Overlaps

University of Central Florida, College of Charleston, Elon, Furman, High Point, Rhodes, Sewanee, University of Miami

If You Apply To ›

Rollins: Early decision I and II, early action, regular decision. SATs or ACTs: optional. Accepts the Common Application with supplement.

Rose–Hulman Institute of Technology

5500 Wabash Avenue, Terre Haute, IN 47803

Rose–Hulman provides that rare combination of technical education and personal attention. Only Caltech, Clarkson, and Harvey Mudd offer comparable intimacy and a technical academic environment. Nearby Indiana State and Saint Mary-of-the-Woods help mitigate the skewed gender ratio. RHIT is among the few engineering schools that encourage study abroad and boast significant athletic opportunities.

Rose–Hulman Institute of Technology may not be as well-known as Caltech, MIT, or even Carnegie Mellon, but it was the first private college to offer an undergraduate degree in chemical engineering, and it continues to innovate. If you can handle the lopsided male/female ratio and the limited list of majors (all in engineering, mathematics, and the sciences; international studies is available only as a second major), Rose–Hulman is committed to offering "an unparalleled undergraduate

Website: www.rose-hulman.edu
Location: Suburban
Private
Total Enrollment: 2,334
Undergraduates: 2,294

(continued)

Male/Female: 76/24
Financial Aid: 99%
Pell Grant: 11%
Expense: Pr $ $
Student Loans: 55%
Average Debt: $ $ $ $
Applicants: 6,097
Accepted: 77%
Enrolled: 13%
Grad in 6 Years: 78%
Returning First-years: 92%
Academics: ✑ ✑ ✑
Social: 🗩
Q of L: ★ ★
Admissions: (800) 248-7448
Email Address:
   admissions@rhit.edu

Strong Programs:
Chemical Engineering
Civil Engineering
Computer Science
Electrical Engineering
Mathematics
Mechanical Engineering
Optical Engineering
Physics

STEM experience characterized by hands-on learning, exceptional career outcomes, a supportive community, and top-ranked faculty." Students are smart and motivated, and they love using their computers for work and play. "We are all dorks," says a senior. "Some of us just hide it better than others."

Established in 1874 and co-ed since 1995, Rose–Hulman is the oldest private engineering school west of the Alleghenies. Its benefactors were Chauncey Rose, an entrepreneur who brought the railroad to Indiana, and the Hulman family, who owned the Indianapolis Motor Speedway for 74 years and gave their fortune to the school in 1971. The 1,300-acre campus includes numerous trees, rolling hills, and a lake. A new $102.3 million "Innovation Grove" district, expected to open in 2027, will offer students opportunities for internships, collaborations on real-world engineering projects, and the chance to engage with cutting-edge health care technology.

General education requirements at Rose–Hulman include math, physics, chemistry, and humanities and social sciences. In the first quarter, first-years must take a Foundations for Success course that covers such topics as time management and study skills. All majors have a senior capstone design or thesis project.

"You have to push yourself academically," says one civil engineering major, adds another, "The academic climate is one of shared hardship; the boat may feel like it's sinking but you're in it together." Forty-two percent of classes have fewer than 20 students. Mechanical engineering, computer science, chemical engineering, and computer engineering are the most popular majors. Civil engineering, math, and physics

> **"The [academic] boat may feel like it's sinking but you're in it together."**

are also strong, and the school's optical engineering major is uncommon at the undergraduate level. A major in engineering design gives students a chance to work on projects with real clients. Regardless of which discipline you choose, odds are you'll find faculty members willing to help, and according to a biomedical engineering major, "The quality of instruction is revolutionary!" Through the Rose Squared program, qualifying students can earn a master's degree in a variety of majors along with their undergraduate degree in four years.

Since only a handful of graduate students are enrolled, teaching assistants don't teach classes, and opportunities to get involved with faculty research abound. The Interdisciplinary Research Collaborative gives selected students the chance to pursue ongoing research projects for 10 weeks during the summer. The Rose Research Fellows program offers paid research experiences to first- and second-year students, and the Rose–Hulman Ventures allows students to work on real client projects in a rapid prototyping facility. The ESCALATE living/learning community introduces first-years to the principles of entrepreneurial and business success. Rose–Hulman is increasing its emphasis on global education, and students have the option of enrolling in international studies as a complement to their primary major. The school also offers exchange programs and courses that combine traditional on-campus coursework with a two- to three-week trip at the end of the quarter. When it comes time to start the job search, "Career services works with every student individually to assist them in finding the right job for them," cheers a senior.

> *The Interdisciplinary Research Collaborative gives selected students the chance to pursue ongoing research projects for 10 weeks during the summer.*

At Rose–Hulman, says a junior, students come from "different countries, communities, religions, cultures, and yet we all come together to form the tight-knit community we have." Twenty-nine percent of undergrads are Indiana natives, and 8 percent come from abroad. Black students make up 3 percent of the student body, Asian Americans 8 percent, Hispanics/Latinos 5 percent, and multiracial students 6 percent. "Diversity is increasingly celebrated," reports a student. Still, a female student bemoans the fact that women make up just 24 percent of the student body. "As a woman on campus, I do feel it sometimes," she admits. Beyond that, political and social issues don't usually play a big role on campus. Merit scholarships are available, averaging $27,200, but there are no athletic awards.

Fifty-seven percent of students live on campus; first-years and sophomores are guaranteed rooms in the residence halls, and a new residence hall, opened in 2025, accommodates 160 first-year students. "We're allowed to do almost anything to the rooms, like add lofts or decks to gain space," says a civil engineering major. Most upperclassmen move into Greek houses or find other off-campus digs. For meals, there's a traditional cafeteria as well as two restaurant-style dining facilities. One enthusiastic senior says, "Rose–Hulman genuinely offers the best college food I have had." The campus and the surrounding area are safe, according to students, and they praise the mental-health support. "We have really good counselors in the counseling center ready to help at any time," says a chemical engineering major.

The town of Terre Haute (population 60,000) has some restaurants and bars ("[It's] often described as a bar town with a college problem," jokes a senior), a mall, a couple of Starbucks locations, and two movie theaters. Various groups, including the Greek organizations and Habitat for Humanity, help the town out with service projects. Greek life draws 29 percent of both men and women. Fraternity parties are a staple of weekend social life. When it comes to drinking, a civil engineering major reports, campus policies emphasize safety, and "the only places where alcohol is actively discouraged are the freshman halls." Everyone looks forward to Greatest Floor (a 24-hour competition between residence halls), basketball games against DePauw, and the homecoming bonfire. Students say the best weekend excursions are road trips to Chicago, Cincinnati, Indianapolis, or St. Louis, all within a few hours' drive.

> **"Everyone is just so gosh darn polite here."**

Varsity teams (the Fightin' Engineers) play in Division III; football, men's and women's soccer, cross-country, and golf are some of the strongest teams. Competitive tech teams like the Rocketry Club, Human Powered Vehicle Team, Team Rose Motorsports, and Cyber Defense Team are strong, but if you're envisioning Rose–Hulman students as pasty-faced lab dwellers, you're misinformed. About half of the student body participates in club sports and intramurals, with basketball, volleyball, and pickleball the most popular.

Students committed to careers in engineering or the sciences will find a topflight education at this technical school with a distinctive Midwestern feel. While Rose–Hulman "doesn't have that big-school pride" so common in this part of the country, students say the "charming and homey" community feel created by the intimate classes and the school's small size more than makes up for that. "Everyone is just so gosh darn polite here," gushes a first-year, while a sophomore says, "Rose–Hulman's institutional personality is the weird quiet kid that could change the world."

> *Through the Rose Squared program, qualifying students can earn a master's degree in a variety of majors along with their undergraduate degree in four years.*

Overlaps

Case Western, Colorado School of Mines, U of I at Urbana–Champaign, Ohio State, Purdue, Rensselaer, Rochester Institute of Technology, Worcester Polytechnic

If You Apply To ›

Rose–Hulman: Early action, regular decision. SATs or ACTs: optional. Accepts the Common Application.

Rutgers–The State University of New Jersey

65 Davidson Road, Piscataway, NJ 08854

One of only nine American universities founded during the colonial period, Rutgers is the dominant public university in the Garden State. Originally chartered as Queens College but subsequently renamed for Revolutionary War hero and benefactor Henry Rutgers. Everything is available: engineering, business, pharmacy, the liberal arts, and the nation's largest women's college. Well known as the birthplace of football.

Website: www.rutgers.edu
Location: Small City
Public
Total Enrollment: 43,671
Undergraduates: 35,051
Male/Female: 50/50
Financial Aid: 83%
Pell Grant: 27%
Expense: Pub $ $ $ $
Student Loans: 49%
Average Debt: $ $
Applicants: 43,347
Accepted: 65%
Enrolled: 27%
Grad in 6 Years: 85%
Returning First-years: 93%
Academics: ✑ ✑ ✑ ✑
Social: 🌑 🌑 🌑
Q of L: ★ ★ ★
Admissions: (848) 445-4636
Email Address:
admissions@ugadm.rutgers
.edu

Strong Programs:
Agricultural Sciences
Business
Fine Arts
Mathematics
Pharmacy
Philosophy
Psychology
Women and Gender Studies

Rutgers played the first college football game against the College of New Jersey (now Princeton) in 1869—and won.

Proud of traditions that extend back to its founding in 1766, this flagship public university of New Jersey likes to compare itself to a city with multiple neighborhoods, each with its own particular identity. With roughly 60,000 full-time undergraduate students spread across three regional campuses in New Brunswick, Newark, and Camden, Rutgers is all about choice. Choices between more than 150 undergraduate majors and 4,000-plus courses. Choices about which of the more than 500 student organizations catch your fancy. Even choices about which of its many libraries, computer labs, and student centers to frequent. "Rutgers is a place that gives students opportunities to do and be whatever they want," says a senior.

Seventy-five percent of full-time undergraduates (more than 35,000) enroll in Rutgers–New Brunswick, which is itself a collection of five residential sub-campuses strung out along the Raritan River and linked by a free university bus system that allows students to move easily among the various units for classes, housing, and social life. The historical core is the College Avenue campus, which boasts architectural gems dating to the American Revolution and is home to the huge School of Arts and Sciences. In addition to the football stadium, the Busch campus hosts the engineering and pharmacy schools, while Cook offers a bucolic setting for the School of Environmental and Biological Sciences. Douglass, with its Georgian colonial architecture, is home to the Douglass Residential College, the largest women's college in the country. Livingston, with its extensive array of solar panels, is home to the business school, the basketball arena, and a movie theater.

Among the undergraduate majors offered at Rutgers–New Brunswick, the most popular include psychology, computer science, biological sciences, information sciences, and human resources management. Perhaps surprisingly, philosophy is internationally renowned. Students universally praise fine arts, agricultural sciences, business, mathematics, and the six-year pharmacy program. The

> **"Professors understand that you are at Rutgers to do more than take classes."**

"incredible resources and opportunities" at Douglass Residential College make the women and gender studies major a good bet, according to an English major. Workloads vary across disciplines, and students generally find them ambitious but manageable. "The sense of community in classes is very strong," says one senior. "Students like to help each other out, and professors understand that you are at Rutgers to do more than take classes." Faculty members all have office hours, and first-year students are taught by regular professors. As at any big state university, classes can be large, although 40 percent have fewer than 20 students. A sophomore reports that "even in those 200-person lecture halls, my professors know my name and are super flexible when it comes to finding time to meet with struggling students."

In an effort to reverse the perennial exodus of New Jersey high school superstars from the state, Rutgers offers a wide range of special academic programs, including the state-of-the-art (and highly selective) Honors College, whose members pursue specialized courses, fulfill service requirements, and complete a cumulative capstone project during their senior year. Interdisciplinary living/learning communities offer live-in faculty that draw students with common interests ranging from various cultural and ethnic identities to meteorology. Biology students have the run of the 360-acre Rutgers Ecological Preserve and Natural Teaching Area, and the Aresty Research Center supports students seeking to engage in research early in their undergraduate career. Entering students have the option of a research-based first-year seminar where they work closely with a faculty member. A junior singles out the Road to Wall Street Program that "provides finance majors with one-on-one mentoring with people currently working on Wall Street." Rutgers is home to more than 175 specialized research centers and institutes dedicated to topics ranging from ancient Roman art to mountain gorillas. Rutgers also offers undergraduate study abroad in more than 30 countries, from France and Greece to Thailand. As for career, health, and other student support services, an English major reports, "The services are strong, but students have to reach out for them."

Although the administration has been attempting to increase the number of out-of-staters, 93 percent of Rutgers–New Brunswick students hail from the Garden State. Nevertheless, the student body reflects the substantial diversity of the state itself, with a good mix of students from cities, suburbs, farms, and seaside communities, and students take pride in their heterogeneity. "Our diversity spans interests, race, gender, class, sexual orientation, religion, and politics," says a management major. "It is the best part of Rutgers." Students of color account for just over half of undergraduates, including 7 percent Black, 16 percent Hispanic/Latino, 33 percent Asian American, and 4 percent multiracial. Seven percent of undergrads come from abroad. Over 300 students receive athletic scholarships in 22 sports; merit scholarships average $8,700.

On-campus housing in New Brunswick typically accommodates 41 percent of full-time students and is readily available on all five sub-campuses. "The rooms are large, and every room comes with a microwave and fridge/freezer combination," reports a music education major. Other on-campus housing options include apartment complexes with kitchens and living rooms. "We have four dining halls, and there are many cafés and food vendors on campus that accept meal swipes," notes one sophomore. "Most people can find a place they are happy eating at regularly." In part because of its Office for Violence Prevention and Victim Assistance, Rutgers has become a national leader in confronting sexual assault on campus. The university also offers a special dormitory for students who are trying to overcome addictions to drugs and alcohol. "The university is generally safe," says an urban planning major. "Access to emergency services is easy and plentiful."

Social life happens both on and off campus. The Greek scene is located off campus near College Avenue, and a sophomore notes, "Only 11 percent of students are involved in Greek life, so we are definitely not 'go Greek or go home.' People party in apartments, bars, houses, and dorms, and there is no single party culture." Another reports, "The RAs are really effective about enforcing alcohol policies." Each sub-campus has its own student center with such diversions as pinball machines, pool tables, bowling alleys, and a snack bar, and the Rutgers University Programming Association sponsors films, performances, and other events. As a major city, New Brunswick offers an array of nearby restaurants and theaters. For those who want to hit the road for fun, New York City and Philadelphia are each only about an hour's drive or train ride, and students flood the Jersey Shore in springtime.

Funky social rituals include Hot Dog Day, which features rides and free hot dogs, and Beats on the Banks, which brings a major rapper or other artist to campus. Given that Rutgers likes to remind the world that it was the birthplace of college football, homecoming is a big deal—with tailgate parties in the stadium parking lot, tons of food (including roast pigs and whole sides of beef), continuous music, and thousands of revelers. Students participating in the Homecoming Bed Races decorate twin beds on wheels and race them down College Avenue for charity. An annual 24-hour dance marathon, which raises money for a children's cancer charity, is another proud tradition.

Varsity, intramural, and club sports fill whatever gap is left by the social scene. Rutgers played the first college football game against the College of New Jersey (now Princeton) in 1869—and won. Now, Rutgers's 20 varsity Scarlet Knights teams

"The services are strong, but students have to reach out for them."

"We are definitely not 'go Greek or go home.'"

compete in Division I in the powerhouse Big Ten. Men's and women's basketball and lacrosse, men's wrestling, and women's soccer, rowing, and field hockey are nationally ranked. "Rutgers likes to pretend that Penn State is our rival, even though they don't care about us," confesses a management major. "So that is fun." Students can also take their pick of more than 50 club sports and dozens of intramural leagues and tournaments.

Rutgers has the usual abundance of people and programs characteristic of a large state university coupled with loyal support from the state's legislature and private sector and tuition that is relatively affordable. Students express irritation about the bus system ("not enough buses," "they leak when it rains"), but most appreciate the fact that, as a public land grant university, Rutgers offers them a huge range of professional and other academic options from which to choose. An exercise science major concludes, "Students at Rutgers have the whole world at their fingertips."

If You Apply To ›

Rutgers: Early action, regular decision. Accepts the Common Application for first-year students. Apply to particular school. Arts applicants must interview, audition, or submit portfolio. Please consult Rutgers's website for the most up-to-date information regarding standardized test requirements.

University of St Andrews: See page 374.

College of Saint Benedict and Saint John's University

37 South College Avenue, St. Joseph, MN 56374

The College of Saint Benedict (CSB) and Saint John's University (SJU) are throwbacks to the way colleges were 50 years ago: women and men on separate campuses and copious amounts of school spirit. Founded by Benedictines, with monastic communities still active on both campuses. More than 80 percent of students are from Minnesota, but global perspectives and study abroad are big emphases.

Remember when women's colleges had nearby brother schools, when dorms were single-sex, and when visitors of the opposite gender were only welcome at certain times? Doesn't ring a bell? Well, you might ask your grandparents. Or you could visit the College of Saint Benedict and Saint John's University. These two single-sex campuses—all-female CSB and all-male SJU—are five miles apart, but they share a president, as well as a common heritage and mission: students and faculty join together in a shared liberal arts education, guided by Benedictine principles. The schools' small sizes and respect for tradition give rise to a tight-knit community. Even if these schools are not high on your list, you might want to take a tour anyway. Visitors are given a loaf of their fabled Johnnie Bread to take with them. Says one happy biology major, "I like to refer to the CSBSJU network as a tight-knit family."

Founded in 1857 by what is now one of the largest men's Benedictine monasteries in the world, Saint John's now operates as an independent entity. It occupies 2,600 pristine acres in rural Minnesota, an area filled with forests, lakes, and the wide-open spaces perfect for outdoorsy types. The two colleges are connected

Website: www.csbsju.edu
Location: Small Town
Private
Total Enrollment: 2,816
Undergraduates: 2,748
Male/Female: 51/49
Financial Aid: 100%
Pell Grant: 26%
Expense: Pr $ $
Student Loans: 67%
Average Debt: $ $ $ $
Applicants: 3,874
Accepted: 83%
Enrolled: 22%
Grad in 6 Years: 76%

by a free and frequent shuttle bus. Alongside a 137-year-old quadrangle erected by monks is a strikingly modern church designed by Marcel Breuer. Saint Benedict, established in 1913 by Benedictine sisters, is a cohesive 800-acre campus composed of redbrick buildings and cobblestone walks. Together, the colleges have invested millions in facilities in recent years, including a major renovation of the SJU library that added a Learning Commons.

Saint Benedict and Saint John's share a joint academic program through which students take classes together on both campuses. The core curriculum, known as the Integrations Curriculum, aims to give students a cohesive, interdisciplinary, and hands-on education. It features components like a first-year seminar, experiential learning such as study abroad or service learning, and an electronic portfolio that ties together students' four years.

The global business leadership program prepares students to be leaders in a global economy and is the most popular major, followed by accounting, nursing, and biology. Programs in political science, music, and chemistry are also well regarded. The interdisciplinary environmental studies program is enhanced by access to the area's natural resources and one of the largest solar farms in the upper Midwest. The theology program benefits from abundant resources, including the Hill Museum & Manuscript Library, one of the foremost microfilm collections of centuries-old handwritten manuscripts. "Many of the classes are centered on discussion, so everyone is playing a critical role in the learning process," says a chemistry major. Very few classes have more than 30 students, and some fill up fast. The small classes encourage a community atmosphere and strong student/faculty ties. "Professors work avidly with students on a regular basis," says a psychology major. The college has phased out eight majors, including gender studies, theater, and some foreign languages, along with several minors to direct resources to higher demand programs, such as economics and computer science.

For those seeking respite from Minnesota winters, the colleges offer faculty-led, semester-long international study programs in various countries on six continents, in which 45 percent of students take part. Numerous shorter trips are also offered during semester and summer breaks. "Study abroad is a big part of our culture here," says a biology major, "and your scholarships will transfer over to your study abroad, making it affordable." The McNeely Center for Entrepreneurship provides classes, coaching, and assistance to budding entrepreneurs from a range of disciplines. The program's Entrepreneurial Scholars travel to Silicon Valley and China/Hong Kong, and all of them start their own entrepreneurial ventures. Undergraduate research is becoming more prevalent (47 percent of students participate), and there is an endowed summer research program in the health and medical areas. Exceptional first-year students are invited to join the colleges' honors program, and upper-class students may also apply.

"Students value community and look out for each other," says a sophomore. "We all share a sense of brotherhood and sisterhood." Forty-four percent of students, known as "Bennies" and "Johnnies," are Roman Catholic, 84 percent are from Minnesota, and most are white. Black students constitute 3 percent of the student body, Hispanics/Latinos 9 percent, and Asian Americans 3 percent. International students account for 4 percent of the student population. A senior notes that despite the homogeneity on campus, the schools offer "a lot of programming events encouraging students to learn about diversity." Politically, a junior says, "We encompass all viewpoints, from ultraconservative to ultraliberal." To become more inclusive, CSB and SJU have both adopted policies explicitly

The residence halls are staffed partly by members of the monastic communities, but students aren't made to feel like a nun is watching their every move.

(continued)

Returning First-years: 86%
Academics: ✍ ✍ ✍
Social: 🗩 🗩 🗩
Q of L: ★ ★ ★
Admissions: (800) 544-1489
Email Address:
  admissions@csbsju.edu

Strong Programs:
Accounting
Biology
Environmental Studies
Global Business Leadership
Music
Nursing
Political Science
Psychology

welcoming students who "consistently live and identify" as "gender fluid or nonbinary" to study at either college, regardless of the gender they were assigned at birth. Merit scholarships averaging $30,200 are available, but there are no athletic scholarships.

Ninety percent of students live on campus; seniors wishing to move off campus must apply for permission. "The progression to nicer housing as you get older is a rite of passage," says a senior. The residence halls are staffed partly by members of the monastic communities, but students aren't made to feel like a nun is watching their every move. On-campus apartments, such as Flynntown, provide a more independent living area for juniors and seniors. Students can choose from four dining halls on either campus, and most report the fare to be tasty and diverse. Campus security gets good reviews, and a sophomore says, "We have bystander intervention training programs on a variety of concerns, such as eating disorders and domestic violence."

"The social scene on campus is great," says a communication major. "The bars in town are always busy and very fun." The Joint Events Council organizes regular weekday and weekend social events, including student performances, comedians, magicians, and concerts. Students 21 and older are allowed to consume alcohol in their rooms or at SJU's on-campus pub, Brother Willie's, named after a deceased brother known as the Night Abbot who dispensed spiritual and worldly wisdom to students. There are no fraternities or sororities, and parties tend to be small affairs. Each year, students look forward to the Festival of Cultures, the Maple Syrup Festival, the Fruit at the Finish Triathlon, the Senior Farewell, and spring break trips involving community service. Also popular is the annual Pines music festival, which welcomes the spring with a day of concerts featuring popular Christian musicians. Says a sophomore, "Off campus, there are many things to do in St. Cloud and also in St. Joseph, such as parties, coffee shops, restaurants, shopping, and movies." Seventy-four percent of students engage in community service, often through Campus Ministry programs. St. Cloud is a few minutes away, and the Twin Cities are 70 miles southeast.

The CSB Bennies field 11 Division III teams, and the SJU Johnnies boast 12. The football team is a perennial powerhouse, and its rivalry with St. Thomas is as strong as ever. Curiously enough, a team of guys known as the Rat Pack gets students psyched up for games. Men's golf, women's softball, and men's track and field make regular national tournament appearances. Nonvarsity students can participate in a variety of club and intramural sports, and activities like kayaking and indoor rock climbing, offered through the Outdoor Leadership Center, are popular year-round.

Students who attend CSB and SJU revel in the schools' small-town setting, their traditions, and the grounding that comes from their shared Benedictine values. Perhaps more than anything, they treasure the community spirit that allows them to grow both individually and together. "We have a strong sense of school pride and alumni connection," says one happy student. "Once a Bennie or a Johnnie, always a Bennie or a Johnnie."

If You Apply To ›

St. Benedict and St. John's: Early action I and II, regular decision. SATs or ACTs: optional. Accepts the Common Application with supplement. CSB accepts applications from students who consistently live and identify as women, regardless of the gender assigned to them at birth. SJU accepts applications from students who consistently live and identify as men, regardless of the gender assigned to them at birth.

St. John's College

Annapolis Campus: 60 College Avenue, Annapolis, MD 21401
Santa Fe Campus: 1160 Camino Cruz Blanca, Santa Fe, NM 87505

Books, books, and more books is what you'll get at St. John's—from Thucydides to Tolstoy, Euclid to Einstein. St. John's attracts smart, intellectual, and nonconformist students who like to talk (and debate) about books and ideas. Academically rigorous. One of the few institutions with two coequal campuses. Students admitted to one can spend time at the other. St. John's is a croquet powerhouse.

With no majors, departments, or lectures (in the traditional sense) and a combined total of fewer than 1,000 students on its two campuses, St. John's College is about as far from the typical postsecondary experience as you can get. The Annapolis campus traces its roots to King William's School—the Maryland colony's "free" school—founded in 1696, making it the third oldest college in the country after Harvard and William & Mary. In 1964, St. John's opened a second campus in Santa Fe, New Mexico, to facilitate a doubling of enrollment and offer its super serious students a change of scenery. While the campuses may be a thousand miles apart, the Johnnies who populate them share an all-consuming quest for knowledge in the classical tradition. Their true teachers are the Great Books' authors, about 200 of the most influential thinkers over the last 3,000 years, including Plato, Shakespeare, Nietzsche, Austen, Du Bois, Woolf, and more. "Students at St. John's College aspire to join the great conversations that began in the primeval forests and have expanded to what we think we know today," says a sophomore. "We appreciate the value of tradition and its role in education."

Physically, the two St. John's campuses are more than just two time zones from one another. The colonial brick structures of the small campus in Annapolis, where the central classroom building dates from 1742, sit in the city's historic district. With the Maryland state capitol and the U.S. Naval Academy around the corner, this campus exudes old-world charm, and its location at the confluence of the Severn River and the Chesapeake Bay allows students to participate in sailing, crew, and individual sculling. The Santa Fe campus, which is 100 percent solar-powered, stands on 250 landlocked acres in the sun-drenched capital of New Mexico, just two and a half miles from downtown. The adobe-style buildings reflect Spanish and Native American traditions, and their perch in the Sangre de Cristo Mountains offers beautiful views of the city below. Students at St. John's in Santa Fe can get back to nature in nearby state and national forests, which offer hiking, mountain biking, kayaking, snowboarding, and skiing. Students may attend both campuses during their academic careers, and about 10 percent do so.

The St. John's curriculum, known as "the program," has every student read 200 Great Books in roughly chronological order. All students major in liberal arts, discussing the books in seminars, writing papers about them, and debating the riddles of human existence that they raise. All classes have no more than 21 students and are led by tutors, who would be tenured professors anywhere else but here are just the most advanced students. "The classroom is a space where if you have done the work, you are equal to everyone else, including the tutors who have Ph.D.s from outstanding institutions," explains a junior. Another student warns, "Someone who is not willing to be assertive in class could have a hard time at St. John's." In a snub to the general trend in American academia toward more and more specialization, each tutor is required to teach any subject within the

> **"We appreciate the value of tradition and its role in education."**

Annapolis Website:
www.sjc.edu
Location: Small City
Private
Total Enrollment: 577
Undergraduates: 487
Male/Female: 51/49
Financial Aid: 95%
Pell Grant: 17%
Expense: Pr $
Student Loans: 96%
Average Debt: $ $
Applicants: 1,059
Accepted: 44%
Enrolled: 28%
Grad in 6 Years: 60%
Returning First-years: 85%
Academics: ✍ ✍ ✍ ✍ ½
Social: 🎭 🎭 🎭
Q of L: ★ ★ ★ ★
Admissions: (800) 727-9238
Email Address: annapolis
.admissions@sjc.edu

Strong Programs:
Classics
Liberal Arts
Literature
Philosophy
Physics

Santa Fe Website:
www.sjc.edu
Location: Small City
Private
Total Enrollment: 415
Undergraduates: 364
Male/Female: 50/50
Financial Aid: 97%
Pell Grant: 36%
Expense: Pr $
Student Loans: 52%
Average Debt: $ $
Applicants: 397
Accepted: 53%

Annapolis students relish their intramural teams, with names like the Druids and the Spartans.

Readings are from primary sources only: math from Euclid and Ptolemy, physics from Maxwell, psychology from Freud.

curriculum. "Because St. John's is not a research institution, the tutor's only job is teaching and engaging with students," says one junior. Both campuses follow a curriculum that would have delighted 19th-century English poet and educator Matthew Arnold, who argued that the goal of education is "to know the best which has been thought and said in the world."

The curriculum includes four years of mathematics, two years of ancient Greek and French, three years of laboratory science, two years of music, and, of course, four years of Great Books seminars. First-year students study the Greeks, sophomores advance through the Romans and the Renaissance, juniors cover the 17th and 18th centuries, and seniors do the 19th and 20th centuries. Readings are from primary sources only: math from Euclid and Ptolemy, physics from Maxwell, psychology from Freud, and so on. The assumption is that the Great Books can stand on their own, representing the highest achievements of human intellect. Importantly, juniors and seniors also take seven-week electives, called preceptorials, where they study a book or topic one-on-one with a tutor. Electives include in-depth courses in computer science that may involve building a simple computer or, in typical St. John's fashion, delving into Richard Feynman's writings on the nature of computer language. In their final semester, seniors write a 20- to 60-page critical essay on a topic of their choice and must pass an hour-long oral examination by a committee of three tutors.

"There is a real sense of community and a collaborative feel to all of the academic work we do," says one sophomore. "Our class conversations carry over into the dining hall, the quad, the common rooms, and coffee shop." While there are no multiple-choice tests and no formal exams, courses are rigorous with a heavy load of reading every week and lots of writing. Since everyone's doing the same thing, there's a lot of pressure not to slack off. St. John's prefers that all eight semesters be completed in residence—meaning no heading off campus for internships or the like, unless it's during the summer break, when every student is guaranteed funding for a summer internship. Study abroad is also offered in the summer through partnerships

"Someone who is not willing to be assertive in class could have a hard time at St. John's."

that send Johnnies to international institutions that have programs that align with the St. John's mission, including in Italy, France, the U.K. and beyond. "A lot of students go to Rome to spend summer reading and having seminars at Rome Institute of Liberal Arts," says a sophomore. Most alumni end up in graduate school—St. John's is one of the top feeders to Ph.D. programs and law schools.

A fifth of St. John's students are transfers from more conventional colleges—a true act of devotion, since St. John's requires everyone to begin as a first-year. A "discussion-based" application option allows applicants to be evaluated almost entirely by face-to-face interviews with admissions counselors and faculty and by participation in a college seminar. The reasons students choose St. John's are never simple, but the common thread is a fierce love of learning. One junior says, "St. John's students are an eclectic mix. Most tend to be creative, intelligent, and curious." The vast majority of students at both campuses are out-of-staters; international students represent 2 percent of the student body. In Annapolis, 9 percent are Hispanic/Latino, 3 percent are Asian American, 1 percent are Black, and 6 percent are multiracial, while in Santa Fe those groups account for 11 percent, 1 percent, 1 percent, and 7 percent, respectively. One student says, "you will not find a lot of activism at St. John's, but we still consider many economic and political issues."

Nearly all students live in the college's co-ed dorms on both campuses; first-years and sophomores are required to reside on campus. In Annapolis, the six "historic" residence halls from the 18th and 19th centuries are arranged around a central quad, while the two modern halls face College Creek. "If you are a fan of Hogwarts you will probably like the Annapolis campus," says a junior. In Santa Fe, the dorms are small, modern units clustered around courtyards. Most students get singles or divided double rooms. Upperclassmen typically live off campus in apartments and group houses. Meals at both campuses get average reviews. As for student services, "Mental health help is accessible 24/7, and there is no cap on the amounts of weekly meetings," reports a junior. "Career services are also prevalent." St. John's matches Pell Grants with an equivalent scholarship and offers merit scholarships averaging $14,700 to $20,300. Additionally, institutional and Federal grants will cover tuition for first-year students from families with annual incomes of $75,000 or less and typical assets.

"Rather than having a full-blown mid-2000s-movie party scene, Johnnies are much more likely to be found on the quad chatting as they smoke cigarettes and share a beer," says a junior. A senior adds, "We don't have any Greek organizations (besides study groups for reading ancient Greek!)." Drinking is a favored release for Johnnies, who have, of course, read Plato's Symposium and are familiar with the likes of François Rabelais ("Drink constantly. You will never die."). Still, hard liquor is not allowed on campus. Off campus, "Annapolis is a cool place to hang out. There are lots of restaurants and bars open late," notes one student. Road trips to Washington, D.C., Baltimore, New York, and Assateague State Park are options for Annapolis students with cars. In Santa Fe, nearby blues and jazz clubs are popular.

Favorite annual events on both campuses include Lola's, a casino night sponsored by the senior class; the Arc party, held to celebrate the sophomores' completion of the Old Testament; and the Achilles Rager that celebrates finishing the *Iliad*. "Almost every month, there's a waltz event, where we do swing dancing, Lindy hop, polka, and waltz," says one student. Reality, a three-day festival of food, games, and general debauchery, is thrown for the seniors the weekend before commencement. "Sometimes we wear togas," hints a junior. Intercollegiate club teams in crew, sailing, fencing, and croquet are available in Annapolis. The Annapolis Cup croquet match against the Naval Academy each spring includes a genteel lawn party to which the Midshipmen don crisp croquet white while the Johnnies sport uniforms that have ranged from kilts to Viking-wear. Annapolis students relish their intramural teams, with names like the Druids and the Spartans. Santa Fe students compete in intercollegiate archery, badminton, fencing, and more, as well as in a handful of club sports. The nearby Rio Grande and Chama rivers offer excellent white-water canoeing, kayaking, and rafting, while the Hueco Tanks area offers rock climbing and bouldering; the Taos Ski Valley and Ski Santa Fe are excellent in the winter months. The Outdoor Programs Office organizes trips and makes athletic equipment available for use.

> "A lot of students go to Rome to spend summer reading and having seminars at Rome Institute of Liberal Arts."

The rigorous St. John's program isn't for everyone—a sophomore recommends interested students "do their research, know who they are and what they want, and whether they will be willing to commit to all of this." Those who do commit are as passionate about learning as their peers at other schools are about basketball rivalries. And while those larger colleges and universities try to keep pace with today's rapid changes, St. John's cherishes its traditions—including the mandate that seniors wear formal academic dress to their oral examinations, which are open to the public. As one happy Johnnie reflects, "A heated discussion about Plato on the grassy knoll is the type of sight that reminds me why I love this place."

Overlaps

Bard, University of Chicago, Columbia, Kenyon, University of Maryland, Reed, St. John's Santa Fe, William & Mary

If You Apply To ›

St. John's: Early decision I and II, early action, regular decision. SATs or ACTs: optional. Accepts the Common Application with supplement or Discussion-Based Application. Apply to one campus only.

St. John's University and College of St. Benedict: See page 612.

St. Lawrence University

23 Romoda Drive, Canton, NY 13617

St. Lawrence is perched far up in the North Country, closer to Ottawa and Montreal than to Syracuse. The remote Adirondack location breeds camaraderie, and St. Lawrence students share a special bond. Compare to Allegheny and Hobart and William Smith. Environmental studies is the crown jewel: Where else can you live, learn, and work in a Mongolian-style yurt?

Website: www.stlawu.edu
Location: Small Town
Private
Total Enrollment: 1,939
Undergraduates: 1,916
Male/Female: 48/52
Financial Aid: 75%
Pell Grant: 23%
Expense: Pr $ $ $
Student Loans: 60%
Average Debt: $ $ $ $
Applicants: 6,089
Accepted: 54%
Enrolled: 13%
Grad in 6 Years: 79%
Returning First-years: 91%
Academics: ✍ ✍ ✍
Social: 🗩 🗩 🗩
Q of L: ★ ★ ★
Admissions: (315) 229-5261
Email Address:
  admissions@stlawu.edu

Strong Programs:
Biology
Business in the Liberal Arts
Canadian Studies
Environmental Studies
Finance
Global Studies
Psychology
Statistics

St. Lawrence University attracts snow lovers who place equal value on their experiences inside and outside the classroom. Its upstate New York location in St. Lawrence County offers quick access to both pristine ski slopes and rugged hiking trails—and to the bright lights of Ottawa and Montreal. A flood of construction has helped to make the campus almost as breathtaking as the natural beauty that surrounds it. And intimate classes mean it's as easy to form friendships with faculty members as it is with fellow students.

Hiking trails, a river, and a university-owned golf course surround St. Lawrence's buildings, many of which date from the late 19th century, and sit on a 1,000-acre tract; facilities are clustered, so even the most distant facilities are only a 10-minute walk from one another. St. Lawrence recently completed a $30 million investment in facilities, renovating residence halls and other student spaces to enhance the living-learning experience. The LEED Gold–certified Johnson Hall of Science supports the biology, chemistry, biomedical sciences, pre-health chemistry, biochemistry, neuroscience, and psychology programs.

St. Lawrence, founded in 1856 by members of the progressive Universalist Church but now nonsectarian, offers a liberal arts education, placing a premium on small classes and team teaching. The general education curriculum consists of courses across the liberal arts and sciences as well as an environmental literacy requirement. Everyone participates in the two-semester First-Year Program (FYP), which emphasizes critical-thinking, research, and communication skills.

> **"The academic climate at St. Lawrence is both intellectually engaging and supportive."**

Students enroll in an FYP course based on academic interest and live with their classmates in the same residential community. FYP professors also serve as academic advisors. "This program creates an instant living and learning community the moment you step on campus, and students within FYPs become like family," says one student. Optional Sophomore Seminars involve intensive advising, teas and coffees with professors, and ample volunteer and hands-on learning opportunities, including course-related field trips.

"The academic climate at St. Lawrence is both intellectually engaging and supportive," says a finance and business major. Economics, business in the liberal arts (an unusual major that rejects the notion of business as a stand-alone area of study), psychology, political science, environmental studies, and performance and communication arts are the most popular majors. Programs in political science, conservation biology, statistics, and global studies are notable, and befitting St. Lawrence's location,

Canadian studies is also a specialty. Newer majors include biomedical sciences, data science, and cybersecurity. Students in the signature environmental studies program are encouraged to pursue combined majors that integrate the study of environmental issues with substantial study in one of 10 other fields, such as geology, psychology, English, or sociology. The Center for the Environment offers education and advocacy opportunities to all students. Courses demand that students pay attention and keep up with their work, but students say competition is hardly a concern. Full professors teach even the introductory courses and make themselves available for extra help; 66 percent of all classes have fewer than 20 students. "My professors are always looking for new ways to challenge students," comments a biology and physics major.

In an effort "to make the world our classroom," St. Lawrence encourages students to spend time away from campus, and 61 percent do so. "Starting from a summer course in Ireland, going to a semester abroad in China, and finishing with an internship-intensive semester in New York—there are numerous options for students to make their experience at St. Lawrence full of exploration," cheers a political science major. The school offers international programs in more than 20 countries and an Adirondack Semester near Tupper Lake, about an hour from campus. Under this program, a small group of students live and study in a yurt village in a park, where they learn wilderness survival skills and take courses on topics such as environmental philosophy and nature writing. The St. Lawrence University Fellowship Program offers housing and $4,500 stipends to selected students for summer research; a majority of students pursue research and nearly 100 percent pursue some form of experiential learning, including internships. Students give high ratings to the Center for Career Excellence, especially its Laurentians Investing in Networking and Careers (LINC) mentorship program. "The LINC program connects sophomores with alumni working in their field of interest," explains a participant.

> "The LINC program connects sophomores with alumni working in their field of interest."

SLU students are "highly motivated and social people with a drive to succeed," says a math and psychology major. Forty percent of Laurentians are New Yorkers, and 11 percent are international. Diversity can be a challenge in the North Country, and just 2 percent of students are Black, 6 percent are Hispanic/Latino, 2 percent are Asian American, and 2 percent are multiracial. Politically, the campus is "liberal but not aggressively so," reports a senior. The university awards merit scholarships averaging $33,200 to top students and hands out around 40 athletic scholarships for Division I men's and women's ice hockey.

Virtually all students live on campus, and seniors have it best, with access to "spacious townhouses that sit along the golf course," says a sophomore. The LEED-certified Kirk Douglas Hall (named for the Class of 1939 grad and Spartacus star) offers spacious single, double, and triple rooms. Over a dozen theme houses and two theme floors are also an option. The food in the main dining hall is said to have "greatly improved," with accommodations for vegans, vegetarians, and other special diets and themed dinners served once a month. The university's rural campus is "generally very safe," says a senior. And a biomedical sciences and public health major says, "If you ever need to talk to someone, the mental health services are really good."

University-sponsored social activities include a campus pub, first-run movies, and the student-run Java Barn music venue. With 9 percent of the men and 23 percent of the women joining fraternities and sororities, Greek groups are a presence but not a dominant force in campus social life. Students 21 and over are permitted to drink on campus. "There is a very lively party culture at St. Lawrence," says a history major, but students report that alcohol policies are effective and parties rarely get out of hand.

Everyone participates in the two-semester First-Year Program (FYP), which emphasizes critical-thinking, research, and communication skills.

The charming town of Canton doesn't offer much in the way of nightlife, but it does have a selection of bars, restaurants, and shops and a twice-weekly farmers market; Potsdam, 10 minutes away, offers more. Ottawa and Montreal, where there's better shopping and dining (and where the drinking age is lower), are easily accessible for weekend road trips. But students say the most popular pastimes include skiing, hiking, rock climbing, and kayaking down the Grasse River (when it's not frozen over), and students make the most of St. Lawrence's Adirondack backyard. "You can rent out gear for free from the Outdoor Program, which allows students to try new things without having to worry about expenses," cheers a junior. Favorite annual traditions include Peak Weekend in the fall, when students, faculty, and staff summit all 46 of the Adirondack High Peaks.

In varsity sports, the Division I Skating Saints hockey teams are the top draw, especially when the opponent is archrival Clarkson. "Hockey is a massive event," confirms a sophomore. Solid Division III teams include men's and women's lacrosse, men's soccer, and men's and women's cross-country and track and field; the squash, alpine skiing, and co-ed riding teams are strong, too.

"There is a very lively party culture at St. Lawrence."

The golf course doubles as a running route in warmer weather and a cross-country ski trail during the winter. Over half of the students participate in 25-plus club sports and a variety of intramurals; available sports range from club hockey to ultimate Frisbee, co-ed soccer, and an annual fall quadathlon.

St. Lawrence makes up for frigid winters with the warmth of a close-knit, caring community. As the frenzied pace of construction winds down and academic standards and career preparation are ratcheted up, St. Lawrence is a school on the rise, especially for those wanting to get back to nature. "With 150 clubs, so many different departments, traveling opportunities, trips, theme houses, Greek life, and so much more," cheers a happy sophomore, "you can never get tired of the campus and the bunch of personalities you find here."

Overlaps

Allegheny, Colby, Dickinson, Gettysburg, Hobart and William Smith, Kenyon, Skidmore, Union

If You Apply To ›

St. Lawrence: Early decision, early action, regular decision. SATs or ACTs: optional. Accepts the Common Application with supplement.

Saint Louis University

1 North Grand Boulevard, St. Louis, MO 63103

SLU is a pleasant oasis amid the bustle of midtown St. Louis, and both the campus and the surrounding neighborhood have been spiffed up in recent decades. In addition to strengths in premed and entrepreneurship, SLU has an unusual specialty in aviation science. Competes with Loyola Chicago and Marquette for bragging rights among Midwestern Jesuit institutions.

Website: www.slu.edu
Location: City Outskirts
Private
Total Enrollment: 13,307
Undergraduates: 8,101
Male/Female: 41/59

Within sight of St. Louis's famed Gateway Arch, the historical gateway to the American West, sits Saint Louis University, which in 1818 became the first university established west of the Mississippi River. The school's academic atmosphere is shaped by the tradition of its founders, the Society of Jesus (Jesuits); administrators ensure that each student receives personal care and attention and expect graduates to contribute to society and lead efforts for social change. Students, in turn, find an atmosphere where their faith is encouraged. SLU offers students numerous nationally recognized programs, from health sciences to business and, of course, theology. "SLU is the type of university that prepares the whole person to go out into the world," says a first-year.

The SLU campus features pedestrian walkways, lush greenery, fountains, and sculptures, as well as signature Saint Louis University arched gateways at all entrances. Cupples House, a beautiful old mansion in the middle of campus, houses 19th-century furniture and an art gallery—and is just a short walk from the modern Busch Student Center. The center is home to a bookstore, eateries, lounges, and conference facilities. Numerous campus renovations and additions have been undertaken in recent years, including the $50 million Interdisciplinary Science and Engineering Building.

In keeping with SLU's strong Jesuit commitment to education in the broadest sense, all undergrads must complete core curriculum requirements in philosophy, theology, cultural diversity, communication, mathematics, science, and other foundational disciplines. First-year students participate in summer orientation and a seminar "designed to ignite their passion for scholarship." The most popular majors include nursing, exercise science, health sciences, and biology. Many students take advantage of premed advising, and five- and six-year direct entry programs allow students to earn advanced degrees in occupational therapy, athletic training, and physical therapy. Business and entrepreneurship majors benefit from the Chaifetz Center for Entrepreneurship, which offers innovation challenges, competitions, and networking events like Billicon Valley. Philosophy and theology are outstanding programs, and SLU attracts scholars from around the globe with one of the world's most complete microfilm collections of Vatican documents. SLU is also home to America's first certified college of aviation and offers degree programs in aviation management and flight science, a legacy of the days when St. Louis was an aviation hub. (Remember Charles Lindbergh's *Spirit of St. Louis*?) Engineering offerings are solid, too.

> "[SLU students are] friendly and pretty laid-back."

The academic climate at SLU is competitive, and one student says, "This school sets high standards for its students, thereby creating opportunities for a good learning environment." Nearly forty percent of undergraduate classes have fewer than 20 students, but the quality of teaching varies greatly, students say. About a third of SLU undergrads study outside of the United States in nearly 50 approved programs across the globe. In Madrid, Spain, SLU has one of the largest and most charming American campuses in Europe. The Micah Program is a living/learning program integrated around themes of peace, justice, and service—it takes its name from the biblical prophet Micah, who spoke out against social injustice in ancient Israel.

SLU students tend to be "friendly and pretty laid-back," says a senior, but "most take school seriously." Many undergraduates come from private, religiously affiliated high schools; 15 percent are Roman Catholic. Forty-two percent hail from the Show-Me State, while 14 percent come from abroad. Black students constitute 9 percent of the student body, Asian Americans 12 percent, Hispanics/Latinos 10 percent, and multiracial students 5 percent. Consistent with SLU's Jesuit heritage, human rights and inclusion are prominent issues of debate. The school offers athletic scholarships and merit scholarships.

Fifty-four percent of undergraduates live on campus, and about half of the first-year students take part in residential learning communities centered on a specific theme or interest. Upperclassmen can move into spacious courtyard-style apartments, but many opt for less expensive apartments off campus. "The dorms are sufficient," one student says. "They're nothing to brag about." Meals at the university's 20 on-campus dining locations are reportedly tasty, with vegetarian, vegan, halal, and gluten-free options available. Students say they feel safe on campus thanks to an active public safety department and the continuing improvement of surrounding neighborhoods.

(continued)

Financial Aid: 99%
Pell Grant: 24%
Expense: Pr $ $
Student Loans: 50%
Average Debt: $ $ $
Applicants: 15,377
Accepted: 81%
Enrolled: 14%
Grad in 6 Years: 80%
Returning First-years: 88%
Academics: ✍ ✍ ✍
Social: 🍷 🍷
Q of L: ★ ★ ★
Admissions: (314) 977-2500
Email Address:
  admission@slu.edu

Strong Programs:
Business
Engineering
Exercise Science
Flight Science
Health Sciences
Nursing
Philosophy
Theology

In Madrid, Spain, SLU has one of the largest and most charming American campuses in Europe.

The school's academic
atmosphere is shaped
by the tradition of its
founders, the Society
of Jesus (Jesuits).

Social life at SLU includes campus events, such as movies in the Quad, dances, and Greek parties, and the plethora of restaurants and coffee shops in St. Louis, as well as movie theaters, museums, bars, sporting events, and nightlife. A student says, "The social life is very active. Students know how to juggle personal with academic lives." Greek life at SLU—unusual for a Jesuit institution—claims more than 1,800 men and women. Students say most parties take place in off-campus apartments or at an off-campus fraternity house, and despite the rules limiting alcohol on campus, it's common in the apartments. Homecoming in the fall and the VIBE concert in the spring feature bands, club-sponsored booths, and vendors. Atlas Week is a weeklong celebration of diversity that includes the Parade of Nations, cultural performances, speakers, and the Billiken World Festival. True to tradition, Sunday evening mass is usually packed with students of all beliefs, and more than 75 percent of students participate in community service and outreach projects. Road trips to Kansas City, Chicago, and schools like the University of Illinois and Indiana University are also popular.

"The social life is very active."

SLU has no varsity football team, but other Billiken squads more than compensate for this deficit. (A billiken was a charm doll and a common good-luck charm in the early 1900s. A popular sportswriter of the time said the charm resembled the then-football coach, and the name stuck.) Teams compete in the Division I Atlantic 10 Conference, and the Billiken's men's soccer, basketball, and baseball teams and women's soccer, basketball, and volleyball teams are the most competitive. For weekend warriors, the Simon Recreation Center boasts a 40-meter pool, six racquetball courts, and loads of equipment. Sand volleyball and flag football are popular intramural sports.

Saint Louis University is winning students' devotion and increasing its national visibility by offering a slew of strong programs. The Jesuit education prepares students to work for a more just and humane world. "SLU is a good choice for its relatively moderate-sized classrooms, its dedication toward a Jesuit mission, and its enjoyable learning environment," says a senior.

Overlaps

Creighton, University of Dayton, U of I at Urbana–Champaign, Loyola University Chicago, Marquette, University of Missouri, WashU in St. Louis, Xavier (OH)

If You Apply To ›

SLU: Early decision I and II, early action, regular decision. SATs or ACTs: optional. Accepts the Common Application with supplement. Apply to particular programs.

St. Mary's College of Maryland

47645 College Drive, St. Mary's City, MD 20686

A public liberal arts institution of the same breed as Mary Washington, UNC Asheville, and much larger William & Mary. The college's historic but sleepy environs are 90 minutes from D.C. and Baltimore on Maryland's western shore. With the Chesapeake Bay close at hand, St. Mary's College is a haven for sailors and nature enthusiasts. Maryland's public honors college is a well-kept secret beyond the state's borders.

Thirty-one years ago, St. Mary's College of Maryland was just another public college, albeit one with a gorgeous waterfront campus in the oldest continuously inhabited English settlement in the New World. In 1992, the state of Maryland decided to make St. Mary's College its public honors college—and the rest, as they often say around here, is history. Students can easily design their own majors, undertake independent research projects, or work closely with professors to investigate whatever interests them.

St. Mary's College has never been connected with any religious denomination and takes its name from its founding in 1840 in St. Mary's City, the original capital of Maryland. The campus sits on a peninsula in southern Maryland where the Potomac River meets the Chesapeake Bay. Not surprisingly, it has an excellent center for estuary research, as well as a strong working relationship with the Chesapeake Biological Laboratory; the school even has its own marina on the St. Mary's River, with a shoreline that gets beautiful sunset views. Architectural styles range from colonial to modern buildings, though the land on which the campus is built belongs to an 1,100-acre national historic landmark, commemorating Maryland's first colonial settlement. For that reason, students may step over archaeological digs as they stroll to class.

The college's core curriculum, known as LEAD (Learning through Experiential and Applied Discovery), emphasizes hands-on experience and career development alongside breadth in the liberal arts. Entering students take a writing-intensive, discussion-focused First Year Seminar. They may choose from two dozen topics—ranging from The Attention Economy to The War on Science—taught by professors from every discipline at the college. To fulfill gen-ed requirements, students can select a LEAD Inquiry, a set of linked classes that explores a theme, such as Public and Environmental Health, Climate, or Justice, from different disciplinary perspectives. Students also progress through a series of courses over their four years on leadership, teamwork, and career development. Additionally, the Honors College Promise guarantees that every student will have access to a research, internship, or study abroad experience. All seniors complete a capstone requirement, usually in the form of a yearlong research project known as the St. Mary's Project.

Biology is among the most popular majors and one of the more difficult programs; students can spend time on the college's research boat when they tire of the lab. Students also sign up in droves for psychology, environmental studies, and economics. Anthropology, chemistry, biochemistry, and English are traditional strengths, and the standout music department includes prize-winning pianist Brian Ganz. The college also offers majors in business administration and management, performing arts, and marine science. Aside from the 25-plus established majors (which include eight cross-disciplinary study areas), more freethinking types may design their own majors.

"Because of the nature of an honors college, all students who attend St. Mary's are academically focused, and there is a common goal to succeed," explains a senior. Sixty-nine percent of classes have fewer than 20 students, and professors are said to be accessible and well respected. "Professors at St. Mary's are always engaged in research and like to involve students in the process," says a psychology major.

St. Mary's College offers study abroad programs, including semester or yearlong opportunities with James Cook University in Australia; University College Dublin in Ireland; Akita International University in Japan; University of Ljubljana in Slovenia; multiple options in Thailand, South Korea, Morocco, Bhutan, Italy, the UK, and more; as well as a rotating list of short-term faculty-led programs during semester breaks. "Seize the opportunity to go abroad," recommends a psychology major, "because SMCM is very helpful with making sure you have the materials and info you need." The Washington Program places students in top summer internships with the government, nonprofits, and think tanks in Washington, D.C., and offers mentoring from alumni.

Eighty-nine percent of undergraduates come from Maryland, which gives the campus a homegrown feel; less than 1 percent come from foreign countries. Students

Website: www.smcm.edu
Location: Rural
Public
Total Enrollment: 1,603
Undergraduates: 1,589
Male/Female: 40/60
Financial Aid: 66%
Pell Grant: 22%
Expense: Pub $ $ $
Student Loans: 50%
Average Debt: $ $
Applicants: 3,401
Accepted: 69%
Enrolled: 17%
Grad in 6 Years: 70%
Returning First-years: 86%
Academics: ✍ ✍ ✍ ✍
Social: 🍷 🍷 🍷
Q of L: ★ ★ ★ ★
Admissions: (240) 895-5000
Email Address:
   admissions@smcm.edu

Strong Programs:
Anthropology
Biochemistry
Biology
Chemistry
English
Environmental Studies
Music
Psychology

> "All students who attend St. Mary's are academically focused."

The student-run Programs Board organizes events like concerts, comedians, and costume parties.

acknowledge that campus diversity, while growing, has a long way to go. Black students account for 11 percent of the student body, Hispanics/Latinos 9 percent, Asian Americans 3 percent, and multiracial students 6 percent. A senior praises the DeSousa-Brent Program, which "is for students from underrepresented groups . . . and provides guidance and support in shaping them into leaders." A sociology major comments that politically conservative students "might have a tough time fitting in." St. Mary's College is more expensive than other publics in Maryland but much less expensive than the private liberal arts colleges with which it also competes. Qualified students receive merit scholarships worth an average of $5,100. There are no athletic awards.

Campus housing is guaranteed for all four years, but students report that facilities need updates. Eighty-two percent of full-time students live on campus. Most residence halls are co-ed, although open (gender-neutral) housing is available; apartments and townhouses are reserved for upperclassmen. Off-campus housing options include old farmhouses and riverside cottages for rent. "The Great Room (our cafeteria) is one of the best parts about living on campus and one of the reasons you frequently see seniors still on unlimited meal plans," cheers a senior. Regarding campus safety, a student says, "I feel incredibly safe as a woman on my campus, and the Title IX office takes things really seriously here."

St. Mary's College doesn't have fraternities or sororities, and its secluded peninsular location means there's little nightlife off campus, but one senior confirms, "The fun that happens on campus is more than enough to make up for that!" The student-run Programs Board organizes events like concerts, comedians, and costume parties, and for the culture-hungry, there are also theaters, an art gallery, lectures, and films on campus. Students

"It's virtually impossible to graduate without knowing how to sail."

report that the party scene is limited and alcohol policies are strictly enforced. The St. Mary's River offers a wealth of outdoor activities. "Most days if we aren't in class, you'll find us paddleboarding, sailing, kayaking, swimming, or just studying on the docks. On nice days, there's a summer-camp atmosphere to it all," says one student. Another adds, "It's virtually impossible to graduate without knowing how to sail." The waterfront also becomes the focus of campuswide activities, including the bamboo boat race held each fall, Bay-to-Bay Service Day and the Bottom County music festival in April, and the end-of-year World Carnival.

The college fields 23 varsity Seahawks teams, most of which compete in the Division III United East Conference; men's and women's lacrosse, men's soccer, field hockey, women's rowing, and men's and women's swimming are among the most successful, and numerous other sports have earned tournament berths in recent years. The college also boasts a nationally ranked sailing program. About a quarter of the students take part in recreational sports; floor hockey, dodgeball, and soccer are favorite intramurals, while rugby, ultimate Frisbee, and equestrian are the most popular club sports.

St. Mary's College has worked hard to establish itself as one of the nation's premier public liberal arts colleges. Though its small size and remote location can feel confining to some, students leave with a solid grounding in the liberal arts—and the close bonds that they forge with friends during peaceful days on the St. Mary's River. For those looking to be part of an intellectual community in a small-town setting, St. Mary's College just might be a place to set sail.

If You Apply To ›

St. Mary's: Early decision I and II, early action, regular decision. SATs or ACTs: optional. Accepts the Common Application with supplement.

One Winooski Park, Colchester, VT 05439

Liberal arts college founded by Edmundites located near a top college town with breathtaking views of the Adirondack and Green Mountains. Cheerful, service-oriented academic community with most students being New Englanders. Proximity to Burlington helps make for vibrant social scene. Easy access to Montreal and to some of the best skiing and snowboarding in the East.

Saint Michael's College carries the distinction of being the only Edmundite institution of higher learning in the world. The college was established by the Society of Saint Edmund, a group of French Catholic priests who took Saint Edmund, Archbishop of Canterbury, as their spiritual inspiration. The Society maintains an on-campus presence, and the influence of the patron saint can be found in the college's dedication to meaningful residential experiences, comprehensive liberal arts, and social justice. A junior says, "Saint Michael's teaches students to go out into the world and work to make it a better place."

Founded in 1904, Saint Michael's sits on 440 acres overlooking Vermont's Green Mountains and the Winooski River. Just five minutes from Burlington, the campus features redbrick architecture, themed gardens, a central quad, a 340-acre natural area, and even a working farm. To the east, Mount Mansfield—Vermont's tallest peak—provides a spectacular backdrop. The Dion Family Student Center and Quad Commons residence hall overlook the mountains and use geothermal heating and cooling, among other green technologies.

Under the core curriculum, all students take five courses: Purposeful Learning, which aids in the transition to college, First-Year Seminar, Fundamental Philosophical Questions, Study of Christian Traditions and Thought, and Junior Seminar. Seniors complete a capstone project as part of a senior seminar in their major. Students also meet requirements in the areas of Intellectual Exploration (liberal arts and sciences), Edmundite Tradition, and Professional Competencies, which encourage experiential learning.

Saint Michael's offers a plethora of solid programs, including business, psychology, education, biology, environmental science, and religious studies. Neuroscience is a top draw, too, and majors in cybersecurity, equity studies, and digital marketing are also available. The Institute for Global Engagement is a hub of international activity providing opportunities for international advocacy, a Peace Corps prep program, internationally oriented student clubs, and more. The Leahy Institute for the Environment also provides collaborative learning experiences. A 3–2 engineering program with nearby University of Vermont and a prepharmacy program are popular, and a 4+1 Master's in Teaching program allows education majors to earn a master's degree and teaching license in just one additional year. Students may also take advantage of cross-registration options with Champlain College.

> **"It's a running joke that St. Mike's students will hold the door for you even if you're a mile away."**

"My classroom experiences have ranged from OK to legitimately transformative," says an English major. "Most of the time, it just feels like I'm getting a good education." Seventy-three percent of classes have fewer than 20 students and only a handful have more than 30; many are taught in a discussion-based format. Students praise professors for their knowledge and willingness to make themselves available.

Website: www.smcvt.edu
Location: Small City
Private
Total Enrollment: 1,142
Undergraduates: 1,083
Male/Female: 46/54
Financial Aid: 99%
Pell Grant: 25%
Expense: Pr $
Student Loans: 66%
Average Debt: $ $ $ $
Applicants: 2,788
Accepted: 85%
Enrolled: 12%
Grad in 6 Years: 73%
Returning First-years: 80%
Academics: ✐ ✐ ✐
Social: 🗩 🗩 🗩 🗩
Q of L: ★ ★ ★
Admissions: (800) 762-8000
Email Address:
admission@smcvt.edu

Strong Programs:
Biology
Business
Education
Environmental Science
Neuroscience
Prepharmacy
Psychology
Religious Studies

"Due to the small class sizes, you get to know your professors on a deeper level," observes an English major, and student support services generally receive favorable reviews.

Students in the Honors Program take specialized core courses and a colloquium, live in honors housing, and complete a senior honors project in their major. A hefty 31 percent of Saint Michael's students take part in undergraduate research, and each year, about 50 students receive stipends for full-time work as research partners with faculty during the summer. More than 100 study abroad options include such far-flung locales as Argentina, Ghana, India, Tanzania, and Denmark.

On campus, says a senior, "It's a running joke that St. Mike's students will hold the door for you even if you're a mile away." A good portion of the student body is Catholic. Black students account for only 4 percent of the student body, Hispanics/Latinos 6 percent, Asian Americans 2 percent, and multiracial students 3 percent. Typically, about 29 percent come from Vermont and 4 percent from foreign countries. Student organizations like the Diversity Coalition and Martin Luther King Jr. Society put on events throughout the year to support inclusion on campus, as does the Institute for Equity & Justice, which was founded in 2023 in response to advocacy from a group of students, staff, and faculty. The political atmosphere is heavily liberal. The college offers merit awards averaging $29,000 to qualified students, and more than 100 athletic scholarships are available in 18 of the college's 20-plus varsity sports. The St. Mike's Community Commitment covers tuition for families making up to $100,000.

Students are required to spend all four years on campus in the residence halls, which a sophomore says "creates a sense of community among the different classes." All first-year students are housed in living/learning communities organized around four main themes: leadership, service, wellness, and approaches to transition. Residence halls include traditional dorms with double and single rooms, suites with shared living spaces, townhouses, and apartment-style accommodations. Campus dining options include an unlimited meal plan at the Green Mountain Dining Room; meals are said to be "decently good" but repetitive. Students report feeling safe on campus, and while there have been instances of sexual assault, says one student, the school "always informs us of what steps they are taking to protect the community and hold those who were responsible accountable."

Socially, says a sophomore, "there's a good mix of hanging out on campus, going downtown, and going skiing or hiking with friends." Even without Greek life, there is a lively party scene. Apart from senior housing, the campus is dry, and students describe a no-pressure, safety-oriented attitude toward drinking. Campuswide activities include comedians, coffeehouse music and poetry performances, and talent shows. Every Friday and Saturday night, the college hosts the Weekend Grilling Program, which provides free food between 11 p.m. and 1 a.m. Fall and spring concerts are popular campus events, and students relish the annual P-Day (Preparation Day) tradition, when "the whole school dresses up in funny outfits then goes to the field [complex] where the school has brought in all sorts of fun activities," according to an English major. Popular excursions "are to downtown Burlington or to the mountains and great outdoors like Mount Mansfield or Camel's Hump," says one student. Montreal is just 90 minutes away.

Nearby Burlington (population 45,000) is "a great college town, as it contains two other colleges: UVM and Champlain," a sophomore says. "The area [offers] a fun atmosphere to eat, shop, and go out." Saint Michael's students receive a free bus pass that will take them downtown, and the Saint Michael's Cultural Pass gives students unlimited access to performances at Burlington's Flynn Theater for little or no

"Due to the small class sizes, you get to know your professors on a deeper level."

cost. An unrestricted (and deeply discounted) season pass to Sugarbush Ski Resort is available as well. Most students get involved in at least one service program through MOVE (Mobilization of Volunteer Efforts) over the course of their college careers.

The majority of Saint Michael's Division II sports compete in the Northeast-10 Conference. Competitive Purple Knights teams include alpine skiing, men's and women's lacrosse and ice hockey, and men's basketball. Varsity outdoor track was added in 2025. Club and intramural programs draw 40 percent of students and include the Adventure Sports Center, which organizes about 75 outings per semester, including sea kayaking, rock and ice climbing, white-water rafting, and other outdoor pursuits.

Saint Michael's College attracts students who appreciate the unique vision inspired by Saint Edmund so many years ago—not to mention the beautiful Vermont setting—and who want to use their education for the betterment of the world. An English major reflects, "St. Mike's is a weird mash-up of progressive, traditional, humble, compassionate people who just want to be good for the world and do the right thing."

St. Olaf College

1520 St. Olaf Avenue, Northfield, MN 55057

Grounded in strong Lutheran traditions, St. Olaf boasts a religiously diverse student body, strong academics, and a global orientation. Has more of a Midwestern feel than crosstown rival Carleton but is a leader among liberal arts colleges in the percentage of students who study abroad. The St. Olaf Choir is world famous. With about 3,000 students, St. Olaf is on the big side of small.

St. Olaf College's home is Northfield, Minnesota, which bills itself as the city of "Cows, Colleges, and Contentment." Founded in 1874 by Norwegian Lutheran immigrants and affiliated with the Evangelical Lutheran Church in America, St. Olaf provides "a balance of academics, extracurricular activities, study abroad, and career-building opportunities [to] develop the whole student intellectually, spiritually, physically, culturally, and emotionally." One Ole (pronounced "Oh-lee") describes her peers as "Minnesota nice" (not, by the way, a characteristic inherited from the not-so-nice 11th-century Norwegian king who became the school's namesake). "I wanted a school with an atmosphere of hard work but without demoralizing competitiveness, and that is what I've found at St. Olaf," remarks a satisfied senior.

The school's meticulously landscaped 350-acre campus is located on Manitou Heights, overlooking the Cannon River valley and the town of Northfield (population 21,000). More than 10,000 trees, native prairie, and a wetlands wildlife area surround the 34 native limestone buildings that form the campus. Holland Hall, built in 1925, was modeled on the Mont-Saint-Michel monastery in France. Regents Hall of Natural and Mathematical Sciences, a 200,000-square-foot science center, earned the prestigious LEED Platinum rating. Newer structures include a 300-bed residence hall and townhouse-style residences housing 140 students.

St. Olaf's social life takes place mostly on campus, and weekend spots include a student-run nightclub called the Pause.

In addition to distribution requirements in a range of liberal arts subjects, St. Olaf's core curriculum includes an Open-Linked-Enduring (OLE) Experience in Practice requirement that asks students to engage in significant hands-on learning, whether through an independent research project, study abroad, an internship, or other faculty-led coursework or experiences. All first-year students complete a first-year seminar and a writing and rhetoric course, requirements that can be fulfilled either by taking individual courses or by signing up for a Conversation Program—an interdisciplinary, team-taught program that brings together students and faculty for a critical exploration of specific topics within their historical, cultural, and social contexts. Programs include Enduring Questions, American Conversations, Asian Conversations, Environmental Conversations, Public Affairs Conversation, and Race Matters. These signature one- to two-year programs "take care of a ton of general requirements, but they are extremely rigorous," cautions one first-year.

Biology, mathematics, psychology, and economics are the most popular majors and among the school's best. The college boasts strong offerings in interdisciplinary areas such as international relations, environmental studies, linguistics, and race and ethnic studies. The music department draws high praise; it offers many performance opportunities with eight school choirs and seven instrumental ensembles. The St. Olaf Choir performs in major venues around the nation and can be heard singing with the Minnesota Orchestra. Dance and chemistry are also notable, and, not surprisingly, Nordic studies is a specialty. The Individual Major allows students to form their own program of study.

"Students are usually expected to take initiative and work on their own."

Academically, "Students are usually expected to take initiative and work on their own but they are always provided with the necessary guidance and resources for them to flourish," says a psychology and Japanese major. Students hold faculty members in high regard for their engaging approaches to teaching. "Many professors also integrate research opportunities, global perspectives and ethical considerations into their teaching," explains a quantitative economics and political science major. Forty-one percent of the classes have fewer than 20 students. The Piper Center for Vocation and Career receives high ratings, especially for its Connections Program trips, which take students to major cities nationwide to network with alumni.

In the last quarter century, St. Olaf has cultivated an international agenda for its students and faculty, and it consistently ranks among the top baccalaureate liberal arts colleges in the country for the percentage of students who study abroad. "St. Olaf has study abroad opportunities on every continent except Antarctica, so there really are Oles all over the globe at any given point in time," cheers a senior. Sixty-nine percent of students participate. In addition to approved partner and exchange programs, St. Olaf offers as many as 100 study abroad programs in more than 40 countries, including faculty-led Global Semester and Environmental Science in Australia and New Zealand programs. Research opportunities are available in all disciplines and are especially robust in the sciences; about half of the students take advantage of them.

"Oles tend to push themselves pretty hard and to be involved in a lot of different things," comments a social studies education and history double major. Forty-seven percent of students hail from Minnesota, and 11 percent come from overseas.

"Oles tend to push themselves pretty hard and to be involved in a lot of different things."

Asian Americans make up 5 percent, Hispanics/Latinos 10 percent, Black students 3 percent, and multiracial students 5 percent, and the college is actively recruiting more students from diverse backgrounds. Sixteen percent of students are Lutheran; chapel services, though not mandatory, are held daily. "There are individuals from different socioeconomic, political, religious, and geographic backgrounds, which allows people to find a community," shares a psychology major. Most students are high achievers from Midwestern public schools, drawn in part by hundreds of merit scholarships, which average $29,000 each year. St. Olaf has a tradition of meeting the full demonstrated need of all admitted students.

Nearly all undergrads reside on campus or in college-owned houses available off campus; 42 percent of the housing is gender-inclusive. All first-years live together in four dedicated dorms, where Junior Counselors on each floor plan fun community activities; upperclassmen enjoy suite-style layouts. Students eat in one large, modern dining hall and rave about the meals: "The food is way better than I ever thought college food could be," cheers a vocal performance major. They can also use their meal plans at neighboring Carleton's two dining halls (and vice versa). Students give good ratings to campus safety and report that efforts to educate the community about campus sexual assault have been effective. "The school is also very good at proactive outreach as they often host wellness events throughout the year," says a first-year of mental health care.

St. Olaf's social life takes place mostly on campus, and weekend spots include a student-run nightclub called the Pause (beloved for its pizza and live entertainment) and a coffeehouse, the Cage. The fine arts department provides many music, theater, and dance performances. "St. Olaf is a dry campus, meaning no alcohol, but the policy isn't strictly enforced," explains a senior, and while there are no fraternities or sororities, a low-key **"The town of Northfield is small but extremely charming."** party scene can be found. The Student Government Association sponsors frequent dances, speakers, and cultural events. The most talked-about annual event, established in 1912, is the three-day Christmas Festival, during which five choirs and the St. Olaf Orchestra combine in televised concerts celebrating Christmas—and the college dining hall serves hearty Scandinavian food.

"The town of Northfield is small but extremely charming, with cute coffee shops, a co-op, parks, amazing thrift shops, and Carleton College nearby," says a sophomore. The town also offers several bars and two breweries. Each September, the locals reenact the failed 1876 attempt by Jesse James to rob the town bank. "Students are actively involved in community mentor, volunteer, and outreach programs," reports a student. For those seeking a taste of city life, buses leave regularly for the twin cities of Minneapolis and St. Paul, less than an hour's drive, where one can experience a shopper's paradise at the huge Mall of America.

St. Olaf has outstanding Division III athletic programs. The Oles men's soccer team regularly brings home conference titles. Men's and women's cross-country and swimming and diving teams are consistently competitive in the Minnesota Intercollegiate Athletic Conference, and the Nordic and Alpine skiing teams have achieved national success. The St. Olaf football team battles rival Carleton for the honor of having the statue in the town's square face the winning campus. The chorus of St. Olaf's fight song is "Um! Yah! Yah!" which has become a popular chant on campus. Students can also take their pick of around 30 club sports and 20 intramurals; broomball—ice hockey played with brooms instead of sticks and shoes rather than skates—is the sport of choice in the winter. The men's and women's ultimate Frisbee club teams are nationally competitive.

For those yearning for a school where community and scholarship exist on the same celebrated plane, St. Olaf could be the right place to spend four years. It's a school where students work hard and are encouraged by good teachers, toughened by Minnesota winters, and nourished by strong moral values and community spirit.

Overlaps

Carleton, Grinnell, Gustavus Adolphus, Luther, Macalester, University of Minnesota, University of St. Thomas, UW–Madison

If You Apply To ›

St. Olaf: Early decision I and II, early action, regular decision. SATs or ACTs: optional. Accepts the Common Application with supplement. Music applicants must submit additional application.

University of San Diego

5998 Alcala Park, San Diego, CA 92110

With a panoramic view of the Pacific Ocean, USD is riding a wave of popularity enhanced by its sun-drenched location. Not to be confused with its public UC counterpart across town, USD is now a popular alternative to Roman Catholic peers the University of San Francisco and Santa Clara. Strong in business, engineering, and study abroad.

Website: www.sandiego.edu
Location: City Center
Private
Total Enrollment: 7,320
Undergraduates: 5,584
Male/Female: 43/57
Financial Aid: 80%
Pell Grant: 31%
Expense: Pr $ $
Student Loans: 40%
Average Debt: $ $
Applicants: 17,010
Accepted: 52%
Enrolled: 12%
Grad in 6 Years: 84%
Returning First-years: 91%
Academics: ✍ ✍ ✍
Social: 🗨 🗨 🗨 🗨
Q of L: ★ ★ ★ ★
Admissions: (619) 260-4506
Email Address:
admissions@sandiego.edu

Strong Programs:
Accountancy
Behavioral Neuroscience
Business Administration
Communication Studies
Engineering
Finance
Marketing
Psychology

Students at the University of San Diego have many reasons to cheer: a beatific oceanside campus, a rich Roman Catholic heritage centered around ethical conduct and compassionate service, and an array of superb academics. "USD is becoming more and more competitive, and the academic programs continue to get better," says one first-year student. "There has never been a better time to come to USD than right now."

Founded in 1949 under the auspices of the local bishop and a religious order, USD occupies 180 acres on a mesa overlooking San Diego's Mission Bay and is only two miles north of downtown. The buildings are designed in 16th-century Spanish Renaissance architectural style in a nod to San Diego's Catholic heritage and the Universidad de Alcalá in Spain. In a fitting architectural juxtaposition, at one end of campus is the Joan B. Kroc (of McDonald's fame) Institute for Peace and Justice; at the other is the Jenny Craig Pavilion, with fitness facilities where you can work off your Big Macs. Recent additions include a wellness center, a basketball practice facility, and a STEM building.

USD's core curriculum focuses on integrating knowledge and experiences from different disciplines. The core encompasses Competencies, such as writing and critical thinking; Foundations courses in theology, philosophy, ethics, and diversity and inclusion; and Explorations courses in five general liberal arts areas. A fourth component, Integrative Learning, is the focus of the first year, when new students join one of five living/learning communities (LLCs): Cultivator, Collaborator, Advocate, Illuminator, and Innovator. In addition to taking a fall-semester course related to the theme of their LLC and living together with their classmates in the residence halls, first-years also have access to a "scholastic assistant," an older student who serves as a mentor and organizes out-of-class activities. Students describe the LLCs as integral to their transition to college life.

> **"There has never been a better time to come to USD than right now."**

USD offers more than 60 degree programs across seven schools: business, leadership and education sciences, law, nursing and health science, arts and sciences, engineering, and peace studies. Some of the most popular undergraduate majors are business administration, finance, real estate, and marketing. Engineering is a traditional strength. Forty-one percent of classes have fewer than 20 students, but none exceed 50. "The classes do a great job of emphasizing the importance of collaboration in projects and in the classroom," says a biomedical engineering major. Professors are accessible and classes aren't taught by TAs. A business administration major explains, "I have had lunch with my professors outside class on many different occasions because they just care about their students so much." Career services receive good ratings, especially for finding internships.

The Honors Program offers small classes and a core curriculum of innovative courses to qualified students. More than 200 students present research projects at

USD's annual undergraduate research conference. Those who overdose on Southern California's ubiquitous blue skies and sunshine may take part in USD's robust study abroad program, which sends 43 percent of students to live and study in more than 30 countries and more than 80 programs, including a permanent program at the University of San Diego Madrid Center in Spain. Nearly half of all undergrads participate in yearlong, semester, summer, or intersession programs.

"The San Diego vibe is truly alive and well on USD's campus," says a business analytics major. "My fellow students are laid-back, fun, and compassionate individuals." Fifty-six percent of undergrads hail from the Golden State, 6 percent are international, and many come from affluent backgrounds. "USD is making strides to become a Hispanic Serving Institution, in order to diversify its student body more," remarks a senior. Currently, Hispanics/Latinos account for 28 percent of the student body, Black students 5 percent, Asian Americans 7 percent, and multiracial students 8 percent. Forty percent of students are Catholic, and students praise the university ministry, which "develops a sense of belonging for all people, not just religious students," says an economics, theology and religious studies major. There is a healthy conservative presence on campus, but one senior notes, "USD really values free speech and the importance of open dialogue for any issue." The school offers merit awards averaging $19,800, and there are more than 100 athletic awards.

Half of all undergraduates live on campus, and all but commuters are required to do so for both their first and second year. All students reside in living/learning communities. Residence halls are a mix of singles, doubles, triples, and limited quads. Apartments range from one room to four bedrooms. When the dinner bell rings, students are well fed. "Meals are delicious," says one junior, and a senior adds, "There is an option to mobile order food and set a pick-up time to ensure the food will be ready during breaks." Campus security is excellent, students say, with officers on duty around the clock. "A huge sexual assault awareness task force has done a lot of good things after a few accusations in the past few years," according to a senior.

> **"The classes do a great job of emphasizing the importance of collaboration."**

Socially, USD offers something for everyone, says a senior. "Want to stay in one night, or go relax at a bonfire on the beach? There will be plenty of people looking to go with you." For those who choose to eschew the sand and waves, USD offers a slate of on-campus activities, including movies, concerts, and mass. The Greek scene attracts 14 percent of the men and 20 percent of the women. Alcohol is allowed only in designated areas for those students of legal age, and "this policy is heavily enforced by the RAs," says a marketing major. Downtown San Diego has plenty to offer: "Whether it's restaurants or going to the beach, bay, downtown, Balboa Park, there is just so much to do, you never get bored," raves a senior. The USD community is big on giving back, too, with more than 300,000 hours of service each year. Popular road trips include Las Vegas and Big Bear.

USD sponsors 17 Division I intercollegiate teams and is a member of the West Coast Conference for all sports except football, which competes in the Pioneer League. Students are especially rowdy when the Torero basketball team takes on rival Gonzaga. Football, baseball, men's soccer, men's golf, women's volleyball, and men's and women's tennis have been competitive in recent years. Twenty-seven percent of students participate in intramural and club sports; among the most popular are ultimate Frisbee, dodgeball, soccer, and lacrosse.

Don't underestimate USD—this small institution offers a rich variety of academic programs, and its students understand that they are living out their college careers in one of the most beautiful spots in the country. What's more, students truly appreciate the sense of community that thrives on campus. As one satisfied

Overlaps

UCLA, UC San Diego, Chapman, Creighton, Gonzaga, Loyola Marymount, Marquette, Santa Clara

senior describes it, "USD is really that place where you can feel home no matter what your background is or where you come from or who you identify as. It is home for everyone, and I can really attest to that value."

University of San Francisco

2130 Fulton Street, San Francisco, CA 94117

Talk about prime real estate: USF is next door to the legendary Haight-Ashbury district, down the street from Golden Gate Park, and within five miles of the Pacific Ocean. Though USF is a Jesuit institution, just a quarter of its students are Roman Catholic. Big emphasis on service learning and social justice.

Website: www.usfca.edu
Location: City Center
Private
Total Enrollment: 7,022
Undergraduates: 5,110
Male/Female: 35/65
Financial Aid: 79%
Pell Grant: 37%
Expense: Pr $ $
Student Loans: 48%
Average Debt: $ $ $ $
Applicants: 24,888
Accepted: 62%
Enrolled: 6%
Grad in 6 Years: 70%
Returning First-years: 84%
Academics: ✍ ✍ ✍
Social: 🗩 🗩 🗩
Q of L: ★ ★ ★ ★
Admissions: (415) 422-6563
Email Address:
admission@usfca.edu

Strong Programs:
Biology
Communications
Computer Science
Entrepreneurship and
  Innovation
Finance
Hospitality Management
Nursing
Psychology

Founded by the Society of Jesus (the Jesuits) in 1855, the University of San Francisco has evolved to reflect the energy and freewheeling spirit of the city that it calls home. Its culturally diverse collection of undergraduates feast on nursing, biology, business, and other academic challenges in a liberal arts setting that encourages them to use their knowledge and experiences to change the world for the better. "The Jesuit progressive attitude is very present," says a communications studies major, "as well as the social justice campaigns that our school is very involved in."

USF's 55 well-kept acres, spotted with beautiful basilica-type buildings and modern facilities, are, as one student puts it, "wedged into the heart of San Francisco." The campus stands atop one of San Francisco's seven hills, adjacent to Golden Gate Park, overlooking San Francisco Bay and the city skyline. The newer Lone Mountain East residence hall houses 600 sophomores in apartment-style units.

The 44-unit Core Curriculum requires students to take courses in six major categories: foundation of communication; math and sciences; humanities; philosophy, theology, and ethics; social sciences; and visual and performing arts. All students take at least one Community Engaged Learning class, which allows them to contribute to local organizations, reflect on justice issues in San Francisco, and strengthen the community while earning class credit. "I took a first-year seminar on opera, and it was one of the best classes I've ever had," raves a happy mathematics major. The Muscat Scholars Program supports incoming first-generation students in their transition to college life, and the Black Achievement Success and Engagement initiative provides a rigorous scholars program, resource center, and a living/learning community for Black-identified students.

Undergraduates at USF choose from more than 100 majors, minors, and interdisciplinary concentrations. The university places a strong emphasis on its preprofessional programs in nursing, science, communications, and business. Nursing, psychology, biology, and computer science are the most popular majors. Data science and entrepreneurship and innovation are also strengths. In the School of Nursing's Simulation Lab, students interact with state-of-the-art mannequins, including adult, pediatrics, and obstetrics, that simulate symptoms and conditions specific to real-life patients and scenarios. The Center for Asia Pacific Studies enhances interdisciplinary majors with an Asian focus, as does the Asian studies program. The visual arts program provides courses in art education, graphic and fine art, drawing, painting, art history, and museum studies. USF has expanded the number of 4+1 pathways for students to earn a master's degree along with their baccalaureate in five years.

Some of the preprofessional majors are quite demanding, and "competition for internships and leadership opportunities can get intense," says an advertising major, but a first-year adds, "The academic climate is relaxed; people are studious but it is not a competition." Forty-two percent of undergraduate classes have fewer than 20 students, and according to a junior, "All USF professors are active in their field" and able to bring real-world experience into the classroom.

> **"People are studious but it is not a competition."**

"Internships and service learning are definitely big parts of the education here at USF," says one senior. Nearby Silicon Valley is a boon for those seeking research or internship opportunities in the tech sector, banking and finance firms, biotech companies, arts organizations, and nonprofits. Qualified students in 17 majors may apply for the Horizon Collective to gain hands-on experience and chart a career pathway in climate and sustainability, health and wellbeing, or AI and technology by tackling real-world issues. The four-year Honors College, open to students in all majors, offers small interdisciplinary seminars, lectures from visiting scholars and artists, and opportunities to apply for funding to conduct research or travel abroad. The "distinctively Jesuit" St. Ignatius Institute living/learning community allows students to study the great books of Western civilization and spend a semester or year studying abroad in Oxford, England. Overall, the university offers more than 100 study abroad programs in 45 countries. "USF also has a partnership with UC San Francisco, so a lot of people are able to do research at the various UCSF campuses," notes a junior.

> *The College Players is the oldest continuously performing college theater group in the West.*

"USF students are very open-minded and adventurous," comments a senior. Seventy percent of undergraduates are from California, and 9 percent hail from abroad. About 29 percent identify as Catholic. Students praise the school's diversity: Asian Americans account for 26 percent of the population, Black students 8 percent, Hispanics/Latinos 22 percent, and multiracial students 10 percent. A sociology major points to "socioeconomic advancement for marginalized communities, environmental and social justice, and LGBTQ+ positivity and acceptance" as popular causes on campus. Admission is need-blind, and USF offers merit scholarships averaging $22,500, as well as athletic scholarships; 37 percent of incoming first-years receive Pell Grants.

> **"Internships and service learning are definitely big parts of the education here at USF."**

Sixty-two percent of undergrads live in campus housing, which is guaranteed for the first two years. After that, most students brave San Francisco's budget-busting rental market, which "can be a struggle," says a senior. On-campus students say the dining facilities offer a range of vegan, vegetarian, and other choices. "Campus safety officers are constantly roaming the campus making sure that the students are safe," reports a student. Adds a first-year, "Counseling and Psychological Services is one of the best services offered on campus."

More than 100 student clubs and organizations provide numerous events and social activities and, says a nursing major, "The party culture is specific to the student involvement or organization." The College Players is the oldest continuously performing college theater group in the West. Fraternities attract 5 percent of the men and sororities draw 9 percent of the women. The school's zero-tolerance policy on underage drinking is strictly enforced. The traditional Night Howl occurs at the end of first-year orientation in the fall: new students gather by the wolf sculpture in front of Gleeson Library and "howl at the moon for good luck," explains a sophomore. In the spring, the Donaroo music festival brings big-name performers to campus. But most socializing takes place off campus, and students take advantage of

> *All students take at least one Community Engaged Learning class, which allows them to contribute to local organizations and reflect on justice issues in San Francisco.*

public transportation to get everywhere from Chinatown and the beach to museums and the symphony. "Living in a city like San Francisco, there is no reason to constrict oneself to the confines of a campus, with so many concerts, bars, nightclubs, and other happenings going on," says a senior.

Varsity athletics provide a popular diversion as well, and the Division I USF Dons compete in the West Coast Conference. Men's soccer and women's cross-country are perennial powerhouses. The university sponsors more than 20 club and intramural sports; the club volleyball, boxing, and judo teams are nationally competitive. Students make ample use of the Koret Health and Recreation Center, which touts an Olympic-size swimming pool, exercise and weight rooms, and a variety of playing courts.

> **"Living in a city like San Francisco, there is no reason to constrict oneself to the confines of a campus."**

In line with its Jesuit tradition, the core mission of USF is to provide a solid liberal arts and preprofessional education that develops students holistically, promotes the common good, and creates "a more humane and just world." Despite the "notoriously expensive" cost of living in San Francisco, students make the most of their time here. "Students at USF truly care about learning and we desire to achieve great things in life," says a kinesiology major. "I haven't met a student who doesn't want to change the world."

If You Apply To ›

USF: Early decision I and II, early action, regular decision. SATs or ACTs: optional. Accepts the Common Application with supplement.

Santa Clara University

500 El Camino Real, Santa Clara, CA 95053

Santa Clara is a selective midsized California university now drawing increased national attention. Gorgeous Silicon Valley campus is within easy reach of San Francisco, and the large endowment also contributes to an air of prosperity. A well-developed core curriculum keeps students focused on basic academic and other values. Offers engineering and business in addition to the liberal arts.

Steeped in history and tradition, Santa Clara University was founded by the Society of Jesus (Jesuits) in 1851 with a mission that emphasizes a commitment to academics and the community. The class schedule is based on 10-week quarters, classes stay small and intimate, and the curriculum focuses on an expanding global society. "Santa Clara's personality is warm, friendly, inquisitive, and passionate about social justice," says a marketing major. Add to that the infinite opportunities for networking and internships in Silicon Valley, and Santa Clara offers a well-rounded educational experience.

SCU's old-world charm includes 106 acres complete with lush green lawns, palm trees, and luscious rose gardens, accented by authentic Spanish architecture. The Mission Gardens, replete with olive trees, are a beautiful escape from the pressures of school. The famous classic mission church was rebuilt in 1926 in the design of the six previous churches that were destroyed by seemingly biblical disasters ranging from fires to floods. Newer structures include the Sobrato

Campus for Discovery and Innovation, a massive $300 million facility housing the university's STEM programs.

The Core Curriculum provides "a humanistic education that leads toward an informed, ethical engagement with the world." It prescribes courses in three broad categories—Foundations, Explorations, and Integrations. Foundations includes classes in critical thinking, writing, languages, math, and religion. Explorations builds on Foundations and includes options from ethics, diversity, and civic engagement, to arts, natural sciences, religion, and others. Integration's Core Pathways program supplements the major and core curriculum by offering 24 sets of courses with innovative common themes across disciplines, such as design, hunger and poverty, justice and the arts, and values in science and technology; students choose one Pathway and complete three or four courses. All first-year students are members of a Residential Learning Community (RLC) and take two-quarter sequences of Critical Thinking & Writing and Cultures & Ideas linked to their RLC. Students must complete a requirement that involves community service, and most majors require a capstone experience or senior project.

> **"Santa Clara's personality is warm, friendly, inquisitive, and passionate about social justice."**

In addition to liberal arts, Santa Clara offers preprofessional programs in engineering and business. Engineering students can opt for a dual-degree program that allows them to get a bachelor's and master's degree in five years. The Leavey School of Business is renowned along the West Coast, with finance, economics, and marketing all strong. In the College of Arts and Sciences, communication and psychology remain popular. Other notable majors include environmental science, environmental studies, public health science, bioengineering, and computer science and engineering.

While courses are challenging, students say the quarter system gives them more control over the intensity of their workload. "Every 10 weeks you can change your workload to something that fits best for you," explains a public health science major. Small classes—43 percent enroll fewer than 20 students—taught by full professors allow plenty of time for one-on-one interaction. Students in all fields opt to engage in research supervised by a faculty member, much of it subsidized by grants. "It's very easy to get research or TA positions," says an economics major. "If you want to be a big fish in a small pond, SCU is a great choice."

For students looking for more of a challenge, the honors program places 65 to 70 selected first-years in seminar-style classes, and an endowed scholarship sponsors one student's junior year at Mansfield College, Oxford University. The LEAD (Leadership, Excellence, and Academic Development) Scholars Program invites students whose parents did not attend college to join a small community of peers who work closely with faculty and staff to cultivate leadership skills. The study abroad program is extensive, with options in over 40 countries on every continent except Antarctica. Those seeking professional experience find ample assistance at the Career Center, which offers mock interviews,

> **"If you want to be a big fish in a small pond, SCU is a great choice."**

résumé edits, cover letter help, goal setting, and more. "I cannot stress enough how much of a perk Silicon Valley is for going to SCU," enthuses a sophomore. "Internship opportunities are endless."

According to a psychology major, Santa Clara students are "very driven and 'go, go, go' all the time." About half of undergraduates are Roman Catholic, and religion, while not intrusive, is a force in many aspects of campus life. The campus ministry provides counseling and opportunities for spiritual development, and many students are active in local volunteer organizations. Fifty-eight percent of undergraduates hail from California, and 7 percent come from foreign countries. The student

(continued)

Enrolled: 18%
Grad in 6 Years: 88%
Returning First-years: 94%
Academics: ✍ ✍ ✍
Social: 🌑 🌑 🌑 🌑
Q of L: ★ ★ ★ ★
Admissions: (408) 554-4700
Email Address:
  admission@scu.edu

Strong Programs:
Bioengineering
Computer Science and
  Engineering
Economics
Environmental Science
Environmental Studies
Finance
Public Health Science

Fall Concert, the Global Village celebration, and the Gonzaga basketball game are favorite annual events.

body on this liberal campus is almost evenly split between public school graduates and alumni of religiously affiliated or other private schools. Twenty-one percent of the students are Asian American, 3 percent are Black, 20 percent are Hispanic/Latino, and 9 percent are multiracial, but socioeconomically, the school is much less diverse, with just 10 percent of incoming first-year students receiving Pell Grants. "Our school is quite posh," concedes an accounting major. "Being located in the heart of Silicon Valley, there is a lot of luxury." Merit-based academic awards averaging $16,400, and over 100 athletic scholarships are available to those who qualify. The Johnson Scholars Program rewards up to 10 outstanding incoming students with four-year, full-tuition scholarships and special opportunities to develop leadership skills.

Almost all first-years and sophomores live on campus before packing up and heading for shared houses or apartments for the last two years; roughly half of all undergrads reside in campus housing. All first-year students, including commuters, participate in one of the nine Residential Learning Communities, living in themed dorms and taking courses with students who share similar academic or social interests. The campus offers one central dining hall. "Everything is made fresh," says an environmental science major, "and we have a killer salad bar for those who like their veggies." Students give good ratings to campus safety. "I think people feel safe on and around campus because of the location," reports a junior.

Santa Clara ended its support of fraternities and sororities, but Greek organizations and a lively off-campus party scene persist, albeit independently. On-campus social life is led by the nearly 200 student organizations that coordinate events,

> "Being located in the heart of Silicon Valley, there is a lot of luxury."

making it "easy to join in on the fun," says a senior. The Bronco is a sports and recreation area where students can hang out, play billiards, and enjoy a late-night meal. Fall Concert, the Global Village celebration, the Gonzaga basketball game, and the Love Jones talent show are favorite annual events. The town of Santa Clara is mostly residential. For those who want to bask in the sun, Santa Cruz is only 20 miles away. San Francisco lies within 45 minutes, and other short road trips include Napa Valley, Monterey, and Palo Alto.

The Santa Clara Broncos compete in Division I; men's and women's soccer and basketball, women's volleyball, men's tennis, and baseball are among the more successful programs. Women's soccer recently claimed the national title. Intramural and club sports, including soccer, volleyball, sailing, and more, draw the enthusiastic participation of a third of the undergraduates. "Every patch of grass usually has someone either chucking a Frisbee or kicking a ball around," says a political science major.

Santa Clara University is a warm place in every sense of the word. The physical setting is comfortable and scenic. More important, the SCU community gives meaning to the traditional Jesuit ideals of infusing morality and ethics into strong and coherent academics. Students say they are reminded of all this daily by their school's nickname: "Claradise."

Overlaps

Boston College, UC Berkeley, UC Davis, UCLA, Cal Poly–San Luis Obispo, Loyola Marymount, University of San Diego, University of Southern California

If You Apply To ›

SCU: Early decision I and II, early action, regular decision. Accepts the Common Application with supplement. Please consult Santa Clara's website for the most up-to-date information regarding standardized test requirements.

Sarah Lawrence College

1 Mead Way, Bronxville, NY 10708

A free-spirited sister of East Coast alternative institutions like Bard and Bennington where individualism reigns supreme. Though co-ed, women significantly outnumber men. Strong in the humanities and visual and performing arts, Sarah Lawrence takes its inspiration from the Oxford University tutorial system. Nationally known for creative writing and filmmaking. Full of quirky, headstrong intellectuals who hop the train to New York City with ease.

Sarah Lawrence College attracts creative, curious, and highly motivated individuals who are both critical thinkers and devotees of independent learning. They love literature and the arts and take pride in their academic prowess. Indeed, freedom and exploration are valued more highly than any tradition here. Yet students also appreciate the things that have always been constants here, such as the emphasis on small classes and one-on-one conferences with professors. As a senior studying theater and sociology attests, what makes Sarah Lawrence stand out is that "students are given full agency and autonomy over their education."

Established in 1926 as a women's college and named after the wife of a founder, Sarah Lawrence went co-ed in 1968. The campus sits on a quaint, 44-acre tract in the city of Yonkers called Lawrence Park West, a wealthy Westchester County community close to the village of Bronxville, where even the public library boasts Oriental rugs and fireplaces. On campus, the prevailing architectural theme is English Tudor, including the mansion from the founder's converted estate. The landscape is hilly and green, with more than a hundred types of trees and abundant rock outcroppings. Because the school's founders believed that there should be as little physical separation as possible between life and work, many classrooms, dormitory suites, and faculty offices are all housed in the same buildings. Though its holdings are small—fewer than 350,000 volumes—the cozy library is charming. The remodeled HUB center for Humanity, Understanding, and Belonging and the Barbara Walters Campus Center (named for one of the school's most famous alumnae) provide spaces for student organizations, socializing, campus dining, and community events.

Students focus on any of nearly 50 disciplines, and regardless of what they choose to study, all students at Sarah Lawrence become intimately acquainted with the written word; writing begins in the first year and continues across the curriculum for the next three. General education requirements include credits in at least three of four academic areas, leaving lots of room for students to dabble in whatever strikes their fancy. Though there are formal grades, more important is the student's portfolio of work, accompanied by in-depth, written evaluations from professors, filed twice a year. To ease the transition to college, all first-years take a First-Year Studies seminar, choosing from more than 30 topics. The professor of their chosen course becomes their "don," the person who often guides their academic development throughout their four years.

"The academic climate is creative and driven."

"The academic climate is creative and driven," says a journalism and gender studies major. Despite challenging academics, a senior adds, "Competition between students is low because everybody's course of study is so individualized." Indeed, every student designs their own program of study, and almost no subject is out of bounds. Writing, psychology, filmmaking, and visual and performing arts are among the college's traditional strengths, and other popular concentrations include literature and art history. Aspiring psychologists may participate in fieldwork at the college's Early Childhood Center. The premed program, more structured than other offerings, places nearly all eligible graduates into medical school.

The majority of classes are roundtable seminars, with 77 percent of them enrolling fewer than 20 students. "Our discussions are always so fruitful because I'm not getting lectured at," shares a writing and literature student. Most students take three courses per semester, and professors meet one-on-one with their students weekly or biweekly in a system modeled after Oxford University's tutorials, so there's no time to slack off—or fall behind. "The professors are so passionate," cheers a public policy analysis student. Perhaps because of the college's emphasis on personal relationships with professors, even the registration process requires deep thought: students interview teachers to ensure that courses fit into their academic plans and that the professor is someone they respect and want to study with.

All students at Sarah Lawrence conduct research as part of their one-on-ones with professors. The Sarah Lawrence Center for the Urban River is a facility on the banks of the Hudson River that affords research opportunities for students pursuing environmental and social sciences. Students are encouraged to study abroad, and the college runs its own semester, yearlong, and summer study abroad programs in such locales as Oxford, London, Paris, Havana, Tokyo, Osaka, and Florence, Italy. Twenty-one percent of students undertake some sort of international experience. Those interested in service learning may participate in the Intensive Semester in Yonkers, in which they take three classes in Yonkers centered on the history of the city and community empowerment while also working with local nonprofit organizations. "Sarah Lawrence's Community Leadership Internship Program is a fantastic way to develop one's leadership skills and gather professional experience," says a liberal arts student.

> **"[The] Community Leadership Internship Program is a fantastic way to develop one's leadership skills."**

Sarah Lawrence students "are not afraid to express themselves artistically, verbally, or with their clothing," describes a senior. Nineteen percent of undergrads are natives of New York State—the bulk from nearby New York City—and 6 percent come from abroad. Five percent of students are Black, 5 percent Asian American, 12 percent Hispanic/Latino, and 7 percent multiracial. The student body is 80 percent female, and many undergrads come from affluent families. A senior comments, "It can be difficult for students from working-class backgrounds and first-generation college students" to find their place on campus. Political and social issues ranging from racism and human rights to climate change attract much attention here, and students are "more than happy to start a protest," says one student. Notes a junior, "It is very much left leaning." Merit scholarships averaging $28,500 are available to qualified students.

Nearly all students live in the "eclectic" campus housing, which is available to all full-time students. Campus food receives fair reviews, and there are plenty of options for students with special dietary needs. Campus security is strong, and students report that sexual harassment and assault policies and support services are effective. Career Services also receives student praise for "connecting current students with alumni, and hosting internship fairs and networking events," observes a junior studying creative writing.

> **"Sarah Lawrence does not have any Greek life, nor does it want to."**

With a plethora of student organizations hosting on-campus activities, and the school's proximity to New York City, social life is varied and active. Theater fans and aspiring actors flock to discounted Broadway shows, and clubs, bars, museums, and concert halls also beckon. "Sarah Lawrence does not have any Greek life, nor does it want to," affirms a junior. College policies require party hosts who serve alcohol to register, and a dance and literature student says party culture is "not a defining part" of campus life. Favorite traditions include the annual fall screening of *The Princess Bride* to honor star and Sarah Lawrence alum Cary Elwes, fall and spring formals, and a midnight breakfast, served during the last week of each semester.

The Sarah Lawrence Gryphons, named for a mythical figure that is part lion and part eagle, field 16 teams that compete in the Division III Skyline Conference. Women's soccer and tennis, and men's basketball are recent conference champs, and women's swimming is also competitive. "We have very unofficial rivalries with Vassar and Bard—more ironic than not," claims a senior. The intramural program revolves around one-day invitational events—squash matches, dodgeball tournaments, fitness challenges—rather than league play.

Sarah Lawrence offers a close-knit community for writers, artists, and creative thinkers in a lush setting just outside the hustle and bustle of Manhattan. "The education students get at Sarah Lawrence is unlike any other. You can truly have it all here," says a writing student. "You can play sports and perform in the theater. You can study botany and poetry at the same time."

Overlaps

Bard, Mount Holyoke, NYU, Oberlin, Reed, Skidmore, Smith, Vassar

If You Apply To ›

Sarah Lawrence: Early decision I and II, early action, regular decision. SATs or ACTs: optional. Accepts the Common Application.

Scripps College: See page 156.

Seattle University

901 12th Avenue, Seattle, WA 98122

Unlike the University of Washington, Seattle University is a stone's throw from downtown and within walking distance of the waterfront. Jesuit tradition guarantees a nurturing environment and student growth both academically and in experiential learning. The university is a national institution that remains true to its Pacific Northwestern roots. Out-of-staters are drawn as much by the city of Seattle as by the university itself.

Although Seattle has cultivated a reputation based largely on software, Starbucks lattes, and perpetually gray skies, the city is also home to Seattle University, a vibrant institution founded by the Society of Jesus (Jesuits) in 1891 that attracts 4,000 undergraduates. With strong preprofessional programs and a commitment to social and spiritual engagement, SU continues to express its mission to empower leaders for a just and humane world.

SU now has two urban campuses. In summer 2025, SU subsumed the former Cornish College of Arts in the South Lake Union neighborhood of Seattle, just a mile and a half from the main campus. The First Hill campus, bordered by busy city streets, is a 50-acre urban sanctuary in the heart of Seattle. The university's diverse buildings are united by a recurring theme of red brick and light-filled atriums. The

Website: www.seattleu.edu
Location: City Center
Private
Total Enrollment: 5,595
Undergraduates: 3,995
Male/Female: 39/61
Financial Aid: 92%
Pell Grant: 28%
Expense: Pr $ $
Student Loans: 65%

(continued)

Average Debt: $

Applicants: 8,468

Accepted: 77%

Enrolled: 14%

Grad in 6 Years: 73%

Returning First-years: 84%

Academics: ✑ ✑ ✑

Social: 🗩 🗩 🗩

Q of L: ★ ★ ★ ★

Admissions: (206) 220-8040

Email Address:
admissions@seattleu.edu

Strong Programs:
Biology
Computer Science
Criminal Justice
Diagnostic Ultrasound
Engineering
Finance
Marketing
Nursing

Dining options get rave reviews for being local, seasonal, organic, sustainable, and made to order.

Chapel of St. Ignatius is a prize-winning building designed by Steven Holl around the concept of a "gathering of different lights." Special areas like the Ethnobotanical Garden and Japanese American Remembrance Garden highlight native plants and local history. The art deco–style Main Campus Center is listed with the National Register of Historic Places. The Seattle University Museum of Art is being constructed following a gift from property developer Richard Hedreen of his $300 million art collection. The newly named Cornish College of the Arts at Seattle University sits on about four acres in downtown Seattle and offers 11 fine arts degrees, along with more than 10,000 square feet in production space, a state-of-the-art auditorium, playhouse, performance hall, and gallery.

The 60-credit University Core Curriculum introduces all students to the "unique tradition of Jesuit liberal education" and aims to develop the whole person for a life of service, providing a foundation for questioning and learning in any major or profession. The core features seminars in writing, quantitative reasoning and creative expression, humanities, social sciences, and natural sciences, as well as coursework in philosophy and theology. Incoming students complete a first-year seminar built around a central theme or problem (enrollment is limited to 19 students), and seniors must complete a capstone course.

> **"Many of our majors require some sort of internship."**

SU students choose from more than 70 undergraduate degree programs across five of SU's seven academic colleges. SU's most popular majors are also some of its best: nursing, business/management, computer science, and kinesiology. The B.S. degree in diagnostic ultrasound is a particular specialty, and criminal justice, engineering, and biology are also strengths. Six-year, dual-degree programs in which one of 14 majors can be combined with law are also available. Previously on the quarter system, SU has transitioned to a semester system. Forty percent of classes have fewer than 20 students, but almost none have more than 50.

More than 450 community-engaged learning courses are offered each year, and about a quarter of students participate. Motivated students may enroll in the University Honors program, which employs Socratic dialogue with the Jesuit tradition of challenging students to learn for themselves and offers three concurrent classes in every term. The program makes extensive use of the seminar format and focuses on the history of ideas, with tracks in Intellectual Traditions; Society, Policy, and Citizenship; and Innovations. According to a strategic communications major, "Many of our majors require some sort of internship, and professors are more than willing to get students connected with opportunities in the area." When students want to escape Seattle's dreary skies and near-constant drizzle, they can take part in the university's study abroad program. Twenty-five percent of students pack their bags for programs offered in 50 nations around the world. SU also sends approximately 20 students to the National Conference for Undergraduate Research each year as part of a robust undergraduate research program.

"Everyone at this school believes in making the world a better place in their own way," comments a communication and media major. Nineteen percent of undergraduates are Catholic. Fifty-two percent hail from Washington, and 7 percent are from other nations. Black students constitute 11 percent of the student body, Asian Americans 37 percent, Hispanics/Latinos 16 percent, Pacific Islanders 4 percent, and Native Americans 2 percent. The university, like its host city, has a reputation for progressive liberalism.

> **"Everyone at this school believes in making the world a better place in their own way."**

"We're all feminists, agents against racism, and allies," says a sophomore, adding, "As a queer student, I feel more than safe—I feel embraced." Merit scholarships worth an average of $27,200 are awarded annually, and athletes vie for more than 250 scholarships.

Fifty-five percent of SU students live in university housing. Students are required to live on campus through their sophomore year; after that, housing is not guaranteed. A biology major says, "The surrounding area is very expensive, so most students who move off campus share bedrooms in apartments or townhouses." Dining options, on the other hand, get rave reviews for being local, seasonal, organic, sustainable, made to order, and, in the words of one student, "delicious, Instagram-ready food." Students report feeling safe on campus, day and night.

With more than 140 student clubs and organizations, there are plenty of opportunities to socialize on campus. Consistent with Jesuit tradition, there are no fraternities or sororities, and one student says, "Not a whole lot of drinking occurs on campus." Instead, students head off campus to enjoy Seattle's vibrant nightlife. "We are right next to Capitol Hill, which is the famous arts district/nightlife neighborhood," explains a sophomore. "Everything is walkable." Students can take advantage of the city's ubiquitous coffeehouses, eateries, shops, and concert venues.

SU's Redhawks compete in the West Coast Conference (and Division I). Men's and women's soccer and softball have been competitive in recent years. Basketball, baseball, and soccer games against the University of Washington draw crowds. SU's Championship Field has been completely refurbished and is a practice facility for the 2026 FIFA Men's World Cup. Intramural and club sports sign up 30 percent of students; popular options include flag football, softball, and crew.

With its emphasis on the liberal arts, experiential learning, and Jesuit principles, SU affords students an experience "which focuses on educating the entire person," according to one junior. For those students who are not averse to hard work and overcast skies, Seattle University might be an inspired choice—just be sure to pack a raincoat.

Overlaps

Chapman, Elon, Gonzaga, University of Oregon, University of the Pacific, Santa Clara, University of Washington, Western Washington

If You Apply To ›

Seattle: Early action, regular decision. SATs or ACTs: optional. Accepts the Common Application. Application includes optional question about gender identity.

Skidmore College

815 North Broadway, Saratoga Springs, NY 12866

Founded in 1903 as a "young women's industrial club" that offered courses in everything from typewriting to music and folk dancing, now co-ed Skidmore College still excels in exploration rooted in creativity, especially in the fine and performing arts. More recently it has become known for strong science programs. Compare to Connecticut College, Vassar, and Wheaton (MA). Unique wooded campus gives the feel of living in a forest.

Skidmore College serves up solid academics with a decidedly nontraditional flair. "Everything we do at Skidmore is driven by our belief that Creative Thought Matters," says the administration. "It's an inclusive philosophy that takes work and vulnerability." At Skidmore, freedom of speech, thought, and expression thrives in small classes where thought-provoking discussion is encouraged by supportive and accessible faculty. "The college has a charm, sort of like a summer camp," says a junior. Thanks to an emphasis on interdisciplinary learning, students can "have diverse interests and be able to dabble in anything," a senior says.

Website: www.skidmore.edu
Location: Small City
Private
Total Enrollment: 2,668
Undergraduates: 2,668
Male/Female: 40/60
Financial Aid: 57%

In 1961, as enrollment surged, Skidmore traded its Victorian campus in the heart of Saratoga Springs for 750 acres on the northwest edge of town. Since then, the campus has grown to more than 50 buildings on 1,200 acres, and the student body has doubled in size (men were welcomed in 1971). While contemporary in style, the newer buildings on Skidmore's Jonsson campus reflect the Victorian heritage of the school's original Scribner campus. Covered walkways connect the residential, academic, and social centers, and the prevailing views are of surrounding mountains, woods, and fields. The college has implemented geothermal heating and cooling in half of its buildings and generates more than 15 percent of its power from a nearby hydroelectric dam and its own solar array. A new tennis and wellness center opened in 2025.

Skidmore's First-Year Experience includes a classwide summer reading project and a choice from among more than 40 Scribner Seminars. These seminars are typically capped at 16 students and taught by professors who also serve as mentors and advisors. Seminar topics are broad and varied, in keeping with Skidmore's 41 majors; recent offerings include The Business of Food, and Latinx Expression: Color in Culture. Students in each seminar receive guidance and support from an upper-class peer mentor, and themes raised in the summer reading crop up again during the year in campuswide programming.

The most popular majors at Skidmore are in the social sciences, business and marketing, psychology, and visual and performing arts. Nearly one-third of students major in the physical and life sciences. Students in biology, environmental science, environmental studies, and geoscience courses often conduct fieldwork in the college's 300-acre North Woods, a natural laboratory. Skidmore augments liberal arts and sciences offerings with preprofessional majors in business, education studies, health and human physiological sciences, and social work, not to mention cooperative and dual-degree programs in engineering, business administration, accounting, finance, physical and occupational therapy, and nursing, offered in conjunction with such institutions as Clarkson, Dartmouth, NYU, and Syracuse.

"Skidmore is a very collaborative working environment. Professors challenge students to constantly improve communication skills by working with other students and submitting work in both written and oral forms," explains a sophomore.

> **"Skidmore is a very collaborative working environment."**

"Professors are super engaged, prepared, and willing to meet with students during office hours," adds an English and theater major. Seventy-six percent of classes have fewer than 20 students. Skidmore's Summer Collaborative Research Program provides roughly 80 students a funded opportunity to work individually with faculty mentors for up to 10 weeks on original research in disciplines ranging from biology to business. "There are lots of opportunities for hands-on experience," shares an economics major. "In our sciences, almost all the equipment can be operated by students." Internships are popular, too, with 85 percent of students doing at least one during their college years, often with funding from the school. Students also speak highly of the 120 approved off-campus study options in 45 countries, especially Skidmore-run programs in France, England, and New Zealand. Forty-seven percent of the students spend at least one semester abroad.

Skidmore's Summer Collaborative Research Program provides roughly 80 students a funded opportunity to work individually with faculty mentors.

"When describing my peers to friends at home I call them granola, a bit alternative, kind, creative, open to new experiences, a bit strange sometimes (in an interesting way), and expressive," says a junior. Students hail primarily from New York (31 percent), Massachusetts, New Jersey, Connecticut, and California; 8 percent come from foreign countries. Asian Americans constitute 6 percent of the student body, Hispanics/Latinos 11 percent, Black students 4 percent, and multiracial students 6 percent. "Politically, Skidmore is a very liberal campus," attests a psychology and philosophy major. Limited awards for academic merit are available, although there are no athletic scholarships. Additionally, the college commits to meeting the full demonstrated financial need of all enrolled students.

Ninety percent of Skidmore students live on campus. Most residence hall floors are co-ed, but students can choose options such as women, quiet, or substance-free floors. "Housing is great. It's guaranteed all four years, and the on-campus apartments are unbelievably nice," says a student. Most buildings have carpeting, air-conditioning, and cozy window seats. Some upperclassmen move to apartments—whether on campus in the Northwoods Village Apartments or the Sussman Village Apartments or off campus in Saratoga Springs. The Murray-Aikins Dining Hall provides students with fresh, healthy, allergy-inclusive options, including Chicken Finger Fridays and themed meals (think: Game of Thrones-inspired). "I have friends visit me from other schools and demand to be sneaked into our dining hall," boasts a first-year. In fact, Skidmore's dining services has won the American Culinary Federation's gold medal for culinary excellence eight times. Career and mental health services also get high marks from students.

"Most of the social life revolves around campus clubs and organizations," reports a chemistry major. "Since we don't have Greek life, we don't have the stereotypical party scene on campus." Skidmore's more traditional activities, which have continued even after a half century of coeducation, include Club Fair, Winter Carnival, and the National College Comedy Festival. Newer traditions include a student-run tribute concert; the Big Green Scream, which ushers in the men's and women's basketball seasons; and Pack the Rink, which marks the beginning of the men's ice hockey season.

The nearby Adirondacks and Green Mountains make Skidmore a haven for backpackers, skiers, and members of the popular Outdoors Club. The old resort town of Saratoga Springs, with its healing waters, antique shops, and eateries, offers plenty of culture, including the Saratoga Performing Arts Center, an annual Victorian Streetwalk, and Chowderfest events. Students reach out to the community through BenefAction, a volunteer group connected to several local agencies and schools. The best road trips include Albany, New York City, and Boston.

Skidmore's men's and women's varsity teams (the Thoroughbreds) compete in Division III; the men's and women's basketball and tennis teams have claimed Liberty League championships in recent years. The riding program has won 11 Intercollegiate Horse Show Association national championships. About 20 club and intramural sports are available as well.

Skidmore continues to win the hearts of motivated students with gorgeous scenery, caring faculty, and its flexibility, openness, and receptivity to growth. "Our school motto is 'Creative Thought Matters' and I've found that message to be very true in Skidmore," says an economics major. "They encourage interdisciplinary collaboration through classes and research. Students often double major or major and minor in very different things, and fresh perspectives are always welcome."

> **"I have friends visit me from other schools and demand to be sneaked into our dining hall."**

> *The college has implemented geothermal heating and cooling in half of its buildings.*

> ### Overlaps
> **Bates, Bowdoin, Colby, Colgate, Connecticut College, Hamilton, Oberlin, Vassar**

If You Apply To ›

Skidmore: Early decision I and II, regular decision. SATs or ACTs: optional. Accepts the Common Application.

10 Elm Street, Northampton, MA 01063

With a total enrollment of about 2,800, Smith is one of the largest top women's colleges, strong in the sciences and the arts, and the first women's college to offer engineering. Liberal Northampton provides sophisticated social life, and membership in the Five College Consortium adds depth and breadth all around. Compare to Bryn Mawr.

Website: www.smith.edu

Location: Small City

Private

Total Enrollment: 2,814

Undergraduates: 2,537

Male/Female: 0/100

Financial Aid: 85%

Pell Grant: 20%

Expense: Pr $ $ $

Student Loans: 51%

Average Debt: $

Applicants: 8,666

Accepted: 21%

Enrolled: 35%

Grad in 6 Years: 89%

Returning First-years: 94%

Academics: ✎ ✎ ✎ ✎

Social: 🗨 🗨 🗨

Q of L: ★ ★ ★ ★

Admissions: (413) 585-2500

Email Address:
admission@smith.edu

Strong Programs:

Art History

Biology

Dance

Engineering

Government

Landscape Studies

Music

Psychology

Heaven only knows what Sophia Smith would think of the women's college she founded in 1871 with the hope it would be "pervaded by the Spirit of Evangelical Christian Religion." There are still Evangelicals at Smith, but today they join the rest of their schoolmates in crusading against racism, classism, sexism, and homophobia. Though the all-female school remains strongly committed to its liberal arts mission, it is also focused on placing women at the forefront of science and technology. Students here have the opportunity to become leaders in the male-dominated field of engineering or pursue interdisciplinary fields such as landscape studies or the study of women and gender. "Smith has an open curriculum, a great college town, and a very strong science program," says one sophomore.

Smith is in the small city of Northampton, an artsy and politically progressive oasis within an hour's drive of the Berkshire Mountains. The 147-acre campus sparkles with many gardens, Paradise Pond, and a plant house. Buildings cover a range of styles from late 18th century to modern, and the college has successfully retained its historic atmosphere while keeping facilities up to date. The college's science and engineering building, Ford Hall, earned LEED Gold Certification and

> **"Smith has an open curriculum, a great college town, and a very strong science program."**

boasts a myriad of high-tech equipment, including two electron microscopes. Smith's three libraries house one of the largest collections of any liberal arts college in the country. The renovated, state-of-the-art Neilson Library, redesigned by Maya Lin (of Vietnam Veterans Memorial fame), is the intellectual heart of the campus.

With the exception of at least one writing course, Smith students have unusual freedom to plan a course of study. They must take half of their credits outside of their major, and first-year students can take small seminars on topics such as Rebellious Women or The Art of Travel. Students can expand their academic options by registering for courses at any of the other Five College Consortium member schools: Amherst, Hampshire, Mount Holyoke, and UMass Amherst.

Popular majors recently have included those in the social sciences, biological life sciences, psychology, visual and performing arts, and ethnic and gender studies. Science majors enjoy numerous opportunities to assist professors with their research. The Picker Engineering Program, the country's first women-only, accredited engineering program, offers an ambitious engineering curriculum taught within the full depth and breadth of the liberal arts. Those who complete it are highly sought after: recent graduates have headed to prestigious graduate programs at Cornell, Harvard, MIT, Princeton, and other colleges; received highly competitive National Science Foundation fellowships; and have been quickly snatched up by employers. Smith's art history department is among the best in the nation and enjoys access to the college's superb museum. Dance and music are notable as well. Landscape studies, which focuses on the relationship between humans and natural and built environments, is a first-of-its-kind undergraduate program among liberal arts colleges.

Be ready to hit the books hard with your fellow Smithies. Coursework is described as "very intense and very difficult," although the atmosphere is "not too competitive because we all want to grow together," according to one student. Students generally refrain from discussing grades, choosing instead to focus on helping each other. Smith's student-run honor system, which covers everything from exams to library checkout, is widely praised and enforced. All courses are taught by professors, and 67 percent of them have fewer than 20 students. Students seem to be pleased with the quality of teaching. "My professors have all been accessible and supportive as well as open-minded and articulate," says a sophomore.

Eligible students may enter the Smith Scholars program and embark on one or two years of independent study or extra college research for full credit. The STRIDE program allows first-years and sophomores to become paid research assistants to professors. Students are also enthusiastic about the opportunity to take part in Smith's legendary study abroad program, which sends interested members of the junior class to their choice of several countries for at least a semester. The Praxis program allows each student to participate in at least one summer internship funded by the college. More than 100 older students are enrolled in the groundbreaking Ada Comstock Scholars Program for women returning to college.

Smithies are "women who know what they want and know how to get things done," says a government major. Eighteen percent of undergraduates hail from Massachusetts, and 14 percent come from abroad. Black students account for 5 percent of the student body, Asian Americans 10 percent, Hispanics/Latinas 12 percent, and multiracial students 6 percent. Nobody disputes that Smith is a liberal place, with social issues of

> "[Classes are] not too competitive because we all want to grow together."

the day dominating conversations, though some students are surprised to find themselves in such a freewheeling atmosphere. With its $2.7 billion endowment, Smith has deeper pockets than many of its competitors. And though it's got a hefty price tag, the school meets the full demonstrated financial need of admitted students and has replaced loans with grants in all need-based financial aid packages. It also offers merit-based awards that average $22,800 annually.

Housing at Smith, which consists of 41 houses (not dorms), is universally adored and is home to 98 percent of students. "The house system builds strong community, and each house has its own traditions," a student explains. Each house accommodates from 10 to 100 students and functions as a self-governing unit, responsible for everything from visiting hours to weekend parties and concerts. The atmosphere is less that of a sorority than of an extended family. Classes are mixed in each house, and first-year students easily mingle with seniors. Alternative options include food cooperatives, language-themed housing, and an apartment complex. There are several dining locations on campus open at specific times for breakfast, lunch, and dinner on the weekdays and brunch and dinner on the weekends, and the food gets good reviews. Some houses even have family-style Thursday dinners to which students invite faculty members.

You will not be greeted with a rocking social scene at Smith, but there are plenty of parties to be had and great places to visit. "The student organizations on campus are pretty good at organizing events like movie nights and sundae parties," says a senior. The five-college system sponsors a free bus service that runs to the other four campuses of the consortium, which offer a broad range of social and cultural

> "Northampton is one of my favorite places."

opportunities. Students say the alcohol policies are getting stricter, and IDs are checked and hands are stamped at campus parties. Smith also offers time-honored traditions like Mountain Day in the fall, when the president cancels class for a day of hiking and bonding, complete with brown-bag lunches.

Northampton is a college town of about 30,000 that is known for its freewheeling culture and funky bohemianism. The town is home to multiple subcultures and is generally tolerant of everyone. "Northampton is one of my favorite places," says a senior. "It's small and artsy, has multiple venues for music and dance, a dance club, bowling alley, and a lot of great restaurants. There is never a lack of nightlife." The Jandon Center for Community Engagement assists student volunteers with finding long-term placements and short-term projects in Northampton, the surrounding communities, and on campus. The New England countryside has numerous special charms, including ski slopes only an hour away. The best road trips are to Boston (two hours) or New York City (three hours).

Smith has a long tradition of success in Division III athletics; the college was the first women's college to join the NCAA and still places a premium on recruiting strong athletes. The Pioneer crew, basketball, soccer, and field hockey teams are competitive in the New England Women's and Men's Athletic Conference. Smith's multimillion-dollar sports complex features indoor tennis and track facilities and a six-lane swimming pool. Interhouse competitions include everything from kickball and inner-tube water polo to rugby.

"It can be hard to adapt to the environment of a women's college," acknowledges one senior. "But it's been the most valuable thing I've ever done." The spirit of the college's founder, Sophia Smith, lives on at this eclectic, open-minded institution where women don lab coats, power suits, combat boots, and even white dresses at graduation. This "community of close, intelligent, interesting, and compassionate women" readies them to be and do just about anything.

If You Apply To ›

Smith: Early decision I and II, regular decision. SATs or ACTs: optional. Accepts the Common Application with supplement. Accepts applications from students whose birth certificates reflect their gender as female or who identify as female.

University of the South (Sewanee)

735 University Avenue, Sewanee, TN 37383

Easily mistaken for an Oxford or a Cambridge plunked down in the highlands of Tennessee. Traditions loom large at Sewanee, including its honor code and ties to the Episcopal Church. Long known as a force in Southern literature, Sewanee is also strong in environmental studies and economics and encourages study abroad. Trying to move beyond its image as an old, Southern college, but diversity remains a challenge. If you have a horse, bring it along.

The University of the South, known affectionately as Sewanee, was founded in 1857 when a group of southern Episcopal bishops saw the need for a distinguished center of learning in the region. After a hiatus brought on by the Civil War, it opened its doors in 1868 with the financial backing of Anglican parishes in England and a starter library donated by Oxford and Cambridge. Traditions thrive—academic gowns are sartorially chic, and the two semesters are Advent and Easter—even as the university works to modernize.

Sewanee—a name of indeterminate Native American origin most likely tied to its geography—is located atop Tennessee's Cumberland Plateau, between Chattanooga and Nashville. The atmosphere is like "attending Oxford in England," a first-year student says, "only with mountains!" Stately English Gothic buildings are carved from beige-and-pink sandstone native to the region, and each has plenty of space, as the school spreads out over a 13,000-acre forested plot fondly known as "the Domain." Particularly noteworthy structures are St. Luke's Chapel and All Saints' Chapel and Convocation Hall, built in 1886.

As part of Sewanee's general education program, students pursue seven learning objectives in their first two years: Reading Closely, Understanding the Arts, Seeking Meaning, Exploring Past and Present, Observing and Experimenting, Cross-Cultural Comprehension, and Encountering Perspectives. The First-Year Experience program includes early exploration of campus opportunities, completion of a general education course, and a weekly seminar focused on transitioning to college. All students take a writing-intensive course, and must complete a capstone experience, which may include a traditional comprehensive exam, a project, research presentation, or a performance.

> "My fellow students are driven, kind, outdoorsy, and fun-loving."

Psychology, economics, English, and biology are the most popular majors, along with international and global studies, an interdisciplinary program with faculty from 14 departments. The strength of Sewanee's English department is nationally recognized, thanks in part to a bequest from playwright Tennessee Williams. The Sewanee Review—the oldest continuously published literary quarterly in the United States—and the Sewanee Writers' Conference enhance the department's reputation, as does a new major in creative writing. The sciences are strong, especially the many forms of environmental studies, given the campus's rich natural setting. The Integrated Program in the Environment encompasses six majors and six minors that incorporate coursework in the natural and social sciences, humanities, and fine arts. Prehealth and preprofessional programs are highly regarded; students applying to medical, dental, and veterinary schools enjoy high acceptance rates. Although Sewanee does not offer a business major, its economics and finance majors can be paired with a prebusiness program that offers special experiential learning opportunities and a business minor with finance, managerial, and international tracks.

Students report that the coursework is challenging and intensive, but the atmosphere breeds camaraderie. "Students will frequently hole up in the library or in a classroom together studying for tests or writing essays," explains a sophomore. Sixty-six percent of courses enroll fewer than 20 students, and the faculty receives rave reviews. "The professors here are top-notch and have absolutely made my experience," cheers a politics major. Most professors wear black academic gowns in the classroom and beyond, as do many members of Sewanee's signature honor society, the Order of the Gown. "People wear gowns around sometimes," concurs a junior. Sewanee also takes its honor code very seriously. Violations—such as lying, cheating, or stealing—usually result in suspension. Sewanee is "steeped in tradition that almost all students abide by, no matter how archaic," a sophomore says.

The Sewanee Pledge initiative promises three benefits to all undergraduates: funding for a summer internship or research opportunity, access to a semester-long study abroad program at no additional tuition cost, and a graduation guarantee that provides an additional year of study tuition-free to students who are unable to complete a single major within four years.

> "Many students [are] actively involved in social justice and progressive causes."

Overall, 45 percent of students study abroad in their choice of more than 400 approved programs; the Sewanee Semester in Spain and short-term summer programs tend to draw the most interest.

"My fellow students are driven, kind, outdoorsy, and fun-loving," describes a senior. Twenty-four percent of Sewanee's students are Tennessee natives, though many of the rest come from the Southeast; 4 percent are international. As a school in

(continued)

Student Loans: 43%
Average Debt: $ $ $
Applicants: 4,703
Accepted: 57%
Enrolled: 18%
Grad in 6 Years: 80%
Returning First-years: 89%
Academics: ✍ ✍ ✍ ✍
Social: 🗩 🗩 🗩
Q of L: ★ ★ ★ ★
Admissions: (800) 522-2234
Email Address:
  admiss@sewanee.edu

Strong Programs:
Creative Writing
Economics
English
Environmental Studies
International and Global
  Studies
Politics
Prehealth
Psychology

The Sewanee Outing Program sponsors outdoor adventures like caving, kayaking, and mountaineering.

the South, the atmosphere can be quite familial—almost a quarter of entering first-years are legacies. Still, one senior argues, Sewanee students are not simply a "large group of privileged preps." One student calls it "weird and goofy, like a productive summer camp." The student body is 18 percent Episcopalian and overwhelmingly Christian, although students of all faiths are welcomed. Students of color have a small presence on campus, with Black students making up 4 percent of the student body, Asian Americans 1 percent, Hispanics/Latinos 5 percent, and multiracial students 3 percent. "Sewanee's student body generally leans very liberal, with many students actively involved in social justice and progressive causes," says one senior. Each year, the school hands out merit scholarships averaging $26,700, and socioeconomic diversity is gradually rising.

Virtually all Sewanee students live in the residence halls, and students report that while the quality of the facilities varies, the community atmosphere is tight-knit and welcoming. "What's most cool is we have theme houses, which allow students to live with people with similar interests," cheers a junior. McClurg Dining Hall serves a wide variety of food and accommodates students' requests. Life on the Mountain is peaceful and "students most always feel safe and secure," according to one junior. Students receive training in alcohol and sexual misconduct intervention strategies, and for mental health care, "CAPS (Counseling and Psychological Services) provides support, including specialized options like grief groups, and serves as an additional advocate for student's well-being," says an economics major.

Fraternities and sororities are a big deal here, with a substantial majority of students—52 percent of the men and 65 percent of the women—signing up. The

"Essentially, [Sewanee is] a magical castle in the forest where everyone knows each other."

university enforces an open-door policy for on-campus events, which makes Greek parties more inclusive. "Greek life rules the social scene, but university-funded programs help keep life from becoming one long frat-a-thon," remarks a student. Drinking is a fact of life, but a sophomore reports that with a medical amnesty policy and other measures, "the main focus is safety." Annual Fall and Spring Party weekends draw alumni and friends back to campus, and students also enjoy the Perpetual Motion dance performances and Sewaneroo music festival. Popular road trips include Atlanta, Nashville, and Chattanooga, so it helps to have a car. Nearby lakes, waterfalls, and caverns also offer rafting, hiking, camping, and other active day trips.

Varsity sports are popular at Sewanee, where the Tigers compete in Division III. Football is probably the favorite sport on campus—games are important social events. While a once-popular cheer dating to the 1890s ("Tigers, Tigers, leave 'em in the lurch. Down with the heathens and up with the Church. Yea, Sewanee's Right!") isn't often heard at games nowadays, the YSR abbreviation ("Yea, Sewanee's right!") persists, usually being shouted at the end of the school's alma mater and other moments that call for a burst of school spirit. "The Sewanee-Rhodes rivalry is one of the most exciting traditions on campus and spans all sports," cheers a senior. The men's and women's tennis teams dominate the Southern Athletic Association, each winning the conference title every year in which they have competed, and men's and women's golf, men's and women's lacrosse, and soccer have also been successful. The equestrian team regularly ranks among the top teams in the country. About a third of students join intramurals, club sports, or the Sewanee Outing Program, which sponsors outdoor adventures like caving, kayaking, and mountaineering.

Sewanee's small size offers students plenty of opportunity to really make a difference. The rich traditions tap into the university's long history and give the campus a life and personality all its own. "Essentially, [it's] a magical castle in the forest where everyone knows each other. We call it 'The Hogwarts of the South' for a reason," says a happy English major. "There's a strong sense of belonging here, cultivated through shared experiences, traditions, and a campus culture that blends the whimsical and the intellectual."

University of South Carolina

Columbia, SC 29208

Among public flagship universities in the South, USC struggles against the image of being one giant step behind UNC at Chapel Hill. The university boasts one of the top international business programs in the nation. Criminal justice is also a specialty. Unlike Clemson, USC is in a major city. Check out the Honors College, which is one of the best anywhere.

Whether it's football or international business, students at the University of South Carolina are game—after all, they're the Gamecocks, and like their mascot, they've got plenty of fighting spirit. Students love to cheer on the school's football and basketball teams, especially if the opponent is longtime rival Clemson. South Carolina is working hard to give its campus a more cosmopolitan feel through academic programs with a strong global focus and initiatives such as the Student Council on Diversity and Inclusion.

South Carolina's main campus is located in the heart of Columbia (population 145,000), which also happens to be the state capital. Government buildings and downtown businesses are within an easy walk, allowing students to secure internships or even part-time jobs during the school year. The old section of the campus, which dates to the school's 1801 founding, includes the glorious oak-lined Horseshoe; 10 of its 19th-century buildings are now listed in the National Register of Historic Places. The $250 million Innovista complex integrates public and private sector research in high-tech facilities. The massive, $210 million Campus Village complex houses 1,800 students, a dining facility, and academic support spaces.

Regardless of the program in which they enroll, students must complete the Carolina Core, a series of distribution requirements that includes courses in problem solving, writing, foreign language, global citizenship and multicultural understanding, and scientific literacy (among others). USC has been a national leader in developing initiatives to support the first-year transition, such as the required three-hour University 101 seminar.

> **"The courses are challenging and the environment is laid-back."**

According to one student, University 101 is "an incredible class. You learn about student skills, time management, all the resources at USC, and have a ton of fun." To build community, there's the First-Year Reading Experience, in which entering students read the same book before coming to campus, then discuss it in small groups upon arrival.

South Carolina offers a slew of undergraduate degree programs; business is the most popular, followed by majors in health professions, biological sciences, psychology, engineering, and communication/journalism. With South Carolina's coastal economy depending on foreign trade, the university has developed a top-notch

Website: www.sc.edu
Location: City Center
Public
Total Enrollment: 34,677
Undergraduates: 29,015
Male/Female: 40/60
Financial Aid: 63%
Pell Grant: 19%
Expense: Pub $ $ $
Student Loans: 53%
Average Debt: $ $ $
Applicants: 52,703
Accepted: 60%
Enrolled: 23%
Grad in 6 Years: 79%
Returning First-years: 92%
Academics: ✑ ✑ ✑
Social: 🗩 🗩 🗩
Q of L: ★ ★ ★
Admissions: (803) 777-7700
Email Address: admissions-ugrad@sc.edu

Strong Programs:
Biological Sciences
Criminal Justice
Exercise Science
Global Studies
International Business
International Studies
Nursing
Psychology

international business program, as well as notable majors in international studies and global studies. Students in the journalism and mass communications program benefit from an excellent film library right on campus, while budding marine scientists may study and do research at a 17,000-acre facility about three hours away. Art students, neglected at many universities, here have access to the latest cameras, editing stations, and computers, as well as pottery kilns and other necessary equipment. Musicians enjoy a four-level building with a music and performance library, rehearsal rooms, recording studios, and a 250-seat lecture hall. The English program benefits from sizable collections of research material on F. Scott Fitzgerald and Ernest Hemingway. An unusual minor in medical humanities gives doctors-to-be an introduction to the ethical, cultural, legal, economic, and political factors that affect medical practice today.

"For the most part, the courses are challenging and the environment is laid-back," says one senior. A classmate adds, "Students share notes, study together, and help out others." Thirty-four percent of undergraduate classes have fewer than 20 students, and the quality of teaching is generally high: "All my professors are passionate about what they teach and do a great job of sharing their passion with us," one student says. Unlike many honors programs that focus on lower-division education, USC's Honors College provides curricular and research opportunities across all four years. About 600 courses are available annually through the Honors College, which serves more than 2,000 students. Nineteen percent of undergraduates study, intern, volunteer, or conduct independent research abroad, taking advantage of programs offered in more than 60 different countries.

USC draws students from all 50 states and more than 100 countries; 60 percent of undergrads are in-staters and 1 percent are international. Ten percent of students are Black, 4 percent are Asian American, 7 percent are Hispanic/Latino, and 4 percent are multiracial. "It is the norm to be involved with at least two or three student organizations and to be very active on campus," says one student. Another cites education funding and LGBTQ rights as hot-button issues. The university awards merit scholarships averaging $4,800 as well as athletic scholarships. The Gamecock Guarantee promises to cover tuition and fees for low-income South Carolina residents who are the first in their family to attend college.

"Most social life takes place off campus."

All first-year students live on campus in nearly two dozen living/learning communities, ranging from academic fields like business and engineering to special interests like sustainability and leadership. "I loved living on campus," recalls one junior. "It was so easy to walk to class from my residence hall." After the first year, housing can be expensive and difficult to get, students say, and only 29 percent of all undergrads reside on campus. Dining options range from fast-food stands to all-you-can-eat lines, with plenty of vegetarian and healthy choices—and, of course, some junk food, too. "You will never go hungry," promises one student. Students report feeling safe while roaming campus.

"Most social life takes place off campus," says a psychology major. "We have cool bars and restaurants close to campus that are geared toward younger people." Thirty percent of South Carolina's men and 36 percent of the women go Greek, and their chapters provide much of the weekend social life on campus. Despite school policies, some underage students "sneak [alcohol] in and are not bothered if they behave themselves," says a speech/language pathology major. Still, concerned about binge and underage drinking, administrators have increased funding for alternative activities, such as films, dance performances, theatrical productions, concerts, and comedy shows. And with more than 400 student groups on campus, everyone should be able to find a niche. Downtown Columbia offers more theaters, a comedy club, a performing arts center, and Five Points, a strip boasting several bars. Outdoorsy types appreciate the beaches an hour and a half away, as well as the mountain ranges four hours north for hiking, skiing, and camping.

Fall football weekends are always a big deal at South Carolina, which competes in the Division I Southeastern Conference. The enduring rivalry with the Clemson Tigers is one of the oldest and most colorful in college sports, with festivities beginning weeks in advance; their annual game (the Palmetto Bowl) has been played for more than a century. "We do an annual Tiger Burn, where the engineering students build a 30-foot-tall tiger and burn it to the ground before the big game," says one Gamecock. "That's really fun!" Winter weekends welcome another of USC's strong sports, basketball, played in the 342,000-square-foot Colonial Center. The women's basketball team has been a perennial powerhouse, bringing home numerous SEC championships and the national title in 2024. USC's baseball and women's golf, soccer, and softball teams are competitive, too. Students can also choose from dozens of club and intramural sports or dip into the indoor and outdoor pools at the Strom Thurmond Fitness and Wellness Center, which features an indoor track, basketball and racquetball courts, and a climbing wall.

School spirit remains as strong as ever at South Carolina's flagship university, but the pace of change is picking up. Yet even as its academic focus grows increasingly global, USC has a more personal feel than many state universities, thanks to its special emphasis on student support and diversity of all types. Perhaps that's why Gamecocks say no place could be finer.

> **"We do an annual Tiger Burn, where the engineering students build a 30-foot-tall tiger and burn it to the ground."**

If You Apply To ›

South Carolina: Early action, regular decision. Accepts the Common Application with supplement. Please consult South Carolina's website for the most up-to-date information regarding standardized test requirements.

University of Southern California

University Park, Los Angeles, CA 90089

USC's old handle: "The University of Spoiled Children." USC's new handle: highly selective West Coast university with preeminent programs in cinematic arts and business. The region's only major private university that also has a top football team. L.A.'s answer to NYU with way more Heisman Trophies.

Once dismissed as little more than an academic bastion of privilege and training ground for the Los Angeles corporate community, the University of Southern California has come into its own as a West Coast destination for students seeking the advantages of study in a center for the arts, technology, communication, and international trade. The school's lush campus and prime Los Angeles location have led to a flood of applicants, making it continually tougher to win admission. Students cheer on national championship teams and give high marks to the Trojan alumni network as well. Often accused of being elitist, USC, founded in 1880, continues to populate the next generation of Los Angeles business leaders.

USC's University Park campus has an unmistakably upscale vibe and offers a mix of traditional ivy-covered and modern structures, arranged around fountains

Dining halls offer plenty of options, including an international buffet in the Parkside complex.

and reflecting pools, well shaded from the Southern California sun. Sitting on 226 parklike acres, just minutes from downtown Los Angeles, USC is a veritable urban oasis. Newer additions to campus include the $700 million, 2,700-bed USC Village, a student housing project, as well as a neighborhood revitalization effort that includes eight residential colleges, a Gothic-style dining hall, and two dozen retail stores.

USC's Core Curriculum, aimed at sharpening critical thinking and communication skills, requires nine courses: six general education, two intensive writing, and one diversity. Students with high GPAs and test scores may choose the Thematic Option—a.k.a. the "Traumatic Option"—in place of regular general education courses. The 200 or so who do get smaller classes with some of the university's best teachers and a handpicked group of writing instructors. First-years may also join one of the school's Learning Communities, groups of 20 students with common academic interests, such as business, medicine, technology, or languages. Each community takes four common courses during the first year and meets with a dedicated faculty mentor and staff advisor three to six times a semester. The First Generation Plus Student Success Center serves as a resource hub supporting first-generation, undocumented, former foster youth, and transfer students.

USC offers undergraduates the chance to pursue degrees not only in the Dornsife College of Letters, Arts, and Sciences, but also at any of its 20 professional schools and schools of the arts—an advantage that students appreciate. "The flexibility to take classes from different professional schools really highlights the emphasis here on interdisciplinary studies," says a cinema and media studies major. In fact, USC strongly encourages students to pursue double majors or a combination of majors and minors in unrelated academic fields, which means business majors may minor in bioethics, or Russian and art history majors may study the music industry or business too. Majors in business, social sciences, visual and performing arts, engineering, and communication are strong and enroll the most students. The cinematic arts, film, and television production major is first-rate, and architecture is highly regarded. The progressive degree program allows students to apply to a master's-level program during their junior year; depending on the field, one can earn a bachelor's and master's degree in as little as 10 semesters.

> "My professors . . . are normally my first line of defense when I need advice."

The academic climate is challenging, and students report that while there is some "friendly competition," their classmates are mostly supportive of each other. Sixty-one percent of undergraduate classes enroll fewer than 20 students, but the quality of teaching varies, especially in some introductory courses for first-years, which can be huge. Advising and career services get mixed reviews. An English major says, "My biggest support system at USC has been my professors, and they are normally my first line of defense when I need advice." The Discovery Scholars program honors original research and creativity among undergraduates, and the Global Scholars program singles out students who excel both at home and abroad. USC offers more than 50 semester- and yearlong study abroad programs in nearly 30 countries in addition to several short-term options offered during summer and winter breaks and the May term.

USC students are perhaps best characterized by a sense of "ambitious drive," says one senior. Most pride themselves on their ability to maintain decent grades along with an active social life. Sixty-two percent of USC undergrads come from within the state, and 13 percent come from foreign countries. This left-leaning campus is racially diverse, with Black students making up 7 percent of the student body, Hispanics/Latinos 23 percent, Asian Americans 23 percent, and multiracial students 6 percent. Hundreds of merit scholarships, averaging $19,200, are awarded each year, as are more than 100 athletic awards. USC also meets 100 percent of students' demonstrated financial need and is need-blind

> "The entire Los Angeles area is full of fun things to do."

in its admissions. Undergraduates from families with annual incomes of $80,000 or less qualify for free tuition.

Thirty-six percent of USC undergrads live on campus. All first-year students are housed in residential colleges, which are led by faculty masters in residence and serve as a hub for social life. Since swimming pools, tennis courts, carpeting, microwaves, refrigerators, and air-conditioning are just some of the luxuries to be found in USC dorms, not to mention the USC Village, it's no wonder more upperclassmen would like to stay on campus. But because there isn't enough space for everyone, students typically move after their first year to fraternity and sorority houses or apartments, which are just a short walk away. Dining halls offer plenty of options, including an international buffet in the Parkside complex. Some nearby areas are rather rough, but thanks to USC's police department, which regularly patrols the campus and surrounding neighborhood, most students say they've never felt unsafe. "USC has made sure that, with regard to sexual assault, all students know where to seek help and access tools to deal with this issue," notes a senior.

The on-campus social scene revolves around activities organized by student clubs, fraternity parties on "The Row," sporting events, the annual Springfest concert, and the Los Angeles Times Festival of Books in the spring. A modest portion of students go Greek. Several fraternities have severed ties with the university following the enactment of new rules imposed in the wake of a series of sexual assault accusations stemming from fraternity parties. Though L.A. is hardly a college town in any traditional sense, it does offer an endless variety of bars, clubs, shopping, and cultural experiences. As a junior points out, "The entire Los Angeles area is full of fun things to do if you're willing to hop on a train or take an Uber." Whether you're looking for an internship at a law firm or a movie studio, you want to learn to surf, or you're eager to check out a new band before they get signed to a major label, L.A. delivers. Famous Venice Beach is just a few miles from USC's campus, and in the winter months, students can reach the San Gabriel Mountains (and its ski resorts) in less than an hour (by car, not by skis). USC students are also active in the community, tutoring in 10 local schools through the Joint Educational Project.

"We are drawing an academically competitive and involved student body."

Now in the Big Ten Conference, USC's Trojan athletics teams have won many national championships, including men's indoor track and field in 2025. Women's beach volleyball, golf, and basketball and men's water polo are also competitive. Two of USC's biggest schoolwide traditions center on the ol' pigskin. The first is Troy Week—the week leading up to the UCLA game—which culminates with the Conquest pep rally and concert in the middle of campus. Then there's the Weekender, when USC students take off en masse for northern California to see their beloved Trojans face off against Stanford or Berkeley. Throngs of USC undergrads, alumni, and fans gather in San Francisco's Union Square for a huge pep rally featuring the band, cheerleaders, and university personalities.

USC is a university on the move, though its progress has recently been marred by well-publicized scandals involving athletics, admissions, and sexual abuse. "We are drawing an academically competitive and involved student body," says a geography and communication major. Pack your sunscreen, flip-flops, and some assertiveness, and you'll fit right in. Shrinking violets, on the other hand, should probably look elsewhere.

Overlaps

Boston University, UC Berkeley, UCLA, UC San Diego, Cornell University, NYU, Northwestern, Stanford

If You Apply To ›

USC: Early action, regular decision. SATs or ACTs: optional. Accepts the Common Application.

Southern Methodist University

6425 Boaz Lane, Dallas, TX 75205

SMU is best known for business, the performing arts, and an abundance of school spirit. Go-getter mentality is pervasive, and students benefit from internships and other opportunities in nearby Dallas. Picture-book campus five miles from downtown adds to its appeal. Methodist, but mainly in name.

Website: www.smu.edu
Location: City Outskirts
Private
Total Enrollment: 9,662
Undergraduates: 7,145
Male/Female: 49/51
Financial Aid: 72%
Pell Grant: 9%
Expense: Pr $ $
Student Loans: 29%
Average Debt: $ $ $ $
Applicants: 15,245
Accepted: 63%
Enrolled: 18%
Grad in 6 Years: 84%
Returning First-years: 91%
Academics: ✍ ✍ ✍
Social: 🍷 🍷 🍷
Q of L: ★ ★ ★ ★
Admissions: (800) 323-0672
Email Address:
  ugadmission@smu.edu

Strong Programs:
Biology
Business
Economics
Engineering
English
Finance
History
Visual and Performing Arts

Southern Methodist University is looking beyond its long-standing characterization as a training ground for the business elite of Dallas. Admissions standards are on the rise, and recent years have brought an updated curriculum that emphasizes interdisciplinary study, a new residential model, and, in the words of one senior, "tons of new campus buildings." The highly regarded Cox School of Business sets the no-nonsense tone for SMU's success-driven academic climate. Although founded in 1911 by what is now the United Methodist Church, SMU is nondenominational; 12 percent of students are Methodist, and all faiths are welcomed.

SMU's well-landscaped campus is situated in the suburb of University Park, located "five minutes from downtown Dallas and within 30 minutes of everything else," according to one student. Flower beds, fountains, and neatly trimmed lawns surround stately brick buildings, most of them collegiate Georgian. Dallas Hall, with its four-story rotunda, is the centerpiece. The Meadows Museum houses one of the finest collections of Spanish art outside Spain, and SMU is the only private college in the country to host a presidential library on its main campus, the George W. Bush Presidential Center. The Ford Hall for Research and Innovation serves as an interdisciplinary research hub for faculty, students, and industry partners to collaborate on complex problems.

The Common Curriculum combines coursework in a range of disciplines with hands-on experiences and is designed to prepare students to be flexible, lifelong learners. Required courses include writing, critical reasoning, quantitative reasoning, and a variety of arts and sciences "breadth" courses. Students say they find ample time to explore their interests. "There is a lot of room to double or even triple major," explains a biology and math major. The Office of Engaged Learning supports students who wish to undertake capstone-level projects on campus or abroad, such as extended research, service projects, internships, and entrepreneurial start-ups; participants can apply for fellowships of up to $2,000.

> **"Some of my professors have practically been my life coaches."**

Students hail the Cox School of Business (including its Caruth Institute for Entrepreneurship) and the Meadows School of the Arts, which turns out professional artists, actors, singers, and dancers, as SMU's strongest suits. Some of the most popular fields of study are finance, economics, biology, accounting, and applied physiology and sport management, an interdisciplinary program that teaches the biological basis of health while offering the business skills needed in the health and fitness industries. Engineers have access to top-of-the-line research labs and an extensive co-op program thanks to the proximity of hundreds of high-tech companies, including AT&T and Texas Instruments. The Tower Center for Political Studies focuses on international relations and comparative politics, while the Tate Lecture Series gives students a chance to interact with national and international figures, such as Smithsonian Institution leader Lonnie G. Bunch III, *New York Times* columnist David Brooks, and award-winning actor and activist Marlee Matlin. As for the humanities, English and history are particularly strong, and SMU publishes *Southwest Review*, the third-oldest continuously published literary quarterly in the nation. Communications and journalism are popular majors. SMU was the first university in the South to offer a major in human rights.

SMU prides itself on small classes; 54 percent of undergraduate courses have fewer than 20 students. "Some of my professors have practically been my life coaches," says an advertising major. "They've helped me excel in classes and prepare for interviews. They've provided recommendation letters and answered my emails at two in the morning. They never stop caring for their students." Most classes are taught by full-time faculty, and teaching assistants provide extra help. The student-staffed Altshuler Learning Enhancement Center offers tutoring and workshops.

The top 10 percent of each incoming class is invited to join the University Honors Program, which features small seminars on topics not offered broadly. Study abroad programs take about a quarter of undergrads around the world; faculty-led options are available in 14 locations. Each year, 20 to 25 exceptional incoming students are named President's Scholars and awarded full-tuition scholarships as well as opportunities to study abroad and participate in an annual retreat in Taos. Dallas-area employers also offer thousands of internships and learning opportunities to SMU students yearly.

A marketing major describes SMU students as passionate and driven to succeed, adding, "There's a big go-getter mentality all throughout campus." Forty-six percent of undergraduates are from the Lone Star State, and 4 percent come from outside of the U.S. Diversity among the student population has increased over the past decade, and currently Hispanics/Latinos account for 18 percent of the student body, Asian Americans 8 percent, Black students 5 percent, and multiracial students 5 percent. A senior reports that, politically, there is a "pretty good mix" of views on campus. SMU offers merit scholarships averaging $29,400, as well as roughly 200 athletic scholarships in 17 sports. Just 9 percent of entering first-years qualify for a Pell Grant.

Half of the undergrads live on campus; first- and second-year students are required to live in one of 11 Residential Commons, each of which has a resident faculty member, intended to integrate academic, residential, and social experiences. SMU Service House residents engage in community service in disadvantaged neighborhoods across Dallas. All residence halls are co-ed by floor, and options include single and double rooms, some with their own bathrooms. The traditional, all-you-can-eat meal plans include dining dollars that can be used at the two main dining halls and at on-campus fast-dining options like Chick-fil-A, Sushic, and Panera Bread. "Now that I live off campus, I actually miss the food in the SMU dining halls," says a student. Campus security is said to be strong, and students praise the Not On My Campus campaign aimed at raising awareness of the issue of sexual assault.

When the weekend comes, the more than 200 student groups sponsor speakers and other diversions. "Social life at SMU is vibrant both on and off campus," says a sophomore. Forty-four percent of the women join sororities, and 38 percent of the men pledge fraternities. "Greek organizations have off-campus parties, since SMU is technically a dry campus," notes a senior. Dallas has plenty to offer in terms of social life: "Whether it's exploring the Deep Ellum and Bishop Arts districts or going out in Uptown, we never get bored here," says a management major. Hundreds of students volunteer with more than 70 nonprofits in the greater Dallas area, and service trips over spring break are popular, too. Highlights of the campus calendar include PerunaPalooza, a birthday carnival in honor of the Mustang mascot (a pony). Students mark the end of the fall semester with the Celebration of Lights featuring holiday lights and carols at Dallas Hall. Favorite road trips are to Austin, with its

"There's a big go-getter mentality all throughout campus."

abundance of restaurants, bars, and live music, and South Padre, Texas, a popular spring break spot with a great beach.

Football games are a big deal here—after all, this is Texas—and SMU students get riled up for the annual battle against Texas Christian University for possession of the Iron Skillet. For home games, Mustang fans enjoy one of the best tailgate parties in Texas through Boulevarding, which features family activities, music, and food on the main quad. "Boulevarding on game days is the most fun tailgating experience in the South!" cheers an environmental studies major. When basketball season arrives, students camp out with their friends to get tickets, and "The Mob" spirit group packs into the student section of Moody Coliseum. The SMU Mustangs compete in the Division I Athletic Coast Conference. The equestrian team has brought home national championships. Men's and women's golf and tennis, men's swimming and diving, and women's rowing are recent conference champions. About a third of the students participate each year in club sports and the intramural program, which offers more than 18 individual and team sporting activities.

> "Boulevarding on game days is the most fun tailgating experience in the South!"

"SMU is a relatively small school that has a big school feel," says a senior. "We still have a blast before home football games, we have big parties, and we have incredible school spirit." Although known for its striking campus and success-oriented students, SMU offers solid preprofessional training along with an active social life and ample opportunities to give back to the city of Dallas. The result is an environment where future industry moguls, problem solvers, performers, and artists alike can find space to grow.

Overlaps

Baylor, University of Miami (FL), University of Southern California, UT Austin, Texas Christian, Tulane, Vanderbilt, Wake Forest

If You Apply To ›

Southern Methodist: Early decision I and II, early action, regular decision. SATs or ACTs: optional. Accepts the Common Application with supplement.

Southwestern University

1001 E University Avenue, Georgetown, TX 78626

The oldest institution of higher education in Texas, Southwestern is one of its top liberal arts colleges. Compare to more conservative Austin College and much larger Trinity University. Southwestern prides itself on individual attention and down-to-earth friendliness, with emphasis on interdisciplinary and inquiry-based learning. Participation in the Paideia program adds spice to the learning environment.

Website: www.southwestern.edu
Location: Suburban
Private
Total Enrollment: 1,423
Undergraduates: 1,423
Male/Female: 45/54
Financial Aid: 98%

In a state known for political conservatism and an assumption that bigger is better, Southwestern University stands out like a monadnock. Small and agile, it pursues a flexible and innovative brand of teaching and learning in a culture where the liberal arts are not always appreciated. "You learn to express and defend your opinions," says one student. "I learned how to think."

Founded in 1840, five years before Texas became a state, Southwestern sits on 700 acres at the edge of the rolling Texas Hill Country, although the city of Austin has expanded to meet Georgetown. The Texas limestone buildings, built in the Romanesque style, date from the early 20th century, and there are plenty of lush lawns and towering oak trees. Southwestern's commitment to sustainability includes an agreement with the city of Georgetown that allows it to use 100 percent wind power for the campus's electrical needs. The university has several ongoing renovation and construction projects, including a new, mixed-use first-year residence hall, a welcome center, and more.

To graduate, Southwestern students must complete a First-Year Seminar and satisfy requirements in several liberal arts areas, as well as language and culture, social justice, fitness and recreational activity, and a capstone experience. First-year seminars introduce students to the Paideia program, which gives them a chance to explore interests that may fall outside their major. A sociology and English double major explains, "It's nice to be able to get a taste of how others may see and understand the world in various other disciplines." The university has bolstered academic advising, assigning every incoming student to a professional academic advisor, followed by a faculty or staff advisor after their first year.

The most popular majors are also some of Southwestern's strongest: psychology, communication studies, kinesiology, and business, which is taught as one of the liberal arts. In the Sarofim School of Fine Arts, where pottery is a specialty, student work approaches graduate-level quality. Theatre, environmental studies, and sociology are also strengths. Political science and STEM majors alike benefit from SU's proximity to Austin, the state capital and a hub of tech innovation. Interdisciplinary minors are available in data science, health studies, and design thinking.

"Because class sizes are small, discussions tend to be lively and personal—there's no hiding in the back row," says a psychology and business major. Seventy-one percent of SU classes have fewer than 20 students, and professors are appreciated for their willingness to help students with course concepts and research opportunities. "There's genuine mentorship woven into every course," says a sophomore. Academic support and career services are highly praised as well, from departmental student mentors to the comprehensive resources offered by the Center for Career and Professional Development, including one-on-one counseling, alumni panels, and campuswide internship and job fairs. "I definitely feel prepared for life after college because everything is a process that has been put in motion since I arrived my first semester," says a junior.

SU encourages undergraduate research (about half of the students participate), and each year holds a symposium to showcase students' scholarly endeavors. The King Creativity Fund provides grants to support up to 20 "innovative and visionary projects" each academic year. For study abroad, 27 percent of students take advantage of faculty-led programs in England, Spain, France, and Argentina, among others. The university also sponsors an internship program in Washington, D.C., and an arts apprenticeship program in New York City.

Eighty-seven percent of Southwestern students come from Texas, and many are the first in their families to go to college. "Although there is some cultural diversity," says a sophomore, "many students that belong to minority groups have expressed the difficulties of being a person of color on this campus." Hispanics/Latinos are the largest minority group at SU, making up 30 percent of the student body; Black students add 6 percent, Asian Americans 3 percent, and multiracial students 4 percent. Two percent come from foreign countries. Students describe a sometimes volatile mix of conservative and liberal political views on campus. "The CDSJ (Coalition for Diversity and Social Justice) is a fantastic umbrella organization that has a place for everyone to get involved and be an activist on and off campus," says a computer science major.

> "Because class sizes are small, discussions tend to be lively and personal."

> "There's genuine mentorship woven into every course."

(continued)

Pell Grant: 29%
Expense: Pr $ $
Student Loans: 60%
Average Debt: $ $ $
Applicants: 6,313
Accepted: 43%
Enrolled: 14%
Grad in 6 Years: 73%
Returning First-years: 81%
Academics: ✍ ✍ ✍
Social: 🗩 🗩 🗩
Q of L: ★ ★ ★
Admissions: (512) 863-1200
Email Address:
  admission@southwestern
  .edu

Strong Programs:
Biology
Business
Communication Studies
Environmental Studies
Kinesiology
Psychology
Studio Art

Annual traditions include SING, a talent competition between student organizations.

Eligible students receive scholarships based on academic performance, averaging $28,400 annually; talent awards are also available for fine arts majors, though there are no athletic scholarships.

Three-quarters of SU students live in the residence halls, where the number of stars increases as you get older—juniors and seniors usually get apartment-style facilities with their own bedrooms, bathrooms, and kitchens. Meals at the central, all-you-can-eat Mabee Commons dining hall are getting "somewhat better than they'd been in recent years," according to a senior. Students do enjoy the nearby Cove's coffee bar and late-night grill. Students can also swipe their "Pirate cards" at pizzerias and other local merchants. Students say they generally feel safe on campus, but the administration's handling of sexual assault cases has been a hot-button issue. Mental health counseling gets average reviews.

"Southwestern's social life isn't totally quiet—there is a party scene on campus—but it tends to be smaller and more low-key than what you'll find in Austin," says a sophomore. Almost all the social life at Southwestern takes place on campus, and the school sponsors activities like retro game nights, carnival nights, and free concerts. Southwestern has a strong Greek system, drawing 31 percent of the men and 28 percent of the women, "but you do not have to be Greek to have a fabulous social life," says a sociology major. Students 21 and older are permitted to consume alcohol in designated areas on campus. Annual traditions include SING, a talent competition between student organizations; the spring concert on the mall; and Late Night Breakfast, in which "faculty and staff serve students breakfast during finals week while karaoke and other fun stuff happens!"

Georgetown (population 78,000), the county seat, caters mainly to families, but things are getting more exciting thanks to the expanding bar and restaurant options, weekly farmers markets, and live music on Friday evenings. The city's historic downtown and the popular Blue Hole swimming area are both within walking distance of campus, and students enjoy bike trails along the San Gabriel River. "Georgetown offers a lot of natural beauty," says a communication major. Forty-two percent of students get involved in the community through service learning and volunteer work. The bars and clubs of Austin's Sixth Street are just a half hour away, and San Antonio, College Station, Dallas, and Houston aren't that much farther.

The Southwestern Pirates field 20 Division III varsity sports. The school is a member of the Southern Collegiate Athletic Conference; men's soccer, track and field, golf, and tennis, and women's tennis, soccer, and volleyball are all competitive. Games against archrival Trinity in San Antonio always draw crowds. Fifty-three percent of students compete in intramural and club sports, with flag football, basketball, sand volleyball, and pickleball being among the most popular.

With its emphasis on in-depth and student-centered learning, Southwestern is doing its best to push the frontiers of liberal arts instruction in the 21st century. "Southwestern has a long history and a lot of potential," says an English major. "Students tangibly shape the culture, and you will see your impact if you choose to make one." In a state where things tend to be huge and overwhelming, Southwestern University is out to show that good things can come in small packages.

> **"There is a party scene on campus—but it tends to be smaller and more low-key than what you'll find in Austin."**

If You Apply To ›

Southwestern: Early decision, early action, regular decision. SATs or ACTs: optional. Accepts the Common Application with supplement.

Spelman College: See page 38.

Stanford University

450 Jane Stanford Way, Stanford, CA 94305

If you're looking for an Eastern counterpart to Stanford, think Duke with a touch of MIT mixed in. Stanford's big-time athletics, preprofessional feel, and laid-back atmosphere set it apart from Ivy League competitors. In contrast to the hurly-burly of Bay Area rival Berkeley, Stanford's aura is upscale, spacious, and green. Bring your bike and a pair of sunglasses, and leave your ego behind.

You might think the only difference between Stanford and the Ivy League is a couple hundred extra sunny days each year. You'd be wrong. From the red-tiled roofs to the lush greenery and California vibe, Stanford is a world away from the Gothic intellectual vibes of the Ivies. Virtually all the great Eastern universities began as places to ponder the meaning of life, with European institutions as their models. Stanford, by contrast, built its academic reputation around science and engineering, fields conducive to American ingenuity and industry, and only later cultivated excellence in the humanities and social sciences. In this sense, Stanford is, without a doubt, the nation's first great "American" university. Now one of the most super-selective universities in the country—turning down 24 of every 25 applicants—Stanford has begun to increase the size of its entering classes and intends to expand its dormitories and number of faculty proportionately until it reaches a new comfort level.

The differences between Stanford and other institutions it competes against for the country's top high school seniors are evident everywhere, from the architecture to the curriculum. The school's mission-style buildings look outward to the world at large rather than inward to ivy-covered courtyards. And unlike its Colonial-era predecessors, Stanford—founded in 1885 by railroad magnate and politician Leland Stanford (who drove in the golden spike marking the completion of the first transcontinental railroad across the U.S.) and his wife Jane Stanford in memory of their son Leland Jr.—has been co-ed from the beginning. During its centennial, the school became the first U.S. university to successfully launch a billion-dollar capital campaign; today Stanford's endowment is $36 billion. Some architectural critics say the campus looks like the world's biggest Mexican restaurant, even though Frederick Law Olmsted, designer of New York City's Central Park, planned many of the buildings. The campus stretches from the foothills of the Santa Cruz Mountains to the edge of Palo Alto in the heart of Silicon Valley, smack in the middle of earthquake country. The campus is nationally recognized as "bicycle friendly" and is outfitted with 12 miles of bike lanes, 19,000 bike parking spaces, and free bike repair stations.

Stanford requires first-year students to take two civic, liberal, and global education courses, and then all students complete 11 in a series called Ways of Thinking/ Ways of Doing, which includes aesthetic and interpretive inquiry, social inquiry, scientific analysis, formal reasoning, applied quantitative reasoning, exploring difference and power, ethical reasoning, and creative expression. Stanford also requires writing and rhetoric courses and one year of a foreign language. More than 200

> **"Overall, professors do seem to care about the students."**

Website: www.stanford.edu
Location: Suburban
Private
Total Enrollment: 17,086
Undergraduates: 7,554
Male/Female: 48/52
Financial Aid: 88%
Pell Grant: 16%
Expense: Pr $ $ $
Student Loans: 12%
Average Debt: $ $
Applicants: 57,326
Accepted: 4%
Enrolled: 82%
Grad in 6 Years: 92%
Returning First-years: 98%
Academics: ✍ ✍ ✍ ✍ ✍
Social: 🗩 🗩 🗩 🗩
Q of L: ★ ★ ★ ★ ★
Admissions: (650) 723-2091
Email Address:
admission@stanford.edu

Strong Programs:
Biology
Communication
Computer Science
Earth Systems
Engineering
International Relations
Marine Science
Public Policy

optional, small-group Introductory Seminars are available to first-years and sopho-mores, covering topics like The Data Scientist as Detective and The Global Refugee Crisis; one student credits these courses with helping first-years "develop relation-ships with really engaging professors."

Computer science is the most popular major on campus, followed by human biology, economics, symbolic systems, and engineering, especially mechanical engi-neering. Stanford has developed a spate of interdisciplinary programs, notably inter-national relations, public policy, and earth systems; the latter is an interdisciplinary environmental science major. The Haas Center for Public Service offers more than 130 service-learning courses in a wide range of disciplines, while the well-regarded com-munication department offers paid positions at various California media outlets. The Stanford Hopkins Marine Station is located on a mile of coastland in Pacific Grove, next to the Monterey Bay Aquarium, and offers courses in marine and biological sciences.

Don't let Stanford's California location fool you into thinking studying is optional—it's more like a full-time job. "People are always working together on proj-ects and assignments. This might be because it is intense, and many students do take on a heavy workload," one student says. Stanford's faculty ranks among the best in the nation, with impeccable credentials, and most departments boast a nationally known name or two. Class sizes are generally small, with 70 percent enrolling fewer than 20 students. "Overall, professors do seem to care about the students. They are definitely accessible, almost all having open office hours," says one computer sci-ence major.

For students inclined to study abroad, programs are offered at Stanford's campus in Cape Town, South Africa, as well as several other locations around the globe, including Australia, Chile, Japan, and Germany. Forty-eight percent of each gradu-ating class takes advantage of these programs. Closer to home, the Stanford-in-Washington program allows 60 students to live, study, and intern in the nation's capital each quarter, and a similar program is offered in New York City. The Summer Research College is designed to create community among undergraduates engaged in full-time summer research on campus, and there are three honors programs. Three-quarters of students undertake independent study projects with faculty. For those seeking additional academic support, the Schwab Learning Center—named after alum Charles Schwab of financial services fame—offers services for students with learning disabilities and ADHD.

> **"Junior year, I lived in an old faculty mansion for 30 students that had a Thai chef."**

Stanford students may be Olympic champions and future Rhodes scholars, but students say there isn't a sense of elitism on campus. One notes, "People are a bit quirky, but everyone is generally happy and easy to get along with." Forty-three percent are from California, while international students represent 13 percent of the population. More than half of undergraduates identify as students of color: Asian Americans account for 29 percent, Hispanics/Latinos 17 percent, Black stu-dents 7 percent, and multiracial students 10 percent. Students on this liberal campus are keen to be heard, and recent hot topics include "divestment from Israel, divestment from fossil fuels, and race relations," according to one senior. Admissions are need-blind, and the university guarantees to meet the full demonstrated finan-cial need of every domestic admit. Academic scholarships are based on need (mean-ing no merit awards), attendance is free for students from families with incomes of less than $100,000, and Stanford has lowered parent contributions for families with incomes of less than $150,000. The university also awards hundreds of athletic scholarships every year.

First-years must live on campus, and Stanford guarantees housing for four years; 96 percent of students stay on campus, in part because of the lack of affordable off-campus options in extraordinarily expensive Silicon Valley. As students gain seniority, a lottery system decides where they'll live. "Junior year, I lived in an old faculty mansion for 30 students that had a Thai chef," one student says. The multimillion-dollar Governor's Corner complex includes all-oak fixtures, homey rooms with views of the foothills, microwave ovens in the kitchenettes, and Italian leather sofas in the lounges. Dorm dwellers must sign up for a meal plan. "Campus security is quite good. We have an AlertSU program that texts emergency messages to the school whenever there is any sort of security violation, and Stanford is extremely well-lit at night," says a first-year student.

Like most things at Stanford, social life and activities vary a great deal, although most take place on campus, with a constant lineup of events and performances. Greek organizations claim 21 percent of the men and 25 percent of the women and provide their share of happy hours and weekend bashes, which are open to all. Underage drinking happens but is kept under control. As one first-year puts it, "Party culture is not exclusively Greek, and social life is not exclusively partying." As tradition goes, Full Moon on the Quad occurs at the first full moon of the fall quarter, during which first-years can become "true Stanford students" by kissing a senior at midnight on the quad. The Viennese Ball is a February event that may make you wish you'd taken ballroom dancing lessons, and Halloween finds students partying at the Mausoleum, the Stanfords' final resting place.

Palo Alto "has a few fun hangouts and is slightly overpriced," a political science major says, and students love to seek refuge in the outdoors—nearby hills are perfect for jogging and biking. Trips to the Sierra Nevada mountains (four hours away) or to the Pacific Coast (45 minutes) are popular, as are jaunts to San Francisco, Los Angeles, or the Napa Valley.

The Stanford Cardinals have a proud athletic tradition that has made it a perennial winner of the Division I Directors' Cup, which recognizes the best overall collegiate athletic program in the country. Men's gymnastics and women's water polo, rowing, and golf and sailing have won have won national titles in the past two years. The baseball team has been to the College World Series, and the football team has become a powerhouse. Men's water polo and women's volleyball, swimming, and diving are also standouts—the school has been a perennial source of Olympic-level swimmers. The annual contest against Pac-12 archrival Cal (Berkeley) is dubbed the "Big Game." The marching band proudly revels in its raucous irreverence, to the delight of students and the dismay of conservative types. For those not drawn to varsity play, Stanford offers more than 30 club sports and intramural activities, and its vast sports complex includes 26 tennis courts, two gymnasiums, a stadium, an 18-hole golf course, and four swimming pools.

Stanford University's sunny demeanor and infectious West Coast optimism offer an appealing alternative to the gloom and gray weather that seem to hang over some of its East Coast counterparts, with the same high-caliber academics and deep athletic traditions that have made them great.

> **"[Palo Alto] has a few fun hangouts and is slightly overpriced."**

If You Apply To ›

Stanford: Single choice early action, regular decision. SATs or ACTs: required. Accepts the Common Application with supplement.

State University of New York

As the second-largest comprehensive university system in the country (after its California State counterpart), the State University of New York provides its 387,000 students with a lavish buffet of educational opportunities, from optometry, fashion, and ceramics to space-age Ph.D.s in nanoscale engineering and everything in between.

The statistics of SUNY (pronounced "SOOney") are awesome. SUNY has an annual operating budget of billions, greater than the gross national product of many countries and larger than the budget of more than a dozen American states. The system encompasses 64 campuses across New York and 21,000 acres of property. It has some 340,000 undergraduates, offers more than 4,350 undergraduate majors, and employs 29,000 faculty members. Every year SUNY's colleges and universities award about 84,000 degrees (66,000 of them to undergraduates), ranging from associate's to Ph.D.s in thousands of academic fields. And it boasts nearly three million living alumni.

Not only does this scale and breadth make SUNY a microcosm of all that American higher education has to offer, but its universities have long been among the most affordable in the U.S. Under New York State's Excelsior Scholarship program, the first of its kind in the country, in-state students from households earning up to $125,000 qualify for reduced tuition at any of the state's two- and four-year institutions.

These statistics are even more remarkable considering that until 1948, the State of New York had no state university at all. That year, the legislature created the State University of New York around a cluster of 29 institutions, the best of which focused on the training of teachers, to handle the flow of returning World War II veterans. A "gentleman's agreement" not to compete with the state's private colleges, which for generations had enjoyed a monopoly on higher education in New York, hindered SUNY's movement into the liberal arts. Not until Nelson A. Rockefeller became governor in 1960, and made higher education expansion a priority, did the State University begin its dramatic growth.

SUNY has since evolved into a vast knowledge network consisting of 14 University Centers and doctorate-granting institutions (think research universities, medical schools, specialized colleges of environmental science and veterinary medicine, and the like); 13 four-year Arts and Sciences Colleges (think liberal arts institutions, offering both undergraduate and graduate programs); seven Technology Colleges, offering both two- and four-year degrees in specialized fields; and 30 locally sponsored Community Colleges.

Consistent with this ambitious enterprise, system leaders have made a concerted effort to recognize and enhance student diversity and to make students of all backgrounds feel welcome. The Office of Diversity, Equity, and Inclusion has helped increase enrollment of students of color. Slightly less than half of the student body—48 percent—continues to be white. Seventeen percent of students are Hispanic/Latino, 11 percent are Black, 9 percent are Asian American, and 3 percent are multiracial. Women account for 56 percent of undergraduates. SUNY has launched numerous initiatives to increase retention and graduation rates among underrepresented students and is now turning its attention to faculty—to the support of historically underrepresented faculty of color in general and of female faculty of all races in STEM fields. SUNY's definition of diversity is sweeping and covers not only race and ethnicity but also religion, sexual orientation, gender identity and expression, age, and socio-economic status. Like many other institutions of higher learning in the U.S., SUNY has also come under scrutiny from the Trump administration and has lost roughly $32 million dollars in federal grant funding, but SUNY's chancellor has stated that the school will continue to stand by its DEI initiatives.

Prospective students apply to SUNY via the system's ApplySUNY portal or the Common App, selecting the campuses where they wish to be considered. Levels of selectivity inevitably vary widely across an institutional network of this size: most SUNY Community Colleges operate on an open-enrollment basis, while SUNY's "U-centers" and specialized programs are among the most competitive public institutions in the nation. Students who earn associate's degrees in a two-year SUNY program are guaranteed the chance to continue their education at a four-year institution (though not necessarily at their first choice). In-state undergraduates pay the same tuition at all SUNY institutions and comparable, if varying, fees. Rates at the Community Colleges are lower and vary. For the roughly 14,000 out-of-state students, who make up 7 percent of the student body, tuition and fees at a SUNY school currently run between $11,000 and $19,600, depending on the type of institution—well within range of other leading public flagships such as UC Berkeley and the University of Michigan.

Mainly for political reasons, the State University of New York chose not to follow the model of other states and build a single, flagship campus like an Austin or a Chapel Hill. Instead, it created four University Centers with undergraduate, graduate, and professional schools—one in each corner of the state. Although each of them considers itself to be a comprehensive university, there has been a certain degree of specialization from the beginning: Albany is strongest in education and public policy, Binghamton is best known for undergraduate arts and sciences, Stony Brook is noted for its hard sciences, and Buffalo maintains a strong reputation in the life sciences and geography. Both Stony Brook and Buffalo are designated by the state as joint flagships of the SUNY system. Critics charge that the decision to forgo a dominant flagship campus for so many decades has diminished SUNY's chances of achieving national prominence, and that the lack of big-time, Division I football and famous Ph.D. programs has affected its reputation. That said, others maintain that somewhere in the labs and libraries of these public powerhouses are lurking the Nobel Prize winners of this century.

SUNY's 13 Arts and Sciences Colleges vary in size and character. Many were founded historically as teachers' colleges and have successfully made the transition into public liberal arts colleges on the small, New England model. They range from Potsdam, the northernmost SUNY campus and one of the oldest colleges in the United States, to Purchase, a suburban campus in Westchester County that specializes in the visual and performing arts, to Old Westbury on Long Island, which began as an experimental institution to serve minority students, older women, and others who had been "bypassed" by more traditional institutions.

The seven Technology Colleges lack the academic prominence of their Arts and Sciences peers, but they play a key role in serving state and regional demand for vocational training by delivering a wide variety of two- and four-year programs. Five of them (Alfred State, Canton, Cobleskill, Delhi, and Morrisville) are concerned primarily with agriculture but also have programs in engineering, nursing, medical technology, data processing, and business administration. Farmingdale offers an extensive range of programs, from ornamental horticulture to aerospace technology. Maritime, founded in 1874, is the oldest maritime academy in the United States.

A little-known feature of the SUNY system is that five of its state-funded programs are lodged in private institutions—four at Cornell University (agriculture and life sciences, human ecology, industrial and labor relations, and veterinary medicine) and one at Alfred University (ceramics). Even though they are attending a private institution, students in these programs pay much lower SUNY-level tuition rates.

Like their peers around the country, SUNY's 30 Community Colleges have traditionally enjoyed a lower profile, but a growing emphasis on vocationalism and the soaring costs of higher education have brought them back into favor. It used to be that students looked to New York's Community Colleges for terminal degrees that could readily apply to the marketplace. Now, an increasing number of students who otherwise would have been packed off to a four-year college are saving money by staying home for the first two years and then transferring within the SUNY system to a four-year college—or even a University Center—to get their bachelor's degrees. More than half of SUNY's Community Colleges offer on-campus housing.

Following are full-length descriptions of SUNY's four University Centers (the University at Albany, Binghamton University, the University at Buffalo, and Stony Brook University) as well as two of the Arts and Sciences Colleges best known beyond New York's borders (Purchase College and the College at Geneseo).

SUNY–University at Albany

1400 Washington Avenue, Albany, NY 12222

Like the rest of the SUNY system, University at Albany is much better than its relative anonymity would suggest. Strong in anything related to public policy, including criminal justice and social welfare. Study abroad programs in Europe and Asia are also strengths. Only 4 percent of undergrads are from outside the Empire State. UAlbany has invested in new architecture, including student housing.

Founded in 1844 to train teachers, UAlbany now offers a bevy of outstanding programs in arts and sciences, business administration, and preprofessional programs, and it is placing increased emphasis on technology. Study abroad is solid, too, but—consistent with its location in the state capital—it's the university's public policy programs that truly shine.

Website: www.albany.edu
Location: Suburban
Public
Total Enrollment: 14,567

(continued)

Undergraduates: 12,017
Male/Female: 45/55
Financial Aid: 64%
Pell Grant: 43%
Expense: Pub $
Student Loans: 66%
Average Debt: $
Applicants: 32,446
Accepted: 69%
Enrolled: 9%
Grad in 6 Years: 64%
Returning First-years: 84%
Academics: ✍ ✍ ✍ ✍
Social: 🗩 🗩 🗩
Q of L: ★ ★ ★
Admissions: (518) 442-5435
Email Address:
ugadmissions@albany.edu

Strong Programs:
Business
Computer Science
Creative Writing
Criminal Justice
Emergency Preparedness,
  Homeland Security, and
  Cybersecurity
Psychology
Public Policy and Management
Social Welfare

A UAlbany weekend starts on Thursday night for many, with off-campus parties or barhopping about town.

Designed by Edward Durrell Stone, who also designed the Kennedy Center and Lincoln Center, UAlbany's main uptown campus is stark, modern, and suburban. Almost all the original academic buildings are clustered in the center of the campus, while some students are housed in symmetrically situated quads named for periods in New York history—Indigenous, Dutch, Colonial, State, and Freedom—and progress clockwise around the campus. New student housing options for upperclassmen include Empire Commons, Freedom Apartments, and Liberty Terrace. The downtown campus primarily houses the university's public policy programs, and the health sciences campus is home to public health programs and research centers. Ongoing construction projects are changing the face of the uptown campus and include a $180 million Emerging Technology and Entrepreneurship Complex, located adjacent to the main campus, and the $200 million AI supercomputing College of Engineering and Applied Sciences building.

UAlbany's general education program consists of 30 credits of distribution requirements, through which students must demonstrate competency in advanced writing, oral discourse, information literacy, and critical thinking. In addition, all first-year students take a required introductory seminar and a course on diversity. For the career-minded, most of UAlbany's preprofessional programs are among the best of any SUNY branch. Students in the public policy and management, social welfare, and criminal justice programs may take advantage of their proximity to the state government to participate in internships. Psychology, anthropology, biology, and homeland security are popular majors, and undergrads are clamoring for admittance to the university's business administration program, which is especially strong in accounting. Students can sign up for one of more than 30 B.A./M.A. programs or opt for a six-year law degree in conjunction with UAlbany Law School. The New York State Writers Institute has enhanced the university's reputation in creative writing. The College of Emergency Preparedness, Homeland Security, and Cybersecurity is the first of its kind in the nation. The new College of Nanotechnology, Science, and Engineering offers nanoscale engineering, environmental science and other programs for undergraduates.

> **"The quality of teaching is excellent overall. There are some superstar professors."**

The academic climate is challenging, and courses tend to be demanding. Classes can be large; just 31 percent enroll fewer than 20 students. Students form study groups to help one another through the coursework, and professors are always available to offer support. "The quality of teaching is excellent overall," a physics major says. "There are some superstar professors and a bad apple here and there, but usually very good instructors." Qualified students can take part in the Honors College, which allows first-years and sophomores to enroll in up to six introductory courses that have been designed by distinguished faculty. The courses emphasize research, service learning, and a creative component. Senior honors students design and complete a yearlong research or creative project. About 12 percent of students take advantage of UAlbany's superior offerings in foreign study, which include programs in 35 countries, plus more than 70 other options available through the SUNY system.

"This campus is friendly and welcoming of individuals of every race and sexual orientation," says a sociology major. Five percent of undergraduates come from states outside New York, and less than 1 percent come from foreign countries. Black students make up 24 percent of the student body, Hispanics/Latinos 20 percent, Asian Americans 10 percent, and multiracial students 4 percent. UAlbany makes available merit scholarships, averaging $3,300, and roughly 200 athletic scholarships in 18 sports. Forty-three percent of first-year students are Pell-eligible. Thanks to New York State's Excelsior Scholarship program, in-state residents whose annual household income does not exceed $125,000 qualify for free tuition.

Forty-five percent of students live in university housing; first-year students are required to live in dorms, where the rooms are described as small but "satisfactory."

Juniors and seniors can choose from a variety of housing options, including the new Empire Commons, which offers four-bedroom apartments. Living/learning communities allow incoming first-years who share similar interests or majors to live together in the same residence hall and take some courses together. Many students move off campus because "the transportation system to and from campus is convenient, and the cost of apartments is as cheap or cheaper than living on campus," explains a junior. Students on the main campus take their meals at the Indian or State quads or at the remodeled Campus Center, while most downtowners live and eat at Alumni Quad. "The Advocacy Center for Sexual Violence is a fantastic resource for students and is quite effective," says a sophomore.

"Our school has a vibrant social life on and off campus," says a senior. "There are multiple clubs and events on campus, and downtown Albany also has a good social scene, such as clubs and restaurants." Students have more than 250 clubs and organizations to choose from, many of which are involved in community service. While most people are serious about their work, a UAlbany weekend starts on Thursday night for many, with off-campus parties or barhopping about town. Students warn that alcohol policies forbidding underage drinking are strict and well enforced. Fraternities and sororities attract just 1 percent of the men and 1 percent of the women, yet they have become the school's main party-throwers. Parkfest is a huge all-school concert that brings in well-known as well as

"There are multiple clubs and events on campus."

up-and-coming bands. The natural resources of the upstate region keep students busy skiing and hiking, and the Student Association owns and operates Dippikill, a wilderness retreat described as UAlbany's "own little Walden" in the Adirondacks. Treks to Montreal and Saratoga are also popular.

As for varsity sports, most Great Danes teams play in the Division I America East Conference. The men's and women's indoor and outdoor track and field teams have dominated the conference, claiming dozens of championships in recent years. Men's and women's lacrosse, men's soccer, and women's basketball are also highly competitive. Intramurals and club sports engender a great deal of student enthusiasm, and participation numbers in the thousands.

The University at Albany is not the concrete, sterile diploma mill its architecture might suggest. It's a place of opportunity for those willing to put in the hours and hard work. As one veteran cautions, "You can find an outlet here for even the most obscure interest, but this is not a school that will educate you when you're not looking."

Overlaps

UC Irvine, George Mason, UMBC, New Jersey Institute of Technology, SUNY–Binghamton, SUNY–Buffalo, SUNY–Stony Brook

If You Apply To ›

SUNY–Albany: Early action, regular decision. Accepts the Common Application with supplement. Please consult SUNY–Albany's website for the most up-to-date information regarding standardized test requirements.

SUNY–Binghamton University

4400 Vestal Parkway E, Binghamton, NY 13902

Binghamton has become one of the premier public universities in the Northeast because of its outstanding academics and commitment to undergraduates. It is writing the rules on how to integrate global awareness and international experiences into undergraduate study. If 100,000 screaming fans on a Saturday afternoon tickles your fancy, head 200 miles southwest to Penn State.

Website: www.binghamton.edu

Location: Suburban

Public

Total Enrollment: 16,847

Undergraduates: 14,318

Male/Female: 48/52

Financial Aid: 63%

Pell Grant: 28%

Expense: Pub $

Student Loans: 52%

Average Debt: $ $

Applicants: 53,007

Accepted: 39%

Enrolled: 16%

Grad in 6 Years: 82%

Returning First-years: 90%

Academics: ✍ ✍ ✍ ✍

Social: 🗩 🗩 🗩

Q of L: ★ ★ ★ ★

Admissions: (607) 777-2171

Email Address:
admit@binghamton.edu

Strong Programs:

Biological Sciences

Business Administration

Computer Science

Economics

Engineering

Foreign Languages

Integrative Neuroscience

Psychology

Annual campus traditions include Stepping on the Coat (to celebrate the arrival of warm weather), the Spring Fling carnival, and Senior Days.

Since its founding in 1946 to serve returning World War II veterans, Binghamton University has offered a private-school experience at a public-school price, even for out-of-staters. With more than 450 clubs and an emphasis on small classes—52 percent of those taken by undergraduates have fewer than 20 students—it's no wonder that students who apply here are also considering schools such as Cornell and NYU. Binghamton offers an intellectually challenging environment with an emphasis on global experiences, including education abroad opportunities in more than 100 countries, area studies programs that focus on specific regions of the world, and the unique Languages Across the Curriculum program. "We don't have to put ourselves in massive amounts of debt and we still come out on top," says a satisfied sophomore.

Binghamton's campus, located in the upstate New York town of Vestal, just a mile west of the city of Binghamton, sits on 930 acres of open grassy space and includes a nature preserve, trails, fountains, and a pond. Most buildings reflect modern architectural design, with continuous upgrades in recent years, including new residential communities, high-tech science and technology buildings, and a $60 million baseball stadium complex. A 13-acre Health Sciences Campus, located a short drive from the main campus, includes the School of Pharmacy, the Decker College of Nursing, and a major health research center.

Students apply to one of the university's five schools with undergraduate programs: the Decker College of Nursing and Health Sciences, the Harpur College of Arts and Sciences, the College of Community and Public Affairs, the School of Management, and the Watson College of Engineering and Applied Science (named for the founder of IBM). Regardless of the school they choose, students face the same general education requirements, which span four categories: language and communication, global vision, liberal arts (including sciences, mathematics, aesthetics, and humanities), and wellness. A first-year transition program pairs first-year students with peer mentors and guides them through experiential learning opportunities and career exploration.

> **"Beating the test is usually more important than beating other students."**

Popular majors include neuroscience, psychology, biology, economics, and accounting. The university offers more than 50 combined bachelor's/master's degree programs, and qualified students are guaranteed entry to the Pharm.D. program. Students have the option to design their own interdisciplinary majors in Harpur College. Binghamton's academic reputation is enhanced by a tough grading policy, which includes pluses and minuses as well as straight letter grades and Fs on the transcripts of failing students rather than no credit. "Students are usually self-motivated and cooperative," says a sophomore. "Beating the test is usually more important than beating other students." According to an electrical engineering and musical theater major, "Binghamton professors aren't just there to teach, give the grade, and call it a day—they love connecting with students."

Global education is central to the Binghamton experience, and about 22 percent of students study abroad. The school operates student exchanges with universities around the world and directly sponsors more than 50 study abroad programs in locations as diverse as the UK, Costa Rica, Japan, Morocco, South Korea, and Australia. "Study abroad at Binghamton is huge!" says an English major. Undergraduate research is also emphasized here (41 percent of students participate), and the invitation-only First-Year Research Immersion program involves enriched courses taught by teams of faculty from multiple STEM disciplines while students laud the Source Project, which introduces humanities and social sciences students to original research. Faculty-supervised independent research, often culminating in a senior honors thesis, is common in Harpur College. The Binghamton University

Scholars Program is a four-year honors program offering special seminars and leadership training to exceptional students, along with opportunities for experiential learning and junior- and senior-year capstone projects.

Although Binghamton offers a top-notch liberal arts and sciences education, word of its excellence has been slow to cross state lines: only 10 percent of undergraduates come from states beyond New York, and another 4 percent hail from foreign nations. By other measures, though, Binghamton's student body is rather diverse: Black students make up 5 percent of the total, Hispanics/Latinos 13 percent, Asian Americans 19 percent, and multiracial students 4 percent. "The biggest social and political issues on campus relate to social equality," a student reports. The university has taken several steps in recent years to create a more inclusive campus environment, including the establishment of an LGBTQ center and the addition of dedicated diversity, equity, and inclusion leadership. Binghamton offers merit scholarships and grants worth an average of $7,400, as well as roughly 300 full or partial athletic scholarships in 21 sports. Under the state's Excelsior Scholarship program, New York residents from families earning $125,000 or less per year qualify for free tuition.

Forty-three percent of Binghamton's students live in college-owned housing. Most of the residence halls have traditional double rooms with bathrooms down the hall or suites with common rooms and shared bathrooms. As one student explains, "Binghamton models the housing system after Oxford. We have six different residential communities, comprised of two to five buildings each. This makes a rather large university seem smaller and more comfortable." One community consists of two apartment-style buildings for upperclassmen. Each community is led by a collegiate professor who helps link students' residential and academic experiences, and each has its own set of traditions. Dining halls have plenty of options, and students report feeling safe while trekking around the university grounds. "The university works hard to make our campus feel like a home; students have enough to worry about, and safety does not need to be one of those things," a senior says. As for career advising, a computer science major says, "Watson Career and Alumni Connections is very helpful, available, and has a wonderfully friendly staff."

When the weekend comes, Binghamton students know how to let off steam. On campus, a senior says, "The options are endless: bowling, concerts, performances, Late Nite Binghamton, sports, and much more." Late Nite Binghamton brings free movies, concerts, and games to campus. Frat parties occur off campus; 15 percent of the men and 16 percent of the women go Greek. One student emphasizes that Greek life is "not something that defines you at this school," and a junior adds, "The Student Association (SA) is a wonderful opportunity to find a massive array of clubs with countless leadership opportunities." While some underage students manage to find alcohol, any caught violating the school's policy "will be taken care of accordingly," says a senior. Annual campus traditions include Stepping on the Coat (to celebrate the arrival of warm weather), the Spring Fling carnival, and Senior Days.

Binghamton's "downtown area is awesome with great restaurants, bars, clubs and various other social spots," says a junior. Also in town, "many students volunteer with local groups, such as food drives and mentoring children," adds a nursing major. Popular road trips include Ithaca and Syracuse, as well as Cortland and Oneonta, about an hour away by car.

> "Study abroad at Binghamton is huge!"

> *Students apply to one of the university's five schools with undergraduate programs.*

> "The Student Association (SA) is a wonderful opportunity to find a massive array of clubs."

> *Binghamton's academic reputation is enhanced by a tough grading policy.*

Binghamton's Bearcats compete in Division I, but the school doesn't field a football team. As a result, perhaps the most significant rivalry is with Cornell in men's lacrosse. Women's basketball, volleyball, and softball and men's cross-country, tennis, and baseball are competitive in the America East Conference. Binghamton's debate team is among the best in the nation, and computer science students excel in the FAA National Design Competition. Intramurals, club sports, and fitness programs attract about 80 percent of the student body.

With a four-year graduation rate that is among the highest of any public university, Binghamton has a reputation for an excellent education at a reasonable price that continues to draw smart New Yorkers—but not as many out-of-staters as it deserves—to its vibrant and growing campus. Despite the hubbub of city life, the university maintains a cozy feel. Says one senior, "When you walk on the campus, you instantly feel at home and a huge sense of camaraderie."

If You Apply To ›

SUNY–Binghamton: Early action, regular decision. SATs or ACTs: optional. Accepts the Common Application with supplement.

SUNY–University at Buffalo

15 Capen Hall, Buffalo, NY 14260

The largest and most academically comprehensive of SUNY's four university centers, Buffalo is also one of the system's two flagship universities, along with Stony Brook. Most students come from western New York and the New York City metro area, and a high percentage commute from home. Working to set itself apart with the visibility that comes from big-time Division I sports, including football. Home of supercomputing center Empire AI.

Part of the mammoth State University of New York system, the University at Buffalo is a standout in medicine, engineering, and computer science, and the university is one of the world's leading supercomputer sites, backed by "a $400 million investment that brings New York State's public and private universities together to advance artificial intelligence." Its resources are large enough to warrant three campuses: North, South, and Downtown. In addition to the sciences, the former private university offers strong professional schools, including a top-ranked school of pharmacy. "UB is like a melting pot," says a premed senior, "but one you need to make the choice of throwing yourself into."

UB traces its heritage to 1846 when it was founded as a private college, led by future U.S. president Millard Fillmore, that evolved into a large university and in 1962 became part of the newly established SUNY system. The university's North Campus, home to most undergraduate programs, stretches across 1,100 acres in the suburbs just outside the city line and boasts buildings designed by world-renowned architects such as I. M. Pei. Meanwhile, the South Campus, along Main Street, favors collegiate ivy-covered buildings and is the home of the schools of architecture, pharmacy, nursing, and public health, as well as UB's highly rated dentistry program. The university provides connecting bus service—known as the UB Stampede—between the North and South campuses. UB's seven main libraries hold more than four million volumes and the James Joyce Collection, the largest Joyce collection in the world. The university continues building and renovating at a steady pace, most recently breaking ground on Agrusa Hall, a new student-focused engineering building on the North Campus.

The general education program, known as the UB Curriculum, includes a small-group UB Seminar for all new students; required coursework in writing, math, and natural sciences; two Pathways courses that allow students to explore interests thematically and globally; and a Capstone e-portfolio aimed at integrating their learning. "First-year seminars and classes help make the college transition a successful and enjoyable one," says a sociology major. The engineering and business management schools are nationally prominent, and architecture is solid, while the English department is notable for its emphasis on poetry. Music, geography, and French are well regarded. Of UB's 150-plus undergraduate majors, some of the most popular are psychology, social sciences, engineering, business/marketing, and nursing. The university offers more than 85 combined bachelor's/master's degrees (such as a five-year business administration B.S./M.B.A. and the only combined occupational therapy program in the SUNY system) and numerous interdisciplinary majors, as well as opportunities for self-designed majors. The UB Startup and Innovation Collaboratory provides students with support and resources to foster entrepreneurship. Many undergrads study abroad, choosing from hundreds of options available through the SUNY system.

Students agree that the academic atmosphere in most disciplines at UB is competitive. "Success through hard work and innovative thinking is really stressed," says an occupational therapy major. "You are measured against your peers in many classes and labs." Class sizes can get quite large, which can be an adjustment for first-years; 35 percent of all undergraduate courses have fewer than 20 students. At a school where graduate education and research get lots of the attention, the faculty are often experts in their field, but the teaching "is really professor-dependent," says a management information systems major. Given the sheer size of the school and the multitude of opportunities, a junior says, "It's easy to get lost or confused." To support students academically and socially, UB offers its Proud to be First initiative for first-generation students, peer-assisted learning, free tutoring for all undergraduates, and the Center for Excellence in Writing. Students say the Career Design Center is among the most helpful support services. Students accepted into the UB Honors College enjoy smaller classes, priority class registration, faculty mentors, and specialized advising.

"Students like to be involved but at the same time are very studious," says one senior. "They also like to party." Eighty-eight percent hail from New York State, 9 percent come from nations outside the U.S., and 43 percent of UB's domestic students are racially/ethnically diverse. The campus is socioeconomically diverse as well, with 47 percent of entering first-years qualifying for Pell Grants. UB's considerable efforts in increasing awareness of diversity include the Intercultural and Diversity Center and the Office of Equity, Diversity, and Inclusion. Regarding hot-button topics of the moment, on campus "people are very politically charged," says one student. Merit scholarships averaging $4,500 are offered to the top incoming students, and athletic scholarships are also available. In-state residents qualify for free tuition under the state's Excelsior Scholarship program, provided their family's annual income is $125,000 or less.

Thirty-four percent of students live on campus in traditional residence halls or apartments for upper-class students; the rest commute from home or find less

The winters are cold in Buffalo, but students can take refuge inside a series of enclosed elevated walkways.

The university offers more than 85 combined bachelor's/ master's degrees.

"UB is like a melting pot, but one you need to make the choice of throwing yourself into."

"Success through hard work and innovative thinking is really stressed."

expensive apartments nearby. Most of the on-campus dwellers reside on the North Campus. Gender-inclusive housing is available for students who wish to live in a mixed-gender housing environment. Students have a smorgasbord of dining choices ranging from three dining halls to more than 35 food courts, restaurants, and snack stops, including local favorite Tim Hortons. "Everything is clean, well organized, with great service and fantastic food," cheers a junior. Students report that security on campus is adequate, and sexual assault cases are "definitely not taken lightly."

A business administration major says social life varies depending on the campus: "North is in the quiet suburbs and everything from there is a commute, South is party central and on the border of a bad neighborhood, and downtown is for medical students but in a great area with much to do." School-sponsored events and activities organized by the more than 500 student organizations keep students busy during the week. Alcohol is allowed on campus for students 21 and over. The Greek system draws less than 1 percent of UB men and 2 percent of women. With Homecoming, Fall/SpringFest, Distinguished Speakers Series, and the Zodiaque Dance Company, there are many arts, culture and group events to participate in. Off campus, "Downtown Buffalo is super fun and young," says a sophomore. Friday night happy hour centers on beer and the city's famed chicken wings. Also popular are the Buffalo AKG Art Museum, with its world-renowned collection of modern art, and the Triple-A baseball Bisons, who play downtown. The two major pro teams, the Buffalo Bills (football) and the Sabres (hockey), are both top draws.

The winters are cold in Buffalo, but students can take refuge inside a series of enclosed elevated walkways that connect most of the North Campus academic buildings. The flip side is that the outlying areas of the city offer great skiing, skating, and snowmobiling—and the ski club even offers free rides to the slopes. Having a car might be a good idea—"to go off campus, it is unfortunately a trek," says one student, but others warn that parking can be a problem on campus. Although most students are content to stay in Buffalo, those who want a change of scenery can drive to Niagara Falls, just a few minutes away, or to Rochester, Cleveland, or Toronto, where the drinking age is lower. "The best road trip is 10 minutes to Canada," says an anthropology and geology double major.

UB has been trying to enhance its visibility by getting its name on the sports pages with teams from 16 sports competing in the Mid-American Conference. It is the only major SUNY unit to field a Division I football team; fans pack into the school's 30,000-seat football stadium. The Bulls women's soccer and volleyball teams and men's and women's track and field and basketball teams are competitive. Intramural sports are popular, especially soccer and Oozefest—a massive mud-volleyball tournament that draws students, faculty, staff, and alumni. "Oozefest is probably our number one tradition," says a senior. "Tons of teams sign up, dress in costume, and start playing early in the morning."

At a university as large as UB, students learn to take initiative with their education, and students here say they appreciate UB's huge range of academic programs, research resources, and social events. Says one satisfied senior, "UB is a school that provides people from all walks of life the opportunity to obtain a quality education and experience diversity firsthand."

The University at Buffalo is one of the world's leading supercomputer sites.

"Downtown Buffalo is super fun and young."

Overlaps

UC Irvine, Cornell University, University of Iowa, University of Pittsburgh, Rutgers, SUNY–Albany, SUNY–Binghamton, SUNY–Stony Brook

If You Apply To ›

University at Buffalo: Early action, regular decision, rolling admissions. Please consult UB's website for the most up-to-date information regarding standardized test requirements. Accepts the Common Application with supplement.

1 College Circle, Geneseo, NY 14454

Geneseo is a preferred option for New Yorkers who want the feel of a private liberal arts college at a public-school price. It is similar in scale to Mary Washington and William & Mary in Virginia, much smaller than Miami of Ohio. Offers business and education in addition to the liberal arts and sciences. Less than 5 percent of the students come from outside New York.

The SUNY–College at Geneseo offers a serious academic environment at an affordable price. Designated as New York's Public Honors College in 2024, this equity-centered college attracts high achievers who "tend to be friendly, liberal, and hardworking," says a junior. Responsive, attentive professors help compensate for the long winters and somewhat isolated location. Excellent preprofessional programs make admission competitive for this most pastoral campus of the State University of New York system.

Geneseo sits in the scenic Genesee Valley of western New York. Founded as a public teacher training college in 1871, it became part of the emerging SUNY system in 1948. The surrounding community has been designated a National Historic Landmark Community. An elementary education major calls the town "small and inviting" and says the historic storefronts and nearby forests and rolling hills make for "beautiful scenery." Campus architecture ranges from Gothic to modern, and recent campus improvements include a new multicultural center and LGBTQ+ lounge and a $40 million renovation of the Milne Library.

General education requirements, dubbed "A Geneseo Education for a Connected World," include foundational courses in scientific and quantitative reasoning, communication, and five courses in participation in a global society. Every student also completes an integrative and applied learning project before graduation, which might involve research, community

> **"The academic climate at Geneseo is rigorous."**

engagement, internships, study abroad, or other opportunities. All first-year students take a writing seminar in a small class, focusing on a theme related to the instructor's discipline. Popular majors include psychology, education, business administration, and biology. Physics, geography, and accounting are also strengths. New and rapidly growing majors include astrophysics; philosophy, politics, and economics; sustainability studies; and sociomedical sciences. Cooperative programs with other SUNY campuses in physical therapy, optometry, engineering, and other fields allow students to finish their graduate degrees a year ahead of schedule.

"The academic climate at Geneseo is rigorous, but the professors and staff provide you with the tools and support needed to succeed," reports a biology major. Thirty-six percent of the classes have fewer than 20 students, and the quality of teaching is said to be generally high, especially in upper-level courses. "Many professors are welcoming and willing to answer questions and interact with students," says an accounting major. Top students are invited to join the prestigious Edgar Fellows scholarship program, which includes a $2,000 annual scholarship, five honors courses, and an opportunity to complete a senior thesis or a research, creative, or service project. Thirty-seven percent of all undergrads undertake research projects. The acclaimed Geneseo Opportunities for Leadership Development program, which is open to all students, seeks to prepare students for college and community leadership

---

Website: www.geneseo.edu
Location: Small Town
Public
Total Enrollment: 3,790
Undergraduates: 3,752
Male/Female: 35/65
Financial Aid: 68%
Pell Grant: 32%
Expense: Pub $
Student Loans: 62%
Average Debt: $ $
Applicants: 15,293
Accepted: 66%
Enrolled: 10%
Grad in 6 Years: 72%
Returning First-years: 87%
Academics: ✍ ✍ ✍
Social: 🗩 🗩 🗩
Q of L: ★ ★ ★ ★
Admissions: (585) 245-5571
Email Address:
admissions@geneseo.edu

Strong Programs:
Accounting
Biology
Business Administration
Communication
Education
Geography
Physics
Psychology

roles via workshops and symposia. Thirteen percent of students study abroad, and the college offers around 60 programs in more than 30 nations; through other SUNY campuses, students have access to more than 900 programs.

"Although there is a small amount of racial diversity, everyone is welcome and accepted on campus," says one student. Ninety-eight percent of Geneseo students are from New York State, and 1 percent come from abroad. Asian Americans make up 3 percent of the student body, Hispanics/Latinos 8 percent, Black students 4 percent, and multiracial students 1 percent. "Politically, there seems to be a 50/50 split based on who I encounter," says a senior, but the political climate doesn't usually get heated. Geneseo offers merit scholarships averaging $2,500 each to qualified first-year students but no athletic awards. New York State's Excelsior Scholarship grants free tuition to in-state students whose families earn up to $125,000 in annual income.

Fifty-seven percent of Geneseo students live in the residence halls and townhouses, where 16 living/learning communities are available for interested students. Rooms are guaranteed for four years, although most juniors and seniors choose to move off campus. The Red Jacket Dining Complex has been renovated, and a senior reports, "Dining is decent, though the plans are a bit overpriced." Students say that, given its small-town location, the campus is safe, and an English major notes that Geneseo has "stepped up its educational resources on sexual consent for incoming students." One senior laments a lack of funding for some student support systems at Geneseo, but adds, "There has been some improvement in the mental health counseling offered."

> "[T]here is a very charming Geneseo social scene."

"We do not have a huge nightlife, but there is a very charming Geneseo social scene," says a psychology major. "There are a lot of activities on campus as well as great festivals and events in the town itself." Fraternities and sororities, which draw 14 percent of the men and 22 percent of the women, set the social tone and host most of the parties. "Greek life is a loud, influential minority," says one student. If Greek life doesn't appeal, students can get involved in any of the more than 180 student organizations or partake in college-sponsored late-night activities at the College Union. Sixty percent of students are active in the community, volunteering thousands of hours of service each year through annual days of service, events like Relay For Life, and numerous student groups. Students also look forward to annual fall and spring festivals, GREAT Day (a celebration of student research, creative work, and talent), and monthly multicultural club dinners and shows.

Adjacent to campus, the town of Geneseo's Main Street has more than 60 shops, restaurants, and cafés. A campus shuttle takes students to a nearby Wegmans supermarket and Walmart. Outdoorsy types appreciate the nearby Letchworth State Park, often referred to as the "Grand Canyon of the East"; rowers enjoy beautiful Conesus Lake, only a 10-minute drive from campus. Popular road trips include Rochester, 30 miles north, and Buffalo, 60 miles west; don't forget your hat, mittens, and parka!

Geneseo's varsity teams, the Knights, compete in Division III. Men's ice hockey and women's basketball are nationally competitive, while men's and women's cross-country and swimming and diving are perennial conference champions. Ice hockey, though, stirs up the most school spirit: "Hockey is huge here," confirms a senior. Thirty-eight percent of Geneseo students participate in intramural and club sports, including broomball, basketball, indoor soccer, and sand volleyball.

The SUNY–College at Geneseo offers students the best of two worlds. Given its size, professors can provide the kind of personal attention normally seen only at private liberal arts colleges; because of its public status, all that attention comes at a bargain price. These factors have made it competitive. "There's a unique energy on

Outdoorsy types appreciate the nearby Letchworth State Park, often referred to as the "Grand Canyon of the East."

All first-year students take a writing seminar in a small class, focusing on a theme related to the instructor's discipline.

Overlaps

University of Delaware, Ithaca, SUNY–Albany, SUNY–Binghamton, SUNY–Buffalo, SUNY–Oswego, Syracuse, University of Rochester

campus," says a satisfied senior, "a sense that if you're willing to put in the effort, there are countless opportunities waiting for you."

Purchase College, SUNY

735 Anderson Hill Road, Purchase, NY 10577

One of the few public institutions that has a strong arts specialty. The visual and performing arts are signature programs, but many students also come to Purchase for a robust range of liberal arts offerings, from environmental studies, biology, and psychology to film and creative writing. Proximity to NYC enhances academic and social opportunities. Eclectic campus life offers funky traditions and an active music scene.

Purchase College, SUNY is a dream come true for aspiring artists of all kinds—an academic environment that provides a strong sense of community yet celebrates individuals for their unique talents and contributions. The liberal arts are well supported here, too, with a growing number of academic opportunities. Purchase's location just 35 miles north of New York City is ideal for its creative, socially conscious students who take full advantage of the endless cultural and professional opportunities the city has to offer. A literature major says, "There's a raw energy that exists on campus—in the students and professors—that I don't think many other colleges have."

Set on a 500-acre wooded estate in an area of upscale Westchester County's most scenic suburbia, Purchase has a campus described by one student as "sleek, modern, ominous, and brick." The college, founded in 1967 to serve as a "cultural gem" in the SUNY system, has earned a national reputation for its instruction in music, dance, theatre, and visual arts. Almost all the faculty members in the School of the Arts are professionals who perform or exhibit regularly in the New York metropolitan area, and the spacious, dazzling facilities here rank among the best in the world. The college also boasts the Neuberger Museum, one of the largest public college museums. The four-theater Performing Arts Center is huge, and dance students practice in a building that contains a dozen studios, whirlpool rooms, and a "body-correction" facility.

> "Dancers, actors, visual artists, and music students pull the most weight as far as campus life is concerned."

Mingling with highly motivated and talented performers and artists can make some students in the School of Liberal Arts and Sciences feel a little out of place, and the academic atmosphere reportedly varies between programs. "Dancers, actors, visual artists, and music students pull the most weight as far as campus life is concerned," opines a student. Even so, about 60 percent of Purchase students pursue liberal arts degrees. Psychology, environmental studies, biology, film, creative writing, and new media have strong reputations, and theatre and performance, dance, and arts management are other popular choices, as are mathematics, computer science, economics, and journalism. Purchase's respected studio composition and studio production programs are offered through the conservatory of music. New majors include law and justice studies and global studies.

Website: www.purchase.edu
Location: Suburban
Public
Total Enrollment: 3,077
Undergraduates: 3,042
Male/Female: 41/59
Financial Aid: 71%
Pell Grant: 41%
Expense: Pub $
Student Loans: 69%
Average Debt: $
Applicants: 7,847
Accepted: 74%
Enrolled: 13%
Grad in 6 Years: 63%
Returning First-years: 80%
Academics: ✍ ✍ ✍
Social: 🗩 🗩 🗩
Q of L: ★ ★ ★
Admissions: (914) 251-6300
Email Address:
  admissions@purchase.edu

Strong Programs:
Biology
Creative Writing
Dance
Environmental Studies
Music
Studio Production
Theatre
Psychology

All Purchase students complete the same core curriculum, which requires coursework in six knowledge areas including the arts and humanities; communication; world languages; mathematics and quantitative reasoning; diversity, equity, and inclusion and social justice; natural sciences and scientific reasoning. A requirement in civic discourse has been added as well. Most new students take an introductory First-Year Seminar. Students in the liberal arts and sciences complete a senior project, which is often research-based, while those in the arts divisions undertake a senior recital or show. Purchase students tend to be serious about their own personal achievements, and with 69 percent of classes enrolling fewer than 20 students, professors are said to be accessible and friendly. "Professors do all they can to assist their students through available office hours, practice questions, and via email," says a chemistry major. Faculty members lead short-term study abroad programs during the summer on such topics as art history and language in Italy and political theater in Prague; affiliated programs in the SUNY system provide access to hundreds of other options.

One student describes Purchase students as "very artsy, politically aware, very alternative and weird." Another adds, "Purchase is a judgment-free zone, and we are proud of that." Eighty percent of students are from New York State, most from New York City and Westchester and Rockland counties. Others are from Long Island, New Jersey, and Connecticut; 2 percent are international. Black students account for 12 percent of the student body, Hispanics/Latinos 29 percent, Asian Americans 4 percent, and multiracial students 6 percent. Forty-one percent of first-years are eligible for Pell Grants. In addition to need-based aid, merit scholarships averaging $3,300 are awarded each year. New York residents from families whose annual incomes are below $125,000 can attend Purchase tuition-free under the state's Excelsior Scholarship program.

Eighty-six percent of Purchase students live on campus, and a student explains, "There are older and newer dorms, and their condition definitely reflects their age." Options are improving, however, with a 300-bed residence hall that recently opened, and plans are in the works to renovate some of the older facilities. With quirky names like Wayback, Farside, and Fort Awesome, the dorms at least sound like fun places to live. Housing in the surrounding suburbs is expensive and hard to find, so many students commute from home. "College food is college food," muses one student of the dining facilities. The college has expanded its resources and educational programming related to student safety.

The campus is a neighbor to the world headquarters of major corporations like IBM and PepsiCo, and the town of Purchase is by no means student-oriented. A campus shuttle takes students to nearby White Plains and Port Chester and to the Metro North station where they can catch a train to the Big Apple. The school has been working in recent years to strengthen campus life, and students say those efforts are paying off. "There is always something happening to keep you entertained here and mostly everyone is a social butterfly," says a psychology major. A lively music scene brings indie and up-and-coming bands to campus throughout the year, and the Performing Arts Center regularly hosts student, faculty, and guest performances. New York artists and celebrities also visit for lectures, performances, and other events. With about 50 active clubs on campus, there is usually something going on in the Student Center (a.k.a. "the Stood"). Fraternities and sororities are definitely out. Purchase is not without its traditions: Afrodisiac and Culture Shock are two annual festivals ("carnival rides, food trucks and vendors, petting zoos, and performances by famous people"), and Pancake Madness happens at the end of each semester with the dining hall serving breakfast at 10 p.m.

Purchase fields 17 varsity sports that compete in the Division III Skyline Conference. The few competitive Panthers teams include men's basketball, men's volleyball, men's and women's tennis, and baseball. Intramural and club sports draw about 30 percent of students and range from the typical basketball and soccer to the not-so-typical Nerf club and circus skills club.

As the "fun, weird cousin of the SUNY schools," as one senior puts it, Purchase is a perfect place to study the arts and still be able to indulge in academics of all kinds or vice versa. "If you want to see talent and also tap into your own talent/creativity, Purchase is definitely the school for you," says a junior. Indeed, the opportunity that Purchase offers for a personalized, diverse education is unique within the SUNY system.

If You Apply To ›

SUNY–Purchase: Early action, rolling admissions. SATs or ACTs: optional. Accepts the Common Application with supplement. Apply to particular school or program. Auditions held for acting, dance, and music. Portfolios required for art and design, creative writing, film, and theater design/technology.

SUNY–Stony Brook University

100 Nicolls Road, Stony Brook, NY 11794

Strategically located 60 miles east of New York City, Stony Brook is one of the academic leaders of the SUNY system. The natural sciences, engineering, and health fields are the major drawing cards. Situated in the lap of Long Island luxury, Stony Brook offers easy access to beachfront playlands. Still caters mainly to students from the New York tristate area.

As one of two flagship universities in the SUNY system, Stony Brook aims to be the model of a student-centered research university. Its three Undergraduate Colleges provide a small college community experience with all the assets of a leading research university. Since its founding in 1957, the public university has made a name for itself with its top-notch programs in the hard sciences. It has also become known for the high quality of its professors and its challenging but supportive learning environment.

The school's location on Long Island's plush North Shore is a powerful enticement. Sitting on 1,040 wooded acres just outside of the small, picturesque village of Stony Brook and only 90 minutes from New York City and half an hour from the beaches of the South Shore, the campus is a conglomeration of redbrick buildings interspersed with several modern brick and concrete designs. Campus beautification and sustainability are priorities, and grass and trees have replaced much of the uninspiring campus concrete. Newer structures include two residence halls and a dining facility.

The Stony Brook Curriculum is based on a series of learning outcomes and is organized into four categories: Demonstrate Versatility, Explore Interconnectedness, Pursue Deeper Understanding, and Prepare for Lifelong Learning. All first-year students—residents and commuters alike—enter the university as members of one of three Undergraduate Colleges: Creativity, Technology, and Innovation; Global Health, Wellness, and Community; and Social Justice, Equity, and Ethics. Each college has its own faculty director, as well as both academic and residential advisors. First-year students participate in theme-based academic and cocurricular programs, which include two small seminar courses.

Strong Programs:
Business Management
Economics
Engineering
Geology
Health Science
Marine Vertebrate Biology
Nursing
Physics

The Roth Pond Regatta, featuring cardboard boat races, is a big social event.

The comprehensive university hospital and research center make health science and nursing strong.

Coming of age in the high-tech era, Stony Brook quickly became recognized for its science departments. Facilities are extensive, and the science faculty includes internationally known researchers. The comprehensive university hospital and research center make health science and nursing strong. The hospital, which has been ranked among the nation's best for teaching, attracts grants and offers many opportunities for research programs for undergrads as well as graduate students. Psychology, biology, health science, and business management are the most popular majors. Engineering, geology, marine vertebrate biology, physics, economics, and globalization studies are also strengths. Stony Brook boasts the first school of communication and journalism in the SUNY system, which is home to the Marie Colvin Center for International Reporting. The art program's fine arts building includes studios and a reference library that complements Stony Brook's beautiful five-theater Staller Center for the Arts and 5,000-square-foot Zuccaire Gallery. Every summer, the Stony Brook Film Festival brings leading and emerging independent filmmakers to campus. A new major in rhetoric and writing has been added.

"Students are often studying at one of our many libraries here into the late hours of the night."

"Students are often studying at one of our many libraries here into the late hours of the night," says a health science and psychology double major. And while the coursework is difficult, "I was able to build connections with many professors and felt guided and supported," says a senior. Classes can be large, with just 36 percent enrolling fewer than 20 students.

An Undergraduate Research and Creative Activities program offers students the opportunity to work on research projects with faculty members from the time they are first-years until they graduate. The WISE (Women in Science and Engineering) Honors Program encourages women entering the university as first-years to pursue study in the sciences, engineering, and mathematics. Students rave about Stony Brook's study abroad programs (England, France, Italy, Japan, and Madagascar are just some of the possibilities). Students can also choose established internships in the fields of policy analysis, political science, psychology, foreign language, or social welfare. University Scholars is a four-year honors program for students who rank at the top of the incoming first-year class that offers specialized support, programming, and events. Students praise the free tutoring and the career advising on campus.

"Career advisors send out weekly emails and host job fairs."

"Career advisors send out weekly emails and host job fairs where you're able to learn about specific jobs and internships for your major and your chosen career," lauds a journalism major.

Students at Stony Brook are "academically driven, intelligent, focused," says a senior. Ninety-two percent of Stony Brook undergraduates hail from New York, and a good portion commute from Long Island homes; 9 percent arrive from foreign countries. The student body is 6 percent Black, 16 percent Hispanic/Latino, 36 percent Asian American, and 3 percent multiracial. As for politics, a health science major says, "I think it's great that students are able to respectfully use their voice to speak out on issues on both the large and small scale." Merit scholarships averaging $3,800 are given out each year, in addition to around 200 athletic scholarships. A sizable 43 percent of Stony Brook undergraduates receive Pell Grants. As at other SUNY schools, in-state students at Stony Brook whose families earn $125,000 or less in annual income enjoy free tuition under the state's Excelsior Scholarship program.

Stony Brook, which has one of the largest residential programs in the SUNY system, has a slew of robust facilities that provide students access to state-of-the-art fitness centers, computing centers, and big-screen TVs. Half of undergrads live in university housing. While residential first-years must take a meal plan, upperclassmen who live in suites on campus either opt for a flexible food-service plan or pay a nominal fee to cook for themselves. Kosher and vegetarian food co-ops keep interested students well supplied with cheap eats. The university's Walk Service Program escorts students around campus at night. "We sit through so many sexual assault lectures and workshops and online courses, and it has honestly helped," says one student.

"Stony Brook isn't much of a party school," says a sophomore, and the university has fairly strict policies on alcohol consumption. The Greek system draws just 2 percent of the men and 3 percent of the women. Because many students go home on the weekends, students say the party scene is low-key, although a junior notes, "Student Engagement is always throwing some sort of event for students who stay." Current and classic movies are screened during the week, along with frequent concerts, plays, and other performances. Annual traditions include the Wolfieland carnival at the start of the school year and the homecoming football game. "In the spring, we have Earthstock, a celebration of nature and recycling, and Strawberry Fest, where there are different strawberry-themed foods for us to try," explains a biomedical engineering major. The Roth Pond Regatta, featuring cardboard boat races, is another big social event.

> **"In the spring, we have . . . Strawberry Fest, where there are different strawberry-themed foods for us to try."**

"Stony Brook is a wealthy residential town that cannot be categorized as a 'college town,'" one student says. Nearby Port Jefferson offers small shops and interesting restaurants, but having a car is helpful—many students make do with trains, and a station is conveniently located at the edge of campus. Beachcombing on the nearby North Shore or on the Atlantic Ocean shore of Long Island and heading into New York City are popular ways to pass the weekends.

Stony Brook's 18 Division I teams compete in the Colonial Athletic Association. The nationally ranked Seawolves women's lacrosse team has dominated the conference in recent years, and other champs include women's basketball, men's cross-country, and baseball. Intramurals, ranging from soccer and flag football to handball and table tennis, provide one of the school's greatest rallying points, and students are also active in more than 40 club sports.

Though Stony Brook is not old enough to have ivy-covered walls, it does offer some of the best academic opportunities in the SUNY system, especially in the sciences. Students tout their school's diversity and creativity, as well as the feeling of hospitality that pervades campus life.

Says a first-year student, "There is a strong sense of community here, and everyone wants to support each other in their endeavors."

Overlaps

UC San Diego, UConn, Georgia Tech, UMass Amherst, NYU, SUNY–Albany, SUNY–Binghamton, SUNY–Buffalo

If You Apply To ›

SUNY–Stony Brook: Early action, regular decision. Accepts the Common Application with supplement. Please consult Stony Brook's website for the most up-to-date information regarding standardized test requirements.

Stetson University

421 N Woodland Boulevard, DeLand, FL 32723

The oldest private university in Florida, Stetson keeps company with the likes of Baylor and Furman among prominent Southern institutions. Established the state's first schools of business, law, and music. Business and music are traditionally the strongest programs. Feels more like a small college than a university.

Website: www.stetson.edu
Location: Small City
Private
Total Enrollment: 3,302
Undergraduates: 2,271
Male/Female: 43/56
Financial Aid: 99%
Pell Grant: 49%
Expense: Pr $ $
Student Loans: 57%
Average Debt: $ $
Applicants: 11,674
Accepted: 72%
Enrolled: 8%
Grad in 6 Years: 62%
Returning First-years: 78%
Academics: ✍ ✍ ✍
Social: 🗩 🗩 🗩
Q of L: ★ ★ ★
Admissions: (386) 822-7100
Email Address:
 admissions@stetson.edu

Strong Programs:
Accounting
Digital Arts
Entrepreneurship
Finance
Health Sciences
Music
Professional Sales
Russian, East European, and
 Eurasian Studies

The Stetson Undergraduate Research Experience program awards funding to students for summer research or creative projects.

Stetson University, founded in 1883 and named for the maker of the famed 10-gallon hat (John B., who was an early benefactor), draws students from across the country with its small size and emphasis on experiential and liberal learning. Once a bastion of conservatism, the school has become more liberal and interfaith since cutting ties with the Southern Baptists in the 1990s. With top-notch business programs and strengths in music, health sciences, psychology, environmental science, and digital arts, and an increased focus on interdisciplinary study, this private Florida university continues to attract students who aren't afraid to wear a variety of hats during their stay.

Located halfway between Orlando and Daytona Beach, Stetson's 185-acre campus features mainly brick structures in Late Victorian and early 20th century revival styles. While some modern buildings are scattered about, the theme is decidedly Southern, complete with century-old sabal palms and live oaks. A science complex has allowed Stetson to expand health sciences, environmental science, pre-health, and other science programs. A new 305-bed residence hall opened in 2026.

Stetson has three undergraduate colleges and schools—music, business administration, and arts and sciences—and its general education requirements apply to all of them. All entering students take a First Year Seminar, which allows them to work closely with Stetson faculty to ease the transition to college. First-years who are undecided on a major participate in the Discovery program, and all students take a Junior Seminar that focuses on personal and social responsibility. Seniors in the College of Arts and Sciences must complete a faculty-mentored capstone research or creative project, while music students perform a senior recital. Additionally, all students must pass four writing or writing-enhanced courses in order to graduate. Through Stetson's new Hatter Ready program, all students participate in experiential hands-on learning, including study abroad, research and internships.

> **"The professors constantly encourage you to take on more projects and research."**

Stetson is known for its business program and particularly majors in accounting, professional sales, finance, and entrepreneurship. Would-be money managers benefit from the award-winning Roland George Investments Program, where they oversee a portfolio worth nearly $7 million in stocks and bonds. Students who hope to work for themselves can tap into the Prince Entrepreneurship Program, which connects them with successful business owners, while the Family Enterprise Center was one of the first in the nation in educating students for work in family businesses. The digital arts program is well regarded for game design, and Russian, East European, and Eurasian studies is a surprising strength. Stetson's music school is notable (ahem) for choral music and public performances in addition to academic programs in theory, composition, music education, and performance. Aspiring lawyers may take advantage of a 3+3 accelerated Bachelor's/J.D. program or a 4+3 direct admission program with Stetson's College of Law.

"Stetson has a positive, well-balanced academic climate," says a computer science major. Seventy-three percent of classes have fewer than 20 students, and group work is common. Professors are always willing to help, and many have worked in the field they are teaching before stepping in front of the lectern. "The professors constantly encourage you to take on more projects and research, if you are interested, and push you within their classes," says an English major.

Students with wanderlust can choose from more than 100 faculty-led, exchange, or affiliate programs, and international internships are an option, too; 14 percent of undergrads typically study abroad. Stetson's honors program incorporates international study, community service, and a senior colloquium and also allows students to create their own majors. Seventy-one percent of students get involved in research. The Stetson Undergraduate Research Experience program awards funding to students for summer research or creative projects with faculty members, and original student work is celebrated at the annual Stetson Showcase.

"The majority of Stetson students are academically minded and community driven," says a health sciences major. Sixty-eight percent of Stetson Hatters come from Florida, and 9 percent hail from foreign countries. Black students constitute 12 percent of the student body, Hispanics/Latinos make up 22 percent, Asian Americans add 2 percent, and multiracial students represent 6 percent. Many come from affluent families, but

"Stetson students are academically minded and community driven."

49 percent of current first-years are Pell-eligible. Students of all faiths and identities are welcomed; the Cross-Cultural Center houses multicultural student organizations. Students describe a mix of political views on campus. Merit scholarships and non-need-based grants averaging $33,700 are awarded each year, and Stetson also hands out athletic scholarships in 18 sports.

Seventy-two percent of undergrads live in the residence halls, since everyone is required to do so through junior year, except for commuters who live at home. "I lived on campus all four years because I loved how connected it made me to my campus and my peers," comments a senior. Stetson's traditional, buffet-style cafeteria is known as the Commons, and students say the meals are usually satisfactory, with sufficient accommodations for those with dietary restrictions. Campus safety receives good ratings. "The campus is well lit at night, and Public Safety is very present," reports a psychology major.

"Greek organizations are usually the place to find parties or connections to party life," says a junior, adding that "music organizations also offer a type of subculture partying." Fraternities attract 18 percent of the men, and sororities draw 17 percent of the women. Hatter Productions and more than 100 student organizations present plenty of other on-campus opportunities for entertainment and activities. Students look forward to

"Stetson is very much a 'what can we do for our students' school."

annual homecoming events, including a talent show, tailgating, and Hatter Howl with live music, food, and carnival games. Ninety percent of students participate in volunteer activities, often through service-learning courses. When your birthday rolls around, it's best to don your bathing suit—it's a popular tradition for fellow students to toss you into the midcampus Holler Fountain.

As for the "adorable, small Southern town" of DeLand (population 43,000), it boasts "shops, galleries, and cafés" but only a handful of bars, so students often head to Orlando (40 minutes from campus) or Daytona Beach (20 minutes) to eat out, shop, or dance the night away. In addition to the omnipresent beaches, Blue Spring and DeLeon Springs offer canoeing and nature watching. Popular road trips include Miami for clubbing and the Keys for camping.

The baseball, women's tennis, and women's beach volleyball programs have been the standard-bearers for Stetson's Division I Hatters, each taking home multiple Atlantic Sun Conference titles in recent years. Men's basketball won its first-ever conference championship in 2024. Women's basketball, men's soccer, and golf are also strong. The football team competes in the Pioneer Football League against the likes of Butler and Davidson. Rowing teams practice on picturesque Lake Beresford. The Hollis Wellness Center offers fitness facilities, and 23 percent of students participate in club and intramural sports, ranging from soccer and surfing to flag football.

Stetson students tip their hats (sorry) to the one-on-one attention freely given at this small Sunshine State university. "Stetson is very much a 'what can we do for our

Overlaps

Baldwin Wallace, University of Central Florida, Drake, University of Florida, Loyola University New Orleans, University of Redlands, Rollins, Valencia

students' school," explains a junior. After four years spent enjoying great weather and forming close friendships with peers and professors, students emerge with solid academic foundations for future work or study.

Stevens Institute of Technology

1 Castle Point Terrace, Hoboken, NJ 07030

Stevens ranks with Clarkson and Worcester Polytechnic among East Coast technical institutes that offer intimacy and personalized education. Youth-oriented Hoboken is a major plus and an easier commute to Manhattan than most places in Brooklyn. Co-op program is a popular option. Plan to work hard.

Website: www.stevens.edu
Location: Small City
Private
Total Enrollment: 6,961
Undergraduates: 4,190
Male/Female: 66/34
Financial Aid: 97%
Pell Grant: 26%
Expense: Pr $ $ $
Student Loans: 60%
Average Debt: $ $ $ $
Applicants: 10,673
Accepted: 48%
Enrolled: 21%
Grad in 6 Years: 87%
Returning First-years: 94%
Academics: ✎ ✎ ✎
Social: 🗩 🗩
Q of L: ★ ★ ★ ★
Admissions: (201) 216-5194
Email Address:
admissions@stevens.edu

Strong Programs:
Biomedical Engineering
Business and Technology
Computer Engineering
Computer Science
Cybersecurity
Mechanical Engineering
Music and Technology
Quantitative Finance

At Stevens Institute of Technology, students accept intense classwork, all-nighters, and trips to the Big Apple as givens. The school is located just across the Hudson River from Manhattan, which means that students have the cultural, athletic, and gastronomic resources of New York City at their fingertips. Engineering and the sciences set the tone on campus. Even business, arts, and humanities programs are taught through the lens of technology, but students seem prepared to take on the challenge of balancing work and play. "At Stevens, you really get out what you put in," says a biomedical engineering major, "and there is enough support to help you achieve your goals."

An eclectic mix of architectural styles compose Stevens's 55-acre campus. Many of the residence halls and administrative buildings are redbrick; classroom and lab facilities range from traditional, ivy-covered brownstones to modern glass-and-steel structures. The ABS Engineering Center houses five labs designed for robotics, naval engineering, structural engineering, hydraulics, and other research. The $256 million University Center Complex boasts two residential towers with outstanding views of Manhattan's skyline.

Stevens was created in 1870 through the will of 19th-century inventor Edwin Augustus Stevens (father of the Jeef Beef, a cast-iron plow popular with New Jersey farmers). It is organized into three schools—the Schaefer School of Engineering and Science, the School of Business, and the School of Humanities, Arts, and Social Sciences—and offers 35 majors. The core curriculum includes a First-Year Experience course for entering students, a set of Foundations courses on writing, leadership and ethics, computing, and entrepreneurship, and Frontiers of Technology courses that expose students to the most important current and emerging technologies. Most seniors take a yearlong capstone course.

> "It's very tech-oriented, with a lot of hands-on group work."

Stevens's programs in biomedical, chemical, civil, computer, electrical, and naval engineering are all highly regarded, as is the major in mechanical engineering, not surprising since the program dates to the school's founding. Business programs are growing in number and popularity and include a major in quantitative finance, rare at the undergraduate level. Other notable majors include artificial intelligence, computer science, cybersecurity, business and technology, music and technology, and visual arts and technology. A five-year co-op program allows engineering and science students to incorporate full-time internships into their studies.

Students describe the academic climate as challenging but supportive. "It's very tech-oriented, with a lot of hands-on group work," says a mechanical engineering major, adding, "It's not for the faint of heart." Thirty-one percent of classes have fewer than 20 students, and students agree that, despite a few professors more interested in their research than their teaching, the quality of instruction is above average. "Many professors come from industry or research backgrounds, which adds a layer of relevance and depth to what we're learning," comments an industrial and systems engineering major.

Professional practice is an important part of the Stevens environment, with nearly all students participating in cooperative education, internships, or mature research and design projects. "What makes Stevens unique is that it blends strong academics with real-world application from day one," says a sophomore. "You're not just learning theory—you're applying it in co-ops, research, clubs, classes, or even the Makerspace." The Pinnacle Scholars Program, which invites top students to participate in faculty-guided research or an international experience during the summer, comes with a stipend of up to $5,000, the option to pursue an accelerated master's degree, and other benefits. Hundreds of short- and long-term study abroad and exchange programs are available, although few students find the time to take advantage of them. Men outnumber women, but one junior sees this as an advantage: "As a female at Stevens, I feel this has actually helped me with holding my own and 'vying with the boys,' as I call it." The Lore-El Center for Women's Leadership offers events ranging from health and wellness activities to leadership conferences and professional dinners with successful women in industry. "The School of Business's job office is exceptional," reports a mechanical engineering major, who adds, "Mental health is fairly well staffed."

Students are "driven, ambitious, and deeply focused on their goals—whether that's launching a startup, getting into grad school, or landing a competitive co-op," says a sophomore. Sixty-five percent of the students at Stevens are from New Jersey; many others come from the greater New York City area, and 4 percent hail from foreign nations. Twenty-one percent of undergraduates are Asian American, 17 percent are Hispanic/Latino, just 3 percent are Black, and 4 percent are multiracial. "Stevens is not a very politically active campus," says a biomedical engineering major. In addition to need-based financial aid, qualified students receive merit-based scholarships that average $23,900. The Clark Scholars and Stevens ACES programs seek to attract more students from underrepresented backgrounds to STEM fields.

Forty-six percent of undergraduates live in housing provided by Stevens, while others find their own off-campus apartments. "Campus has a solid variety of food options," remarks a senior. Students say campus security officers are visible and friendly, and a junior notes that a "Take Back the Night committee works all year to raise awareness for domestic violence and sexual assault."

"The social scene at Stevens is vibrant if you know where to look," says a junior. Thirteen percent of Stevens men join fraternities, and 18 percent of the women pledge sororities. "People like to party here, but they keep it in check," says a quantitative finance major. "Greek houses follow campus policies regarding alcohol and usually hold registered parties where bouncers check IDs." The Founder's Day Ball is a favorite event, along with Winter Wonderland and TechFest, "when we bring in a relatively famous artist to perform at the end of the year," says one student. The annual Innovation Expo features entrepreneurial lectures, a student concert, a Shark Tank–style pitch competition with a $10,000 top prize, and hundreds of cool projects on display. When students leave campus, "Hoboken is a great place to be during college," cheers a senior. "There are many restaurants, bars, and festivals." Plus, Greenwich Village, Times Square, and the bright lights of Broadway are just 15 minutes away on the PATH train. Road trips include Yankee Stadium in the Bronx and Six Flags Great Adventure near Trenton. Beaches and ski slopes are both within a 90-minute drive.

Students cheer enthusiastically when the Division III Stevens Ducks take the pool, field, and court. Most teams compete in the Middle Atlantic Conference, and many have brought home recent conference championships, including men's soccer, men's and women's volleyball, men's and women's lacrosse, and men's and women's basketball, to name just a few. There are also intramural and club teams with basketball, flag football, and kickball being the most popular.

Stevens's urban location and relatively small size can make for fun times, but the emphasis here is on hard work and innovation. "[We are] small but mighty," says a proud student. Stevens graduates go on to make a dent in the world; notable alums include Nobel Laureate Frederick Reines, who detected the subatomic world of the neutrino; Alexander Calder, world-renowned sculptor of mobiles; and Marques Brownlee, well-known YouTuber and tech influencer. "Stevens is a hub for future innovators," concludes an electrical engineering major. "The curriculum and the services are all meant to prepare students for impactful careers in technology-based fields."

If You Apply To ›

Stevens: Early decision I and II, early action, regular decision. Accepts the Common Application with supplement. Please consult Stevens's website for the most up-to-date information regarding standardized test requirements.

Susquehanna University

514 University Avenue, Selinsgrove, PA 17870

Susquehanna offers a refreshing alternative to the cookie-cutter education at many small colleges. Its innovative core curriculum emphasizes personal development and requires students to spend at least two weeks learning off campus. Best known for its business program and big on study abroad. With a more down-to-earth atmosphere than at upscale competitors like Bucknell and Dickinson, it is a national leader in promoting socioeconomic diversity.

"Susquewho?" That's the question many students ask when they're first introduced to this undergraduate institution in rural central Pennsylvania founded in 1858 as a missionary institute; it became a university in 1895. While it may not be a household name, Susquehanna University is earning a reputation as an innovator. "My school defines an educated person as writers who can understand and execute personal finance, scientists who can write poetry and stories, and mathematicians who can think critically about world problems," says a sophomore. Friendly faculty, personal attention, and an emphasis on community make SU a good place to expand your mind. The university's off-campus study requirement makes it a fitting choice for those looking to see more of the world, too.

Susquehanna's campus is beautiful and serene, set on 297 lush acres in the small town of Selinsgrove on the Susquehanna River. Most of the 94 buildings on campus are brick, with Georgian the predominant architectural style. Selinsgrove Hall, built in 1858, and Seibert Hall, built in 1901, are on the National Register of Historic Places. A 14-acre, 12,000-panel solar array supplies nearly a third of the campus's electricity.

Susquehanna's Central Curriculum emphasizes coursework in five areas: Richness of Thought (fine arts and math); Natural World; Human Interactions (history, sociology, ethics, and language); Intellectual Skills (writing, oral presentation, and teamwork); and Connections (an off-campus, cross-cultural experience matched with diversity classes). All first-year students participate in an orientation program, and take a Writing and Thinking course as well as a First-Year Seminar that helps them make the transition to college-level work. Finally, all students take a capstone course or practicum in their major.

The prestigious Weis School of Business draws the most Susquehanna students, thanks in part to the fact that it guarantees its students an international internship and offers a semester-long London Program exclusively for business majors. Biology, communications, creative writing, and education are other popular majors; psychology and music are solid. Susquehanna is increasingly recognized for its science programs, especially biochemistry, environmental science, and biomedical sciences. Newer options include minors in sustainability management and church music. SU students may also pursue 3–2 engineering degrees in partnership with Case Western Reserve, Columbia, and WashU in St. Louis.

> "The Career Development Center does a lot of work with alumni networking to help students get ready for their professional life."

Sixty-four percent of classes at SU have fewer than 20 students, and student/faculty interaction is one of Susquehanna's strong points. Students describe academics as challenging. "Professors truly care about students and preparing them for post-graduation, which really shows through faculty-student interactions, especially outside of the classroom," says a sports media communications major. Students enjoy a bevy of support services, too. "The Career Development Center does a lot of work with alumni networking to help students get ready for their professional life," says a publishing and editing major. And a biochemistry major notes, "The campus as a whole definitely emphasizes taking care of your mental and physical health."

To fulfill their curricular Connections requirement, students utilize the GO (Global Opportunities) program, which requires them to study away from campus for at least two weeks and to reflect on their experiences when they return. Students choose from more than 130 options—a third of which are semester-long programs—on six continents; nearly all students study abroad, and those who don't head to locations across the U.S. As a senior explains, "The goal is for students to experience a new culture before they graduate, and this requirement adds to the culture of diversity at Susquehanna." Most students also complete internships as a crucial part of their education and future job searches. About 10 percent of students join the Susquehanna Honors Program, which entails a sequence of special courses and projects, off-campus opportunities, and an honors living/learning community.

At Susquehanna, students are "driven, friendly people who form a very strong and tight-knit community," says a senior. Sixty-two percent of SU students are from Pennsylvania, and the majority attended public high school; 1 percent of students are international. Seven percent are Black, 7 percent are Hispanic/Latino, 2 percent are Asian American, and 3 percent are multiracial; diversity education is an area of emphasis on campus. A senior describes the political climate as "pretty evenly split," and for the most part discussions are "cordial and respectful." Merit scholarships

(continued)

Applicants: 5,554
Accepted: 81%
Enrolled: 14%
Grad in 6 Years: 77%
Returning First-years: 86%
Academics: ✍ ✍ ✍
Social: 🗩 🗩 🗩
Q of L: ★ ★ ★ ★
Admissions: (570) 372-4260
Email Address:
suadmiss@susqu.edu

Strong Programs:
Biomedical Sciences
Business
Communication Studies
Creative Writing
Management
Music
Psychology

Favorite campus traditions include a Thanksgiving dinner at which faculty members serve students.

averaging $39,500 are available for resident Einsteins, but there are no athletic scholarships.

All Susquehanna students are required to live on campus, except for the 11 percent who are commuters. First-year students are assigned to four traditional residence halls. After the first year, students partake in a lottery system to choose from a variety of options, including suites, townhouses, on-campus apartments, and Greek houses. One student says food in the main cafeteria "can be hit or miss, but when it's good, it's good." Students report that the campus feels secure, and a sophomore adds, "Campus Safety, the Violence Intervention and Prevention Center, and our Green Dot bystander training program promote a safer culture."

"The campus hosts a ton of different events for students," says an accounting and management major. Charlie's, the school coffeehouse, offers activities like open-mic, trivia, and football-and-wings nights, while Trax, the on-campus nightclub, serves alcohol to those of age. Eighteen percent of the men and 13 percent of the women belong to fraternities and sororities, respectively, but Greeks and parties do not dominate the social scene. Homecoming, Halloween on the Ave.— "where the local community trick-or-treats at our Greek life houses," explains a student—and Spring Carnival are the big annual events. Favorite campus traditions include a Thanksgiving dinner at which faculty members serve students "the best meal of the year," a candlelight Christmas service, and Senior Hike, when the university president leads seniors to the top of nearby Mount Mahanoy.

Outside the university, Selinsgrove is "small and quaint," with several restaurants and stores. SU was originally founded in 1858 to prepare students for the ministry, and the university's commitment to the community has remained strong.

Each year, much of the student population volunteers on significant community service projects. In the surrounding countryside, "it's not uncommon to see an Amish family go by in their horse and buggy," says a student. The Susquehanna River and nearby state parks draw students to kayak, hike, and picnic. For those with cars, Penn State is an hour away.

The Susquehanna River Hawks field 23 Division III teams, plus cheerleading. Baseball, field hockey, football, and men's and women's track and field all have brought home Landmark Conference titles since 2023. Students also enjoy a diverse recreational sports program consisting of 10 club sports and a variety of intramurals. The crew, equestrian, and ice hockey clubs sign up the most students, while flag football, co-ed soccer, and cornhole are among the most popular intramurals.

At Susquehanna, "Students are challenged to take initiative with their learning" in a friendly, open environment, says a senior. From interning with local organizations to taking classes on the other side of the globe, the firsthand exposure to diverse experiences and perspectives that SU students receive makes Susquehanna worthwhile—and a name worth learning.

Overlaps

Dickinson, Elizabethtown, Gettysburg, Juniata, Lycoming, Muhlenberg, Penn State, Ursinus

If You Apply To ›

Susquehanna: Early decision, early action I and II, regular decision. SATs or ACTs: optional. Accepts the Common Application with supplement. Creative writing, graphic design, and studio art applicants must submit portfolio. Music applicants must audition.

500 College Avenue, Swarthmore, PA 19081

Don't mistake Swarthmore for a miniature version of an Ivy League school. Swat is more intellectual (and liberal) than its counterparts in New Haven and Cambridge. The college's honors program gives hardy souls a taste of graduate school, which is where legions of Swatties invariably end up. Geekier than Wesleyan, more grounded than Reed, and more collaborative than just about anywhere.

Swarthmore College's leafy green campus may be just 11 miles from Philadelphia, but students often don't have the time or the inclination to make the jaunt. That's because they have opted for one of the country's most self-consciously intellectual undergraduate environments. Swatties are bright, hardworking, and eclectic in their interests, and campus life is fabled for its intensity. But the intensity doesn't come from huge amounts of coursework (à la Yale) as much as the self-imposed drive of talented students who want to do lots of things simultaneously—from academics to social protests to rugby—and do them well. "Our commitment to interdisciplinary self-discovery starts on day one," say administrators. "The first semester is pass-fail, so students can learn adjust to college life without the pressure of letter grades." Students agree: "Swat is a truly intellectual place where people love ideas with all of their hearts," says a philosophy major.

Swarthmore was founded in 1864 by the liberal Hicksite branch of the Religious Society of Friends (Quakers) in Philadelphia and named after a 17th-century English manor house that was a center of the early Quaker movement. Swarthmore's 425-acre suburban campus is a nationally registered arboretum, distinguished by rolling wooded hills. Multistory buildings with natural stone exteriors from local quarries, shaped roofs, and cornices are the norm, fostering a quiet, collegiate atmosphere. Newer structures demonstrate Swarthmore's commitment to sustainability: The Dining and Community Commons (DCC) project includes the Dining Center—with 800 solar panels on the roof—Sharples Commons, and a geoexchange plant that provides carbon-free heating, cooling, and electricity to campus.

Students are required to take three courses in each of the college's three divisions—humanities, natural sciences and engineering (unusual for a liberal arts college), and social sciences—and at least two of the three must be in different departments. Swatties must also demonstrate foreign language competency, fulfill a physical education requirement (which includes a swimming test), and take three writing courses from at least two divisions. Optional first-year seminars emphasize close interaction with faculty members. The most popular majors are sociology and anthropology, computer and information sciences, biology, and mathematics and statistics. Engineering, English, and philosophy are also strong, and students give high marks to majors in visual and performing arts. A new major has been added in philosophy, politics, and economics. Cross-registration is offered with nearby Bryn Mawr, Haverford, and Penn.

At Swarthmore there is no class rank or dean's list, and there is a big emphasis on group projects. A first-year explains, "While the courses are generally very challenging, the environment of Swat is not competitive at all. You will often see students reminding each other of assignments, giving each other tips on how to succeed, and studying in the library together." Indeed, the administration has encouraged

> **"Swat is a truly intellectual place where people love ideas with all of their hearts."**

Website: www.swarthmore.edu
Location: Suburban
Private
Total Enrollment: 1,620
Undergraduates: 1,620
Male/Female: 48/52
Financial Aid: 54%
Pell Grant: 16%
Expense: Pr $ $ $ $
Student Loans: 18%
Average Debt: $ $ $
Applicants: 13,065
Accepted: 8%
Enrolled: 44%
Grad in 6 Years: 92%
Returning First-years: 94%
Academics: ✐ ✐ ✐ ✐ ✐
Social: 🗩 🗩 🗩
Q of L: ★ ★ ★ ★
Admissions: (610) 328-8300
Email Address:
admissions@swarthmore.edu

Strong Programs:
Biology
Computer Science
Engineering
English
Mathematics
Philosophy
Political Science
Visual and Performing Arts

a spirit of collegiality by sprinkling small lounges and cappuccino bars around the dorms and academic spaces. Class sizes are intimate as well, with 71 percent enrolling fewer than 20 students. "All the classes are taught by professors, many of them world-class, and they are always accessible and very, very friendly," says a classics and fine arts double major. Aside from teaching, Swarthmore professors also serve as advisors, and students are also assigned to Student Academic Mentors, who shepherd them through the first year on campus.

The acclaimed two-year honors program features small seminars or independent study and collaborative relationships between students and professors. Setting it apart from any other program in the United States are the written and oral examinations, which are reviewed by external faculty at the end of the senior year and gauge the students' ability to hold their own with experts in the field. One student describes honors as "like a pre-Ph.D. program"; indeed, Swarthmore is among the top five institutions in the nation for the proportion of graduates who go on to earn Ph.D.s, at 22 percent. A third of Swarthmore students study abroad in more than 250 programs in countries such as France, Japan, Poland, and Spain. Roughly two-thirds of students get involved with faculty-guided research or independent creative projects. A sophomore adds, "We have a great group of networked alumni who are always willing to help students, especially with externships, in which students stay with their Swat alum host family one week before winter break and shadow them."

"Ultimately, we are all nerds here," a history major says. "Each of us in our own way has found a place where our passionate, geekiest interests are validated, appreciated, and celebrated by our fellow Swatties." Swarthmore is home to a diverse student body; 12 percent are Pennsylvania residents and 14 percent are international. Ten percent of students are Black, 17 percent Asian American, 16 percent Hispanic/Latino, and 11 percent multiracial.

"All the classes are taught by professors, many of them world-class."

Consistent with its Quaker roots, Swarthmore encourages students to be as educated as possible on issues of cultural, racial, and socioeconomic pluralism, and the entire community is brought into decisions on issues such as socially responsible investments and the pay scale of campus workers. Liberals far outnumber conservatives, students say, but students on both sides are keen to stand up for issues they are passionate about. Swarthmore is need-blind in its admissions and meets 100 percent of admitted students' demonstrated financial need. In an effort to reduce the burden of debt, the college joined the ranks of schools that have replaced loans with grants in their financial aid packages. In addition, every student receives an $800 credit at the start of each academic year to fund the purchase of textbooks from the campus bookstore.

Ninety-five percent of undergraduates live on campus, and housing is guaranteed for all four years. "The dorms each have their own personality," says a senior, "and for the most part, they are quite comfortable and well maintained." Dining options are said to be diverse and plentiful, if not always gourmet level, and a handful of local eateries are also covered by the meal plan. Campus safety personnel are "quick to respond in any circumstance," and a sophomore says, "We have a very active Title IX office that works on prevention and resolution equally."

Most social life at Swarthmore takes place on campus, and it often begins late, since students hit the books until 10 or 11 p.m. and then head out for fun. "In order to receive funding from the Social Affairs Committee, an event has to be open to all members of campus," explains an economics major. "Because of this regulation, you don't have to worry about getting in to a party or having to pay for most events." The college banned fraternities and sororities in 2019 but allows students of legal age to have alcohol on campus, and one student says, "Campus police are not disciplinarians. They want students to be safe." Annual traditions include the McCabe Mile, where participants take a break from studying for midterms by running 18 laps around the basement stacks of the McCabe Library, and Primal Scream, where everyone screams at midnight the night before final exams.

Students' biggest complaints include lack of sleep and too much work, self-imposed or otherwise. When not studying, Swatties are often volunteering in Philadelphia or the nearby smaller city of Chester. The Eugene Lang Center for Civic and Social Responsibility has made Swarthmore a national force in the area of service learning. "Swarthmore is characterized by a genuine will to do good in the world," an engineering major says. The village of Swarthmore, known as the "'Ville," has some stores, a pizza parlor, and a Chinese restaurant. Students say there's not much in the way of off-campus social activity. For that, they take the 20-minute train ride from the on-campus train station into downtown Philadelphia, where many temptations await, including concerts, dance clubs, museums, and four professional sports teams. The King of Prussia mall, with a movie theater and department stores, isn't far either.

With Swarthmore's focus on academics, athletics aren't a high priority. The school scrapped its football program because the need to recruit enough men to remain competitive in the increasingly intense Division III environment was undermining efforts to recruit students with other interests and talents. Men's basketball and swimming have won Centennial Conference championships in recent years. Other competitive Garnet teams include men's track and field and men's and women's tennis. Any victory over archrival Haverford will have Swatties swelling with pride. Intramurals and club sports are available, and the women's rugby team's annual Prom Dress Rugby match against Ursinus is a beloved event. In the Crum Regatta, student-made boats float in nearby Crum Creek—Swarthmore's answer to the America's Cup.

"The dorms each have their own personality."

Swarthmore is a place where the administration supports the student body completely, and students are given a voice in a variety of issues ranging from faculty hiring decisions to making campuswide policies. Students who want to take an active role in their education beyond the classroom door may find the right fit here. Says a student, "We really are dedicated to learning just because we like to learn, not because we want the A."

Overlaps

Amherst, Bowdoin, Carleton, Harvard, Pomona, Princeton, Williams, Yale

If You Apply To ›

Swarthmore: Early decision I and II, regular decision. SATs or ACTs: optional. Accepts the Common Application with supplement.

Syracuse University

900 South Crouse Avenue, Syracuse, NY 13244

Syracuse defines itself as a student-centered research university. World renowned in communications, Syracuse is also strong in architecture, biology, economics, the arts, and psychology. The university has been a national leader in promoting socioeconomic diversity. Basketball provides solace during snowy winter nights.

Anyone who has watched college sports on TV is familiar with the bright-orange color associated with Syracuse University. They've seen the screaming fans and the stadium overflowing with cheering hordes. But beyond all the athletic fanfare is passion of another sort: in recent years, the university has launched academic programs and

Website: www.syracuse.edu
Location: Small City
Private

(continued)

Total Enrollment: 19,778

Undergraduates: 14,961

Male/Female: 44/56

Financial Aid: 81%

Pell Grant: 19%

Expense: Pr $ $ $

Student Loans: 46%

Average Debt: $ $ $ $

Applicants: 44,480

Accepted: 46%

Enrolled: 19%

Grad in 6 Years: 84%

Returning First-years: 90%

Academics: ✍ ✍ ✍

Social: 🗩 🗩 🗩

Q of L: ★ ★ ★

Admissions: (315) 443-3611

Email Address:
  orange@syr.edu

Strong Programs:
Architecture
Biology
Communications/Journalism
Geography
Management
Sport Management
Television, Radio, and Film
Visual and Performing Arts

The Syracuse Orange football team rocks the spacious JMA Dome, cheered on by their fruit-inspired mascot, Otto the Orange.

research initiatives in emerging areas such as global enterprise technology, eSports communication and management, bio-inspired science, and artificial intelligence, and it has invested in new faculty hires, facility upgrades, and expanded course offerings.

The Syracuse campus is located on a hill overlooking the city of Syracuse in central New York State. The character and mixture of architectural styles depict a continuously changing campus, which is grassy, full of trees, and surrounded by residential neighborhoods. Twenty-five of the university's 140 buildings are listed in the National Register of Historic Places. Many schools and colleges have restructured facilities to accommodate more faculty/student research.

General education requirements vary by school and college, but students can expect challenging coursework across the board. "Each school at Syracuse has its own academic climate," says a civil engineering major, "and some are more competitive than others," but classes are usually small; 61 percent have fewer than 20 students. Several of the schools subscribe to the Arts and Sciences core requirements, which include coursework in the sciences, math, social sciences, humanities, and contemporary issues. All entering first-year students participate in a one-credit seminar course on issues of identity, belonging, and student success in addition to a writing seminar. Students also take at least one course that fulfills an inclusion, diversity, equity, and accessibility requirement.

"Each school at Syracuse has its own academic climate."

The S. I. Newhouse School of Public Communications is a superstar of Syracuse's academic programs, offering eight majors and opportunities for dual majors. Journalism and the television, radio, and film major are two of the school's strengths. Additionally, Syracuse's programs in architecture, business, psychology, and visual and performing arts, especially drama, are popular and well regarded. Also well-known is the Maxwell School of Citizenship and Public Affairs, whose faculty members teach sought-after undergraduate courses in economics, history, political science, international relations, and other social sciences. The College of Arts and Sciences is the largest college at Syracuse and offers recognized programs in geography, writing and rhetoric, philosophy, and chemistry. "As a STEM student, I've found the academic climate to be surprisingly collaborative," says a biochemistry major. The faculty gets generally good reviews. Notes a student, "Their enthusiasm for the subjects they teach is contagious, making even challenging subjects more engaging."

Teaming with NASA, the university has a $3 million virtual aerospace engineering facility—one of three in the nation—where students have helped design a reusable space launch vehicle. Syracuse students have also participated in NASA's reduced-gravity student flight programs. Integrated learning majors, including forensic science, ethics, and digital humanities, allow students to experience hands-on involvement in pressing current issues. The university offers an honors program for particularly motivated students, and many students participate in undergraduate research and community-based projects. Nearly 50 percent study abroad; Syracuse has centers in England, France, Italy, Spain, and Chile. But students can enroll in their choice of more than 100 other programs in 60 locations. The university also offers semester-long academic and internship programs at its centers in Los Angeles, New York City, and Washington, D.C. Students praise the university's support services. "The alumni network is incredible and they help students every chance that they can," lauds a television, radio, and film major.

Thirty-two percent of enrolled students are from New York State, mostly from New York City and Long Island; 9 percent are international. Syracuse welcomes veterans and students connected to the military, who make up more than 6 percent of the student body. Students of color are also well represented, with Black students making up 8 percent of the student body, Asian Americans 8 percent, Hispanics/Latinos 13 percent, and multiracial students 5 percent. Administrators say that Syracuse has invested more funds in scholarships that primarily benefit underrepresented students and that it remains committed to admissions policies that have made the school a national leader in promoting socioeconomic diversity. "Syracuse has made immense strides in bringing minority voices to the forefront of the conversations on diversity issues," reports a student. Athletes are well supported with over 450 athletic scholarships in 16 sports. Merit scholarships average over $15,900.

Fifty-four percent of undergraduates live in university housing, which is described as comfortable and well maintained. Students are required to live on campus for their first two years; all first-years reside in residence halls on North Campus. South Campus offers apartment-style facilities. Living/learning communities and theme housing are popular options, as well. "I was in the engineering learning community, where I met my closest friends," says a senior. "These people were my ultimate support system." The campus offers more than 20 eateries, including five residential dining centers. "There are always plenty of options and they cater to all dietary restrictions," says a civil engineering major. As for safety, the university provides a transport/escort service for students studying late on campus and 24/7 on-site security in all campus housing.

> "Greek life definitely plays a huge role on this campus."

With 25 percent of men and 41 percent of women joining fraternities and sororities, respectively, "Greek life definitely plays a huge role on this campus," a student notes. However, says another, "Whatever a student wants to do on a weekend, there are so many options for them to do it." Orange After Dark puts on late-night activities like movie nights, bowling, and laser tag. Students also enjoy the annual Juice Jam, Block Party, and Martin Luther King Jr. celebrations.

Students generally enjoy the city of Syracuse with its excellent art museum, theaters, music venues, festivals, and restaurants. Around 70 percent are involved in the community through internships and volunteer work. While students complain about lack of parking, if they tire of the life in Syracuse, several quaint country towns are nearby, as are multiple ski resorts. Destiny USA, about 10 minutes away, is the country's sixth-largest shopping center. Popular road trips include Skaneateles Lake, Ithaca, Niagara Falls, Montreal, and Rochester.

Athletics are another cornerstone of student life at Syracuse. "Whether you are a socialite who loves Greek life or a nerd who loves science, on game days we're all bleeding orange," says one senior. The Syracuse Orange football team rocks the spacious JMA Dome, cheered on by their fruit-inspired mascot, Otto the Orange, and 42,000 fans. Men's soccer, women's rowing, and men's and women's track

> "On game days we're all bleeding orange."

and field are consistently strong, and there's a lively Duke–Syracuse basketball rivalry. About 85 percent of students also get involved in more than 60 club and intramural programs ranging from basketball and flag football to volleyball.

From a supportive alumni network to special academic partnerships with NASA and opportunities to study abroad or volunteer right at home, students at Syracuse know they've got something special. "[The school] has a great balance between the energy and resources of a large university and the close-knit feel of a smaller liberal arts college," says a senior. The wintry climate may be cold and snowy, but the ubiquitous bright-orange paraphernalia all over campus is enough to warm anyone. "Orange is more than a color—it is a way of life," says a physics and political science double major. "Syracuse students are all in."

Overlaps

Boston College, Boston University, Carnegie Mellon, Clemson, Drexel, University of Michigan, Northeastern, Penn State

If You Apply To ›

Syracuse: Early decision I and II, regular decision. Accepts the Common Application. Please consult Syracuse University's website for the most up-to-date information regarding standardized test requirements. Apply to particular program; can apply to single, dual, or combined programs. Applicants to art and architecture programs must submit portfolio. Applicants to drama and music programs must audition.

Knoxville, TN 37996

UT is in the middle of the pack among its Southeastern rivals—behind Florida, U of Georgia, and UNC; ahead of Alabama, Arkansas, and Ole Miss. As the only major public university in Tennessee, UT comes close to being all things to all students. Strong in business, engineering, architecture, and offers research opportunities. One of the few Southern flagship universities located in a major city.

Website: www.utk.edu
Location: City Center
Public
Total Enrollment: 33,954
Undergraduates: 29,542
Male/Female: 46/54
Financial Aid: 40%
Pell Grant: 22%
Expense: Pub $ $
Student Loans: 41%
Average Debt: $ $ $
Applicants: 59,764
Accepted: 42%
Enrolled: 27%
Grad in 6 Years: 74%
Returning First-years: 92%
Academics: ✍ ✍ ✍
Social: 🌢 🌢 🌢 🌢
Q of L: ★ ★ ★
Admissions: (865) 974-1111
Email Address:
  admissions@utk.edu

Strong Programs:
Architecture
Biology
Business
Engineering
Kinesiology
Nursing
Psychology
Supply Chain Management

Students at the University of Tennessee put a premium on school spirit, athletics, and academics—typically in that order. In the fall, boisterous fans pack into one of the nation's largest on-campus football stadiums to watch the Volunteers play against national powerhouses like Alabama, Arkansas, and Florida. Also competitive is the SEC-dominating women's basketball and men's baseball teams. "Bleeding orange is the only way to go!" cheers one happy denizen. Amid this excitement, it's easy to forget that UT also prides itself on a number of strong academic programs.

Set in the foothills of the Great Smoky Mountains, UT, whose roots date to 1794, is in the heart of east Tennessee's urban hub. The 920-acre campus has an array of architectural styles ranging from Gothic to Georgian to modern. Particularly noteworthy is the Hodges Library—the largest one in the state—built in the shape of a ziggurat. The university has spent approximately $1 billion in the last decade on new construction, renovations, and landscaping improvements. Streets that once ran through the center of campus have been transformed into landscaped pathways, and several parking lots have been replaced by grassy lawns. Other new projects include the new Torchbearer residential hall and the recently opened $129 million Zeanah Engineering Complex.

UT's general education requirements are fairly extensive and include courses in written and oral communications, quantitative reasoning, arts and humanities, cultures and civilizations, social sciences, and natural sciences, plus a foreign language or multicultural studies. Many strong academic programs are in preprofessional fields, most notably business (particularly supply chain management), architecture, engineering, and nursing. On the liberal arts side, marketing, psychology, and finance are popular majors. The modern foreign languages and literatures major allows students to combine a concentration in a language, such as German, Spanish, or Japanese, with one in international business.

"Some classes are harder than anything I could imagine."

Academic competition varies, as does course difficulty. "Some classes are harder than anything I could imagine, and some require little effort," says one junior. Large lectures are commonplace, and students report occasional problems with registration because preference is given to seniors. Even so, the university has bolstered academic advising, tutoring, and career services in recent years, and graduation rates have been on the rise. Professors receive mixed reviews: "I have had some really good professors and some mediocre ones," a supply chain management major says.

UT is the managing partner of Oak Ridge National Laboratory—the federal government's largest nonweapons lab, located a few miles away—which enhances science and technology offerings and involves 350 students and faculty in disciplines as diverse as English and physics. About 2 percent of undergraduates are members of the university-wide Chancellor's Honors program, and most of UT's colleges also offer honors tracks. UT established the Haslam Scholars program for

15 of the university's top students; selection criteria include scholastic achievement, leadership potential, and special talents. Haslam scholars enjoy such benefits as study groups mentored by top UT faculty, a study abroad experience, and research support. Students wishing to study abroad select from programs in more than 60 countries on six continents. The most popular options are short-term, faculty-led programs that provide students the opportunity to study under the guidance of a faculty member during the summer terms.

UT students are "levelheaded but tend to get a little crazy on the weekends," says a student. Sixty-three percent of undergraduates are homegrown Tennesseans, and 1 percent are international. Enrollment of students of color remains low—Black students account for 4 percent of undergrads, Hispanics/Latinos 7 percent, Asian Americans 4 percent, and multiracial students 5 percent—but the university has hired a vice chancellor of access and engagement to promote and improve campus diversity. Financial aid opportunities have been generous, with thousands of merit scholarships available (averaging $6,400) and more than 200 athletic scholarships in 20 sports.

Twenty-nine percent of UT students live on campus. Although a few older buildings remain, the university built several new residence halls as part of a recent multiphase housing development plan. Each of the dorms has a residence hall association, which for a token fee provides checkout of sports equipment, games, cooking utensils, and other useful items. First-years may choose from several living/learning communities and dine in any of over 30 spots on campus. Remote alarm units and the LiveSafe mobile app allow students to report a crime from anywhere on campus, and the university has developed comprehensive sexual assault awareness and prevention programs.

> **"I have had some really good professors."**

Students say that the social life is "very important" and active both on and off campus. Greek attracts 20 percent of the men and 37 percent of the women. The social calendar is dotted with numerous major events, including homecoming, the Carnicus and All Sing skit and singing competitions, and Knoxville's Dogwood Arts Festival. True to their name, Volunteers also like to get involved in community service projects. Cumberland Avenue (a.k.a. The Strip), a few blocks away, offers a lively variety of bars and eateries.

Still, nothing compares to the sea of orange that engulfs the campus on Saturday afternoons in the fall. More than 100,000 people jam the football stadium to see the Volunteers take on their Southeastern Conference rivals. Students liken football in Knoxville to religion, and according to one, "'Alabama' is a four-letter word" in these parts. UT has claimed multiple team national championships—baseball won its first in 2024—and more than 200 team SEC titles in its history. Recent conference champs include men's basketball and tennis and women's soccer and swimming and diving. The intramural program attracts roughly a quarter of undergraduates, and the most popular sports are flag football, indoor and outdoor soccer, basketball, and softball.

With its athletic prowess well established, administrators and students are hoping that UT can develop a comparable reputation for its academics. In its quest to climb the ranks of public research universities, UT is transforming its campus with a spate of new construction and ever-increasing academic resources. In the meantime, many will find the growing opportunities here at the "Big Orange" to be well worth the squeezing.

True to their name, Volunteers also like to get involved in community service projects.

The university has bolstered academic advising, tutoring, and career services in recent years.

Overlaps

University of Alabama, Auburn, Clemson, CU Boulder, University of Georgia, University of Kentucky, University of Missouri, University of South Carolina

If You Apply To ›

UT: Early action, regular decision. SATs or ACTs: required. Accepts the Common Application. Audition required for music applicants.

110 Inner Campus Drive, Austin, TX 78712

UT Austin regularly lands on any list of the nation's top public universities, and its Plan II honors program is among the most renowned liberal arts experiences anywhere. Offering a unique mix of culture, food, and entertainment, Austin is one of the country's great college towns. As the Texas capital, it serves as a proving ground for aspiring politicians and tech entrepreneurs, even as state lawmakers increasingly take aim at diversity initiatives, faculty control of the curriculum, and other traditional academic values. Supercompetitive admissions for out-of-staters. Where else can you spend time watching bats?

Website: www.utexas.edu
Location: City Center
Public
Total Enrollment: 50,718
Undergraduates: 40,554
Male/Female: 42/58
Financial Aid: 44%
Pell Grant: 27%
Expense: Pub $ $
Student Loans: 36%
Average Debt: $
Applicants: 72,885
Accepted: 27%
Enrolled: 47%
Grad in 6 Years: 89%
Returning First-years: 97%
Academics: 🖋 🖋 🖋 🖋
Social: 🍷 🍷 🍷 🍷
Q of L: ★ ★ ★ ★
Admissions: (512) 475-7399
Email Address: admissions@ austin.utexas.edu

Strong Programs:
Architecture
Business
Communication
Computer Science
Engineering
English
Radio, Television, and Film
Social Work

The University of Texas at Austin has come a long way from where it began in 1883 as a small school with only one building, eight teachers, two departments, and 221 students. Today, the campus is a Texas-sized home to more than 40,000 full-time undergraduates. From its extensive academic programs to its powerful athletic teams to its location in one of the nation's ultimate college towns, UT Austin has everything a Longhorn could ask for. "Our university is a diverse community with amazing opportunities for success," says a junior.

A 431-acre oasis near downtown Austin, replete with rolling hills, trees, creeks, and fountains, the campus features buildings ranging from "old, distinguished" limestone structures to contemporary Southwest architecture. The iconic UT Tower is adorned with a large clock and chimes (a lifesaver for the disorganized) and is illuminated in Longhorn orange after big athletic wins. From the steps of the Tower, one can see the verdant Austin hills and the state capitol. The outstanding library system holds more than 10 million volumes located in 17 different libraries across campus. Newer facilities include a basketball and rowing training facility.

"My professors are above and beyond my expectations."

All undergraduates complete a 42-hour core curriculum that requires coursework in English composition, humanities, American and Texas government, American history, social sciences, math, science and technology, and visual and performing arts. Entering first-year students are expected to participate in a small-group community their first semester and take a First-Year Signature Course, which is usually taught by a senior professor and introduces them to academic discussion and analysis of issues from an interdisciplinary perspective.

The list of academic strengths at UT Austin is daunting. Undergraduate offerings in accounting, advertising, architecture, communication, finance, marketing, radio-television-film, and social work are first-rate. Engineering and computer science programs are excellent and continue to expand. The English department is huge (nearly 60 tenure-track professors), and students give it high marks. UT's McDonald Observatory, based in West Texas, boasts one of the world's largest telescopes. Students say the academic climate is competitive and demanding. "There are many rigorous majors that have accelerated courses or competitive programs," says a student. Many UT classes are quite large, but 37 percent have fewer than 20 students. UT is a research university, so the professors are often busy in the laboratories. They do, however, have office hours. "My professors are above and beyond my expectations," says a psychology major. "Their own interest in their topics is obvious, and the determination to aid the students is admirable." Under pressure from conservative politicians, the university recently opened a School of Civic

Leadership with the goal of attracting more conservative students, and it has taken steps to weaken faculty governance and foster public scrutiny of course offerings.

The Plan II liberal arts honors program, a national model, is one of the oldest honors programs in the country and one of the best academic deals anywhere. It offers qualified students a flexible curriculum, top-notch professors, small seminar courses, and individualized counseling and provides them with all of the advantages of a large university in a small-college atmosphere. Business, communication, engineering, liberal arts, and natural sciences honors programs are also available. Being in the capital city should have its advantages, and it does. Nearly 200 UT undergrads work for lawmakers in the Texas Legislature, only a 10-minute walk from campus. Internships with the likes of Apple, Meta, Amazon, Google, and Samsung in the city's rapidly expanding tech sector (nicknamed Silicon Hills) are just as popular. Engineering majors can alternate work and study in the co-op program. The Sanger Learning Center offers sessions with learning specialists, peer tutoring, coaching on public speaking, and other academic help. Study abroad options are available in 100 countries.

UT students are "intelligent, involved, and proactive in their education," says a senior. Given the university's stellar academic profile, it's no surprise that admission here has become exceedingly difficult for out-of-staters. Ninety percent of UT undergraduates are Texans, and 5 percent hail from outside the U.S. Historically, UT has been integral in the careers of renowned Texas politicians, and students are active in voicing their opinion on a wide range of issues. Hispanic/Latino students account for 28 percent of undergrads, Asian Americans 26 percent, Black students 5 percent, and multiracial students 4 percent. The university offers welcome programs, social and educational events, and peer mentoring. It also awards merit scholarships averaging $3,900, as well as hundreds of athletic scholarships. In addition, UT Austin now provides full-tuition scholarships to in-state undergraduates whose families make $100,000 or less per year and smaller awards to those with incomes of up to $125,000.

"Football games pull the student body together and give us a chance to show our school spirit."

Only 18 percent of undergrads live in university-owned housing, but the school has purchased additional properties near campus, adding over 700 beds, and is currently building a new residence hall with about 1,000 beds. "Most of the dorms are old," says a student, "but they have nice facilities." Residence halls offer a variety of living options based on common social and educational interests. Apartments and condos close to campus are lovely—and very expensive. More reasonably priced digs can be found in other parts of town. But be forewarned: UT life requires lots of walking, especially for commuters, though free shuttle stops are scattered about, and UT students can ride the Capital Metro buses and shuttles for free with their student ID. As for food, there is a wide variety of options, including healthy, vegetarian, kosher, and vegan fare. Security can be a concern (Austin is an urban area after all), but students report feeling safe on campus, thanks to active and highly visible campus police.

The university's student event planning organization hosts concerts, movies, and social events. The Cactus Café is an iconic venue with live musical acts. It also boasts the world's only collection of orange-topped pool tables in its arcade and bowling alley. The Texas Union at the center of campus is a hub for student gamers with the state-of-the-art Alienware Longhorn Esports Lounge. For those more interested in octaves than eight balls, the Performing Arts Center has five theaters and attracts nationally known performers. There are also more than 1,300 student organizations from which to choose. Fourteen percent of the men and 7 percent of the women go Greek. Annual festivals include Forty Acres Fest, a sprawling carnival of the campus organizations. And Texas Independence Day provides an occasion for celebration in March.

As the state capital, Austin is hardly a typical college town, but it is one of the best. "I love it," exclaims a junior. "It has a great live music scene and is beautiful."

Nightlife centers on nearby downtown, which is full of bars, restaurants, and buskers of all types, and the well-known music scene that features everything from blues to jazz to rock to folk, as well as the Austin City Limits and South by Southwest festivals. Along with live music, bat-watching is one of Austin's most popular activities—the city is known as "Bat City" after the colony of Mexican free-tailed bats that lives under the Congress Avenue Bridge in the spring and summer. It's the largest urban bat colony in North America. Halloween draws an estimated 80,000 costumed revelers to Sixth Street (and sometimes up its lampposts). When the weather gets too muggy (quite often in spring and summer), students head for off-campus campgrounds, lakes, and parks. The most popular road trips are to San Antonio or Dallas. For spring break, students travel to Padre Island, if not New Orleans.

Athletics are as vital as oxygen for most Texans, so it shouldn't come as a shock that the annual operating expenses of UT Austin's athletic department exceed $250 million—or that the university has joined the lucrative Division I Southeastern Conference. Students especially look forward to the annual Texas–Oklahoma rivalry football game played in the Cotton Bowl Stadium in Dallas. "Football games pull the student body together and give us a chance to show our school spirit," says one student. Bevo XV, the famed UT mascot, is the latest in a long line of live longhorn steer mascots to be a fixture on football Saturdays and at events throughout the year. The basketball programs have a new arena in the Moody Center. Softball and men's swimming and diving won national titles in 2025. UT's extensive intramural and club sports program rounds up 25 percent of students and offers weekend athletes access to the same great facilities that the big-time jocks use.

> **"There are many rigorous majors that have accelerated courses or competitive programs."**

UT Austin may seem overwhelming because of its imposing size, but students say the school spirit and sense of community found here make it feel smaller. UT prides itself on having one of the most reasonably priced tuitions in the country for a flagship public research university. It also offers one of the best all-around educational experiences a student could ask for, especially if you make it into Plan II Honors. Whether UT can sustain its traditional excellence in the face of current assaults by conservative politicians on tenure and academic freedom, however, remains to be seen. Stay tuned.

Overlaps

Baylor, Duke, University of Houston, MIT, NYU, Rice, Texas A&M, Vanderbilt

If You Apply To ›

UT Austin: Early action, regular decision. SATs or ACTs: required. Accepts the Common Application. Apply either to institution as a whole or particular program. Certain departments have additional requirements.

University of Texas at Dallas

800 W Campbell Road, Richardson, TX 75080

A rising star in the Lone Star State, UT Dallas is now the most selective of the regional campuses of the UT system. Has put on a full-court press to attract top students in science, technology, and business—and is growing its liberal arts offerings. Good living conditions and a serious honors program. Chess is a big deal, and football here is of the flag variety. Political interference in academic and governance policies is problematic.

The University of Texas at Dallas has a brainy reputation, known by many as the university established in 1961 by founders of Texas Instruments, the technology giant that introduced the pocket calculator to the world. It was initially a graduate research center, especially in the areas of space sciences and astrophysics, but it did not begin awarding undergraduate degrees until 1975, and admitted its first class in 1990. Since then, the university has grown as a four-year university with an emphasis on engineering, mathematics, the sciences, and the management of new technologies. While STEM majors are what the university is best known for, its reputation in the arts and social sciences is growing. And there remains an indie-film feel to its futuristic campus, its quirky Comet mascot, and ubiquitous "Keep UTD Nerdy" merchandise.

UT Dallas is situated on 650 rolling acres in the Dallas suburb of Richardson. Most buildings are positioned around a central mall that features blooming trees, flower beds, fountains, and reflecting pools. The predominant architectural style is modern, and many buildings are interconnected by a series of glass sky bridges. The Natural Science and Engineering Research Laboratory is playfully referred to as the "mermaid building" for its iridescent blue, green, and magenta shingles, which resemble fish scales. "The new student union is just one example of how UTD is continuing to grow and invest in the student experience," cheers a senior.

To graduate, students must complete a general education curriculum consisting of coursework across a broad range of liberal arts and sciences disciplines. All incoming students take a small-group First-Year Seminar, learn about campus resources, and receive peer mentoring. "UTD is a young, vibrant, and promising institution," raves one senior. "Even freshmen have the chance to create new organizations and traditions, work in real labs with full professors, and be in contact with top administrators."

> **"Most professors . . . will take time out of their day to answer your questions."**

UTD boasts highly respected programs in speech, language, and hearing sciences; information technology and systems; biomedical engineering; and neuroscience. STEM fields account for more than half of UTD's 66 undergraduate degree programs, and students praise virtually all of the university's programs in the hard sciences and technology, especially engineering and computer science. The innovative Harry W. Bass School of Arts, Technology, and Emerging Communication, which blends humanities with science and technology, offers a popular B.A. degree as well as concentrations in animation and games and media arts and design with a focus on emerging technologies. The Jindal School of Management offers a solid menu of business programs, and a handful of majors in the social sciences and humanities are available. Some of UTD's most popular majors include computer science; biology; and business administration. More than 40 undergraduate programs offer a fast-track option that allows qualified seniors to take graduate courses to earn a master's degree.

"The academic climate is rigorous and can be highly competitive," says an economics major, but a computer science major adds, "There are many mentor programs available" that help struggling students. The Undergraduate Success Scholars program "exists to help students from specific backgrounds to gain the resources and opportunities to succeed," explains a senior. Just 24 percent of undergraduate classes enroll fewer than 20 students. "Most professors, especially STEM professors, will take time out of their day to answer your questions," says a mechanical engineering major. As part of broad efforts to shape academic policies at Texas public universities, state political leaders have reduced the role of UT Dallas faculty members in university governance. Qualified students may take part in the Wildenthal Honors College, which houses seven programs that grant students access to personal mentoring and special social and academic opportunities. The program is valuable

Website: www.utdallas.edu
Location: Suburban
Public
Total Enrollment: 24,418
Undergraduates: 18,688
Male/Female: 55/45
Financial Aid: 69%
Pell Grant: 32%
Expense: Pub $ $
Student Loans: 31%
Average Debt: $
Applicants: 31,789
Accepted: 65%
Enrolled: 20%
Grad in 6 Years: 76%
Returning First-years: 90%
Academics: ✍ ✍ ✍
Social: 🗩 🗩 🗩
Q of L: ★ ★ ★
Admissions: (972) 883-2270
Email Address:
   admission@utdallas.edu

Strong Programs:
Animation and Game
   Development
Arts, Technology, and
   Emerging Communication
Biology
Computer Science
Engineering
Information Technology and
   Systems
Neuroscience
Psychology

because it allows students "to get to know the professors better and open the door to new opportunities for research and just meeting more cool people," enthuses one first-year student. The Undergraduate Research Program provides stipends for students to pursue short-term research proposals, while the Institute for Innovation and Entrepreneurship promotes cross-disciplinary academic and student startup programs. Students rave about the study abroad options, which are available in about 50 countries. The McDermott Scholars program offers a four-year full ride plus stipends for international travel, field trips, and other benefits; up to 20 first-year students are selected every year.

Given the student body's heavy interest in STEM fields, one senior says, "Most people here are fairly nerdy to some extent, but we like it that way!" Ninety-three percent of undergraduates hail from the Lone Star State and 5 percent from abroad. Black students account for 6 percent of the student body, Asian Americans 43 percent, Hispanics/Latinos 18 percent, and multiracial students 4 percent. "Politically, this school is more left leaning," says a computer science major, adding that due to Texas's ban on DEI initiatives at public universities, "a lot of resources that existed for women, the LGBTQ+ community, and minority groups are being removed as we speak, so there is uproar about that." The university hands out merit scholarships averaging $9,900 and athletic scholarships in 17 sports. UTD covers full tuition and mandatory fees for Texas residents whose families earn $100,000 or less per year; 32 percent of incoming first-years receive Pell Grants. The Academic Bridge Program helps more than 130 high-potential students from underserved schools make the transition to college-level academics with personal advising, mentoring, and tutoring.

> "Most people here are fairly nerdy to some extent, but we like it that way!"

Twenty-two percent of undergrads live on campus in suite-style residence halls and apartment-style housing. "The first-year dorms are the epitome of excellent college housing," says one student. New students can choose to participate in a living/learning community (LLC) where they live in the same residence hall, attend classes together, and participate in group activities. A bevy of dining options is available, including choices for the health conscious. Students rate campus security highly, and for mental health care, "UTD offers six free counseling sessions, which is a good starting point," notes a neuroscience and psychology major.

Students say the social scene is tame. "There isn't much of a party culture, though there are events frequently throughout the week," explains a psychology and child learning and development major. The Greek system attracts only 3 percent of the men and 4 percent of the women, and the university is said to be "fairly strict" when it comes to enforcing alcohol policies. Popular traditions include Weeks of Welcome, homecoming, and the annual Oozeball tournament (that's mud volleyball, for the uninitiated). Richardson is "pleasant and relaxed," says a senior. Students frequent the Northside restaurants across the street from campus and get involved with the locals through community service projects. When it's time for off-campus fun, "Dallas is one of the most exciting cities in the country," crows a senior. "If you're willing to drive into town, you have access to a massive arts scene and some amazing food!"

> "Dallas is one of the most exciting cities in the country."

UTD may be one of the few places in Texas where football isn't considered a way of life. In fact, "our 'football' team [is] a world-renowned chess team," says a first-year. The university does have 17 other varsity sports, along with a co-ed eSports team. In 2025, UTD moved up to Division II and joined the Lone Star Conference, and historically, men's basketball, soccer, and cross-country, and women's golf and tennis have been competitive. Temoc, the student-designed official mascot, is a "slightly creepy" blue-skinned comet-in-human-form (try spelling it backward!)

"that people love and write fanfics about," shares a first-year. The juggernaut chess team has made a record 20 appearances in the President's Cup (the "final four" of college chess). About 14 percent of students take part in intramural and club sports. Popular activities include flag football, basketball, spikeball, and soccer.

Although efforts by state political leaders to meddle in academic and governance are issues at all Texas universities, UTD continues to appeal to those students seeking challenging coursework, access to undergraduate research in top-notch facilities, and administrators who value their input. "Sure, UTD is a relatively new university, but there is enough tradition to be proud of," reasons a biomedical engineering major. And for many, the mix of STEM and the growing liberal arts offerings is a reason to cheer. "People here are building robots, doing research, or coding apps, but you also see students making short films, composing music, or designing video games," says a happy senior. "That mix is part of what makes it feel different." Students here aren't bound by tradition—they're creating it.

If You Apply To ›

UT Dallas: Early action, rolling admissions. Accepts the Common Application. Please consult UT Dallas's website for the most up-to-date information regarding standardized test requirements.

Texas A&M University

400 Bizzell Street, College Station, TX 77843

Coming to Texas A&M is like joining a big family with more than 65,000 full-time members. In addition to fanatical school spirit, Texas A&M offers leading programs in the natural sciences, engineering, and business. To succeed in this mass of humanity, students must find their academic niche. The student body is 95 percent Texan, and out-of-staters should be prepared for serious culture shock that now includes attacks on traditional academic values and practices by conservative politicians.

Known for top-notch science and engineering programs and unsurpassed school spirit, Texas A&M opened in 1876 as the state's first public institution of higher education: a land, air, and sea grant college with a military training focus. "Because Texas A&M began as a military academy, it was built on a foundation of leadership, discipline, and love of country," says an administrator. Today, this school of more than 50,000 full-time undergrads is focused on teaching, research, and service, boasts a massive endowment, and enjoys innumerable traditions. When they're not studying for rigorous classes, Aggies may be found at Midnight Yell before each home and away football game or yelling—as the saying around campus goes, "Aggies don't cheer, we yell!"—for their teams at other high-energy athletic events.

"Aggieland" is one of the largest university campuses in the country (5,200 acres)—something apparent to students every time they walk or bike to class or take the student-driven buses. The campus combines historic brick buildings from the turn of the 20th century with new, modern facilities shaded by live oak trees. Students enjoy many green spaces on campus, including Aggie Park, a 20-acre outdoor recreational space that includes a lake, an outdoor amphitheater, and public Wi-Fi. Newer construction includes an academic and wellness center, a nuclear engineering education building, and more.

With more than 1,300 student-led clubs and organizations to choose from, students should have little trouble fitting in.

Studying, working, and volunteering sometimes take students far from Aggieland.

The general education requirements include communication; math; life and physical sciences; language, philosophy, and culture; creative arts; American history; government; and social/behavioral sciences. Entering students participate in Hullabaloo U, a first-year experience class introducing them to the school. While Texas A&M is best known for its agriculture, engineering, and veterinary medicine colleges, the university is cultivating a strong liberal arts program and a highly competitive business school. Psychology, biomedical science, mechanical engineering, and communication tend to be the most popular majors. The fine arts programs in visual performance studies, dance science, philosophy, and classics are also strong.

Students generally agree that while academics are taken seriously here, the climate is, in the words of a junior, "definitely collaborative." Teaching assistants and grad students are often found behind lecterns, and 27 percent of classes have more than 50 students. Undergraduate research is, unsurprisingly, important here, and getting involved is "as easy as emailing a professor and starting that conversation," says a biomedical engineering major. Highly motivated students also recommend the University Honors Program as a good way to make friends and enjoy perks like "priority registration, access to smaller classes with better professors, and networking with the brightest minds here at Texas A&M," according to one participant. Studying, working, and volunteering sometimes take students far from Aggieland—Texas A&M is a leader among American public universities in sending students abroad, mostly in short-term programs; more than 100 faculty-led programs are available, along with hundreds of other options through partnerships and exchange programs worldwide. Like other public universities in the state, Texas A&M has recently come under pressure from conservative lawmakers to curtail faculty advocacy of concepts linked to diversity and other liberal values. In a well-publicized incident, a philosophy professor was told to remove passages from Plato's *Symposium* from a course syllabus because it discussed aspects of love and sexuality.

"College Station is a model college town."

Ninety-five percent of undergraduates are from Texas, and just 1 percent come from other countries. Even if you're not from Texas, Aggies are known for their friendliness. Says one, "From your first tour on campus to the day you graduate, no matter who you are, you'll be greeted with a smile and a 'Howdy!'" Black students make up 2 percent of the student body, Asian Americans 14 percent, Hispanics/Latinos 26 percent, and multiracial students 4 percent. Athletes compete for hundreds of scholarships, while scholars vie for thousands of merit awards averaging $4,900. The university has locked in its tuition rate through spring 2027, but out-of-staters may be subject to tuition increases.

Texas A&M has seven different residence hall styles, two apartment complexes, and a variety of floorplans that range from cheap and not-so-comfortable to expensive and cushy (with private bathrooms and in-unit laundry machines), but they accommodate only 18 percent of undergrads. A communication major recommends the university's first-year living/learning communities as a chance to "meet people with similar interests as you" and because "applying for one can help guarantee a spot to live on campus." Most upperclassmen live in the numerous apartments and houses in College Station or its twin city, Bryan, and the university runs an extensive bus system throughout the community. Dining halls, fast-food chains, snack shops, and food trucks are all over campus. "I'm never afraid on campus that my things will get stolen or that I will be in danger," says a nonprofit management major.

"You could write a book—and many have—about all the traditions we have here."

When it comes to social life, a junior advises, "It is imperative that you join a student organization in order to make Texas A&M feel a little smaller and to really find your niche and purpose." With more than 1,300 student-led clubs and organizations to choose from, students should have little trouble fitting in. With such a large student body, neither Greek life nor partying define the social scene. Students appreciate the amenities of the surrounding area, especially in the Northgate district and Century Square, which offer ample restaurants, bars, and shops. "College Station is a model college town," asserts a senior. Students are actively involved in the community, and the Big Event, which draws thousands of Aggies each year, is the nation's largest student-run, one-day community service event. Those seeking a getaway can drive an hour and a half to either Houston or Austin, and the beaches of the Gulf Coast beckon.

Texas A&M is practically synonymous with tradition. Boasts one senior, "You could write a book—and many have—about all the traditions we have here." Favorites include the 12th Man, in which all students stand for the entirety of every football game as a symbol of their loyalty and readiness to take the field, and Aggie Muster, held in more than 275 locations around the world to remember alumni who died within the year. There's also the 400-plus member Fightin' Texas Aggie Band. The famous Corps of Cadets is one of the largest uniformed leadership training programs in the country, with about 2,000 cadets. Although just a fraction of the student body, the Corps remains the single most important keeper of the spirit and traditions of Aggieland.

Athletics, whether on the varsity level or for recreation, are at the top of almost anyone's list here. The school's 20 varsity teams compete in the ultracompetitive Division I Southeastern Conference (SEC), where they face powerhouses such as Alabama and Georgia. Texas A&M has won several national titles (the latest being men's outdoor track and field and women's volleyball in 2025) and 33 conference championships.

Women's tennis and golf have also won recent conference championships. Up to 100,000 football fans rock Kyle Field with cries of "Gig 'em, Aggies," or "Whoop!" Basketball, flag football, racquetball, and soccer are among the most popular sports in the well-organized and extensive intramural program.

Despite its size, Texas A&M manages to feel familial to students. "A great school will challenge and nurture you to become an individual who is ready to conquer any problem in the world—and that right there is Texas A&M," says one happy biology major. Recent pressure from conservative Texas lawmakers has called into question some of the academic values that have made the university such a school in the past. But for now, with all those varied educational opportunities and memorable traditions worth cheering (that is to say, "yelling") about, it's no wonder students here are so devoted to their "Aggie Family." Unless, of course, they're into Plato.

Overlaps

University of Florida, University of Georgia, Ohio State, University of Oklahoma, Penn State, UT Austin, UT Dallas, Texas Tech

If You Apply To ›

Texas A&M: Rolling admissions. SATs or ACTs: optional. Accepts the Common Application with supplement. Apply to particular schools or programs. Primarily committed to state residents.

Texas Christian University

2800 South University Drive, Fort Worth, TX 76109

The personalized private alternative to Texas-sized state universities. Tuition is less, and the student body less affluent, than that at archrival SMU. Though affiliated with the Disciples of Christ, TCU goes lighter on religion than, say, Baylor. Strengths include business, communication, and the fine arts. Strong sense of community and school spirit.

The traditional lighting of the Christmas tree (featuring carols, hot chocolate, cookies, Santa, reindeer, and even fireworks) is always a special event.

You know a school has spirit (if that's the right word) when its students paint themselves purple to cheer raucously for a spiky toad. Although outsiders might be baffled by such a display, Texans know these folks are TCU fans cheering for the home team (officially known as the Texas Christian University Horned Frogs) at a Saturday afternoon football game. There's a true sense of school spirit and solidarity here. And TCU may seem more accessible than rivals Southern Methodist and Baylor. Enthuses a junior, "It has that classic campus feel with beautiful buildings, spirited football games, and tons of purple frogs!"

One of the first co-ed colleges west of the Mississippi, TCU was founded on the Texas prairie in 1873 by two brothers, Addison and Randolph Clark, to "promote literary and scientific education" and develop character on the Texas prairie. The spacious 302-acre campus is kept in almost perfect condition and features tree-lined walkways and grassy areas. Nearby is a lovely residential neighborhood not too far from the shops and restaurants of downtown Fort Worth. The campus boasts an eclectic mix of architecture, ranging from neo-Georgian to contemporary. Newer facilities include two East Campus residence halls and a dining hall, the Harrison Family Football Performance Center, and the Simpson Family Athletics Restoration and Wellness Center.

Students choose their majors from 117 disciplines, with the core curriculum embodying the base of the liberal arts education and advancing the TCU mission, "to think and act as ethical citizens in a global community." The core curriculum emphasizes critical thinking and is divided into four areas: critical and creative thinking; quantitative and scientific reasoning; communication; and responsible citizenship. There are first-year seminar courses along with a student

> **"It has that classic campus feel with beautiful buildings, spirited football games, and tons of purple frogs!"**

orientation and Frog Camp (an optional summer camp that emphasizes team building and school spirit). "Frog Aides is a freshman leadership cohort that opens up so many doors on campus and beyond," recommends a political science major. TCU's standout programs are business, nursing, biology, strategic communication, education, and fine arts. TCU boasts a 100 percent placement rate for their graduates who earn a teaching certification. In the Neeley School of Business, selected upperclassmen manage a $1.75 million investment portfolio. The university also offers an innovative dance program with a ballet major, a strong theatre internship program, and majors in ranch management and youth advocacy and educational studies.

"TCU is a hard university. Classes are fun, but you are in for work," says a sports broadcasting major, adding "Professors really care and often know you by name." Classes are frequently small, with 39 percent enrolling fewer than 20 students, and many professors take on the role of mentors, as do academic advisors. Top achievers may be invited to join the honors college, living together in the honors dorm their first year and pursuing individual research opportunities as part of their honors thesis senior year. "Honors classes are focused more on critical thinking, ethics, and human connections rather than definitions and formulas," explains one participant. Forty percent of students choose to study abroad and can choose from 20 countries in their pick of more than 50 programs, including faculty-led options. Career services, which are specific to each college, get high marks.

Students at TCU are "driven, involved, and generally friendly," says a junior. "Most people are passionate about something. Which could range from academics, sports, Greek life, or service." The student body is fairly homogeneous; 48 percent are from Texas, many from affluent, conservative families. Black students account for 4 percent of the student body, Hispanics/Latinos 19 percent, Asian

Americans 3 percent, and multiracial students 4 percent; 5 percent of students are international. Lack of diversity is a top concern among students, but a junior notes that TCU has been "taking a lot more interest in diversity and inclusion efforts within everything from recruitment and admissions to first-year experience programs." This is hardly an activist campus, and although TCU is affiliated with the Christian Church (Disciples of Christ), the atmosphere is not overtly religious. TCU provides merit awards averaging $22,300 and more than 300 athletic scholarships.

Students are required to live on campus their first two years, and overall, 48 percent live in university-owned housing. "All residence halls have recently been remodeled and there are no 'gross' or 'old' residence halls," shares a junior. Most juniors and seniors, however, move off campus, and fraternity and sorority members may live in their Greek houses after their first year. Campus meals receive satisfactory reviews. An evening safety escort service, Froggy Five-O, takes you wherever you want to go on campus, and students say they feel safe. The annual, weeklong It's On Us campaign works to raise awareness of sexual assault, and a senior says, "I am proud of TCU for addressing it head-on."

Greek life is important at TCU; 49 percent of the men and 62 percent of the women join Greek organizations. They party in the esprit de corps tradition, but there's plenty of fun left on campus and in Fort Worth to keep the non-Greek Frogs hopping, such as movie nights, concerts, food trucks, and sports games. "Alcohol violations are a big deal," says a student, and involve a three-strike system. Students look forward to the fall concert each year that brings big-name acts to campus, and the traditional lighting of the Christmas tree (featuring carols, hot chocolate, cookies, Santa, reindeer, and even fireworks) is always a special event. "Fort Worth is cultured and has plenty of things to do," says a senior. "The stockyards let you get in touch with the inner country in you, and no one should miss a visit to Billy Bob's, the world's largest honky-tonk." Dallas is only 45 minutes to the east; other road trips include Austin, San Antonio, and the Gulf Coast.

TCU fields 22 varsity athletic programs, which compete—and excel—in the tough Big 12 Conference. "The Baylor and SMU rival football games are always super exciting each year," cheers one eager Frog. Rifle, men's tennis, and beach volleyball have won recent NCAA championships. Women's basketball, women's soccer, men's tennis, and beach volleyball are also strong. Intramural and club sports, from flag football and basketball to pickleball and elite dance, are popular with students as well.

From its student-friendly admissions process to its dedication to supporting and developing students once they hop onto campus, TCU is an accessible university offering a personalized educational experience. The school's warm students have no shortage of purple pride. As one junior says, "TCU is full of rah-rah school spirit and a student body that never fails to say, 'Go Frogs!'"

Overlaps

Auburn, Baylor, University of Oklahoma, Southern Methodist, UT Austin, Texas A&M, Tulane, Vanderbilt

If You Apply To ›

TCU: Early decision I and II, early action, regular decision. Accepts the Common Application. Optional Freedom of Expression question allows space for any information not included elsewhere in application. Please consult TCU's website for the most up-to-date information regarding standardized test requirements.

2500 Broadway, Lubbock, TX 79409

A child of the remote West Texas plains, Texas Tech is emerging from the large shadow of Texas A&M as one of the state's top research universities. It takes big-time sports to be on the map in Texas, and the Red Raiders—aided by the caped Masked Rider on horseback—have taken up the challenge. Bills itself as smaller and more personal than UT or A&M.

Website: www.ttu.edu

Location: City Center

Public

Total Enrollment: 34,912

Undergraduates: 29,505

Male/Female: 50/50

Financial Aid: 85%

Pell Grant: 25%

Expense: Pub $

Student Loans: 48%

Average Debt: $ $ $

Applicants: 34,356

Accepted: 73%

Enrolled: 27%

Grad in 6 Years: 69%

Returning First-years: 85%

Academics: ✐ ✐ ✐

Social: 💬 💬 💬

Q of L: ★ ★ ★

Admissions: (806) 742-1480

Email Address:
admissions@ttu.edu

Strong Programs:
Agriculture
Animal Science
Communication Studies
Education
Marketing
Mechanical Engineering
Music
Wind Energy

Texas Tech University has come a long way from its humble beginnings. Founded as Texas Technological College in 1923, the school opened its doors two years later in the West Texas city of Lubbock with fewer than 1,000 students. Today, Texas Tech has 13 colleges and schools, including a School of Veterinary Medicine and a School of Law, and eight academic locations. Hosting more than 29,000 full-time undergraduates, it aspires to become a distinguished research university on the national level. "We are enjoying increasing emphasis on undergraduate research, service learning, and community engagement," administrators say.

Tech's campus sits on more than 1,800 acres and features impressive landscaping and Spanish Renaissance–style red-tile-roofed buildings. The university has invested over $900 million in improving campus facilities since 2016. Tech has a slew of unique facilities on its campus, including an Agri-STEM Complex and a USDA Cotton Classification Complex. Newer construction includes the Academic Sciences Building and a renovation and expansion of the Texas Tech National Ranching Heritage Center.

The university offers more than 150 degree programs. Tech's comprehensive core curriculum requirements span all of the colleges and schools and include the usual arts and sciences courses; some majors involve a capstone course as well. Mechanical engineering, marketing, communication studies, biology, and management are some of the most popular majors, and the education, animal science, wind energy, and music programs are also

"We are enjoying increasing emphasis on undergraduate research."

well regarded. The university studies major, which allows students to integrate three customizable areas of study, is a popular option. New majors include human-centered AI, construction engineering technology, event management, and more.

Despite Tech's massive size, 79 percent of classes have fewer than 50 students. As at many large research universities, a junior reports, academic rigor and quality of instruction "really depend on the teacher and the level of the class." Graduate assistants may lead discussion sections or labs, but they aren't the main force at the lectern. An optional First Year Raider Experience program helps with the transition from high school to college.

Students are able to get involved in research through the True Scholars program, which also provides funding. Outstanding first-year students may enroll in Tech's Honors College, which offers personalized mentorship, a living/learning community, and special course offerings. They can also work on research projects, either independently (with a professor's guidance) or as part of a student/faculty team. For those yearning to leave the hardscrabble plains of West Texas, Texas Tech's footprint expands far beyond Lubbock, including a campus in Costa Rica. Around 5 percent of students go abroad to study in more than 50 countries; approximately 20 percent of those are first-generation students. "Tech students want to learn and excel and push those around them to do the same," says a student.

The Tech student body is largely homegrown; 90 percent hail from the Lone Star State, and 2 percent come from foreign nations. Black students account for 6 percent of the undergraduate population, Hispanics/Latinos 30 percent, Asian Americans 3 percent, and multiracial students 5 percent. Administrators say the number of first-generation students has doubled over the past decade. According to a public relations major, "A majority of students identify as Republican." Tech offers merit scholarships worth an average of $4,500 as well as athletic awards. Elite chess players can vie for a handful of scholarships as well. The Red Raider Guarantee offers free tuition and fees to qualified first-years who are Texas residents and whose families earn less than $80,000 per year. The $10K Degree Completion Program allows students with at least 80 credit hours to earn their degree for as little as $10,000.

Only 23 percent of the students at Tech live in the 20 residence halls, and first-years are required to do so. "The dorms are the ultimate college experience," enthuses one senior. Co-ed, single-sex, and quiet study dorms are available, as are 18 living/learning communities. Dining options are plentiful, and a junior says, "Whether you're a vegetarian or on a protein diet, you'll eat well here." A safe-ride shuttle service offers students added levels of security and convenience, and the Risk Intervention and Safety Education office is working to prevent sexual violence and support personal wellness on campus.

More than 500 student organizations offer plenty of activities to keep students busy on campus. Twelve percent of the men pledge fraternities and 16 percent of the women join sororities, so a sizable contingent heads to the parties at Greek Circle, although students say Greek groups don't dominate the social scene. Since most students live off campus, that's where most of the weekend action is. "Most partying happens at places like bars or house parties," explains a junior. Lubbock's Depot District is a popular destination, as most bars and clubs admit anyone 18 and over. Annual traditions at Texas Tech include homecoming, complete with a bonfire and parade; the Carol of Lights near the end of the fall semester; and Arbor Day, when hundreds of students gather to plant flowers across campus. The city of Lubbock (population 260,000) offers numerous opportunities to get involved with the community through work with the Boys & Girls Clubs of America, United Way, animal shelters, or Bible study at local churches. Popular road trips include any of the four nearby lakes (for picnicking, boating, or camping), skiing in New Mexico (four hours away), and anywhere the Red Raiders are competing.

The Division I Red Raiders are members of the Big 12 Conference. When the football team takes the field, the Masked Rider, replete with red-and-black cape and cowboy hat, motivates the crowd by galloping up and down the sidelines, and "fans throw tortillas on the field at kickoff," says a sophomore. Men's basketball, men's and women's track and field, soccer, softball, and women's tennis have brought home titles recently. The university's livestock and meat-judging teams have won several national championships. Intramural and club sports, which attract thousands of undergraduates, include everything from soccer and flag football to pickleball and sand volleyball.

Texas Tech has grown and thrived over the past century. Students should come prepared for the heat, the relative isolation of the West Texas Plains, and the effort it often takes to be more than a number at any school of this size. Those who do, says a public relations major, will be rewarded by a strong sense of community and school pride: "Everyone is friendly here at Texas Tech because we're all part of something bigger than ourselves."

Annual traditions at Texas Tech include homecoming, complete with a bonfire and parade, and the Carol of Lights near the end of the fall semester.

The $10K Degree Completion Program allows students with at least 80 credit hours to earn their degree for as little as $10,000.

Overlaps

University of Arkansas, University of Houston, University of Oklahoma, Texas A&M, Texas State, UT Austin, UT Dallas, UT San Antonio

If You Apply To ›

Texas Tech: Rolling admissions. Accepts the Common Application. Please consult Texas Tech's website for the most up-to-date information regarding standardized test requirements.

University of Toronto: See page 361.

Trinity College

300 Summit Street, Hartford, CT 06106

Long known for both its quality academics and its well-to-do students, Trinity is shaking up its admissions practices and emerging as a national leader in efforts to diversify its student body. Abundant community-based learning and service opportunities take imaginative advantage of the school's urban setting. Trinity joins Lafayette, Smith, Swarthmore, and Union as a small liberal arts college that offers engineering.

Website: www.trincoll.edu
Location: City Center
Private
Total Enrollment: 2,189
Undergraduates: 2,165
Male/Female: 49/51
Financial Aid: 72%
Pell Grant: 12%
Expense: Pr $ $ $
Student Loans: 42%
Average Debt: $ $ $ $
Applicants: 6,396
Accepted: 34%
Enrolled: 27%
Grad in 6 Years: 85%
Returning First-years: 90%
Academics: ✎ ✎ ✎ ✎
Social: 🗩 🗩 🗩 🗩
Q of L: ★ ★ ★
Admissions: (860) 297-2180
Email Address: admissions
.office@trincoll.edu

Strong Programs:
American Studies
Biology
Economics
Engineering
Human Rights Studies
Neuroscience
Political Science
Psychology

For students at Trinity College, the learning experience doesn't stop at the campus borders. At first glance, the small liberal arts college and the large city of Hartford, Connecticut, seem like an uneasy match. But instead of insulating itself from outside problems, Trinity takes advantage of its surroundings by using Hartford as its classroom. At the college's downtown Liberal Arts Action Lab, community partners team up with students and faculty to research and propose solutions to problems facing the city. On campus, academic standards continue to rise, and students graduate with a strong liberal arts background. "Students are the priority here," says one senior.

Trinity was founded in 1823 by Connecticut Episcopalians as an alternative to Congregationalist Yale. Splendid Gothic-style stone buildings decorate Trinity's 100-acre campus. The large, grassy quadrangle is perfect for tossing a Frisbee or relaxing on warm spring and fall afternoons. Along with revitalizing the neighborhood that surrounds it, Trinity's campus is undergoing its own revitalization. Newer facilities include the Gruss Music Center, the Crescent Center for Arts and Neuroscience, and several athletic fields. Classroom facilities in some of the college's original buildings have been renovated, and the Crescent Street Townhouses provide accommodations for 340 upperclassmen.

Trinity's general education requirements include distribution courses across the liberal arts and sciences, as well as demonstrated proficiency in writing, mathematics, and a foreign language. The First-Year Seminar emphasizes writing, speaking, and critical thinking; the seminar instructor serves as students' academic advisor. Five Gateway programs give selected first-year students a chance to study in-depth topics from interdisciplinary perspectives through a multi-semester sequence of courses. Offerings include InterArts, Interdisciplinary Science, Community Action, Humanities, and Global Health Humanities, which one student calls "phenomenal—very challenging and rewarding." A global engagement requirement can be completed by coursework or study abroad.

> **"[The Gateway programs are] phenomenal—very challenging and rewarding."**

Popular majors at Trinity include economics, political science, psychology, and public policy and law. Human rights studies is notable, and students say the school's small engineering program is strong. Accelerated bachelor's/master's degree programs are available in American studies and neuroscience. Trinity's close ties to the community are also apparent in the curriculum; students can take courses on urban development and the history of the city of Hartford or choose from service-learning courses that incorporate opportunities to work with more than 80 local community service organizations.

Faculty/student collaboration is a tradition at Trinity. Two-thirds of students work with professors on research and scholarly papers, and many students join their mentors to present findings at symposia. "The academic climate is small, discussion driven, opportunity driven, and [a] supporting community," says a junior. Sixty-nine percent of classes have fewer than 20 students. Students say that professors have high expectations of them, and most go the extra mile to provide support.

More than half of the students seek internships in government (including the Legislative Internship Program at the nearby state capital), nonprofit organizations, and businesses in Hartford (the insurance capital of the world). Trinity's study-away program, in which 52 percent of students take part, includes the college's own international program sites in four cities, ranging from Cape Town to Vienna, as well as more than 90 approved and affiliated programs. Other enticing choices include the Trinity/La MaMa Performing Arts program in New York City and the Washington Semester in D.C.

Although the school has had a reputation for enrolling, in the words of a sophomore, "prep school students from privileged families," it is moving away from its traditionally heavy penchant for New England boarding school grads, seeking to diversify the student body. Thirteen percent of Trinity students are Connecticut natives; an increasing number come from California, and 14 percent are international. Asian Americans currently account for 4 percent of the student body, Hispanics/Latinos 9 percent, Black students 6 percent, and multiracial students 4 percent. "For the majority, we are very liberal," says a human rights and political science major. Athletic scholarships are not available and merit awards are limited, but Trinity does provide special financial packages to replace student loans for students with the most need. The college also guarantees to meet students' full demonstrated need for four years.

Eighty-two percent of Trinity's students live in the co-ed dorms. First-years are grouped into "nests" of 60 to 75 students, aimed at creating a more intimate sense of community. Students report that meals at Mather, Trinity's renovated dining hall, are adequate, with options for those with special tastes and needs, and the à la carte and grab-and-go items at the Bistro and the Cave provide alternatives. "Campus safety officers are always around to make sure our students feel safe," says a senior.

"The social life revolves around on-campus activity," a sophomore says. Students praise the Entertainment Activities Council, which brings in comedians and musical performers and organizes parties, study breaks, and community service days. "The campus dances are very popular with the entire student body," says a senior. The Underground Coffeehouse and the Bistro's weekly comedy nights are also student favorites. But the action on Thursday, Friday, and Saturday nights is mostly at the Greek houses (25 percent of the men and 21 percent of the women join up). Students say alcohol is not hard to come by, but "the campus policies on alcohol are fairly severe on underage drinkers and abusers," says a student. Spring Weekend brings bands to campus for a three-day party outdoors. Popular road trips include Montreal, Boston, New York City, and the beaches and mountains of Maine.

"Hartford has a terrific assortment of restaurants, ranging from cheap but delicious ethnic fare to upscale, parent-friendly places," says a philosophy major. A college-sponsored "culture van" takes students downtown to catch a show at the Bushnell or visit the Wadsworth Atheneum, the nation's oldest public art museum. A professional soccer team and a citywide bike-share program were recently introduced. "We have both a beautiful rural campus and are located in a capital city,"

Spring Weekend brings bands to campus for a three-day party outdoors.

"We have both a beautiful rural campus and are located in a capital city."

Accelerated bachelor's/master's degree programs are available in American studies and neuroscience.

Splendid Gothic-style stone buildings decorate Trinity's 100-acre campus.

opines a senior. "Our location provides us with endless cultural opportunities and fun things to do as well as educational access to internships." The Office of Community Service and Civic Engagement helps coordinate such opportunities, and students have created and run organizations that provide housing, tutoring, meals, and other services to youth, families, and senior citizens.

Trinity's Bantams compete in Division III, and both men's and women's squash are powerhouses, and men's basketball won its first national championship in 2025. Other solid programs include men's ice hockey, football, and women's lacrosse. Homecoming typically brings Wesleyan or Amherst to campus for football. About half of the students take part in the intramural and club sports programs.

> "The campus dances are very popular with the entire student body."

With its dual emphasis on traditional liberal arts education and civic engagement, Trinity aims to prepare students to be independent thinkers ready to make a difference both locally and globally. And students here have taken their civic responsibility to heart. At Trinity, an English major says, "Students are pushed to reshape the way they think and tackle challenges to make an impact in their community."

If You Apply To ›

Trinity College: Early decision I and II, regular decision. SATs or ACTs: optional. Accepts the Common Application with optional essay supplement that encourages applicants to write about their interest in Trinity.

Trinity College Dublin: See page 377.

Trinity University

1 Trinity Place, San Antonio, TX 78212

One of the few national liberal arts colleges in a major city, Trinity is twice as big as nearby rivals Austin College and Southwestern University. Like Lafayette, Union, Smith, Swarthmore, and that other Trinity, it is also a rare small liberal arts college that offers engineering. Strong in business, health care administration, and education. San Antonio offers superb internships and runs neck and neck with Austin as the most desirable city in Texas.

Trinity University is a small school with big bucks, with one of the nation's largest educational endowments, over $2 billion, for a school its size. The wealth is used unashamedly to lure capable students with bargain tuition rates and to entice talented professors from around the nation. The result? A student body composed of smart, ambitious men and women and a stellar faculty. Students here enjoy challenges but still manage a laid-back Texas attitude. "Our uniqueness stems from our diversity, rigorous academic programs, and community focus all rolled into one," says a senior.

Trinity was founded in 1869 in a small central Texas town just after the end of the Civil War. In 1952, the school moved to its current location, a residential area about three miles from downtown San Antonio, one of the most beautiful cities in the Southwest. The 125-acre campus, located on what was once a rock quarry, is a National Historic District filled with the Southern architecture of O'Neil Ford. Everything fits the school's aesthetically pleasing and somewhat well-to-do image, from the uniform redbrick buildings to the stately pathways that wind along gorgeous green lawns and through immaculate gardens spotted with Henry Moore sculptures. Trinity's most dominant landmark is Murchison Tower, which rises in the center of campus and is visible from numerous vantage points throughout San Antonio. The Chapman-Halsell-Dicke Complex, completed in 2024, features student-focused spaces in the Halsell and Chapman Centers, alongside Dicke Hall, which serves as the front door to the Humanities.

Trinity's general education curriculum, called Pathways, contains five signature curricular elements: the First-Year Experience, Core Capacities, Approaches to Creation and Analysis, Interdisciplinary Discoveries, and Experiential Learning. Trinity has a highly praised education department, with a five-year master of arts in teaching program, and a good advising program for students interested in health professions. Trinity's business-related programs are some of its best

> **"Trinity is rigorous in the way that everyone seems to be doing research or internships."**

and most popular; the engineering, computer science, and psychology programs are strong too. Neuroscience, finance, accounting, and engineering science enroll the most students. Budding journalists and advertisers can try their hand at broadcasting through internships with the communication department's television and radio stations. The five-year accounting program allows students to serve an internship with the big four accounting firms in offices around the nation while earning a salary and receiving college credit. The Cultures and Languages Across the Curriculum program features classes such as business, communication, modern languages, and education taught in languages that include Chinese, Japanese, Spanish, and Russian.

"Trinity is rigorous in the way that everyone seems to be doing research or internships, or have three majors," comments a political science major. But the instructors are supportive, and small classes—69 percent have fewer than 20 students—allow for more interaction. "Every professor I've had has known me by name," says a business and communication double major. "Professors are not only experts in their fields but also deeply committed to their students." A team of professional academic advisors work with incoming first-year students until they declare their majors, at which point students are assigned to a faculty advisor within their department. Students can participate in research projects with faculty mentors, including in the Summer Undergraduate Research Fellowship. "The Arts, Letters, and Enterprise program is pretty much business for nonprofits," explains a junior. "The best part is its internship matching program [with] San Antonio with nonprofits." Students also recommend study abroad, which is offered in more than 50 countries.

"Students at Trinity are really energetic," says a senior. "They're engaged, curious, and passionate about a wide range of interests," adds another. Seventy-eight percent of Trinity undergraduates are Texans, and 5 percent are international. The school is fairly diverse ethnically; Hispanics/Latinos account for 25 percent, Asian Americans 8 percent, Black students 4 percent, and multi-

> **"Every professor I've had has known me by name."**

racial students 6 percent. Politically, students say the population leans liberal, and "topics such as racial justice, equity and inclusion, climate change, and free speech often spark active conversations," observes a senior. "The campus community generally values respectful debate." Merit scholarships averaging $26,600 are available to academically gifted students; there are no athletic scholarships.

Students are required to live on campus through junior year. In fact, 79 percent of the students live in the residence halls, which one student describes as "fantastic,

(continued)

Applicants: 12,504
Accepted: 26%
Enrolled: 21%
Grad in 6 Years: 84%
Returning First-years: 93%
Academics: ✐ ✐ ✐
Social: 🗨 🗨 🗨
Q of L: ★ ★ ★
Admissions: (800) 874-6489
Email Address:
  admissions@trinity.edu

Strong Programs:
Biology
Business
Computer Science
Economics
Education
Engineering
Neuroscience
Psychology

Students look forward to Fiesta, a weeklong celebration of San Antonio's mixed culture featuring bands, dancing, food, and drink.

with walk-in closets, private balconies, suite-style rooms, and a cleaning service." Still, students echo one classmate, who says, "housing day is routinely one of the most stressful days on campus," as securing a preferred room can be difficult. A university-owned apartment complex is an option for upperclassmen, but most seniors find their own places off campus. Campus dining is "delicious," according to a student. "I've been eating on campus for four years, and I'm still not sick of the food." A junior says students feel safe and "the university police are constantly monitoring the campus." Other student services also receive praise. "We have great advising and mental health services that are all free and easily accessible for students," says an accounting major.

With more than 100 clubs hosting weekend events, there are plenty of activities to keep students busy. The university sponsors a lecture series that brings notable politicians and public figures to campus. Beer and wine may be consumed on campus by those of legal age in upper-class residence halls. Approximately 25 percent of undergraduates are involved in local fraternity and sorority organizations, which hold parties in Greek houses just off campus. "Students love Nacho Hour and Milk and Cookies every Wednesday and Thursday," says a junior. During birthdays, friends dunk the celebrant in the main campus fountain. Students also look forward to Fiesta, a weeklong celebration of San Antonio's mixed culture featuring bands, dancing, food, and drink, as well as an annual block party, Chocolate Fest, and TigerFest.

San Antonio, with its famed River Walk replete with interesting restaurants, receives a well-deserved thumbs-up from students. It doesn't hurt that the city is home to several other colleges. "My friends and I love exploring the San Antonio food scene," cheers a senior. "There are also fun things to do like the zoo, the botanical gardens, museums, the missions, downtown, farmer's markets, etc." Students get involved in city life by contributing more than 88,000 hours of community service every year. The Trinity University Volunteer Action Community connects students with local volunteer opportunities. The city's beautiful, warm weather provides plenty of activities for the students year-round, but there are also many fun road trips. The funky state capital of Austin is 90 miles north, and students can also road-trip to the Texas Gulf Coast and the Hill Country.

> **"My friends and I love exploring the San Antonio food scene."**

Trinity's 18 varsity sports teams compete in the Division III Southern Athletic Association as of fall 2025. Prior to joining the SAA, the Tigers men's and women's tennis teams and the track and field teams brought home recent conference championships, and the baseball team is nationally competitive. Students enjoy a variety of intramural and club sports, including flag football, ultimate Frisbee, and sand volleyball.

A big state and big money give students at this small university many of the advantages of a larger school, from strong preprofessional offerings and accomplished professors to plentiful research opportunities. But a senior says it's Trinity's emphasis on people and the rich heritage of its location that make it a special place: "Trinity's strong sense of community as well as its San Antonio roots provide a great culture."

Overlaps

Austin College, Colorado College, Denison, Furman, Lafayette, Macalester, Skidmore, Southwestern

If You Apply To ›

Trinity University: Early decision I and II, early action, regular decision. Accepts the Common Application with supplement. Please consult Trinity's website for the most up-to-date information regarding standardized test requirements.

100 E Normal Avenue, Kirksville, MO 63501

Widely regarded as Missouri's de facto honors college, Truman has more in common with private institutions than with nondescript regional publics. Occupies a public ivy niche like Miami of Ohio and William & Mary. Rural setting encourages strong focus on academics, including lots of undergraduate research. Less than a quarter of the students are from out of state, mainly from Illinois.

Truman State University, Missouri's only public liberal arts college, attracts high achievers from across the Show-Me State. Founded in 1867 as a regional teacher training institution, the school became a statewide university in 1985 and 11 years later took the name of the only Missourian to serve as a president of the United States. Indeed, since shifting to a liberal arts and sciences mission, Truman has worked to become a "public ivy" on the order of Miami University (OH) or William & Mary. True, the small town of Kirksville, Missouri, is no Williamsburg, Virginia—or even Oxford, Ohio. But the school's relative isolation makes it easier to concentrate on academics. "Truman is a fairly inexpensive school that has an amazing reputation," states an accounting major. "This brings students who are extremely hardworking but also want an affordable education."

Truman is located in the northeastern corner of Missouri, about 200 miles from both Kansas City and St. Louis. The flower-laden campus includes approximately 40 buildings on 210 acres, many of which are Georgian in style—in fact, the oldest portion of the campus, dating to 1873, is modeled on Thomas Jefferson's design for the University of Virginia. The Robison Planetarium and Multimedia Theater is one of the campus's newer facilities.

Truman's general education curriculum—The Dialogues—emphasizes practical skills and experiences alongside breadth in the liberal arts and sciences. Highlights of the curriculum include a common experience for incoming first-year students, consisting of a Self and Society seminar, as well as a requirement that seniors take a capstone course in their major. In addition, all students are encouraged to complete at least one hands-on learning experience, such as study abroad, an internship, or undergraduate research. First-year students participate in Truman Week, a five-day program designed to help them adjust to college life.

> **"Truman brings students who are extremely hardworking but also want an affordable education."**

The most popular major is business administration; biology, exercise science, and health sciences round out the list of programs with the highest enrollment. An interdisciplinary studies major allows students to combine coursework from two or more disciplines to create a specialized major. Nursing is a traditional strength, and there are also solid five-year programs for students interested in education or accounting, which culminate in the awarding of bachelor's and master's degrees. Majors in data science, cannabis and natural medicinals, and environmental science are among recently added programs.

Students describe an academic climate that is "supportive and collaborative." Sixty-two percent of classes have fewer than 20 students, which makes access to top-notch professors the norm and "allows for complex and mature discussions of course material," explains a sophomore. Students praise the career center, and a first-year notes, "There are tons of seminars to talk about practical ways to improve your hirability."

Website: www.truman.edu
Location: Rural
Public
Total Enrollment: 2,514
Undergraduates: 2,459
Male/Female: 39/61
Financial Aid: 91%
Pell Grant: 30%
Expense: Pub $
Student Loans: 45%
Average Debt: $
Applicants: 2,883
Accepted: 84%
Enrolled: 26%
Grad in 6 Years: 69%
Returning First-years: 85%
Academics: ✎ ✎ ✎
Social: 🗩 🗩 🗩
Q of L: ★ ★ ★
Admissions: (660) 785-4114
Email Address:
  admissions@truman.edu

Strong Programs:
Accounting
Biology
Business Administration
Data Science
Education
Exercise Science
Nursing
Psychology

Students seeking to challenge themselves beyond the regular curriculum can sign up for the Honors Scholar Program, which requires them to complete at least five rigorous courses of their choosing in a range of disciplines. Twenty percent of students partake in study abroad opportunities available via roughly 500 programs in more than 65 countries around the world. Forty percent of students conduct independent research or collaborate with faculty members on research projects, and Truman typically sends one of the largest delegations of undergraduates to the annual National Conference on Undergraduate Research.

"I would call Truman a nerd school," says a physics and mathematics double major. "Nearly everyone at Truman is there to learn first, so education and work take priority over almost everything else." Seventy-seven percent of Truman students are native to Missouri, and 10 percent hail from abroad. "The majority of students are from middle-class, white homes," notes a sociology major. "There is a need for improvement in diversity." Hispanic/Latino students represent 4 percent of the student body, Asian Americans 2 percent, Black students 2 percent, and multiracial students 3 percent. A political science major categorizes the low-key political climate as "slightly left of center." Merit scholarships are available to qualified students; the average award is $7,800. The school also hands out roughly 300 athletic scholarships. Additionally, the Truman Access Grant provides funding to a limited number of students who have unmet need after their federal financial aid and Truman scholarship award have been packaged.

Thirty-two percent of Truman students live on campus in the residence halls. Students say it's easy to get a room, but most move off campus after their sophomore year. "Campus food is as good as can be expected for mass-produced buffet-style dining," opines a senior. Students report feeling safe on their rural campus, and Truman has invested in mental health counseling services and created campuswide wellness initiatives. A nursing major agrees, "Truman has made an incredible change in how it approaches the topic of mental health."

Social life at Truman is robust, according to students. "Because of Truman's semi-isolated location, the Student Activities Board brings in various musicians, comedians, YouTube stars, speakers, and performers to campus for free," explains a first-year. The Greek system plays an integral part in Truman's social life—22 percent of men and 17 percent of women sign up—but there are also 200 other student organizations to choose from. Since the campus is dry, says an exercise science major, "Most parties take place off campus, where they're hosted by Greek organizations, athletic teams, or one of the bars in town." Students also venture out on road trips to St. Louis, Kansas City, various destinations in Iowa, and Quincy, Illinois. Everyone looks forward to homecoming and Oktoberfest (featuring free root beer) in the fall and the Final Blowout carnival in the spring, with wacky games, inflatables, free food, and prizes. "Two traditions that stick out to me are giving the Harry S. Truman statue a penny for good luck on your test," notes a senior. "The second is kissing in the sunken garden is a sign of future marriage."

The town of Kirksville (population 17,600) grows on you, say students. "All of the essentials of a college town are present, including a Walmart, a bowling alley, a good movie theater, and a beautiful state park," a business administration major says. Two-thirds of students take advantage of various opportunities to get involved in volunteer work and service learning. The Big Event is a popular one-day service event that brings more than 1,500 campus volunteers to Kirksville. Truman hosts 12 service organizations, which provide thousands of hours of service every year.

When not exercising their academic muscles, Truman's Bulldogs, members of the Great Lakes Valley Conference, are succeeding in the pool and on the playing field. The men's and women's swim teams have won multiple Division II titles, and the football, men's and women's basketball, and women's track and field teams are also competitive. The success of the forensics team, the school's longest-running cocurricular activity and winner of several state titles, speaks for itself. Roughly a quarter of the students participate in the 20 intramural events offered per semester, which include everything from basketball and soccer to pickleball and baggo (a.k.a. cornhole).

"With some of the highest admissions standards of any public university in the state, Truman has a distinct culture of academic excellence," says a student. Indeed, Truman offers challenging academics pursued within a close-knit community. Though its rural Missouri location can feel isolating, its affordable price certainly makes it worth considering.

Overlaps

Bradley, Creighton, University of Minnesota–Morris, University of Missouri, Missouri State, The College of New Jersey, Saint Louis University, SUNY–Geneseo

If You Apply To ›

Truman State: Rolling admissions. Accepts the Common Application with supplement. Please consult Truman's website for the most up-to-date information regarding standardized test requirements.

Tufts University

Medford, MA 02155

One of the smallest and most undergraduate-focused of the major research universities, Tufts is known for its global focus and emphasis on civic engagement. Strengths run the gamut from classics and philosophy to engineering and international relations. Located just outside student-friendly Boston, it begs comparison to Brown as well as to other top urban schools such as Georgetown, Northwestern, and WashU. The Experimental College lets students take nontraditional courses for credit.

Website: www.tufts.edu
Location: City Outskirts
Private
Total Enrollment: 13,599
Undergraduates: 7,126
Male/Female: 43/55
Financial Aid: 81%
Pell Grant: 13%
Expense: Pr $ $ $ $
Student Loans: 26%
Average Debt: $ $
Applicants: 34,432
Accepted: 11%
Enrolled: 46%
Grad in 6 Years: 94%
Returning First-years: 96%
Academics: ✍ ✍ ✍ ✍
Social: 🌑 🌑 🌑

Founded in 1852 by Universalist businessman Charles Tufts, and once considered a backup for those who couldn't get into an Ivy, Tufts University isn't a safety school anymore. Applications are up dramatically, propelling Tufts into the ranks of the more selective schools in the country. With its strong academics, high-achieving student body, and attractive setting, some might say that not much more separates Tufts from its illustrious neighbors, Harvard and MIT, than a few stops on the T. Says one senior, "Tufts's institutional personality is like a jumbo-sized bubble filled with a civically engaged, conscientious, and passionate community and student body."

Tufts's 150-acre, tree-lined campus on Walnut Hill overlooks the heart of nearby Boston and is a striking scene. The main campus, with its brick and stone buildings, sits on the Medford/Somerville boundary. Medford, the fifth-oldest city in the country, was a powerful shipbuilding center during the 19th century. Somerville lies adjacent to the Tufts campus, and in 1776, the first American flag was raised on its Prospect Hill. Notable campus facilities include the LEED Gold–certified Science and Engineering Complex.

Undergraduate teaching is what attracts students to Tufts. They get highly personalized attention from faculty, and they enjoy wide freedom to pursue independent study and to complete research and internships for credit. Tufts students also get a healthy diet of traditional academic fare. For liberal arts students, distribution

(continued)

Q of L: ★ ★ ★ ★
Admissions: (617) 627-3170
Email Address:
 undergraduate
 .admissions@tufts.edu

Strong Programs:
Biology
Child Study and Human
 Development
Classics
Computer Science
Economics
Engineering
International Relations
Philosophy

University-sponsored activities include concerts, plays, and free movies on weekend nights.

The Civic Semester program sends incoming students to engage in experiential learning and social justice issues in Peru or Thailand.

requirements include a world civilization course in addition to art, English, language and culture, social sciences, humanities, natural sciences, and math. Engineers must take eight courses in the arts, humanities, and social sciences, with one of those fulfilling a writing requirement. The most popular majors include biology, computer science, international relations, and economics. Tufts also boasts strong classics and philosophy departments, and there is an excellent child study and human development program. Interdisciplinary programs, such as data science, civic studies, and human factors engineering (or engineering psychology), are growing in popularity. With the university's acquisition of the School of the Museum of Fine Arts in Boston, students can earn a B.F.A. in interdisciplinary studio art or pursue a five-year program that combines the B.F.A. with a B.A. or B.S. degree in another field within the School of Arts and Sciences.

Tufts has two popular programs in which students who need a break from being on the receiving end of knowledge can develop and teach courses. The first, the Experimental College, annually offers more than 100 nontraditional, full-credit courses on topics ranging from Pharmacology and Therapeutics to The Ethics of Voluntourism that are taught by students, faculty, and outside lecturers. The second, Explorations seminars, connects students with a faculty member who doubles as an advisor; these courses are a way for first-years to get to know each other and ease into the college experience.

> **"My fellow students are civically engaged, intellectually curious, collaborative, and socially aware."**

"The academic climate at Tufts is a very stimulating one that really motivates you to find your passion and dig deep into research and the intricacies of different disciplines," says an economics major, and students agree that the atmosphere is supportive. "No two students here are the same, which creates a collaborative community rather than a cutthroat environment," says a child study and human development major. Fifty-nine percent of classes have fewer than 20 students, and most courses are taught by full professors. "Professors at Tufts are extremely accommodating and willing to help," says a senior. "If students reach out or attend office hours and put in the effort, professors will meet the students halfway."

The Tisch College of Civic Life is praised for offering "really great opportunities," says a computer science and environmental studies major, from the Civic Semester program that sends incoming students to engage in experiential learning and social justice issues in Peru or Thailand, to the Tufts Prison Initiative and the Tisch Scholars leadership program. Tufts also offers a Washington Semester, exchanges with Swarthmore and Spelman, and cross-registration at several Boston schools. Forty-five percent of undergrads study abroad. Students may choose to spend their summer at Tufts's overseas campus in Talloires, France, embark on a semester or year abroad at one of nearly 200 preapproved programs, or select one of Tufts's own full-immersion programs in 10 locations around the globe.

> **"Professors at Tufts are extremely accommodating and willing to help."**

"My fellow students are civically engaged, intellectually curious, collaborative, and socially aware," says a junior. Twenty percent of undergrads hail from Massachusetts; California, New York, and New Jersey are also well represented. The university's reputation in international relations attracts a respectable number of international students (17 percent) and Americans living abroad. Asian American students make up 17 percent of the population, Hispanics/Latinos 10 percent, Black students 6 percent, and multiracial students 8 percent. "Politically, there's a strong progressive presence on campus, but there's room for respectful debate and differing opinions," says a senior. Very few merit-based scholarships are available, and there are no athletic scholarships, but the new Tufts Tuition Pact guarantees free tuition for U.S. families earning less than $150,000.

Forty-one percent of students live on campus. Accommodations in the Uphill and Downhill (the two quads joined by a great expanse of grass and trees) campus dorms vary from long hallways of double rooms to apartment-like suites, old houses, and co-ops—and a good-natured rivalry exists between the two areas. First-years and sophomores must live on campus in the dorms, while juniors and seniors compete in a lottery or move to apartments just a short walk from campus. "Tufts is very accommodating and has a streamlined process for accommodations," a student notes. All first-year students are required to have the unlimited meal plan, and the dining services get good reviews. The campus police department is said to be effective, and a chemical engineering major reports that an ongoing dialogue is "pushing the administration in the right direction for handling sexual assault on campus, and positive changes have been made." Students also speak positively about other services, including career advising and mental health support.

According to an international relations major, "Tufts is not a party school, but there are many opportunities to be social on campus." Tufts has earned a national reputation for its programs to promote the "responsible" use of alcohol and has revised multiple policies governing the Greek system, including delaying rush until sophomore year. Currently, 12 percent of the men and 12 percent of the women join fraternities and sororities. University-sponsored activities include concerts, plays (Aidekman Arts Center stages 15 to 20 productions each year), and free movies on weekend nights. Several a cappella groups thrive at Tufts, and a favorite student group is the Tufts Dance Collective, where "groups of students practice goofy dances all semester" and put on two shows per year that draw big crowds. Other major campus events include homecoming and a Halloween tradition when "everyone puts pumpkins in hard-to-reach places all over campus," explains a sophomore. Spring Fling, an outdoor concert that helps students relax before final exams, is also popular.

While suburban Medford may not be exciting for those of college age, the T metro system extends to the Tufts campus, so it's easy to make a quick jaunt to "student city" (a.k.a. Boston) for work or play. Davis Square in Somerville is even closer and provides plenty of restaurants, nightlife, and music stores. The largest student organization by far, with more than 1,000 students, is the Leonard Carmichael Society, the umbrella group for volunteer activities ranging from adult literacy and blood drives to work with the homeless and victims of domestic violence.

Tufts fields 29 teams in the Division III New England Small College Athletic Conference (NESCAC). The Jumbos (named after PT Barnum's famous circus elephant) men's soccer, men's lacrosse, rowing, and field hockey all won national titles in 2025. Sixteen percent of students play in intramural and club sports. The Tufts Sabermetrics team, which grew out of the Experimental College, is a national powerhouse in competitions that apply sophisticated statistical techniques to the sport of baseball.

Tufts is experiencing a modern-day renaissance. This, along with a swelling applicant pool, makes Tufts a much hotter school than it was just a few years ago. And its proximity to Boston, an intellectual and educational mecca, makes it even more attractive. "You get the small liberal arts feel with access to a big city's energy, culture, and professional opportunities," cheers a senior. "In the end, you graduate not only with a Tufts degree that's respected and meaningful, but also with lasting friendships and memories."

Tufts boasts strong classics and philosophy departments, and there is an excellent child study and human development program.

"Tufts is not a party school, but there are many opportunities to be social on campus."

Overlaps

Brown, Cornell University, Dartmouth, Harvard, Northwestern, Penn, WashU in St. Louis, Wesleyan

If You Apply To ›

Tufts: Early decision I and II, regular decision. Accepts the Common Application with supplement. Portfolio required for applicants to School of the Museum of Fine Arts. Application includes optional gender identity field. Please consult Tufts's website for the most up-to-date information regarding standardized test requirements.

6823 St. Charles Avenue, New Orleans, LA 70118

The map may say that Tulane is in the South, but it has the temperament of an East Coast institution. Similar number of undergraduates as Emory and Vanderbilt among leading Southeastern universities. Tulane has developed a strong emphasis on interdisciplinary research and community service, both academic and practical.

Website: www.tulane.edu
Location: City Center
Private
Total Enrollment: 11,012
Undergraduates: 7,248
Male/Female: 38/62
Financial Aid: 69%
Pell Grant: 11%
Expense: Pr $ $ $
Student Loans: 27%
Average Debt: $ $
Applicants: 32,069
Accepted: 14%
Enrolled: 40%
Grad in 6 Years: 86%
Returning First-years: 93%
Academics: ✍ ✍ ✍
Social: 💬 💬 💬 💬
Q of L: ★ ★ ★
Admissions: (800) 873-9283
Email Address: undergrad
.admission@tulane.edu

Strong Programs:
Architecture
Business
Environmental Sciences
International Studies
Latin American Studies
Natural Sciences
Political Economy
Public Health

Once a staid, genteel choice for students seeking a traditional education, Tulane University has rebranded itself with a focus on interdisciplinary research, scholarship, and community service. It now attracts service-minded and research-oriented students from all 50 states who choose from more than 150 service-learning opportunities. Tulane promises a solid education to those who are ready to take up residence in the Big Easy. "To attend Tulane is to be a resident of one of the most unique cities in the world," cheers a senior. "The flexibility, service opportunities, and city itself make it different from any other school in the country."

Tulane is unusual in that it was created as a public medical college in 1834 but then privatized in 1884 thanks to the beneficence of businessman Paul Tulane. The school's 110-acre campus sits in an attractive residential area of uptown New Orleans, about 15 minutes from the French Quarter and the business district. The administration building, Gibson Hall, faces St. Charles Avenue, where one of the nation's last streetcar lines still clatters past mansions. Across the street is Audubon Park, a 385-acre spread where students jog, walk, study, or watch the sun set over the Mississippi River. The buildings of gray limestone and pillared brick, separated by southern live oak trees, are modeled after the neo-collegiate/Creole mixture indigenous to Louisiana institutional-type structures. One point of pride is the university's 13 Tiffany windows, one of the largest collections anywhere. Recently added facilities include new homes for the School of Science & Engineering and School of Architecture, a new aquatics center, and the Commons dining facility.

Tulane remains committed to its mission as a major research university that emphasizes undergraduate opportunities. All undergrads enroll in the Newcomb-Tulane College, which coordinates academic experiences and support. Students complete a rigorous set of core curriculum requirements that includes a service-learning course as well as a public service project, which can take the form of a research project, internship, study abroad program, or honors thesis. Several programs help first-years make the transition from high school to college, such as TIDES (Tulane Interdisciplinary Experience Seminars), where students connect with a peer mentor and take a small-group course on topics as varied as yoga, J. R. R. Tolkien, and New Orleans cemetery architecture.

> **"To attend Tulane is to be a resident of one of the most unique cities in the world."**

Together, five schools—architecture, business, liberal arts, public health and tropical medicine, and science and engineering—offer more than 75 undergraduate majors. "You can take classes in all five and major across schools," explains a political science major. The most popular programs include business, psychology, social sciences, and biological sciences. Tulane's strength lies in the natural sciences, environmental sciences, architecture, and the humanities; international programs in general and Latin American studies in particular are strong. The Stone Center for Latin American studies offers more than 150 courses taught by 70 faculty members. An interdisciplinary program in political economy (economics, political science, and philosophy) stands out among the social sciences and is very popular with prelaw students. Environmental studies majors benefit from the ByWater Institute, where faculty members and students work together to study and preserve Louisiana's waterways and coast.

"Since students can really tailor their curriculum to their interests, people are usually pretty diligent about their studies," observes a mathematics and sociology double major. Sixty-one percent of classes have fewer than 20 students; graduate instructors teach some beginning-level classes in English, foreign languages, and math. But a senior says, "All of my professors have brought real-world experience to their subjects in the classroom." About 22 percent of students join the highly acclaimed honors program. Tulane offers more than 100 study abroad programs in 40 nations, including one-semester programs in locations such as Thailand to study community public health and Senegal to study international development. Even first-year students go abroad, with more than 150 who study at partner universities ranging from the American University of Paris to Temple University in Japan.

Tulane manifests a somewhat Southern feel in a sophisticated and cosmopolitan institution. "My classmates are passionate and driven to accomplish great feats in research, technology, service, and many other things," says a finance and international development major. Twelve percent of undergraduates are Louisiana residents, and 5 percent come from outside the U.S. Despite the diversity of its host city, Tulane's student body is fairly homogeneous: 6 percent are Black, 11 percent are Hispanic/Latino, 6 percent are Asian American, and 5 percent are multiracial. A senior characterizes the "average Tulane student" as "white, affluent, politically center-to-liberal, and from a large city or a surrounding suburb." The university awards hundreds of merit scholarships, averaging $19,400, and over 100 athletic scholarships.

"Crawfest has live music all day and buckets of free crawfish!"

Tulane guarantees and expects students to live on campus for their first three years. Currently, 56 percent of undergrads do so. Many upperclassmen opt to move off campus, but the university opened two new residence halls in 2025 completing The Village, on-campus housing that was funded by what an administrator says is "the largest capital investment in Tulane's history." The recently opened Dining Room at the Commons is the university's main dining facility, offering 10 meal stations with rotating menus. A monthly farmers market and food trucks that accept the school's meal plan enhance students' options. Tulane has beefed up its counseling staff and programming to combat sexual assault, and a late-night shuttle service transports students safely to and from campus.

"Tulane has a rich social scene both on and off-campus," says a public health major. "It's hard not to when you call New Orleans home." Fraternities and sororities are a presence—42 percent of the men and 53 percent of the women join—but do not dominate the social life, and there are more than 200 student organizations on campus. "Crawfest and Bookfest are my favorite festivals on campus," says an English and political economy major. "Crawfest has live music all day and buckets of free crawfish!" The New Orleans Book Festival draws best-selling authors. Playing host to about 130 festivals every year, "New Orleans itself never stops partying!" boasts a student. Mardi Gras is such a celebration that classes are suspended for two days and students from all over the country pour in to celebrate. Road-trip destinations include the Gulf Coast, Austin, Houston, and the Florida panhandle.

While schoolwork is taken seriously at Tulane, so are sports. Football and men's and women's basketball and tennis are solid, and the baseball team has a big following. The university fields 17 Green Wave teams that compete in the Division I American Athletic Conference. Club and intramural sports are big, and students can also opt for weight work, squash, or swimming, among other options, at the Reily Student Recreation Center.

Rich in tradition, Tulane is a forward-looking school where the possibilities seem endless. And like its hometown, it is an energetic melting pot of interests and activity. As one senior puts it, "Tulane is a mixture of New Orleans soul, Southern hospitality, and college student swagger." Those seeking a dynamic, service-oriented education in a vibrant city need look no further. C'est si bon!

If You Apply To ›

Tulane: Early decision I and II, early action, regular decision. Accepts the Common Application with supplement. Please consult Tulane's website for the most up-to-date information regarding standardized test requirements.

University of Tulsa

800 S Tucker Drive, Tulsa, OK 74104

Tulsa is a modestly priced private university in an area of the country dominated by large and less expensive public universities. Blessed by a substantial oil-fueled endowment, TU combines the academics of a small liberal arts college with the resources of a private research university. Engineering and computer science are strong; music and English literature are also unlikely strengths. New Great Books curriculum for honors students is special.

Website: www.utulsa.edu

Location: City Outskirts

Private

Total Enrollment: 3,439

Undergraduates: 2,573

Male/Female: 48/52

Financial Aid: 99%

Pell Grant: 34%

Expense: Pr $

Student Loans: 45%

Average Debt: $ $

Applicants: 6,631

Accepted: 58%

Enrolled: 15%

Grad in 6 Years: 69%

Returning First-years: 92%

Academics: ✑ ✑ ✑

Social: 🗨 🗨 🗨

Q of L: ★ ★

Admissions: (918) 631-2307

Email Address:

admission@utulsa.edu

The University of Tulsa is a small, private university with a technical bent and a strong international reputation. Known for its engineering and science programs, including petroleum engineering and geosciences, TU argues that quality education in all fields should be firmly grounded in the arts and sciences. The university offers a strong emphasis on undergraduate research and hands-on work experience, and a strong peer tutoring program works to assure that no one gets lost. "TU is a small university with big-school opportunities," says a junior nursing student.

Founded in 1894 under Presbyterian auspices in what was then Indian Territory, TU occupies a 210-acre campus three miles from downtown Tulsa with a striking view of the city's skyline from the steps of the neo-Gothic McFarlin Library. The university's more than 90 buildings run the architectural gamut from 1930s-vintage Collegiate Gothic to contemporary, all variations on a theme of yellow Tennessee limestone dubbed "TU stone." The Lorton Performance Center is TU's showcase facility for the performance arts.

The university has been mired in a budget-inspired personality crisis over the past decade. After embarking on an ill-conceived effort in 2019 to de-emphasize the arts and sciences in favor of its professional schools, including its well-regarded college of engineering and business and a new college of health science, a new administration moved aggressively beginning in 2021 to restore TU's traditional balance of the arts and humanities with professional and technical studies. But by fall 2025, TU's administration was in flux again in the face of a $31 million deficit in its 2026 budget. Some staff was laid off, administration costs slashed, and a hiring freeze put in place. An honors

> **"TU is a small university with big-school opportunities."**

program that offered an unusual four-year Great Books curriculum has been restructured. It remains to be seen if some of the arts and sciences majors, such as music, philosophy, and religion, that had previously been rescued from the chopping block, will continue. Stay tuned.

General education requirements, known as the Tulsa Curriculum, include a series of Core courses that foster skills in math, language, and critical thinking, as well as 25 hours of Block courses, which are introductory courses in the humanities, fine arts, social sciences, and natural sciences. Most students take six hours of formal writing instruction and at least three hours of math. All TU students are encouraged to study a foreign language, but the number of credits required varies by type of degree. In addition to its well-established and internationally recognized petroleum engineering and geosciences programs, TU offers solid majors in computer science, nursing, biochemistry, psychology, accounting, and exercise and sports science. Tulsa is one of 77 schools in the nation that trains America's Cyber Corps, the first line of defense against computer hackers and terrorists, and the university has added a B.S. degree in cybersecurity. The English department has some impressive resources at its disposal in McFarlin Library's special collections, which boast letters, manuscripts, and other materials by 19th- and 20th-century authors. Students in the international engineering/science and language program earn both a B.S. in engineering or science and a B.A. in a foreign language in five years. Psychology, biology, mechanical engineering, and exercise and sports science are the most popular majors.

Courses are rigorous, and students say the workload can be heavy, but classmates are always willing to help one another out. Sixty-two percent of classes enroll fewer than 20 students, and professors are praised for being approachable and accommodating of student needs. "I rarely feel intimidated to ask questions, and the professors usually know students by name," praises a biology major. Students also give high ratings to the university's academic support resources, including workshops, subsidized tutoring sessions, and grad students who serve as academic counselors, helping with goal setting, study tips, and time-management skills. The CaneCareers Job Placement Guarantee promises that if students who complete a professional development program are not subsequently employed or enrolled in graduate school within six months of graduation, the university will cover the cost of tuition for one semester in one of TU's master's degree programs.

"I have had a high-paying internship ever since my freshman year."

The Tulsa Undergraduate Research Challenge offers outstanding opportunities to conduct cutting-edge research with faculty mentors and has produced dozens of national scholarship winners. Eight percent of students study abroad for a semester, short term, or summer; short-term programs include a nursing and technology course in Scotland, an athletic training course in Ireland, and a tropical biology course in Costa Rica. "Tulsa puts high emphasis on the vital role summer internships can play in one's academic career," says an enthusiastic senior. "I have had a high-paying internship ever since my freshman year."

"TU has that Midwestern charm to it," says a junior. "It is a culture of high-achieving but kind people who push you to be your best." Fifty-seven percent of Tulsa's students are from Oklahoma; most others are from the Midwest and Southwest, with many hailing from Texas and Missouri. Ten percent are international. The student body is 6 percent Black, 11 percent Hispanic/Latino, 6 percent Asian American, 4 percent Native American, and 8 percent multiracial. Students describe the campus as "moderately liberal," and a junior says TU is "not a hotbed for political activism." A bevy of merit and athletic scholarships are available for qualified students. Thirty-four percent of incoming first-years qualify for Pell Grants.

Campus traditions include the ringing of the college's cupola bell by each senior after their last final exam.

Sixty-five percent of students reside in campus housing; most first-years and sophomores are required to do so, and while some upperclassmen move off campus, many choose to stay because of the school's six luxury apartment villages. A marketing major says, "Our worst dorms are nicer than the newest dorms on many state school campuses." The Student Union food court was renovated, and students can also choose from cafeteria and bar-and-grill options, but many students describe the cafeteria food as, simply, "bad." Students give administrators credit for adopting a more transparent approach to the issue of sexual assault. "We are always informed when an assault is reported," notes a media studies major.

The social life at TU is surprisingly robust, if not raucous, thanks to hundreds of student organizations and a healthy Greek life. The university sponsors regular social events, and students enjoy simply hanging with friends at small gatherings too. The Greek organizations claim 21 percent of TU men and 17 percent of the women, and the frats host registered parties that are limited to a preauthorized guest list. Student-initiated policies govern drinking on campus and are well enforced. Campus traditions include the ringing of the college's cupola bell by each senior after their last final exam. Other big events include the homecoming bonfire and football game and the Lights On concert.

Nearby parks and lakes please outdoor enthusiasts. Downtown Tulsa offers symphony, ballet, opera, museums, and an annual St. Patrick's Day celebration. "Tulsa is such a vibrant city and is booming every day," says a senior, who recommends the Brookside and Cherry Street districts and concerts at Cain's Ballroom. Sixty-two percent of students volunteer with groups like Habitat for Humanity, Reading Partners, and the Community Food Bank of Eastern Oklahoma. The Bricktown section of Oklahoma City and nearby casinos, along with more distant Dallas, St. Louis, and Kansas City, are popular road trips.

> "Tulsa is such a vibrant city and is booming every day."

In Oklahoma, sports are important, to say the least. The Division I Golden Hurricane compete in the American Athletic Conference in 17 intercollegiate sports. Students get riled up when the football team is pitted against rivals Oklahoma and Oklahoma State and when the basketball team suits up against Memphis and SMU. Men's and women's tennis, track and field, and cross-country are also competitive, as is the softball team. Many students take advantage of TU's club sports and intramural offerings; the most popular are flag football and volleyball.

Its ongoing academic identity issues notwithstanding, TU for now remains a private research university that allows students to pursue the kind of education they would get at a small liberal arts college while pursuing options in professional fields such as engineering, business, and the health sciences. It is doing so with an explicit focus on its students. As one speech pathology major puts it, "The university is always doing things to improve student life and to make all students feel like they are seen and that they belong."

Overlaps

Baylor, Creighton, Lehigh, Rice, Saint Louis University, Southern Methodist, Texas Christian, WashU in St. Louis

If You Apply To ›

Tulsa: Early decision, early action I and II, rolling admissions. Accepts the Common Application with supplement. Please consult Tulsa's website for the most up-to-date information regarding standardized test requirements.

807 Union Street, Schenectady, NY 12308

Union is split down the middle between liberal arts and engineering. That means its center of gravity is more toward the technical side than places like Lafayette, Trinity, and Tufts, but less so than Clarkson and Rensselaer. Big commitment to undergraduate research. Schenectady has become livelier, and there are outdoor getaways in all directions. Relatively anonymous because it does not fit into conventional categories.

Founded way back in 1795, Union College is one of the oldest nondenominational liberal arts colleges in the country. Its name reflects the founders' desire to create a welcoming, unifying academic community open to the region's diverse religious and national groups. More than 225 years later, engineering and the liberal arts go hand in hand as Union "provides a rigorous, holistic, and immersive education that emphasizes integration, innovation, inclusion, and reflection for every student." Undergraduate research has deep roots at Union, starting in the mid-20th century when a chemistry professor began involving students in his colloid chemistry investigations. Today, "Union has a unique blend of a liberal arts environment with strong STEM programs, which creates a well-rounded academic experience," says a happy junior.

Union's 100-acre campus sits on a hill overlooking Schenectady, which played a pivotal role in the Industrial Revolution as a transportation and manufacturing center. The campus was designed in 1813 by French architect and landscaper Joseph Jacques Ramée, whose vision took shape in brownstone and red brick, with plenty of white arches, pilasters, and lacy green trees. The campus plan also includes eight acres of formal gardens and woodlands. The eye-catching, 16-sided Nott Memorial, a National Historic Landmark described as "a feat of high Victorian Gothic," is a meeting, study, and exhibition center. The Mohawk Harbor, a new $50 million arena featuring a 2,200-seat ice hockey rink, opened in fall 2025.

> **"Union has a unique blend of a liberal arts environment with strong STEM programs."**

To fulfill Union's general education requirements, students take core courses in their first and second years that promote reading, writing, and analytical skills, including a required interdisciplinary First-Year Preceptorial followed by a Sophomore Research Seminar. They also take courses spread among social science, humanities, linguistic and cultural competency, quantitative and mathematical reasoning, and natural and applied science or engineering. All students must complete a senior thesis or senior seminar paper to graduate.

Among Union's most popular majors are economics, mechanical engineering, biology, and psychology. Students also flock to strong programs in geology, computer science, English, and history; the latter department is home to Union's most esteemed lecturer, Stephen Berk, whose course on the Holocaust and 20th Century Europe is a hot ticket. Each year, about 50 incoming first year students are named Union Scholars. The designation extends the First-Year Preceptorial to two terms and gives students access to independent study projects, departmental honors programs, and expanded study abroad options. Eighty percent of all Union students conduct undergraduate research en route to their degrees. "It is very easy to get involved and work closely with a professor," says a junior. Each spring Union cancels classes one afternoon for the Steinmetz Symposium so that students can present scholarly projects in a professional conference atmosphere.

Website: www.union.edu
Location: Small City
Private
Total Enrollment: 2,031
Undergraduates: 2,031
Male/Female: 53/47
Financial Aid: 92%
Pell Grant: 14%
Expense: Pr $ $ $ $
Student Loans: 57%
Average Debt: $ $ $ $
Applicants: 8,210
Accepted: 44%
Enrolled: 14%
Grad in 6 Years: 81%
Returning First-years: 90%
Academics: ✍ ✍ ✍ ✍
Social: 🌐 🌐 🌐
Q of L: ★ ★ ★
Admissions: (518) 388-6112
Email Address:
  admissions@union.edu

Strong Programs:
Biology
Computer Science
Economics
English
Geology
History
Mechanical Engineering
Psychology

Interdisciplinary study is the norm at Union, with established programs in bioengineering, Latin American and Caribbean studies, law and public policy, and Russian and Eastern European studies, to name a few. The college's Kelly Adirondack Center, 10 minutes from campus, features the 15,000-item Adirondack Research Library and is a boon to students interested in environmental research and stewardship. The educational studies program allows aspiring teachers to complete courses and fieldwork required for secondary school certification in a variety of subjects. The Leadership in Medicine program, a joint program with Clarkson University's Union Graduate College and Albany Medical College, gives students the opportunity to earn a bachelor's degree, an M.S. in health management or an M.B.A. in health systems administration, and a medical degree in eight years.

"The academic climate at Union College is challenging but manageable, with a strong emphasis on critical thinking and hands-on learning," reports a biomedical engineering major. A sophomore adds, "We are very lucky to have stellar professors who are always looking to be active in the lives of their pupils." Sixty-nine percent of classes have fewer than 20 students, and students can expect to see full professors at the lecterns rather than teaching assistants. Union operates on a trimester system, which means thrice-a-year exams and a late start to summer jobs—but also the opportunity to concentrate on just three courses a term. More terms also means more opportunities for independent study and internships, either in the state capital of Albany, 20 minutes away, or in Washington, D.C. By the time graduation rolls around, 60 percent of students have studied abroad, many of them in faculty-led, three-week "mini terms" during winter or summer break.

"The academic climate at Union College is challenging but manageable."

Thirty-two percent of Union students are New Yorkers, and 11 percent are international. Four percent of students are Black, 11 percent are Hispanic/Latino, 7 percent are Asian American, and 4 percent are multiracial, but the school has been working to boost these numbers. A junior says "Socioeconomic and geographic diversity are growing." A senior describes the political climate as "rather balanced." Union awards hundreds of merit scholarships averaging $22,000, and it meets the full demonstrated financial need of admitted students. Athletic grants are available to Division I ice hockey players.

Ninety percent of Union students live on campus. The Minerva house system (named after the Roman goddess of wisdom) is aimed at getting students and faculty members to contribute to Union's social, residential, and intellectual life—and, students say, at decreasing the influence of the Greek system, which draws 10 percent of the men and 12 percent of the women. "The dorms are fine, pretty typical, but the apartments for seniors and all the theme houses are very nice," reports a student. Students recommend West, which is co-ed by room and thus very social, as well as Fox and Davidson, where first years and sophomores live in suites. Dining options consist of four main eating areas, and the quality of meals "really depends on the day," says a first-year. "Campus police watch out very closely for the safety of students," says a sociology major. And a biomedical engineering major points out, "There is a wide range of health services available, such as therapy dogs, nutrition counseling, and physicals."

"The majority of social life is on campus," says a student. "There are Minerva events and on-campus movies as well as typical fraternity parties." Campus events also include comedians, concerts, and speakers. Despite these alternatives and strictly enforced alcohol policies, most students agree that "Greek life dominates," as one student asserts. "Two of the biggest campus traditions are Lobsterfest and Springfest," reports a biomedical engineering major. "During Lobsterfest, every student gets a whole lobster, which is pretty unique." Springfest brings live performers to campus.

Off campus, Schenectady, whose name derives from the Mohawk word for "the place beyond the pines," is an old-line industrial city that is within walking distance of campus where students can explore shops, including a bookstore, catch a movie, or enjoy performances at Proctors, a historic theater showcasing a range of acts including traveling Broadway shows. Union also offers volunteer opportunities to connect Union students with local partners. The popular grant-funded Science and Technology Entry Program pairs historically underrepresented and economically disadvantaged students in grades 7–12 with Union students for college preparation and increased participation in STEM. Nearby, Saratoga Springs boasts restaurants, jazz clubs, horse racing, and Skidmore College. Popular road trips include Boston, Montreal, New York, and the ski slopes of nearby Vermont.

"Two of the biggest campus traditions are Lobsterfest and Springfest."

Union's athletic teams (recently renamed the Garnet Chargers) compete in Division III, aside from men's and women's ice hockey, both of which are Division I. Union is also competitive in men's and women's soccer and swimming and women's basketball, lacrosse, softball, and volleyball. Intramural and club sports include teams in everything from volleyball and broomball to ultimate Frisbee and fly-fishing.

Union's mission has been constantly evolving for more than two centuries, and it continues to adapt to meet the needs and interests of students and faculty. It retains its commitment to a strong core liberal arts curriculum while acknowledging the increasing effects of globalization and technology. As one happy sophomore puts it, at Union, "The campus community is welcoming, the faculty is supportive, and the academic opportunities are abundant."

If You Apply To ›

Union: Early decision I and II, early action, regular decision. SATs or ACTs: optional. Accepts the Common Application.

Ursinus College

601 E Main Street, Collegeville, PA 19426

Ursinus is the smallest of the cohort of eastern Pennsylvania liberal arts colleges that includes Franklin & Marshall, Lafayette, and Muhlenberg. The plus side is more attention from faculty and more emphasis on independent and outside-the-box learning. The setting is suburban, and Philly is within arm's reach.

Although it is a secular institution, Ursinus College, founded in 1869, takes its name from a 16th-century German Calvinist, Zacharias Ursinus, who directed that students should "examine all things and keep what is good." In recent years, Ursinus has reinvigorated its liberal arts roots—expanding its offerings and restructuring its core curriculum to emphasize questions of human existence and to prepare students "not simply to make a living, but to make a life of purpose." What hasn't changed is the close-knit feel of the school. "Ursinus's culture is one of inquisitive learning through experimentation and discussion with peers that brings students together in a small campus atmosphere," muses a senior.

Ursinus is in Collegeville (so named before the school was founded), about 25 miles west of Philadelphia and 10 miles from the green, rolling hills of Valley Forge National Park. Buildings on the 170-acre campus are mostly constructed of

Website: www.ursinus.edu
Location: Suburban
Private
Total Enrollment: 1,487
Undergraduates: 1,487
Male/Female: 52/48
Financial Aid: 98%
Pell Grant: 28%
Expense: Pr $ $
Student Loans: 74%
Average Debt: $ $ $ $

(continued)

Applicants: 3,304
Accepted: 92%
Enrolled: 13%
Grad in 6 Years: 73%
Returning First-years: 87%
Academics: ✍ ✍ ✍
Social: 🌣 🌣 🌣
Q of L: ★ ★ ★
Admissions: (610) 409-3200
Email Address:
  admission@ursinus.edu

Strong Programs:
Applied Economics
Biology
English
Environmental Studies
Health and Exercise Physiology
International Relations
Politics
Psychology

Pennsylvania fieldstone; many have had their interiors upgraded and their exteriors preserved and restored. Actors and dancers benefit from rehearsal and exhibition space in the Kaleidoscope Performing Arts Center. Newer additions include the 42,500-square-foot Innovation and Discovery Center.

Ursinus's core curriculum, called Quest: Open Questions Open Minds, is intended to engage students in deep inquiry and reflection on four central themes: identifying personal values, living in communities, understanding the world, and making life-shaping decisions. The core begins with the Common Intellectual Experience—a two-semester course taken in the first year that explores works ranging from Plato to Hindu scripture to Ta-Nehisi Coates. Additional components include interdisciplinary coursework, an experiential learning project (an independent research or creative project, an internship, study abroad, student teaching, or civic engagement), and a Core Capstone course in the senior year.

Students choose among more than 35 majors, with the most popular being biology, applied economics, health and exercise physiology, psychology, and neuroscience. The environment and sustainability program is strong, providing students access to the college's organic farm and the Whittaker Environmental Research Station. Ursinus also offers solid programs in English, politics, and international relations. Classes are small—64 percent have fewer than 20 students—and students are mostly pleased with the quality of teaching, especially since there are no teaching assistants. According to a psychology and international relations double major, the academic climate is "rigorous in some disciplines and very laid-back in others, but mostly the professors expect a high level of work and motivation from the students."

> **"Many Summer Fellows end up extending their research into honors research senior year."**

Each year, 70 to 80 rising juniors and seniors get fellowships from the school to fund full-time summer research projects with a faculty member. "Many Summer Fellows end up extending their research into honors research senior year," explains a senior. The Parlee Center for Science and the Common Good aims to help students understand and explain the ethical, political, and cultural impacts of their scientific work, offering a speaker series, a student fellows program, internships, and summer research opportunities. The U-Imagine Center for Integrative and Entrepreneurial Studies and the Melrose Center for Global Civic Engagement offer similar programming. Ursinus students can choose to study abroad, both in programs designed and run by the college and in affiliate programs. The Philadelphia Experience places selected students in a residence hall in Philadelphia for a semester to take courses with Ursinus faculty, along with their choice of an internship or independent research project.

"Our students have many different interests," says an applied economics major. "A football player may also be in the men's a cappella group. A theater star may also do honors biology research." Sixty-two percent of students are from Pennsylvania, and less than 1 percent are from foreign countries, with most others hailing from New York, New Jersey, and other Mid-Atlantic and New England states. Black students make up 10 percent of the student body, Asian Americans 3 percent, Hispanics/Latinos 8 percent, and multiracial students 5 percent. Both sides of the political aisle are represented on campus, and a first-year describes the atmosphere as "calm," with students "discussing their opinions together." Non-need-based scholarships and grants averaging $31,800 are available each year, but no athletic scholarships are offered.

> *Student-run special interest housing is available for those who share social or academic interests.*

Ninety percent of students at Ursinus live in college housing, which adds to the feeling of community. Upperclassmen quickly grab the Main Street houses, a string of Victorian-era homes comprising the Residential Village across the street from campus, while first-years are clustered in BPS and BWC (short for Beardwood-Paisley-Stauffer and Brodbeck-Wilkinson-Curtis, respectively), which have generously sized rooms. Reimert Hall is the party dorm. Student-run special interest housing is available, too, for those who share social or academic interests. At the main dining hall, Wismer, "the meals are actually good ninety-nine percent of the time," says a first-year student, and "they have options that are vegan and vegetarian and food that is free of seven main allergens as well." A junior reports, "Campus Safety is always seen around campus mingling with students and gaining their respect and trust."

Much of the social life occurs on campus, including performances, themed cuisine nights, and craft nights organized by the student activities board. Greek life draws 4 percent of the men and 8 percent of the women, and parties hosted by fraternities and sports teams are a popular weekend diversion. Registered on-campus parties are monitored by student "social hosts" who check IDs and make sure things don't get out of hand. "A lot of drinking goes on," reports a junior. Homecoming is a favorite tradition in the fall, and in the spring, students look forward to the annual Bear Bash concert and Airband, "a big charity lip-synching and performing event," says an English major. Sixty-five percent of students perform regular volunteer work.

The town of Collegeville is just 10 blocks long—and Ursinus takes up five of those—but a politics major says it offers "a few good bars and restaurants to entertain students." Frequent school-sponsored shuttles take students to the shops, restaurants, sporting events, and festivals of Philadelphia, less than an hour away. Many students with cars escape to the Jersey Shore during warmer months.

Ursinus students love their Division III sports. For those seeking post collegiate careers in coaching, Ursinus is a well-known stepping stone to those positions, thanks in part to a tight network of loyal alumni who tap each other for opportunities. The Bears field strong teams in men's and women's basketball, men's lacrosse, and women's swimming and field hockey. Intramural and club sports draw 40 percent of students, and the annual women's Prom Dress Rugby encounter with Swarthmore is always a big hit.

Ursinus may not be in the center of a big metropolitan area, and it doesn't offer big-time sports, but the college compensates for its lack of size with the feeling that students, faculty, and staff are one big family. "The special thing about Ursinus is the people," says a biology major. "Everyone—the students, professors, and staff—is so friendly and open and just wants you to succeed." Good old Zacharias would be proud.

> "The professors expect a high level of work and motivation from the students."

Overlaps

Allegheny, Drexel, Gettysburg, Muhlenberg, Temple, Washington & Jefferson, Washington College, Wheaton (MA)

If You Apply To ›

Ursinus: Early decision I and II, early action, regular decision. SATs or ACTs: optional. Accepts the Common Application.

University of Utah

201 Presidents Circle, Salt Lake City, UT 84112

One of the oldest universities west of the Mississippi, the University of Utah sits in the region's only major city. Science and professional programs such as business and engineering are traditional strengths. Has positioned itself as a more accessible alternative to California's public higher education system—with plenty of academic opportunities and school spirit to go around. Applications have doubled in the last decade, and out-of-state enrollment is on the rise.

Students look forward to the Grand Kerfuffle, which brings major musical acts to campus every spring.

In addition to being the flagship institution of the state's higher education system, the University of Utah is a major national scientific research center. Founded in 1850, the university is unusual in its ability to offer students the advantages of living in a city while at the same time maintaining a connection with nature. Utah has recently increased its focus on the undergraduate experience by beefing up academic programs and building new residential facilities, including a $51 million student life center. Applications have surged as a result, and students say enthusiasm for their school is higher than ever. "We have the school spirit, the drive to transform the world, and the resources and connections needed for students to succeed," cheers one senior.

Set in the foothills of the Wasatch Mountains near the shores of the Great Salt Lake, the university enjoys a picturesque location a half-hour drive from "the greatest snow on earth." Occupying 1,500 well-landscaped acres with nearly as many kinds of trees as undergraduates, the campus doubles as the state's arboretum. The university's structures range from historic 19th-century buildings to state-of-the-art modern facilities. The Impact and Prosperity Epicenter, housing nearly 800 students, opened in 2024. The $97 million Skaggs Applied Science Building, supporting education and research in aerospace, biotechnology, data science, semiconductor technology, hazardous weather forecasting, and air quality, opened in July 2025.

Utah students choose from a comprehensive academic menu, including more than 100 undergraduate majors, and the U does not skimp on general education requirements. Students must take classes in writing, American institutions, math, statistics, and intellectual explorations, which include two courses in the humanities, sciences, social sciences, or fine arts, as well as fulfill international and diversity course requirements.

"Professors care about what they teach their students and want them to learn."

Utah is renowned for its research in biomedical engineering, and majors in business administration, entrepreneurship, international studies, and social work are strong. The Lassonde Entrepreneur Institute offers training to budding entrepreneurs, 400 of whom get to reside in the $45 million Lassonde Studios, featuring the sort of pods and shared spaces characteristic of high-tech workplaces. An unusual major in quantitative analysis of markets and organizations was developed jointly by the business school and the department of economics. Programs in ballet and modern dance are also well regarded. Students interested in video game development or digital animation may pursue a major in computer science with an entertainment arts and engineering emphasis or a major in games. The most popular majors include psychology, communication, biology, and health and kinesiology.

The academic climate can be challenging, but in general "the workload is fairly manageable," according to one sophomore. Introductory courses often enroll hundreds of students, with smaller discussion sections led by graduate student teaching assistants. Overall, 42 percent of classes have fewer than 20 students. Students report that the quality of teaching varies by department, but for the most part, says a business major, "professors care about what they teach their students and want them to learn." The LEAP (Learning Engagement Achievement Progress) learning community involves a two-semester sequence of courses led by faculty and peer advisors; roughly a third of incoming students participate. Those seeking a more challenging curriculum and the chance to write a thesis may apply to the Honors College.

The Undergraduate Research Opportunities Program provides a $1,200 stipend and educational programming for students who assist with a faculty member's research or creative project or who carry out a project of their own under the supervision of a faculty member. "There is so much research going on at the U and so many opportunities to get involved with it," cheers a junior. Additionally, students can study abroad via some 500 programs offered in more than 50 countries.

Utah's students are a mostly middle-class, fairly homogeneous lot; 64 percent of undergraduates are Utah residents, and nearly all attended public schools. A growing number of students are arriving from out of state, especially Californians who feel shut out by the higher education system back home; 5 percent come from abroad. Black students make up just 1 percent of the student population, Asian Americans 6 percent, Hispanic/Latino 14 percent, and multiracial students 6 percent. Students describe their fellow Utes as "friendly" and "supportive" and say the political climate is diverse and sometimes polarized. A substantial percentage of Utah students are Mormon. Says a sociology major, "U students are pretty all across the spectrum politically, with most being moderately liberal." Utah offers merit scholarships averaging $7,400, and athletic scholarships are available in 20 sports. Additionally, the Native Student Scholarship Program covers costs not met by scholarships and grants for undergraduates who are enrolled members in one of Utah's federally recognized tribes.

Only 18 percent of students live on campus, but those who do seem to be pleased with the housing facilities, many of which were built to accommodate visitors during the 2002 Olympics. Off-campus apartments within walking distance of the campus are plentiful. Students are also generally satisfied with the food, though edibility varies based on which campus eatery you choose. At lunchtime, local food trucks usually line up around the Marriott Library plaza, a popular gathering place. Students report feeling safe on campus, and the university has increased the number of staff dedicated to Title IX issues. The career center and mental health counseling also get good reviews.

The on-campus social scene is becoming ever livelier with the influx of out-of-state students. Participation in Greek life is an increasingly popular option; currently, 8 percent of the men and 11 percent of the women join fraternities and sororities. "From lectures, concerts, dance performances, and late-night Crimson Nights parties, there is something for everyone," a student says. Students also look forward to the Grand Kerfuffle, which brings major musical acts to campus every spring.

Utah's proximity to the mountains means that "much of the social life is recreational," according to one junior. Favorite road trips take students to Las Vegas, Lake Powell, and nearby ski resorts (with slopeside bus service available from the school). Salt Lake City isn't exactly a college town, but a junior says, "The nightlife in SLC downtown is great if you are over 21." Adjacent to campus, the Latter-day Saints Institute of Religion sponsors dances and other social activities with a decidedly conservative bent. There are also centers for other faiths, notably Jewish and Roman Catholic. Cultural activities include the respected Utah Symphony, several dance companies, opera, and, of course, the Mormon Tabernacle Choir.

> "There is so much research going on at the U and so many opportunities to get involved with it."

Utah's teams compete in the Division I Big 12 Conference, and football and basketball bring students together in the MUSS—Mighty Utah Student Section—where cheers are loudest during the "Holy War" rivalry football game against Brigham Young. Cross-country, co-ed skiing, women's basketball, men's golf and lacrosse, and women's gymnastics and softball make regular NCAA tournament appearances. In addition to the university's dozens of club sports and intramurals (canoe battleship, anyone?), the Outdoor Adventure Program offers backpacking, river running, mountain biking, and skiing trips.

Students say that academic quality, diversity, and the residential experience are all on the rise at Utah. "People are here to learn, and there is a strong focus on

Overlaps

University of Arizona, Arizona State, Brigham Young, CU Boulder, U of I at Chicago, Utah State, Utah Valley, University of Washington research and advancement," says a family, community, and human development major. It's also one of the few places where you can find nationally recognized professional programs within easy reach of nationally recognized skiing.

Vanderbilt University

2305 West End Avenue, Nashville, TN 37203

Strongest and most selective of schools that still find a way to blend Southern hospitality with modern, cutting-edge academics in an urban setting. Vandy has become more diverse in recent years, geographically and otherwise. More selective than Emory and now comparable to Duke and Rice among leading schools south of the Mason–Dixon line. One of the few major universities where both academics and athletics are top-notch.

Website: www.vanderbilt.edu
Location: City Center
Private
Total Enrollment: 12,845
Undergraduates: 7,166
Male/Female: 47/53
Financial Aid: 92%
Pell Grant: 15%
Expense: Pr $ $ $
Student Loans: 17%
Average Debt: $ $
Applicants: 45,409
Accepted: 6%
Enrolled: 61%
Grad in 6 Years: 94%
Returning First-years: 96%
Academics: ✑ ✑ ✑ ✑
Social: 🗩 🗩 🗩 🗩
Q of L: ★ ★ ★ ★
Admissions: (800) 288-0432
Email Address:
  admissions@vanderbilt.edu

Strong Programs:
Biological Sciences
Computer Science
Economics
Education
Engineering

Once a quiet, conservative school in the heart of the South known as a preferred choice for Atlanta and Birmingham elites, Vanderbilt University has diversified its student body and brought a more cosmopolitan atmosphere to campus. Coats, ties, and pearls may be giving way to Commodore fan gear at football games these days, but the university continues to succeed in marrying Old South gentility with modern attitudes. The result is a relaxed, friendly culture that makes the rigorous academic environment easier to handle. "Students looking for a balance between great academics and a solid social life need to look at Vandy," counsels a history major.

Established in 1873 by railroad and shipping magnate Cornelius ("the Commodore") Vanderbilt, the university's 340-acre tract in Nashville is an arboretum and includes Peabody College, the central section of which is listed on the National Register of Historic Places. On the main campus, art and sculptures dot the landscape, and architectural styles range from Gothic to modern glass and brick. The Sarratt Student Center serves as a social hub, with a movie theater, Rand Dining Hall, a pub, and offices for student organizations. The West End neighborhood has been transformed with the addition of four new residential colleges in recent years.

> "Students looking for a balance between great academics and a solid social life need to look at Vandy."

Undergraduates choose one of four schools—College of Arts and Science, School of Engineering, Blair School of Music, or Peabody College of Education and Human Development—but everyone takes their core liberal arts courses in the College of Arts and Science, where the writing program is a standout. Immersion Vanderbilt, a graduation requirement, calls for every undergraduate to undertake an immersive learning experience (such as internships, fieldwork, or performances) culminating in a final project. First-year students take two core seminars, Being Human and Science, Technology, and Values, which allow students to explore various topics in small groups with close faculty interaction.

Engineering, education, and music are particular strengths at Vandy. Popular majors include economics; medicine, health, and society; human and organizational development; computer science; engineering (especially mechanical); and biological sciences. Education majors who enroll at Peabody College are required to double major, usually in a liberal arts field. Many students interested in financial careers declare an economics major and pursue a business minor. The university has added an interdisciplinary major in climate studies.

"The academic climate of Vanderbilt is absolutely collaborative," an elementary education major says. "It provides the academic rigor I was hoping for without any of the cutthroat aspect I was afraid would accompany such an academically challenging school." Fifty-nine percent of courses have fewer than 20 students, and in the classroom, Vanderbilt students abide by the school's honor system, which dates from 1875. The system governs all aspects of academic conduct and makes it possible for professors to give unproctored exams. Students rave about the faculty. "Many professors go out of their way to encourage students to get involved with research and internship opportunities," comments a junior.

Internship opportunities abound in Nashville, particularly in state government, healthcare management, the tech sector, and, of course, the music industry. Sixty-three percent of students, from all four undergraduate schools, participate in research, and many copublish articles. The campus is home to more than 100 interdisciplinary centers and institutes. Vanderbilt's study abroad program typically attracts about 40 percent of students and offers the chance to spend a summer, a semester, or a year on one of seven continents via more than 120 programs. The optional "Maymester" allows students to spend four weeks on a single project, helpful for double majors or those who'd like to embark on a short-term internship or overseas trip.

The campus is home to more than 100 interdisciplinary centers and institutes.

Twelve percent of undergraduates are from Tennessee, and 11 percent are international, coming from more than 50 countries. Asian Americans account for 19 percent of the student body, Black students 9 percent, Hispanics/Latinos 11 percent, and multiracial students 6 percent. Students report that a diverse mix of political views are represented on campus. "I would not describe Vanderbilt as an activist campus per se, but there have been several rallies and protests," observes an English major. Vanderbilt employs a need-blind admissions process, meets full demonstrated need for all admitted students, and offers loan-free financial aid packages for students with demonstrated need. In addition, Vanderbilt provides full-tuition scholarships for students whose families earn up to $150,000. Many households who earn more than $150,000 still receive an Opportunity Vanderbilt award for as much as $70,000, depending on income. It also awards over 200 athletic scholarships.

"[Dining facilities] always provide a delicious array of options."

Eighty-four percent of Vanderbilt undergraduates live in campus housing. All first-year students live together in 10 Commons houses and take part in Vanderbilt Visions, a living/learning initiative designed to foster a sense of community among new students. Each first-year is assigned to a Visions group, which has about 18 students, a faculty advisor, and an upper-class peer mentor. In addition to meeting with their group once a week during the fall semester, students have opportunities to get to know the faculty who live in the various Commons houses. Students also compete in the Commons Cup. A junior explains, "You and your house compete in intramurals, sustainability, community service, and academics over the course of the whole year." Six residential colleges for upper-class students are available as well. Other options for older students include 10-person townhouses, six-room suites, theme dorms, and school-owned apartments.

Education majors who enroll at Peabody College are required to double major, usually in a liberal arts field.

Vanderbilt has 19 dining facilities that "always provide a delicious array of options," according to a junior, and all campus residents are required to buy a meal plan. Dining services include special facilities and an app serving students with food allergies. The Taste of Nashville program allows students to use their meal money at two dozen local restaurants. Students report feeling safe on campus, thanks to an active security department that "watches out for Vanderbilt students and keeps us safe." As for sexual assault awareness and prevention, one student says Vanderbilt "is facing this issue head-on," especially through the efforts of the Project Safe Center.

Twenty-four percent of the women and 28 percent of the men join the Greek system; while many Greek parties are open to the entire campus, the effort to encourage mixing between the groups is not always successful. "Fraternities and sororities start the social scene," a senior says, "but certainly don't encompass all aspects of Vanderbilt's social life." The first-year Commons campus is dry, but of-age students are allowed to have alcohol elsewhere on campus, although open containers are banned in public and kegs are also taboo. As at many colleges, one student says, "underage students can find loopholes." Students get involved in more than 500 student organizations. Favorite Vanderbilt traditions are the Commodore Quake and Rites of Spring music festivals, as well as Founders Walk at the end of move-in weekend, where new incoming students walk through campus while upperclassmen welcome them with cheers.

Vanderbilt's proximity to Music City USA provides plenty of diversions. "Nashville is so much fun," cheers one senior. "The list of excellent restaurants, bars, shopping, and live music venues is endless." Country music fans won't want to miss the Hall of Fame. Beyond Nashville's borders are the Great Smoky Mountains and state parks with picnic facilities, beautiful lakes, and skiing in the winter. The best road trips are to Memphis (home of Elvis), New Orleans (for Mardi Gras), and Louisville (for the Kentucky Derby). Students also engage in the local community through a variety of service-oriented programs. Alternative Spring Break, which takes students to more than 30 service sites across the country for volunteer work during spring break, is Vandy's largest student-run organization.

"Nashville is so much fun!"

Vanderbilt may be the smallest—and the only private—institution in the competitive and football-crazy Division I Southeastern Conference, but there is no shortage of enthusiasm among Commodore fans. Vandy reconfigured its athletic program some years ago to cut costs. Instead of losing ground (as many feared), the programs have thrived. The baseball team is a perennial contender for the national title, while the men's golf and women's soccer and bowling are recent conference champs. Football won the 2024 Birmingham Bowl. There are 30-plus club sports for weekend jocks, as well as more than 40 intramural sports leagues.

Vanderbilt sits squarely among the top universities in the nation and has capitalized on its unique blend of Southern charm and scholarly achievement to attract students from around the country and beyond. Four years here do carry a steep before-financial-aid sticker price; witness a tongue-in-cheek campus slogan, "Vanderbilt: It Even Sounds Expensive." But for many, investing in a Vanderbilt education is money well spent.

Overlaps

Duke, Emory, Harvard, Northwestern, Penn, Rice, WashU in St. Louis, Yale

If You Apply To ›

Vanderbilt: Early decision I and II, regular decision. Accepts the Common Application with supplement. Apply to particular school or program. Audition required for music applicants. Please consult Vanderbilt's website for the most up-to-date information regarding standardized test requirements.

Vassar College

124 Raymond Avenue, Poughkeepsie, NY 12604

Vassar is a thriving, highly selective institution where traditional strengths in humanities and the arts are matched by robust offerings in the natural and social sciences as well as languages. Open curriculum offers students the freedom and flexibility to pursue diverse passions and discover new interests. Long at the forefront of national efforts to promote socioeconomic diversity in selective schools.

Are you a scientist who composes music in your spare time? Or perhaps an actor who enjoys dissecting Plato and Aristotle? If so, you may feel at home at Vassar, a distinguished liberal arts college just 70 miles north of New York City. Known for its curricular flexibility, tolerance, and commitment to diversity, Vassar attracts a community of intellectually curious and creative individuals. "I really wanted to go to a small, artsy college with a diverse student body and great academic programs," says a film and English double major. "Vassar checked all those boxes."

Vassar was founded in 1861 by a brewer named Matthew Vassar to provide women an education equal to that once only available to men. It is hard to imagine that Vassar once considered picking up and moving to Yale in the 1960s rather than become a co-ed institution, but it did begin admitting men in 1969 and remains in its picturesque location just outside Poughkeepsie, New York, where its 1,000-acre campus is an arboretum. Daffodils bloom in the spring, and the autumn foliage is breathtaking. Encircled by a fieldstone wall, the campus also boasts an astronomical observatory, a state-of-the-art physics building, a farm with an ecological field station, and an art center with 21,000 works, from ancient Egyptian to modern times. The architecture is predominantly neo-Gothic, with buildings also designed by notables such as Marcel Breuer, Eero Saarinen, and James Renwick.

> **"Vassar students are always trying to do their personal best."**

Vassar has no core curriculum and no distribution requirements. Indeed, academic flexibility is paramount. That said, all students must choose one first-year writing seminar from nearly 50 courses taught across the curriculum, as well as one course that requires significant quantitative analysis. Students must also demonstrate intermediate-level proficiency in one of the 20 languages taught at Vassar.

The most popular majors include psychological science, biology, English, and economics. The biology building houses electron microscopes, including a recently acquired next-generation $1 million confocal microscope, while music students are spoiled by a grand collection of Steinway pianos sprinkled across the campus. Drama, film, art, and international studies are also strengths, as are interdisciplinary majors such as science, technology, and society and data science and society. Regardless of their course of study, students find the academic climate rigorous. "Vassar students are always trying to do their personal best—they're seeking to engage more deeply with each subsequent assignment," says a senior. Small classes and tutorials are the norm, and exams are given under an honor system. Since Vassar has no graduate students or research-only faculty, all classes are taught by professors who "are easy to interact with, and office hours are a must," urges a mathematics major.

About 45 percent of students study abroad via 200 programs offered in more than 60 countries prior to graduation. Vassar allows students to use their financial aid packages to support study away from campus. Also highly regarded is the

Website: www.vassar.edu
Location: Small City
Private
Total Enrollment: 2,406
Undergraduates: 2,406
Male/Female: 38/62
Financial Aid: 55%
Pell Grant: 23%
Expense: Pr $ $ $ $
Student Loans: 43%
Average Debt: $
Applicants: 12,447
Accepted: 19%
Enrolled: 29%
Grad in 6 Years: 91%
Returning First-years: 95%
Academics: ✍ ✍ ✍ ✍
Social: 🍷 🍷 🍷
Q of L: ★ ★ ★ ★
Admissions: (845) 437-7300
Email Address:
admissions@vassar.edu

Strong Programs:
Art
Biology
Drama
English
Film
Neuroscience
Political Science
Science, Technology, and
  Society

college's Undergraduate Research Summer Institute, which offers stipends for students to work one-on-one with faculty members on scientific projects, either on or off campus. The Ford Scholars program offers opportunities for student/faculty collaboration in the humanities and social sciences. Most students participate in some sort of off-campus internship or community-based fieldwork for credit during the academic year. Dual-degree programs with partner universities are available in several disciplines, including engineering and public health. A B.A./M.B.A. program with SUNY–New Paltz launched in 2025. "Career advising is super helpful with ways to find internships and jobs," says a psychology and film double major.

According to an economics major, Vassar attracts "curious, creative, and socially conscious people" who generally share progressive points of view. Vassar's LGBTQ community is visible and active, and a biology major notes, "People usually introduce themselves with their gender pronouns." Thirty-one percent of students are native New Yorkers, and 6 percent are international. Asian Americans make up 12 percent of the student body, Black students 4 percent, Hispanics/Latinos 14 percent, and multiracial students 8 percent. The school's ALANA Center supports students of color and other ethnic and cultural groups. Vassar has been a leader among elite private schools in promoting socioeconomic diversity on campus, and the college recently launched The Vassar Institute for the Liberal Arts, a public classroom where scholars, community members, and students engage with each other in dialogue and debate about the issues of the day. The college offers need-blind admissions for first-year applicants who are U.S. citizens or permanent residents and guarantees to meet the full demonstrated financial need of admits; it also eliminates or reduces loans for students from low-income households.

"Career advising is super helpful with ways to find internships and jobs."

Housing is guaranteed for four years, and 97 percent of students live on campus, where there's an eclectic mix of nine dorms. All but one are co-ed. "Some dorms are really modern and sparkling," says a junior. "Others have a vintage college feel, with traditional wood paneling, trim, and floors." The word is that Lathrop is the best dorm for first-years, but no halls are reserved strictly for first-year students. Seniors favor the college-owned townhouses (five-person suites) and the four-person Terrace Apartments, both with kitchens and living rooms. Campus dining has improved considerably, students say, with recent renovations, expanded options, and late-night hours. Students report that their open campus feels safe, and a psychology major says, "Conversations about consent in all realms of college life are common, and there are multiple systems in place to report sexual assault and help survivors." Mental health services are also solid, students say.

Absent a Greek system, social life revolves around campus films, lectures, concerts, and small parties hosted in senior apartments or townhouses. "We are not a dry campus, as our founder did brew beer," quips a biology major; parties must be registered with campus security. Performing arts groups provide an important social outlet too. "Comedy shows, concerts and art shows are popular," adds a sophomore. The city of Poughkeepsie has undergone a renaissance in recent years and features the world's longest elevated pedestrian bridge (212 feet tall and 1.28 miles long, in case you're wondering), which offers stunning views of the Hudson Valley. Restaurants and shops are within walking distance of campus, and malls and movie theaters aren't much farther away, but a junior says, "Poughkeepsie is not explored by students as much as it should be." In warmer weather, Mohonk State Park offers hiking and other outdoor diversions. Also close by are Franklin D. Roosevelt's Hyde Park (for history) and the Culinary Institute of America (for gourmet meals prepared by students). If students feel confined on campus, says a sophomore, "Luckily, it's really easy to get to NYC via Metro North or Amtrak [trains]."

Traditions are big at Vassar. Students can still unwind after a hard day of classes with afternoon tea in the Rose Parlor of the historic Main Building. And on Founder's Day in May, the entire community celebrates Matthew Vassar's birthday with music, carnival rides, food, and a day out on the grass. Fireworks and a movie cap off the festivities. "The best part is that there's a theme each year for everyone to dress up as," cheers a math major. "One theme was 'medieval fairytale,' where everyone dressed up as knights, maidens, fairies, and many other creative things."

Vassar's Division III varsity squads (the Brewers) compete in the Liberty League. Competitive teams include men's and women's volleyball, soccer, basketball, tennis, swimming and diving, track and field, and rugby, as well as field hockey. Intramural sports are offered at two levels, competitive and recreational, and there are also club sports. Teams face off in everything from basketball and soccer to ultimate Frisbee.

> **"We are not a dry campus, as our founder did brew beer."**

While Vassar continues to offer a menu of high-quality liberal arts courses emphasizing interdisciplinary connections, the college has also embraced technology and diversity, helping to create an atmosphere where individual passions shine. Says one contented Brewer, "We take the time to enjoy college for what it is—a serious, but not too serious, time of life for learning and development."

If You Apply To ›

Vassar: Early decision I and II, regular decision. SATs or ACTs: optional. Accepts the Common Application with supplement. "Your Space" section of application allows candidates room to show something else about themselves.

University of Vermont

194 South Prospect Street, Burlington, VT 05401

For an out-of-stater sizing up public universities, there could hardly be a more appealing place than UVM. The size is manageable, Burlington is a quintessential college town, and Lake Champlain and the Green Mountains are on your doorstep. UVM feels like a private university, but, alas, it is also priced like one. Attracts a mix of party animals and serious scholars.

With its beautiful setting, wide academic offerings, and abundance of clubs and cocurricular pursuits, the University of Vermont draws students from across the state and around the country. And, says a math major, they're not all granola types with a penchant for soy milk and snowboarding. While it's a public school, UVM's academics, research opportunities, and price tag are more akin to those of a private institution. Generous financial aid packages, investment in infrastructure, and a growing emphasis on hands-on learning experiences are helping to ensure that Vermont remains both affordable and relevant amid increasing competition from schools of both types.

Chartered in 1791, UVM was the fifth college to be established in New England. UVM's picturesque campus sits on the shores of Lake Champlain in Burlington, virtually a stone's throw from the Canadian border. Architectural styles range from colonial to high Victorian Gothic and functional modern; the oldest structures, in the center of the campus, are recognized on the National Registry of Historic Places. Newer additions to the campus include a state-of-the-art, $104 million STEM complex, a residential complex, and an integrated arts center.

Students enjoy the Fallfest, Winterfest, and Springfest concerts every year.

UVM began as a private university but attained quasi-public status in 1862 with the passage of the Morrill Land-Grant College Act and a merger with a public agricultural college. Today, UVM's seven undergraduate colleges and schools set their own curricula grounded in the liberal arts. All students across the university must complete the Catamount Core Curriculum, which includes general education courses in quantitative reasoning, sustainability, diversity, and global citizenship, and all first-year students must fulfill a three-credit foundational writing and information literacy requirement.

Some of the most popular majors are in natural resources and conservation, health sciences, biology, and business/marketing. Animal science, biomedical engineering, data science, and food systems are also strengths. Premed, nursing, and prevet students benefit from the research and teaching capabilities of Vermont's fine medical school in the heart of campus, as well as from a seven-year program with the vet school at Tufts. Nearly 40 accelerated master's programs allow undergrads to begin working toward advanced degrees. How tough is the academic environment? "It really depends on the course of study that you choose," says one student. Forty-one percent of classes enroll fewer than 20 students, and professors are said to be accessible and supportive. A junior says, "Professors do an excellent job of combining curricula with a sense of purpose. Everything we do here is worthwhile."

> **"Everything we do here is worthwhile."**

Special programs for first-years include four-day TREK programs, in which students, led by upper-class mentors, go hiking or biking, do community service, or take a leadership skills development course before classes start. In the College of Arts & Sciences, students are enthusiastic about the First-Year Seminar program, which places first-years together in groups of 10 to 15 in a writing-intensive, discussion-oriented seminar taught by a professor who is also each student's advisor. Students in the Honors College write a senior thesis, and an environmental studies major notes, "There are lots of opportunities for undergraduates to get involved in professors' research because we have a relatively small population of grad students." Through the Vermont Legislative Research Service, undergraduate public policy students provide state legislators with policy briefs on current issues. Eighteen percent of all undergrads go abroad; UVM offers 500 options in nearly 70 countries.

> **"There are lots of opportunities for undergraduates to get involved in professors' research."**

"Many UVM students like to be outdoors in all seasons," reports a public communication major, and they tend to be highly involved in extracurriculars. Twenty-two percent of UVM undergraduates are native Vermonters, and 1 percent are international. Hispanics/Latinos make up 6 percent of the student body, Asian Americans 3 percent, Black students less than 1 percent, and multiracial students 4 percent. The lack of racial and other diversity is a common complaint, and social justice and environmental issues also receive attention on campus. "Student activism is very frequent here, and there are constantly conversations about how we can make the university a better place," observes a community and international development major. The university offers merit scholarships averaging $16,000 and nearly 200 athletic awards in 20 sports. The Catamount Commitment covers tuition and fees for qualifying in-state students from low-income families.

Fifty-six percent of UVM undergrads live in campus housing; they are required to do so for their first two years. All students living on campus are affiliated with a residential learning community, with options ranging from Outdoor Experience to Leadership and Social Change to the popular Wellness Environment. "Living in the res hall is a ton of fun, and it's an awesome environment to meet new people," says an animal science major. Students express appreciation for the university's efforts to serve local, organic, and sustainable options at four dining halls and several retail and café locations. A political science and history major notes, "At UVM, we talk about sexual assault, and because of that, we have a high level of reporting when compared to other schools."

Four percent of UVM men and 5 percent of women join Greek groups, so when the weekend comes, college-sponsored movies, dances, craft nights, and coffeehouses help keep things lively. Students enjoy the Fallfest, Winterfest, and Springfest concerts every year, and the Naked Bike Ride is a notable biannual tradition, according to a senior: "On the last day of classes each semester, hundreds of people gather at midnight to run or bike naked around a campus green."

Much of the fun also happens on nearby ski slopes, mountain trails, and waterways and in Burlington itself, especially the Church Street pedestrian mall, where the music scene draws top talent and is always bustling. "You can spend your Friday night at a gourmet restaurant, an off-Broadway theater production, or barhopping around town and still be atop a mountain skiing the very next morning," says a junior. Indeed, the energetic downtown boasts symphonies, art galleries, chic shopping, and lively bars and restaurants, and Lake Champlain is only five minutes away. Forty-four percent of students volunteer in the local community, often through service-learning courses. As much as they love their little city, students do look forward to occasionally getting out of town. A favorite road trip is Montreal—90 minutes away—with its even bigger music scene and a drinking age of 18. The Outing Club is one of UVM's most popular student organizations, as the nearby Green Mountains, White Mountains, and Adirondacks offer prime hiking, backpacking, and rock climbing.

UVM fields a number of highly competitive Division I Catamount ("cat of the mountains") teams. The men's ice hockey team is the school's pride and joy, having ranked as high as second nationally. Students get access to tickets before the general public, a nice perk, since games are always sold out. There is no football team, but women's basketball and field hockey claimed America East championships in 2025. Men's and women's soccer, lacrosse, and men's basketball are also competitive. The ski team is a perennial powerhouse, winning 38 Eastern Intercollegiate Ski Association titles. Thirty percent of students participate in dozens of intramural and club sports, with broomball, ice hockey, and soccer proving to be popular, along with less traditional options like canoe battleship and eSports.

Students at UVM may be laid-back, but they're also curious, caring, open-minded, active, and willing to work hard. They view extracurricular involvement as critical to the undergraduate experience, and at UVM, they find abundant opportunities to engage both inside and outside the classroom. Says one junior, "It's hard to describe the energy that ignites everything we do."

Special programs for first-years include four-day TREK programs, in which students, led by upper-class mentors, go hiking or biking and do community service.

Overlaps

CU Boulder, UConn, UMass Amherst, University of New Hampshire, Northeastern, St. Lawrence, SUNY–Binghamton, Syracuse

If You Apply To ›

UVM: Early decision I and II, early action, regular decision. Accepts the Common Application with supplement. Apply to individual schools or programs. Please consult UVM's website for the most up-to-date information regarding standardized test requirements.

800 E Lancaster Avenue, Villanova, PA 19085

Set in an upscale suburb, Villanova is becoming increasingly popular as Philadelphia's answer to Boston College. As at BC, about 70 percent of the students are Roman Catholic (compared with about half at Georgetown). The troika of business, engineering, and nursing are popular at 'Nova. Downtown Philadelphia is a quick hop away by train. Newly famous as the alma mater of Pope Leo XIV.

Website: www.villanova.edu
Location: Suburban
Private
Total Enrollment: 8,320
Undergraduates: 6,731
Male/Female: 46/54
Financial Aid: 74%
Pell Grant: 12%
Expense: Pr $ $ $ $
Student Loans: 43%
Average Debt: $ $ $ $
Applicants: 23,256
Accepted: 27%
Enrolled: 28%
Grad in 6 Years: 92%
Returning First-years: 95%
Academics: ✍ ✍ ✍
Social: 🗩 🗩 🗩
Q of L: ★ ★ ★
Admissions: (610) 519-4000
Email Address:
 gotovu@villanova.edu

Strong Programs:
Biology
Communication
Economics
Engineering
Finance
Nursing
Social Sciences

Villanova University takes pride in its Augustinian heritage, emphasizing intellectual, professional, and spiritual growth as a path to "transforming hearts and minds." It's the school where Robert Prevost, the Chicago-born Pope Leo XIV, earned a B.S. in mathematics in 1977. It has all the trappings of a vintage Roman Catholic university, from strong academics to deeply rooted traditions and rivalries and students firmly dedicated to their faith and service to others. Says one junior, "There are times I walk out of a class at Villanova and just have to stop for a second to take it all in and appreciate what an amazing opportunity I've been afforded."

Founded in 1842 by the community-focused Order of Saint Augustine, Villanova's lush campus of more than 260 acres is situated along Philadelphia's suburban Main Line. Old stone buildings, well-kept lawns, and secluded, tree-lined walkways are a reminder of the campus's historical roots, while several newer buildings are LEED certified. Recent construction includes a major project that has transformed 14 acres of parking lots into a bustling area featuring new residence halls, eateries, and a performing arts center, all linked to the campus core by a pedestrian bridge. Villanova is in the midst of adding further enhancements to the campus, including a new 150,000-square-foot home for the Falvey Library.

Undergraduates may enroll in the College of Liberal Arts and Sciences, the Villanova School of Business, the College of Engineering, or the Fitzpatrick College of Nursing. All students follow a liberal arts core curriculum. First-year students take the yearlong Augustine and Culture Seminar (ACS) and are housed with their ACS classmates or in optional themed learning communities in the residence halls. In the first semester, they read works from the ancient, medieval, and Renaissance periods—ranging from the Greeks and Saint Augustine to the Middle Ages and Shakespeare. In the second semester, students explore works from the Early Modern, Enlightenment, Romantic, Modernist, and Contemporary eras.

> **"The courses are rigorous and are often discussion-oriented."**

Finance, engineering, nursing, and economics are all strong and popular at Villanova, as are the social sciences, biology, and communication programs. Additional undergraduate programs include majors in gender and women's studies and Arab and Islamic studies, as well as minors in global health, counseling, and business law and corporate governance. Forty-four percent of undergraduate classes have fewer than 20 students. "The courses are rigorous and are often discussion-oriented and reading- and writing-intensive," says one communication major. Another student says, "Villanova professors go the extra mile for their students through office hours, research, and personal conversations." An honors program is available to about 300 students. Forty percent of students study abroad each year; communication and computer science students can apply for semester-long internships at the Vatican in Rome.

"The students who attend Villanova are passionate and devoted," says a sophomore. "They care about their work, but, more importantly, they care about their community." Many are from the East Coast, and 23 percent hail from Pennsylvania; 2 percent come from foreign countries. Black students account for 6 percent of the student body, Hispanics/Latinos 11 percent, Asian Americans 7 percent, and multiracial students 4 percent. "We're not an extremely political campus," one student muses, "although social justice issues like poverty, hunger, and homelessness are all big issues." Merit scholarships are available, averaging $28,800, as are more than 200 athletic scholarships in 24 sports.

Housing on campus is guaranteed for three years, and 93 percent of undergraduates call the residence halls home. "Rooms are great at Villanova," says one senior. "My first and second year, I had a sink in my room so I didn't have to walk down the hall to wash my face or brush my teeth." First-years live primarily on the South Campus Circle, while juniors and seniors choose residence halls on the main campus or apartment-style housing on West Campus via lottery system. Most seniors move to houses and apartments in the surrounding neighborhoods. The university offers more than a dozen campus eateries, which serve everything from pizza to Chinese food, wraps, and vegetarian and vegan menus. "Food at Villanova is delicious," says a student. "Tons of variety with so many options I sometimes don't know which one to choose."

> *The university offers more than a dozen campus eateries, which serve everything from pizza to Chinese food.*

"I have never had a dull weekend at Villanova because there is always something going on. If you are looking to party, you can. If you are looking to just chill, you can do that, too," a student explains. Weekend social life centers around campus events and parties, some sponsored by Greek groups, which claim 9 percent of the men and 20 percent of the women. Students get together with friends at the student center on Fridays and Saturdays for Late Night at Villanova events, such as comedians, bands, open-mic nights, and dance parties. Juniors and seniors tend to spend evenings at bars along the local Main Line or in Philadelphia, just 12 minutes away by train. The city's entertainment and cultural opportunities include museums and pro sports, as well as events at numerous other colleges and universities, from La Salle and Temple to Drexel, Penn, and St. Joseph's.

"Everyone works hard, plays hard, and still finds time to give back to the community."

Despite the tough courses, a senior says, "Everyone works hard, plays hard, and still finds time to give back to the community." Indeed, Villanova students volunteer roughly 250,000 hours of service each year. About 400 students participate in service trips over the fall and spring breaks, volunteering for projects like building houses and assisting victims of natural disasters. Each fall, Villanova hosts the largest annual student-run Special Olympics event in the world, drawing thousands of athletes, coaches, and volunteers from across campus and the local community.

> *Villanova is the school where Robert Prevost, the Chicago-born Pope Leo XIV, earned a B.S. in mathematics in 1977.*

When they are not out socializing or serving their community, Villanova students are cheering for the men's basketball team. Men's and women's basketball, cross-country, and women's swimming and diving and softball are competitive in the Big East Conference. Club sports and intramurals are a big draw, and popular activities include basketball, flag football, soccer, and men's ice hockey.

Despite the changes in the world around it, Villanova continues its devotion to its students, community, and strong traditions, both academic and spiritual. The administration has set its sights on making Villanova one of the premier Catholic institutions, up there with Notre Dame, Georgetown, and Boston College (and the only one to turn out a pope). While taking pride in tradition, it recognizes that its continuing improvements to campus facilities and ongoing development of educational and cocurricular programs will help its students remain competitive in the workplace and the world beyond.

Overlaps

Boston College, Fordham, Georgetown, Lehigh, Northeastern, Notre Dame, Penn, UVA

If You Apply To ›

Villanova: Early decision I and II, early action, regular decision. Accepts the Common Application. Apply to a particular school or program. Please consult Villanova's website for the most up-to-date information regarding standardized test requirements.

190 McCormick Road, Charlottesville, VA 22903

When Southern literary icon William Faulkner famously wrote "The past is never dead. It's not even past," he might very well have been thinking about the University of Virgina. Founded by Thomas Jefferson, whose academic values and architectural visions are a continuing presence. Relatively small for a top-notch public flagship, UVA combines high-quality, innovative academics and a vibrant social scene that is spirited in multiple senses of the word. Nestled in the culturally rich town of Charlottesville just 100 miles from Washington and 60 miles from Richmond.

Website: www.virginia.edu
Location: Small City
Public
Total Enrollment: 23,350
Undergraduates: 17,031
Male/Female: 45/55
Financial Aid: 53%
Pell Grant: 22%
Expense: Pub $ $ $ $
Student Loans: 30%
Average Debt: $
Applicants: 58,951
Accepted: 17%
Enrolled: 40%
Grad in 6 Years: 96%
Returning First-years: 98%
Academics: ✍ ✍ ✍ ✍ ✍
Social: 🗩 🗩 🗩 🗩
Q of L: ★ ★ ★ ★ ★
Admissions: (434) 982-3200
Email Address:
  undergradadmission@
  virginia.edu

Strong Programs:
Biology
Commerce
Computer Science
Economics
Engineering
Global Studies
Psychology
Sociology

Easily one of the most prestigious public schools in the nation, the University of Virginia is known to all in Charlottesville as Mr. Jefferson's University. Not just any Mr. Jefferson, mind you, but *the* Mr. Jefferson, author of the Declaration of Independence. Of all his accomplishments, Jefferson was arguably proudest of UVA—he even asked that his epitaph speak to his role in creating the university in 1819 rather than his presidency of the United States. This legacy has come under increasing scrutiny in light of growing public awareness of some of Jefferson's racist views and ownership of hundreds of slaves. In response, the university has sought to "contextualize" its Jeffersonian legacy and remove the names of persons who supported the Confederate cause from places of honor on campus.

Located just east of the Blue Ridge Mountains in central Virginia, UVA's campus (the "Grounds") is dotted with historic buildings designed by Jefferson himself. At the core is Jefferson's "academical village," with majestic white pillars and extensive brickwork. The village rises around a rectangular terraced green, known as the Lawn, which is flanked by two rows of identical one-story rooms reserved for undergraduate student leaders. Behind the buildings are public gardens, while the Rotunda, a half-scale model of the Roman Pantheon, overlooks the Lawn and stands as a symbol of the Enlightenment belief in secularism and freedom. Countering all this Jeffersonian stateliness are newer, state-of-the-art classrooms and residence halls that offer all the latest technological bells and whistles, and the abstract Memorial to Enslaved Laborers, created to honor the 4,000 enslaved people who built and sustained UVA.

UVA isn't just an elite public school; it holds its own against the best private schools as well, especially in the areas of business, engineering, and global studies. Sociology and the life sciences draw praise as well. Majors enrolling the most students are in the liberal arts, social sciences, engineering, and business/marketing. The majority of incoming first-years enroll in the College of Arts and Sciences, but undergraduates may also enroll in the schools of Architecture, Engineering, Nursing, or Education and Human Development. After their first year, about 350 students are accepted into the McIntire School of Commerce, UVA's undergraduate business school. Not surprisingly, competition for these spots is tough. A five-year program for aspiring teachers yields a B.A. from the College of Arts and Sciences and a Master of Teaching degree from UVA's Curry School of Education and Human Development. The Batten School of Leadership and Public Policy trains students for public service careers in both domestic and international arenas and offers a five-year bachelor/master of public policy. Students may also pursue a degree in the new School of Data Science.

> **"UVA definitely has an intense academic climate."**

"UVA definitely has an intense academic climate, as students are always in the libraries studying," says a government and history double major. Virginia requires students in arts and sciences to complete the College Curriculum, which features three categories of coursework: Engagements (a yearlong sequence of small first-year seminars), Literacies (language, rhetoric, computation, and data analysis), and Disciplines (21 credits in a range of liberal arts areas). Although 47 percent of classes enroll fewer than 20 students, lower-level classes can be huge, with as many as 500 people. A senior explains that, especially in upper-level courses, "Most professors are willing to schedule appointments as you might need and are excited to connect with their students." Special programs for first-years include University Seminars, which are taught by some of the school's best faculty and limited to 18 students in order to encourage interactive learning and intensive discussion.

Highly capable students may win admission to the Echols Scholars program, which allows about 200 top-entering first-years the chance to pursue academic exploration without the constraints of distribution or major-field requirements. Echols students also live together for their first year. The Rodman Scholars program in the School of Engineering and Applied Science selects its members based on top academic performance and leadership. An intensive two-week January term provides additional opportunities for research seminars, interdisciplinary coursework, and study abroad. Twenty-six percent of undergrads go abroad to study, conduct research, or intern in their choice of more than 65 countries. Career advising gets high marks: "Career advising is mandatory in many classes through the UVA Career Center, and they provide a lot of help with interview prep and pre-professional advising," says a junior.

Students instituted Virginia's notable honor system in 1842 after no one owned up to shooting a professor on the Lawn. The residence halls, student council, and Judiciary Committee remain student-run to this day—and they really put the brakes on lying, cheating, or stealing. The honor code remains integral to the culture here. A classics major says, "Our honor code is more than just some words scribbled on paper—it's a way of life and a bond of trust between you, your peers, and faculty."

"Career advising is mandatory in many classes through the UVA Career Center."

Admission is competitive. Seventy percent of undergraduates are Virginians, and 5 percent are international. The rest hail from all 50 states. Eight percent of UVA students are Black, 20 percent are Asian American, 8 percent are Hispanic/Latino, and 6 percent are multiracial. "Students at UVA generally are fairly serious about academics, competitive, and very motivated," says a junior, who adds that due to the underrepresentation of various groups, "the culture can sometimes feel exclusive." Despite some current political headwinds, UVA still has support programs for LGBTQ+ students and Black students, and has multicultural and interfaith centers. Students describe a mix of political views on campus but say the student body leans liberal. UVA is one of only a handful of public universities in the nation that practices need-blind admissions and meets 100 percent of all admitted students' demonstrated financial need. The school hands out hundreds of athletic scholarships each year, along with merit awards worth an average of $4,900 each. In-state students from families with incomes of less than $100,000 attend tuition-free.

Forty-one percent of students at Virginia live on campus, including about 800 who bunk in the three residential colleges: Brown College at Monroe Hill, Hereford College, and International Residential College. Hereford's contemporary architecture has been described by the *New York Times* as "proudly, almost defiantly modern," in contrast to most of the other campus buildings. First-year residence halls are said to be the nicest on campus, and incoming students get first pick for housing. Fifty-four top seniors win the honor of living in spartan rooms along the Lawn, and among the outer set of rooms, called the range, students can visit room #13, which was occupied for a semester by Edgar Allan Poe in 1826 before he was suspended for nonpayment of tuition. "Most upperclassmen live off Grounds, and there is a chaotic rush to get good housing beginning as early as September of the year prior," complains a junior. Meal plans are required for first-years, and campus fare receives decent reviews. After UVA initiated and updated several programs aimed at education and prevention of sexual assault, "Our administration is increasing the normalcy of talking about [it], and I do think it is helping," reflects a junior. As for general safety, a student reports, "We have campus police, Charlottesville police, and an Ambassadors watch program all looking out for the safety of students."

"UVA only has a party scene on the weekends," says a junior, "as students are too busy with schoolwork during the week." About 30 percent of students join fraternities or sororities; Greek parties happen off campus. Mr. Jefferson founded UVA as a place where students could come together to "drink from the cup of knowledge," but because fraternity rush is dry and parties must have guest lists, there's less quaffing of other brews going on. Still, determined Virginians haven't stopped metamorphosing into Rowdy Wahoos when the sun goes down—the nickname comes from a long-ago school cheer about a fish that can drink twice its weight. For nondrinkers and those under 21, the student-run University Programs Council and nearly 900 clubs and other organizations offer movies, concerts, social hours, and other booze-free options. "There are a lot of ways to meet new people," cheers a foreign affairs major. Most students are "highly involved" in multiple extracurriculars.

"Almost everything here is a tradition," remarks one student. Favorites include Lighting of the Lawn, featuring a cappella performances and an orchestrated light show on the Rotunda that kicks off the holiday season, and Foxfield, in which students dress up and host catered parties prior to attending a steeplechase horse race each April. Sporting events are popular, with enthusiastic students and fans donning orange and blue. Streaking the Lawn is a rite of passage, students say. We would like to tell you more about the various secret societies, but we can't—for one thing, they're secret!

As for Charlottesville (population 44,000), it's "the perfect college town," says an anthropology major, and often a pleasant surprise for those coming from larger urban areas. There are restaurants and bars; gorgeous vineyards and wineries; and plenty of shops, theaters, and other cultural attractions. Students congregate at the Corner, a commercial strip adjacent to campus boasting several popular bars. They also immerse themselves in community service in the area; UVA's nationally recognized Madison House coordinates the activities of a host of volunteer groups. Outdoorsy folks can hike, bike, ski, and sightsee in the nearby Blue Ridge Mountains, or simply daydream while strolling Skyline Drive. Popular road trips include Washington, D.C., Richmond, and anywhere the Cavaliers are playing football, basketball, or soccer.

Big-time Atlantic Coast Conference basketball has long been an integral part of UVA life, and the men's team claimed the national championship title in 2019. The Cavaliers field several other competitive Division I teams as well: women's swimming and diving and rowing and men's lacrosse and tennis are all recent national champions. Competitions get especially heated when Virginia Tech's Hokies come to town. A junior comments, "Our rivalry with Virginia Tech is hilarious and an excellent way to bond two very different people together as peers." There are also dozens of intramural sports leagues or tournaments, in everything from flag football to inner-tube water polo, and more than 65 club sports.

At UVA, the social life is as vigorous as the academics are rigorous, and the friendships that are formed here last far beyond the college years. "We have a deep

Thomas Jefferson asked that his epitaph speak to his role in creating the university in 1819.

"Our honor code is more than just some words scribbled on paper."

Overlaps

UC Berkeley, Cornell University, George Mason, Georgetown, University of Michigan, Penn, Virginia Tech, William & Mary history and are a school that's steeped in traditions," comments a government major "If you want to get an amazing education while also being able to let loose, UVA is the place for you!"

Virginia Tech

800 Drillfield Drive, Blacksburg, VA 24061

Offers a unique blend of high tech and Southern hospitality. Engineering has always been its calling card, but business and architecture are popular. Admission is competitive for out-of-state applicants. Blacksburg is a nice college town but far from the population centers near the coast. Hokie Nation loves its football team. Compare to Clemson, Georgia Tech, and Purdue.

Officially known as the Virginia Polytechnic Institute and State University, Virginia Tech is a land grant university that offers a slate of solid academic programs, competitive Division I athletics, and storied traditions. Engineering, business, and architecture attract top students from around the country who are proud to be part of the "Hokie Nation." A senior says, "Even in a school with [over] 30,000 students, I feel like I'm in a small town with 200 people. Everyone here is so friendly."

Founded in 1872, Virginia Tech's campus is set on a plateau in the scenic Blue Ridge Mountains and occupies 3,000 acres that come complete with a duck pond, hiking trails, and a 250-year-old plantation that operates as a museum. Students enjoy unlimited outdoor recreation thanks to the proximity of the Jefferson National Forest, the Appalachian Trail, the scenic Blue Ridge Parkway, and the majestic old New River. The campus buildings are an attractive mix of gray limestone structures, colonial-style brick, and modern cement buildings, and the campus continues to undergo renovations and additions.

Virginia Tech is best known for its first-rate technical and professional training. For undergrads with an appetite for engineering, Tech has programs for every taste, including aerospace, chemical, computer, mining, ocean, and more. The Pamplin College of Business, which offers a notable major in hospitality and tourism management, is also prominent. The five-year architecture program is considered one of the nation's best, and the industrial design major is strong too. The most popular majors include engineering (especially mechanical), biology, business information technology, and finance. Though no longer Tech's centerpiece, the College of Agriculture and Life Sciences remains strong, especially in animal science. Students in the College of Natural Resources and Environment can choose from solid majors in forestry, meteorology, sustainable biomaterials, and wildlife conservation. The humanities tend not to fare as well in the university's high-tech environment. The university also has a tradition of excellence in the performing arts, and the school's theater group has won numerous awards.

> "My professors seemed to really care about what I was pursuing and how I was learning."

Website: www.vt.edu
Location: Small Town
Public
Total Enrollment: 36,034
Undergraduates: 30,114
Male/Female: 56/44
Financial Aid: 59%
Pell Grant: 13%
Expense: Pub $ $ $
Student Loans: 45%
Average Debt: $ $ $
Applicants: 52,296
Accepted: 55%
Enrolled: 25%
Grad in 6 Years: 86%
Returning First-years: 93%
Academics: ✑ ✑ ✑
Social: 🗩 🗩 🗩
Q of L: ★ ★ ★ ★
Admissions: (540) 231-6267
Email Address:
admissions@vt.edu

Strong Programs:
Animal Science
Architecture
Business
Engineering
Forestry
Hospitality and Tourism
  Management
Industrial Design
Meteorology

A junior describes the academic climate as "rigorous but very encouraging." The general education program, known as Pathways, requires students to take coursework in several liberal arts areas and gives students the option of pursuing interdisciplinary Pathways minors or hands-on learning experiences, like research or study abroad, to fulfill their gen-eds. Introductory class size tends to be large—sometimes well into the hundreds. Most of the big lecture classes are taught by full-time faculty, though discussions and grading are generally handled by teaching assistants. A senior says, "For the most part, my professors seemed to really care about what I was pursuing and how I was learning, not just performing." The roughly 1,700 students who participate in the Honors College are guaranteed access to top faculty and research opportunities.

The nationally acclaimed Small Business Institute enables faculty-led groups of business majors to work with local merchants, analyze their problems, and make suggestions on how to increase profits. Each year, about 500 students (mostly engineers) take advantage of Tech's co-op program, getting paid for real-world work experience. The Corps of Cadets, a tradition since the university's founding in 1872, offers a unique opportunity for students who wish to combine leadership training with an academic major. The 1,100 Cadets who enroll follow a structured military lifestyle, living together in the Corps's dedicated residence halls and wearing uniforms to class. In addition to choosing between a military/ROTC track and a citizen-leader track, Cadets can earn a minor in leadership. Sixty-nine percent of undergrads conduct research, and for the 28 percent who aspire to study abroad, Tech offers more than 200 programs in 60 nations around the globe.

According to a senior, Virginia Tech students are "down-to-earth, reasonable, and fun people." Seventy-four percent of undergraduates call Virginia home, and 5 percent arrive from abroad. Not surprisingly, the admissions office is inundated with out-of-state applicants, which means stiff competition for the slots available to non-Virginians. Tech's relative isolation from major cities is a drag on minority recruitment: Black students represent 6 percent, Hispanics/Latinos 10 percent, Asian Americans 14 percent, and multiracial students 6 percent of the student body. "For a school in southwest Virginia, the political climate on campus is refreshingly balanced," says a sophomore. Students looking at pricey Northeastern technical schools will find Tech a real bargain. The university hands out more than 400 athletic scholarships in addition to thousands of merit awards averaging $3,600. The Funds for the Future program aims to offset tuition increases for low-income undergraduates.

First-years and the Corps of Cadets are required to live on campus, but overcrowding has been an issue in recent years as enrollment continues to increase. "You need to look for housing early," warns a student. Currently, 33 percent of all undergrads reside in campus-owned housing. After their first year, most students move into nearby off-campus apartment complexes. Dining services receive enthusiastic reviews for variety, taste, and options for special diets. "Virginia Tech offers many classes to learn how to protect yourself and make yourself knowledgeable about the issue of sexual assault," notes a sophomore.

Leisure-time favorites include bowling and billiards in the student center, club activities, and school-sponsored plays, concerts, arts and crafts fairs, and dances. Thirteen percent of the men and 19 percent of the women join fraternities and sororities, and students say Greek groups do not dominate social life. Some of the most important annual events include the Ring Dance (when juniors receive their school rings) and the Corps of Cadets military ball. Service is a big emphasis, and many students get involved in the local community. "Blacksburg has many great restaurants within walking distance of campus, as well as a discount movie theater and the farmers market every weekend," says a neuroscience major. For real big-city

Leisure-time favorites include bowling and billiards in the student center, club activities, and more.

"Blacksburg has many great restaurants within walking distance of campus."

The College of Agriculture and Life Sciences remains strong, especially in animal science.

action, Washington, D.C., and Richmond are four and three hours away by car, respectively. Given that the school is nestled in the Blue Ridge Mountains, hiking, biking, caving, and water sports are popular pastimes, too.

Virginia Tech competes in the Division I Atlantic Coast Conference, and the football team's multiple appearances in postseason bowl games have cheered alumni and hiked applications. The annual big game pits the Hokies against the Cavaliers of the University of Virginia. Men's wrestling and men's and women's basketball and track and field have also performed well in recent years. Tech's extensive recreational program boasts more than 40 intramural and 30 club sports, with everything from football to horseshoes and underwater hockey—a recent rage.

Virginia Tech encourages students to "invent the future," and that's just what today's citizens of the Hokie Nation aim to do. By taking advantage of Tech's particular blend of high-tech learning and Southern hospitality, students have countless opportunities to gain industry experience, travel abroad, and spend four years with like-minded peers.

Overlaps

Clemson, CU Boulder, Georgia Tech, James Madison, Penn State, Purdue, Texas A&M, UVA

If You Apply To ›

Tech: Early action, regular decision. Accepts the Common Application with supplement. Music applicants must audition. Please consult Virginia Tech's website for the most up-to-date information regarding standardized test requirements.

Wabash College

301 W Wabash Avenue, Crawfordsville, IN 47933

Wabash and Hampden–Sydney in Virginia are the last of the all-male breed. With steady enrollment, lots of tradition, and plenty of money in the bank, Wabash sees no reason to change. Intense bonding is an important part of the Wabash experience, and few co-ed schools can match the loyalty of Wabash alumni. The Gentleman's Rule says it all.

Wabash College was founded in Indiana in 1832 by transplanted Ivy Leaguers who shared the Enlightenment's optimistic view of human nature and envisioned a "classical and English high school rising into a college as soon as the wants of the country demand." Their vision proved to be 20/20. All-male Wabash has not only prospered but also remained true to its academic and social traditions, including the Gentleman's Rule of self-responsibility that students continue to live by. "Wabash College has a culture that has not changed for 50 years. It can be a hard school to fit into if you do not meet the status quo, but it also is a brotherhood," says a junior.

"Classes at Wabash are hard."

The 94-acre Wabash campus is characterized by redbrick, white-columned, Georgian-style buildings (three are originals from the 1830s). Located in the heart of Crawfordsville, a small town of about 16,000, Wabash is surrounded by grass and tall trees that are part of the gorgeous Fuller Arboretum. A new Latino Community Center opened in fall 2025.

The Wabash educational program has certainly proved itself over the years. This small college has amassed an impressive list of alumni: executives of major corporations, doctors, lawyers, and many Ph.D.s. Wabash alumni are typically faithful to their school in the form of generous donations. On a per-capita basis, the school's

Website: www.wabash.edu
Location: Small Town
Private
Total Enrollment: 866
Undergraduates: 866
Male/Female: 100/0
Financial Aid: 99%
Pell Grant: 27%
Expense: Pr $
Student Loans: 63%
Average Debt: $ $ $
Applicants: 2,199
Accepted: 63%
Enrolled: 18%
Grad in 6 Years: 77%
Returning First-years: 93%
Academics: ✍ ✍ ✍
Social: 🗩 🗩
Q of L: ★ ★ ★

(continued)

Admissions: (800) 345-5385
Email Address:
 admissions@wabash.edu

Strong Programs:
 Biology
 Chemistry
 Economics
 English
 Religion
 Rhetoric
 Theater

$421 million endowment makes it one of the wealthiest in the nation. General education requirements include courses from a wide variety of fields—natural and behavioral sciences, literature and fine arts, mathematics, and language studies, as well as a course in global citizenship, justice, and diversity. All first-years participate in a community service project during orientation and take a tutorial in the fall that is designed to focus them on reading, writing, and class participation, followed by a colloquium titled Enduring Questions in the spring. All seniors must complete comprehensive examinations in their final semester, consisting of two days of written exams in their major and an hour-long oral exam on their overall liberal arts experience.

Philosophy, politics, and economics (PPE); biology; economics; and rhetoric draw the most majors at Wabash, and high accolades go to the chemistry, biology, and English departments. Religion and theater are traditional strengths. Those who can't satisfy their high-tech interests at Wabash can opt for a 3–2 program in engineering with Columbia, Washington University in St. Louis, or Purdue. "Classes at Wabash are hard," a PPE major acknowledges. "They tell you that before you come here, but they really are hard." Seventy-one percent of classes have fewer than 20 students, and a political science and religion double major explains, "Professors here challenge you but they always want to see you succeed." Students roundly praise the Quantitative Skills Center and the Writing Center for their assistance with classwork, as well as career services for connecting them with internships, jobs, and influential alumni. Seventy-nine percent of students participate in at least one internship during their time at Wabash.

"Professors are always looking for students to help them with their research," says a PPE major. And paid, full-time research positions with faculty are a popular summertime pursuit, particularly among students in the sciences. About half of the students study abroad via semester-long programs offered by third-party providers as well as cross-cultural immersion-learning courses at Wabash that include short-term travel components—at no

"Professors are always looking for students to help them with their research."

extra cost to students. WabashX initiatives provide hands-on experience in three interdisciplinary fields: democracy and public discourse; global health; and innovation, business, and entrepreneurship. Participating students engage in such opportunities as academic summits, internships, consulting projects, volunteer work, and travel abroad. They also enjoy access to dedicated coworking space in the Fusion 54 center in downtown Crawfordsville, where they can interact with local business leaders.

Wabash students are "driven and ready to get their stuff done," affirms a biology major. Most come from public high schools in Indiana, but 22 percent come from other states, and 9 percent hail from foreign countries. Black students represent 4 percent of the student body, Hispanics/Latinos 13 percent, Asian Americans 1 percent, and multiracial students 3 percent. A biology major reports that "the student body tends to lean right," and a senior adds, "We are able to have genuine and calm conversations about our differences and what we believe." Merit awards averaging $33,000 are available to qualified students.

For housing, the college offers five residence halls, two lodges, two duplex-style townhomes, and 10 fraternity houses; all students are required to live on campus all four years. Dorm residents must eat in the dining hall. "Food is hit or miss depending on where and when you eat on campus," says a sophomore. Wabash addresses the topics of sexual assault and gender-based violence during new student orientation and leadership development activities throughout the year. The college has beefed up counseling and mental health services in recent years. "Our counseling center is free to students and is usable as many times as possible," notes a biology major.

Chapel Sing, where first-years compete to see who can best sing the lengthy school song, is a favorite ritual.

As for the surrounding town of Crawfordsville, "There is a surprising amount of stuff in town," one student says. "Golf courses, all the food you need, some stores—you got mainly everything except a big bar scene." On campus, 59 percent of the students join the school's 10 fraternities. "Greek organizations are the social life on campus. No one else throws parties," says a sophomore. Students say there is a noticeable divide between fraternity brothers and "independents." As for drinking on campus, students describe policies as generally loose, as long as students are behaving responsibly. Weekend trips to Purdue and Indiana University are popular. Traditions are taken seriously at Wabash, from homecoming to not passing beneath certain archways on campus, and "painting the senior bench your fraternity colors," shares a senior. Chapel Sing, where first-years compete to see who can best sing the lengthy school song, is a favorite ritual, but undoubtedly the biggest is the school's long-standing rivalry with DePauw, which dates to 1890 and is capped off every year by the football game that decides who gets to keep the prized Monon Bell. Wabash has won 10 of the last 15 rivalry games.

That competitive spirit extends to all the Little Giants' (so named because the 1904 football team was said to be performing above its weight) Division III athletic programs. The wrestling team is a perennial contender for the national title, while the basketball team won the 2024 and track team the 2024 and 2025 North Coast Athletic Conference championships. Baseball and soccer are also competitive. About half of the students participate in intramural and club sports, including basketball, flag football, soccer, and softball.

"Brotherhood is at the core of the college."

Traditions have not changed much since the school's founding back in the 1830s and still play an important part in the lives of the men at Wabash. Some students complain about the lack of women and culture in the surrounding area, but many are happy with the college's intensive, rigorous programs and expanding opportunities for interdisciplinary study and hands-on experiences. "Brotherhood is at the core of the college," says a senior. "You will develop lifelong friendships with not just current students but also past and future students, developing a network that is unmatched."

Overlaps

Denison, DePauw, Hampden–Sydney, Indiana University, Kalamazoo, Purdue, Texas A&M, Wooster

If You Apply To ›

Wabash: Early decision, early action, regular decision. SATs or ACTs: optional. Accepts the Common Application with supplement.

Wake Forest University

1834 Wake Forest Road, Winston-Salem, NC 27109

Wake Forest's Baptist heritage and Winston-Salem location give it a more down-home flavor than Duke or Emory. But take out your magnifying glass and you'll also find one of the nation's most innovative institutions. It was Wake, not Brown or Tufts, that became the first leading private university to go test-optional for the SAT and ACT back in 2008. Holds its own in big-time Atlantic Coast Conference sports with schools five times its size. The strong Greek system dominates the social scene.

Long one of the top private schools in the Southeast, Wake Forest has transformed its regional recognition into a national reputation. The university is best known for basketball, but its solid academics are its real strength. Students work hard, hence

Website: www.wfu.edu
Location: Suburban
Private
Total Enrollment: 8,051
Undergraduates: 5,413
Male/Female: 45/55
Financial Aid: 65%
Pell Grant: 8%
Expense: Pr $ $ $ $
Student Loans: 22%
Average Debt: $ $ $
Applicants: 18,727
Accepted: 22%
Enrolled: 36%
Grad in 6 Years: 89%
Returning First-years: 93%
Academics: ✐ ✐ ✐ ✐
Social: 🗩 🗩 🗩
Q of L: ★ ★ ★
Admissions: (336) 758-5201
Email Address:
admissions@wfu.edu

Strong Programs:
Business and Enterprise
  Management
Communication
Economics
Finance
Politics and International
  Affairs
Psychology

Favorite events include a midnight concert by the school orchestra every Halloween, with members in full costume.

the nickname "Work Forest," but the university's size and strong Greek system mean it's also easy to establish close friendships. "Wake Forest is the best of both worlds," says a political science major. "Academics are challenging, and you're surrounded by motivated and intelligent peers. At the same time, students pride themselves on being social."

Located in the Central Piedmont region of North Carolina, Wake Forest was founded in 1834 by the North Carolina Baptist Convention in Wake Forest, near Raleigh. It moved to Winston-Salem in 1956 and in 1986 replaced formal ties to the Baptists with a "fraternal" relationship. The university's 340-acre campus features flowers, wooded trails, and stately magnolias. There are more than 40 Georgian-style buildings constructed of old Virginia brick with granite trim. The campus is bordered by the lush, 148-acre Reynolda Gardens annex, which features a formal garden, greenhouses, and one of the first collections of Japanese cherry trees in the U.S. Wake Downtown is a 115,000-square-foot, STEM-focused space adjacent to Wake's School of Medicine in downtown Winston-Salem. Newer additions include the 180,000-square-foot Wake Forest Wellbeing Center, housing fitness and recreation facilities as well as offices for student health services.

To graduate from Wake Forest, students must complete a standard distribution of liberal arts courses in addition to taking an introductory first-year seminar and satisfying a 21st Century Stewardship course with options ranging from ethical inquiry to world culture. The most popular programs include finance, communication, economics, psychology, and biology; the School of Business is highly regarded. Wake has an unusual number of interdisciplinary centers and programs for an institution of its size. The innovative Center for Entrepreneurship sponsors programs such as Startup Lab, which allows students to develop business concepts into commercial ventures with the help of seed capital. The Interdisciplinary Arts Center brings together students, faculty, and staff for arts collaborations with subject matter ranging from romance languages to neuroscience.

> **"Academics are challenging, and you're surrounded by motivated and intelligent peers."**

Students agree that courses at Wake Forest are rigorous, but a history and psychology double major says, "I have been impressed by how collaborative Wake students are." Sixty-four percent of undergraduate classes have fewer than 20 students. Faculty members get high marks; graduate assistants teach some labs and health classes, but otherwise professors are at the lectern. "I've been told by professors, department heads, and academic advisors that their first goal for me is that I learn the material and have enriching experiences while at school," says a physics major. "It's very refreshing to have faculty who put the emphasis on this rather than grades." The Office of Personal and Career Development takes a four-year approach to helping students prepare for future careers.

Undergraduates at Wake Forest have plenty of opportunities to participate in faculty-mentored research, and Richter Scholarships fund select independent study or research projects that involve travel away from campus. The Pro Humanitate Institute allows students to put their skills and knowledge to work helping the community; the center takes its name from the school's motto, which means "In Service to Humanity." Exceptionally able students may qualify for the Honors in Arts and Sciences distinction by taking three or more honors seminars during their first three years. The Wake Washington Center gives selected undergraduates the chance to live, study, intern, and network in the nation's capital for a semester. And for those who wish to spread their wings internationally, Wake Forest's residential study centers in Copenhagen, London, Vienna, and on the Grand Canal in Venice beckon. Wake Forest offers more than 400 semester, summer, and yearlong study abroad programs in more than 70 countries worldwide.

"Students at Wake Forest are highly driven," says a senior. Eighty-three percent of undergraduates hail from outside North Carolina, including 6 percent who come from foreign countries. The university's move to de-emphasize the SAT and ACT was one of its many efforts to boost lagging diversity, but success has been limited. Currently, Black students make up 6 percent of the undergraduate population, Asian Americans add 5 percent, Hispanics/Latinos contribute 10 percent, and multiracial students represent 5 percent. Although the university meets 98 percent of admitted students' demonstrated financial need, it is weak on socioeconomic diversity, with a mere 8 percent of first-years qualifying for Pell Grants. Still, Wake Forest offers an early action option specifically designed for first-generation college students. Merit scholarships averaging $17,100 are awarded to eligible students, in addition to around 200 athletic scholarships.

> **"I have been impressed by how collaborative Wake students are."**

Seventy-five percent of students live on campus, as they are required to do for their first three years. In addition to all-gender restrooms across campus, the university now offers gender-neutral housing options and has increased the size and visibility of its LGBTQ Center. Dining options have improved recently, students say: "There are two standard cafeterias, as well as a Starbucks, Chick-fil-A, Moe's, Subway, and other options." One student complains, "Campus security could be better. There is a fair amount of crime in certain areas of campus." Students say sexual assault is not a prevalent issue, but the Safe Office is an effective resource for those who need it.

The Wake Washington Center gives selected undergraduates the chance to live, study, intern, and network in the nation's capital for a semester.

Twenty-eight percent of men and 65 percent of women go Greek, and Greek life dominates the social scene. Fraternities and sororities do not have houses on campus, but they throw open parties in dorm lounges or in off-campus houses. "Other organizations, such as Student Union, make a huge effort to bring other social options, such as concerts, movies, and events, to campus," says a student. The school's honor code helps to keep rowdy behavior in check; as one student cautions, "If you are caught with alcohol and you are under 21, there are strict consequences." Everyone enjoys the annual homecoming festivities, and after the Demon Deacons score big athletic victories, students roll the quad in toilet paper to celebrate. Other favorite events include a midnight concert by the school orchestra every Halloween, with members in full costume, and Lilting Banshees comedy troupe shows. Another Wake Forest tradition is Hit the Bricks, an eight-hour relay race benefitting cancer research that runs along the brick pathways of Hearn Plaza. Popular road trips are to the beach or the mountains; Chapel Hill, Durham, and Raleigh are each 100 miles away, and Atlanta and the Washington/Baltimore areas are about a five-hour drive.

> **"[The Student Union brings] social options, such as concerts, movies, and events, to campus."**

The city of Winston-Salem is rich in culture, with a symphony, a Christmastime "Moravian love feast," film festivals, multiple art museums, a thriving arts district, and the well-known University of North Carolina School of the Arts. It's also home to the corporate headquarters of another Southern specialty: Krispy Kreme Doughnuts. "Winston is a very suburban town with a lot of young families and a Southern feel," a student says. The town also has a strong music scene, with live bands playing regularly at downtown venues. Popular volunteer activities include Project Pumpkin, a trick-or-treat night on campus for underprivileged children.

The Interdisciplinary Arts Center brings together students, faculty, and staff for arts collaborations.

Wake Forest sports teams became known as the oxymoronic Demon Deacons after a major victory over Duke in 1922 when, in the words of the editor of the school newspaper, they "fought like demons." Basketball is the undisputed king at Wake Forest—think Chris Paul and Tim Duncan—and is perennially strong in the rough-and-tumble Division I Atlantic Coast Conference. Other solid teams include men's and women's soccer, men's tennis and baseball, and women's golf. Of course, virtually any contest against in-state rival UNC at Chapel Hill is guaranteed to get students excited. Intramural and club sports are also offered—soccer, basketball, and floor hockey are some of the most popular—and according to a senior, "Fun supersedes talent."

A spirit of engagement pervades the Wake Forest experience, as well as an underdog mentality when compared with competitors that are bigger, slightly more famous, or located in places like Chapel Hill or Atlanta instead of Winston-Salem. The Deacs always punch above their weight. As one student puts it, "We are a small school with big school spirit."

If You Apply To ›

Wake Forest: Early decision I and II, early action, regular decision. SATs or ACTs: optional. Accepts the Common Application with supplement.

Warren Wilson College

701 Warren Wilson Road, Swannanoa, NC 28778

Among a handful of schools where students combine academics, community engagement, and on-campus work that helps keep tuition down. Roots in the culture of Appalachia combine with a strong international and social justice orientation to give Warren Wilson its distinctive flavor. Setting in the mountains of western North Carolina is tough to beat. Campus atmosphere ranges from liberal to far-out alternative.

Warren Wilson is a small liberal arts college flush with engaging quirks. It promotes global perspectives while maintaining its roots in Appalachian culture. It puts students to work (including on the campus farm) and makes service learning a central part of the educational experience. "Every major is designed for learning in action and includes a carefully designed sequence of experiences integrating theory with practice," say administrators. The school is also at the forefront of the "green" movement, having divested its endowment from fossil fuels in 2020, and the college has opened the Center for Working Lands, which uses campus forest, fields, and streams to showcase new practices in climate change mitigation, prevention, and resilience. In 2025, Warren Wilson reduced tuition by 40 percent to further the institution's goal of being "a place of radical inclusion." In the words of a senior, "My school is wild. It is a big old 'take that' to the status quo. It is a group of people who are going to change the world."

Founded by the Presbyterian Church in 1894 as the Asheville Farm School, Warren Wilson College initially provided formal schooling for "mountain boys." In 1967, it transformed into a four-year, co-ed liberal arts college that, while still maintaining its Presbyterian heritage, welcomes students of all backgrounds. WWC is located 15 minutes from downtown Asheville in the lush Swannanoa Valley of the Blue Ridge Mountains.

> **"The academic climate is intimate, inclusive, and experiential."**

Its 1,132-acre campus features formal gardens, fruit and vegetable gardens, a 300-acre farm, and approximately 16 miles of hiking trails. Consistent with campus culture, the wood-and-stone buildings are small in scale and built in an architectural style that emphasizes natural earth tones accented by extensive stonework by traditional Appalachian stonemasons.

The signature feature of the WWC curriculum is its unique experiential education program, which combines liberal arts coursework, community engagement, campus work, internships, and capstone research. To graduate, students must participate in community engaged courses where they volunteer with more than 100 community organizations tackling issues like food security, homelessness, education, and the environment. Warren Wilson is also one of 10 four-year Federal Work Colleges in the nation that require all residential students to work on campus—a practice that helps keep tuition down. To fulfill their work requirement, students choose to spend 10 to 16 hours every week working in crews that range from blacksmithing and recycling projects to IT services, photography, and keeping the college farm going. To meet general education requirements, WWC students take a broad range of liberal arts courses and all first-year students enroll in the writing-intensive First-Year Seminar, which includes introductory service-learning experiences. In addition, every undergraduate major requires a culminating capstone project.

Students may choose from 22 majors, 17 minors, and 13 concentrations. Some of the most popular majors are environmental studies, conservation biology, sociology/anthropology, and art. Ecological forestry is a unique strength; sustainable agriculture and creative writing are also strong. Majors have been added recently in media and communications, animal science, data science, and international and social justice; majors in chemistry, mathematics, and global studies have been discontinued. Students give high marks to the social work major and the natural sciences, especially biology. The popular outdoor leadership major prepares students to lead outdoor adventure education programs, focusing on both technical skills like backpacking and rock climbing and interpersonal skills like leadership and counseling. Appalachian studies, a minor within the International and Social Justice Studies program, serves as a catalyst for local cultural activities.

"The academic climate is intimate, inclusive, and experiential," says a philosophy major. "Really committing for the work program is a unique aspect of our school." Classes are small, and a first-year says, "Our faculty members are highly accessible, and many of them live on campus." An honors track is open to high-achieving students in several majors. Internship opportunities are incorporated into all programs, and 45 percent of students study abroad during their time at WWC. Faculty-led programs involve a semester-long course on campus, followed by two to three weeks on an international "field experience." Qualified students may also study for a semester or two in countries such as China, Finland, Germany, Japan, and South Korea. Academic advising is offered through the Center for Engaged Learning and Careers.

"There are different bubbles at WWC," says a social work major of the students. "Some athletes, some musicians, some artists, some farmers, some outdoor recreation people, some down to earth folks and some academically focused people." Thirty-seven percent of students hail from North Carolina, and 3 percent are international. Black students account for 5 percent, Hispanics/Latinos 9 percent, Asian Americans 1 percent, and multiracial students 4 percent. Upon graduation, most students go into service professions, such as teaching or working for environmental or other nongovernmental organizations. "Students here are really passionate about climate change, sustainability, and environmental justice," says a data science major. "It's a big part of the campus culture," which leans liberal. A solid 45 percent of first-years are Pell-eligible, and merit scholarships are available. Under the school's

The outdoor program is the largest on campus and sponsors weekly hiking, camping, skiing, or other excursions.

"Students here are really passionate about climate change, sustainability, and environmental justice."

To fulfill their work requirement, students choose to spend 10 to 16 hours every week working in crews.

North Carolina Free Tuition Plan, all North Carolina residents who qualify for federal or state need-based financial aid will have the rest of their tuition covered by the college for all four years. Students are paid at least $3,000 per year toward tuition for their work on campus through the school's Work Program.

Eighty-seven percent of students live in the dorms, which an environmental studies major describes as "adequate." The 36-bed, LEED Platinum–certified EcoDorm incorporates solar heating and natural ventilation and is made of hardwoods milled on campus. Other theme housing options are also available. Students have one main dining hall and three cafés to choose from; the vegetarian and vegan fare at Cowpie is said to be particularly tasty. Students say they feel safe on campus, and the Queer Resource Center provides support for the large LGBTQIA+ community on campus and education on gender and sexuality. "The mental health office was particularly useful to me," says an anthropology major, "They offer free counseling services to every student."

In the absence of Greek organizations, students create plenty of ways to have fun and blow off steam on campus. "The social scene has more of a farm-school vibe, with parties sometimes happening at the farm barn," says a first-year student.

> "The social scene has more of a farm-school vibe, with parties sometimes happening at the farm barn."

The outdoor program is the largest on campus and sponsors weekly hiking, camping, skiing, or other excursions. Students 21 and over who wish to imbibe must bring their own beer to parties. Popular events include the student-run Warren Wilson Circus and homecoming. On Work Day, classes are canceled so students and faculty can work together on campus projects and enjoy a pig roast, courtesy of the campus farm crew.

Only 15 minutes away, Asheville "has great restaurants, art galleries, and a fun downtown scene that offers a nice break from campus life," offers one student. A transportation crew provides rides into town for grocery runs and special events. Thanks to the college's community engagement requirement, students take an active role in their surroundings through volunteer work. WWC sponsors short-term engagement projects during vacation breaks, and popular road trips include Atlanta and the beaches of South Carolina.

In a state famed for its rabid sports fans, many Warren Wilson students are conspicuously nonchalant about athletics, and sports have not been a big emphasis here. Nevertheless, the college joined NCAA's Division III in 2024 and has added women's rugby and triathlon, and men's and women's volleyball and track and field. The Fighting Owls boast strong men's and women's basketball, soccer, and cross-country teams. The varsity cycling and mountain biking teams are nationally competitive. Intramural and club sports are options as well.

Success at Warren Wilson is measured not only by grades but also by community service and a sense of stewardship. "One of the most beautiful things about Wilson is that it is a college where I can help pull a calf during a winter calving season in a beautiful valley, then head up to my Latin American Cinema class," says a happy student. Those who aren't afraid to get their hands dirty will see this small liberal arts college as a valuable place that combines the notion of thinking globally with acting locally. "It's not for everybody," admits an anthropology major, "but it's great for those who are looking for a unique and untraditional college experience."

Overlaps

Appalachian State, Bard, Bennington, College of the Atlantic, Guilford, Hampshire, UNC Asheville, UNC Greensboro

If You Apply To ›

Warren Wilson: Early decision, early action, rolling admissions. SATs or ACTs: optional. Accepts the Common Application with supplement. Application includes fields to indicate preferred name, gender, and gender pronouns.

University of Washington

1410 NE Campus Parkway, Seattle, WA 98195

UW wows visitors with its sprawling parklike campus in hugely popular Seattle. Washington is tougher than University of Oregon for out-of-state admission but not as hard as UC heavyweights Berkeley or UCLA. In addition to breathtaking views, location near both the coast and mountains makes for strong marine and environmental studies programs.

The University of Washington, referred to affectionately as "the Udub," has cemented its reputation as a solid research institution, and its over 30,000 full-time undergraduates benefit from traditional strengths in business, health, and natural sciences. Students here understand that size and its consequent anonymity are the prices that must be paid for the wealth of opportunities that await them, although First-Year Interest Groups and a four-year honors program help make the university feel smaller. Those looking for an extra-personal touch might want to investigate UW's campuses in Tacoma and Bothell, where average class sizes are smaller. But if the Seattle campus is your focus, one senior hints, just "learn to work the system."

UW was founded in 1861, prior to statehood, by prominent Seattle-area residents as the Territorial University of Washington. Today, the UW campus in Seattle blends Gothic architecture and the lush, green landscape of the Pacific Northwest. It features several distinctive landmarks. Red Square sits atop the Central Plaza parking garage and features the Broken Obelisk, a 26-foot-high steel sculpture gifted to the university by the Virginia Wright Fund. All of the university's energy comes from renewable resources, and UW has reduced its overall energy use. New facilities include an interdisciplinary engineering building.

Undergraduates in both professional and liberal arts programs must fulfill standard, university-wide distribution requirements to graduate. Individual schools and colleges also have their own requirements. First-year students are given special attention via the First-Year Interest Group (FIG) program, which offers a chance to meet, discuss, and study with other first-years who have similar interests. Each FIG consists of 20 to 25 students who share a cluster of classes (which fulfill graduation requirements) and includes a weekly seminar led by a junior or senior peer advisor.

"The academic climate is often quite competitive."

Many of UW's diverse undergraduate strengths correspond with its excellent graduate programs. The competitive business major, for example, benefits from the university's highly regarded business school and is one of the most popular majors, along with psychology, biology, computer science (which is tops in the country in producing female graduates), and political science. Students majoring in public health, pharmacy, and nursing profit from access to facilities and faculty at the medical school, an international leader in cancer and heart research, cell biology, and organ transplants. English and drama are traditional strengths in the humanities. Also recommended for undergraduates are marine biology, environmental studies, architecture, and most engineering programs, especially human centered design and engineering, and bioengineering. Reflecting the focus on natural resources in Washington's economy, the program in fisheries is excellent, as are earth and atmospheric sciences, including oceanography.

UW follows a quarter system, which means academics are challenging and fast-paced. "The academic climate is often quite competitive with students striving to

Website: www.washington.edu
Location: City Center
Public
Total Enrollment: 43,408
Undergraduates: 30,141
Male/Female: 43/57
Financial Aid: 69%
Pell Grant: 26%
Expense: Pub $ $ $
Student Loans: 25%
Average Debt: $
Applicants: 69,166
Accepted: 39%
Enrolled: 27%
Grad in 6 Years: 85%
Returning First-years: 95%
Academics: ✎ ✎ ✎ ✎
Social: 🌑 🌑 🌑
Q of L: ★ ★ ★
Admissions: (206) 543-9686
Email Address:
askuwadm@uw.edu

Strong Programs:
Architecture
Business
Computer Science
Drama
Engineering
Environmental Studies
Informatics
Oceanography

be the best out of their peers," says a communication major. A common complaint is "having to apply to a major. It is already hard to get into UW, but then once you do, you might not even get into your desired major," explains a senior. Entry into preprofessional and STEM-related programs is particularly difficult, and students say you might want to have a backup plan. Twenty-seven percent of undergraduate classes have more than 50 students. "Faculty members often compensate for large class sizes by making themselves extremely accessible," says a public health major, and many professors are tops in their field.

For those interested in skirting the masses, UW's Honors Program offers small classes on interesting subjects taught by fine professors. "All of my best experiences and opportunities have been through the Honors Program: from scholarships to the Honors Living Learning Community in the residence halls, to Honors-specific study abroad courses," cheers a sophomore. "The Community Learning and Engagement Center is helpful for finding community and experiential learning opportunities," offers a communication major. Twenty percent of undergraduates study abroad via more than 90 faculty-led programs and have options at more than 70 partner institutions across the globe. A program in experiential learning encourages students to find internships, and a variety of classes give students the opportunity to volunteer as part of their coursework. In addition, a political science major recommends students check out "the Undergraduate Research Symposium. UW has so many opportunities for students of any level to get involved in the research process."

Sixty-seven percent of undergraduates are state residents, but it now has a notably large proportion of international students, at 12 percent. The student body is 27 percent Asian American, 10 percent Hispanic/Latino, 4 percent Black, and 8 percent multiracial. The campus, like its host city, is politically liberal. Students, says a senior, "are go-getters and active in the world around them."

> **"UW has so many opportunities for students of any level to get involved in the research process."**

Merit-based scholarships averaging $4,300 per year are available to high-achieving students, and the university also doles out more than 450 athletic scholarships. The Washington College Grant provides free or reduced tuition for in-state students from low- and middle-income families who meet certain requirements. The grant is funded in part by a statewide tax on Washington-based businesses like Amazon and Microsoft that depend on highly skilled workers.

Twenty-six percent of students live in the school's 12 co-ed dorms, including 74 percent of first-years. "The residence halls are really new and nice facilities for the most part. The main drawback is that they are pretty expensive," says a junior. Most students live off campus in Seattle or other parts of King County. Each dorm has its own cafeteria and fast-food line based on a debit card system. The Husky Union Building also offers a dining hall, espresso bar (don't forget, this is Seattle!), writing center, sun deck, and lounges, not to mention a bowling alley, gaming lounge, student-run bike shop, and more. Regarding campus safety, a first-year cautions, "Since campus is in an urban area, you really have to be careful at night." Career services gets mixed reviews with one student finding it "underwhelming."

With a large commuter population, "Many people describe feeling that it is difficult to meet people in classes and find their communities through clubs, interest groups, Greek life, etc.," says a community, environment, and planning major. On campus, the social scene tends to be defined by the Greeks and the 1,000-plus student organizations that sponsor various activities. Approximately 4,000 students join a combined total of nearly 65 fraternities and sororities. Alcohol is allowed on campus for students 21 and over, but marijuana is not (despite being legal in the state of Washington), and students report that policies are strictly enforced. One tradition everyone looks forward to is Dawg Daze in the fall, which "consists of

200-plus events to welcome first-year students and returning students from their summer vacations," explains a communication major. "Outside of campus, Capitol Hill is a popular spot for nightlife," shares a psychology and business administration double major. "It's just two stops away on the Link light rail and offers a variety of bars and clubs." The Seattle Center and other venues host outstanding operas, symphonies, touring shows, and major league sports.

But who needs pro sports with UW's Division I Huskies around, who compete in the Big Ten conference? Husky Fever breaks out on every football weekend, and the stands are always packed for UW's team, especially when Washington State comes to town to vie for the coveted Apple Cup. Men's and women's rowing won recent national championships, while men's soccer and track and field and women's softball are competitive. UW offers more than 35 club sports and 30 intramural leagues in which 30 percent of students compete. More than anything else, the great outdoors defines the University of Washington. The campus offers breathtaking views of Lake Washington and the Cascade and Olympic mountains. Outdoor pastimes for students include boating, hiking, camping, and skiing, all found nearby, and Canada is close enough for road trips to Vancouver. The weather is consistently temperate, and natives insist that the city's reputation for rain is undeserved. Then again, the sports stadium has an overhang to protect spectators from showers.

> **"UW strikes a balance between academic ambition and laid-back West Coast culture."**

"UW strikes a balance between academic ambition and laid-back West Coast culture," says a junior. "It's a place where you need to take initiative, but once you do, there are countless opportunities and support systems." While some students will not appreciate the occasionally impersonal academics, many students can overlook these obstacles for the big picture of the University of Washington—one that takes in more than just the beautiful scenery.

Overlaps

UC Berkeley, UCLA, UC San Diego, UC Santa Barbara, U of I at Urbana–Champaign, University of Michigan, NYU, UT Austin

If You Apply To ›

Washington: Regular decision. SATs or ACTs: optional. Accepts the Common Application.

Washington & Jefferson College

60 S Lincoln Street, Washington, PA 15301

Premed Central would be as accurate a name as any for W&J, which has one of the nation's highest proportions of students who go on to medical school and women who earn STEM doctorates. Law school and business school are also popular destinations, and undergraduates in all fields pack their bags to conduct independent research in far-flung locales through the innovative Magellan Project.

Wannabe doctors and lawyers would be well-advised to give Washington & Jefferson College a look. This small Pennsylvania college, founded in 1781 by Presbyterian ministers, is renowned for its preprofessional programs, and graduates are almost guaranteed acceptance into medical, health-related, and STEM graduate programs. At the same time, the college's curriculum is growing more interdisciplinary and international in scope and putting more emphasis on independent student work. Classes remain small here, and students enjoy an active social life thanks to a hearty Greek scene and the nearby city of Pittsburgh.

Website: www.washjeff.edu
Location: Small Town
Private
Total Enrollment: 1,288
Undergraduates: 1,288
Male/Female: 54/46
Financial Aid: 100%

(continued)

Pell Grant: 39%

Expense: Pr $

Student Loans: 77%

Average Debt: $ $ $

Applicants: 3,947

Accepted: 81%

Enrolled: 13%

Grad in 6 Years: 70%

Returning First-years: 81%

Academics: ✍ ✍ ✍

Social: 🗨 🗨 🗨

Q of L: ★ ★

Admissions: (724) 223-6025

Email Address:

admission@washjeff.edu

Strong Programs:
Accounting
Biological Sciences
Business Administration
Chemistry
Communication Arts
Economics
English
Psychology

Flannel Fest in the fall brings in activities and treats, and students look forward to the Spring Concert.

The campus, like the student body, is tight-knit: more than 50 buildings sit on 65 acres in a small town about 30 miles outside of Pittsburgh. W&J is the 11th-oldest college in the country and houses the eighth-oldest college building, which was built in 1793. The school got its name following the merger shortly after the Civil War of two colleges whose names you can probably discern. The prevailing architectural style is traditional colonial/Georgian, though modern structures have been added at a rapid pace during the past two decades.

Students at W&J are required to either double major or pursue a major and minor. An ethical leadership component is integrated into a range of liberal arts and sciences classes on offer, and students must demonstrate proficiency in writing, speaking, reading, quantitative reasoning, foreign language, and use of information technology. Every first-year student enrolls in a first-year seminar selecting from multiple course options, and all students complete a practical experience (PREX), which may involve an internship, service project, guided on-campus student employment, advanced research projects, or self-designed experiences. All graduating seniors take part in a capstone experience.

Given that W&J is a magnet for students who plan to pursue M.D.s, J.D.s, and M.B.A.s, some of the school's most popular majors are business administration, accounting, psychology, and computing and information studies. English, communication arts, economics, and biology are also strong, and a nursing major has been added. An entrepreneurship minor gives students the chance to interact with founders of Fortune 500 companies, and the interdisciplinary computing and information studies major offers five concentrations: data science, computer science, digital media, interaction design, and web and mobile technologies. A thematic major allows students to design their own course of study. Rare among liberal arts colleges are the 3–4 programs with the Pennsylvania Colleges of Optometry and Podiatry. More technically minded students can take advantage of 3–2 engineering programs with Case Western Reserve, Columbia, University of Pittsburgh, and WashU in St. Louis.

> **"Because it is such a small campus, you know everyone in your academic field very well."**

W&J's formula for success starts with individual attention in small classes; 73 percent of classes have fewer than 20 students, and a junior says professors "work tirelessly to ensure a safe and challenging classroom environment." Students agree that the academic climate is tough, especially for those on the premed and prelaw tracks, but as a business major points out, "Because it is such a small campus, you know everyone in your academic field very well." In addition to faculty advisors and peer mentors, a Student Success Consultant meets with students one-on-one to guide them through their first year.

The Magellan Project provides funding for approximately 100 first-years, sophomores, and juniors to put their liberal arts education to work each year through self-designed summer research projects or internships that involve domestic or international travel. Past projects have included the Hawaiian Biome Comparison and ecotourism in New Zealand. "The Magellan Project is by far the best opportunity that W&J offers," enthuses one participant. The Washington Fellows Program is an honors program that provides participating students a bevy of special opportunities to interact with distinguished faculty, alumni, and guests. "If you're in the art department, you can also have the privilege of going on all-expenses paid art trips to see museums, plays, etc., through the Hugh Taylor Art Endowment," says a communications and Spanish major. During the May term, students find brief apprenticeships in prospective career areas, take a short-term tour abroad, or engage in nontraditional coursework. Eleven percent of students study abroad, and the Office of Global Education offers more than 30 approved options in more than 20 countries. A robust alumni mentorship program matches students with alumni in careers or locations of interest.

W&J students describe their classmates as "goal-oriented" and "willing to help others." Students agree that a lack of diversity is notable. Seventy-four percent of students hail from Pennsylvania, and many are from neighboring states in the Northeast; 1 percent are international. Six percent of students are Black, 6 percent are Hispanic/Latino, 2 percent are Asian American, and 7 percent are multiracial. "Socioeconomically and politically, there is some diversity," says a biology major. Merit scholarships average $12,300, but there are no athletic scholarships. A notable 39 percent of students qualify for Pell Grants.

Students can live in either co-ed or single-sex dorms, and 86 percent of students live on campus. Housing is guaranteed for four years, and students say the first-year dorms are "adequate," but the choices get better with academic rank and include suite-style and apartment options for upperclassmen. Living/Learning communities, such as Substance Free House, STEM House, and others are available. Campus meals get mostly positive reviews. "The dining facilities have become healthier and offer more options for students with dietary needs," comments a biology major. W&J has launched bystander awareness training and a student group of peer advocates to help educate the community on preventing sexual violence. Mental health counseling services get positive reviews from students.

"There is little social scene on campus as most students are local and tend to go home on the weekends," says a biology major. But a communications major begs to differ, "W&J has increasingly made on-campus fun more of a priority in recent years. Every Friday the college hosts 'Feel-Good Fridays,' in which a fun mini-event takes place around lunchtime, which can range from spinning a wheel to earn a prize, or getting a free donut." Flannel Fest in the fall brings in activities and treats, and students look forward to the Spring Concert. Greek life draws 20 percent of the men and 32 percent of the women, and chapter parties are said to be "very inclusive and welcoming." At the Inside Scoop, students enjoy big-screen televisions, Netflix, pool tables, and a student-run café that gives away free food and milkshakes every weekend. There are also numerous student organizations to join, from the outdoors club to the student theater company.

Not all students share the administration's appreciation for "the unique characteristics of the western Pennsylvania milieu." Some complain that there is nothing to do in Washington, a former steel/mining town of 13,000, now hit by hard times. While relations with the locals can be a bit strained, students try to assuage this by actively volunteering in the community. One student says, "Most people just make the drive to Pittsburgh," which is 30 minutes away; the University of Pittsburgh and Penn State are popular destinations for more diverse social opportunities.

Just about anyone has a shot at the Division III varsity sports at W&J, where the teams are known, naturally, as the Presidents. Recent Presidents' Athletic Conference champions include baseball and women's lacrosse; men's and women's golf, football, and women's basketball are competitive. Half of students participate in club teams and intramural and recreational sports, including flag football, basketball, and ultimate Frisbee.

With expanding academic options and the freedom to self-design experiences abroad, W&J is opening more and more doors for students. Students praise the education they receive and the school's close-knit environment. As one sophomore sums up, "If you want to get into med school, law school, or grad school, W&J is a great launching pad."

Overlaps

Allegheny, Beloit, Duquesne, Gustavus Adolphus, Illinois Wesleyan, Juniata, Kalamazoo, Lake Forest

If You Apply To ›

W&J: Early decision, regular decision. SATs or ACTs: not considered. Accepts the Common Application with supplement.

204 W Washington Street, Lexington, VA 24450

The ninth oldest university in the U.S., historically rooted W&L is one of the most selective small colleges in the South, rivaled only by Davidson. W&L supplements the liberal arts with strong programs in business and journalism. Picture-postcard campus is three hours from Washington, D.C. Honor System thrives. Greek participation is robust.

Website: www.wlu.edu
Location: Small City
Private
Total Enrollment: 2,241
Undergraduates: 1,886
Male/Female: 49/51
Financial Aid: 53%
Pell Grant: 14%
Expense: Pr $ $ $
Student Loans: 26%
Average Debt: $ $ $
Applicants: 8,213
Accepted: 14%
Enrolled: 41%
Grad in 6 Years: 94%
Returning First-years: 97%
Academics: ✎ ✎ ✎ ✎
Social: 🍷 🍷 🍷
Q of L: ★ ★ ★ ★
Admissions: (540) 458-8710
Email Address:
admissions@wlu.edu

Strong Programs:
Accounting
Business Administration
Cognitive and Behavioral
 Science
Economics
Engineering
Journalism
Political Science
Poverty and Human Capability
 Studies

Washington and Lee University, which shares the town of Lexington, Virginia, with the Virginia Military Institute, has always epitomized Southern gentility. The long-standing "Speaking Tradition" ensures at least casual communication between members of the W&L community when they pass one another on the well-manicured grounds. Hallmark traditions, like the Honor System and Speaking Tradition, remain central to campus life, even as the community grows more diverse and reflective of the modern world. Incoming classes in recent years are increasingly diverse. Nearly four decades after women were first admitted, today's atmosphere is more 21st century—as befits one of the South's leading liberal arts colleges. Says a senior, "Each individual walks away with a unique sense of what it means to be an honorable, thoughtful, civilized participant in a global society."

Founded in 1749, W&L is named after George Washington, whose donation to the school in 1796 saved it from dire financial straits, and Robert E. Lee, who was president of the college from 1865 until his death in 1870. After an agonizing year-long discussion, university trustees voted in 2021 to retain Lee as part of the school's name. They also stripped Lee's name from the campus chapel

> **"The academic climate at W&L is very collaborative."**

(where he is buried near the remains of his horse Traveller) and announced a number of steps designed to "expand diversity and inclusion." Among them, the university established the DeLaney Center for Southern Race, Culture, and Politics, which promotes teaching and research on race and Southern identity.

W&L's wooded campus sits atop a hill of lush green lawns, sweeping from one national landmark to another. The iconic Colonnade features stately redbrick structures with white Doric columns and the prevailing architectural style is Greek Revival, although the physical face of the campus is changing. The school recently opened the $13.5 million Ruscio Center for Global Learning, the Williams School of Commerce, Economics, and Politics building, and the Lindley Center for Student Wellness.

General education requirements account for one-third of a student's coursework and include a first-year writing seminar and courses in literature, fine arts, history, philosophy, religion, science and math, social science, foreign language, and physical education. Students must also complete four credits of experiential learning. The Spring Term is a four-week, one course immersive experience during which students pursue research or creative projects, field-based learning, and international study. Forty percent of students spend time overseas at some point, traveling to destinations in more than 40 countries.

Although a standard liberal arts program remains the foundation of W&L's curriculum, the university offers excellent preprofessional programs, particularly in business and accounting, through the Williams School of Commerce, Economics, and Politics, as well as in journalism and engineering. Political science and government, history, cognitive and behavioral science, and biochemistry are popular choices as well. Students pursuing pre-law or pre-health paths benefit from strong advising, personal faculty mentorship, and relevant experiential opportunities. The Shepherd Program remains a national leader in poverty and human capability studies, offering a minor in poverty studies that requires students to complete an eight-week summer internship with an organization focused on poverty-related issues. The program combines "intellectual pursuits with the real world in a way that makes one's education both tangible and more meaningful," says one participant.

"The academic climate at W&L is very collaborative," says an economics major, "with professors encouraging students to work together and lean on each other through their studies." Classes are small—80 percent have fewer than 20 students—and there are no teaching assistants. Says an economics and Spanish major, "I have never had a class with more than 24 students during my four years here, and I have never left a class without a professor knowing my name." Well-qualified students can apply for the Summer Research Scholars Program, which offers students roughly 150 paid fellowships for assisting professors in research or doing their own. The famous Honor System lends a relaxed feeling to the otherwise rigorous academic climate. Tests and final exams are taken without faculty supervision; doors remain unlocked, laptops stay on desks, and library stacks are open 24 hours a day. Counseling and career services are highly praised. "The career counselors make an effort to get to know each student on an individual basis to position students for success," says a junior.

"At W&L, students are invested in each other and want to see each other succeed," says an economics major. Eleven percent of W&L students are native Virginians, and students from northeast of D.C. are well represented; international students make up 6 percent of the population. Amid ongoing efforts to increase diversity of all types, Black students currently account for 5 percent of the student body, Hispanics/Latinos 9 percent, Asian Americans 5 percent, and multiracial students 4 percent. Though the atmosphere is still more traditional than at most leading liberal arts colleges, the days of rock-ribbed conservatism are gone. "Politically, W&L is split fairly evenly between conservative and liberal mindsets," says a junior. "W&L as an institution is intentional in supporting students of color, queer students, international students, and people who come from low-income backgrounds."

"The career counselors make an effort to get to know each student on an individual basis."

W&L's Johnson Scholarship Program awards merit scholarships covering tuition, room, and board to approximately 10 percent of each entering class. Johnson Scholars also receive funding of up to $10,000 to support summer experiences like travel, internships, and research projects. Merit scholarships average $51,200. As a Division III school, W&L does not offer athletic scholarships. The university has need-blind admissions, and it guarantees to meet the full demonstrated financial need—without loans—of all admitted students. For those whose families earn less than $150,000 annually, the W&L Promise program provides full-tuition grants. With these initiatives, socioeconomic diversity is slowly increasing, but the majority of students still come from wealthy backgrounds. Still, a first-generation student urges, "We need diverse students at Washington and Lee, and the support system from the university is in place to welcome them."

Seventy-four percent of students reside on campus, as they are required to do for their first three years. Students spend their first year in co-ed dorms. Many sophomores move into Greek houses or theme houses, while juniors and seniors opt for apartment- and townhouse-style accommodations. "The housing options are newly renovated and really nice," cheers one student. First-year students must purchase a

*Hallmark traditions,
like the Honor
System and Speaking
Tradition, remain
central to campus life.*

meal plan, and dining options get good reviews. Students say the Honor System, campus security personnel, and thorough training programs on preventing and responding to sexual assault contribute to their feelings of safety on campus.

"Greek culture is pervasive," explains a cognitive and behavioral science major, and a senior adds, "The social scene at W&L is very inclusive with social events being open to everyone." Seventy-two percent of both the men and women take part in Greek life. Favorite annual events include the formal Fancy Dress Ball (a.k.a. "prom for college") and the Black Ball, sponsored by the Student Association for Black Unity. While underage drinking is banned in the dorms, students insist that their peers "like to party and drink." Friday Underground, a weekly coffeehouse with free food, coffee, and student performances, has proven to be a popular social alternative. W&L's mock political convention for the party out of power, held every four years, has predicted past presidential nominees with uncanny accuracy.

The school's scenic location in the midst of the Appalachian Mountains means an abundance of activities for nature lovers, including hunting, fishing, camping,

"The social scene at W&L is very inclusive with social events being open to everyone."

mountain biking, skiing, and tubing on the rivers. The Outing Club, the largest student organization on campus, organizes day trips throughout the year and lengthier excursions during school breaks. Lexington, a "quiet, friendly town that has much history to offer," also offers a few bars, two movie theaters, and several restaurants. Washington, D.C., Richmond, Charlottesville, and Roanoke are easily reached by car for weekend trips.

W&L offers 24 varsity sports at the Division III level, and most teams participate in the Old Dominion Athletic Conference. In recent years, the Generals have taken home conference championships in men's and women's lacrosse, women's tennis and basketball, men's golf and soccer, and men's and women's tennis. The university sponsors approximately 25 club and intramural sports, ranging from flag football and basketball to pickleball and ping-pong.

"Washington and Lee is an institution with a lot of history, but per our motto [non incautus future], we are 'not unmindful of the future,'" says an English major. A sense of history and tradition does pervade the campus, from the liberal arts curriculum to the time-tested Honor System. W&L continues to focus on preparing students to succeed in a more globally interconnected world. According to a biology major, one thing remains constant: "W&L is a tight-knit community with trust and honor at the forefront."

Overlaps

Dartmouth, Davidson, Duke, Middlebury, University of Richmond, UVA, Wake Forest, William & Mary

If You Apply To ›

W&L: Early decision I and II, regular decision. SATs or ACTs: optional. Accepts the Common Application with supplement.

Washington College

300 Washington Avenue, Chestertown, MD 21620

A small liberal arts college with strengths in the sciences, business management, pre-med, writing, and environmental science, Washington College is one of the oldest schools in the country. The college has George Washington as its éminence grise. Chestertown is small and quaint, so students make their own fun. Known for its Center for Environment & Society as well as its commitment to sustainability.

Chartered in 1782 in the closing days of the American Revolution, Washington College was the first college to be established in the newly independent United States and the first to adopt a thoroughly secular mission: educating citizens, patriots, and leaders for the new democracy. It takes its name from George Washington, who never slept in any of its dorms but who did make a modest founding grant of 50 guineas and served as a trustee. His spirit looms over the campus as strongly as that of "Mr. Jefferson" at UVA. One of the first things first-year students do upon arrival is sign the Honor Code (Washington students cannot tell lies). "Washington College is a home, and it is an unbelievably special place," cheers a happy history major. "Like any family we have our issues, but at the end of the day I have never been in another place where I have felt this encouraged and supported."

Washington College sits on 112 acres adjacent to downtown Chestertown, a quiet community of 5,100 on the Chester River on the eastern shore of Chesapeake Bay. Most buildings are redbrick, Georgian-style structures connected by old brick walkways and enhanced by large shade trees. The historic heart of the campus is the green where commencement is held and where a bronze statue of you-know-who keeps watch. The Gibson Center of the Arts, the Toll Science Center, and the Hodson Commons mix large expanses of glass with traditional red brick. The college has invested millions in renovations and new facilities in recent years, including several residence halls, as well as the Casey Academic Center.

First-year students begin their studies with a required First-Year Seminar course in which they develop their reading, writing, research, discussion, and presentation skills. In addition to standard distribution requirements, students must also complete a senior capstone experience that, depending on their major field, can take the form of a comprehensive exam, thesis, scientific research project, theatrical production, or portfolio of writing or artwork.

The most popular majors are also among the strongest and include business management, biology/premed, psychology, environmental science and studies, and pre-engineering. The college's notable writing program is embedded in all disciplines, and the Rose O'Neill Literary House is a cultural hub where students can discuss poetry and literature over a cup of tea and freshly baked cookies; it has a long-standing tradition of bringing writers such as Jericho Brown, R.O. Kwon, and Natalie Diaz to campus. Seniors from all disciplines may submit writing portfolios to vie for the Sophie Kerr Prize. Named after a popular American writer of the early 20th century, it is the largest undergraduate literary prize in the country and gives the school its annual 15 minutes of fame in the national media. The 2025 winner took home a check for just over $74,000. A new School of Global Business, Economics, and Social Impact will launch in fall 2026.

Not surprisingly, Washington College is also a wonderful place to study history and American studies. "When you are on campus, you feel the history," enthuses one student. The Starr Center for the Study of the American Experience, located in the old Custom House on the Chester River, helps students study the culture of the Native Americans who once populated the area, trace the Revolutionary War campaigns in the Chesapeake region, and explore the history of the African American experience on the Eastern Shore through the Center's Chesapeake Heartland Program. What's more, notes a senior, the Center offers "internships that pay well and give [students] hands-on work in the humanities." Washington also takes advantage of its rural setting and nearby waterways to offer a strong program in environmental science and studies. The Center for Environment & Society promotes stewardship of the area's natural resources, including a Chesapeake Semester that offers hands-on experience in the watershed and a trip to Costa Rica for comparative study. The River and

Field Campus, located 10 minutes from the college's main campus, is a 5,000-acre living laboratory for avian, environmental, and archaeological research and has a number of dual-degree programs including 3–2 programs in environmental studies with Duke University, engineering with Columbia, and nursing with the University of Maryland.

Students report that most of their instruction comes from full professors who are easily accessible, and 86 percent of classes have fewer than 20 students. "Because of smaller class sizes, professors tend to cater their instruction to the interests of the students when possible," says an international studies and anthropology double major. Washington College operates on a four-credits-per-course basis, with three hours of classes and students expected to work on their own for the fourth. "Classes are challenging and require a high level of work in order to excel," comments an environmental science major. Every first-year is assigned to a peer mentor who is trained to help them adjust to college life.

The Presidential Fellows program offers special academic opportunities to the top 20 percent of entering first-years. Washington students can study abroad in programs offered in more than 30 countries. Short-term, faculty-led study-abroad options are available during summer and winter breaks. The school's proximity to Washington, D.C., Philadelphia, and Baltimore affords excellent access to internships. In recent years, Washington students have interned at the National Archives, the U.S. Congress, and the Smithsonian. A junior notes, "Our Career Center is one of the best resources we have on-campus." Adds another junior, "It has access to a pool of money for covering internship costs (housing, transportation, etc)."

> "Professors tend to cater their instruction to the interests of the students when possible."

"Students at Washington College are warm and welcoming," states an English and sociology major. Forty-four percent of students at Washington are from Maryland, and 1 percent hail from other countries. "The college has made efforts to foster a more inclusive community," says a political science major, "including hiring more diverse faculty and staff, offering scholarships to students from underrepresented backgrounds, and implementing programs to promote cultural awareness." Black students represent 9 percent of the student body, Hispanics/Latinos 10 percent, and Asian Americans 3 percent. A human development major says, "Politically, there are students that support different sides, and this is where we are the most diverse." Merit scholarships averaging $36,100 annually are available; there are no athletic scholarships. The Washington Scholars program awards full scholarship funding to high-achieving, high-need students.

All students are guaranteed on-campus housing for all four years, and 84 percent take up the offer. Rooms are assigned through a lottery with numbers based on class year. A sophomore reports that "not all dorms are created equal, but none of them are completely unacceptable." Corsica is among the choicest in a cluster of dorms located on what students call the "Western Shore," overlooking the athletic fields. Meals at the dining hall are all-you-can-eat, and a senior claims, "The dining hall has greatly improved during my time here," in terms of quality and options for vegans and vegetarians. Students give decent ratings to campus safety and efforts to raise awareness about sexual assault.

According to a senior, Washington's social life is "focused on community involvement and academic pursuits rather than partying." There are occasional off-campus house parties, but most social life takes place on campus, much of it coordinated by the school's 80-plus student organizations. The Student Events Board sponsors concerts, film series, open-mic nights, silent discos, bonfires, and other entertainment. Four percent of the men belong to fraternities and 6 percent of the women to sororities. The Crab Feast, put on by Phi Delta Theta, is popular, as is the all-campus picnic. By far the biggest social event of the year is the formal Birthday Ball in February in honor of you-know-who's birthday. "We love our namesake!" cheers an English major. Students 21 and over are allowed to imbibe on campus, and students say alcohol policies are focused on student safety. A junior says, "Chestertown is quirky and charming, with historic buildings, music, food, art, and boutique shopping," but students seeking more active nightlife head for Annapolis, Baltimore, Philadelphia, or Washington, D.C.

Washington's Shoremen and Shorewomen compete in the Division III Centennial Conference. Men's and women's rowing and the co-ed sailing team are nationally competitive, and men's soccer has reached the NCAA Final Four. Students turn out in huge numbers for the annual War on the Shore, when the men's lacrosse team takes on its biggest rival, Salisbury University. Students also can join intramural and club sports; basketball, Frisbee, volleyball, and soccer are popular offerings. "Our cornhole tournament is a student favorite," say administrators. Held once a month, Outdoor Adventure trips, like rock climbing, cycling, and crabbing and fishing charters, are widely anticipated.

"Our Career Center is one of the best resources we have on-campus."

After managing to be around for more than 240 years without making much of a splash beyond Chesapeake Bay, Washington College now seems bent on making a name for itself in academic areas where it has a comparative advantage, especially business, the sciences, and the environment. "There is an emphasis on learning and growing, rather than perfection," says a senior, "which makes Washington College a place where students feel comfortable to make mistakes, ask questions, and reach new heights intellectually." George would probably approve.

Overlaps

Allegheny, University of Delaware, Goucher, University of Maryland, Muhlenberg, St. Mary's College of Maryland, Transylvania, Ursinus

If You Apply To ›

Washington College: Early decision, early action, regular decision. SATs or ACTs: optional. Accepts the Common Application.

Washington University in St. Louis

1 Brookings Drive, St. Louis, MO 63130

Washington University in St. Louis has secured a place among the country's outside-the-Ivy-walls elite schools, half a step behind Northwestern, on the shoulder of Vanderbilt, and a half step ahead of Emory. Core strength in the biological sciences with a halo effect from its top-ranked medical school; also top-notch in business. Preprofessional orientation, yet encourages exploration and collaboration.

Though it's always been well recognized regionally, Washington University in St. Louis long ago established itself as a truly national institution—with a friendly, relaxed Midwestern feel that differentiates it from the high-strung Eastern Ivies. WashU "students and faculty believe in the power of collaboration and that bringing voices from all backgrounds to the table allows us to break new ground." Applications have skyrocketed, and with a hefty $12 billion endowment, strong preprofessional programs, and an emphasis on research, it's not hard to see why. An architecture major says, "WashU is a high-end, collaborative research institution

Website: www.wustl.edu
Location: City Outskirts
Private
Total Enrollment: 14,237
Undergraduates: 7,509
Male/Female: 47/53
Financial Aid: 52%

Every spring, the whole campus turns out for the century-old Thurtene Carnival, the oldest student-run philanthropic festival in the country.

dedicated more to the growth of its students than the growth of its own personal brand."

WashU was founded in 1853 and given its name to honor George Washington and his service to the country. Its 169-acre campus adjoins Forest Park, one of the nation's largest urban parks. Buildings are constructed in the collegiate Gothic style, mostly in red Missouri granite and white limestone, with plenty of climbing ivy, gargoyles, and arches. The state-of-the-art Knight and Bauer Halls are home to the Olin Business School and include classrooms designed to enhance student and faculty interaction. As part of a major construction initiative on the east end of campus, the university built four new academic and multiuse facilities for arts and engineering, expanded the campus art museum, and added a new dining pavilion and the Sumers Welcome Center.

Undergraduates enroll in one or more of WashU's five divisions—arts and sciences, architecture, art, business, or engineering. General education requirements vary by school and program. The university's offerings in the natural sciences, particularly biology and chemistry, have long been notable, especially among those on the premed track. Bio majors benefit from efforts to integrate undergraduate research into activities at WashU's

> **"[WashU] students and faculty believe in the power of collaboration."**

outstanding medical school, which provides significant opportunities to conduct advanced laboratory research with faculty. WashU's business, engineering, architecture, and design programs are traditional strengths as well, and biomedical engineering has become a specialty. Double majors are encouraged, and interdisciplinary majors, such as philosophy-neuroscience-psychology and business and computer science, are growing rapidly. New majors have been added in public health and society and data science.

Each academic division offers options for incoming first-years to acclimate to the university environment and explore their options. In Arts & Sciences, for instance, students may take first-year seminars on diverse topics, such as Memory Studies or Literature and Celebrity. Similarly, the Olin Business School's Foundations of Business Course, taught by senior faculty, focuses on a different topic each week. Students in the Beyond Boundaries program take team-taught, cross-disciplinary courses across the university's five divisions in their first year that address big societal, intellectual, technological, and scientific challenges before moving into the division of their choice as sophomores. Those seeking even broader horizons may study in their choice of more than 50 different countries, and 33 percent do so, often through faculty-led programs during the summer. Students report that it's easy to get involved with WashU's extensive research projects. "WashU's Office of Undergraduate Research fully funded my trip to a national conference in Washington, D.C., where I gave an oral presentation," enthuses an anthropology major.

Students agree that classes are rigorous, but "everyone is supportive of each other's academic journeys and are willing to share as many resources as possible," says an educational studies major. "Students are not cutthroat," which is a key factor setting it apart from its Ivy League competitors. Those who are struggling will find plenty of help from teaching assistants (who conduct review sessions), academic advisors, study groups, and even a 24-hour peer counseling service called Uncle Joe's. Students also praise the writing center as helpful. Sixty-five percent of classes have fewer than 20 students, and undergrads have uncommon access to one-on-one mentoring relationships with top faculty. A junior says, "It is so obvious that the instructors are incredibly passionate about what they are teaching," adding they are also "immensely personable and accommodating."

WashU "students are friendly, driven, and change-oriented," says a senior. Seventy-seven percent of undergraduates are out-of-staters, with a large contingent from Eastern states like New York and New Jersey, and another 10 percent are international. Black students account for 9 percent, Hispanics/Latinos 13 percent, Asian Americans 21 percent, and multiracial students 6 percent. "The student body here is pretty diverse, not just racially, but socioeconomically," says an educational studies major, and a biomedical engineering student adds, "WashU is a very politically active campus and every political group has representation."

A limited number of academic scholarships averaging $44,600 are awarded each year, but there are no athletic scholarships. As part of its efforts to become more socioeconomically diverse, WashU has adopted a need-blind admissions policy for domestic first-year applicants. The university has also replaced loans with grants and scholarships for students in addition to awarding them more than $3,500 in grants to offset costs like the purchase of a personal computer. WashU meets the full demonstrated financial need of admitted students, and in recent years, it has increased the proportion of first-year students who qualify for Pell Grants (25 percent). For students from Missouri and southern Illinois with family incomes less than $75,000 per year, the WashU Pledge covers tuition, fees, housing, and food for four years.

Sixty-nine percent of WashU students live in campus housing, including the co-ed dormitories known as residential colleges. "The rooms are larger than your average dorm room, and we have Tempur-Pedic mattresses," boasts a student. "If that doesn't qualify us as best housing, I don't know what would." First-years and most sophomores live on the "South 40" (40 acres located on the south end of the main campus); first-years are guaranteed rooms, and gender-inclusive housing is available as an option. Juniors and seniors may live in university-owned apartments, and some choose true off-campus digs in the nearby neighborhoods of University City and Clayton, where apartments are reasonably priced. Meal plans may be used in any of the dining centers, which students say are excellent. "Food on campus is great, with many options to choose from thanks to five local restaurants that came to campus," cheers a senior. Students give good ratings to campus safety, which is aided by a comfort dog program that includes four therapy dogs who "have become beloved members of the campus community and make frequent appearances at campus events to support the mental health of all students."

Socially, "There can be a party presence on campus for you if you want to pursue it, but the Delmar Loop is the place to go to eat out with friends," says an accounting major. WashU students pride themselves on being able to balance work and play, and on weekends, movies, fraternity parties, and concerts tear them away from their books. Every spring, the whole campus turns out for the century-old Thurtene Carnival, the oldest student-run philanthropic festival in the country. Student groups—especially fraternities and sororities, which attract 17 percent of both men and women—build booths, sell food, and put on plays; profits are donated to a children's charity. Four student-led cultural shows—Diwali, Lunar New Year Festival, Black Anthology, and Carnaval—are always well attended. St. Louis's annual hot air balloon race is a favorite event: "Anywhere you are on campus you can see hot air balloons overhead," enthuses a senior. Alcohol policies emphasize safe and responsible drinking, and students say that, in that regard, they are effective.

WashU offers robust recreational options because of its location abutting Forest Park: a golf course, an ice-skating rink, a zoo, a lake with boat rentals, art and history museums, an outdoor theater, and a science center are all within a short walk. So, too, are the restaurants, bars, shops, and galleries of the Delmar Loop. The St. Louis Blues, Cardinals, and City SC attract pro hockey, baseball, and soccer fans, and the city is also home to the addictive Ted Drewes frozen custard. The school runs a free shuttle service to parts of St. Louis not within walking distance and offers a Metro

"The instructors are incredibly passionate about what they are teaching."

Pass for free access to the city's bus and light-rail systems. "St. Louis is often described as the largest small town you will ever visit or the smallest big city you will ever see," says a sophomore. "I appreciate St. Louis because there is plenty to do without it being overwhelming." Community service programs such as Each One Teach One, in partnership with the city's schools, attract a sizable number of students. The best road trips include Chicago, Nashville, Memphis, and Lake of the Ozarks, as well as Columbia, Missouri—home of the University of Missouri.

The WashU Bears compete in Division III, and women's tennis, men's and women's track and field, and women's soccer have all brought home recent national championships. Men's and women's soccer and outdoor track and field, and women's softball have won University Athletic Association Conference titles. A quarter of the students compete in 40 club sports or play intramural sports, ranging from badminton, racquetball, and flag football to pocket billiards and ultimate Frisbee.

> **"The Delmar Loop is the place to go to eat out with friends."**

High school counselors say that your best chances of getting accepted at WashU are either by opting for early decision or being cherry-picked off the waitlist. But however they get there, students find WashU both academically challenging and personally supportive. As one senior reflects, "The sense of community among the student body is palpable, and attending this university is a friendly reminder that you can climb to the top while still lifting others around you."

If You Apply To ›

WashU: Early decision I and II, regular decision. Accepts the Common Application with supplement. Apply to one of five undergraduate schools. Portfolio is required for applicants to College of Art and recommended for applicants to College of Architecture. Please consult WashU's website for the most up-to-date information regarding standardized test requirements.

Wellesley College

106 Central Street, Wellesley, MA 02481

There is no better recipe for popularity than first-rate academics and a postcard-perfect campus on the outskirts of Boston. That formula keeps Wellesley atop the women's college pecking order—along with superb programs in economics and the natural sciences. Among leading women's colleges, only Barnard accepts a lower percentage. Over half of undergraduates are students of color.

Wellesley College is not just the best women's college in the nation—it's one of the best colleges in the nation, period. With a history dating to 1870 and an alumnae roster that includes Hillary Rodham Clinton, Diane Sawyer, and the late Madeleine Albright, Wellesley should be at the top of the list for high achievers who are seeking the benefits of an all-women's college. Wellesley women excel in whatever field they choose, including traditional male bastions like economics and the sciences. "Wellesley's personality is intense, thoughtful, supportive, and unapologetically smart," says a psychology major.

Nestled in a Boston suburb, the Wellesley campus, one of the most beautiful anywhere, occupies 500 rolling acres of cultivated and natural areas, including Lake Waban. Campus buildings range in architectural style from Gothic (with stone towers and brick quadrangles) to state-of-the-art science, arts, and sports facilities. A

22-acre arboretum and botanical garden features a wide variety of trees and plants. The Davis Museum houses 11 galleries, a cinema, and a café. The five campus libraries, which include an academic art library, boast more than a million volumes. Several facilities have been renovated under the Wellesley Campus Renewal Plan, including the student services building, the Science Center, and the main campus library.

Wellesley has distribution requirements that include units in language and literature; visual arts, music, theater, film, and video; social and behavioral analysis; epistemology and cognition; religion, ethics, and moral philosophy; historical studies; natural and physical science; and mathematical modeling and problem-solving. In addition, students complete an experiential learning requirement and take a first-year writing class, a foreign language, and courses in multiculturalism, quantitative reasoning and data literacy, and physical education.

With its hefty $2.9 billion endowment (the largest among the nation's all-female colleges and universities) and lavish facilities, Wellesley offers a top-of-the-line educational experience. Some of the most popular majors are economics, computer science, psychology, and political science. Economics is known as the powerhouse; in fact, Wellesley has produced most of the country's high-ranking female economists. Biology is also strong, and students in biochemistry work with faculty on DNA research. Nearly two dozen interdepartmental majors are available in fields ranging from peace and justice studies to chemical physics to a notable program in international relations. Anything Wellesley women find lacking in their curriculum can probably be found at MIT, where they have full cross-registration privileges. Wellesley students can also take courses at nearby Babson College and Olin College of Engineering.

> "Wellesley's personality is intense, thoughtful, supportive, and unapologetically smart."

"The academic climate at Wellesley is academically rigorous and collaborative," observes an American studies major. "Students and professors alike are incredibly passionate about learning and often bring their personal experiences and identities into discussion-based classes." Under the honor system, students may take their finals, unsupervised, at any time during exam week. Class sizes are almost always small. Professors are highly respected and make themselves readily available. "The professors here open and easy to talk to," says an economics and psychology double major. First-years have both faculty advisors and peer mentors. Students give rave reviews to Wellesley's career services, which "offers amazing advising, resume help, mock interviews, and connects students with internships and alumnae across industries," says a psychology major. "Mental Health Services is also strong," says a junior. In an effort to alleviate first-year students' stress about grades as they adjust to Wellesley's rigorous atmosphere, the college employs a shadow-grading policy, in which their first-semester grades do not appear on their academic transcripts.

Seventy-seven percent of students conduct undergraduate research or independent study, and grants from private foundations have allowed Wellesley to add innovative programs, including independent research tutorials for advanced science students and fellowship funding for joint student/faculty projects. "One of the most defining aspects of my Wellesley experience has been research through the First-Year Apprentice Program (FYAP)," cheers a psychology major. About half of the students study abroad through 180 approved programs, including Wellesley-run programs in France and Italy. Through the Albright Institute, 40 students each year are chosen to be Albright Fellows, attending classes with both Wellesley and visiting professors, then completing a funded summer internship abroad; past Fellows have interned with the U.S. State Department, the European Union Chamber of Commerce, and the Human Rights Education and Monitoring Center.

The closest thing Wellesley has to sororities are nonresidential societies, which sometimes host parties.

(continued)

Applicants: 8,714
Accepted: 14%
Enrolled: 48%
Grad in 6 Years: 92%
Returning First-years: 97%
Academics: ✍ ✍ ✍ ✍ ✍
Social: 🗨 🗨 🗨
Q of L: ★ ★ ★ ★
Admissions: (781) 283-2270
Email Address:
admission@wellesley.edu

Strong Programs:
Biochemistry
Biology
Computer Science
Economics
International Relations
Peace and Justice Studies
Political Science
Psychology

What are Wellesley women like? A sophomore says, "Think Beyoncé: empowered, smart, and driven." Only 13 percent of students are from Massachusetts, other students come from every state and more than 50 countries; 13 percent are international. Eight percent are Black, 26 percent are Asian American, 14 percent are Hispanic/Latina, and 8 percent are multiracial. "There's strong representation of BIPOC students, international students, and first-generation college students," reports a psychology major, and an American studies major adds, "Topics like labor rights, gender and sexuality, and international human rights frequently come up in both academic and activist spaces." Financial aid awards are based on need—meaning few merit scholarships—but admissions for U.S. citizens and permanent residents are need-blind, and Wellesley meets the full calculated need of admitted students. Wellesley has also eliminated loans for families with incomes below $100,000 per year and has reduced loans for others.

"Wellesley is academically rigorous and collaborative."

Residence life at Wellesley is a step ahead of most institutions. Virtually every student lives on campus, and residence halls feature high-ceilinged living rooms, hardwood floors, fireplaces, walk-in closets, kitchenettes with microwaves, and even grand pianos. First-years are housed in the same halls as upperclasswomen, and juniors and seniors are generally granted single rooms. Peer tutors also live in each hall and are trained to tutor in specific subjects, as well as in study skills and time management. Meal cards are valid in all dining halls and at the campus snack bar. "We have a dining hall that is vegetarian and kosher, as well as one that is nut-free," says a sophomore. Campus security is strong, and a junior notes, "Sexual assault cases are minimal on campus, but students have access to a number of resources for sexual education and reporting."

Wellesley's social scene tends to be quiet, although as a junior says, "There's a good mix of on-campus events: themed dances, cultural nights, org parties, outdoor movie nights, and club events." The Lulu Chow Wang Campus Center, referred to affectionately as "Lulu," is a hub of activity day and night, with its student-run pub, Café Hoop, and coffeehouse. The closest thing Wellesley has to sororities are nonresidential societies, which sometimes host parties, for arts and music, literature, Shakespeare, politics, and general lectures. "Many students also socialize off-campus, especially with friends at Babson, Olin, and MIT," says a junior.

"There's strong representation of BIPOC students, international students, and first-generation college students."

Wellesley is chock-full of traditions, the most endearing of which include Flower Sunday (where first-years are paired with older students in a welcome ceremony), step-singing (an all-campus sing-along on the chapel steps), Spring Weekend (with a big-name band and comedian), and a hoop-rolling contest by seniors in their graduation robes. The winner of this contest will supposedly be the first in her class to achieve her goals, and she gets off to a flying start when her classmates toss her in the lake. The lake is also the site of Lake Day, when students take a break from classes to enjoy a festival held on the lawn. Service is a key component of the Wellesley community, dating back to the college's inception. Wellesley's motto, Non ministrari sed ministrare, translates to "Not to be served but to serve."

The town of Wellesley is an upper-crust Boston suburb without many amenities for students. "Be forewarned," cautions a student, "Wellesley is a snobby town of rich people." Still, when it comes to weekend fun, Wellesley is in a prime location. Not even half an hour away, Boston attracts students with all manner of social opportunities. Cambridge—with Harvard Square, MIT frat parties, and lots of clubs and cafés—is accessible by an hourly school shuttle that runs on weekdays and weekends. There is also a commuter rail station located a short walk from campus. Cape Cod, Providence, and the Vermont and New Hampshire ski slopes are close by car.

Many students balance their academic schedule with Division III athletics, intramurals, and club sports. The rowing team is a perennial contender for the national title. Other top Blue teams include swimming and diving, soccer, and volleyball. The big athletic rival is Smith College, another of the Seven Sisters group of great women's colleges. The sports center, named the Nannerl Keohane Sports Center in honor of Wellesley's 11th president (who went on to run Duke), offers an Olympic-size pool; squash, racquetball, and tennis courts; dance studios; a weight room; and an indoor track. Harvard's Head of the Charles crew race and the Boston Marathon—Wellesley's "Scream Tunnel" is legendary among runners worldwide—share honors as the most popular spectator sports of the year.

When it comes to academics, Wellesley women are serious. Their school is competitive with all but the top three Ivies. Many of them enjoy the traditions of the school and appreciate the idyllic atmosphere for contemplation but know they are poised to dominate whatever field they enter. "Female empowerment isn't served with dinner, and we don't get confidence boosts for dessert," muses one student. "But somehow, after just a few years here, all my ideas about what's actually possible and how much I'm truly capable of have changed."

Overlaps

Amherst, Barnard, Cornell, Pomona, Princeton, Swarthmore, Williams, Yale

If You Apply To ›

Wellesley: Early decision I and II, regular decision. Accepts the Common Application with supplement. Accepts applications from students who live as women and consistently identify as female, as well as students who were assigned female at birth and identify as nonbinary. Please consult Wellesley's website for the most up-to-date information regarding standardized test requirements.

Wesleyan University

45 Wyllys Avenue, Middletown, CT 06459

Usually compared to Amherst or Williams, Wesleyan is really more like Swarthmore. The key differences: Wesleyan is twice as big and a little more streetwise. Wes students are progressive, politically minded, and fiercely independent. Multicultural specialties like ethnomusicology, film studies, and East Asian studies add spice to the scene. New York and Boston are both two hours away but not easily accessible on public transportation.

Whether they're engrossed in academics, debating social issues, or civically engaged in community service, Wesleyan students seem to do things with a passion and intensity that helps set this school apart. "There's an energy on this campus; for me, it's a spirit of creativity and political energy," a sophomore explains. In recent years, a significant number of Wesleyan alumni have gone on to make their mark in the high-tech world and the entertainment industry, including *Hamilton* creator Lin-Manuel Miranda, whose earlier Broadway hit, *In the Heights*, had its origins as a sophomore theater production.

Wesleyan was founded in 1831 when Methodists teamed up with local citizens to create a college, and diversity here begins with the campus architecture. The nucleus of this stately university is a century-old row of lovely brownstones that look out over the football field. The rest of the buildings can be described as

Website: www.wesleyan.edu
Location: Small City
Private
Total Enrollment: 3,194
Undergraduates: 3,059
Male/Female: 48/52
Financial Aid: 43%
Pell Grant: 14%
Expense: Pr $ $ $ $
Student Loans: 27%
Average Debt: $ $

(continued)

Applicants: 14,389
Accepted: 16%
Enrolled: 35%
Grad in 6 Years: 92%
Returning First-years: 95%
Academics: ✍ ✍ ✍ ✍ ✍
Social: 🍷 🍷 🍷
Q of L: ★ ★ ★
Admissions: (860) 685-3000
Email Address:
  admission@wesleyan.edu

Strong Programs:
Astronomy
East Asian Studies
Economics
English
Film Studies
Molecular Biology and
  Biochemistry
Music
Science and Technology
  Studies

"eclectic" and range from mod-looking dorms of the '50s and '60s to the beautiful and ultramodern Center for the Arts. Dozens of Wesleyan-owned wood-frame houses serve as senior residences that look freshly plucked from Main Street, USA. The Gordon Career Center is situated in the heart of the campus and features a multipurpose career commons. The libraries have more than a million volumes, practically unheard-of at a school this size. Whenever you happen to walk past the brightly lit, glass-walled study room of Sci-Li (the science library), you're apt to see numerous students huddled over their books. A new, state-of-the-art science building is expected to open in fall 2026.

Wesleyan's curriculum ensures the relevance of liberal arts education in the 21st century by offering seminars for first-year students and clustering courses to help students reach their academic objectives. Students are expected to take a minimum of three courses in each of three areas—humanities and the arts, social and behavioral sciences, and natural sciences and mathematics. They can choose from among nearly 50 majors, and at the end of their first year, students may apply to major in one of Wesleyan's competitive, interdisciplinary colleges, including the College of Letters (European literature, history, and philosophy), the College of Social Studies (history, government, political and social theory, and economics), and the College of Science and Technology Studies (which allows students to do advanced work in a science discipline while studying science and medicine through a philosophical, sociohistorical lens). Other interdisciplinary colleges offering linked majors include the Bailey College of the Environment, the College of Integrative Sciences, the College of Design and Engineering Studies, and the College of Educational Studies. The first-rate College of Film and the Moving Image enjoys an international reputation. The College of East Asian Studies, another strength, offers advanced language courses and study abroad with a focus on cultural fluency, and it boasts an authentic Japanese tearoom.

> **"There's an energy on this campus; for me, it's a spirit of creativity and political energy."**

Many of Wesleyan's more popular majors—economics, psychology, government, and computer science—are also some of its strongest. Music, film studies, astronomy, and science and technology studies are also standouts. But even the smaller departments attract attention. Ethnomusicology, including African drumming and dance, is a stunning specialty; students can be found reclining on the wide, carpeted bleachers at the World Music Hall or watching a dozen musicians play the Indonesian gamelan. The math department emphasizes problem-solving in small groups rather than interminable lectures dedicated to theory. Undergraduates in the sciences and psychology work alongside faculty in their research laboratories and frequently earn the opportunity to publish in scientific journals. The Shapiro Center for Creative Writing and Criticism offers instruction from some of the world's most distinguished authors, while the Allbritton Center for the Study of Public Life provides Wesleyan Political Engagement Grants to bolster student-driven civic engagement initiatives. Students can also take advantage of dual-degree programs in engineering with Dartmouth, Caltech, and Columbia.

The men's basketball team made it to the NCAA Final Four in 2025.

"Wesleyan's academic climate is built on collaboration and flexibility across disciplines," says a government major, adding that the flexibility cuts down on competition. The university has used its wealth to attract highly rated faculty members who are expected to be scholar-teachers: academic superstars who juggle groundbreaking research, engaging lectures, and personal student attention at the same time—and they seem to pull it off. "The relationships with the faculty members always extend beyond the classrooms—at their house, in restaurants, even in random outskirts," cheers a computer science major. Wesleyan strives to keep its classes small, and 74 percent of the courses have fewer than 20 students. "With popular classes, you have to be persistent, but you can get in," a history major says. If beseeching is not your style, studying abroad may be a temporary tonic to registration headaches. Thirty-nine percent of students take advantage of programs available in all areas of the world; internships are also popular.

Wesleyan's excellent reputation and strong recruiting network attract students from all over, ensuring the mash-up of viewpoints that makes it such a vital place. "Three words to describe the typical Wesleyan student: open-minded, driven, and quirky," offers a biology major. Adds a neuroscience major, "We're always willing to have a conversation and explore something new." Ten percent of undergraduates are Connecticut natives, and 10 percent hail from foreign nations. The student body is 6 percent Black, 11 percent Hispanic/Latino, 9 percent Asian American, and 7 percent multiracial. Students are mostly liberal and vocal about hot-button social and political issues. "Inclusion—both on and off campus—is always the goal of student activism," says a government major. Wesleyan has ended preferences for legacy students and meets students' full demonstrated financial need—without loans—for eligible students regardless of family income.

Housing is guaranteed for four years, and most first-year students are consigned to singles or doubles in the campus dorms. Upperclassmen who want to live off campus must apply for permission (very few do). "The housing system at Wesleyan is really unique. It's based on a system of progressive independence, so every year you have more freedom and more responsibility," explains a student. Upperclassmen enjoy townhouses for four or five students, as well as college-owned houses and apartments. Campus dining gets good reviews: "Vegetarians love Wesleyan and so do meat eaters. There is an option for everyone," one student says. Students

"The relationships with the faculty members always extend beyond the classrooms."

report feeling safe on campus and say the university has taken an active role in sexual assault prevention. Most services get good student reviews: "A lot of people go to our mental health services office, who offer group and individual sessions," reports a German major. "They also offer events throughout the semester such as de-stress nights, Drag-Queen Bingo, and therapy dogs and goats."

Greek membership is nominal, with just 4 percent of students joining the three co-ed fraternities and one sorority. Consistent with the university's encouragement of independence, students bear a large part of the responsibility for policing themselves. "There is definitely a drinking/party culture, but there is absolutely no pressure to participate," says one senior. Activities abound from comedy performances to a cappella groups, films, plays, bands, lectures, parties, and events planned by the nearly 300 student groups. "The social scene at Wesleyan is very much a 'choose your own adventure' environment," says a junior. Major events on the social calendar include WesRave, a silent dance party on Foss Hill, and the Spring Fling outdoor festival. And who could forget Undies in Olin, when "students strip to their underwear in Olin Library during admitted student tours in the spring," says a senior.

Middletown is a small city within easy driving distance of Hartford and New Haven, but it is off the beaten track of steady public transportation (like trains). It has undergone a renaissance in recent years, and students cheer the myriad ethnic restaurants available. "Middletown isn't a bad place for college," says a student. "There are bars on Main Street that cater to a college crowd. Plus, there is a diverse collection of restaurants, which is great for when the family comes to visit." Wes students contribute a great deal of time to community service and help maintain a peaceful, beneficial relationship with the town. And Wesleyan's rural surroundings afford the much-appreciated opportunity to jog through the countryside, swim at nearby Wadsworth Falls, or pick apples in the local orchards. To get off campus, "You usually need a car or a friends with a car (which you will easily find because so many students bring cars)," says a senior. Good road trips include New York and Boston, each two hours away, and decent ski areas and beaches just under an hour away.

The Wesleyan Cardinals compete in the Division III New England Small College Athletic Conference (NESCAC) and field 30 varsity teams. The men's basketball team made it to the NCAA Final Four in 2025. The men's crew team won the 2024 IRA National Championship, and women's crew is also strong. Football, women's tennis, men's lacrosse, and women's volleyball have won recent conference titles. Annual encounters with "Little Three" rivals Williams and Amherst lure even the most serious student out of the library and into the action. Recreational sports are popular: 38 percent of students compete in four intramural and 13 club sports. Rugby is strong, and the ultimate Frisbee club (the "Nietzsch Factor," named after a former star player's dog, not a misspelling of the philosopher) almost always trounces challengers.

> **"Three words to describe the typical Wesleyan student: open-minded, driven, and quirky."**

The key to Wesleyan's success seems to be the fostering of an intellectual milieu where independent thinking and an appreciation of differences are omnipresent. As a senior puts it, "The people here can be quirky and weird while simultaneously being incredibly talented and high-achieving students." Indeed, the Wesleyan experience means liberal learning in a climate of individual freedom—a freedom that encourages motivated students who stay on task to explore and excel in a supportive, welcoming atmosphere. Abundant opportunities are open to students willing to take advantage of them, which is precisely what these doers do.

Overlaps

Brown, UC Berkeley, Cornell University, Harvard, Tufts, Vassar, Williams, Yale

If You Apply To ›

Wesleyan: Early decision I and II, regular decision. SATs or ACTs: optional. Accepts the Common Application with supplement.

West Virginia University

1 Waterfront Place, Morgantown, WV 26506

Surrounded by the likes of Ohio, Pennsylvania, and Virginia, West Virginia has traditionally exported its best students to other states for college. But WVU also attracts its share of out-of-staters, some drawn to its one-of-a-kind forensics program. The honors program is a must for top students, and the university has solid programs in professional fields ranging from health sciences to engineering. But recent serious cuts in undergraduate academic programs will determine where the university goes from here.

Website: www.wvu.edu
Location: Small City
Public
Total Enrollment: 20,656
Undergraduates: 16,811
Male/Female: 49/51
Financial Aid: 66%
Pell Grant: 26%

West Virginia University earned the right to be the state's flagship land grant university in the wake of the Civil War as the only one in the state to offer research and doctoral-degree programs. The university is still recovering from a budget shortfall in 2023 that resulted in deep faculty and academic program cuts, but a new president was appointed in July 2025 and the university reports the retention rate has improved and enrollment has increased by more than 7 percent. And despite the cuts, WVU has over 450 student organizations, and 18 intercollegiate varsity athletic programs. It also is a leader of research in petroleum and natural gas engineering, forensic science, and rural health.

WVU is situated in the picturesque mountains of north-central West Virginia, a few miles from the Pennsylvania border and overlooking the Monongahela River. A driverless rail system connects the campus's three areas—the older downtown, the more modern Evansdale, and the health sciences area. Ten of the ivy-covered Morgantown buildings, dating mainly from the 19th century, are listed on the National Register of Historic Places; many of their interiors have been restored or renovated. Reynolds Hall, a 186,000-square-foot business and economics complex, features academic, residential, and recreational space.

All WVU students must complete the General Education Foundations program, which consists of coursework in eight areas: composition and rhetoric, science and technology, mathematics and quantitative skills, society and connections, human inquiry and the past, the arts and creativity, global studies and diversity, and a special focus area drawing on a subject of personal interest. For many students, fulfilling the special focus area requirement leads to a minor or even a second major. All incoming students take a First-Year Seminar that covers study skills, university and community support services, goal setting, and career planning.

West Virginia offers more than 130 majors that span 14 colleges and schools, the best of which are engineering (particularly energy-related) and the allied health sciences (medical technology, physical therapy, nursing, and occupational therapy). The most popular majors are in business/marketing, engineering, health professions, and biological/life sciences. WVU was the first school in the nation to offer a degree in forensic science, and it now offers forensic biology, forensic chemistry, and a forensic examiner major. Additional programs of note include undergraduate majors in strategic communications, management information systems, health informatics, and information management physics. Nursing and exercise physiology are strong programs as well. Forty-four percent of undergraduate classes have fewer than 20 students, and students say the difficulty of WVU academics depends largely on the classes they take. "Certain classes and a segment of the student population create a competitive climate," explains a senior. The Honors College offers small classes, special housing, and early registration to the top 5 percent of WVU students. Study abroad programs are available in more than 70 countries through a variety of faculty-led, partner, and exchange options.

WVU students describe their classmates as friendly, helpful, boisterous, and "sometimes rowdy." Though WVU attracts students from all U.S. states and more than 100 countries, its appeal is primarily regional. Forty-seven percent of undergraduates are in-staters, and 2 percent are international; sizable contingents arrive from western Pennsylvania, Maryland, and New Jersey. Black students represent 3 percent of undergrads, Hispanics/Latinos 5 percent, Asian Americans 2 percent, and multiracial students 6 percent. The university offers thousands of merit scholarships, worth an average of $9,000, and hundreds of athletic awards.

Twenty-two percent of WVU's undergraduates live on campus. Most dorms are co-ed; the older ones are known for their character, while the newer residential complexes in Evansdale have larger rooms and luxuries like air-conditioning. Living/learning communities are available in areas ranging from forensics and creative arts to innovation and the environment. "Off-campus housing is plentiful, but rent is high because demand is high," cautions a senior. Students complain that meals in the four main dining halls are "incredibly overpriced" and parking on campus can be difficult, although the local Morgantown Mountain Line buses take students to all university housing for free. Despite "frequent events highlighting awareness for women's issues,

> "Certain classes and a segment of the student population create a competitive climate."

> "Little else can compare to singing 'Country Roads' with the student body."

(continued)

Expense: Pub $ $
Student Loans: 63%
Average Debt: $ $ $ $
Applicants: 20,150
Accepted: 77%
Enrolled: 26%
Grad in 6 Years: 64%
Returning First-years: 83%
Academics: ✐ ✐
Social: 🗩 🗩 🗩 🗩
Q of L: ★ ★ ★
Admissions: (304) 293-2121
Email Address:
 wvuadmissions@mail.wvu
 .edu

Strong Programs:
Biology
Criminology
Engineering
Exercise Physiology
Forensic Sciences
Health Sciences
Nursing
Psychology

The annual Welcome Week offers hundreds of activities, including a free FallFest concert.

particularly sexual assault," a sophomore says, many students feel that the university has been doing a "less-than-satisfactory job addressing individual cases once they have been brought to light."

Morgantown is a small city of 30,000 with a college-town feel and plenty of community service opportunities. "This town revolves around the university and provides so much for the students," says a senior. The school has worked hard to curtail underage drinking, banning alcohol in the dorms and placing restrictions on Greek parties and rush activities, although students report that these efforts haven't slowed down the off-campus party scene. Roughly 6 percent of the men and 5 percent of the women go Greek. Social life on campus often centers on the free food, movies, bands, and comedians offered Thursday through Saturday by the school-sponsored WVUp All Night program. The annual Welcome Week offers hundreds of activities, including a free FallFest concert, and Mountaineer Week showcases the customs of Appalachia. For those with cars, road trips to Pittsburgh, Columbus, and Washington, D.C., are quick and easy.

West Virginians are passionate about Mountaineers football. "Every football game is a festival in some way," says a senior, and a sophomore adds, "Little else can compare to singing 'Country Roads' with the student body" after every home victory. The rifle team is a powerhouse, having won 20 NCAA championships, the most recent in 2025. West Virginia also fields competitive Division I Big 12 teams in men's and women's basketball and soccer, along with women's gymnastics and men's wrestling. Intramural and club sports are popular, especially basketball, flag football, and dodgeball. The cricket club team has won several national championships. Students also enjoy easy access to nearby hiking, white-water rafting, and skiing.

UWV continues to be dedicated to academic preparation and research that will improve the lives of citizens not only in West Virginia but also across the globe. Still, this mission is facing headwinds as the impact of what the administration calls its "academic transformation" continues to play out. Whether the changes will succeed in closing the budget gap and ensuring that UWV remains a solid choice for a wide range of students remains to be seen. Stay tuned.

If You Apply To ›

West Virginia: Rolling admissions. Accepts the Common Application with supplement. Please consult West Virginia's website for the most up-to-date information regarding standardized test requirements.

Westmont College

955 La Paz Road, Santa Barbara, CA 93108

A Christian liberal arts college, Southern California style. Westmont academics are taught from an unapologetically Christian perspective, but overall climate is more laid-back than at other evangelical powerhouses like Wheaton (IL) and Gordon. Nationally known for kinesiology. Almost everyone gets financial aid, but cultural homogeneity is an issue. Shorts and sandals are the norm, and Santa Barbara's picturesque surf and sand beckon nearby.

Westmont College prides itself on offering students a strong grounding in the liberal arts while remaining faithful to its motto, Christus Primatum Tenens ("Christ holding preeminence")—"We combine rigorous academics and a deep love for God," say administrators. Unlike many Christian colleges, Westmont has never had ties to any particular Protestant denomination and sees itself as part of a worldwide evangelical tradition embracing a range of theological perspectives (90 percent of students are Christian). Faculty members, all practicing Christians, take pride in presenting competing lifestyles and value systems to challenge and nurture students' faith. "The biggest difference that I've seen from transferring from a huge university to Westmont is the intentionality behind the professors' hearts," says a happy senior. "They actually care for the students."

Founded in 1937, Westmont sits on a former estate nestled in the Santa Barbara foothills of the Santa Ynez Mountains along the Pacific Coast. The campus, which has been periodically evacuated due to Old Testament-like wildfires and flooding, boasts a Mediterranean-style residence, gardens, and buildings crafted of sandstone and other local natural materials. Newer construction includes the Fletcher Jones Foundation Center for Engineering and the Westmont Keith Center, currently being renovated to help expand the popular nursing program.

In addition to attending chapel three times a week, Westmont students undertake an extensive general education program grounded in the Christian liberal arts tradition. The program includes courses in biblical literature and history; justice, reconciliation, and diversity; standard distribution requirements; and a skills component that includes writing- and speech-intensive courses and foreign language. Students then undertake one of two Compassionate Action options aimed at applying their faith to society. All seniors complete a capstone experience.

> "[Professors] actually care for the students."

One of Westmont's most popular majors is kinesiology—the interdisciplinary study of the art and science of human movement or, as Westmont faculty are wont to put it, "God's greatest creation: the human body." The economics and business major, which requires students to study abroad twice, is a noteworthy draw, as are biology and nursing. The religious studies department boasts several respected scholars, which is a good thing, since so many of their courses are required for graduation. Music is well-funded and strong, as is art, which focuses on the fine arts and art history. Newer majors include engineering and data analytics. Fifty-nine percent of classes have fewer than 20 students, and a senior says, "The small population allows for students to bond closely." All classes are taught by regular faculty members, who are described by one psychology major as "interactive, attentive, and highly empathetic." Students have good things to say about Westmont's career advising and other support services; the psychological counseling center has added staff and expanded its hours.

Students are invited to engage in undergraduate research independently or with a professor, and many present their work at biannual Research Symposia. The Augustinian Scholars Program offers generous four-year scholarships to roughly a third of incoming first-years, who engage in seminars that explore Christian intellectual traditions and higher education as a Christian calling. A semester-long program in social entrepreneurship based in downtown Santa Barbara involves project-based internships. Westmont prides itself on fostering global perspectives; 60 percent of students study abroad, often in programs led by Westmont faculty, and financial aid can be applied to foreign study. "I had the opportunity to go to Turkey, Greece, North Macedonia, and Italy to study the life of the Apostle Paul," raves a graphic arts major.

A sophomore describes fellow students as "generally laid-back, friendly, outdoorsy, and bubbly." Seventy-two percent of Westmont students come from California, while others mainly come from other Western states, often from middle- and upper-middle-class Christian homes. "At least racially, the college has been

<table>
<tr><td>Website: www.westmont.edu</td></tr>
<tr><td>Location: Small City</td></tr>
<tr><td>Private</td></tr>
<tr><td>Total Enrollment: 1,312</td></tr>
<tr><td>Undergraduates: 1,293</td></tr>
<tr><td>Male/Female: 42/58</td></tr>
<tr><td>Financial Aid: 97%</td></tr>
<tr><td>Pell Grant: 28%</td></tr>
<tr><td>Expense: Pr $ $</td></tr>
<tr><td>Student Loans: 59%</td></tr>
<tr><td>Average Debt: $ $ $</td></tr>
<tr><td>Applicants: 2,483</td></tr>
<tr><td>Accepted: 77%</td></tr>
<tr><td>Enrolled: 16%</td></tr>
<tr><td>Grad in 6 Years: 70%</td></tr>
<tr><td>Returning First-years: 85%</td></tr>
<tr><td>Academics: ✍ ✍ ✍</td></tr>
<tr><td>Social: 🌑 🌑 🌑</td></tr>
<tr><td>Q of L: ★ ★ ★ ★</td></tr>
<tr><td>Admissions: (800) 777-9011</td></tr>
<tr><td>Email Address:
 admissions@westmont.edu</td></tr>
</table>

Strong Programs:
Art
Biology
Communications
Economics and Business
Engineering
Kinesiology
Music
Religious Studies

> *A semester-long program in social entrepreneurship based in downtown Santa Barbara involves project-based internships.*

increasing its diversity over the years," says a senior, "but it is still predominantly white and evangelical Christian. Students who are from abroad or who have different faiths may struggle at Westmont." Two percent of students come from outside the United States. Hispanics/Latinos make up 23 percent of students, Asian Americans 5 percent, and multiracial students 9 percent, while Black students account for just 3 percent. The campus political climate is usually low-key, although a student confesses, "Issues of race, LGBTQ+, and abortion are difficult topics at Westmont College." Generous merit scholarships average $26,500 per year, and athletic scholarships are available as well.

All students are required to live on campus for all four years, with only a few exceptions. The dorms at Westmont are clean, well-maintained, and conveniently located. The Global Leadership Center, where every room has its own bathroom, gives priority to seniors and students who engage in leadership and study abroad programs. Westmont has a single all-day dining facility, imaginatively known as the Dining Commons, where, as a communication major puts it, "the food is pretty good as far as cafeteria food goes." Fridays are "Farm Fresh," featuring veggies from the campus's own garden, managed by students minoring in environmental studies. Students give the college high ratings for campus safety.

Consistent with their Christian values, all Westmont students engage in community service projects. Through the student-run Potter's Clay program, students spend their spring break working with contractors, doctors, and other professionals in Ensenada, Mexico. The Urban Initiative sends teams to work with local nonprofit organizations in U.S. cities. On campus, the Westmont Activities Council sponsors intramurals, dances,

> **"[Students are] generally laid-back, friendly, outdoorsy, and bubbly."**

and other events. "Socializing may look like going swing dancing or to a movie rather than to a party," says a chemistry and biology major. Alcohol is banned on campus, but a communication major says that "students are allowed to drink off campus if they are of legal age." Students complain that parking is a problem, but a campus shuttle allows ready access to Santa Barbara's many options, ranging from coffee shops and shopping to hiking, surfing, and beach volleyball. Westmont traditions include the annual Spring Sing musical skit competition between dorms, and Midnight Madness, a rally that gets students excited about the upcoming basketball season.

Basketball is among the school's 15 varsity teams (the Warriors) that compete in the NCAA's Division II. "The annual rivalries are games against Azusa or Biola," says a senior, cheering, "#BEATBIOLA!" Baseball captured the Pacific West Conference championship in 2025. Men's and women's basketball, and women's volleyball and soccer are also strong. Popular intramural and club sports include basketball, volleyball, and ultimate Frisbee, drawing 30 percent of students.

Westmont students laugh at their stereotypes ("drinking smoothies from the local Blenders store") and occasionally bristle at the chapel requirements ("more a burden than a time with God"), but most welcome these as part of the fabric that makes Westmont's friendly, close-knit, and caring community possible. "People who come to Westmont actually want to do something in life," says a senior, "and statistics show that they get it done."

Overlaps

Azusa Pacific, Baylor, Biola, California Lutheran, Gordon, Pepperdine, Point Loma, Wheaton (IL)

If You Apply To ›

Westmont: Early action I and II, rolling admissions. Accepts the Common Application with supplement. Applicants must agree to Community Life Statement. Please consult Westmont's website for the most up-to-date information regarding standardized test requirements.

Wheaton College (IL)

501 College Avenue, Wheaton, IL 60187

Wheaton is at the top of the academic heap in evangelical education, challenged only by Pepperdine (with its Malibu digs) and traditional competitors such as Gordon and Calvin. Students must not only follow Wheaton's stringent code of conduct but also affirm their personal faith in Jesus Christ. Wheaton's low tuition makes it relatively affordable. The worldly temptations of Chicago hover less than an hour away.

Wheaton College combines academic rigor and evangelical orthodoxy with a firm commitment to the liberal arts, preparing students "to build the church and benefit society worldwide 'For Christ and His Kingdom.'" It is one of only two major evangelical schools in the *Fiske Guide* with an admissions process that requires students to be professing Christians (see also Gordon College), and its Community Covenant prohibits the use of alcohol, tobacco, and drugs. Though most young adults would chafe under such restrictions, Wheaties take it all in stride. "There's an emphasis on tradition and culture," says an elementary education major. "We are openly Christian, and students on this campus are really passionate and really kind and caring."

Wheaton was founded in 1860 by evangelical abolitionists and was a stop on the Underground Railroad. Today the college is nondenominational, and its verdant, 80-acre campus is an oasis of sorts in the midst of one of Chicago's oldest and most established suburbs. The castle-like Blanchard Hall, completed in 1927, keeps watch over the community from atop the front campus hill; when couples get engaged, they climb to the top of the tower to share their news by ringing the bell. Nearby sits Billy Graham Hall, which houses a museum and the college archives, making it a hub for research on American evangelicalism. (The late evangelist was a Wheaton alumnus.) A $62 million expansion of the Armerding Center for Music and the Arts has added a 648-seat concert hall, among other performing arts spaces.

Sporting one of the largest endowments among the nation's evangelical schools (around $610 million), Wheaton offers students a generous bevy of programs and facilities. General education requirements ("Christ at the Core") include a broad array of thematic coursework, as well as a first-year seminar, an advanced seminar, and a senior capstone experience. The most popular majors are business and economics, psychology, English, communication, and biology. Music, and biblical and theological studies are considered strengths. Motivated students may opt for 3–2 dual-degree programs in nursing and engineering or choose from 11 accelerated, five-year master's degree programs ranging from teaching and theology to Old Testament archaeology. In the classroom, there's an emphasis on teamwork, and a biology major calls the atmosphere "serious but collaborative." The quality of teaching varies, but students get "the benefit of Christian professors who provide a stimulating intellectual experience in light of the Christian faith," according to one junior.

> **"We are openly Christian, and students on this campus are really passionate and really kind and caring."**

Students have the opportunity to participate in research at Argonne National Laboratory, just down the road, and for those seeking a truly global experience, there's study abroad in more than 30 countries, including special Wheaton programs in China, England, France, Germany, and more. "Study abroad programs are quite common to the Wheaton experience," a student says, describing them as

Website: www.wheaton.edu
Location: Suburban
Private
Total Enrollment: 2,874
Undergraduates: 2,150
Male/Female: 45/55
Financial Aid: 91%
Pell Grant: 22%
Expense: Pr $
Student Loans: 47%
Average Debt: $ $
Applicants: 1,866
Accepted: 90%
Enrolled: 33%
Grad in 6 Years: 85%
Returning First-years: 93%
Academics: ✐ ✐ ✐
Social: 🌢 🌢 🌢
Q of L: ★ ★ ★ ★
Admissions: (800) 222-2419
Email Address:
admissions@wheaton.edu

Strong Programs:
Applied Health Sciences
Biblical and Theological
  Studies
Business and Economics
Communication
English
Music
Philosophy
Theater

"superb and life-changing." Those concerned with social justice, a definite focus at Wheaton, may be interested in the Human Needs and Global Resources program, which sends students to developing countries for six months to work on projects such as building roads and schools. Summer study in several scientific fields is available at the Black Hills Science Station. For incoming first-year students, the required two-week Wheaton Passage program combines on-campus orientation with an off-campus experience intended to facilitate community-building and self-discovery. Options include a wilderness track (backpacking, canoeing, or rock climbing), a Northwoods track (arts and outdoor activities or equestrian training at Honey Rock), and an urban track (city adventures and urban studies in downtown Chicago or the city's Woodlawn neighborhood). A Wheaton Passage track for transfer students explores Chicago's diverse neighborhoods.

"The student body is extremely motivated and high-achieving," says one student. "They desire to encourage their peers to pursue excellence in their God-given gifts." Twenty-seven percent of Wheaton students hail from Illinois, and 4 percent come from overseas. Eight percent are missionary kids and 4 percent are third-culture kids. Black students comprise 3 percent of the student body, Hispanics/Latinos make up 8 percent, Asian Americans add 10 percent, and multiracial students account for 6 percent. With both conservative and liberal students represented on campus, students say the political climate is active and sometimes tense. Wheaton's Community Covenant shuns "homosexual behavior and all other sexual relations outside the bounds of marriage between a man and woman"; thus, LGBTQ issues have been controversial. "LGBTQ students struggle to find a voice or place on campus," comments a student. There are no athletic scholarships, but merit awards averaging $23,200 are awarded to qualified students.

Ninety-one percent of Wheaton students live in campus housing, and well-kept accommodations range from single-sex dorms with traditional double rooms and bathrooms down the hall to college-owned houses and apartments. Opposite-sex visitation is limited to certain hours on certain days, though "each semester, dorms are allowed two 'raids' to their opposite floor," says an education major. Everyone eats in Anderson Commons, where, one student says, "everything is made from scratch." Students report feeling safe on campus. "Our Title IX coordinator on campus is an active participant in Wheaton's discourse and daily life. Besides this, Wheaton does not often acknowledge issues of sexual assault publicly or openly," remarks a senior.

"We have a lot of fun here, but all alcohol-free fun."

Since Wheaton lacks fraternities and sororities, and because students agree to abstain from alcohol, drugs, and tobacco, the social life revolves around other tamer pursuits. "We have a lot of fun here, but all alcohol-free fun," says a psychology major. The College Union plans events like talent shows, roller disco, and an annual President's Ball. A junior says, "The town of Wheaton is a friendly suburb with nice restaurants and a good bike trail, but it's pretty much closed down by nine p.m." A commuter train near campus whisks students to downtown Chicago in 45 minutes, where restaurants, blues clubs, theaters, museums, shopping, and professional sports are in abundance. Favorite traditions include Missions in Focus week, which brings missionary organizations and Christian speakers to campus, and the individual dorm floors' own traditions, one of which includes an annual root beer kegger.

Wheaton's 21 varsity athletic teams (the Thunder) compete in Division III; football and men's and women's basketball, soccer, and swimming are among the strongest teams. Football, basketball, and soccer games "are always exciting and well attended," says one student, especially if the opponent is Augustana College. The debate and chess teams are competitive, too. Forty-four percent of students play intramural and club sports. And while it's not an athletic competition per se, juniors and seniors do get excited about decorating "the Bench," a reinforced concrete slab that is the subject of an ongoing and often rough-and-tumble game of keep-away.

Wheaton College remains "committed to the principle that truth is revealed by God through Christ, in whom is hidden all the treasures of wisdom and knowledge." Students believe that their school's dedication to Christianity only strengthens the bonds they develop with one another and their understanding of the broader world. "The Wheaton education is hard to duplicate," says one student. "Learning at Wheaton truly does prepare you for Christ and His kingdom."

If You Apply To ›

Wheaton (IL): Early action I and II, regular decision I and II. Accepts the Common Application with supplement. Please consult Wheaton's website for the most up-to-date information regarding standardized test requirements.

Wheaton College (MA)

26 E Main Street, Norton, MA 02766

Although its address says it's in Massachusetts, Wheaton is actually closer to Providence than to Boston. But getting to either by train is quick and easy. One of the few nationally known institutions in the area that is still not supercompetitive. Curriculum includes interdisciplinary, hands-on, and project-based work in addition to traditional courses. Smaller than Skidmore, comparable to Connecticut College.

Wheaton College offers students plenty of opportunities to make their academic marks. Since 2000, more than 250 Wheaton students have received national fellowships, and the college remains among the top 10 liberal arts colleges for Fulbright scholars. Increasingly focused on experiential learning, Wheaton makes sure its students shine outside the classroom, too. Says one satisfied senior, "Wheaton's commitment to supporting its students to leverage their liberal arts education and change the world permeates all aspects of life on campus."

The college was founded in 1834 by Laban Wheaton, a judge and U.S. congressman, in memory of his daughter. Established to offer high-quality education to women, Wheaton has been co-ed since 1988. The school's relatively rural location offers few distractions from intellectual pursuits. Its 400-acre campus blends Georgian brick buildings and modern structures set among beautiful lawns and shade trees. The two halves of the campus (upper and lower) are separated by Peacock Pond, which probably qualifies as the only heated duck pond on any American campus. The renovated Discovery Center houses the nursing program.

Wheaton's Compass curriculum supports a broad foundation of knowledge and shows students how to make linkages between disciplines. In their first year, all students take a reading- and writing-intensive interdisciplinary course taught by a faculty team representing different academic fields. As sophomores, students undertake a required hands-on learning experience, such as a research or service project, a study abroad program, or an internship. In addition, throughout their four years, students pursue a Mentored Academic Pathway—a personal academic plan guided by faculty and staff advisors—and develop a portfolio reflecting on their experiences and showcasing their work.

Business and management, psychology, biology, and history are Wheaton's most popular majors. Programs in the arts are well recognized—impressive given the school's

(continued)

Chemistry
Economics
Neuroscience
Political Science
Psychology
Visual Art

For the Head of the Peacock race, students build vessels (no boats allowed) and race them across Peacock Pond.

small size—and the chemistry department is also strong. A B.S. in nursing offers a state-of-the-art simulation center and labs. Students interested in interdisciplinary study can choose majors like neuroscience or theater and English dramatic literature, or they may design their own majors. Several Liberal Education and Professional Success (LEAP) interdisciplinary certificate paths, which serve as a bridge between the liberal arts and careers, are available as an add-on to the Compass Curriculum, including criminal justice; design and fabrication; food industry; galleries, libraries, archives, and museums; and stem cell research. Dual-degree programs with Dartmouth, Emerson, and other institutions are available in engineering, business, communication, religion, and optometry. The Center for Global Education offers more than 100 approved study abroad programs in more than 45 countries around the world; the WheaGo Global program allows students to start their first semester in Spain, Switzerland, Australia, Greece, or France. One unique option sends students and a faculty member to Royal Thimphu College in Bhutan for a semester; the king of Bhutan happens to be a Wheaton alumnus.

According to a psychology major, "Critical thinking, intensive writing, and collaborative projects are part of almost every class, which allows for in-depth exploration of concepts, themes, and lessons." Sixty-one percent of Wheaton's classes have fewer than 20 students. "Professors are open to feedback and are available to talk outside the classroom," says a junior. Aside from a faculty advisor, students get a staff mentor and two peer advisors, known as preceptors. The Life and Career Design Institute sets students up with a Career Navigator to aid students as they explore various career paths and to help them secure internships. The center awards summer fellowships ranging from $2,000 to $5,000 to students pursuing unpaid internships, research opportunities, or service projects, ensuring that, in the words of one senior, "students never have to worry about choosing between a paycheck and a professional experience."

> **"Critical thinking, intensive writing, and collaborative projects are part of almost every class."**

Forty-one percent of Wheaton students come from Massachusetts, and 4 percent hail from foreign nations. The student body is largely white and affluent. Black students account for 5 percent, Hispanics/Latinos 8 percent, Asian Americans 4 percent, and multiracial students 5 percent. Students are said to be friendly and open to differing views; politically, the campus leans left. "Wheaton's legacy as a former women's college means that people are very attuned to feminist and gender issues," explains a senior. "These are issues that students rally around." Merit scholarships averaging $37,200 are available, but there are no athletic awards.

As might be expected on this small, suburban campus, virtually everyone (93 percent) lives in one of Wheaton's dorms or theme houses. All students are guaranteed housing for four years; first-years live in doubles or triples, and upperclassmen try their luck in the lottery system. "Housing is livable, but some of the facilities are getting old," comments a sophomore. The renovated dining halls are bright and spacious, and the biggest winners of all are the ducks, which thrive on the leftover bread students toss into Peacock Pond. "There's a big push for local, fresh, and organic produce," says a junior. The administration has increased the number of mental health counselors, and students say they feel safe on campus and that campus safety officers are visible and active.

> **"People are very attuned to feminist and gender issues."**

Social life at Wheaton includes dances, concerts, lectures, parties on campus, and other activities organized by the more than 100 student groups. Students unwind at the college's student center, which offers a café, dance studio, and sun deck for afternoon study breaks. There are no sororities or fraternities here, but there is a party scene, as a junior explains: "Theme houses and suites do throw down quite often." Students say they appreciate the school's "Safety Always Matters Most" approach to drinking. The biggest event of the year is Spring Weekend, featuring live bands, outdoor barbecues, and the Head of the Peacock race, where students build vessels (no boats allowed) and race them across Peacock Pond. "The winner gets to take our president on a victory lap around the pond," cheers a first-year. And it's an unofficial tradition to go for a swim in the pond at least once before graduation.

The town of Norton, just outside campus, draws students with services opportunities, such as a Big Brother Big Sister program, hospital visits, and academic tutoring, but there's little to do otherwise, students say. "It's a very quiet town, and most students stay on campus rather than venture off into Norton," says a student. Relatively convenient access to two state capitals livens up the social scene. "We're 20 minutes from Providence and 40 minutes from Boston. If you can't find something to do on the weekend, you're just looking for something to complain about," remarks a student.

The Life and Career Design Institute sets students up with a Career Navigator.

The Wheaton Lyons compete in Division III. The Lyons nickname honors Mary Lyon, the 19th-century educational pioneer who established Wheaton's first curriculum and later founded Mount Holyoke. Recent conference champs include men's soccer and women's cross-country. Women's swimming and diving is also strong. The athletic facility boasts an eight-lane swimming pool, a field house, and an 850-seat arena for basketball or volleyball. Popular club and intramural sports include rugby, ultimate Frisbee, soccer, and basketball.

"We text with deans, have lunch with professors."

Students at Wheaton take an active role in campus planning and college operations, as well as in their community. "We don't just have coffee in the café," says a political science major. "We text with deans, have lunch with professors, coffee with advisors, a beer with our favorite professor. These kinds of relationships are the Wheaton way. They supplement the intellectual energy and debate that takes place among students." Indeed, students here take pride in their achievements inside and outside the classroom while striving to preserve the school's friendly, small-town feel.

Overlaps

Clark, Connecticut College, Kalamazoo, UMass Amherst, Ohio Wesleyan, Roanoke, Ursinus

If You Apply To ›

Wheaton (MA): Early decision I and II, early action I and II, regular decision. SATs or ACTs: optional. Accepts the Common Application with supplement. Application includes question on gender identity.

Whitman College

345 Boyer Avenue, Walla Walla, WA 99362

Whitman has quietly established itself as one of the West's leading liberal arts colleges. Don't bother with the umbrella: Walla Walla (a.k.a. W2) is in sunny eastern Washington. Whitman's small-town location creates tight-knit community spirit and alumni loyalty. While true to its liberal arts heritage, Whitman has no traditional business program but has expanded its curriculum with minors in finance and data science. Combines outdoorsy camaraderie with the slower pace of life in the rural Northwest.

You don't have to own a Frisbee to succeed at Whitman, but if you've got one, bring it along—you'll find a campus full of friendly students eager to toss it back to you. Though it isn't well-known outside the Pacific Northwest, Whitman offers a solid liberal arts education along with plenty of fun for outdoorsy types. Students are down-to-earth and feel a deep loyalty to one another—and to their school.

Website: www.whitman.edu
Location: Small Town
Private
Total Enrollment: 1,510

(continued)

Undergraduates: 1,510
Male/Female: 42/57
Financial Aid: 96%
Pell Grant: 21%
Expense: Pr $ $ $
Student Loans: 40%
Average Debt: $ $
Applicants: 7,243
Accepted: 38%
Enrolled: 14%
Grad in 6 Years: 81%
Returning First-years: 89%
Academics: ✍ ✍ ✍ ✍
Social: 🍷 🍷 🍷
Q of L: ★ ★ ★ ★
Admissions: (509) 527-5176
Email Address:
admission@whitman.edu

Strong Programs:
Astronomy
Biochemistry, Biophysics, and
 Molecular Biology
Economics
English
Environmental Studies
Neuroscience
Psychology

When the weather is nice, students gather on Ankeny Field to study, toss a Frisbee, or relax.

Whitman was founded in 1882, initially under religious auspices, and named in honor of Marcus and Narcissa Whitman, missionaries to the Cayuse Indians (and promoters of white colonialism) who were killed in 1847 following more than a decade of increasingly contentious interactions between their mission settlement and the tribal members. Everything important is within walking distance of campus, including the main drag of Walla Walla (which means "many waters" in the Cayuse language), which once won a national Best Main Street award. The 117-acre campus, which features colonial buildings and modern facilities, sits at the foot of the Blue Mountains, surrounded by golden wheat fields and vineyards. Beyond the town are gorgeous mountains, rivers, and forests. On campus, the recently opened Third Space Center, designed for students from historically marginalized communities, offers a community room, a dining room, and a full kitchen stocked with global staples.

All Whitman students complete the General Studies Program, which includes both a first-year seminar and distribution requirements in various disciplines. The first-year program revolves around a two-semester sequence of learning, with the first semester focused on exploring complex questions and the second on making persuasive written and spoken arguments. Depending on their major, all seniors must either complete a written senior thesis and oral defense or pass comprehensive written and oral exams in their major; Whitman was the first U.S. higher learning institution to require seniors to take comprehensive exams.

> **"Students are very immersed in their academic life."**

Biology, psychology, economics, and computer science are the most popular majors, along with environmental studies, English, and the interdisciplinary major in biochemistry, biophysics, and molecular biology, which are also some of the best programs. Whitman also boasts an astronomy program, unusual among small colleges. New majors include neuroscience and ethics and society, while new minors include finance; data science; and law, culture, and the humanities. Whitman has 3–2 programs in engineering, oceanography, forestry, and environmental management, offered in partnership with institutions like Caltech, Columbia, Duke, and the University of Washington.

"Students are very immersed in their academic life and follow-up conversations outside of the classroom," comments a senior. Classes are generally small; 69 percent have fewer than 20 students, and an environmental studies major reports, "Professors are extremely knowledgeable in their fields and are excited to get to know their students."

Whitman also has an extensive Asian art collection, and additional coursework in Chinese language and Asian studies is available through a summer program in China. Forty percent of Whitman students study off campus, most packing their bags for one of the more than 80 semester- and yearlong programs that are offered in 40-plus countries. Financial aid packages can be applied to all approved programs. Students may also take urban studies terms within the U.S. in Philadelphia and Washington, D.C. "Semester in the West is Whitman's signature program," explains an environmental studies and politics major. "Students travel across the American West and meet with activists, environmentalists, ranchers, Native Americans, and

> **"[Whitties are] outdoorsy activists."**

lawmakers to discuss local issues." During the daylong Whitman Undergraduate Conference, student scholarship and creativity are celebrated with presentations, posters, and performances. Highly competitive Whitman Internship Grants award up to $5,500 to selected students to pursue unpaid internships in the U.S. or abroad.

Thirty-three percent of students are from Washington State, and many of the rest hail from the suburbs of Western cities, notably San Francisco and Portland;

14 percent arrive from overseas. Whitties are "outdoorsy activists," says a psychology major. "Generally, students are kindhearted and authentic." The student body leans liberal, and recent activism has focused on increasing diversity on campus. Currently, 6 percent of students are Asian American, 13 percent are Hispanic/Latino, 3 percent are Black, and 7 percent are multiracial. The Glover Alston Intercultural Center helps support diversity and intercultural awareness on campus. There are numerous merit scholarships averaging $19,300 but no athletic awards. Whitman meets the full financial need of students from Washington State.

Seventy percent of Whitman students live in campus housing; first-years and sophomores are required to do so. In the newest residence hall, Stanton, "the accommodations feel like a resort," says a student, who adds that "the older buildings are comfortable and in good shape." Several theme houses are available for students who share interests such as writing, fine arts, environmentalism, and spirituality. Meals in the main dining hall get enthusiastic reviews. "I rarely get tired of the food, and it's easy to stay healthy on the meal plan, which is a rare find at a college," cheers a psychology major. A junior reports that "Whitman security is available 24/7 to support students," and measures like safety escorts, bystander intervention training, and "sober roamers" who watch over their classmates at registered on-campus parties help keep the campus community safe.

The social life at Whitman revolves around on-campus activities, such as theatrical productions and events held by more than 80 student clubs, as well as fraternity or off-campus house parties. Eighteen percent of both the men and the women go Greek, and according to a physics major, "Greek life at Whitman is very relaxed." When the weather is nice, students gather on Ankeny Field to study, toss a Frisbee, or relax, and watch-

ing the sun set over the wheat fields is a popular pastime. "There is a surprisingly large population that smokes marijuana socially," says a student, noting that the substance is legal for those 21 and over in the state of Washington. "It's very accepted, yet people don't feel pressured to smoke." Big annual events include the spring Renaissance Faire and the Whitsquatch music and art festival, featuring student bands and popular musicians.

Walla Walla (population 34,000) is located in a valley in the center of agricultural southeastern Washington and supports a symphony, community playhouse, art galleries, two rodeos, and a hot-air balloon festival, not to mention a state penitentiary. "The area is small and quaint—a great place to explore local wineries or try out new restaurants," says a senior. About 30 percent of students get involved in community service opportunities. Outdoor pursuits are important in this part of the country, where autumn is gorgeous, winter sporadically snowy, and spring delightfully warm. Hiking, biking, and backpacking are minutes away, and whitewater rafting and rock climbing are popular on weekends. Two ski centers and other recreational areas are within an hour's drive, and Seattle (260 miles) and Portland (235 miles) offer a welcome change of scenery.

The Whitman Blues compete in Division III. Men's tennis has brought home over a dozen Northwest Conference championships in recent years. Men's and women's basketball are nationally competitive, and everyone looks forward to the annual rivalry game against Whitworth University (the "Battle of the Whits"). Women's swimming, men's and women's tennis, men's golf, and baseball are solid, too. The majority of students play club and intramural sports. Club lacrosse and rugby tournaments draw crowds, as does "Onionfest," a regional ultimate Frisbee tournament. Rock climbers can challenge themselves at the world-class Climbing Center.

Whitman was the first U.S. higher learning institution to require seniors to take comprehensive exams.

Overlaps

Carleton, Colorado College, Kenyon, Lewis & Clark, Macalester, Occidental, University of Puget Sound, Reed

"If you're choosing a liberal arts school in the Northwest," says a student, "choose Whitman!" Indeed, students seeking a traditional liberal arts education with a strong sense of community and a healthy dose of outdoor fun would do well to heed this enthusiastic Whittie's advice. And they don't need an umbrella.

Whittier College

13406 E Philadelphia Street, Whittier, CA 90602

Whittier's Quaker heritage brings a touch of the East to suburban L.A. Less selective than Occidental and the Claremont Colleges, Whittier lures ethnically and socioeconomically diverse students with a bevy of academic scholarships and a welcoming community. Whittier's functional campus lacks the opulence of the Claremonts and the panache of Pepperdine. Check out the Whittier Scholars option.

Website: www.whittier.edu
Location: Suburban
Private
Total Enrollment: 797
Undergraduates: 767
Male/Female: 41/52
Financial Aid: 85%
Pell Grant: 12%
Expense: Pr $
Student Loans: 66%
Average Debt: $ $ $
Applicants: 4,393
Accepted: 84%
Enrolled: 6%
Grad in 6 Years: 60%
Returning First-years: 66%
Academics: ✍ ✍ ✍
Social: 🗩 🗩 🗩
Q of L: ★ ★ ★ ★
Admissions: (888) 200-0369
Email Address:
admission@whittier.edu

Strong Programs:
Biology
Business Administration
Child Development
English
Kinesiology
Political Science
Psychology

Founded in 1887 by members of the Religious Society of Friends (Quakers), Whittier College is a global training ground for a diverse student body interested in standing up for social justice and making a positive impact in the world. Whittier students can be found all around the world, studying in dozens of foreign countries. And when they return to the Whittier campus, they have access to caring faculty and classmates who "want to be liberally educated and enjoy the small-campus vibe," reports a mathematics-business major.

Located just 18 miles from downtown Los Angeles, the college, whose name is inspired by Quaker poet John Greenleaf Whittier, is perched on a hill overlooking the town of Whittier, California, with the San Gabriel Mountains rising up from the horizon. The 73-acre campus is a pleasant mixture of modern buildings tucked between the red-roofed, white-walled Spanish traditionals. Its landmark building, Deihl Hall, includes a digital audio/video computer lab for languages. A four-foot-high granite monument stands on the north campus lawn honoring Whittier's most famous alum, former president Richard Nixon. The state-of-the-art Science & Learning Center is the latest addition to campus.

Whittier offers its undergraduates two major curricular programs: the traditional Liberal Education Program and, the path less taken, the Whittier Scholars Program. Most students take the first option, in which they fulfill distribution requirements that emphasize written communication and quantitative reasoning. Students are required to fulfill experiential learning requirements through courses in natural science, creative expression, culture and language, historical inquiry, and engaging

> **"[Whittier students] want to be liberally educated and enjoy the small-campus vibe."**

diversity. Through their four years, students take three Life Labs. The first-year lab introduces the students to Whittier, the second addresses career and educational opportunities in their major, and in the third, students work with faculty in their major to build resumes and/or portfolios based on their post-graduate interests. Whittier offers more than 50 majors, the strongest and most popular of which include business administration, psychology, kinesiology, English, biology, and child development.

The second curricular option, the Whittier Scholars Program, is the college's signature program. Students are relieved of most general requirements and start from square one with the help of a faculty advisor to design their own major. Recent self-designed majors have included urban community studies, cultural nutrition, and film and humanities. The program is highly regarded because of the more active role it allows students to play and the freedom it affords them in pursuing their interests.

All students, no matter which curriculum they choose, must fulfill a yearlong first-year writing requirement, choosing their preferences from a variety of seminars. First-years also attend a series of speakers who discuss topics relevant to student coursework and take part in the Exploring Los Angeles series, which includes trips to museums and cultural events. Seniors complete a capstone requirement.

Whittier ended its formal affiliation with the Quakers in the 1940s, but the prevailing spirit of community hearkens back to their traditions. A biology major says, "Whittier provides a positive learning environment where students are actively encouraged to get involved." Sixty-six percent of classes have fewer than 20 students, and first-years are taught by full professors. "For the most part, the quality of the teaching has been very intense but very rewarding," says a student. For those looking to add global scope to their college experience, semester-long and short-term study abroad options include destinations like Paris, Rome, Cape Town, and Beijing; many programs are faculty-led. What's more, every student who studies abroad in a Whittier-approved program receives an automatic Global Poet Scholarship worth $2,000.

The Turner Residence Hall entices many students with panoramic views of Los Angeles.

"Students at Whittier are mostly liberal and are passionate about social justice and national politics," says a senior. Seventy-one percent of undergraduates come from California, while 13 percent arrive from abroad. Diversity is taken seriously here. Whittier draws a good portion of students—including many commuters—from nearby communities east of Los Angeles, and the school's Latino population has grown by more than 20 percent in the last decade as local demographics have shifted. Currently, Hispanic/Latino students represent 51 percent of the student body, while Black students add 4 percent, Asian Americans 4 percent, and multiracial students 7 percent. "Tolerance is a big watchword on campus," a junior says, and the college's Office of Inclusive Excellence provides an array of resources and programming to support diversity. In addition to need-based aid, the college awards merit scholarships averaging $32,700.

"[Uptown Whittier is] a perfect place for a night on the town with friends."

Fifty-two percent of Whittier students live on campus. The Turner Residence Hall entices many students with panoramic views of Los Angeles. "The first-year residence halls are older with limited air-conditioning," reports a history and music major. Many first-years choose to participate in living/learning communities organized around particular academic or social interests. Campus residents take their meals at the Campus Inn dining hall (known as the CI), where the food is said to be typical college fare. The Spot, Whittier's popular campus coffeehouse, includes a nightclub called—logically enough—the Club. Students give high ratings to campus safety.

Whittier students can be found all around the world, studying in dozens of foreign countries.

Ten social societies (they're not called fraternities or sororities here) attract 10 percent of the men and 10 percent of the women but hardly dominate the social scene. Their dances, however, which frequently feature live entertainment, are welcomed by all. Whittier has a fairly strict alcohol policy, students say. Popular annual events include the Whittfest concert in the spring, the Midnight Breakfast served by professors during second-semester finals, and Sportsfest, which is a campuswide competition in which dorms compete in a variety of athletic, intellectual, and wacky games and events. The most important campus landmark is the Rock, which sits near the front of campus and is given fresh coats of paint by countless aspiring artists.

For many, a favored diversion is road tripping, everywhere from Disneyland to the California beaches. Other common destinations include Joshua Tree, San Diego, and Las Vegas. For nightlife closer to campus, Los Angeles looms large. The local community, known as Uptown Whittier, offers quaint shops, restaurants, a movie theater, and cobblestone sidewalks, and a senior calls it "a perfect place for a night on the town with friends." It's also a place for community-minded students to get involved.

Johnny Poet is Whittier's pen-wielding mascot (inspired by the school's namesake). The Poets compete in Division III, where both the men's and women's basketball teams reached the Southern California Intercollegiate Athletic Conference (SCIAC) Postseason Tournament in 2025. Volleyball is also competitive. In 2022 the school eliminated its 115-year-old football program as well as men's and women's golf and men's lacrosse. Intramurals are a big draw, especially pickleball, kickball, volleyball, and basketball.

The students at Whittier have created a supportive, intimate environment where people work together and celebrate their diversity. And with the opportunity to design their own majors, students here are active in their own education but get plenty of support along the way. Says a sophomore, "I have no doubt that I have faculty, staff, and administrators advocating for me and cheering me on toward my personal goals."

If You Apply To ›

Whittier: Early action, rolling admission. SATs or ACTs: not considered. Accepts the Common Application.

Willamette University

900 State Street, Salem, OR 97301

Willamette is strategically located next door to the Oregon state capitol and 50 minutes from Portland. Comparable in size to Whitman and U of Puget Sound, and smaller than Lewis & Clark, Willamette offers extensive study abroad enhanced by ties to Asia. Well-known in the West but is still developing a national reputation to equal that of competitors such as Lewis & Clark.

Willamette University was founded in 1842 in the Willamette Valley by a Methodist missionary to the Oregon territory as the first university in the West. Students frequently take advantage of their proximity to the state's executive, judicial, and legislative offices as well as a nearby hospital for internships, jobs, or off-campus learning experiences. A comprehensive study abroad program carries students to destinations around the globe. On campus, students find a more personal atmosphere than larger universities nearby and appreciate the low-key yet challenging academic milieu. One satisfied chemistry major says, "This is the place where you can grow as a student, leader, and person as you pursue your passions."

The 61-acre campus is home to abundant trees (testimony to Oregon's frequent rain), small wildlife, and occasionally steelhead salmon that splash around in Mill Stream, which runs between WU's redbrick academic buildings. The college-owned forest at Zena is a 305-acre outdoor laboratory about a 10-minute drive from campus that hosts regular student and faculty research in biology, sustainability, art, and other fields. The university's LEED Gold–certified Ford Hall features large, collaborative learning spaces and faculty offices.

All students at Willamette (pronounced "Will-AM-it") take the first-year College Colloquium seminar, study in a language other than English, and satisfy an equity, diversity, and inclusion course requirement. They also complete coursework in five liberal arts categories: math and sciences, natural sciences, social sciences, humanities, and arts. In addition, students take capstone senior seminars, often culminating in research or thesis projects. The most popular majors are environmental science; economics; politics, policy, law, and ethics; and data science. Other particularly strong programs include chemistry; Japanese studies; music; theatre; public health; and history. The "rigorous and competitive" combined degree programs include business (3–2 B.A./M.B.A.), law (3–3 B.A./J.D.), and data science (3–1 B.S./M.S.) and integrate the liberal arts and professional education. Willamette's merger with Pacific Northwest College of Art, the region's oldest school of art and design, in 2021 significantly expanded offerings in these areas.

> "This is the place where you can grow as a student, leader, and person as you pursue your passions."

Academics are rigorous, but students don't compete for grades. "Professors do not seek to make classes difficult for no reason," says a politics, policy, law and ethics major. "Instead, they strategically push us to explore new ideas and question our most deeply held beliefs." Classes are "incredibly intimate," the student adds; 75 percent have fewer than 20 students. And for those seeking additional support, "Tutors are available in every subject, for free, and there is a writing center within which students can arrange appointments for help with papers or academic projects," reports a senior.

When students aren't reading or writing papers, undergraduate research opportunities in every discipline beckon; the university awards more than 75 undergraduate research grants each year. Eighteen percent of students participate in a robust study abroad program that sends them to their choice of more than 45 nations, and Willamette also benefits from its colocation with the U.S. campus of Tokyo International University.

Willamette students are "passionate, outgoing, and outspoken," says a senior. "There is recognition that students can act as agents of change in a multitude of ways." Thirty-one percent of WU students are native Oregonians, and much of the remainder comes from Western states, notably California and Washington; 2 percent are international. Black students make up 2 percent of the student body, Hispanics/Latinos 15 percent, Asian Americans 4 percent, and multiracial students 9 percent. Social justice issues spark discussion on the "left-leaning" campus, and the Student Center for Equity and Empowerment supports students from underrepresented groups. Willamette offers talent and academic merit scholarships each year averaging $27,200; there are no athletic awards.

Sixty-eight percent of Willamette students live in campus housing, which is social and convenient to classes and parties. "Willamette's dorms are not remarkable, but they provide incredible experiences for fostering community," says a student. Juniors and seniors may move off campus, and "living in Salem is quite cheap," says an upperclassman. The student-owned and -operated Bistro offers a coffeehouse atmosphere and is a popular alternative to cafeteria fare. "All of the food is fresh, local, and made on campus by staff that students grow to know personally," explains a senior. Students report that the university has taken a strong stance on responding to and educating the community about sexual assault and providing mental health support.

> "Professors do not seek to make classes difficult for no reason."

(continued)

Accepted: 77%
Enrolled: 14%
Grad in 6 Years: 71%
Returning First-years: 87%
Academics: ✍ ✍ ✍
Social: 🗩 🗩 🗩
Q of L: ★ ★ ★ ★
Admissions: (503) 370-6303
Email Address:
  bearcat@willamette.edu

Strong Programs:
Biology
Data Science
Economics
History
Japanese Studies
Music
Politics, Policy, Law, and Ethics
Public Health

The student-owned and -operated Bistro offers a coffeehouse atmosphere.

"The social scene at Willamette is best described as a choose-your-own-adventure," describes a junior, from free movies and lectures on campus, open-mic nights at the Bistro, dance parties (salsa or swing), or performances by the music and theatre departments. Nine percent of Willamette men and 12 percent of the women go Greek, but students say that Greeks don't dominate the social scene. When it comes to drinking, "Parties happen, but [students] are remarkably well-behaved," a student says. Annual social highlights include the Black Tie Affair formal dance, a spring music festival, and a student-run luau held by the Hawai'i Club for more than three decades. "There is a tradition of throwing your friends into Mill Stream on their birthday," says a junior.

Downtown Salem is a short walk from campus. "It has tons to offer, from restaurants, live music and theater, movies, arcades, escape rooms, etc.," cheers a senior. Riverfront Park provides "a gorgeous green space right on the Willamette River with miles worth of hiking trails, an amphitheater, play-structures and more." Also nearby are the Cascade Mountains and beaches of Newport and Lincoln City (an hour's drive), skiing and snowboarding on Mount Hood or in the high desert town of Bend (three hours), and the cosmopolitan cities of Portland (50 minutes) and Seattle (about four hours north). Willamette students remain true to the school motto, "Not unto ourselves alone are we born," volunteering tens of thousands of hours each year with various community organizations.

The Willamette Bearcats compete in Division III, and baseball and women's basketball are recent Northwest Conference champions. Men's and women's track and field, women's lacrosse and triathlon and men's golf are also strong. The annual football game against Linfield draws big crowds, and games against Pacific Lutheran are also well attended. Club sports range from the competitive (soccer, rugby, and ultimate Frisbee) to the recreational (badminton, volleyball, table tennis, eSports, and more), and intramurals are another popular option.

Willamette may be the best little school you've never heard of, at least if you're from outside the California–Oregon–Washington corridor. "Willamette is unabashedly itself," says one student. "Community members from all backgrounds feel very comfortable being themselves and embracing who they are." The school's close-knit community is strengthened by its emphasis on service and by warm, supportive faculty members who push students to achieve.

If You Apply To ›

Willamette: Early decision, early action, regular decision. SATs or ACTs: optional. Accepts the Common Application. Applicants have the option of providing information about their gender and sexual identity.

William & Mary

Williamsburg, VA 23187

Founded in 1693 by royal charter and named after the reigning British monarchs at the time, William & Mary offers an ideal mix of research and liberal arts. With 7,000 undergraduates, it is larger than Mary Washington and Richmond, smaller and more intellectual than the University of Virginia. W&M boasts one of the top graduation rates among public universities and the highest percentage of graduates who go on to earn Ph.D.s. Williamsburg, capital of the former colony of Virginia, is more exciting for tourists than for college students.

Traditions abound at William & Mary, yet this historic university—the second-oldest in the nation after Harvard—continues to evolve. It has graduated three former U.S. presidents—Thomas Jefferson, James Monroe, and John Tyler. Rival UVA prides itself on being "Mr. Jefferson's" university, but W&M is quick to remind the Cavaliers that it educated Mr. Jefferson in the first place. "Students at William & Mary choose to attend the university for its intense academic rigor, strong sense of community, rich history, and legacy of traditions," says one senior.

A profusion of azaleas and crape myrtle adds splashes of color to William & Mary's finely manicured campus, located about 150 miles southeast of Washington, D.C. The campus is divided into three sections and includes Lake Matoaka, the oldest human-made lake in Virginia, and a wooded wildlife preserve, which is filled with trails and widely used by the science departments. The Historic Campus is a grouping of three colonial structures still in use. The oldest and most striking is the Wren Building, which was constructed between 1695 and 1700 and is the country's oldest college building and arguably one of the loveliest. The Old Campus buildings date from the '20s and '30s, and New Campus, where ground was first broken in the '60s, is home to a recreation center and the new Arts Quarter. Crim Dell, a wooded area with a small pond spanned by an old-style wooden bridge, is one of the most romantic spots on any campus.

William & Mary, which was founded as a private college and did not go public until 1906, created Phi Beta Kappa in December of 1776. The honor code, established by Thomas Jefferson in 1779, demands much from the university's students. W&M's College Curriculum includes two first-year seminars: one "big ideas" course and one reading- and writing-intensive course, both of which are offered in every academic discipline. Students must also take coursework in a range of liberal arts areas, with a particular emphasis

> **"I like to call it the Goldilocks university . . . because it's not too big, not too small."**

on interdisciplinary perspectives, and fulfill requirements in global perspectives; difference, equity, and justice; and foreign language proficiency. All seniors complete a capstone project. The Charles Center for Academic Excellence facilitates honors programs, research opportunities, and applied learning opportunities. "Through this summer research program, I gained skills related to statistical analysis, writing, presenting, and study design," says a psychology major.

At William & Mary, STEM majors have increased by 46 percent over the past 10 years, and in 2025, W&M opened the School of Computing, Data Sciences & Physics to provide increased opportunities for faculty and students to "generate new knowledge and expand understanding" in these fields. Business, government, biology, human health and physiology, and psychology are among the most popular majors, and computer science, economics, neuroscience, and international relations are well regarded. New majors include coastal and marine sciences and public health. Aspiring engineers can study the engineering physics and applied design (EPAD) physics concentration or sign up for a 3–2 program with Columbia University. W&M's joint degree program with the University of St Andrews in Scotland is one of the few international undergraduate joint degrees available in the U.S. "It changed my life," raves a senior. "St Andrews is my favorite place on earth."

"In terms of academics, I have been challenged more than I have ever been in my whole life," reports a government major. Adds another student, "It is not 'cool' to do poorly in class." Nevertheless, students say the prevailing culture is one of cooperation and support. "There's a phrase here: TWAMP. It stands for the Typical William & Mary Person," explains a music major. "This kinda sums up the fun-loving, caring, thoughtful, and passionate nature of students here. Everyone cares about academics but is also happy and supportive of others." Faculty members are said to be supportive as well. "Professors have often encouraged me to be bold and

Because William & Mary is a state-supported university, 60 percent of its undergraduates are Virginians.

controversial with my ways of thinking," says a junior. Forty-six percent of classes have fewer than 20 students, although a few introductory lectures have more than 100, and nearly all classes are taught by faculty, not graduate students.

Students rave about W&M's study abroad options, and 60 percent participate. "There are tons of opportunities to study abroad that are fit for every student: from semester-long programs to programs over summer and winter breaks that last between two and eight weeks and even spring break study abroad opportunities," reports a senior. The top 10 percent of first-year students are designated Monroe Scholars and receive summer research stipends to support independent projects. Eighty-five percent of students participate in some sort of faculty-mentored research experience. Students cheer the Cohen Career Center, which helps first-years and sophomores identify and pursue career interests.

Because William & Mary is a state-supported university, 60 percent of its undergraduates are Virginians, hailing largely from wealthier counties in the northern part of the state; 4 percent are international. Asian Americans now account for 11 percent of the students, Hispanics/Latinos 9 percent, Black students 4 percent, and multiracial students 8 percent. "Students at W&M have a wide variety of political and social views," says a government major. "There is a relatively large vocal group who voices their opinions on pro-LGBTQ, pro-choice, and pro-union causes," reports a sociology major. Like many older colleges, W&M has begun to grapple with its historical ties to slavery, including the renaming of several buildings and restoration of the Bray School, said to be the oldest existing schoolhouse for Black children. The Hearth: Memorial to the Enslaved, serves as a local hub for community building on campus.

Students report feeling safe on campus and cheer the services provided. Several student-led groups address issues of sexual assault. The Haven program features peers trained to talk to sexual assault survivors. "Our new wellness center offers all kinds of resources for physical and mental health," says a linguistics and music major. The McLeod Tyler Wellness Center houses health, counseling, recreation, and other services ranging from mindfulness workshops and yoga sessions to fitness classes. It operates the Counseling Center and Student Health Center. Merit scholarships averaging $6,100 are disbursed to qualified undergrads, and over 250 athletic scholarships are also offered.

In 2025, William & Mary opened five new and refurbished residence halls, with all residences being upgraded with air conditioning over the next few years. A new dining hall is slated to open in 2026. "There is so much construction going on right now to add more facilities to the school—which we desperately need," shares a junior. Fifty-eight percent of undergrads occupy campus housing, which is required for the first two years. Special-interest housing is available—there are eight language houses—and life in a fraternity or sorority house is an option. As for campus dining, a new dining vendor is bringing improved food services that are reportedly receiving good reviews.

"The social scene is active on campus," says a senior. "There is always an organization hosting an event, fundraiser, or concert of some kind." Indeed, students can enjoy the soothing voices of one of the many a cappella groups, dance the night away at fraternity parties, grab a midnight snack at the Sadler Center, or watch the latest dance or theater performance at the Glenn Close Theatre (named for the acclaimed actor, a William & Mary alum). Twenty-four percent of the men and 26 percent of the women join Greek organizations, which host most of the on-campus parties. "Greek life is an option, but it by no means dictates social life, which is nice," says a government major. A senior counsels, "Don't come to William & Mary if you're looking for a party school!" The university has strict policies against underage drinking, but students say if they behave safely, they stay out of trouble.

Traditions are the stuff of which William & Mary is made. "It's honestly why I'm still here," gushes an English major. "I love the lore and the cute town." Perhaps the most cherished is the annual Yule Log Ceremony in the Wren Courtyard, where students sing carols and hear the president read a holiday story. On Charter Day, bells chime and students celebrate the distinguished history of their more than 330-year-old institution. Each year, first-years walk through the Wren Building for Opening Convocation, where they're greeted by cheering upperclassmen and faculty. As they graduate, they pass through the Wren in the other direction. Multiple secret societies are known to exist; their activities are, well, secret, but rumored to be generally philanthropic in nature.

Anyone who gets restless can always step across the street to Merchants Square, a pedestrian mall lined with dozens of restaurants, coffee shops, and more. Students can also picnic at Colonial Williamsburg, jog down Duke of Gloucester Street (a.k.a. "DOG Street"), or study in a beautiful garden. "Eventually, you don't raise an eyebrow when colonial reenactors are behind you at the grocery store buying beer," quips one senior. Nightlife is a hit-or-miss affair (mostly miss), although volunteer opportunities abound and 70 percent of students participate. Richmond, Norfolk, and Virginia Beach—a favorite springtime mecca—are about an hour's drive; Washington, D.C., and the Shenandoah Mountains are also popular road trips.

Each year, more than 500 Tribe athletes compete on 23 Division I teams. Women's field hockey, tennis, basketball, and swimming and men's cross-country and football have been consistently competitive in recent years. Over 450 intramural teams and more than 40 club sports, such as rowing and ultimate Frisbee, attract a large percentage of the student body.

William & Mary is reminiscent of the dual-faced Roman god Janus, ever mindful of its rich historical legacy but also keenly aware of new academic and cultural forces swirling about. As a place to look both ways, W&M is, as one student puts it, "happy, quirky, intelligent, and proud." A happy senior describes it this way: "I like to call it the Goldilocks university in Virginia because it's not too big, not too small, and has all the opportunities that come with being a public institution." In other words, for many students, it's just right.

If You Apply To ›

William & Mary: Early decision I and II, regular decision. SATs or ACTs: optional. Accepts the Common Application with supplement.

Williams College

880 Main Street, Williamstown, MA 01267

Running neck and neck with Amherst on the selectivity chart, Williams sits on a campus of surpassing beauty in the foothills of the Berkshires. Making serious efforts to broaden racial, ethnic, and socioeconomic diversity. The campus art museum, one of the best anywhere, anchors strong arts programs. Locals hail the splendid isolation of Williamstown as a way to build community.

Williams College vies with rival Amherst for possession of both the color purple—they each use it on team uniforms and in their logos—and the distinction of being one of the top liberal arts colleges in the United States. (Amherst was founded in

Website: www.williams.edu
Location: Rural
Private
Total Enrollment: 2,120
Undergraduates: 2,071
Male/Female: 47/52
Financial Aid: 58%
Pell Grant: 19%
Expense: Pr $ $ $ $
Student Loans: 21%
Average Debt: $
Applicants: 15,411
Accepted: 8%
Enrolled: 43%
Grad in 6 Years: 97%
Returning First-years: 97%
Academics: ✍ ✍ ✍ ✍ ✍
Social: 🗩 🗩 🗩
Q of L: ★ ★ ★ ★
Admissions: (413) 597-2211
Email Address:
  admission@williams.edu

Strong Programs:
Art History
Biology
Computer Science
Economics
Environmental Studies
Mathematics
Political Science
Studio Art

Favorite traditions include homecoming, Winter Carnival, and Spring Fling.

1821 by a breakaway group of Williams students, along with the school's then-president.) Nestled in a small hamlet in the Berkshires, Williams is the more isolated of the two, but students say that makes for a more intimate sense of community. "I knew I wanted a small liberal arts college where I wouldn't get lost in the crowd," says a senior. "The school is nerdy and quirky and active all rolled into one." School spirit abounds, and when not gazing at the purple mountains' majesty, students at Williams are digging into their studies with fervor.

Williams was established in 1793 as a "western counterpart" to Harvard and Yale under a bequest from the estate of landowner Ephraim Williams. The college's buildings constitute a veritable omnium-gatherum of architectural styles, from the elegantly simple Federal design of the original West College to contemporary structures by Charles Moore and William Rawn. The brick and gray stone buildings are arranged in loosely organized quads, which are both enclosed and open to nature. Newer additions include the 113,000-square-foot, eco-friendly Wachenheim Science Center, housing the mathematics and statistics, psychology, and geosciences departments, and the college's multicultural hub, the Davis Center.

The Williams curriculum emphasizes interdisciplinary studies and personalized teaching. Distribution requirements include at least three courses in each of the school's three divisions: languages and arts, social studies, and sciences and mathematics. Students must also fulfill requirements in writing, quantitative and formal reasoning, and difference, power, and equity; pick a major from 37 options; pass four quarters of phys ed; spend at least six semesters in residence; and participate in Winter Study every January, when they may take a course, complete a research project, or travel abroad.

One of Williams's greatest strengths is in art, which benefits from the Williams College Museum of Art (one of the finest college art museums in America) that will be housed in a new building in 2027. The Clark Art Institute and MASS MoCA, a nearby center for contemporary visual, performing, and media arts, are also minutes away. Williams was one of the first liberal arts colleges to establish an environmental studies program, which is enhanced by fieldwork opportunities in the 2,600-acre, college-owned Hopkins Forest. Popular majors include economics, mathematics, psychology, computer science, political science, and English. Students seeking a change of pace, especially during the bitter and blustery winter, can pack their bags for more than 180 programs, including short-term, faculty-led study tours and an innovative yearlong program organized with Oxford's Exeter College in England.

> **"Tutorials are basically all critical engagement all the time."**

There are only two small graduate programs at Williams—in art history and development economics—so graduate students are few and far between, and you'll never find them teaching a class. Roughly two-thirds of Williams students sign up for courses taught in the Oxford tutorial format: two students and a faculty member meet each week, with the students alternating who has to do independent work, like an essay, lab report, or art piece, and who gets to critique it. "Tutorials are basically all critical engagement all the time," explains a political science major, because students learn to communicate, collaborate, and defend their ideas. And while academics at Williams are rigorous, the environment is supportive. "Professors knew my name from day one," says a history and political science major. About half of the students conduct research with faculty, and Williams offers more than 300 funded summer research positions across all disciplines. A senior says alumni "go out of their way to help Williams students succeed" by setting them up with internships and other opportunities.

Students at Williams are accomplished. One student says, "I know people who can read *Harry Potter* in Latin, translate rap songs into Arabic, and sight-read

'Rocket Man' perfectly on the piano." Just 14 percent of students are in-staters, and another 10 percent are international. Black students make up 6 percent of the student body, Asian Americans add 12 percent, Hispanics/Latinos represent 14 percent, and multiracial students comprise 7 percent. Politically, Williams leans left, and students say there is a small but dedicated group of student activists on campus. Many students come from affluent backgrounds, which, according to a junior, lends a certain "New England boarding school" vibe to campus, but Williams has a need-blind admissions process for domestic applicants, and socioeconomic diversity has been slowly increasing. All financial aid is need-based—there are no merit or athletic scholarships—and the college guarantees to meet the full demonstrated need of all admitted students. Furthermore, Williams offers all-grant financial aid packages, meaning that students who receive financial aid don't need loans or to fulfill work-study requirements.

Ninety-two percent of students live on campus; housing is guaranteed for four years, and only seniors are eligible to move out. "Most of the dorms are nice, or at least charming," says an English and Africana studies major. First-years live in groups of 25 to 35 students each (known as "entries") along with three or four junior advisors, who serve as big siblings, mentors, and sounding boards. After the first year, students have an affiliation with one of four upperclassmen residential neighborhoods and enter their housing draw. Campus dining offers three dining halls with friendly staff and satisfying meals, and small co-ops are available for seniors who want to cook for themselves. In addition to required trainings and other college programming, a student says, "Multiple student groups host events throughout the year to keep up the conversation surrounding the prevention of sexual assault."

Fraternities and sororities were abolished long ago, but that hasn't stopped Williams students from partying. "The party culture is centered around athletic teams, performance groups, and cultural affinity groups," explains an economics major. The college requires registration of parties over a certain size and mandates availability of food and nonalcoholic beverages whenever alcohol is present. Favorite traditions include homecoming, Winter Carnival, and Spring Fling. The most beloved tradition is Mountain Day, held on a Friday in October. Which day it will be is a well-kept secret, broken only when the college president sends out an email canceling classes and church bells begin tolling at 8 a.m. Students picnic on the campus's main lawn, then choose from a variety of hikes, including one to the top of Mount Greylock, where hot cider and doughnuts are waiting on the summit.

The small village of Williamstown (population 7,800), adjacent to campus, is "sort of the quintessential New England town," says a student. The Log is a popular hangout for pizza and live performances, and students frequent a few cafés and an independent movie theater, but the town isn't exactly a hot spot for social life. The Clark Art Institute, within walking distance of campus, possesses one of the finest collections of Renoir and Degas in the nation, as well as a great library. The college theater is home to the Williamstown Theatre Festival in the summer, which often features Broadway stars. Nearby slopes and trails beckon, offering skiing, cycling, and backpacking. Civilization—in the form of Albany, New York—is just an hour's drive. Other popular destinations include New York City and Boston (both accessible by train from Albany or three hours by car).

With 32 varsity teams and an active club sports program, athletics are more like an established religion here than an extracurricular activity. The Ephs (short for founder Ephraim) are a perennial winner of the Division III Directors' Cup, awarded

Overlaps

Amherst, Brown, Columbia, Cornell University, Dartmouth, Harvard, Penn, Yale

annually to the school with the strongest overall athletic program. Recent New England Small College Athletic Conference champions include football, men's crew, and men's and women's swimming and diving. Williams competes against Amherst and Wesleyan in the Little Three, "although Williams sports are super strong, and it usually is no contest!" cheers a senior. Intramurals are a popular option for those seeking less competitive athletic diversions.

It takes a special kind of student to be happy at Williams. Those who delight in the life of the mind and don't mind trading the amenities found at more urban schools for a small, intimate community will no doubt bleed purple by the time they leave. Says a senior, "I've never been more engaged in what I'm learning than here at Williams."

If You Apply To ›

Williams: Early decision, regular decision. Accepts the Common Application with supplement. Please consult Williams's website for the most up-to-date information regarding standardized test requirements.

University of Wisconsin–Madison

500 Lincoln Drive, Madison, WI 53706

Madison draws nearly a third of its students from out of state, a higher proportion than many other leading Midwestern public universities. Why brave the cold? Reasons include top programs in an array of professional fields and several innovative living/learning programs. There's also the pleasure of life in Madison, a combination state capital/college town in the mold of Austin, Texas. Sky-high retention rates.

Website: www.wisc.edu

Location: City Center

Public

Total Enrollment: 46,008

Undergraduates: 35,196

Male/Female: 46/54

Financial Aid: 57%

Pell Grant: 21%

Expense: Pub $ $

Student Loans: 33%

Average Debt: $ $

Applicants: 65,933

Accepted: 45%

Enrolled: 29%

Grad in 6 Years: 90%

Returning First-years: 96%

Academics: ✑ ✑ ✑ ✑

Social: 🗩 🗩 🗩 🗩

Q of L: ★ ★ ★ ★

Admissions: (608) 262-3961

Email Address:
onwisconsin@admissions.wisc.edu

For more than 175 years, the University of Wisconsin has been guided by the Progressive-era philosophy of the "Wisconsin Idea" that the purpose of a great state university is to seek truth and apply the resulting knowledge to the benefit of the students and society as a whole. Such a philosophy has turned Wisconsin, which dates to 1848, into one of the world's leading universities—one where more than 35,000 full-time undergraduates take advantage of high-level academics and a rich array of resources. State funding is back on the rise after years of deep budget cuts, and Wisconsin remains a place where professional and other programs are outstanding. Just bring a strong desire to learn—and a very warm coat.

Described by one Madison student as "architecturally olden with a modern touch," the mainly brick campus is distinctive. It spreads out over 936 hilly, tree-covered acres and across an isthmus between two glacial lakes, Mendota and Monona. From atop Bascom Hill, the center of campus, you look east past the statue of Lincoln and the liberal arts buildings, down to a library mall that was the scene of many a political dem-

> **"You have to be fairly strong and confident [here]. No one holds your hand."**

onstration during the '60s. Farther east, you see rows of State Street pubs and restaurants and the bleached dome of the Wisconsin state capitol. On the other side of the hill, another part of campus, dedicated to the agricultural and health sciences, twists along Lake Mendota. But students from both sides of the hill congregate in the old student union, Memorial Union, where political arguments and backgammon games can rage all night. Outside on the union's veranda, students can look out at the sailboats in summer or iceboats in winter. Morgridge Hall provides state-of-the-art facilities for cross-disciplinary studies in data, technology, and computing.

Distribution requirements vary among the different schools and academic departments, but they are uniformly rigorous, with science and math courses required for B.A. students and a foreign language for virtually everyone. All students must fulfill a three-part graduation requirement in quantitative reasoning, communication, and ethnic studies. Students who prefer the academic road less traveled can opt for the Integrated Liberal Studies certificate program, which allows them to fulfill several gen eds with a series of related, interdisciplinary courses rather than taking electives at random.

Madison's academic climate is demanding. "There are a lot of smart people studying here," notes one student. The list of first-rate academic programs at Madison would constitute a college catalog elsewhere. Some highlights include education, agriculture, communication, biological sciences, and social sciences. The most popular majors are computer science, business, psychology, and data science. Due to overcrowding, some of the strongest fields, such as business and engineering, have more selective admissions criteria than others. Although many classes are large, 42 percent have fewer than 20 students. Professors at Madison are certainly among the nation's best, with National Academy of Science members and Guggenheim fellows scattered liberally among the departments.

While the university's size can be daunting, harried first-years aren't left to fend for themselves. The university offers several first-year programs designed to ease the transition into college life. A first-year seminar encourages students to examine learning strategies; connect with faculty, staff, and peers; and become familiar with campus resources. First-Year Interest Groups (FIGs) consist of 20 first-year students who may live in the same residence hall or "residential neighborhood" and who also enroll in a cluster of three classes together. Each FIG cluster of courses has a central theme; the central or "synthesizing" course integrates content from the other two classes. After their first year, many students participate in internships, and 24 percent study abroad in countries ranging from France, Brazil, India, and Israel to Thailand. Forty-four percent conduct undergraduate research.

If there is a common characteristic among Madison undergraduates, it is assertiveness. "It's easy to get lost in the crowd here, so you have to be fairly strong and confident," declares one student. "No one holds your hand." The flip side is that "anyone can fit in, you just have to find your own niche." Forty-nine percent of undergraduates hail from Wisconsin, and 9 percent are international. The school is a heartland of progressive politics, and Madison's reputation as a haven for liberals remains intact. "Students here are called liberal because they are eager and willing to change and are continually looking for newer and better ideas," explains one activist. Asian Americans make up 11 percent of the student body, Hispanics/Latinos 9 percent, Black students 3 percent, and multiracial students 5 percent. Academic merit scholarships averaging $7,200 are available, along with more than 300 athletic scholarships. Madison covers tuition for eligible students whose family income is $65,000 or less. Members of Wisconsin American Indian tribes are guaranteed to have their full in-state tuition costs met.

Twenty-five percent of undergrads, mostly first-years, reside in university housing. Dorms are either co-ed or single sex and come equipped with laundry facilities, game rooms, and lounges. Most also have a cafeteria. The student union offers two meal plans, and there are plenty of restaurants and fast-food places nearby. Escort services for those walking and those needing a ride help keep students safe on campus. A variety of programs and groups, such as U Got This!, are working to educate the community on preventing sexual assault and supporting survivors.

Madison covers tuition for eligible students whose family income is $65,000 or less.

"Frat parties are a very popular break from the bar scene."

All students must fulfill a three-part graduation requirement in quantitative reasoning, communication, and ethnic studies.

One old standby for social life that is still as popular as ever is the student union, which hosts bands, shows, and so forth and provides a great atmosphere in which to hang out. There are more film clubs than anyone can follow, and everyone has a favorite bar. Nine percent of the men and 8 percent of the women go Greek. "Frat parties are a very popular break from the bar scene," quips one expert on both options. Madison (a.k.a. Madtown) is an excellent college town and has been the stomping ground for many fine rock 'n' roll and blues bands on the road to fame. Volunteering is a tradition here; the university consistently tops the list for providing the Peace Corps with the most entrants of any college or university in the nation. Nature enthusiasts can lose themselves in the university's 12,000-acre nature preserve or hit nearby ski slopes.

The students at this Big Ten school show "tons of interest" in sports, especially hockey and football, in which the Badgers battle Minnesota's Gophers for the trophy of Paul Bunyan's Axe. The formidable women's ice hockey and volleyball teams claimed recent national titles, and the school has produced its share of Big Ten champions as well in men's cross-country and ice hockey. Bucky Badger apparel, emblazoned with slogans ranging from the urbane to the decidedly uncouth, is ubiquitous. However, the much-acclaimed marching band may outdo all the teams in popularity. Recreational sports are another favorite pastime, with dozens of intramurals and more than 40 club sports offered at varying levels of competitiveness.

Despite fervent efforts in recent years by politicians with narrow and instrumentalist views of higher education to scuttle the Wisconsin Idea, Madison remains one of the best and most well-rounded flagship state universities anywhere. It is a school that students sum up as "diverse, intellectual, fashionable, and moderately hedonistic." And these are the qualities that attract bright and energetic students from everywhere. "You feel you're accepted for who you are no matter what," says one student. "It's so nice to just be yourself."

If You Apply To ›

Wisconsin: Early action, regular decision. Accepts the Common Application. Please consult Wisconsin's website for the most up-to-date information regarding standardized test requirements.

Wittenberg University

200 W Ward Street, Springfield, OH 45504

Wittenberg is an outpost of cozy Midwestern friendliness. Less national than Denison or Wooster, Witt has plenty of old-fashioned school spirit and powerhouse Division III athletic teams. Top students should aim for the honors program, which provides a chance for independent research. Witt doles out plenty of merit scholarships to above-average students. The university is trying to dig out from an ongoing financial struggle.

Founded in 1845 by German Lutheran immigrants and named after the city where Martin Luther launched the Protestant Reformation, Wittenberg University remains true to its faith by emphasizing strong student/faculty relationships—and making sure that students don't get too settled in their campus comfort zone. In fact, Wittenberg requires all students to complete a community service experience before they graduate. "The campus is beautiful, it's a great school, and it's so obvious how much everyone here loves it," gushes an education major.

The Wittenberg campus is classic Midwestern collegiate, with a mixture of 1800s and Gothic-inspired buildings on 114 rolling acres in a designated arboretum in southwestern Ohio. The redbrick Myers residence hall, with picturesque white pillars and an open-air dome dating from the 19th century, stands at the center. Many of the campus's buildings are showing their age, although the $40 million Health, Wellness, and Athletics Complex features a full-size indoor turf field surrounded by a running track, among other facilities.

Wittenberg's Connections core curriculum emphasizes a solid liberal arts background, with coursework ranging from scientific inquiry to U.S. diversity and equity to creative process. A required First-Year Seminar in the fall helps students transition from high school to college. All students must complete one civic engagement experience, such as an academic course that incorporates volunteer work, as well as two other hands-on learning experiences, which may include research, internships, study abroad, or leadership experiences. Finally, seniors create a culminating reflection that connects their experiences over their four years.

An ongoing financial crisis and declining enrollment have prompted the school to cut five majors—including music, music education, German, Spanish, and East Asian studies—and reduce faculty and staff. The university's accreditation status is under review with a determination due in 2027. Despite this, students give high marks to the education program, which is among the most popular majors, along with biology, business, exercise science, and psychology. Health-related fields, especially nursing and other prehealth professional programs, are particularly well regarded. Other notable programs include environmental science, English, and international studies. Wittenberg also offers 3–2 engineering programs with Columbia University and Case Western Reserve, and a dual degree physics and engineering program with Indiana Tech. The academic climate is described as "challenging but friendly," and study groups are common, according to one junior. Professors are roundly praised for their teaching styles and willingness to make themselves available outside the classroom. "The instruction is wonderful, well-thought-out, and flawlessly executed," affirms an early education major. Sixty percent of classes have fewer than 20 students. As long as students declare their major on time and complete all courses with a C or better, the college guarantees a degree in four years—and will pay for any additional necessary courses.

The Compass program combines nine different student support services in one collaborative space in the Thomas Library and is intended, in part, to improve the college's retention and graduation rates. In addition to offering academic support, Compass connects students to research, community service, and internship opportunities, and students contribute over 25,000 hours of community service each year. A University Honors Program enrolls 15 percent of students, who conduct independent research culminating in a senior thesis, and individual departments offer ample opportunities to work on research with faculty members. In fact, 50 percent of students partake in undergraduate research. Wittenberg encourages students to take a semester or a year away from campus, and 20 percent do so, both in the U.S. and abroad. Most students pack their bags for the college's own faculty-led semesters in Germany and Costa Rica, although a multitude of other partner programs are available. Wittenberg's Local Government Management Internship Program is an option for those interested in public service.

"Witt students are proactive," says a junior. "We are constantly championing new causes, whether through community service or fundraising. We are always on the go!" Nowadays, Lutherans represent just 6 percent of the student body. Seventy-nine percent of Wittenberg students are native Ohioans, and less than 1 percent hail from other countries. Many others are from nearby states like Indiana, Michigan,

> "The campus is beautiful, it's a great school."

Favorite annual events include Wittfest, a campus festival and concert with games, food, prizes, and socializing before finals.

and Pennsylvania. Black students make up 13 percent of the student body, Hispanics/Latinos 6 percent, Asian Americans 1 percent, and multiracial students 4 percent. The Diversity Center houses student awareness organizations to help support underrepresented groups on campus. Students say the campus is fairly evenly split between conservatives and liberals, and both groups are vocal. Wittenberg is generous in awarding merit scholarships, which average $28,200; there are no athletic scholarships. A substantial 43 percent of incoming first-years receive Pell Grants. The Wittenberg College Access Program provides special financial aid packages to academically talented students from low-income families.

Eighty-three percent of students reside on Wittenberg's hilly campus; first-years and sophomores are required to do so. After that, most juniors and seniors choose houses and apartments owned by the school in the surrounding neighborhood—the "Wittenburbs," as students like to say. "Dorms are spacious and air-conditioned," a student explains, "with options for all-girl, honors, and substance-free housing." Those in need of sustenance (perhaps to fuel all-night study sessions) select from a variety of dining options that students call "acceptable," including vegetarian and low-fat items. To mitigate sexual assault on campus, the university has implemented bystander awareness and response training programs.

When not engaged in their studies, students at Wittenberg can choose among more than 50 student organizations, performing arts groups, and intramurals. Greek life is a big emphasis, with 7 percent of men and 9 percent of women belonging to fraternities and sororities. When the weekend rolls around, social life centers on parties in houses, dorm rooms, and apartments on or near campus. Greek groups, the Union Board, and the Residence Hall Association bring in guest speakers, movies, comedians, and concerts. Favorite annual events include Greek Week, homecoming ("the alumni involvement is incredible"), W Day, and Wittfest, a campus festival and concert with games, food, prizes, and socializing before finals. "It is open to the community, but all the students go," a senior says. "It resembles a carnival, and at night there's a big concert on the lawn." Springfield (population 59,000) is a struggling blue-collar city, but it's beginning to show signs of revival. The city offers movie theaters, restaurants, a brewery, a performing arts center, and plenty of service opportunities. "There are definitely some gems in Springfield, and every now and then, my friends and I like to get off campus to explore," comments a finance major. Popular road trips include Dayton (30 minutes), Columbus (45 minutes), and Cincinnati (90 minutes).

> **"The instruction is wonderful, well-thought-out, and flawlessly executed."**

Wittenberg's athletic teams (the Tigers) are competitive in Division III, and rivalries with Allegheny, Wabash, and the College of Wooster really get students riled up, especially when the football team takes the field. Women's volleyball, cross-country, and track and field have won North Coast Athletic Conference titles. Men's golf won its 30th NCAC title in 2025. Intramurals and club sports are a huge draw, too, with sports such as crew, racquetball, and rugby. Nearby state parks offer swimming, camping, biking trails, and picnics in the warmer months and skiing in the winter.

While not as well-known as many of its bigger Midwestern brethren, Wittenberg has plenty to offer those students who decide to attend, including a solid honors program, an active Greek scene, and serious Division III athletics. And with an increased focus on student support and diversifying its academic offerings, the school is slowly extending its regional reach.

Overlaps

Baldwin Wallace, Capital University, Denison, Miami (OH), Ohio Northern, Ohio Wesleyan, Otterbein, Wooster

If You Apply To ›

Wittenberg: Early decision, early action, rolling admissions. SATs or ACTs: optional. Accepts the Common Application with supplement.

Wofford College

429 N Church Street, Spartanburg, SC 29303

Located in Spartanburg and with roughly 1,800 undergraduates, Wofford is strong in the life sciences and study abroad. Compare with Furman and Presbyterian. The college is one of the smallest institutions to compete in Division I football, and Greek life dominates the traditional social scene. Diversity is a constant challenge. Where else do first-year students get their own personal librarian?

Wofford students take pride in combining a well-rounded curriculum built on traditional strengths in the sciences with career-related internships and study abroad. The college has taken bold steps to increase—and diversify—enrollment while lowering the student/faculty ratio. Legend has it that a pair of green eyes can be seen at night over a painting in Main Building, where every student takes at least one class. Students study hard under the "eyes of Old Main" and form lasting friendships with peers and faculty members. "We are bright, driven individuals who learn to utilize our skills to the best of our potential to make the world around us a better place," says a junior.

Wofford is located near the heart of Spartanburg (population 38,000), a mid-sized city in the northwest corner of South Carolina, and it is affiliated with the United Methodist Church. Founded in 1854, it's one of fewer than 200 existing American colleges that opened before the Civil War, and it still operates on its original campus, a National Historic District. Azaleas, magnolias, and dogwoods surround the distinctive, twin-towered Main Building and four original faculty homes on the 180-acre campus, which is also a nationally recognized arboretum. Newer additions to campus include the sustainably designed Chandler Center for Environmental Studies and a 150-bed residence hall.

> **"The academic climate at Wofford is very competitive."**

Wofford requires courses in English, fine arts, foreign languages, humanities, science, history, philosophy, cultural perspectives, math, and wellness. First-years take a required Liberal Arts Seminar 101 course in the fall that hones their reading, writing, and discussion skills; recent offerings have included Confronting Climate Change, Victorian Women Behaving Badly, and Muslims in America. All first-years are also assigned a Student Success Team that includes an academic advisor, a student peer leader, a staff guide, and a personal librarian.

Traditionally, Wofford's strongest and most attractive programs have been in the life sciences, which turn out about a third of its graduates. Every year, two dozen of the school's graduates go on to graduate medical or dental programs; another two dozen go on to law school. Business programs (especially when combined with a second major in Chinese, French, German, or Spanish) and English, with its emphasis on creative writing, are solid, and government is also strong. Some of the most popular majors are biology, finance, psychology, and accounting. Prospective engineers may apply for 3–2 programs with Clemson or New York's Columbia University. Fifty-six percent of classes enroll fewer than 20 students, and students agree that, across the board, the workload tends to be heavy. "I would say the academic climate at Wofford is very competitive in the sense that students feel pressured to excel," says a sophomore.

"Professors encourage students to come visit their office about both class and personal concerns," says a psychology major. "Many help students secure research positions, internships, and other opportunities." Indeed, special enrichment

<table>
<tr><td>Website: www.wofford.edu</td></tr>
<tr><td>Location: Small City</td></tr>
<tr><td>Private</td></tr>
<tr><td>Total Enrollment: 1,800</td></tr>
<tr><td>Undergraduates: 1,800</td></tr>
<tr><td>Male/Female: 48/51</td></tr>
<tr><td>Financial Aid: 99%</td></tr>
<tr><td>Pell Grant: 21%</td></tr>
<tr><td>Expense: Pr $ $</td></tr>
<tr><td>Student Loans: 50%</td></tr>
<tr><td>Average Debt: $ $ $</td></tr>
<tr><td>Applicants: 4,459</td></tr>
<tr><td>Accepted: 52%</td></tr>
<tr><td>Enrolled: 18%</td></tr>
<tr><td>Grad in 6 Years: 83%</td></tr>
<tr><td>Returning First-years: 91%</td></tr>
<tr><td>Academics: ✑ ✑ ✑</td></tr>
<tr><td>Social: 🗩 🗩</td></tr>
<tr><td>Q of L: ★ ★ ★</td></tr>
<tr><td>Admissions: (864) 597-4130</td></tr>
<tr><td>Email Address:
admission@wofford.edu</td></tr>
<tr><td>Strong Programs:
Accounting
Biology
Business
English
Finance
Government
Psychology
Spanish</td></tr>
</table>

opportunities abound at Wofford. The Presidential Seminar brings together 20 out-standing seniors from different disciplines to discuss readings from classical and contemporary essays on philosophy, politics, and the complexities of human nature. The Career Center connects students to internships, entrepreneurship opportuni-ties, and other pre-professional services. A quarter of Wofford students participate in some form of study abroad, embarking on programs in more than 50 coun-tries. Short-term, faculty-led programs are offered during the January term, while semester- and yearlong options are available through approved partners; students can often apply financial aid toward program costs. Every year, one Presidential International Scholar travels around the world, all expenses paid, to study an issue of global importance for a semester.

Fifty-four percent of students hail from South Carolina and just 2 percent from abroad. Black students make up 7 percent of the student population, Asian Americans 3 percent, Hispanics/Latinos 6 percent, and multiracial students 4 percent. Conservative white students from middle- to upper-class backgrounds make up the majority, and students note that the low level of racial diversity has been a source of tension on campus. "Wofford's administration is a lot more liberal and encourages diversity, whereas Wofford students and alums often show distaste or frustration toward more socially liberal and inclusive endeavors," comments a student. Merit scholarships averaging $26,600 are available to qualified students, and there are also athletic scholarships in 19 sports.

Ninety-two percent of Wofford's students live on campus, where first-years get doubles in Greene Hall and the recently renovated Marsh Hall or four-person suites in Carlisle Hall. A biology major explains, "Each year that you are at Wofford, the housing situation gets better and better, culmi-nating in the Village—a fantastic apartment community for the seniors." About a quarter of first-years join living/learning communities so they can live with classmates who share their academic interests. A senior says meals in Wofford's three main dining facilities are "getting better each year." Campus secu-rity gets mixed reviews. "Sexual assault is an issue on Wofford's campus because most cases go unreported," says a junior, who also credits the administration with increasing the visibility of Title IX staff and resources "so more cases will be reported." The Center for Wellness and Counseling Services has been remodeled and addi-tional mental health counselors hired to meet increased demand from students.

The Greek system is a huge force in Wofford's social life, enlisting 34 percent of the men and 50 percent of the women. The Johnson Greek Village features individ-ual houses for fraternities, sororities, and multicultural organizations and serves as the social center of campus. Most Greek groups host parties every Friday and Saturday—with some kicking off the weekend on Thursday. "The school wants to shut down underage drinking, and they're cracking down on it," warns one student. The Student Affairs Committee offers campuswide events like comedians and music for those uninterested in the Greek system. "Spring Weekend is much anticipated at Wofford, as there are bands, cookouts, shaving-cream fights, and a beach volleyball tournament," says a student. Off campus, Spartanburg is home to six other colleges. Students say it's not a great college town, but there are some fun hangouts and occa-sional street fairs and concerts. Almost every Wofford student participates in some type of community-based learning. Terrier Play Day brings kids from the commu-nity to campus for a fair with booths and games. For a change of pace, students can head to Greenville, Atlanta, and Charlotte.

The Division I Wofford Terriers compete in the Southern Conference and have produced a number of competitive teams, including football; women's volleyball;

and men's basketball, which brought home the 2025 conference title, and games against rival Furman always draw crowds. The school's quiz bowl and chartered financial analyst teams are nationally competitive. Students are also active in intramural, recreational, and club sports, and some of the most popular programs include Terrier Tag (a cross between football and rugby), soccer, and pickleball.

A former Wofford chaplain was fond of saying, "You don't come to Wofford—you join it." And students say that's true, citing the close-knit community and intimate student/faculty relationships fostered by the school's small size. Although administrative efforts to build a more diverse, inclusive campus have been met with some resistance, the status quo here is slowly changing. "Wofford is in a period of transition currently, but I don't think that's a negative," reflects an English major. "Wofford is interested in creating citizens of our world who will foster improvement, and I see Wofford as an institution focused on moving forward while still preserving tradition."

If You Apply To ›

Wofford: Early decision I and II, early action, regular decision. SATs or ACTs: optional. Accepts the Common Application.

The College of Wooster

1189 Beall Avenue, Wooster, OH 44691

Despite its status as a modest Midwestern college with fewer than 2,000 students, Wooster is renowned in academic circles around the globe. Access is relatively easy, but graduating requires students to complete an independent study project in their senior year—earning a coveted Tootsie Roll. More intellectually intense than competitors such as Denison. Prioritizes mentorship and prides itself on turning students into real scholars.

Instead of telling students what to think, the College of Wooster focuses on teaching students how to do it themselves through what it calls its "research-based liberal arts curriculum." From the first-year seminar to the final day when seniors hand in their theses, the college paves each student's path to independence. The emphasis here is on global perspectives, mentored research, cross-collaboration between departments and majors, and the heritage that stems from its origin as a college founded in 1866 by Scottish Presbyterians. The one-on-one attention from faculty makes Wooster an intellectual refuge in the rural countryside of Ohio. "Wooster is full of quirky, fascinating, and deeply passionate students, faculty, and staff who are lifelong learners and who cultivate a variety of hobbies and interests," says a senior.

Located in the city of Wooster, Ohio, the college's hilltop campus is spread over 240 acres, with many campus buildings designed in the English–collegiate Gothic style and constructed of cream-colored brick. More recent buildings are trimmed in Indiana limestone or Ohio sandstone. The central arch and two towers of Kauke Hall (the central building in Quinby Quadrangle, the square around which the college grew) make it stand out. The Gault Library for Independent Study offers a private carrel for each senior in the humanities and social sciences. A $40 million renovation of the student center centralized student support services, updated the dining hall, and expanded space for student clubs and relaxation.

What goes on behind the facades of Wooster's attractive buildings is even more impressive than the structures themselves. The required First-Year Seminar, limited to 15 students per section, introduces students to intensive writing, critical thinking, and interdisciplinary study. In addition to the first-year seminar, Wooster requires coursework in arts and humanities, history and social sciences, and mathematical and natural sciences, as well as in global and cultural perspectives, religious perspectives, and a foreign language. The curriculum culminates with a yearlong senior Independent Study project.

At Wooster, "students develop specific and deep academic interests," says an English major. Among the most popular majors are psychology, biology, computer science, neurology, and political science. Business economics and global and international studies are also strengths. Several optional Pathway programs in interdisciplinary areas allow students to explore broader academic and career interests. Sixty-four percent of classes enroll fewer than 20 students, and only a few introductory courses have teaching assistants, who run review sessions and offer extra help. Students praise faculty members for their devotion to teaching, and a history major says, "Mentorship and collaboration are pervasive across campus."

Indeed, mentored undergraduate research is the heart of a Wooster education, highlighted by paid opportunities in the Applied Methods and Research Experience, APEX Fellowships, the Sophomore Research Program, and other internships. The Independent Study (IS) required of all seniors lets students explore subjects they're passionate about with one-on-one faculty guidance. "The research skills you develop are second to none,"

"Wooster is full of quirky, fascinating, and deeply passionate students."

affirms one student. IS has become such a part of Wooster that each year, seniors celebrate IS Monday—the day they turn in their projects—with a campuswide parade led by bagpipers. Completion of the IS earns you a Tootsie Roll to eat or keep for posterity next to your diploma. "It's a day all Wooster graduates will always remember!" a senior says. The college awards funds each year for student research, travel, or materials to support thesis work. The APEX (Advising, Planning, and Experiential Learning) center combines several offices related to student and career services and helps coordinate internships, study abroad, tutoring, and peer mentoring. When Wooster's remote locale gets too confining, students may choose from semester-long programs in more than 40 countries worldwide or short-term TREK programs led by Wooster faculty during spring and summer breaks.

Spring Fest brings games, a zip line, and food trucks to campus.

Wooster students are "very hardworking and focused, while also knowing how to have hobbies and fun," says a biochemistry and molecular biology major. Adds a music education and German studies major, "We are often very nerdy, and interest in activities such as RPGs, anime, and so on is quite common." As the college's reputation spreads, it's becoming more selective. Black students constitute 10 percent of the student body, Asian Americans 4 percent, Hispanics/Latinos 5 percent, and multiracial students 4 percent. Wooster has a notable international flavor—14 percent of students hail from more than 60 foreign nations, while 34 percent come from Ohio.

"[Students are] often very nerdy, and interest in activities such as RPGs, anime, and so on is quite common."

"It feels really good to be seen and heard, and with so many clubs focused on first-gen students, sexual orientation, political thought, and so on, you can really find your people," cheers a senior. Politically, the campus is "overall quite liberal," says a junior. Merit awards averaging $35,800 are available, and students are admitted without regard for financial need.

All students live on Wooster's campus in 14 co-ed dorms, where rooms are small but mostly "acceptable." "Wooster is in the process of updating older dorms so they can be modern and ADA friendly," reports a communication studies major. Students seriously committed to service may apply to live in one of the college's 30 residential program houses, each of which is affiliated with a community group. Meals are served in the Lowry Center dining hall and get average reviews. When it comes to responding to the issue of campus sexual assault, a neuroscience major says, "The school is constantly improving and is transparent about its effectiveness." But in general, students say that given Wooster's location "in the middle of cornfields," safety isn't an issue. The college reports it has increased access and programs for students, faculty, and staff, but one student opines, "Mental health counseling is notoriously difficult to obtain."

Students say they enjoy the "quaint and friendly" town of Wooster, a 10-minute walk from campus. "The downtown area offers an excellent social scene for going to brunch, hanging out with friends, and going to the farmers market on Saturdays," says a senior. Still, the majority of social life is campus-based. Visiting lecturers and student performances keep students busy on weekdays, while a senior says, "Campus offices regularly host popular recreational events, such as music festivals, the eagerly-anticipated Casino Night, and other events." Two major weekend hangouts on campus are the Underground, a bar and dance club that hosts well-known bands, and the Alley, featuring multi-purpose activity space and free arcade games. The college has no national Greek organizations, but local "sections" draw 12 percent of the men and "clubs" attract 20 percent of the women. Students say the party scene is low-key and no one is pressured to drink alcohol. Cleveland is a one-hour drive.

The school's Scottish heritage is on display in its kilted bagpipe band and its Scottish dancers, who perform during Scot Saturdays, Scot Spirit Day in the fall, and other big events throughout the year. "Every student leaves Wooster with a love for bagpipes," enthuses a sociology major. Other annual traditions include an outdoor music festival and the Culture Show during International Education Week in the fall and Spring Fest, which brings games, a zip line, and food trucks to campus. When it snows—which it does quite often in Wooster—students descend upon the Kauke arch and fill it with snow, a tradition that goes back decades.

Wooster fields Division III teams in 23 sports. Fighting Scots basketball is a spectator favorite, especially when the opponent is rival Wittenberg. Baseball, men's and women's track and field, women's soccer, and men's basketball are standouts in the North Coast Athletic Conference. Moot Court and Model UN have been successful in regional and national competitions. Club and intramural sports sign up students in droves; soccer, basketball, pickleball, dodgeball, and softball are particularly popular.

The College of Wooster is nationally recognized for its commitment to mentored research, its international focus, and its encouragement of independent thinking. The distinctive independent study requirement actively shapes both the individual student experience and the campus atmosphere. "Getting to go through something like that together creates a really unique personality at our school," says a senior. "IS is a really big thing at Wooster, and it has shaped the way I will go forward in life."

"Every student leaves Wooster with a love for bagpipes."

Overlaps

Denison, Dickinson, Kenyon, Macalester, Oberlin, Ohio Wesleyan, Whitman

If You Apply To ›

Wooster: Early decision I and II, early action, regular decision. SATs or ACTs: optional. Accepts the Common Application.

Worcester Polytechnic Institute

100 Institute Road, Worcester, MA 01609

Small and innovative, WPI is anything but a stodgy technical institute. The WPI Plan is hands-on and project-based and takes a humanistic view of engineering. Emphasizes teamwork instead of competition. Global focus unusual for a STEM school. WPI enrolls fewer students than Rensselaer but has more undergraduates than MIT.

Website: www.wpi.edu
Location: Small City
Private
Total Enrollment: 6,301
Undergraduates: 5,330
Male/Female: 67/33
Financial Aid: 99%
Pell Grant: 15%
Expense: Pr $ $
Student Loans: N/A
Average Debt: N/A
Applicants: 12,559
Accepted: 60%
Enrolled: 18%
Grad in 6 Years: 90%
Returning First-years: 94%
Academics: ✍ ✍ ✍
Social: 🗩 🗩 🗩
Q of L: ★ ★ ★ ★
Admissions: (508) 831-5286
Email Address:
admissions@wpi.edu

Strong Programs:
Aerospace Engineering
Architectural Engineering
Bioinformatics and
  Computational Biology
Biomedical Engineering
Computer Science
Interactive Media and Game
  Development
Mechanical Engineering
Robotics Engineering

As a pioneer in STEM education, Worcester Polytechnic Institute has built a solid reputation, particularly for its engineering programs. But with its ever-expanding academic curriculum (including business studies, interactive media and game development, and more), surprising devotion to music and theater, and dedication to hands-on undergraduate experiences, WPI has broadened the definition of what it means to be a techie haven. As an administrator explains, "The university's tradition of academic achievement and practical application is reflected in its motto, Lehr und Kunst, or 'Theory and Practice.'" More than anything, it's WPI's intentionally humanistic approach to science and engineering that really sets it apart. As an industrial engineering major explains, "WPI's culture is one that allows students to be themselves. Everyone is involved in STEM and finds learning awesome."

WPI, established in 1865, is the third-oldest independent science and engineering school in the nation. Its compact 95-acre campus is set atop one of Worcester's "seven hills" on the residential outskirts of town and borders two parks and the historic Highland Street District, where local merchants and students come together to form the neighborhood community. Old English stone buildings complete with creeping ivy are focal points of the architecture, but modern facilities have moved in to claim their own space on the immaculately kept grounds, including the Innovation Studio, featuring high-tech classrooms, makerspaces, and labs, as well as a 140-bed residence hall.

WPI's curriculum remains remarkably broad and flexible for a high-powered technological university. The intent of WPI's unique educational philosophy of theory and practice is to build self-confidence and social skills, to nurture well-rounded students interested in using their knowledge to improve the world, and, especially, to develop teamwork. First-years have the option of signing up for a two-term Great Problems Seminar, which a junior calls "a great way to get one's feet wet with project-based learning." Standard course distribution requirements vary by major but include classes in engineering, math, and science, as well as a humanities and arts requirement. The Interactive Qualifying Project (IQP) is a distinctive requirement that has students apply technical knowledge to one of society's problems, usually working in teams of two to four students with a faculty advisor. The Major Qualifying Project (MQP) requirement serves as a capstone in which students work on a truly professional-level problem in their major course of study. "It is a great opportunity to actually create something and also a great project to put on your résumé for post college," cheers a sophomore. Many IQPs and MQPs involve corporate, nonprofit, or government sponsors, to whom students present their research findings and recommendations.

> "WPI's culture is one that allows students to be themselves."

The most popular majors are mechanical engineering, computer science, electrical and computer engineering, and robotics engineering. Aerospace engineering and architectural engineering are traditional strengths, as are interdisciplinary programs such as interactive media and game development (IMGD) and bioinformatics and computational biology. The school launched the nation's first undergraduate robotics engineering program, which has grown to include M.S. and Ph.D. programs. WPI has a FinTech program also offering B.S., M.S., and Ph.D. degrees. A rare fire protection engineering combined B.S./M.S. program now also includes an explosion protection engineering program. Many biomedical engineering majors do their projects at UMass Medical and Tufts's veterinary school, as well as at local hospitals. Math and science types can pick up middle or high school teaching credentials through the university's STEM Education Center. Creative writing, music, and drama are offered as minors, and well over 300 students participate in 30 musical and theatrical groups on campus.

An academic year at WPI consists of four terms, each lasting seven weeks, which means courses are fast-paced and intense, but a chemical engineering major calls it "a good system if you're an organized person." Students take three courses per term, and although some introductory classes enroll more than 100 students, most classes are small—66 percent have fewer than 20 students. Professors are generally praised for having "a very good mix of theoretical knowledge and practical workplace experience," says an aerospace major. To further promote cooperation and cohesiveness, the only recorded grades are A, B, C, or No Record. Failing grades do not appear on transcripts, and the school does not compute GPAs or class ranks. Because of this, says a biochemistry major, "students are not overly competitive with one another."

WPI also offers a distinctive Global Projects Program, in which students travel to more than 50 off-campus project centers run by resident faculty advisors across the U.S. and around the world, working in teams to solve a real-world problem for a local sponsor. More than 80 percent of students take advantage of the program, most of them to fulfill their IQP or MQP requirements, while 63 percent of students study abroad. Every incoming first-year is eligible for a Global Project Scholarship of up to $5,000 to support participation in the program. Super motivated students can also complete Individually Sponsored Residential Projects, in which they design their own independent, off-campus study project under the direction of a faculty member, in addition to their other project work. The co-op program enables students to take time away from the classroom to pursue paid, full-time work experience, which may add on extra time to their degree program. "WPI offers an insurmountable arsenal of resources for students to take advantage of," cheers a computer science major.

Of the students, a senior says, "We are goofy, determined, hardworking, and just fun. We all know what we want and really work toward it but have a lot of fun in achieving that goal." Forty-six percent of undergraduates are Massachusetts natives, and 6 percent come from abroad. "The campus is not very diverse on socioeconomic status," says a senior. Black students account for 3 percent of the students, Hispanics/Latinos 9 percent, Asian Americans 13 percent, and multiracial students 4 percent. Men outnumber women 3 to 2. A chemical engineering major calls the student body "relatively apolitical," since "students in general are much more interested in impacting the world through science, technology, and engineering than through political activism." Merit scholarships averaging $22,100 are doled out annually, but there are no athletic scholarships.

Forty-five percent of all undergrads live in campus housing, which a senior says "is generally good and rooms are nice and spacious." Co-ed halls offer traditional and suite-style options, while on-campus apartments and smaller houses make for more homelike living. Upperclassmen tend to move to Greek houses or off-campus apartments. Students can take their meals in the main dining hall, food court, or on-campus restaurant. "Mental health services have become increasingly impressive in the recent years," A senior notes. "WPI's Center for Well-Being has been an amazing place for students to relax, take a break, and think about their well-being."

Social life is usually a good mix of on- and off-campus activities. "There are many ways to socialize at WPI, through opportunities like our very safe Greek Life culture, as well as events hosted by different groups," says a junior. Student-organized coffeehouses, game nights, concerts, improv shows, and movies are popular, as are Greek parties. Twenty-two percent of the men join fraternities, and 27 percent of the women enter sororities. On campus, "Parties hosted by Greek organizations are monitored and safe," shares a student. A century-old campus tradition is the Goat's Head Rivalry, a yearlong grudge match between the first-year and sophomore classes that includes the Pennant Rush, a rope pull next to Salisbury Pond, and a WPI trivia competition. The prize? A bronze goat's head trophy with the winning class's year engraved on it.

While not exactly a tourist destination, Worcester does offer many clubs and restaurants, an art museum, and a large multipurpose arena that hosts concerts and sporting events. It's also home to the minor league baseball team, the WooSox. "The Student Activities Office will have weekend day trips [to] Wachusett Mountain, all different types of fruit picking, bowling, the Boston Aquarium, etc.," a sophomore says. Several nearby colleges, including Clark and Holy Cross, provide even more social and academic opportunities. Boston and Hartford are both an hour's drive, as are ski resorts and beaches.

> "WPI offers an insurmountable arsenal of resources for students to take advantage of."

The WPI Engineers compete in Division III sports and field several strong teams. Women's rowing was the varsity eight national champion in 2024, and indoor track and field also won two recent national championships. Men's basketball and soccer, and men's and women's swimming and diving are also competitive. "There is always an annual Worcester State University versus WPI midnight basketball game, which is always a fun social event," cheers an industrial engineering major. Eighty percent of the student body participate in intramural and recreational sports, with underwater hockey being a particular favorite among more than 40 club sports.

One of WPI's chants is fittingly mathematic: "E to the x, d-y, d-x, e to the ix, d-x; cosine, secant, tangent, sine; 3.14159; e-i, radical, pi; fight 'em, fight 'em, WPI!" If you know what any of that stuff means, you'll fit right in.

Overlaps

Carnegie Mellon, UMass Amherst, MIT, Northeastern, Purdue, Rensselaer, Rochester Institute of Technology, Stevens Institute of Technology

If You Apply To ›

WPI: Early decision I and II, early action I and II, regular decision. SATs or ACTs: optional. Accepts the Common Application.

Xavier University of Louisiana

1 Drexel Drive, New Orleans, LA 70125

The only historically Black college with Roman Catholic ties, Xavier is bigger than a small college but smaller than most universities. Competes with Howard, LSU, Morehouse, and Spelman. Strong in pharmacy and the physical sciences and nationally known for turning out future doctors, pharmacists, and science teachers. Five percent of students are Catholic. Location in New Orleans is a big plus.

As the nation's only historically Black and Catholic college, Xavier University of Louisiana has a stellar reputation for graduating a wealth of scientists, aspiring medical professionals, and future leaders. A small New Orleans college, Xavier prepares students for their chosen careers while providing a strong foundation in the liberal arts and a supportive community. Says one English major: "Xavier is where future leaders are made."

Xavier, a.k.a. XULA, was established as a university in 1925 by Katharine Drexel and the Sisters of the Blessed Sacrament. Drexel, a former Philadelphia socialite and niece of Drexel University founder Anthony J. Drexel, devoted her life to the education of African Americans and Native Americans, and she was canonized in 2000 by Pope John Paul II. Xavier is located near the heart of New Orleans in a quiet neighborhood dotted with bungalows. The focal point of the campus is the Library Resource Center, which, with its green roof and stately neo-Gothic architectural style, has become a landmark for those traveling by car from the New Orleans airport to the French Quarter. An enclosed campus green mutes the urban feel of the encroaching city, and yellow-brick buildings have been erected among the historic limestone structures. Since 2005's Hurricane Katrina, XULA has gone on a $130 million renovation and building spree that includes the state-of-the-art Pharmacy Pavilion, the Convocation Center, and the stunning St. Katharine Drexel Chapel designed by renowned Argentine architect César Pelli.

Xavier's core curriculum, known as XCore, consists of three stages, beginning with Foundations courses in the first year that orient students to the university, basic skills like college writing, and the city of New Orleans. The second stage, Explorations, requires classes in several liberal arts categories ranging from theology and scientific reasoning to African American heritage and legacies. In the third stage, Engagements, students take two interdisciplinary seminars, each focusing on a different "big idea" or global issue, such as corporate social responsibility and food security. Finally, all students complete a senior capstone course in their major.

The university maintains its reputation as one of the most effective teaching institutions anywhere; the Center for the Advancement of Teaching and Faculty Development works to improve pedagogy across the curriculum. Nearly 60 percent of undergraduates major in a science-related field; biology and psychology are the most popular majors, along with chemistry (including prepharmacy), business, and public health sciences. "If you want to go into medicine, I would recommend Xavier," explains a student. "They have one of, if not the best, premed programs for minority students." Xavier is a leading institution nationally in the number of Black alumni who graduate from medical school, and the university has announced plans to establish its own medical school. Xavier is also among the top producers of Black pharmacists. Fitting for its location, Xavier offers a music major with a concentration in jazz studies. New programs include majors in robotics and mechatronics engineering and African American and diaspora studies. In addition to the many internships available, Xavier offers cooperative education programs in all fields and study abroad programs around the world.

"I would describe the academic climate as competitive in terms of obtaining internships," says one student, "but collaborative as well because most students here are willing to help one another with their studies." Priests and nuns teach and help run the school, though the notably diverse faculty and staff are composed of laypeople. Fifty-eight percent of classes have fewer than 20 students. "Teachers are accessible and give personalized attention," says one senior, "especially in upper-level courses." Academic tutoring, and academic and career advising are well supported, and there is a strong emphasis on community service.

Website: www.xula.edu
Location: City Center
Private
Total Enrollment: 2,882
Undergraduates: 2,560
Male/Female: 25/75
Financial Aid: 72%
Pell Grant: 66%
Expense: Pr $
Student Loans: 98%
Average Debt: $
Applicants: 10,260
Accepted: 69%
Enrolled: 12%
Grad in 6 Years: 48%
Returning First-years: 71%
Academics: ✍ ✍ ✍
Social: 🗩 🗩 🗩
Q of L: ★ ★ ★
Admissions: (504) 520-7388
Email Address:
  apply@xula.edu

Strong Programs:
Biology
Business
Chemistry
Education
Music
Prepharmacy
Psychology
Public Health Sciences

> **"Xavier is where future leaders are made."**

Frequent forums and town-hall meetings give students a chance to discuss social and political concerns.

"Students are focused, self-motivated, driven, engaged, empowered, and very straightforward about what they want to achieve," comments a biology major. For a historically Black college, XULA's student body is quite diverse. Eighty percent of undergrads are Black, 2 percent are Asian American, 4 percent are Hispanic/Latino, 4 percent are multiracial, and 1 percent are white. Xavier has achieved a national reputation for its programs to reach out to local high schools to identify and nurture talented students of color. Thirty-one percent of students are from Louisiana, primarily the New Orleans area, and the balance come from 40 other states. Many are second- or third-generation Xavierites. Three percent come from abroad. Frequent forums and town-hall meetings give students a chance to discuss social and political concerns. A limited number of academic awards are available to qualified students, as are athletic scholarships. A substantial 66 percent of incoming first-years are eligible for Pell Grants.

Ninety percent of Xavier's first-year students live in the contemporary-looking residence halls, three of which are same-sex. Overall 67 percent of students live in campus housing. Students report being mostly satisfied with the dining options: "The dining hall gets the job done," says a student. As a major city, New Orleans experiences a fair amount of crime, so campus security is a top priority, with highly visible officers who provide rides back to the dorms after late-night study sessions; the XULASafe App includes safety options such as a mobile blue light location alert, emergency preparedness resources, and more.

Athletic events and activities organized by student clubs offer some entertainment on campus, and, as a junior explains, "Every Friday, we have Live Music Friday, where we have music on the yard during lunchtime." Popular annual events include Homecoming and Spring Fest. Otherwise, given the endless options for socializing and nightlife in New Orleans, the social scene on campus tends to be quiet.

"Xavier students from all over the country revel in the New Orleans culture and bond over it," remarks a sociology major. Fraternities and sororities attract just 3 percent of the men and 7 percent of the women, and since Xavier is a dry campus, Greek parties usually happen at off-campus venues. As for road trips, students head to Baton Rouge, Houston, Atlanta, and Miami.

Xavier's Gold Rush (men's) and Gold Nuggets (women's) varsity sports teams compete along with the 2024 National Cheerleading Association winning co-ed cheer team in the NAIA Division I and are enthusiastically supported, especially when the opponent is crosstown rival Dillard University. Competitive teams include men's and women's basketball, track and field, rowing, baseball, softball, women's cross-country, women's volleyball, and men's and women's soccer. Those interested in recreational sports can sign up for intramural basketball, flag football, and volleyball, among others.

"Xavier is a cradle for overachieving Black students to come together and challenge each other," opines a history major. "It is an environment that celebrates and supports high academic performance and achievement." With a mind for the future, Xavier stays true to its beginnings as a historically Black and Catholic university and to its mission of preparing students to work toward "a more just and humane society."

Overlaps

Benedict, Claflin, Hampton, Howard, Louisiana State, Morehouse, Spelman, Tuskegee

If You Apply To ›

Xavier: Rolling admissions. Accepts the Common Application with supplement. Please consult Xavier's website for the most up-to-date information regarding standardized test requirements.

Yale University

New Haven, CT 06520

Yale is the middle-sized member of the Ivy League's big three: bigger than Princeton, smaller than Harvard. Its widely imitated residential college system helps Yale strike a balance between being a research university and an undergraduate college. New Haven isn't New York, but it has a relatively lively urban scene. Plan to work hard.

Founded in 1701 by Connecticut Congregationalists concerned about "backsliding" among their counterparts at a certain school in Cambridge, Massachusetts, Yale has long been recognized as one of the world's finest private universities and one of the few Ivy League schools focused on undergraduates. Students here remain as dedicated to their studies as ever and tend to carry their achievements lightly. And thanks to Yale's residential college system, this huge research university feels like more of a home for its students. "Yale students are truly happy to be here," says a sophomore. "Everyone has a massive crush on Yale, and that makes all the difference in living and working here for four years."

Yale's campus looks like the traditional archetype—magnificent courtyards, imposing quadrangles, Gothic buildings designed by James Gamble Rogers, and Harkness Tower, a 216-foot spire. Most of the residential colleges date to the 1930s. The university, which bears the name of early benefactor Elihu Yale, has increased its full-time undergraduate enrollment over the last few years and opened two new residential colleges. The Greenberg Engineering Teaching Concourse offers state-of-the-art spaces for undergraduate teaching and collaboration; together with the Yale Center for Engineering Innovation and Design and the Tsai Center for Innovative Thinking at Yale, it forms an "innovation corridor" on campus. The Kline Tower, Yale's tallest building, recently was renovated to become a hub for mathematical, statistical, and data-driven research.

Inside Yale's wrought-iron gates, academic programs are superb across the board, with arts and humanities programs especially outstanding. With tradition ever-present on campus, the Puritan work ethic remains. Graduating from Yale demands 36 courses—nine a year—rather than the 32 courses required at most other colleges. Students agree that despite all the hard work, the academic environment is not based on competition. "Students are not only willing but eager to work together to complete problem sets and study for tests," explains a junior. "Being in such a supportive environment really facilitates learning."

> **"Everyone has a massive crush on Yale, and that makes all the difference in living here for four years."**

Although Yale has 13 professional schools and a Graduate School of Arts and Sciences, Yale College—the undergraduate arts and sciences division—remains the university's heart and soul. Virtually all professors teach undergraduates, and the professional schools' resources—especially architecture, fine arts, drama, and music—are available to them as well. Yale's superb economics department, replete with budding hedge fund managers and management consultants, offers the most popular undergraduate major, followed by computer science, history, and psychology. History offers one of the most demanding programs, including a mandatory 30- to 50-page senior essay. The English department is routinely at the vanguard of literary theory, while an outstanding interdisciplinary humanities major includes the study of the medieval, Renaissance, and modern periods. The global affairs major includes a senior capstone project in which small groups of students are assigned to

Website: www.yale.edu
Location: Small City
Private
Total Enrollment: 15,121
Undergraduates: 6,753
Male/Female: 48/51
Financial Aid: 64%
Pell Grant: 25%
Expense: Pr $ $ $ $
Student Loans: 12%
Average Debt: $
Applicants: 57,517
Accepted: 4%
Enrolled: 70%
Grad in 6 Years: 96%
Returning First-years: 99%
Academics: ✍ ✍ ✍ ✍ ✍
Social: 💬 💬 💬
Q of L: ★ ★ ★
Admissions: (203) 432-9316
Email Address: student.questions@yale.edu

Strong Programs:
Architecture
Biological Science
Drama
Economics
Engineering
English
Fine Arts
Music

a policy task force where they apply their academic training to a specific real-world problem. Most labs and classrooms are located on Science Hill. Yale has spent half a billion dollars on science and engineering facilities in recent years. The biological science departments are excellent, and its students' interests range from biomedical engineering research to preparation for medical school. Architecture and modern languages, especially French and Chinese, are first-rate, and the school's Center for the Study of Globalization is renowned as well. "Yale places a special interest on interdisciplinary learning, so you never feel burdened to one singular academic path," says an ethics, politics, and economics major.

High-achieving first-years with a particularly strong appetite for the humanities can enroll in Directed Studies, a yearlong, three-course program that examines the literature, philosophy, history, and politics of Western tradition. Prospective DSers, who must apply in May or June of their senior year in high school, should be prepared for some serious bonding with their books—they don't dub it "Directed Suicide" for nothing. Nearly all science and engineering majors do research with faculty members in any of the more than 1,200 labs on campus; many are doing their own research as early as the summer after their first year. "Professors love having undergrads in their labs as mentees," says a molecular, cellular, and developmental biology major. Yale's Science, Technology, and Research Scholars Program offers research and mentorship opportunities, career planning, and other specialized support for historically underrepresented students, including women, minorities, and those from economically disadvantaged backgrounds.

> **"Students are not only willing but eager to work together."**

Despite its reverence for tradition, Yale doesn't require any specific courses for graduation, and it doesn't have a core curriculum. Instead, students must take two classes in humanities and arts, social sciences, and sciences, along with two courses that emphasize writing and another two that emphasize quantitative reasoning. Yale also mandates intermediate-level mastery of a foreign language. Most undergraduates take advantage of hundreds of study, internship, and research opportunities offered around the world. "Yale works hard to make study abroad affordable for every student," says a political science major. "I spent a summer abroad in Siena, Italy, and, best of all, the entire experience was covered by my Yale financial aid." The Yale in London program is popular, as are summer sessions abroad for intensive language study.

> *Yale has long been recognized as one of the world's finest private universities and one of the few Ivy League schools focused on undergraduates.*

Introductory-level classes at Yale can be large lectures, accompanied by small discussion sections typically led by graduate teaching fellows, although first-year seminars are offered each year on a wide range of topics, and as a junior explains, each "often involves a highly prestigious faculty member teaching to a small group." Upper-level seminars are small and plentiful. Of the 1,000 classes offered each semester, 73 percent have fewer than 20 students. "The quality of education is simply unmatched," boasts a junior. "I can expect for my history professors to provide their first account into meeting world leaders, the political science department to consistently have politicians speaking, or an economics professor to be up for a new Nobel Prize." Some of the most popular courses, such as John Gaddis's Cold War history class, seem more like performances, students say, and James Rothman, winner of the Nobel Prize in Physiology or Medicine, lives in one of Yale's residential colleges. Even with the big names, says a mechanical engineering major, "The academic climate at Yale is very collaborative."

"Yalies are passionate about the things they are involved in and fully invest themselves in those passions," observes a junior. Eighty-three percent of undergraduates are from outside of Connecticut, including many from the Northeast and 11 percent from other countries, and the student body is evenly split along gender lines. Black students make up 9 percent of students, Hispanics/Latinos 17 percent, Asian Americans

22 percent, and multiracial students 7 percent. One student from a rural background mentions a "stark socioeconomic divide," griping, "It's hard to feel like you truly belong when wealth is such a visible and unspoken norm." Yalies aren't shy about expressing their opinions. "Students are politically active and strive to make changes they feel are necessary," says a chemical engineering major. No merit or athletic awards are available, but the university admits students without regard to financial need and meets the full demonstrated need of all its undergraduate students, who are not expected to take out loans. Families making less than $200,000 receive need-based scholarships that cover tuition, while families earning up to $100,000 receive aid that also covers additional expenses, such as room and board.

The 14 residential colleges that serve as Yale's dorms are the focal points for undergraduate social life and central to the distinct culture of Yale. "Yale's dorms are like palaces," cheers one student. Endowed by Yale graduate Edward S. Harkness (who also began the house system at Harvard) and modeled on those at Oxford and Cambridge, Yale's colleges provide intimate living/learning communities, creating the atmosphere of a small liberal arts college within a large research university. A senior says they are "similar to the house system at Hogwarts in the Harry Potter series." Each college has a library, dining hall, "butteries" that sell late-night food, and special facilities such as a gym, photography darkroom, or small theater. All colleges also have their own head of college and dean who live in the college, as well as affiliated faculty members who can help undergraduates struggling to adapt to the rigors of life at Yale. Residential colleges organize social and cultural events, such as teas where prominent public figures meet with groups of students. The dining halls serve good meals and multiple options. A senior notes, "We have an iPhone app that tells you the menu in each dining hall each night."

Much of each residential college's distinctive identity comes from its architecture. Some buildings are fashioned in a craggy, fortress-like Gothic style, while others are done in the more open colonial style, with red brick and green shutters as the prevailing motif. All colleges have their own special nooks and crannies with cryptic inscriptions paying tribute to illustrious Yalies of generations past. First-years in 10 of the 14 colleges

> **"Yale places a special interest on interdisciplinary learning."**

live together on the Old Campus, the historic 19th-century quadrangle, before moving into their colleges as sophomores; first-years in the other four colleges live in their college from the start. Students generally live in suites with a living room and single or double bedrooms, but many seniors get singles. Some upper-level students move into New Haven, although 80 percent of students choose to stay on campus all four years. Despite New Haven's urban character, students say that they feel physically safe. A female biochemistry major adds, "There have been sexual assaults on campus, and, fortunately, the school's administration has been responding swiftly." Adds another student, "On the mental health front, Yale has invested significantly in student well-being."

In addition to identifying with their colleges, many Yale students identify strongly with extracurricular groups, clubs, and organizations, spending most of their waking hours outside class at the newspaper, radio station, or computer center. Particularly clubby are the a cappella singing groups, whose members do everything from drinking together on certain weeknights to touring together during spring break. Most famous are the Whiffenpoofs, who serenade at Mory's Temple Bar and are the oldest collegiate a cappella group, founded in 1909. Many of Yale's mysterious secret societies, such as Skull and Bones, have their own mausoleum-like clubhouses and issue invitations to those with the right qualifications (like being a Bush). There are also the Yale Anti-Gravity Society (jugglers), improv comedy groups, and a multitude of other organizations.

> *Graduating from Yale demands 36 courses—nine a year—rather than the 32 courses required at most other colleges.*

Though studying takes the lion's share of their time, students find ways to unwind. About 10 percent of Yalies belong to a fraternity or sorority, and Greek parties are open to all. "There is no pressure to get involved in a party culture," says a first-year. The undergraduate Yale Symphony Orchestra puts on an original show every Halloween that fills Woolsey Hall with students in costume. First-years gather for an annual holiday dinner that features a procession of culinary treats known as the Parade of Comestibles. The evening of the first large snowfall of the season brings the annual snowball fight on Old Campus. Spring Fling brings well-known artists for a huge outdoor concert. For the artistically inclined, there are numerous concerts and film screenings on the weekends. The Tony Award–winning Yale Repertory Theater depends heavily on graduate school talent but always brings in a few top stage stars each season and offers reduced-price student passes.

The Yale campus is in the middle of downtown New Haven (population 138,000), a once-gritty small city that is riding the crest of a resurgence that, in the words of a junior, has made it "the perfect blend of manageable quaintness and urban opportunity." Natural history and art museums on and near campus, especially the Yale University Art Gallery and the British Art Center, are excellent. The city's long-standing theatrical tradition continues at two grand old theater and concert halls a block from campus. Shops, bars, and restaurants lie within easy walking distance. Locals will swear that Pepe's on Wooster Street was the first (and best!) pizza parlor in the country. Once-testy relations between students and locals are improving. "The city definitely caters to students to make them feel welcome and safe," says a biochemistry major, and about 60 percent of Yale undergrads reciprocate by doing volunteer work in town through Dwight Hall, the largest student-run college community service organization in the country. "Community service is part of the fabric that makes Yale what it is," says a senior. "It's a major part of student life and culture." For those seeking big-city excitement, Metro North trains run almost hourly to New York, and visiting Boston is nearly as easy.

Yale fields a full complement of 34 athletic teams (the Bulldogs), which play in Division I. Recent Ivy League champions include men's basketball, women's lacrosse, and women's sailing. More than half the student body takes part in intramural competition among the residential colleges; the winning college gets the coveted Tying Cup. The annual Harvard–Yale football game—known simply as The Game—is an occasion for tailgating by thousands of blue-clad students, whether it takes place in New Haven or Cambridge. Yale's Mock Trial team is consistently a top performer at national championships.

Yale is one of America's oldest institutions of higher learning, and students and graduates here take seriously the intonation, "For God, for country, and for Yale." For proof, just remember that among its alumni, Yale counts the presidents or former presidents of about 70 other colleges and universities and five U.S. presidents. As the university progresses into its fourth century, its past and former students continue to make their marks on the world and give credit to their experience at the school. "Yale has helped me grow in ways I never expected—both intellectually and personally," cheers an ethics, politics, and economics major. "The students here are deeply passionate about what they do, and that energy is contagious. You're surrounded by people who care, not just about their own goals, but about the world around them."

If You Apply To ›

Yale: Single-choice early action, regular decision. SATs or ACTs: required. Accepts the Common Application with supplement.

Acknowledgments

FISKE GUIDE TO COLLEGES STAFF

Editor: Edward B. Fiske
Managing Editor: Lisa Chambers
Contributing Editor: Bruce G. Hammond

One of the joys of producing the *Fiske Guide to Colleges* each year is the opportunity to work with talented writers and editors committed to helping college-bound students navigate the increasingly chaotic world of college admissions today. Such a task requires mobilizing the talents, energy, and ideas of many people, and I am grateful to have benefited from an abundance of all three.

My gratitude starts with the overall editorial vision and support of Dominique Raccah, the visionary founder of Sourcebooks, and her close associates Todd Stocke and Anna Michels. It is a joy to work with Lisa Chambers, the managing editor, who can always be counted on to bring vision, competence, and an upbeat attitude to any task at hand. Likewise, I am grateful for the sure editorial oversight of Sophia Ellinas. In addition, Sarah Otterness, Bret Kehoe, and Tina George guided the production process; Kirsten Clawson kept our timelines in check; while Jay Farahani provided crucial technical support. I also continue to be grateful for the support of Bruce G. Hammond, my longtime coauthor of the *Fiske Guide to Getting Into the Right College* and other books about college admissions.

For many years I have benefited from the wise guidance of the high school college counselors who serve on our Editorial Advisory Group and provide counsel on current issues in college admissions. Their names are listed on the next page. Special thanks go out this year to Rich Avitabile, Nancy Beane, Lauren Cook, Ralph Figueroa, Crys Latham, Candice Mackey, Jan Russell, Lisa Sohmer, Anna Takahashi, Chris Teare, and Alyson Tom for their insights on some specific editorial issues. Thanks also to Joe Klunder who has once again provided valuable editorial assistance. And thanks to Carolyn Barr, Gary Coulter, Jesse Schatz, and Jack Shull for advice on the new section on international schools with English-language programs.

In the final analysis, the *Fiske Guide to Colleges* is dependent on the contributions of the thousands of students and college administrators who took the time to answer detailed and demanding questionnaires. Their candor and cooperation are deeply appreciated. While I, of course, accept full responsibility for the final product, the quality and usefulness of the book is a testimony to their thoughtful reflections on the colleges and universities with which they are associated.

Edward B. Fiske
Chapel Hill, NC
March 2026

EDITORIAL ADVISORY GROUP

Richard Avitabile, Middletown, DE
Gerimae Bassichis, Port St. Lucie, FL
Nancy Beane, Atlanta, GA
Sam Bigelow, Concord, MA
Carolyn Blair, Clayton, MO
Robin Boren, Englewood, CO
Lauren Cook, San Francisco, CA
Ralph Figueroa, Albuquerque, NM
Carol Gill, Mount Kisco, NY
Peggy Hoch, Palo Alto, CA
Marcia Hunt, Fort Lauderdale, FL
Marsha Irwin, San Francisco, CA

Matt Lane, Ross, CA
Crys Latham, Washington, D.C.
Katrin Muir Lau, Houston, TX
Candice Mackey, Los Angeles, CA
Judy Muir, Houston, TX
Gay S. Pepper, Naples, FL
Jan Russell, Moraga, CA
Lisa Sohmer, Indian Rocks Beach, FL
Anna Takahashi, East Palo Alto, CA
Chris Teare, Madison, CT
Alyson Tom, Palo Alto, CA
Mark van Warmerdam, Danville, CA

About the Authors

In 1980, when he was Education Editor of the *New York Times*, **Edward B. Fiske** sensed that college-bound students and their families needed better information on which to base their educational choices. Thus was born what soon evolved into the *Fiske Guide to Colleges*. A native of Philadelphia, Fiske graduated from Wesleyan University with high honors and earned master's degrees from Columbia University and Princeton Theological Seminary. In addition to the *Fiske Guide*, he is the author of numerous books on college admissions as well as *Smart Schools, Smart Kids*, a study of current school reform efforts. Fiske left the *Times* in 1991 to pursue his interest in education in developing countries. He lived in Cambodia, New Zealand, and South Africa and wrote about education for UNESCO, the World Bank, the Academy for Educational Development, and other international organizations. Fiske lives in Chapel Hill, North Carolina, with his wife, Helen Ladd, a professor emerita at Duke University. They are coauthors of *When Schools Compete: A Cautionary Tale, Elusive Equity: Education Reform in Post-Apartheid South Africa*, and *Handbook of Research in Education Finance and Policy*.

An award-winning editor and nonfiction writer, **Lisa Chambers**'s appreciation of and belief in higher education started as a child growing up on college campuses with her parents, who were academics and administrators. Chambers graduated cum laude with a B.A. and M.A. in English from the University of Pennsylvania and earned an M.F.A. in creative writing from Goddard College. She has spent much of her career in magazine publishing, as the executive editor of *Closer* weekly and managing editor of *TV Guide* magazine. In addition to her editorial leadership roles, she works as a writer, editor, and consultant for colleges and universities. She lives in New York's Hudson Valley.

Invitation to Readers

The *Fiske Guide to Colleges* welcomes comments from readers on the write-ups contained in the Guide, as well as suggestions regarding ways that we could better serve our readers. Please send your comments to:

Fiske Guide to Colleges
Email: fiskesupport@sourcebooks.com

Thanks for your interest in the *Fiske Guide*.

FISKE'S

College Admission Pledge
for Students

I have accepted the fact that my parents or guardians are clueless. I am serene. I will betray not a tremor when they offer opinions or advice, no matter how laughable. My soul will be light as a feather when my parents elbow their way to the front of my college tour and talk the guide's ear off. I am serene.

Going to college is a stressful time for my parents, even though they are not the ones going. I recognize that neurosis is beyond anyone's control. Each week, I will calmly reassure them that I am working on my essays, have registered for my tests, am finishing my applications, have scheduled my interviews, am aware of all deadlines, and will have everything done in plenty of time. I will smile good-naturedly as my parent asks four follow-up questions at College Night.

I will try not to say "no" simply because my parents say "yes," and I will remain open to the possibility, however improbable, that they may have a point. I may not be fully conscious of my anxieties about the college search—the fear of being judged and the fear of leaving home are both strong. I don't really want to get out of here as much as I say I do, and it is easier to put off thinking about the college search than to get it done. My parents are right about the importance of being proactive, even if they do get carried away.

Though the college search belongs to me, I will listen to my parents or guardians. They know me better than anyone else, and they are the ones who will pay most of the bills. Their ideas about what will be best for me are based on years of experience in the real world. I will seriously consider what they say as I form my own opinions.

I must take charge of the college search. If I do, the nagging will stop, and everyone's anxiety will go down. My parents have given me a remarkable gift—the ability to think and do for myself. I know I can do it with a little help from them.

FISKE'S

College Admission Pledge
for Parents and Guardians

I am resigned to the fact that my child's college search will end in disaster. I am serene. Deadlines will be missed and scholarships will be lost as my child lounges under pulsating headphones or stares transfixed at an iPhone for hours at a time. I am a guardian and I know nothing. I am serene.

Confronted with endless procrastination, my impulse is to take control—to register for tests, plan visits, schedule interviews, and get applications. It was I who asked those four follow-up questions at College Night—I couldn't help myself. And yet I know that everything will be fine if I can summon the fortitude to relax. My child is smart, capable, and perhaps a little too accustomed to me jumping in and fixing things. I will hold back. I will drop hints and encourage, then back off. I will facilitate rather than dominate. The college search won't happen on my schedule, but it will happen.

I will not get too high or low about any facet of the college search. By doing so, I give it more importance than it really has. My child's self-worth may already be too wrapped up in getting an acceptance letter. I will attempt to lessen the fear rather than heighten it.

I will try not to say "no" simply because my child says "yes," and I will remain open to the possibility, however improbable, that my child has the most important things under control. I understand that my anxiety comes partly from a sense of impending loss. I can feel my child slipping away. Sometimes I hold on too tightly or let social acceptability cloud the issue of what is best.

I realize that my child is almost ready to go and that a little rebellion at this time of life can be a good thing. I will respect and encourage independence, even if some of it is expressed as resentment toward me. I will make suggestions with care and try to avoid unnecessary confrontation.

Paying for college is my responsibility. I will take a major role in the search for financial aid and scholarships and speak honestly to my child about the financial realities we face.

I must help my child take charge of the college search. I will try to support without smothering, encourage without annoying, and consult without controlling. The college search is too big to be handled alone—I will be there every step of the way.

Notes

Notes

Notes

Notes